# The
# New York
# State
# Directory

2021/2022

# The
# New York
# State
# Directory

Grey House
Publishing

AMENIA, NY 12501

PRESIDENT: Richard Gottlieb
PUBLISHER: Leslie Mackenzie
EDITORIAL DIRECTOR: Laura Mars
EDITORIAL RESEARCH: Krystal Dos Santos; Olivia Parsonson
PRODUCTION MANAGER: Kristen Hayes
MARKETING DIRECTOR: Jessica Moody

Grey House Publishing, Inc.
4919 Route 22
Amenia, NY 12501
518.789.8700
FAX 518.789.0545
www.greyhouse.com
e-mail: books @greyhouse.com

The New York State directory. — [1st ed.] (1983)-

Annual
ISSN: 0737-1314

1. New York (State)—Officials and employees—Directories. 2. Government executives—New York (State)—Directories. 3. Legislators—New York (State)—Directories.

JK3430 .N52
353.9747002

ISBN: 978-1-64265-816-3

# TABLE OF CONTENTS

# INTRODUCTION

This 2021/2022 edition of *The New York State Directory* is a comprehensive guide to public officials and private sector organizations and individuals who influence public policy in the state of New York. Fully updated with current addresses and office holders, this edition includes dozens of four-color maps—Demographic and Congressional Maps that show population, race, employment, home value, education, income, voter distribution, and break outs of New York's congressional districts.

## Arrangement

*The New York State Directory* includes 45 chapters, arranged in eight sections, plus Appendices. A list of detailed sources appears in the Organization of Data that follows this introduction.

**Section One** includes three chapters: Executive Branch, Legislative Branch, and the Judicial Branch of New York State government. This section profiles the public officials in the state's executive departments, administrative agencies, and court system. Detailed listings of departments and agencies appear in Section Two.

**Section Two** includes 25 chapters covering the most significant public policy issue areas from Agriculture to Veterans & Military. Arranged in alphabetical order, each Policy Area chapter identifies the state, local, and federal agencies and officials that formulate or implement policy. Each chapter ends with a list of Private Sector experts and advocates who influence the policy process.

**Section Three** is comprised of four chapters with state and local government information: Public Information Offices; U.S. Congress Membership & Committees; County Government; and Municipal Government.

**Section Four** includes three chapters—lists and contact information for Political Parties and Political Action Committees, and a Lobbying How-to Guide.

**Section Five** has one Business chapter—Chambers of Commerce and Economic & Industrial Development Organizations. All listings have valuable contact information and key executives.

**Section Six** is News Media—detailed listings for Newspapers, News Services, News Magazines, News Radio and News Television stations that serve New York State. Listings include current contact information, plus valuable key executives.

**Section Seven** covers Education in two chapters—New York State Colleges & Universities, and Public School Districts in the state.

**Section Eight** includes 246 current, comprehensive Biographies of all New York state lawmakers: Executive; New York Senate; New York Assembly; U.S. Senate; and U.S. House of Representatives. All profiles include office addresses with phone numbers, fax numbers and email addresses, making it easy to contact these influential individuals.

## Appendices and Indexes

- **Financial Plan Overview:** Cash Disbursements by Department, projected to FY 2025.

- **Demographic & Reference Maps:** four-color maps that show physical features, federal lands and Indian reservations, racial breakdown, age, income, education, congressional districts, and more.

- **Three Indexes:** Name Index; Organization Index; and Geographic Index.

Every reasonable effort has been made to ensure that information in *The New York State Directory* is as accessible and accurate as possible. Organizational, agency, and key official updates and verification were made as late as March 2021. Continuing assistance and cooperation from state, regional, county, municipal, and federal officials and staff have helped make *The New York State Directory* a unique and valuable resource. We are grateful to these individuals and the private sector sources listed for their generous contributions of time and insight.

In addition to this latest edition of the *Directory,* Grey House offers a companion volume, *Profiles of New York State.* This comprehensive volume provides demographic, economic, religious, geographic, and historical details on the more than 2,500 places that make up New York state—counties, cities, towns, villages, boroughs, and Indian reservations. In addition, *Profiles of New York State* includes chapters on Education, Ancestry, Hispanic & Asian Populations, Climate, plus four-color maps, comparative statistics and rankings.

# ORGANIZATION OF DATA

## Section 1: New York State Branches of Government

*Executive Branch.* Outlines key staff in the Governor's and Lieutenant Governor's offices and senior officials in New York state executive departments and agencies. Biographies for the senior executive branch officials appear in the Biographies section at the back of the book.

*Legislative Branch.* Covers the state Senate and Assembly leadership, membership, administrative staff, and standing committees and subcommittees. Committee listings include the Chairperson, Ranking Minority Member, Majority and Minority committee members, committee staff, and key Senate or Assembly Majority and Minority staff assignments. Biographies with district office information for Senators and Assembly members appear in the Biographies section at the back of the book.

*Judicial Branch.* Identifies the state courts, judges who currently sit on these courts, and the clerk of each court. Includes the Court of Appeals, Appellate Division courts, Supreme Court, Court of Claims, New York City courts, county courts, district courts and city courts outside New York City. The county judge section identifies the specific court with which the judge is associated.

## Section 2: Policy Areas

This section classifies New York state government activity into 25 major policy areas. Each policy area lists key individuals in the New York state government, federal government, and the private sector who have expertise in the area of government activity. All entries show organization name, individual name, title, address, telephone number, and fax number. Internet and e-mail addresses are included where available.

Each policy area includes the following information:

### New York State
*Governor's Office.* Identifies the Governor's legal and program staff assigned to the policy area.

*Executive Department & Related Agencies.* Provides a complete organizational description of the primary state departments and agencies responsible for the policy area. Also includes those state departments and agencies whose activities relate to the policy area.

*Corporations, Authorities & Commissions.* Covers independent public and quasi-private sector agencies in the state, as well as intrastate bodies to which New York sends a representative.

*Legislative Standing Committees.* Lists committees and subcommittees which oversee governmental activities in that policy area, their respective chairpersons, and ranking minority members.

### U.S. Government
*Executive Departments & Related Agencies.* Identifies federal departments and agencies located in or assigned to the New York region.

*U.S. Congress.* Lists congressional committees which oversee federal activities in that policy area, their respective chairpersons, ranking minority members, and NY delegation members.

### Private Sector Sources
Includes an alphabetized list of public interest groups, trade and professional associations, corporations, and academia, with the associated individuals who have expertise in the policy area.

## Section 3: State & Local Government Public Information

*Public Information Offices.* Lists key contacts in state government public information offices and libraries.

*U.S. Congress.* Lists all New York State delegates to the Senate and the House of Representatives with their Washington, DC office, phone and fax numbers, and e-mail addresses. Biographies with district office information for each New York Senator and Representative appear in the *Biographies* section at the back of the book. Provides a comprehensive list of all Senate and House standing, select, and special committees and subcommittees. Each committee and subcommittee entry includes the chairperson, ranking minority member, and assigned members from the New York delegation.

*County Government.* Identifies senior government officials in all New York counties.

*Municipal Government.* Identifies senior public officials for cities, towns, and villages in New York with populations greater than 20,000. All New York City departments are included in the city listing.

## Section 4: Political Parties & Related Organizations

*Political Parties.* Lists statewide party officials and county chairpersons for the Conservative, Democratic, Independence and Republican parties.

*Political Action Committees.* Lists registered political action committees and their treasurers.

*Lobbying How-To Guide.*

## Section 5: Business

*Chambers of Commerce.* Lists contact information for chambers of commerce, and economic and industrial development organizations and their primary officials.

## Section 6: News Media

Identifies daily and weekly newspapers in New York, major news services with reporters assigned to cover state government, radio stations with a news format, and television stations with independent news staff. Newspapers are categorized by the primary city they serve. Staff listings include managing, news, and editorial page editors, and political reporters. News service entries include bureau chiefs and reporters. Radio and television entries include the news director.

## Section 7: Education

*SUNY and Other Universities and Colleges.* Includes the board of trustees, system administration, the four University Centers, and all colleges and community colleges in the SUNY system; the central administration and all colleges in the CUNY system; and independent colleges and universities. Each college includes the name of its top official, usually the president or dean, as well as address, telephone number and Internet address.

*Public School Administrators.* Lists school district administrators by county and school district. The New York City School's subsection includes officials in the Chancellor's office. Following are BOCES District Superintendents by supervisory district and the education administrators of schools operated by the state or other public agencies.

## Section 8: Biographies

Includes political biographies of all individuals representing New York state's Executive Branch, New York state Assembly members, New York state Senate members, US Senators from New York, and US Representatives from New York

## Appendices

**Financial Plan Overview**
*Cash Disbursements By Function—All Government Funds.* Provides information excerpted from the New York State FY 2022 Executive Budget Financial Plan.

**Demographic & Reference Maps**
Populated Places, Transportation & Physical Features
Federal Lands & Indian Reservations
Congressional Districts
Population
Percent White
Percent Black
Percent Asian
Percent Hispanic
Median Age
Median Household Income
Median Home Value
High School Graduates
College Graduates
Voted for Joe Biden in 2020
Core Based Statistical Areas, Counties, and Independent Cities

**Indexes**

*Name Index.* Includes every official and executive name listed in *The New York State Directory*.

*Organizations Index.* Includes the names of the top three organization levels in all New York state executive departments and agencies, as well as public corporations, authorities, and commissions. In addition, this index includes all organizations listed in the Private Sector section of each policy chapter, as well as lobbyist organizations and political action committees, chambers of commerce, newspapers, news services, radio and television stations, SUNY and CUNY locations, and private colleges.

*Geographic Index.* Includes the organizations listed in the *Government and Private Sector Organizations Index* (see above) arranged by the city location.

# ACRONYMS

| | |
|---|---|
| AAA | Automobile Association of America |
| AAAA | Army Aviation Association of America |
| AARP | American Association of Retired Persons |
| AFA | Air Force Association |
| AFL-CIO | American Federation of Labor/Congress of Industrial Organizations |
| AFSA | Air Force Sergeants Association |
| AFSCME | American Federation of State, County & Municipal Employees |
| AFWOA | Air Force Women Officers Association |
| AHRC | Association for the Help of Retarded Children |
| AIA | American Institute of Architects |
| AIVF | Association of Independent Video & Filmmakers |
| AMAC | Association for Metroarea Autistic Children |
| AMSUS | Association of Military Surgeons of the US |
| ASPCA | American Society for the Prevention of Cruelty to Animals |
| AUSA | Association of the US Army |
| | |
| BAC | Bricklayers & Allied Craftsmen |
| BIANYS | Brain Injury Association of NYS |
| BLS | Bureau of Labor Statistics |
| BOCES | Board of Cooperative Educational Services |
| | |
| CASES | Center for Alternative Sentencing & Employment Services |
| CBVH | Commission for the Blind & Visually Handicapped |
| CGR | Center for Governmental Research |
| CHIP | Community Housing Improvement Program |
| CIO | Chief Information Office |
| COA | Commissioned Officers Association |
| COMPA | Committee of Methadone Program Administrators |
| COPE | Committee on Political Education |
| CPB | Customs & Border Protection |
| CPR | Institute for Conflict Prevention and Resolution |
| CSD | Central School District |
| CUNY | City University of New York |
| | |
| DHS | Department of Homeland Security |
| | |
| FEGS | Federation Employment & Guidance Service |
| FEMA | Federal Emergency Management Agency |
| FRA | Fleet Reserve Association |
| FRIA | Friends & Relatives of Institutionalized Aged |
| | |
| HANNYS | Hunger Action Network of New York State |
| HFA | Housing Finance Agency |
| | |
| IBPAT | International Brotherhood of Painters & Allied Trades |
| IBT | International Brotherhood of Teamsters |
| ILGWU | International Ladies' Garment Workers' Union |
| IOLA | Interest on Lawyers Account |
| IUE | International Union of Electrical, Radio & Machine Workers |
| IUOE | International Union of Operating Engineers |
| | |
| MADD | Mothers Against Drunk Driving |
| MBBA | Municipal Bond Bank Agency |
| MCA | Military Chaplains Association |
| MCL | Marine Corps League |
| MOAA | Military Officers Association of America |
| MOPH | Military Order of the Purple Heart |
| MTA | Metropolitan Transportation Authority |

| | |
|---|---|
| NAIFA | North American Insurance & Finance Association |
| NERA | National Enlisted Reserve Association |
| NGAUS | National Guard Association of the US |
| NLN | National League for Nursing |
| NLUS | Navy League of the US |
| NMFA | National Military Family Association |
| NOFA | Northeast Organization Farming Association |
| NOW | National Organization for Women |
| NRA | National Reserve Association |
| NYC | New York City |
| NYANA | New York Association for New Americans |
| NYAPRS | New York Association of Psychiatric Rehabilitation Services |
| NYATEP | New York Association of Training & Employment Professionals |
| NYCCT | New York Community College Trustees |
| NYS | New York State |
| NYSARC | New York State Association for Retarded Citizens |
| NYSANA | New York State Association of Nurse Anesthetists |
| NYSHESC | New York State Higher Education Services Corp |
| NYSIR | New York State Insurance Reciprocal |
| NYSID | New York State Industries for the Disabled |
| NYSSMA | New York State School Music Association |
| NYSEG | New York State Electric & Gas Corporation |
| NYSTEC | New York State Technology Enterprise Corporation |
| NYSTEA | New York State Transportation Engineering Alliance |
| NYU | New York University |
| | |
| OOA | Office of Administration |
| | |
| PAC | Political Action Committee |
| PACE | Political Action for Candidates' Election |
| PAF | Political Action Fund |
| PAT | Political Action Team |
| PBA | Patrolmen's Benevolent Association |
| PCNY | Police Conference of New York |
| PEF | Political Education Fund - and - Public Employees Federation |
| PRLDEF | Puerto Rican Legal Defense and Education Fund |
| PSRC | Professional Standards Review Council |
| | |
| RCIL | Resource Center for Independent Living |
| RID | Rid Intoxicated Drivers |
| RIOC | Roosevelt Island Operating Corporation |
| ROA | Reserve Officers Association |
| | |
| SCAA | Schuyler Center for Analysis & Advocacy |
| SEMO | State Emergency Management Office |
| SENSES | Statewide Emergency Network for Social & Economic Security |
| SIFMA | Securities Industry and Financial Markets Association |
| SONYMA | State of New York Mortgage Agency |
| SUNY | State University of New York |
| | |
| UNYAN | United New York Ambulance Network |
| USWA | United Steel Workers of America |
| | |
| VESID | Vocational & Educational Services for Individuals with Disabilities Office |
| VFW | Veterans of Foreign Wars |
| VISN | Veterans Integrated Service Network |
| VWIN | Veterans Widows International Network |
| | |
| WHEDCO | Women's Housing & Economic Development Corporation |

# Section 1:
# BRANCHES OF GOVERNMENT

# EXECUTIVE BRANCH

*This chapter provides a summary of officials in the Executive Branch. For a more detailed listing of specific executive and administrative departments and agencies, refer to the appropriate policy area in Section 2 or to the Organizations Index. Biographies for the senior Executive Branch officials appear in a separate section in the back of the book.*

## NEW YORK STATE

**Governor (also see Governor's Office):**
  Andrew M Cuomo . . . . . . . . . . . . . . . . . . . . . . . **518-474-8390**
**Lieutenant Governor:**
  Kathleen C Hochul . . . . . . . . . . . . . . . . . . . . . . **581-402-2292**
**Chief Information Officer & Director, Office of Information Technology Services (also see CIO Office & Office of Information Technology Services):**
  Angelo Riddick . . . . . . . . . . . . . . . . . . . . . . . . . **518-408-2140**
**Comptroller (also see State Comptroller, Office of the):**
  Thomas P DiNapoli . . . . . . . . . . **518-474-4044 or 212-383-1600**
**Attorney General (also see Law Department):**
  Letitia James . . . . . . . . . . . . . . . **212-416-8000 or 518-776-2000**
**Secretary of State (also see State Department):**
  Rossana Rosado . . . . . . . . . . . . . **518-486-9844 or 212-417-5800**

## Governor's Office
Executive Chamber
State Capitol
Albany, NY 12224
518-474-8390
Web site: www.governor.ny.gov; www.ny.gov

Governor:
  Andrew M Cuomo . . . . . . . . . . . . . . . . . . . . . . . . . . . .518-474-8390
Secretary to the Governor:
  Melissa DeRosa . . . . . . . . . . . . . . . . . . . . .518-474-4246 or 212-681-4580
Counsel to the Governor:
  Kumiki Gibson . . . . . . . . . . . . . . . . . . . . . .518-474-8343 or 212-681-4580
Chief of Staff:
  Jill DesRosiers . . . . . . . . . . . . . . . . . . . . . .518-474-8390 or 212-681-4580
Director, Communications:
  Peter Ajemian . . . . . . . . . . . . . . . . . . . . . . .518-474-8418 or 212-681-4640

## Office of the Secretary
Secretary to the Governor:
  Melissa DeRosa . . . . . . . . . . . . . . . . . . . . .518-474-4246 or 212-681-4580
Director, State Operations and Infrastructure:
  Kelly Cummings . . . . . . . . . . . . . . . . . . . . . . . . . . . .518-486-9871
Chief of Staff:
  Jill DesRosiers . . . . . . . . . . . . . . . . . . . . . .518-474-8390 or 212-681-4580
Special Counsel to the Governor:
  Judith Mogul . . . . . . . . . . . . . . . . . . . . . . . . . . . . . .518-408-2051
Special Counsel & Senior Advisor to the Governor:
  Elizabeth Garvey . . . . . . . . . . . . . . . . . . . . . . . . . . . .212-681-4580
Deputy Director of State Operations:
  Christian Jackstadt . . . . . . . . . . . . . . . . . . . . . . . . . .212-681-4586
Deputy Secretary for Intergovernmental Affairs:
  Jesse Campoamor . . . . . . . . . . . . . . . . . . . . . . . . . . .518-486-1100
Executive Deputy Secretary:
  Joseph Rabito . . . . . . . . . . . . . . .518-473-5704 or 212-681-4580
Deputy Secretary for Civil Rights:
  Vacant . . . . . . . . . . . . . . . . . . . . .518-486-1214 or 212-681-4580
Chairman of Energy & Finance for New York:
  Richard L. Kauffman . . . . . . . . . . . . . . . . . . . . . . . . .518-486-9746
Deputy Secretary, Education:
  Daniel Fuller . . . . . . . . . . . . . . . . . . . . . . . . . . . . . .518-486-9699

Deputy Secretary, Energy & Environment:
  Ali Zaidi . . . . . . . . . . . . . . . . . . . . .518-408-2552 or 212-681-5840
Deputy Secretary, Food & Agriculture:
  Patrick Hooker . . . . . . . . . . . . . . . . . . . . . . . . . . . . .518-486-3960
Deputy Secretary, Financial Services and Taxation:
  Niall O'Hegarty
Deputy Secretary, Health & Human Services:
  Richard Beker . . . . . . . . . . . . . . . . .518-408-2500 or 212-681-4580
Deputy Secretary, Labor:
  Vacant . . . . . . . . . . . . . . . . . . . . . .518-486-1214 or 212-681-4584
Deputy Secretary, Public Safety:
  Jeremy Schockett . . . . . . . . . . . . . . . . . . . . . . . . . . .518-474-3522
Deputy Secretary, Transportation:
  Christopher O'Brien . . . . . . . . . . . . . . . . . . . . . . . . . .518-473-6745
Director of Policy:
  David Yassky . . . . . . . . . . . . . . . . . . . . . . . . . . . . . .518-408-2576

### Communications
Director, Communications:
  Peter Ajemian . . . . . . . . . . . . . . . .518-474-8418 or 212-681-4640

### Counsel
Counsel to the Governor:
  Kumiki Gibson . . . . . . . . . . . . . . . .518-474-8343 or 212-681-4580
First Assistant Counsel:
  R Nadine Fontaine . . . . . . . . . . . . . . . . . . . . . . . . . .518-474-8434

## New York City Office
  633 Third Avenue, 38th Floor, New York, NY 10017
  212-681-4580
Governor:
  Andrew M Cuomo . . . . . . . . . . . . . . . . . . . . . . . . . . .518-474-8390

## Washington Office of the Governor
  444 North Capitol Street NW, Suite 301, Washington, DC 20001
  202-434-7100
Director:
  Alexander Cochran . . . . . . . . . . . . . . . . . . . . . . . . . .202-434-7100

## Lieutenant Governor's Office
Executive Chamber
State Capitol
Albany, NY 12224
518-402-2292  Fax: 518-474-1513

633 Third Avenue
New York, NY 10017
212-681-4580

Lieutenant Governor:
  Kathleen C Hochul . . . . . . . . . . . . . . . . . . . . . . . . . .518-402-2292
Chief of Staff:
  Jeffrey Lewis . . . . . . . . . . . . . . . . . . . . . . . . . . . . . .518-402-2292
Deputy Chief of Staff:
  Melissa Bochenski . . . . . . . . . . . . . . . . . . . . . . . . . .518-402-2292
Director, Communications:
  Haley Viccaro . . . . . . . . . . . . . . . . . . . . . . . . . . . . . .518-402-2292
Director, External Affairs:
  Rachel Swack . . . . . . . . . . . . . . . . . . . . . . . . . . . . . .518-202-2292

## EXECUTIVE DEPARTMENTS AND RELATED AGENCIES

### Aging, Office for the
2 Empire State Plaza
Albany, NY 12223-1251
844-697-6321 or 800-342-9871  Fax: 518-474-0608
e-mail: nysofa@aging.ny.gov
Web site: www.aging.ny.gov

*Offices and agencies generally appear in alphabetical order, except when specific order is requested by listee.*

Director:
  Greg Olsen
Executive Deputy Director:
  Vacant . . . . . . . . . . . . . . . . . . . . . . . . . . . . .518-474-7012
Counsel:
  Vacant . . . . . . . . . . . . . . . . . . . . . . . . . . . . .518-474-0388
Deputy Director, Agency Operations:
  John Cochran . . . . . . . . . . . . . . . . . . . . . . . . .518-474-7012
Deputy Director, Division of Aging Network Operations:
  Jack Lynch . . . . . . . . . . . . . . . . . . . . . . . . . .518-473-4808
Deputy Director, Division of Policy, Planning, Program & Outcomes:
  Laurie Pferr . . . . . . . . . . . . . . . . . . . . . . . . .518-474-7012
Public Information Officer:
  Reza Mizbani . . . . . . . . . . . . . . . . . . . . . . . . .518-474-7181
  e-mail: reza.mizbani@aging.ny.gov
Director of Aging Projects:
  Kelly Mateja . . . . . . . . . . . . . . . . . . . . . . . . .518-473-7424
Assistant Counsel:
  Stephen Syzdek . . . . . . . . . . . . . . . . . . . . . . . .518-474-5041
State Long Term Care Ombudsman:
  Claudette Royal . . . . . . . . . . . . . . . . . . . . . . . .800-342-9871

## Agriculture & Markets Department
10B Airline Drive
Albany, NY 12235
518-457-4188 or 800-554-4501  Fax: 518-457-3087
e-mail: info@agriculture.ny.gov
Web site: www.agriculture.ny.gov

Commissioner:
  Richard Ball . . . . . . . . . . . . . . . .518-457-8876 or 518-457-4188
First Deputy Commissioner:
  Steve McGrattan . . . . . . . . . . . . . . . . . . . . . . .518-457-2771
Deputy Commissioner:
  Kevin King . . . . . . . . . . . . . . . . . . . . . . . . . .518-485-2771
  e-mail: kevin.king@agriculture.ny.gov
Deputy Commissioner:
  Jackie Moody-Czub . . . . . . . . . . . . . . . . . . . . . .518-485-7728
  e-mail: jackie.moody-czub@agriculture.ny.gov
Deputy Commissioner:
  Jennifer Trodden . . . . . . . . . . . . . . . . . . . . . . .518-485-7728
  e-mail: jennifer.trodden@agriculture.ny.gov
General Counsel:
  Scott Wyner . . . . . . . . . . . . . . . . . . . . . . . . .518-457-1059
  e-mail: scott.wyner@agriculture.ny.gov
Public Information Officer:
  Jola Szubielski . . . . . . . . . . . . .518-485-7728 or 518-457-3136
  fax: 518-457-3087
  e-mail: jola.szubielski@agriculture.ny.gov

## New York State Liquor Authority (Division of Alcoholic Beverage Control)
105 W 125th Street
New York, NY 10027
518-474-3114
Web site: www.sla.ny.gov

80 South Swan Street
Suite 900
Albany, NY 12210-8002
518-474-3114
Fax: 518-402-4015

535 Washington Street
Suite 303
Buffalo, NY 14203
518-474-3114
Fax: 716-847-3435

Chairman:
  Vincent G Bradley . . . . . . . . . . . . . . . . . . . . . .518-473-6559
Commissioner:
  Greeley T Ford . . . . . . . . . .518-474-3114 or 212-961-8300
Commissioner:
  Lily M Fan . . . . . . . . . . . . . . . . . . . . . . . . . .518-474-3114
Deputy Commissioner, Licensing:
  Adam Roberts . . . . . . . . . . . . . . . . . . . . . . . .518-474-3114
  e-mail: adam.roberts@sla.ny.gov
Secretary to the Authority:
  Thomas Donohue . . . . . . . . . . . . . . . . . . . . . . .518-474-3114
  e-mail: Thomas.Donohue@sla.ny.gov
Executive Deputy Commissioner:
  Sharif Kabir . . . . . . . . . . . . . . . . . . . . . . . . .518-474-3114
  e-mail: Sharif.Kabir@sla.ny.gov
Director, Enforcement:
  Joseph Finelli . . . . . . . . . . . . . . . . . . . . . . . .518-474-3114
  e-mail: Joseph.Finelli@sla.ny.gov
Director, Public Affairs:
  William Crowley . . . . . . . . . . .518-474-3114 or 518-474-4875
  fax: 518-473-9565
  e-mail: William.Crowley@sla.ny.gov
Director, Administration:
  Kimberly Ciccone . . . . . . . . . . . . . . . . . . . . . .518-474-3114
  e-mail: Kimberly.Ciccone@sla.ny.gov
Counsel to the Authority:
  Vacant . . . . . . . . . . . . . . . . . . . . . . . . . . . .518-474-3114

## Alcoholism & Substance Abuse Services, Office of
1450 Western Avenue
Albany, NY 12203-3526
518-473-3460
e-mail: communications@oasas.ny.gov
Web site: www.oasas.ny.gov

501 7th Avenue
8th Floor
New York, NY 10018-5903
646-728-4533

Commissioner:
  Arlene González-Sánchez . . . . . . . . . . . . . . . . . . .518-457-2061
Executive Deputy Commissioner:
  Sean M Byrne . . . . . . . . . . . . . . . . . . . . . . . . .518-485-2337
Director, Office of the Medical Director:
  Marc Manseau . . . . . . . . . . . . . . . . . . . . . . . . .518-457-5989
General Counsel:
  Trisha Schell-Guy . . . . . . . . . . . . . . . . . . . . . .518-485-2312
Associate Commissioner, Division of Prevention & Problem Gambling Services:
  Patricia Zuber-Wilson . . . . . . . . . . . . . . . . . . . .518-457-4384
Associate Commissioner, Fiscal Administration Division:
  Vittoria Parry . . . . . . . . . . . . . . . . . . . . . . . .518-457-5312
Associate Commissioner, Treatment & Recovery:
  Patricia Lincourt
Associate Commissioner, Quality Assurance & Performance Improvement Division:
  Keith McCarthy . . . . . . . . . . . . . . . . . . . . . . . .518-485-2250
Associate Commissioner, Outcome Management & System Information Division:
  Vacant . . . . . . . . . . . . . . . . . . . . . . . . . . . .518-485-2322
Director, Government Affairs & Federal Policy:
  Tracey Collins . . . . . . . . . . . . . . . . . . . . . . . .518-485-1484
Director, Office of Public Information & Communications:
  Edison Alban
Director, Health Initiatives:
  Peggy Bonneau . . . . . . . . . . . . . . . . . . . . . . . .518-457-5989
Director, Office of NYC Operations, Affirmative Action and Bureau of Statewide Field Operations:
  Manuel Mosquera . . . . . . . . . . . . . . . . . . . . . . .646-728-4720

*Offices and agencies generally appear in alphabetical order, except when specific order is requested by listee.*

## Financial Services Department
One State Street
New York, NY 10004-1511
212-480-6400 or 800-342-3736
e-mail: public-affairs@dfs.ny.gov
Web site: www.dfs.ny.gov

One Commerce Plaza
Albany, NY 12257
Fax:

Walter Mahoney Office Building
65 Court Street, Room 7
Buffalo, NY 14202
Fax:

Superintendent:
Linda A Lacewell . . . . . . . . . . . . . . . . . . . . . . . . . . . . . .212-709-3500
Chief Information Officer:
Vacant . . . . . . . . . . . . . . . . . . . . . . . . . . . . . . . . . . . . . .212-709-5420
Director, Criminal Investigations Bureau:
Ricardo Velez . . . . . . . . . . . . . . . . . . . . . . . . . . . . . . . .212-709-3500
Director, Frauds:
Frank Orlando . . . . . . . . . . . . . . . . . . . .212-480-6074/fax: 212-709-3555
Director, Capital Markets Division:
Anna Taam . . . . . . . . . . . . . . . . . . . . .212-480-5071/fax: 212-480-6085

## Budget, Division of the
State Capitol
Room 128
Albany, NY 12224-0341
518-474-2300
e-mail: dob.sm.press@budget.ny.gov
Web site: www.budget.ny.gov

Director:
Robert F. Mujica . . . . . . . . . . . . . . . . . . . . . . . . . . . . . .518-474-2300
Deputy Director:
Sandra Beattie . . . . . . . . . . . . . . . . . . . . . . . . . . . . . . . .518-474-2300
Deputy Director:
Charles Williams . . . . . . . . . . . . . . . . . . . . . . . . . . . . . .518-474-2300
Press Officer:
Freeman Klopott . . . . . . . . . . . . . . . . . . . . . . . . . . . . . .518-473-3885

## CIO & Office of Information Technology Services (ITS)
State Capitol
Empire State Plaza
P.O. Box 2062
Albany, NY 12220-0062
518-402-3899 or 844-891-1786
e-mail: fixit@its.ny.gov
Web site: www.its.ny.gov

Chief Information Officer/Director of Information Technology Services:
Angelo Riddick . . . . . . . . . . . . . . . . . . . . . . . . . .518-408-2140
Executive Deputy Chief Information Officer:
Karen Geduldig . . . . . . . . . . . . . . . . . . . . . . . . . . . . . .518-473-9450
Chief Technology Officer:
Rajiv Rao . . . . . . . . . . . . . . . . . . . . . . . . . . . . . . . . . .518-486-9200
Chief General Counsel:
David Green . . . . . . . . . . . . . . . . . . . . . . . . . . . . . . . .518-408-2484
Acting Chief Data Officer:
John Rager
Director, Administration:
Theresa Papa . . . . . . . . . . . . . . . . . . . . . . . . . . . . . . .518-408-2484
Chief Information Security Officer:
Karen Sorady . . . . . . . . . . . . . . . . . . . . . . . . . . . . . . .518-242-5200

Director, Public Information:
Vacant . . . . . . . . . . . . . . . . . . . . . . . . . . . . . . . . . . . . .518-402-3899

## Children & Family Services, Office of
52 Washington Street
Rensselaer, NY 12144-2834
518-473-7793  Fax: 518-486-7550
e-mail: info@ocfs.ny.gov
Web site: ocfs.ny.gov

Commissioner:
Sheila Poole . . . . . . . . . . . . . . . . . . . . . . . . . . . . .518-473-8437
e-mail: info@ocfs.ny.gov
Assistant Commissioner, Communications:
Monica Mahaffey . . . . . . . . . . . . . . . . . . . . . . . . . . . . .518-473-7793
e-mail: info@ocfs.ny.gov
Associate Commissioner, Administration/Human Resources:
Mary Carli . . . . . . . . . . . . . . . . . . . . .518-486-6942 or 518-402-3211
Deputy Commissioner, Child Welfare & Community Service:
Lisa Ghartey Ogundimu . . . . . . . . . . . . . . . . . . . . . . .518-474-3377
Deputy Commissioner, Juvenile Justice & Opportunity for Youth:
Felicia Reid . . . . . . . . . . . . . . . . . . . . . . . . . . . . . . . . .518-473-1786
Associate Commissioner, Blind & Visually Handicapped Commission:
Brian Daniels . . . . . . . . . . . . . . . . . . . . . . . . . . . . . . .518-474-7812
e-mail: brian.daniels@ocfs.state.ny.us

## Council on Children & Families . . . . . . . . . . . . . . .fax: 518-473-2570
52 Washington Street, West Building, Suite 99, Rensselaer, NY 12144
518-474-5522 or 518-473-3652  Fax: 518-473-2570
e-mail: council@ccf.ny.gov
Web site: www.ccf.ny.gov
Executive Director:
Renée L Rider . . . . . . . . . . . . . . . . . . . . .518-473-3652/fax: 518-473-2570
e-mail: renee.rider@ccf.ny.gov
Deputy Director & Counsel:
Elana Marton . . . . . . . . . . . . . . . . . . . . .518-473-3652/fax: 518-473-2570
e-mail: elana.marton@ccf.ny.gov
Project Director, Head Start Collaboration:
Patricia Persell . . . . . . . . . . . . . . . . . . . . . . . . . . . . . .518-474-9352
e-mail: patricia.persell@ccf.ny.gov
Policy Analyst & Kids Count Director:
Cate Teuten Bohn

## Civil Service Department
Empire State Plaza, Agency Building One
9th Floor
Albany, NY 12239
518-457-2487 or 877-697-5627
e-mail: pio@cs.ny.gov
Web site: www.cs.ny.gov

Commissioner:
Lola W Brabham . . . . . . . . . . . . . . . . . . . . . . . . . . . . .518-457-2487
Assistant Commissioner, Strategic Planning and Management:
Vacant . . . . . . . . . . . . . . . . . . . . . . . . . . . . . . . . . . . . .518-457-2487
Deputy Commissioner, Operations:
Rebecca Corso . . . . . . . . . . . . . . . . . . . . . . . . . . . . . .518-473-9539
Deputy Commissioner, Administration:
Daquetta Jones
Special Counsel:
Marc Hannibal . . . . . . . . . . . . . . . . . . . . . . . . . . . . . .518-473-2624
Deputy Commissioner, Municipal and Local Government Services:
Joe Cavazos . . . . . . . . . . . . . . . . . . . . . . . . . . . . . . . .518-473-5022
Director, Financial Administration:
Dominique Choute . . . . . . . . . . . . . . . . . . . . . . . . . . . .518-473-2269
Director, Employee Benefits Division:
James DeWan . . . . . . . . . . . . . . . . . . . . . . . . . . . . . . .518-473-1977
Director, Human Resources & Administrative Planning:
Valerie Morrison . . . . . . . . . . . . . . . . . . . . . . . . . . . . .518-473-4306

*Offices and agencies generally appear in alphabetical order, except when specific order is requested by listee.*

Director, Communications:
   Jian Paolucci . . . . . . . . . . . . . . . . . . . . . . . . . . . . . . . . . . . 518-457-9375
   e-mail: pio@cs.state.ny.us

**Civil Service Commission**
   Web site: www.cs.ny.gov/commission
President:
   Vacant . . . . . . . . . . . . . . . . . . . . . . . . . . . . . . . . . . . . . . . 518-457-3701
Commissioner:
   Lola W Brabham . . . . . . . . . . . . . . . . . . . . . . . . . . . . . . . 518-473-6326
Commissioner:
   Vacant . . . . . . . . . . . . . . . . . . . . . . . . . . . . . . . . . . . . . . . 518-473-9539

**Consumer Protection, Division of**
One Commerce Plaza
99 Washington Aveue
Albany, NY 12231-0001
518-474-8583 or 800-697-1220  Fax: 518-473-9055
e-mail: info@dos.ny.gov
Web site: www.dos.ny.gov/consumerprotection

Executive Deputy Director:
   Aiesha Battle . . . . . . . . . . . . . . . . . . . . . . . . . . . . . . . . . . 518-474-2363

**Corrections & Community Supervision Department**
1220 Washington Avenue
Building 2, State Campus
Albany, NY 12226-2050
518-457-8126
Web site: www.doccs.ny.gov

Acting Commissioner:
   Anthony J Annucci . . . . . . . . . . . . . . . . . . 518-457-1748 or 518-457-8134
Assistant Commissioner & Executive Assistant:
   Melissa Coolidge . . . . . . . . . . . . . . . . . . . . . . . . . . . . . . 518-457-1281
Acting Deputy Commissioner, Administrative Services:
   Stephen Brandow . . . . . . . . . . . . . . . . . . . . . . . . . . . . . . 518-457-8188
Deputy Commissioner, Correctional Facility Operations:
   James O'Gorman . . . . . . . . . . . . . . . . . . . . . . . . . . . . . . 518-457-8138
Deputy Commissioner, Health Services Division/Chief Medical Officer:
   John Morely, MD . . . . . . . . . . . . . . . . . . . . . . . . . . . . . . 518-457-7073
Deputy Commissioner, Program Services:
   Jeffrey McKoy . . . . . . . . . . . . . . . . . . . . . . . . . . . . . . . . 518-457-5555
Public Information Officer:
   Thomas Mailey . . . . . . . . . . . . . . . . . . . . . . . . . . . . . . . . 518-457-8182

**Council on the Arts**
300 Park Avenue South
10th Floor
New York, NY 10010
212-459-8800
e-mail: info@arts.ny.gov
Web site: www.arts.ny.gov

Chair:
   Katherine Nicholls
Executive Director:
   Mara Manus . . . . . . . . . . . . . . . . . . . . . . . . . . . . . . . . . . 212-459-8808
   e-mail: mara.manus@arts.ny.gov
Deputy Director, Programs:
   Megan White . . . . . . . . . . . . . . . . . . . . . . . . . . . . . . . . . 212-459-8806
   e-mail: megan.white@arts.ny.gov
Director, Agency Operations/HR Liaison:
   Brenda K Brown . . . . . . . . . . . . . . . . . . . . . . . . . . . . . . 212-459-8827
   e-mail: brenda.brown@arts.ny.gov
Deputy Director, Operations & General Counsel:
   Abigail Young . . . . . . . . . . . . . . . . . . . . . . . . . . . . . . . . 212-459-8832
   e-mail: Abigail.Young@arts.ny.gov

Director, Compliance Unit:
   Tracy Hamilton . . . . . . . . . . . . . . . . . . . . . . . . . . . . . . . 212-459-8822
   e-mail: tracy.hamilton@arts.ny.gov
Manager, Information Technology Services:
   Lenn Savoca Ditman . . . . . . . . . . . . . . . . . . . . . . . . . . . 212-459-8810
   e-mail: lenn.ditman@arts.ny.gov
Director, Public Information:
   Ronni Reich . . . . . . . . . . . . . . . . . . . . . . . . . . . . . . . . . . 212-459-8859
   e-mail: ronni.reich@arts.ny.gov

**Criminal Justice Services, Division of**
80 South Swan Street
Albany, NY 12210
518-457-5837 or 800-262-3257  Fax: 518-457-3089
e-mail: InfoDCJS@dcjs.ny.gov
Web site: www.criminaljustice.ny.gov

Executive Deputy Commissioner:
   Michael C Green . . . . . . . . . . . . . . . . . . . . . . . . . . . . . . 518-457-1260
Deputy Commissioner, Program Development & Funding:
   Jeffrey Bender . . . . . . . . . . . . . . . . . . . . . . . . . . . . . . . . 518-457-8462
   e-mail: funding@dcjs.ny.gov
First Deputy Commissioner:
   Mark White . . . . . . . . . . . . . . . . . . . . . . . . . . . . . . . . . . 518-457-1260
Acting Deputy Commissioner & Counsel:
   Michael Flaherty . . . . . . . . . . . . . . . . . . . . . . . . . . . . . . 518-457-4181
Deputy Commissioner, Public Safety:
   Michael Wood . . . . . . . . . . . . . . . . . . . . . . . . . . . . . . . . 518-457-6985
Deputy Commissioner, Justice Research & Performance:
   Terry Salo . . . . . . . . . . . . . . . . . . . . . . . . . . . . . . . . . . . 518-457-7301
Director, Public Information:
   Janine Kava . . . . . . . . . . . . . . . . . . . . . . . . . . . . . . . . . . 518-457-8828
   e-mail: janine.kava@dcjs.ny.gov
Director, Finance:
   Brad Stevens . . . . . . . . . . . . . . . . . . . . . . . . . . . . . . . . . 518-457-6105
Director, Human Resources Management:
   Karen Davis . . . . . . . . . . . . . . . . . . . . . . . . . . . . . . . . . . 518-485-1704

**Developmental Disabilities Planning Council**
99 Washington Avenue
Suite 1230
Albany, NY 12210
518-486-7505 or 800-395-3372
e-mail: information@ddpc.ny.gov
Web site: www.ddpc.ny.gov

Chairperson:
   Vacant . . . . . . . . . . . . . . . . . . . . . . . . . . . . . . . . . . . . . . 800-395-3372
Vice Chairperson:
   Vacant . . . . . . . . . . . . . . . . . . . . . . . . . . . . . . . . . . . . . . 800-395-3372
Executive Director:
   Sheila M Carey . . . . . . . . . . . . . . . . . . . . . . . . . . . . . . . 518-486-7505
   e-mail: sheila.carey@ddpc.ny.gov

**Education Department**
State Education Building
89 Washington Avenue
Albany, NY 12234
518-474-3852
Web site: www.nysed.gov

Interim Commissioner & University President:
   Betty A Rosa . . . . . . . . . . . . . . . . . . . . . . . . . . . . . . . . . 518-474-5844
Executive Deputy Commissioner:
   Vacant . . . . . . . . . . . . . . . . . . . . . . . . . . . . . . . . . . . . . . 518-473-8381
Assistant Commissioner, Public Affairs:
   Emily DeSantis . . . . . . . . . . . . . . . . . . . . . . . . . . . . . . . 518-474-1201

*Offices and agencies generally appear in alphabetical order, except when specific order is requested by listee.*

Acting Counsel & Deputy Commissioner, Legal Affairs:
Aaron Baldwin . . . . . . . . . . . . . . . . . . . . . . . . . . . . . .518-474-6400
e-mail: legal@nysed.gov
Deputy Commissioner, Higher Education:
William Murphy . . . . . . . . . . . . . . . . . . . . . . . . . . . . . .518-486-3633
Deputy Commissioner, Cultural Education Office:
Mark Schaming. . . . . . . . . . . . . . . . . . . . . . . . . . . . . . .518-474-5976
Deputy Commissioner, Office of the Professions:
Sarah Benson . . . . . . . . . . . . . . . . . . . . . . . . . . . . . . .518-486-1765
Senior Deputy Commissioner, Office of P-12 Education Policy:
Kimberly Wilkins . . . . . . . . . . . . . . . . . . . . . . . . . . . . .518-474-3862
e-mail: nysedp12@nysed.gov
Deputy Commissioner, Adult Career & Continuing Education Services
(ACCES):
Kevin Smith . . . . . . . . . . . . . . . . . . . . . . . . . . . . . . . .518-474-2714
e-mail: accesadm@nysed.gov
Deputy Commissioner, Performance Improvement & Management Services:
Sharon Cates-Williams. . . . . . . . . . . . . . . . . . . . . . . . . .518-473-4706
Chief Financial Officer:
Phyllis Morris . . . . . . . . . . . . . . . . . . . . . . . . . . . . . . .518-474-7751

## Elections, State Board of
40 North Pearl Street
Suite 5
Albany, NY 12207-2729
518-474-6220 or 518-474-8100  Fax: 518-486-4068
e-mail: info@elections.ny.gov
Web site: www.elections.ny.gov

Co-Chair:
Peter S Kosinski . . . . . . . . . . . . . . . . . . . .518-474-8100 or 518-474-6236
Co-Chair:
Douglas A Kellner . . . . . . . . . . . . . . . . . . . . . . . . . . . .518-474-8100
Commissioner:
Andrew J Spano . . . . . . . . . . . . . . . . . . . . . . . . . . . . .518-474-8100
Commissioner:
Vacant. . . . . . . . . . . . . . . . . . . . . . . . . .518-474-8100 or 518-474-6236
Co-Executive Director:
Todd Valentine. . . . . . . . . . . . . . . . . . . .518-474-6336 or 518-474-6236
fax: 518-474-1008
Co-Executive Director:
Robert A Brehm . . . . . . . . . . . . . . . . . . . .518-474-6336 or 518-474-8100
fax: 518-474-1008
Special Counsel:
Kimberly A Galvin. . . . . . . . . . . . . . . . .518-474-6367 or 518-474-2063
fax: 518-486-6627
Administrative Officer:
Vacant . . . . . . . . . . . . . . . . . . . . . . . .518-474-6336/fax: 518-474-1008
Director, Election Operations:
Thomas E Connolly. . . . . . . . . . . . . . . .518-473-5086/fax: 518-486-4546
Director, Public Information:
John W Conklin. . . . . . . . . . . . . . . .518-474-1953/fax: 518-473-8315
e-mail: info@elections.ny.gov
Chief Enforcement Counsel:
Vacant. . . . . . . . . . . . . . . . . . . . . . . . . . . . . . . . . . .518-486-7858
e-mail: enforcement@elections.ny.gov

## Empire State Development Corporation
633 Third Avenue
Floor 37
New York, NY 10017
212-803-3100  Fax: 212-803-3131
Web site: www.esd.ny.gov

625 Broadway
Albany, NY 12245
518-292-5100

95 Perry Street
Suite 500
Buffalo, NY 14203
716-846-8200
Fax: 716-846-8260

President & CEO, Commissioner:
Eric Gertler. . . . . . . . . . . . . . . . . . . . .212-803-3700 or 518-292-5100
e-mail: president@esd.ny.gov
Chief Operating Officer & Deputy Commissioner:
Kevin Younis . . . . . . . . . . . . . . . . . . . . . . . . . . . . . .212-803-3100
Chief Financial Officer:
Elaine Kloss
Chief of Staff & EVP of State Marketing Strategy:
Richard Newman
Executive Vice President, Administration:
Ed Hamilton . . . . . . . . . . . . . . . . . . . . . . . . . . . . . .212-803-3700
Executive Vice President, Legal & General Counsel:
Elizabeth Fine. . . . . . . . . . . . . . . . . . . . . . . . . . . . . .212-803-3100

## Employee Relations, Governor's Office of
2 Empire State Plaza
Albany, NY 12223
518-473-3130  Fax: 518-486-7304
e-mail: info@goer.ny.gov
Web site: www.goer.ny.gov

Director:
Michael N Volforte . . . . . . . . . . . . . . . .518-474-6988/fax: 518-486-7304
Deputy Director, Contract Negotiations & Administration:
Vacant . . . . . . . . . . . . . . . . . . . . . . . .518-473-3130/fax: 518-486-7304
Deputy Counsel:
Amy Petragnani. . . . . . . . . . . . . . . . . . .518-474-4090/fax: 518-486-7304
Administrative Officer:
Dawn M LaPointe . . . . . . . . . . . . . . . . .518-473-3467/fax: 518-473-6725

## Environmental Conservation Department
625 Broadway
Albany, NY 12233-0001
518-402-8044
e-mail: contact@dec.ny.gov
Web site: www.dec.ny.gov

Commissioner:
Basil Seggos . . . . . . . . . . . . . . . . . . . .518-402-8545/fax: 518-402-8541
Executive Deputy Commissioner:
Judy Drabicki. . . . . . . . . . . . . . . . . . . .518-402-8560/fax: 518-402-9016
Deputy Commissioner & General Counsel:
Thomas Berkman. . . . . . . . . . . . . . . . . .518-402-8543/fax: 518-402-9018
Deputy Commissioner, Hearings & Mediation:
Louis Alexander . . . . . . . . . . . . . . . . . .518-402-8537/fax: 518-402-9016
Deputy Commissioner, Administration, Management, Budget & Operations:
Jeffrey Stefanko. . . . . . . . . . . . . . . . . .518-402-9401/fax: 518-402-9016
Deputy Commissioner, Public Protection & Regional Affairs:
Steve Smith . . . . . . . . . . . . . . . . . . . . .518-402-8549/fax: 518-402-9016
Deputy Commissioner, Remediation & Materials Management:
Martin Brand . . . . . . . . . . . . . . . . . . . .518-402-9401/fax: 518-402-9016
Deputy Commissioner, Water & Watershed Resources Office:
James Tierney . . . . . . . . . . . . . . . . . . .518-402-2794/fax: 518-402-8541
Deputy Commissioner, Public Affairs:
Erica Ringewald . . . . . . . . . . . . . . . . . .518-402-8000/fax: 518-402-9016
e-mail: pressoffice@dec.ny.gov
Deputy Commissioner, Air Resources, Climate Change & Energy:
Jared Snyder . . . . . . . . . . . . . . . . . . . .518-402-2794/fax: 518-402-9016

## General Services, Office of
Corning Tower
36th Floor

*Offices and agencies generally appear in alphabetical order, except when specific order is requested by listee.*

Empire State Plaza
Albany, NY 12242
518-474-3899
e-mail: comments@ogs.ny.gov
Web site: www.ogs.ny.gov

Commissioner:
  RoAnn Destito....................518-474-5991/fax: 518-486-9179
Executive Deputy Commissioner:
  Daniel Cunningham...........................518-473-6953
Deputy Commissioner, Administration & Operations:
  Eric S McShane..............................518-474-3199
Deputy Commissioner, Design & Construction:
  Margaret Larkin.............................518-474-0337
Deputy Chief Procurement Officer:
  Susan Filburn...............518-473-5294/fax: 518-474-2437
Deputy Commissioner, Legal Services & Counsel:
  Bradley Allen..............518-474-5988/fax: 518-473-4973
Director, Real Estate Planning & Development Group:
  James Sproat...............................518-474-4944
Director, Communications:
  Heather Groll...............518-474-5987/fax: 518-486-9179
  e-mail: heather.groll@ogs.ny.gov

## Health Department
Corning Tower
Empire State Plaza
Albany, NY 12237
518-474-2011 or 518-474-7354
e-mail: dohweb@health.ny.gov
Web site: www.health.ny.gov

Commissioner:
  Howard A Zucker, MD, JD.....................518-474-2011
Executive Deputy Commissioner:
  Lisa J Pino, MA, JD.........................518-474-2011
Assistant Commissioner, Governmental & External Affairs:
  Estibaliz Alonso............................518-473-1124
Deputy Health Cluster CIO:
  Linh Le
Deputy Commissioner, Office of Health Insurance Programs/NYS Health
  Executive Director:
  Donna Frescatore............................518-474-3018
General Counsel:
  Richard J Zahnleuter........................518-474-7553
Deputy Commissioner, Public Health:
  Vacant......................................518-473-0771
Director, Health Emergency Preparedness:
  Michael J Primeau...........................518-474-2893
Director, AIDS Institute:
  Johanne Morne, E, MS...........518-474-6399 or 212-417-5500
Director, Center for Community Health:
  Nora Yates..................................518-473-4371
Director, Family Health:
  Lauren Tobias...............................518-474-6968
Deputy Commissioner, Primary Care & Health Systems Management:
  Vacant......................................518-474-1686
Director, The Wadsworth Center:
  Vacant......................518-474-3157/fax: 518-474-3439
  e-mail: jill.taylor@health.ny.gov
Assistant Commissioner, Public Affairs:
  Gary Holmes.................................518-474-7354
Deputy Director, Governmental Affairs:
  Michelle Newman.........................518-474-7354 x1
Director, Public Information:
  Jonah Bruno.................................518-474-7354

## Homeland Security & Emergency Services, Division of
1220 Washington Avenue
Building 7A
Suite 710
Albany, NY 12242
518-242-5000  Fax: 518-322-4978
Web site: www.dhses.ny.gov

633 Third Avenue
32nd Floor
New York, NY 10017
212-867-7060

Commissioner:
  Patrick A Murphy............................518-242-5103
State Fire Administrator, Office of Fire Prevention and Control:
  Francis J Nerney, Jr........................518-474-6746
  e-mail: fire@dhses.ny.gov
Director, Office of Emergency Management:
  Matt Franklin..............518-292-2301/fax: 518-322-4978
Deputy Commissioner:
  Dan O'Hara
Director, Office of Interoperable & Emergency Communications:
  Michael Sprague............................518-242-8275
  e-mail: dhses.oiec@dhses.ny.gov
Public Information Officer:
  Kristin Devoe..............................518-242-5153

### Office of Counter Terrorism
  1220 Washington Avenue, Building 7A, Suite 710, Albany, NY 12226
  518-242-5000
  Web site: www.dhses.ny.gov
Public Safety Coordinator:
  Dan Albert..................................518-242-5000
Assistant Director, Infrastructure Protection:
  Brian Wright................................518-242-5000
Program Officer, Office of Counter Terrorism:
  Jennifer Margulies.........................518-242-5000

## Housing & Community Renewal, Division of
Hampton Plaza
38-40 State Street
Albany, NY 12207
866-ASK-DHCR or 212-480-6700  Fax: 866-275-3427
e-mail: hcrinfo@nyshcr.org
Web site: www.nyshcr.org

641 Lexington Avenue
New York, NY 10022
866-275-3427

535 Washington Street
Electric Tower
Suite 105
Buffalo, NY 14203
Fax:

Commissioner:
  RuthAnne Visnauskas
Executive Deputy Commissioner & Chief Operating Officer:
  Betsy Mallow...............................866-275-3427
President, Office of Housing Preservation:
  Mark Colon.................................866-275-3427
Senior Vice President, Multifamily Finance:
  Nicole Ferreira
  e-mail: OCRinfo@nyshcr.org
General Counsel:
  Linda Manley

*Offices and agencies generally appear in alphabetical order, except when specific order is requested by listee.*

Senior Vice President, Single Family & Community Development:
  Dina Levy
Chief of Staff:
  Gabriella Green

## Hudson River Valley Greenway
625 Broadway
4th Floor
Albany, NY 12207
518-473-3835
e-mail: hrvg@hudsongreenway.ny.gov
Web site: www.hudsongreenway.ny.gov

### Greenway Conservancy for the Hudson River Valley
Chairman:
  Kevin M Burke . . . . . . . . . . . . . . . . . . . . . . . . . . . . . . . .518-473-3835
Executive Director:
  Scott Keller . . . . . . . . . . . . . . . . . . . . . . . . . . . . . . . . . .518-473-3835

### Hudson River Valley Greenway Communities Council
Council Chair:
  Barnabas McHenry, Esq. . . . . . . . . . . . . . . . . . . . . . .518-473-3835
Executive Director:
  Scott Keller . . . . . . . . . . . . . . . . . . . . . . . . . . . . . . . . . .518-473-3835

## Human Rights, State Division of
1 Fordham Plaza
4th Floor
Bronx, NY 10458
718-741-8400 or 888-392-3644  Fax: 718-741-8318
e-mail: infobronx@dhr.ny.gov
Web site: www.dhr.ny.gov

Interim Commissioner:
  Johnathan J Smith . . . . . . . . . . . . . . . . . . . . . . . . . . . .718-741-8326
Chief Administrative Law Judge:
  Lilliana Estrella-Castillo . . . . . . . . . . . . . . . . . . . . . . . .718-741-8342
Deputy Commissioner, Regional Affairs & Federal Programs:
  Gina N Martinez . . . . . . . . . . . . . . . . . . . . . . . . . . . . . .718-741-8324
Deputy Commissioner, Enforcement:
  Melissa Franco . . . . . . . . . . . . . . . . . . . . . . . . . . . . . . .718-741-8326
Director, Brooklyn Region:
  William Lamot . . . . . . . . . . . . . . . . . . . . . . . . . . . . . . .718-722-2385
  e-mail: infobrooklyn@dhr.ny.gov
General Counsel:
  Caroline Downey . . . . . . . . . . . . . . . . . . . . . . . . . . . . .718-741-8398
Director, External Relations:
  Vacant . . . . . . . . . . . . . . . . . . . . . . . . . . . . . . . . . . . . . .718-741-8400

## Inspector General (NYS), Office of the
Empire State Plaza
Building 2
16th Floor
Albany, NY 12223
518-474-1010 or 212-635-3150  Fax: 518-486-3745
Web site: www.ig.ny.gov

61 Broadway
Suite 2100
New York, NY 10006
212-635-3150
Fax: 212-809-1630

State Inspector General:
  Letizia Tagliafierro . . . . . . . . . . . . . . . . . .212-635-3150 or 518-474-1010
  e-mail: inspector.general@ig.ny.gov
Executive Deputy Inspector General:
  Spencer Freedman . . . . . . . . . . . . . . . . . .212-635-3150 or 518-474-1010

Special Deputy Inspector General:
  Philip Foglia . . . . . . . . . . . . . . . . . . . . . . . . . . . . . . . . .212-635-3150
Special Deputy, Communications & External Affairs:
  Vacant . . . . . . . . . . . . . . . . . . . . . . . . . . . .518-474-1010 or 212-635-3150

## Insurance Fund (NYS)
One Watervliet Avenue Ext
Albany, NY 12206-1629
518-437-6400
Web site: www.nysif.com

199 Church Street
New York, NY 10007-1100
212-587-5435

Executive Director & CEO:
  Eric Madoff . . . . . . . . . . . . . . . . . . . . . . . . . . . . . . . . .518-437-5220
Chief Operating Officer & Deputy Executive Director:
  Shirley Stark
Chief Financial Officer:
  Willaim Gratrix
General Attorney:
  Tanisha Edwards, Esq
Director, Administration:
  Patricia Carroll

### Insurance Fund Board of Commissioners
Chair:
  Kenneth R Theobalds . . . . . . . . . . . . . . . .518-437-6400 or 518-437-5220
Vice Chair:
  Barry Swidler . . . . . . . . . . . . . . . . . . . . . . .518-437-6400 or 518-437-5220

## Labor Department
W.A. Harriman Campus
Building 12
Albany, NY 12240
518-457-9000 or 888-469-7365  Fax: 518-457-6908
e-mail: nysdol@labor.ny.gov
Web site: www.labor.ny.gov

Commissioner:
  Roberta Reardon . . . . . . . . . . . . . . . . . . . . . . . . . . . . .518-457-9000
Executive Deputy Commissioner:
  Nathaalie Carey . . . . . . . . . . . . . . . . . . . . . . . . . . . . . .518-457-4318
Acting Counsel:
  Jill Archambault
Acting Deputy Commissioner, Administration:
  Jack Dougherty
Acting Associate Deputy Commissioner, Employment Security:
  Lars Thompson
Deputy Commissioner, Workforce Development:
  Karen Coleman . . . . . . . . . . . . . . . . . . . . . . . . . . . . . .518-457-4317
Acting Deputy Commissioner, Worker Protection:
  Milan Bhatt
Associate Commissioner, Communications:
  Peter Brancato . . . . . . . . . . . . . . . . . . . . . . . . . . . . . . .518-457-5519

## Law Department
28 Liberty Street
New York, NY 10005
212-416-8000 or 800-771-7755
Web site: www.ag.ny.gov

State Capitol
Albany, NY 12224-0341
518-776-2000
Fax: 518-650-9401

*Offices and agencies generally appear in alphabetical order, except when specific order is requested by listee.*

Attorney General:
    Letitia James..........................212-416-8000 or 518-776-2000
Chief of Staff:
    Ibrahim Khan ...................................................212-416-8050
Chief Operating Officer:
    Jonathan Pinn ..................................................212-416-8050
Solicitor General:
    Barbara Underwood ...............212-416-8016 or 518-776-2002
Chief Deputy Attorney General, Criminal Justice:
    José Maldonado ................................................212-416-8050
Executive Deputy Attorney General, Economic Justice:
    Chris D'Angelo.................................................212-416-8050
Chief Deputy Attorney General, Social Justice:
    Meghan Faux ...................................................212-416-8050
Executive Deputy Attorney General, Regional Offices:
    Vacant .............................................................716-853-8451
Executive Deputy Attorney General, State Counsel:
    Orelia Merchant ...............................................212-416-8050
Director, Public Affairs & Press Secretary:
    Nicholas Paolucci ..................212-416-8060/fax: 212-416-6005
    e-mail: nyag.pressoffice@ag.ny.gov

## New York State Gaming Commission
1 Broadway Center
P.O. Box 7500
Schenectady, NY 12301-7500
518-388-3300
e-mail: info@gaming.ny.gov
Web site: www.gaming.ny.gov

Executive Director:
    Robert Williams ...............................................518-388-3400
General Counsel:
    Edmund Burns ..................................................518-388-3408
Director, Lottery Division:
    Gweneth Dean....................................................518-388-3352
Director, Communications:
    Brad Maione.....................................................518-388-3415
Gaming Commissioner:
    John A Crotty ...................................................518-388-3400
Gaming Commissioner:
    Peter J Moschetti, Jr ..........................................518-388-3400
Gaming Commissioner:
    John J Poklemba ...............................................518-388-3400
Gaming Commissioner & Chair:
    Barry Sample.....................................................518-388-3400
Gaming Commissioner:
    Jerry Skurnik....................................................518-388-3400

## Mental Health, Office of
44 Holland Avenue
Albany, NY 12229
518-474-4403 or 800-597-8481
Web site: www.omh.ny.gov

Commissioner:
    Ann Marie T Sullivan, MD.........................518-474-4403
Executive Deputy Commissioner:
    Christopher Tavella, PhD ...........518-474-7056/fax: 518-473-4690
Deputy Commissioner & General Counsel:
    Mark Noordsy.....................................................518-474-1331
Chief Medical Officer:
    Thomas Smith, MD.............................212-330-1650 x 360
Deputy Commissioner & Chief Fiscal Officer:
    Emil Slane .......................................................518-474-3631
Director, Center for Human Resource Management:
    J Lynn Heath ......................518-474-0171/fax: 518-474-7536
Director, Public Information:
    James Plastiras..................518-474-6540/fax: 518-473-3456

## NYS Office for People with Developmental Disabilities
44 Holland Avenue
Albany, NY 12229
866-946-9733 or 518-473-1997
Web site: www.opwdd.ny.gov

Commissioner:
    Theodore Kastner ..............................................518-473-1997
Executive Deputy Commissioner:
    Roger Bearden ......................518-473-1997 or 518-474-9897
General Counsel:
    Joshua Olsen .....................................................518-473-1873
Director, Audit Services:
    James Nellegar ..................................................518-474-4376
Director, Advocacy Services:
    Dixie Yonkers....................................................518-402-4213
Director, Communications & Public Affairs:
    Vacant.............................................................518-474-6601
    e-mail: communications.office@opwdd.ny.gov

## Military & Naval Affairs, Division of
330 Old Niskayuna Road
Latham, NY 12110-3514
518-786-4581 or 518-489-6188  Fax: 518-786-4649
e-mail: ng.ny.nyarng.list.dmnawm@mail.mil
Web site: www.dmna.ny.gov

Adjutant General:
    Major Gen Raymond F Shields Jr ......................518-786-4502
Chief of Staff:
    Col Steven Rowe ..............................................518-786-4502
Commander, Army National Guard:
    Col David Piwowarski
Legal Counsel:
    Vacant.............................................................518-786-4541
Director, Governmental & Community Affairs:
    James M Huelle.................................................518-786-4580
Director, Public Affairs:
    Eric Durr .......................518-786-4581/fax: 518-786-4649
Director, Budget & Finance:
    Robert A Martin ...............................................518-786-4514

## Motor Vehicles Department
6 Empire State Plaza
Albany, NY 12228
518-486-9786
Web site: dmv.ny.gov

Commissioner:
    Mark JF Schroeder
Executive Deputy Commissioner:
    Theresa L Egan ....................518-474-0846/fax: 518-474-0712
Deputy Commissioner, Administration:
    Gregory J Kline...................518-474-6876/fax: 518-474-0712
Deputy Commissioner & Counsel:
    Timothy B Lennon .................518-473-1965/fax: 518-474-0712
Deputy Commissioner, Operations & Customer Service:
    Heriberto Barbot.................518-474-0846/fax: 518-474-0712
Deputy Commissioner, Policy, Safety & Driver Licensing:
    Janet Ho ..........................................................518-474-0846
Deputy Commissioner, Compliance:
    Thomas P Higgins................................................518-474-8328
Director, Driver Safety Programs:
    Vacant.............................................................518-473-7197
Assistant Commissioner, Communications & Marketing:
    Lisa Koumjian .....................518-473-7000/fax: 518-473-1930

*Offices and agencies generally appear in alphabetical order, except when specific order is requested by listee.*

## NYSTAR - Division of Science, Technology & Innovation
633 Third Avenue
37th Floor
New York, NY 10017
518-292-5700  Fax: 518-292-5794
e-mail: NYSTARSupport@esd.ny.gov
Web site: www.esd.ny.gov/NYSTAR

625 Broadway
Albany, NY 12245
518-292-5100

95 Perry Street
Suite 500
Buffalo, NY 14203
716-846-8200

Director:
  Matthew Watson.................................518-292-5700
Executive Vice President, Public Affairs & Strategic Initiatives:
  Kay Wright ....................518-292-5700/fax: 518-292-5798
Executive Vice President, Legal & General Counsel:
  Elizabeth Fine.................................518-292-5700

## Parks, Recreation & Historic Preservation, NYS Office of
625 Broadway
Albany, NY 12207
518-474-0456  Fax: 518-474-4492
Web site: www.parks.ny.gov

Commissioner:
  Erik Kulleseid.................................518-474-0443
Executive Deputy Commissioner:
  Tom Alworth
  fax: 518-474-4492
Deputy Commissioner, Finance & Administration:
  Vacant
Director, Operations & Programs:
  Marc Talluto.................................518-474-0440
Deputy Commissioner, Historic Preservation:
  Daniel Mackay.................................518-268-2171
Special Assistant to the Commissioner:
  Andy Fyfe.................................518-474-1748
General Counsel:
  Paul Laudato.................................518-474-0414
Park Police/Director, Law Enforcement:
  Vacant.................518-474-4029 or 845-786-2781
  fax: 518-408-1032
Public Information Officer:
  Dan Keefe.................................518-486-1868
Deputy Public Information Officer:
  Brian Nearing.................................518-486-1868

## Parole Board, The
Corrections & Community Supervision
1220 Washington Avenue
Building 2
Albany, NY 12226
518-473-9548  Fax: 518-473-6037
Web site: doccs.ny.gov

Acting Commissioner:
  Anthony J Annucci.................518-457-1748 or 518-457-8134
Deputy Commissioner & Counsel:
  Vacant.................................518-485-9613
Director, Public Information:
  Thomas Mailey.................................518-457-8182

Chairwoman, Board of Parole:
  Tina M Stanford, Esq.............518-473-9548 or 518-473-9400
Director, Internal Operations:
  Vacant.................................518-408-3473

## Prevention of Domestic Violence, Office for the
80 South Swan Street
11th Floor, Room 1157
Albany, NY 12210
518-457-5800  Fax: 518-457-5810
e-mail: opdvpublicinfo@opdv.ny.gov
Web site: www.opdv.ny.gov

90 Church Street
13th Floor
New York, NY 10007
212-417-4477
Fax: 212-417-4972

Executive Director:
  Kelli Owens ....................518-457-5800 or 518-457-5916
Director, NYC Program:
  Sujata Warrier.................212-417-4477/fax: 518-417-4972
Counsel:
  Ellen Schell.................................518-457-5757
Director, Bureau of Public Awareness & Prevention:
  Suzanne Cecala.................................518-457-5744
  e-mail: suzanne.cecala@opdv.ny.gov

## Public Employment Relations Board
Empire State Plaza
Agency Bldg 2, 18th & 20th Floors
PO Box 2074
Albany, NY 12220-0074
518-457-2578  Fax: 518-457-2664
e-mail: perbinfo@perb.ny.gov
Web site: www.perb.ny.gov

55 Hanson Place
Suite 700
Brooklyn, NY 11217
718-722-4545

The Electric Tower
535 Washington Street
Suite 302
Buffalo, NY 14203
716-847-3449

Chair:
  John Wirenius.................................518-457-2578
Deputy Chair:
  Sarah G Coleman.................................518-457-2578
Executive Director, Office of Administration:
  Jonathan O'Rourke.................................518-457-2676
General Counsel:
  David P Quinn.................................518-457-2678
Director, Conciliation Office:
  Kevin B Flanigan.................................518-457-2690
Director, Employment Practices & Representation:
  Melanie Wlasuk.................................518-457-5973

## Public Service Commission
NYS Dept of Public Service
Empire State Plaza
Building 3
Albany, NY 12223-1350

*Offices and agencies generally appear in alphabetical order, except when specific order is requested by listee.*

518-474-7080  Fax: 518-474-2838
Web site: www.dps.ny.gov

Chair:
  John B Rhodes
Commissioner:
  Diane X Burman . . . . . . . . . . . . . . . . . .518-408-1978/fax: 518-473-2838
Commissioner:
  Tracey A Edwards. . . . . . . . . . . . . . . . .518-474-2523/fax: 518-473-2838
Commissioner:
  John B Howard
Secretary to the Commission:
  Michelle L Phillips . . . . . . . . . . . . . . .518-474-6530/fax: 518-474-9842
  e-mail: secretary@dps.ny.gov
General Counsel:
  Robert Rosenthal. . . . . . . . . . . . . . . . . . . . . . . . . . . . . .518-474-2510
Acting Director, Consumer Services Office:
  Bruce Alch . . . . . . . . . . . . . . . . . . . . . . . . . . . . . . . . .212-837-7244
Director, Electric, Gas & Water:
  Tammy Mitchell . . . . . . . . . . . . . . . . . . . . . . . . . . . . . .518-486-2483
Director, Office of Administration:
  Donald Duvall . . . . . . . . . . . . . . . . .518-474-2508/fax: 518-474-0413
Director, Telecommunications:
  Debra LaBelle . . . . . . . . . . . . . . . . .518-474-1668/fax: 518-474-5616
Director, Accounting & Finance:
  Doris Stout . . . . . . . . . . . . . . . . . . .518-474-4508 or 212-417-2136
Director, Public Affairs:
  James Denn . . . . . . . . . . . . . . . . . . .518-474-7080/fax: 518-473-2838
  e-mail: james.denn@dps.ny.gov

## Real Property Tax Services, Office of

NYS Dept of Tax & Finance
WA Harriman State Campus
Building 8A
Albany, NY 12227
518-457-7377 or 518-591-5232
Web site: www.tax.ny.gov

Commissioner:
  Michael R Schmidt. . . . . . . . . . . . . . . .518-530-4081 or 518-474-2982
Secretary of Board & Assistant Deputy Commissioner:
  Vacant
State Board Member:
  Scott C Becker . . . . . . . . . . . . . . . . . .518-474-3793 or 518-591-5232
State Board Member:
  Samuel J Casella. . . . . . . . . . . . . . . . .518-474-3793 or 518-591-5232
State Board Member (Chair):
  Matthew Rand . . . . . . . . . . . . . . . . . .518-474-3793 or 518-591-5232

## State Comptroller, Office of the

110 State Street
15th Floor
Albany, NY 12236
518-474-4044  Fax: 518-473-3004
e-mail: contactus@osc.state.ny.us
Web site: www.osc.state.ny.us

59 Maiden Lane
New York, NY 10038
212-383-1600

State Comptroller:
  Thomas P DiNapoli . . . . . . . . . . . . . . .518-474-4044 or 212-383-1600
First Deputy Comptroller:
  Pete Grannis. . . . . . . . . . . . . . . . . . . .518-474-2909 or 212-681-4469
Chief of Staff:
  Shawn Thompson . . . . . . . . . . . . . . . . . . . . . . . . . . . . . .518-474-4044
Chief Information Officer:
  Robert Loomis . . . . . . . . . . . . . . . . . . . . . . . . . . . . . . .518-486-4349

Deputy Comptroller, Diversity Programs:
  Nancy Hernandez
Director, Communications:
  Jennifer Freeman . . . . . . . . . . . . . . . . .518-474-4015 or 212-383-2501
  e-mail: jfreeman@osc.state.ny.us
Deputy Comptroller, Payroll, Accounting & Revenue Services:
  David Hasso
Deputy Comptroller, Human Resources:
  Karim Adeen-Hasan . . . . . . . . . . . . . . . . . . . . . . . . . . . .518-474-5512
Inspector General, Internal Audit:
  Stephen Hamilton . . . . . . . . . . . . . . . . . . . . . . . . . . . . .518-408-4906
General Counsel:
  Nelson Sheingold . . . . . . . . . . . . . . . . . . . . . . . . . . . . . .518-474-3444
Executive Deputy Comptroller, Operations:
  John Traylor . . . . . . . . . . . . . . . . . . . . . . . . . . . . . . . . .518-402-4103
Deputy Comptroller, City of New York:
  Ken Bleiwas . . . . . . . . . . . . . . . . . . . . . . . . . . . . . . . . .212-383-3900
  e-mail: osdc@osc.state.ny.us
Deputy Comptroller, Budget & Policy Analysis:
  Robert Ward . . . . . . . . . . . . . . . . . . . . . . . . . . . . . . . . .518-473-4333
Assistant Comptroller, Intergovernmental & Community Affairs:
  Erin Stevens. . . . . . . . . . . . . . . . . . .518-402-3234/fax: 518-408-3852

## State Department

One Commerce Plaza
99 Washington Avenue
Albany, NY 12231-0001
518-474-4750  Fax: 518-474-4597
e-mail: info@dos.ny.gov
Web site: www.dos.ny.gov

123 William Street
New York, NY 10038-3804
212-417-5800
Fax: 212-417-2383

Secretary of State:
  Rossana Rosado . . . . . . . . . . . . . . . . .518-486-9844 or 212-417-5800
First Deputy Secretary of State:
  Daniel Shapiro . . . . . . . . . . . . . . . . . . . . . . . . . . . . . . .518-474-4750
Executive Deputy Secretary of State:
  Brendan C Hughes . . . . . . . . . . . . . . . . . . . . . . . . . . . . .518-474-0050
General Counsel:
  Linda Baldwin . . . . . . . . . . . . . . . . . .518-474-6740/fax: 518-473-9211
Deputy Secretary, Licensing:
  Charles Fields . . . . . . . . . . . . . . . . . . . . . . . . . . . . . . . .518-473-2728
Deputy Secretary of State, Local Government Services:
  Mark Pattison. . . . . . . . . . . . . . . . . .518-473-3355/fax: 518-474-6572
  e-mail: mark.pattison@dos.ny.gov
Deputy Secretary, Communications & Community Affairs:
  Vacant . . . . . . . . . . . . . . . . . . . . . . .518-486-9846/fax: 518-474-4765
  e-mail: info@dos.state.ny.us

## State Police, Division of

1220 Washington Avenue
Building 22
Albany, NY 12226-2252
518-457-2180 or 518-457-6811
e-mail: nyspmail@troopers.ny.gov
Web site: www.troopers.ny.gov

Superintendent:
  Keith M Corlett. . . . . . . . . . . . . . . . . . . . . . . . . . . . . . .518-457-6721
First Deputy Superintendent:
  Kevin P Bruen . . . . . . . . . . . . . . . . . .518-457-6711/fax: 518-485-7505
First Deputy Counsel:
  Steve Hogan. . . . . . . . . . . . . . . . . . . .518-457-6137/fax: 518-485-1164
Deputy Superintendent, Administration:
  Christopher Fiore . . . . . . . . . . . . . . . . . . . . . . . . . . . . . .518-457-6622

*Offices and agencies generally appear in alphabetical order, except when specific order is requested by listee.*

Deputy Superintendent, Employee Relations:
Steven G James . . . . . . . . . . . . . . . . . . . . .518-457-3572/fax: 518-485-7505
Deputy Superintendent, Professional Standards Bureau:
Patrick J Regan . . . . . . . . . . . . . . . . . . . . . . . . . . . . . . .518-457-6621
Deputy Superintendent, Internal Affairs:
Scott M Crosier. . . . . . . . . . . . . . . . . . . . . . . . . . . . . . .518-485-6018
Director, Public Information:
Beau Duffy . . . . . . . . . . . . .518-457-2180/fax: 518-485-7818
e-mail: pio@troopers.ny.gov

## Tax Appeals, Division of
Agency Building 1
Empire State Plaza
Albany, NY 12223
518-266-3000  Fax: 518-271-0886
e-mail: dta@dta.ny.gov
Web site: www.dta.ny.gov

### Tax Appeals Tribunal
President & Commissioner:
Roberta Moseley Nero . . . . . . . . . . . . . . . . . . . . . . . . .518-266-3050
Commissioner:
Anthony Giardina . . . . . . . . . . . . . . . . . . . . . . . . . . . .518-266-3050
Commissioner:
Deirdre K Scozzafava. . . . . . . . . . . . . . . . . . . . . . . . . .518-266-3050
Counsel:
Timothy J Alston. . . . . . . . . . . . . . . . . . . . . . . . . . . . .518-266-3052
Secretary to the Tribunal:
Jean A McDonnell . . . . . . . . . . . . . . . . . . . . . . . . . . . .518-266-3036

### Administrative Law Judges & Officers
Supervising Administrative Law Judge:
Herbert M Friedman, Jr. . . . . . . . . . . . . . . . . . . . . . . . .518-266-3000
Presiding Officer:
Vacant . . . . . . . . . . . . . . . . . . . . . . . . . . . . . . . . . . .518-266-3000

## Taxation & Finance Department
W.A. Harriman Campus
Building 9
Albany, NY 12227
518-457-4242 or 518-457-2244  Fax: 518-457-2486
Web site: www.tax.ny.gov

Commissioner:
Michael R Schmidt. . . . . . . . . . . . . . . . . . . . . . . . . . .518-457-2244
Executive Deputy Commissioner:
Andrew D Morris . . . . . . . . . . . . . . .518-530-4444 or 518-530-5000
Deputy Commissioner & Counsel:
Amanda Hiller . . . . . . . . . . . . . . . .518-457-3746 or 518-530-5300
fax: 518-457-8247
Deputy Commissioner & State Treasurer:
Christopher Curtis . . . . . . . . . . . . . . .518-474-4250/fax: 518-402-4118
Deputy Commissioner, Criminal Investigations:
Argi O'Leary. . . . . . . . . . . . . . . . . . . . . . . . . . . . . . .518-530-5348
Deputy Commissioner, Tax Policy Analysis:
Scott Palladino . . . . . . . . . . . . . . . .518-457-4357 or 518-530-5344
Deputy Commissioner, Processing & Taxpayer Services:
Michael Shollar. . . . . . . . . . . . . . . . . . . . . . . . . . . . .518-530-5320
Chief Fiscal Officer & Budget/Management Analysis:
Eric Mostert . . . . . . . . . . . . . . . . .518-485-5080 or 518-530-4000
Director, Public Information:
Geoffrey Gloak . . . . . . . . . . . . . . . . . . . . . . . . . . . . .518-457-7377

## Temporary & Disability Assistance, Office of
40 North Pearl Street
Albany, NY 12243
518-473-1090 or 518-474-9516  Fax: 518-486-6255
e-mail: nyspio@otda.ny.gov
Web site: www.otda.ny.gov

Commissioner:
Michael P Hein . . . . . . . . . . . . . . . . .518-474-4152/fax: 518-486-6255
Executive Deputy Commissioner:
Barbara C Guinn. . . . . . . . . . . . . . . . . . . . . . . . . . . . .518-474-9425
Deputy Commissioner, Child Support Services:
Eileen Stack . . . . . . . . . . . . . . . . . . . . . . . . . . . . . . .518-474-9425
Deputy Commissioner, Administrative Services Division:
Eric Schwenzfeier. . . . . . . . . . . . . . . . . . . . . . . . . . . .518-473-3912
Deputy Commissioner, Shelter Oversight & Compliance Division:
Cheryl Contento . . . . . . . . . . . . . . . . . . . . . . . . . . . .518-486-4040
Deputy Commissioner, Housing Refugee Services & Disability
Determinations:
Linda Glassman . . . . . . . . . . . . . . . . . . . . . . . . . . . .518-486-1012
Deputy Commissioner, Office of Administrative Hearings:
Roy Esnard . . . . . . . . . . . . . . . . . . . . . . . . . . . . . . .718-923-4334
General Counsel:
Krista Rock . . . . . . . . . . . . . . . . . . . . . . . . . . . . . . .518-474-9502
Director, Intergovernmental Affairs:
Judi West. . . . . . . . . . . . . . . . . . . . . . . . . . . . . . . . .518-474-7420
Director, Public Information:
Anthony Farmer. . . . . . . . . . . . . . . .518-474-9516/fax: 518-486-6935
e-mail: nyspio@otda.ny.gov

## Transportation Department
50 Wolf Road
Albany, NY 12232
518-457-6195  Fax: 518-457-5583
Web site: www.dot.ny.gov

Commissioner:
Marie Therese Dominguez. . . . . . . . . . . . . . . . . . . . . . .518-457-4422
Assistant Commissioner, Operations & Asset Management:
Sam Zhou . . . . . . . . . . . . . . . . . . . . . . . . . . . . . . . .518-457-9684
Chief Counsel, Legal Affairs Division:
Jan McLachlan . . . . . . . . . . . . . . . . . . . . . . . . . . . . .518-457-2411
Executive Deputy Commissioner, Policy & Planning Division:
Ron Epstein. . . . . . . . . . . . . . . . . . . . . . . . . . . . . . .518-457-2320
Director, Administrative Services Division:
Grace Boss . . . . . . . . . . . . . . . . . . . . . . . . . . . . . . .518-457-6300
Director, Audit:
Theresa Vottis. . . . . . . . . . . . . . . . . . . . . . . . . . . . . .518-457-1590
Chief Engineer, Engineering Division:
Nicolas Choubah. . . . . . . . . . . . . . . . . . . . . . . . . . . .518-457-4430
Director, Communications Office:
Joseph Morrissey . . . . . . . . . . . . . . . . . . . . . . . . . . . .518-457-6400

## Veterans' Affairs, Division of
2 Empire State Plaza
17th Floor
Albany, NY 12223
518-474-6114 or 888-838-7697  Fax: 518-473-0379
e-mail: dvainfo@veterans.ny.gov
Web site: www.veterans.ny.gov

Director:
Vacant. . . . . . . . . . . . . . . . . . . . . . . . . . . . . . . . . . .518-474-6114
Executive Deputy Director:
Joel Evans . . . . . . . . . . . . . . . . . . . . . . . . . . . . . . . .518-474-6114
Secretary to the Director:
Mary Quay . . . . . . . . . . . . . . . . . . . . . . . . . . . . . . . .518-474-6114
e-mail: m.quay@veterans.ny.gov
Deputy Director, VA Programs:
Benjamin Pomerance . . . . . . . . . . . . . . . . . . . . . . . . .518-474-6114
Counsel:
Jonathan Fishbein . . . . . . . . . . . . . . . . . . . . . . . . . . .518-474-6114
Deputy Director, Eastern Region:
Vacant. . . . . . . . . . . . . . . . . . . . . . . . . . . . . . . . . . .718-722-2584
Deputy Director, Western Region:
Vacant. . . . . . . . . . . . . . . . . . . . . . . . . . . . . . . . . . .716-847-3414

*Offices and agencies generally appear in alphabetical order, except when specific order is requested by listee.*

## Victim Services, Office of
55 Hanson Place
10th Floor
Brooklyn, NY 11217
718-923-4325 or 800-247-8035  Fax: 718-923-4347
Web site: www.ovs.ny.gov

Alfred E Smith Building
80 S Swan Street
2nd Floor
Albany, NY 12210
518-457-8727
Fax: 518-457-8658

Director:
    Elizabeth Cronin, Esq . . . . . . . . . . . . . . . . . . . . . . . . . . . . . 518-485-5719
General Counsel/Legal Unit:
    John Watson . . . . . . . . . . . . . . . . . . . . 518-457-8066/fax: 518-457-8658
Deputy Director, Administration:
    Virginia Miller . . . . . . . . . . . . . . . . . . . . . . . . . . . . . . . . . . . 518-457-8003
Grants & Victim Assistance Programs:
    Chet Fiske . . . . . . . . . . . . . . . . . . . . . . . . . . . . . . . . . . . . . . 518-457-5001
Director, Public Information:
    Janine Kava . . . . . . . . . . . . . . . . . . . . . . . . . . . . . . . . . . . . . 518-457-8828
    e-mail: janine.kava@dcjs.ny.gov
Deputy Director, Claims:
    Maureen Fahy . . . . . . . . . . . . . . . . . . . . . . . . . . . . . . . . . . . . 518-457-8050

## Welfare Inspector General, Office of NYS
Empire State Plaza
Agency Bldg 2
16th Floor
Albany, NY 12223
518-474-1010 or 800-367-4448  Fax: 518-486-3745
e-mail: inspector.general@ig.ny.gov
Web site: www.owig.ny.gov

Welfare Inspector General:
    Letizia Tagliafierro . . . . . . . . . . . . . . . . . . 212-635-3150 or 518-474-1010
Chief Investigator:
    Joseph Bucci . . . . . . . . . . . . . . . . . . . . . . . 718-923-4290 or 518-474-1010
Confidential Assistant/Office Manager:
    Joy Quiles . . . . . . . . . . . . . . . . . . . . . . . . . 718-923-4290 or 518-474-1010
    fax: 718-923-4310

## Workers' Compensation Board
328 State Street
Schenectady, NY 12305-2318
518-408-0469 or 877-632-4996  Fax: 518-473-1415
e-mail: general_information@wcb.ny.gov
Web site: www.wcb.ny.gov

Executive Director:
    MaryBeth Woods . . . . . . . . . . . . . . . . . . . . . . . . . . . . . . . . . 518-408-0469
Chair, Board of Commissioners:
    Clarissa M Rodriguez . . . . . . . . . . . . . . . 518-408-0469/fax: 518-473-1415
Vice Chair:
    Freida Foster . . . . . . . . . . . . . . . . . . . . . 518-408-0469/fax: 518-473-1415
Secretary to the Board:
    Kim McCarroll . . . . . . . . . . . . . . . . . . . . . . . . . . . . . . . . . . . 518-402-6070
Chief, Security:
    Sylvio Mantello . . . . . . . . . . . . . . . . . . . 518-486-0373/fax: 518-402-6100
General Counsel:
    David Wertheim . . . . . . . . . . . . . . . . . . . 518-486-9564/fax: 518-402-0113
    e-mail: officeofgeneralcounsel@wcb.ny.gov
Director, Public Information:
    Melissa Stewart . . . . . . . . . . . . . . . . . . . 518-408-0469/fax: 518-473-1415
    e-mail: publicinfo@wcb.ny.gov
Advocate for Injured Workers:
    Vacant . . . . . . . . . . . . . . . . . . . . . . . . . . 800-580-6665 or 518-474-8182
    fax: 518-486-7510
    e-mail: advinjwkr@wcb.ny.gov
Fraud Inspector General:
    Vacant . . . . . . . . . . . . . . . . . . . . . . . . . . . . . . . . . . . . . . . . . 800-367-4448

*Offices and agencies generally appear in alphabetical order, except when specific order is requested by listee.*

# LEGISLATIVE BRANCH SENATE

*Members of the Senate welcome e-mail correspondence from the public. They may reply by e-mail, or by mail when more extensive follow-up is necessary. Please include both an e-mail and mailing address in all correspondence. Biographies of Senate Members appear in a separate section in the back of the book.*

## STATE SENATE LEADERSHIP

**State Capitol**
**Albany, NY 12247**
**Web site: www.nysenate.gov**

### ADMINISTRATION

**Alejandra N Paulino** . . . . . . . . . . . . . . . 518-455-2051/fax: 518-455-3332
*Title:* Secretary of the Senate

**Michelle Cameron** . . . . . . . . . . . . . . . . . 518-455-2201/fax: 518-455-6742
*Title:* Director, Appointments Office

**Michael Fallon** . . . . . . . . . . . . . . . . . . . . . . . . . . . . . . 518-455-2246
*Title:* Director, Chamber Operations

**Robert Tiberia** . . . . . . . . . . . . . . . . . . . . . . . . . . . . . . 518-455-2245
*Title:* Deputy Journal Clerk

**Ryan McLeod** . . . . . . . . . . . . . . . . . . . . . . . . . . . . . . . . 518-455-2521
*Title:* Supervisor, Legislative Services

**James Giliberto** . . . . . . . . . . . . . . . . . . . . . . . . . . . . . 518-455-2468
*Title:* Legislative Librarian, Legislative Library

**Stephen F Slagen** . . . . . . . . . . . . . . . . . . . . . . . . . . . . 518-455-2338
*Title:* Sergeant-at-Arms

**Nicholas Parrella** . . . . . . . . . . . . . . . . . . . . . . . . . . . . 518-455-7150
*Title:* Director, Student Programs Office

**Tracy Starr** . . . . . . . . . . . . . . . . . . . . . . . . . . . . . . . . . 518-455-3145
*Title:* District Office Coordinator

**Donna Schmidt** . . . . . . . . . . . . . . . . . . . . . . . . . . . . . . 518-455-3376
*Title:* Assistant Personnel Officer

**James Bell** . . . . . . . . . . . . . . . . . . . . . . . . . . . . . . . . . . 518-455-2313
*Title:* Director, Technology Services

### REPUBLICAN CONFERENCE LEADERSHIP

**Robert G Ortt (R, C, IP)** . . . . . . . . . . . . . . . . . . . . . . . . . . . . . . . .
*e-mail:* ortt@nysenate.gov
*Title:* Minority Leader

**Joseph A Griffo (R, C, IP)** . . . . . . . . . . . . . . . . . . . . . . . . . . . . . . .
*Title:* Assistant Minority Leader

**Thomas F O'Mara (R, C, IP)** . . . . . . . . . . . . . . . . . . . . . . . . . . . . .
*e-mail:* omara@nysenate.gov
*Title:* Ranking Member, Finance Committee

**Patty Ritchie (R, C, IP)** . . . . . . . . . . . . . . . . . . . . . . . . . . . . . . . . .
*e-mail:* ritchie@nysenate.gov
*Title:* Chair, Senate Minority Conference

**Andrew J Lanza (R, C, IP, RFM)** . . . . . . . . . . . . . . . . . . 518-455-3334
*e-mail:* lanza@nysenate.gov
*Title:* Deputy Minority Leader

**Sue Serino (R, C, IP)** . . . . . . . . . . . . . . . . . . . . . . . . . . . . . 518-455-3161
*e-mail:* serino@nysenate.gov
*Title:* Vice Chair, Senate Minority Conference

**Patrick M Gallivan (R, C, IP)** . . . . . . . . . . . . . . . . . . . . . . . 518-455-3471
*e-mail:* gallivan@nysenate.gov
*Title:* Minority Whip

### REPUBLICAN CONFERENCE STAFF

**Robert Farley** . . . . . . . . . . . . . . . . . . . . . . . . . . . . . . . . . 518-986-2037
*Title:* Senior Counsel to the Republican Conference

**Vacant** . . . . . . . . . . . . . . . . . . . . . . . . . . . . . . . . . . . . . . . 518-455-2533
*Title:* Counsel

**Dawn Harrington** . . . . . . . . . . . . . . . . . . . . . . . . . . . . . . . 518-455-2381
*Title:* Director of Administration

**Robin Mueller** . . . . . . . . . . . . . . . . . . . . . . . . . . . . . . . . . . . . . . . . . . .
*Title:* Special Assistant to Republican Conference Leader

**Shawn M MacKinnon** . . . . . . . . . . . . . . . . . . . . . . . . . . . . 518-455-2675
*Title:* Secretary to the Finance Committee

**Joseph Conway** . . . . . . . . . . . . . . . . . . . . . . . . . . . . . . . . . . . . . . . . .
*Title:* Director, Republican Conference

**Scott M Reif** . . . . . . . . . . . . . . . . . . . . . . . . . . . . . . . . . . . 518-455-3545
*Title:* Director, Communications

**Ryan McLeod** . . . . . . . . . . . . . . . . . . . . . . . . . . . . . . . . . . 518-455-2550
*Title:* Supervisor, Legislative Services

### DEMOCRATIC CONFERENCE LEADERSHIP

**Andrea Stewart-Cousins (D/IP/WF)** . . . . . . . . . . . . . . . . . 518-455-2585
*e-mail:* scousins@nysenate.gov
*Title:* Temporary President and Majority Leader

**Michael Gianaris (D)** . . . . . . . . . . . . . . . . . . . . . . . . . . . . 518-455-3486
*e-mail:* gianaris@nysenate.gov
*Title:* Deputy Majority Leader

**Toby Ann Stavisky (D)** . . . . . . . . . . . . . . . . . . . . . . . . . . . 518-455-3461
*e-mail:* stavisky@nysenate.gov
*Title:* Vice Chair of Majority Conference

**Brian A Benjamin (D)** . . . . . . . . . . . . . . . . . . . . . . . . . . . . 518-455-2441
*e-mail:* bbenjamin@nysenate.gov
*Title:* Senior Assistant Majority Leader

**Jose M Serrano (D, WF)** . . . . . . . . . . . . . . . . . . . . . . . . . . 518-455-2795
*e-mail:* serrano@nysenate.gov
*Title:* Chair of the Majority Conference

**Kevin S Parker (D, WF)** . . . . . . . . . . . . . . . . . . . . . . . . . . . 518-455-2580
*e-mail:* parker@nysenate.gov
*Title:* Majority Whip

**Timothy M Kennedy (D, IP, WF)** . . . . . . . . . . . . . . . . . . . . 518-455-2426
*e-mail:* kennedy@nysenate.gov
*Title:* Chair of Majority Program Development Committee

**Joseph P Addabbo, Jr (D)** . . . . . . . . . . . . . . . . . . . . . . . . . 518-455-2322
*e-mail:* addabbo@nysenate.gov
*Title:* Majority Deputy Whip

**Liz Krueger (D, WF)** . . . . . . . . . . . . . . . . . . . . . . . . . . . . . 518-455-2297
*e-mail:* lkrueger@nysenate.gov
*Title:* Chair of the Senate Finance Committee

**Neil D Breslin (D, IP, WF)** . . . . . . . . . . . . . . . . . . . . . . . . . 518-455-2225
*e-mail:* breslin@nysenate.gov
*Title:* Vice President Pro Tempore

*Offices and agencies generally appear in alphabetical order, except when specific order is requested by listee.*

**John C Liu (D)** . . . . . . . . . . . . . . . . . . . . . . . . . . . . . . 518-455-2210
*e-mail:* liu@nysenate.gov
*Title:* Majority Assistant Whip

**Gustavo Rivera (D, WF)** . . . . . . . . . . . . . . . . . . . 518-455-3395
*e-mail:* grivera@nysenate.gov
*Title:* Assistant Majority Leader on House Operations

**Brad Hoylman (D, WF)** . . . . . . . . . . . . . . . . . . . . . 518-455-2451
*e-mail:* hoylman@nysenate.gov
*Title:* Assistant Majority Leader on Conference Operations

**Leroy Comrie (D)** . . . . . . . . . . . . . . . . . . . . . . . . . . 518-455-2701
*e-mail:* comrie@nysenate.gov
*Title:* Deputy Majority Leader, State/Federal Relations

**Roxanne J Persaud (D)** . . . . . . . . . . . . . . . . . . . . . 518-455-2788
*e-mail:* persaud@nysenate.gov
*Title:* Majority Conference Secretary

**Todd Kaminsky (D)** . . . . . . . . . . . . . . . . . . . . . . . . 518-455-3401
*e-mail:* kaminsky@nysenate.gov
*Title:* Liaison to the Executive Branch

**Shelley Mayer (D, WF)** . . . . . . . . . . . . . . . . . . . . . 518-455-2031
*e-mail:* smayer@nysenate.gov
*Title:* Deputy Majority Leader, Senate/Assembly Relations

### DEMOCRATIC CONFERENCE STAFF

**Loren Amor** . . . . . . . . . . . . . . . . . . . . . . . . . . . . . . . 518-455-2800
*Title:* Director, Intergovernmental Affairs

**Vacant** . . . . . . . . . . . . . . . . . . . . . . . . . . . . . . . . . . . . . .
*Title:* Special Assistant

**Christopher T Higgins** . . . . . . . . . . . . . . . . . . . . . 518-455-2711
*Title:* Deputy Counsel

**Laura Manno** . . . . . . . . . . . . . . . . . . . . . . . . . . . . . . . .
*Title:* Director, Majority Operations

**Felix Muniz** . . . . . . . . . . . . . . . . . . . . . . . . . . . . . . . . .
*Title:* Director, Finance

**Peter Mooney** . . . . . . . . . . . . . . . . . . . . . . . . . . . . . 518-455-2501
*Title:* Director, Minority Conference Services

**Jonathan R Heppner** . . . . . . . . . . . . . . . . . . . . . . . 518-455-2415
*Title:* Press Secretary

### STATE SENATE ROSTER

*Multiple party abbreviations following the names of legislators indicate that those legislators ran as the Senate candidate for each identified party.*
*Source: NYS Board of Elections. Party abbreviations: Conservative (C), Democrat (D), Green (G), Independent (IP), Liberal (L), Reform (RFM), Republican (R), Working Families (WF)*

**Joseph P Addabbo, Jr (D)** . . . . . . . . . . 518-455-2322/fax: 518-426-6875
*District:* 15 *Room:* 811 LOB *e-mail:* addabbo@nysenate.gov
*Title:* Majority Deputy Whip
*Committees:* Aging; Civil Service & Pensions; Domestic Animal Welfare; Education; Racing, Gaming & Wagering (Chair); State-Native American Relations; Veterans, Homeland Security & Military Affairs
*Senior Staff:* Anthony Giudice

**Fred Akshar (R, C, IP, RFM)** . . . . . . . 518-455-2677/fax: 518-426-6720
*District:* 52 *Room:* 805 LOB *e-mail:* akshar@nysenate.gov
*Committees:* Alcoholism & Substance Abuse; Codes; Crime Victims, Crime & Correction; Elections; Labor; Disabilities; Civil Service & Pensions
*Senior Staff:* Emmanuel Priest

**Jamaal T Bailey (D)** . . . . . . . . . . . . . . . . . . . . . . 518-455-2061
*District:* 36 *Room:* 707 LOB *e-mail:* bailey@nysenate.gov
*Title:* Chair of Committee on Codes
*Committees:* Codes (Chair); Children & Families; Finance: Judiciary; Mental Health Rules; Joint Senate Task Force on Opioids, Addition & Overdose Prevention
*Senior Staff:* Jason Laidley

**Brian A Benjamin (D)** . . . . . . . . . . . . . 518-455-2441/fax: 518-426-6809
*District:* 30 *Room:* 517 LOB *e-mail:* bbenjamin@nysenate.gov
*Title:* Senior Assistant Majority Leader
*Committees:* Budget & Revenues (Chair); Codes; Finance; Health; Rules; Transportation; Joint Senate Task Force on Opioids, Addiction & Overdose Prevention
*Senior Staff:* Kercena A Dozier

**Alessandra Biaggi (D, WF)** . . . . . . . . . . . . . . . . . . . 518-455-3595
*District:* 34 *Room:* 905 LOB *e-mail:* biaggi@nysenate.gov
*Title:* Chair of Committee on Ethics and Internal Governance
*Committees:* Agriculture; Codes; Ethics & Internal Governance (Chair); Health; Investigations & Government Operations; Legislative Women's Caucus; Judiciary; Rules
*Senior Staff:* Maya Moskowitz

**George M Borrello (R, C, IP)** . . . . . . . . . . . . . . . . . . . . .
*District:* 57 *Room:* *e-mail:* borrello@nysenate.gov
*Committees:* Agriculture; Banks; Procurement & Contracts; Aging; Finance; Internet & Technology; Local Government
*Senior Staff:* Lisa Hill

**Phil Boyle (R)** . . . . . . . . . . . . . . . . . . . . . . . . . . . 518-455-3411
*District:* 4 *Room:* 814 LOB *e-mail:* pboyle@nysenate.gov
*Committees:* Higher Education; Judiciary; Domestic Animal Welfare; Energy & Telecommunications; Ethics & Internal Governance; Health; Rules; Housing, Construction & Community Development
*Senior Staff:* Sarah Schreiner

**Neil D Breslin (D, IP, WF)** . . . . . . . . . . 518-455-2225/fax: 518-426-6807
*District:* 44 *Room:* 430 CAP *e-mail:* breslin@nysenate.gov
*Title:* Vice President Pro Tempore
*Committees:* Banks; Ethics & Internal Governance; Finance; Cities; Insurance (Chair); Judiciary; Legislative Commission on Rural Resources; Rules; NYS Legislative Ethics Commission
*Senior Staff:* Vacant

**Jabari Brisport (D)** . . . . . . . . . . . . . . . . . . . . . . . . . . . .
*District:* 25 *Room:* *e-mail:* brisport@nysenate.gov
*Committees:* Children & Families; Banks; Codes; Housing, Construction & Community Development; Libraries; New York City Education
*Senior Staff:* Vacant

**John E Brooks (D)** . . . . . . . . . . . . . . . 518-455-2765/fax: 518-426-6925
*District:* 8 *Room:* 513 LOB *e-mail:* brooks@nysenate.gov
*Title:* Chair of Committee on Veterans, Homeland Security and Military Affairs
*Committees:* Education; Insurance; Local Government; Mental Health & Developmental Disabilities; Veterans, Homeland Security & Military Affairs (Chair)
*Senior Staff:* Joe Agovino

**Samra G Brouk (D, WF)** . . . . . . . . . . . . . . . . . . . . . . . . . . .
*District:* 55 *Room:* *e-mail:* brouk@nysenate.gov
*Committees:* Mental Health; Aging; Alcoholism & Substance Abuse; Education; Elections; Health; Women's Issues
*Senior Staff:* Vacant

**Leroy Comrie (D)** . . . . . . . . . . . . . . . 518-455-2701/fax: 518-455-2816
*District:* 14 *Room:* 617 LOB *e-mail:* comrie@nysenate.gov
*Title:* Deputy Majority Leader, State/Federal Relations
*Committees:* Cities; Consumer Protection; Corporations, Authorities & Commissions (Chair); Finance; Racing, Gaming & Wagering; Rules
*Senior Staff:* Andrew Taranto

*Offices and agencies generally appear in alphabetical order, except when specific order is requested by listee.*

**Jeremy A Cooney (D, WF)** . . . . . . . . . . . . . . . . . . . . . . . . .
*District:* 56  *Room:*  *e-mail:* cooney@nysenate.gov
*Committees:* Cities; Codes; Insurance; Cultural Affairs, Tourism, Parks & Recreation; Higher Education; Procurement & Contracts; Transportation
*Senior Staff:* Vacant

**Simcha Felder (D)** . . . . . . . . . . . . . . . .518-455-2754/fax: 518-426-6931
*District:* 17  *Room:* 504 LOB  *e-mail:* felder@nysenate.gov
*Committees:* Administrative Regulations Review Commission (Chair); Aging; Disabilities; Mental Health; New York Education; Social Services
*Senior Staff:* Sheri Toiv

**Patrick M Gallivan (R, C, IP)** . . . . . . . 518-455-3471/fax: 518-426-6949
*District:* 59  *Room:* 512 LOB  *e-mail:* gallivan@nysenate.gov
*Title:* Minority Whip
*Committees:* Codes; Crime Victims, Crime & Correction; Finance; Health; Labor; Transportation; Joint Senate Task Force on Opioids, Addiction & Overdose Prevention
*Senior Staff:* Jim Ranney

**James Gaughran (D)** . . . . . . . . . . . . . . . 518-455-3250/fax: 518-426-6785
*District:* 5  *Room:* 848 LOB  *e-mail:* gaughran@nysenate.gov
*Title:* Chair, Committee on Local Government
*Committees:* Energy & Telecommunications;Corporations, Authorities & Commissions; Higher Education; Local Government (Chair); Racing, Gaming & Wagering; Investigations & Government Operations
*Senior Staff:* Marissa Espinoza

**Michael Gianaris (D)** . . . . . . . . . . . . . . . 518-455-3486/fax: 518-426-6929
*District:* 12  *Room:* 427 CAP  *e-mail:* gianaris@nysenate.gov
*Title:* Deputy Majority Leader
*Committees:* Rules
*Senior Staff:* Alexander Marion

**Andrew Gounardes (D)** . . . . . . . . . . . . 518-455-3270/fax: 518-426-6782
*District:* 22  *Room:* 409 LOB  *e-mail:* gounardes@nysenate.gov
*Title:* Chairman of Committee on Civil Service and Pensions
*Committees:* Civil Service & Pensions (Chair); Cities; Consumer Protection; Insurance; Higher Education; Judiciary; Labor
*Senior Staff:* Sarah Anders

**Joseph A Griffo (R, C, IP)** . . . . . . . . . . 718-455-3334/fax: 518-426-6921
*District:* 47  *Room:* 413C CAP  *e-mail:* griffo@nysenate.gov
*Title:* Assistant Minority Leader
*Committees:*
*Senior Staff:* Alex Gerould

**Pete Harckham (D)** . . . . . . . . . . . . . . . .518-455-2340/fax: 518-426-6786
*District:* 40  *Room:* 812 LOB  *e-mail:* harckham@nysenate.gov
*Title:* Chairman of Committee on Alcoholism and Substance Abuse
*Committees:* Alcoholism & Substance Abuse (Chair); Domestic Animal Welfare; Energy & Telecommunications; Environmental Conservation; Finance; Veterans, Homeland Security & Military Affairs; Women's Issues
*Senior Staff:* Vacant

**Pamela Helming (R, C, IP)** . . . . . . . . . . . . . . . . . . . . . . .518-455-2366
*District:* 54  *Room:* 517 LOB  *e-mail:* helming@nysenate.gov
*Committees:* Agriculture; Commerce, Economic Development & Small Business; Housing, Construction & Community Development; Legislative Commission on Rural Resources; Racing, Gaming & Wagering; Cultural Affairs, Tourism, Parks & Recreation; Insurance
*Senior Staff:* Vacant

**Michelle Hinchey (D, WF)** . . . . . . . . . . . . . . . . . . . . . . . . . . . . . . .
*District:* 46  *Room:*  *e-mail:*
*Committees:* Agriculture (Chair); Alcoholism & Substance Abuse; Commerce, Economic Development & Small Business; Cultural Affairs, Tourism, Parks & Recreation; Energy & Telecommunications; Environmental Conservation; Local Government
*Senior Staff:* Jesse Meyer

**Brad Hoylman (D, WF)** . . . . . . . . . . . . 518-455-2451/fax: 518-426-6846
*District:* 27  *Room:* 413 LOB  *e-mail:* hoylman@nysenate.gov
*Title:* Assistant Majority Leader on Conference Operations
*Committees:* Cities; Cultural Affairs, Tourism, Parks & Recreation; Finance; Health; Judiciary (Chair); Rules
*Senior Staff:* Aaron Ghitelman
*Chairman of Committee on Cities:* Robert Jackson (D, WF)
*Senior Staff:* Chris Nickell

**Daphne Jordan (R, C, IP, RFM)** . . . . . . . . . . . . . . . . . . . .518-455-2381
*District:* 43  *Room:* 508 LOB  *e-mail:* jordan@nysenate.gov
*Committees:* Agriculture; Libraries; Women's Issues; Racing, Gaming & Wagering; State-Native American Relations; Legislative Women's Caucus; Procurement & Contracts; Veterans, Homeland Security & Military Affairs
*Senior Staff:* Vacant

**Todd Kaminsky (D)** . . . . . . . . . . . . . . . . 518-455-3401/fax: 518-426-6914
*District:* 9  *Room:* 307 LOB  *e-mail:* kaminsky@nysenate.gov
*Title:* Liason to the Executive Branch
*Committees:* Codes; Budget & Revenue; Environmental Conservation (Chair); Health; Investigations & Government Operations; Transportation; Ethics & Internal Governance
*Senior Staff:* Spencer MacDonald

**Anna M Kaplan (D, IP, WF)** . . . . . . . . 518-455-2170/fax: 518-426-6787
*District:* 7  *Room:* 805 LOB  *e-mail:* kaplan@nysenate.gov
*Title:* Chair of Committee on Commerce, Economic Development and Small Business
*Committees:* Commerce, Economic Development & Small Business (Chair); Environmental Conservation; Procurement & Contracts; Judiciary; Transportation; Women's Issues; Legislative Women's Caucus; Alcoholism & Substance Abuse
*Senior Staff:* Sean Ross Collins

**Brian Kavanagh (D, WF)** . . . . . . . . . . . 518-455-2625/fax: 518-426-6956
*District:* 26  *Room:* 515 LOB  *e-mail:* kavanagh@nysenate.gov
*Title:* Chair of Committee on Housing, Construction and Community Development
*Committees:* Codes; Consumer Protection; Elections; Energy & Telecommunications; Environmental Conservation; Housing, Constructions & Community Development (Chair); Social Services
*Senior Staff:* Stanley Davis

**Timothy M Kennedy (D, IP, WF)** . . . . . 518-455-2426/fax: 518-426-6851
*District:* 63  *Room:* 708 LOB  *e-mail:* kennedy@nysenate.gov
*Title:* Chair of Majority Program Development Committee
*Committees:* Banks; Energy & Telecommunications; Finance; Insurance; Cities; Rules; State-Native American Relations (Chair); Transportation
*Senior Staff:* Emily Reid

**Liz Krueger (D, WF)** . . . . . . . . . . . . . . . 518-455-2297/fax: 518-426-6874
*District:* 28  *Room:* 416 CAP  *e-mail:* lkrueger@nysenate.gov
*Title:* Chair of the Senate Finance Committee
*Committees:* Budget & Revenues; Finance (Chair); Legislative Women's Caucus; Rules
*Senior Staff:* Justin Flagg

**Andrew J Lanza (R, C, IP, RFM)** . . . . 518-455-3215/fax: 518-426-6852
*District:* 24  *Room:* 708 LOB  *e-mail:* lanza@nysenate.gov
*Title:* Deputy Minority Leader
*Committees:* Cities; Ethics & Internal Governance; Judiciary; New York City Education; Rules
*Senior Staff:* Vacant

**John C Liu (D)** . . . . . . . . . . . . . . . . . . . . . . . . . . . . . . . . .518-455-2210
*District:* 11  *Room:* 802 LOB  *e-mail:* liu@nysenate.gov
*Title:* Majority Assistant Whip
*Committees:* Alcoholism & Substance Abuse; Budget & Revenues; Education; Finance; New York City Education (Chair); Rules; Transportation
*Senior Staff:* Vacant

*Offices and agencies generally appear in alphabetical order, except when specific order is requested by listee.*

**John W Mannion (D)**............................................
*District:* 50  *Room:*  *e-mail:* mannion@nysenate.gov
*Title:* Chair of Committee on Disabilities
*Committees:* Disabilities (Chair); Environmental Conservation; Education;
Children & Families; Civil Service & Pensions; Internet & Technology;
Housing, Construction & Community Development
*Senior Staff:* Vacant

**Mike Martucci (R, C, IP)**....................................
*District:* 42  *Room:*  *e-mail:* martucci@nysenate.gov
*Committees:* Commerce, Economic Development & Small Business;
Children & Families; Cities; Corporations, Authorities & Commissions;
Disabilities; Housing, Construction & Community Development
*Senior Staff:* Jane Kunzweiler

**Mario R Mattera (R, C, IP)**...............................
*District:* 2  *Room:*  *e-mail:* mattera@nysenate.gov
*Committees:* Consumer Protection; Corporations, Authorities &
Commissions; Labor; Transportation
*Senior Staff:* Vacant

**Rachel May (D, WF)**............................518-455-2838
*District:* 53  *Room:* 803 LOB  *e-mail:* may@nysenate.gov
*Committees:* Aging (Chair); Agriculture; Cities; Legislative Commission on
Rural Resources; Environmental Conservation; Elections; Legislative
Women's Caucus; State-Native American Relations; Banks
*Senior Staff:* Jessica Bumpus

**Shelley Mayer (D, WF)**............518-455-2031/fax: 518-426-6860
*District:* 37  *Room:* 509 LOB  *e-mail:* smayer@nysenate.gov
*Title:* Deputy Majority Leader, Senate/Assembly Relations
*Committees:* Corporations, Authorities & Commissions; Education (Chair);
Elections; Cities; Rules; Legislative Women's Caucus; Labor; Racing,
Gaming & Wagering;
*Senior Staff:* Emiljana Ulaj

**Zellnor Myrie (D)**.............................518-455-2410
*District:* 20  *Room:* 903 LOB  *e-mail:* myrie@nysenate.gov
*Title:* Chair of Committee on Elections
*Committees:* Codes; Consumer Protection; Crime Victims, Crime &
Correction; Elections (Chair); Housing, Construction & Community
Development; Judiciary; Social Services
*Senior Staff:* Matt Baer

**Thomas F O'Mara (R, C, IP)**........518-455-2091/fax: 518-426-6976
*District:* 58  *Room:* 406 LOB  *e-mail:* omara@nysenate.gov
*Title:* Ranking Member, Finance Committee
*Committees:* Finance; Codes; Investigations & Government Operations;
Insurance; Judiciary; Rules; Energy & Telecommunications
*Senior Staff:* Vacant

**Peter Oberacker (R, C)**.....................................
*District:* 51  *Room:*  *e-mail:* oberacker@nysenate.gov
*Committees:* Alcoholism & Substance Abuse; Internet & Technology;
Education; Health; Higher Education; Judiciary
*Senior Staff:* Jeff Bishop

**Robert G Ortt (R, C, IP)**............518-455-2024/fax: 518-426-6987
*District:* 62  *Room:* 617 LOB  *e-mail:* ortt@nysenate.gov
*Title:* Minority Leader
*Committees:* Rules; State-Native American Relations
*Senior Staff:* Andrew Dugan

**Anthony H Palumbo (R)**....................................
*District:* 1  *Room:*  *e-mail:* palumbo@nysenate.gov
*Committees:* Codes; Ethics & Internal Governance; Environmental
Conservation; Investigations & Government Operations; Judiciary; Mental
Health
*Senior Staff:* Vacant

**Kevin S Parker (D, WF)**............518-455-2580/fax: 518-426-6843
*District:* 21  *Room:* 504 CAP  *e-mail:* parker@nysenate.gov
*Title:* Majority Whip
*Committees:* Higher Education; Banks; Energy & Telecommunications
(Chair); Finance; Insurance; Internet & Technology; Rules
*Senior Staff:* Raven Robinson

**Roxanne J Persaud (D)**.......................518-455-2788
*District:* 19  *Room:* 409 LOB  *e-mail:* persaud@nysenate.gov
*Title:* Majority Conference Secretary
*Committees:* Children & Families; Commerce, Economic Development &
Small Business; Labor; Social Services (Chair); Transportation; Legislative
Women's Caucus; Joint Senate Task Force on Opioids, Addiction &
Overdose Prevention; Cities
*Senior Staff:* Owen Johnson

**Jessica Ramos (D, WF)**........................518-455-2529
*District:* 13  *Room:* 415 LOB  *e-mail:* ramos@nysenate.gov
*Committees:* Labor; Commerce, Economic Development & Small Business;
Corporations, Authorities & Commissions; Labor (Chair); Legislative
Women's Caucus; New York City Education; Internet & Technology;
Agriculture
*Senior Staff:* Esther Rosario

**Edward A Rath III (R)**......................................
*District:* 61  *Room:*  *e-mail:* rath@nysenate.gov
*Committees:* Elections; Local Government; Budget & Revenue; Cities;
Health; Labor
*Senior Staff:* Gabriella Rogers

**Elijah Reichlin-Melnick (D, WF)**.........................
*District:* 38  *Room:*  *e-mail:* reichlin@nysenate.gov
*Title:* Chair of Committee on Procurement & Contracts
*Committees:* Procurement & Contracts (Chair); Consumer Protection; Local
Government; Education; Transportation; Investigations & Government
Operations; Veterans, Homeland Security & Military Affairs
*Senior Staff:* Massimo Cordella

**Patty Ritchie (R, C, IP)**............518-455-3438/fax: 518-426-6740
*District:* 48  *Room:* 412 LOB  *e-mail:* ritchie@nysenate.gov
*Title:* Chair, Senate Minority Conference
*Committees:* Elections; Energy & Telecommunications; Finance; Legislative
Commission on Rural Resources; Veterans, Homeland Security and Military
Affairs; Legislative Women's Caucus
*Senior Staff:* Vacant

**Gustavo Rivera (D, WF)**....................................
*District:* 33  *Room:* 502 CAP  *e-mail:* grivera@nysenate.gov
*Title:* Assistant Majority Leader on House Operations
*Committees:* Crime Victims, Crime & Corrections; Finance; Health (Chair);
Housing, Construction & Community Development; Mental Health;
Alcoholism & Substance Abuse; Higher Education; Finance
*Senior Staff:* Valeria Munt

**Sean M Ryan (D)**...........................................
*District:* 60  *Room:*  *e-mail:* ryan@nysenate.gov
*Title:* Assistant Minority Whip
*Committees:* Libraries; Education; Health; Labor; Commerce, Economic
Development & Small Business; Crime Victims, Crime & Correction;
Housing, Construction & Community Development
*Senior Staff:* Vacant

**Julia Salazar (D, WF)**.......................518-455-2177
*District:* 18  *Room:* 711B LOB  *e-mail:* salazar@nysenate.gov
*Committees:* Children & Families; Finance; Health; Housing, Construction &
Community Development; Women's Issues (Chair); Crime Victims, Crime &
Correction (Chair); Budget & Revenue; Legislative Women's Caucus
*Senior Staff:* Sihem Mellah-Sliker

*Offices and agencies generally appear in alphabetical order, except when specific order is requested by listee.*

**James Sanders Jr (D)** . . . . . . . . . . . . . . 518-455-3531/fax: 518-426-6859
*District:* 10 *Room:* 711 LOB *e-mail:* sanders@nysenate.gov
*Committees:* Banks (Chair); Commerce, Economic Development & Small
Business; Cultural Affairs, Tourism, Parks & Recreation; Insurance; Labor;
Veterans, Homeland Security & Military Affairs; Procurement & Contracts
*Senior Staff:* AnnMarie Costella

**Diane J Savino (D, IP)** . . . . . . . . . . . . 518-455-2437/fax: 518-426-6943
*District:* 23 *Room:* 315 LOB *e-mail:* savino@nysenate.gov
*Title:* Chair of Committee on Internet and Technology
*Committees:* Civil Service & Pensions; Codes; Finance; Internet &
Technology (Chair); Labor; Rules; Joint Senate Task Force on Opioids,
Addiction & Overdose Prevention; Banks; Legislative Women's Caucus
*Senior Staff:* Vacant

**Luis R Sepulveda (D)** . . . . . . . . . . . . . . 518-455-2511/fax: 518-426-6845
*District:* 32 *Room:* 608 LOB *e-mail:* sepulveda@nysenate.gov
*Committees:*
*Senior Staff:* Tahirih Anthony

**Sue Serino (R, C, IP)** . . . . . . . . . . . . . . . . . . . . . . . . . . 518-455-2945
*District:* 41 *Room:* 613 LOB *e-mail:* serino@nysenate.gov
*Title:* Vice Chair, Senate Minority Conference
*Committees:* Aging; Insurance; Social Services; Finance; Transportation;
Legislative Women's Caucus; Cultural Affairs, Tourism, Parks & Recreation
*Senior Staff:* Vacant

**Jose M Serrano (D, WF)** . . . . . . . . . . . . 518-455-2795/fax: 518-426-6886
*District:* 29 *Room:* 420C CAP *e-mail:* serrano@nysenate.gov
*Title:* Chair of the Majority Conference
*Committees:* Aging; Cultural Affairs, Tourism, Parks & Recreation (Chair);
Environmental Conservation; Women's Issues; Veterans, Homeland Security
& Military Affairs
*Senior Staff:* Vacant

**James Skoufis (D)** . . . . . . . . . . . . . . . . 518-455-3290/fax: 518-426-6784
*District:* 39 *Room:* 815 LOB *e-mail:* skoufis@nysenate.gov
*Committees:* Judiciary; Corporations, Authorities & Commissions; Finance;
Investigations & Government Operations (Chair); Labor; Transportation
*Senior Staff:* Jess Gulotta

**Toby Ann Stavisky (D)** . . . . . . . . . . . . . 518-455-3461/fax: 518-426-6857
*District:* 16 *Room:* 913 LOB *e-mail:* stavisky@nysenate.gov
*Title:* Vice Chair of Majority Conference
*Committees:* Education; Ethics & Internal Governance; Finance; Higher
Education (Chair); Judiciary; Racing, Gaming, & Wagering; Legislative
Women's Caucus
*Senior Staff:* Pierce Brix

**Daniel G Stec (R)** . . . . . . . . . . . . . . . . . . . . . . . . . . . . . . . .
*District:* 45 *Room:* *e-mail:* stec@nysenate.gov
*Committees:* Children & Families; Environmental Conservation; Banks;
Education; Health; Libraries
*Senior Staff:* Vacant

**Andrea Stewart-Cousins (D/IP/WF)** . . 518-455-2585/fax: 518-426-6811
*District:* 35 *Room:* 907 LOB *e-mail:* scousins@nysenate.gov
*Title:* Temporary President and Majority Leader
*Committees:* Legislative Women's Caucus; Rules (Chair)
*Senior Staff:* Vacant

**James Tedisco (R, C)** . . . . . . . . . . . . . . 518-455-2181/fax: 518-426-6821
*District:* 49 *Room:* 515 LOB *e-mail:* tedisco@nysenate.gov
*Committees:* Banks; Education; Mental Health; Finance; Consumer
Protection; Commerce, Economic Development & Small Business; New
York City Education
*Senior Staff:* Adam Kramer

**Kevin Thomas (D)** . . . . . . . . . . . . . . . . 518-455-3260/fax: 518-426-6783
*District:* 6 *Room:* 808 LOB *e-mail:* thomas@nysenate.gov
*Title:* Chair of Committee on Consumer Protection
*Committees:* Banks; Consumer Protection (Chair); Finance; Health; Local
Government; Internet & Technology
*Senior Staff:* Emily Mancini

**Alexis Weik (R, C)** . . . . . . . . . . . . . . . . . . . . . . . . . . . . . . . . . . .
*District:* 3 *Room:* *e-mail:* weik@nysenate.gov
*Committees:* Budget & Revenue; Social Services; Civil Service & Pensions;
Social Sorcia Services; Education; Women's Issues; Veterans, Homeland
Security & Military Affairs
*Senior Staff:* Vacant

## STATE SENATE STANDING COMMITTEES

### Administrative Regulations Review Commission (ARRC)
Chair:
Simcha Felder (D) . . . . . . . . . . . . . . . . . . . . . . . . . . . . . .718-253-2015

**Membership**

**Minority**

**Majority**

### Aging
Chair:
Rachel May (D, WF) . . . . . . . . . . . . . . . . . . . . . . . . . . .518-455-2838
Ranking Minority Member:
Sue Serino (R, C, IP) . . . . . . . . . . . . . . . . . . . . . . . . . . .518-455-2945

**Committee Staff**
Legislative Director:
Eric Vandervort . . . . . . . . . . . . . . . . . . . . . . . . . . . . . . .518-455-2838

**Membership**

**Majority**
| | |
|---|---|
| Joseph P Addabbo, Jr | Samra G Brouk |
| Simcha Felder | Jose M Serrano |

**Minority**
George M Borrello

### Agriculture
Chair:
Michelle Hinchey (D, WF)
Ranking Minority Member:
George M Borrello (R, C, IP)

**Committee Staff**
Committee Clerk:
Alyvia Lewter . . . . . . . . . . . . . . . . . . . . . . . . . . . . . . .518-455-2400

**Key Senate Staff Assignments**
Counsel:
Kyle Pero . . . . . . . . . . . . . . . . . . . . . . . . . . . . . . . . . . .518-455-2400

**Membership**

**Majority**
| | |
|---|---|
| Alessandra Biaggi | Jabari Brisport |
| Leroy Comrie | Rachel May |
| Jessica Ramos | |

**Minority**
| | |
|---|---|
| Daphne Jordan | Pamela Helming |

### Alcoholism & Substance Abuse
Chair:
Pete Harckham (D) . . . . . . . . . . . . . . . . . . . . . . . . . . .518-455-2340
Ranking Minority Member:
Peter Oberacker (R, C)

**Membership**

**Majority**
| | |
|---|---|
| Samra G Brouk | Michelle Hinchey |
| Anna M Kaplan | Gustavo Rivera |

*Offices and agencies generally appear in alphabetical order, except when specific order is requested by listee.*

Legislative
Branch

**Minority**
Fred Akshar

## Banks
Chair:
James Sanders Jr (D)................................518-455-3531
Ranking Minority Member:
George M Borrello (R, C, IP)

### Committee Staff
**Key Senate Staff Assignments**
Counsel:
Vacant............................................518-455-3531
Legislative Director:
Paul Alexander...................................518-455-3531

### Membership

**Majority**
| | |
|---|---|
| Neil D Breslin | Jabari Brisport |
| Timothy M Kennedy | Rachel May |
| Kevin S Parker | Diane J Savino |
| Kevin Thomas | |

**Minority**
| | |
|---|---|
| Daniel G Stec | James Tedisco |

## Budget & Revenues
Chair:
Brian A Benjamin (D)...........................518-455-2441
Ranking Minority Member:
Alexis Weik (R, C)

### Membership

**Majority**
| | |
|---|---|
| Todd Kaminsky | Liz Krueger |
| John C Liu | Julia Salazar |

**Minority**
Edward A Rath III

## Children & Families
Chair:
Jabari Brisport (D)
Ranking Minority Member:
Daniel G Stec (R)

### Membership

**Majority**
| | |
|---|---|
| Jamaal T Bailey | John W Mannion |
| Roxanne J Persaud | Julia Salazar |

**Minority**
Mike Martucci

## Cities 1
Chair:
Robert Jackson (D, WF)........................518-455-2041
Ranking Minority Member:
Andrew J Lanza (R, C, IP, RFM)..............518-455-3215

### Committee Staff
Committee Clerk:
Vacant............................................518-455-2041

**Majority**
| | |
|---|---|
| Leroy Comrie | Andrew Gounardes |
| Brad Hoylman | Roxanne J Persaud |

**Minority**
Mike Martucci

## Cities 2
Chair:
Jeremy A Cooney (D, WF)......................518-455-2041
Ranking Minority Member:
Joseph A Griffo (R, C, IP)

### Membership

**Majority**
| | |
|---|---|
| Neil D Breslin | Timothy M Kennedy |
| Rachel May | Shelley B Mayer |

**Minority**
Edward A Rath III

## Civil Service & Pensions
Chair:
Andrew Gounardes (D).........................518-455-3270
Ranking Minority Member:
Fred Akshar (R, C, IP, RFM)

### Committee Staff
Legislative Counsel:
Mary Robyn Cotrona ..........................518-455-3270

**Key Senate Staff Assignments**

### Membership

**Majority**
| | |
|---|---|
| Joseph P Addabbo, Jr | Robert Jackson |
| John W Mannion | Diane J Savino |

**Minority**
Alexis Weik

## Codes
Chair:
Jamaal T Bailey (D) ...........................518-455-2061
Ranking Minority Member:
Anthony H Palumbo (R)

### Committee Staff
Committee Counsel:
Noel Mendez....................................518-455-2061

### Membership

**Majority**
| | |
|---|---|
| Brian A Benjamin | Alessandra Biaggi |
| Jabari Brisport | Jeremy A Cooney |
| Todd Kaminsky | Brian Kavanagh |
| Zellnor Myrie | Diane J Savino |

**Minority**
| | |
|---|---|
| Fred Akshar | Patrick M Gallivan |
| Thomas F O'Mara | |

## Commerce, Economic Development & Small Business
Chair:
Anna M Kaplan (D, IP, WF)...................518-455-2170
Ranking Minority Member:
Mike Martucci (R, C, IP) ......................518-455-2366

### Committee Staff
Legislative Director:
Joseph Erdman .................................518-455-2170

**Key Senate Staff Assignments**
Counsel:
Rebecca Sheehan ..............................518-455-2170

*Offices and agencies generally appear in alphabetical order, except when specific order is requested by listee.*

**Membership**

**Majority**

Michelle Hinchey          Roxanne J Persaud
Jessica Ramos             Sean M Ryan
James Sanders Jr

**Minority**

Pamela Helming            James Tedisco

## Consumer Protection
Chair:
Kevin Thomas (D) . . . . . . . . . . . . . . . . . . . . . . . . . . . .518-455-3260
Ranking Minority Member:
Mario R Mattera (R, C, IP). . . . . . . . . . . . . . . . . . . . .518-455-2181

**Committee Staff**
Legislative Director:
Tamina Bramer. . . . . . . . . . . . . . . . . . . . . . . . . . . . .518-455-3260

**Membership**

**Majority**

Andrew Gounardes          Brian Kavanagh
Zellnor Myrie             Elijah Reichlin-Melnick

**Minority**

James Tedicso

## Corporations, Authorities & Commissions
Chair:
Leroy Comrie (D) . . . . . . . . . . . . . . . . . . . . . . . . . . . .518-455-2701
Ranking Minority Member:
Mario R Mattera (R, C, IP)

**Committee Staff**
Legislative Director:
Christopher Labarge. . . . . . . . . . . . . . . . . . . . . . . . . .518-455-2701

**Key Senate Staff Assignments**
Counsel:
Paul Nichols . . . . . . . . . . . . . . . . . . . . . . . . . . . . . . .518-455-2701

**Membership**

**Majority**

James Gaughran            Shelley Mayer
Jessica Ramos             James Skoufis

**Minority**

Mike Martucci

## Crime Victims, Crime & Correction
Chair:
Julia Salazar (D, WF) . . . . . . . . . . . . . . . . . . . . . . . . .518-455-2677
Ranking Minority Member:
Fred Akshar (R, C, IP, RFM) . . . . . . . . . . . . . . . . . . . .518-455-2677

**Committee Staff**
Legislative Director:
Shantalee Martinez. . . . . . . . . . . . . . . . . . . . . . . . . . .518-455-2511

**Key Senate Staff Assignments**
Legislative Counsel:
Oshire Zak . . . . . . . . . . . . . . . . . . . . . . . . . . . . . . . .518-455-2511

**Membership**

**Majority**

Jamaal T Bailey           Zellnor Myrie
Gustavo Rivera            Sean M Ryan

**Minority**

Partick M Gallivan

## Cultural Affairs, Tourism, Parks & Recreation
Chair:
Jose M Serrano (D, WF). . . . . . . . . . . . . . . . . . . . . . . .518-455-2795
Ranking Minority Member:
Sue Serino (R, C, IP) . . . . . . . . . . . . . . . . . . . . . . . . .518-455-2215

**Committee Staff**
Committee/Legislative Director:
Andrew Postiglione . . . . . . . . . . . . . . . . . . . . . . . . . .518-455-2795

**Membership**

**Majority**

Jeremy A Cooney           Michelle Hinchey
Brad Hoylman              James Sanders Jr

**Minority**

Pamela Helming

## Disabilities
Chair:
John W Mannion (D)

**Membership**

**Majority**

John E Brooks             Simcha Felder
Brad Hoylman              Roxanne J Persaud

**Minority**

Fred Akshar               Mike Martucci

## Education
Chair:
Shelley Mayer (D, WF). . . . . . . . . . . . . . . . . . . . . . . .518-455-2031
Ranking Minority Member:
James Tedisco (R, C)

**Committee Staff**
Committee Director:
Georgia Asciutto. . . . . . . . . . . . . . . . . . . . . . . . . . . . .518-455-2031
Legislative Counsel:
Andrew Buder. . . . . . . . . . . . . . . . . . . . . . . . . . . . . . .518-455-2031
Legislative Director:
Martha Mahoney. . . . . . . . . . . . . . . . . . . . . . . . . . . . .518-455-2031

**Membership**

**Majority**

Joseph P Addabbo, Jr      John E Brooks
Samra G Brouk             Robert Jackson
John C Liu                John W Mannion
Elijah Reichlin-Melnick   Sean M Ryan
Toby Ann Stavisky

**Minority**

Joseph A Griffo           Peter Oberacker
Daniel G Stec             Alexis Weik

## Elections
Chair:
Zellnor Myrie (D) . . . . . . . . . . . . . . . . . . . . . . . . . . . .518-455-2410
Ranking Minority Member:
Edward A Rath III (R)

**Committee Staff**
Counsel/Legislative Director:
Chaka Laguerre. . . . . . . . . . . . . . . . . . . . . . . . . . . . . .518-455-2410

**Membership**

**Majority**

Samra G Brouk             Brian Kavanagh
Rachel May                Shelley Mayer

*Offices and agencies generally appear in alphabetical order, except when specific order is requested by listee.*

Minority
  Patty Ritchie

## Energy & Telecommunications
Chair:
  Kevin S Parker (D, WF) . . . . . . . . . . . . . . . . . . . . . . . 518-455-2580
Ranking Minority Member:
  Patty Ritchie (R, C, IP) . . . . . . . . . . . . . . . . . . . . . . . 518-455-3438

### Committee Staff
Committee Director:
  Joshua Jones . . . . . . . . . . . . . . . . . . . . . . . . . . . . . . . 518-455-2580
Legislative Director:
  Tamara Tucker . . . . . . . . . . . . . . . . . . . . . . . . . . . . . . 518-455-2580

### Membership

Majority
  James Gaughran            Pete Harckham
  Michelle Hinchey          Brian Kavanagh
  Timothy M Kennedy

Minority
  Phil Boyle                Thomas F O'Mara

## Environmental Conservation
Chair:
  Todd Kaminsky (D) . . . . . . . . . . . . . . . . . . . . . . . . . . 518-455-3401
Ranking Minority Member:
  Daniel G Stec (R)

### Committee Staff
Legislative Director/Counsel:
  Brielle Christian . . . . . . . . . . . . . . . . . . . . . . . . . . . . 518-455-3401

### Membership

Majority
  Pete Harckham             Michelle Hinchey
  Anna M Kaplan             Brian Kavanagh
  John W Mannion            Rachel May
  Jose M Serrano

Minority
  Anthony H Palumbo         Patty Ritchie

## Ethics & Internal Governance
Chair:
  Alessandra Biaggi (D, WF) . . . . . . . . . . . . . . . . . . . . 518-455-3595
Ranking Minority Member:
  Anthony H Palumbo (R)

### Committee Staff
Legislative Director:
  Jordine Jones . . . . . . . . . . . . . . . . . . . . . . . . . . . . . . 518-455-3595

### Membership

Majority
  Neil D Breslin            Todd Kaminsky
  Toby Ann Stavisky

Minority
  Phil Boyle                Andrew J Lanza

## Finance
Chair:
  Liz Krueger (D, WF) . . . . . . . . . . . . . . . . . . . . . . . . . 518-455-2297
Ranking Minority Member:
  Thomas F O'Mara (R, C, IP)

### Committee Staff
Secretary to the Committee:
  Shawn M MacKinnon . . . . . . . . . . . . . . . . . . . . . . . . 518-455-3565

Key Senate Staff Assignments
Director of Budget Studies:
  Peter Drao . . . . . . . . . . . . . . . . . . . . . . . . . . . . . . . . 518-455-3563
Counsel:
  Steven Rodway

### Membership

Majority
  Jamaal T Bailey           Brian A Benjamin
  Neil D Breslin            Leroy Comrie
  Pete Harckham             Brad Hoylman
  Timothy M Kennedy         John C Liu
  Kevin S Parker            Gustavo Rivera
  Julia Salazar             Diane J Savino
  James Skoufis             Toby Ann Stavisky
  Kevin Thomas

Minority
  George M Borrello         Patrick M Gallivan
  Joseph A Griffo           Patty Ritchie
  Sue Serino                James Tedisco

## Health
Chair:
  Gustavo Rivera (D, WF) . . . . . . . . . . . . . . . . . . . . . . 518-455-3395
Ranking Minority Member:
  Patrick M Gallivan (R, C, IP) . . . . . . . . . . . . . . . . . . 518-455-3471

### Committee Staff
Committee Director:
  Kristin Sinclair . . . . . . . . . . . . . . . . . . . . . . . . . . . . . 518-455-3395
Policy Analyst:
  Jay Baez . . . . . . . . . . . . . . . . . . . . . . . . . . . . . . . . . . 518-455-3395
Counsel:
  Latoya Matthew . . . . . . . . . . . . . . . . . . . . . . . . . . . . 518-455-3395

### Membership

Majority
  Brian A Benjamin          Alessandra Biaggi
  Samra G Brouk             Brad Hoylman
  Todd Kaminsky             Rachel May
  Sean M Ryan               Julia Salazar
  Kevin Thomas

Minority
  Phil Boyle                Peter Oberacker
  Edward A Rath III         Daniel G Stec

## Higher Education
Chair:
  Toby Ann Stavisky (D) . . . . . . . . . . . . . . . . . . . . . . . 518-455-3461
Ranking Minority Member:
  Phil Boyle (R)

### Committee Staff
Legislative Director:
  Jan Dorman . . . . . . . . . . . . . . . . . . . . . . . . . . . . . . . 518-455-3461
Democratic Senior Counsel:
  Dan Leinung . . . . . . . . . . . . . . . . . . . . . . . . . . . . . . 518-455-2821

### Membership

Majority
  Jeremy A Cooney           James Gaughran
  Andrew Gounardes          Robert Jackson
  John C Liu                Kevin S Parker
  Gustavo Rivera

Minority
  Joseph A Griffo           Peter Oberacker

*Offices and agencies generally appear in alphabetical order, except when specific order is requested by listee.*

## Housing, Construction & Community Development
Chair:
Brian Kavanagh (D, WF) . . . . . . . . . . . . . . . . . . . . . . . . . .518-455-2625
Ranking Minority Member:
Pamela Helming (R, C, IP)

### Committee Staff
Legislative Assistant:
Cleveland Stair . . . . . . . . . . . . . . . . . . . . . . . . . . . . . . . . .518-455-2625

### Membership

#### Majority
| | |
|---|---|
| Jabari Brisport | Robert Jackson |
| John W Mannion | Zellnor Myrie |
| Gustavo Rivera | Sean M Ryan |
| Julia Salazar | |

#### Minority
| | |
|---|---|
| Phil Boyle | Mike Martucci |

## Insurance
Chair:
Neil D Breslin (D, IP, WF) . . . . . . . . . . . . . . . . . . . . . . . . . .518-455-2225
Ranking Minority Member:
Pamela Helming (R, C, IP)

### Committee Staff
Legislative Director:
Matthew Barron . . . . . . . . . . . . . . . . . . . . . . . . . . . . . . . . .518-455-2225

### Membership

#### Majority
| | |
|---|---|
| John E Brooks | Jeremy A Cooney |
| Andrew Gounardes | Pete Harckham |
| Timothy M Kennedy | Kevin S Parker |
| James Sanders Jr | |

#### Minority
| | |
|---|---|
| Thomas F O'Mara | Sue Serino |

## Internet & Technology
Chair:
Diane J Savino (D, IP) . . . . . . . . . . . . . . . . . . . . . . . . . .518-455-2437
Ranking Minority Member:
Peter Oberacker (R, C)

### Committee Staff
Legislative Counsel:
Richard Mulvaney . . . . . . . . . . . . . . . . . . . . . . . . . . . . . . .518-455-2437

### Membership

#### Majority
| | |
|---|---|
| John W Mannion | Kevin S Parker |
| Jessica Ramos | Kevin Thomas |

#### Minority
| |
|---|
| George M Borrello |

## Investigations & Government Operations
Chair:
James Skoufis (D) . . . . . . . . . . . . . . . . . . . . . . . . . . . . . .518-455-3290
Ranking Minority Member:
Thomas F O'Mara (R, C, IP)

### Committee Staff
Counsel:
Sara DiBernardo . . . . . . . . . . . . . . . . . . . . . . . . . . . . . . . .518-455-3290

### Membership

#### Majority
| | |
|---|---|
| Alessandra Biaggi | James Gaughran |
| Todd Kaminsky | Elijah Reichlin-Melnick |

#### Minority
| |
|---|
| Anthony H Palumbo |

## Judiciary
Chair:
Brad Hoylman (D, WF) . . . . . . . . . . . . . . . . . . . . . . . . . . .518-455-2451
Ranking Minority Member:
Phil Boyle (R)

### Committee Staff
Legislative Director:
Kendall Jacobsen . . . . . . . . . . . . . . . . . . . . . . . . . . . . . . .518-455-2451

### Membership

#### Majority
| | |
|---|---|
| Jamaal T Bailey | Alessandra Biaggi |
| Neil D Breslin | Andrew Gounardes |
| Anna M Kaplan | Zellnor Myrie |
| James Skoufis | Toby Ann Stavisky |
| Kevin Thomas | |

#### Minority
| | |
|---|---|
| Andrew J Lanza | Thomas F O'Mara |
| Peter Oberacker | Anthony H Palumbo |

## Labor
Chair:
Jessica Ramos (D, WF) . . . . . . . . . . . . . . . . . . . . . . . . . . .518-455-2529
Ranking Minority Member:
Patrick M Gallivan (R, C, IP)

### Committee Staff
Committee Director:
Samantha Acevedo . . . . . . . . . . . . . . . . . . . . . . . . . . . . . .518-455-2529

### Membership

#### Majority
| | |
|---|---|
| Andrew Gounardes | Robert Jackson |
| Shelley Mayer | Roxanne J Persaud |
| Sean M Ryan | James Sanders Jr |
| Diane J Savino | James Skoufis |

#### Minority
| | |
|---|---|
| Fred Akshar | Mario R Mattera |
| Edward A Rath III | |

## Legislative Commission on Rural Resources
Chair:
Rachel May (D, WF) . . . . . . . . . . . . . . . . . . . . . . . . . . . . .518-455-2838
Ranking Minority Member:
Pamela Helming (R, C, IP) . . . . . . . . . . . . . . . . . . . . . . . .518-455-2366

### Membership

#### Majority
| |
|---|
| Neil D Breslin |

#### Minority
| |
|---|
| Patty Ritchie |

## Local Government
Chair:
James Gaughran (D) . . . . . . . . . . . . . . . . . . . . . . . . . . . . .518-455-3250
Ranking Minority Member:
Edward A Rath III (R)

**Committee Staff**
Legislative Director/Committee Clerk:
Vacant..........................................518-455-3250
Counsel:
Jennifer Slagen-Bobersky......................518-455-3250

**Membership**

**Majority**
John E Brooks                Michelle Hinchey
Elijah Reichlin-Melnick      Kevin Thomas

**Minority**
George M Borrello

## Mental Health
Chair:
Samra G Brouk (D, WF)
Ranking Minority Member:
James Tedisco (R, C)

**Committee Staff**
Committee Director:
John Koury....................................518-455-2991
Legislative Director:
Brian Coffin..................................518-455-2991

**Membership**

**Majority**
Jamaal T Bailey              John E Brooks
Simcha Felder                Gustavo Rivera

**Minority**
Anthony H Palumbo

## Procurement & Contracts
Chair:
Elijah Reichlin-Melnick (D, WF)
Ranking Minority Member:
George M Borrello (R, C, IP)

**Membership**

**Majority**
Leroy Comrie                 Jeremy A Cooney
Anna A Kaplan                James Sanders Jr

**Minority**
Daphne Jordan

## Racing, Gaming & Wagering
Chair:
Joseph P Addabbo, Jr (D).....................518-455-2322
Ranking Minority Member:
Daphne Jordan (R, C, IP, RFM)................518-455-2381

**Committee Staff**
Committee Director:
Shanna Cassidy...............................518-455-2322

**Membership**

**Majority**
Brian A Benjamin             James Gaughran
Shelley Mayer                Toby Ann Stavisky

**Minority**
Pamela Helming

## Rules
Chair:
Andrea Stewart-Cousins (D/IP/WF)............518-455-2585

Ranking Minority Member:
Robert G Ortt (R, C, IP)

**Membership**

**Majority**
Joseph A Addabbo Jr          Jamaal T Bailey
Brian A Benjamin             Alessandra Biaggi
Neil D Breslin               Leroy Comrie
Michael Gianaris             Timothy M Kennedy
Liz Krueger                  John C Liu
Shelley B Mayer              Kevin S Parker
Diane J Savino

**Minority**
Phil Boyle                   Patrick M Gallivan
Joseph A Griffo              Andrew J Lanza
Thomas F O'Mara              Patty Ritchie

## Social Services
Chair:
Roxanne J Persaud (D)........................518-455-2788
Ranking Minority Member:
Alexis Weik (R, C)

**Committee Staff**
Committee Director:
Dennis Weakley, Jr...........................518-455-2788

**Membership**

**Majority**
Simcha Felder                Brian Kavanagh
Zellnor Myrie                Jose M Serrano

**Minority**
Sue Serino

## Transportation
Chair:
Timothy M Kennedy (D, IP, WF)................518-455-2426
Ranking Minority Member:
Joseph A Griffo (R, C, IP)

**Committee Staff**
Committee Clerk:
Meg Brown....................................518-455-2426
Legislative Director:
Richard Rodgers..............................518-455-2426

**Membership**

**Majority**
Jeremy A Cooney              Todd Kaminsky
Anna M Kaplan                John C Liu
Roxanne J Persaud            Jessica Ramos
Elijah Reichlin-Melnick      James Skoufis

**Minority**
Patrick M Gallivan           Mario R Mattera
Sue Serino

## Veterans, Homeland Security & Military Affairs
Chair:
John E Brooks (D)............................518-455-2765
Ranking Minority Member:
Patty Ritchie (R, C, IP)

**Committee Staff**
Committee Clerk:
Christine Schoeffler.........................518-455-2765
Legislative Director:
Francis Palasieski...........................518-455-2765

*Offices and agencies generally appear in alphabetical order, except when specific order is requested by listee.*

**Membership**

**Majority**

| | |
|---|---|
| Joseph P Addabbo, Jr | Pete Harckham |
| Elijah Reichlin-Melnick | James Sanders Jr |
| Jose M Serrano | |

**Minority**

| | |
|---|---|
| Daphne Jordan | Alexis Weik |

## Women's Issues
Chair:
Julia Salazar (D, WF).............................518-455-2177
Ranking Minority Member:
Daphne Jordan (R, C, IP, RFM)

**Committee Staff**
Legislative Director:
Guillermo Martinez................................518-455-2177

**Membership**

**Majority**

| | |
|---|---|
| Samra G Brouk | Pete Harckham |
| Anna M Kaplan | Jose M Serrano |

**Minority**

Alexis Weik

## SENATE SELECT & SPECIAL COMMITTEES & SPECIAL TASK FORCES

## Joint Senate Task Force On Opioids, Addiction & Overdose Prevention
Co-Chair:
Pete Harckham (D, WF)
Co-Chair:
Gustavo Rivera (D, WF)

**Membership**

**Majority**

| | |
|---|---|
| Jamaal T Bailey | Brian A Benjamin |
| Rachel May | Roxanne J Persaud |
| Diane J Savino | |

**Minority**

Patrick M Gallivan

## Legislative Women's Caucus
Treasurer:
Toby Ann Stavinsky (D)

**Membership**

**Majority**

| | |
|---|---|
| Alessandra Biaggi | Anna M Kaplan |
| Liz Krueger | Rachel May |
| Shelley B Mayer | Roxanne J Persaud |
| Jessica Ramos | Julia Salazar |
| Diane J Savino | Andrea Stewart-Cousins |

**Minority**

| | |
|---|---|
| Pamela Helming | Daphne Jordan |
| Patty Ritchie | Sue Serino |

## Libraries
Chair:
Sean M Ryan (D)
Ranking Minority Member:
Daphne Jordan (R, C, IP, RFM)

**Membership**

**Majority**

| | |
|---|---|
| Jabari Brisport | John E Brooks |
| Brad Hoylman | Diane J Savino |

**Minority**

Daniel G Stec

## New York City Education Subcommittee
Chair:
John C Liu (D) ....................................518-455-2210
Ranking Minority Member:
Andrew J Lanza (R, C, IP, RFM)....................518-455-3215

**Membership**

**Majority**

| | |
|---|---|
| Jabari Brisport | Simcha Felder |
| Robert Jackson | Jessica Ramos |

**Minority**

James Tedisco

## State-Native American Relations
Chair:
Timothy M Kennedy (D, IP, WF)....................518-455-2426
Ranking Minority Member:
Daphne Jordan (R, C, IP, RFM).....................518-455-2381

**Membership**

**Majority**

| | |
|---|---|
| Joseph P Addabbo, Jr | Rachel May |
| Gustavo Rivera | |

**Minority**

Robert G Ortt

*Offices and agencies generally appear in alphabetical order, except when specific order is requested by listee.*

## LEGISLATIVE BRANCH ASSEMBLY

### STATE ASSEMBLY LEADERSHIP

*Members of the Assembly welcome e-mail correspondence from the public. They may reply by e-mail, or by mail when more extensive follow-up is necessary. Please include both an e-mail and mailing address in all correspondence. Biographies of Assembly Members appears in a separate section in the back of the book.*

**State Capitol**
**Albany, NY 12248**
**Web site: nyassembly.gov**

### ADMINISTRATION

**Mary-Anne E Dandles** ..............518-455-4242/fax: 518-455-4935
*Title:* Clerk of the Assembly

**Wayne P Jackson** ..................518-455-3797/fax: 518-455-4445
*Title:* Sergeant-at-Arms, Chamber

**Morgan E Weinberg**......................518-455-5767
*Title:* Director, Communication Information Services (CIS)

**Amy Metcalfe** ....................518-455-4411/fax: 518-455-4298
*Title:* Director, Administration

**Kathleen McCarty**....................518-455-4704/fax: 518-455-4705
*Title:* Director, Internship Program

**Mike Gaffney** .....................518-455-5165/fax: 518-455-4741
*Title:* Director, Document Room

**Robin Marilla**....................518-455-4218/fax: 518-455-5175
*Title:* Public Information Officer

**Vacant**............................518-455-2468/fax: 518-426-6901
*Title:* Reference Librarian, Legislative Library

**Edward J Harris** .................518-455-5190/fax: 518-455-4517
*Title:* Director, Operations

### MAJORITY LEADERSHIP

**Carl E Heastie (D)** .................518-455-3791/fax: 518-455-4812
*e-mail:* Speaker@nyassembly.gov
*Title:* Speaker

**Crystal D Peoples-Stokes (D)** ......................518-455-5005
*e-mail:* PeopleC@nyassembly.gov
*Title:* Majority Leader

**Helene E Weinstein (D)** ......................518-455-5462
*e-mail:* WeinstH@nyassembly.gov
*Title:* Chair, Ways & Means Committee

**Catherine Nolan (D)** ...........................518-455-4851
*e-mail:* NolanC@nyassembly.gov
*Title:* Deputy Speaker

**Jeffrion L Aubry (D)**...............518-455-4561/fax: 518-455-4565
*e-mail:* AubryJ@nyassembly.gov
*Title:* Speaker Pro Tempore

**N Nick Perry (D)** .............................518-455-4166
*e-mail:* PerryN@nyassembly.gov
*Title:* Assistant Speaker Pro Tempore

**Phil Ramos (D)**..........................631-435-3214
*e-mail:* ramosp@nyassembly.gov
*Title:* Assistant Speaker

**Vivian E Cook (D)**..........................518-455-4203
*e-mail:* CookV@nyassembly.gov
*Title:* Chair, Committee on Standing Committees

**Michaelle C Solages (D)** ..........................518-455-5185
*e-mail:* solagesm@nyassembly.gov
*Title:* Deputy Majority Leader

**Alicia Hyndman (D)** ..........................518-455-5606
*e-mail:* hydmana@nyassembly.gov
*Title:* Assistant Majority Leader

**William Colton (D)** ..........................518-455-5828
*e-mail:* ColtonW@nyassembly.gov
*Title:* Majority Whip

**José Rivera (D)**..........................518-455-5414
*e-mail:* RiveraJ@nyassembly.gov
*Title:* Deputy Majority Whip

**Stacey Pheffer Amato (D)** ..........................518-455-4621
*e-mail:* amatos@nyassembly.gov
*Title:* Assistant Majority Whip

**Pamela J Hunter (D)**..........................518-455-4897
*e-mail:* hunterp@nyassembly.gov
*Title:* Chair, Majority Conference

**Jaime R Williams (D)**..........................518-455-5821
*e-mail:* williamsja@nyassembly.gov
*Title:* Vice Chair, Majority Conference

**Pat Burke (D)** ..........................518-455-5676
*e-mail:* burkep@nyassembly.gov
*Title:* Secretary, Majority Conference

**Patricia Fahy (D)**..........................518-455-5444
*e-mail:* fahyp@nyassembly.gov
*Title:* Chair, Majority Steering

**Monica P Wallace** ..................518-455-4474/fax: 518-455-4727
*e-mail:* wallacem@nyassembly.gov
*Title:* Vice Chair, Majority Steering

**Inez E Dickens (D)**..........................518-455-5402
*e-mail:* dickens1@nyassembly.gov
*Title:* Chair, Majority Program

**Al Taylor (D)** ..........................518-455-5411
*e-mail:* taylora@nyassembly.gov
*Title:* Chair, Majority House Operations

**Maritza Davila (D)**..................518-455-5537/fax: 518-455-5789
*e-mail:* DavilaM@nyassembly.gov
*Title:* Chair, Puerto Rican/Hispanic Task Force

### MAJORITY STAFF

**Jevonni Brooks-Dennis**.............518-455-3791/fax: 518-455-4812
*Title:* Chief of Staff to the Speaker

**Mike Whyland** ....................518-455-3791/fax: 518-455-4812
*Title:* Press Secretary to the Speaker

**Paul Tearno**......................518-455-4736/fax: 518-455-5428
*Title:* Director, Index Operations

**Joanne Barker**...........................................
*Title:* Counsel to the Majority

*Offices and agencies generally appear in alphabetical order, except when specific order is requested by listee.*

**Blake Washington** . . . . . . . . . . . . . . . . . . . . . . . . . . . . . . . . . . . . . . .
*Title:* Secretary to the Committee on Ways & Means

## MINORITY LEADERSHIP

**William A Barclay (R, I, C)** . . . . . . . . . . . . . . . . . . . . . . . . 518-455-3751
*e-mail:* barclaW@nyassembly.gov
*Title:* Minority Leader

**Andy Goodell (R, C, I)** . . . . . . . . . . . . . . . . . . . . . . . . . . . . 518-455-4511
*e-mail:* goodella@nyassembly.gov
*Title:* Minority Leader Pro Tempore

**Mary Beth Walsh (R, C, I)** . . . . . . . . . . . . . . . . . . . . . . . . . 518-455-4627
*e-mail:* walshm@nyassembly.gov
*Title:* Assistant Minority Leader Pro Tempore

**Stephen Hawley (R, C, I)** . . . . . . . . . . . . . . . . . . . . . . . . . . 518-455-5811
*e-mail:* HawleyS@nyassembly.gov
*Title:* Deputy Minority Leader

**Ken Blankenbush (R)** . . . . . . . . . . . . . . . . . . . . . . . . . . . . . 518-455-5878
*e-mail:* blankenbushk@nyassembly.gov
*Title:* Assistant Minority Leader

**Philip A Palmesano (R, C, I)** . . . . . . . . . . . . . . . . . . . . . . . 518-455-5952
*e-mail:* palmesanop@nyassembly.gov
*Title:* Assistant Minority Leader

**Michael Montesano (R, C)** . . . . . . . . . . 518-455-5716/fax: 518-455-5970
*e-mail:* montesanom@nyassembly.gov
*Title:* Minority Whip

**Karl Brabenec (R)** . . . . . . . . . . . . . . . . 518-455-5791/fax: 518-455-4644
*e-mail:* brabeneckM@nyassembly.gov
*Title:* Deputy Minority Whip

**David DiPietro (R, C, I)** . . . . . . . . . . . . 518-455-5991/fax: 518-455-5929
*e-mail:* dipietrod@nyassembly.gov
*Title:* Assistant Minority Whip

**Michael J Norris (R, I)** . . . . . . . . . . . . . . . . . . . . . . . . . . . . 518-455-5741
*e-mail:* norrism@nyassembly.gov
*Title:* Chair, Minority Conference

**Jake Ashby (R, C, I)** . . . . . . . . . . . . . . . . . . . . . . . . . . . . . 518-455-5565
*e-mail:* ashbyj@nyassembly.gov
*Title:* Vice Chair, Minority Conference

**Brian Manktelow (R, C, I)** . . . . . . . . . . . . . . . . . . . . . . . . . 518-455-5784
*e-mail:* manktelowb@nyassembly.gov
*Title:* Secretary, Minority Conference

**David G McDonough (R, C, I)** . . . . . . . . . . . . . . . . . . . . . . 518-455-4633
*e-mail:* mcdonoughd@nyassembly.gov
*Title:* Chair, Minority Joint Conference Committee

**Melissa Miller (R, C)** . . . . . . . . . . . . . . . . . . . . . . . . . . . . . 518-455-4611
*e-mail:* millerml@nyassembly.gov
*Title:* Vice Chair, Minority Joint Conference Committee

**Angelo J Morinello (R, C, I)** . . . . . . . . 518-455-5797/fax: 518-455-5289
*e-mail:* morinelloa@nyassembly.gov
*Title:* Chair, Steering Committee

**Brian D Miller (R, I)** . . . . . . . . . . . . . . . . . . . . . . . . . . . . . 518-455-5783
*e-mail:* millerb@nyassembly.gov
*Title:* Vice Chair, Steering Committee

**Kevin M Byrne (R, C)** . . . . . . . . . . . . . . . . . . . . . . . . . . . . 518-455-4684
*e-mail:* byrneK@nyassembly.gov
*Title:* Chair, Program Committee

**Michael J Fitzpatrick (R, C, I)** . . . . . . . . . . . . . . . . . . . . . 518-455-5772
*e-mail:* fitzpatrickM@nyassembly.gov
*Title:* Vice Chair, Program Committee

**Vacant** . . . . . . . . . . . . . . . . . . . . . . . . . . . . . . . . . . . . . . . . . . 518-455-0000
*Title:* Chair, Minority House Operations

**Edward P Ra (R)** . . . . . . . . . . . . . . . . . . . . . . . . . . . . . . . . 518-455-5841
*e-mail:* rae@nyassembly.gov
*Title:* Ranking Minority Member, Ways & Means

## MINORITY STAFF

**Judy Skype** . . . . . . . . . . . . . . . . . . . . . . . . . . . . . . . . . . . . . 518-455-3751
*Title:* Chief of Staff

**Vacant** . . . . . . . . . . . . . . . . . . . . . . . . . . . . . . . . . . . . . . . . . . 518-455-4211
*Title:* Deputy Chief of Staff

**Michael Fraser** . . . . . . . . . . . . . . . . . . 518-455-3751/fax: 518-455-3750
*Title:* Director, Minority Communications

**Michael Daly** . . . . . . . . . . . . . . . . . . . . . . . . . . . . . . . . . . . . 518-455-5002
*Title:* Director, Minority Research & Program Development

**Rebecca Dower** . . . . . . . . . . . . . . . . . . 518-455-5161/fax: 518-455-4550
*Title:* Director, Minority Ways & Means Staff

## STATE ASSEMBLY ROSTER

*Multiple party abbreviations following the names of legislators indicate that those legislators ran as the Assembly candidate for each identified party. Source: NYS Board of Elections. Party abbreviations: Conservative (C), Democrat (D), Green (G), Independent (I), Liberal (L), Republican (R), Right to Life (RL), Veterans (VE), Working Families (WF)*

**Peter J Abbate, Jr (D)** . . . . . . . . . . . . . . . . . . . . . . . . . . . . 518-455-3053
*District:* 49   *Room:* 839 LOB   *e-mail:* abbatep@nyassembly.gov
*Committees:* Aging; Asian Pacific American Task Force; Banks; Consumer Affairs & Protection; Governmental Employees (Chair); Labor

**Thomas J Abinanti (D)** . . . . . . . . . . . . . . . . . . . . . . . . . . . . 518-455-5753
*District:* 92   *Room:* 744 LOB   *e-mail:* abinantit@nyassembly.gov
*Committees:* Codes; Environmental Conservation; Health; Judiciary; People with Disabilities (Chair)
*Senior Staff:* Vacant

**Khaleel M Anderson (D)** . . . . . . . . . . . . . . . . . . . . . . . . . . . 718-327-1845
*District:* 31   *Room:*   *e-mail:* andersonk@nyassembly.gov
*Committees:* Banks; Children & Families; Energy; Insurance; People with Disabilities; Subcommittee on Banking in Underserved Communities (Chair)
*Senior Staff:* Vacant

**Joe Angelino (R)** . . . . . . . . . . . . . . . . . . . . . . . . . . . . . . . . 607-648-6080
*District:* 122   *Room:*   *e-mail:* angelinoj@nyassembly.gov
*Committees:* Banks; Corporations, Authorities & Commissions; People with Disabilities; Oversight, Analysis & Investigation; Tourism, Parks, Art & Sports Development

**Jake Ashby (R, C, I)** . . . . . . . . . . . . . . . . . . . . . . . . . . . . . 518-455-5777
*District:* 107   *Room:* 720 LOB   *e-mail:* ashbyj@nyassembly.gov
*Title:* Vice Chair, Minority Conference
*Committees:* Aging; Health; Ways & Means; Racing & Wagering; Ethics & Guidance; Veterans' Affairs

**Jeffrion L Aubry (D)** . . . . . . . . . . . . . . 518-455-4561/fax: 518-455-4565
*District:* 35   *Room:* 646 LOB   *e-mail:* AubryJ@nyassembly.gov
*Title:* Speaker Pro Tempore
*Committees:* Governmental Employees; Rules; Social Services; Ways & Means; Black, Puerto Rican, Hispanic & Asian Legislative Caucus; Puerto Rican/Hispanic Task Force
*Senior Staff:* Diana Hernandez

*Offices and agencies generally appear in alphabetical order, except when specific order is requested by listee.*

**William A Barclay (R, I, C)**..........................518-455-5841
*District:* 120  *Room:* 444 LOB  *e-mail:* BarclaW@nyassembly.gov
*Title:* Minority Leader
*Committees:* Rules
*Senior Staff:* Jennifer Cook

**Brian Barnwell (D)** ...............518-455-4755/fax: 518-455-5032
*District:* 30  *Room:* 921 LOB  *e-mail:* BarnwellB@nyassembly.gov
*Committees:* Aging; Asian Pacific American Task Force; Banks; Agriculture;
Labor; Real Property Taxation; Puerto Rican/Hispanic Task Force; Veterans'
Affairs; Commission on State-Local Relations (Chair)

**Didi Barrett (D)** ....................518-455-5177/fax: 518-455-5418
*District:* 106  *Room:* 841 LOB  *e-mail:* barrettd@nyassembly.gov
*Committees:* Agriculture; Environmental Conservation; Mental Health; Task
Force on Women's Issues; Tourism, Parks, Arts & Sports Development;
Veterans' Affairs (Chair); Women's Caucus (Chair); Puerto Rican/Hispanic
Task Force

**Charles Barron (D)**.................................518-455-5912
*District:* 60  *Room:* 532 LOB  *e-mail:* barronc@nyassembly.gov
*Committees:* Aging; Subcommittee on Community Integration (Chair);
Economic Development, Job Creation, Commerce & Industry; Energy;
Health; Housing; Social Services; Black, Puerto Rican, Hispanic & Asian
Legislative Caucus
*Senior Staff:* Viola Plummer

**Michael Benedetto (D)** ...........................518-455-5296
*District:* 82  *Room:* 836 LOB  *e-mail:* benedettom@nyassembly.gov
*Committees:* Education (Chair); Labor; Puerto Rican/Hispanic Task Force;
Rules; Subcommittee on Oversight of Minority & Women-Owned Business
Enterprises; Subcommittee on Retention of Homeownership & Stabilization
of Affordable Housing; Ways & Means
*Senior Staff:* John Collazzi

**Rodneyse Bichotte Hermelyn (D)**...................518-455-5385
*District:* 42  *Room:* 727 LOB  *e-mail:* bichotter@nyassembly.gov
*Committees:* Banks; Education; Subcommittee on Oversight of MWBEs
(Chair); Governmental Operations; Health; Higher Education; Housing;
Black, Puerto Rican, Hispanic & Asian Legislative Caucus; Task Force on
Women's Issues; Women's Caucus
*Senior Staff:* Lisa Derrick

**Ken Blankenbush (R)** ...........518-455-5797/fax: 518-455-5289
*District:* 117  *Room:* 322 LOB  *e-mail:* blankenbushk@nyassembly.gov
*Title:* Assistant Minority Leader
*Committees:* Agriculture; Corporations, Authorities & Commissions;
Insurance; Energy; Rules; Ways & Means; Commission on Skills
Development & Career Education
*Senior Staff:* Brian Peck

**Karl Brabenec (R)** ................518-455-5991/fax: 518-455-5929
*District:* 98  *Room:* 329 LOB  *e-mail:* brabeneck@nyassembly.gov
*Title:* Deputy Minority Whip
*Committees:* Aging; Rules; Election Law; Labor; Commission on
Government Administration; Ways & Means
*Senior Staff:* Joseph Coleman

**Edward C Braunstein (D)** .......518-455-5425/fax: 518-455-4648
*District:* 26  *Room:* 842 LOB  *e-mail:* braunsteine@nyassembly.gov
*Committees:* Rules; Cities (Chair); Health; Judiciary; Ways & Means
*Senior Staff:* David Fischer

**Harry B Bronson (D)** ..............................518-455-4527
*District:* 138  *Room:* 824 LOB  *e-mail:* bronsonh@nyassembly.gov
*Committees:* Ways & Means; Economic Development, Job Creation,
Commerce & Industry (Chair); Education; Labor; Transportation
*Senior Staff:* Jen Skoog-Harvey

**Keith P Brown (R)**.................................518-455-5397
*District:* 12  *Room:*  *e-mail:* brownk@nyassembly.gov
*Committees:* Alcoholism & Drug Abuse; Environmental Conservation;
Housing; Judiciary; Social Services

**Chris Burdick (D)** .................................
*District:* 93  *Room:*  *e-mail:* burdickc@nyassembly.gov
*Committees:* Correction; Environmental Conservation; Housing; People with
Disabilities; Veterans' Affairs; Subcommittee on Employment Opportunities
for People with Disabilities (Chair)

**Kenny Burgos (D)**.................................
*District:* 85  *Room:*  *e-mail:* burgosk@nyassembly.gov
*Committees:* Correction; Consumer Affairs & Protection; Election Law;
Labot; Transportation; Subcommittee on Transitional Services (Chair)

**Pat Burke (D)** .....................................518-455-4691
*District:* 142  *Room:* 323 LOB  *e-mail:* burkep@nyassembly.gov
*Title:* Secretary, Majority Conference
*Committees:* Banks; Environmental Conservation; Tourism, Parks, Arts &
Sports Development; Economic Development, Job Creation, Commerce &
Industry; Science & Technology

**Marianne Buttenschon (D)**..........518-455-5454/fax: 518-455-5928
*District:* 119  *Room:* 528 LOB  *e-mail:*
*Committees:* Agriculture; Banks; Economic Development, Job Creation,
Commerce & Industry; Export Trade (Chair); Higher Education; Veterans'
Affairs; Legislative Women's Caucus; Education; Task Force on Women's
Issues

**Kevin M Byrne (R, C)** ..............................518-455-5783
*District:* 94  *Room:* 318 LOB  *e-mail:* ByrneK@nyassembly.gov
*Title:* Chair, Program Committee
*Committees:* Governmental Operations; Health; Insurance; Labor;
Transportation; Ways & Means; Commission on Council on Health Care
Financing

**Marjorie Byrnes (R, C)**.............518-455-5562/fax: 518-455-5918
*District:* 133  *Room:* 723 LOB  *e-mail:* byrnesm@nyassembly.gov
*Committees:* Children & Families; Health; Housing; Judiciary; Small
Business; Women's Caucus; Ethics & Guidance

**Kevin A Cahill (D)**.................................518-455-4436
*District:* 103  *Room:* 716 LOB  *e-mail:* CahillK@nyassembly.gov
*Committees:* Economic Development, Job Creation, Commerce & Industry;
Health; Higher Education; Insurance (Chair); Ways & Means; Examining
Socio-Economic Responses to People with Substance Use Disorders
*Senior Staff:* Laurie Wheelock

**Robert C Carroll (D)**...............518-455-5377/fax: 518-455-5592
*District:* 44  *Room:* 557 LOB  *e-mail:* CarrollR@nyassembly.gov
*Committees:* Cities; Corporations, Authorities & Commissions; Election
Law; Energy; Environmental Conservation; Tourism, Parks, Arts & Sports
Development; Subcommittee on Museums & Cultural Institutions (Chair)

**Sarah Clark (D)** ...................................
*District:* 136  *Room:*  *e-mail:* Clarks@nyassembly.gov
*Committees:* Aging; Children & Families; Higher Education; Local
Governments; Small BUsiness; Task Force on Women's Issues;
Subcommittee on Tuition Assistance Program (Chair)

**William Colton (D)** ................................518-455-5828
*District:* 47  *Room:* 733 LOB  *e-mail:* coltonw@nyassembly.gov
*Title:* Majority Whip
*Committees:* Asian Pacific American Task Force; Correction; Environmental
Conservation; Governmental Employees; Labor; Rules; Ways & Means
*Senior Staff:* Wenyi Zhuang

**William Conrad (D)**................................
*District:* 140  *Room:*  *e-mail:* conradw@nyassembly.gov
*Committees:* Education; Energy; Local Governments; Science & Technology;
Tourism, Parks, Arts & Sports Development; Subcommittee on Volunteer
Emergency Services (Chair)

**Vivian E Cook (D)**.................................518-455-4203
*District:* 32  *Room:* 939 LOB  *e-mail:* cookv@nyassembly.gov
*Title:* Chair, Committee on Standing Committees
*Committees:* Codes; Corporations, Authorities & Commissions; Housing;
Insurance; Rules; Ways & Means; Black, Puerto Rican, Hispanic & Asian

*Offices and agencies generally appear in alphabetical order, except when specific order is requested by listee.*

Legislative Caucus; Women's Caucus; Puerto Rican/Hispanic Task Force;
Task Force on Women's Issues
*Senior Staff:* Joyce Nanci Corker

**Catalina Cruz (D)** . . . . . . . . . . . . . . . . . . . . . . . . . . .518-455-4567
*District:* 39  *Room:* 523 LOB  *e-mail:* cruzc@nyassembly.gov
*Committees:* Aging; Children & Families; Codes; Ethics & Guidance;
Judiciary; Labor; Small Business; Black, Puerto Rican, Hispanic & Asian
Legislative Caucus; Legislative Women's Caucus; Puerto Rican/Hispanic TF;
TF on Women's Issues; TF on New Americans (Chair)

**Michael Cusick (D)** . . . . . . . . . . . . . . . . . . . . . . . . . . .518-455-5526
*District:* 63  *Room:* 724 LOB  *e-mail:* CusickM@nyassembly.gov
*Committees:* Energy (Chair); Governmental Employees; Higher Education;
Veterans' Affairs; Ways & Means

**Steven Cymbrowitz (D)** . . . . . . . . . . . . . . . . . . . . . . .518-455-5214
*District:* 45  *Room:* 943 LOB  *e-mail:* CymbroS@nyassembly.gov
*Committees:* Codes; Environmental Conservation; Health; Housing (Chair);
Insurance
*Senior Staff:* Leonid Markh

**Taylor Darling (D)** . . . . . . . . . . . . . . . . . . . . . . . . . . .518-455-5861
*District:* 18  *Room:* 833 LOB  *e-mail:* darlingT@nyassembly.gov
*Committees:* Black, Puerto Rican, Hispanic & Asian Legislative Caucus;
Children & Families; Eonomic Development, Job Creation, Commerce &
Industry; Local Governments; Small Business; Transportation; Women's
Caucus; People with Disabilities; TF on Women's Issues

**Maritza Davila (D)**. . . . . . . . . . . . . . .518-455-5537/fax: 518-455-5789
*District:* 53  *Room:* 637 LOB  *e-mail:* DavilaM@nyassembly.gov
*Title:* Chair, Puerto Rican/Hispanic Task Force
*Committees:* Alcoholism & Drug Abuse; Children & Families; Correction;
Economic Dvlpmnt, Job Creation, Commerce & Industry; Housing; Social
Services; Black, Puerto Rican, Hispanic & Asian Caucus; Women's Caucus;
Puerto Rican/Hispanic TF (Chair); TF Women's Issues
*Senior Staff:* Joseph Yanis

**Carmen N De La Rosa (D)**. . . . . . . . . . . . . . . . . . . . . .518-455-5807
*District:* 72  *Room:* 538 LOB  *e-mail:* delaRosac@nyassembly.gov
*Committees:* Banks; Corporations, Authorities & Commissions; Correction;
Housing; Labor; Mental Health; Black, Puerto Rican, Hispanic & Asian
Legislative Caucus; Women's Caucus; Puerto Rican/Hispanic Task Force;
Task Force on Women's Issues

**Joe DeStefano (R, C, I)** . . . . . . . . . . . . .518-455-4901/fax: 518-455-5908
*District:* 3  *Room:* 430 LOB  *e-mail:* destefanoj@nyassembly.gov
*Committees:* Aging; Alcoholism & Drug Abuse; Governmental Employees;
Labor; Transportation

**Inez E Dickens (D)**. . . . . . . . . . . . . . . . . . . . . . . . . . .518-455-4793
*District:* 70  *Room:* 819 LOB  *e-mail:* DickensI@nyassembly.gov
*Title:* Chair, Majority Program
*Committees:* Aging; Banks; Black, Puerto Rican, Hispanic & Asian
Legislative Caucus; Education; Libraries & Education Technology; Puerto
Rican/Hispanic TF; Real Property Taxation; Small Business; Women's
Caucus; Task Force on Women's Issues; Rules

**Erik M Dilan (D)** . . . . . . . . . . . . . . . . . . . . . . . . . . . .518-455-5821
*District:* 54  *Room:* 639 LOB  *e-mail:* DilanE@nyassembly.gov
*Committees:* Agriculture; Black, Puerto Rican, Hispanic & Asian Legislative
Caucus; Ways & Means; Corporations, Authorities & Commissions; Energy;
Housing; Insurance; Puerto Rican/Hispanic Task Force
*Senior Staff:* Videsh Persaud

**Jeffrey Dinowitz (D)** . . . . . . . . . . . . . .518-455-5965/fax: 518-455-4437
*District:* 81  *Room:* 831 LOB  *e-mail:* DinowiJ@nyassembly.gov
*Committees:* Election Law; Health; Codes (Chair); Puerto Rican/Hispanic
Task Force; Rules; Ways & Means
*Senior Staff:* Randi Martos

**David DiPietro (R, C, I)** . . . . . . . . . . . . . . . . . . . . . . .518-455-5314
*District:* 147  *Room:* 543 LOB  *e-mail:* DiPietroD@nyassembly.gov
*Title:* Assistant Minority Whip
*Committees:* Insurance; Labor; Small Business; Transportation; Commission
on Government Administration
*Senior Staff:* Christine Gierlinger

**Michael Durso (R)** . . . . . . . . . . . . . . . . . . . . . . . . . . . .
*District:* 9  *Room:*   *e-mail:* dursom@nyassembly.gov
*Committees:* Alcoholism & Drug Abuse; Environmental Conservation;
Labor; Science & Technology; Commission on Skills Development & Career
Education

**Simcha Eichenstein (D)**. . . . . . . . . . . . .518-455-5721/fax: 518-455-5948
*District:* 48  *Room:* 548 LOB  *e-mail:* EichensteinS@nyassembly.gov
*Committees:* Aging; Cities; Housing; Real Property Taxation; Social
Services; Outreach & Oversight of Senior Citizen Programs; Governmental
Employees

**Steve Englebright (D)** . . . . . . . . . . . . . . . . . . . . . . . . .518-455-4804
*District:* 4  *Room:* 621 LOB  *e-mail:* EngleS@nyassembly.gov
*Committees:* Environmental Conservation (Chair); Energy; Higher
Education; Rules; Science & Technology
*Senior Staff:* Maria Hoffman

**Harvey Epstein (D)** . . . . . . . . . . . . . . . . . . . . . . . . . . .518-455-5506
*District:* 74  *Room:* 427 LOB  *e-mail:* epsteinh@nyassembly.gov
*Committees:* Agriculture; Environmental Conservation; Governmental
Operations; Higher Education; Housing; Retention of Homeownership &
Stabilization of Affordable Housing (Chair); People with Disabilities

**Patricia Fahy (D)**. . . . . . . . . . . . . . . . . . . . . . . . . . . . .518-455-4178
*District:* 109  *Room:* 452 LOB  *e-mail:* FahyP@nyassembly.gov
*Title:* Chair, Majority Steerig
*Committees:* Codes; Environmental Conservation; Higher Education; Task
Force on Women's Issues; Tourism, Parks, Arts & Sports Development;
Transportation; Women's Caucus; Economic Development, Job Creation,
Commerce & Industry

**Charles D Fall (D)** . . . . . . . . . . . . . . . . . . . . . . . . . . . .518-455-4677
*District:* 61  *Room:* 534 LOB  *e-mail:*
*Committees:* Aging; Black, Puerto Rican, Hispanic & Asian Legislative
Caucus; Cities; Consumer Affairs & Protection; Corporations, Authorities &
Commissions; Tourism, Parks, Arts & Sports Development; Governmental
Employees

**Nathalia Fernandez (D)** . . . . . . . . . . . . . . . . . . . . . . .518-455-5844
*District:* 80  *Room:* 530 LOB  *e-mail:* fernandezn@nyassembly.gov
*Committees:* Alcoholism & Drug Abuse; Black, Puerto Rican, Hispanic &
Asian Legis. Caucus; Cities; Mental Health; Oversight, Analysis &
Investigation; Social Services; Tourism, Parks, Arts & Sports Devt.;
Women's Caucus; Examining Socio-Economic Resp.

**Michael J Fitzpatrick (R, C, I)** . . . . . . .518-455-5021/fax: 518-455-4394
*District:* 8  *Room:* 458 LOB  *e-mail:* FitzpatrickM@nyassembly.gov
*Title:* Vice Chair, Program Committee
*Committees:* Agriculture; Higher Education; Housing; Ways & Means; Banks
*Senior Staff:* Kathy Albrecht

**Phara Souffrant Forrest (D)** . . . . . . . . . . . . . . . . . . . . . . . .
*District:* 57  *Room:*   *e-mail:* souffrantforrestp@nyassembly.gov
*Committees:* Aging; Consumer Affairs & Protection; Higher Education;
Insurance; Social Services; Task Force on Women's Issues; Subcommittee on
Intergenerational Care (Chair)

**Christopher S Friend (R, C, I)** . . . . . . . . . . . . . . . . . . .518-455-4538
*District:* 124  *Room:* 938 LOB  *e-mail:* friendc@nyassembly.gov
*Committees:* Agriculture; Education; Corporations, Authorities &
Commissions; Economic Development, Job Creation, Commerce & Industry;
Local Governments; Science & Technology
*Senior Staff:* Scott Esty

---

*Offices and agencies generally appear in alphabetical order, except when specific order is requested by listee.*

**Mathylde Frontus (D)**............................518-455-4811
*District:* 46  *Room:* 324 LOB  *e-mail:* frontusm@nyassembly.gov
*Committees:* Aging; Black, Puerto Rican, Hispanic & Asian Legislative
Caucus; Children & Families; Mental Health; Tourism, Parks, Arts, & Sports
Development; Transportation; Women's Caucus; Economic Development,
Job Creation, Commerce & Industry

**Sandy Galef (D)** ...................518-455-5348/fax: 518-455-5728
*District:* 95  *Room:* 641 LOB  *e-mail:* GalefS@nyassembly.gov
*Committees:* Corporations, Authorities & Commissions; Election Law;
Governmental Operations; Health; Real Property Taxation (Chair); Task
Force on Women's Issues; Women's Caucus
*Senior Staff:* Jennifer Fields-Tawil

**Emily Gallagher (D)**............................518
*District:* 50  *Room:*  *e-mail:* gallaghere@nyassembly.gov
*Committees:* Alcoholism & Drug Abuse; Consumer Affairs & Protection;
Election Law; Small Business; Transportation; Task Force on Women's
Issues

**Jeff Gallahan (R)** .............................
*District:* 131  *Room:*  *e-mail:* gallahanj@nyassembly.gov
*Committees:* Aging; Children & Families; Local Governments; Racing &
Wagering; Tourism, Parks, Arts & Sports Development; Commission on
Solid Waste Management

**Jarett Gandolfo (R)** ...........................
*District:* 7  *Room:*  *e-mail:* gandolfoj@nyassembly.gov
*Committees:* Alcoholism & Drug Abuse; Higher Education; Insurance;
Mental Health; Racing & Wagering

**Jodi Giglio (R)**...............................
*District:* 2  *Room:*  *e-mail:* giglioj2@nyassembly.gov
*Committees:* Consumer Affairs & Protection; Economic Development, Job
Creation, Commerce & Industry; Governmental Employees; Labor; Tourism,
Parks, Art & Sports Development; Commission on Water Resource Needs of
New York

**Joseph M Giglio (R, C, I)**..........................518-455-5241
*District:* 148  *Room:* 525 LOB  *e-mail:* GiglioJ@nyassembly.gov
*Committees:* Codes; Correction; Ethics & Guidance; Rules
*Senior Staff:* Heidi Hartley

**Deborah J Glick (D)** ...........................518-455-4841
*District:* 66  *Room:* 717 LOB  *e-mail:* GlickD@nyassembly.gov
*Committees:* Environmental Conservation; Governmental Operations; Higher
Education (Chair); Rules; Task Force on Women's Issues; Ways & Means;
Women's Caucus
*Senior Staff:* Sarah Sanchala

**Jessica Gonzalez-Rojas (D)**.......................
*District:* 34  *Room:*  *e-mail:* gonzalezrojasj@nyassembly.gov
*Committees:* Cities; Children & Families; Corporations, Authorities &
Commissions; Environmental Conservation; Social Services; Asian Pacific
American TF; Black, Puerto Rican, Hispanic & Asian Caucus; Women's
Caucus; New Americans TF; Women's Issues

**Andy Goodell (R, C, I)** ..............518-455-4511/fax: 518-455-4328
*District:* 150  *Room:* 446 LOB  *e-mail:* goodella@nyassembly.gov
*Title:* Minority Leader Pro Tempore
*Committees:* Cities; Governmental Operations; Social Services; Commision
on Administrative Regulations Review
*Senior Staff:* Michele Krege

**Richard N Gottfried (D)**............518-455-4941/fax: 518-455-5939
*District:* 75  *Room:* 822 LOB  *e-mail:* GottfriedR@nyassembly.gov
*Committees:* Asian Pacific American Task Force; Health (Chair); Higher
Education; Rules; Examining Socio-Economic Responses to People with
Substance Use Disorders
*Senior Staff:* Wendi Paster

**Judy Griffin (D)**..............................518-455-4656
*District:* 21  *Room:* 432 LOB  *e-mail:* griffinj@nyassembly.gov
*Committees:* Alcoholism & Drug Abuse; Economic Development, Job
Creation, Commerce & Industry; Environmental Conservation; Governmental
Employees; Higher Education; Women's Caucus; Task Force on Women's
Issues

**Aileen M Gunther (D)** ..........................518-455-5355
*District:* 100  *Room:* 826 LOB  *e-mail:* GuntheA@nyassembly.gov
*Committees:* Agriculture; Environmental Conservation; Health; Mental
Health (Chair); Puerto Rican/Hispanic Task Force; Racing & Wagering; Task
Force on Women's Issues; Women's Caucus; Examining Socio-Economic
Responses to People with Substance Use Disorders

**Stephen Hawley (R, C, I)** ............518-455-5811/fax: 518-455-5558
*District:* 139  *Room:* 521 LOB  *e-mail:* HawleyS@nyassembly.gov
*Title:* Deputy Minority Leader
*Committees:* Agriculture; Insurance; Rules; Subcommittee on Women
Veterans; Veterans' Affairs; Ways & Means

**Carl E Heastie (D)** .................518-455-3791/fax: 518-455-4812
*District:* 83  *Room:* 932 LOB  *e-mail:* speaker@nyassembly.gov
*Title:* Speaker
*Committees:* Rules (Chair); Black, Puerto Rican, Hispanic & Asian
Legislative Caucus
*Senior Staff:* Jevonni Brooks

**Andrew Hevesi (D)** ...........................518-455-4926
*District:* 28  *Room:* 844 LOB  *e-mail:* HevesiA@nyassembly.gov
*Committees:* Banks; Codes; Health; Labor; Children & Families (Chair);
Examining Socio-Economic Responses to People with Substance Use
Disorders
*Senior Staff:* Brent Weitzberg

**Pamela J Hunter (D)**............................518-455-5383
*District:* 128  *Room:* 553 LOB  *e-mail:* HunterP@nyassembly.gov
*Title:* Chair, Majority Conference
*Committees:* Black, Puerto Rican, Hispanic & Asian Caucus; Energy;
Insurance; Social Services; Subcommittee on Women Veterans (Chair);
Transportation; Veterans' Affairs; Examining Socio-Economic Responses to
People with Substance Use Disorders

**Alicia Hyndman (D)** ...........................518-455-4451
*District:* 29  *Room:* 820 LOB  *e-mail:* hyndmana@nyassembly.gov
*Title:* Assistant Majority Leader
*Committees:* Black, Puerto Rican, Hispanic & Asian Caucus; Economic
Development, Job Creation, Commerce & Industry; Education; Governmental
Operations; Ways & Means; Task Force on Women's Issues; Transportation;
Women's Caucus; Asian Pacific American Task Force

**Chantel Jackson (D)**...........................
*District:* 79  *Room:*  *e-mail:* jacksonc@nyassembly.gov
*Committees:* Cities; Education; Mental Health; Alcoholism & Drug Abuse;
Small Business; Task Force on Women's Issues; Subcommittee on Micro
Business (Chair)

**Jonathan G Jacobson (D)**.........................518-455-5593
*District:* 104  *Room:* 628 LOB  *e-mail:* jacobsonj@nyassembly.gov
*Committees:* Cities; Election Law; Insurance; Labor; Local Governments;
Transportation; Election Day Operations & Voter Disenfranchisement (Chair)

**Kimberly Jean-Pierre (D)**...........518-455-5787/fax: 518-455-3976
*District:* 11  *Room:* 742 LOB  *e-mail:* jeanpierrek@nyassembly.gov
*Committees:* Banks; Black, Puerto Rican, Hispanic & Asian Caucus;
Children & Families; Corporations, Authorities & Commissions; Education;
Examining Socio-Economic Responses to People with Substance Use
Disorders; Task Force on Women's Issues; Women's Caucus
*Senior Staff:* Brendan Cunningham

**Josh Jensen (R)**...............................
*District:* 134  *Room:*  *e-mail:* jensenj@nyassembly.gov
*Committees:* Corporations, Authorities & Commissions; Health; Housing;
Libraries & Education Technology

*Offices and agencies generally appear in alphabetical order, except when specific order is requested by listee.*

**Billy Jones (D)** . . . . . . . . . . . . . . . . . . . . . . . . . . . .518-455-5943
*District:* 115 *Room:* 551 LOB *e-mail:* jonesb@nyassembly.gov
*Committees:* Aging; Agriculture; Economic Development, Job Creation, Commerce & Industry; Small Business; Tourism, Parks, Arts & Sports Development; Subcommittee on Agriculture Economic Development and Farmland Protection (Chair); Veterans' Affairs

**Latoya Joyner (D)** . . . . . . . . . . . . . . . .518-455-5671/fax: 518-455-5461
*District:* 77 *Room:* 441 LOB *e-mail:* joynerl@nyassembly.gov
*Committees:* Aging; Black, Puerto Rican, Hispanic & Asian Caucus; Education; Housing; Judiciary; Labor (Chair); Peurto Rican/Hispanic Task Force; Task Force on Women's Issues; Ways & Means; Women's Caucus

**Anna R Kelles (D)**. . . . . . . . . . . . . . . . . . . . . . . . . . . . .
*District:* 125 *Room:* *e-mail:* kellesa@nyassembly.gov
*Committees:* Agriculture; Correction; Economic Development, Job Creation, Commerce & Industry; Environmental Conservation; Local Governments; Task Force on Women's Issues; Subcommittee on Agricultural Production & Technology (Chair)

**Ron Kim (D)** . . . . . . . . . . . . . . . . . . . .518-455-5411/fax: 518-455-4650
*District:* 40 *Room:* 419 LOB *e-mail:* KimR@nyassembly.gov
*Committees:* Aging (Chair); Black, Puerto Rican, Hispanic & Asian Legislative Caucus; Corporations, Authorities & Commissions; Education; Governmental Operations; Housing; Puerto Rican/Hispanic Task Force
*Senior Staff:* Tony Cao

**Kieran Michael Lalor (R, C, I)**. . . . . . . . . . . . . . . . . .518-455-5725
*District:* 105 *Room:* 531 LOB *e-mail:* LalorK@nyassembly.gov
*Committees:* Banks; Corporations, Authorities & Commissions; Economic Development, Job Creation, Commerce & Industry; Governmental Operations; Small Business; Commission on State-Local Relations
*Senior Staff:* Kira Gorman

**Charles D Lavine (D)** . . . . . . . . . . . . .518-455-5456/fax: 518-455-5467
*District:* 13 *Room:* 713 LOB *e-mail:* LavineC@nyassembly.gov
*Committees:* Codes; Ethics & Guidance; Insurance; Judiciary (Chair); Rules
*Senior Staff:* Tara Butler-Sahai

**Michael Lawler (R)** . . . . . . . . . . . . . . . . . . . . . . . . . . . .
*District:* 97 *Room:* *e-mail:* lawlerm@nyassembly.gov
*Committees:* Aging; Banks; Education; Governmental Operations; Housing; Commission on Critical Transportation Choices

**John Lemondes (R)** . . . . . . . . . . . . . . . . . . . . . . . . . . . .
*District:* 126 *Room:* *e-mail:* lemondesj@nyassembly.gov
*Committees:* Banks; Corporations, Authorities & Commissions; Economic Development, Job Creation, Commerce & Industry; Environmental Conservation

**Jennifer Lunsford (D)** . . . . . . . . . . . . . . . . . . . . . . . . . . . .
*District:* 135 *Room:* *e-mail:* lunsfordj@nyassembly.gov
*Committees:* Children & Families; Economic Development, Job Creation, Commerce & Industry; Environmental Conservation; Libraries & Education Technology; Local Governmenta; Task Force on Women's Issues

**Donna A Lupardo (D)**. . . . . . . . . . . . . .518-455-5431/fax: 518-455-5693
*District:* 123 *Room:* 828 LOB *e-mail:* LupardoD@nyassembly.gov
*Committees:* Agriculture (Chair); Economic Development, Job Creation, Commerce & Industry; Higher Education; Rules; Task Force on Women's Issues; Transportation; Women's Caucus
*Senior Staff:* Gloria Poff

**William B Magnarelli (D)** . . . . . . . . . . . . . . . . . . . . .518-455-4826
*District:* 129 *Room:* 830 LOB *e-mail:* MagnarW@nyassembly.gov
*Committees:* Economic Development, Job Creation, Commerce & Industry; Education; Oversight, Analysis & Investigation; Rules; Transportation (Chair); Rules
*Senior Staff:* Christine Slocum

**Zohran Mamdani (D)** . . . . . . . . . . . . . . . . . . . . . . . . . . . .
*District:* 36 *Room:* *e-mail:* mamdaniz@nyassembly.gov
*Committees:* Aging; Cities; Election Law; Energy; Real Property Taxation; Asain Pacific American Task Force (Co-Chair)

**Brian Manktelow (R, C, I)**. . . . . . . . . . . . . . . . . . . . . . .518-455-5655
*District:* 130 *Room:* 629 LOB *e-mail:* manktelowb@nyassembly.gov
*Title:* Secretary, Minority Conference
*Committees:* Banks; Environmental Conservation; Local Governments; Small Business; Veterans' Affairs

**John T McDonald III (D)**. . . . . . . . . . .518-455-4474/fax: 518-455-4727
*District:* 108 *Room:* 417 LOB *e-mail:* McDonaldJ@nyassembly.gov
*Committees:* Alcoholism & Drug Abuse; Higher Education; Insurance; Local Governments; Real Property Taxation; Ways & Means; Health; Oversight, Analysis & Investigation (Chair)
*Senior Staff:* Shalyn Ranellone

**David G McDonough (R, C, I)** . . . . . . .518-455-4633/fax: 518-455-5559
*District:* 14 *Room:* 443 LOB *e-mail:* mcdonoughd@nyassembly.gov
*Title:* Chair, Minority Joint Conference Committee
*Committees:* Consumer Affairs & Protection; Education; Health; Subcommittee on Child Product Safety; Subcommittee on Regulated Mortgage Lenders; Transportation; Veterans' Affairs; Commission on Critical Transportation Choices
*Senior Staff:* Lynette Liverani

**Karen McMahon (D)** . . . . . . . . . . . . . . . . . . . . . . . . . . .518-455-4618
*District:* 146 *Room:* 631 LOB *e-mail:* mcmahonk@nyassembly.gov
*Committees:* Higher Education; Libraries & Education Technology; Judiciary; People with Disabilities; Transportation; Women's Caucus; Task Force on Women's Caucus

**Demond Meeks (D)**. . . . . . . . . . . . . . . . . . . . . . . . . . . .
*District:* 137 *Room:* *e-mail:* meeksd@nyassembly.gov
*Committees:* Children & Families; Cities; Governmental Operations; Housing; Insurance; Subcommittee on Insurer Investments & Market Practices in Underserved Areas

**John K Mikulin (R, C, I)** . . . . . . . . . . . . . . . . . . . . . . .518-455-5341
*District:* 17 *Room:* 550 LOB *e-mail:* mikulinj@nyassembly.gov
*Committees:* Banks; Consumer Affiars & Protection; Education; Election Law; Codes

**Brian D Miller (R, I)**. . . . . . . . . . . . . . . . . . . . . . . . . . .518-455-5334
*District:* 101 *Room:* 544 LOB *e-mail:* millerb@nyassembly.gov
*Title:* Vice Chair, Steering Committee
*Committees:* Agriculture; Consumer Affairs & Protection; Environmental Conservation; Real Property Taxation; Transportation

**Melissa Miller (R, C)**. . . . . . . . . . . . . . . . . . . . . . . . . . .518-455-3028
*District:* 20 *Room:* 426 LOB *e-mail:* MillerML@nyassembly.gov
*Title:* Vice Chair, Minority Joint Conference Committee
*Committees:* People with Disabilities; Aging; Children & Families; Education; Environmental Conservation; Health; Mental Health; Women's Caucus

**Marcela Mitaynes (D)** . . . . . . . . . . . . . . . . . . . . . . . . . . . .
*District:* 51 *Room:* *e-mail:* mitaynesm@nyassembly.gov
*Committees:* Banks; Children & Families; Education; Judiciary; Transportation; Task Force on Women's Issues; Subcommittee on Regulated Mortgage Lenders (Chair)

**Michael Montesano (R, C)**. . . . . . . . . .518-455-4684/fax: 518-455-5477
*District:* 15 *Room:* 437 LOB *e-mail:* Montesanom@nyassembly.gov
*Title:* Minority Whip
*Committees:* Codes; Ethics & Guidance; Judiciary; Oversight, Analysis & Investigation; Ways & Means; Rules
*Senior Staff:* Ida McQuair

**Angelo J Morinello (R, C, I)** . . . . . . . . . . . . . . . . . . . .518-455-5284
*District:* 145 *Room:* 721 LOB *e-mail:* morinelloa@nyassembly.gov
*Title:* Chair, Steering Committee
*Committees:* Codes; Economic Development, Job Creation, Commerce & Industry; Labor; Tourism, Parks, Arts & Sports Development; Veterans' Affairs; Commission on Toxic Substances & Hazardous Wastes

Legislative Branch

*Offices and agencies generally appear in alphabetical order, except when specific order is requested by listee.*

**Yuh-Line Niou (D)**.....................................518-455-3640
*District:* 65  *Room:* 818 LOB  *e-mail:* niouy@nyassembly.gov
*Committees:* Asian Pacific American Task Force; Banks; Black, Puerto Rican, Hispanic & Asian Caucus; Consumer Affairs & Protection; Housing; Insurance; Libraries & Education Tech; TF on Women's Issues; Women's Caucus; Corp., Authorities & Commissions

**Catherine Nolan (D)**.............................518-455-4851
*District:* 37  *Room:* 739 LOB  *e-mail:* nolanc@nyassembly.gov
*Title:* Deputy Speaker
*Committees:* Puerto Rican/Hispanic Task Force; Rules; Task Force on Women's Issues; Veterans' Affairs; Ways & Means; Women's Caucus
*Senior Staff:* Kathleen Whynot

**Michael J Norris (R, I)**.........................518-455-4601
*District:* 144  *Room:* 718 LOB  *e-mail:* norrism@nyassembly.gov
*Title:* Chair, Minority Conference
*Committees:* Election Law; Judiciary; Rules; Ways & Means; Transportation

**Daniel J O'Donnell (D)**..........................518-455-5603
*District:* 69  *Room:* 712 LOB  *e-mail:* OdonnellD@nyassembly.gov
*Committees:* Codes; Education; Environmental Conservation; Puerto Rican/Hispanic Task Force; Tourism, Parks, Arts & Sports Development (Chair)

**Steven Otis (D)** ...................518-455-4897/fax: 518-455-4861
*District:* 91  *Room:* 327 LOB  *e-mail:* OtisS@nyassembly.gov
*Committees:* Corporations, Authorities & Commissions; Education; Environmental Conservation; Science & Technology; Local Governments; Puerto Rican/Hispanic Task Force
*Senior Staff:* Debra Lagapa

**Philip A Palmesano (R, C, I)** ........518-455-5791/fax: 518-455-4644
*District:* 132  *Room:* 320 LOB  *e-mail:* palmesanop@nyassembly.gov
*Title:* Assistant Minority Leader
*Committees:* Correction; Corporations, Authorities & Commissions; Energy; Insurance; Ways & Means; Commission on Rural Resources; Legislative Task Force on Demographic Research & Reapportionment
*Senior Staff:* Sperry Navone

**Amy Paulin (D)** .....................................518-455-5585
*District:* 88  *Room:* 422 LOB  *e-mail:* PaulinA@nyassembly.gov
*Committees:* Corporations, Authorities & Commissions (Chair); Education; Health; Puerto Rican/Hispanic Task Force; Rules; Task Force on Women's Issues; Women's Caucus

**Crystal D Peoples-Stokes (D)** ......................518-455-5005
*District:* 141  *Room:* 926 LOB  *e-mail:* peoplec@nyassembly.gov
*Title:* Majority Leader
*Committees:* Black, Puerto Rican, Hispanic & Asian Caucus; Rules; Women's Caucus; Women's Issues
*Senior Staff:* Mark Boyd

**N Nick Perry (D)** ..................518-455-4166/fax: 518-455-5478
*District:* 58  *Room:* 736 LOB  *e-mail:* perryn@nyassembly.gov
*Title:* Assistant Speaker Pro Tempore
*Committees:* Banks; Black, Puerto Rican, Hispanic & Asian Legislative Caucus; Codes; Labor; Rules; Transportation; Ways & Means
*Senior Staff:* Joyce Elie

**Stacey Pheffer Amato (D)** .........................518-455-4292
*District:* 23  *Room:* 827 LOB  *e-mail:* amatos@nyassembly.gov
*Title:* Assistant Majority Whip
*Committees:* Consumer Affairs & Protection; Corporations, Authorities & Commissions; Governmental Employees; Racing & Wagering; Science & Technology; Veterans' Affairs; Task Force on Women's Issues; Women's Caucus

**Victor M Pichardo (D)**..............................518-455-5511
*District:* 86  *Room:* 602 LOB  *e-mail:* PichardoV@nyassembly.gov
*Committees:* Black, Puerto Rican, Hispanic & Asian Caucus; Banks (Chair); Higher Education; Housing; Small Business; Social Services; Puerto Rican/Hispanic Task Force

**J Gary Pretlow (D)** .................518-455-5291/fax: 518-455-5447
*District:* 89  *Room:* 845 LOB  *e-mail:* PretloJ@nyassembly.gov
*Committees:* Codes; Black, Puerto Rican, Hispanic & Asian Caucus; Codes; Insurance; Puerto Rican/Hispanic Task Force; Racing & Wagering (Chair); Rules; Ways & Means

**Dan Quart (D)** .....................................518-455-4794
*District:* 73  *Room:* 741 LOB  *e-mail:* quartd@nyassembly.gov
*Committees:* Alcoholism & Drug Abuse; Asian Pacific American TF; Commission on Administrative Regulations Review (Chair); Consumer Affairs & Protection; Corporations, Authorities & Commissions; Correction; Judiciary; Tourism, Parks, Arts & Sports Development
*Senior Staff:* Amanda Wallwin

**Edward P Ra (R)** ...................518-455-4627/fax: 518-455-4643
*District:* 19  *Room:* 546 LOB  *e-mail:* rae@nyassembly.gov
*Title:* Ranking Minority Member, Ways & Means
*Committees:* Ways and Means; Rules

**Jenifer Rajkumar (D)** ...............................
*District:* 38  *Room:*   *e-mail:* rajkumarj@nyassembly.gov
*Committees:* Aging; Consumer Affairs & Protection; Judiciary; SMall Business; Veterans' Affairs; Task Force on Women's Issues; Subcommittee on Diversity in Law (Chair)

**Phil Ramos (D)** ....................518-455-5185/fax: 518-455-5236
*District:* 6  *Room:* 648 LOB  *e-mail:* ramosp@nyassembly.gov
*Title:* Assistant Speaker
*Committees:* Aging; Black, Puerto Rican, Hispanic & Asian Legislative Caucus; Education; Local Governments; Puerto Rican/Hispanic Task Force; Subcommittee on Students with Special Needs; Ways & Means
*Senior Staff:* Edith Richiez

**Michael Reilly (R)** .................518-455-4495/fax: 518-455-4501
*District:* 62  *Room:* 428 LOB  *e-mail:* reillym@nyassembly.gov
*Committees:* Education; Governmental Employees; Cities; Codes; Higher Education; Housing

**Karines Reyes (D)** ..................518-455-5102/fax: 518-455-3693
*District:* 87  *Room:* 325 LOB  *e-mail:* reyesk@nyassembly.gov
*Committees:* Aging; Alcoholism & Drug Abuse; Black, Puerto Rican, Hispanic & Asian Legislative Caucus; Health; Labor; Puerto Rican/Hispanic Task Force; Social Services; Women's Caucus

**Diana C Richardson (D)**............................518-455-5262
*District:* 43  *Room:* 834 LOB  *e-mail:* district43@nyassembly.gov
*Committees:* Banks; Black, Puerto Rican, Hispanic & Asian Legislative Caucus; Corporations, Authorities & Commissions; Labor; Mental Health; Small Business; Task Force on Women's Issues

**Jonathan Rivera (D)** ...............................
*District:* 149  *Room:*   *e-mail:* riverajd@nyassembly.gov
*Committees:* Election Law; Energy; Housing; Local Governments; Tourism, Parks, Art & Sports Development; Subcommittee on Regional Tourism Development (Chair)

**José Rivera (D)**.....................518-455-5414/fax: 518-455-5322
*District:* 78  *Room:* 536 LOB  *e-mail:* riveraj@nyassembly.gov
*Title:* Deputy Majority Whip
*Committees:* Aging; Agriculture; Black, Puerto Rican, Hispanic & Asian Legislative Caucus; Insurance; Puerto Rican/Hispanic Task Force; Small Business

**Robert J Rodriguez (D)** ............................518-455-4781
*District:* 68  *Room:* 729 LOB  *e-mail:* Rrodriguez@nyassembly.gov
*Committees:* Banks; Black, Puerto Rican, Hispanic & Asian Caucus; Corporations, Authorities & Commissions; Housing; Labor; Mental Health; Puerto Rican/Hispanic Task Force; Task Force on Demographic Research & Reapportionment (Chair); Ways & Means

**Daniel Rosenthal (D)**..............................518-455-4404
*District:* 27  *Room:* 431 LOB  *e-mail:* rosenthald@nyassembly.gov
*Committees:* Aging; Health; Insurance; Labor; Real Property Taxation; Social Services; Task Force on Food, Farm & Nutrition Policy (Chair)

*Offices and agencies generally appear in alphabetical order, except when specific order is requested by listee.*

**Linda B Rosenthal (D, WF)**.........................518-455-5802
*District:* 67  *Room:* 627 LOB  *e-mail:* RosentL@nyassembly.gov
*Committees:* Agriculture; Codes; Health; Housing; Subcommittee on
Renewable Energy; Social Services (Chair); Subcommittee on Tuition
Assistance Program; Subcommittee on Women's Health; Task Force on
Women's Issues; Women's Caucus
*Senior Staff:* Lauren Schuster

**Nily Rozic (D, WF)** ...............................518-455-5172
*District:* 25  *Room:* 547 LOB  *e-mail:* RozicN@nyassembly.gov
*Committees:* Asian Pacific American Task Force; Consumer Affairs &
Protection; Corporations, Authorities & Commissions; Correction; Labor; TF
on Women's Issues; Ways & Means; Women's Caucus; Black, Puerto Rican,
Hispanic & Asian Caucus; Puerto Rican/Hispanic TF

**John Salka (R, C)** ................................518-455-4807
*District:* 121  *Room:* 529 LOB  *e-mail:*
*Committees:* Children & Families; Economic Development, Job Creation,
Commerce & Industry; Health; Higher Education; Commission on
State-Local Relations

**Angelo Santabarbara (D)**........................518-455-5197
*District:* 111  *Room:* 654 LOB  *e-mail:* SantabarbaraA@nyassembly.gov
*Committees:* Agriculture; Commission on Rural Resources (Chair); Energy;
Governmental Employees; Mental Health; Racing & Wagering;
Subcommittee on Autism Spectrum Disorders (Chair); Veterans' Affairs
*Senior Staff:* Nicole Parisi

**Nader J Sayegh (D)** ...............518-455-3662/fax: 518-455-5499
*District:* 90  *Room:* 326 LOB  *e-mail:*
*Committees:* Banks; Black, Puerto Rican, Hispanic & Asian Legislative
Caucus; Cities; Education; Health; Racing & Wagering; Real Property
Taxation; Subcommittee on Students with Special Needs (Chair)

**Colin Schmitt (R, C, I)** ..........................518-455-5441
*District:* 99  *Room:* 433 LOB  *e-mail:* schmittc@nyassembly.gov
*Committees:* Housing; Insurance; Labor; Local Governments

**Rebecca A Seawright (D)**........................518-455-5676
*District:* 76  *Room:* 650 LOB  *e-mail:* SeawrightR@nyassembly.gov
*Committees:* Banks; Codes; Corporations, Authorities & Commissions;
Education; Judiciary; Puerto Rican/Hispanic Task Force; Ways & Means;
Women's Caucus
*Senior Staff:* Audrey Tannen

**Amanda Septimo (D)**.............................
*District:* 84  *Room:*   *e-mail:* septimoa@nyassembly.gov
*Committees:* Agriculture; Banks; Education; Environmental Conservation;
Veterans' Affairs; Task Force on Women's Issues

**Gina Sillitti (D)** ................................
*District:* 16  *Room:*   *e-mail:*
*Committees:* Economic Development, Job Creation, Commerce & Industry;
Election Law; Local Governments; Tourism, Parks, Art & Sports
Development; Transportation; Task Force on Women's Issues; Subcommittee
on Occupational Licenses (Chair)

**Jo Anne Simon (D)** ..............................518-455-5426
*District:* 52  *Room:* 435 LOB  *e-mail:* simonj@nyassembly.gov
*Committees:* Consumer Affairs & Protection; Education; Ethics & Guidance
(Chair); Higher Education; Labor; Legislative Ethics (Chair); Transportation;
Women's Caucus
*Senior Staff:* Susannah Pasquantonio

**Matthew Simpson (R)** ............................
*District:* 114  *Room:*   *e-mail:* simpsonm@nyassembly.gov
*Committees:* Environmental Conservation; Local Governments; Social
Services; Tourism, Parks, Arts & Sports Development

**Doug Smith (R)** .................................518-455-5937
*District:* 5  *Room:* 545 LOB  *e-mail:* smithd@nyassembly.gov
*Committees:* Aging; Education; Energy; Higher Education; Housing

**Robert Smullen (R, C)** ...........................518-455-5393
*District:* 118  *Room:* 527 LOB  *e-mail:* smullenr@nyassembly.gov
*Committees:* Banks; Economic Development, Job Creation, Commerce &
Industry; Environmental Conservation; Higher Education; Social Services

**Michaelle C Solages (D)** ............518-455-4465/fax: 518-455-5560
*District:* 22  *Room:* 619 LOB  *e-mail:* SolagesM@nyassembly.gov
*Title:* Deputy Majority Leader
*Committees:* Asian Pacific American Task Force; Black, Puerto
Rican/Hispanic Task Force; Libraries & Education Technology; Racing &
Wagering; Social Services; Women's Issues; Women's Caucus

**Phil Steck (D)** ....................518-455-5931/fax: 518-455-5840
*District:* 110  *Room:* 702 LOB  *e-mail:* SteckP@nyassembly.gov
*Committees:* Alcoholism & Drug Abuse (Chair); Labor; Health; Insurance;
Judiciary; Oversight, Analysis & Investigation

**Steve Stern (D)**..................................518-455-5732
*District:* 10  *Room:* 919 LOB  *e-mail:* sterns@nyassembly.gov
*Committees:* Aging; Banks; Economic Development, Job Creation,
Commerce & Industry; Energy; Insurance; Veterans' Affairs

**Al Stirpe (D)** .....................518-455-4505/fax: 518-455-5593
*District:* 127  *Room:* 622 LOB  *e-mail:* StirpeA@nyassembly.gov
*Committees:* Agriculture; Alcoholism & Drug Abuse; Economic
Development, Job Creation, Commerce & Industry; Higher Education; Small
Business (Chair)
*Senior Staff:* Courtenay Ruddy

**Chris Tague (R, C, I)** ............................518-455-5363
*District:* 102  *Room:* 937 LOB  *e-mail:* taguec@nyassembly.gov
*Committees:* Agriculture; Election Law; Environmental Conservation; Real
Property Taxation; Tourism, Parks, Arts & Sports Development

**Michael Tannousis (R)** ..........................
*District:* 64  *Room:*   *e-mail:* tannousism@nyassembly.gov
*Committees:* Aging; Cities; Codes; Governmental Employees; Judiciary;
Commission on Solid Waste Management; Commission on Toxic Substances
& Hazardous Wastes

**Al Taylor (D)** ...................................518-455-5491
*District:* 71  *Room:* 633 LOB  *e-mail:* taylora@nyassembly.gov
*Title:* Chair, Majority House Operations
*Committees:* Aging; Banks; Black, Puerto Rican, Hispanic & Asian
Legislative Caucus; Cities; Education; Election Law; Housing; Puerto
Rican/Hispanic Task Force

**Fred W Thiele Jr (I, D, WF)**......................518-455-5997
*District:* 1  *Room:* 837 LOB  *e-mail:* ThieleF@nyassembly.gov
*Committees:* Environmental Conservation; Local Governments (Chair);
Oversight, Analysis & Investigation; Rules; Transportation
*Senior Staff:* Lisa Lombardo

**Clyde Vanel (D)** ..................518-455-4711/fax: 518-455-3740
*District:* 33  *Room:* 454 LOB  *e-mail:* vanelc@nyassembly.gov
*Committees:* Asian Pacific American Task Force; Banks; Black, Puerto
Rican, Hispanic & Asian Caucus; Children & Families; Codes; Corporations,
Authorities & Commissions; Racing & Wagering; Science & Technology

**Mark Walczyk (R, C, I)** ..........................518-455-5545
*District:* 116  *Room:* 940 LOB  *e-mail:* walczykm@nyassembly.gov
*Committees:* Cities; Commission on Rural Resources; Correction; Energy;
Higher Education; Social Services; Transportation

**Latrice Walker (D)** ..............................518-455-4466
*District:* 55  *Room:* 746 LOB  *e-mail:* WalkerL@nyassembly.gov
*Committees:* Black, Puerto Rican, Hispanic & Asian Caucus; Codes;
Correction; Election Law (Chair); Housing; Judiciary; Puerto Rican/Hispanic
Task Force; Women's Caucus; Women's Issues
*Senior Staff:* Nayemai-Isis McIntosh Green

*Offices and agencies generally appear in alphabetical order, except when specific order is requested by listee.*

**Monica P Wallace (D)** . . . . . . . . . . . . . . 518-455-5921/fax: 518-455-3962
*District:* 143   *Room:* 821 LOB   *e-mail:* wallacem@nyassembly.gov
*Title:* Vice Chair, Majority Steering
*Committees:* Judiciary; Local Governments; Governmental Operations;
Science & Technology; Task Force on Women's Issues; Veterans' Affairs;
Women's Caucus; Transportation

**Mary Beth Walsh (R, C, I)** . . . . . . . . . . . . . . . . . . 518-455-5772
*District:* 112   *Room:* 725 LOB   *e-mail:* walshm@nyassembly.gov
*Title:* Assistant Minority Leader Pro Tempore
*Committees:* Education; Judiciary; Libraries & Education Technology;
Mental Health; Women's Caucus

**Helene E Weinstein (D)** . . . . . . . . . . . . . . . . . . . . 518-455-5462
*District:* 41   *Room:* 923 LOB   *e-mail:* weinsth@nyassembly.gov
*Title:* Chair, Ways & Means Committee
*Committees:* Rules; Task Force on Women's Issues; Ways & Means (Chair);
Women's Caucus
*Senior Staff:* Yehuda Schupper

**David I Weprin (D)** . . . . . . . . . . . . . . . . . . . . . . . 518-455-5806
*District:* 24   *Room:* 526 LOB   *e-mail:* WeprinD@nyassembly.gov
*Committees:* Asian Pacific American Task Force; Banks; Codes; Correction
(Chair); Judiciary; Puerto Rican/Hispanic Task Force; Ways & Means

**Jaime R Williams (D)** . . . . . . . . . . . . . . . . . . . . . . 518-455-5211
*District:* 59   *Room:* 456 LOB   *e-mail:* williamsja@nyassembly.gov
*Title:* Vice Chair, Majority Conference
*Committees:* Agriculture; Black, Puerto Rican, Hispanic & Asian Caucus;
Consumer Affairs & Protection; Environmental Conservation; Governmental
Operations; Task Force on Women's Issues; Transportation; Women's
Caucus; Puerto Rican/Hispanic Task Force

**Carrie Woerner (D)** . . . . . . . . . . . . . . . 518-455-5404/fax: 518-455-3727
*District:* 113   *Room:* 502 LOB   *e-mail:* woernerc@nyassembly.gov
*Committees:* Agriculture; Commission on Rural Resources; Commission on
SKills Development & Career Education (Chair); Local Governments;
Racing & Wagering; Small Business; Task Force on Women's Issues;
Tourism, Parks, Arts & Sports Development; Women's Caucus
*Senior Staff:* Mark Luciano

**Kenneth Zebrowski (D)** . . . . . . . . . . . . . . . . . . . . 518-455-5735
*District:* 96   *Room:* 424 LOB   *e-mail:* ZebrowskiK@nyassembly.gov
*Committees:* Ethics & Guidance; Governmental Employees; Governmental
Operations; Judiciary; Rules; Subcommittee on Emerging Workforce;
Ways & Means
*Senior Staff:* Edward Bresnan

**Stefani Zinerman (D)** . . . . . . . . . . . . . . . . . . . . . . . . . . . . . . . . . . .
*District:* 56   *Room:*    *e-mail:* zinermans@nyassembly.gov
*Committees:* Aging; Agriculture; Labor; People with Disabilities; Task Force
on Women's Issues; Tourism, Parks, Arts & Sports Development;
Subcommittee on Emerging Workforce (Chair)

## STATE ASSEMBLY STANDING COMMITTEES

## Aging
Chair:
  Ron Kim (D) . . . . . . . . . . . . . . . . . . . . . . . . . . . . . . 518-455-4527

**Committee Staff**
Associate Counsel:
  Benjamin Decker

  **Key Assembly Staff Assignments**
  Majority Program Analyst:
    Vacant . . . . . . . . . . . . . . . . . . . . . . . . . . . . . . 518-455-4928

## Membership

  **Majority**
  | | |
  |---|---|
  | Peter J Abbate, Jr | Brian Barnwell |
  | Charles Barron | Sarah Clark |

| | |
|---|---|
| Catalina Cruz | Inez E Dickens |
| Simcha Eichenstein | Charles D Fall |
| Phara Souffrant Forrest | Mathylde Frontus |
| Billy Jones | Zohran Mamdani |
| Jenifer Rajkumar | Phil Ramos |
| Karines Reyes | José Rivera |
| Daniel Rosenthal | Steve Stern |
| Al Taylor | Stefani Zinerman |

**Minority**
| | |
|---|---|
| Jake Ashby | Karl Brabenec |
| Joe DeStefano | Jeff Gallahan |
| Mike Lawler | Melissa Miller |
| Doug Smith | Michael Tannousis |

## Agriculture
Chair:
  Donna A Lupardo (D) . . . . . . . . . . . . . . . . . . . . . . . . 518-455-5431

## Committee Staff
Clerk:
  Vacant

  **Key Assembly Staff Assignments**
  Majority Program & Legislative Analyst:
    Robert Stern . . . . . . . . . . . . . . . . . . . . . . . . . . . 518-455-4928
  Committee Assistant:
    Emily Sischo
  Assisstant Secretary for Program & Policy:
    Giovanni Warren

## Membership

  **Majority**
  | | |
  |---|---|
  | Brian Barnwell | Didi Barrett |
  | Marianne Buttenschon | Erik M Dilan |
  | Harvey Epstein | Aileen M Gunther |
  | Billy Jones | Anna R Kelles |
  | José Rivera | Linda B Rosenthal |
  | Angelo Santabarbara | Amanda Septimo |
  | Al Stirpe | Jamie R Williams |
  | Carrie Woerner | Stefani Zinerman |

  **Minority**
  | | |
  |---|---|
  | Ken Blankenbush | Michael J Fitzpatrick |
  | Christopher S Friend | Stephen Hawley |
  | Brian D Miller | Chris Tague |

## Alcoholism & Drug Abuse
Chair:
  Phil Steck (D) . . . . . . . . . . . . . . . . . . . . . . . . . . . . 518-455-5802

## Committee Staff
Clerk:
  Vacant

  **Key Assembly Staff Assignments**
  Legislative Analyst:
    Katherine Jesaitis
  Assistant Secretary for Program & Policy:
    Jennifer Sacco
  Associate Counsel:
    Vacant

## Membership

  **Majority**
  | | |
  |---|---|
  | Maritza Davila | Nathalia Fernandez |
  | Emily Gallagher | Judy Griffin |
  | Chantel Jackson | John T McDonald III |
  | Dan Quart | Karines Reyes |
  | Al Stirpe | |

*Offices and agencies generally appear in alphabetical order, except when specific order is requested by listee.*

**Minority**

Keith P Brown
Joe DeStefano
Michael Durso
Jarett Gandolfo

## Banks

Chair:
Victor M Pichardo (D) . . . . . . . . . . . . . . . . . . . . . . . . . . . .518-455-5735

**Committee Staff**

Clerk:
Vacant

**Key Assembly Staff Assignments**

Majority Principal Analyst:
Peter Hoffman. . . . . . . . . . . . . . . . . . . . . . . . . . . . . . . . . .518-455-4928
Majority Associate Counsel:
Teri Kleinmann. . . . . . . . . . . . . . . . . . . . . . . . . . . . . . . . . .518-455-4928
Assistant Secretary for Program & Policy:
Aaron Suggs

### Membership

**Majority**

Peter J Abbate, Jr
Khaleel M Anderson
Brian Barnwell
Rodneyse Bichotte Hermelyn
Marianne Buttenschon
Pat Burke
Carmen N De La Rosa
Inez E Dickens
Andrew Hevesi
Kimberly Jean-Pierre
Marcela Mitaynes
Yuh-Line Niou
N Nick Perry
Diana C Richardson
Robert J Rodriguez
Nader J Sayegh
Rebecca A Seawright
Amanda Septimo
Steve Stern
Al Taylor
Clyde Vanel
David I Weprin

**Minority**

Joe Angelino
Michael J Fitzpatrick
Keiran Michael Lalor
Mike Lawler
John Lemondes
Brian Manktelow
John K Mikulin
Robert Smullen

## Children & Families

Chair:
Andrew Hevesi (D). . . . . . . . . . . . . . . . . . . . . . . . . . . . . . .518-455-5118

**Committee Staff**

Associate Counsel:
Vacant
Legislative Director:
Christina Philo

**Key Assembly Staff Assignments**

Assistant Secretary for Program & Policy:
Jennifer Sacco

### Membership

**Majority**

Khaleel M Anderson
Sarah Clark
Catalina Cruz
Taylor Darling
Maritza Davila
Mathylde Frontus
Jessica Gonzalez-Rojas
Kimberly Jean-Pierre
Jennifer Lunsford
Demond Meeks
Marcela Mitaynes
Clyde Vanel

**Minority**

Marjorie Byrnes
Jeff Gallahan
Melissa Miller
John Salka

## Cities

Chair:
Edward C Braunstein (D) . . . . . . . . . . . . . . . . . . . . . . . . .518-455-5425

**Committee Staff**

Clerk:
Iris Figueras

**Key Assembly Staff Assignments**

Majority Deputy Secretary:
Julia Mallalieu
Director, Minority Counsel Staff:
Edmund Wick. . . . . . . . . . . . . . . . . . . . . . . . . . . . . . . . . . .518-455-4262

### Membership

**Majority**

Robert C Carroll
Simcha Eichenstein
Charles D Fall
Nathalia Fernandez
Jessica Gonzalez-Rojas
Chantel Jackson
Zohran Mamdani
Jonathan G Jacobson
Demond Meeks
Nader J Sayegh
Al Taylor

**Minority**

Andy Goodell
Michael Reilly
Michael Tannousis
Mark Walczyk

## Codes

Chair:
Jeffrey Dinowitz (D). . . . . . . . . . . . . . . . . . . . . . . . . . . . .518-455-4477

**Committee Staff**

Clerk:
Carolyn Wildman . . . . . . . . . . . . . . . . . . . . . . . . . . . . . . . .518-455-4477

**Key Assembly Staff Assignments**

Senior Team Counsel:
Marty Rosenbaum . . . . . . . . . . . . . . . . . . . . . . . . . . . . . .518-455-4313
Associate Counsel:
Jonathan Bailey . . . . . . . . . . . . . . . . . . . . . . . . . . . . . . . .518-455-4313
Majority Principal Analyst:
Nathaniel Jenkins
Executive Secretary:
Vacant

### Membership

**Majority**

Thomas J Abinanti
Vivian E Cook
Catalina Cruz
Steven Cymbrowitz
Patricia Fahy
Andrew Hevesi
Charles D Lavine
Daniel J O'Donnell
N Nick Perry
J Gary Pretlow
Linda B Rosenthal
Rebecca A Seawright
Clyde Vanel
Latrice Walker
David I Weprin

**Minority**

Joseph M Giglio
John K Mikulin
Michael Montesano
Angelo J Morinello
Michael Reilly
Michael Tannousis

## Consumer Affairs & Protection

Chair:
Nily Rozic (D, WF). . . . . . . . . . . . . . . . . . . . . . . . . . . . . .518-455-4545

**Committee Staff**

Clerk:
Christopher Bauer

**Key Assembly Staff Assignments**

Program Counsel & Secretary:
Vacant
Associate Counsel:
Teri Kleinmann

*Offices and agencies generally appear in alphabetical order, except when specific order is requested by listee.*

## Membership

### Majority

| | |
|---|---|
| Peter J Abbate, Jr | Kenny Burgos |
| Charles D Fall | Phara Souffrant Forrest |
| Emily Gallagher | Yuh-Line Niou |
| Stacey Pheffer Amato | Dan Quart |
| Jenifer Rajkumar | Jo Anne Simon |
| Jaime R Williams | |

### Minority

| | |
|---|---|
| Jodi Giglio | David G McDonough |
| John K Mikulin | Brian D Miller |

## Corporations, Authorities & Commissions

Chair:
    Amy Paulin (D) . . . . . . . . . . . . . . . . . . . . . . . . . . . . 518-455-5585

### Committee Staff

Clerk:
    Anais Vasquez

#### Key Assembly Staff Assignments

Majority Assistant Secretary for Program & Policy:
    Vacant
Minority Associate Counsel:
    David Gordon

### Membership

#### Majority

| | |
|---|---|
| Robert C Carroll | Vivian E Cook |
| Carmen N De La Rosa | Erik M Dilan |
| Charles D Fall | Sandy Galef |
| Jessica Gonzalez-Rojas | Kimberly Jean-Pierre |
| Ron Kim | Yuh-Line Niou |
| Steven Otis | Stacey Pheffer Amato |
| Dan Quart | Diana C Richardson |
| Robert J Rodriguez | Nily Rozic |
| Rebecca A Seawright | Clyde Vanel |

#### Minority

| | |
|---|---|
| Joe Angelino | Ken Blankenbush |
| Christopher S Friend | Josh Jensen |
| Kieran Michael Lalor | John Lemondes |
| Philip A Palmesano | |

## Correction

Chair:
    David I Weprin (D) . . . . . . . . . . . . . . . . . . . . . . . . . . . 518-455-5806

### Committee Staff

#### Key Assembly Staff Assignments

Majority Counsel:
    Dianna Goodwin . . . . . . . . . . . . . . . . . . . . . . . . . 518-455-4313
Legislative Analyst:
    Tahirih Anthony

### Membership

#### Majority

| | |
|---|---|
| Chris Burdick | Kenny Burgos |
| William Colton | Maritza Davila |
| Carmen N De La Rosa | Anna R Kelles |
| Dan Quart | Nily Rozic |
| Latrice Walker | |

#### Minority

| | |
|---|---|
| Joseph M Giglio | Philip A Palmesano |
| Mark Walczyk | |

## Economic Development, Job Creation, Commerce & Industry

Chair:
    Harry B Bronson (D) . . . . . . . . . . . . . . . . . . . . . . . . . 518-455-4767

### Committee Staff

Committee Clerk:
    Patrice Mago . . . . . . . . . . . . . . . . . . . . . . . . . . . . 518-455-4767

#### Key Assembly Staff Assignments

Legislative Director:
    Vanessa Komarnicki . . . . . . . . . . . . . . . . . . . . . . . . 518-455-4767
Assistant Secretary for Program & Policy:
    Giovanni Warren

### Membership

#### Majority

| | |
|---|---|
| Charles Barron | Pat Burke |
| Marianne Buttenschon | Kevin A Cahill |
| Taylor Darling | Maritza Davila |
| Patricia Fahy | Mathylde Frontus |
| Judy Griffin | Alicia Hyndman |
| Billy Jones | Anna R Kelles |
| Jennifer Lunsford | Donna A Lupardo |
| William B Magnarelli | Gina Sillitti |
| Steve Stern | Al Stirpe |

#### Minority

| | |
|---|---|
| Christopher S Friend | Jodi Giglio |
| Kieran Michael Lalor | John Lemondes |
| Angelo J Morinello | John Salka |
| Robert Smullen | |

## Education

Chair:
    Michael Benedetto (D) . . . . . . . . . . . . . . . . . . . . . . . . 518-455-5296

### Committee Staff

Committee Clerk:
    Brittany Stinson . . . . . . . . . . . . . . . . . . . . . . . . . . 518-455-4851

#### Key Assembly Staff Assignments

Assistant Secretary for Program & Policy:
    Maria Volpe-McDermott
Associate Counsel:
    Benjamin Decker

### Membership

#### Majority

| | |
|---|---|
| Rodneyse Bichotte Hermelyn | Harry B Bronson |
| Marianne Buttenschon | William Conrad |
| Inez E Dickens | Alicia Hyndman |
| Chantel Jackson | Kimberly Jean-Pierre |
| Latoya Joyner | Ron Kim |
| William B Magnarelli | Marcela Mitaynes |
| Daniel J O'Donnell | Steven Otis |
| Amy Paulin | Phil Ramos |
| Diana C Richardson | Nader J Sayegh |
| Rebecca A Seawright | Amanda Septimo |
| Jo Anne Simon | Al Taylor |

#### Minority

| | |
|---|---|
| Christopher S Friend | Mike Lawler |
| David G McDonough | John K Mikulin |
| Melissa Miller | Michael Reilly |
| Doug Smith | Mary Beth Walsh |

## Election Law

Chair:
    Latrice Walker (D) . . . . . . . . . . . . . . 518-455-5456/fax: 518-455-5467

---

*Offices and agencies generally appear in alphabetical order, except when specific order is requested by listee.*

**Committee Staff**

Executive Secretary:
Vacant

**Key Assembly Staff Assignments**

Majority Program Analyst:
Matthew Aumand . . . . . . . . . . . . . . . . . . . . . . . . . . . . . . . . 518-455-4313
Majority Assistant Secretary:
Vacant
Majority Counsel:
Vacant

## Membership

**Majority**

| | |
|---|---|
| Kenny Burgos | Robert C Carroll |
| Jeffrey Dinowitz | Sandy Galef |
| Emily Gallagher | Jonathan G Jacobson |
| Zohran Mamdani | Jonathan Rivera |
| Gina Sillitti | Al Taylor |

**Minority**

| | |
|---|---|
| Karl Brabenec | John K Mikulin |
| Michael J Norris | Chris Tague |

## Energy

Chair:
Michael Cusick (D) . . . . . . . . . . . . . . . . . . . . . . . . . . . . 518-455-5526

**Committee Staff**

Clerk:
Sharon Grobe . . . . . . . . . . . . . . . . . . . . . . . . . . . . . . . . . 518-455-5526

**Key Assembly Staff Assignments**

Legislative Analyst:
Vacant

## Membership

**Majority**

| | |
|---|---|
| Khaleel M Anderson | Charles Barron |
| Robert C Carroll | William Conrad |
| Erik M Dilan | Steve Englebright |
| Pamela J Hunter | Zohran Mamdani |
| Jonathan Rivera | Angelo Santabarbara |
| Steve Stern | |

**Minority**

| | |
|---|---|
| Ken Blankenbush | Philip A Palmesano |
| Doug Smith | Mark Walczyk |

## Environmental Conservation

Chair:
Steven Englebright (D) . . . . . . . . . . . . . . . . . . . . . . . . . 518-455-4804

**Committee Staff**

Clerk:
Nancy Rissacher . . . . . . . . . . . . . . . . . . . . . . . . . . . . . . . 518-455-4804

**Key Assembly Staff Assignments**

Principal Legislative Analyst:
Vacant
Associate Counsel:
Henry Tranes

## Membership

**Majority**

| | |
|---|---|
| Thomas J Abinanti | Didi Barrett |
| Chris Burdick | Pat Burke |
| Robert C Carroll | William Colton |
| Steven Cymbrowitz | Harvey Epstein |
| Patricia Fahy | Deborah J Glick |
| Jessica Gonzalez-Rojas | Judy Griffin |

| | |
|---|---|
| Aileen M Gunther | Anna R Kelles |
| Jennifer Lunsford | Karen McMahon |
| Daniel J O'Donnell | Steven Otis |
| Amanda Septimo | Fred W Thiele Jr |
| Jaime R Williams | |

**Minority**

| | |
|---|---|
| Keith P Brown | Michael Durso |
| John Lemondes | Brian Manktelow |
| Brian D Miller | Matthew Simpson |
| Robert Smullen | Chris Tague |

## Ethics & Guidance

Chair:
Jo Anne Simon (D) . . . . . . . . . . . . . . . . . . . . . . . . . . . . 518-455-5014

## Membership

**Majority**

| | |
|---|---|
| Catalina Cruz | Charles D Lavine |
| Kenneth Zebrowski | |

**Minority**

| | |
|---|---|
| Jake Ashby | Marjorie Byrnes |
| Joseph M Giglio | Michael Montesano |

## Governmental Employees

Chair:
Peter J Abbate, Jr (D) . . . . . . . . . . . . . . . . . . . . . . . . . . 518-455-3053

**Committee Staff**

Committee Clerk:
Christine Eppelmann . . . . . . . . . . . . . . . . . . . . . . . . . . . . 518-455-3053

**Key Assembly Staff Assignments**

Majority Assistant Secretary:
Jennifer Best . . . . . . . . . . . . . . . . . . . . . . . . . . . . . . . . . . 518-455-4311
Associate Counsel:
Christopher Greenidge

## Membership

**Majority**

| | |
|---|---|
| Jeffrion L Aubry | William Colton |
| Michael Cusick | Simcha Eichenstein |
| Charles D Fall | Judy Griffin |
| Stacey Pheffer Amato | Angelo Santabarbara |
| Kenneth Zebrowski | |

**Minority**

| | |
|---|---|
| Joe DeStefano | Jodi Giglio |
| Michael Reilly | Michael Tannousis |

## Governmental Operations

Chair:
Kenneth Zebrowski (D) . . . . . . . . . . . . . . . . . . . . . . . . . 518-455-5668

**Committee Staff**

Clerk:
Jessica Marsico

**Key Assembly Staff Assignments**

Majority Assistant Secretary:
Aaron Suggs
Associate Counsel:
Nathan Kerstein
Committee Analyst:
Vacant

## Membership

**Majority**

| | |
|---|---|
| Rodneyse Bichotte Hermelyn | Harvey Epstein |
| Sandy Galef | Deborah J Glick |

*Offices and agencies generally appear in alphabetical order, except when specific order is requested by listee.*

|  |  |
|---|---|
| Alicia Hyndman | Ron Kim |
| Demond Meeks | Monica P Wallace |
| Jaime R Williams | |

**Minority**

|  |  |
|---|---|
| Kevin M Byrne | Andy Goodell |
| Kieran Michael Lalor | Mike Lawler |

## Health

Chair:
Richard N Gottfried (D) . . . . . . . . . . . . 518-455-4941/fax: 518-455-5939

### Committee Staff

Clerk:
Vacant . . . . . . . . . . . . . . . . . . . . . . . . . . . . . . . . . . 518-455-4941

#### Key Assembly Staff Assignments
Majority Assistant Secretary:
Jennifer Best
Majority Senior Analyst:
Anthony Kergaravat
Associate Counsel:
Janice Nieves

### Membership

#### Majority

|  |  |
|---|---|
| Thomas J Abinanti | Charles Barron |
| Rodneyse Bichotte Hermelyn | Edward C Braunstein |
| Kevin A Cahill | Steven Cymbrowitz |
| Jeffrey Dinowitz | Sandy Galef |
| Aileen M Gunther | Andrew Hevesi |
| John T McDonald III | Amy Paulin |
| Karines Reyes | Daniel Rosenthal |
| Linda B Rosenthal | Nader J Sayegh |
| Michaelle C Solages | Phil Steck |

#### Minority

|  |  |
|---|---|
| Jake Ashby | Kevin M Byrne |
| Marjorie Byrnes | Josh Jensen |
| David G McDonough | Melissa Miller |
| John Salka | |

## Higher Education

Chair:
Deborah J Glick (D) . . . . . . . . . . . . . . . . . . . . . . . . . . 518-455-4841

### Committee Staff

Clerk:
Louise Mahon . . . . . . . . . . . . . . . . . . . . . . . . . . . . . . 518-455-4841
Legislative Director:
Charles LeDuc . . . . . . . . . . . . . . . . . . . . . . . . . . . . . 518-455-4841

#### Key Assembly Staff Assignments
Associate Counsel:
Vacant
Legislative Analyst:
Ginnie Farrell

### Membership

#### Majority

|  |  |
|---|---|
| Rodneyse Bichotte Hermelyn | Marianne Buttenschon |
| Kevin A Cahill | Sarah Clark |
| Michael Cusick | Steve Englebright |
| Harvey Epstein | Patricia Fahy |
| Phara Souffrant Forest | Richard N Gottfried |
| Judy Griffin | Alicia Hyndman |
| Donna A Lupardo | John T McDonald III |
| Karen McMahon | Victor M Pichardo |
| Jo Anne Simon | Al Stirpe |

#### Minority

|  |  |
|---|---|
| Michael J Fitzpatrick | Jarett Gandolfo |

|  |  |
|---|---|
| Michael Reilly | John Salka |
| Doug Smith | Robert Smullen |
| Mark Walczyk | |

## Housing

Chair:
Steven Cymbrowitz (D) . . . . . . . . . . . . . . . . . . . . . . . . 518-455-5214

### Committee Staff

Clerk:
Lena DeThomasis

#### Key Assembly Staff Assignments
Analyst:
Vacant
Assistant Secretary, Program & Policy:
Giovanni Warren
Associate Counsel:
Patrick Totaro

### Membership

#### Majority

|  |  |
|---|---|
| Charles Barron | Rodneyse Bichotte Hermelyn |
| Chris Burdick | Vivian E Cook |
| Maritza Davila | Carmen N De La Rosa |
| Erik M Dilan | Simcha Eichenstein |
| Harvey Epstein | Latoya Joyner |
| Ron Kim | Demond Meeks |
| Yuh-Line Niou | Victor M Pichardo |
| Jonathan Rivera | Robert J Rodriguez |
| Linda B Rosenthal | Al Taylor |
| Latrice Walker | |

#### Minority

|  |  |
|---|---|
| Keith P Brown | Marjorie Byrnes |
| Michael J Fitzpatrick | Josh Jensen |
| Mike Lawler | Michael Reilly |
| Colin Schmitt | Doug Smith |

## Insurance

Chair:
Kevin A Cahill (D) . . . . . . . . . . . . . . . . . . . . . . . . . . . 518-455-4436

### Committee Staff

Committee Clerk:
Vacant

#### Key Assembly Staff Assignments
Majority Assistant Secretary:
Jennifer Best . . . . . . . . . . . . . . . . . . . . . . . . . . . . . . 518-455-4311
Legislative Analyst:
Fletcher Whyland
Associate Counsel:
Christopher Greenidge

### Membership

#### Majority

|  |  |
|---|---|
| Khaleel M Anderson | Vivian E Cook |
| Steven Cymbrowitz | Erik M Dilan |
| Phara Souffrant Forrest | Pamela J Hunter |
| Jonathan G Jacobson | Charles D Lavine |
| John T McDonald III | Demond Meeks |
| Yuh-Line Niou | J Gary Pretlow |
| José Rivera | Daniel Rosenthal |
| Phil Steck | Steve Stern |
| Jaime R Williams | |

#### Minority

|  |  |
|---|---|
| Ken Blankenbush | Kevin M Byrne |
| David DiPietro | Jarett Gandolfo |
| Stephen Hawley | Philip A Palmesano |

*Offices and agencies generally appear in alphabetical order, except when specific order is requested by listee.*

Colin Schmitt

## Judiciary
Chair:
Charles D Lavine (D) . . . . . . . . . . . . . . 518-455-5965/fax: 518-455-4437

### Committee Staff
Clerk:
Sarah Beaver

#### Key Assembly Staff Assignments
Counsel:
Vacant . . . . . . . . . . . . . . . . . . . . . . . . . . . . . 518-455-4313

### Membership

#### Majority
| | |
|---|---|
| Thomas J Abinanti | Edward C Braunstein |
| Catalina Cruz | Latoya Joyner |
| Karen McMahon | Marcela Mitaynes |
| Dan Quart | Jenifer Rajkumar |
| Rebecca A Seawright | Phil Steck |
| Monica P Walker | Monica P Wallace |
| David I Weprin | Kenneth Zebrowski |

#### Minority
| | |
|---|---|
| Kevin P Brown | Marjorie Byrnes |
| Michael Montesano | Michael J Norris |
| Michael Tannousis | Mary Beth Walsh |

## Labor
Chair:
Latoya Joyner (D) . . . . . . . . . . . . . . . . . . . . . . . . 518-455-5668

### Committee Staff
Clerk:
Vacant . . . . . . . . . . . . . . . . . . . . . . . . . . . . . 518-455-5668

#### Key Assembly Staff Assignments
Majority Assistant Secretary:
Jennifer Best . . . . . . . . . . . . . . . . . . . . . . . . 518-455-4311
Associate Counsel:
Cheyenne James

### Membership

#### Majority
| | |
|---|---|
| Peter J Abbate, Jr | Brian Barnwell |
| Michael Benedetto | Harry B Bronson |
| Kenny Burgos | William Colton |
| Catalina Cruz | Carmen N De La Rosa |
| Andrew Hevesi | Jonathan G Jacobson |
| N Nick Perry | Phil Ramos |
| Karines Reyes | Diana C Richardson |
| Robert J Rodriguez | Daniel Rosenthal |
| Nily Rozic | Jo Anne Simon |
| Phil Steck | Stefani Zinerman |

#### Minority
| | |
|---|---|
| Karl Brabenec | Kevin M Byrne |
| Joe DeStefano | David DiPietro |
| Michael Durso | Jodi Giglio |
| Angelo J Morinello | Colin Schmitt |

## Libraries & Education Technology
Chair:
Kimberly Jean-Pierre (D) . . . . . . . . . . . 518-455-5177/fax: 518-455-5418

### Committee Staff
Clerk:
Vacant

#### Key Assembly Staff Assignments
Majority Program Analyst:
Steve McCutcheon . . . . . . . . . . . . . . . . . . . . . . 518-455-3786
Assistant Secretary, Program & Policy:
Christian Malanga

### Membership

#### Majority
| | |
|---|---|
| Inez E Dickens | Jennifer Lunsford |
| Karen McMahon | Yuh-Line Niou |
| Michaelle C Solages | |

#### Minority
| | |
|---|---|
| Josh Jensen | Mary Beth Walsh |

## Local Governments
Chair:
Fred W Thiele Jr (I, D, WF) . . . . . . . . . . . . . . . . . . . . . . . 518-455-4826

### Committee Staff
Committee Director/Clerk:
Craig Swiecki . . . . . . . . . . . . . . . . . . . . . . . . . . . . . 518-455-4826

#### Key Assembly Staff Assignments
Assistant Secretary, Program & Policy:
Michael Hernandez
Senior Legislative Analyst:
Vacant

### Membership

#### Majority
| | |
|---|---|
| Sarah Clark | William Conrad |
| Taylor Darling | Jonathan G Jacobson |
| Anna R Kelles | Jennifer Lunsford |
| Steven Otis | Phil Ramos |
| Jonathan Rivera | Gina Sillitti |
| Monica P Wallace | Carrie Woerner |

#### Minority
| | |
|---|---|
| Christopher S Friend | Jeff Gallahan |
| Brian Manktelow | Colin Schmitt |
| Matthew Simpson | |

## Mental Health
Chair:
Aileen M Gunther (D) . . . . . . . . . . . . . . . . . . . . . . . . 518-455-5355

### Committee Staff
Legislative Director/Committee Clerk:
Vacant . . . . . . . . . . . . . . . . . . . . . . . . . . . . . 518-455-5102

#### Key Assembly Staff Assignments
Majority Program Analyst:
Willie Sanchez . . . . . . . . . . . . . . . . . . . . . . . . . . 518-455-3786
Associate Counsel:
Janice Nieves

### Membership

#### Majority
| | |
|---|---|
| Didi Barrett | Carmen N De La Rosa |
| Nathalia Fernandez | Mathylde Frontus |
| Chantel Jackson | Diana C Richardson |
| Robert J Rodriguez | Angelo Santabarbara |

#### Minority
| | |
|---|---|
| Jarett Gandolfo | Melissa Miller |
| Mary Beth Walsh | |

## Oversight, Analysis & Investigation
Chair:
John T McDonald III (D) . . . . . . . . . . . 518-455-3662/fax: 518-455-5499

*Offices and agencies generally appear in alphabetical order, except when specific order is requested by listee.*

**Membership**

**Majority**

| | |
|---|---|
| Nathalia Fernandez | William B Magnarelli |
| Phil Steck | Fred W Thiele Jr |

**Minority**

| | |
|---|---|
| Joe Angelino | Michael Montesano |

## People with Disabilities

Chair:
Thomas J Abinanti (D) . . . . . . . . . . . . . . . . . . . . . . . . . . . . 518-455-5441

**Membership**

**Majority**

| | |
|---|---|
| Khaleel M Anderson | Chris Burdick |
| Taylor Darling | Harvey Epstein |
| Karen McMahon | Stefani Zinerman |

**Minority**

| | |
|---|---|
| Joe Angelino | Melissa Miller |

## Racing & Wagering

Chair:
J Gary Pretlow (D) . . . . . . . . . . . . . . . . 518-455-5291/fax: 518-455-5447

**Committee Staff**

Clerk:
Vacant

**Key Assembly Staff Assignments**
Majority Assistant Secretary:
Jennifer Best . . . . . . . . . . . . . . . . . . . . . . . . . . . . . . . . . 518-455-4311
Associate Counsel:
Christopher Greenidge

**Membership**

**Majority**

| | |
|---|---|
| Aileen M Gunther | Stacey Pheffer Amato |
| Angelo Santabarbara | Nader J Sayegh |
| Michaelle C Solages | Clyde Vanel |
| Carrie Woerner | |

**Minority**

| | |
|---|---|
| Jake Ashby | Jeff Gallahan |
| Jarett Gandolfo | |

## Real Property Taxation

Chair:
Sandy Galef (D) . . . . . . . . . . . . . . . . . . . . . . . . . . . . . . . 518-455-5348

**Committee Staff**

Legislative Director/Clerk:
Vacant . . . . . . . . . . . . . . . . . . . . . . . . . . . . . . . . . . . . . . 518-455-5348

**Key Assembly Staff Assignments**
Majority Program Analyst:
Vacant . . . . . . . . . . . . . . . . . . . . . . . . . . . . . . . . . . . . . . 518-455-4363
Secretary, Program & Counsel:
Cindy Ceniviva

**Membership**

**Majority**

| | |
|---|---|
| Brian Barnwell | Inez E Dickens |
| Simcha Eichenstein | Zohran Mamdani |
| John T McDonald III | Daniel Rosenthal |
| Nader J Sayegh | |

**Minority**

| | |
|---|---|
| Brian D Miller | Chris Tague |

## Rules

Chair:
Carl E Heastie (D) . . . . . . . . . . . . . . . . . 518-455-3791/fax: 518-455-4812

**Membership**

**Majority**

| | |
|---|---|
| Jeffrion L Aubry | Michael Benedetto |
| Edward C Braunstein | William Colton |
| Vivian E Cook | Maritza Davila |
| Inez E Dickens | Jeffrey Dinowitz |
| Steve Englebright | Deborah J Glick |
| Richard N Gottfried | Charles D Lavine |
| Donna A Lupardo | William B Magnarelli |
| Catherine Nolan | Amy Paulin |
| Crystal D Peoples-Stokes | N Nick Perry |
| J Gary Pretlow | Fred W Thiele Jr |
| Helene E Weinstein | Kenneth Zebrowski |

**Minority**

| | |
|---|---|
| William A Barclay | Ken Blankenbush |
| Karl Brabenec | Joseph M Giglio |
| Stephen Hawley | Michael Montesano |
| Michael J Norris | Edward P Ra |

## Science & Technology

Chair:
Steven Otis (D)

**Membership**

**Majority**

| | |
|---|---|
| Pat Burke | William Conrad |
| Steve Englebright | Stacey Pfeffer Amato |
| Clyde Vanel | Monica P Wallace |

**Minority**

| | |
|---|---|
| Michael Durso | Christopher S Friend |

## Small Business

Chair:
Al Stirpe (D) . . . . . . . . . . . . . . . . . . . . . . . . . . . . . . . . . 518-455-5997

**Committee Staff**

**Key Assembly Staff Assignments**
Legislative Analyst:
Debra Jenkins

**Membership**

**Majority**

| | |
|---|---|
| Sarah Clark | Catalina Cruz |
| Taylor Darling | Inez E Dickens |
| Emily Gallagher | Chantel Jackson |
| Billy Jones | Victor M Pichardo |
| Jenifer Rajkumar | Diana C Richardson |
| José Rivera | Carrie Woerner |

**Minority**

| | |
|---|---|
| Marjorie Byrnes | David DiPietro |
| Kieran Michael Lalor | Brian Manktelow |

## Social Services

Chair:
Linda B Rosenthal (D, WF) . . . . . . . . . . . . . . . . . . . . . . . . 518-455-4926

**Committee Staff**

Executive Director/Clerk:
Vacant . . . . . . . . . . . . . . . . . . . . . . . . . . . . . . . . . . . . . . 518-455-4926

**Key Assembly Staff Assignments**
Majority Assistant Secretary:
Vacant . . . . . . . . . . . . . . . . . . . . . . . . . . . . . . . . . . . . . . 518-455-4371

*Offices and agencies generally appear in alphabetical order, except when specific order is requested by listee.*

Majority Associate Counsel:
Jennifer Sacco
Senior Analyst:
Jennifer Marrero

### Membership

**Majority**

| | |
|---|---|
| Jeffrion L Aubry | Charles Barron |
| Maritza Davila | Simcha Eichenstein |
| Nathalia Fernandez | Phara Souffrant Forrest |
| Jessica Gonzalez-Rojas | Pamela J Hunter |
| Victor M Pichardo | Karines Reyes |
| Daniel Rosenthal | Michaelle C Solages |

**Minority**

| | |
|---|---|
| Keith P Brown | Andy Goodell |
| Matthew Simpson | Robert Smullen |
| Mark Walczyk | |

## Tourism, Parks, Arts & Sports Development

Chair:
Daniel J O'Donnell (D). . . . . . . . . . . . . . . . . . . . . . . . . . .518-455-4755

### Committee Staff

Clerk:
Cheryl Myers . . . . . . . . . . . . . . . . . . . . . . . . . . . . . . . .518-455-4755

**Key Assembly Staff Assignments**
Majority Assistant Secretary:
Aaron Suggs. . . . . . . . . . . . . . . . . . . . . . . . . . . . . . .518-455-4355
Majority Program Analyst:
Yolanda Bostic Williams . . . . . . . . . . . . . . . . . . . . . .518-455-4928

### Membership

**Majority**

| | |
|---|---|
| Didi Barrett | Pat Burke |
| Robert C Carroll | William Conrad |
| Patricia Fahy | Charles D Fall |
| Nathalia Fernandez | Mathylde Frontus |
| Billy Jones | Dan Quart |
| Jonathan Rivera | Gina Sillitti |
| Carrie Woerner | Stefani Zinerman |

**Minority**

| | |
|---|---|
| Joe Angelino | Jeff Gallahan |
| Jodi Giglio | Angelo J Morinello |
| Matthew Simpson | Chris Tague |

## Transportation

Chair:
William B Magnarelli (D). . . . . . . . . . . . . . . . . . . . . . . .518-455-5606

### Committee Staff

Clerk:
Vacant. . . . . . . . . . . . . . . . . . . . . . . . . . . . . . . . . . . . .518-455-5606

**Key Assembly Staff Assignments**
Majority Principal Analyst:
Vacant. . . . . . . . . . . . . . . . . . . . . . . . . . . . . . . . . . .518-455-4881
Majority Associate Counsel:
Vacant. . . . . . . . . . . . . . . . . . . . . . . . . . . . . . . . . . .518-455-4881

### Membership

**Majority**

| | |
|---|---|
| Harry B Bronson | Kenny Burgos |
| Taylor Darling | Patricia Fahy |
| Mathylde Frontus | Emily Gallagher |
| Pamela J Hunter | Alicia Hyndman |
| Jonathan G Jacobson | Donna A Lupardo |
| Karen McMahon | Marcela Mitaynes |
| N Nick Perry | Gina Sillitti |

| | |
|---|---|
| Jo Anne Simon | Fred W Thiele Jr |
| Monica P Wallace | Jaime R Williams |

**Minority**

| | |
|---|---|
| Kevin M Byrne | Joe DeStefano |
| David DiPietro | David G McDonough |
| Brian D Miller | Michael J Norris |
| Mark Walczyk | |

## Veterans' Affairs

Chair:
Didi Barrett (D). . . . . . . . . . . . . . . . . . . . . . . . . . . . . . .518-455-4545

### Committee Staff

Clerk:
Vacant. . . . . . . . . . . . . . . . . . . . . . . . . . . . . . . . . . . . .518-455-4545

**Key Assembly Staff Assignments**
Majority Program Analyst:
Joanne Martin. . . . . . . . . . . . . . . . . . . . . . . . . . . . . .518-455-4355
Assistant Secretary, Program & Policy:
Aaron Suggs

### Membership

**Majority**

| | |
|---|---|
| Brian Barnwell | Chris Burdick |
| Marianne Buttenschon | Michael Cusick |
| Pamela J Hunter | Billy Jones |
| Catherine Nolan | Stacey Pheffer Amato |
| Jenifer Rajkumar | Angelo Santabarbara |
| Amanda Septimo | Steve Stern |
| Monica P Wallace | |

**Minority**

| | |
|---|---|
| Jake Ashby | Stephen Hawley |
| Brian Manktelow | David G McDonough |
| Angelo J Morinello | |

## Ways & Means

Chair:
Helene E Weinstein (D) . . . . . . . . . . . . . . . . . . . . . . . . .518-455-5462

### Committee Staff

Chief Economist:
Inbong Kang PhD. . . . . . . . . . . . . . . . . . . . . . . . . . . . .518-455-5462

**Key Assembly Staff Assignments**
Director of Economic & Tax Studies:
Vacant

### Membership

**Majority**

| | |
|---|---|
| Jeffrion L Aubry | Michael Benedetto |
| Edward C Braunstein | Harry B Bronson |
| Kevin A Cahill | William Colton |
| Vivian E Cook | Michael Cusick |
| Erik M Dilan | Jeffrey Dinowitz |
| Deborah J Glick | Alicia Hyndman |
| Latoya Joyner | William B Magnarelli |
| John T McDonald III | Catherine Nolan |
| N Nick Perry | J Gary Pretlow |
| Phil Ramos | Robert J Rodriguez |
| Nily Rozic | Rebecca A Seawright |
| David I Weprin | Kenneth Zebrowski |

**Minority**

| | |
|---|---|
| Jake Ashby | Ken Blankenbush |
| Karl Brabanec | Michael J Fitzpatrick |
| Stephen Hawley | Michael Montesano |
| Michael J Norris | Philip A Palmesano |
| Edward P Ra | |

*Offices and agencies generally appear in alphabetical order, except when specific order is requested by listee.*

## ASSEMBLY TASK FORCES & CAUCUS

### Food, Farm & Nutrition, Task Force on
Chair:
Daniel Rosenthal (D) . . . . . . . . . . . . . . . . . . . . . . . . 518-455-5545
Principal Analyst:
Robert Stern . . . . . . . . . . . . . . . . . . . . . . . . . . . . . . 518-455-5203

### Puerto Rican/Hispanic Task Force
Chair:
Maritza Davila (D) . . . . . . . . . . . . . . . . . . . . . . . . . . 518-455-5514
Legislative Director:
Guillermo Martinez. . . . . . . . . . . . . . . . . . . . . . . . . . 518-455-3608

### Skills Development & Career Education, Legislative Commission on
Assembly Chair:
Carrie Woerner (D). . . . . . . . . . . . . . . . . . . . . . . . . . 518-455-4527

### State-Federal Relations, Legislative Task Force on
Chair:
Erik M Dilan (D). . . . . . . . . . . . . . . . . . . . . . . . . . . . 518-455-5172
Program Manager:
Vacant

### Women's Issues, Task Force on
Chair:
Rebecca A Seawright (D). . . . . . . . . . . . . . . . . . . . . . 518-455-4466

*Offices and agencies generally appear in alphabetical order, except when specific order is requested by listee.*

# JUDICIAL BRANCH

## COURT OF APPEALS

*The Court of Appeals is the highest court in New York State, hearing both civil and criminal appeals. This court consists of the Chief Judge and six Associate Judges. Judges are appointed by the Governor for fourteen-year terms or until age seventy, whichever comes first. The Court of Appeals receives direct appeal on matters where the only question relates to the constitutionality of a State or Federal statute. The Court also establishes policy for administration of the New York State Unified Court System.*

### Court of Appeals

20 Eagle Street
Albany, NY 12207
518-455-7700
Web site: www.nycourts.gov/ctapps/

Clerk of the Court/Legal Counsel:
    John P Asiello.....................................518-455-7700
    e-mail: coa@courts.state.ny.us
Deputy Clerk:
    Heather Davis....................................518-455-7700
Public Information Officer:
    Gary Spencer....................................518-455-7711
Chief Judge:
    Janet DiFiore

#### Associate Judges

Jenny Rivera                    Leslie E Stein
Paul G Feinman                  Rowan D Wilson
Michael J Garcia               Eugene M Fahey

## APPELLATE DIVISIONS

*The Appellate Divisions of the Supreme Court exist for each of New York State's four Judicial Departments. Each Judicial Department is comprised of one or more of the State's twelve judicial districts and has Governor appointed Presiding and Associate Justices. The Presiding Justice serves the duration of his/her term as a Supreme Court Justice. Associate Justices serve for the shorter of a five-year term or the balance of their term. Supreme Court Justices are required to retire at age seventy, unless they become "Certificated" by the Administrative Board of the Courts. Justices may serve after age seventy under Certification for two-year terms, until age seventy-six. The Appellate Divisions review appeals from the Superior Court decisions in civil and criminal cases, and from Appellate Terms and County Courts in civil cases.*

### 1st Department
**Judicial Districts 1, 12**
Courthouse
27 Madison Avenue
New York, NY 10010
212-340-0400
Web site: www.nycourts.gov/courts/ad1/index.shtml

Clerk of the Court:
    Susanna Molina Rojas ...........................212-340-0400
Presiding Justice:
    Rolando T Acosta

#### Associate Justices

Lizbeth Gonzalez               Barbara R Kapnick
Ellen Gesmer                   David Friedman
Angela M Mazzarelli            Jeffrey K Oing
Dianne T Renwick               Tanya R Kennedy
Sallie Manzanet-Daniels        Anil C Singh
Cynthia S Kern                 Judith J Gische
Troy K Webber                  Peter H Moulton
Manuel J Mendez

### 2nd Department
**Judicial Districts 2, 9, 10, 11, 13**
45 Monroe Place
Brooklyn, NY 11201
718-875-1300
Web site: www.nycourts.gov/courts/ad2/index.shtml

Clerk of the Court:
    Aprilanne Agostino .................718-722-6324 or 718-722-6307
    fax: 212-419-8457
    e-mail: ad2clerk@nycourts.gov
Acting Presiding Justice:
    William F Mastro

#### Associate Justices

Colleen Duffy                  Hector D LaSalle
Cheryl E Chambers              Mark C Dillon
Robert J Miller                Reinaldo E Rivera
Angela G Iannacci              Linda Christopher
Francesca E Connolly           Sylvia O Hinds-Radix
Leonard B Austin               Valerie Brathwaite Nelson
Paul Wooten                    William F Mastro
Betsy Barros

### 3rd Department
**Judicial Districts 3, 4, 6**
Capitol Station
PO Box 7288
Albany, NY 12224-0288

---

*Offices and agencies generally appear in alphabetical order, except when specific order is requested by listee.*

518-471-4777  Fax: 518-471-4750
e-mail: AD3ClerksOffice@nycourts.gov
Web site: www.nycourts.gov/ad3/

Clerk of the Court:
   Robert D Mayberger . . . . . . . . . . . . . . . .518-471-4777/fax: 518-471-4750
   e-mail: ad3clerksoffice@nycourts.gov
Presiding Justice:
   Elizabeth A Garry

## Associate Justices

| | |
|---|---|
| Molly Reynolds Fitzgerald | John P Colangelo |
| Michael C Lynch | Sharon A. M. Aarons |
| Christine M Clark | John C Egan Jr |
| Stan L Pritzker | |

## 4th Department
**Judicial Districts 5, 7, 8**
50 East Avenue
Suite 200
Rochester, NY 14604
585-530-3100
Web site: www.nycourts.gov/courts/ad4/

Clerk of the Court:
   Mark W Bennett . . . . . . . . . . . . . . . . .585-530-3100/fax: 585-530-3247
Presiding Justice:
   Gerald J Whalen

## Associate Justices

| | |
|---|---|
| Edward D Carni | John M Curran |
| Brian F DeJoseph | Nancy E Smith |
| John V Centra | Erin M Peradotto |
| Stephen K Lindley | Joanne M Winslow |
| Shirley Troutman | Patrick H NeMoyer |

## SUPREME COURT

*The Supreme Court consists of twelve Judicial Districts, which are comprised of County Courts within NYS (See County Court information in related section). Justices are elected by their Judicial Districts for fourteen-year terms, unless they reach age seventy before term expiration. Justices may serve beyond age seventy if Certificated (see Apellate Divisions for definition). The Supreme Court generally hears cases outside the jurisdiction of other courts, such as: civil matters with monetary limits exceeding that of the lower courts; divorce, separation and annulment proceedings; equity suits; and criminal prosecutions of felonies.*

## 1st Judicial District
**New York County**
Administrative Judge, Civil:
   Deborah Kaplan . . . . . . . . . . . . . . . . . . . . . . . . . . . . .646-386-3600
Administrative Judge, Criminal:
   Ellen N Biben . . . . . . . . . . . . . . . . . . . . . . . . . . . . . .646-386-4083
Chief Clerk, Civil Branch:
   Denis Reo . . . . . . . . . . . . . . . . . .646-386-3030 or 646-386-3600
Chief Clerk, Criminal Branch:
   Christopher DiSanto . . . . . . . . . . . . . . . . . . . . . . . . . .646-386-3900

### Judges

| | |
|---|---|
| Stephen Antignani | Nancy M Bannon |
| Suzanne Adams | Lisa Headley |
| Arlene P Bluth | Phillip Hom |
| James Burke | Anthony Cannataro |
| Gregory Carro | Maragret A Chan |
| Abraham Clott | David Cohen |
| Matthew F Cooper | Daniel Conviser |
| James d'Auguste | Tandra Dawson |
| Ta-Tanisha D James | Mark Dwyer |

| | |
|---|---|
| Carol R Edmead | Erika Edwards |
| Arthur F Engoron | Shawn T Kelly |
| Curtis Farber | Thomas Farber |
| Lyle E Frank | Kathy J King |
| Richard Latin | Paul A Goetz |
| Shlomo S Hagler | Roger Hayes |
| Gilbert C Hong | Melissa Jackson |
| Debra James | Douglas E Hoffman |
| Deborah A Kaplan | Laurence L Love |
| Diane Kiesel | Robert M Mandelbaum |
| Judith McMahon | Felicia A Mennin |
| Juan Merchan | Guy Mitchell |
| Joel M Cohen | Kelly O'Neill Levy |
| Frank P Nervo | Andrew Borrok |
| Herbert J Adlerberg | Louis L Nock |
| Althea Drysdale | Andrea Masley |
| Barry Ostrager | W Franc Perry |
| Dakota Ramseur | Michael J Obus |
| Barbara Jaffe | Ruth Pickholz |
| Eileen Ann Rakower | Mary V Rosado |
| Robert R Reed | Neil Ross |
| Lori S Sattler | Verna L Saunders |
| Jennifer Schecter | Ann Scherzer |
| Carol Sharpe | Francis A Kahn III |
| Michelle Sweeting | O Peter Sherwood |
| Alexander M Tisch | Michael L Katz |
| Adam Silvera | John J Kelley |
| Robert Stolz | Gerald Lebovits |
| Laura Ward | Maxwell Wiley |
| Lynn R Kotler | Cassandra Mullen |
| Gayle Roberts | |

## 2nd Judicial District
**Kings County**
Administrative Judge, Criminal:
   Matthew D'Emic
Administrative Judge, Civil:
   Lawrence S Knipel . . . . . . . . . . . . . . . . . . . . . . . . . . . .718-675-7699
Chief Clerk, Criminal Division:
   Daniel Alessandrino . . . . . . . . . . . . . . . . . . . . . . . . . . .347-296-1076
Chief Clerk, Civil Division:
   Charles A Small, Esq. . . . . . . . . . . . . . . . . . . . . . . . . . .718-675-7699

### Judges

| | |
|---|---|
| Rachel Adams | Loren Baily-Schiffman |
| Thomas P Aliotta | Reginald Boddie |
| Theresa Ciccotto | Gloria M Dabiri |
| Genine D Edwards | Pamela L Fisher |
| Robin S Garson | Bernard Graham |
| Lara Genovesi | Dawn Jimenez-Salta |
| Kathy King | Lawrence Knipel |
| Donald Kurtz | Carl L Landicino |
| Katherine A Levine | Lisa Ottley |
| Mark I Partnow | Michael L Pesce |
| Eric I Prus | Karen B Rothenberg |
| Leon Ruchelsman | Wayne P Saitta |
| Kenneth P Sherman | Debra Silber |
| Ellen M Spodek | Marsha L Steinhardt |
| Peter Sweeney | Jeffrey Sunshine |
| Delores J Thomas | Wavny Toussaint |
| Richard Velasquez | Carolyn Wade |
| Sylvia G Ash | Michelle Weston |

## 3rd Judicial District
**Albany, Columbia, Greene, Rensselaer, Schoharie, Sullivan & Ulster Counties**
Chief Administrative Judge:
   Lawrence K Marks . . . . . . . . . . . . . . . . .518-285-8300/fax: 518-285-6169

*Offices and agencies generally appear in alphabetical order, except when specific order is requested by listee.*

District Administrative Judge:
Gerald W Connolly
e-mail: 3rdjdadministration@nycourts.gov

## Judges

| | |
|---|---|
| Christopher E Cahill | Andrew G Ceresia |
| Gerald W Connolly | Lisa M Fisher |
| James Gilpatric | Michael Mackey |
| Richard J McNally Jr | Richard Mott |
| Christina Ryba | Stephan G Schick |
| Raymond J Elliott, III | Julian Schreibman |

## 4th Judicial District
**Counties: Clint, Essex, Frankln, Fultn, Hamiltn, Montg, St Lawr, Saratga, Schenectady, Warren & Wash**

Administrative Judge:
Felix J Catena . . . . . . . . . . . . . . . . . . . . 518-285-5099/fax: 518-453-8988
District Executive:
Joanne B Haelen, Esq. . . . . . . . . . . . . . 518-285-5099/fax: 518-453-8988

### Judges

| | |
|---|---|
| Martin D Auffredou | Thomas Buchanan |
| Peter Feldstein | Joseph Sise |
| Christine M Clark | Philip V Cortese |
| Felix J Catena | John T Ellis |
| Mary M Farley | John S Hall, Jr. |
| Kathleen B Hogan | Robert G Main, Jr |
| Robert J Muller | Mark L Powers |
| Stan L Pritzker | David B Krogmann |

## 5th Judicial District
**Herkimer, Jefferson, Lewis, Oneida, Onondaga & Oswego Counties**

Administrative Judge:
James P Murphy . . . . . . . . . . . . . . . . . . 315-671-1100/fax: 315-671-1175
District Executive:
Donald C Doerr, Esq. . . . . . . . . . . . . . . 315-671-2111/fax: 315-671-1175
e-mail: 5thjdadministration@nycourts.gov

### Judges

| | |
|---|---|
| Brian F DeJoseph | Bernadette T Clark |
| Bob Antonacci | Gordon J Cuffy |
| Scott DelConte | John J Elliott |
| Erin P Gall | Gregory R Gilbert |
| Donald A Greenwood | Richard V Hunt |
| Martha Walsh Hood | Deborah H Karalunas |
| Patrick F MacRae | James P McClusky |
| Charles C Merrell | David A Murad |
| Anthony J Paris | Norman W Seiter, Jr |
| Norman I Siegel | Kevin G Young |

## 6th Judicial District
**Broome, Chemung, Chenango, Cortland, Delaware, Madison, Otsego, Schuyler, Tioga & Tompkins Counties**

Administrative Judge:
Eugene D Faughan . . . . . . . . . . . . . . . . 607-240-5350/fax: 212-295-4927
District Executive:
Porter L Kirkwood. . . . . . . . . . . . . . . . 607-240-5350/fax: 212-295-4927
e-mail: 6jd-res@nycourts.gov

### Judges

| | |
|---|---|
| Ferris D Lebous | Donald F Cerio, Jr |
| Julie A Campbell | Joseph A McBride |
| Jeffrey A Tait | Eugene D Faughnan |
| Brian D Burns | John C Rowley |

## 7th Judicial District
**Cayuga, Livingston, Monroe, Ontario, Seneca, Steuben, Wayne & Yates Counties**

Administrative Judge:
Craig J Doran . . . . . . . . . . . . . . . . . . . . . . . . . . . . . . . . . .585-371-3266
District Executive:
Ronald Pawelczak. . . . . . . . . . . . . . . . . . . . . . . . . . . . . . . .585-371-3266

### Judges

| | |
|---|---|
| John J Ark | Elma A Bellini |
| Ken Fisher | Evelyn Frazee |
| Thomas E Moran | Robert B Wiggins |
| John Owen | Gail A Donofrio |
| Craig J Doran | Daniel J Doyle |
| John B Gallagher, Jr | Debra H Martin |
| Thomas Stander | J Scott Odorisi |
| James J Piampiano | Alex R Renzi |
| Charles Schiano, Jr | Judith Sinclair |
| Ann Marie Taddeo | William Taylor |
| Victoria M Argento | John L DeMarco |
| Frederick G Reed | W Patrick Falvey |
| Daniel G Barrett | |

## 8th Judicial District
**Allegany, Cattaraugus, Chautauqua, Erie, Genesee, Niagara, Orleans & Wyoming Counties**

Administrative Judge:
Paula L Feroleto . . . . . . . . . . . . . . . . . . . . . . . . . . . . . . . .716-845-2505
District Executive:
Andrew B Isenberg, Esq . . . . . . . . . . . . 716-845-2505/fax: 716-845-7500
e-mail: aisenber@nycourts.gov

### Judges

| | |
|---|---|
| Tracey A Bannister | M William Boller |
| Ralph A Boniello, III | Christopher J Burns |
| Russell P Buscaglia | Frank Caruso |
| Deborah A Chimes | Emilio Colaiacovo |
| Diane Y Devlin | James H Dillon |
| Paula L Feroleto | Daniel J Furlong |
| Joseph R Glownia | Mark J Grisanti |
| Deborah A Haendiges | Lynn W Keane |
| Richard C Kloch, Sr | Frederick J Marshall |
| John L Michalski | Mark A Montour |
| Henry J Nowak | John F O'Donnell |
| Jeannette Ogden | Catherine Nugent Panepinto |
| Sharon S Townsend | Frank A Sedita III |
| Shirley Troutman | Donna M Siwek |
| Mary Slisz | Dennis E Ward |
| Timothy J Walker | Paul B Wojtaszek |
| Gerald J Whalen | |

## 9th Judicial District
**Dutchess, Orange, Putnam, Rockland & Westchester Counties**

Administrative Judge:
Kathie E Davidson . . . . . . . . . . . . . . . . . . . . . . . . . . . . . . .914-824-5840
District Executive:
James M McAllister . . . . . . . . . . . . . . . 914-824-5840/fax: 914-995-4946
e-mail: 9thjdadministration@nycourts.gov

### Judges

| | |
|---|---|
| James W Hubert, Jr | Catherine M Bartlett |
| Robert M Berliner | Robert M DiBella |
| James D Pagones | Susan Cacace |
| Susan M Capeci | Nicholas De Rosa |
| Kathie Davidson | Robert M Dibella |
| Lawrence H Ecker | Robert H Freehill |
| Victor G Grossman | Linda S Jamieson |
| Joan B Lefkowitz | Gerald E Loehr |
| Lewis J Lubell | Paul I Marx |
| Robert A Onofry | Janet C Malone |
| Maria G Rosa | James T Rooney |
| Sandra B Sciortino | Mary H Smith |
| Bruce E Tolbert | Maria S Vazquez-Doles |
| Sam D Walker | Gretchen Walsh |

Charles D Wood

## 10th Judicial District
**Nassau & Suffolk Counties**
Administrative Judge, Nassau:
 Norman St. George . . . . . . . . . . . . . . . 513-493-3000/fax: 516-493-3390
Administrative Judge, Suffolk:
 Andrew A Crecca . . . . . . . . . . . . . . . . . 631-208-5600/fax: 631-853-7741

### Judges

| | |
|---|---|
| Thomas Adams | Richard Ambro |
| Anna Anzalone | Paul J Baisley, Jr |
| Stacy D Bennett | Angelo A Delligatti |
| Antonio Brandveen | Jeffrey S Brown |
| Stephen A Bucaria | Norman Janowitz |
| Julianne Capetola | Mark Cohen |
| John B Collins | William J Condon |
| Andrew A Crecca | R Bruce Cozzens, Jr |
| Edmund Dane | Vito M DeStefano |
| Arthur M Diamond | Timothy S Driscoll |
| Elizabeth H Emerson | Thomas Feinman |
| William G Ford | John Michael Galasso |
| Jerry Garguilo | Sharon Gianelli |
| Jeffrey A Goodstein | Howard Heckman |
| C Randall Hinrichs | Gary Knobel |
| Anthony Marano | Robert A McDonald |
| Karen Murphy | Daniel Palmieri |
| John J Leo | Jack L Libert |
| Joseph Lorintz | H Patrick Leis III |
| Anthony Parga | Randy Sue Marber |
| Roy S Mahon | W Gerard Asher |
| Jerome C Murphy | James McCormack |
| Carol MacKenzie | Joseph C Pastoressa |
| Peter Mayer | Denise F Molia |
| Robert F Quinlan | Athur Pitts |
| David T Reilly | William B Rebolini |
| Denise Sher | Joseph A Santorelli |
| Leonard Steinman | Helen Voutsinas |
| Thomas F Whelan | Hope Zimmerman |

## 11th Judicial District
**Queens County**
Administrative Judge, Criminal:
 Joseph Zayas
Administrative Judge, Civil:
 Marguerite A Grays
Cheif Clerk, Criminal:
 William Reyes. . . . . . . . . . . . . . . . . . . . . . . . . . . . . . . . 718-298-1408
Chief Clerk, Civil:
 Tamara Kersh . . . . . . . . . . . . . . . . . . . . . . . . . . . . . . . . 718-298-1150

### Judges

| | |
|---|---|
| Michael B Aloise | Pam B Jackman Brown |
| Evelyn L Braun | Cheree A Buggs |
| Richard L Buchter | Denis J Butler |
| Anna Culley | Timothy J Dufficy |
| David Elliot | Joseph J Esposito |
| Marguerite A Grays | Darrell L Gavrin |
| Rudolph E Greco, Jr | Marcia Hirsch |
| Kenneth C Holder | Ronald D Hollie |
| Kevin Kerrigan | Stephen A Knopf |
| Phyllis Orlikoff Flug | Barry Kron |
| Robert Kohm | Daniel Lewis |
| Richard Latin | Leslie Leach |
| Charles Lopresto | John B Latella |
| Leonard Livote | Lee A Mayersohn |
| Orin R Kitzes | Robert J McDonald |
| Salvatore J Modica | Peter J O'Donoghue |
| Jodi Orlow | Margaret Parisi McGowan |
| Steven W Paynter | Leslie Purificacion |
| Valerie Brathwaite Nelson | Bernice D Siegal |

| | |
|---|---|
| Frederick D R Sampson | Barry Schwartz |
| Janice A Taylor | Carmen Velasquez |
| William A Viscovich | Allan B Weiss |
| Douglas S Wong | |

## 12th Judicial District
**Bronx County**
Administrative Judge, Civil:
 Doris M Gonzalez. . . . . . . . . . . . . . . . . . . . . . . . . . . . 718-618-1400
Administrative Judge, Criminal:
 Robert Torres . . . . . . . . . . . . . . . . . . . . . . . . . . . . . . . 718-618-3700
Chief Clerk, Civil:
 Tracy Pardo. . . . . . . . . . . . . . . . . . . . . . . . . . . . . . . . . 718-618-1400
Chief Clerk, Criminal:
 Michelle Foggie . . . . . . . . . . . . . . . . . . . . . . . . . . . . . 718-681-3000

### Judges

| | |
|---|---|
| Harold A Adler | Efrain Alvarado |
| Ben Barbato | Steven L Barrett |
| Miriam R Best | Raymond L Bruce |
| Denis J Boyle | John W Carter |
| Joseph E Capella | Margaret L Clancy |
| Mitchell J Danziger | Laura G Douglas |
| Ralph A Fabrizio | Ruben Franco |
| Ethan Greenberg | Stanley B Green |
| Michael A Gross | Doris M Gonzalez |
| Wilma Guzman | Nicholas J Iacovetta |
| Robert T Johnson | Judith S Lieb |
| Martin Marcus | La Tia W Martin |
| Douglas E McKeon | Armando Montano |
| Julia I Rodriguez | Betty Owen Stinson |
| Norma Ruiz | Lucindo Suarez |
| Howard Sherman | Fernando Tapia |
| Troy K Webber | Kenneth L Thompson, Jr |
| Alison Y Tuitt | George R Villegas |
| Alvin M Yearwood | |

## 13th Judicial District
**Richmond County**
Administrative Judge, Civil & Criminal:
 Desmond A Green. . . . . . . . . . . . . . . . . . . . . . . . . . . . 718-675-8700
Chief Clerk, Civil & Criminal:
 Kenneth Fay . . . . . . . . . . . . . . . . . . . . . . . . . . . . . . . . 718-675-8700

### Judges

| | |
|---|---|
| Judith McMahon | Catherine M DiDomenico |
| Kim Dollard | Philip G Minardo |
| Desmond A Green | Leonard P Rienzi |
| Stephen J Rooney | Barbara I Panepinto |
| Charles Troia | |

**COURT OF CLAIMS**

*The Court of Claims is a special trial court that hears and determines only claims against the State of New York. Court of Claims judges are appointed by the Governor for nine-year terms. Certain judges of this court, as designated herein by an \*, also serve as acting Supreme Court Justices for the assigned judicial district.*

### Court of Claims
Robert Abrams Justice Building
Capitol Station
PO Box 7344
Albany, NY 12224
518-432-3411
Web site: http://ww2.nycourts.gov/COURTS/nyscourtofclaims

Clerk of the Court:
 Eileen F Fazzone, Esq. . . . . . . . . . . . . . . . . . . . . . . . . 518-432-3411

*Offices and agencies generally appear in alphabetical order, except when specific order is requested by listee.*

Presiding Judge:
Richard E Sise....................................518-432-3435

## Judges

| | |
|---|---|
| Glen T Bruening | Francis T Collins |
| W Brooks DeBow | James H Ferreira |
| Diane L Fitzpatrick | Judith A Hard |
| Kathleen B Hogan | Michael E Hudson |
| Gina Lopez Summa | Christopher J McCarthy |
| Debra A Martin | Frank P Milano |
| Stephen J Mignano | Renee Forgensi Minarik |
| Edwina G Mendelson | Richard Platkin |
| Walter Rivera | Jeanette Rodriguez-Morick |
| Carmen Victoria St. George | J. David Sampson |
| Catherine C Schaewe | Faviola A Soto |
| David A Weinstein | |

## NEW YORK CITY COURTS

*New York City has its own Civil, Criminal and Family courts, separate from the County Court system. The NYC Civil Court hears civil cases involving amounts up to $25,000, and its judges are elected for ten-year terms. The NYC Criminal Court conducts trials of misdemeanors and violations. Criminal Court judges act as magistrates for all criminal offenses and are appointed by the City's Mayor for ten-year terms. The NYC Family Court hears matters involving children and families, such as: child protection, delinquency, domestic violence, guardianship, parental rights and spousal and child support. Family Court judges are appointed by the City's Mayor for ten-year terms. Certain judges of the Civil Court, as designated herein by an \*, are also assigned to serve in other courts.*

## Civil Court, NYC

Chief Clerk:
Alia Razzaq.....................................646-386-5700
Administrative Judge:
Anthony Cannataro................................646-386-5700

### Bronx County
851 Grand Concourse, Bronx, NY 10451
Clerk of the County:
Gladys Maldonado................718-618-2500 or 718-618-2561

### Kings County
141 Livingston St, Brooklyn, NY 11201
Clerk of the County:
Joseph Minogue...................347-404-9133 or 374-404-9123

### New York County
111 Centre St, New York, NY 10013
Clerk of the County:
Ananias Grajales ................646-386-5730 or 646-386-5600

### Queens County
89-17 Sutphin Blvd, Jamaica, NY 11435
Clerk of the County:
Birdena Frye.....................718-262-7300 or 718-262-7138

### Richmond County
927 Castleton Ave, Staten Island, NY 10310
Clerk of the County:
Deborah Tortorice ...............718-675-8458 or 718-675-8455

### Judges

| | |
|---|---|
| Elena Baron | Sharon Bourne-Clarke |
| Joy F Campanelli | Marian Doherty |
| Denise Dominguez | Connie Morales |
| Cenceria P Edwards | Jill R Epstein |
| John Howard-Algarin | Rachel Freier |
| Robin S Garson* | Emily Morales-Minerva |
| Dweynie Paul | Patria Frias-Colon |
| Ira R Greenberg | Fidel Gomez |

| | |
|---|---|
| Rupert V Barry | David Hawkins |
| Gina Levy Abadi | Nicholas W Moyne |
| Matthew P Blum | John C V Katsanos |
| Ally Shahabuddeen | Judy Kim |
| Odessa Kennedy | Leslie Stroth |
| Sabrina Kraus | Consuelo Melendez-Mallafre |
| Richard Tsai | Carol Ruth Feinman |
| Laurentina McKetney-Butler | Hilary Gingold |
| Jose A Padilla, Jr | Phaedra F Perry |
| Wendy Li | Brenda Rivera |
| Sandra Roper | Debra S Samuels |
| Naita A Semaj-Williams | Claudia Lanzetta |
| Alan Schiff | Myrna Socorro |
| Marissa Soto | Robert J Helbock |
| Carolyn Walker-Diallo* | Evon M Asforis |
| Kenneth Barany | Howard J Baum |
| Karen Bacdayan | Bernadette G Black |
| Miriam Breier | David Bryan |
| Heela Capell | Daniele Chinea |
| Hannah Cohen | Norma Jean Jennings |
| Marc Finkelstein | Thomas M Fitzpatrick |
| Christel Garland | Cheryl J Gonzales |
| Arlene H Hahn | David Harris |
| Shorab Ibrahim | Malaika Scott-McLaughlin-Bland |
| Anne Katz | Sergio Jimenez |
| Jeannine Baer Kuzniewski | Krysztof Lach |
| Lydia C Lai | John S Lansden |
| Diane Lutwak | Kevin C McClanahan |
| Steven Weissman | Kimberly S Slade |
| Clifton Nembhard | Eleanora Ofshtein |
| Frances Ortiz | Julie Poley |
| Maria Ressos | Enedina P Sanchez |
| Bruce E Scheckowitz | Michelle D Schreiber |
| Marcia J Sikowitz | Brenda Spears |
| Jack Stoller | Kimon C Thermos |
| Bryant Tovar | Juliet P Howard |
| Michael L Weisberg | Steven A Weissman |
| Elizabeth J Tao | |

## Criminal Court, NYC

Chief Clerk:
Justin A Barry, Esq ...............646-386-4500/fax: 212-374-4835
Administrative Judge:
Tamiko A Amaker ................................646-386-4500

### Bronx County
215 E 161st St., Bronx, NY 10451
Borough Chief Clerk:
William Kalish ..................718-618-2460/fax: 718-537-5164

### Kings County
120 Schermerhorn St, Brooklyn, NY 11201
Borough Chief Clerk:
James Smoot ....................347-404-9400/fax: 718-643-5234

### New York County
100 Centre St, New York, NY 10013
Borough Chief Clerk:
Arlethia Howard .................646-386-4511/fax: 212-374-5293

### Queens County
125-01 Queens Blvd, Kew Gardens, NY 11415
Borough Chief Clerk:
Carey Wone......................718-298-0792/fax: 718-520-4712

### Richmond County
26 Central Ave, Staten Island, NY 10301
Borough Chief Clerk:
Ada Molina .....................718-675-8558/fax: 718-390-8405

### Judges

| | |
|---|---|
| Alexander M Calabrese* | Charlotte Davidson |

*Offices and agencies generally appear in alphabetical order, except when specific order is requested by listee.*

George A Grasso*  Kevin B McGrath, Jr*
Alan J Meyer*  Michael J Yavinsky*

## Family Court, NYC
Chief Clerk:
  Doreen M Hanley . . . . . . . . . . . . . . . . . . . . 646-386-5170 or 212-374-3700
  fax: 212-374-3257
Administrative Judge:
  Jeanette Ruiz

### Bronx County
  900 Sheridan Ave, Bronx, NY 10451
  e-mail: bronxfamilycourt@nycourts.gov
  Clerk of Court:
    Vacant . . . . . . . . . . . . . . . . . . . . . . . 718-618-2098/fax: 718-590-7875

### Kings County
  330 Jay St, Brooklyn, NY 11201
  e-mail: kingsfamilycourt@nycourts.gov
  Clerk of Court:
    Vacant . . . . . . . . . . . . . . . . . . . . . . . 347-401-9610/fax: 347-401-9609

### New York County
  60 Lafayette St, New York, NY 10013
  e-mail: manhattanfamilycourt@nycourts.gov
  Clerk of Court:
    Juan Paez . . . . . . . . . . . . . . . . . . . . . . 646-386-5200/fax: 212-416-1428

### Queens County
  151-20 Jamaica Ave, Jamaica, NY 11432
  e-mail: queensfamilycourt@nycourts.gov
  Clerk of Court:
    Vacant . . . . . . . . . . . . . . . . . . . . . . . 718-298-0197/fax: 212-401-9234

### Richmond County
  100 Richmond Terrace, Staten Island, NY 10301
  e-mail: richmondfamilycourt@nycourts.gov
  Clerk of Court:
    Vacant . . . . . . . . . . . . . . . . . . . . . . . 718-675-8800/fax: 718-390-5247

### Judges
| | |
|---|---|
| Maria Arias | Elizabeth Barnett |
| Alan Beckoff | Tracey Bing |
| Ashley Black | Sarah Cooper |
| Diane Costanzo | Ben Darvil, Jr. |
| Tandra L Dawson | Jacqueline Deane |
| Peter DeLizzo | Catherine M DiDomenico |
| Alicea Elloras-Ally | Adetokunbo Fasanya |
| Lisa Friederwitzer | Melody Glover |
| Carol Goldstein | Alma Gomez |
| Connie Gonzalez | Ronna Gordon-Galchus |
| Ilana Gruebel | Alison Hamanjian |
| Douglas E Hoffman | Anne-Marie Jolly |
| David Kaplan | Dean Kusakabe |
| Lynn Leopold | Karen Lupuloff |
| Ruben Martino | Michael Milsap |
| Margaret Morgan | Robert Mulroy |
| Mildred Negron | Emily M Olshansky |
| Peter Passidomo | Jane Pearl |
| Valerie Pels | Joan Piccirillo |
| Erik Pitchal | Elenor C Reid |
| Clark V Richardson | Gayle P Roberts |
| Fiordaliza Rodriguez | Emily Ruben |
| Jeanette Ruiz | Helene Sacco |
| Monica Shulman | Gilbert Taylor |
| Javier Vargas | Judith Waksberg |
| Amanda White | Karen Wolff |

## COUNTY COURTS

*NYS has three types of courts designated at a county level: County Court, Family Court and Surrogate's Court. The County Court is authorized to handle criminal prosecutions of offenses committed within the county and hears civil cases involving amounts up to $25,000. County Court judges are elected for ten-year terms. The Family Court hears matters involving children and families (for types of court matters see NYC Courts). Family Court judges are elected for ten-year terms. The Surrogate's Court hears cases involving the affairs of decedents, including the probate of wills, and administration of estates and adoptions. Surrogates are elected for ten-year terms. This section also includes Supreme Court clerks and their addresses. Additional information and a list of judges for the NYS Supreme Court is provided in the related Section.*

## Albany County

### Judges
  County:
    Peter A Lynch
  County:
    William Carter

### County Court
  Albany County Judicial Center, 6 Lodge Street, Albany, NY 12207
  Chief Clerk:
    Charles E Diamond . . . . . . . . . . . . . . 518-285-8777/fax: 518-436-3986

### Family
  30 Clinton Ave, Albany, NY 12207
  Chief Clerk:
    Nala Woodward . . . . . . . . . . . . . . . . 518-285-8600/fax: 518-238-4344

### Supreme Court & Surrogate
  Courthouse, Rm 102, 16 Eagle St, Albany, NY 12207
  Chief Clerk:
    Stacy L Petit . . . . . . . . . . . . . . . . . . . 518-285-8989/fax: 518-453-8697

## Allegany County

### Judges
  Multi-Bench:
    Thomas P Brown
  Multi-Bench:
    Terrence M Parker

### Supreme, County, Family & Surrogate's Courts. fax: 585-268-7090
  7 Court St, Belmont, NY 14813-1084
  585-268-5800  Fax: 585-268-7090
  Chief Clerk-Family:
    Heather Kunz . . . . . . . . . . . . . . . . . . . . . . . . . . . . 585-449-3424
    e-mail: hkunz@nycourts.gov
  Chief Clerk-County/Supreme:
    Jenise Cicirello . . . . . . . . . . . . . . . . . . . . . . . . . . . 585-449-3462
    e-mail: jcicirel@nycourts.gov
  Chief Clerk-Surrogate's:
    Dorine Jacobs . . . . . . . . . . . . . . . . . . . . . . . . . . . . 585-449-3464
    e-mail: dgjacobs@nycourts.gov

## Bronx County

### Judges
  Surrogate:
    Nelida Malavè-González

### COUNTY & FAMILY COURTS: See New York City Courts

### Supreme & Surrogate's Courts
  851 Grand Concourse, Bronx, NY 10451
  Chief Clerk-Surrogate:
    Elix R Madera-Fliegelman

*Offices and agencies generally appear in alphabetical order, except when specific order is requested by listee.*

## Broome County

### Judges
County:
  Joseph Cawley
Family (Supervising):
  Rita Connerton
Surrogate:
  David H Guy
County:
  Kevin P Dooley
Family:
  Mark H Young

### County, Family
65 Hawley St, P.O. Box 1766, Binghamton, NY 13902-1766
Chief Clerk-County:
  Judith Osburn . . . . . . . . . . . . . . . . . .607-240-5800/fax: 607-240-5940
Chief Clerk-Family:
  Cheryl Lidell Obenauer. . . . . . . . . . .607-240-5799/fax: 607-240-5904

### Surrogate & Supreme Court
92 Court St, Binghamton, NY 13901
Chief Clerk-Surrogate:
  Rebecca A Malmquist . . . . . . . . . . . . . . . . . . . . . . . . . .607-240-5789

## Cattaraugus County

### Judges
Multi-Bench:
  Moses M Howden
Multi-Bench:
  Ronald D Ploetz

### Family Court
One Leo Moss Dr, Olean, NY 14760
Chief Clerk:
  Kyle C O'Connor . . . . . . . . . . . . . . . . . . . . . . . . . . . . .716-379-6616
  e-mail: kcoconno@nycourts.gov

### Supreme, County & Surrogate's Courts
Courthouse, 303 Court St, Little Valley, NY 14755
Chief Clerk-Supreme:
  Verna Dry. . . . . . . . . . . . . . . . . . . . . . . . . . . . . . . . . . .716-379-6639
  e-mail: vdry@nycourts.gov
Chief Clerk-Surrogate:
  Judith Zlockie. . . . . . . . . . . . . . . . . . . . . . . . . . . . . . . .716-379-6638
  e-mail: jzlockie@nycourts.gov

## Cayuga County

### Judges
Multi-Bench (Acting):
  Mark H Fandrich

### Family Court
157 Genesee St, Auburn, NY 13021
Chief Clerk:
  Jamie Gleason. . . . . . . . . . . . . . . . . .315-237-6400/fax: 315-237-6401
  e-mail: cayugafamilycourt@courts.state.ny.us

## Chautauqua County

### Judges
Surrogate:
  Stephen W Cass
Family:
  Jeffrey Piazza
Family:
  Michael Sullivan
County:
  David Foley

### Family Court
2 Academy St, Ste 5, Mayville, NY 14757
Chief Clerk:
  David Travis. . . . . . . . . . . . . . . . . . . . . . . . . . . . . . . . .716-753-4100
  e-mail: dtravis@nycourts.gov

### Supreme & County Courts
County Courthouse, 3 North Erie St, P.O. Box 292, Mayville, NY
14757-0292
Chief Clerk:
  Tracie Lorenzo . . . . . . . . . . . . . . . . . . . . . . . . . . . . . . .716-753-4835
  e-mail: tlorenzo@nycourts.gov

### Surrogate Court
Gerace Bldg, Courthouse, PO Box C, Mayville, NY 14757
Chief Clerk:
  Lana Huston . . . . . . . . . . . . . . . . . .716-753-4339/fax: 716-753-4600

## Chemung County

### Judges
Family:
  Mary M Tarantelli
Multi-Bench:
  Richard W Rich
Surrogate:
  Christopher P Baker

### Family Court
203-209 William St, P.O. Box 588, Elmira, NY 14902-0558
Chief Clerk:
  Caitlin A McGurgan . . . . . . . . . . . . .607-873-9500/fax: 212-884-8950
  e-mail: chemungfamilycourt@nycourts.gov

### Supreme & County Courts
203 Lake St., Hazlett Bldg, Elmira, NY 14902-0588
Chief Clerk:
  Samantha Pike. . . . . . . . . . . . . . . . . .607-873-9450/fax: 646-963-6605

### Surrogate Court
203-205 Lake St, P.O. Box 588, Elmira, NY 14902-0588
Chief Clerk:
  Laurie Hubbard . . . . . . . . . . . . . . . . .607-837-9440/fax: 646-963-6606
  e-mail: 6jdchmsurr@courts.state.ny.us

## Chenango County

### Judges
Multi-Bench:
  Frank B Revoir

### Supreme, County, Family & Surrogate's Courts
13 Eaton Ave, Norwich, NY 13815
Chief Clerk:
  Kimberly S Sitts . . . . . . . . . . . . . . .607-337-1457/fax: 917-522-3477
  e-mail: ksitts@nycourts.gov
Deputy Chief Clerk:
  Abigail Rogers

## Clinton County

### Judges
Family:
  Timothy J Lawliss
County:
  Keith Bruno
Surrogate:
  William Favreau

### Supreme, County, Family & Surrogate's Courts
137 Margaret St, Plattsburgh, NY 12901
e-mail: clintonsupremeco@nycourts.gov

*Offices and agencies generally appear in alphabetical order, except when specific order is requested by listee.*

Chief Clerk-Family:
   Cathy Williams....................................518-536-3820
   e-mail: clintonfamily@nycourts.gov
Chief Clerk-County/Supreme:
   Denise Durkin.....................................518-536-3840
   e-mail: clintonsupremeco@nycourts.gov
Chief Clerk-Surrogate:
   Lise Johnson .....................................518-536-3830
   e-mail: clintonsurrogate@nycourts.gov

## Columbia County

**Judges**
County:
   Richard Koweek
County:
   Jonathan D Nichols

## Supreme, County, Family & Surrogate's Courts
401 Union Street, Hudson, NY 12534
Chief Clerk:
   Nicole Austin-Best ...............518-267-3150/fax: 518-267-3126
Chief Clerk-Surrogate:
   Kimberly Jorgensen ...........................518-267-3150

## Cortland County

**Judges**
County:
   David C Alexander
County:
   Julie A Campbell

## Supreme, County, Family & Surrogate's Courts
Courthouse, 46 Greenbush St, Ste 301, Cortland, NY 13045-2725
Chief Clerk:
   Emily Stith....................607-218-3320/fax: 646-963-6452
   e-mail: CortlandSC@nycourts.gov
Deputy Chief Clerk:
   Steven Tillotson ................607-218-3320/fax: 646-963-6452

## Delaware County

**Judges**
Multi-Bench:
   Richard D Northrup Jr
Family:
   Gary A Rosa

## Supreme, County, Family & Surrogate's Courts
Courthouse, 3 Court St, Delhi, NY 13753
Chief Clerk-County/Supreme:
   Kelly Reynolds ................607-746-2131/fax: 646-963-6402
Chief Clerk-Surrogate:
   Lisa Hulse .....................607-746-2126/fax: 646-963-6403
Chief Clerk-Family:
   Lori Metzko....................607-746-2298/fax: 646-963-6400

## Dutchess County

**Judges**
County:
   Jessica Segal
County:
   Edward McLoughlin
Surrogate:
   Michael G Hayes

## Supreme, County & Surrogate's Courts
Courthouse, 10 Market St, Poughkeepsie, NY 12601
Chief Clerk-Surrogate:
   Erica DeTraglia, Esq. ............845-431-1770/fax: 845-476-3659

Chief Clerk-County/Supreme:
   Michael Thompson ..............845-431-1710/fax: 845-431-1743

## Erie County

**Judges**
Family:
   Brenda Freedman
Family:
   Mary G Carney
Family:
   Kevin M Carter
County:
   James F Bargnesi
Family:
   Sharon LoVallo
County:
   Sheila DiTullio
Family:
   Kelly Brinkworth
Family:
   Deanne Tripi
Surrogate:
   Acea M Mosey
Family:
   Margaret O Szczur
County:
   Kenneth Case
County:
   Susan Egan
County:
   Suzanne Maxwell Barnes

## Family Court
One Niagara Plz, Buffalo, NY 14202
Chief Clerk:
   Kelly Buckley ...................716-845-7444/fax: 716-845-7546
   e-mail: kbuckley@nycourts.gov

**Surrogate's Court** ..............................fax: 716-845-7565
Erie County Hall, 92 Franklin St, Buffalo, NY 14202
716-845-2560 Fax: 716-845-7565
Chief Clerk-Surrogate:
   Kathleen A Downing .............716-845-2568/fax: 716-845-7565
   e-mail: kdowning@nycourts.gov

## Supreme & County Court
25 Delaware Ave, Buffalo, NY 14202
Deputy Chief Clerk-County/Supreme:
   Billie Jo Zakia...................716-845-9301/fax: 716-851-3293
   e-mail: kkelley@nycourts.gov

## Essex County

**Judges**
Multi-Bench:
   Richard B Meyer

## Supreme, County, Family & Surrogate's Courts
Courthouse, 7559 Court St, P.O. Box 217, Elizabethtown, NY 12932
Chief Clerk-Surrogate:
   Mary Ann Badger ...............518-873-3384/fax: 518-451-8740
Chief Clerk-Family:
   Jaime Valachovic ................518-873-3320/fax: 518-873-3626
Chief Clerk-Supreme/County:
   Eileen Gonzalez .................518-873-3370/fax: 518-451-8738

## Franklin County

**Judges**
Multi-Bench:
   Robert G Main, Jr

*Offices and agencies generally appear in alphabetical order, except when specific order is requested by listee.*

Family:
  Derek P Champagne

## Supreme, County, Family & Surrogate's Courts
Courthouse, 355 W Main St, Malone, NY 12953
Chief Clerk-Surrogate:
  Martha A LaBarge .............................518-353-7350
  e-mail: FranklinSurrogate@nycourts.gov
Deputy Chief Clerk-Family:
  Emily Cartwright ..............................518-353-7360
  e-mail: FranklinFamily@nycourts.gov
Chief Clerk-Supreme/County:
  Fawn Tatro ....................................518-353-7340
  e-mail: FranklinSupremeCo@nycourts.gov

## Fulton County

### Judges
County/Surrogate:
  Michael W Smrtic
Family:
  James Gerard McAuliffe, Jr

### Supreme, County, Family & Surrogate's Courts
223 W Main St, Johnstown, NY 12095
Chief Clerk-County/Supreme:
  Nancy Garavelli ...............518-736-5539/fax: 518-762-5078
Chief Clerk-Surrogate:
  Donna Austin ..................518-736-5697/fax: 518-762-6372
Chief Clerk-Family:
  Lisa Tricozzi ..................518-706-3260/fax: 518-451-8745

## Genesee County

### Judges
Family:
  Thomas D Williams
County:
  Charles Zambito

### Supreme, County, Family & Surrogate's Courts
County Courts Facility, 1 W Main St, Batavia, NY 14020
Chief Clerk-Family:
  Laurie Johnston.................585-201-5743/fax: 585-371-3956
  e-mail: ljohnsto@nycourts.gov
Chief Clerk-County/Supreme:
  Nicole Desmond ................585-201-5727/fax: 585-344-8517
  e-mail: ndesmond@nycourts.gov
Chief Clerk-Surrogate:
  Michele Westfall-Owens..........585-201-5733/fax: 585-344-8517
  e-mail: mawestfa@nycourts.gov

## Greene County

### Judges
Multi-Bench:
  Charles M Tailleur
Multi-Bench:
  Terry J Wilhelm

### Supreme, County, Family & Surrogate's Courts
Courthouse, 320 Main St, Catskill, NY 12414
Chief Clerk-County/Supreme:
  Ellen Brower....................................518-625-3160
Chief Clerk-Surrogate:
  Heather Sheehan..............................518-625-3150
Chief Clerk-Family:
  Erin Scott .....................................518-625-3180

## Hamilton County

### Judges
Multi-Bench:
  Tatiana N Coffinger

### County, Family & Surrogate's Courts
139 White Birch Lane, P.O. Box 780, Indian Lake, NY 12842
Chief Clerk:
  Araina Eldridge.................518-648-5411/fax: 518-453-8687

## Herkimer County

### Judges
County/Surrogate:
  John H Crandall
Family:
  Thaddeus J Luke

### Family Court
County Office & Court Facility, 301 N Washington St, Ste 2501,
  Herkimer, NY 13350
Chief Clerk:
  Lynn M Kohl....................315-619-3400/fax: 315-266-4534

### Supreme, County & Surrogate's Courts
County Office & Court Facility, 301 N Washington St, Herkimer, NY
13350
Chief Clerk-County/Supreme:
  Therese Soules .................315-619-3400/fax: 315-266-4683

## Jefferson County

### Judges
Family:
  Eugene J Langone
County/Surrogate:
  David A Renzi
Supreme:
  James P McClusky

### County, Family & Surrogate's Courts
163 Arsenal St, Watertown, NY 13601
Chief Clerk-Family:
  Valerie Boyle ..................315-785-3001/fax: 315-266-4776
Chief Clerk-Surrogate:
  Dawn E Bast ...................315-785-3019/fax: 315-785-5194

### Supreme Court
State Office Bldg, 317 Washington St, Watertown, NY 13601
Chief Clerk-County/Supreme:
  Deanna L Morse.................315-221-5818 or 315-785-3044
  fax: 315-266-4779

## Kings County

### Judges
Surrogate:
  Margarita Lopez Torres
Surrogate:
  Harriet L Thompson

### COUNTY & FAMILY COURTS: See New York City Courts

### Supreme Court
Civil: 360 Adams St, Criminal: 320 Jay St, Brooklyn, NY 11201
Chief Clerk-Criminal:
  Daniel M Allessandrino
Chief Clerk-Civil:
  Charles A Small, Esq............................718-675-7699

### Surrogate's Court
2 Johnson St, Brooklyn, NY 11201

*Offices and agencies generally appear in alphabetical order, except when specific order is requested by listee.*

Chief Clerk-Surrogate:
Doreen Quinn.....................347-404-9700 or 347-404-9690

## Lewis County

**Judges**
Multi-Bench:
Daniel R King

**Supreme, County, Family & Surrogate's Courts**
Courthouse, 7660 N State St, 3rd Flr, Lowville, NY 13367
Chief Clerk-County/Supreme/Surrogate:
Melissa J Lopez.................315-376-5345/fax: 315-671-6084
Chief Clerk-Family:
Lacey E Northrup ...............315-376-5380/fax: 315-671-6083

## Livingston County

**Judges**
Multi-Bench:
Kevin G Van Allen
Multi-Bench:
Jennifer M Noto
Multi-Bench:
Thomas E Moran

**Supreme, County, Family & Surrogate's Courts**
Courthouse, 2 Court St, Geneseo, NY 14454-1030
Chief Clerk-Family:
Sonya Poormon
Chief Clerk-Supreme/County:
Jose Cruzado
Chief Clerk-Surrogate:
Nannette Galvin

## Madison County

**Judges**
County:
Patrick J O'Sullivan
Multi-Bench:
Michael St Leger

**Supreme, County, Family & Surrogate's Courts**
Courthouse, 138 N Court St, P.O. Box 545, Wampsville, NY 13163-0545
Chief Clerk-Family:
Dinquia M Sanchez..............315-231-5314/fax: 646-963-6589
e-mail: madisonfamilycourt@courts.state.ny.us
Chief Clerk-Surrogate:
Vacant.......................315-231-5321/fax: 646-963-6594

## Monroe County

**Judges**
Family:
James E Walsh
Family:
James A Vazzana
County:
Vincent Dinolfo
County:
Sam L Valleriani
County:
Michael L Dollinger
County:
Douglas A Randall
Family:
Joseph G Nesser
Family:
John Gallagher
Family:
Dandrea L Ruhlmann

Family:
Alecia J Mazzo
Family:
Fatimat O Reid
Family:
Stacey M Romeo
Surrogate:
Christopher S Ciaccio

**Supreme, County, Family & Surrogate's Courts**. fax: 585-371-3313
Hall of Justice, 99 Exchange Blvd, Rochester, NY 14614
585-371-3310  Fax: 585-371-3313
Chief Clerk-Surrogate:
Mark L Annunziata.........................585-371-3289
e-mail: mannunzi@nycourts.gov
Chief Clerk-County:
Lisa Preston.................585-371-3758/fax: 585-371-3780
e-mail: lpreston@nycourts.gov
Chief Clerk-Family:
Vacant ....................585-371-3544/fax: 585-371-3585
e-mail: monroefamilycourt@nycourts.gov

## Montgomery County

**Judges**
County:
Felix J Catena
Family:
Philip V Cortese
Surrogate:
Guy P Tomlinson

**Supreme, County, Family & Surrogate's Courts**
Courthouse, 58 Broadway, P.O. Box 1500, Fonda, NY 12068-1500
Chief Clerk-Surrogate:
Alison Thomas-Oravsky, Esq. .......518-853-8108/fax: 518-853-8230
Chief Clerk-Family:
Laurie Furnare..................518-853-8133/fax: 518-238-4370
Chief Clerk-County/Supreme:
Timothy J Riley.................518-853-4516/fax: 518-853-3596

## Nassau County

**Judges**
County:
Felice Muraca
County:
Terence P Murphy
County:
Meryl J Berkowitz
County:
Robert G Bogle
County:
Angelo A Delligatti
County (Supervising):
Teresa K Corrigan
Family:
Eileen Daly-Sapraicone
Family:
Linda K Mejias
County:
Helene F Gugerty
Family:
Danielle M Peterson
Family (Supervising):
Ellen R Greenberg
County:
Patricia A Harrington
Family:
Robin M Kent

*Offices and agencies generally appear in alphabetical order, except when specific order is requested by listee.*

Family:
    Ayesha K Brantley
County:
    William J O'Brien
Surrogate:
    Margaret C Reilly
County:
    Robert A Schwartz
Multi-Bench:
    Tammy Robbins
County:
    Francis D Ricigliano
Family:
    Conrad D Singer

### County & Surrogate's Courts
262 Old Country Rd, Mineola, NY 11501
516-493-3710
Chief Clerk-County:
    Donald F Vetter . . . . . . . . . . . . . . . . . . . . . . . . .516-493-3700
Chief Clerk-Surrogate:
    Debra Keller Leimbach . . . . . . . . . . . . . . . . . . . . .516-493-3805

### Family Court
1200 Old Country Rd, Westbury, NY 11590
Chief Clerk:
    Rosalie Fitzgerald. . . . . . . . . . . . . . . . . . . . . . . . . .516-493-4000

### Supreme Court
Supreme Court Bldg, 100 Supreme Court Dr, Mineola, NY 11501
Deputy Chief Clerk:
    Leonard Ambruso. . . . . . . . . . . . . . . . . . . . . . . . . .516-493-3401

## New York County

### Judges
Surrogate:
    Nora S Anderson

### COUNTY & FAMILY COURTS: See New York City Courts

### Supreme Court, Civil Term
60 Centre St, New York, NY 10007
Chief Clerk:
    Denis Reo . . . . . . . . . . . . . . . . . . . . . . . . . . . . . . . .646-386-3600

### Supreme Court, Criminal Term
100 Centre St, New York, NY 10013
Chief Clerk:
    Christopher DiSanto. . . . . . . . . . . . . . . . . . . . . . . . .646-386-3001

### Surrogate's Court
31 Chambers St, New York, NY 10007
Chief Clerk:
    Diana Sanabria . . . . . . . . . . . . . . . . . . . . . . . . . . . .646-386-5000

## Niagara County

### Judges
Family:
    Kathleen Wojtaszek-Gariano
County:
    Matthew J Murphy
County:
    Caroline Wojtaszek

### County, Family & Surrogate's Courts
Courthouse, 175 Hawley St, Lockport, NY 14094
Chief Clerk-Family:
    Deborah Drake . . . . . . . . . . . . . . . . .716-280-6500/fax: 716-439-7170
    e-mail: ddrake@nycourts.gov

Chief Clerk-County/Supreme:
    Michael C Veruto, Esq. . . . . . . . . . . . .716-371-4000/fax: 716-371-4040
    e-mail: mveruto@nycourts.gov
Chief Clerk-Surrogate:
    Angela Stamm-Philipps, Esq. . . . . . . .716-280-6460/fax: 716-280-6480

### County, Supreme & Family Courts
Delsignore Civic Bldg, 775 Third St, Niagara Falls, NY 14301

## Oneida County

### Judges
Family:
    Randall B Caldwell
County:
    Robert L Bauer
County (Supervising):
    Michael L Dwyer
Surrogate:
    Louis P Gigliotti
Family:
    James R Griffith
Family:
    Paul M Deep
Family:
    Julia M Brouillette

### Supreme, County & Family Courts
Courthouse, 200 Elizabeth St, Utica, NY 13501
Chief Clerk-Supreme/County:
    Jeanne Natale
    fax: 315-798-6047
Chief Clerk-Family (Acting):
    David Primo . . . . . . . . . . . . . . . . . . . .315-266-4444/fax: 315-266-4421

### Surrogate's Court
County Office Bldg, 800 Park Ave, 8th Fl, Utica, NY 13501
Deputy Chief Clerk:
    Kelly A Fuller. . . . . . . . . . . . . .315-266-4550 or 315-266-4309 (Rome)
    fax: 315-266-4703

## Onondaga County

### Judges
County:
    Matthew J Doran
County:
    Stephen J Dougherty
Family:
    Christina F DeJoseph
Family:
    Julie A Cecile
Family:
    Michele Pirro Bailey
Family:
    Martha E Mulroy
Surrogate:
    Mary Keib Smith
County:
    Thomas J Miller

### Supreme, Family & Surrogate's Courts
401 Montgomery St., Syracuse, NY 13202
Chief Clerk-Family:
    David Primo, Esq. . . . . . . . . . . . . . . . .315-671-2005/fax: 315-671-1165
Chief Clerk-County/Supreme:
    James E Makowiec. . . . . . . . . . . . . . .315-671-1030 or 315-671-1020
    fax: 315-671-1191
Chief Clerk-Surrogate:
    Eileen A Casey, Esq. . . . . . . . . . . . . .315-671-2100/fax: 315-671-1162

Judicial Branch

## Ontario County

**Judges**
Multi-Bench:
Frederick G Reed
Multi-Bench:
Brian D Dennis
Family:
Kristina A Karle
Family (Acting):
Jacqueline E Sisson

**Supreme, County, Family & Surrogate's Courts**
Courthouse, 27 N Main St, Canandaigua, NY 14424-1459
Chief Clerk-Supreme/County:
Marcilyn Morrisey . . . . . . . . . . . . . 585-412-5300/fax: 585-412-5327
Chief Clerk-Surrogate:
Vacant . . . . . . . . . . . . . . . . . . . . . . . . . . . . . . . . . . 585-412-5301
Chief Clerk-Family:
Linda M DiStefano . . . . . . . . . . . . . 585-412-5299/fax: 585-412-5327
e-mail: ontariofamilycourt@nycourts.gov

## Orange County

**Judges**
County:
Craig Stephen Brown
County:
William L DeProspo
County:
Catherine Bartlett
Supreme:
Robert A Onofry
Supreme:
Sandra Sciortino

**Supreme, County & Family Courts**
285 Main St, Goshen, NY 10924
Chief Clerk-County/Supreme/Family:
Lynn McKelvey . . . . . . . . . . . . . . . . . . . . . . . . . . . . 845-476-3500

## Orleans County

**Judges**
Multi-Bench:
Sanford A Church

**Supreme, County, Family & Surrogate's Courts**
Courthouse Square, 1 S Main St, Ste 3, Albion, NY 14411-1497
Chief Clerk-Surrogate:
Jamie Summers . . . . . . . . . . . . . . . . . . . . . . . . . . . . 585-283-6658
e-mail: jsummers@nycourts.gov
Chief Clerk-Family:
Laurie A Bower . . . . . . . . . . . . . . . . . . . . . . . . . . . . 585-283-6656
e-mail: lbower@nycourts.gov
Chief Clerk-County/Supreme:
Kristin Nicholson . . . . . . . . . . . . . . . . . . . . . . . . . . . 585-283-6657
e-mail: knichols@nycourts.gov

## Oswego County

**Judges**
Surrogate:
Spencer Ludington
County:
Walter W Hafner, Jr
County:
Karen M Brandt Brown
Family:
Thomas Benedetto
Family:
Allison J Nelson

**Family Court**
Public Safety Ctr, 39 Churchill Rd, Oswego, NY 13126
Chief Clerk-Family:
Kathleen L Halstead . . . . . . . . . . . . 315-207-7533/fax: 315-266-4770

**Supreme, County & Surrogate's Courts**
Courthouse, 25 E Oneida St, Oswego, NY 13126
Chief Clerk-Surrogate:
Judy M Livingston . . . . . . . . . . . . . . 315-207-7566/fax: 315-266-4784
Chief Clerk-County/Supreme:
Amy Fox . . . . . . . . . . . . . . . . . . . . . 315-207-7500/fax: 315-266-4519

## Otsego County

**Judges**
Multi-Bench:
John F Lambert

**Supreme, County & Surrogate's Courts**
197 Main St, Cooperstown, NY 13326
Chief Clerk-County/Supreme:
Michael McGovern . . . . . . . . . . . . . . 607-322-3140/fax: 646-963-6663
e-mail: mmcgove1@nycourts.gov
Chief Clerk-Surrogate:
Lisa Weite . . . . . . . . . . . . . . . . . . . . 607-322-3148/fax: 607-240-5966
e-mail: lweite@nycourts.gov

**Family Court**
County Annex Building, 32 Chestnut Street, Cooperstown, NY 13326
Chief Clerk-Family:
Karen A Nichols . . . . . . . . . . . . . . . . 607-322-3130/fax: 607-240-5548
e-mail: otsegofamilycourt@nycourts.gov

## Putnam County

**Judges**
Family:
Joseph J Spofford
Surrogate:
James T Rooney

**Supreme, County & Family Courts**
20 County Center, Carmel, NY 10512
Chief Clerk-Supreme/County/Family:
Lisa D'Angelo . . . . . . . . . . . . . . . . . 845-208-7800/fax: 845-208-7869

**Surrogate's Court**
44 Gleneida Ave, Carmel, NY 10512
Chief Clerk-Surrogate:
Irene Muller . . . . . . . . . . . . . . . . . . . 845-208-7860/fax: 845-431-1936

## Rensselaer County

**Judges**
Family:
Catherine Cholakis
Family:
Elizabeth Marie Walsh
Surrogate:
Paul V Morgan, Jr
County:
Debra J Young
County:
Jennifer Sober

**Family Court**
1504 Fifth Ave, Troy, NY 12180
Chief Clerk:
Barbara Cottrell . . . . . . . . . . . . . . . . 518-435-5515/fax: 518-285-8504

**Supreme, County & Surrogate's Courts** . . . . . . . . fax: 518-285-5077
Courthouse, 80 Second Street, Troy, NY 12180

---

*Offices and agencies generally appear in alphabetical order, except when specific order is requested by listee.*

Chief Clerk-Surrogate:
Susan Wilson..................518-285-6100/fax: 518-272-5452
e-mail: RensselaerSurrogateCourt@nycourts.gov
Chief Clerk-County/Supreme:
Richard F Reilly, Jr. ..............518-285-5025/fax: 518-285-5077

## Rockland County

### Judges
Surrogate:
Keith J Cornell
County:
Kevin F Russo
County:
Rolf M Thorsen
County:
Larry J Schwartz
Family:
Sherri L Eisenpress
Family:
Rachel E Tanguay

### Supreme, County, Family & Surrogate's Courts. fax: 845-638-5312
1 South Main St, New City, NY 10956
845-483-8310 Fax: 845-638-5312
Chief Clerk-Family:
Anna Kosovych.................845-483-8210/fax: 845-638-5319
Chief Clerk-County/Supreme:
Robert Fritz....................845-483-8310/fax: 845-638-5312
Chief Clerk-Surrogate:
Eileen Horan ...................845-483-8260/fax: 914-358-8067

## Saratoga County

### Judges
Family:
Amy J Knussman
Surrogate:
Richard Kupferman
County:
James A Murphy III
Family:
Paul Pelagalli

### Family Court
35 W High St, Ballston Spa, NY 12020
Chief Clerk:
Dennis Bruce...................518-451-8888/fax: 518-453-5942

### Supreme, County & Surrogate's Courts
30 McMaster St, Building 3, Ballston Spa, NY 12020
Chief Clerk-Surrogate:
Lisa Hastings...................518-451-8830/fax: 518-453-8693
Chief Clerk-County/Supreme:
Carianne Brimhall...............518-451-8840/fax: 518-453-5937

## Schenectady County

### Judges
County:
Matthew J Sypniewski
Surrogate:
Vincent W Versaci
Family:
Jill S Polk
Family:
Mark W Blanchfield
Family:
Kevin A Burke

### Family Court
County Office Bldg, 620 State St, Schenectady, NY 12305

Deputy Chief Clerk:
Lawrencia Colon.................518-285-8435/fax: 518-393-1565

### Supreme, County & Surrogate's Courts
Courthouse, 612 State St, Schenectady, NY 12305
Chief Clerk-Surrogate:
Amy Stone.....................518-285-8455/fax: 518-451-8732
Chief Clerk-County/Supreme:
David Cardona .................518-285-8401/fax: 518-451-8731

## Schoharie County

### Judges
Multi-Bench:
George R Bartlett, III

### Supreme, County, Family & Surrogate's Courts
Courthouse, 290 Main St, PO Box 669, Schoharie, NY 12157
Chief Clerk:
F Christian Spies .................518-453-6998 or 518-453-6892

## Schuyler County

### Judges
Multi-Bench:
Matthew C Hayden

### Supreme, County, Family & Surrogate's Courts
Courthouse, 105 9th St, Unit 35, Watkins Glen, NY 14891
Chief Clerk-Family:
Amanda Riley ...................607-228-3352/fax: 646-963-6590
e-mail: alriley@courts.state.ny.us
Chief Clerk-County/Supreme:
Michele Ormsbee ...............607-228-3350/fax: 646-963-6590
Chief Clerk-Surrogate:
Jack Miller.....................607-228-3351/fax: 646-963-6590

## Seneca County

### Judges
County:
Daniel J Doyle
Family:
Jason L Cook
Multi-Bench:
Barry L Porsch

### Supreme, County, Family & Surrogate's Courts
Courthouse, 48 W Williams St, Waterloo, NY 13165
Chief Clerk-Family:
Lori Breese .....................315-835-6231/fax: 315-835-6234
e-mail: senecafamilycourt@nycourts.gov
Chief Clerk-Supreme/County:
Susan Maleski...................315-835-6229/fax: 315-835-6234
Chief Clerk-Surrogate:
Lindsey Sholly .................315-835-6232/fax: 315-835-6234

## St Lawrence County

### Judges
Family:
Cecily L Morris
County:
Gregory P Storie
Surrogate:
John F Richey

### Supreme, County, Family & Surrogate's Courts
Courthouse, 48 Court St, Canton, NY 13617
Chief Clerk-County/Supreme:
Neika Mayo....................315-379-2219/fax: 315-379-2423

*Offices and agencies generally appear in alphabetical order, except when specific order is requested by listee.*

Chief Clerk-Family:
Rhonda Poupore . . . . . . . . . . . . . . . .315-379-2410/fax: 315-386-3197
Chief Clerk-Surrogate:
Debra Dow . . . . . . . . . . . . . . . . . . . .315-379-2217/fax: 315-379-2372

## Steuben County

### Judges
Family:
Chauncey J Watches
Multi-Bench:
Philip J Roche
Multi-Bench:
Patrick F McAllister

### Supreme, County, Family & Surrogate's Courts
Courthouse, 3 E Pulteney Sq, Bath, NY 14810
Chief Clerk-Family:
April L Din . . . . . . . . . . . . . . . . . . . .607-622-8218/fax: 607-622-8239
e-mail: steubenfamilycourt@nycourts.gov
Chief Clerk-Surrogate:
Sara A Barefoot. . . . . . . . . . . . . . . . .607-622-8221/fax: 607-622-8243
Chief Clerk-Supreme/County:
Jodi Wood . . . . . . . . . . . . . . . . . . . . .607-622-8219/fax: 607-622-8244

## Suffolk County

### Judges
County/Acting Surrogate:
Stephen L Braslow
County/Acting Family:
Philip Goglas
County:
Fernando Camacho
County:
Joseph Farneti
County:
Mark Cohen
County:
James C Hudson
County:
John Iliou
County:
James F Quinn
County:
Timothy Mazzei
County:
David A Morris
County:
John H Rouse
County:
Anthony S Senft, Jr

### Supreme Court
1 Court St, Riverhead, NY 11901
Chief Clerk:
Vacant. . . . . . . . . . . . . . . . . . . . . . . . . . . . . . . . . .631-852-2334

### Surrogate's Court
320 Center Dr, Riverhead, NY 11901
Deputy Chief Clerk:
Amy E Campbell . . . . . . . . . . . . . . . . . . . . . . . . . . . .631-852-1746

## Sullivan County

### Judges
County:
James R Farrell
Supreme:
Stephan G Schick

### Surrogate's & Family Courts
Government Center, 100 North St, Monticello, NY 12701
Chief Clerk-Surrogate:
Rita Guarnaccia. . . . . . . . . . . . . . . . .845-791-3500/fax: 845-481-9337
Chief Clerk-Family:
Christina Benson. . . . . . . . . . . . . . . . .845-791-3505/fax: 845-476-3620

### Supreme & County Court
Courthouse, 414 Broadway, Monticello, NY 12701
Chief Clerk-Supreme/County:
Sarah Katzman . . . . . . . . . . . . . . . . . .845-791-3540/fax: 845-791-6170

## Tioga County

### Judges
Multi-Bench:
Gerald Keene

### Supreme County, Family & Surrogate's Courts
Court Annex, 20 Court St, PO Box 10, Owego, NY 13827
Chief Clerk-Family:
Vacant. . . . . . . . . . . . . . . . . . . . . . . .607-689-6077/fax: 646-963-6399
Chief Clerk-Surrogate:
Deborah A Stone Pellinger . . . . . . . . .607-689-6099/fax: 646-963-6398
Chief Clerk-Supreme/County:
Janean Cook . . . . . . . . . . . . . . . . . . . .607-689-6102/fax: 212-401-5970

## Tompkins County

### Judges
Multi-Bench:
John C Rowley
Multi-Bench:
Joseph R Cassidy

### Supreme, County, Family & Surrogate's Courts
Courthouse, 320 N Tioga St, Ithaca, NY 14850
Chief Clerk-Surrogate:
Lori S Decker . . . . . . . . . . . . . . . . . . .607-216-6655/fax: 212-457-2952
Chief Clerk-County/Supreme:
Mary C Hodges . . . . . . . . . . . . . . . . . .607-216-6630 or 607-216-6610
fax: 212-401-9071
Chief Clerk-Family:
Adel Terris . . . . . . . . . . . . . . . . . . . . .607-216-6640/fax: 212-457-2951
e-mail: tpkfamily@nycourts.gov

## Ulster County

### Judges
County:
Bryan Rounds
Family:
Marianne O Mizel
Family:
Keri Savona
Surrogate:
Sara McGinty
Family:
Anthony McGinty

### Family Court
2 Development Court, Kingston, NY 12401
Chief Clerk:
Elaine Stinemire . . . . . . . . . . . . . . . . .845-481-9430/fax: 845-483-8114
e-mail: ulsterfamilycourt@nycourts.gov

### Supreme & County Courts
Courthouse, 285 Wall St, Kingston, NY 12401
Chief Clerk:
Claudia Jones . . . . . . . . . . . . . . . . . . .845-481-9375/fax: 845-476-3619

---

*Offices and agencies generally appear in alphabetical order, except when specific order is requested by listee.*

**Surrogate's Court**
240 Fair St, Kingston, NY 12401
Chief Clerk:
Linda McCluskey . . . . . . . . . . . . . . . 845-481-9338/fax: 845-483-8427
e-mail: ulstersurrogatecourt@nycourts.gov

## Warren County

### Judges
Family:
Paulette M Kershko
Family:
Ted M Wilson
County/Surrogate:
Robin A Smith

### Supreme, County, Family & Surrogate's Courts
Municipal Center, 1340 State Route 9, Lake George, NY 12845
Chief Clerk-Family:
Katherine Thompson . . . . . . . . . . . . . . . . . . . . . . . . . . 518-480-6305
e-mail: warrenfamily@nycourts.gov
Chief Clerk-Surrogate:
Deborah Ricci . . . . . . . . . . . . . . . . . . . . . . . . . . . . . . . 518-480-6360
e-mail: warrensurrogate@nycourts.gov
Deputy Chief Clerk-County/Supreme:
Sheila Kent . . . . . . . . . . . . . . . . . . . . . . . . . . . . . . . . . 518-480-6335

## Washington County

### Judges
Multi-Bench:
Adam D Michelini
Multi-Bench:
Kelly S McKeighan

### Supreme, County, Family & Surrogate's Courts
Courthouse, 383 Broadway, Fort Edward, NY 12828
Chief Clerk-County/Supreme:
Tricia Robarge. . . . . . . . . . . . . . . . . . 518-746-2521/fax: 518-746-2519
Chief Clerk-Family:
Nicole Hoag . . . . . . . . . . . . . . . . . . . 518-746-2501/fax: 518-746-2503
Chief Clerk-Surrogate:
Rachel Finnegan . . . . . . . . . . . . . . . . 518-746-2545/fax: 518-285-4389

## Wayne County

### Judges
Multi-Bench:
Richard M Healy
Multi-Bench:
John B Nesbitt
Multi-Bench:
Daniel G Barrett

### Supreme, County, Family & Surrogate's Courts
Hall of Justice, 54 Broad St, Rm 106, Lyons, NY 14489
Chief Clerk-Surrogate:
Christina Herman . . . . . . . . . . . . . . . 315-665-8119/fax: 315-665-8110
Chief Clerk-Family:
Corinne Sergeant. . . . . . . . . . . . . . . . 315-665-8115/fax: 315-665-8106
e-mail: waynefamilycourt@nycourts.gov
Chief Clerk-Supreme/County:
Adriane Kidder . . . . . . . . . . . . . . . . . 315-665-8117/fax: 315-665-8112

## Westchester County

### Judges
County:
Helen M Blackwood
County:
Susan M Capeci

County:
Susan Cacace
County:
George E Fufido, Jr
Surrogate:
Brandon R Sall
County:
Susan Kettner
County:
Anne E Minihan
County:
David S Zuckerman
Family:
Arlene Katz

### Supreme, County & Family Courts
111 Dr Martin Luther King Jr Blvd, White Plains, NY 10601
Chief Clerk-Family:
Vacant . . . . . . . . . . . . . . . . . . . . . . . 914-824-5500/fax: 914-824-5860
Chief Clerk-County/Supreme:
Lakisha C Hickson . . . . . . . . . . . . . . . 914-824-5300 or 914-824-5400
fax: 914-824-5873

### Surrogate's Court
111 Dr Martin Luther King Jr Blvd, 19th Fl, White Plains, NY 10601
Chief Clerk:
Johanna K O'Brien . . . . . . . . . . . . . . 914-824-5656/fax: 914-358-8042

## Wyoming County

### Judges
Multi-Bench:
Michael Mohun
Multi-Bench:
Keith Kibler

### Supreme, County, Family & Surrogate's Courts
Courthouse, 147 N Main St, Warsaw, NY 14569
Deputy Chief Clerk-Surrogate:
Michelle Zastempowski . . . . . . . . . . . 585-228-3217/fax: 585-228-3230
e-mail: jbaker@nycourts.gov
Chief Clerk-Family:
Rachel Maston. . . . . . . . . . . . . . . . . . 585-228-3229/fax: 585-228-3230
e-mail: rmaston@nycourts.gov
Chief Clerk-County/Supreme:
Betty Fisher . . . . . . . . . . . . . . . . . . . 585-228-3199/fax: 585-228-3236
e-mail: rmmiller@nycourts.gov

## Yates County

### Judges
Multi-Bench:
Jason L Cook

### Supreme, County, Family & Surrogate's Courts
Courthouse, 415 Liberty St, Penn Yan, NY 14527
Chief Clerk-Supreme/County:
Carol B Winslow. . . . . . . . . . . . . . . . 315-835-6308/fax: 315-835-6309
Chief Clerk-Family:
Tammy James . . . . . . . . . . . . . . . . . . 315-835-6314/fax: 315-835-6320
e-mail: yatesfamilycourt@nycourts.gov
Chief Clerk-Surrogate:
Vanessa V Smith . . . . . . . . . . . . . . . . 315-835-6321/fax: 315-835-6322

## DISTRICT COURTS

*District Courts exist in Nassau County and in five western towns of Suffolk County. District Courts have civil jurisdiction up to $15,000, and criminal jurisdiction for misdemeanors, violations and lesser offenses. Judges are elected for six-year terms by their judicial districts.*

*Offices and agencies generally appear in alphabetical order, except when specific order is requested by listee.*

## Nassau County

### 1st, 2nd & 4th District Courts
99 Main St, Hempstead, NY 11550
516-493-4200
District Executive:
Paul Lamanna, Esq...........................516-493-3001

### Judges
Supervising Judge:
Elizabeth Fox-McDonough

| | |
|---|---|
| Valerie Alexander | David W McAndrews |
| James M Darcy | Andrew M Engel |
| Scott Fairgrieve | Tricia M Ferrell |
| Joseph Girardi | David Goodsell |
| Darlene D Harris | William Hohauser |
| Douglas J Lerose | Martin J Massell |
| Ignatius L Muscarella | Paul Meli |
| Colin F O'Donnell | Anthony W Paradiso |
| Andrea Phoenix | Robert E Pipia |
| Erica L Prager | Scott H Siller |
| Joy M Watson | |

## Suffolk County
Chief Clerk:
Michael Paparatto................................631-852-2568

### 1st District Court, Criminal Term.............fax: 631-853-4505
John P Cohalan, Jr Court Complex, 400 Carleton Ave, P.O. Box 9073,
Central Islip, NY 11722
631-208-5775 Fax: 631-853-4505

### 2nd District Court...........................fax: 631-854-1127
30 East Hoffman Avenue, Lindenhurst, NY 11757
631-208-5775 Fax: 631-854-1127

### 3rd District Court ..........................fax: 631-854-4549
1850 New York Ave, Huntington Station, NY 11746
631-208-5775 Fax: 631-854-4549

### 4th District Court...........................fax: 631-853-5951
Veterans' Memorial Highway, Hauppauge, NY 11788
631-208-5775 Fax: 631-853-5951

### 5th District Court...........................fax: 631-854-9681
3105 Veterans Memorial Hwy, Ronkonkoma, NY 11779
631-208-5775 Fax: 631-854-9681

### 6th District Court...........................fax: 631-854-1444
150 W Main St, Patchogue, NY 11772
631-208-5775 Fax: 631-854-1444

### Judges
Supervising Judge:
Karen Kerr

| | |
|---|---|
| John J Andrews | Toni A Bean |
| Pierce F Cohalan | Carl J Copertino |
| Richard T Dunne | James P Flanagan |
| Alfred Graf | Patricia Grant Flynn |
| C Stephen Hackeling | Paul E Hennings |
| Jennifer A Henry | Gaetan B Lozito |
| James Malone | James F Matthews |
| James McDonaugh | Derrick Robinson |
| Eric Sachs | James A Saladino |
| John P Schettino | Garrett W Swenson, Jr |

## CITY COURTS OUTSIDE NEW YORK CITY

*City Courts outside New York City have civil jurisdiction up to $15,000 and criminal jurisdiction over misdemeanors or lesser offenses. City Court judges are either elected or appointed for terms of ten years for full-time judges and six years for part-time judges.*

## Albany

### Judges
Multi-Bench:
William G Keith
Criminal:
Joshua Farrell
Criminal:
Holly Trexler
Multi-Bench:
Helena Heath
Criminal:
John Reilly

### Civil Court
Albany City Hall, Room 209, 24 Eagle Street, Albany, NY 12207
Chief Clerk:
Anthony Mancino...............518-453-4640/fax: 518-453-8679
e-mail: albanycivilcourt@nycourts.gov

### Criminal Court
Public Safety Bldg, 1 Morton Ave, Albany, NY 12202
Chief Clerk:
Anthony Mancino...............518-453-5520/fax: 518-453-8990
e-mail: albanycriminalcourt@nycourts.gov

### Traffic Court
Albany City Hall Basement, 24 Eagle St, Albany, NY 12207
Chief Clerk:
Anthony Mancino...............518-453-4630/fax: 518-453-8699
e-mail: albanytrafficcourt@nycourts.gov

## Amsterdam

### Judges
William J Mycek                    Lisa W Lorman

### Civil & Criminal Courts
Public Safety Bldg, Rm 208, 1 Guy Park Ave Ext, Amsterdam, NY 12010
Acting Chief Clerk:
Tammy Beck...................518-842-9510/fax: 518-453-8646

## Auburn

### Judges
Kristin L Garland                  David B Thurston

### Civil & Criminal Courts
157 Genesee St, Auburn, NY 13021
Chief Clerk:
Deborah L Robillard..............315-237-6420/fax: 315-237-6421
e-mail: auburncitycourt@nycourts.gov

## Batavia

### Judges
Durin B Rogers                     Thomas Burns

### Civil & Criminal Courts
Facility Bldg, 1 W Main St, Batavia, NY 14020
Chief Clerk:
Jennifer Wallace ................585-201-5760/fax: 585-371-3954
e-mail: jwallace@nycourts.gov

## Beacon

### Judges
Rebecca S Mensch                   Timothy G Pagones

### Civil & Criminal Courts
1 Municipal Plz, Ste 2, Beacon, NY 12508
Chief Clerk:
Margaret Connaughton...........845-431-1900/fax: 845-431-1736

*Offices and agencies generally appear in alphabetical order, except when specific order is requested by listee.*

## Binghamton

**Judges**

Carol A Cocchiola      William C Pelella
Daniel L Seiden

**Civil & Criminal Courts**

City Hall, Governmental Plz, 38 Hawley St, 5th Fl, Binghamton, NY 13901
Chief Clerk:
Jennifer L B Katz . . . . . . . . . . . . . . . 607-240-4272/fax: 607-240-5946
e-mail: sbaker@nycourts.gov

## Buffalo

**Judges**

| | |
|---|---|
| Lenora Foote-Beavers | Patrick M Carney |
| Betty Calvo-Torres | Debra L Givens |
| Craig D Hannah | Shannon M Heneghan |
| Kevin J Keane | Andrew C LoTempio |
| Peter J Savage, III | JaHarr Pridgen |
| Diane Wray | Barbara Johnson-Lee |
| Robert T Russell Jr | Phillio Dabney |

**Civil & Criminal Courts** . . . . . . . . . . . . . . . . . . . . . . fax: 716-847-8257

50 Delaware Ave, Buffalo, NY 14202
716-845-2600  Fax: 716-847-8257
Chief Clerk:
Erika Webb. . . . . . . . . . . . . . . . . . . . . . . . . . . . . . . .716-845-2654
e-mail: ewebb@nycourts.gov

## Canandaigua

**Judges**

Jacqueline Sisson      David J Whitcomb

**Civil & Criminal Courts** . . . . . . . . . . . . . . . . . . . . . . fax: 585-412-5172

City Hall, 2 N Main St, Canandaigua, NY 14424
585-412-5170  Fax: 585-412-5172
Chief Clerk:
Katherine Watkins. . . . . . . . . . . . . . .585-412-5170/fax: 585-412-5172

## Cohoes

**Judges**

Eric Galarneau      Thomas Marcelle

**Civil, Criminal & Traffic Courts**

City Hall, 97 Mohawk St, Cohoes, NY 12047
Chief Clerk:
Allison Polemeropoulos . . . . . . . . . . 518-453-5501/fax: 518-233-8202
e-mail: cohoescitycourt@nycourts.gov

## Corning

**Judges**

George J Welch, Jr      Mathew K McCarthy

**Civil & Criminal Courts**

500 Nasser Civic Ctr Plz, Ste 101, Corning, NY 14830
Chief Clerk:
Colleen A Flanagan. . . . . . . . . . . . . .607-654-6033/fax: 607-654-6030
e-mail: corningcitycourt@nycourts.gov

## Cortland

**Judges**

Lawrence J Knickerbocker      Elizabeth A Burns

**Civil & Criminal Courts**

City Hall, 25 Court St, Cortland, NY 13045

Chief Clerk:
Diana L Davis . . . . . . . . . . . . . . . . . .607-218-3300/fax: 607-218-3299

## Dunkirk

**Judges**

Rachel E Roberts (Acting)      John M Kuzdale

**Civil & Criminal Courts**

City Hall, 342 Central Ave, Dunkirk, NY 14048-2122
Chief Clerk:
Jean Dill . . . . . . . . . . . . . . . . . . . . . .716-366-2055/fax: 716-366-3622
e-mail: jdill@nycourts.gov

## Elmira

**Judges**

Steven W Forrest      Peter F Finnerty

**Civil & Criminal Courts**

317 E Church St, Elmira, NY 14901
e-mail: elmiracitycourt@courts.state.ny.us
Chief Clerk:
Casey Johnson. . . . . . . . . . . . . . . . . .607-837-9520/fax: 212-401-9240
e-mail: elmiracitycourt@courts.state.ny.us

## Fulton

**Judges**

David H Hawthorne      James M Nicholson

**Civil & Criminal Courts**

Municipal Bldg, 141 S First St, Fulton, NY 13069
e-mail: fulton_city@courts.state.ny.us
Chief Clerk:
Maureen Ball. . . . . . . . . . . . . . . . . . .315-207-7231/fax: 315-266-4753
e-mail: mball@courts.state.ny.us

## Geneva

**Judges**

William J Hart      Elisabeth A Toole
Leslie Cohen-Hickey

**Civil & Criminal Courts**

255 Exchange St, Geneva, NY 14456
Chief Clerk:
Josephine Guard . . . . . . . . . . . . . . . .315-237-6575/fax: 315-237-6415

## Glen Cove

**Judges**

Richard J McCord

**Civil & Criminal Courts**

13 Glen St, Glen Cove, NY 11542
Chief Clerk:
Stacey Gallo . . . . . . . . . . . . . . . . . . .516-403-2441/fax: 516-403-2457

## Glens Falls

**Judges**

Gary C Hobbs      Nikki J Moreschi

**Civil & Criminal Courts**

City Hall, 42 Ridge St, 3rd Fl, Glens Falls, NY 12801
Chief Clerk:
Lisa Ghenoiu . . . . . . . . . . . . . . . . . . . . . . . . . . . . . . .518-480-6365
e-mail: GlensFallsCity@nycourts.gov

*Offices and agencies generally appear in alphabetical order, except when specific order is requested by listee.*

## Gloversville

**Judges**
Traci DiMezza              Cory Dalmata

**Civil & Criminal Courts**
City Hall, 3 Frontage Rd, Gloversville, NY 12078
Acting Chief Clerk:
  Stephen Russo ............................518-706-3320
  e-mail: GloversvilleCity@nycourts.gov

## Hornell

**Judges**
Jennifer L Donlon          David E Coddington

**Civil & Criminal Courts**
82 Main St, Ste 101, Hornell, NY 14843
Chief Clerk:
  Love Griffin ..............607-590-3314/fax: 607-590-3316
  e-mail: hornellcity@nycourts.gov

## Hudson

**Judges**
John Connor, Jr            Brian J Herman

**City Court**
701-B Union St, Hudson, NY 12534
Chief Clerk:
  Jamie Empire...............518-267-3082/fax: 212-457-2682
  e-mail: hudsoncitycourt@nycourts.gov

## Ithaca

**Judges**
Seth J Peacock             Richard M Wallace

**Civil & Criminal Courts**
118 E Clinton St, Ithaca, NY 14850
Chief Clerk:
  Vacant ....................607-216-6660/fax: 607-240-5821
  e-mail: ithacacitycourt@nycourts.gov

## Jamestown

**Judges**
John L LaMancuso           Frederick A Larson

**Civil & Criminal Courts**
Municipal Bldg, 200 E 3rd St, Jamestown, NY 14701
Chief Clerk:
  Lisa Cannon ...............716-483-7561/fax: 716-483-7519
  e-mail: lmeacham@nycourts.gov

## Johnstown

**Judges**
Michael C Viscosi          Brett A Preston

**Civil & Criminal Courts**
City Hall, 33-41 E Main St, Ste 105, Johnstown, NY 12095
Chief Clerk:
  Stephen Russo...............518-706-3310/fax: 578-453-8651
  e-mail: JohnstownCity@nycourts.gov

## Kingston

**Judges**
Lawrence E Ball            Philip W Kirschner

**City Court**
Kingston City Court, 1 Garraghan Dr, Kingston, NY 12401

Chief Clerk:
  Nicole Murphy .............845-481-9350/fax: 845-483-8113
  e-mail: kingstoncitycourt@nycourts.gov

## Lackawanna

**Judges**
Kenneth Szyszkowski        Gary N Violanti

**Civil & Criminal Courts**
City Hall, 714 Ridge Rd, Lackawanna, NY 14218
Chief Clerk:
  Carol Williams .............716-845-7216/fax: 716-845-7599
  e-mail: cawillia@nycourts.gov

## Little Falls

**Judges**
Joy Malone                 Mark Rose

**Civil & Criminal Courts**
City Hall, 659 E Main St, Little Falls, NY 13365
Chief Clerk:
  Judith Bowman .............315-619-3408/fax: 315-266-4711

## Lockport

**Judges**
William J Watson           Thomas M DiMillo

**Civil & Criminal Courts**
1 Locks Plz, Lockport, NY 14094
716-280-6205
Chief Clerk:
  Laura Peters...............716-280-6207/fax: 716-439-6684
  e-mail: cjwagner@nycourts.gov

## Long Beach

**Judges**
Corey E Klein              William Miller

**Civil & Criminal Courts**
1 W Chester St, Long Beach, NY 11561
516-442-8544
Chief Clerk:
  Robert Davis...............................516-442-8555

## Mechanicville

**Judges**
Jeffrey N Bagnoli          Constantine F DeStefano

**Civil & Criminal Courts**
City Hall, 36 N Main St, Mechanicville, NY 12118
Chief Clerk:
  Francine Baker .............518-453-5959/fax: 518-453-8678

## Middletown

**Judges**
Steven W Brockett          Richard J Guertin

**Civil & Criminal Courts**
2 James St, Middletown, NY 10940
Chief Clerk:
  Diane S Gould.............845-476-3630/fax: 845-570-5072

## Mount Vernon

**Judges**
Lyndon D Williams          William Edwards
Nichelle A Johnson         Adam Seiden

*Offices and agencies generally appear in alphabetical order, except when specific order is requested by listee.*

**Civil & Criminal Courts**
2 Roosevelt Square N, 2nd Fl, Mount Vernon, NY 10550
Chief Clerk:
Lawrence Darden . . . . . . . . . . . . . . 914-831-6440/fax: 914-358-8027

## New Rochelle

**Judges**
Matthew J Costa                    Eileen Songer McCarthy
Jared R Rice

**Civil & Criminal Courts**
475 North Ave, New Rochelle, NY 10801
Chief Clerk:
James Generoso. . . . . . . . . . . . . . . . 914-358-8000/fax: 914-358-8098

## Newburgh

**Judges**
Peter M Kulkin                     Paul D Trachte
Joanne M Forbes

**Civil & Criminal Courts**
300 Broadway, Newburgh, NY 12550
Chief Clerk:
Jasmin Reyes-Finch . . . . . . . . . . . . . 845-483-8100/fax: 845-565-0230

## Niagara Falls

**Judges**
Chief Judge:
Mark A Violante
Danielle Restaino                  James J Faso, Jr
Diane Vitello

**Civil & Criminal Courts**
1925 Main Street, Niagara Falls, NY 14305
716-371-4100
Chief Clerk:
Deonna Mazur. . . . . . . . . . . . . . . . .716-371-4131/fax: 716-371-4048
e-mail: dmazur@nycourts.gov

## North Tonawanda

**Judges**
Shawn P Nickerson                  Katherine Alexander

**Civil & Criminal Courts**
City Hall, 216 Payne Ave, North Tonawanda, NY 14120
Chief Clerk:
Jennifer Steele. . . . . . . . . . . . . . . . .716-845-7240/fax: 716-743-1754
e-mail: jasteele@nycourts.gov

## Norwich

**Judges**
Michael J Genute                   Patrick Flanagan

**Civil & Criminal Courts**
13 Eaton Ave, Norwich, NY 13815
Chief Clerk:
Vacant. . . . . . . . . . . . . . . . . . . . . . . .607-337-1457/fax: 917-522-3477

## Ogdensburg

**Judges**
Marcia L LeMay                     Keith S Massey, Jr

**Civil & Criminal Courts**
330 Ford St, Ogdensburg, NY 13669
Chief Clerk:
Lisa Marie Meyer . . . . . . . . . . . . . .315-393-3941/fax: 315-393-6839

## Olean

**Judges**
William J Gabler                   Nicholas DiCerbo

**Civil & Criminal Courts**
101 E State St, Olean, NY 14760
Chief Clerk:
Heather Marcellin . . . . . . . . . . . . . .716-379-6660/fax: 716-379-6678
e-mail: hmarcell@nycourts.gov

## Oneida

**Judges**
Michael J Misiaszek

**Civil & Criminal Courts**
Municipal Bldg, 108 Main St, Oneida, NY 13421
Chief Clerk:
Lynne Mondrick . . . . . . . . . . . . . . . .315-266-4740/fax: 646-963-6435
e-mail: oneidacitycourt@courts.state.ny.us

## Oneonta

**Judges**
Lucy P Bernier                     Donald J Schwartz

**Civil & Criminal Courts**
Public Safety Bldg, 81 Main St, Oneonta, NY 13820
Chief Clerk:
Catherine J Tisenchek. . . . . . . . . . . .607-376-5380/fax: 646-963-6433

## Oswego

**Judges**
James M Metcalf                    Thomas A Reynolds

**Civil & Criminal Courts**
Conway Municipal Center, 20 W Oneida St, Oswego, NY 13126
Chief Clerk:
Cassie Kinney . . . . . . . . . . . . . . . . .315-207-7251/fax: 315-266-4752
e-mail: osw_city_ct@courts.state.ny.us

## Peekskill

**Judges**
Lissette G Fernandez               Reginald J Johnson

**Civil & Criminal Courts**
2 Nelson Ave, Peekskill, NY 10566
Chief Clerk:
Concetta (Tina) Cardinale. . . . . . . . .914-831-6480/fax: 914-736-1889

## Plattsburgh

**Judges**
Timothy G Blatchley                Matthew G Favro

**Civil & Criminal Courts**
24 US Oval, Plattsburgh, NY 12903
Chief Clerk:
Kimberly Crow . . . . . . . . . . . . . . . . .518-536-3870/fax: 518-453-8624
e-mail: PlattsburghCity@nycourts.gov

## Port Jervis

**Judges**
James M Hendry III                 Matthew D Witherow

**Civil & Criminal Courts**
20 Hammond St, Port Jervis, NY 12771
Chief Clerk:
Catherine Quinn . . . . . . . . . . . . . . . .845-476-3700/fax: 845-476-3691

*Offices and agencies generally appear in alphabetical order, except when specific order is requested by listee.*

## Poughkeepsie

**Judges**
Frank M Mora                    Scott L Volkman

**Civil & Criminal Courts**
62 Civic Ctr Plz, Poughkeepsie, NY 12601
Chief Clerk:
Lori Conners . . . . . . . . . . . . . . . . . . . . . . . . . . . . . . . . . . . . 845-483-8200

## Rensselaer

**Judges**
Linda Blom Johnson              Kathleen Robichaud

**Civil & Criminal Courts**
City Hall, 62 Washington Street, Rensselaer, NY 12144
Chief Clerk:
Barbara Agans . . . . . . . . . . . . . . . . . . 518-453-4680/fax: 518-453-8996
e-mail: rensselaercitycourt@nycourts.gov

## Rochester

**Judges**
Melissa L Barrett               Charles F Crimi, Jr
Maija C Dixon                   Jack Elliott
Teresa D Johnson                Michael C Lopez
Stephen T Miller                Caroline Morrison
Nicole D Morris                 Ellen Yacknin

**Civil Court** . . . . . . . . . . . . . . . . . . . . . . . . . . . . . . fax: 585-371-3427
99 Exchange Boulevard, Rm 6, Rochester, NY 14614
585-371-3412  Fax: 585-371-3427
Chief Clerk:
Eugene Crimi

**Criminal Court** . . . . . . . . . . . . . . . . . . . . . . . . . . . fax: 585-371-3430
123 Public Safety Bldg, Rochester, NY 14614
585-371-3413  Fax: 585-371-3430
Chief Clerk:
Eugene Crimi

## Rome

**Judges**
Gregory J Amoroso               John C Gannon

**Civil & Criminal Courts**
100 W Court St, Rome, NY 13440
Chief Clerk:
Matthew Brown . . . . . . . . . . . . . . . . . 315-266-4700/fax: 315-266-4705
e-mail: RomeCity@nycourts.gov

## Rye

**Judges**
Joseph L Latwin                 Valerie Livingston

**Civil & Criminal Courts**
21 McCullough Pl, Rye, NY 10580
Chief Clerk:
Antoinette Cipriano . . . . . . . . . . . . . 914-831-6400/fax: 914-831-6546

## Salamanca

**Judges**
William J Gabler                Matthew Swenson

**Civil & Criminal Courts**
225 Wildwood Ave, Salamanca, NY 14779
Chief Clerk:
Stella Johnston . . . . . . . . . . . . . . . . 716-379-6670/fax: 716-379-6676
e-mail: ssjohnst@nycourts.gov

## Saratoga Springs

**Judges**
Francine R Vero                 Jeffrey D Wait

**Civil & Criminal Courts**
City Hall, 474 Broadway, Saratoga Springs, NY 12866
Chief Clerk:
Casey Scatena . . . . . . . . . . . . . . . . . . . 518-451-8780/fax: 518-453-8686

## Schenectady

**Judges**
Teneka E Frost                  Carl G Falotico
Mark J Caruso                   Robert W Hoffman

**Civil Court**
City Hall, 105 Jay St, Schenectady, NY 12305
Chief Clerk:
Rebecca I Rose . . . . . . . . . . . . . . . . . 518-453-6989/fax: 518-285-8983

**Criminal Court**
531 Liberty St, Schenectady, NY 12305
Chief Clerk:
Rebecca I Rose . . . . . . . . . . . . . . . . . 518-453-6989/fax: 518-453-8983

## Sherrill

**Judges**
James W Betro

**Civil & Criminal Courts**
373 Sherrill Rd, Sherrill, NY 13461
Chief Clerk:
Vacant . . . . . . . . . . . . . . . . . . . . . . . . 315-266-4381/fax: 315-266-4384

## Syracuse

**Judges**
Vanessa E Bogan                 James H Cecile
Erica T Clarke                  Felicia Pitts Davis
Mary Anne Doherty               Anne L Magnarelli
Shadia Tadros                   Derrek T Thomas

**Civil & Criminal Courts**
505 S State St, Syracuse, NY 13202-2104
Deputy Chief Clerk:
Valerie L James . . . . . . . . . . . . . . . . . 315-671-2700 or 315-671-2782
fax: 315-671-2741

## Tonawanda

**Judges**
Chief Judge:
Mark Saltarelli
Dean Lilac

**Civil & Criminal Courts** . . . . . . . . . . . . . . . . . . . . . fax: 716-845-7590
200 Niagara St, Tonawanda, NY 14150
716-845-2160  Fax: 716-845-7590
Deputy Chief Clerk:
Stacey Bush . . . . . . . . . . . . . . . . . . . . 716-845-2165/fax: 716-845-7590
e-mail: sbush@nycourts.gov

## Troy

**Judges**
Christopher T Maier             Jill Kehn
Matthew J Turner

**Civil & Criminal Court**
51 State St, 2nd & 3rd Floors, Troy, NY 12180

*Offices and agencies generally appear in alphabetical order, except when specific order is requested by listee.*

Chief Clerk:
  Karen DeBenedetto . . . . . . . . . . . . . . . . . . . . . . . . . . . . . 518-453-5900
  e-mail: TroyCityCourt@nycourts.gov

## Utica

### Judges
F Christopher Giruzzi          Ralph J Eannace
Joseph A Saba, Jr

### Civil & Criminal Courts
411 Oriskany St W, Utica, NY 13502
Chief Clerk:
  Donna K Lynskey . . . . . . . . . . . . . . . . . . . . . . . . . . . . . . 315-266-4600

## Watertown

### Judges
Anthony M Neddo                Eric T Swartz

### Civil & Criminal Courts
Municipal Bldg, 245 Washington St, Watertown, NY 13601
Chief Clerk:
  Benjamin Cobb . . . . . . . . . . . . . . . . . 315-785-7785/fax: 315-266-4783

## Watervliet

### Judges
Thomas Lamb                    Susan B Reinfurt

### Civil & Criminal Courts
2 - 15th St, Watervliet, NY 12189
Chief Clerk:
  Robin Robillard . . . . . . . . . . . . . . . . . 518-453-5550/fax: 518-453-8995
  e-mail: watervlietcitycourt@nycourts.gov

## White Plains

### Judges
John P Collins                 Jo Ann Friia
Lynette V Spaulding            Eric P Press

### Civil & Criminal Courts
77 S Lexington Ave, White Plains, NY 10601
Chief Clerk:
  Eileen Byrne . . . . . . . . . . . . . . . . . . . . 914-824-5675/fax: 914-824-5858

## Yonkers

### Judges
Thomas Quinones                Karen N Best
Arthur J Doran, III            Elena Goldberg Velazquez
Evan Inlaw                     Verris B Shako
Daniel P Romano

### Civil & Criminal Courts
100 S Broadway, Yonkers, NY 10701
Chief Clerk:
  Marisa Garcia . . . . . . . . . . . . . . . . . . 914-831-6450/fax: 914-377-6395

*Offices and agencies generally appear in alphabetical order, except when specific order is requested by listee.*

# Section 2:
# POLICY AREAS

# AGRICULTURE

## NEW YORK STATE

### GOVERNOR'S OFFICE

**Governor's Office**
Executive Chamber
State Capitol
Albany, NY 12224
518-474-8390  Fax: 518-474-1513
Web site: www.ny.gov

Governor:
    Andrew M Cuomo . . . . . . . . . . . . . . . . . . . . . . . . . . . . . .518-474-8390
Secretary to the Governor:
    Melissa DeRosa . . . . . . . . . . . . . . . .518-474-4246 or 212-681-4580
Counsel to the Governor:
    Kumiki Gibson . . . . . . . . . . . . . . . . . . . . . .518-474-8343 or 212-681-4580
Chief of Staff:
    Jill DesRosiers . . . . . . . . . . . . . . . . . . . . .518-474-8390 or 212-681-4580
Director, Communications:
    Peter Ajemian . . . . . . . . . . . . . . . . . . . . .518-474-8418 or 212-681-4640
Deputy Secretary, Food & Agriculture:
    Patrick Hooker . . . . . . . . . . . . . . . . . . . . . . . . . . . . . . . .518-486-3960
Chairman of Energy & Finance for New York:
    Richard L. Kauffman . . . . . . . . . . . . . . . . . . . . . . . . . . .518-486-9746

### EXECUTIVE DEPARTMENTS AND RELATED AGENCIES

**Agriculture & Markets Department**
10B Airline Drive
Albany, NY 12235
518-457-4188 or 800-554-4501  Fax: 518-457-3087
e-mail: info@agriculture.ny.gov
Web site: www.agriculture.ny.gov

Commissioner:
    Richard Ball . . . . . . . . . . . . . . . . . . . .518-457-8876 or 518-457-4188
First Deputy Commissioner:
    Steve McGrattan . . . . . . . . . . . . . . . . . . . . . . . . . . . . . .518-457-2771
Deputy Commissioner:
    Kevin King . . . . . . . . . . . . . . . . . . . . . . . . . . . . . . . . . . .518-485-2771
Deputy Commissioner:
    Jackie Moody-Czub . . . . . . . . . . . . . . . . . . . . . . . . . . . .518-485-7728
Internal Auditor:
    Adam Roberts . . . . . . . . . . . . . . . . . . . . . . . . . . . . . . . . .518-485-7728
Agency Emergency Management Coordinator:
    Vacant . . . . . . . . . . . . . . . . . . . . . . . . . . . . . . . . . . . . . . .518-457-2771
Director, Intergovernmental Affairs:
    Geoff Palmer . . . . . . . . . . . . . . . . . . . . . . . . . . . . . . . . .518-457-2771
    e-mail: geoff.palmer@agriculture.ny.gov
Special Assistant:
    Frank Rooney . . . . . . . . . . . . . . . . . . . . . . . . . . . . . . . . .518-485-7728
    e-mail: frank.rooney@agriculture.ny.gov
Public Information Officer:
    Jola Szubielski . . . . . . . . . . . . . . . . . .518-485-7728 or 518-457-3136
    fax: 518-457-3087
    e-mail: jola.szubielski@agriculture.ny.gov

**Agricultural Development Division**
Director, Agricultural Development:
    Vacant . . . . . . . . . . . . . . . . . . . . . . . . . . . . . . . . . . . . . . .518-457-7076
Access To Healthy Foods:
    Jonathan Thomson . . . . . . . . . . . . . . . . . . . . . . . . . . . . .518-485-8902
    e-mail: jonathan.thomson@agriculture.ny.gov

Marketing & Promotion:
    Sue Santamarina . . . . . . . . . . . . . . . . . . . . . . . . . . . . . .518-457-7229
    e-mail: sue.santamarina@agriculture.ny.gov
Economic Development Specialist:
    Tim Pezzolesi . . . . . . . . . . . . . . . . . . . . . . . . . . . . . . . . .518-457-8883
    e-mail: tim.pezzolesi@agriculture.ny.gov

    **Agricultural Districts**
    Manager:
        Bob Somers. . . . . . . . . . . . . . . . . . . . . . . . . . . . . . . .518-457-3738
        e-mail: bob.somers@agriculture.ny.gov

**Animal Industry** . . . . . . . . . . . . . . . . . . . . . . . . . . .fax: 518-485-7773
Director:
    Dr. David Smith . . . . . . . . . . . . . . . . . . . . . . . . . . . . . . .518-457-3502
    e-mail: david.smith@agriculture.ny.gov

**Counsel's Office** . . . . . . . . . . . . . . . . . . . . . . . . . .fax: 518-457-8842
Counsel:
    Scott Wyner . . . . . . . . . . . . . . . . . . . . . . . . . . . . . . . . . .518-457-1059
    e-mail: scott.wyner@agriculture.ny.gov

**Fiscal Management** . . . . . . . . . . . . . . . . . . . . . . .fax: 518-485-7750
Director:
    Lisa Brooks. . . . . . . . . . . . . . . . . . . . . . . . . . . . . . . . . . .518-457-2080

**Food Laboratory** . . . . . . . . . . . . . . . . . . . . . . . . .fax: 518-485-8097
Director:
    Dr. Maria Ishida . . . . . . . . . . . . . . . . . . . . . . . . . . . . . .518-457-4477
    e-mail: maria.ishida@agriculture.ny.gov
Assistant Director:
    Debra Oglesby . . . . . . . . . . . . . . . . . . . . . . . . . . . . . . . .518-485-5012
Associate Food Chemist:
    Robert Sheridan . . . . . . . . . . . . . . . . . . . . . . . . . . . . . . .518-457-8885
    e-mail: robert.sheridan@agriculture.ny.gov
Associate Food Chemist:
    Virginia Greene. . . . . . . . . . . . . . . . . . . . . . . . . . . . . . .518-485-8098

**Food Safety & Inspection** . . . . . . . . . . . . . . . . .fax: 518-485-8986
Director:
    John Luker . . . . . . . . . . . . . . . . . . . . . . . . . . . . . . . . . . .518-457-4492
Assistant Director:
    Vacant . . . . . . . . . . . . . . . . . . . . . . . . . . . . . . . . . . . . . . .518-457-5382

    **Field Operations**
    Director, Field Operations:
        Erin Sawyer . . . . . . . . . . . . . . . . . . . . . . . . . . . . . . .518-457-5380
        e-mail: erin.sawyer@agriculture.ny.gov
    *Brooklyn* . . . . . . . . . . . . . . . . . . . . . . . . . . . . . . .fax: 718-722-2510
        55 Hanson Place, Rm 378, Brooklyn, NY 11217-1583
        Chief Inspector:
            Richard Olson . . . . . . . . . . . . . . . . . . . . . . . . . . .718-722-2876
    *Buffalo* . . . . . . . . . . . . . . . . . . . . . . . . . . . . . . . .fax: 716-847-3155
        535 Washington Ave, Ste 203, Buffalo, NY 14203
        Supervising Inspector:
            Dan Gump . . . . . . . . . . . . . . . . . . . . . . . . . . . . . .716-847-3185
    *Hauppauge*
        Suffolk State Ofc Bldg, Veterans' Memorial Hwy, Happauge, NY
        11787
        631-952-3079
        Vacant
    *Rochester* . . . . . . . . . . . . . . . . . . . . . . . . . . . . . .fax: 716-424-1248
        1530 Jefferson Rd, Rochester, NY 14623
        585-427-2273  Fax: 716-424-1248
        Supervising Food Inspector:
            Evelyn Ahrens . . . . . . . . . . . . . . . . . . . . . . . . . . .585-427-0200
    *Syracuse* . . . . . . . . . . . . . . . . . . . . . . . . . . . . . . .fax: 315-487-1064
        Art & Home Center, New York State Fairgrounds, Syracuse, NY
        13209
        Supervising Food Regional Supervisor:
            Vacant . . . . . . . . . . . . . . . . . . . . . . . . . . . . . . . . .315-487-0852

*Offices and agencies generally appear in alphabetical order, except when specific order is requested by listee.*

Policy Areas

**Human Resources** . . . . . . . . . . . . . . . . . . . . . . . . . . fax: 518-457-8852
Director:
    Mark Vanderpoel . . . . . . . . . . . . . . . . . . . . . . . . . .518-457-3216
    e-mail: mark.vanderpoel@agriculture.ny.gov

**Information Systems** . . . . . . . . . . . . . . . . . . . . fax: 518-457-7815
Director:
    Vacant . . . . . . . . . . . . . . . . . . . . . . . . . . . . . . . . .518-457-7368

**Kosher Law Enforcement**
Director:
    Rabbi Aaron Metzger . . . . . . . . . . . . . . . . . . . . . .718-722-2852
    e-mail: kosher@agriculture.ny.gov

**Land & Water Resources** . . . . . . . . . . . . . . . . fax: 518-457-3412
  10B Airline Drive, Albany, NY 12235
  518-457-3738  Fax: 518-457-3412
  Web site: www.nys-soilandwater.org
Executive Director:
    Michael Latham . . . . . . . . . . . . . . . . . . . . . . . . . .518-457-3738
    e-mail: michael.latham@agriculture.ny.gov

**Milk Control & Dairy Services** . . . . . . . . . . . . . . fax: 518-485-8730
Director:
    Casey McCue . . . . . . . . . . . . . . . . . . . . . . . . . . .518-457-1772
    e-mail: casey.mccue@agriculture.ny.gov
Market Research Information & Reporting:
    David Del Cogliano . . . . . . . . . . . . . . . . . . . . . . . .518-457-1772
    e-mail: david.delcogliano@agriculture.ny.gov

**New York City Office** . . . . . . . . . . . . . . . . . . . . . fax: 718-722-2510
  55 Hanson Place, Brooklyn, NY 11217-1583
Chief, Food Safety & Inspection:
    Richard Olson . . . . . . . . . . . . . . . . . . . . . . . . . . .718-722-2876

**Plant Industry** . . . . . . . . . . . . . . . . . . . . . . . . . . fax: 518-457-1204
Director:
    Christopher Logue . . . . . . . . . . . . . . . . . . . . . . . .518-457-2087
    e-mail: christopher.logue@agriculture.ny.gov

**Soil & Water Conservation Committee** . . . . . . . . fax: 518-457-3412
  10B Airline Drive, Albany, NY 12235
  518-457-3738  Fax: 518-457-3412
  Web site: www.nys-soilandwater.org
Chair:
    Dale Stein . . . . . . . . . . . . . . . . . . . . . . . . . . . . . .518-457-3738

**State Fair** . . . . . . . . . . . . . . . . . . . . . . . . . . . . . fax: 315-487-9260
  581 State Fair Blvd, Syracuse, NY 13209
  315-487-7711  Fax: 315-487-9260
  Web site: www.nysfair.org
Director:
    Troy Waffner . . . . . . . . . . . . . . . . . . . . . . . .315-487-7711 x1200

**Statistics** . . . . . . . . . . . . . . . . . . . . . . . . . . . . . . fax: 518-453-6564
  Fax: 518-453-6564
  Web site: www.nass.usda.gov
State Statistician:
    Vacant . . . . . . . . . . . . . . . . . . . . . . . . . . . . . . . . .518-487-5570

**Weights & Measures** . . . . . . . . . . . . . . . . . . . . . . fax: 518-457-5693
  4 Burnett Blvd, Rm 216, Poughkeepsie, NY 12603
Director:
    Michael Sikula . . . . . . . . . . . . . . . . . . . . . . . . . . .518-457-3146
    e-mail: mike.sikula@agriculture.ny.gov

## NEW YORK STATE LEGISLATURE

*See Legislative Branch in Section 1 for additional Standing Committee and Subcommittee information.*

**Assembly Standing Committees**

**Agriculture**
Chair:
    Donna A Lupardo (D) . . . . . . . . . . . . . . . . . . . . . .518-455-5431

**Assembly Task Force**

**Food, Farm & Nutrition, Task Force on**
Chair:
    Daniel Rosenthal (D) . . . . . . . . . . . . . . . . . . . . . .518-455-5545

**Senate Standing Committees**

**Agriculture**

**Senate/Assembly Legislative Commissions**

**Legislative Commission on Rural Resources**
Chair:
    Rachel May (D, WF) . . . . . . . . . . . . . . . . . . . . . . .518-455-2366

## U.S. GOVERNMENT

### EXECUTIVE DEPARTMENTS AND RELATED AGENCIES

**Commodity Futures Trading Commission**
Three Lafayette Centre
1155 21st Street Northwest
Washington, DC 20581
202-418-5000  Fax: 202-418-5521
e-mail: questions@cftc.gov
Web site: www.cftc.gov

**Eastern Region**
  140 Broadway, New York, NY 10005
  646-746-9700
Regional Counsel:
  Vacant

**US Commerce Department**
1401 Constitution Avenue NW
Washington, DC 20230
202-482-2000
Web site: www.commerce.gov

**National Oceanic & Atmospheric Administration**
  1401 Constitution Avenue NW, Room 5128, Washington, DC 20230

  **National Weather Service, Eastern Region**
  630 Johnson Avenue, Suite 202, Bohemia, NY 11716
  631-244-0100
  e-mail: erhwebmaster@noaa.gov
  Web site: www.weather.gov/erh/
  Director, Eastern Region:
    Jason Tuell, Ph.D. . . . . . . . . . . . . . . . . . . . . . .631-244-0101
    e-mail: jason.tuell@noaa.gov
  Regional Program Manager:
    John Koch . . . . . . . . . . . . . . . . . . . . . . . . . . . .631-244-0104
    e-mail: john.koch@noaa.gov
  Regional Program Manager:
    Jeff Waldstreicher . . . . . . . . . . . . . . . . . . . . . .631-244-0131
    e-mail: jeff.waldstreicher@noaa.gov
  Chief, Meteorological Services Division:
    John Guiney . . . . . . . . . . . . . . . . . . . . . . . . . . .631-244-0121
    e-mail: john.guiney@noaa.gov
  Chief, Hydrologic Services Division:
    Vacant . . . . . . . . . . . . . . . . . . . . . . . . . . . . . . .631-244-0111

*Offices and agencies generally appear in alphabetical order, except when specific order is requested by listee.*

Chief, Scientific Services Division:
Kenneth Johnson . . . . . . . . . . . . . . . . . . . . . . . . . . . . . .631-244-0136
e-mail: kenneth.johnson@noaa.gov

## US Department of Agriculture
1400 Independence Avenue SW
Washington, DC 20250
202-720-2791
Web site: www.usda.gov

### Agricultural Marketing Service
1445 Federal Drive, Montgomery, AL 36107
334-223-7488
e-mail: amsadministratoroffice@ams.usda.gov

#### Dairy Programs
Web site: www.ams.usda.gov/about-ams/programs-offices/dairy-program
*Northeast Marketing Area*
302A Washington Avenue Extension, Albany, NY 12203-7303
e-mail: maalbany@fedmilk1.com
Web site: www.fmmone.com
Chief, Market Information:
Lorrie Warren Cashman. . . . . . . . . . . . . . . . . . . . .518-452-4410

#### Specialty Crops Program
*SC Inspection Division—Jamaica Office* . . . . . . . . fax: 718-558-8628
158-15 Liberty Avenue, Room 4022, Jamaica, NY 11433
718-558-8632  Fax: 718-558-8628
Officer-in-Charge:
Jagarnauth Persaud . . . . . . . . . . . . . . . . . . . . . . . .718-558-8632
*SC Inspection Division—Bronx Office* . . . . . . . . . . . fax: 718-589-5108
275B New York City Terminal Market, Bronx, NY 10474-7351
718-991-7665  Fax: 718-589-5108
Officer-in-Charge:
Anthony Georgiana . . . . . . . . . . . . . . . . . . . . . . . .718-991-7665

#### USDA-AMS Poultry Grading Branch
*Gastonia Region—New York Office* . . . . . . . . . . . . . fax: 518-459-5163
21 Aviation Road, Albany, NY 12205
Coordinator:
Vacant . . . . . . . . . . . . . . . . . . . . . . . . . . . . . . . . . .518-457-2090

### Agricultural Research Service

#### Northeast Area
*Ithaca NY Research Units*
*Robert W Holley Center for Agriculture & Health*
583 Tower Road, Ithaca, NY 14853
607-255-5480
Center Director & Research Leader:
Leon V Kochian. . . . . . . . . . . . . . . . . . . . . . . . . . .607-255-5480
e-mail: leon.kochian@ars.usda.gov
*Geneva NY Research Units*
*Plant Genetic Resources & Grape Genetic Research Units* . . . . . . . fax:
315-787-2483
Grape Genetics Research Unit, USDA, ARS, 630 West North Street,
Geneva, NY 14456
315-787-2340  Fax: 315-787-2483
Research Leader:
Gan-Yuan Zhong . . . . . . . . . . . 315-787-2482/fax: 315-787-2483
e-mail: ganyuan.zhong@ars.usda.gov

### Animal & Plant Health Inspection Service

#### Plant Protection Quarantine (PPQ) Programs-Eastern Region . . . . fax:
919-855-7611
920 Main Campus Drive, Suite 150, Raleigh, NC 27606-5202
919-855-7600  Fax: 919-855-7611
Plant Health Director:
Vacant
*Avoca Work Unit*
8237 Kanona Road, Avoca, NY 14809-9729

607-566-2212
Director:
Daniel J Kepich . . . . . . . . . . . . . . . . . . . . . . . . . . . .607-566-2212
e-mail: daniel.j.kepich@aphis.usda.gov
*Buffalo Work Station*
1 Peace Bridge Plaza, Suite 314, Buffalo, NY 14213
Entomologist:
Stephen Young. . . . . . . . . . . . . . . . . . . . . . . . . . . . .607-329-6351
e-mail: stephen.t.young@aphis.usda.gov
*Canandaigua Work Station*
3037 County Road 10, Canandaigua, NY 14424
Senior PPQ Officer:
Cynthia Estey . . . . . . . . . . . . . . . . . . . . . . . . . . .585-394-0525 x5
e-mail: cynthia.a.estey@aphis.usda.gov
*Champlain Work Station* . . . . . . . . . . . . . . . . . . . . . . fax: 585-394-8367
217 West Service Road, Champlain, NY 12919
PPQ Officer:
Thomas Colarusso . . . . . . . . . . . . . . . . . . . . . . . . .518-298-5529
e-mail: thomas.w.colarusso@aphis.usda.gov
*Ellicottville Work Station*
8 Martha Street, Ellicottville, NY 14731
PPQ Officer:
Jacqueline Klahn . . . . . . . . . . . . . . . . . . . . . . . . . .716-699-8954
e-mail: jacquelineklahn@aphis.usda.gov
*JFK International Airport Inspection Station*
230-59 International Airport Center Blvd, Suite 100, Jamaica, NY
11413
718-553-3500
Supervisory PPQ Officer:
Joanne Alba-Foster . . . . . . . . . . . . . . . . . . . . . . . .718-553-3503
*New York State Office*
500 New Karner Road, Suite 2, Albany, NY 12205-3857
State Plant Health Director:
Diana Hoffman . . . . . . . . . . . . . . . . . . . . . . . . . . .518-218-7510
e-mail: diana.l.hoffman@aphis.usda.gov
*Oneida Work Station*
248 Main Street, 1st Floor, Oneida, NY 13421
Senior PPQ Officer:
Paul F Wrege . . . . . . . . . . . . . . . . . . . . . . . . . . . . .315-361-4281
e-mail: paul.f.wrege@usda.gov
*Westhampton Beach Work Station* . . . . . . . . . . . . . fax: 631-288-6021
4 Stewart Avenue, Westhampton Beach, NY 11978-1103
PPQ Officer:
William Hsiang . . . . . . . . . . . . . . . . . . . . . . . . . . .631-288-4191
e-mail: william.w.hsiang@aphis.usda.gov

### Veterinary Services
*NY Animal Import Center* . . . . . . . . . . . . . . . . . . . . . fax: 718-553-3572
200 Drury Lane, Rock Tavern, NY 12575
718-553-3570  Fax: 718-553-3572
Director:
Renee Oleck. . . . . . . . . . . . . . . . . . . . . . . . . . . . . .845-838-5500
e-mail: vspsnic@aphis.usda.gov
*New York Area Office*
500 New Karner Road, 2nd Floor, Albany, NY 12205
Center Director, Veterinary Services:
Dr Roxanne C Mullaney . . . . . . 518-218-7540/fax: 518-218-7545
e-mail: vspsny@aphis.usda.gov

### Cornell Cooperative Extension Service
Cornell University, Roberts Hall, Room 365, Ithaca, NY 14853

### Farm Service Agency, New York State Office . . . fax: 315-477-6323
441 South Salina Street, Suite 536, Syracuse, NY 13202
State Executive Director:
James Barber. . . . . . . . . . . . . . . . . . . . . . . . . . . . . .315-477-6300
e-mail: james.barber@ny.usda.gov

### Food & Nutrition Service
Web site: www.fns.usda.gov

---

*Offices and agencies generally appear in alphabetical order, except when specific order is requested by listee.*

Policy Areas

**Northeast Regional Office**
10 Causeway Street, Room 501, Boston, MA 02222-1069
617-565-6370
Acting Regional Administrator:
    Kurt Messner . . . . . . . . . . . . . . . . . . . . . . . . . . . . . . . . . . . . . .617-565-6370

**New York City Field Office**
201 Varick Street, Room 609, New York, NY 10014
212-620-6307
Section Chief:
    Denise Thomas . . . . . . . . . . . . . . . . . . . . . . . . . . . . . .212-620-6338

## Food Safety & Inspection Service
Web site: www.fsis.usda.gov

## National Agricultural Statistics Service-NY Field Office . . . . . fax: 800-591-3834
10B Airline Drive, Albany, NY 12235
800-821-1276 or 518-457-5570  Fax: 800-591-3834
Web site: www.nass.usda.gov
State Statistician:
    Blair Smith . . . . . . . . . . . . . . . . . . . . . . . . . . . . . . . . . . . .518-457-5570

## Office of the Inspector General, Northeast Region . . . . . . . . . . fax: 212-264-8416
26 Federal Plaza, Room 1409, New York, NY 10278-0004
Special Agent-in-Charge:
    William Squires . . . . . . . . . . . . . . . . . . . . . . . . . . . . . . .212-264-8400

## Rural Development
Web site: www.rd.usda.gov/ny

**New York State Regional Office** . . . . . . . . . . . . . . . . fax: 315-477-6438
441 South Salina Street, Suite 357, Syracuse, NY 13202-2541
315-477-6400 or TTY:315-477-6447  Fax: 315-477-6438
Acting State Director:
    Scott Collins . . . . . . . . . . . . . .315-477-6437/fax: 855-477-8540
Eastern Region Area Director:
    Ronda Falkena . . . . . . . . . . . . . . . . . . . . . . . . . . . .845-343-1872 x4
Northern Region Area Director:
    Brian Murray . . . . . . . . . . . . . . . . . . . . . . . . . . . . . . .315-386-2401 x4
Western Region Area Director:
    Jim Walfrand . . . . . . . . . . . . . . . . . . . . . . . . . . . . . . .585-343-9167 x4

## USDA/GIPSA, Packers & Stockyards Programs Eastern
**Regional Office** . . . . . . . . . . . . . . . . . . . . . . . . . . . fax: 404-562-5848
75 Ted Turner Drive SW, Suite 230, Atlanta, GA 30303
404-562-5840  Fax: 404-562-5848
Regional Director:
    Elkin Parker . . . . . . . . . . . . . . . . . . . . . . . . . . . . . . . .404-562-5840
    e-mail: elkin.w.parker@usda.gov

---

## US Department of Homeland Security (DHS)
Web site: www.dhs.gov

## Customs & Border Protection (CBP)
877-227-5511
Web site: www.cbp.gov

**Agricultural Inspections (AI)**
*Albany, Port of* . . . . . . . . . . . . . . . . . . . . . . . . . . . . .fax: 518-431-0203
445 Broadway, Room 216, Albany, NY 12207
518-431-0200  Fax: 518-431-0203
Port Director:
    Andrew Wescott . . . . . . . . . . . . .518-431-0200/fax: 518-431-0203
*Alexandria Bay* . . . . . . . . . . . . . . . . . . . . . . . . . . . .fax: 315-482-5304
46735 Interstate Route 81, Alexandria Bay, NY 13607
315-482-2065  Fax: 315-482-5304
Supervisory CBP Officer:
    Darren Erwin . . . . . . . . . . . . . . . . . . . . . . . . . . . . .315-482-2681
    e-mail: darren.r.erwin@cbp.dhs.gov
*Binghamton Airport* . . . . . . . . . . . . . . . . . . . . . . . . .fax: 607-763-4292
2534 Airport Road, Box 4, Johnson City, NY 13790

607-763-4294  Fax: 607-763-4292
Port Director:
    Vacant
*Buffalo, Port of*
726 Exchange Street, Suite 400, Buffalo, NY 14210
Supervisory CBP Officer:
    Gary Friedman
*Champlain, Port of* . . . . . . . . . . . . . . . . . . . . . . . . .fax: 518-298-8395
237 West Service Road, Champlain, NY 12919
518-298-8311  Fax: 518-298-8395
Port Director:
    Paul Mongillo . . . . . . . . . . . . . . . . . . . . . . . . . . .518-298-8311
*JFK International Airport Area Office* . . . . . . . . . . .fax: 718-487-5191
John F. Kennedy International Airport, Building #77, Jamaica, NY 11430
718-487-5164  Fax: 718-487-5191
Public Affairs Officer:
    Anthony Bucci . . . . . . . . . . . . . . . . . . . . . . . . . . .646-733-3275
    e-mail: anthony.bucci@cbp.dhs.gov
*Massena, Port of*
30M Seaway International Bridge, PO Box 207, Rooseveltown, NY 13683
315-769-3091
Tribal Liaison Officer:
    Tracey S. Casey . . . . . . . . . . . . . . . . . . . . . . . . . . .315-769-3091
*Ogdensburg, Port of*
Ogdensburg Bridge Plaza, 104 Bridge Approach Road, Ogdensburg, NY 13669
315-393-1390
Port Director:
    Wade Davis . . . . . . . . . . . . . . . . . . . . . . . . . . . . . .313-393-1390
*Rochester, Port of* . . . . . . . . . . . . . . . . . . . . . . . . . .fax: 585-263-5828
1200 Brooks Avenue, Rochester, NY 14624
585-263-6293  Fax: 585-263-5828
Port Director:
    Ronald Menz . . . . . . . . . . . . . . . . . . . . . . . . . . . . . .585-263-6293
*Syracuse, Port of*
152 Air Cargo Road, Suite 201, North Syracuse, NY 13212
315-455-8446
Port Director:
    David Harris . . . . . . . . . . . . . . . . . . . . . . . . . . . . . .315-455-8446
*Trout River, Port of* . . . . . . . . . . . . . . . . . . . . . . . . .fax: 518-483-3717
17013 State Route 30, Constable, NY 12926
518-483-0821  Fax: 518-483-3717
Public Affairs Liaison:
    Richard Misztal . . . . . . . . . . . . . . . . . . . . . . . . . . .716-626-0400

## U.S. CONGRESS

*See U.S. Congress Chapter for additional Standing Committee and Subcommittee information.*

## House of Representatives Standing Committees

### Agriculture
Committee Chair:
    K. Michael Conaway (R-TX-11)
Ranking Member:
    Collin C. Peterson (D-MN-07)

### Appropriations
Chair:
    Harold Rogers (R-KY)
Ranking Minority Member:
    Nita Lowey (D-NY)
New York Delegate:
    Steve Israel (D)
New York Delegate:
    Jose E Serrano (D)

*Offices and agencies generally appear in alphabetical order, except when specific order is requested by listee.*

**Subcommittee**

*Agriculture, Rural Development, FDA & Related Agencies*
Chair:
Robert Aderholt (R-AL) . . . . . . . . . . . . . . . . . . . . . 202-225-2638
Ranking Member:
Sam Farr (D-CA)

## Senate Standing Committees

### Agriculture, Nutrition & Forestry
Chair:
Pat Roberts (R-KS)
Ranking Member:
Debbie Stabenow (D-MI)

### Appropriations
Chair:
Thad Cochran (R-MS) . . . . . . . . . . . . . . . . . . . . . . . . 202-224-5054
Vice Chair:
Barbara A. Mikulski (D-MD)

**Subcommittee**

*Agriculture, Rural Development, FDA & Related Agencies*
Chair:
Jerry Moran (R-KS). . . . . . . . . . . . . . . . . . . . . . . . 202-224-6521
Ranking Member:
Jeff Merkley (D-OR)

## PRIVATE SECTOR

### Agricultural Affiliates
3568 Snders Settlement Road, Sanborn, NY 14132
562-522-1736
*Advise & inform agriculture industry on labor issues & related public policy*
Paul Baker, Executive Director

### American Farmland Trust, New York Office
112 Spring Street, Suite 207, Saratoga Springs, NY 12866
518-581-0078  Fax: 518-581-0079
Web site: www.farmland.org/newyork
*Advocacy & education to protect farmland & promote environmentally sound farming practices*
David Haight, New York State Director
Tammey Holtby, Operations Coordinator

### American Society for the Prevention of Cruelty to Animals (ASPCA)
424 East 92nd Street, New York, NY 10128-6804
212-876-7700 or 888-666-2279
e-mail: publicinformation@aspca.org
Web site: www.aspca.org
*Promoting humane treatment of animals, education & advocacy programs & conducting statewide anti-cruelty investigation & enforcement*
Matthew Bershadker, President & Chief Executive Officer

### Associated New York State State Food Processors Inc
150 State Street, Rochester, NY 14614
585-256-4614
Web site: www.nyfoodprocessors.org
Jeffrey Hartline, President

### Birds Eye Foods Inc
399 Jefferson Road, Parsippany, NJ 07054
800-432-3102
Web site: www.birdseye.com
*Produces & markets processed food products*
Mike Barkley, Executive Vice President

### Christmas Tree Farmers Association of New York Inc
PO Box 705, Salem, NY 12865
518-854-7386  Fax: 518-854-7387
e-mail: info@ctfany.org
Web site: www.christmastreesny.org
*Producer of fresh Christmas trees & evergreen wreaths*
Mary Jeanne Packer, Executive Director

### Consumers Union
101 Truman Avenue, Yonkers, NY 10703-1057
914-378-2000  Fax: 914-378-2900
Web site: www.consumerreports.org; www.consumersunion.org
*Advocacy and policy to improve consumer products and address food safety issues, including genetically engineered food, microbial safety of food, toxic chemical issues, pesticides, integrated pest management, sustainable agriculture*
Jean Halloran, Director, Food Policy Initiatives

### Community & Regional Development Institute (CaRDI)
275 Warren Hall, Cornell University, Ithaca, NY 14853
607-255-9510  Fax: 607-255-2231
e-mail: cardi@cornell.edu
Web site: www.cardi.cals.cornell.edu
*Provides research, training, education & policy analysis on community & regional development issues*
Jennifer Jensen, Communications & Outreach Coordinator

### Cornell Cooperative Extension, Pesticide Management Education Program
5142 Comstock Hall, Cornell University, Ithaca, NY 14853-0901
607-255-1866  Fax: 607-255-3075
e-mail: rdg5@cornell.edu
Web site: pmep.cce.cornell.edu
*Provides training materials, outreach & information on pesticides and pests*
Ronald D Gardner, Program Coordinator

### Cornell Cooperative Extension, Agriculture & Food Systems Program
272 Morrison, Cornell University, New York, NY 14853
607-255-2878
e-mail: tro2@cornell.edu
Web site: www.cce.cornell.edu
*Research to enhance the food systems and agricultural resources of New York*
Tom Overton, Associate Director, Agriculture & Life Sciences

### Cornell University, Department of Applied Economics & Management
Warren Hall, Ithaca, NY 14853
607-255-4576
Web site: www.dyson.cornell.edu
*Agricultural economics*
William Lesser, Interim Director
Andrew Novakovic, Associate Director for Engagement

### Cornell University, FarmNet Program
Dept of Applied Economics & Management, 415 Warren Hall, Ithaca, NY 14853-7801
607-255-4121 or 800-547-3276  Fax: 607-254-7435
e-mail: nyfarmnet@cornell.edu
Web site: www.nyfarmnet.org
*Farm family resource library; financial & family consultations; workshops for agricultural services professionals & farmers*
Ed Stachr, Executive Director

*Offices and agencies generally appear in alphabetical order, except when specific order is requested by listee.*

**Cornell University, PRO-DAIRY Program**
College of Agriculture & Life Sciences, 272 Morrison Hall, Ithaca, NY 14853
607-255-2878  Fax: 607-255-1335
e-mail: tro2@cornell.edu
Web site: www.prodairy.cals.cornell.edu
*Applied research and extension education program for dairy farmers in New York*
Tom Overton, Program Director

**Dairy Farmers of America Northeast**
5001 Brittonfield Parkway, Syracuse, NY 13057
315-431-1352 or 816-801-6455
Web site: www.dfamilk.com
*Markets, sells & processes milk and dairy products*
Brad Keating, Senior Vice President & Chief Operating Officer

**Empire State Honey Producers Association**
437 Hurley Road, Brasher Falls, NY 13613
315-769-2566
Web site: www.eshpa.org
*Association for beekeepers in New York State serving to protect & promote the honey bee and honey production*
Mark Berninghausen, President

**Empire State Potato Growers Inc**
PO Box 566, Stanley, NY 14561-0566
585-526-5356 or 877-697-7837  Fax: 585-526-6576
Web site: www.empirepotatogrowers.com
*To foster the potato industry in NYS*
Melanie Wickham, Executive Director

**Farm Sanctuary**
3100 Aikens Road, PO Box 150, Watkins Glen, NY 14891
607-583-2225  Fax: 607-583-2041
Web site: www.farmsanctuary.org
*Farm animal rescue & protection; public information programs & advocacy for the humane treatment of animals*
Gene Baur, President

**Farmedic Training Program**
20 Church Street, PO Box 5670, Cortland, NY 13045
800-822-3747
e-mail: farmedic@mcneilandcompany.com
Web site: www.farmedic.com
*Training programs for emergency providers & agricultural workers to reduce mortality, injury & property loss from agricultural emergencies*
Dave Denniston, Executive Director

**Farmers' Market Federation of NY**
117 Highbridge Street, Fayetteville, NY 13066
315-400-1447  Fax: 844-300-6809
*Education & services for New York farmers' market managers, farmers & sponsors.*
Diane Eggert, Director

**Food Industry Alliance of New York State Inc**
130 Washington Avenue, Albany, NY 12210
518-434-1900  Fax: 518-434-9962
Web site: www.fiany.com
*Association of retail grocery, cooperative, wholesale & supplier/manufacturer food companies*
Michael Rosen, President & CEO

**Fund for Animals (The)**
200 West 57th Street, New York, NY 10019
212-757-3425 or 888-405-3863  Fax: 212-246-2633
e-mail: info@fundforanimals.org
Web site: www.fundforanimals.org
*Animal protection through education, advocacy programs & hands-on veterinary care*
Marian Probst, Chair

**Garden Gate Greenhouse**
11649 West Perrysburg Road, Perrysburg, NY 14129
716-532-6282
*Greenhouse plant production*
Gary Patterson, President

**Global Gardens Program, New York Botanical Garden (The)**
2900 Southern Blvd, Bronx, NY 10458-5126
718-817-8700  Fax: 718-220-6504
Web site: www.nybg.org
*Promoting understanding of ethnic diversity & the interconnectedness of cultures through gardening*
Gregory Long, Chief Executive Officer

**GreenThumb**
100 Gold Street, Suite 3100, New York, NY 10038
212-602-5300  Fax: 212-602-5334
e-mail: greenthumbinfo@parks.nyc.gov
Web site: www.greenthumbnyc.org
*Development & preservation of community gardens; workshops addressing a variety of topics including gardening, farming & community organizing*
Bill LoSasso, Director

**Greenmarket/Council on the Environment of NYC**
100 Gold Street, Suite 3300, New York, NY 10038
212-788-7900  Fax: 212-788-7913
Web site: www.grownyc.org
*Promotes regional sustainable agriculture & improves access to locally grown agricultural products*
Marcel Van Ooyen, Executive Director

**Hill, Gosdeck & McGraw LLC**
99 Washington Avenue, Suite 400, Albany, NY 12210
518-463-5449  Fax: 518-463-0947
e-mail: jeffhill@hgmlobby.com
*Workers compensation, group self insurance and food industry regulation*
Jeffrey L Hill, Partner

**Humane Society of the United States, New York State**
200 West 57th Street, Suite 705, New York, NY 10019
917-331-7187
Web site: www.humanesociety.org
*Promotes humane treatment of animals; abuse & violence prevention; animal rescue & disaster preparedness*
Brian Shapiro, State Director

**Long Island Farm Bureau**
104 Edwards Avenue, Suite 3, Calverton, NY 11933
631-727-3777  Fax: 631-727-3721
e-mail: askus@lifb.com
Web site: www.lifb.com
*Seeks to provide protection for the agricultural industries in Long Island and New York State*
Karen Rivara, President

**Long Island Nursery & Landscape Association Inc**
136 Everett Road, Albany, NY 12205
518-694-5540 or 516-249-0545  Fax: 518-427-9495
e-mail: info@linla.org
Web site: www.linla.org
*Non-profit organization representing Long Island's horticulture industry*
Carol Saporito, President

**National Potato Board**
**McCormick Farms Inc**
4189 Route 78, Bliss, NY 14024
585-322-7274  Fax: 585-322-7495
*Crop farm*
Jim McCormick, President & CEO

---

*Offices and agencies generally appear in alphabetical order, except when specific order is requested by listee.*

**My-T Acres Inc**
8127 Lewiston Road, Batavia, NY 14020
585-343-1026 Fax: 585-343-2051
*Vegetable crops & grain*
Peter Call, Co-Owner

**NOFA-NY Certified Organic LLC**
840 Upper Front Street, Binghamton, NY 13905-1542
607-724-9851 Fax: 607-724-9853
e-mail: certifiedorganic@nofany.org
Web site: www.nofany.org
*Organic farming certification*
Lori Kenyon, Certification Director

**NY Farms!**
125 Williams Road, Candor, NY 13743
607-659-3710 Fax: 607-659-3710
*Aims to promote farming, protect farmland & improve food systems in New York State*
Mary Jeanne Packer, Executive Director

**NYS Agricultural Society**
1818 Linwood Road, Linwood, NY 14486
315-727-5449
e-mail: ann@nysagsociety.org
Web site: www.nysagsociety.org
*Provides education, leadership & recognition programs to develop, promote & enhance the agriculture industry of New York State*
Ann Shephard, Executive Secretary

**NYS Arborists**
136 Everett Road, Albany, NY 12205
518-694-5507 Fax: 518-935-9436
e-mail: info@nysarborists.com
Web site: www.nysarborists.com
*Association representing arborists & educators; promotes education & research about trees & conservation*
Trevor Hall, President

**NYS Association for Food Protection**
5372 Summit Avenue, Lowville, NY 13367
315-404-0133
e-mail: amyr.nysafp@gmail.com
Web site: www.nysafp.com
*Association made up of food manufacturing, equipment supply, academia, government and retail all serving to enable exchange of information on food supply protection.*
Amy Rhodes, Executive Secretary

**NYS Association of Veterinary Technicians Inc**
PO Box 760, Glenmont, NY 12077
518-779-0775
Web site: www.nysavt.org
*Association supporting the veterinary technician profession*
Donna Meier, President

**NYS Berry Growers Association**
630 West North Street, Geneva, NY 14456
315-787-2404
e-mail: nysbga@gmail.com
Web site: www.nysbga.org
*Provides information to and connects berry growers from large wholesale family farms to independent farm stands and small pick-your-own operations, across New York State. The NYSBGA also advocates on behalf of berry growers to the NYS legislature.*
Robin Catalano, Communications Manager
Karen Wilson, Office Manager
Paul Baker, Executive Director

**NYS Cheese Manufacturers Association, Department of Food Science**
Cornell University, 116 Stocking Hall, Ithaca, NY 14853
607-255-2892 Fax: 607-255-7619
e-mail: jgg3@cornell.edu
Web site: www.nyscheesemakers.com
*Cheese manufacturing education & product promotion*
Janene Lucia, Secretary

**NYS Grange**
100 Grange Place, Cortland, NY 13045
607-756-7553 Fax: 607-756-7757
e-mail: nysgrange@nysgrange.org
Web site: www.nysgrange.org
*Advocacy, education & services for farm, rural & suburban families*
Kathy E Miller, Director

**NYS Horticultural Society**
630 West North Street, Geneva, NY 14456
315-787-2404 Fax: 315-787-2216
e-mail: nyshs@hotmail.com
Web site: www.nyshs.org
*Advocacy, education & member services for the New York State fruit industry*
Paul Baker, Executive Director

**NYS Nursery/Landscape Association**
136 Everett Road, Albany, NY 12205
518-694-4430 Fax: 518-694-4431
e-mail: info@nysnla.com
Web site: www.nysnla.com
*Trade association representing the nursery & landscape business professionals of New York State*
Holly Cargill-Cramer, Executive Director

**NYS Turfgrass Association**
PO Box 612, Latham, NY 12110
518-783-1229 or 800-873-8873 Fax: 518-783-1258
e-mail: nysta@nysta.org
Web site: www.nysta.org
*Provides education & research for individuals in the turfgrass & grounds industry*
Elizabeth Seme, Executive Director

**NYS Vegetable Growers Association Inc**
8351 Lewiston Road, Batavia, NY 14020
585-993-0775
e-mail: nysvegetablegrowers@gmail.com
Web site: www.nysvga.org
*Produce industry education & product promotion*
Brian Reeves, President

**NYS Weights & Measures Association**
7660 State Street, Lowville, NY 13367
315-377-2069 Fax: 315-376-5874
Web site: www.nyswma.com
*Promote uniformity in measure accuracy, enforcement standards & legal requirements*
Barbara J Cooper, Director

**National Coffee Association**
45 Broadway, Suite 1140, New York, NY 10006
212-766-4007 Fax: 212-766-5815
Web site: www.ncausa.org
*Represents & supports the nation's coffee industry*
William Murray, President & Chief Executive Officer

**National Grape Cooperative-Welch Foods Inc**
300 Baker Avenue, Suite 101, Concord, MA 01742
978-371-1000 or 800-340-6870 Fax: 978-371-3879
Web site: www.welchs.com
*Manufacturer of juices, jams & jellies.*
Bradley Irwin, President & Chief Executive Officer

*Offices and agencies generally appear in alphabetical order, except when specific order is requested by listee.*

## New York Agriculture in the Classroom

Cornell University, Dept of Horticulture, 134 Plant Science Building, Ithaca, NY 14853
518-480-1978
e-mail: nyaitc@cornell.edu
Web site: www.agclassroom.org
*Program serving to improve agricultural literacy by collaborating with community educators & farmers to raise awareness about agricultural production & food systems*
Katie Bigness, Coordinator

## New York Apple Association Inc

7645 Main Street, PO Box 350, Fishers, NY 14453-0350
585-924-2171  Fax: 585-924-1629
Web site: www.nyapplecountry.com
*Promotes NYS apples & apple products*
James Allen, President & CEO

## New York Beef Industry Council Inc

PO Box 250, Westmoreland, NY 13490
315-339-6922  Fax: 315-339-6931
Web site: www.nybeef.org
*Non-profit organization conducting beef promotion & enhancing opportunities for cattle producers in NYS*
Carol Gillis, Executive Director

## New York Center for Agricultural Medicine & Health, Bassett Healthcare

1 Atwell Road, Cooperstown, NY 13326
800-343-7527 or 607-547-6023  Fax: 607-547-6087
Web site: www.nycamh.com
*Occupational health & medicine in agriculture*
John May, MD, Deputy Director

## New York Farm Bureau

159 Wolf Road, PO Box 5330, Albany, NY 12205-0330
518-436-8495 or 800-342-4143  Fax: 518-431-5656
e-mail: info@nyfb.org
Web site: www.nyfb.org
*Resources, education, advocacy, services & programs for the agricultural industry & community*
Jeff Kirby, Executive Director

## New York Corn & Soybean Growers Association

PO Box 133, Silver Springs, NY 14550
585-689-2321
Web site: www.nycornsoy.org
*Grassroots organization focused on advancing the interests of corn & soybean producers*
Steve Van Voorhis, President

## New York Holstein Association

957 Mitchell Street, Ithaca, NY 14850
607-273-7591 or 800-834-4644  Fax: 607-273-7612
Web site: www.nyholsteins.com
*Dairy breed association serving to promote & develop Holstein breed cattle*
Patricia G Gifford, Executive Manager

## New York Pork Producers Coop

5146 Transit Road, Depew, NY 14043
716-697-3031
Web site: www.newyorkpork.org
*Education & promotion of pork industry in NY*
Krista Jaskier, Executive Secretary/State Contact

## New York Seed Improvement Project, Cornell University, Plant Breeding Department

Cornell University, 240 Emerson Hall, Ithaca, NY 14853
607-255-9869  Fax: 607-255-9048
e-mail: pma3@cornell.edu
Web site: www.plbrgen.cals.cornell.edu
*Provides seed certification for the state of NY & develops seed stocks for certified seed growers*
Phil Atkins, Manager

## New York State Association of Agricultural Fairs Inc

67 Verbeck Avenue, Schaghticoke, NY 12154
518-753-4956  Fax: 518-753-0208
e-mail: carousels4@aol.com
Web site: www.nyfairs.org
*Utilizes fairs to promote agricultural development in NYS*
Norma W Hamilton, Executive Secretary

## New York State Maple Producers Association Inc

301 Myron Road, Syracuse, NY 13219
315-877-5795  Fax: 315-488-0459
e-mail: office@nysmaple.com
Web site: www.nysmaple.com
*Promoting quality maple products through education and research.*
Helen Thomas, Executive Director

## New York State Veterinary Medical Society

100 Great Oaks Blvd, Suite 127, Albany, NY 12203
518-869-7867 or 800-876-9867
e-mail: staff@nysvms.org
Web site: www.nysvms.org
*Association for veterinarians in NYS*
Jennifer Mauer, Executive Director

## New York Thoroughbred Breeders Inc

57 Phila Street, Saratoga Springs, NY 12866
518-587-0777  Fax: 518-587-1551
e-mail: info@nytbreeders.org
Web site: www.nytbreeders.org
Jeffrey Cannizzo, Executive Director

## New York Wine & Grape Foundation

800 South Main Street, Suite 200, Canandaigua, NY 14424
585-394-3620  Fax: 585-394-3649
e-mail: info@newyorkwines.org
Web site: www.newyorkwines.org
*Promotion of winery products & tours; research for wine & grape related products*
James Trezise, President

## Northeast Dairy Foods Association Inc

427 South Main Street, North Syracuse, NY 13212
315-452-6455  Fax: 315-452-1643
*Full service trade association representing the dairy processing, manufacturing & distribution industry of New York & surrounding states*
Bruce W Krupke, Executive Vice President

## Northeast Organic Farming Association of New York

1423 Hathaway Drive, Farmington, NY 14425
585-271-1979  Fax: 585-271-7166
e-mail: info@nofany.org
Web site: www.nofany.org
*Association of farmers, gardeners & consumers promoting a sustainable food system in NYS through education, advocacy & organic food production*
Nancy Apolito, Interim Executive Director

*Offices and agencies generally appear in alphabetical order, except when specific order is requested by listee.*

**Community & Economic Development**
**PathStone Corporation**
400 East Avenue, Rochester, NY 14607
585-340-3300 or 800-888-6770
Web site: www.pathstone.org
*Provides services, advocacy & assistance for farmworker, rural & urban communities*
Thomas Bergin, Administrator of Corporate Communication

**Public Markets Partners/Baum Forum**
5454 Palisade Avenue, Bronx, NY 10471
718-884-5716
Web site: www.baumforum.org
*Organizes educational programs & events designed to address farming issues, promote regional agriculture & encourage healthy food systems*
Hilary Baum, President

**Regional Farm & Food Project**
PO Box 621, Saratoga Springs, NY 12866
518-858-6866
*Non-profit organization focused on building supply & demand for local food products and providing resources for farmers & consumers in the greater Hudson-Mohawk Valley region*
Suzanne Carreker-Voigt, Chair

**Seneca Foods Corporation**
3736 South Main Street, Marion, NY 14505
315-926-8100  Fax: 315-926-8300
e-mail: webmaster@senecafoods.com
Web site: www.senecafoods.com
*Fruit & vegetable food products*
Kraig H Kayser, President & CEO

**NYS Bar Association**
**Special Committee on Animals & the Law**
1 Elk Street, Albany, NY 12207
518-463-3200  Fax: 518-463-5993
Web site: www.nysba.org
*Provides resources & programs about animal law & related issues*
Natalie A Carraway, Chair

**Tea Association of the USA Inc**
362 5th Avenue, Suite 801, New York, NY 10001
212-986-9415  Fax: 212-697-8658
e-mail: info@teausa.com
Web site: www.teausa.com
*Trade association for the tea industry*
Peter Goggi, President

**United Dairy Cooperative Services Inc**
12 North Park Street, Seneca Falls, NY 13148
315-568-2750  Fax: 315-568-2752
*Management, accounting & payroll services to agriculture industry*
Robert Nichols, President

**Upstate Niagara Cooperative Inc**
25 Anderson Road, Buffalo, NY 14225
716-892-3156  Fax: 716-892-3157
e-mail: emailus@upstateniagara.com
Web site: www.upstateniagara.com
*Markets milk & dairy products*
Lawrence Webster, Chief Executive Officer

Policy Areas

*Offices and agencies generally appear in alphabetical order, except when specific order is requested by listee.*

# BANKING AND FINANCE

## NEW YORK STATE

### GOVERNOR'S OFFICE

**Governor's Office**
Executive Chamber
State Capitol
Albany, NY 12224
518-474-8390  Fax: 518-474-1513
Web site: www.ny.gov

Governor:
  Andrew M Cuomo . . . . . . . . . . . . . . . . . . . . . . . . . . . . . . . .518-474-8390
Secretary to the Governor:
  Melissa DeRosa . . . . . . . . . . . . . . . . . . . .518-474-4246 or 212-681-4580
Counsel to the Governor:
  Kumiki Gibson . . . . . . . . . . . . . . . . . . . . .518-474-8343 or 212-681-4580
Chief of Staff:
  Jill DesRosiers . . . . . . . . . . . . . . . . . . . . .518-474-8390 or 212-681-4580
Deputy Secretary for General Government Financial Services:
  Vacant . . . . . . . . . . . . . . . . . . . . . . . . . . . . . . . . . . . . .518-474-5442
Director, Communications:
  Peter Ajemian . . . . . . . . . . . . . . . . . . . . . .518-474-8418 or 212-681-4640

### EXECUTIVE DEPARTMENTS AND RELATED AGENCIES

**Financial Services Department**
One State Street
New York, NY 10004-1511
212-480-6400 or 800-342-3736
e-mail: public-affairs@dfs.ny.gov
Web site: www.dfs.ny.gov

One Commerce Plaza
Albany, NY 12257
Fax:

Walter Mahoney Office Building
65 Court Street, Room 7
Buffalo, NY 14202
Fax:

Superintendent:
  Maria T. Vullo . . . . . . . . . . . . . . . . . . . . . . . . . . . . . . . .212-709-3500
Acting Chief of Staff:
  Dan Burstein . . . . . . . . . . . . . . . . . . . . . . . . . . . . . . . . .212-709-1651
Director, Administration & Operations:
  Chad Loshbaugh . . . . . . . . . . . . . . . . . . . . . . . . . . . . . . .518-473-0365
General Counsel:
  Celeste Koeleveld . . . . . . . . . . . . . . . . . . . . . . . . . . . . . .212-356-2300
Executive Deputy Superintendent, Enforcement:
  Matthew L. Levine
Executive Deputy Superintendent, Communications & Strategy:
  Richard A. Loconte
Special Assistant to the Superintendent:
  Jennifer L. Smith
Senior Public Information Specialist:
  Ronald Klug . . . . . . . . . . . . . . . . . . . . . . . . . . . . . . . . . .212-709-1691
Consumer Representative, State Charter Advisory Board:
  Vacant . . . . . . . . . . . . . . . . . . . . . . . . . . . . . . . . . . . . .212-709-3500

**Banking Division**
Deputy Superintendent:
  Vacant . . . . . . . . . . . . . . . . . . . . . . . . . . . . . . . . . . . . .212-709-1690

**Insurance Division**
Chief, Life Insurance Bureau:
  Gail Keren . . . . . . . . . . . . . . . . . . . . . .212-480-5030/fax: 212-480-5329
Chief, Health Insurance Bureau:
  Vacant . . . . . . . . . . . . . . . . . . . . . . . . . . . . . . . . . . . . .518-486-2970
Chief Insurance Examiner 3:
  Michael Maffei . . . . . . . . . . . . . . . . . . . . . . . . . . . . . . . .212-480-5023

**Financial Frauds & Consumer Protection Division**
Director, Frauds:
  Frank Orlando . . . . . . . . . . . . . . . . . . . .212-480-6074/fax: 212-709-3555
Assistant Director, Frauds:
  Angelo Carbone . . . . . . . . . . . . . . . . . . . . . . . . . . . . . . .212-480-5688

**Capital Markets Division**
Director, Capital Markets:
  Vacant . . . . . . . . . . . . . . . . . . . . . . . . . .212-480-5071/fax: 212-480-6085

**Real Estate Finance Division**
Deputy Superintendent, Mortgage Banking:
  Rhonda Ricketts . . . . . . . . . . . . . . . . . . . . . . . . . . . . . . .212-709-5540

---

**Law Department**
28 Liberty Street
New York, NY 10005
212-416-8000 or 800-771-7755
Web site: www.ag.ny.gov

State Capitol
Albany, NY 12224-0341
518-776-2000
Fax: 518-650-9401

Attorney General:
  Letitia James . . . . . . . . . . . . . . . . . . . . . .212-416-8000 or 518-776-2000
Director, Public Information:
  Shawn Morris . . . . . . . . . . . . . . . . . . . .518-776-2357/fax: 518-650-9401
Press Secretary:
  Fernando Aquino . . . . . . . . . . . . . . . . . .212-416-8060/fax: 212-416-6005
  e-mail: nyag.pressoffice@ag.ny.gov

**Economic Justice**
Executive Deputy Attorney General:
  Siobhan Kennedy . . . . . . . . . . . . . . . . . . . . . . . . . . . . . .212-416-8050

**Antitrust Bureau**
Bureau Chief:
  Eric J Stock . . . . . . . . . . . . . . . . . . . .212-416-8262/fax: 212-416-6015
  e-mail: eric.stock@ag.ny.gov

**Consumer Frauds & Protection Bureau**
Bureau Chief:
  Jane Azia . . . . . . . . . . . . . . . . . . . . . .212-416-8300/fax: 212-416-8003

**Internet Bureau**
Bureau Chief:
  Kathleen McGee . . . . . . . . . . . . . . . . .212-416-8433/fax: 212-416-8369
  e-mail: ifraud@ag.ny.gov

**Investor Protection Bureau**
Bureau Chief:
  Chad Johnson . . . . . . . . . . . . . . . . . . .212-416-8225/fax: 212-416-8816

**Real Estate Finance Bureau**
Bureau Chief:
  Marissa Piesman . . . . . . . . . . . . . . . . .212-416-8102/fax: 212-416-8136

*Offices and agencies generally appear in alphabetical order, except when specific order is requested by listee.*

## CORPORATIONS, AUTHORITIES AND COMMISSIONS

### New York State Homes & Community Renewal
641 Lexington Ave
New York, NY 10022
866-275-3427
e-mail: hcrinfo@nyshcr.org
Web site: www.nyshcr.org

Hampton Plaza
38-40 State Street
Albany, NY 12207
518-473-2526

Commissioner/CEO:
  RuthAnne Visnauskas
Executive Deputy Commissioner & Chief Operating Officer:
  Betsy Mallow . . . . . . . . . . . . . . . . . . . . . . . . . . . . . . . . . . . . . . .866-275-3427
President, Office of Housing Preservation:
  Mark Colon. . . . . . . . . . . . . . . . . . . . . . . . . . . . . . . . . . . . . . . .866-275-3427
General Counsel:
  Adam Schuman. . . . . . . . . . . . . . . . . . . . . . . . . . . . . . . . .212-480-6700
Chief of Staff:
  Meredith Levine . . . . . . . . . . . . . . . . . . . . . . . . . . . . . . . . .212-480-6700
Director, Fair Housing & Equal Opportunity:
  Wanda Graham . . . . . . . . . . . . . . . . . . . . . . . . . . . . . . . . . .212-480-6700

## NEW YORK STATE LEGISLATURE

*See Legislative Branch in Section 1 for additional Standing Committee and Subcommittee information.*

### Assembly Standing Committees

#### Banks
Chair:
  Vacant . . . . . . . . . . . . . . . . . . . . . . . . . . . . . . . . . . . . . . . . . . .518-455-5735

### Senate Standing Committees

#### Banks
Chair:
  James Sanders Jr (D). . . . . . . . . . . . . . . . . . . . . . . . . . . . . . .518-455-3531
Ranking Minority Member:
  Robert E. Antonacci (R, C, IP). . . . . . . . . . . . . . . . . . . . . . .518-455-3511

## U.S. GOVERNMENT

## EXECUTIVE DEPARTMENTS AND RELATED AGENCIES

### Export Import Bank of the United States
Web site: www.exim.gov

**Northeast Regional Office** . . . . . . . . . . . . . . . . . . . . . fax: 212-809-2687
  Ted Weiss Federal Building, 290 Broadway, 13th Floor, New York, NY 10007
  212-809-2650  Fax: 212-809-2687
Regional Director:
  Gregory Smith. . . . . . . . . . . . . . . . . . . . . . . . . . . . . . . . . . .212 809 2652

### Federal Deposit Insurance Corporation
877-275-3342
Web site: www.fdic.gov

**Division of Depositor and Consumer Protection**
  350 Fifth Avenue, Suite 1200, New York, NY 10118-0110

800-334-9593 or 917-320-2500
Regional Director:
  John Vogel
Deputy Regional Director:
  John P Conneely

### Federal Reserve System

**Federal Reserve Bank of New York**
  33 Liberty Street, New York, NY 10045
  212-720-5000
  e-mail: general.info@ny.frb.org
  Web site: www.newyorkfed.org
President:
  William C Dudley
First Vice President:
  Michael Strine
Chair:
  Emily K Rafferty

### National Credit Union Administration
Web site: www.ncua.gov

**Albany Region**
  9 Washington Square, Washington Avenue Extension, Albany, NY 12205
  518-862-7400
Regional Director:
  L J Blankenberger . . . . . . . . . . . . . . . . . . .518-862-7400/fax: 518-862-7420

### US Treasury Department
Web site: www.treasury.gov

**Comptroller of the Currency**
  Web site: www.occ.treas.gov

  **Northeastern District Office** . . . . . . . . . . . . . . . . . . . . .fax: 212-790-4058
  340 Madison Avenue, 5th Floor, New York, NY 10173-0002
  212-790-4000  Fax: 212-790-4058
  Deputy Comptroller:
    Kristin Kiefer . . . . . . . . . . . . . . . . . .212-790-4001/fax: 212-790-4058
  Associate Deputy Comptroller:
    Maureen Whalen . . . . . . . . . . . . . . . . . . . . . . . . . . . .212-790-4061
  District Counsel:
    Jonathan Rushdoony . . . . . . . . . . . . . . . . . . . . . . . . .212-790-4010

**US Mint**
  Web site: www.usmint.gov
Plant Manager:
  Ellen McCullom . . . . . . . . . . . . . . . . . . . . . . . . . . . . . . . . .845-446-6200

## U.S. CONGRESS

*See U.S. Congress Chapter for additional Standing Committee and Subcommittee information.*

### House of Representatives Standing Committees

**Financial Services**
Chair:
  Jeb Hensarling (R-TX)
Ranking Member:
  Maxine Waters (D-CA)
New York Delegate:
  Peter T. King (R)
New York Delegate:
  Carolyn B. Maloney (D)
New York Delegate:
  Nydia M. Velazquez (D)
New York Delegate:
  Gregory W. Meeks (D)

*Offices and agencies generally appear in alphabetical order, except when specific order is requested by listee.*

Policy Areas

## Senate Standing Committees

### Banking, Housing & Urban Affairs
Chair:
  Richard Shelby (R-AL) . . . . . . . . . . . . . 202-224-5744/fax: 202-224-3416
Ranking Member:
  Sherrod Brown (D-OH)
New York Delegate:
  Charles E Schumer (D) . . . . . . . . . . . . . . . . . . . . . . . . . 202-224-6542

## PRIVATE SECTOR

**American Express Company**
200 Vesey Street, New York, NY 10285-3106
212-640-2000  Fax: 212-640-0404
Web site: www.americanexpress.com
*Consumer lending, travel services, proprietary database marketing, insurance underwriting & investment services*
Stephen Lemson, Vice President, State & Government Affairs

**American International Group Inc**
175 Water Street, New York, NY 10038
212-770-7000
Web site: www.aig.com
*International business, insurance & financial services*
Phil Fasano, Chief Information Officer

**Antalek & Moore Insurance Agency**
340 Main Street, Beacon, NY 12508
845-245-6216 or 800-860-7176  Fax: 845-831-5631
*Provides insurance & risk management services*
Patrick C Moore, Partner

**Apple Bank for Savings**
122 East 42nd Street, 9th Fl, New York, NY 10168
914-902-2775
Web site: www.applebank.com
*Personal & business banking services*
Steven C Bush, President & Chief Executive Officer

**Astoria Bank**
1 Astoria Bank Plaza, Lake Success, NY 11042-1085
516-327-3000  Fax: 516-327-7860
Alan P Eggleston, Senior Executive Vice President

**Bank of Akron**
46 Main Street, Akron, NY 14001
716-542-5401 or 877-542-5401  Fax: 716-542-5510
Web site: www.bankofakron.com
*Director - Independent Bankers Association of New York State (IBANYS); personal & business banking; financial services*
E Peter Forrestel, II, President & Chief Executive Officer

**Brown Brothers Harriman & Co**
140 Broadway, New York, NY 10005-1101
212-483-1818
Web site: www.bbh.com
*Provides private banking & investment management services*
Andrew P Hofer, Managing Director/Head of Taxable Portfolio Management

**Canandaigua National Bank & Trust Co**
72 South Main Street, Canandaigua, NY 14424
585-394-4260 or 800-724-2621  Fax: 585-396-1355
e-mail: ghamlin@cnbank.com
Web site: www.cnbank.com
*Full service banking*
George W Hamlin, Chairman, Trust Officer & Senior Policy Advisor
Frank H Hamlin, President & Chief Executive Officer

**Capital One Bank**
275 Broadhollow Road, Melville, NY 11747
631-844-1376
Web site: www.capitalone.com
Heidi Joseph, Regional Executive

**Citigroup Inc**
388 Greenwich Street, New York, NY 10013
212-559-1000 or 800-285-3000
Web site: www.citigroup.com
*Commercial & retail banking*
Michael L Corbat, Chief Executive Officer

**The Clearing House Association, LLC**
1114 Avenue of the Americas, 17th Floor, New York, NY 10036
212-613-0100  Fax: 212-612-9253
e-mail: tchinfo@theclearinghouse.org
Web site: www.theclearinghouse.org
*Electronic funds transfer*
James Aramanda, President & Chief Executive Officer

**Community Bank N.A.**
5790 Wildewaters Parkway, Suite 170, Syracuse, NY 13214
315-445-2282 or 800-388-4679
Web site: www.communitybankna.com
*Personal & business banking*
Mark Tryniski, President & Chief Executive Officer

**Cornell University, Economics Department**
404 Uris Hall, Ithaca, NY 14853
607-255-4254  Fax: 607-255-2818
e-mail: lb19@cornell.edu
Web site: www.economics.cornell.edu
*Economic research; microeconomic theory & financial economics*
Lawerence Blume, Chair

**Deutsche Bank**
60 Wall Street, New York, NY 10005
212-250-2500
Web site: www.db.com
*Investment, private & commercial banking; wealth & asset management*
Dr. Marcus Schenck, Chief Financial Officer

**Federal Home Loan Bank of New York**
101 Park Avenue, New York, NY 10178-0599
212-681-6000  Fax: 212-441-6890
Web site: www.fhlbny.com
*Provides credit products, correspondent services & community lending programs for members*
Jose R. Gonzalez, President & Chief Executive Officer

**Financial Services Forum**
601 Thirteenth Street NW, Suite 750 South, Washington, DC 20005
202-457-8765  Fax: 202-457-8769
Web site: www.financialservicesforum.org
*Organization consisting of CEOs of sixteen of the largest financial institutions in the US*
Brian T Moynihan, Chair

**Goldman Sachs & Co**
200 West Street, 29th Floor, New York, NY 10282
202-902-1000
Web site: www.goldmansachs.com
*Investment banking & management*
Lloyd C Blankfein, Chairman & Chief Executive Officer

**HSBC USA Inc**
452 Fifth Avenue, New York, NY 10018
212-525-5000
Web site: www.us.hsbc.com
*Commercial & retail banking*
Mark Zaeske, Chief Financial Officer

*Offices and agencies generally appear in alphabetical order, except when specific order is requested by listee.*

**IRX Therapeutics Inc**
140 West 57th St, Ste 3D, New York, NY 10019
212-582-1199  Fax: 212-582-3659
Web site: www.irxtherapeutics.com
Jeffrey Hwang, President/Chief Operating Officer

**Independent Bankers Association of NYS**
19 Dove Street, Suite 101, Albany, NY 12210
518-436-4646  Fax: 518-436-4648
Web site: www.ibanys.net
*Represents New York's independent community banks*
John J Witkowski, President & Chief Executive Officer

**JPMorgan Chase & Co**
270 Park Avenue, New York, NY 10017-2070
212-464-1909
Web site: www.jpmorganchase.com
*Financial services, investment banking & asset management*
Jamie Dimon, Chairman & Chief Executive Officer

**KeyBank**
65 Dutch Hill Road, Orangeburg, NY 10962
845-398-2280 or 845-365-5890  Fax: 845-365-5890
Web site: www.key.com
*Retail & commercial banking; investment management*
Ruth Mahoney, Market President

**Kudlow & Company LLC**
301 Tahmore Drive, Fairfield, CT 06825
203-228-5050  Fax: 203-228-5040
e-mail: svarga@kudlow.com
Web site: www.kudlow.com
*Economic research & consulting services*

**Lake Shore Savings**
128 East Fourth Street, Dunkirk, NY 14048
716-366-4070  Fax: 716-366-2965
e-mail: dave.mancuso@lakeshoresavings.com
Web site: www.lakeshoresavings.com
*Personal & business banking with focus on mortgage, real estate, commercial & consumer loans*
Daniel Reininga, President & Chief Executive Officer

**M&T Bank Corporation**
One M&T Plaza, 345 Main Street, Buffalo, NY 14203-2399
716-842-4470  Fax: 716-842-5839
e-mail: rwilmers@mtb.com
Web site: www.mtb.com
*Commercial, savings & mortgage banking services*
Robert G Wilmers, Chairman & Chief Executive Officer

**MBIA Insurance Corporation**
1 Manhattanville Road, Suite 301, Purchase, NY 10577
914-273-4545
Web site: www.mbia.com
*Municipal bond insurance & specialized financial services*
Jay Brown, Chief Executive Officer

**Mallory Factor Inc**
555 Madison Avenue, New York, NY 10022
212-350-0000  Fax: 212-350-0001
*Consulting & financial services*
Mallory Factor, President

**Merrill Lynch & Co Inc**
4 World Financial Center, 250 Vesey Street, New York, NY 10080
800-637-7455
Web site: www.ml.com
*Securities, capital markets & financial services*
Andy M Sieg, Managing Director

**Morgan Stanley**
1585 Broadway Avenue, New York, NY 10036
212-761-4000  Fax: 212-762-7994
Web site: www.morganstanley.com
*Investment banking, asset management & financial services*
James Gorman, Chairman & Chief Executive Officer

**Municipal Credit Union**
22 Cortlandt Street, New York, NY 10007-3107
212-238-3512
Web site: www.nymcu.org
*Credit union serving members in New York*
Kam Wong, President & Chief Executive Officer

**NBT Bancorp Inc.**
PO Box 351, Norwich, NY 13815
607-337-2265 or 800-628-2265
e-mail: customerservice@nbtbank.com
Web site: www.nbtbank.com
*Commercial banking*
Martin A Dietrich, President & Chief Executive Officer

**National Federation of Community Development Credit Unions**
39 Broadway, Suite 2140, New York, NY 10006-3063
212-809-1850  Fax: 212-809-3274
e-mail: info@cdcu.coop
Web site: www.cdcu.coop
*Association of credit unions serving lower-income people & communities*
Cathie Mahon, President & Chief Executive Officer

**Navicore Solutions**
200 US Highway 9, Manalapan, NJ 07726
800-992-4557
Web site: www.navicoresolutions.org
*Credit counseling & debt management services*
Diane Gray, Vice President of Counseling & Education

**New York Bankers Association**
99 Park Avenue, 4th Floor, New York, NY 10016-1502
212-297-1600  Fax: 212-297-1658
e-mail: msmith@nyba.com
Web site: www.nyba.com
*Association providing education, advocacy & services for the banking industry of New York State*
Michael P Smith, President & Chief Executive Officer

**New York Community Bank**
615 Merrick Avenue, Westbury, NY 11590
877-786-6560
Web site: www.mynycb.com
Joseph R. Ficalora, President & Chief Executive Officer

**New York Credit Union Association**
1021 Watervliet-Shaker Road, PO Box 15118, Albany, NY 12212-5118
518-437-8100 or 800-342-9835  Fax: 518-437-8284
e-mail: info@nycua.org
Web site: www.nycua.org
*Supports & advocates for credit unions throughout NYS*
William J Mellin, President & Chief Executive Officer

**New York Stock Exchange**
11 Wall Street, New York, NY 10005
212-656-3000
Web site: www.nyse.com
Anthony J Albanese, Chief Regulatory Officer

**Norddeutsche Landesbank Girozentrale**
1114 Avenue of the Americas, 20th Floor, New York, NY 10036
212-398-7300  Fax: 212-812-6860
Web site: www.nordlb.com
Christian Jagenberg, Executive Vice President & General Manager

*Policy Areas*

---

*Offices and agencies generally appear in alphabetical order, except when specific order is requested by listee.*

**North Country Savings Bank**
127 Main Street, Canton, NY 13617
315-386-4533  Fax: 315-386-3739
Web site: www.northcountrysavings.com
Victoria A Oakes, Assistant Vice President

**Pioneer Savings Bank**
21 Second Street, Troy, NY 12180
518-687-5400  Fax: 518-274-1060
Web site: www.pioneerbanking.com
Thomas L. Amell, President & Chief Executive Officer

**Securities Industry & Financial Markets Association (SIFMA)**
120 Broadway, 35th Floor, New York, NY 10271
212-313-1200  Fax: 212-313-1301
e-mail: inquiry@sifma.org
Web site: www.sifma.org
*Association representing the securities industry of the United States*
Kenneth E Bentsen Jr., President & Chief Executive Officer

**Sullivan & Cromwell**
125 Broad Street, New York, NY 10004-2498
212-558-4000  Fax: 212-558-3588
Web site: www.sullcrom.com
*Bank regulation & acquisition law*
H Rodgin Cohen, Partner & Senior Chairman
Joseph Shenker, Partner & Chairman

**TD Bank N.A.**
1 Old Loudon Road, Latham, NY 12110
518-785-8628
Web site: www.tdbank.com
*Commercial, retail & investment banking*
Gail Jefferson, Assistant Vice President

**Tompkins Financial Corporation**
110 North Tioga Street, PO Box 460, Ithaca, NY 14851
607-273-3210  Fax: 607-273-0063
e-mail: sromaine@tompkinstrust.com
Web site: www.tompkinsfinancial.com
*$5.5 Billion financial services holding company headquartered in Ithaca, NY. Parent company to Tompkins Trust Company, The Bank of Castile and Mahopac National Bank, as well as Tompkins Insurance Services & Tompkins Financial.*
Stephen S Romaine, President & Chief Executive Officer

**Ulster Savings Bank**
180 Schwank Drive, Kingston, NY 12401
845-338-6322 or 866-440-0391  Fax: 845-339-9008
Web site: www.ulstersavings.com
*Banking services including consumer loans, commercial mortgages & online banking*
Glenn Sutherland, Interim President & Chief Executive Officer

**Valley National Bank**
1455 Valley Road, Wayne, NJ 07470
973-686-5034 or 800-522-4100  Fax: 973-694-2261
e-mail: rfraser@valleynationalbank.com
Web site: www.valleynationalbank.com
*Full-service banking, cash management, municipal leasing & public finance*
Ronald Fraser, First Vice President, Municipal & Government

**White & Case LLP**
1155 Avenue of the Americas, New York, NY 10036-2787
212-819-8200  Fax: 212-354-8113
e-mail: dwall@whitecase.com
Web site: www.whitecase.com
*Advises domestic & foreign banks on the nature & structure of their operations & activities in the US & abroad*
Duane D Wall, Partner of Counsel

# COMMERCE, INDUSTRY & ECONOMIC DEVELOPMENT

## NEW YORK STATE

### GOVERNOR'S OFFICE

## Governor's Office
Executive Chamber
State Capitol
Albany, NY 12224
518-474-8390  Fax: 518-474-1513
Web site: www.ny.gov

Governor:
  Andrew M Cuomo . . . . . . . . . . . . . . . . . . . . . . . . . . . . . .518-474-8390
Secretary to the Governor:
  Melissa DeRosa . . . . . . . . . . . . . . . . . . . . .518-474-4246 or 212-681-4580
Counsel to the Governor:
  Jill DesRosiers . . . . . . . . . . . . . . . . . . . . . .518-474-8343 or 212-681-4580
Deputy Secretary for General Government Financial Services:
  Vacant . . . . . . . . . . . . . . . . . . . . . . . . . . . . . . . . . . . .518-474-5442
First Assistant Counsel:
  R Nadine Fontaine . . . . . . . . . . . . . . . . . . . . . . . . . . . . . .518-474-8434
Chief of Staff:
  Jill DesRosiers . . . . . . . . . . . . . . . . . . . . . .518-474-8390 or 212-681-4580
Director, Communications:
  Peter Ajemian . . . . . . . . . . . . . . . . . . . . . . .518-474-8418 or 212-681-4640

### EXECUTIVE DEPARTMENTS AND RELATED AGENCIES

## New York State Liquor Authority (Division of Alcoholic Beverage Control)
80 South Swan Street
Suite 900
Albany, NY 12210-8002
518-474-3114
Web site: www.sla.ny.gov

317 Lenox Avenue
New York, NY 10027
Fax:

535 Washington Street
Suite 303
Buffalo, NY 14203
518-474-3114
Fax: 716-847-3435

Chairman:
  Vincent G Bradley . . . . . . . . . . . . . . . . . .212-961-8300 or 518-474-3114
Commissioner:
  Greeley T Ford . . . . . . . . . . . . . . . . . . . . . .212-961-8300 or 518-474-3114
Director, Enforcement:
  Joseph Finelli . . . . . . . . . . . . . . . . . . . . . . . . . . . . . . . .518-474-3114
  e-mail: Joseph.Finelli@sla.ny.gov
Counsel to the Authority:
  Vacant . . . . . . . . . . . . . . . . . . . . . . . . . . . . . . . . . . . . .518-474-3114

## Administration
Secretary to the Authority:
  Thomas Donohue . . . . . . . . . . . . . . . . . . . . . . . . . . . . . .518-474-3114
  e-mail: Thomas.Donohue@sla.ny.gov
Deputy Commissioner, Administration:
  Chad Loshbaugh . . . . . . . . . . . . . . . . . . . . . . . . . . . . . . .518-473-0365

Director, Administration:
  Kimberly Ciccone . . . . . . . . . . . . . . . . . . . . . . . . . . . . . .518-474-3114
  e-mail: Kimberly.Ciccone@sla.ny.gov
Director, Public Affairs:
  William Crowley . . . . . . . . . . . . . . . . . . . .518-474-3114 or 518-474-4875
  fax: 518-473-9565
  e-mail: William.Crowley@sla.ny.gov

## Licensing & Enforcement

**Albany (Zone II)**
80 S Swan St, Ste 900, Albany, NY 12210-8002
Director, Enforcement:
  Joseph Finelli . . . . . . . . . . . . . . . . . . . . . . . . . . . . . . . .518-474-3114
  e-mail: Joseph.Finelli@sla.ny.gov
Deputy Counsel:
  Lisa Bonacci . . . . . . . . . . . . . . . . . . . . . . . . . . . . . . . . .518-474-3114
Director, Information Technology:
  Michael Drake . . . . . . . . . . . . . . . . . . . .518-474-3114 or 518-474-8704
  fax: 518-402-4015

**Buffalo (Zone III)**
Iskalo Electric Tower, 535 Washington St, Ste 303, Buffalo, NY 14203
Deputy Commissioner, Licensing:
  David L Edmunds Jr. . . . . . . . . . . . . . . . . . . . . . . . . . . . .716-847-3001
Supervising Beverage Control Investigator:
  Gary Bartikofsky . . . . . . . . . . . . . . . . . . . . . . . . . . . . . .716-847-3035

**New York City (Zone I)**
317 Lenox Avenue, New York, NY 10027
Deputy Chief Executive Officer:
  Michael Jones . . . . . . . . . . . . . . . . . . . . . . . . . . . . . . . .212-961-8300
Supervising Beverage Control Investigator:
  Franklin Englander . . . . . . . . . . . . . . . . . . . . . . . . . . . . .212-961-8376

## Budget, Division of the
State Capitol
Room 128
Albany, NY 12224-0314
518-474-2300
e-mail: dob.sm.press@budget.ny.gov
Web site: www.budget.ny.gov

Director:
  Robert F. Mujica . . . . . . . . . . . . . . . . . . . . . . . . . . . . . .518-474-2300
Deputy Director:
  Sandra Beattie . . . . . . . . . . . . . . . . . . . . . . . . . . . . . . . .518-474-2300
Deputy Director:
  Charles Williams . . . . . . . . . . . . . . . . . . . . . . . . . . . . . . .518-474-2300
Press Officer:
  Morris Peters . . . . . . . . . . . . . . . . . . . . . . . . . . . . . . . . .518-473-3885
  e-mail: dob.sm.press@budget.ny.gov

## Consumer Protection, Division of
One Commerce Plaza
99 Washington Avenue
Albany, NY 12231-0001
518-474-8583 or 800-697-1220  Fax: 518-473-9055
e-mail: info@dos.ny.gov
Web site: www.dos.ny.gov/consumerprotection/

Executive Deputy Director:
  Aiesha Battle . . . . . . . . . . . . . . . . . . . . . . . . . . . . . . . . .518-474-2363

## Empire State Development Corporation
633 Third Avenue
Floor 37
New York, NY 10017
212-803-3100  Fax: 212-803-3131
Web site: www.esd.ny.gov

*Offices and agencies generally appear in alphabetical order, except when specific order is requested by listee.*

Policy Areas

625 Broadway
Albany, NY 12245
518-292-5100

95 Perry Street
Suite 500
Buffalo, NY 14203
716-846-8200
Fax: 716-846-8260

President & CEO, Commissioner:
   Howard Zemsky.....................212-803-3700 or 518-292-5100
   e-mail: president@esd.ny.gov
Chief Operating Officer & Deputy Commissioner:
   Kevin Younis ................................212-803-3100
Executive Vice President, Administration:
   Ed Hamilton .......................................212-803-3700
Chief of Staff & EVP of State Marketing Strategy:
   Richard Newman
Chief Financial Officer:
   Elaine Kloss

## Law Department
28 Liberty Street
New York, NY 10005
212-416-8000 or 800-771-7755
Web site: www.ag.ny.gov

State Capitol
Albany, NY 12224-0341
518-776-2000
Fax: 518-650-9401

Attorney General:
   Letitia James.......................212-416-8000 or 518-776-2000
Chief of Staff:
   Ibrahim Khan ...............................212-416-8050
Press Secretary:
   Fernando Aquino..................212-416-8060/fax: 212-416-6005
   e-mail: nyag.pressoffice@ag.ny.gov
Solicitor General:
   Vacant...........................212-416-8016 or 518-776-2002

### Economic Justice
Executive Deputy Attorney General:
   Siobhan Kennedy ...............................212-416-8050

#### Antitrust Bureau
Bureau Chief:
   Eric J Stock .....................212-416-8282/fax: 212-416-6015

#### Consumer Frauds Bureau
Bureau Chief:
   Jane Azia .......................212-416-8300 or 518-776-2307
   fax: 212-416-6003

#### Internet Bureau
Bureau Chief:
   Kathleen McGee ................212-416-8433/fax: 212-416-8369

#### Investor Protection Bureau
Bureau Chief:
   Chad Johnson ..................212-416-8225/fax: 212-416-8816

### State Counsel
Executive Deputy Attorney General:
   Vacant..........................................212-416-8050

#### Claims Bureau
Bureau Chief:
   Katharine Brooks ................518-776-2300 or 212-416-8500

## NYSTAR - Division of Science, Technology & Innovation
625 Broadway
8th Floor
Albany, NY 12245
518-292-5700  Fax: 518-292-5794
e-mail: NYSTARSupport@esd.ny.gov
Web site: www.esd.ny.gov/nystar

Director:
   Matthew Watson...........................518-292-5700
Executive Vice President, Public Affairs & Strategic Initiatives:
   Kay Wright ......................518-292-5700/fax: 518-292-5798
Executive Vice President, Legal & General Counsel:
   Elizabeth Fine ....................................518-292-5700

### Centers for Advanced Technology

#### Center for Advanced Ceramic Technology at Alfred University
2 Pine Street, Alfred, NY 14802-1296
e-mail: cactinfo@alfred.edu
Web site: cact.alfred.edu
Director:
   Dr Matthew M Hall..............607-871-2486/fax: 607-871-3469
   e-mail: hallmm@alfred.edu

#### Center for Advanced Materials Processing at Clarkson Univ
CAMP, Box 5665, Potsdam, NY 13699-5665
Web site: www.clarkson.edu/camp
Director:
   S V Babu ......................315-268-2336/fax: 315-268-7615
   e-mail: babu@clarkson.edu

#### Center for Advanced Tech in Biomedical & Bioengineering
University at Buffalo, 701 Ellicott St, Buffalo, NY 14203
Web site: www.bioinformatics.buffalo.edu/cat
Co-Director:
   Alexander N. Cartwright PhD .....................716-645-0312
Co-Director:
   Marnie LaVigne PhD ...........................716-645-0312

#### Sensor CAT-Diagnostic Tools & Sensor Systems
SUNY Stony Brook, Suffolk Hall, Room 115B, Stony Brook, NY 11794-3717
e-mail: sensor@ece.sunysb.edu
Web site: sensorcat.sunysb.edu
Director:
   Serge Luryi.....................631-632-1368 or 631-632-8420
   fax: 631-632-8529

#### Center for Emerging & Innovative Sciences
Univ of Rochester, Taylor Hall, 260 Hutchinson Rd, Rochester, NY 14627-0194
Web site: www.ceis.rochester.edu
Director:
   Mark Bocko ..................................585-275-0547
   e-mail: mark.bocko@seas.rochester.edu

#### Center for Advanced Information Management
Columbia University, 630 W 168th St, Bldg 130, New York, NY 10032
Director:
   George Hripcsak .................212-305-2944/fax: 212-305-0196

#### Center for Advanced Technology in Life Science Enterprise
Cornell University, 130 Biotechnology Bldg, Ithaca, NY 14853-2703
Web site: www.biotech.cornell.edu/cat
Director:
   George Grills ...............................607-255-9693
   e-mail: biotech@cornell.edu

#### Center for Advanced Technology in Photonics Applications
CUNY, Steinman Hall T606, 160 Convent Avenue, New York, NY 10031
Director:
   David T. Crouse, PhD ............212-650-5330/fax: 212-650-7760

*Offices and agencies generally appear in alphabetical order, except when specific order is requested by listee.*

**Center for Advanced Tech in Telecommunications at Polytech Univ**
5 MetroTech Center, 9th Floor, Brooklyn, NY 11201
Director:
    Shivendra S Panwar . . . . . . . . . . . . . . . 718-260-3050 or 718-260-3740
    fax: 718-260-8687

**Center for Automation Technologies & Systems at Rensselaer**
CII 8011, 110 8th Street, Troy, NY 12180
Web site: www.cats.rpi.edu
Director:
    John Wen . . . . . . . . . . . . . . . . . . . . . 518-276-8744/fax: 518-276-4897

**Center for Advanced Medical Biotechnology**
Biotechnology Building, 2nd Floor, Stony Brook, NY 11790
Web site: www.biotech.sunysb.edu
Director:
    Clinton T Rubin PhD . . . . . . . . . . . . . 631-632-8521/fax: 631-632-8577

**Center for Computer Applications & Software Engineering**
Syracuse University, 2-212 Ctr for Science & Tech, Syracuse, NY 13244
Director:
    Pramod Varshney . . . . . . . . . . . . . . . 315-443-1060/fax: 315-443-4745
    e-mail: varshney@syr.edu

**Center in Nanomaterials and Nanoelectronics**
251 Fuller Road, Albany, NY 12203
Director:
    Michael Fancher . . . . . . . . . . . . . . . . 518-437-8686/fax: 518-437-8687

**Future Energy Systems CAT at Rensselaer Polytechnic Inst**
110 8th Street, Troy, NY 12180
e-mail: cfes@rpi.edu
Web site: www.rpi.edu/cfes
Director:
    Dr. Jian Sun . . . . . . . . . . . . . . . . . . . 518-276-8297/fax: 518-276-6844
    e-mail: jsun@ecse.rpi.edu

**Integrated Electronics Engineering Center at Binghamton**
IEEC, Vestal Pkwy East, PO Box 6000, Binghamton, NY 13902-6000
e-mail: ieec@binghamton.edu
Web site: www.binghamton.edu/ieec/
Director:
    Daryl Santos . . . . . . . . . . . . . . . . . . . 607-777-4769/fax: 607-777-4683

## Regional Technology Development Centers

**Alliance for Manufacturing & Technology**
59 Court St, 6th Fl, State St Entrance, Binghamton, NY 13901
e-mail: info@amt-mep.org
Web site: www.amt-mep.org
Executive Director:
    Edward Gaetano . . . . . . . . . . . . 607-774-0022 x304/fax: 607-774-0026

**Center for Economic Growth**
30 Pearl Street, Ste 100, Albany, NY 12207
e-mail: ceg@ceg.org
Web site: www.ceg.org
President/CEO:
    F Michael Tucker . . . . . . . . . . . . . . . 518-465-8975/fax: 518-465-6681
    e-mail: miket@ceg.org

**Central New York Technology Development Organization**
445 Electronics Pkwy, Ste 206, Liverpool, NY 13088
Web site: www.tdo.org
President/CEO:
    Robert I Trachtenberg . . . . . . . . . . . . 315 425-5144/fax: 315-233-1259
    e-mail: rtrachtenberg@tdo.org

**Council for Interntl Trade, Tech, Education & Communication**
Peyton Hall, Box 8561, Main St, Clarkson University, Potsdam, NY 13669
Web site: www.citec.org
Executive Director:
    William P. Murray . . . . . . . . . . 315-268-3778 x29/fax: 315-268-4432

**High Technology of Rochester**
150 Lucius Gordon Drive, Suite 100, West Henrietta, NY 14586
Web site: www.htr.org
President:
    Jim Sendall . . . . . . . . . . . . . . . . . . . . . . . . . . . . . . . 585-214-2400
    e-mail: info@htr.org

**Hudson Valley Technology Development Center**
1450 Route 300, Building 1, Newburgh, NY 12550
Web site: www.hvtdc.org
Executive Director:
    Thomas G Phillips, Sr . . . . . . . 845-391-8214 x3006/fax: 845-845-8218
    e-mail: tom.phillips@hvtdc.org

**Industrial & Technology Assistance Corp**
39 Broadway, Suite 100, New York, NY 10006
Web site: www.itac.org
President:
    Sara Garretson . . . . . . . . . . . . . . . . . 212-809-3900/fax: 646-588-5156
    e-mail: sgarretson@itac.org

**Long Island Forum for Technology**
510 Grumman Road West, Bay Shore, NY 11706
e-mail: info@lift.org
Executive Director:
    William Wahlig . . . . . . . . . . . . . . . . . 631-969-3700/fax: 631-846-2789
    e-mail: bwahlig@lift.org

**Mohawk Valley Applied Technology Corp**
207 Genesee St, Ste 405, Utica, NY 13501
Web site: www.mvatc.com
President:
    Paul MacEnroe . . . . . . . . . . . . . . . . . 315-793-8050/fax: 315-793-8057

**INSYTE Consulting (Western NY Technology Development Ctr)**
726 Exchange St, Ste 812, Buffalo, NY 14210
Web site: www.insyte-consulting.com
President:
    Benjamin Rand . . . . . . . . . . . . . . . . . 716-636-3626/fax: 716-845-6418
    e-mail: brand@insyte-consulting.com

## State Department
One Commerce Plaza
99 Washington Avenue
Albany, NY 12231-0001
518-474-4750  Fax: 518-474-4597
e-mail: info@dos.ny.gov
Web site: www.dos.ny.gov

123 William St
New York, NY 10038-3804
212-417-5800
Fax: 212-417-2383

Secretary of State:
    Rossana Rosado . . . . . . . . . . . . . . . . . 518-486-9844 or 212-417-5800
First Deputy Secretary of State:
    Daniel Shapiro . . . . . . . . . . . . . . . . . . . . . . . . . . . . . 518-474-4750
Deputy Secretary of State, Public Affairs:
    Vacant . . . . . . . . . . . . . . . . . . . . . . . . . . . . . . . . . . . .212-417-5800
Assistant Secretary of State, Communications:
    Vacant . . . . . . . . . . . . . . . . . . . . . . 518-474-4752/fax: 518-474-4597
    e-mail: info@dos.state.ny.us
General Counsel:
    Linda Baldwin . . . . . . . . . . . . . . . . . . 518-474-6740/fax: 518-473-9211
Deputy Secretary of State, Local Government & Community Services:
    Robert Elliott . . . . . . . . . . . . . . . . . . . 518-486-9888/fax: 518-474-6572

*Offices and agencies generally appear in alphabetical order, except when specific order is requested by listee.*

Policy Areas

## Licensing Services Division
Deputy Secretary of State:
Marcos Vigil . . . . . . . . . . . . . . .518-473-2728/fax: 518-473-2730
e-mail: licensing@dos.state.ny.us

### Administrative Rules Division
Manger, Publications:
Maribeth St. Germain . . . . . . . . . . . .518-474-6957/fax: 518-473-9055
e-mail: adminrules@dos.state.ny.us

### Cemeteries Division
Director:
Richard D Fishman . . . . . . . . . . . . . . .518-474-6226 or 212-417-5713
fax: 518-473-0876
e-mail: cemeteries@dos.state.ny.us

### Corporations, State Records & UCC Division
Director:
Sandra J. Tallman . . . . . . . . . . . . . . .518-473-2492/fax: 518-474-1418
e-mail: corporations@dos.ny.gov

## Taxation & Finance Department
W.A. Harriman Campus
Building 9
Albany, NY 12227
518-457-4242 or 518-457-2244  Fax: 518-457-2486
Web site: www.tax.ny.gov

Commissioner:
Vacant . . . . . . . . . . . . . . . . . . . . . . . .518-457-2244
Executive Deputy Commissioner:
Nonie Manion. . . . . . . . . . . . . .518-530-4444 or 518-530-5000
Deputy Commissioner & Counsel:
Amanda Hiller . . . . . . . . . . . .518-457-3746 or 518-530-5300
fax: 518-457-8247
Director, Conciliation & Mediation Services:
Robert Farrelly . . . . . . . . . . . . . . . . . .518-485-8063
Director, Executive Correspondence & Legislative Affairs:
Maryann Tucker . . . . . . . . . . . . . . . . .518-457-2398
Director, Public Information:
Geoffrey Gloak . . . . . . . . . . . . . . . . . .518-457-7377

## Office of Processing & Taxpayer Services (OPTS)
Deputy Commissioner:
Edward Chaszczewski . . . . . . . . . . . . . . . . . . . . . . . . . .518-530-5320

### Human Resources Management
Director:
Valerie DeBerry . . . . . . . . . . . . . . . . . . . . . . . . . .518-457-2786

## Office of Budget & Management Analysis
Chief Fiscal Officer:
Eric Mostert . . . . . . . . . . . . . . . . .518-485-5080 or 518-530-4000

### Planning & Management Analysis Bureau
Director:
Mary Ellen Nagengast . . . . . . . . . . . . . . . . . .518-457-8660

## Office of Processing & Taxpayer Services
Deputy Commissioner:
Edward Chaszczewski . . . . . . . . . . . . . . . . . . . . . . . . . .518-530-5320

## Office of State Treasury
Deputy Commissioner & State Treasurer:
Christopher Curtis . . . . . . . . . . . . . . .518-474-4250/fax: 518-402-4118

## Office of Criminal Enforcement
Deputy Commissioner, Criminal Investigations:
Argi O'Leary. . . . . . . . . . . . . . . . . . . . . . . . . . . .518-530-5348

### Audit Division
Director:
Joe Carzo . . . . . . . . . . . . . . . . . . . . . . . . . .518-451-8910

## Collections & Civil Enforcement
Deputy Commissioner:
Argi O'Leary . . . . . . . . . . . . . . . . . . . . . . . . . . . . . .518-591-1980

## Office of Tax Policy Analysis
Deputy Commissioner:
Robert D Plattner . . . . . . . . . . . . . . . .518-457-4357 or 518-530-5344

## CORPORATIONS, AUTHORITIES AND COMMISSIONS

## Central New York Regional Market Authority
2100 Park St
Syracuse, NY 13208
315-422-8647  Fax: 315-422-6897
Web site: cnyrma.com

Commissioner of Agricultural Markets:
Richard Ball . . . . . . . . . . . . . . . . . . . . . .518-457-8876 or 518-457-4188
Commissioner's Representative:
Troy Waffner . . . . . . . . . . . . . . . . . . . . . . . . . .315-422-8647

## Development Authority of the North Country
317 Washington Street
Watertown, NY 13601
315-661-3200
e-mail: info@danc.org
Web site: www.danc.org

Chair:
Gary Turck . . . . . . . . . . . . . . . . . . . . . . . . .315-661-3200
Executive Director:
James Wright . . . . . . . . . . . . . . . . . . . . . . . . .315-661-3200
Deputy Executive Director:
Thomas R Sauter. . . . . . . . . . . . . . . . . . . . . . . .315-661-3200
e-mail: tsauter@danc.org
Director, Engineering:
Carrie Tuttle. . . . . . . . . . . . . . . . . . .315-661-3210/fax: 315-786-2971
Telecom Division Manager:
David Wolf . . . . . . . . . . . . . . . . . . . . . . . .315-661-3200
e-mail: oatn@danc.org
Landfill Superintendent:
Steve McElwain . . . . . . . . . . . . . . . . . . . . . . .315-661-3230
Director, Regional Development:
Michelle Capone. . . . . . . . . . . . . . . . . . . . . . . .315-661-3200

## Great Lakes Commission
2805 S Industrial Hwy
Ste 100
Ann Arbor, MI 48104-6791
734-971-9135  Fax: 734-971-9150
e-mail: teder@glc.org
Web site: www.glc.org

Chairman:
Jon W Allan . . . . . . . . . . . . . . . . . . . . . . . . .517-284-5035
e-mail: allanj@michigan.gov
Vice Chair:
Jon W Allan . . . . . . . . . . . . . . . . . . . . . . . . .517-284-5035
e-mail: allanj@michigan.gov
New York State Commissioner:
Basil Seggos . . . . . . . . . . . . . . . . .518-402-8540/fax: 518-402-8541
Executive Director:
Tim A Eder . . . . . . . . . . . . . . . . . . . . . . . . .734-971-9135
e-mail: teder@glc.org
Deputy Director:
Thomas R Crane . . . . . . . . . . . . . . . . . . . . . . . .734-971-9135
e-mail: tcrane@glc.org

*Offices and agencies generally appear in alphabetical order, except when specific order is requested by listee.*

CIO:
   Stephen J Cole . . . . . . . . . . . . . . . . . . . . . . . . . . . . .734-971-9135
   e-mail: scole@glc.org
Program Director:
   Victoria Pebbles . . . . . . . . . . . . . . . . . . . . . . . . . . . .734-971-9135
   e-mail: vpebbles@glc.org
Communications Director:
   Beth Wanamaker. . . . . . . . . . . . . . . . . . . . . . . . . . . . . .734-971-9135
   e-mail: beth@glc.org
Policy Director:
   Matthew Doss . . . . . . . . . . . . . . . . . . . . . . . . . . . . . . .734-971-9135
   e-mail: mdoss@glc.org

## United Nations Development Corporation

Two United Nations Plaza, 27th Fl
New York, NY 10017
212-888-1618  Fax: 212-588-0758
e-mail: info@undc.org
Web site: www.undc.org

Chair, Board of Directors:
   George Klein. . . . . . . . . . . . . . . . . . . . . . . . . . . . . . . .212-888-1618
Sr VP & General Counsel/Secretary:
   Robert Cole. . . . . . . . . . . . . . . . . . . . . . . . . . . . . . . . .212-888-1618
Vice President:
   Kenneth Coopersmith . . . . . . . . . . . . . . . . . . . . . . . . . .212-888-1618
Controller/Treasurer:
   Jorge Ortiz. . . . . . . . . . . . . . . . . . . . . . . . . . . . . . . . . .212-888-1618

## NEW YORK STATE LEGISLATURE

*See Legislative Branch in Section 1 for additional Standing Committee and Subcommittee information.*

## Assembly Standing Committees

### Cities
Chair:
   Edward C Braunstein (D) . . . . . . . . . . . . . . . . . . . . . . .518-455-5425

### Consumer Affairs & Protection
Chair:
   Nily Rozic (D, WF). . . . . . . . . . . . . . . . . . . . . . . . . . . .518-455-4545

### Corporations, Authorities & Commissions
Chair:
   Amy Paulin (D). . . . . . . . . . . . . . . . . . . . . . . . . . . . . . .518-455-5585

### Economic Development, Job Creation, Commerce & Industry
Chair:
   Harry B Bronson (D) . . . . . . . . . . . . . . . . . . . . . . . . . .518-455-4767

### Small Business
Chair:
   Vacant. . . . . . . . . . . . . . . . . . . . . . . . . . . . . . . . . . . . .518-455-5997

## Assembly Task Forces

### University-Industry Cooperation, Task Force on
Chair:
   Vacant. . . . . . . . . . . . . . . . . . . . . . . . . . . . . . . . . . . . .518-455-0000
Coordinator:
   Maureen Schoolman . . . . . . . . . . . . . . .518-455-3632/fax: 518-455-4175

## Senate Standing Committees

### Cities
Chair:
   Robert Jackson (D, WF). . . . . . . . . . . . . . . . . . . . . . . .518-455-2041

Ranking Minority Member:
   Andrew J Lanza (R, C, IP, RFM). . . . . . . . . . . . . . . . . . .518-455-3215

### Commerce, Economic Development & Small Business
Chair:
   Anna M Kaplan (D, IP, WF). . . . . . . . . . . . . . . . . . . . .518-455-2170
Minority Member:
   Pamela Helming (R, C, IP). . . . . . . . . . . . . . . . . . . . . .518-455-2366

### Consumer Protection
Chair:
   Kevin Thomas (D) . . . . . . . . . . . . . . . . . . . . . . . . . . . .518-455-3260
Minority Member:
   James Tedisco (R, C) . . . . . . . . . . . . . . . . . . . . . . . . . .518-455-2181

### Corporations, Authorities & Commissions
Chair:
   Leroy Comrie (D). . . . . . . . . . . . . . . . . . . . . . . . . . . . .518-455-2701

## Senate/Assembly Legislative Commissions

### Legislative Commission on Rural Resources
Ranking Minority Member:
   Pamela Helming (R, C, IP). . . . . . . . . . . . . . . . . . . . . .518-455-2366
Chair:
   Frank Skartados (D) . . . . . . . . . . . . . . . .518-455-5762/fax: 518-455-5593

## U.S. GOVERNMENT

## EXECUTIVE DEPARTMENTS AND RELATED AGENCIES

## Commodity Futures Trading Commission
Web site: www.cftc.gov

**Eastern Region**
   140 Broadway, New York, NY 10005
   646-746-9700
Regional Counsel:
   Lenel Hickson Jr. . . . . . . . . . . . . . . . . . .646-746-9700/fax: 646-746-9938

## Consumer Product Safety Commission
301-504-7923 or 800-504-0124  Fax: 301-504-0124
Web site: www.cpsc.gov

**Eastern Regional Center**
   201 Varick Street, Room 903, New York, NY 10014
   212-620-4120
Acting Director:
   Vacant

## Export Import Bank of the United States
Web site: www.exim.gov

**Northeast Regional Office** . . . . . . . . . . . . . . . . . . . . .fax: 212-809-2687
   Ted Weiss Federal Building, 290 Broadway, 13th Floor, New York, NY 10007
   212-809-2650  Fax: 212-809-2687
Regional Director:
   Gregory Smith . . . . . . . . . . . . . . . . . . .212-809-2652/fax: 212-809-2687

## Federal Trade Commission
212-607-2829  Fax: 212-607-2822
Web site: www.ftc.gov

**Northeast Regional Office** . . . . . . . . . . . . . . . . . . . . .fax: 212-607-2822
   1 Bowling Green, New York, NY 10004
   877-382-4357  Fax: 212-607-2822
Regional Director:
   William H. Efron . . . . . . . . . . . . . . . . . . . . . . . . . . . .212-607-2829

*Offices and agencies generally appear in alphabetical order, except when specific order is requested by listee.*

## Small Business Administration
Web site: www.sba.gov

**Region II New York**..........................fax: 212-264-4963
26 Federal Plaza, Suite 3108, New York, NY 10278
212-264-1450  Fax: 212-264-4963
Regional Administrator:
Kellie LeDet
Regional Communications Director:
Rita Chappelle

### District Offices
*Buffalo* ....................................fax: 716-551-4418
130 South Elmwood Avenue, Suite 540, Buffalo, NY 14202
716-551-4301  Fax: 716-551-4418
District Director:
Franklin J Sciortino ..........716-551-4305/fax: 716-481-1974
e-mail: franklin.sciortino@sba.gov
*New Jersey* ..................................fax: 973-645-6265
2 Gateway Center, Suite 1501, Newark, NJ 07102
973-645-2434  Fax: 973-645-6265
District Director:
Alfred Titone ..............973-645-3680/fax: 202-481-6560
e-mail: alfred.titone@sba.gov
*New York City*...............................fax: 212-264-4963
26 Federal Plaza, Suite 3100, New York, NY 10278
212-264-4354  Fax: 212-264-4963
District Director:
Beth Goldberg
*Syracuse* ...................................fax: 315-471-9288
224 Harrison Street, Suite 506, Syracuse, NY 13202
315-471-9393  Fax: 315-471-9288
District Director:
Bernard J Paprocki
e-mail: bernard.paprocki@sba.gov

### New York Small Business Development Center
State University of New York, 10 North Pearl Street, Albany, NY 12246
800-732-7232 or 518-944-2840
Chair:
Brad Rosenstein

## US Commerce Department
Web site: www.commerce.gov

### Census Bureau
Web site: www.census.gov

**New York Region**...........................fax: 212-584-3402
32 Old Slip, 9th Floor, New York, NY 10005
212-584-3400 or 800-991-2520  Fax: 212-584-3402
e-mail: new.york.regional.office@census.gov
Regional Director:
Jeff T. Behler...................212-584-3400/fax: 212-584-3402

### Economic Development Administration
Web site: www.eda.gov

**Philadelphia Region (includes New York)**
The Curtis Center, 601 Walnut Street, Suite 140 South, Philadelphia, PA 19106
Regional Director:
Linda Cruz-Carnall ..............215-597-4603/fax: 215-597-1063

### Minority Business Development Agency
Web site: www.mbda.gov

**New York Region**
26 Federal Plaza, New York, NY 10278
212-264-3262

**New York Business Center**
535 Fifth Avenue, 16th Floor, New York, NY 10017

646-821-4008
Project Director:
Paul Sawyer

**South Bronx Business Center**
555 Bergen Avenue, 3rd Floor, Bronx, NY 10455
718-732-7540
Project Director:
Sharon Higgins

**Williamsburg Business Center**
12 Heyward Street, 2nd Floor, Brooklyn, NY 11211
718-522-5620
Contact:
Yehuda Turner

## National Oceanic & Atmospheric Administration

### National Weather Service, Eastern Region
630 Johnson Avenue, Suite 202, Bohemia, NY 11716
Web site: www.weather.gov/erh/
Director:
Jason Tuell
e-mail: jason.tuell@noaa.gov
Deputy Director:
Mickey J Brown ...............................631-244-0100
Regional Program Manager:
John Koch....................................631-244-0104
e-mail: john.koch@noaa.gov
Regional Program Manager:
Jeff Waldstreicher............................631-244-0131
e-mail: jeff.waldstreicher@noaa.gov
Scientific Services Division Chief:
Kenneth Johnson
e-mail: kenneth.johnson@noaa.gov
Meteorological Services Division Chief:
John Guiney ..................................631-244-0121
e-mail: john.guiney@noaa.gov

### National Weather Service
Center for Environmental Science & Tech, 251 Fuller Road, Suite B-300, Albany, NY 12203-3640
Science & Operations Officer:
Warren Snyder ................................518-435-9580

## US Commercial Service - International Trade Administration
Web site: www.trade.gov

### Buffalo US Export Assistance Center
130 South Elmwood Avenue, Suite 530, Buffalo, NY 14202
e-mail: office.buffalo@trade.gov
Web site: www.export.gov/newyork/bflorochsyr
Director:
Rosanna Masucci ...............716-551-4191/fax: 716-551-5290
e-mail: rosanna.masucci@trade.gov

### Harlem US Export Assistance Center.............fax: 212-860-6203
163 West 125th Street, Suite 901, New York, NY 10027
212-860-6200  Fax: 212-860-6203
e-mail: office.harlem@trade.gov
Web site: www.export.gov/newyork/harlem
USEAC Director:
K L Fredericks..................212-860-6200/fax: 212-860-6203
e-mail: kl.fredericks@trade.gov

### Long Island US Export Assistance Center
Commercial Service Long Island, PO Box 423, Old Westbury, NY 11568-0210
e-mail: officelongislandny@trade.gov
Web site: www.export.gov/newyork/longisland
Director:
Susan Sadocha ................................516-427-9117
e-mail: susan.sadocha@trade.gov

*Offices and agencies generally appear in alphabetical order, except when specific order is requested by listee.*

**New York US Export Assistance Center**
Ted Weiss Federal Building, 290 Broadway, Suite 1312, New York, NY 10007
USEAC Director:
Carmela Mammas . . . . . . . . . . . . . . . 212-809-2676/fax: 212-809-2687
e-mail: carmela.mammas@trade.gov

## US Department of Agriculture

### Rural Development
Web site: www.rd.usda.gov

**New York State Office**. . . . . . . . . . . . . . . . . . . . . . . . .fax: 315-477-6438
441 South Salina Street, Suite 357, Syracuse, NY 13202-2541
315-477-6400  Fax: 315-477-6438
Acting New York State Director:
Scott Collins . . . . . . . . . . . . . . . . . . . . . . . . . . . . .315-477-6437
Special Projects Coordinator:
Christopher Stewart

## US Justice Department
Web site: www.justice.gov

**Antitrust Division-New York Field Office** . . . . . . . fax: 212-335-8021
26 Federal Plaza, Room 3630, New York, NY 10278-0004
212-335-8000  Fax: 212-335-8021
e-mail: newyork.atr@usdoj.gov
Chief:
Jeffrey Martino
Assistant Chief:
Stephen J. McCahey

**Civil Division-Commercial Litigation Branch**
950 Pennsylvania Avenue NW, Washington, DC 20530-0001
202-514-2000
e-mail: civil.feedback@usdoj.gov
Principal Deputy Assistant Attorney General:
Benjamin C Mizer

**Community Relations Service**
600 East Street NW, Suite 6000, Washington, DC 20530
202-305-2935
e-mail: askcrs@usdoj.gov
Acting Director:
Paul Monteiro

**Community Relations Service-Northeast & Caribbean Region**
26 Federal Plaza, Suite 36-118, New York, NY 10278
CRS Conciliator:
Linda Ortiz

## US Securities & Exchange Commission
Web site: www.sec.gov

**New York Regional Office**
200 Vesey Street, Suite 400, New York, NY 10281-1022
212-336-1100
e-mail: newyork@sec.gov
Regional Director:
Andrew Calamari . . . . . . . . . . . . . . . . . . . . . . . . . . . . . .212-336-1100

**Enforcement Division**
Director:
Andrew Ceresney . . . . . . . . . . . . . . . . . . . . . . . . . . . .202-551-4500

**Investment Management**
Director:
David Grim . . . . . . . . . . . . . . . . . . . . . . . . . . . . . . . . .202-551-6720

*See U.S. Congress Chapter for additional Standing Committee and Subcommittee information.*

### House of Representatives Standing Committees

**Energy & Commerce**
Chair:
Fred Upton (R-MI)
Ranking Member:
Frank Pallone (D-NJ)
New York Delegate:
Eliot L. Engel (D) . . . . . . . . . . . . . . . . . . . . . . . . . . . .202-225-2464
New York Delegate:
Paul Tonko (D)
New York Delegate:
Yvette Clarke (D)
New York Delegate:
Chris Collins (R)

**Foreign Affairs**
Chair:
Edward R. Royce (R-CA)
Ranking Member:
Eliot L. Engel (D-NY)
New York Delegate:
Gregory W. Meeks (D)
New York Delegate:
Brian Higgins (D)
New York Delegate:
Grace Meng (D)
New York Delegate:
Lee M. Zeldin (R)
New York Delegate:
Daniel Donovan (R)

**Small Business**
Chair:
Steve Chabot (R-OH)
Ranking Member:
Nydia Velazquez (D-NY)
New York Delegate:
Richard Hanna (R)
New York Delegate:
Chris Gibson (R)
New York Delegate:
Grace Meng (D)
New York Delegate:
Yvette Clarke (D)

### Joint Senate & House Standing Committees

**Economic Committee, Joint**
Chair:
Daniel Coats (R-IN)
Vice Chair:
Pat Tiberi (R-OH)
Ranking Member:
Carolyn Maloney (D-NY)

### Senate Standing Committees

**Commerce, Science & Transportation**
Chair:
John Thune (R-SD) . . . . . . . . . . . . . . . . . . . . . . . . . . . .202-224-2321
Ranking Member:
Bill Nelson (D-FL)

*Offices and agencies generally appear in alphabetical order, except when specific order is requested by listee.*

Policy Areas

**Finance**
Chair:
   Orrin G. Hatch (R-UT) . . . . . . . . . . . . . . . . . . . . . . . . . . 202-224-5251
Ranking Member:
   Ron Wyden (D-OR)

**Foreign Relations**
Chair:
   Bob Corker (R-TN) . . . . . . . . . . . . . . . . . . . . . . . . . . . . 202-224-3344
Ranking Member:
   Ben Cardin (D-MD)

**Small Business & Entrepreneurship**
Chair:
   David Vitter (R-LA) . . . . . . . . . . . . . . . . . . . . . . . . . . . 202-224-4623
Ranking Member:
   Jeanne Shaheen (D-NH)

## PRIVATE SECTOR

**Altria Client Services**
677 Broadway, Suite 1207, Albany, NY 12207
518-431-8090
Web site: www.altria.com
*Manufacturing & marketing of foods, tobacco, alcoholic beverages*
Martin J Barrington, Chairman & Chief Executive Officer

**American Chemistry Council**
One Commerce Plaza, 99 Washington Avenue, Suite 701, Albany, NY 12210
518-432-7835  Fax: 518-426-2276
e-mail: steve_rosario@americanchemistry.com
Web site: www.americanchemistry.com
Stephen Rosario, Director, Northeast Region

**American Council of Engineering Companies of NY (ACEC New York)**
6 Airline Drive, Albany, NY 12205
518-452-8611  Fax: 518-452-1710
e-mail: acecny@acecny.org
Web site: www.acecny.org
*Business association for consulting engineering firms*
Jay J Simson, President

**American Institute of Architects (AIA) New York State Inc**
50 State Street, 5th Floor, Albany, NY 12207
518-449-3334  Fax: 518-426-8176
e-mail: aianys@aianys.org
Web site: www.aianys.org
*Architectural regulations, state policy, smart growth & affordable housing*
Georgi Ann Bailey, Executive Director

**American Management Association International**
1601 Broadway, New York, NY 10019
212-586-8100 or 877-566-9441  Fax: 212-891-0368
Web site: www.amanet.org
*Business education & management training programs for individuals & organizations*
Edward T Reilly, President & Chief Executive Officer

**Associated Builders & Contractors, Empire State Chapter**
6369 Collamer Road East, Syracuse, NY 13057
315-463-7539 or 800-477-7743  Fax: 315-463-7621
e-mail: empire@abcnys.org
Web site: www.abcnys.org
*Merit shop construction trade association*
Brian Sampson, President

**Associated General Contractors of America, NYS Chapter**
10 Airline Drive, Suite 203, Albany, NY 12205-1025
518-456-1134  Fax: 518-456-1198
e-mail: agcadmin@agcnys.org
Web site: www.agcnys.org
*Represents contractors & companies in the construction industry*
Michael J Elmendorf II, President & Chief Executive Officer

**Association Development Group Inc**
136 Everett Road, Albany, NY 12205
518-465-7085  Fax: 518-427-9495
e-mail: info@adgcommunications.com
Web site: www.adgcommunications.com
*Association management, communications, education & training, strategic planning, leadership & membership support, advocacy, database design*
Kathleen A Van De Loo, President & Chief Executive Officer

**Association for a Better New York**
355 Lexington Avenue, 8th Floor, New York, NY 10017
212-370-5800  Fax: 212-661-5877
Web site: www.abny.org
*Networking & advocacy for the development of businesses & communities in New York*
Angela Pinsky, Executive Director

**Better Business Bureau of Metropolitan New York**
30 East 33rd Street, 12th Floor, New York, NY 10016
212-533-6200  Fax: 212-477-4912
e-mail: inquiry@newyork.bbb.org
Web site: www.bbb.org/new-york-city
*Membership organization promoting ethical business practices*
Claire Rosenzweig, President & Chief Executive Officer

**Brown & Kelly, LLP**
800 Main Place Tower, 350 Main Street, Buffalo, NY 14202
716-854-2620  Fax: 716-854-0082
Kenneth A. Krajewski, Managing Partner

**Building Contractors Association**
451 Park Avenue South, 4th Floor, New York, NY 10016
212-683-8080  Fax: 212-683-0404
e-mail: johare@ny-bca.com
Web site: www.ny-bca.com
*Association representing construction organizations in New York*
John O'Hare, Assistant Managing Director

**Building Industry Association of NYC Inc**
3130 Amboy Road, Staten Island, NY 10306
718-720-3070  Fax: 718-720-3088
e-mail: jessica@webuildnyc.com
Web site: www.webuildnyc.com
Jessica Fortino, Executive Officer

**Business Council for International Understanding**
1501 Broadway, Suite 2300, New York, NY 10018
212-490-0460  Fax: 212-697-8526
Web site: www.bciu.org
*Promotes relationships between business & government leaders & provides services to develop international commerce & trade*
Peter J Tichansky, President & Chief Executive Officer

**Business Council of New York State Inc**
152 Washington Avenue, Albany, NY 12210
518-465-7511 or 800-358-1202  Fax: 518-465-4389
e-mail: heather.briccetti@bcnys.org
Web site: www.bcnys.org
*Business organization representing the interests of firms in New York State*
Heather C. Briccetti, President & Chief Executive Officer

*Offices and agencies generally appear in alphabetical order, except when specific order is requested by listee.*

Policy Areas

## Center for Economic Growth Inc

39 North Pearl Street, Suite 100, Albany, NY 12207
518-465-8975  Fax: 518-465-6681
e-mail: ceg@ceg.org
Web site: www.ceg.org
*Business membership non-profit promoting economic & business development in the Capital Region and Tech Valley*
Michael J. Hickey, Interim President & Chief Executive Officer

## Columbia University, Technology Ventures

80 Claremont Avenue, 4th Floor, New York, NY 10027
212-854-8444  Fax: 212-854-8463
e-mail: techventures@columbia.edu
Web site: www.techventures.columbia.edu
*Identifies & patents new products & transfers inventions from academic research to industry organizations*
Orin Herskowitz, Executive Director

## Conference Board (The)

845 Third Avenue, New York, NY 10022-6600
212-759-0900 or 212-339-0345
e-mail: matteo.tonello@conferenceboard.org
Web site: www.conference-board.org
*Research for business*
Matteo Tonello, Vice President & Managing Director

## Construction Contractors Association of the Hudson Valley Inc

330 Meadow Avenue, Newburgh, NY 12550
845-562-4280  Fax: 845-562-1448
e-mail: info@ccahv.com
Web site: www.ccahv.com
*Association representing commercial & industrial building contractors in Hudson Valley*
A. Alan Seidman, Executive Director

## Consumers Union

101 Truman Avenue, Yonkers, NY 10703-1057
914-378-2000  Fax: 914-378-2900
Web site: www.consumerreports.org; www.consumersunion.org
*Publisher of Consumer Reports magazine; independent, nonprofit organization serving consumers through marketplace testing & research*
Marta Tellado, President & Chief Executive Officer

## Cornell University, Economics Department

404 Uris Hall, Ithaca, NY 14853
607-255-4254  Fax: 607-255-2818
e-mail: lb19@cornell.edu
Web site: www.economics.cornell.edu
*Economic research; microeconomic theory & financial economics*
Lawerence Blume, Chair

## Dale Carnegie & Associates Inc

780 Third Avenue, New York, NY 10017
212-750-4455 or 800-231-5800
*Executive leadership training*
Joseph K. Hart, President & Chief Executive Officer

## Davis Polk & Wardwell

450 Lexington Avenue, New York, NY 10017
212-450-4000  Fax: 212-701-5800
e-mail: gencoun@davispolk.com
Web site: www.davispolk.com
*Securities litigation & antitrust law*
Charles S. Duggan, General Counsel

## Development Counsellors International

215 Park Avenue South, 14th Floor, New York, NY 10003
212-725-0707  Fax: 212-725-2254
Web site: www.aboutdci.com
*Marketing services for economic development & tourism*
Andrew T Levine, President & Chief Creative Officer

## EVCI Career Colleges Holding Corp

1 Van Der Donck Street, Yonkers, NY 10701-7049
914-623-0700  Fax: 914-964-8222
*Owns & operates accredited career & college centers in NY & PA emphasizing business, technology & allied health programs*
Vacant, President & Chief Executive Officer

## Eastern Contractors Association Inc

6 Airline Drive, Albany, NY 12205-1095
518-869-0961  Fax: 518-869-2378
e-mail: info@ecainc.org
Web site: www.ecainc.org
*Trade association of union signatory general contractors and subcontractors, suppliers, and service firms engaged in commercial, industrial and institutional construction throughout eastern New York.*
Todd G Helfrich, President & Chief Executive Officer
Laura Regan, Vice-President

## Eastman Kodak Company

343 State Street, Rochester, NY 14650
585-724-4000 or 866-563-2533
Web site: www.kodak.com
*Manufactures & markets imaging systems & related services*
Terry Taber, Senior Vice President & Chief Technical Officer

## Empire Center for New York State Policy

100 State Street, Suite 600, Albany, NY 12207
518-434-3100  Fax: 518-434-3130
e-mail: info@empirecenter.org
Web site: www.empirecenter.org
*An independent non-profit organization working to foster economic growth & freedom in New York State through research & education*
Edmund J McMahon, President

## Empire State Restaurant & Tavern Association Inc

12 Sheridan Avenue, Albany, NY 12207
518-436-8121  Fax: 518-436-7287
e-mail: esrta@verizon.net
Web site: www.esrta.org
*Grassroots organization promoting the interests of on-premise beverage alcohol licensees*
Scott Wexler, Executive Director

## Empire State Society of Association Executives Inc

120 Defreest Drive, Suite 1, Troy, NY 12180
518-463-1755  Fax: 518-463-5257
e-mail: vanessa@essae.org
Web site: www.essae.org
*Education, information, research & networking for professional staff of trade, business & professional associations*
Vanessa E. LaClair, Executive Director

## Eric Mower & Associates

211 West Jefferson Street, Syracuse, NY 13202
315-466-1000  Fax: 315-466-2000
e-mail: csteenstra@mower.com
Web site: www.mower.com
*Marketing communications & issues management*
Chris Steenstra, Managing Partner

## NYS Bar Assn, Antitrust Law Section
## Federal Trade Commission

1 Bowling Green, Suite 318, New York, NY 10004
212-607-2829
Edith Ramirez, Chair

---

*Offices and agencies generally appear in alphabetical order, except when specific order is requested by listee.*

**Food Industry Alliance of New York State Inc**
130 Washington Avenue, Albany, NY 12210
518-434-1900  Fax: 518-434-9962
e-mail: michael@fiany.com
Web site: www.fiany.com
*Association of retail grocery, cooperative, wholesale &*
*supplier/manufacturer food companies*
Michael Rosen, President & Chief Executive Officer

**General Contractors Association of NY**
60 East 42nd Street, Suite 3510, New York, NY 10165-3598
212-687-3131  Fax: 212-808-5267
e-mail: info@gcany.net
Web site: www.gcany.com
*Heavy construction, transportation*
Denise M. Richardson, Executive Director

**Gilbert Tweed Associates Inc**
415 Madison Avenue, 20th Floor, New York, NY 10017
212-758-3000  Fax: 212-832-1040
e-mail: spinson@gilberttweed.com
Web site: www.gilberttweed.com
*Executive searches in public transit, transportation, energy, utilities,*
*communication & insurance*
Stephanie L Pinson, President

**NYS Bar Assn, Intellectual Property Law Section**
**Hartman & Winnicki, PC**
West 115 Century Road, Suite 120, Paramus, NJ 07652
201-967-8040  Fax: 201-967-0590
e-mail: rick@ravin.com
Web site: www.hartmanwinnicki.com
Richard L. Ravin, Member

**IBM Corporation**
1 New Orchard Road, Armonk, NY 10504-1722
914-499-1900
Web site: www.ibm.com
*Technology & business consulting company*
Virginia M. Rometty, President & Chief Executive Officer

**International Flavors & Fragrances Inc**
521 West 57th Street, New York, NY 10019-2960
212-765-5500  Fax: 212-708-7132
Web site: www.iff.com
*Creates & manufactures flavors & fragrances for consumer products*
Andreas Fibig, Chairman & Chief Executive Officer

**Macy's Inc**
151 West 34th Street, New York, NY 10001
212-494-3000
*Retail department/specialty stores*
Edward Jay Goldberg, Senior Vice President Government & Consumer
  Affairs

**Manhattan Institute for Policy Research**
52 Vanderbilt Avenue, 2nd Floor, New York, NY 10017
212-599-7000  Fax: 212-599-3494
e-mail: communications@manhattan-institute.org
Web site: www.manhattan-institute.org
*Produces & promotes research on taxes, welfare, education & other public*
*policy issues*
Lawrence J. Mone, President

**Manufacturers Association of Central New York**
5788 Wildewaters Parkway, Suite 5, Syracuse, NY 13214
315-474-4201  Fax: 315-474-0524
e-mail: kburns@macny.org
Web site: www.macny.org
*Association of manufacturers providing training, networking opportunities,*
*advocacy, purchasing solutions, resources & services for members*
Karyn Burns, Vice President, Communications & Government Relations

**NYS Bar Assn, Business Law Section**
**Menaker & Herrmann LLP**
10 East 40th Street, New York, NY 10016
212-545-1900  Fax: 212-545-1656
e-mail: info@mhjur.com
Web site: www.mhjur.com
*Offers counsel in Antitrust, Corporate/Commercial Transactions,*
*Commercial Litigation, Commodities, Futures & Derivatives*
Samuel F. Abernethy, Partner

**Mid-Hudson Pattern for Progress**
3 Washington Center, Newburgh, NY 12550
845-565-4900  Fax: 845-565-4918
e-mail: rdegroat@pfprogress.org
Web site: www.pattern-for-progress.org
*Regional planning, research & policy development*
Jonathan Drapkin, President & Chief Executive Officer

**NY Society of Association Executives Inc (NYSAE)**
322 Eighth Avenue, Suite 702, New York, NY 10001-8001
212-206-8230  Fax: 212-645-1147
e-mail: info@nysaenet.org
Web site: www.nysaenet.org
*Association dedicated to advancing the interests of members of not-for-profit*
*organizations in metropolitan NY*
Joel A. Dolci, President & Chief Executive Officer

**NYS Association of Electrical Contractors**
PO Box 807, Latham, NY 12110
518-852-0154 or 800-724-1904  Fax: 518-713-2627
e-mail: jfm@nysaec.org
Web site: www.nysaec.org
*Represents the interests of electrical contractors*
Jay Mangione, Executive Director

**NYS Builders Association Inc**
152 Washington Avenue, Albany, NY 12210
518-465-2492  Fax: 518-465-0635
e-mail: info@nysba.com
Web site: www.nysba.com
*Advocates for the advancement of the building & housing industry; provides*
*programs, research & education for members*
Lewis Dubuque, Executive Vice President

**NYS Building & Construction Trades Council**
50 State Street, 3rd Floor, Albany, NY 12207
518-435-9108  Fax: 518-435-9204
e-mail: nybuildingtrades@me.com
Web site: www.nybuildingtrades.com
*Represents the interests & protects the rights of unionized construction*
*workers in New York*
James Cahill, President

**NYS Clinical Laboratory Association Inc**
394 Waverly Avenue, Brooklyn, NY 11238
718-857-0414  Fax: 718-857-5628
e-mail: info@nyscla.org
Web site: www.nyscla.com
*Not-for-profit trade association dedicated to advancing the business interests*
*of New York State's clinical laboratory industry*
Thomas Rafalsky, President

**NYS Economic Development Council**
111 Washington Avenue, 6th Floor, Albany, NY 12210
518-426-4058  Fax: 518-426-4059
e-mail: mcmahon@nysedc.org
Web site: www.nysedc.org
*Economic development professionals membership organization*
Brian T. McMahon, Executive Director

*Offices and agencies generally appear in alphabetical order, except when specific order is requested by listee.*

**NYS Society of Certified Public Accountants**
14 Wall Street, 19th Floor, New York, NY 10005
800-537-3635  Fax: 866-495-1354
e-mail: jbarry@nysscpa.org
Web site: www.nysscpa.org
*Advocacy & information for the certified public accountants of New York State*
Joanne S. Barry, Executive Director

**NYS Trade Adjustment Assistance Center**
81 State Street, Suite 4, Binghamton, NY 13901
607-771-0875 or 844-279-0705  Fax: 607-724-2404
e-mail: info@nystaac.org
Web site: www.nystaac.org
*Offers aid to New York manufacturers & service companies that are competing with foreign imports*
Louis G. McKeage, Director

**National Association of Black Accountants, NY Chapter**
PO Box 2791, Grand Central Station, New York, NY 10163
212-969-0560  Fax: 646-349-9620
e-mail: info@nabany.org
Web site: www.nabany.org
*Represents the interests of African Americans & other minorities in the fields of accounting, auditing, business, consulting, finance & information technology*
Rosalind P. Danner, President

**National Federation of Independent Business**
100 State Street, Suite 440, Albany, NY 12207
518-434-1262 or 609-989-8777  Fax: 518-426-8799
e-mail: mike.durant@nfib.org
Web site: www.nfib.com/new-york/
*Small business advocacy; supporting pro-small business candidates at the state & federal levels*
Michael P. Durant, State Director

**New York Association of Convenience Stores**
130 Washington Avenue, Suite 300, Albany, NY 12210-2219
518-432-1400  Fax: 518-432-7400
e-mail: info@nyacs.org
Web site: www.nyacs.org
*Serves New York State's convenience store industry*
Jim Calvin, President

**New York Biotechnology Association (The)**
205 East 42nd Street, 14th Floor, New York, NY 10017
212-433-2623  Fax: 212-433-0779
Web site: www.newyorkbio.org
*Promotes the development & growth of NYS-based biotechnology and life science research organizations through the provision of services & information*
Nathan P. Tinker, PhD, Executive Director

**New York Building Congress**
44 West 28th Street, 12th Floor, New York, NY 10001-4212
212-481-9230  Fax: 212-447-6037
e-mail: info@buildingcongress.com
Web site: www.buildingcongress.com
*Membership association dedicated to advancing New York City's construction industry*
Richard T. Anderson, President

**New York Business Development Corporation**
50 Beaver Street, Suite 500, Albany, NY 12207
518-463-2268  Fax: 518-463-0240
e-mail: mackrell@nybdc.com
Web site: www.nybdc.com
*Small business lending; loan programs*
Patrick J. MacKrell, President & Chief Executive Officer

**New York Mercantile Exchange Inc**
1 North End Avenue, New York, NY 10282-1101
212-299-2000  Fax: 212-301-4568
Web site: www.cmegroup.com
*Commodity trading*
Terrence A. Duffy, Executive Chairman & President

**New York State Auto Dealers Association**
37 Elk Street, Albany, NY 12207
518-463-1148  Fax: 518-432-1309
Web site: www.nysada.com
*Association representing vehicle dealers in New York State*
Robert Vancavage, President

**New York State Restaurant Association**
409 New Karner Road, Suite 202, Albany, NY 12205
518-452-4222 or 800-452-5212  Fax: 518-452-4497
e-mail: info@nysra.org
Web site: www.nysra.org
*Promotes and protects the food service industry in New York State*
Melissa Autilio Fleischut, President & Chief Executive Officer

**New York Technology Council**
307 West 38th Street, 13th Floor, New York, NY 10018
646-435-1088
e-mail: info@nytech.org
Web site: www.nytech.org
*Promotes New York City's technology industry*
Erik Grimmelmann, President & Chief Executive Officer

**New York University Stern School of Business, Berkley Center for Entrepreneurship & Innovation**
40 West Fourth Street, Suite 400, New York, NY 10012
212-998-0070
Web site: www.stern.nyu.edu
*Programs & services designed to provide venture development assistance to NYU students, researchers & entrepreneurs*
Luke Williams, Executive Director

**Northeast Equipment Dealers Association Inc**
128 Metropolitan Park Drive, Liverpool, NY 13088
315-457-0314 or 800-932-0607  Fax: 315-451-3548
e-mail: rgaiss@ne-equip.com
Web site: www.ne-equip.org
*Association of agricultural, industrial & outdoor power equipment dealers in the Northeast region of the US*
Ralph Gaiss, Executive VP & CEO

**Partnership for New York City**
One Battery Park Plaza, 5th Floor, New York, NY 10004-1479
212-493-7400 or 212-493-7548  Fax: 212-344-3344
Web site: www.pfnyc.org
*Business organization working in partnership with government, labor & the nonprofit sectors to develop New York City's economy*
Kathryn S. Wylde, President & Chief Executive Officer

**Pepsi Co**
700 Anderson Hill Road, MD 3/1-311, Purchase, NY 10577
914-253-2000  Fax: 914-253-2070
Web site: www.pepsi.com
*Manufactures, sells & distributes soft drinks, concentrates, syrups, snack foods & beverages*
Indra K. Nooyi, Chairman & Chief Executive Officer

**Perry Davis Associates**
25 West 45th Street, Suite 1405, New York, NY 10036
212-840-1166  Fax: 212-840-1514
e-mail: perry@perrydavis.com
Web site: www.perrydavis.com
*Economic development, training, fundraising & management consulting for nonprofit organizations*
Perry Davis, President

*Offices and agencies generally appear in alphabetical order, except when specific order is requested by listee.*

**Printing Industries Alliance**
636 North French Road, Suite 1, Amherst, NY 14228
716-691-3211 or 800-777-4742  Fax: 716-691-4249
e-mail: tfreeman@pialliance.org
Web site: www.pialliance.org
*Trade association providing services & support for the graphic communications industry of NY, Northern NJ & Northwestern PA*
Timothy Freeman, President

**NYS Bar Assn, Multi-jurisdictional Practice Cmte**
**Proskauer Rose LLP**
11 Times Square, New York, NY 10036
212-969-3000  Fax: 212-969-2900
e-mail: info@proskauer.com
Web site: www.proskauer.com
Klaus Eppler, Partner

**Public Policy Institute of NYS Inc**
152 Washington Avenue, Albany, NY 12210
518-465-7511  Fax: 518-432-4537
Web site: www.ppinys.org
*Conducts & publishes research on NYS economic development issues*
Heather C. Briccetti, President & Chief Executive Officer

**Regional Plan Association**
4 Irving Place, 7th Floor, New York, NY 10003
212-253-2727  Fax: 212-253-5666
e-mail: twright@rpa.org
Web site: www.rpa.org
*Association seeking to enhance economic development & quality of life in the New York metropolitan region through advocacy & research*
Thomas K. Wright, President

**Retail Council of New York State**
258 State Street, Albany, NY 12210
518-465-3586 or 800-442-3589  Fax: 518-465-7960
Web site: www.retailcouncilnys.com
*Serves retailers, merchants & other goods & services providers based in New York State*
Ted Potrikus, President & Chief Executive Officer

**Software & Information Industry Association**
1090 Vermont Avenue NW, 6th Floor, Washington, DC 20005-4095
202-289-7442  Fax: 202-289-7097
Web site: www.siia.net
*Issues affecting the software & information industry, in particular electronic commerce & the digital marketplace*
Ken Wasch, President

**Support Services Alliance Inc**
165 Main Street, Oneida, NY 13421
315-363-6584
*Payroll services for businesses*
Steven Cole, Chief Executive Officer

**The New York State Society of Professional Engineers Inc (NYSSPE)**
6 Airline Drive, Suite 114, Albany, NY 12205
518-283-7490  Fax: 518-283-7495
Web site: www.nysspe.org
*Represents professional engineers in NYS & promotes the ethical practice of engineering*
Anthony Fasano, Executive Director

**UHY Advisors**
4 Tower Place, Executive Park, 7th Floor, Albany, NY 12203
518-449-3171  Fax: 518-449-5832
e-mail: hfoote@uhy-us.com
Web site: www.uhy-us.com
*Professional financial, tax, business & tax advisory services for mid-sized to larger companies*
Howard Foote, Managing Director & Chief Financial Officer

**Wegmans Food Markets Inc**
1500 Brooks Avenue, PO Box 30844, Rochester, NY 14603-0844
585-464-4760 or 800-934-6267  Fax: 585-464-4669
Web site: www.wegmans.com
Mary Ellen Burris, Senior Vice President, Consumer Affairs

**Women's Business Center of New York State**
200 Genesee Street, Utica, NY 13502
315-733-9848 or 877-844-9848  Fax: 315-733-0247
e-mail: nywbc@aol.com
Web site: www.nywbc.org
*Dedicated to helping women reach their entrepreneurial goals & aspirations through assistance & training*
Donna L. Rebisz, Project Director

**Women's Venture Fund Inc**
220 Fifth Avenue, 9th Floor, New York, NY 10001
212-563-0499
e-mail: info@wvf-ny.org
*Provides support for women entrepreneurs through training, advisory services, loans & technical assistance*
Maria Otero, President & Founder

**Zogby Analytics**
901 Broad Street, Utica, NY 13501
315-624-9642
Web site: www.zogbyanalytics.com
*Polling, surveys, focus groups, market research studies & data analysis for businesses & communities*
Jonathan Zogby, Chief Executive Officer

*Offices and agencies generally appear in alphabetical order, except when specific order is requested by listee.*

# CORPORATIONS, AUTHORITIES & COMMISSIONS

## NEW YORK STATE

### Adirondack Park Agency
1133 NYS Route 86
PO Box 99
Ray Brook, NY 12977
518-891-4050  Fax: 518-891-3938
Web site: www.apa.ny.gov

Chair:
  Leilani Ulrich ........................................518-891-4050
Executive Director:
  Terry Martino .......................................518-891-4050
Counsel:
  James Townsend.....................................518-891-4050
Public Relations:
  Keith McKeever .....................................518-891-4050

### Agriculture & NYS Horse Breeding Development Fund
1 Broadway Center
Schenectady, NY 12305
518-388-0178  Fax: 518-388-2791
e-mail: info@nysirestakes.com
Web site: www.nysirestakes.com

Executive Director:
  M. Kelly Young

### Albany County Airport Authority
Albany International Airport
Administration Building
2nd Floor
Albany, NY 12211
518-242-2222 x1  Fax: 518-242-2641
e-mail: info@albanyairport.com
Web site: www.albanyairport.com

Chief Executive Officer:
  John A O'Donnell PE .........................518-242-2222 x1
Chief Financial Officer:
  William O'Reilly................................518-242-2222 x1
Director, Public Affairs:
  Douglas I. Myers...............................518-242-2222 x1
Counsel:
  Peter F Stuto....................................518-242-2222 x1
Airport Planner:
  Stephen A Iachetta.............................518-242-2222 x1
Administrative Services:
  Liz Charland ....................................518-242-2222 x1

### Albany Port District Commission
106 Smith Blvd, Admin Bldg
Port of Albany
Albany, NY 12202
518-463-8763  Fax: 518-463-8767
e-mail: portofalbany@portofalbany.us
Web site: www.portofalbany.us

Chair:
  Georgette Steffens.................................518-463-8763
General Manager:
  Richard Hendrick ................................518-463-8763
  e-mail: rhendrick@portofalbany.us

Counsel:
  Thomas Owens .....................................518-694-0910

### Atlantic States Marine Fisheries Commission
1050 N. Highland Street
Ste 200 A-N
Arlington, VA 22201
703-842-0740  Fax: 703-842-0741
e-mail: info@asmfc.org
Web site: www.asmfc.org

Chair (NH):
  Douglas E Grout ..................................603-868-1095
  e-mail: douglas.grout@wildlife.nh.gov
Vice Chair (NY):
  James Gilmore......................................631-444-0433
Governor's Appointee, New York:
  Emerson C Hasbrouck, Jr .......................631-928-1524
Executive Director:
  Robert E Beal .....................................703-842-0740
  e-mail: rbeal@asmfc.org
Director Communications:
  Tina Berger .......................................703-842-0740
  e-mail: tberger@asmfc.org

### Battery Park City Authority (Hugh L Carey)
One World Financial Center, 24th Fl
200 Liberty Street
New York, NY 10281
212-417-2000  Fax: 212-417-2001
e-mail: info.bpc@bpca.ny.gov
Web site: www.bpca.ny.gov

Chairman & CEO:
  Dennis Mehiel.....................................212-417-2000
President & Chief Operating Officer:
  Shari Hyman .....................212-417-4205/fax: 212-417-4153
Vice Chair:
  Donald Cappocia..................................212-417-2000
Member:
  Hector Batista ....................................212-417-2000
Member:
  Lester Petracca ...................................212-417-2000
Member:
  Martha J Gallo....................................212-417-2000
VP External Relations:
  Robin Forst .......................212-417-2276/fax: 212-417-2279
  e-mail: robin.forst@bpca.ny.gov

### Brooklyn Navy Yard Development Corporation
63 Flushing Ave, Unit #300
Bldg 292, 3rd Fl
Brooklyn, NY 11205
718-907-5900  Fax: 718-643-9296
e-mail: info@brooklynnavyyard.org
Web site: www.brooklynnavyyard.org

Chair:
  Henry Gutman......................................718-907-5900
President & Chief Executive Officer:
  David Ehrenberg...................................718-907-5900
Executive Vice President/Chief Operating Officer:
  Elliot S. Matz ....................................718-907-5900
General Counsel:
  Paul Kelly ........................................718-907-5900
EVP/Chief of Staff:
  Clare Newman ....................................718-907-5900
Senior Vice President, External Affairs:
  Richard Drucker ..................................718-907-5900

Policy Areas

*Offices and agencies generally appear in alphabetical order, except when specific order is requested by listee.*

## Buffalo & Fort Erie Public Bridge Authority (Peace Bridge Authority)

One Peace Bridge Plaza
Buffalo, NY 14213-2494
716-884-6744  Fax: 716-884-2089
Web site: www.peacebridge.com

Chair (US):
   William Hoyt . . . . . . . . . . . . . . . . . . . .716-884-6744/fax: 716-883-7246
Vice Chair (Canada):
   Anthony M Annunziata . . . . . . . . . . . . . .716-884-6744/fax: 716-883-7246
General Manager:
   Ron Rienas . . . . . . . . . . . . . . . . . . . . . . . . . . .716-884-6744

## Capital District Regional Off-Track Betting Corporation

510 Smith St
Schenectady, NY 12305
518-344-5266 or 800-292-2387  Fax: 518-370-5460
e-mail: customerservice@capitalotb.com
Web site: www.capitalotb.com

Chair:
   Marcel Webb . . . . . . . . . . . . . . . . . . . . . . . .518-344-5225
Board Secretary & Director:
   F James Mumpton . . . . . . . . . . . . . . . . . . . . .518-344-5225
President & Chief Executive Officer:
   John F Signor . . . . . . . . . . . . . . . . . . . . . . .518-344-5225
VP, Corporate Operations:
   Tod Grenci . . . . . . . . . . . . . . . . . . . . . . . . .518-344-5408
VP, Legal Affairs/General Counsel:
   Robert Hemsworth . . . . . . . . . . . . . . . . . . . .518-344-5298
VP, Finance/Comptroller:
   Nancy Priputen-Madrian . . . . . . . . . . . . . . . . .518-344-5233
VP, Human Resources:
   Robert Dantz . . . . . . . . . . . . . . . . . . . . . . . .518-344-5301

## Capital District Regional Planning Commission

One Park Place
Suite 102
Albany, NY 12205
518-453-0850  Fax: 518-453-0856
e-mail: cdrpc@cdrpc.org
Web site: www.cdrpc.org

Executive Director:
   Rocco A Ferraro . . . . . . . . . . . . . . . . . . . . . .518-453-0850
   e-mail: rocky@cdrpc.org
Financial Officer:
   Tim Canty . . . . . . . . . . . . . . . . . . . . . . . . . .518-453-0850

## Capital District Transportation Authority

110 Watervliet Ave
Albany, NY 12206
518-437-8300 or 518-482-8822  Fax: 518-437-8318
Web site: www.cdta.org

Chair:
   David M Stackrow . . . . . . . . . . . . . . . . . . . . .518-437-8311
Vice Chair:
   Georgeanna Nugent Lussier . . . . . . . . . . . . . . . .518-437-8311
CEO:
   Carm Basile . . . . . . . . . . . . . . . . .518-437-6840/fax: 518-437-8349
   e-mail: carmb@cdta.org
General Counsel:
   Amanda A Avery . . . . . . . . . . . . . .518-437-8315/fax: 518-437-8318
   e-mail: amandaa@cdta.org

VP, Finance & Administration:
   Michael P Collins . . . . . . . . . . . . . . .518-437-8330/fax: 518-437-8347
   e-mail: mikec@cdta.org
Director of Transportation:
   Frederick C Gilliam . . . . . . . . . . . . . .518-437-8372/fax: 518-437-8328
   e-mail: fredg@cdta.org
VP, Planning & Infrastructure:
   Christopher G Desany . . . . . . . . . . . . .518-437-8320/fax: 518-437-8328
   e-mail: chrisd@cdta.org

## Catskill Off-Track Betting Corporation

Park Place
Box 3000
Pomona, NY 10970
845-362-0407  Fax: 845-362-0419
e-mail: otb@interbets.com
Web site: www.interbets.com

President:
   Donald J Groth . . . . . . . . . . . . . . . . . . . . . . .845-362-0400

## Central New York Regional Market Authority

2100 Park St
Syracuse, NY 13208
315-422-8647  Fax: 315-422-6897

Commissioner of Agricultural Markets:
   Richard Ball . . . . . . . . . . . . . . .518-457-8876 or 518-457-4188
Commissioner's Representative:
   Troy Waffner . . . . . . . . . . . . . . . . . . . . . . . .315-422-8647

## Central New York Regional Transportation Authority

200 Cortland Ave
PO Box 820
Syracuse, NY 13205-0820
315-442-3400  Fax: 315-442-3337

Chair, Board of Directors:
   Brian M Schultz . . . . . . . . . . . . . . . . . . . . . .315-442-3300
CEO:
   Richard Lee . . . . . . . . . . . . . . . . . . . . . . . . .315-442-3360
VP, Finance:
   Christine LoCurto . . . . . . . . . . . . . . . . . . . . .315-442-3355
Counsel:
   Barry Shulman . . . . . . . . . . . . . . . . . . . . . . .315-442-3400

## Central Pine Barrens Joint Planning & Policy Commission

624 Old Riverhead Road
Westhampton Beach, NY 11978
631-288-1079  Fax: 631-288-1367
e-mail: info@pb.state.ny.us
Web site: www.pb.state.ny.us

Chair & Governor's Appointee & Region 1 Director DEC:
   Peter A Scully . . . . . . . . . . . . . . . . . . . . . . .631-288-1079
Member & Suffolk County Executive:
   Steve Bellone . . . . . . . . . . . . . . . . . . . . . . .631-288-1079
Member & Brookhaven Town Supervisor:
   Edward P. Romaine . . . . . . . . . . . . . . . . . . . .631-288-1079
Member & Riverhead Town Supervisor:
   Sean M Walter . . . . . . . . . . . . . . . . . . . . . . .631-288-1079
Member & Southampton Town Supervisor:
   Anna E Throne-Holst . . . . . . . . . . . . . . . . . . .631-288-1079

## City University Construction Fund

555 W 57th St, 10th Fl
New York, NY 10019

*Offices and agencies generally appear in alphabetical order, except when specific order is requested by listee.*

212-541-0171  Fax: 212-541-0175

Interim Executive Director:
  Judith Bergtraum. . . . . . . . . . . . . . . . . . . . . . . . . . . . . . . . .646-664-2605
  e-mail: iris.weinshall@mail.cuny.edu
Counsel:
  Frederick Schaffer. . . . . . . . . . . . . . . . . . . . . . . . . . . . . . . .646-664-9210

## Delaware River Basin Commission
25 State Police Drive
PO Box 7360
West Trenton, NJ 08628-0360
609-883-9500  Fax: 609-883-9522
Web site: www.nj.gov/drbc

New York Member/Vice Chair:
  Andrew M. Cuomo. . . . . . . . . . . . . . . . . . . . . . . . . . . . . . . . .518-474-8390
Executive Director:
  Steve Tambini . . . . . . . . . . . . . . . . . . . . . . . . . . . . . . .609-883-9500 x200
  e-mail: steve.tambini@drbc.nj.gov
Commission Secretary & Assistant General Counsel:
  Pamela Bush . . . . . . . . . . . . . . . . . . . . . . . . . . . . . . .609-883-9500 x203
  e-mail: pamela.bush@drbc.nj.gov
General Counsel:
  Kenneth J Warren . . . . . . . . . . . . . . . . . . . . . . . . . . . . . . . .484-383-4834
  e-mail: kwarren@warrenenvcounsel.com
Communications Manager:
  Clarke Rupert. . . . . . . . . . . . . . . . . . . . . . . . . . . . . . .609-883-9500 x260

## Development Authority of the North Country
317 Washington Street
Watertown, NY 13601
315-661-3200
e-mail: info@danc.org
Web site: www.danc.org

Chair:
  Gary Turck . . . . . . . . . . . . . . . . . . . . . . . . . . . . . . . . . . . . .315-661-3200
Executive Director:
  James Wright . . . . . . . . . . . . . . . . . . . . . . . . . . . . . . . . . . .315-661-3200
Deputy Executive Director:
  Thomas R Sauter. . . . . . . . . . . . . . . . . . . . . . . . . . . . . . . .315-661-3200
Director, Engineering:
  Carrie Tuttle . . . . . . . . . . . . . . . . . . . . . . . . . . . . . . . . . . .315-661-3210
Telecom Division Manager:
  David Wolf . . . . . . . . . . . . . . . . . . . . . . . . . . . . . . . . . . . .315-661-3200
  e-mail: oatn@danc.org
Landfill Superintendent:
  Steve McElwain . . . . . . . . . . . . . . . . . . . . . . . . . . . . . . . .315-661-3230
Director, Regional Development:
  Michelle Capone. . . . . . . . . . . . . . . . . . . . . . . . . . . . . . . .315-661-3200

## Empire State Development Corporation
633 Third Avenue
Floor 37
New York, NY 10017
212-803-3100  Fax: 212-803-3131
Web site: www.esd.ny.gov

625 Broadway
Albany, NY 12245
518-292-5100

95 Perry Street
Suite 500
Buffalo, NY 14203
716-846-8200
Fax: 716-846-8260

President & CEO, Commissioner:
  Howard Zemsky . . . . . . . . . . . . . . . . . . . . .212-803-3700 or 518-292-5100
  e-mail: president@esd.ny.gov
Chief Operating Officer & Deputy Commissioner:
  Kevin Younis . . . . . . . . . . . . . . . . . . . . . . . . . . . . . . . . . .212-803-3100
Executive Vice President, Administration:
  Ed Hamilton . . . . . . . . . . . . . . . . . . . . . . . . . . . . . . . . . .212-803-3700
Chief Financial Officer:
  Elaine Kloss
Chief of Staff & EVP of State Marketing Strategy:
  Richard Newman

## Great Lakes Commission
2805 S Industrial Hwy
Ste 100
Ann Arbor, MI 48104-6791
734-971-9135  Fax: 734-971-9150
e-mail: teder@glc.org
Web site: www.glc.org

Chairman:
  Jon W Allan . . . . . . . . . . . . . . . . . . . . . . . . . . . . . . . . . . .517-284-5035
  e-mail: allanj@michigan.gov
New York State Commissioner:
  Basil Seggos . . . . . . . . . . . . . . . . . . .518-402-8540/fax: 518-402-8541
Executive Director:
  Tim A Eder . . . . . . . . . . . . . . . . . . . . . . . . . . . . . . . . . . .734-971-9135
  e-mail: teder@glc.org
Deputy Director:
  Thomas R Crane . . . . . . . . . . . . . . . . . . . . . . . . . . . . . . .734-971-9135
  e-mail: tcrane@glc.org
CIO:
  Stephen J Cole . . . . . . . . . . . . . . . . . . . . . . . . . . . . . . . .734-971-9135
  e-mail: scole@glc.org
Program Director:
  Victoria Pebbles . . . . . . . . . . . . . . . . . . . . . . . . . . . . . . .734-971-9135
  e-mail: vpebbles@glc.org
Communications Director:
  Beth Wanamaker. . . . . . . . . . . . . . . . . . . . . . . . . . . . . . .734-971-9135
  e-mail: beth@glc.org
Policy Director:
  Matthew Doss . . . . . . . . . . . . . . . . . . . . . . . . . . . . . . . . .734-971-9135
  e-mail: mdoss@glc.org

## Hudson River-Black River Regulating District
Hudson River Area Office
350 Northern Blvd, Ste 304
Albany, NY 12204
518-465-3491  Fax: 518-432-2485
e-mail: hrao@hrbrrd.com
Web site: www.hrbrrd.com

Chair:
  Mark M Finkle . . . . . . . . . . . . . . . . . . . . . . . . . . . . . . . . .518-465-3491
Executive Director (Acting):
  Richard J Ferrara. . . . . . . . . . . . . . . . . . . . . . . . . . . . . . .518-465-3491
Chief Engineer:
  Robert S Foltan . . . . . . . . . . . . . . . . . . . . . . . . . . . . . . . .518-465-3491
Chief Fiscal Officer:
  Richard J Ferrara. . . . . . . . . . . . . . . . . . . . . . . . . . . . . . .518-465-3491
General Counsel:
  Robert P Leslie . . . . . . . . . . . . . . . . . . . . . . . . . . . . . . . .518-465-3491

## Interest on Lawyer Account (IOLA) Fund of the State of NY
11 East 44th St
Ste 1406
New York, NY 10017

*Offices and agencies generally appear in alphabetical order, except when specific order is requested by listee.*

Policy Areas

646-865-1541 or 800-222-4652  Fax: 646-865-1545
e-mail: iolaf@iola.org
Web site: www.iola.org

Chair:
　Mary Rothwell Davis . . . . . . . . . . . . . . . . . . . . . . . . . .646-865-1541
Executive Director:
　Christopher O'Malley. . . . . . . . . . . . . . . . . . . . . . . . . .646-865-1541
General Counsel:
　Christine M Fecko . . . . . . . . . . . . . . . . . . . . . . . . . . .646-865-1541
Director of Administration:
　Michele D Agard . . . . . . . . . . . . . . . . . . . . . . . . . . . .646-865-1541

## Interstate Environmental Commission
2800 Victory Blvd
6S-106
Staten Island, NY 10314
718-982-3792  Fax: 718-698-8472
e-mail: iecmail@iec-nynjct.org
Web site: www.iec-nynjct.org

Chair (CT):
　Patricia Sesto. . . . . . . . . . . . . . . . . . . . . . . . . . . . . .212-967-1414
Vice Chair (NY):
　Judith L Baron . . . . . . . . . . . . . . . . . . . . . . . . . . . . .212-967-1414
Vice Chair (NJ):
　John M Scagnelli . . . . . . . . . . . . . . . . . . . . . . . . . . . .212-967-1414
Senior Manager:
　Evelyn R Powers. . . . . . . . . . . . . . . . . . . . . . . . . . . . .212-967-1414

## Interstate Oil & Gas Compact Commission
PO Box 53127
900 NE 23rd St
Oklahoma City, OK 73152-3127
405-525-3556  Fax: 405-525-3592
e-mail: iogcc@iogcc.state.ok.us
Web site: www.iogcc.ok.gov

Chair:
　Governor Mary Fallin (OK) . . . . . . . . . . . . . . . . . . . . .405-525-3556
Vice Chair:
　David Porter . . . . . . . . . . . . . . . . . . . . . . . . . . . . . .405-525-3556
Executive Director:
　Mike Smith . . . . . . . . . . . . . . . . . . . . . . . . . . . . . . .405-525-3556
New York State Official Representative:
　Bradley J Field . . . . . . . . . . . . . . . . . . . . . . . . . . . .518-402-8076
Communications Manager:
　Carol Booth. . . . . . . . . . . . . . . . . . . . . . . . . . . . . . .405-525-3556

## Lake George Park Commission
75 Fort George Rd
PO Box 749
Lake George, NY 12845
518-668-9347  Fax: 518-668-5001
e-mail: info@lgpc.state.ny.us
Web site: www.lgpc.state.ny.us

Chair:
　Bruce E Young . . . . . . . . . . . . . . . . . . . . . . . . . . . . .518-668-9347
Executive Director:
　David Wick. . . . . . . . . . . . . . . . . . . . . . . . . . . . . . .518-668-9347
　e-mail: dave@lgpc.state.ny.us
Counsel:
　Eileen Haynes . . . . . . . . . . . . . . . . . . . . . . . . . . . . .518-668-9347
Director of Law Enforcement:
　F. Joe Johns. . . . . . . . . . . . . . . . . . . . . . . . . . . . . .518-668-9347
　e-mail: jjohns@lgpc.state.ny.us

Director, Operations:
　Keith Fish . . . . . . . . . . . . . . . . . . . . . . . . . . . . . . .518-668-9347
　e-mail: keith@lgpc.state.ny.us

## Lawyers' Fund for Client Protection
119 Washington Ave
Albany, NY 12210
518-434-1935 or 800-442-FUND  Fax: 518-434-5641
e-mail: info@nylawfund.org
Web site: www.nylawfund.org

Chair:
　Eric A Seiff . . . . . . . . . . . . . . . . . . . . . . . . . . . . . .518-434-1935
Vice Chair:
　Nancy Burner . . . . . . . . . . . . . . . . . . . . . . . . . . . . .518-434-1935
Executive Director & Counsel:
　Timothy O'Sullivan . . . . . . . . . . . . . . . . . . . . . . . . . .518-434-1935

## Legislative Bill Drafting Commission
Capitol, Rm 308
Albany, NY 12224
518-455-7500  Fax: 518-455-7598

Commissioner:
　Randall G Bluth . . . . . . . . . . . . . . . . . . . . . . . . . . . .518-455-7506
　e-mail: bluth@lbdc.state.ny.us

## Legislative Retrieval System . . . . . . . . . . . . . . . . . . .fax: 518-455-7679
1450 Western Ave, Albany, NY 12203
800-356-6566  Fax: 518-455-7679
Director:
　Burleigh McCutcheon. . . . . . . . . . . . . . . . . . . . . . . . .518-455-7672
　e-mail: mccutcheon@lbdc.state.ny.us

## MTA (Metropolitan Transportation Authority)
2 Broadway
New York, NY 10004
212-878-7000  Fax: 212-878-7264
Web site: www.mta.info

Chairman/CEO:
　Thomas F. Prendergast . . . . . . . . . . . . . . . . . . . . . . . .212-878-7200
Director of Security:
　Raymond Diaz . . . . . . . . . . . . . . . . . . . . . . . . . . . . .212-878-7155
Vice President, Government & Community Relations:
　Lois Tendler . . . . . . . . . . . . . . . . . . . . . . . . . . . . . .212-878-7160
Senior Director, Human Resources/Retirement:
　Margaret M. Connor
CAO/Employee Relations:
　Anita Miller. . . . . . . . . . . . . . . . . . . . . . . . . . . . . . .212-878-7438
Auditor General:
　Michael J Fucilli . . . . . . . . . . . . . . . . . . . . . . . . . . . .212-878-7000
Director, Special Project Development & Planning:
　William Wheeler. . . . . . . . . . . . . . . . . . . . . . . . . . . . .212-878-7278
Chief Financial Officer:
　Robert E. Foran
General Counsel:
　Jerome F Page . . . . . . . . . . . . . . . .212-878-7313/fax: 212-878-7050
Chief of Staff:
　Donna Evans . . . . . . . . . . . . . . . . . . . . . . . . . . . . . .212-878-7206
Director, External Communications:
　Adam Lisberg . . . . . . . . . . . . . . . . . . . . . . . . . . . . . .212-878-7440

## MTA Bridges & Tunnels
2 Broadway
22nd Floor
New York, NY 10004-2801
646-252-7000  Fax: 646-252-7408
Web site: www.mta.info/bandt

*Offices and agencies generally appear in alphabetical order, except when specific order is requested by listee.*

Chairman/CEO:
Thomas F. Prendergast . . . . . . . . . . . . . . . . . . . . . . . . . . . . .212-878-7200
President:
Donald Spero . . . . . . . . . . . . . . . . . . . . . . . . . . . . . . . . . .212-360-3100
Chief Engineer:
Joseph Keane . . . . . . . . . . . . . . . . . . . . . . . . . . . . . . . . .212-878-7200
Vice President, Administration:
Sharon Gallo-Kotcher . . . . . . . . . . . . . . . . . . . . . . . . . . . . . .212-360-3015
Vice President, Operations:
Patrick Parisi . . . . . . . . . . . . . . . . . . . . . . . . . . . . . . . . . . . .212-878-7200
Chief Procurement Officer:
Gavin Masterson . . . . . . . . . . . . . . . . . . . . . . . . . . . . . . . .646-252-7084
Vice President, Staff Services & Chief of Staff:
Albert Rivera . . . . . . . . . . . . . . . . . . . . . . . . . . . . . . . . . .646-252-7421
Chief Financial Officer (Acting):
Mildred Chua . . . . . . . . . . . . . . . . . . . . . . . . . . . . . . . . . .646-252-7132
General Counsel:
M. Margaret Terry . . . . . . . . . . . . . . . . . . . . . . . . . . . . . .212-878-7200
Manager, Public Affairs:
Judith Glave . . . . . . . . . . . . . . . . . . . . . . . . . . . . . . . . . .646-252-7276

## MTA Bus Company
2 Broadway
New York, NY 10004
212-878-7174  Fax: 212-878-0205
Web site: www.mta.info/busco

Chairman/CEO:
Thomas F. Prendergast . . . . . . . . . . . . . . . . . . . . . . . . . . . . .212-878-7200
President:
Darryl Irick . . . . . . . . . . . . . . . . . . . . . . . . . . . . . . . . . . .212-878-7174

## MTA Capital Construction Program
2 Broadway
8th Floor
New York, NY 10002
646-252-4575
Web site: www.mta.info/capital

Chairman/CEO:
Thomas F. Prendergast . . . . . . . . . . . . . . . . . . . . . . . . . . . . .212-878-7200
President:
Dr Michael Horodniceanu . . . . . . . . . . . . . . . . . . . . . . . . .646-252-4277
Chief of Staff:
Ayala Malinovitz . . . . . . . . . . . . . . . . . . . . . . . . . . . . . . . .646-252-4011
Senior Director, Government & Community Affairs:
Richard Mulieri . . . . . . . . . . . . . . . . . . . . . . . . . . . . . . . . .646-252-4197
Executive Vice President:
William Goldstein . . . . . . . . . . . . . . . . . . . . . . . . . . . . . . . .646-252-4277
Senior Vice President &  General Counsel:
Evan Eisland . . . . . . . . . . . . . . . . . . . . . . . . . . . . . . . . . .646-252-4274
Senior Director/Chief Procurement Officer:
David Cannon . . . . . . . . . . . . . . . . . . . . . . . . . . . . . . . . . .646-252-2321
Vice President/Chief Engineer:
Mike Kyriacou . . . . . . . . . . . . . . . . . . . . . . . . . . . . . . . .646-252-4500
Senior Vice President & Program Executive, East Side Access:
Alan Paskoff . . . . . . . . . . . . . . . . . . . . . . . . . . . . . . . . .212-967-0118
Senior Vice President & Program Executive, 2nd Ave Subway:
William Goodrich . . . . . . . . . . . . . . . . . . . . . . . . . . . . . . .212-510-2661
VP & Program Executive, #7 Subway Line Extension:
Mark Schiffman . . . . . . . . . . . . . . . . . . . . . . . . . . . . . . . .646-252-3723
Director, System Safety & Security:
Eric Osnes . . . . . . . . . . . . . . . . . . . . . . . . . . . . . . . . . .646-252-4556
Vice President, Program Controls & Quality Safety:
Raymond Schaeffer . . . . . . . . . . . . . . . . . . . . . . . . . . . . .646-252-5393
Vice President, Planning, Development & External Relations:
Joseph Petrocelli . . . . . . . . . . . . . . . . . . . . . . . . . . . . . .646-252-3813

## MTA Long Island Rail Road
Jamaica Station
Jamaica, NY 11435
718-558-7400  Fax: 718-558-8212
Web site: www.mta.info/lirr

Chairman/CEO:
Thomas F. Prendergast . . . . . . . . . . . . . . . . . . . . . . . . . . . . .212-878-7200
President:
Patrick A Nowakowski . . . . . . . . . . . . . . . . . . . . . . . . . . . .718-558-8252
Executive Vice President:
Albert Cosenza . . . . . . . . . . . . . . . . . . . . . . . . . . . . . . .718-558-7993
e-mail: accosen@lirr.org
Chief Information Officer:
Scott Dieterich . . . . . . . . . . . . . . . . . . . . . . . . . . . . . . .718-588-8166
Vice President, General Counsel & Secretary:
Richard Gans . . . . . . . . . . . . . . . . . . . . . . . . . . . . . . . . .718-558-8264
Vice President, Labor Relations:
Michael Chirillo . . . . . . . . . . . . . . . . . . . . . . . . . . . . . . .718-558-7405
Vice President, Market Development & Public Affairs:
Joseph Calderone . . . . . . . . . . . . . . . . . . . . . . . . . . . . . .718-558-7301
Vice President, ESA/Special Projects:
John Coulter . . . . . . . . . . . . . . . . . . . . . . . . . . . . . . . . .718-558-7363
e-mail: jwcoult@lirr.org
Director, System Safety:
Frank Lo Presti . . . . . . . . . . . . . . . . . . . . . . . . . . . . . . .718-558-7711
General Manager, Public Affairs:
Susan McGowan . . . . . . . . . . . . . . . . . . . . . . . . . . . . . . .718-558-7400

## MTA Metro-North Railroad
2 Broadway
New York, NY 10004
212-340-2677  Fax: 212-340-4995
Web site: www.mta.info/mnr

Chairman/CEO:
Thomas F. Prendergast . . . . . . . . . . . . . . . . . . . . . . . . . . . . .212-878-7200
President:
Joseph Giulietti . . . . . . . . . . . . . . . . . . . . . . . . . . . . . . . . .212-340-2677
General Counsel:
Seth Cummins . . . . . . . . . . . . . . . . . . . . . . . . . . . . . . . .212-340-4933
VP, Finance & Informational Systems:
D. Kim Porcelain . . . . . . . . . . . . . . . . . . . . . . . . . . . . . .212-340-2636
Senior VP, Operations:
Robert Lieblong . . . . . . . . . . . . . . . . . . . . . . . . . . . . . . . .212-499-4300
Senior Director, Capital Planning & Program:
John Kennard . . . . . . . . . . . . . . . . . . . . . . . . . . . . . . . . .212-340-2500
Chief of Staff & Operations:
David Treasure . . . . . . . . . . . . . . . . . . . . . . . . . . . . . . . .212-340-2677
Chief Safety & Security Officer:
Anne Kirsch . . . . . . . . . . . . . . . . . . . . . . . . . . . . . . . . . .212-340-4913
Senior Director, Capital Programs:
Timothy McCartney . . . . . . . . . . . . . . . . . . . . . . . . . . . . .212-340-4913
Vice President, Business Operations:
Thomas Tendy . . . . . . . . . . . . . . . . . . . . . . . . . . . . . . . .212-672-1251
Senior Director, Corporate & Public Affairs:
Mark Mannix . . . . . . . . . . . . . . . . . . . . . . . . . . . . . . . . .212-340-2142

## MTA New York City Transit
2 Broadway
New York, NY 10004
718-330-3000  Fax: 718-596-2146
Web site: www.mta.info/nyct

Chairman/CEO:
Thomas F. Prendergast . . . . . . . . . . . . . . . . . . . . . . . . . . . . .212-878-7200
President:
Veronique Hakim . . . . . . . . . . . . . . . . . . . . . . . . . . . . . . .646-252-5800
Chief Transportation Officer:
Herbert Lambert . . . . . . . . . . . . . . . . . . . . . . . . . . . . . . .718-330-3000

*Offices and agencies generally appear in alphabetical order, except when specific order is requested by listee.*

Policy Areas

Vice President, Labor Relations:
   Christopher Johnson . . . . . . . . . . . . . . . . . . . . . . . . .718-330-3000
Vice President, Corporate Communications:
   Paul Fleuranges. . . . . . . . . . . . . . . . . . . . . . . . . . . . .646-252-5873
Vice President, Technology & Information Services:
   Signey Gellineau. . . . . . . . . . . . . . . . . . . . . . . . . . . . .718-330-3000
Vice President & General Counsel:
   Martin Schnabel . . . . . . . . . . . . . . . . . . . . . . . . . . . . .718-694-3900
Director, Labor Relations:
   Andrew Paul . . . . . . . . . . . . . . . . . . . . . . . . . . . . . . . .646-252-5880

## MTA Office of the Inspector General
2 Penn Paza, 5th Fl
New York, NY 10121
212-878-0000 or 800-682-4448  Fax: 212-878-0003
e-mail: complaints@mtaig.org
Web site: www.mtaig.state.ny.us

Inspector General:
   Barry L Kluger . . . . . . . . . . . . . . . . . . . . . . . . . . . . . .212-878-0000

## Nassau Regional Off-Track Betting Corporation
139 Liberty Ave
Mineola, NY 11501
516-572-2800  Fax: 516-572-2840
e-mail: webmaster@nassauotb.com
Web site: www.nassauotb.com

President:
   Joseph G. Cairo, Jr.. . . . . . . . . . . . . . . . . . . . . . . . . .516-572-2800
Director, Facilities Development:
   John J Sparacio . . . . . . . . . . . . . . . . . . . . . . . . . . . . .516-572-2800

## New England Interstate Water Pollution Control Commission
Wannalancit Mills
650 Suffolk Street
Suite 410
Lowell, MA 01854
978-323-7929  Fax: 978-323-7919
e-mail: mail@neiwpcc.org
Web site: www.neiwpcc.org

Chair (ME):
   Michael Kuhns . . . . . . . . . . . . . . . . . . . . . . . . . . . . .978-323-7929
Vice Chair (MA):
   Douglas Fine . . . . . . . . . . . . . . . . . . . . . . . . . . . . . . .978-323-7929
Commissioner, New York State:
   Basil Seggos . . . . . . . . . . . . . . . . . . . . . . . . . . . . . . .518-402-8545
Executive Director:
   Ronald F Poltak . . . . . . . . . . . . . . . . . . . . . . . . . . . . .978-323-7929
   e-mail: rpoltak@neiwpcc.org
Deputy Director:
   Susan Sullivan. . . . . . . . . . . . . . . . . . . . . . . . . . . . . .978-323-7929
   e-mail: ssullivan@neiwpcc.org

## New York City Housing Development Corporation
110 William St
10th Fl
New York, NY 10038
212-227-5500  Fax: 212-227-6865
e-mail: info@nychdc.com
Web site: www.nychdc.com

Chairperson:
   Vicki Been . . . . . . . . . . . . . . . . . . . . . . . . . . . . . . . .212-863-6100
President:
   Gary D Rodney. . . . . . . . . . . . . . . . . . . . . . . . . . . . . .212-227-3600

Executive VP/COO & General Counsel:
   Richard Froehlich . . . . . . . . . . . . . . . . . . . . . . . . . . .212-227-7435
Executive VP, Real Estate:
   Paula R Carethers . . . . . . . . . . . . . . . . . . . . . . . . . . .212-227-6846
Senior Vice President, Portfolio Management:
   Teresa Gigliello. . . . . . . . . . . . . . . . . . . . . . . . . . . . .212-227-9133
Vice President, Loan Servicing:
   Karen Santiago . . . . . . . . . . . . . . . . . . . . . . . . . . . . .212-227-7494
Chief Credit Officer:
   Mary Horn. . . . . . . . . . . . . . . . . . . . . . . . . . . . . . . . .212-227-9724
Communications/Press Office:
   Vacant. . . . . . . . . . . . . . . . . . . . . . . . . . . . . . . . . . . .212-227-2644

## New York City Residential Mortgage Insurance Corporation
Chair:
   Vicki Been . . . . . . . . . . . . . . . . . . . . . . . . . . . . . . . .212-863-6100
President:
   Gary D Rodney. . . . . . . . . . . . . . . . . . . . . . . . . . . . . .212-227-3600

## New York City School Construction Authority
30-30 Thomson Ave
Long Island City, NY 11101-3045
718-472-8000  Fax: 718-472-8840
Web site: www.nycsca.org

Chair/Chancellor:
   Carmen Farina. . . . . . . . . . . . . . . . . . . . . . . . . . . . . .718-472-8000
President & Chief Executive Officer:
   Lorraine Grillo . . . . . . . . . . . . . . . . . . . . . . . . . . . . .718-472-8001
Executive Vice President & General Counsel:
   Ross J Holden . . . . . . . . . . . . . . . . . . . . . . . . . . . . . .718-472-8220
VP, Finance:
   Marianne Egri . . . . . . . . . . . . . . . . . . . . . . . . . . . . . .718-472-8012
VP, Construction Management:
   Vacant. . . . . . . . . . . . . . . . . . . . . . . . . . . . . . . . . . . .718-472-8359
VP, Architecture & Engineering:
   E Bruce Barrett, RA . . . . . . . . . . . . . . . . . . . . . . . . . .718-472-8710
VP, Administration:
   Rebecca Fraley-Corrado. . . . . . . . . . . . . . . . . . . . . . .718-472-8149

## New York Convention Center Operating Corporation
655 W 34th St
New York, NY 10001-1188
212-216-2000  Fax: 212-216-2588
e-mail: moreinfo@javitscenter.com
Web site: www.javitscenter.com

Chair:
   Henry Silverman. . . . . . . . . . . . . . . . . . . . . . . . . . . . .212-216-2130
President/CEO:
   Alan Steel . . . . . . . . . . . . . . . . . . . . . . . . . . . . . . . . .212-216-2000
SVP/Chief Financial Officer:
   John Menapace. . . . . . . . . . . . . . . . . . . . . . . . . . . . . .212-216-2369
SVP/General Counsel:
   Bradley Siciliano. . . . . . . . . . . . . . . . . . . . . . . . . . . . .212-216-2125
SVP, Sales & Marketing:
   Doreen Guerin. . . . . . . . . . . . . . . . . . . . . . . . . . . . . .212-216-2335

## New York Metropolitan Transportation Council
25 Beaver St
Ste 201
New York, NY 10004
212-383-7200  Fax: 212-383-2418
e-mail: nymtc-web@dot.ny.gov
Web site: www.nymtc.org

Interim Executive Director:
   Lisa Daglian . . . . . . . . . . . . . . . . . . . . . . . . . . . . . . .212-383-7200

*Offices and agencies generally appear in alphabetical order, except when specific order is requested by listee.*

Acting Director, Administration:
   Nina Del Senno . . . . . . . . . . . . . . . . . . . . . . . . . .212-383-2402
      e-mail: nina.delsenno@dot.ny.gov
Director, Planning:
   Gerard J Bogacz . . . . . . . . . . . . . . . . . . . . . . . . .212-383-7260
      e-mail: gerry.bogacz@dot.ny.gov
PIO:
   Stacy Graham-Hunt . . . . . . . . . . . . . . . . . . . . . . . . . .212-383-7203
      e-mail: stacy.graham-hunt@dot.ny.gov

## New York Power Authority
123 Main Street
Mailstop 10-H
White Plains, NY 10601-3170
914-681-6200  Fax: 914-390-8190
e-mail: info@nypa.gov
Web site: www.nypa.gov

Chairman:
   John R. Koelmel . . . . . . . . . . . . . . . . . . . . . . . . . . . .914-287-3636
President & Chief Executive Officer:
   Gil C Quiniones . . . . . . . . . . . . . . . . . . . . . . . . . .914-287-3501
SVP, Corporate Affairs:
   Rocco Iannarelli . . . . . . . . . . . . . . . . . . . . . . . . .518-433-6700
Chief Operating Officer:
   Edward A Welz. . . . . . . . . . . . . . . . . . . . . . . . . . . .518-433-6700
EVP & General Counsel:
   Justin E Driscoll . . . . . . . . . . . . . . . . . . . . . . . . .914-681-6200

## New York State Assn of Fire Districts
PO Box 1419
Massapequa, NY 11758
631-947-2079 or 800-520-9594  Fax: 631-207-1655
Web site: www.firedistnys.com

President:
   Anthony J Gallino. . . . . . . . . . . . . . . . . . . . . . . . . .631-831-6875
      e-mail: president@afdsny.org
First Vice President:
   Thomas Rinaldi. . . . . . . . . . . . . . . . . . . . . . . . . . .518-664-6538
      e-mail: 1vp.president@afdsny.org
Second Vice President:
   Frederick Senti Jr . . . . . . . . . . . . . . . . . . . . . . . . .516-486-3023
      e-mail: 2vp.president@afdsny.org
Secretary & Treasurer:
   Joseph P DeStefano . . . . . . . . . . . . . . . . . . . . . . . .631-947-2079
      e-mail: dacomish@aol.com
Counsel:
   William N Young. . . . . . . . . . . . . . . .800-349-2904 or 518-456-6767
      fax: 518-456-4644
      e-mail: byoung@yfkblaw.com

## New York State Athletic Commission
123 William St
2nd Floor
New York, NY 10038
212-417-5700  Fax: 212-417-4987
e-mail: info@dos.ny.gov
Web site: www.dos.ny.gov/athletic

Chair:
   Tom Hoover . . . . . . . . . . . . . . . . . . . . . . . . . . . . .212-417-5700

## New York State Board of Law Examiners
Corporate Plaza Bldg 3
254 Washington Ave Ext
Albany, NY 12203-5195

518-453-5990  Fax: 518-452-5729
Web site: www.nybarexam.org

Chair:
   Diane F Bosse. . . . . . . . . . . . . . . . . . . . . . . . . . . .518-453-5990
Executive Director:
   John J McAlary. . . . . . . . . . . . . . . . . . . . . . . . . . .518-453-5990

## New York State Bridge Authority
Mid-Hudson Bridge Plaza
PO Box 1010
Highland, NY 12528
845-691-7245  Fax: 845-691-3560
e-mail: info@nysba.ny.gov
Web site: www.nysba.ny.gov

Chair:
   Richard A. Gerentine . . . . . . . . . . . . . . . . . . . . . . .845-691-7245
Vice Chair:
   Joseph Ramaglia . . . . . . . . . . . . . . . . . . . . . . . . . .845-691-7245
Executive Director:
   Joseph Ruggiero . . . . . . . . . . . . . . . . . . . . . . . . . .845-691-7245
Director, IT:
   Gregory J Herd . . . . . . . . . . . . . . . . . . . . . . . . . . .518-828-4107
Director, Toll Collections & Operations:
   Wayne V Ferguson . . . . . . . . . . . . . . . . . . . . . . . . .845-691-7245

## New York State Commission of Correction
80 South Swan St
12th Fl
Albany, NY 12210
518-485-2346  Fax: 518-485-2467
e-mail: infoscoc@scoc.ny.gov
Web site: www.scoc.ny.gov

Chairman:
   Thomas A Beilein
Commissioner & Chair, Medical Review Board:
   Thomas J Loughren
Commissioner & Chair, Citizen's Policy & Complaint Review Counsel:
   Allen Riley
Assistant to Chair:
   Patricia Amati
Counsel:
   Brian Callahan
Director, Operations:
   Terry Moran
      e-mail: Terry.Moran@scoc.ny.gov

## New York State Commission on Judicial Nomination
c/o Greenberg Traurig LLP
54 State Street
Albany, NY 12207
518-689-1400  Fax: 518-689-1499
Web site: www.nysegov.com/cjn/

Chair:
   Vacant. . . . . . . . . . . . . . . . . . . . . . . . . . . . . . . .212-735-3680
Counsel:
   Henry Greenberg. . . . . . . . . . . . . . . . . . . . . . . . . .518-689-1400
      e-mail: greenbergh@gtlaw.com

## New York State Commission on the Restoration of the Capitol
Corning Tower, 31st Fl
Empire State Plaza
Albany, NY 12242
518-473-0341  Fax: 518-486-5720

*Offices and agencies generally appear in alphabetical order, except when specific order is requested by listee.*

Executive Director:
  Andrea J Lazarski . . . . . . . . . . . . . . . . . . . . . . . . . . . . .518-473-0341
  e-mail: andrea.lazarski@ogs.ny.gov

## New York State Disaster Preparedness Commission
Building 7A, Suite 710
1220 Washington Ave
Albany, NY 12242
518-242-5000
Web site: www.dhses.ny.gov/oem/disaster-prep

NYS Div. of Homeland Sec./Emerg. Serv.
633 Third Ave.
32nd Fl.
New York, NY 10017
212-867-7060

Chairman:
  Roger L. Parrino, Sr.

## New York State Dormitory Authority
515 Broadway
Albany, NY 12207-2964
518-257-3000 Fax: 518-257-3100
e-mail: dabonds@dasny.org
Web site: www.dasny.org

One Penn Plaza
52nd Fl
New York, NY 10119-0098
212-273-5000
Fax: 212-273-5121

539 Franklin St
Buffalo, NY 14202-1109
716-884-9780
Fax: 716-884-9787

Chair:
  Alfonso L Carney Jr . . . . . . . . . . . . . . . .518-257-3000/fax: 518-257-3100
President/CEO:
  Paul T Williams Jr. . . . . . . . . . . . . . . . .518-257-3180/fax: 518-257-3183
Vice President:
  Michael T Corrigan . . . . . . . . . . . . . . .518-257-3192/fax: 518-257-3183
Acting Chief Financial Officer:
  Linda H Button . . . . . . . . . . . . . . . . . .518-257-3562/fax: 518-257-3100
General Counsel:
  Michael Cusack. . . . . . . . . . . . . . . . .518-257-3120/fax: 518-257-3101
Managing Director, Construction:
  Stephen D Curro, PE . . . . . . . . . . . . . .518-257-3271/fax: 518-257-3100
  e-mail: scurro@dasny.org
Managing Director, Public Finance & Portfolio Monitoring:
  Portia Lee. . . . . . . . . . . . . . . . . . .518-257-3362/fax: 518-257-3100
  e-mail: plee@dasny.org
Public Information Officer:
  John Chirlin. . . . . . . . . . . . . . . . . . . . . . . . . . . . . . . .518-257-3380
  e-mail: jchirlin@dasny.org

## New York State Energy Research & Development Authority
17 Columbia Circle
Albany, NY 12203-6399
518-862-1090 Fax: 518-862-1091
e-mail: info@nyserda.ny.gov
Web site: www.nyserda.ny.gov

Chairman:
  Richard L. Kauffman . . . . . . . . . . . . . . . . . . . . . . . . . . . . .518-486-9746
President & CEO:
  John B Rhodes. . . . . . . . . . . . . . . . . . . . . . . . . . . .518-862-1090 x3278
General Counsel:
  Noah C Shaw. . . . . . . . . . . . . . . . . . . . . . . . . . . . .518-862-1090 x3280
Program Manager, Economic Development & Community Outreach:
  Kelly Tyler . . . . . . . . . . . . . . . . . . . . . . . . . . .716-842-1522 x 3005
  e-mail: kelly.tyler@nyserda.ny.gov
Director, Communications:
  Kate Muller. . . . . . . . . . . . . . . .518-862-1090 x3582/fax: 518-862-1091
  e-mail: kate.muller@nyserda.ny.gov

## New York State Environmental Facilities Corp
625 Broadway
Albany, NY 12207-2997
518-402-6924 or 800-882-9721  Fax: 518-486-9323
e-mail: press@efc.ny.gov
Web site: www.nysefc.org

President/CEO:
  Sabrina M Ty . . . . . . . . . . . . . . . . . . . . . . . . . . . . . . . .518-402-6951
Legal Division/General Counsel:
  James R Levine. . . . . . . . . . . . . . . . . . . . . . . . . . . . . . .518-402-6969
Director, Engineering & Program Management:
  Timothy P Burns. . . . . . . . . . . . . . . . . . . . . . . . . . . . . .518-402-7396
Director, Technical Advisory Services:
  Vacant . . . . . . . . . . . . . . . . . . . . . . . . . . . . . . . . . . . .518-402-7461
Director, PIO:
  Jon Sorensen . . . . . . . . . . . . . . . . . . . . . . . . . . . . . . . .518-402-6924
Controller & Director, Corporate Operations:
  Michael Malinoski . . . . . . . . . . . . . . . . . . . . . . . . . . . . .518-486-9267

## New York State Gaming Commission
1 Broadway Center
P.O. Box 7500
Schenectady, NY 12301-7500
518-388-3300
e-mail: info@gaming.ny.gov
Web site: www.gaming.ny.gov

Gaming Commissioner:
  Peter J Moschetti, Jr . . . . . . . . . . . . . . . . . . . . . . . . . . . .518-388-3400
Gaming Commissioner:
  Todd R. Snyder. . . . . . . . . . . . . . . . . . . . . . . . . . . . . . .518-388-3400
Gaming Commissioner & Chair:
  Barry Sample. . . . . . . . . . . . . . . . . . . . . . . . . . . . . . . .518-388-3400
Gaming Commissioner:
  John A Crotty . . . . . . . . . . . . . . . . . . . . . . . . . . . . . . . .518-388-3400
Gaming Commissioner:
  John J Poklemba . . . . . . . . . . . . . . . . . . . . . . . . . . . . . .518-388-3400
Executive Director:
  Robert Williams . . . . . . . . . . . . . . . . . . . . . . . . . . . . . .518-388-3400
Director, Communications:
  Brad Maione . . . . . . . . . . . . . . . . . . . . . . . . . . . . . . . .518-388-3415

## Joint Commission on Public Ethics (JCOPE)
540 Broadway
Albany, NY 12207
518-408-3976  Fax: 518-408-3975
e-mail: jcope@jcope.ny.gov
Web site: www.jcope.ny.gov

Executive Director:
  Seth Agata. . . . . . . . . . . . . . . . . . . . . . . . . . . . . . . . . .518-408-3976
Chair:
  Daniel J Horwitz. . . . . . . . . . . . . . . . . . . . . . . . . . . . . .518-408-3976
General Counsel:
  Monica Stamm . . . . . . . . . . . . . . . . . . . . . . . . . . . . . . .518-408-3976

*Offices and agencies generally appear in alphabetical order, except when specific order is requested by listee.*

Chief of Staff:
   Kevin T Gagan . . . . . . . . . . . . . . . . . . . .518-408-3976/fax: 518-408-3975

## New York State Financial Control Board
123 William St
23rd Fl
New York, NY 10038-3804
212-417-5046  Fax: 212-417-5055
e-mail: nysfcb@fcb.state.ny.us
Web site: www.fcb.state.ny.us

Acting Executive Director:
   Jeffrey Sommer. . . . . . . . . . . . . . . . . . . . . . . . . . . . . .212-417-5066
Deputy Director, Expenditure & Covered Organization Analysis:
   Dennis DeLisle . . . . . . . . . . . . . . . . . . . . . . . . . . . . . .212-417-5069
Deputy Director, Finance & Capital Analysis:
   Jewel A Douglas. . . . . . . . . . . . . . . . . . . . . . . . . . . . . .212-417-5067
Acting Deputy Director, Economic & Revenue Analysis:
   Martin Fischman. . . . . . . . . . . . . . . . . . . . . . . . . . . . . .212-417-5068
Associate Director, Administration:
   Mattie W Taylor . . . . . . . . . . . . . . . . . . . . . . . . . . . . . .212-417-5053

## New York State Higher Education Services Corp (NYSHESC)
99 Washington Ave
Albany, NY 12255
888-697-4372
Web site: www.hesc.ny.gov

Executive Vice President & Acting President:
   Elsa Magee . . . . . . . . . . . . . . . . . . . . .518-474-5592/fax: 518-474-5593
   e-mail: elsa.magee@hesc.ny.gov
Director, Training & Information Services:
   Teresa Gehrer . . . . . . . . . . . . . . . . .518-402-6429/fax: 518-474-2839
Director, Federal Relations:
   Frank Ballmann. . . . . . . . . . . . . . . . . . . . . . . . . . . . . .202-721-1186
   e-mail: frank.ballmann@hesc.ny.gov
Director, Audit:
   Matt Downey. . . . . . . . . . . . . . . . . . . .518-473-2287/fax: 518-486-6515
   e-mail: matt.downey@hesc.ny.gov
General Counsel:
   Thomas Brennan . . . . . . . . . . . . . . . . .518-473-1585/fax: 518-486-6515
   e-mail: thomas.brennan@hesc.ny.gov
Communications/PIO:
   Vacant. . . . . . . . . . . . . . . . . . . . . . . .518-474-5592 or 518-474-5775
   fax: 518-474-5593
Director, Federal Operations:
   Victor Stucchi . . . . . . . . . . . . . . . . . .518-486-5885/fax: 518-402-3276
   e-mail: victor.stucchi@hesc.ny.gov
Administrative Officer & CFO:
   Warren Wallin . . . . . . . . . . . . . . . . . . .518-486-5885/fax: 518-474-4301
   e-mail: warren.wall@hesc.ny.gov

## New York State Homes & Community Renewal
641 Lexington Ave
New York, NY 10022
866-275-3427
e-mail: hcrinfo@nyshcr.org
Web site: www.nyshcr.org

Hampton Plaza
38-40 State Street
Albany, NY 12207
518-473-2526

Commissioner/CEO:
   RuthAnne Visnauskas

Executive Deputy Commissioner & Chief Operating Officer:
   Betsy Mallow . . . . . . . . . . . . . . . . . . . . . . . . . . . . . . .866-275-3427
President, Office of Housing Preservation:
   Mark Colon. . . . . . . . . . . . . . . . . . . . . . . . . . . . . . . . .866-275-3427
General Counsel:
   Adam Schuman. . . . . . . . . . . . . . . . . . . . . . . . . . . . . .212-480-6700
Chief of Staff:
   Meredith Levine . . . . . . . . . . . . . . . . . . . . . . . . . . . . .212-480-6700
Director, Fair Housing & Equal Opportunity:
   Wanda Graham . . . . . . . . . . . . . . . . . . . . . . . . . . . . . .212-480-6700
Public Information:
   . . . . . . . . . . . . . . . . . . . . . . . . . . . . . . . . . . . . . . . . .212-872-0338

## New York State Judicial Conduct Commission
61 Broadway
12th Floor
New York, NY 10006
646-386-4800  Fax: 646-458-0037
e-mail: cjc@cjc.ny.gov
Web site: www.cjc.ny.gov

Corning Tower
Suite 2301
Empire State Plaza
Albany, NY 12223
518-453-4600
Fax: 518-486-1850

Chair:
   Joseph W Belluck . . . . . . . . . . . . . . . . . . . . . . . . . . . .646-386-4800
Vice Chair:
   Paul B Harding . . . . . . . . . . . . . . . . . . . . . . . . . . . . . .646-386-4800
Administrator & Counsel:
   Robert H Tembeckjian . . . . . . . . . . . . . . . . . . . . . . . . .646-386-4800
Deputy Administrator in Charge, Albany Office:
   Cathleen Cenci . . . . . . . . . . . . . . . . . . . . . . . . . . . . . .518-453-4600
Deputy Administrator in Charge, Rochester Office:
   John J Postel . . . . . . . . . . . . . . . . . . . . . . . . . . . . . . .585-232-5756
Deputy Administrator in Charge, New York City Office:
   Mark Levine . . . . . . . . . . . . . . . . . . . . . . . . . . . . . . . .646-386-4800
Deputy Administrator, Litigation:
   Edward Lindner . . . . . . . . . . . . . . . . . . . . . . . . . . . . . .518-474-5617
Clerk:
   Jean M Savanyu, Esq . . . . . . . . . . . . . . . . . . . . . . . . . .646-386-4800

## New York State Law Reporting Bureau
17 Lodge Street
Albany, NY 12207
518-453-6900  Fax: 518-426-1640

State Reporter:
   William J Hooks. . . . . . . . . . . . . . . . . . . . . . . . . . . . . .518-453-6900
Deputy State Reporter:
   Katherine D LaBoda, Esq. . . . . . . . . . . . . . . . . . . . . . . .518-453-6900
   e-mail: Reporter@courts.state.ny.us
Assistant State Reporter:
   Cara J Broussea, Esq. . . . . . . . . . . . . . . . . . . . . . . . . .518-453-6900
   e-mail: Reporter@courts.state.ny.us

## New York State Law Revision Commission
80 New Scotland Ave
Albany, NY 12208
518-472-5858  Fax: 518-445-2303
e-mail: nylrc@albanylaw.edu
Web site: www.lawrevision.state.ny.us

Chairman:
   Peter J. Kiernan. . . . . . . . . . . . . . . . . . . . . . . . . . . . . .518-408-2051

*Offices and agencies generally appear in alphabetical order, except when specific order is requested by listee.*

Policy Areas

Executive Director:
Rose Mary Bailly ................................518-472-5858
Chairman:
Vincent G Bradley ..............518-474-3114 or 212-961-8300
Commissioner:
Greeley T Ford ..................518-474-3114 or 212-961-8300
Counsel to the Authority:
Vacant .........................................518-474-3114
Commissioner:
Lily M Fan .....................................518-474-3114
Director, Public Affairs:
William Crowley ..............518-474-3114 or 518-474-4875
fax: 518-473-9565
e-mail: William.Crowley@sla.ny.gov

## New York State Olympic Regional Development Authority

Olympic Center
2634 Main Street
Lake Placid, NY 12946
518-523-1655  Fax: 518-523-9275
e-mail: info@orda.org
Web site: www.orda.org/corporate

President & CEO:
Ted Blazer .................................518-523-1655 x201
e-mail: blazer@orda.org
Vice President:
Jeffrey Byrne ..............................518-523-1655 x203
e-mail: byrne@orda.org
Olympic Center Manager:
Dennis Allen ...............................518-523-1655 x222
e-mail: allen@orda.org
Director, Corporate Development:
Jeff Potter .....................................518-523-1655
e-mail: jpotter@orda.org
Director, Events:
Katie Million ...............................518-523-1655 x212
e-mail: kmillion@orda.org
Director, Finance:
Padraig Power ...............................518-523-1655 x217
e-mail: ppower@orda.org
Communications Manager:
Jon Lundin ....................................518-523-1655
e-mail: jlundin@orda.org

## New York State Teachers' Retirement System

10 Corporate Woods Dr
Albany, NY 12211-2395
518-447-2900 or 800-348-7298  Fax: 518-447-2695
e-mail: media@nystrs.org
Web site: www.nystrs.org

Executive Director:
Thomas K Lee...................................518-447-2726
General Counsel:
Joseph J. Indelicato, Jr........................518-447-2722
Actuary:
Richard Young ................................518-447-2692
Managing Director Operations:
Kevin Schaefer ................................518-447-2730
Director, Member Relations:
Sheila Gardella ...............................518-447-2684
Manager, Public Information:
John Cardillo ...................518-447-4743/fax: 518-447-2875
e-mail: john.cardillo@nystrs.org
Managing Director, Real Estate:
David C. Gillian ...............................518-447-2751

## New York State Thoroughbred Breeding & Development Fund Corporation

One Broadway Center
Suite 601
Schenectady, NY 12305
518-388-0174  Fax: 518-344-1235
e-mail: nybreds@nybreds.com
Web site: www.nybreds.com

Executive Director:
Tracy Egan ....................................518-388-0174

## New York State Thruway Authority

200 Southern Blvd
PO Box 189
Albany, NY 12201
518-436-2700  Fax: 518-436-2899
Web site: www.thruway.ny.gov

Chair:
Joanne M Mahoney...............................518-436-3000
Interim Executive Director:
Maria Lehman..................................518-436-2900
General Counsel:
Gordon Cuffy ..................................518-436-2840
CFO:
Matt Howard...................................518-436-2840
Director, Media Relations & Communications:
Jennifer Givner ...............................518-471-5300

### New York State Canal Corporation

Web site: www.canals.ny.gov
Interim Executive Director:
Maria Lehman ...............518-436-3055/fax: 518-471-5023
Director of Canals:
Brian U. Stratton..............................518-436-3055

## New York State Tug Hill Commission

Dulles State Office Bldg
317 Washington St
Watertown, NY 13601
315-785-2380  Fax: 315-785-2574
e-mail: tughill@tughill.org
Web site: www.tughill.org

Chair:
Jan Bogdanowicz ...............................315-785-2380
Executive Director:
Katie Malinowski...............................315-785-2570
e-mail: katie@tughill.org

## Niagara Falls Bridge Commission

5365 Military Rd
Lewiston, NY 14092
716-285-6322 or 905-354-5641  Fax: 716-282-3292
e-mail: general_inquiries@niagarafallsbridges.com
Web site: www.niagarafallsbridges.com

Chair:
Linda L McAusland .............................716-285-6322
Vice Chair:
Russell G Quarantello..........................716-285-6322
Treasurer:
Harry R Palladino .............................716-285-6322
Secretary:
John Lopinski .................................716-285-6322

*Offices and agencies generally appear in alphabetical order, except when specific order is requested by listee.*

## Niagara Frontier Transportation Authority

181 Ellicott St
Buffalo, NY 14203
716-855-7300 or 800-622-1220  Fax: 716-855-6655
Web site: www.nfta.com

Chair:
  Sister Denise A. Roche
Executive Director:
  Kimberley A Minkel................................716-855-7470
Chief Financial Officer:
  John Cox.........................................716-855-7300
General Counsel:
  David J State.....................................716-855-7686
Director, Aviation:
  William Vanecek..................................716-630-6030
Director, Human Resources:
  Karen Novo.......................................716-855-7343
Director, Public Transit:
  Thomas George...................................716-855-7390
Director, Engineering:
  Michael Bykowski.................................716-855-7389
Director, Public Affairs:
  C Douglas Hartmayer.............................716-855-7420
Chief, NFTA Police:
  George W. Gast...................................716-855-7666

## Northeastern Forest Fire Protection Commission

21 Parmenter Terrace
PO Box 6192
China Village, ME 04926
207-968-3782  Fax: 207-968-3782
e-mail: info@nffpc.org
Web site: www.nffpc.org

Executive Committee Chair:
  Steven Sinclair...................................802-241-3680
  e-mail: ssinclair@vermont.gov
Executive Director/Center Manager:
  Thomas G Parent.................................207-968-3782
  e-mail: necompact@fairpoint.net
Operations Committee, Chair:
  Rick Vollick......................................413-770-1235
  e-mail: rvollick@gmail.com
New York Fire Prevention & Education:
  Andrew Jacob....................................518-402-8840
  e-mail: atjacob@gw.dec.state.ny.us

## Ogdensburg Bridge & Port Authority

One Bridge Plaza
Ogdensburg, NY 13669
315-393-4080  Fax: 315-393-7068
e-mail: obpa@ogdensport.com
Web site: www.ogdensport.com

Chair:
  Samuel J LaMacchia..............................315-393-4080
Executive Director:
  Wade A Davis....................................315-393-4080
  e-mail: wadavis@ogdensport.com

## Ohio River Valley Water Sanitation Commission

5735 Kellogg Ave
Cincinnati, OH 45230
513-231-7719  Fax: 513-231-7761
e-mail: info@orsanco.org
Web site: www.orsanco.org

New York State Commissioner:
  Douglas E Conroe................................513-231-7719
New York State Commissioner:
  Michael P Wilson.................................513-231-7719
New York State Commissioner:
  Basil Seggos......................................518-402-8545
Executive Director:
  Richard Harrison.........................513-231-7719 ext 105
  e-mail: rharrison@orsanco.org
Source Water Protection/Emergency Response/External Relations:
  Jerry Schulte............................513-231-7719 ext 104
  e-mail: jschulte@orsanco.org
Communications Coordinator:
  Lisa Cochran............................513-231-7719 ext 102
  e-mail: lcochran@orsanco.org

## Port Authority of New York & New Jersey

4 World Trade Center
150 Greenwich Street
New York, NY 10007
212-435-7000  Fax: 212-435-4032
Web site: www.panynj.gov

Chair, New Jersey:
  John J Degnan...................................212-435-7000
Vice Chair, New York:
  Scott H Rechler...................................212-435-7000
Executive Director:
  Patrick Foye.....................................212-435-7271
Director World Trade Center Operations:
  Hugh P McCann..................................212-435-7887
Director, Government & Community Affairs - NY (Acting):
  Ian R Van Praagh................................212-435-6903
Assistant General Counsel:
  Carlene V McIntyre..............................212-435-3515
Chief Financial Officer:
  Elizabeth McCarthy..............................212-435-7738
Director Media Relations:
  Ron Marsico.....................212-435-7777/fax: 212-435-4032
Director, Public Safety/Superintendent of Police:
  Michael A Fedorko...............................212-435-7000
Chief Engineer:
  James A Starace.................................212-435-7449
Office of Secretary:
  Karen E Eastman.................................212-435-6528

## Port of Oswego Authority

1 East Second St
Oswego, NY 13126
315-343-4503  Fax: 315-343-5498
e-mail: shipping@portoswego.com
Web site: www.portoswego.com

Chairman:
  Terrence Hammill.................................315-343-4503
Executive Director & CEO:
  Zelko N. Kirincich.............................315-343-4503 x111
Manager, Administrative Services/Facility Security Officer:
  William Scriber...............................315-343-4503 x108
  e-mail: wscriber@portoswego.com
Supervisor of Marina Operations:
  Bernie Bacon.....................................315-343-1967
  e-mail: oswegomarina@yahoo.com

## Rochester-Genesee Regional Transportation Authority-RTS

1372 E Main St
PO Box 90629
Rochester, NY 14609

*Offices and agencies generally appear in alphabetical order, except when specific order is requested by listee.*

**103**

585-654-0200 or 585-288-1700  Fax: 585-654-0224
Web site: www.myrts.com

Chief Executive Officer:
  Bill Carpenter . . . . . . . . . . . . . . . . . . . . . . . . . . . .585-654-0200
Chief Operating Officer:
  Miguel A Velazquez. . . . . . . . . . . . . . . . . . . . . . . . .585-654-0200
Chief Financial Officer:
  Scott Adair . . . . . . . . . . . . . . . . . . . . . . . . . . . . . .585-654-0200
General Counsel/CAO:
  Daniel DeLaus . . . . . . . . . . . . . . . . . . . . . . . . . . . .585-654-0200
Public Information Officer:
  Tom Brede. . . . . . . . . . . . . . . . . . . . . . . . . . . . . . .585-654-0730

## Roosevelt Island Operating Corporation (RIOC)
591 Main St
Roosevelt Island, NY 10044
212-832-4540  Fax: 212-832-4582
e-mail: information@rioc.ny.gov

President/CEO:
  Charlene M Indelicato . . . . . . . . . . . . . . . . . . . . . .212-832-4540 x319
Director Island Operations:
  Cyril Opperman . . . . . . . . . . . . . . . . . . . . . . . . . .212-832-4583
  e-mail: cyril.opperman@rioc.ny.gov
VP/General Counsel:
  Donald D. Lewis . . . . . . . . . . . . . . . . . . . . . . . . . .212-832-4540 x311
  e-mail: donald.lewis@rioc.ny.gov
VP/Chief Financial Officer:
  Frances Walton . . . . . . . . . . . . . . . . . . . . . . . . . . .212-832-4540 x350
Director Public Safety:
  Captain Estrella Suarez. . . . . . . . . . . . . . . . . . . . . .212-832-4545
  e-mail: keith.guerra@rioc.ny.gov

## State University Construction Fund
353 Broadway
Albany, NY 12246
518-320-3200  Fax: 518-443-1008
Web site: www.sucf.suny.edu

General Manager:
  Robert M Haelen. . . . . . . . . . . . . . . . . . . . . . . . . .518-320-1502
Associate Counsel:
  Terese Meagher. . . . . . . . . . . . . . . . . . . . . . . . . . .518-320-1746

## Suffolk Regional Off-Track Betting Corporation
425 Oser Ave
Ste 2
Hauppauge, NY 11788
631-853-1000  Fax: 631-853-1086
e-mail: customerservice@suffolkotb.com
Web site: www.suffolkotb.com

President/CEO:
  Philip C. Nolan . . . . . . . . . . . . . . . . . . . . . . . . . . .631-853-1000
Vice President:
  Anthony Pancella . . . . . . . . . . . . . . . . . . . . . . . . . .631-853-1000
General Counsel:
  James McManmon . . . . . . . . . . . . . . . . . . . . . . . . .631-853-1000
Director Governmental & Public Affairs:
  Debbie Pfeiffer . . . . . . . . . . . . . . . . . . . . . . . . . . .631-853-1000

## Thousand Islands Bridge Authority
PO Box 428, Collins Landing
43530 Interstate 81
Alexandria Bay, NY 13607

315-482-2501 or 315-658-2281  Fax: 315-482-5925
e-mail: info@tibridge.com
Web site: www.tibridge.com

Chair:
  Robert Barnard . . . . . . . . . . . . . . . . . . . . . . . . . . .315-482-2501
Executive Director:
  Robert G Horr, III . . . . . . . . . . . . . . . . . . . . . . . . .315-482-2501
  e-mail: roberthorr@tibridge.com
Legal Counsel:
  Dennis Whelpley . . . . . . . . . . . . . . . . . . . . . . . . . .315-482-2501

## Uniform State Laws Commission
c/o Coughlin & Gerhart LLP
99 Corporate Drive
PO Box 2059
Binghamton, NY 13902-2039
607-723-9511  Fax: 607-723-1530

Chair:
  Richard B Long. . . . . . . . . . . . . . . . . . . . . . . . . . .607-821-2202
  e-mail: rlong@cglawoffices.com
Member:
  Sandra Stern . . . . . . . . . . . . . . . . . . . . . . . . . . . .212-207-8150
Member:
  Norman L. Greene . . . . . . . . . . . . . . . . . . . . . . . . .212-661-5030
Member:
  Justin L. Vigdor . . . . . . . . . . . . . . . . . . . . . . . . . .585-232-5300 ext 228
Member:
  Mark F Glaser. . . . . . . . . . . . . . . . . . . . . . . . . . . .518-689-1413

## United Nations Development Corporation
Two United Nations Plaza, 27th Fl
New York, NY 10017
212-888-1618  Fax: 212-588-0758
e-mail: info@undc.org
Web site: www.undc.org

Chair, Board of Directors:
  George Klein. . . . . . . . . . . . . . . . . . . . . . . . . . . . .212-888-1618
Sr VP & General Counsel/Secretary:
  Robert Cole . . . . . . . . . . . . . . . . . . . . . . . . . . . . .212-888-1618
Controller/Treasurer:
  Jorge Ortiz. . . . . . . . . . . . . . . . . . . . . . . . . . . . . .212-888-1618
Vice President:
  Kenneth Coopersmith . . . . . . . . . . . . . . . . . . . . . . .212-888-1618

## Waterfront Commission of New York Harbor
39 Broadway, 4th Fl
New York, NY 10006
212-742-9280  Fax: 212-480-0587
Web site: www.wcnyh.org

Commissioner, New York:
  Ronald Goldstock . . . . . . . . . . . . . . . . . . . . . . . . .212-742-9280
Commissioner, New Jersey:
  Michael Murphy . . . . . . . . . . . . . . . . . . . . . . . . . .212-742-9280
Executive Director:
  Walter M Arsenault . . . . . . . . . . . . . . . . . . . . . . . .212-905-9201
General Counsel:
  Phoebe S Sorial. . . . . . . . . . . . . . . . . . . . . . . . . . .212-742-8965

## Western Regional Off-Track Betting Corp
8315 Park Road
Batavia, NY 14020
585-343-3750  Fax: 585-343-6873
e-mail: info@westernotb.com
Web site: www.westernotb.com

*Offices and agencies generally appear in alphabetical order, except when specific order is requested by listee.*

Chair:
  Richard D Bianchi . . . . . . . . . . . . . . . . . . . . . . . . . . . . . . .585-343-3750
President & Chief Executive Officer:
  Michael D Kane . . . . . . . . . . . . . . . . . . . . . . . . . . . . . . . . .585-343-3750
VP-Administration:
  William R White. . . . . . . . . . . . . . . . . . . . . . . . . . . . . . . . .585-343-3750
General Counsel:
  Henry Wojtaszek. . . . . . . . . . . . . . . . . . . . . . . . . . . . . . . . .585-343-3750

Director, Video Gaming:
  Mark Wolf. . . . . . . . . . . . . . . . . . . . . . . . . . . . . . . . . . . . .585-343-3750
Communications/Mutuels Manager:
  James Haas . . . . . . . . . . . . . . . . . . . . . . . . . . . . . . . . . . . .585-343-3750
Manager, Branch Operations:
  Edward Merriman. . . . . . . . . . . . . . . . . . . . . . . . . . . . . . . . .585-343-3750

*Offices and agencies generally appear in alphabetical order, except when specific order is requested by listee.*

# CRIME & CORRECTIONS

## NEW YORK STATE

## GOVERNOR'S OFFICE

### Governor's Office
Executive Chamber
State Capitol
Albany, NY 12224
518-474-8390  Fax: 518-474-1513
Web site: www.ny.gov

Governor:
  Andrew M Cuomo . . . . . . . . . . . . . . . . . . . . . . . . . . . . . . . . .518-474-8390
Secretary to the Governor:
  Melissa DeRosa . . . . . . . . . . . . . . . . . . . . .518-474-4246 or 212-681-4580
Counsel to the Governor:
  Kumiki Gibson . . . . . . . . . . . . . . . . . . . . . . .518-474-8343 or 212-681-4580
First Assistant Counsel:
  R Nadine Fontaine . . . . . . . . . . . . . . . . . . . . . . . . . . . .518-474-8434
Chief of Staff:
  Jill DesRosiers . . . . . . . . . . . . . . . . . . . . .518-474-8390 or 212-681-4580
Director, Communications:
  Peter Ajemian . . . . . . . . . . . . . . . . . . . . . . .518-474-8418 or 212-681-4640

## EXECUTIVE DEPARTMENTS AND RELATED AGENCIES

### Corrections & Community Supervision Department
1220 Washington Avenue
Building 2, State Campus
Albany, NY 12226-2050
518-457-8126
Web site: www.doccs.ny.gov

Acting Commissioner:
  Anthony J Annucci. . . . . . . . . . . . . . . . . .518-457-8134 or 518-457-1748
Deputy Commissioner & Counsel:
  Kevin Bruen . . . . . . . . . . . . . . . . . . . . . . . . . . . . . . . .518-485-9613
Assistant Commissioner & Executive Assistant:
  Melissa Coolidge . . . . . . . . . . . . . . . . . . . . . . . . . . . .518-457-1281
Deputy Commissioner, Health Services Division/Chief Medical Officer:
  Carl Koenigsmann, MD . . . . . . . . . . . . . . . .518-457-7073
Deputy Commissioner, Program Services:
  Jeffrey McKoy . . . . . . . . . . . . . . . . . . . . . . . . . . . .518-457-5555
Asst Commissioner, Program Services:
  Catherine Jacobsen . . . . . . . . . . . . . . . . . . . . . . . . .518-408-5825
Director, Public Information:
  Thomas Mailey . . . . . . . . . . . . . . . . . . . . . . . . . . . . .518-457-8182

### Administrative Services
Acting Deputy Commissioner:
  Stephen Brandow . . . . . . . . . . . . . . . . . . . . . . . . . . .518-457-8188
Assistant Commissioner:
  Thomas Corcoran . . . . . . . . . . . . . . . . . . . . . . . . . . .518-457-7135

#### Budget & Finance Division
Director:
  Sandy Downey . . . . . . . . . . . . . . . . . . . . . . . . . . . . . .518-457-5562

#### Diversity Management
Director:
  Deborah E. Nazon . . . . . . . . . . . . . . . . . . . . . . . . . .518-485-5806

#### Human Resources Management Division
Director, Personnel:
  Darren Ayotte . . . . . . . . . . . . . . . . . . . . . . . . . . . . . .518-457-9887

#### Support Operations
550 Broadway, Menands, NY 12204
Director:
  Nannette Ferri . . . . . . . . . . . . . . . . . . . . . . .518-436-7886 x3015

### Inmate Grievance
Director:
  Karen Bellamy . . . . . . . . . . . . . . . . . . . . . . . . . . . . . .518-457-1885
Deputy Commissioner, Correctional Industries & Accreditation:
  Osbourne A McKay . . . . . . . . . . . . . . . . . . . . . . . . . .518-485-2858

### Internal Controls
Director:
  Peter Berezny . . . . . . . . . . . . . . . . . . . . . . . . . . . . . . .518-485-1394
Special Assistant for Labor Relations:
  John Shipley . . . . . . . . . . . . . . . . . . . . . . . . . . . . . . . .518-457-7291

### Training Academy
1134 New Scotland Rd, Albany, NY 12208
Director:
  Joseph Tewksbury . . . . . . . . . . . . . . . . . . . . . . . . . .518-489-9072

## Correctional Facility Operations
Deputy Commissioner:
  James O'Gorman . . . . . . . . . . . . . . . . . . . . . . . . . . . .518-457-8138
Assistant Commissioner:
  Patricia Le Coney . . . . . . . . . . . . . . . . . . . . . . . . . . .518-457-5902
Chief of Investigations & Inspector General:
  Vernon Fonda . . . . . . . . . . . . . . . . . . . . . . . . . . . . . . .518-457-2653
Associate Commissioner, Population Management:
  Ann Marie McGrath . . . . . . . . . . . . . . . . . . . . . . . . . .518-457-7261

### Correctional Industries Division . . . . . . . . . . . . . . . . .fax: 518-436-6007
Corcraft Products, 550 Broadway, Albany, NY 12204
Fax: 518-436-6007
Web site: www.corcraft.org
Director:
  Michael Hurt . . . . . . . . . . . . . . . . . . . . . . . . . . .518-436-6321 x2305

### Facilities
#### Adirondack Correctional Facility
  196 Ray Brook Rd, Box 110, Route 86, Ray Brook, NY 12977-0110
  Superintendent:
    Jeffrey Tedford . . . . . . . . . . . . . . . . . . . . . . . . . .518-891-1343
#### Albion Correctional Facility
  3595 State School Rd, Albion, NY 14411
  Superintendent:
    William Powers . . . . . . . . . . . . . . . . . . . . . . . . . .585-589-5511
#### Altona Correctional Facility
  555 Devils Den Rd, Altona, NY 12910
  Superintendent:
    John Demars. . . . . . . . . . . . . . . . . . . . . . . . . . . . .518-236-7841
#### Attica Correctional Facility
  639 Exchange Street, Attica, NY 14011-0149
  Superintendent:
    Mark Bradt. . . . . . . . . . . . . . . . . . . . . . . . . . . . . .585-591-2000
#### Auburn Correctional Facility
  135 State St, Auburn, NY 13024
  Superintendent:
    Harold Graham. . . . . . . . . . . . . . . . . . . . . . . . . . .315-253-8401
#### Bare Hill Correctional Facility
  Caller Box #20 181 Brand Rd, Malone, NY 12953
  Superintendent:
    Bruce Yelich . . . . . . . . . . . . . . . . . . . . . . . . . . . . .518-483-8411
#### Bayview Correctional Facility
  550 West 20th St, New York, NY 10011
  Superintendent:
    Vacant . . . . . . . . . . . . . . . . . . . . . . . . . . . . . . . . . .212-255-7590
#### Beacon Correctional Facility
  50 Camp Beacon Rd, PO Box 780, Beacon, NY 12508-0780
  Superintendent:
    Gail Thomas. . . . . . . . . . . . . . . . . . . . . . . . . . . . . .845-831-4200

*Offices and agencies generally appear in alphabetical order, except when specific order is requested by listee.*

**Bedford Hills Correctional Facility**
247 Harris Rd, Bedford Hills, NY 10507
Superintendent:
Sabina Kaplan . . . . . . . . . . . . . . . . . . . . . . . . . . . 914-241-3100

**Butler Correctional Facility**
PO Box 388, 14001 Westbury Cutoff Rd, Red Creek, NY 13143
Superintendent:
Sheryl Zenzen . . . . . . . . . . . . . . . . . . . . . . . . . . 315-754-8001

**Cape Vincent Correctional Facility**
36560 Route 12E, Box 599, Cape Vincent, NY 13618
Superintendent:
Patricia LeConey . . . . . . . . . . . . . . . . . . . . . . . . . 315-654-4100

**Cayuga Correctional Facility**
PO Box 1150, 2202 Route 38A, Moravia, NY 13119-1150
Superintendent:
David Stallone . . . . . . . . . . . . . . . . . . . . . . . . . . . 315-497-1110

**Chateaugay Correctional Facility**
PO Box 320, 7874 Route 11, Chateaugay, NY 12920
Superintendent:
Michael Lira . . . . . . . . . . . . . . . . . . . . . . . . . . . . . 518-497-3300

**Clinton Correctional Facility**
PO Box 2000, 1156 Route 374, Cook St, Dannemora, NY 12929
Superintendent:
Thomas LaValley . . . . . . . . . . . . . . . . . . . 518-492-2511 x2099

**Collins Correctional Facility**
PO Box 490, Middle Rd, Collins, NY 14034-0490
Superintendent:
Michael Graziano . . . . . . . . . . . . . . . . . . . . . . . . . 716-532-4588

**Coxsackie Correctional Facility**
11260 Route 9W, Box 200, West Coxsackie, NY 12051-0200
Superintendent:
Daniel Martuscello . . . . . . . . . . . . . . . . . . . . . . . . 518-731-2781

**Downstate Correctional Facility**
121 Red Schoolhouse Rd, PO Box 445, Fishkill, NY 12524-0445
Superintendent:
Ada Perez . . . . . . . . . . . . . . . . . . . . . . . . . . . . . . . 845-831-6600

**Eastern NY Correctional Facility**
30 Institution Rd, Box 338, Napanoch, NY 12458-0338
Superintendent:
Thomas Griffin . . . . . . . . . . . . . . . . . . . . . . . . . . . 845-647-7400

**Edgecombe Correctional Facility**
611 Edgecombe Ave, New York, NY 10032-4398
Superintendent:
Shelda Washington . . . . . . . . . . . . . . . . . . . . . . . . 212-923-2575

**Elmira Correctional Facility**
1879 Davis St, PO Box 500, Elmira, NY 14902-0500
Superintendent:
Paul Chappius . . . . . . . . . . . . . . . . . . . . . . . . . . . . 607-734-3901

**Fishkill Correctional Facility**
18 Strack Dr, PO Box 307, Prospect Street, Beacon, NY 12508
Superintendent:
William Connolly . . . . . . . . . . . . . . . . . . . . . . . . . 845-831-0400

**Five Points Correctional Facility**
Caller Box 400, 6000 State Rte 96, Romulus, NY 14541
Superintendent:
Michael Sheahan . . . . . . . . . . . . . . . . . . . . . . . . . 607-869-5111

**Franklin Correctional Facility**
62 Bare Hill Rd, PO Box 10, Malone, NY 12953
Superintendent:
Darwin LaClair . . . . . . . . . . . . . . . . . . . . . . . . . . . 518-483-6040

**Gouverneur Correctional Facility**
112 Scotch Settlement Rd, PO Box 370, Gouverneur, NY 13642-0370
Superintendent:
Elizabeth O'Meara . . . . . . . . . . . . . . . . . . . . . . . . 315-287-7351

**Gowanda Correctional Facility**
PO Box 350, South Rd, Gowanda, NY 14070-0350
Superintendent:
John Lempke . . . . . . . . . . . . . . . . . . . . . . . . . . . . . 716-532-0177

**Great Meadow Correctional Facility**
11739 State Rte 22, Box 51, Comstock, NY 12821

Superintendent:
Steve Racette . . . . . . . . . . . . . . . . . . . . . . . . . . . . 518-639-5516

**Green Haven Correctional Facility**
594 Rte 216, Stormville, NY 12582
Superintendent:
William Lee . . . . . . . . . . . . . . . . . . . . . . . . . . . . . . 845-221-2711

**Greene Correctional Facility**
PO Box 8, 165 Plank Rd, Coxsackie, NY 12051-0008
Superintendent:
Brandon Smith . . . . . . . . . . . . . . . . . . . . . . . . . . . 518-731-2741

**Groveland Correctional Facility**
7000 Sonyea Rd, PO Box 50, Sonyea, NY 14556
Superintendent:
Sandra Amoia-Kowalczyk . . . . . . . . . . . . . . . . . . . 585-658-2871

**Hale Creek ASACTC**
279 Maloney Rd, Johnstown, NY 12095
Superintendent:
David Hallenbeck . . . . . . . . . . . . . . . . . . . . . . . . . 518-736-2094

**Hudson Correctional Facility**
Box 576, 56 East Court St, Hudson, NY 12534-0576
Superintendent:
Donna Lewin . . . . . . . . . . . . . . . . . . . . . . . . . . . . . 518-828-4311

**Lakeview Shock Incarceration Correctional Facility**
9300 Lake Ave, PO Box T, Brocton, NY 14716
Superintendent:
Malcolm Cully . . . . . . . . . . . . . . . . . . . . . . . . . . . . 716-792-7100

**Lincoln Correctional Facility**
31-33 West 110th St, New York, NY 10026-4398
Superintendent:
Wendy Featherstone . . . . . . . . . . . . . . . . . . . . . . . 212-860-9400

**Livingston Correctional Facility**
7005 Sonyea Rd, PO Box 49, Sonyea, NY 14556-0049
Superintendent:
Michelle Artus . . . . . . . . . . . . . . . . . . . . . . . . . . . . 585-658-3710

**Marcy Correctional Facility**
PO Box 5000, 9000 Old River Rd, Marcy, NY 13403
Superintendent:
Charles Kelly . . . . . . . . . . . . . . . . . . . . . . . . . . . . . 315-768-1400

**Mid-State Correctional Facility**
PO Box 216, 9005 Old River Rd, Marcy, NY 13403-0216
Superintendent:
John Colvin . . . . . . . . . . . . . . . . . . . . . . . . . . . . . . 315-768-8581

**Mohawk Correctional Facility**
6100 School Road, PO Box 8451, Rome, NY 13440
Superintendent:
Paul Gonyea . . . . . . . . . . . . . . . . . . . . . . . . . . . . . 315-339-5232

**Monterey Shock Incarceration Correctional Facility**
2150 Evergreen Hill Rd, RD #1, Beaver Dams, NY 14812-9718
Superintendent:
Leroy Fields . . . . . . . . . . . . . . . . . . . . . . . . . . . . . . 607-962-3184

**Moriah Shock Incarceration Correctional Facility**
PO Box 999, Mineville, NY 12956-0999
Superintendent:
Bruce McCormick . . . . . . . . . . . . . . . . . . . . . . . . . 518-942-7561

**Mt McGregor Correctional Facility**
1000 Mt McGregor Rd, Box 2071, Wilton, NY 12831-5071
Superintendent:
William Haggett . . . . . . . . . . . . . . . . . . . . . . . . . . 518-587-3960

**Ogdensburg Correctional Facility**
One Correction Way, Ogdensburg, NY 13669-2288
Superintendent:
Larry Frank . . . . . . . . . . . . . . . . . . . . . . . . . . . . . . 315-393-0281

**Orleans Correctional Facility**
3595 Gaines Basin Rd, Albion, NY 14411
Superintendent:
Sandra Dolce . . . . . . . . . . . . . . . . . . . . . . . . . . . . . 585-589-6820

**Otisville Correctional Facility**
57 Sanitorium Rd, Box 8, Otisville, NY 10963-0008
Superintendent:
Kathleen Gerbing . . . . . . . . . . . . . . . . . . . . . . . . . 845-386-1490

*Policy Areas*

*Offices and agencies generally appear in alphabetical order, except when specific order is requested by listee.*

**Queensboro Correctional Facility**
47-04 Van Dam St, Long Island City, NY 11101-3081
Superintendent:
  Dennis Breslin . . . . . . . . . . . . . . . . . . . . . . . . . . . . 718-361-8920
**Riverview Correctional Facility**
PO Box 158, 1110 Tibbits Dr, Ogdensburg, NY 13669
Superintendent:
  Calvin Rabsatt . . . . . . . . . . . . . . . . . . . . . . . . . . . . 315-393-8400
**Rochester Correctional Facility**
470 Ford St, Rochester, NY 14608-2499
Superintendent:
  Sheryl Zenzen . . . . . . . . . . . . . . . . . . . . . . . . . . . . 585-454-2280
**Shawangunk Correctional Facility**
200 Quick Rd, PO Box 750, Wallkill, NY 12589-0750
Superintendent:
  Joseph Smith . . . . . . . . . . . . . . . . . . . . . . . . . . . . 845-895-2081
**Sing Sing Correctional Facility**
354 Hunter St, Ossining, NY 10562
Superintendent:
  Michael Capra . . . . . . . . . . . . . . . . . . . . . . . . . . . . 914-941-0108
**Southport Correctional Facility**
236 Bob Masia Dr, PO Box 2000, Pine City, NY 14871
Superintendent:
  Stephen Wenderlich . . . . . . . . . . . . . . . . . . . . . . . . 607-737-0850
**Sullivan Correctional Facility**
Box 116, 325 Riverside Dr, Fallsburg, NY 12733-0116
Superintendent:
  Patrick Griffin . . . . . . . . . . . . . . . . . . . . . . . . . . . . 845-434-2080
**Taconic Correctional Facility**
250 Harris Rd, Bedford Hills, NY 10507-2498
Superintendent:
  Patty Nelson . . . . . . . . . . . . . . . . . . . . . . . . . . . . 914-241-3010
**Ulster Correctional Facility**
750 Berme Rd, PO Box 800, Napanoch, NY 12458
Superintendent:
  Jerome Nicolato . . . . . . . . . . . . . . . . . . . . . . . . . . 845-647-1670
**Upstate Correctional Facility**
PO Box 2000, 309 Bare Hill Rd, Malone, NY 12953
Superintendent:
  David Rock . . . . . . . . . . . . . . . . . . . . . . . . . . . . 518-483-6997
**Wallkill Correctional Facility**
50 McKenderick Rd, PO Box G, Wallkill, NY 12589-0286
Superintendent:
  Timothy Laffin Sr . . . . . . . . . . . . . . . . . . . . . . . . . . 845-895-2021
**Washington Correctional Facility**
72 Lock 11 Lane, Box 180, Comstock, NY 12821-0180
Superintendent:
  Tim Sheehan . . . . . . . . . . . . . . . . . . . . . . . . . . . . 518-639-4486
**Watertown Correctional Facility**
23147 Swan Rd, Watertown, NY 13601-9340
Superintendent:
  Barry McArdle . . . . . . . . . . . . . . . . . . . . . . . . . . . . 315-782-7490
**Wende Correctional Facility**
3040 Wende Rd, PO Box 1187, Alden, NY 14004-1187
Superintendent:
  Dale Artus . . . . . . . . . . . . . . . . . . . . . . . . . . . . 716-937-4000
**Willard Drug Treatment Center**
7116 County Route 132, PO Box 303, Willard, NY 14588
Superintendent:
  Ricky Bartlett . . . . . . . . . . . . . . . . . . . . . . . . . . . . 607-869-5500
**Woodbourne Correctional Facility**
99 Prison Rd, PO Box 1000, Woodbourne, NY 12788
Superintendent:
  Robert Cunningham . . . . . . . . . . . . . . . . . . . . . . . 845-434-7730
**Wyoming Correctional Facility**
3203 Dunbar Rd, PO Box 501, Attica, NY 14011
Superintendent:
  David Unger . . . . . . . . . . . . . . . . . . . . . . . . . . . . 585-591-1010

**Security Staffing Unit**
Director:
  Philip Battiste . . . . . . . . . . . . . . . . . . . . . . . . . . . . 518-485-5407
**Special Operations**
Director, Corrections Emergency Response Team (Cert):
  Col. Dennis Bradford . . . . . . . . . . . . . . . . . . . . . . . 518-457-2006
Director, CIU:
  James O'Gorman . . . . . . . . . . . . . . . . . . . . . . . . . . 518-457-2006
Director, Special Housing/Inmate Disciplinary Program:
  Albert Prack . . . . . . . . . . . . . . . . . . . . . . . . . . . . 518-457-2337

## Health Services Division
Deputy Commissioner/Chief Medical Officer:
  Carl Koenigsmann, MD . . . . . . . . . . . . . . . . . . . . . 518-457-7073
Assistant Commissioner, Health Services:
  Elizabeth Ritter . . . . . . . . . . . . . . . . . . . . . . . . . . . 518-445-6176

**Correctional Health Services**
Director:
  Nancy Lyng . . . . . . . . . . . . . . . . . . . . . . . . . . . . 518-445-6176

**Dental Services**
Director:
  Mary D'Silva DDS . . . . . . . . . . . . . . . . . . . . . . . . . 518-445-6176

**Mental Health**
Director:
  Doris Ramirez-Romero . . . . . . . . . . . . . . . . . . . . . . 518-445-6071

## Population Management
Chief of Investigations:
  Vernon Fonda . . . . . . . . . . . . . . . 518-457-2653 or 518-457-2653

**Management Information Services**
Director/CIO:
  Thomas Herzog . . . . . . . . . . . . . . . . . . . . . . . . . . . 518-457-2540

**Program Planning, Research & Evaluation**
Director:
  Paul Korotkin . . . . . . . . . . . . . . . . . . . . . . . . . . . . 518-408-0424

## Program Services
Deputy Commissioner:
  Jeffrey McKoy . . . . . . . . . . . . . . . . . . . . . . . . . . . . 518-457-5555
Assistant Commissioner:
  Catherine Jacobsen . . . . . . . . . . . . . . . . . . . . . . . . 518-408-5825

**Education**
Director:
  Linda Hollmen . . . . . . . . . . . . . . . . . . . . . . . . . . . . 518-402-0092

**Guidance & Counseling**
Director:
  Joanne Nigro . . . . . . . . . . . . . . . . . . . . . . . . . . . . 518-402-1789

**Library Services**
Supervising Librarian:
  Barbara Ost . . . . . . . . . . . . . . . . . . . . . . . . . . . . 518-485-7109

**Ministerial, Family & Volunteer Services**
Director:
  Cheryl V Morris . . . . . . . . . . . . . . . . . . . . . . . . . . . 518-402-1700

**Substance Abuse Treatment Services**
Director:
  Rachael Young . . . . . . . . . . . . . . . . . . . . . . . . . . . 518-402-1745

## Victim Services, Office of
AE Smith Building
80 S Swan Street
2nd Floor
Albany, NY 12210

*Offices and agencies generally appear in alphabetical order, except when specific order is requested by listee.*

518-457-8727 or 800-247-8035  Fax: 518-457-8658
Web site: www.ovs.ny.gov

55 Hanson Place
10th Floor
Brooklyn, NY 11217
718-923-4325
Fax: 718-923-4347

Director:
    Elizabeth Cronin, Esq . . . . . . . . . . . . . . . . . . . . . . . . . . .518-485-5719
Deputy Director, Administration:
    Virginia Miller . . . . . . . . . . . . . . . . . . . . . . . . . . . . . .518-457-8003
Brooklyn Investigations Unit, Crime Compensation:
    Claudette Christian Bullock . . . . . . . . . . . . . . . . . .718-923-4348
Albany Investigations Unit, Crime Compensation:
    Karen Senez . . . . . . . . . . . . . . . . . . . . . . . . . . . . . . . .518-457-8060
General Counsel/Legal Unit:
    John Watson . . . . . . . . . . . . . . . . .518-457-8066/fax: 518-457-8658
Director, Public Information:
    Janine Kava. . . . . . . . . . . . . . . . . . . . . . . . . . . . . . . . .518-457-8828
    e-mail: janine.kava@dcjs.ny.gov

## Criminal Justice Services, Division of

80 South Swan Street
Albany, NY 12210
518-457-5837 or 800-262-3257  Fax: 518-457-3089
e-mail: InfoDCJS@dcjs.ny.gov
Web site: www.criminaljustice.ny.gov

Executive Deputy Commissioner:
    Michael C Green. . . . . . . . . . . . . . . . . . . . . . . . . . . . .518-457-1260
Director, Workforce Diversity & Equity Program Unit:
    Wanda Troche. . . . . . . . . . . . . . . . . . . . . . . . . . . . . .518-485-7962
Director, Public Information:
    Janine Kava. . . . . . . . . . . . . . . . . . . . . . . . . . . . . . . . .518-457-8828
    e-mail: janine.kava@dcjs.ny.gov

### Administration Office

First Deputy Commissioner:
    Mark Bonacquist. . . . . . . . . . . . . . . . . . . . . . . . . . . . .518-457-1260

#### Administrative Services
Director:
    Vacant. . . . . . . . . . . . . . . . . . . . . . . . . . . . . . . . . . . . .518-457-4168

#### Human Resources Management
Director:
    Karen Davis . . . . . . . . . . . . . . . . . . . . . . . . . . . . . . . .518-485-1704

#### State Finance & Budget
Director, Finance:
    Brad Stevens. . . . . . . . . . . . . . . . . . . . . . . . . . . . . . . .518-457-6105
Director, Internal Audit & Compliance:
    Bob Wright. . . . . . . . . . . . . . . . . . . . . . . . . . . . . . . . .518-485-5823

### Advisory Groups

#### Juvenile Justice Advisory Group
Chair:
    John E. Carter, Jr. . . . . . . . . . . . . . . . . . . . . . . . . . . . .518-457-3670

#### NYS Motor Vehicle Theft & Insurance Fraud Prevention Board
Chair:
    Michael C Green. . . . . . . . . . . . . . . . . . . . . . . . . . . . .518-485-8462

### Office of Legal Services
Deputy Commissioner & Counsel:
    John Czajka. . . . . . . . . . . . . . . . . . . . . . . . . . . . . . . . .518-457-4181

### Missing & Exploited Children Clearinghouse
Director:
    Vacant. . . . . . . . . . . . . . . . . . . . . . . . . . . . . . . . . . . .518-485-7641

## Commission on Forensic Science
Chair:
    Michael C Green, Esq.

### Office of Forensic Services
Director:
    Brian J Gestring . . . . . . . . . . . . . . . . . . . . . . . . . . . . .518-457-4181

## Office of Criminal Justice Operations
Deputy Commissioner:
    Joe Morrissey . . . . . . . . . . . . . . . . . . . . . . . . . . . . . . .518-485-2995

### Office of Operations
Assistant Director:
    Vacant. . . . . . . . . . . . . . . . . . . . . . . . . . . . . . . . . . . .518-457-6050
Chief, Operations:
    Vacant. . . . . . . . . . . . . . . . . . . . . . . . . . . . . . . . . . . .518-485-7688

## Office of Internal Audit and Compliance

## Office of Justice Research & Performance
Deputy Commissioner:
    Terry Salo . . . . . . . . . . . . . . . . . . . . . . . . . . . . . . . . .518-457-7301

## Office of Public Safety
Deputy Commissioner:
    Michael Wood518-457-6985

### Law Enforcement Agency Accreditation Council
Chair:
    Marvin Fisher

### Municipal Police Training Council
Chair:
    Sheriff Ronald G. Spike

### Security Guard Advisory Council (SGAC)
Chair:
    Robert S Tucker

### State Committee for Coordination of Police Services for Elderly (TRIAD)

## Office of Program Development & Funding
Deputy Commissioner:
    Vacant. . . . . . . . . . . . . . . . . . . . . . . . . . . . . . . . . . . .518-457-8462
    e-mail: funding@dcjs.ny.gov

## Office of Sex Offender Management
Director:
    Vacant. . . . . . . . . . . . . . . . . . . . . . . . . . . . . . . . . . . .518-457-6985

## Gun Involved Violence Elimination (GIVE) Initiative
Director:
    Vacant. . . . . . . . . . . . . . . . . . . . . . . . . . . . . . . . . . . .518-485-7923

## Inspector General (NYS), Office of the
Empire State Plaza
Building 2
16th Floor
Albany, NY 12223
518-474-1010 or 800-367-4448  Fax: 518-486-3745
Web site: www.ig.ny.gov

61 Broadway
Suite 2100
New York, NY 10006
212-635-3150
Fax: 212-809-1630

*Offices and agencies generally appear in alphabetical order, except when specific order is requested by listee.*

State Inspector General:
    Letizia Tagliafierro....................212-635-3150 or 518-474-1010
    e-mail: inspector.general@ig.ny.gov
Executive Deputy Inspector General:
    Spencer Freedman ..................212-635-3150 or 518-474-1010
Chief Investigator:
    Robert Werner.........................................212-635-3150
Special Deputy, Communications & External Affairs:
    Vacant................................518-474-1010 or 212-635-3150

## Law Department

28 Liberty Street
New York, NY 10005
212-416-8000 or 800-771-7755
Web site: www.ag.ny.gov

State Capitol
Albany, NY 12224-0341
518-776-2000
Fax: 518-650-9401

Attorney General:
    Letitia James....................212-416-8000 or 518-776-2000
Acting Chief Operating Officer:
    Joshua Carr.........................................212-416-8050
Press Secretary:
    Fernando Aquino..................212-416-8060/fax: 212-416-6005
    e-mail: nyag.pressoffice@ag.ny.gov

### Appeals & Opinions

Solicitor General:
    Vacant...........................212-416-8016 or 518-776-2002
Deputy Solicitor General, Criminal Appeals:
    Nikki Kowalski.......................................212-416-8370
Deputy Solicitor General:
    Anisha Dasgupta.....................................212-416-8921
Deputy Solicitor General:
    Steven Wu.......................212-416-6312/fax: 212-416-8962

#### Law Library
Chief, Library Services:
    Patricia Partello.................518-776-2566/fax: 518-915-7737
Legal Support Analyst:
    Vacant ............................212-416-8012/fax: 212-416-6130

### Criminal Justice

Executive Deputy Attorney General:
    Kelly Donovan ......................................212-416-8050

#### Criminal Enforcement & Financial Crimes Bureau
Bureau Chief:
    Gary Fishman....................212-416-8750 or 518-776-2370

#### Medicaid Fraud Control Unit
120 Broadway, 13th Fl, New York, NY 10271-0007
Deputy Attorney General:
    Amy Held ......................212-417-5250/fax: 212-417-4284

#### Guns, Gangs & Drugs Initiative
Special Deputy Attorney General:
    Carl J Boykin ......................................315-793-2502

### Economic Justice

Executive Deputy Attorney General:
    Siobhan Kennedy ...................................212-416-8050
Deputy Attorney General:
    Virginia Chavez Romano ...........................212-416-8389

#### Antitrust Bureau
Bureau Chief:
    Eric J Stock....................212-416-8282/fax: 212-416-6015

### Consumer Frauds Bureau
Bureau Chief:
    Jane Azia.......................212-416-6067/fax: 212-416-6003

### Social Justice

Executive Deputy Attorney General:
    Vacant ........................212-416-8075/fax: 212-416-8942

#### Civil Rights Bureau
Bureau Chief:
    Lourdes Rosado.................212-416-8250/fax: 212-416-8074

### Investigations

Chief, Investigations:
    Dominick Zarrella..................212-416-6328 or 518-486-4540
    fax: 212-416-8773

### State Counsel

#### Civil Recoveries Bureau
Bureau Chief:
    John Cremo.....................518-776-2173/fax: 518-915-7731

#### Claims Bureau
Bureau Chief:
    Katharine Brooks..................518-776-2300 or 212-416-8500

#### Litigation Bureau
Bureau Chief:
    Jeffrey Dvorin ....................518-776-2300 or 212-416-8610

#### Real Property Bureau
Bureau Chief:
    Alison Crocker ......................................518-776-2700

## Parole Board, The

Corrections & Community Supervision
1220 Washington Avenue
Building 2
Albany, NY 12226
518-473-9400  Fax: 518-473-6037
Web site: www.parole.ny.gov; doccs.ny.gov

### Executive Office

Acting Commissioner:
    Anthony J Annucci...................518-457-8134 or 518-457-1748
Secretary to the Chair:
    Rachael Seguin .....................................518-473-9548
Director, Public Information:
    Thomas Mailey......................................518-457-8182
Administrative Assistant:
    Lorraine Morse ..................518-473-5424/fax: 518-473-6037

### Administrative Services

Director, Human Resource Management:
    Barbara Farley.......................................518-473-3901
Labor Relations Representative:
    Vacant ............................................518-474-5612

### Clemency Unit

97 Central Ave, Albany, NY 12206
Director:
    Donald Fries ........................................518-485-8953

### Information Services

Director:
    John Armitage ...................518-445-7558/fax: 518-445-7553

### Office of Counsel

Deputy Commissioner & Counsel:
    Kevin Bruen .......................................518-485-9613

*Offices and agencies generally appear in alphabetical order, except when specific order is requested by listee.*

## Parole Operations Unit
Deputy Commissioner, Community Supervision:
    Vacant . . . . . . . . . . . . . . . . . . . . . . . . . . . . . . . . . . . . . . . . . . . .212-239-5730
Director, Internal Operations:
    Vacant . . . . . . . . . . . . . . . . . . . . . . . . . . . . . . . . . . . . . . . . . . . .518-408-3473
Deputy Director, Sex Offenders Mgmt Unit:
    Mary Osborne . . . . . . . . . . . . . . . . . . . . . . . . . . . . . . . . . . . . . .518-473-5572
Regional Dir-Region I:
    Michael Falk . . . . . . . . . . . . . . . . . . . . . . . . . . . . . . . . . . . . . . .212-736-9880
Regional Dir-Region II:
    Milton Brown . . . . . . . . . . . . . . . . . . . . . . . . . . . . . . . . . . . . . .718-558-5227
Regional Dir-Region III:
    Steven Claudio . . . . . . . . . . . . . . . . . . . . . . . . . . . . . . . . . . . . .914-654-8690
Regional Dir-Region IV:
    Michael Burdi . . . . . . . . . . . . . . . . . . . . . . . . . . . . . . . . . . . . . .518-459-7469
Regional Dir-Region V:
    Eugenio Russi . . . . . . . . . . . . . . . . . . . . . . . . . . . . . . . . . . . . . .585-232-6927

## Policy Analysis
Director:
    Michael R Buckman . . . . . . . . . . . . . . . . . . . . . . . . . . . . . . . .518-445-6071

## Victim Impact Unit . . . . . . . . . . . . . . . . . . . . . . .fax: 518-493-9659
Parole Officer:
    Barbara Tobin . . . . . . . . . . . . . . . . . . . . . . . . . . . . . . . . . . . . . .518-486-4400
Parole Officer:
    Christine Robinson . . . . . . . . . . . . . . . . . . . . . . . . . . . . . . . . .518-486-4400

## Prevention of Domestic Violence, Office for the
80 South Swan Street
11th Floor, Room 1157
Albany, NY 12210
518-457-5800  Fax: 518-457-5810
e-mail: opdvpublicinfo@opdv.ny.gov
Web site: www.opdv.ny.gov

90 Church St
13th Floor
New York, NY 10007
212-417-4477
Fax: 212-417-4972

Executive Director:
    Gwen Wright . . . . . . . . . . . . . . . . . . . . . . .518-457-5800 or 518-457-5916
Director, Bureau of Public Awareness & Prevention:
    Suzanne Cecala . . . . . . . . . . . . . . . . . . . . . . . . . . . . . . . . . . . .518-457-5744
    e-mail: suzanne.cecala@opdv.ny.gov

## State Police, Division of
1220 Washington Avenue
Building 22
Albany, NY 12226-2252
518-457-2180 or 518-457-6811
e-mail: nyspmail@troopers.ny.gov
Web site: www.troopers.ny.gov

Superintendent:
    George P Beach, II . . . . . . . . . . . . . . . . . . . . . . . . . . . . . . . . .518-457-6721
First Deputy Superintendent:
    Kevin P Bruen . . . . . . . . . . . . . . . . . . . .518-457-6711/fax: 518-485-7505
First Deputy Counsel:
    Steve Hogan . . . . . . . . . . . . . . . . . . . . . .518-457-6137/fax: 518-485-1164

### Administration
Director:
    Vacant . . . . . . . . . . . . . . . . . . . . . . .518-457-6622/fax: 518-485-5051

#### Forensic Investigation Center
Director, Staff Inspector:
    Gerald M Zeosky . . . . . . . . . . . . . . . .518-457-2466/fax: 518-457-2477

### Public Information
Director:
    Beau Duffy . . . . . . . . . . . . . . . . . . . . .518-457-2180/fax: 518-485-7818
    e-mail: pio@troopers.ny.gov

### Employee Relations
Deputy Superintendent:
    Steven G James . . . . . . . . . . . . . . . . . . .518-457-3572/fax: 518-485-7505

#### Human Resources
Deputy Superintendent:
    Bryon Christman . . . . . . . . . . . . . . . .518-485-5044/fax: 518-485-2293

#### State Police Academy
Director:
    Major Ellwood A Sloat, Jr . . . . . . . . .518-457-7254/fax: 518-485-1454

### Field Command
Deputy Superintendent:
    Vacant . . . . . . . . . . . . . . . . . . . . . . . . .518-457-6554/fax: 518-457-4779

### Internal Affairs
Deputy Superintendent:
    Scott M Crosier . . . . . . . . . . . . . . . . . . . . . . . . . . . . . . . . . . . .518-485-6018

## CORPORATIONS, AUTHORITIES AND COMMISSIONS

### New York State Commission of Correction
80 South Swan St
12th Fl
Albany, NY 12210
518-485-2346  Fax: 518-485-2467
e-mail: infoscoc@scoc.ny.gov
Web site: www.scoc.ny.gov

Chairman:
    Thomas A Beilein
Commissioner & Chair, Medical Review Board:
    Thomas J Loughren
Commissioner & Chair, Citizen's Policy & Complaint Review Council:
    Allen Riley
Assistant to Chair:
    Patricia Amati
Counsel:
    Brian Callahan
Director, Operations:
    Terry Moran
    e-mail: Terry.Moran@scoc.ny.gov

## NEW YORK STATE LEGISLATURE

*See Legislative Branch in Section 1 for additional Standing Committee and Subcommittee information.*

### Assembly Standing Committees

#### Alcoholism & Drug Abuse
Chair:
    Phil Steck . . . . . . . . . . . . . . . . . . . . . . . . . . . . . . . . . . . . . . . . . .518-455-5802

#### Codes
Chair:
    Jeffrey Dinowitz (D) . . . . . . . . . . . . . . . . . . . . . . . . . . . . . . . .518-455-4477

#### Correction
Chair:
    David I. Weprin (D) . . . . . . . . . . . . . . . . . . . . . . . . . . . . . . . . .518-455-5806

*Offices and agencies generally appear in alphabetical order, except when specific order is requested by listee.*

Policy Areas

## Senate Standing Committees

### Codes
Chair:
Jamaal T Bailey (D) ............................518-455-2061
Ranking Minority Member:
Andrew J Lanza (R, C, IP, RFM)....................518-455-3215

### Crime Victims, Crime & Correction
Ranking Minority Member:
Fred Akshar (R, C, IP, RFM) ......,.............518-455-2677

## U.S. GOVERNMENT

## EXECUTIVE DEPARTMENTS AND RELATED AGENCIES

### US Justice Department
Web site: www.justice.gov

### Bureau of Alcohol, Tobacco, Firearms & Explosives
Web site: www.atf.gov

New York Field Division........................fax: 646-335-9061
Financial Square, 32 Old Slip, Suite 3500, New York, NY 10005
646-335-9060  Fax: 646-335-9061
e-mail: nydiv@atf.gov
Special Agent-in-Charge:
Delano Reid
Public Information Officer:
Charles Mulham

### Drug Enforcement Administration - New York Task Force
99 10th Avenue, New York, NY 10011
212-337-3900
Web site: www.dea.gov
Special Agent-in-Charge:
James J. Hunt
Associate Special Agent-in-Charge:
Wilbert L Plummer...............................212-337-2901
Public Information Officer:
Erin Mulvey ....................................212-337-2906

### Federal Bureau of Investigation - New York Field Offices
Web site: www.fbi.gov

Albany.........................................fax: 518-431-7463
200 McCarty Avenue, Albany, NY 12209
518-465-7551  Fax: 518-431-7463
Web site: www.fbi.gov/albany
Special Agent-in-Charge:
Andrew Vale....................................518-465-7551

Buffalo........................................fax: 716-843-5288
One FBI Plaza, Buffalo, NY 14202-2698
716-856-7800  Fax: 716-843-5288
Web site: www.fbi.gov/buffalo
Special Agent-in-Charge:
Adam S. Cohen..................................716-856-7800

New York City
26 Federal Plaza, 23rd Floor, New York, NY 10278-0004
212-384-1000 or 212-384-2100
Assistant Director-in-Charge:
Diego Rodriguez...............................212-384-1000

### Federal Bureau of Prisons
Web site: www.bop.gov

Brooklyn Metropolitan Detention Center..........fax: 718-840-5005
80 29th Street, Brooklyn, NY 11232
718-840-4200  Fax: 718-840-5005

Warden:
Frank Strada ...................718-840-4200/fax: 718-840-5005
CCM New York.................................fax: 718-840-4207
100 29th Street, Brooklyn, NY 11232
718-840-4219  Fax: 718-840-4207

Federal Correctional Institution at Otisville .......fax: 845-386-6727
Two Mile Drive, PO Box 600, Otisville, NY 10963
845-386-6700  Fax: 845-386-6727
Warden:
Monica Recktenwald

Metropolitan Correctional Center................fax: 646-836-7751
150 Park Row, New York, NY 10007
646-836-6300  Fax: 646-836-7751
Warden:
Maureen Baird

Ray Brook Federal Correctional Institution
128 Ray Brook Road, Ray Brook, NY 12977
Warden:
Donald Hudson ..................518-897-4000/fax: 518-897-4216

### Secret Service - New York Field Offices

Albany
7 Southwoods Blvd, Suite 305-A, Albany, NY 12211
Resident Agent-in-Charge:
William Leege ................................518-427-0400

Buffalo
598 Main Street, Suite 300, Buffalo, NY 14202
Special Agent-in-Charge:
Tracy Gast....................................716-551-4401

JFK/LGA
230-59 Rockaway Blvd, Suite 265, Springfield Gardens, NY 11413
718-553-0911
Resident Agent-in-Charge:
John McQuade.................................718-553-0911

Melville
145 Pinelawn Road, Suite 200N, Melville, NY 11747
631-293-4028
Resident Agent-in-Charge:
Farrell Dolan.................................631-293-4028

New York City
335 Adams Street, 32nd Floor, Brooklyn, NY 11201
718-840-1000
Special Agent-in-Charge:
Robert J. Sica...............................718-840-1000

Rochester
100 Chestnut Street, Suite 1820, Rochester, NY 14604
585-232-4160
Special Agent:
Joel Blackerby ..............................585-232-4160

Syracuse ......................................fax: 315-448-0302
100 South Clinton Street, Suite 1371, Syracuse, NY 13261
315-448-0304  Fax: 315-448-0302
Resident Agent-in-Charge:
Timothy Kirk ................................315-448-0304

White Plains
140 Grand Street, Suite 801, White Plains, NY 10601
914-682-6300
Resident Agent-in-Charge:
Jeff Wood....................................914-682-6300

*Offices and agencies generally appear in alphabetical order, except when specific order is requested by listee.*

## US Attorney's Office - New York

**Eastern District** . . . . . . . . . . . . . . . . . . . . . . . . . . . . . fax: 718-254-7508
271 Cadman Plaza East, Brooklyn, NY 11201
718-254-7000 Fax: 718-254-7508
US Attorney:
   Robert L. Capers . . . . . . . . . . . . . . 718-254-7000/fax: 718-254-7508
Assistant United States Attorney:
   James R. Cho. . . . . . . . . . . . . . . . 718-254-6519/fax: 718-254-7508
Assistant United States Attorney:
   Joseph Anthony Marutollo . . . . . . . . . 718-254-6288/fax: 718-254-7508
Assistant United States Attorney:
   Elliot M. Schachner. . . . . . . . . . . . . 718-254-6053/fax: 718-254-7508
Executive Assistant United States Attorney:
   William J. Muller . . . . . . . . . . . . . . 718-254-7000/fax: 718-254-7508
Assistant United States Attorney, Criminal Division:
   Zainab Ahmad
Deputy Chief, Civil Division:
   Gail Matthews
Chief of Affirmative Civil Enforcement, Civil Division:
   John Vagelatos

**Northern District** . . . . . . . . . . . . . . . . . . . . . . . . . . . fax: 315-448-0689
315-448-0672 Fax: 315-448-0689
  *Albany*
   445 Broadway, Room 218, Albany, NY 12207-2924
   Assistant United States Attorney:
    Thomas Spina Jr.
  *Binghamton* . . . . . . . . . . . . . . . . . . . . . . . . . fax: 607-773-2901
   319 Federal Building, 15 Henry Street, Binghamton, NY 13901
   607-773-2887 Fax: 607-773-2901
   Assistant United States Attorney:
    Miro Lovric
  *Plattsburgh* . . . . . . . . . . . . . . . . . . . . . . . . . fax: 518-314-7811
   14 Durkee Street, Suite 340, Plattsburgh, NY 12901
   518-314-7800 Fax: 518-314-7811
   Assistant United States Attorney:
    Elizabeth Horsman
  *Syracuse* . . . . . . . . . . . . . . . . . . . . . . . . . . . fax: 315-448-0689
   100 South Clinton Street, PO Box 7198, Syracuse, NY 13261-7198
   315-448-0672 Fax: 315-448-0689
   United States Attorney:
    Richard S. Hartunian . . . . . . . . . . . . . . . . . . . 315-448-0672
   Assistant United States Attorney:
    Tamara B. Thomson. . . . . . . . . . . . . . . . . . . . 315-448-0672
   Assistant United States Attorney, Chief Civil Division:
    Thomas Spina Jr.
   Assistant United States Attorney, Chief Criminal Division:
    Elizabeth C. Coombe
   Administrative Officer:
    Martha Stratton. . . . . . . . . . . . 315-448-0672/fax: 315-448-0689

**Southern District** . . . . . . . . . . . . . . . . . . . . . . . . . . fax: 212-637-2685
1 St. Andrew's Plaza, New York, NY 10007
212-637-2200 Fax: 212-637-2685
  *New York City*
   United States Attorney:
    Preet Bharara
   Deputy United States Attorney:
    Joon H. Kim. . . . . . . . . . . . . . . . . . . . . . . . 212-637-2200
   Chief, Criminal Division:
    Daniel Stein . . . . . . . . . . . . . . . . . . . . . . . . 212-637-2200
   Chief, Civil Division:
    Sara L. Shudofsky . . . . . . . . . . . . . . . . . . . . 212-637-2800
   Deputy Chief, Criminal Division:
    Andrew Dember. . . . . . . . . . . . . . . . . . . . . . 212-637-2200
   Assistant United States Attorney, Civil Division:
    Rebecca Martin . . . . . . . . . . . . . . . . . . . . . . 212-637-2800
  *White Plains*
   300 Quarropas Street, White Plains, NY 10601-4150
   914-993-1900 or 914-993-1916

Assistant United States Attorney, White Plains Co-Chief:
   Perry Carbone . . . . . . . . . . . . . . . . . . . . . . . . . . 914-993-1900

**Western District**
  *Buffalo* . . . . . . . . . . . . . . . . . . . . . . . . . . . . . fax: 716-551-3052
   138 Delaware Avenue, Buffalo, NY 14202
   716-843-5700 Fax: 716-551-3052
   United States Attorney:
    William J. Hochul, Jr.
   Assistant United States Attorney, Appellate Division Chief:
    Joseph J. Karaszewski
   Assistant United States Attorney, Civil Division Chief:
    Mary Pat Fleming . . . . . . . . . . . . . . . . . . . . 716-843-5867
   Assistant United States Attorney, Criminal Division Chief:
    Joseph M. Guerra, III. . . . . . . . . . . . . . . . . . . 716-843-5824
   Assistant United States Attorney, National Security Coordinator:
    Anthony M. Bruce . . . . . . . . . . . . . . . . . . . . 716-843-5886
   Assistant United States Attorney, General Crimes Section Chief:
    Michael DiGiacomo
   Administrative Officer:
    Amy L. Smith. . . . . . . . . . . . . . . . . . . . . . . 716-843-5700
  *Rochester* . . . . . . . . . . . . . . . . . . . . . . . . . . . fax: 585-263-6226
   100 State Street, Suite 500, Rochester, NY 14614
   585-263-6760 Fax: 585-263-6226
   Assistant United States Attorney-in-Charge:
    Richard A. Resnick . . . . . . . . . . . . . . . . . . . . 585-263-6760

## US Marshals' Service - New York

**Eastern District**
  *Brooklyn*
   US Courthouse, 225 Cadman Plaza, Brooklyn, NY 11201
   718-260-0440
   United States Marshal:
    Charles Dunne
  *Central Islip*
   100 Federal Plaza, Central Islip, NY 11722
   631-712-6000
   United States Marshal:
    Charles Dunne

**Northern District**
  *Albany*
   James T. Foley Courthouse, 445 Broadway, Albany, NY 12201
   518-472-5401
   United States Marshal:
    David McNulty
  *Binghamton*
   US Courthouse & Federal Building, 15 Henry Street, Binghamton,
    NY 13902
   607-773-2723
   United States Marshal:
    David McNulty
  *Syracuse*
   100 South Clinton Street, Syracuse, NY 13261
   315-473-7601
   United States Marshal:
    David McNulty
  *Utica*
   Alexander Pirnie Federal Building, 10 Broad Street, Room 213,
    Utica, NY 13501
   315-793-8109
   United States Marshal:
    David McNulty

**Southern District**
500 Pearl Street, New York, NY 10007
United States Marshal:
  Michael Greco. . . . . . . . . . . . . . . 212-331-7200/fax: 212-637-6130

**Western District**
  *Buffalo*
   2 Niagara Street, Buffalo, NY 14202

*Offices and agencies generally appear in alphabetical order, except when specific order is requested by listee.*

716-348-5300
United States Marshal:
    Charles Salina
**Rochester**
    US Courthouse, 100 State Street, Room 2240, Rochester, NY 14614
585-263-5787
United States Marshal:
    Charles Salina

## US Parole Commission
90 K Street NE, 3rd Floor, Washington, DC 20530
Chairman:
    J. Patricia Wilson Smoot . . . . . . . . . . . . . . . . . . . . . . . . . 202-346-7000

### U.S. CONGRESS

*See U.S. Congress Chapter for additional Standing Committee and Subcommittee information.*

## House of Representatives Standing Committees

### Judiciary
Chair:
    Bob Goodlatte (R-VA)
Ranking Member:
    John Conyers, Jr. (D-MI)
New York Delegate:
    Hakeem Jeffries (D)
New York Delegate:
    Jerrold Nadler (D) . . . . . . . . . . . . . . . . . . . . . . . . . . . . 202-225-5635

> **Subcommittee**
> *Crime, Terrorism, Homeland Security & Investigations*
> Chair:
>     Jim Sensenbrenner, Jr. (R-WI)
> Ranking Member:
>     Sheila Jackson Lee (D-TX) . . . . . . . . . . . . . . . . . . . 202-225-3816

## Senate Standing Committees

### Judiciary
Chair:
    Chuck Grassley (R-IA) . . . . . . . . . . . . . . . . . . . . . . . . . 202-224-3744
Ranking Member:
    Patrick Leahy (D-VT)
New York Delegate:
    Charles Schumer (D) . . . . . . . . . . . . . . . . . . . . . . . . . . 202-224-6542

### PRIVATE SECTOR

## American Society for the Prevention of Cruelty to Animals (ASPCA)
424 East 92nd Street, New York, NY 10128-6804
212-876-7700 or 888-666-2279
e-mail: publicinformation@aspca.org
Web site: www.aspca.org
*Promoting humane treatment of animals, education & advocacy programs & conducting statewide anti-cruelty investigation & enforcement*
Matthew Bershadker, President & Chief Executive Officer

## Associated Licensed Detectives of New York State
PO Box 13684, Albany, NY 12212
518-621-4517 or 800-417-0710  Fax: 518-621-4516
e-mail: info@aldonys.org
Web site: www.aldonys.org
*Membership association representing the interests of the NYS private investigation industry*
Gil Alba, President

## Ballard Spahr LLP New York
919 Third Avenue, 37th Floor, New York, NY 10022
212-223-0200  Fax: 212-223-1942
e-mail: stillmanc@ballardspahr.com
Web site: www.ballardspahr.com
*White collar criminal law*
Charles A. Stillman, Partner

## Berkshire Farm Center & Services for Youth
13640 State Route 22, Canaan, NY 12029
518-781-4567  Fax: 518-781-0507
e-mail: info@berkshirefarm.org
Web site: www.berkshirefarm.org
*Child welfare agency for troubled youth & families*
Timothy Giacchetta, President & Chief Executive Officer

## CUNY John Jay College of Criminal Justice
899 10th Avenue, New York, NY 10019
212-237-8600  Fax: 212-237-8607
e-mail: jtravis@jjay.cuny.edu
Web site: www.jjay.cuny.edu
*Criminal justice, police & fire science, forensic science & psychology, international criminal justice, public administration*
Jeremy Travis, President

## Center for Alternative Sentencing & Employment Services (CASES)
151 Lawrence Street, 3rd Floor, Brooklyn, NY 11201
212-553-6300  Fax: 718-596-3872
e-mail: info@cases.org
Web site: www.cases.org
*Advocacy for the use of community sanctions designed to improve behavioral health & public safety*
Joel Copperman, President & Chief Executive Officer

## Center for Law & Justice
Pine West Plaza, Building 2, Washington Ave. Exit, Albany, NY 12205
518-427-8361  Fax: 518-427-8362
e-mail: cflj@verizon.net
Web site: www.cflj.org
*Advocacy for fair treatment of disadvantaged & low-income NY communities in the legal & criminal justice systems; referrals, workshops, outreach & education*
Dr. Alice P. Green, Executive Director

## Coalition Against Domestic Violence, NYS
119 Washington Avenue, Albany, NY 12210
518-482-5465  Fax: 518-482-3807
e-mail: vasquez@nyscadv.org
Web site: www.nyscadv.org
*Domestic violence prevention; training, technical assistance, events & publications*
Tammy Van Epps, President

## Coalition Against Sexual Assault (NYS)
28 Essex Street, Albany, NY 12206
518-482-4222  Fax: 518-482-4248
e-mail: jzannoni@nyscasa.org
Web site: www.nyscasa.org
*Advocacy, public education, technical assistance & training*
Joanne Zannoni, Executive Director

## Correctional Association of New York
2090 Adam Clayton Powell Blvd, Suite 200, New York, NY 10027
212-254-5700  Fax: 212-473-2807
Web site: www.correctionalassociation.org
*Advocates for improved prison conditions & a fair criminal justice system*
Laura Davidson, Director of Operations and Human Resources

---

*Offices and agencies generally appear in alphabetical order, except when specific order is requested by listee.*

**NYS Bar Assn, Public Trust & Confidence in the Legal System**
**Debevoise & Plimpton LLP**
919 Third Avenue, New York, NY 10022
212-909-6000  Fax: 212-909-6836
Web site: www.debevoise.com
Tom Orewyler, Head of Communications

**Education & Assistance Corporation Inc**
50 Clinton Street, Suite 107, Hempstead, NY 11550
516-539-0150  Fax: 516-539-0160
e-mail: lelder@eacinc.org
Web site: www.eacinc.org
*Advocacy, education & counseling programs & services for youth, seniors, families & communities in need*
Lance W. Elder, President & Chief Executive Officer

**Fortune Society (The)**
29-76 Northern Boulevard, Long Island City, NY 11101
212-691-7554  Fax: 212-255-4948
e-mail: sgoldstein@fortunesociety.org
Web site: www.fortunesociety.org
*Founded in 1967, The Fortune Society's mission is to support successful reentry from incarceration and promote alternatives to incarceration. Services include Alternative to Incarceration Programs, Education, Employment, Family Services, & more.*
JoAnne Page, President & CEO
Sherry Goldstein, Vice President, Agency Operations
Stanley Richards, Executive Vice President

**Hofstra University, School of Law**
121 Hofstra University, Hempstead, NY 11549-1210
516-463-5858
e-mail: hofstralaw@hofstra.edu
*Antitrust, criminal law, evidence*
Eric Lane, Dean

**Law Offices of Stanley N Lupkin**
98 Cutter Mill Road, Suite 227N, Great Neck, NY 11021
516-482-1223
*Corporate, criminal & financial investigations, integrity monitorships*
Stanley N. Lupkin, Partner

**Legal Action Center**
225 Varick Street, 4th Floor, New York, NY 10014
212-243-1313 or 800-223-4044  Fax: 212-675-0286
e-mail: lacinfo@lac.org
Web site: www.lac.org
*Promotes alternatives to incarceration & advocates for policies that address issues relating to alcohol/drug abuse, HIV/AIDS & criminal justice*
Paul N. Samuels, President & Director

**Legal Aid Society**
199 Water Street, New York, NY 10038
212-557-3300  Fax: 212-509-8761
Web site: www.legal-aid.org
*Criminal defense & appeals*
Seymour W. James, Jr., Attorney-in-Chief

**NYS Bar Assn, Criminal Justice Section**
**Michael T Kelly, Esq**
207 Admirals Walk, Buffalo, NY 14202
716-361-5828  Fax: 866-574-0725
Sean Patrick Kelly, Attorney

**Mothers Against Drunk Driving (MADD) of NYS**
33 Walt Whitman Road, Suite 210W, Huntington Station, NY 11746
631-547-6233 or 877-MADD-Help  Fax: 631-547-6235
e-mail: ny.state@madd.org
Web site: www.madd.org/ny
*The mission of Mothers Against Drunk Driving is to end drunk driving, help fight drugged driving, support the victims of these violent crimes, and prevent underage drinking.*
Richard Mallow, Executive Director

**NYS Association of Chiefs of Police Inc**
2697 Hamburg Street, Schenectady, NY 12303
518-355-3371  Fax: 518-356-5767
Web site: www.nychiefs.org
*Association of police chiefs dedicated to maintaining law & order in NYS*
Margaret Ryan, Executive Director

**NYS Correctional Officers & Police Benevolent Association Inc**
102 Hackett Blvd, Albany, NY 12209
518-427-1551 or 888-484-7279  Fax: 518-426-1635
e-mail: nyscopba@nyscopba.org
Web site: www.nyscopba.org
*Promotes the interests of New York State's correctional officers*
Michael B. Powers, President

**NYS Council of Probation Administrators**
PO Box 2, 272 Broadway, Albany, NY 12203
518-487-5200  Fax: 518-487-5204
e-mail: info@nyscopa.com
Web site: www.nyscopa.com
*Works to advance the interests of probation administrators in NYS, provide information on probation & develop strategies for crime prevention*
Joy Bennett, President

**NYS Defenders Association**
194 Washington Avenue, Suite 500, Albany, NY 12210-2314
518-465-3524  Fax: 518-465-3249
Web site: www.nysda.org
*Criminal defense*
Jonathan E. Gradess, Executive Director

**NYS Deputies Association Inc**
61 Laredo Drive, Rochester, NY 14624
585-247-9322  Fax: 585-247-6661
e-mail: executivedirector@nysdeputy.org
Web site: www.nysdeputy.org
Thomas H. Ross, Executive Director

**NYS Law Enforcement Officers Union, Council 82, AFSCME, AFL-CIO**
Hollis V Chase Building, 63 Colvin Avenue, Albany, NY 12206
518-489-8424 or 800-724-0482  Fax: 518-435-1523
e-mail: c82@council82.org
Web site: www.council82.org
*Union representing New York State's law enforcement officers & professionals; provides advocacy, support & research assistance for its members*
James Lyman, Executive Director

**NYS Sheriffs' Association**
27 Elk Street, Albany, NY 12207
518-434-9091  Fax: 518-434-9093
e-mail: pkehoe@nysheriffs.org
Web site: www.nysheriffs.org
*Not-for-profit corporation dedicated to providing support for sheriffs in NYS*
Peter R. Kehoe, Executive Director

Policy Areas

*Offices and agencies generally appear in alphabetical order, except when specific order is requested by listee.*

## New York State Law Enforcement Council
One Hogan Place, New York, NY 10013
212-335-8927  Fax: 212-335-3808
*Advocates for NY's law enforcement community & works to enhance the quality of justice & safety in NY*
Kate Hogan, Chair

## Osborne Association
809 Westchester Avenue, Bronx, NY 10455
718-707-2600  Fax: 718-707-3102
e-mail: info@osborneny.org
Web site: www.osborneny.org
*Career/educational counseling, job referrals & training for recently released prisoners, substance abuse treatment, case management, HIV/AIDS counseling, family services, parenting education, re-entry services, housing placement assistance*
Elizabeth A. Gaynes, President & Chief Executive Officer

## Pace University, School of Law, John Jay Legal Services Inc
78 North Broadway, White Plains, NY 10603
914-422-4333  Fax: 914-422-4391
e-mail: gflint@law.pace.edu
Web site: www.law.pace.edu/john-jay-legal-services
*Law school client representation clinical program specializing in the areas of criminal trial advocacy, disability rights litigation/transactional representation, immigration & investor rights/securities arbitrations*
Margaret M. Flint, Executive Director

## Patrolmen's Benevolent Association
125 Broad Street, 11th Floor, New York, NY 10004-2400
212-298-9100 or 212-349-7560
e-mail: rzink@nycpba.org
Web site: www.nycpba.org
*NYC patrolmen's union*
Patrick J. Lynch, President

## Police Conference of NY Inc (PCNY)
112 State Street, Suite 1120, Albany, NY 12207
518-463-3283  Fax: 518-463-2488
e-mail: pcnyinfo@pcny.org
Web site: www.pcny.org
*Advocacy for law enforcement officers*
Richard Wells, President

## Prisoners' Legal Services of New York
41 State Street, Suite M112, Albany, NY 12207
518-445-6050
*Protects the rights of prisoners & advocates for humane prison conditions*
Karen L. Murtagh, Executive Director

## Remove Intoxicated Drivers (RID-USA Inc)
1013 Nott Street, PO Box 520, Schenectady, NY 12301
518-372-0034 or 888-283-5144  Fax: 518-370-4917
Web site: www.rid-usa.org
*Victims' rights, alcohol policy & public awareness*
Doris Aiken, President

## Rochester Interfaith Jail Ministry Inc
2 Riverside Street, Rochester, NY 14613
585-458-5423
*Support services for ex-offenders, the incarcerated & their families*
Robert Crystal, Director

## Services for the UnderServed (SUS)
305 Seventh Avenue, 10th Floor, New York, NY 10001
212-633-6900
e-mail: info@sus.org
Web site: www.sus.org
*Disabilities services & support, substance abuse treatment & counseling, shelters & homelessness prevention services, low-income & supported housing*
Donna Colonna, Chief Executive Officer

## Stony Brook Drinking Driver Program LLC
PO Box 263, Holtsville, NY 11742
631-716-2001  Fax: 631-716-4439
e-mail: classes@stonybrookddp.com
Web site: www.stonybrookddp.com
*Drinking & driving education & prevention*
Judith Forde, Director

## Trooper Foundation-State of New York Inc
3 Airport Park Blvd, Latham, NY 12110-1441
518-785-1002  Fax: 518-785-1003
e-mail: rmincher@nystf.org
Web site: www.nystrooperfoundation.org
*Provides training, education, programs & services for NYS Police*
Rachael L. Mincher, President

## Vera Institute of Justice
233 Broadway, 12th Floor, New York, NY 10279-1299
212-334-1300  Fax: 212-941-9407
e-mail: contactvera@vera.org
Web site: www.vera.org
*Works to ensure fair & equitable systems of justice & safety through research, technical assistance & demonstration projects*
Nicholas Turner, President & Director

## Women's Prison Association & Home Inc
110 Second Avenue, New York, NY 10003
646-292-7740  Fax: 646-292-7763
e-mail: info@wpaonline.org
Web site: www.wpaonline.org
*Community corrections & family preservation programs*
Georgia Lerner, Executive Director

*Offices and agencies generally appear in alphabetical order, except when specific order is requested by listee.*

# EDUCATION

## NEW YORK STATE

### GOVERNOR'S OFFICE

**Governor's Office**
Executive Chamber
State Capitol
Albany, NY 12224
518-474-8390  Fax: 518-474-1513
Web site: www.ny.gov

Governor:
  Andrew M Cuomo . . . . . . . . . . . . . . . . . . . . . . . . . . .518-474-8390
Secretary to the Governor:
  Melissa DeRosa . . . . . . . . . . . . . . . . . .518-474-4246 or 212-681-4580
Counsel to the Governor:
  Kumiki Gibson . . . . . . . . . . . . . . . . . . . . .518-474-8343 or 212-681-4580
Director of Policy:
  David Yassky . . . . . . . . . . . . . . . . . . . . . . . . . . . .518-408-2576
Deputy Secretary, Education:
  Daniel Fuller . . . . . . . . . . . . . . . . . . . . . . . . . . . . .518-474-9883
Chief of Staff:
  Jill DesRosiers . . . . . . . . . . . . . . . . . . . . .518-474-8390 or 212-681-4580
Director, Communications:
  Peter Ajemian . . . . . . . . . . . . . . . . . . . . .518-474-8418 or 212-681-4640

### EXECUTIVE DEPARTMENTS AND RELATED AGENCIES

**Board of Regents**
89 Washington Ave
EB, Rm 110
Albany, NY 12234
518-474-5889  Fax: 518-486-2405
e-mail: regentsoffice@nysed.gov
Web site: www.regents.nysed.gov

Chancellor:
  Betty A Rosa (2018) . . . . . . . . . . . . . . . . . . . . . . . . .518-474-5889
    e-mail: Regent.Rosa@nysed.gov
Vice Chancellor:
  T. Andrew Brown (2017) . . . . . . . . . . . . . . . . . . . . .585-454-3667
    e-mail: Regent.Brown@nysed.gov
Education Commissioner, USNY President:
  MaryEllen Elia . . . . . . . . . . . . . . . . . . . . . . . . . . . .518-474-5844
Secretary to the Board:
  Anthony Lofrumento . . . . . . . . . . . . . . . . . . . . . . . . .518-474-5889
Member:
  James E Cottrell (2019) . . . . . . . . . . . . . . . . . . . . . .718-270-2331
    e-mail: regent.cottrell@nysed.gov
Member:
  Luis O Reyes (2021) . . . . . . . . . . . . . . . . . . . . . . . . .518-474-5889
    e-mail: Regent.Reyes@nysed.gov
Member:
  Josephine Finn (2019) . . . . . . . . . . . . . . . . . . . . . . . .518-474-5889
Member:
  Kathleen M Cashin (2020) . . . . . . . . . . . . . . . . . . . . .518-474-5889
    e-mail: regent.cashin@nysed.gov
Member:
  Elizabeth S. Hakanson . . . . . . . . . . . . . . . . . . . . . . . .518-474-5889
    e-mail: Regent.Hakanson@nysed.gov
Member:
  Judith Johnson (2020) . . . . . . . . . . . . . . . . . . . . . . . .518-474-5889
    e-mail: regentchapey@nysed.gov

Member:
  Wade S Norwood (2019) . . . . . . . . . . . . . . . . . . . . . .585-436-2944
    e-mail: regent.norwood@nysed.gov
Member:
  Catherine Collins (2020) . . . . . . . . . . . . . . . . . . . . . . .518-474-5889
    e-mail: regent.collins@nysed.gov
Member:
  Judith Chin (2018) . . . . . . . . . . . . . . . . . . . . . . . . . .518-474-5889
    e-mail: regent.chin@nysed.gov
Member:
  Christine D Cea (2019) . . . . . . . . . . . . . . . . . . . . . . . .718-494-5306
    e-mail: regent.Cea@nysed.gov
Member:
  Nan Eileen Mead . . . . . . . . . . . . . . . . . . . . . . . . . .518-474-5889
    e-mail: Regent.Mead@nysed.gov
Member:
  Beverly Ourderkirk (2020) . . . . . . . . . . . . . . . . . . . . .315-375-8596
    e-mail: regent.ouderkirk@nysed.gov
Member:
  James R Tallon, Jr (2017) . . . . . . . . . . . . . . . . . . . . . .212-494-0777
    e-mail: regent.tallon@nysed.gov
Member:
  Roger B Tilles (2020) . . . . . . . . . . . . . . . . . . . . . . . . .516-364-2533
    e-mail: regent.tilles@nysed.gov
Member:
  Lester W Young, Jr (2020) . . . . . . . . . . . . . . . . . . . . .718-722-2796
    e-mail: regent.young@nysed.gov

**Children & Family Services, Office of**
52 Washington Street
Rensselaer, NY 12144-2834
518-473-7793  Fax: 518-486-7550
e-mail: info@ocfs.ny.gov

Commissioner:
  Sheila Poole . . . . . . . . . . . . . . . . . . . . . . . . . . . . .518-473-8437
    e-mail: info@ocfs.ny.gov
Assistant Commissioner, Communications:
  Monica Mahaffey . . . . . . . . . . . . . . . . . . . . . . . . . .518-473-7793
Bureau of Policy Analysis:
  Rayana Gonzales . . . . . . . . . . . . . . . . . . . . . . . . . .518-473-1776
Deputy Commissioner, Juvenile Justice & Opportunity for Youth:
  Felicia Reid . . . . . . . . . . . . . . . . . . . . . . . . . . . . . .518-473-1786
Deputy Commissioner, Child Welfare & Community Service:
  Lisa Ghartey Ogundimu . . . . . . . . . . . . . . . . . . . . . . .518-474-3377
Director of Regional Operations:
  Jim Hart . . . . . . . . . . . . . . . . . . . . . . . . . . . . . . . .518-473-1790

**Regional Operations**
Deputy Commissioner, Childcare Services:
  Janice Molnar . . . . . . . . . . . . . . . . . . . . . . . . . . . . .518-486-6247
Acting Associate Commissioner, Youth Programs & Services:
  Joseph Tomassone . . . . . . . . . . . . . . . . . . . . . . . . . .518-486-6766

**Education Department**
State Education Building
89 Washington Avenue
Albany, NY 12234
518-474-3852
Web site: www.nysed.gov

Interim Commissioner & University President:
  Betty A Rosa . . . . . . . . . . . . . . . . . . . . . . . . . . . . . .518-474-5844
Executive Deputy Commissioner:
  Vacant . . . . . . . . . . . . . . . . . . . . . . . . . . . . . . . . .518-473-8381
Assistant Commissioner, Public Affairs:
  Emily DeSantis . . . . . . . . . . . . . . . . . . . . . . . . . . . .518-474-1201
Chief Financial Officer:
  Phyllis Morris . . . . . . . . . . . . . . . . . . . . . . . . . . . . .518-474-7751

*Offices and agencies generally appear in alphabetical order, except when specific order is requested by listee.*

Policy Areas

Acting Counsel & Deputy Commissioner, Legal Affairs:
    Aaron Baldwin .................................518-474-6400
    e-mail: legal@nysed.gov

## Cultural Education Office
Cultural Education Center, 222 Madison Avenue, Albany, NY 12230
Web site: www.oce.nysed.gov
Deputy Commissioner:
    Mark Schaming...................................518-474-5976

### Educational Television & Public Broadcasting
Acting Director:
    Thomas Ruller ...............................518-474-5862
    e-mail: tom.ruller@nysed.gov

### State Archives
e-mail: archinfo@mail.nysed.gov
Assistant Commissioner & State Archivist:
    Thomas Ruller ................518-474-6926 or 518-473-7091
    e-mail: tom.ruller@nysed.gov
Archivist, Scheduling and State Agency Services:
    Richard Sloma .................518-474-6926 or 518-473-4715
    e-mail: richard.sloma@nysed.gov
Director, Archival Services:
    Maria Holden ...................518-474-6276 or 518-474-4856
    e-mail: maria.holden@nysed.gov
Head of Research Services:
    James Folts ..................................518-474-8955
    e-mail: archref@nysed.gov
Coordinator, State Records Center:
    Maggi Gonsalves ................518-457-4801 or 518-457-1040
    e-mail: records@nysed.gov
Head, Local Government Advisory Services:
    David Lowry...................................518-474-6926
    e-mail: recmgmt@nysed.gov
Head, Information Services:
    Michelle Arpey ................................518-474-6926
    e-mail: archinfo@nysed.gov
Educational Programs:
    Julie Daniels....................518-473-8495 or 518-474-6926
    e-mail: archedu@nysed.gov

### State Library
Cultural Education Center, 222 Madison Avenue, Albany, NY 12230
Web site: www.nysl.nysed.gov
Assistant Commissioner & State Librarian:
    Bernard Margolis .............................518-474-5930
    e-mail: bernard.margolis@nysed.gov
Unit Head, Technical Services & Systems:
    Liza Duncan .................................518-474-5946
    e-mail: liza.duncan@nysed.gov
Library Development:
    Carol Ann Desch ..............................518-474-7196
    e-mail: carol.desch@nysed.gov
Talking Book & Braille Library, BARD:
    Michael Whitney ..............................518-473-6178

### State Museum Office
Web site: www.nysm.nysed.gov
Director:
    Mark A Schaming..............................518-474-5812
    e-mail: nysmweb@nysed.gov
Coordinator, Public Programs:
    Nicole LaFountain............................518-474-0575
    e-mail: nicole.lafountain@nysed.gov

### Research and Collections
Director:
    Dr. John P Hart...............................518-474-5816
    e-mail: john.hart@nysed.gov
Chief Curator of History:
    Dr. Jennifer Lemak............................518-474-5842
    e-mail: jennifer.lemak@nysed.gov

Collections Database Manager:
    Ellen Stevens ...............................518-408-1522
    e-mail: ellen.stevens@nysed.gov
State Archaeologist:
    Dr.Christina B Reith.........................518-402-5975
    e-mail: christina.reith@nysed.gov

## Office of Curriculum & Instruction

## Office of Performance Improvement & Management Services/Chief Financial Office
Web site: www.oms.nysed.gov
Deputy Commissioner:
    Sharon Cates-Williams........................518-473-4706
Chief Financial Officer:
    Vacant......................................518-474-7751
Facilities & Business Services:
    Vacant......................................518-474-7770
Human Resources Management:
    Vacant......................................518-474-5215
    e-mail: hr@nysed.gov
    Grant Finance:
        Sarah Martin................................518-474-4875
        e-mail: grantsweb@nysed.gov
Director, Audit Services:
    Thalia Melendez ................518-473-4516/fax: 518-473-0259
    e-mail: oas@nysed.gov
Director, Education Finance:
    Brian Cechnicki .............................518-486-2422
State Review Officer:
    Justyn Bates ................................518-485-9373
Director, Special Education Fiscal Services - Rate Setting Unit:
    Suzanne Bolling ...............518-474-3227/fax: 518-486-3606
    e-mail: rateweb@nysed.gov
Director, STAC (Systems to Track & Account for Children):
    Steven Wright...................518-486-4887 or 518-474-7116
    fax: 518-402-5047

### Information Technology Services
Chief Information Officer:
    Karen Starke ..................518-486-5311/fax: 518-474-2519
Assistant Director:
    Ken Mason ...................................518-474-4640

## Office of P-12 Education Policy
89 Washington Avenue, EB West 2nd Fl Mezzanine, Albany, NY 12234
e-mail: nysedp12@mail.nysed.gov
Web site: www.p12.nysed.gov
Senior Deputy Commissioner:
    Kimberly Wilkins.............................518-474-3862
Basic Educational Data System (BEDS):
    Vacant......................................518-474-7965
Office of Early Learning:
    Meg McNiff..................................518-474-5807
    e-mail: oel@nysed.gov
Assistant Commissioner, Office of Innovation & School Reform:
    Cheryl Atkinson .............................518-473-8852
Native American Education:
    Vacant......................................518-474-0537
    *Child Nutrition Knowledge Center*
    Lead Contact:
        Vacant .....................................518-473-8781
    *Educational Management Services*
    Lead Contact:
        Vacant .....................................518-474-6541
    *Facilities & Planning*
    Acting Director:
        Rosanne Groff ...............518-474-3906 or 518-473-8486
    *Grants Management*
    Lead Contact:
        Maureen Lavare............................518-474-3936

*Offices and agencies generally appear in alphabetical order, except when specific order is requested by listee.*

Lead Contact:
David Frank . . . . . . . . . . . . . . . . . . . . . . . . . . . . . .518-474-1762
Assistant Commissioner:
Renee Rider . . . . . . . . . . . . . . . . . . . . . . . . . . .518-474-4817
Lead Contact:
Eric Suhr . . . . . . . . . . . . . . . . . . . . . . . . . . . . . .518-486-1547

## Office of Higher Education
89 Washington Ave, Room 977 EB Annex, Albany, NY 12234
e-mail: hedepcom@nysed.gov
Web site: www.highered.nysed.gov
Deputy Commissioner:
William Murphy . . . . . . . . . . . . . . . . . . . . . . . . . . . .518-486-3633

### Office of College and University Evaluation
Executive Director:
Vacant . . . . . . . . . . . . . . . . . . . . . .518-474-1551/fax: 518-474-7468
e-mail: ocueinfo@nysed.gov

### Office of Postsecondary Access, Support and Success
Executive Director:
Stanley S Hansen Jr. . . . . . . . . . . . . .518-474-3719/fax: 518-474-7468
e-mail: kiap@nysed.gov

### Office of Teaching Initiatives
Assistant Director:
Ann Jasinski . . . . . . . . . . . . . . . . . . . . . . . . . . . . . .518-474-3901

## Office of the Professions . . . . . . . . . . . . . . . . . . . .fax: 518-474-3863
89 Washington Avenue, 2nd Floor, West Mezzanine, Albany, NY 12234
Fax: 518-474-3863
Web site: www.op.nysed.gov
Deputy Commissioner:
Sarah Benson . . . . . . . . . . . . . . . . . . . . . . . . . . . . . .518-486-1765

### Office of Professional Discipline

### Registration Unit

### Professional Licensing Services
Director:
Susan Naccarato . . . . . . . . . . . .518-474-3817 x340/fax: 518-402-5265
e-mail: opdpls@nysed.gov

## Office of Adult Career & Continuing Education Services
(ACCES) . . . . . . . . . . . . . . . . . . . . . . . . . . . . . . . . .fax: 518-474-8802
89 Washington Avenue, Room 460 EBA, Albany, NY 12234
Fax: 518-474-8802
Web site: www.acces.nysed.gov
Deputy Commissioner:
Kevin Smith . . . . . . . . . . . . . . . . . . . . . . . . . . . . . . .518-474-2714
Assistant Commissioner:
Deborah Brown-Johnson . . . . . . . . . . .518-402-3955/fax: 518-473-6073
e-mail: accesadm@nysed.gov
Director, Proprietary School Supervision:
Vacant . . . . . . . . . . . . . . . . . . . .518-474-3969/fax: 518-473-3644
e-mail: BPSS@nysed.gov
Director, Adult Education Program & Policy:
Vacant . . . . . . . . . . . . . . . . . . . .518-474-8892/fax: 518-474-0319
e-mail: AEPP@nysed.gov
Director, Operations:
Deborah Brown-Johnson . . . . . . . . . . .518-474-2714/fax: 518-474-8802
e-mail: accesadm@nysed.gov

### Fiscal & Administrative Services
Coordinator:
Vacant . . . . . . . . . . . . . . . . . . . . . . . . . . . . . . . . . .518-486-4038

### Vocational Rehabilitation Administration
Statewide Corodinator, Workforce Development & Business Relations:
Joseph Tedesco . . . . . . . . . . . . . . . . . . . . . . . . . . . . .518-473-6829
e-mail: joseph.tedesco@nysed.gov

Manager, Independent Living Centers:
Robert Gumson . . . . . . . . . . . . . . . . . . . . . . . . . . . . .518-474-2925
e-mail: rgumson@mail.nysed.gov
### Albany District Office
80 Wolf Road, Suite 200, 2nd Floor, Albany, NY 12205
Manager:
Barbara Arisohn . . . . . . . . . . . . . .518-485-5545 or 518-473-8097
fax: 518-457-4562
e-mail: barbara.arisohn@nysed.gov
### Bronx District Office
1215 Zerega Avenue, Bronx, NY 10462
Manager:
Judith Pina . . . . . . . . . . . . . . . . . .718-931-3500 or 718-931-3023
fax: 718-931-4299
### Brooklyn District Office
55 Hanson Place, 2nd Floor, Brooklyn, NY 11217-1578
Manager:
Mark Weinstein . . . . . . . . . . . . . .718-722-6700 or 718-722-6710
fax: 718-722-6714
### Buffalo District Office
508 Main Street, Buffalo, NY 14202
Manager:
Christine Luly . . . . . . . . . . . . . . .716-848-8001 or 716-848-8012
fax: 716-848-8103
### Garden City District Office
711 Stewart Avenue, Suite 4, Garden City, NY 11530
Assistant District Office Manager:
Nick Spinelli . . . . . . . . . . . . . . . .516-227-6800 or 516-227-6802
fax: 516-227-6834
### Hauppauge District Office
State Office Building, 250 Veterans Memorial Highway, Room
3A-12, Hauppauge, NY 11788
Manager:
Sandy Silver . . . . . . . . . . . . . . . .631-952-6357 or 631-952-6350
fax: 631-952-5826
### Malone District Office
209 West Main Stree, Suite 3, Malone, NY 12953
Manager:
Pamela Dority . . . . . . . . . . . . . .518-483-3530/fax: 518-483-3552
e-mail: pamela.dority@nysed.gov
### Manhattan District Office
116 West 32nd Street, 5th Floor, New York, NY 10001
Assistant District Office Manager:
Diane Cox . . . . . . . . . . . . . . . . . .212-630-2300 or 212-630-2317
fax: 212-630-2365
e-mail: diane.cox@nysed.gov
### Mid-Hudson District Office
Manchester Mill Center, 301 Manchester Road, Suite 200,
Poughkeepsie, NY 12603
Regional Coordinator:
Daniel O'Shea . . . . . . . . . . . . . .845-452-5325 or 845-452-4935
fax: 845-452-5336
### Queens District Office
11-15 47th Avenue, Long Island City, NY 11101
Manager:
Magaly Lovell . . . . . . . . . . . . . . .347-510-3100 or 347-510-3138
fax: 718-784-3702
e-mail: magaly.lovell@nysed.gov
### Rochester District Office
109 S Union Street, 2nd Floor, Rochester, NY 14607
Assistant District Office Manager:
Wendy Ford . . . . . . . . . . . . . . . .585-238-2900 or 585-238-2932
fax: 585-325-2001
e-mail: wendy.ford@nysed.gov
### Southern Tier District Office
44 Hawley Street, Binghamton, NY 13901
Regional Coordinator:
Jack Lance . . . . . . . . . . . . . . . . . .607-721-8400 or 607-721-8401
fax: 607-721-8390
e-mail: jlance@mail.nysed.gov

*Offices and agencies generally appear in alphabetical order, except when specific order is requested by listee.*

### Syracuse District Office
333 East Washington Street, Room 230, Syracuse, NY 13202-1428
Manager:
Patrick Sheppard . . . . . . . . . . . . . 315-428-4179 or 315-428-4030
fax: 315-428-4280
e-mail: patrick.sheppard@nysed.gov

### Utica District Office
207 Genesee Street, Utica, NY 13501-2812
Manager:
Judith Petroski . . . . . . . . . . . . . . . 315-793-2536 or 315-793-2553
fax: 315-793-2724
e-mail: judith.petroski@nysed.gov

### White Plains District Office
75 South Broadway, Suite 200, White Plains, NY 10601
Manager:
Linda Schramm . . . . . . . . . . . . . . 914-946-1313 or 914-946-2423
fax: 914-946-1726
e-mail: linda.schramm@nysed.gov

## NYSTAR - Division of Science, Technology & Innovation
625 Broadway
8th Floor
Albany, NY 12245
518-292-5700  Fax: 518-292-5794
e-mail: NYSTARSupport@esd.ny.gov
Web site: www.esd.ny.gov/nystar

Director:
Matthew Watson . . . . . . . . . . . . . . . . . . . . . . . . . . . . . . 518-292-5700
Executive Vice President, Public Affairs & Strategic Initiatives:
Kay Wright . . . . . . . . . . . . . . . . . . . . . 518-292-5700/fax: 518-292-5798
Executive Vice President, Legal & General Counsel:
Elizabeth Fine . . . . . . . . . . . . . . . . . . . . . . . . . . . . . . . 518-292-5700

### Centers for Advanced Technology

#### Center for Advanced Ceramic Technology at Alfred University
2 Pine Street, Alfred, NY 14802-1296
e-mail: cactinfo@alfred.edu
Web site: cact.alfred.edu
Director:
Dr Matthew M Hall . . . . . . . . . . . . . . 607-871-2486/fax: 607-871-3469

#### Center for Advanced Materials Processing at Clarkson Univ
CAMP, Box 5665, Potsdam, NY 13699-5665
Web site: www.clarkson.edu/camp
Director:
S V Babu . . . . . . . . . . . . . . . . . . . . . 315-268-2336/fax: 315-268-7615
e-mail: babu@clarkson.edu

#### Center for Advanced Tech in Biomedical & Bioengineering
Univeristy at Buffalo, 701 Ellicott Street, Buffalo, NY 14203
Web site: www.bioinformatics.buffalo.edu/
Co-Director:
Alexander N. Cartwright PhD . . . . . . . . . . . . . . . . . . . . 716-645-0312
Co-Director:
Marnie LaVigne PhD . . . . . . . . . . . . . . . . . . . . . . . . . . 716-645-0312

#### Sensor CAT-Diagnostic Tools & Sensor Systems
SUNY at Stony Brook, Suffolk Hall, Room 115B, Stony Brook, NY
11794-3717
Web site: sensorcat.sunysb.edu
Director:
Serge Luryi . . . . . . . . . . . . . . . . . . . . 631-632-1368 or 631-632-8420
fax: 631-632-8529

#### Center for Emerging & Innovative Sciences
Univ of Rochester, 2 Taylor Hall, 260 Hutchison Rd, Rochester, NY
14627
Web site: www.ceis.rochester.edu

Director:
Mark Bocko . . . . . . . . . . . . . . . . . . . . . . . . . . . . . . . . 585-275-0547
e-mail: mark.bocko@seas.rochester.edu

#### Center for Advanced Information Management
Columbia University, 630 W 168th St, Bldg 30, New York, NY 10032
Director:
George Hripcsak . . . . . . . . . . . . . . . . 212-305-2944/fax: 212-305-0196

#### Center for Advanced Technology in Life Science Enterprise
Cornell University, 130 Biotechnology Bldg, Ithaca, NY 14853-2703
Web site: www.biotech.cornell.edu/cat
Director:
George Grills . . . . . . . . . . . . . . . . . . . . . . . . . . . . . . . 607-255-9693
e-mail: biotech@cornell.edu

#### Center for Advanced Technology in Photonics Applications
CUNY, Steinman Hall T606, 16D Convent Avenue, New York, NY 10031
Director:
David T. Crouse, PhD . . . . . . . . . . . . . . . . . . . . . . . . . 212-650-5330

#### Center for Automation Technologies & Systems at Rensselaer
CII 8011, 110 8th Street, Troy, NY 12180
Web site: www.cats.rpi.edu
Director:
John Wen . . . . . . . . . . . . . . . . . . . . . 518-276-8744/fax: 518-276-4897

#### Center for Advanced Medical Biotechnology
Biotechnology Building, 2nd Floor, Stony Brook, NY 11790
Web site: www.biotech.sunysb.edu
Director:
Clinton T Rubin PhD . . . . . . . . . . . . . 631-632-8521/fax: 631-632-8577

#### Center for Computer Applications & Software Engineering
Syracuse University, 2-212 Ctr for Science & Tech, Syracuse, NY 13244
Director:
Pramod Varshney . . . . . . . . . . . . . . . 315-443-1060/fax: 315-443-4745
e-mail: varshney@syr.edu

#### Center in Nanomaterials and Nanoelectronics
251 Fuller Road, Albany, NY 12203
Director:
Michael Fancher . . . . . . . . . . . . . . . . 518-437-8686/fax: 518-437-8687

#### Ctr for Advanced Tech in Telecommunications at Polytech Univ
5 MetroTech Center, 9th Floor, Brooklyn, NY 11201
Director:
Shivendra S Panwar . . . . . . . . . . . . . . 718-260-3050 or 718-260-3740
fax: 718-260-3074

#### Future Energy Systems CAT at Rensselaer Polytechnic Inst
110 8th Street, Troy, NY 12180
e-mail: cfes@rpi.edu
Web site: www.rpi.edu/cfes
Director:
Dr. Jian Sun . . . . . . . . . . . . . . . . . . . 518-276-8294/fax: 518-276-6844
e-mail: jsun@ecse.rpi.edu

#### Integrated Electronics Engineering Center at Binghamton
IEEC, Vestal Pkwy East, PO Box 6000, Binghamton, NY 13902-6000
e-mail: ieec@binghamton.edu
Web site: www.binghamton.edu/ieec/
Director:
Daryl Santos . . . . . . . . . . . . . . . . . . . 607-777-4769/fax: 607-777-4683

### Regional Technology Development Centers

#### Alliance for Manufacturing & Technology
69 Court St, 6th Fl, State St Entrance, Binghamton, NY 13901
e-mail: info@amt-mep.org
Web site: www.amt-mep.org
Executive Director:
Edward Gaetano . . . . . . . . . . . . 607-774-0022 x304/fax: 607-774-0026

*Offices and agencies generally appear in alphabetical order, except when specific order is requested by listee.*

**Center for Economic Growth**
30 Pearl St, Ste 100, Albany, NY 12207
e-mail: ceg@ceg.org
Web site: www.ceg.org
President/CEO:
    F Michael Tucker . . . . . . . . . . . . . . . 518-465-8975/fax: 518-465-6681
    e-mail: miket@ceg.org

**Central New York Technology Development Organization**
445 Electronics Pkwy, Ste 206, Liverpool, NY 13088
e-mail: mail@tdo.org
Web site: www.tdo.org
President/CEO:
    Robert I Trachtenberg . . . . . . . . . . . . 315-425-5144/fax: 315-233-1259
    e-mail: rtrachtenberg@tdo.org

**Council for Interntl Trade, Tech, Education & Communication**
Peyton Hall, Box 8561, Main St, Clarkson University, Potsdam, NY 13669
Web site: www.citec.org
Executive Director:
    William P. Murray . . . . . . . . . . . 315-268-3778 x29/fax: 315-268-4432

**High Technology of Rochester**
150 Lucius Gordon Dr, Suite 100, West Henrietta, NY 14586
Web site: www.htr.org
President:
    Jim Sendall . . . . . . . . . . . . . . . . . . . . . . . . . . . . . . . 585-214-2400
    e-mail: info@htr.org

**Hudson Valley Technology Development Center**
1450 Route 300, Building 1, Newburgh, NY 12550
e-mail: info@hvtdc.org
Web site: www.hvtdc.org
Executive Director:
    Thomas G Phillips, Sr . . . . . . . 845-391-8214 x3006/fax: 845-845-8218
    e-mail: tom.phillips@hvtdc.org

**Industrial & Technology Assistance Corp**
39 Broadway, Suite 1110, New York, NY 10006
Web site: www.itac.org
President:
    Sara Garretson . . . . . . . . . . . . . . . . . . 212-809-3900/fax: 646-588-5156
    e-mail: sgarretson@itac.org

**Long Island Forum for Technology**
510 Grumman Road West, Bethpage, NY 11714
e-mail: info@lift.org
Executive Director:
    William Wahlig . . . . . . . . . . . . . . . . . 631-969-3700/fax: 631-846-2789
    e-mail: bwahlig@lift.org

**Mohawk Valley Applied Technology Corp**
207 Genesee St, Ste 405, Utica, NY 13501
President:
    Paul MacEnroe . . . . . . . . . . . . . . . . . 315-793-8050/fax: 315-793-8057

**INSYTE Consulting (Western NY Technology Development Ctr)**
726 Exchange St, Ste 812, Buffalo, NY 14210
Web site: www.insyte-consulting.com
President:
    Benjamin Rand . . . . . . . . . . . . . . . . . 716-636-3626/fax: 716-845-6418

## CORPORATIONS, AUTHORITIES AND COMMISSIONS

# City University Construction Fund
555 W 57th St
11th Fl
New York, NY 10019
212-541-0171  Fax: 212-541-1014

Interim Executive Director:
    Judith Bergtraum . . . . . . . . . . . . . . . . . . . . . . . . . . . . . . 646-664-2605
    e-mail: iris.weinshall@mail.cuny.edu
Counsel:
    Frederick Schaffer . . . . . . . . . . . . . . . . . . . . . . . . . . . . . 646-664-9210

## New York City School Construction Authority
30-30 Thomson Ave
Long Island City, NY 11101-3045
718-472-8000  Fax: 718-472-8840
Web site: www.nycsca.org

Chair/Chancellor:
    Carmen Farina . . . . . . . . . . . . . . . . . . . . . . . . . . . . . . . 718-472-8000
President & Chief Executive Officer:
    Lorraine Grillo . . . . . . . . . . . . . . . . . . . . . . . . . . . . . . . 718-472-8001
Executive Vice President & General Counsel:
    Ross J Holden . . . . . . . . . . . . . . . . . . . . . . . . . . . . . . . 718-472-8220
VP, Finance:
    Marianne Egri . . . . . . . . . . . . . . . . . . . . . . . . . . . . . . . 718-472-8012
VP, Construction Management:
    Vacant . . . . . . . . . . . . . . . . . . . . . . . . . . . . . . . . . . . . . 718-472-8359
VP, Architecture & Engineering:
    E Bruce Barrett, RA . . . . . . . . . . . . . . . . . . . . . . . . . . . 718-472-8710
VP, Administration:
    Rebecca Fraley-Corrado . . . . . . . . . . . . . . . . . . . . . . . . 718-472-8149

## New York State Dormitory Authority
515 Broadway
Albany, NY 12207-2964
518-257-3000  Fax: 518-257-3100
e-mail: dabonds@dasny.org
Web site: www.dasny.org

One Penn Plaza
52nd Fl
New York, NY 10119-0098
212-273-5000
Fax: 212-273-5121

539 Franklin St
Buffalo, NY 14202-1109
716-884-9780
Fax: 716-884-9787

Chair:
    Alfonso L Carney Jr . . . . . . . . . . . . . . . 518-257-3000/fax: 518-257-3100
President/CEO:
    Paul T Williams Jr . . . . . . . . . . . . . . . . . 518-257-3180/fax: 518-257-3183
Vice President:
    Michael T Corrigan . . . . . . . . . . . . . . . . 518-257-3192/fax: 518-257-3183
Acting Chief Financial Officer:
    Linda H Button . . . . . . . . . . . . . . . . . . . 518-257-3562/fax: 518-257-3100
General Counsel:
    Michael Cusack . . . . . . . . . . . . . . . . . . . 518-257-3120/fax: 518-257-3101
Managing Director, Construction:
    Stephen D Curro, PE . . . . . . . . . . . . . . . 518-257-3271/fax: 518-257-3100
    e-mail: scurro@dasny.org
Managing Director, Public Finance & Portfolio Monitoring:
    Portia Lee . . . . . . . . . . . . . . . . . . . . . . . 518-257-3362/fax: 518-257-3100
    e mail: plee@dasny.org
Public Information Officer:
    John Chirlin . . . . . . . . . . . . . . . . . . . . . . . . . . . . . . . . . 518-257-3380
    e-mail: jchirlin@dasny.org

*Offices and agencies generally appear in alphabetical order, except when specific order is requested by listee.*

## New York State Higher Education Services Corp (NYSHESC)
99 Washington Ave
Albany, NY 12255
888-697-4372
Web site: www.hesc.ny.gov

Executive Vice President & Acting President:
Elsa Magee . . . . . . . . . . . . . . . . . . . . . .518-474-5592/fax: 518-474-5593
e-mail: elsa.magee@hesc.ny.gov
Director, Federal Relations:
Frank Ballmann. . . . . . . . . . . . . . . . . . . . . . . . . . . . . . .202-721-1186
e-mail: frank.ballmann@hesc.ny.gov
Director, Audit:
Matt Downey . . . . . . . . . . . . . . . . . . . .518-473-2287/fax: 518-486-6515
e-mail: matt.downey@hesc.ny.gov
General Counsel:
Thomas Brennan . . . . . . . . . . . . . . . . . . .518-473-1585/fax: 518-486-6515
e-mail: thomas.brennan@hesc.ny.gov
Communications/PIO:
Vacant. . . . . . . . . . . . . . . . . . . . . . .518-474-5775 or 518-474-5592
fax: 518-474-5593
Director, Federal Operations:
Victor Stucchi . . . . . . . . . . . . . . . . . . . .518-486-5885/fax: 518-402-3276
e-mail: victor.stucchi@hesc.ny.gov
Administrative Officer & CFO:
Warren Wallin . . . . . . . . . . . . . . . . . . .518-474-7505/fax: 518-474-4301
e-mail: victor.stucchi@hesc.ny.gov
Director, Training & Information Services:
Teresa Gehrer . . . . . . . . . . . . . . . . . . .518-402-6429/fax: 518-474-2839

## New York State Teachers' Retirement System
10 Corporate Woods Dr
Albany, NY 12211-2395
518-447-2900 or 800-348-7298 Fax: 518-447-2695
e-mail: media@nystrs.org
Web site: www.nystrs.org

Executive Director:
Thomas K Lee. . . . . . . . . . . . . . . . . . . . . . . . . . . . . . .518-447-2726
General Counsel:
Joseph J. Indelicato, Jr. . . . . . . . . . . . . . . . . . . . . . . . . . .518-447-2722
Actuary:
Richard Young . . . . . . . . . . . . . . . . . . . . . . . . . . . . . . .518-447-2692
Managing Director Operations:
Kevin Schaefer . . . . . . . . . . . . . . . . . . . . . . . . . . . . . . .518-447-2730
Director, Member Relations:
Sheila Gardella . . . . . . . . . . . . . . . . . . . . . . . . . . . . . . .518-447-2684
Manager, Public Information:
John Cardillo . . . . . . . . . . . . . . . . .518-447-4743/fax: 518-447-2875
Managing Director, Real Estate:
David C. Gillian . . . . . . . . . . . . . . . . . . . . . . . . . . . . . . .518-447-2751
Managing Director, Private Equity:
John W. Virtanen . . . . . . . . . . . . . . . . . . . . . . . . . . . . . .518-447-2751

## State University Construction Fund
353 Broadway
Albany, NY 12246
518-320-3200 Fax: 518-443-1008
Web site: www.sucf.suny.edu

General Manager:
Robert M Haelen. . . . . . . . . . . . . . . . . . . . . . . . . . . . . . .518-320-1502
Associate Counsel:
Terese Meagher. . . . . . . . . . . . . . . . . . . . . . . . . . . . . . .518-320-1746

*See Legislative Branch in Section 1 for additional Standing Committee and Subcommittee information.*

### Assembly Standing Committees

**Education**
Chair:
Michael Benedetto (D) . . . . . . . . . . . . . . . . . . . . . . . . . .518-455-5296

**Higher Education**
Chair:
Deborah J Glick (D) . . . . . . . . . . . . . . . . . . . . . . . . . . . .518-455-4841

**Libraries & Education Technology**
Chair:
Vacant . . . . . . . . . . . . . . . . . . . . . . .518-455-5517/fax: 518-455-5418

### Assembly Task Forces

**Skills Development & Career Education, Legislative Commission on**
Assembly Chair:
Vacant . . . . . . . . . . . . . . . . . . . . . . . . . . . . . . . . . . .518-455-4527

**University-Industry Cooperation, Legislative Task Force on**
Chair:
Vacant . . . . . . . . . . . . . . . . . . . . . . . . . . . . . . . . . . .518-455-0000
Coordinator:
Maureen Schoolman . . . . . . . . . . . . . . . .518-455-3632/fax: 518-455-4175

### Senate Standing Committees

**Education**
Chair:
Shelley Mayer (D, WF). . . . . . . . . . . . . . . . . . . . . . . . . . .518-455-2031
Ranking Minority Member:
Betty Little (R, C, IP) . . . . . . . . . . . . . . . . . . . . . . . . . . .518-455-2811

**Higher Education**
Chair:
Toby Ann Stavisky (D). . . . . . . . . . . . . . . . . . . . . . . . . . .518-455-3461
Ranking Minority Member:
Kennth P. LaValle (R) . . . . . . . . . . . . . . . . . . . . . . . . . . .518-455-3121

### National Archives & Records Administration

**Franklin D Roosevelt Presidential Library & Museum**
4079 Albany Post Road, Hyde Park, NY 12538
846-486-7770
Web site: www.fdrlibrary.marist.edu
Director:
Paul M. Sparrow . . . . . . . . . . . . . . . . . . . . . . . . . . . . . .845-486-7741
e-mail: paul.sparrow@nara.gov

### US Defense Department
Web site: www.defense.gov

### US Military Academy
622 Swift Road, West Point, NY 10996
845-938-4011
Web site: www.usma.edu
Superintendent:
Lt. Gen. Robert L. Caslen, Jr.

*Offices and agencies generally appear in alphabetical order, except when specific order is requested by listee.*

Public Affairs:
  Staff Sgt. Vito Bryant

## US Education Department
Web site: www.ed.gov

**Region 2 - NY, NJ, PR, Vi** . . . . . . . . . . . . . . . . . . . . . fax: 646-428-3904
  32 Old Slip, 25th Floor, New York, NY 10005
  646-428-3906  Fax: 646-428-3904
Communications Director:
  Jacquelyn Pitta . . . . . . . . . . . . . . . . . . . . . . . . . 646-428-3906
Education Program Specialist:
  Taylor Owen Ramsey . . . . . . . . . . . . . . . . . . . . . . 646-428-3906

### Civil Rights
Regional Director:
  Timothy Blanchard . . . . . . . . . . . . . . . . . . . . . . . 646-428-3805
Chief Civil Rights Attorney:
  Rachel Pomerantz . . . . . . . . . . . . . . . . . . . . . . . . 646-428-3835

### Federal Student Aid
Director:
  Robin R. Shinn . . . . . . . . . . . . . . . . . . . . . . . . . . 646-428-3770
Team Leader:
  Susan Ferraiole . . . . . . . . . . . . . . . . . . . . . . . . . . 646-428-3771

### Office of Inspector General
Regional Inspector General, Audit:
  Daniel P. Schultz . . . . . . . . . . . . . . . . . . . . . . . . 646-428-3888
Special Agent-in-Charge:
  Brian Hickey . . . . . . . . . . . . . . . . . . . . . . . . . . . . 646-428-3874

### Office of Management
Human Resources Specialist:
  Vacant

## US Transportation Department
Web site: www.transportation.gov

**US Merchant Marine Academy** . . . . . . . . . . . . . . . fax: 516-773-5774
  300 Steamboat Road, Kings Point, NY 11024
  516-773-5800  Fax: 516-773-5774
  Web site: www.usmma.edu
Superintendent:
  Rear Admiral James A. Helis

### U.S. CONGRESS

*See U.S. Congress Chapter for additional Standing Committee and Subcommittee information.*

## House of Representatives Standing Committees

### Education & the Workforce
Chair:
  John Kline (R-MN) . . . . . . . . . . . . . . . . . . . . . . . . 202-225-2271
Ranking Member:
  Robert C. Scott (D-VA) . . . . . . . . . . . . . . . . . . . . 202-225-8351
New York Delegate:
  Hakeem S. Jeffries (D) . . . . . . . . . . . . . . . . . . . . . 202-225-5936
New York Delegate:
  Elise Stefanik (R) . . . . . . . . . . . . . . . . . . . . . . . . . 202-225-4611

## Senate Standing Committees

### Health, Education, Labor & Pensions
Chair:
  Lamar Alexander (R-TN) . . . . . . . . . . . . . . . . . . . 202-224-4944
Ranking Member:
  Patty Murray (D-WA) . . . . . . . . . . . . . . . . . . . . . . 202-224-2621

### PRIVATE SECTOR

**ASPIRA of New York Inc**
630 9th Avenue, Suite 302, New York, NY 10036
212-564-6880  Fax: 212-564-7152
*Works towards the social advancement of youth in the Puerto Rican & Latino communities through the provision of educational programs & services*
Dr. Mark Gonzalez, Chief Executive Officer

**Advocates for Children of New York Inc**
151 West 30th Street, 5th Floor, New York, NY 10001
212-947-9779  Fax: 212-947-9790
e-mail: info@advocatesforchildren.org
Web site: www.advocatesforchildren.org
*Advocacy for public education for all NYS children*
Kim Sweet, Executive Director

**Africa-America Institute (The)**
420 Lexington Avenue, Suite 1706, New York, NY 10170-0002
212-949-5666  Fax: 212-682-6174
e-mail: aainy@aaionline.org
Web site: www.aaionline.org
*Organization committed to fostering development in Africa through advanced education & professional training*
Amini Kajunju, President & Chief Executive Officer

**Agudath Israel of America**
42 Broadway, 14th Floor, New York, NY 10004
212-797-9000  Fax: 646-254-1600
e-mail: news@agudathisrael.org
*Religious school education; Orthodox Judaism*
Dovid Zwiebel, Executive Vice President

**American Higher Education Development Corporation**
116 Village Blvd, Suite 200, Princeton, NJ 08540
646-569-5681
e-mail: stave@ahed.com
Web site: www.ahed.com
*Acquisition of & investment in post-secondary education institutions*
Stephen Tave, President & Chief Executive Officer

**Associated Medical Schools of New York**
1270 Avenue of the Americas, Suite 606, New York, NY 10020
212-218-4610  Fax: 212-218-4278
e-mail: info@amsny.org
Web site: www.amsny.org
*A consortium of the sixteen medical schools in New York State; advocacy, resources & educational development programs*
Jo Wiederhorn, President & Chief Executive Officer

**Association of Proprietary Colleges**
121 State Street, Albany, NY 12207
518-437-1867  Fax: 518-436-4751
e-mail: apc@apc-colleges.org
Web site: www.apc-colleges.org
*Association representing the proprietary colleges of New York State*
Donna S. Gurnett, Executive Director

**Catholic School Administrators Association of NYS**
525 4th Avenue, Troy, NY 12182
518-273-1205  Fax: 518-273-1206
Web site: www.csaanys.org
Carol Geddis, Executive Director

**Center for Educational Innovation - Public Education Association**
28 West 44th Street, Suite 801, New York, NY 10036
212-302-8800  Fax: 212-302-0088
e-mail: info@the-cei.org
Web site: www.the-cei.org
*Advocacy & public information for NYC public education*
Seymour Fliegel, President

*Offices and agencies generally appear in alphabetical order, except when specific order is requested by listee.*

Policy Areas

**Cerebral Palsy Associations of New York State**
330 West 34th Street, 15th Floor, New York, NY 10001-2488
212-947-5770  Fax: 212-594-4538
e-mail: information@cpofnys.org
Web site: www.cpofnys.org
*Serves individuals with cerebral palsy & other significant disabilities as well as their families through advocacy, technical assistance, publications & networking events*
Susan Constantino, President & Chief Executive Officer

**Coalition of New York State Career Schools (The)**
437 Old Albany Post Road, Garrison, NY 10524
845-788-5070  Fax: 845-788-5071
Web site: www.cnyscs.com
*Licensed trade & business schools in NYS*
Terence M. Zaleski, Executive Director & Counsel

**Commission on Independent Colleges & Universities**
17 Elk Street, PO Box 7289, Albany, NY 12224
518-436-4781  Fax: 518-436-0417
Web site: www.cicu.org
*Association dedicated to promoting the public policy interests of New York State's independent colleges & universities; advocacy, research, publications & programs*
Laura L. Anglin, President

**Conference of Big 5 School Districts**
74 Chapel Street, Albany, NY 12207
518-465-4274  Fax: 518-465-0638
e-mail: big5@big5schools.org
Web site: www.big5schools.org
Georgia M. Asciutto, Executive Director

**Cornell University**
314 Day Hall, Ithaca, NY 14853
607-254-4636  Fax: 607-254-6225
e-mail: info@cornell.edu
Web site: www.cornell.edu
Joel Malina, Vice President for University Relations

**Cornell University, Rural Schools Association of NYS**
Warren Hall 275 Flex, Cornell University, Ithaca, NY 14853
607-255-8709 or 518-250-5710  Fax: 607-254-2896
e-mail: dal295@cornell.edu
Web site: www.cardi.cals.cornell.edu/programs/rsa
*Advocacy for small & rural school districts throughout New York*
David A. Little, Executive Director

**Cornell University, School of Industrial & Labor Relations**
309 Ives Hall, Ithaca, NY 14853
607-255-2762 or 607-255-3276  Fax: 607-255-2185
e-mail: hallock@cornell.edu
Web site: www.ilr.cornell.edu
*Education, workforce preparedness; student peer culture, employee training, recruitment & selection practices*
Kevin Hallock, Dean

**Council of School Supervisors & Administrators**
40 Rector Street, 12th Floor, New York, NY 10006
212-823-2020  Fax: 212-962-6130
e-mail: erminia@csa-nyc.org
Web site: www.csa-nyc.org
Ernest Logan, President

**ExpandED Schools**
1440 Broadway, 16th Floor, New York, NY 10018
646-943-8700
e-mail: info@expandedschools.org
Web site: www.expandedschools.org
*Non-profit organization dedicated to ensuring that all children in NYS have access to quality in-school, after-school & summer programs*
Lucy N. Friedman, President

**Council on the Environment of NYC, Environmental Education**
100 Gold Street, Suite 3300, New York, NY 10038
212-788-7900  Fax: 212-788-7913
Web site: www.grownyc.org
*Environmental education & action training programs for students*
Marcel Van Ooyen, Executive Director

**Fordham University**
441 East Fordham Road, Bronx, NY 10458
718-817-1000
e-mail: president@fordham.edu
Web site: www.fordham.edu
Joseph M McShane, SJ, President

**Jewish Education Project (The)**
520 Eighth Avenue, 15th Floor, New York, NY 10018
646-472-5300  Fax: 646-472-5421
e-mail: info@jewishedproject.org
Web site: www.jewishedproject.org
*Advancing & enhancing Jewish education*
Tara Slone-Goldstein, President

**Learning Leaders**
75 Maiden Lane, Room 801, New York, NY 10038
212-213-3370  Fax: 212-213-0787
*Provides volunteers & parents with resources & training workshops designed to help New York City's public school students develop study, organizational & other school-based skills*
Jane Heaphy, Executive Director

**Library Trustees Association of NYS**
PO Box 11048, Albany, NY 12211
518-445-9505
Web site: www.librarytrustees.org
Patricia Fontanella, President

**MDRC**
16 East 34th Street, 19th Floor, New York, NY 10016-4326
212-532-3200  Fax: 212-684-0832
e-mail: information@mdrc.org
Web site: www.mdrc.org
*Nonprofit research & field testing of education & employment programs for disadvantaged adults & youth*
Gordon Berlin, President

**Museum Association of New York**
265 River Street, Troy, NY 12180
518-273-3400  Fax: 518-273-3416
e-mail: info@manyonline.org
Web site: www.manyonline.org
*An information & advocacy resource for the state's museum community*
Devin Lander, Executive Director

**New York Community Colleges Association of Presidents**
c/o Onondaga Community College, 4585 West Seneca Turnpike, Syracuse, NY 13215-4585
315-498-2214  Fax: 315-469-4475
Kevin Dunn, President

**NYC Board of Education Employees, Local 372/AFSCME, AFL-CIO**
125 Barclay Street, 6th Floor, New York, NY 10007
212-815-1372  Fax: 212-815-1347
Web site: www.local372.org
Shaun D. Francois, President

*Offices and agencies generally appear in alphabetical order, except when specific order is requested by listee.*

**NYS Alliance for Arts Education**
PO Box 2217, Albany, NY 12220-0217
518-473-0823 Fax: 518-486-7329
Web site: www.nysaae.org
*State & local advocacy, professional development, technical assistance & information for educators, organizations, artists, parents & policymakers*
Carol Brown, President

**NYS Association for Health, Physical Education, Recreation & Dance**
77 North Ann Street, Little Falls, NY 13365
315-823-1015 Fax: 315-823-1012
Web site: www.nysahperd.org
*Promoting, educating & creating opportunites for physical education, health, recreation & dance professionals*
James Rose, President

**NYS Association for the Education of Young Children**
230 Washington Avenue Ext, Albany, NY 12203-5390
518-867-3517 Fax: 518-867-3520
e-mail: contactus@nysaeyc.org
Web site: www.nysaeyc.org
*Advocacy, education & support for individuals working in the early care & education profession in NYS*
Kristen Kerr, Executive Director

**NYS Association of School Business Officials**
453 New Karner Road, Albany, NY 12205
518-434-2281 Fax: 518-434-1303
e-mail: asbomail@nysasbo.org
Web site: www.nysasbo.org
*Leadership in the practice of school business management*
Michael J. Borges, Executive Director

**NYS Association of Small City School Districts**
c/o Biggerstaff Law Firm, 1280 New Scotland Road, Slingerlands, NY 12159
518-475-9500 Fax: 518-475-7677
e-mail: reb@biggerstaff-firm.com
Web site: scsd.neric.org
*Advocacy for small city school districts*
Robert Biggerstaff, Executive Director

**NYS Head Start Association**
230 Washington Avenue Ext, Albany, NY 12203
518-452-0897 Fax: 518-452-0898
e-mail: nyshsa@gmail.com
Web site: www.nysheadstart.org
*Educational program designed to meet the needs of low-income children & their families*
Ouida Foster Toutebon, Executive Director

**NYS Public High School Athletic Association**
8 Airport Park Blvd, Latham, NY 12110
518-690-0771 Fax: 518-690-0775
Web site: www.nysphsaa.org
*Promotes fair & safe interschool athletic competition & activities among secondary schools in NYS*
Robert Zayas, Executive Director

**NYS Reading Association**
PO Box 874, Albany, NY 12201-0874
518-741-0032 Fax: 518-741-0032
Web site: www.nysreading.org
*Literacy education advocacy & professional development programs for educators*
Eileen LaSpaluto, President

**Nelson A Rockefeller Inst of Govt, Higher Education Program**
411 State Street, Albany, NY 12203-1003
518-443-5522 or 518-443-5837 Fax: 518-443-5788
e-mail: info@rockinst.suny.edu
Web site: www.rockinst.org
*Accountability & autonomy in public higher education; system governance; performance funding, budgeting, reporting & assessment*
Thomas L. Gais, Director

**New York Community College Trustees (NYCCT)**
State University Plaza, S-123, Albany, NY 12246
518-320-1302 or 518-320-1100 Fax: 518-320-1543
Web site: www.suny.edu/nycct
*Education, advocacy & communication for the trustees of NYS community colleges*
Cynthia Demarest, President & Chief Executive Officer

**New York Library Association (The)**
6021 State Farm Road, Guilderland, NY 12084
518-432-6952 Fax: 518-427-1697
e-mail: info@nyla.org
Web site: www.nyla.org
*Advocacy on behalf of public, college & school libraries on funding & legislation*
Jeremy Johannesen, Executive Director

**New York State Association of Independent Schools**
17 Elk Street, 1st Floor, Albany, NY 12207
518-694-5500 Fax: 518-694-5501
e-mail: mark@nysais.org
Web site: www.nysais.org
*Accreditation & evaluation of member schools, professional development programs, advocacy, information & statistics*
Mark W. Lauria, Executive Director

**New York State Catholic Conference**
465 State Street, Albany, NY 12203-1004
518-434-6195 Fax: 518-434-9796
e-mail: info@nyscatholic.org
Web site: www.nyscatholic.org
*Represents the public policy interests of NYS Bishops in the areas of health, education, welfare & human/civil rights with the objective of achieving justice for all individuals*
Richard E. Barnes, Executive Director

**New York State Congress of Parents & Teachers Inc**
One Wembley Court, Albany, NY 12205-3830
518-452-8808 or 877-569-7782 Fax: 518-452-8105
e-mail: pta.office@nyspta.org
Web site: www.nyspta.org
*Advocates for & promotes education, health & welfare for all children*
Bonnie Russell, President

**New York State Council of School Superintendents**
7 Elk Street, 3rd Floor, Albany, NY 12207-1002
518-449-1063 Fax: 518-426-2229
Web site: www.nyscoss.org
Robert J. Reidy, Jr., Executive Director

**New York State School Boards Association**
24 Century Hill Drive, Suite 200, Latham, NY 12110-2125
518-783-0200 Fax: 518-783-0211
Web site: www.nyssba.org
*Public school leadership advocates*
Timothy G. Kremer, Executive Director

Policy Areas

*Offices and agencies generally appear in alphabetical order, except when specific order is requested by listee.*

**New York State School Music Association (NYSSMA)**
718 The Plain Road, Westbury, NY 11590-5931
516-997-7200 Fax: 516-997-1700
e-mail: executive@nyssma.org
Web site: www.nyssma.org
*Advocacy for quality music education for all students in member school programs*
Steven E. Schopp, Executive Director

**New York State United Teachers/AFT, NEA, AFL-CIO**
800 Troy-Schenectady Road, Latham, NY 12110-2455
518-213-6000 or 800-342-9810 Fax: 518-213-6415
Web site: www.nysut.org
*Represents employees & retirees of NY's public schools, colleges & healthcare facilities*
Karen E. Magee, President

**New York University**
25 West 4th Street, 5th Floor, New York, NY 10012
212-998-6840 Fax: 212-995-4021
e-mail: jhb5@nyu.edu
Web site: www.nyu.edu
*Office of Public Affairs*
John Beckman, Vice President

**Niagara University**
Alumni Hall, Niagara University, NY 14109-2014
716-286-8352 Fax: 716-286-8349
Web site: www.niagara.edu
Timothy M. Downs, Chief Academic Officer

**ProLiteracy Worldwide**
104 Marcellus Street, Syracuse, NY 13204
315-422-9121 or 888-528-2224 Fax: 315-422-6369
e-mail: info@proliteracy.org
Web site: www.proliteracy.org
*Promotes educational programs & services designed to help adults & families gain literacy skills*
Kevin Morgan, President & Chief Executive Officer

**Rensselaer Polytechnic Institute**
110 8th Street, Troy, NY 12180
518-276-2750 Fax: 518-276-3715
e-mail: media@rpi.edu
Web site: www.rpi.edu
*Strategic Communications & External Relations*
Allison Newman, Associate Vice President, External Relations & Administration

**Research Foundation of SUNY**
PO Box 9, Albany, NY 12201-0009
518-434-7000 Fax: 518-434-9108
e-mail: cathy.kaszluga@rfsuny.org
Web site: www.rfsuny.org
*Facilitates research, education & public service at SUNY campuses*
Catherine Kaszluga, Vice President for Strategy & Planning

**Rochester School for the Deaf**
1545 St Paul Street, Rochester, NY 14621
585-544-1240 Fax: 585-544-0383
e-mail: info@rsdeaf.org
Web site: www.rsdeaf.org
*Complete educational program for deaf, blind & physically disabled students in NYS*
Antony A.L. McLetchie, Superintendent & Chief Executive Officer

**Schuyler Center for Analysis & Advocacy (SCAA)**
540 Broadway, Albany, NY 12207
518-463-1896 Fax: 518-463-3364
e-mail: kbreslin@scaany.org
Web site: www.scaany.org
*Advocacy & policy analysis on education, child welfare, health, economic security, mental health, revenue & taxation issues*
Kate Breslin, President & Chief Executive Officer

**School Administrators Association of NYS**
8 Airport Park Blvd, Latham, NY 12110
518-782-0600 Fax: 518-782-9552
e-mail: kcasey@saanys.org
Web site: www.saanys.org
*Advocacy & services for New York State's public school leaders*
Kevin S. Casey, Executive Director

**Sports & Arts in Schools Foundation**
58-12 Queens Blvd, Suite 1, Woodside, NY 11377
718-786-7110 Fax: 718-205-1098
e-mail: info@sasfny.org
Web site: www.sasfny.org
*Organizes activities to help underachieving NYC students build their skills & improve wellness*
James R. O'Neill, Chief Executive Officer

**Syracuse University, Maxwell School of Citizenship & Public Affairs**
200 Eggers Hall, Syracuse, NY 13244-1020
315-443-2252
e-mail: info@maxwell.syr.edu
Web site: www.maxwell.syr.edu
*Education, healthcare, entrepreneurship policies, social welfare, income distribution & comparative social policies*
James B. Steinberg, Dean

**Syracuse University, Office of Government & Community Relations**
Room 2-212, Center for Science & Technology, Syracuse, NY 13244-4100
315-443-3919 Fax: 315-443-3676
e-mail: gcr@syr.edu
Web site: gcr.syr.edu
Eric Persons, Associate Vice President

**Teachers College, Columbia University**
525 West 120th Street, New York, NY 10027
212-678-3000 Fax: 212-678-3682
e-mail: fuhrman@tc.columbia.edu
Web site: www.tc.columbia.edu
*Education policy*
Susan H. Fuhrman, President

**Teaching Matters Inc**
475 Riverside Drive, Suite 1270, New York, NY 10115-0122
212-870-3505 Fax: 212-870-3516
e-mail: inquiry@teachingmatters.org
Web site: www.teachingmatters.org
*Technology planning & professional development for NYC public schools*
Lynette Guastaferro, Executive Director

**United Federation of Teachers**
52 Broadway, New York, NY 10004
212-777-7500
e-mail: mmulgrew@uft.org
Web site: www.uft.org
*Advocacy for education & healthcare professionals*
Michael Mulgrew, President

*Offices and agencies generally appear in alphabetical order, except when specific order is requested by listee.*

**United University Professions**
800 Troy-Schenectady Road, Latham, NY 12110-2424
800-342-4206  Fax: 866-812-9446
e-mail: fkowal@uupmail.org
Web site: www.uupinfo.org
*SUNY labor union of academic & other professional faculty*
Frederick E. Kowal, President

**Western New York Library Resources Council**
Airport Commerce Park East, 4950 Genesee Street, Suite 170, Cheektowaga, NY 14225
716-633-0705  Fax: 716-288-9400
e-mail: sknab@wnylrc.org
Web site: www.wnylrc.org
*Consortium of Western NY libraries dedicated to improving access to information & promoting resource sharing & library interests*
Sheryl Knab, Executive Director

Policy Areas

*Offices and agencies generally appear in alphabetical order, except when specific order is requested by listee.*

## ELECTIONS

### NEW YORK STATE

### GOVERNOR'S OFFICE

**Governor's Office**
Executive Chamber
State Capitol
Albany, NY 12224
518-474-8390 Fax: 518-474-1513
Web site: www.ny.gov

Governor:
  Andrew M Cuomo . . . . . . . . . . . . . . . . . . . . . . . . . . . . . . . 518-474-8390
Secretary to the Governor:
  Melissa DeRosa . . . . . . . . . . . . . . . . . . . . 518-474-4246 or 212-681-4580
Counsel to the Governor:
  Kumiki Gibson . . . . . . . . . . . . . . . . . . . . . 518-474-8343 or 212-681-4580
Chief of Staff:
  Jill DesRosiers . . . . . . . . . . . . . . . . . . . . . 518-474-8390 or 212-681-4580
Director, Communications:
  Peter Ajemian . . . . . . . . . . . . . . . . . . . . . 518-474-8418 or 212-681-4640
Deputy Secretary for Civil Rights:
  Vacant . . . . . . . . . . . . . . . . . . . . . . . . 212-681-4580 or 518-486-1214
First Assistant Counsel:
  R Nadine Fontaine . . . . . . . . . . . . . . . . . . . . . . . . . . . . . 518-474-8434

### EXECUTIVE DEPARTMENTS AND RELATED AGENCIES

**Elections, State Board of**
40 North Pearl Street
Suite 5
Albany, NY 12207-2729
518-474-6220 or 518-474-8100  Fax: 518-486-4068
e-mail: info@elections.ny.gov
Web site: www.elections.ny.gov

Co-Chair:
  Peter S Kosinski . . . . . . . . . . . . . . . . . . . 518-474-8100 or 518-474-6236
Co-Chair:
  Douglas A Kellner . . . . . . . . . . . . . . . . . . . . . . . . . . . . . 518-474-8100
Commissioner:
  Andrew J Spano . . . . . . . . . . . . . . . . . . . . . . . . . . . . . . 518-474-8100
Commissioner:
  Gregory P. Peterson . . . . . . . . . . . . . . . . 518-474-8100 or 518-474-6236
Co-Executive Director:
  Todd Valentine . . . . . . . . . . . . . . . . . . . . 518-474-6336 or 518-474-6236
  fax: 518-474-1008
Co-Executive Director:
  Robert A Brehm . . . . . . . . . . . . . . . . . . . . 518-474-6336 or 518-474-8100
  fax: 518-474-1008
Special Counsel:
  Kimberly A Galvin . . . . . . . . . . . . . . . . . . 518-474-6367 or 518-474-2063
  fax: 518-486-6627
Director, Public Information:
  John W Conklin . . . . . . . . . . . . . . . . . . 518-474-1953/fax: 518-473-8315
  e-mail: info@elections.ny.gov

**Administrative Services**
Administrative Officer:
  Vacant . . . . . . . . . . . . . . . . . . . . . . 518-474-6336/fax: 518-474-1008

**Campaign Finance**
Campaign Finance:
  Campaign Finance/ Compliance Call Center . . . . . . . . . . 518-474-8200 or
  800-458-3453

fax: 518-486-6627
e-mail: cfinfo@elections.ny.gov

**Counsel/Enforcement**
Chief Enforcement Counsel:
  Vacant . . . . . . . . . . . . . . . . . . . . . . . . . . . . . . . . . . . . . . 518-486-7858
  e-mail: enforcement@elections.ny.gov
Special Counsel:
  Kimberly A Galvin . . . . . . . . . . . . . . . . . . 518-474-6367 or 518-474-2063
  fax: 518-486-6627
Co-Counsel:
  Brian M Quail . . . . . . . . . . . . . . . . . . . . . . . . . . . . . . . . 518-474-6367
Deputy Counsel:
  William McCann . . . . . . . . . . . . . . . . . . . . . . . . . . . . . . . 518-474-2063

**Election Operations & Services**
Director:
  Thomas E Connolly . . . . . . . . . . . . . . . . . . 518-473-5086/fax: 518-486-4546
Deputy Director:
  Brendan Lovullo . . . . . . . . . . . . . . . . . . 518-473-5086/fax: 518-486-4546

**Public Information**
Director:
  John W Conklin . . . . . . . . . . . . . . . . . . 518-474-1953/fax: 518-473-8315
  e-mail: info@elections.ny.gov
Deputy Director:
  Thomas E Connolly . . . . . . . . . . . . . . . . . . . . . . . . . . . . . 518-474-1953

**County Boards of Elections**

**Albany** . . . . . . . . . . . . . . . . . . . . . . . . . . . . . . . . fax: 518-487-5077
32 N Russell Road, Albany, NY 12206
Fax: 518-487-5077
e-mail: boardofelections@albanycounty.com
Web site: www.albanycounty.com
Commissioner:
  Matthew J Clyne (D) . . . . . . . . . . . . . . . . . . . . . . . . . 518-487-5060
Commissioner:
  Rachel L Bledi (R) . . . . . . . . . . . . . . . . . . . . . . . . . . . 518-487-5060
Deputy Commissioner:
  Kathleen A Donovan (D) . . . . . . . . . . . . . . . . . . . . . . . 518-487-5060
Deputy Commissioner:
  Ellen Graziano (R) . . . . . . . . . . . . . . . . . . . . . . . . . . . 518-487-5060

**Allegany** . . . . . . . . . . . . . . . . . . . . . . . . . . . . . . . fax: 585-268-9406
6 Schuyler Street, Belmont, NY 14813
Fax: 585-268-9406
e-mail: acboe@alleganyco.com
Web site: www.alleganyco.com
Commissioner:
  Michael J McCormick (D) . . . . . . . . . . . . . . . . . . . . . 585-268-9295
  e-mail: mccormm@alleganyco.com
Commissioner:
  Richard Hollis (R) . . . . . . . . . . . . . . . . . . . . . . . . . . . 585-268-9294
  e-mail: hollisrg@alleganyco.com
Deputy Commissioner:
  Barbara Broughton (D) . . . . . . . . . . . . . . . . . . . . . . . 585-268-9295
  e-mail: broughB@alleganyco.com
Deputy Commissioner:
  Marcy Crawford (R) . . . . . . . . . . . . . . . . . . . . . . . . . 585-268-9294
  e-mail: crawfoMJ@alleganyco.com

**Broome** . . . . . . . . . . . . . . . . . . . . . . . . . . . . . . fax: 607-778-2174
Government Plaza, 60 Hawley Street, P.O. Box 1766, Binghamton, NY
  13902
Fax: 607-778-2174
Web site: www.broomevotes.com
Commissioner:
  John L Perticone (D) . . . . . . . . . . . . . . . . . . . . . . . . . 607-778-2172
Commissioner:
  Oliver N Blaise, III (R) . . . . . . . . . . . . . . . . . . . . . . . . 607-778-2172
Deputy Commissioner:
  Christina Dutko (D) . . . . . . . . . . . . . . . . . . . . . . . . . . 607-778-2172

*Offices and agencies generally appear in alphabetical order, except when specific order is requested by listee.*

Deputy Commissioner:
 Karen A Davis (R) . . . . . . . . . . . . . . . . . . . . .607-778-2172

**Cattaraugus** . . . . . . . . . . . . . . . . . . . . . . . . . . . .fax: 716-938-2775
207 Rock City Street, Suite 100, Little Valley, NY 14755
Fax: 716-938-2775
Web site: www.cattco.org
Commissioner:
 Kevin Burleson (D) . . . . . . . . . . . . . . . . . . .716-938-2404
Commissioner:
 Michael M Brisky (R) . . . . . . . . . . . . . . . . . .716-938-2405
Deputy Commissioner:
 Laura Howard (D) . . . . . . . . . . . . . . . . . . . . .716-938-2403
Deputy Commissioner:
 Cortney Spittler (R) . . . . . . . . . . . . . . . . . . .716-938-2401

**Cayuga** . . . . . . . . . . . . . . . . . . . . . . . . . . . .fax: 315-253-1289
157 Genesee Street (Basement), Auburn, NY 13021
Commissioner:
 Katie Lacey (D) . . . . . . . . . . . . . . . . . . . . . . .315-253-1285
Commissioner:
 Cherl Heary (R) . . . . . . . . . . . . . . . . . . . . . . .315-253-1285
 e-mail: cheary@cayugacounty.us
Deputy Commissioner:
 Deborah Calarco (D) . . . . . . . . . . . . . . . . . . .315-253-1285
Deputy Commissioner:
 Roberta Massarini (R) . . . . . . . . . . . . . . . . . .315-253-1285

**Chautauqua** . . . . . . . . . . . . . . . . . . . . . . .fax: 716-753-4111
7 North Erie St, Mayville, NY 14757
716-753-4580  Fax: 716-753-4111
e-mail: vote@co.chautauqua.ny.us
Web site: www.co.chautauqua.ny.us
Commissioner:
 Norman P Green (D). . . . . . . . . . . . . . . . . . . .716-753-4580
 e-mail: GreenN@co.chautauqua.ny.us
Commissioner:
 Brian C Abram (R). . . . . . . . . . . . . . . . . . . . .716-753-4580
 e-mail: AbramB@co.chautauqua.ny.us
Commissioner:
 Doris Parment (D) . . . . . . . . . . . . . . . . . . . . .716-753-4580
Commissioner:
 Nacole Ellis (R) . . . . . . . . . . . . . . . . . . . . . . .716-753-4580

**Chemung**. . . . . . . . . . . . . . . . . . . . . . . . . . . .fax: 607-737-5499
378 S Main Street, PO Box 588, Elmira, NY 14902-0588
607-737-5475  Fax: 607-737-5499
e-mail: votechemung@co.chemung.ny.us
Web site: www.chemungcounty.com
Commissioner:
 Cindy Emmer (D). . . . . . . . . . . . . . . . . . . . . .607-737-5475
Commissioner:
 Robert D Siglin (R) . . . . . . . . . . . . . . . . . . . .607-737-5475
Deputy Commissioner:
 Mary Collins (D) . . . . . . . . . . . . . . . . . . . . . .607-737-5475
 e-mail: marycollins@co.chemung.ny.us
Deputy Commissioner:
 Linda A Forrest (R) . . . . . . . . . . . . . . . . . . . .607-737-5475
 e-mail: lforrest@co.chemung.ny.us

**Chenango** . . . . . . . . . . . . . . . . . . . . . . . . .fax: 607-337-1766
5 Court Street, Norwich, NY 13815
607-337-1760  Fax: 607-337-1766
e-mail: boe@co.chenango.ny.us
Web site: www.co.chenango.ny.us
Commissioner:
 Carol A Franklin (D) . . . . . . . . . . . . . . . . . . .607-337-1765
 e-mail: carolf@co.chenango.ny.us
Commissioner:
 Mary Lou A Monahan (R) . . . . . . . . . . . . . . .607-337-1764
Deputy Commissioner:
 Carly J Hendricks (D). . . . . . . . . . . . . . . . . . .607-337-1764

Deputy Commissioner:
 Jamie Anderson (R) . . . . . . . . . . . . . . . . . . . .607-337-1764

**Clinton** . . . . . . . . . . . . . . . . . . . . . . . . . . . .fax: 518-565-4508
County Gov't Center, 137 Margaret St, Ste 104, Plattsburgh, NY 12901
Fax: 518-565-4508
Web site: www.clintoncountygov.com
Commissioner:
 Mary R Dyer (D) . . . . . . . . . . . . . . . . . . . . . .518-565-4740
Commissioner:
 Gregory Campbell (R) . . . . . . . . . . . . . . . . . .518-565-4740
Deputy Commissioner:
 Susan R Castine (D) . . . . . . . . . . . . . . . . . . . .518-565-4740
Deputy Commissioner:
 Kara McBrayer (R). . . . . . . . . . . . . . . . . . . . .518-565-4740

**Columbia** . . . . . . . . . . . . . . . . . . . . . . . . . .fax: 518-828-2624
401 State St, Hudson, NY 12534
Fax: 518-828-2624
e-mail: elections@columbiacountyny.com
Web site: www.columbiacountyny.com
Commissioner:
 Virginia Martin (D) . . . . . . . . . . . . . . . . . . . .518-828-3115
Commissioner:
 Jason Nastke (R). . . . . . . . . . . . . . . . . . . . . . .518-828-3115
Deputy Commissioner:
 Hilary Hillman (D) . . . . . . . . . . . . . . . . . . . . .518-828-3115
Deputy Commissioner:
 Kathy L Harter (R) . . . . . . . . . . . . . . . . . . . . .518-828-3115

**Cortland** . . . . . . . . . . . . . . . . . . . . . . . . . . .fax: 607-758-5513
112 River Street, Ste 1, Cortland, NY 13045
607-758-5032  Fax: 607-758-5513
e-mail: elections@cortland-co.org
Commissioner:
 Thomas Henry Brown (D) . . . . . . . . . . . . . . .607-753-5033
 e-mail: tbrown@cortland-co.org
Commissioner:
 Robert C Howe (R). . . . . . . . . . . . . . . . . . . . .607-753-5031
 e-mail: rhowe@cortland-co.org

**Delaware**. . . . . . . . . . . . . . . . . . . . . . . . . . .fax: 607-746-6516
3 Gallant Ave, Delhi, NY 13753
607-832-5321  Fax: 607-746-6516
e-mail: boe.move@co.delaware.ny.us
Web site: www.co.delaware.ny.us
Commissioner:
 Judith Garrison (D). . . . . . . . . . . . . . . . . . . . .607-832-5321
Commissioner:
 William J Campbell (R) . . . . . . . . . . . . . . . . .607-832-5321
Deputy Commissioner:
 Paula Schermerhorn (D). . . . . . . . . . . . . . . . .607-832-5321
Deputy Commissioner:
 Robin L Alger (R) . . . . . . . . . . . . . . . . . . . . .607-832-5321

**Dutchess** . . . . . . . . . . . . . . . . . . . . . . . . . . .fax: 845-486-2483
47 Cannon St, Poughkeepsie, NY 12601
Fax: 845-486-2483
e-mail: dutchesselections@dutchessny.gov
Web site: www.dutchesselections.com
Commissioner:
 Marco Caviglia (D). . . . . . . . . . . . . . . . . . . . .845-486-2473
 e-mail: mcaviglia@dutchessny.gov
Commissioner:
 Erik Haight (R). . . . . . . . . . . . . . . . . . . . . . . .845-486-2473
 e-mail: ehaight@dutchessny.gov
Deputy Commissioner:
 Daniel Miller (D) . . . . . . . . . . . . . . . . . . . . . .845-486-2477
Deputy Commissioner:
 Erin Reverri (R) . . . . . . . . . . . . . . . . . . . . . . .845-486-2475
 e-mail: ereverri@dutchessny.gov

*Offices and agencies generally appear in alphabetical order, except when specific order is requested by listee.*

**Erie** . . . . . . . . . . . . . . . . . . . . . . . . . . . . . .fax: 716-858-8282
134 West Eagle St, Buffalo, NY 14202
Fax: 716-858-8282
Web site: elections.erie.gov
Commissioner:
  Leonard Lenihan (D) . . . . . . . . . . . . . . . . . . . . . .716-858-7787
Commissioner:
  Ralph M Mohr (R) . . . . . . . . . . . . . . . . . . . . . . . .716-858-7786
Deputy Commissioner:
  Arthur O Eve Jr (D) . . . . . . . . . . . . . . . . . . . . . .716-858-8891
Deputy Commissioner:
  Robin Sion (R) . . . . . . . . . . . . . . . . . . . . . . . . . .716-858-8891

**Essex** . . . . . . . . . . . . . . . . . . . . . . . . . . . .fax: 518-873-3479
7551 Court Street, PO Box 217, Elizabethtown, NY 12932
518-873-3474 Fax: 518-873-3479
e-mail: essexelections@co.essex.ny.us
Web site: www.co.essex.ny.us/elect.asp
Commissioner:
  Mark C. Whitney (D) . . . . . . . . . . . . . . . . . .518-873-3475
  e-mail: mwhitney@co.essex.ny.us
Commissioner:
  Allison McGahay (R) . . . . . . . . . . . . . . . . . .518-873-3478
  e-mail: amcgahay@co.essex.ny.us
Deputy Commissioner:
  Holly Rollins (D) . . . . . . . . . . . . . . . . . . . . .518-873-3477
  e-mail: hrollins@co.essex.ny.us
Deputy Commissioner:
  Shona Doyle (R) . . . . . . . . . . . . . . . . . . . . .518-873-3476
  e-mail: sdoyle@co.essex.ny.us

**Franklin** . . . . . . . . . . . . . . . . . . . . . . . . . .fax: 518-481-6018
335 West Main St, Ste 161, Malone, NY 12953-1823
518-481-1663 Fax: 518-481-6018
e-mail: boe@co.franklin.ny.us
Web site: franklincony.org
Commissioner:
  Kelly Cox (D) . . . . . . . . . . . . . . . . . . . . . . . .518-481-1662
  e-mail: kcox@co.franklin.ny.us
Commissioner:
  Tracy Sparks (R) . . . . . . . . . . . . . . . . . . . . .518-481-1661
  e-mail: tsparks@co.franklin.ny.us
Deputy Commissioner:
  Linda S. Maneely (D) . . . . . . . . . . . . . . . . . .518-481-1663
Deputy Commissioner:
  Erin Brockway (R) . . . . . . . . . . . . . . . . . . . .518-481-1663
  e-mail: ebrockway@co.franklin.ny.us

**Fulton** . . . . . . . . . . . . . . . . . . . . . . . . . . . .fax: 518-736-1612
2714 State Highway 29, Ste 1, Johnstown, NY 12095-9946
Fax: 518-736-1612
Web site: www.fultoncountyny.org
Commissioner:
  Lynne Rubscha (D) . . . . . . . . . . . . . . . . . . .518-736-5526
Commissioner:
  Lee A Hollenbeck (R) . . . . . . . . . . . . . . . . .518-736-5526
Deputy Commissioner:
  Michele Miller (D) . . . . . . . . . . . . . . . . . . . .518-736-5526
Deputy Commissioner:
  Theresa E Dugan (R) . . . . . . . . . . . . . . . . . .518-736-5526

**Genesee** . . . . . . . . . . . . . . . . . . . . . . . . . .fax: 585-344-8562
County Bldg One, 15 Main St, PO Box 284, Batavia, NY 14021
Fax: 585-344-8562
e-mail: election@co.genesee.ny.us
Web site: www.co.genesee.ny.us
Commissioner:
  Lorie J Longhany (D) . . . . . . . . . . . . . . . . . .585-344-2550
Commissioner:
  Richard Siebert (R) . . . . . . . . . . . . . . . . . . .585-344-2550
Deputy Commissioner:
  Karen S Gannon (D) . . . . . . . . . . . . . . . . . .585-344-2250

Deputy Commissioner:
  Melissa L Gaebler (R) . . . . . . . . . . . . . . . . . . . . . .585-344-2250

**Greene** . . . . . . . . . . . . . . . . . . . . . . . . . . . .fax: 518-719-3784
411 Main Street, Ste 437, Catskill, NY 12414
Fax: 518-719-3784
e-mail: elections@discovergreene.com
Web site: greenegovernment.com
Commissioner:
  Marie Metzler (D) . . . . . . . . . . . . . . . . . . . .518-719-3550
  e-mail: mmetzler@discovergreene.com
Commissioner:
  Brent Bogardus (R) . . . . . . . . . . . . . . . . . . .518-719-3550
  e-mail: bbogardus@discovergreene.com
Deputy Commissioner:
  Casey McCarthy (D) . . . . . . . . . . . . . . . . . .518-719-3550
Deputy Commissioner (Acting):
  Carol Engelmann (R) . . . . . . . . . . . . . . . . . .518-719-3550

**Hamilton** . . . . . . . . . . . . . . . . . . . . . . . . . .fax: 518-548-6345
Route 8, PO Box 175, Lake Pleasant, NY 12108
Fax: 518-548-6345
e-mail: elections@hamiltoncountyny.gov
Web site: www.hamiltoncounty.com
Commissioner:
  Cathleen E Rogers (D) . . . . . . . . . . . . . . . . .518-548-4684
Commissioner:
  Marie Buanno (R) . . . . . . . . . . . . . . . . . . . .518-548-4684
Deputy Commissioner:
  Jaime Parslow (D) . . . . . . . . . . . . . . . . . . . .518-548-4684
Deputy Commissioner:
  Virginia E Morris (R) . . . . . . . . . . . . . . . . . .518-548-4684

**Herkimer** . . . . . . . . . . . . . . . . . . . . . . . . . .fax: 315-867-1106
109 Mary Street, Suite 1306, Herkimer, NY 13350
315-867-1102 Fax: 315-867-1106
e-mail: boeinfo@herkimercounty.org
Web site: herkimercounty.org
Commissioner:
  Connie L Shepherd (D) . . . . . . . . . . . . . . . . .315-867-1103
Commissioner:
  Louis Patrick Christie (R) . . . . . . . . . . . . . . .315-867-1104
Deputy Commissioner:
  Robert Drumm (D) . . . . . . . . . . . . . . . . . . .315-867-1102
Deputy Commissioner:
  Jennifer Williams (R) . . . . . . . . . . . . . . . . . .315-867-1102

**Jefferson** . . . . . . . . . . . . . . . . . . . . . . . . . .fax: 315-785-5197
175 Arsenal St, 4th Floor, Watertown, NY 13601
Fax: 315-785-5197
Web site: www.co.jefferson.ny.us
Commissioner:
  Babette M. Hall (D) . . . . . . . . . . . . . . . . . . .315-785-3027
Commissioner:
  Jude Seymour (R) . . . . . . . . . . . . . . . . . . . .315-785-3027
Deputy Commissioner:
  Michelle LaFave (D) . . . . . . . . . . . . . . . . . . .315-785-3027
Deputy Commissioner:
  Trina L Kampnich (R) . . . . . . . . . . . . . . . . . .315-785-3027

**Lewis** . . . . . . . . . . . . . . . . . . . . . . . . . . . . .fax: 315-376-2860
7660 N. State St, Lowville, NY 13367
Fax: 315-376-2860
Web site: www.lewiscountyny.org
Commissioner:
  Lindsay Burriss (D) . . . . . . . . . . . . . . . . . . .315-376-5329
  e-mail: lindsayburriss@lewiscounty.ny.gov
Commissioner:
  Ann M Nortz (R) . . . . . . . . . . . . . . . . . . . . .315-376-5329
  e-mail: annortz@lewiscounty.ny.gov
Deputy Commissioner:
  Nicole Demo (D)

*Offices and agencies generally appear in alphabetical order, except when specific order is requested by listee.*

Deputy Commissioner:
  Angela Peters (R)

**Livingston** . . . . . . . . . . . . . . . . . . . . . . . . . . . . . . . . . . . . .fax: 585-243-7015
County Government Ctr, 6 Court St, Rm 104, Geneseo, NY 14454-1043
Commissioner:
  David DiPasquale (D) . . . . . . . . . . . . . . . . . . . . . . . . .585-243-7090
Commissioner:
  Nancy L Leven (R). . . . . . . . . . . . . . . . . . . . . . . . . . . .585-243-7090
Deputy Commissioner:
  Laura Schoonover (D) . . . . . . . . . . . . . . . . . . . . . . . . .585-243-7090
  e-mail: lschoonover@co.livingston.ny.us
Deputy Commissioner:
  Diana Farrell (R). . . . . . . . . . . . . . . . . . . . . . . . . . . . . .585-243-7090

**Madison** . . . . . . . . . . . . . . . . . . . . . . . . . . . . . . . . . . . .fax: 315-366-2532
North Court St, County Office Bldg, PO Box 666, Wampsville, NY 13163
Fax: 315-366-2532
e-mail: boecommissioners@madisoncounty.ny.gov
Commissioner:
  Laura P Costello (D). . . . . . . . . . . . . . . . . . . . . . . . . .315-366-2231
Commissioner:
  Kelley S Hood (R) . . . . . . . . . . . . . . . . . . . . . . . . . . . .315-366-2231
Deputy Commissioner:
  Ann L Jones (D) . . . . . . . . . . . . . . . . . . . . . . . . . . . . . .315-366-2231
Deputy Commissioner:
  Mary Egger (R). . . . . . . . . . . . . . . . . . . . . . . . . . . . . . .315-366-2231

**Monroe** . . . . . . . . . . . . . . . . . . . . . . . . . . . . . . . . . . . . .fax: 585-324-1612
39 Main St West, Rochester, NY 14614
585-753-1550  Fax: 585-324-1612
e-mail: mcboe@monroecounty.gov
Web site: www.monroecounty.gov
Commissioner:
  Thomas F Ferrarese (D) . . . . . . . . . .585-753-1550/fax: 585-753-1531
  e-mail: tFerrarese@monroecounty.gov
Commissioner:
  David Van Varick (R) . . . . . . . . . . . .585-753-1550/fax: 585-753-1521
Deputy Commissioner:
  Colleen Anderson (D). . . . . . . . . . . .585-753-1550/fax: 585-753-1531
Deputy Commissioner:
  Douglas E French (R) . . . . . . . . . . . .585-753-1550/fax: 585-753-1521

**Montgomery** . . . . . . . . . . . . . . . . . . . . . . . . . . . . . . . . . .fax: 518-853-8392
Old Court House, 9 Park St, PO Box 1500, Fonda, NY 12068-1500
518-853-8180  Fax: 518-853-8392
e-mail: boe@co.montgomery.ny.us
Commissioner:
  Jamie M Duchessi (D) . . . . . . . . . . . . . . . . . . . . . . . .518-853-8181
Commissioner:
  Terrance J Smith (R). . . . . . . . . . . . . . . . . . . . . . . . . .518-853-8182
Deputy Commissioner:
  Caroline Swartz (D) . . . . . . . . . . . . . . . . . . . . . . . . . .518-853-8183
Deputy Commissioner:
  Wendy D. Shaver (R). . . . . . . . . . . . . . . . . . . . . . . . .518-853-8183

**Nassau** . . . . . . . . . . . . . . . . . . . . . . . . . . . . . . . . . . . . . .fax: 516-571-2058
240 Old Country Rd, 5th Fl, Mineola, NY 11501
Fax: 516-571-2058
e-mail: fedmil@nassaucountyny.gov
Web site: www.nassaucountyny.gov
Commissioner:
  David J Gugerty (D). . . . . . . . . . . . . . . . . . . . . . . . . .516-571-2411
Commissioner:
  Louis G Savinetti (R) . . . . . . . . . . . . . . . . . . . . . . . . .516-571-2411
Deputy Commissioner:
  Michael Santeramo (D) . . . . . . . . . . . . . . . . . . . . . . .516-571-2411
Deputy Commissioner:
  Carol Demauro Busketta (R) . . . . . . . . . . . . . . . . . . .516-571-2411

**New York City** . . . . . . . . . . . . . . . . . . . . . . . . . . . .fax: 212-487-5349
32 Broadway, 7th Fl, New York, NY 10004

Fax: 212-487-5349
e-mail: electioninfo@boe.nyc.ny.us
Web site: www.vote.nyc.ny.us
Executive Director:
  Michael J Ryan (D) . . . . . . . . . . . . . . . . . . . . . . . . . .212-487-5300
Deputy Executive Director:
  Dawn Sandow (R) . . . . . . . . . . . . . . . . . . . . . . . . . . .212-487-5300
Administrative Manager:
  Pamela Green Perkins (D) . . . . . . . . . . . . . . . . . . . . .212-487-5300
Operations Manager:
  Georgea Kontzamanis (R) . . . . . . . . . . . . . . . . . . . . .212-487-5300
*Bronx* . . . . . . . . . . . . . . . . . . . . . . . . . . . . . . . . . . . . .fax: 718-299-2140
  1780 Grand Concourse, 5th Fl, Bronx, NY 10457
  Fax: 718-299-2140
    e-mail: voterreg@boe.nyc.ny.us
  Commissioner:
    Bianca Perez (D) . . . . . . . . . . . . . . . . . . . . . . . . .718-299-9017
  Commissioner:
    Michael A Rendino (R) . . . . . . . . . . . . . . . . . . . . .718-299-9017
  Deputy Chief Clerk:
    Marricka Scott-McFadden (D) . . . . . . . . . . . . . . . .718-299-9017
  Deputy Chief Clerk:
    Anthony J Ribustello (R). . . . . . . . . . . . . . . . . . . . .718-299-9017
*Kings* . . . . . . . . . . . . . . . . . . . . . . . . . . . . . . . . . . . . .fax: 718-246-5958
  345 Adams St, 4th Fl, Brooklyn, NY 11201
  Commissioner:
    John Flateau (D). . . . . . . . . . . . . . . . . . . . . . . . . .718-797-8800
  Commissioner:
    Simon Shamoun (R). . . . . . . . . . . . . . . . . . . . . . . .718-797-8800
  Deputy Chief Clerk:
    BettyAnn Canizio (D) . . . . . . . . . . . . . . . . . . . . . .718-797-8800
  Chief Clerk:
    Diane Haslett Rudiano (R) . . . . . . . . . . . . . . . . . . .718-797-8800
*New York* . . . . . . . . . . . . . . . . . . . . . . . . . . . . . . . . .fax: 646-638-2047
  200 Varick St, 10th Fl, New York, NY 10014
  Commissioner:
    Alan Schulkin (D) . . . . . . . . . . . . . . . . . . . . . . . . .212-886-2100
  Commissioner:
    Frederic M Umane (R). . . . . . . . . . . . . . . . . . . . . .212-886-2100
    e-mail: fumane@boe.nyc.ny.us
  Chief Clerk:
    Greg Lehman (R). . . . . . . . . . . . . . . . . . . . . . . . . .212-886-2100
  Deputy Chief Clerk:
    William A Allen (D) . . . . . . . . . . . . . . . . . . . . . . .212-886-2100
*Queens* . . . . . . . . . . . . . . . . . . . . . . . . . . . . . . . . . . .fax: 718-459-3384
  118-35 Queens Blvd, Forest Hills, NY 11375
  Commissioner:
    Jose M Araujo (D) . . . . . . . . . . . . . . . . . . . . . . . . .718-730-6730
  Commissioner:
    Michael Michel (R) . . . . . . . . . . . . . . . . . . . . . . . .718-730-6730
  Chief Clerk:
    Barbara Conacchio (D) . . . . . . . . . . . . . . . . . . . . .718-730-6730
  Deputy Chief Clerk:
    Bart Haggerty (R) . . . . . . . . . . . . . . . . . . . . . . . . .718-730-6730
*Richmond* . . . . . . . . . . . . . . . . . . . . . . . . . . . . . . . . .fax: 718-876-0912
  1 Edgewater Plaza, Staten Island, NY 10305
  Fax: 718-876-0912
    e-mail: voterreg@boe.nyc.ny.us
  Commissioner:
    Maria R Guastella (D) . . . . . . . . . . . . . . . . . . . . . .718-876-0079
  Commissioner:
    Ronald Castorina, Jr (R) . . . . . . . . . . . . . . . . . . . . .718-876-0079
  Chief Clerk:
    Sheila Del Giorno (D) . . . . . . . . . . . . . . . . . . . . . .718-876-0079
  Deputy Chief Clerk:
    Anthony Andruili (R) . . . . . . . . . . . . . . . . . . . . . .718-876-0079

**Niagara** . . . . . . . . . . . . . . . . . . . . . . . . . . . . . . . . . . . .fax: 716-438-4054
111 Main Street, Ste 100, Lockport, NY 14094

*Offices and agencies generally appear in alphabetical order, except when specific order is requested by listee.*

716-438-4040  Fax: 716-438-4054
e-mail: ncboe@niagaracounty.com
Web site: www.elections.niagara.ny.us
Commissioner:
Lora A. Allen (D) . . . . . . . . . . . . . . . . . . . . .716-438-4041
e-mail: lora.allen@niagaracounty.com
Commissioner:
Jennifer Fronczak (R) . . . . . . . . . . . . . . . . . .716-438-4040
e-mail: jennifer.fronczak@niagaracounty.org
Deputy Commissioner:
Darryl DiNoto (D) . . . . . . . . . . . . . . . . . . . . .716-438-4041
Deputy Commissioner:
Michael Carney (R) . . . . . . . . . . . . . . . . . . . .716-438-4040

**Oneida** . . . . . . . . . . . . . . . . . . . . .fax: 315-798-6412
Union Station, 321 Main St, 3rd Fl, Utica, NY 13501
Fax: 315-798-6412
e-mail: boardofelections@ocgov.net
Web site: www.ocgov.net
Commissioner:
Jordan S Karp (D) . . . . . . . . . . . . . . . . . . . . .315-798-5761
Commissioner:
Rose Grimaldi (R) . . . . . . . . . . . . . . . . . . . . .315-798-5763
e-mail: rgrimaldi@ocgov.net
Deputy Commissioner:
Carolann N. Cardone (D) . . . . . . . . . . . . . . . .315-798-5765
Deputy Commissioner:
Catherine A Dumka (R) . . . . . . . . . . . . . . . . .315-798-5765

**Onondaga** . . . . . . . . . . . . . . . . . . . .fax: 315-435-8451
1000 Erie Boulevard West, Syracuse, NY 13204
Fax: 315-435-8451
e-mail: elections@ongov.net
Web site: www.ongov.net
Commissioner:
Dustin M. Czarny (D) . . . . . . . . . . . . . . . . . .315-435-3312
Commissioner:
Helen M Kiggins-Walsh (R) . . . . . . . . . . . . . .315-435-3312

**Ontario** . . . . . . . . . . . . . . . . . . . . .fax: 585-393-2941
74 Ontario St, Canandaigua, NY 14424
Fax: 585-393-2941
e-mail: boe@co.ontario.ny.us
Web site: www.co.ontario.ny.us/elections
Commissioner:
Mary Q Salotti (D) . . . . . . . . . . . . . . . . . . . .585-396-4005
e-mail: mary.salotti@co.ontario.ny.us
Commissioner:
Michael J Northrup (R) . . . . . . . . . . . . . . . . .585-396-4005
e-mail: michael.northrup@co.ontario.ny.us
Clerk to Commissioner:
Karen Reed (D) . . . . . . . . . . . . . . . . . . . . . . .585-396-4005
Clerk to Commissioner:
Karen Bodine (R) . . . . . . . . . . . . . . . . . . . . .585-396-4005

**Orange** . . . . . . . . . . . . . . . . . . . . .fax: 845-291-2437
75 Webster Ave, PO Box 30, Goshen, NY 10924
845-360-6500  Fax: 845-291-2437
e-mail: elections@orangecountygov.com
Web site: www.orangecountygov.com
Commissioner:
Susan Bahren (D) . . . . . . . . . . . . . . . . . . . . .845-360-6500
Commissioner:
David C Green (R) . . . . . . . . . . . . . . . . . . . . .845-360-6500
Deputy Commissioner:
Louise Vandemark (D) . . . . . . . . . . . . . . . . . .845-360-6500
Deputy Commissioner:
Courtney Canfield Greene (R) . . . . . . . . . . . . .845-360-6500

**Orleans** . . . . . . . . . . . . . . . . . . . . .fax: 585-589-2771
14012 State Rte 31, Albion, NY 14411

Fax: 585-589-2771
Web site: www.orleansny.com
Commissioner:
Janice E Grabowski (D) . . . . . . . . . . . . . . . . .585-589-3274
e-mail: janice.grabowski@orleansny.com
Commissioner:
Sylvia Shoemaker (R) . . . . . . . . . . . . . . . . . .585-589-3274
Deputy Commissioner:
Eileen Aina (D) . . . . . . . . . . . . . . . . . . . . . . .585-589-3274
Deputy Commissioner:
Dorothy Morgan (R) . . . . . . . . . . . . . . . . . . .585-589-3274

**Oswego** . . . . . . . . . . . . . . . . . . . . .fax: 315-349-8357
185 E Seneca St, Box 9, Oswego, NY 13126
Commissioner:
Richard Atkins (D) . . . . . . . . . . . . . . . . . . . .315-349-8350
Commissioner:
Peggy Bickford (R) . . . . . . . . . . . . . . . . . . . .315-349-8350
Deputy Commissioner:
Teresa Munger (D) . . . . . . . . . . . . . . . . . . . .315-349-8350
Deputy Commissioner:
Marianne B. Ingerson (R) . . . . . . . . . . . . . . .315-349-8350

**Otsego** . . . . . . . . . . . . . . . . . . . . .fax: 607-547-4248
140 County Hwy 33W, Ste 2, Cooperstown, NY 13326
Fax: 607-547-4248
e-mail: boe@otsegocounty.com
Web site: www.otsegocounty.com/depts/boe
Commissioner:
Michael Henrici (D) . . . . . . . . . . . . . . . . . . .607-547-4325
e-mail: henricim@otsegocounty.com
Commissioner:
Lori L Lehenbauer (R) . . . . . . . . . . . . . . . . . .607-547-4247
e-mail: lehenbauerl@otsegocounty.com
Deputy Commissioner:
Victoria A Curtis (D) . . . . . . . . . . . . . . . . . . .607-547-4325
Deputy Commissioner:
Christina A Morrison (R) . . . . . . . . . . . . . . . .607-547-4247

**Putnam** . . . . . . . . . . . . . . . . . . . . .fax: 845-808-1920
25 Old Rte 6, Carmel, NY 10512
Fax: 845-808-1920
e-mail: putnamcountyelections@putnamcountyny.gov
Web site: www.putnamcountyny.com/boe/index.htm
Commissioner:
Catherine Croft (D) . . . . . . . . . . . . . . . . . . . .845-808-1300
Commissioner:
Anthony G Scannapieco, Jr (R) . . . . . . . . . . . .845-808-1300
Deputy Commissioner:
Andrea Basli (D) . . . . . . . . . . . . . . . . . . . . . .845-808-1300
Deputy Commissioner:
Kelly K Primavera (R) . . . . . . . . . . . . . . . . . .845-808-1300

**Rensselaer** . . . . . . . . . . . . . . . . . . . .fax: 518-270-2909
Ned Pattison Govt Ctr, 1600 Seventh Ave, Troy, NY 12180
Fax: 518-270-2909
e-mail: renscoboe@rensco.com
Commissioner:
Edward G McDonough (D) . . . . . . . . . . . . . . .518-270-2990
Commissioner:
Larry A Bugbee (R) . . . . . . . . . . . . . . . . . . . .518-270-2990

**Rockland** . . . . . . . . . . . . . . . . . . . .fax: 845-638-5196
11 New Hempstead Road, New City, NY 10956
845-638-5172  Fax: 845-638-5196
e-mail: voterinfo@co.rockland.ny.us
Web site: www.voterockland.com
Democratic Commissioner of Elections:
Kristen Zebrowski Stavisky (D) . . . . . . . . . . . .845-638-5289
e-mail: staviskk@co.rockland.ny.us

*Offices and agencies generally appear in alphabetical order, except when specific order is requested by listee.*

Republican Commissioner of Elections:
Patricia A. Giblin (R) ............................845-638-5287
e-mail: giblinp@co.rockland.ny.us
Deputy Commissioner of Elections:
Kathleen M. Pietanza (D).......................845-638-5291
e-mail: pietanzk@co.rockland.ny.us
Deputy Commissioner of Elections:
Marino Fontana (R) ............................845-638-5290
e-mail: fontanam@co.rockland.ny.us

**Saint Lawrence** ....................fax: 315-386-2737
80 State Hwy 310, Canton, NY 13617
Fax: 315-386-2737
Web site: www.co.st-lawrence.ny.us
Commissioner:
Jennie H Bacon (D) ...........................315-379-2202
e-mail: jbacon@stlawco.org
Commissioner:
Thomas A Nichols (R) .........................315-379-2202
e-mail: tnichols@stlawco.org
Deputy Commissioner:
Seth Belt (D).................................315-379-2202
e-mail: sbelt@stlawco.org
Deputy Commissioner:
Thomas O Hardiman (R) .......................315-379-2202

**Saratoga** ..........................fax: 518-884-4751
50 W High St, Ballston Spa, NY 12020
Fax: 518-884-4751
e-mail: elections@saratogacountyny.gov
Web site: www.saratogacountyny.gov
Commissioner:
William Fruci (D)..............................518-885-2249
Commissioner:
Roger J Schiera (R) ..........................518-885-2249
Deputy Commissioner:
Carol Turney (D) .............................518-885-2249
Deputy Commissioner:
John Marcellus (R)............................518-885-2249

**Schenectady** .......................fax: 518-377-2716
388 Broadway, Ste E, Schenectady, NY 12305-2520
Fax: 518-377-2716
Web site: www.schenectadycounty.com
Commissioner:
Amy M Hild (D)...............................518-377-2469
Commissioner:
Darlene D Harris (R) .........................518-377-2469
Deputy Commissioner:
Laura Fronk (D) .............................518-377-2469
Deputy Commissioner:
Philip Aydinian (R) ..........................518-377-2469

**Schoharie** .........................fax: 518-295-8419
County Office Bldg, 284 Main St, PO Box 99, Schoharie, NY 12157
Fax: 518-295-8419
e-mail: boe@co.schoharie.ny.us
Commissioner:
Clifford C Hay (D).............................518-295-8388
Commissioner:
Lewis L Wilson (R) . ..........................518-295-8388
Deputy Commissioner:
Richard Shultes (D) ..........................518-295-8388
e mail: rich.shultes@co.schoharie.ny us
Deputy Commissioner:
Sara Davies-Griffin (R) .......................518-295-8388
e-mail: griffins@co.schoharie.ny.us

**Schuyler** ..........................fax: 607-535-8364
County Ofc Bldg, 105 Ninth St, Unit 13, Watkins Glen, NY 14891-9972
Fax: 607-535-8364
e-mail: elections@co.schuyler.ny.us

Commissioner:
John L Vona (D)...............................607-535-8195
Commissioner:
Joseph Fazzary (R)............................607-535-8195
Deputy Commissioner:
Carolyn Elkins (D) ...........................607-535-8195
Deputy Commissioner:
Cindy L Cady (R) .............................607-535-8195

**Seneca** ...........................fax: 315-539-3710
1 DiPronio Dr, Waterloo, NY 13165
Commissioner:
Ruth V Same (D) .............................315-539-1760
e-mail: rsame@co.seneca.ny.us
Commissioner:
Tiffany Folk (R) ..............................315-539-1760
Deputy Commissioner:
Carl J Same (D) ..............................315-539-1760
e-mail: csame@co.seneca.ny.us
Deputy Commissioner:
Sherrill A O'Brien (R) ........................315-539-1760

**Steuben** ..........................fax: 607-664-2376
3 E Pulteney Square, Bath, NY 14810
607-664-2260  Fax: 607-664-2376
e-mail: elections@co.steuben.ny.us
Web site: www.steubencony.org
Commissioner:
Kelly J Penziul (D)............................607-664-2260
Commissioner:
Veronica Olin (R).............................607-664-2260
e-mail: veronica@co.steuben.ny.us
Deputy Commissioner:
Colleen A Hauryski (D) .......................607-664-2260
Deputy Commissioner:
Angelia M Cornish (R).........................607-664-2260

**Suffolk**............................fax: 631-852-4590
Yaphank Ave, PO Box 700, Yaphank, NY 11980
Commissioner:
Anita S Katz (D)..............................631-852-4500
Commissioner:
Nick LaLota (R) ..............................631-852-4500
Deputy Commissioner:
Jeanne O'Rourke (D) .........................631-852-4500
Deputy Commissioner:
Betty Manzella (R)............................631-852-4500

**Sullivan**...........................fax: 845-807-0410
Government Ctr, 100 North St, PO Box 5012, Monticello, NY 12701-5192
Commissioner:
Ann Prusinski (D).............................845-807-0400
Commissioner:
Lori Benjamin (R) ............................845-807-0400
Deputy Commissioner:
Honora Wohl (D) .............................845-807-0400
Deputy Commissioner:
Pam Murran (R) ..............................845-807-0400

**Tioga** .............................fax: 607-687-6348
1062 State Rte 38, PO Box 306, Owego, NY 13827
607-687-8261  Fax: 607-687-6348
e-mail: votetioga@co.tioga.ny.us
Web site: www.tiogacountyny.com
Commissioner:
John J Langan (D) ............................607-687-8261
Commissioner:
Bernadette M Toombs (R) .....................607-687-8261
e-mail: toombsb@co.tioga.ny.us
Deputy Commissioner:
Sandra Saddlemire (D).........................607-687-8261
e-mail: saddlemires@co.tioga.ny.us

*Offices and agencies generally appear in alphabetical order, except when specific order is requested by listee.*

Deputy Commissioner:
   Lin Layman (R) .................................607-687-8261
   e-mail: laymanl@co.tioga.ny.us

**Tompkins** ...........................................fax: 607-274-5533
Court House Annex, 128 E Buffalo St, Ithaca, NY 14850
Commissioner:
   Stephen M DeWitt (D).........................607-274-5522
   e-mail: sdewitt@tompkins-co.org
Commissioner:
   Elizabeth W Cree (R)..........................607-274-5522
   e-mail: ecree@tompkins-co.org
Deputy Commissioner:
   Laura Norman (D) .............................607-274-5522
Deputy Commissioner:
   Kari L Stamm (R)..............................607-274-5522

**Ulster**................................................fax: 845-334-5434
284 Wall Street, Kingston, NY 12401
Fax: 845-334-5434
e-mail: elections@co.ulster.ny.us
Web site: www.co.ulster.ny.us/elections/
Commissioner:
   C Victor Work (D) .............................845-334-5470
Commissioner:
   Thomas F Turco (R)............................845-334-5470
Deputy Commissioner:
   Ashley Dittus (D) .............................845-334-5470
Deputy Commissioner:
   Patty Jacobsen (R) ............................845-334-5470

**Warren** ..............................................fax: 518-761-6480
County Municipal Center, 1340 State Rte 9, 3rd Fl, Lake George, NY
   12845
518-761-6456  Fax: 518-761-6480
e-mail: boe@warrencountyny.gov
Web site: www.warrencountyny.gov/boe
Commissioner:
   Elizabeth J McLaughlin (D).....................518-761-6459
Commissioner:
   Mary Beth Casey (R) ..........................518-761-6458
Deputy Commissioner:
   Kimberly Ross (D).............................518-761-6456
Deputy Commissioner:
   Emily Kladis (R)..............................518-761-6457

**Washington**...........................................fax: 518-746-2179
383 Broadway, Fort Edward, NY 12828
518-746-2180  Fax: 518-746-2179
e-mail: boardofelections@co.washington.ny.us
Commissioner:
   Jeffrey J Curtis (D)............................518-746-2180
Commissioner:
   Leslie Allen (R) ..............................518-746-2180
Deputy Commissioner:
   Melinda Suprenant (D).........................518-746-2180
Deputy Commissioner:
   Thomas Rogers (R)............................518-746-2180

**Wayne**...............................................fax: 315-946-7409
7376 State Route 31, PO Box 636, Lyons, NY 14489
Fax: 315-946-7409
Web site: www.co.wayne.ny.us
Commissioner:
   Mark H Alquist (D) ...........................315-946-7400
Commissioner:
   Marjorie M Bridson (R) ........................315-946-7400
Deputy Commissioner:
   Joyce A Krebbeks (D) .........................315-946-7400
Deputy Commissioner:
   Kelley M Borrelli (R)..........................315-946-7400

**Westchester** .....................................fax: 914-995-3190
25 Quarropas Street, White Plains, NY 10601
Fax: 914-995-3190
e-mail: boe-west@westchestergov.com
Commissioner:
   Reginald A LaFayette (D).........914-995-5700/fax: 914-995-7753
Commissioner:
   Douglas A Colety (R)...........................914-995-5700
Deputy Commissioner:
   Jeannie L Palazola (D) .........................914-995-5700
Deputy Commissioner:
   Dotty DiPalo (R)..............................914-995-5700

**Wyoming**.............................................fax: 585-786-8843
4 Perry Avenue, Warsaw, NY 14569-1329
Fax: 585-786-8843
e-mail: boewyoming@wyomingco.net
Web site: www.wyomingco.net
Commissioner:
   Anna Mae Balmas (D) .........................585-786-8931
Commissioner:
   James E Schlick (R)...........................585-786-8931
Deputy Commissioner:
   Jeanne M Williams (D) ........................585-786-8931
   e-mail: jewilliams@frontiernet.net
Deputy Commissioner:
   Wendy Simpson (R)...........................585-786-8931
   e-mail: wlsimpson@frontiernet.net

**Yates** ...............................................fax: 315-536-5523
417 Liberty St, Ste 1124, Penn Yan, NY 14527
Fax: 315-536-5523
e-mail: boardofelections@yatescounty.org
Commissioner:
   Robert Brechko (D) ...........................315-536-5135
Commissioner:
   Amy J Daines (R) ............................315-536-5135
Deputy Commissioner:
   Sandra P McKay (D) ..........................315-536-5135
Deputy Commissioner:
   Helen J Scarpechi (R)..........................315-536-5135

**Information Technology Unit**
Director, Data Processing/CTO:
   Mark Goldhaber ..............................518-473-4803

## CORPORATIONS, AUTHORITIES AND COMMISSIONS

### Joint Commission on Public Ethics (JCOPE)
540 Broadway
Albany, NY 12207
518-408-3976  Fax: 518-408-3975
e-mail: jcope@jcope.ny.gov
Web site: www.jcope.ny.gov

Executive Director:
   Seth Agata.................................518-408-3976
Chair:
   Daniel J Horwitz.............................518-408-3976
General Counsel:
   Monica Stamm ..............................518-408-3976
Chief of Staff:
   Kevin T Gagan .................518-408-3976/fax: 518-408-3975

## NEW YORK STATE LEGISLATURE

*See Legislative Branch in Section 1 for additional Standing Committee and Subcommittee information.*

---

*Offices and agencies generally appear in alphabetical order, except when specific order is requested by listee.*

## Assembly Standing Committees

### Election Law
Chair:
Rebecca A Seawright . . . . . . . . . . . . . . 518-455-5456/fax: 518-455-5467

## Senate Standing Committees

### Elections
Chair:
Zellnor Myrie (D) . . . . . . . . . . . . . . . . . . . . . . . . . . . . . .518-455-2410
Ranking Minority Member:
Catharine Young (R, C, IP) . . . . . . . . . . . . . . . . . . . . . . .518-455-3563

## Senate/Assembly Legislative Commissions

### Demographic Research & Reapportionment, Legislative Task Force on
Senate Co-Chair:
Michael F Nozzolio (R) . . . . . . . . . . . . . . . . . . . . . . . . . .518-455-2366
Assembly Co-Chair:
Vacant . . . . . . . . . . . . . . . . . . . . . . . . . . . . . . . . . . . . . .518-455-5514
Assembly Program Manager:
Karen Blatt. . . . . . . . . . . . . . . . . . . . .212-618-1100/fax: 212-618-1135
Executive Director:
Frank Tassone . . . . . . . . . . . . . . . . . . .212-618-1110/fax: 212-618-1135

## U.S. GOVERNMENT

## EXECUTIVE DEPARTMENTS AND RELATED AGENCIES

### Federal Election Commission
999 E Street NW
Washington, DC 20463
202-694-1000 or 800-424-9530
e-mail: info@fec.gov
Web site: www.fec.gov

Chair:
Matthew S. Petersen
e-mail: commissionerpetersen@fec.gov
Vice Chair:
Steven T. Walther
e-mail: swalther@fec.gov
Commissioner:
Caroline C. Hunter
e-mail: commissionerhunter@fec.gov
Commissioner:
Ann M. Ravel
e-mail: commissionerravel@fec.gov
Commissioner:
Ellen L. Weintraub
e-mail: commissionerweintraub@fec.gov

### US Commission on Civil Rights
Web site: www.usccr.gov

### EASTERN REGION (includes New York State)
624 9th Street NW, Suite 500, Washington, DC 20425
Regional Director:
Ivy L. Davis . . . . . . . . . . . . . . . . . .202-376-7533 or TTY: 202-376-8116

## U.S. CONGRESS

*See U.S. Congress Chapter for additional Standing Committee and Subcommittee information.*

## House of Representatives Standing Committees

### Oversight & Government Reform
Chair:
Jason Chaffetz (R-UT) . . . . . . . . . . . . . . . . . . . . . . . . . . . .202-225-7751
Ranking Member:
Elijah Cummings (D-MD) . . . . . . . . . . . . . . . . . . . . . . . .202-225-4741
New York Delegate:
Carolyn B. Maloney (D). . . . . . . . . . . . . . . . . . . . . . . . . .202-225-7944

#### Subcommittee
##### Government Operations
Chair:
Mark Meadows (R-NC). . . . . . . . . . . . . . . . . . . . .202-225-6401
Ranking Member:
Gerald Connolly (D-VA). . . . . . . . . . . . . . . . . . . .202-225-1492

### Ethics
Chair:
Charles W. Dent (R-PA). . . . . . . . . . . . . . . . . . . . . . . . . .202-225-6411
Ranking Member:
Linda T. Sanchez (D-CA). . . . . . . . . . . . . . . . . . . . . . . . .202-225-6676

## Senate Standing Committees

### Ethics, Select Committee on
Chair:
Johnny Isakson (R-GA) . . . . . . . . . . . . . . . . . . . . . . . . . .202-224-3643
Vice Chair:
Barbara Boxer (D-CA) . . . . . . . . . . . . . . . . . . . . . . . . . . .202-224-3553

### Homeland Security & Governmental Affairs
Chair:
Ron Johnson (R-WI). . . . . . . . . . . . . . . . . . . . . . . . . . . . .202-224-5323
Ranking Member:
Thomas R. Carper (D-DE) . . . . . . . . . . . . . . . . . . . . . . . .202-224-2441

## PRIVATE SECTOR

### Arthur J Finkelstein & Associates Inc
16 North Astor, Irvington, NY 10533
914-591-8142
*Election polling & consulting*
Arthur J. Finkelstein, President

### Branford Communications
611 Broadway, New York, NY 10012
212-260-9905  Fax: 212-260-9908
*Media consulting; print production & advertising*
Ernest Lendler, President

### Bynum, Thompson, Ryer
2120 L Street NW, Suite 305, Washington, DC 20037
202-263-4383
e-mail: thompson@btrsc.com
Web site: www.btrsc.com
*Campaign communication, strategy & media production*
Jim Thompson, Owner

### CUNY Graduate School, Center for Urban Research
365 5th Avenue, New York, NY 10016-4309
212-817-2030  Fax: 212-817-1575
e-mail: cur@gc.cuny.edu
Web site: www.gc.cuny.edu
*Political participation, voting behavior, NYC politics & urban economic & demographic change*
John Mollenkopf, Director

*Offices and agencies generally appear in alphabetical order, except when specific order is requested by listee.*

**Century Foundation (The)**
1 Whitehall Street, 15th Floor, New York, NY 10004
212-452-7700  Fax: 212-535-7534
e-mail: info@tcf.org
Web site: www.tcf.org
*Research & analysis of domestic & foreign policy issues, including matters relating to education, the workforce, health care, human rights & election reform*
Lucy Muirhead, Vice President, Communications

**Citizen Action of New York**
94 Central Avenue, Albany, NY 12206
518-465-4600  Fax: 518-465-2890
e-mail: info@citizenactionny.org
Web site: www.citizenactionny.org
*Campaign finance reform; health care advocacy & consumer protection; education*
Karen Scharff, Executive Director

**Columbia Law School, Legislative Drafting Research Fund**
435 West 116th Street, New York, NY 10027-7297
212-854-2640 or 212-854-5633  Fax: 212-854-7946
e-mail: rb34@columbia.edu
Web site: www.law.columbia.edu
*State & local government law, property law & election law*
Richard Briffault, Director & Professor of Legislation

**Common Cause/NY**
80 Broad Street, New York, NY 10004
212-691-6421  Fax: 212-807-1809
e-mail: nyoffice@commoncause.org
Web site: www.commoncause.org/states/new-york/
*Campaign finance reform, ballot access, political gift disclosure & public interest lobbying*
Susan Lerner, Executive Director

**Conservative Party of NYS**
325 Parkview Drive, Schenectady, NY 12303
518-356-7882  Fax: 518-356-3773
e-mail: cpnys@nybiz.rr.com
Web site: www.cpnys.org
*Campaign consulting services & funding for Conservative Party political candidates*
Shaun Marie Levine, Executive Director

**Cookfair Media Inc**
536 Buckingham Avenue, Syracuse, NY 13210
315-478-3359  Fax: 315-478-5236
*Campaign media production, print production & advertising*
John R. Cookfair, III, President

**Democratic Congressional Campaign Committee**
430 South Capitol Street SE, Washington, DC 20003
202-863-1500  Fax: 202-485-3436
Web site: www.dccc.org
*Funding for Democratic congressional candidates; campaign strategy*
Ben Ray Lujan, Chair

**Election Computer Services Inc**
197 County Route 7, Pine Plains, NY 12567
518-398-8844 or 212-750-8844
*Computer services, voter lists & direct mail*
Marguerite Terwilliger, Principal

**EMILY's List**
1800 M Street NW, Suite 375N, Washington, DC 20036
202-326-1400  Fax: 202-326-1415
Web site: www.emilyslist.org
*Political network for pro-choice Democratic women political candidates*
Jessica O'Connell, Executive Director

**Harris Poll (The)**
155 Corporate Woods, Rochester, NY 14623
585-272-8400 or 877-919-4765
Web site: www.theharrispoll.com
*Polls on a range of topics, including politics, the economy, health & sports*
Kathy Steinberg, Director

**League of Women Voters of New York State**
62 Grand Street, Albany, NY 12207-2712
518-465-4162  Fax: 518-465-0812
e-mail: laura@lwvny.org
Web site: www.lwvny.org
*Public policy issues forum; good government advocacy*
Laura Ladd Bierman, Executive Director

**Marist Institute for Public Opinion**
Marist College, 3399 North Road, Poughkeepsie, NY 12601
845-575-5050  Fax: 845-575-5111
e-mail: lee.miringoff@marist.edu
Web site: www.maristpoll.marist.edu
*Develops & conducts nonpartisan public opinion polls on elections & issues*
Lee M. Miringoff, Director

**NY League of Conservation Voters/NY Conservation Education Fund**
30 Broad Street, 30th Floor, New York, NY 10004
212-361-6350  Fax: 212-361-6363
e-mail: info@nylcvef.org
Web site: www.nylcvef.org
*Endorsement of pro-environmental candidates; environmental advocacy & education statewide*
Marcia Bystryn, President

**NYC Campaign Finance Board**
100 Church Street, 12th Floor, New York, NY 10007
212-409-1800  Fax: 212-409-1705
Web site: www.nyccfb.info
*Public funding of candidates for NYC elective offices*
Amy M. Loprest, Executive Director

**NYS Right to Life Committee**
41 State Street, Suite M-100, Albany, NY 12207
518-434-1293  Fax: 518-426-1200
e-mail: admin@nysrighttolife.org
Web site: www.nysrighttolife.org
Lori Kehoe, Executive Director

**National Organization for Women, NYS**
150 West 28th Street, Suite 304, New York, NY 10001
212-627-9895  Fax: 212-627-9861
e-mail: nownewyorkstate@gmail.com
Web site: www.nownys.org
*Campaign assistance & funding for political candidates who support women's equality; legislative lobbying on women's issues*
Sonia Ossorio, President

**New School for Social Research, Department of Politics**
6 East 16th Street, Room 711A, New York, NY 10003
212-229-5747 x3090  Fax: 212-229-5473
e-mail: kalyvasa@newschool.edu
Web site: www.newschool.edu
*Political issues & analysis*
Andreas Kalyvas, Chair

**New York Republican State Committee**
315 State Street, Albany, NY 12210
518-462-2601  Fax: 518-449-7443
Jason Weingartner, Executive Director

*Offices and agencies generally appear in alphabetical order, except when specific order is requested by listee.*

**New York State Democratic Committee**
750 Third Avenue, 31st Floor, New York, NY 10017
212-725-8825  Fax: 212-725-8867
Web site: www.nydems.org
Sheila Comar, Executive Commitee Chair

**New York University, Departmentt of Politics**
19 West 4th Street, 2nd Floor, New York, NY 10012-9580
212-998-8500  Fax: 212-995-4184
e-mail: russell.hardin@nyu.edu
Web site: www.politics.as.nyu.edu
*Collective action & social movements; nationalism & ethnic conflict; constitutionalism*
Russell Hardin, Professor of Politics

**New York University, Graduate School of Journalism**
20 Cooper Square, 6th Floor, New York, NY 10003
212-998-7980  Fax: 212-995-4148
e-mail: perri.klass@nyu.edu
Web site: www.journalism.nyu.edu
*Public information & knowledge*
Perri Klass, Director

**New York Wired for Education LLC**
251 Fuller Road, Room B150, Albany, NY 12203
518-462-1780
Web site: www.metrixlearning.com
Brian S. Lee, Chief Executive Officer

**Nostradamus Advertising**
884 West End Avenue, Suite 2, New York, NY 10025
212-581-1362
e-mail: nos@nostradamus.net
Web site: www.nostradamus.net
*Print production, media consulting, direct mail development*
Barry N. Sher, President

**Public Agenda**
6 East 39th Street, 9th Floor, New York, NY 10016
212-686-6610  Fax: 212-889-3461
e-mail: info@publicagenda.org
Web site: www.publicagenda.org
*Nonpartisan, nonprofit organization dedicated to conducting unbiased public opinion research & producing fair-minded citizen education materials*
Will Friedman, President

**SUNY at Albany, Nelson A Rockefeller College**
135 Western Avenue, Albany, NY 12222
518-442-5244  Fax: 518-442-5298
e-mail: hildreth@albany.edu
Web site: www.albany.edu/rockefeller
*Intergovernmental relations; NY state & local government; ethics in government; election systems & voting*
Anne Hildreth, Associate Professor

**SUNY at New Paltz, College of Liberal Arts & Sciences**
1 Hawk Drive, New Paltz, NY 12561-2499
845-257-7869 or 877-696-7411
e-mail: millerj@newpaltz.edu
Web site: www.newpaltz.edu
*Local & state government process & structure; regionalism; politics & election law*
Jeff Miller, Political Science Chair & Associate Professor

**Sheinkopf Communications**
152 Madison Avenue, Suite 1603, New York, NY 10016
212-725-2378  Fax: 212-725-6896
*Strategic message counseling for corporate & political clients*
Hank Sheinkopf, President

**US Term Limits Foundation**
1250 Connecticut Avenue NW, Suite 200, Washington, DC 20036
202-261-3532
Web site: www.termlimits.org
*Works to combat government malpractice*
Howard Rich, Chairman

**Women's Campaign Fund**
718 7th Street NW, 2nd Floor, Washington, DC 20001
202-796-8259
e-mail: info@wcfonline.org
Web site: www.wcfonline.org
*Support for women political candidates & advocacy for more women in government & elected office*
Betsy Mullins, President & Chief Executive Officer

**Women's City Club of New York**
110 West 40th Street, Suite 1002, New York, NY 10018
212-353-8070  Fax: 212-228-4665
e-mail: info@wccny.org
Web site: www.wccny.org
*Nonpartisan, nonprofit activist organization whose mission is to inform public policy & enhance the quality of life for all New Yorkers through education, advocacy & issue analysis*
Jacqueline M. Ebanks, Executive Director

**Working Families Party**
1 Metrotech Center North, 11th Floor, Brooklyn, NY 11217
718-222-3796  Fax: 718-246-3718
Web site: www.workingfamilies.org
Bill Lipton, State Director

**Zogby Analytics**
901 Broad Street, Utica, NY 13501
315-624-9642
Web site: www.zogbyanalytics.com
*Polling, surveys, focus groups, market research studies & data analysis for businesses & communities*
Jonathan Zogby, Chief Executive Officer

Policy Areas

*Offices and agencies generally appear in alphabetical order, except when specific order is requested by listee.*

# ENERGY, UTILITY & COMMUNICATION SERVICES

## NEW YORK STATE

### GOVERNOR'S OFFICE

## Governor's Office
Executive Chamber
State Capitol
Albany, NY 12224
518-474-8390  Fax: 518-474-1513
Web site: www.ny.gov

Governor:
   Andrew M Cuomo . . . . . . . . . . . . . . . . . . . . . . . . . . . . . . .518-474-8390
Secretary to the Governor:
   Melissa DeRosa . . . . . . . . . . . . . . . . . . . .518-474-4246 or 212-681-4580
Counsel to the Governor:
   Kumiki Gibson . . . . . . . . . . . . . . . . . . . .518-474-8343 or 212-681-4580
Chairman of Energy & Finance for New York:
   Richard L. Kauffman . . . . . . . . . . . . . . . . . . . . . . . . .518-486-9746
Chief of Staff:
   Jill DesRosiers . . . . . . . . . . . . . . . . .518-474-8390 or 212-681-4580
Director, Communications:
   Peter Ajemian . . . . . . . . . . . . . . . . . . . .518-474-8418 or 212-681-4640

### EXECUTIVE DEPARTMENTS AND RELATED AGENCIES

## CIO & Office of Information Technology Services (ITS)
State Capitol
Empire State Plaza
P.O. Box 2062
Albany, NY 12220-0062
518-402-3899 or 844-891-1786
e-mail: fixit@its.ny.gov
Web site: www.its.ny.gov

Chief Information Officer & Director:
   Robert H. Samson. . . . . . . . . . . . . . . . . . . . . . . . . . . . . . .518-408-2140
Executive Deputy Chief Information Officer:
   Karen Geduldig. . . . . . . . . . . . . . . . . . . . . . . . . . . . . .518-473-9450
Chief General Counsel:
   Shoshanah Bewlay . . . . . . . . . . . . . . . . . . . . . . . . . . . . .518-408-2484
Director, Public Information:
   Vacant. . . . . . . . . . . . . . . . . . . . . . . . . . . . . . . . . . . . .518-402-3899

### Administration
Chief Operating Officer:
   Ray Rose. . . . . . . . . . . . . . . . . . . . . . . . . . . . . . . . . . . .518-402-7000
Director, Administration:
   Theresa Papa. . . . . . . . . . . . . . . . . . . . . . . . . . . . . . . .518-408-2484
Chief Technology Officer:
   Rajiv Rao . . . . . . . . . . . . . . . . . . . . . . . . . . . . . . . . . .518-486-9200
Acting Chief Data Officer:
   John Rager
Chief Information Security Officer:
   Karen Sorady . . . . . . . . . . . . . . . . . . . . . . . . . . . . . . .518-242-5200
Chief Portfolio Officer:
   Nancy Mulholland . . . . . . . . . . . . . . . . . . . . . . . . . . . . .518-473-9450

## Consumer Protection, Division of
One Commerce Plaza
99 Washington Avenue
Albany, NY 12231-0001

518-474-8583 or 800-697-1220  Fax: 518-473-9055
e-mail: info@dos.ny.gov
Web site: www.dos.ny.gov/consumerprotection/

Executive Deputy Director:
   Aiesha Battle. . . . . . . . . . . . . . . . . . . . . . . . . . . . . . . . .518-474-2363

## Law Department
28 Liberty Street
New York, NY 10005
212-416-8000 or 800-771-7755
Web site: www.ag.ny.gov

State Capitol
Albany, NY 12224-0341
518-776-2000
Fax: 518-650-9401

Attorney General:
   Letitia James. . . . . . . . . . . . . . . . . . . .212-416-8000 or 518-776-2000
Chief of Staff:
   Brian Mahanna . . . . . . . . . . . . . . . . . . . . . . . . . . . . . .212-416-8050
Director, Public Information:
   Shawn Morris . . . . . . . . . . . . . . . . . .518-776-2357/fax: 518-650-9401
Press Secretary:
   Fernando Aquino. . . . . . . . . . . . . . . .212-416-8060/fax: 212-416-6005
   e-mail: nyag.pressoffice@ag.ny.gov

## Economic Justice
Executive Deputy Attorney General:
   Siobhan Kennedy . . . . . . . . . . . . . . . . . . . . . . . . . . . . .212-416-8050

#### Internet Bureau
Bureau Chief:
   Kathleen McGee . . . . . . . . . . . . . . . .212-416-8433/fax: 212-416-8369

## Public Service Commission
NYS Dept of Public Service
Empire State Plaza
Building 3
Albany, NY 12223-1350
518-474-7080  Fax: 518-474-2838
Web site: www.dps.ny.gov

Chair:
   John B Rhodes. . . . . . . . . . . . . . . . . .518-474-2523/fax: 518-473-2838
General Counsel:
   Robert Rosenthal. . . . . . . . . . . . . . . . . . . . . . . . . . . . .518-474-2510
Director, Electric, Gas & Water:
   Tammy Mitchell . . . . . . . . . . . . . . . . . . . . . . . . . . . . . .518-486-2483
Secretary to the Commission:
   Kathleen H Burgess. . . . . . . . . . . . . . . .518-474-6530/fax: 518-474-9842
   e-mail: secretary@dps.ny.gov
Director, Public Affairs:
   James Denn . . . . . . . . . . . . . . . . . . . .518-474-7080/fax: 518-473-2838
   e-mail: james.denn@dps.ny.gov

## Accounting & Finance Office
Director:
   Doris Stout . . . . . . . . . . . . . . . . . . . . . .518-474-4508 or 212-417-2136

## Consumer Policy Office
Director:
   Douglas Elfner. . . . . . . . . . . . . . . . . . . .518-402-5786/fax: 518-473-5685

## Consumer Services Office
Acting Director:
   Bruce Alch . . . . . . . . . . . . . . . . . . . . . . . . . . . . . . . . .212-837-7244
  :
   Consumer Complaints . . . . . . . . . . . .1-800-342-3377/fax: 518-486-7868

*Offices and agencies generally appear in alphabetical order, except when specific order is requested by listee.*

### Electric, Gas & Water Office

Director:
Tammy Mitchell . . . . . . . . . . . . . . . . . . . . . . . . . . . .518-486-2483
Director:
Tammy Mitchell . . . . . . . . . . . . . . . . . . . . . . . . . . . .518-486-2483
Deputy Director, Gas, Water & Steam:
Michael Scott. . . . . . . . . . . . . . . . . . . .518-474-1372/fax: 518-473-4992
Chief, Economic Development & Retail Access:
Bruce Alch. . . . . . . . . . . . . . . . . . . .518-486-2400/fax: 518-473-5204
Chief, Bulk Electric Systems:
Tammy Mitchell . . . . . . . . . . . . . . . . .518-486-2462/fax: 518-473-2420
Chief, Policy Coordination:
William Heinrich. . . . . . . . . . . . . . . . .518-473-3402/fax: 518-473-2420
Chief, Gas Rates & Tariffs:
Thomas Coonan. . . . . . . . . . . . . . . . . .518-473-6694/fax: 518-473-4992
Chief, Gas Policy & Supply:
Cynthia McCarran . . . . . . . . . . . . . . . .518-474-1396/fax: 518-473-4992
Chief, Water:
James Evensen. . . . . . . . . . . . . . . . . . .212-417-2321/fax: 212-417-2324
Chief, Safety, Electric, Gas & Steam:
Gavin S Nicoletta . . . . . . . . . . . . . . . .518-486-2496/fax: 518-473-1498
Chief, Utility Security:
John Sennett. . . . . . . . . . . . . . . . . . . . .518-402-5445/fax: 518-473-5685

### Hearings & Alternative Dispute Resolution Office

Chief Administrative Law Judge:
Elizabeth Liebschutz . . . . . . . . . . . . . .518-474-4521/fax: 518-473-3263

### Industry & Governmental Relations Office

Managing Director:
Michael Corso. . . . . . . . . . . . . . . . . . . . . . . . . . . . . . .518-474-4686

### Office of Administration

Director:
Sorelle Brauth . . . . . . . . . . . . . . . . . . .518-474-2508/fax: 518-474-0413
Adminstrative Management:
Judy Regan . . . . . . . . . . . . . . . . . . . . .518-474-1990/fax: 518-474-0413
Finance & Budget:
Carole Gnacik . . . . . . . . . . . . . . . . . . .518-474-2516/fax: 518-473-9990
Human Resources:
Janice Nissen. . . . . . . . . . . . . . . . . . . .518-486-2626/fax: 518-473-9990
Information Services Director:
Carmela Turpin . . . . . . . . . . . . . . . . . .518-486-4960/fax: 518-473-7815
Internal Audit:
Theresa Schillaci . . . . . . . . . . . . . . . . .518-473-2079/fax: 518-486-6081

### Market & Regulatory Economics Office

Director:
Warren Myers. . . . . . . . . . . . . . . . . . . . . . . . . . . . . . . .518-474-1721

### Office of Telecommunications

Director:
Debra LaBelle . . . . . . . . . . . . . . . . . . .518-474-1668/fax: 518-474-5616

## CORPORATIONS, AUTHORITIES AND COMMISSIONS

### Interstate Oil & Gas Compact Commission

PO Box 53127
900 NE 23rd St
Oklahoma City, OK 73152-3127
405-525-3556  Fax: 405-525-3592
Web site: www.iogcc.ok.gov

Chair:
Governor Mary Fallin (OK) . . . . . . . . . . . . . . . . . . . .405-525-3556
Vice Chair:
David Porter . . . . . . . . . . . . . . . . . . . . . . . . . . . . . . . .405-525-3556
Executive Director:
Mike Smith. . . . . . . . . . . . . . . . . . . . . . . . . . . . . . . . .405-525-3556
New York State Official Representative:
Bradley J Field . . . . . . . . . . . . . . . . . . . . . . . . . . . . . .518-402-8076

Communications Manager:
Carol Booth. . . . . . . . . . . . . . . . . . . . . . . . . . . . . . . . .405-525-3556

### New York Power Authority

123 Main Street
Mailstop 10-H
White Plains, NY 10601-3170
914-681-6200  Fax: 914-390-8190
e-mail: info@nypa.gov
Web site: www.nypa.gov

Chairman:
John R. Koelmel . . . . . . . . . . . . . . . . . . . . . . . . . . . . .914-287-3636
President & Chief Executive Officer:
Gil C Quiniones . . . . . . . . . . . . . . . . . . . . . . . . . . . . .914-287-3501
SVP, Corporate Affairs:
Rocco Iannarelli . . . . . . . . . . . . . . . . . . . . . . . . . . . . .518-433-6700
Chief Operating Officer:
Edward A Welz. . . . . . . . . . . . . . . . . . . . . . . . . . . . . .518-433-6700
EVP & General Counsel:
Justin E Driscoll . . . . . . . . . . . . . . . . . . . . . . . . . . . . .914-681-6200

### New York State Energy Research & Development Authority

17 Columbia Circle
Albany, NY 12203-6399
518-862-1090  Fax: 518-862-1091
e-mail: info@nyserda.ny.gov
Web site: www.nyserda.ny.gov

Chairman:
Richard L. Kauffman . . . . . . . . . . . . . . . . . . . . . . . . . .518-486-9746
President & CEO:
John B Rhodes. . . . . . . . . . . . . . . . . . . . . . . . . .518-862-1090 x3278
General Counsel:
Noah C Shaw. . . . . . . . . . . . . . . . . . . . . . . . . . .518-862-1090 x3280
Program Manager, Economic Development & Community Outreach:
Kelly Tyler. . . . . . . . . . . . . . . . . . . . . . . .716-842-1522 x. 3005
e-mail: kelly.tyler@nyserda.ny.gov
Director, Communications:
Kate Muller. . . . . . . . . . . . . .518-862-1090 x3582/fax: 518-862-1091
e-mail: kate.muller@nyserda.ny.gov

## NEW YORK STATE LEGISLATURE

*See Legislative Branch in Section 1 for additional Standing Committee and Subcommittee information.*

### Assembly Standing Committees

**Energy**
Chair:
Michael Cusick (D). . . . . . . . . . . . . . . . . . . . . . . . . . .518-455-5526

### Senate Standing Committees

**Energy & Telecommunications**
Chair:
Kevin S Parker (D, WF) . . . . . . . . . . . . . . . . . . . . . . . .518-455-2580
Ranking Minority Member:
Patty Ritchie (R, C, IP). . . . . . . . . . . . . . . . . . . . . . . . .518-455-3438

*Offices and agencies generally appear in alphabetical order, except when specific order is requested by listee.*

Policy Areas

## U.S. GOVERNMENT

## EXECUTIVE DEPARTMENTS AND RELATED AGENCIES

### Federal Communications Commission
e-mail: fccinfo@fcc.gov
Web site: www.fcc.gov

**Office of Media Relations** ...................... fax: 866-418-0232
445 12th Street SW, Room CY-C314, Washington, DC 20554
888-225-5322  Fax: 866-418-0232
Director:
Shannon Gilson

### Nuclear Regulatory Commission
Web site: www.nrc.gov

**REGION I (includes New York State)**
2100 Renaissance Blvd, Suite 100, King of Prussia, PA 19406-2713
Regional Administrator:
Daniel Dorman
Deputy Regional Administrator:
David Lew
Senior Public Affairs Officer:
Diane Screnci

### US Department of Agriculture
Web site: www.usda.gov

**Rural Development**
Web site: www.rd.usda.gov/ny

**New York State Office**......................... fax: 315-477-6438
The Galleries of Syracuse, 441 South Salina Street, Suite 357, Syracuse,
NY 13202-2541
TTY: 315-477-6447 or 315-477-6400  Fax: 315-477-6438
Acting State Director:
Scott Collins ............................315-477-6437
Special Projects Coordinator:
Christopher Stewart

**Eastern New York Office** ...................... fax: 855-889-1632
255 Dolson Avenue, Suite 104, Middletown, NY 10940
845-343-1872 x4  Fax: 855-889-1632
Director:
Ronda Falkena................................845-343-1872 x4

**Western New York Office**...................... fax: 607-753-3190
1 North Main Street, 2nd Floor, Cortland, NY 13045
607-753-0851  Fax: 607-753-3190
Director:
Jim Walfrand................................585-343-9167 x4

### US Department of Energy

**Federal Energy Regulatory Commission**

**New York Regional Office**
19 West 34th Street, Suite 400, New York, NY 10001-3006
Regional Engineer:
John Spain

**Office of External Affairs**
888 First Street NE, Washington, DC 20426
866-208-3372
Director:
Leonard Tao ...................202-502-8004/fax: 202-208-2106

### Laboratories

**Brookhaven National Laboratory**
*External Affairs & Stakeholder Relations*
PO Box 5000, Upton, NY 11973-5000
Director, Stakeholder & Community Relations Office:
David Manning
*Office of the Director*
2 Center Street, Upton, NY 11973
Director:
Doon Gibbs

**Knolls Atomic Power Laboratory- KAPL Inc**
2401 River Road, Niskayuna, NY 12309

## U.S. CONGRESS

*See U.S. Congress Chapter for additional Standing Committee and Subcommittee information.*

### House of Representatives Standing Committees

**Appropriations**
Chair:
Harold Rogers (R-KY).............................202-225-4601
Ranking Member:
Nita M. Lowey (D-NY) ..........................202-225-6506
New York Delegate:
Steve Israel (D)................................202-225-3335
New York Delegate:
Jose E. Serrano (D)............................202-225-4361

**Subcommittee**
*Energy & Water Development*
Chair:
Mike Simpson (R-ID) ......................202-225-5531
Ranking Member:
Marcy Kaptur (D-OH)....................202-225-4146

**Energy & Commerce**
Chair:
Fred Upton (R-MI) .............................202-225-3761
Ranking Member:
Frank Pallone (D-NJ) .........................202-225-4671
New York Delegate:
Eliot L. Engel (D)............................202-225-2464
New York Delegate:
Paul Tonko (D)................................202-225-5076
New York Delegate:
Yvette Clarke (D)............................202-225-6231
New York Delegate:
Chris Collins (R).............................202-225-5265

**Subcommittee**
*Energy & Power*
Chair:
Ed Whitfield (R-KY).......................202-225-3115
Ranking Member:
Bobby L. Rush (D-IL)......................202-225-4372
New York Delegate:
Eliot L. Engel (D) .......................202-225-2464
New York Delegate:
Paul Tonko (D) ...........................202-225-5076

**Natural Resources**
Chair:
Rob Bishop (R-UT) ............................202-225-0453
Ranking Member:
Raul M. Grijalva (D-AZ) .....................202-225-2435

*Offices and agencies generally appear in alphabetical order, except when specific order is requested by listee.*

**Subcommittees**

*Energy & Mineral Resources*
Chair:
Doug Lamborn (R-CO) . . . . . . . . . . . . . . . . . . . . . . .202-225-4422
Ranking Member:
Alan Lowenthal (D-CA) . . . . . . . . . . . . . . . . . . . . . .202-225-7924

*Water, Power & Oceans*
Chair:
John Fleming (R-LA). . . . . . . . . . . . . . . . . . . . . . . .202-225-2777
Ranking Member:
Jared Huffman (D-CA) . . . . . . . . . . . . . . . . . . . . . .202-225-5161

## Science, Space & Technology
Chair:
Lamar Smith (R-TX). . . . . . . . . . . . . . . . . . . . . . . . . .202-225-4236
Ranking Member:
Eddie Bernice Johnson (D-TX) . . . . . . . . . . . . . . . . .202-225-8885

**Subcommittee**

*Energy*
Chair:
Randy Weber (R-TX) . . . . . . . . . . . . . . . . . . . . . . .202-225-2831
Ranking Member:
Alan Grayson (D-FL). . . . . . . . . . . . . . . . . . . . . . .202-225-9889

## Senate Standing Committees

### Appropriations
Chair:
Thad Cochran (R-MS) . . . . . . . . . . . . . . . . . . . . . . . . .202-224-5054
Vice Chair:
Barbara A. Mikulski (D-MD). . . . . . . . . . . . . . . . . . . .202-224-4654

**Subcommittee**

*Energy & Water Development*
Chair:
Lamar Alexander (R-TN) . . . . . . . . . . . . . . . . . . . .202-224-4944
Ranking Member:
Dianne Feinstein (D-CA). . . . . . . . . . . . . . . . . . . . .202-224-3841

### Commerce, Science & Transportation
Chair:
John Thune (R-SD). . . . . . . . . . . . . . . . . . . . . . . . . . .202-224-2321
Ranking Member:
Bill Nelson (D-FL) . . . . . . . . . . . . . . . . . . . . . . . . . . .202-224-5274

**Subcommittee**

*Aviation Operations, Safety & Security*
Chair:
Kelly Ayotte (R-NH). . . . . . . . . . . . . . . . . . . . . . . .202-224-3324
Ranking Member:
Maria Cantwell (D-WA) . . . . . . . . . . . . . . . . . . . . .202-224-3441

*Space, Science & Competitiveness*
Chair:
Ted Cruz (R-TX) . . . . . . . . . . . . . . . . . . . . . . . . . .202-224-5922
Ranking Member:
Gary Peters (D-MI) . . . . . . . . . . . . . . . . . . . . . . . .202-224-6221

### Energy & Natural Resources
Chair:
Lisa Murkowski (R-AK). . . . . . . . . . . . . . . . . . . . . . . .202-224-6665
Ranking Member:
Maria Cantwell (D-WA). . . . . . . . . . . . . . . . . . . . . . . .202-224-3441

## PRIVATE SECTOR

### AT&T Corporation
One AT&T Way, Bedminster, NJ 07921
908-234-6507
Web site: www.att.com
*Telecommunications services & systems*
Edward Amoroso, Senior Vice President & Chief Security Officer

### Association of Public Broadcasting Stations of NY Inc
33 Elk Street, Suite 200, Albany, NY 12207
518-462-1590  Fax: 518-462-1390
*Public television*
Peter Repas, Executive Director

### CBS Corporation
51 West 52nd Street, New York, NY 10019-6188
212-975-4321
Web site: www.cbscorporation.com
*TV & radio broadcasting, news, entertainment*
Leslie Moonves, Chairman, President & Chief Executive Officer

### Cable Telecommunications Association of New York, Inc
54 State Street, Suite 800, Albany, NY 12207
518-463-6676  Fax: 518-463-0574
*Advocates for & represents the interests of the cable television industry*
James Reynolds, Director

### Cablevision Systems Corporation
1111 Stewart Avenue, Bethpage, NY 11714-3581
866-200-7273
e-mail: lrosenbl@cablevision.com
Web site: www.cablevision.com
*Owns & operates cable television systems & programming networks; provides telecommunications services*
Lisa Rosenblum, Executive Vice President, Government & Public Affairs

### Central Hudson Gas & Electric Corporation
284 South Avenue, Poughkeepsie, NY 12601
845-452-2700  Fax: 845-486-5658
Web site: www.centralhudson.com
*Delivers natural gas & electricity to consumers*
Michael L. Mosher, President & Chief Executive Officer

### Consolidated Edison Energy
Cooper Station, PO Box 138, New York, NY 10276-0138
800-752-6633
Web site: www.coned.com
John H. Banks III, Vice President, Government & Community Relations

### Constellation Energy
Metro-North Region, 810 7th Avenue, Suite 400, New York, NY 10019
212-885-6400  Fax: 212-883-5888
Web site: www.constellation.com
*Energy services provider*
Joseph Nigro, Chief Executive Officer

### Crane & Parente, PLLC
48 Howard Street, Albany, NY 12207
518-432-8000
*Governmental relations, banking & financial services, corporate law, construction law, energy, utilities, communications, land use, environmental & wireless telecommunications law*
James B. Crane, II, Managing Member

### Empire State Petroleum Association Inc
56 Clifton Country Road, Suite 108, Clifton Park, NY 12065
518-280-6645  Fax: 518-280-6670
Web site: www.eseany.org
*Petroleum industry lobby & trade association*
Thomas J. Peters, Chief Executive Officer

*Offices and agencies generally appear in alphabetical order, except when specific order is requested by listee.*

Policy Areas

**Energy Coalition New York**
1 Commerce Plaza, Albany, NY 12260
518-487-7600
*Electric & natural gas utility companies*
William Y. Crowell III, Executive Director

**Entek Power Services**
11 Satterly Rd, East Setauket, NY 11733
631-751-9800  Fax: 631-980-3759
*Energy consulting*
Harry Davitian, President

**Entergy Nuclear Northeast**
440 Hamilton Avenue, White Plains, NY 10601
914-272-3200  Fax: 914-272-3205
Web site: www.entergy.com
*Operator of nuclear power plants across the US*
John A. Ventosa, Chief Operating Officer, Northern Fleet

**Exxon Mobil Corporation**
1400 Old Country Road, Suite 203, Westbury, NY 11590
516-333-0171
Web site: www.exxonmobil.com
Donald L Clarke, Manager, Public Affairs Northeast

**Frontier, A Citizens Communications Co**
19 John Street, Middletown, NY 10940
845-344-9801  Fax: 845-343-3768
*Full service telecommunications provider*
Ellen Amarosa, Manager

**Fund for the City of New York, Center for Internet Innovation**
121 Avenue of the Americas, 6th Floor, New York, NY 10013-1590
212-925-6675  Fax: 212-925-5675
Web site: www.fcny.org
*Developing technology systems & applications that help advance the operations & performance of NY government & nonprofit organizations*
Mary McCormick, President

**NYS Bar Assn, Electronic Communications Task Force**
**Heslin Rothenberg Farley & Mesiti PC**
5 Columbia Cir, Albany, NY 12203
518-452-5600  Fax: 518-452-5579
e-mail: dpm@hrfmlaw.com
Web site: www.hrfmlaw.com
David P. Miranda, Partner

**Hess Corporation**
1185 Avenue of the Americas, 40th Floor, New York, NY 10036
212-997-8500  Fax: 212-536-8390
Web site: www.hess.com
*Manufactures & markets petroleum products; operates gasoline outlets*
John B. Hess, Chief Executive Officer

**NYS Bar Assn, Media Law Committee**
**Hogan Lovells US LLP**
875 Third Avenue, New York, NY 10022
212-918-3000  Fax: 212-918-3100
e-mail: warren.gorrell@hoganlovells.com
Web site: www.hoganlovells.com
J. Warren Gorrell, Jr., Partner

**Independent Oil & Gas Association of New York**
38 Lake Street, Hamburg, NY 14075
716-202-4688  Fax: 716-202-4689
e-mail: brgill@iogany.org
Web site: www.iogany.org
*Trade association representing oil & natural gas producers, drillers & affiliated service companies*
Bradley Gill, Executive Director

**Independent Power Producers of NY Inc**
194 Washington Avenue, Suite 315, Albany, NY 12210
518-436-3749  Fax: 518-436-0369
e-mail: gavin@ippny.org
Web site: www.ippny.org
*Companies developing alternative, environmentally friendly electric generating facilities*
Gavin J. Donohue, President & Chief Executive Officer

**Komanoff Energy Associates**
11 Hanover Square, 21st Floor, New York, NY 10005
212-260-5237
e-mail: kea@igc.org
Web site: www.carbontax.org
*Energy, utilities & transportation consulting*
Charles Komanoff, Director

**Mechanical Technology Incorporated**
325 Washington Avenue Ext., Albany, NY 12205
518-218-2550  Fax: 518-533-2201
Web site: www.mechtech.com
*New energy technologies, precision measurement & testing instruments*
Kevin G. Lynch, Chairman & Chief Executive Officer

**Municipal Electric Utilities Association**
6652 Hammersmith Drive, East Syracuse, NY 13057
315-453-7851  Fax: 315-453-7849
e-mail: info@meua.org
Web site: www.meua.org
Tony Modafferi, Executive Director

**NY Oil Heating Association**
183 Madison Avenue, Suite 1403, New York, NY 10016
212-695-1380  Fax: 212-594-6583
Web site: www.nyoha.org
*Represents NYC's fuel industry*
Rocco Lacertosa, President & Chief Executive Officer

**New York Press Association**
621 Columbia Street Ext., Suite 1, Cohoes, NY 12047
518-464-6483  Fax: 518-464-6489
e-mail: mkrea@nynewspapers.com
Web site: www.nynewspapers.com
*Weekly community & ethnic newspaper publishers*
Michelle K. Rea, Executive Director

**NY Propane Gas Association**
PO Box 760, Clifton Park, NY 12065
518-383-3823  Fax: 518-383-3824
Web site: www.nypropane.com
*Promotes & represents the interests of New York's propane industry through education & networking*
Rick Cummings, President

**NYS Broadcasters Association**
1805 Western Avenue, Albany, NY 12203
518-456-8888  Fax: 518-456-8943
e-mail: ddonovan@nysbroadcasters.org
Web site: www.nysbroadcasters.org
*Trade association for NYS television & radio stations*
David Donovan, President & Executive Director

**NYS Forum Inc**
24 Aviation Road, Albany, NY 12205
518-438-7414  Fax: 518-438-1416
e-mail: info@nysforum.org
Web site: www.nysforum.org
*Information technology management; assists government officials & entities with knowledge transfer & exchange*
Joan Sullivan, Executive Director

*Offices and agencies generally appear in alphabetical order, except when specific order is requested by listee.*

**NYS Technology Enterprise Corporation (NYSTEC)**
540 Broadway, 3rd Floor, Albany, NY 12207
888-969-7832  Fax: 518-431-7037
e-mail: nystec@nystec.com
Web site: www.nystec.com
*Technology acquisition, technology management & engineering services to government clients & other institutions*
Mike Walsh, President & Chief Executive Officer

**National Economic Research Associates**
1166 Avenue of the Americas, 29th Floor, New York, NY 10036
212-345-3000  Fax: 212-345-4650
Web site: www.nera.com
*Utility & transportation regulation, deregulation & antitrust*
Dr. Andrew Carron, Chairman

**NYS Bar Assn, Public Utility Law Committee**
**National Fuel Gas Company**
6363 Main Street, Williamsville, NY 14221
716-857-7000 or 716-686-6123
Web site: www.nationalfuel.com
*Natural gas distribution, storage, production & marketing*
Ronald J. Tanski, President & Chief Executive Officer

**National Grid**
300 Erie Blvd West, Syracuse, NY 13202
315-428-5430 or 800-642-4272
Web site: www.nationalgridus.com
Chris Murphy, Vice President

**New York Independent System Operator - Not For Profit**
10 Krey Blvd, Rensselaer, NY 12144
518-356-6000 or 518-356-7325  Fax: 518-356-7524
Web site: www.nyiso.com
*Grid operator*
Kevin Lanahan, Vice President, External Affairs

**New York News Publishers Association**
252 Hudson Avenue, Albany, NY 12210
518-449-1667 or 800-777-1667  Fax: 518-449-5053
e-mail: dianenynpa@aol.com
Web site: www.nynpa.com
*Represents NY's daily, weekly & online newspapers; provides training, networking & support*
Diane Kennedy, President

**New York Press Photographers Association**
Church St. Station, PO Box 3346, New York, NY 10008-3346
212-889-6633  Fax: 212-889-6634
e-mail: office@nyppa.org
Web site: www.nyppa.org
Bruce Cotler, President

**Rochester Gas and Electric Corporation**
**New York State Electric & Gas Corporation (NYSEG)**
18 Link Drive, PO Box 5224, Binghamton, NY 13902-5224
607-762-7200 or 800-572-1111
Web site: www.nyseg.com
Philip Thompson, Regional Operations Manager

**New York State Petroleum Council**
150 State Street, Albany, NY 12207
518-465-3563  Fax: 518-465-4022
Web site: www.api.org
*Petroleum industry lobby*
Karen Moreau, Executive Director

**New York State Telecommunications Association Inc**
4 Tower Place, 2nd Floor, Albany, NY 12203
518-443-2700  Fax: 518-443-2810
Web site: www.nysta.com
Robert R. Puckett, President

**New York Technology Council**
307 West 38th Street, 13th Floor, New York, NY 10018
646-435-1088
e-mail: info@nytech.org
Web site: www.nytech.org
*Promotes New York City's technology industry*
Erik Grimmelmann, President & Chief Executive Officer

**Northeast Gas Association**
75 Second Avenue, Suite 510, Needham, MA 02494-2859
781-455-6800  Fax: 781-455-6828
Web site: www.northeastgas.org
*Trade association serving the natural gas industry of the Northeast US through education, training, research, planning & development*
Thomas M. Kiley, President & Chief Executive Officer

**Oil Heat Institute of Long Island**
200 Parkway Drive South, Suite 202, Hauppauge, NY 11788
631-360-0200  Fax: 631-360-0781
Web site: www.ohili.org
*Heating oil industry association*
Kevin M. Rooney, Chief Executive Officer

**Orange & Rockland Utilities Inc**
One Blue Hill Plaza, Pearl River, NY 10965
845-352-6000  Fax: 845-577-6914
Web site: www.oru.com
*Electric & gas utility*
Timothy P. Cawley, President & Chief Executive Officer

**Plug Power Inc**
968 Albany Shaker Road, Latham, NY 12110
518-782-7700  Fax: 518-782-9060
Web site: www.plugpower.com
*Fuel cell research & development for small stationary applications*
Gerard L. Conway, Jr., Vice President of Government Affairs & General Counsel

**Public Utility Law Project of New York Inc**
90 State Street, Suite 601, Albany, NY 12207-1715
518-449-3375 or 800-255-7857  Fax: 518-449-1769
Web site: www.pulp.tc
*Advocacy of universal service, affordability & customer protection for residential utility consumers*
Richard Berkley, Executive Director

**Rochester Gas & Electric Corporation**
89 East Avenue, Rochester, NY 14649-0001
800-295-7323
Web site: www.rge.com
Dick Marion, Economic Development Specialist

**Sithe Global**
757 Third Avenue, 24th Floor, New York, NY 10017
212-351-0000  Fax: 212-351-0880
Web site: www.sitheglobal.com
*Electric generation facility development*
Martin B. Rosenberg, Chief Executive Officer

**Soligent Distribution LLC - East Coast Distribution Center**
3 Security Drive, Suite 303, Cranbury, NJ 08512
609-860-6444
Web site: www.soligent.net
*Solar distribution; solar energy equipment & services*
Jonathan Doochin, Chief Executive Officer

**Spanish Broadcasting System Network Inc**
26 West 56th Street, New York, NY 10019
212-541-9200  Fax: 212-541-9295
Web site: www.spanishbroadcasting.com
*Spanish language FM radio stations*
Eric Garcia, General Manager

*Offices and agencies generally appear in alphabetical order, except when specific order is requested by listee.*

**Verizon Communications**
140 West Street, New York, NY 10013
212-395-1000 or 800-837-4966
Web site: www.verizon.com
*Telecommunications services for northeastern US*
David Lamendola, Director of Government Affairs, NY & CT

**Viacom Inc**
1515 Broadway, New York, NY 10036
212-258-6000
Web site: www.viacom.com
*International media, entertainment*
Philippe Dauman, President & Chief Executive Officer

**Wall Street Journal (The)**
1211 Avenue of the Americas, New York, NY 10036
212-416-2000 or 800-568-7625  Fax: 212-416-2720
Web site: www.wsj.com
Gerard Baker, Editor in Chief

**WNET New York Public Media**
825 Eighth Avenue, New York, NY 10019
212-560-2000 or 212-560-1313  Fax: 212-560-2001
e-mail: programming@thirteen.org
Web site: www.wnet.org
*Producer of arts, public affairs & educational programs; broadcast & online media*
Neal Shapiro, President & Chief Executive Officer

# ENVIRONMENT & NATURAL RESOURCES

## NEW YORK STATE

### GOVERNOR'S OFFICE

**Governor's Office**
Executive Chamber
State Capitol
Albany, NY 12224
518-474-8390  Fax: 518-474-1513
Web site: www.ny.gov

Governor:
    Andrew M Cuomo .................................518-474-8390
Secretary to the Governor:
    Melissa DeRosa ....................518-474-4246 or 212-681-4580
Counsel to the Governor:
    Kumini Gibson ....................518-474-8343 or 212-681-4580
Chairman of Energy & Finance for New York:
    Richard L. Kauffman ..............................518-486-9746
Deputy Secretary, Energy & Environment:
    Ali Zaidi .........................518-408-2552 or 212-681-5840
Chief of Staff:
    Jill DesRosiers ....................518-474-8390 or 212-681-4580
Director, Communications:
    Peter Ajemian.....................518-474-8418 or 212-681-4640

### EXECUTIVE DEPARTMENTS AND RELATED AGENCIES

**Empire State Development Corporation**
633 Third Avenue
Floor 37
New York, NY 10017
212-803-3100  Fax: 212-803-3131
Web site: www.esd.ny.gov

625 Broadway
Albany, NY 12245
518-292-5100

95 Perry Street
Suite 500
Buffalo, NY 14203
716-846-8200
Fax: 716-846-8260

President & CEO, Commissioner:
    Howard Zemsky....................212-803-3700 or 518-292-5100
    e-mail: president@esd.ny.gov
Chief Operating Officer & Deputy Commissioner:
    Kevin Younis ..............................212-803-3100
Chief Financial Officer:
    Elaine Kloss

**Environmental Conservation Department**
625 Broadway
Albany, NY 12233-0001
518-402-8044
e-mail: contact@dec.ny.gov
Web site: www.dec.ny.gov

Commissioner:
    Basil Seggos ...................518-402-8545/fax: 518-402-8541

Executive Deputy Commissioner:
    Kenneth Lynch ...................518-402-8560/fax: 518-402-9016
Deputy Commissioner, Public Affairs:
    Erica Ringewald ..................518-402-8000/fax: 518-402-9016
    e-mail: pressoffice@dec.ny.gov
Deputy Commissioner, Administration, Management, Budget & Operations:
    Jeffrey Stefanko....................518-402-9401/fax: 518-402-9016
Director, Internal Audit & Investigation:
    Ann Lapinski......................518-402-8184/fax: 518-496-9957

**Air Resources, Climate Change & Energy Office**
Deputy Commissioner:
    Jared Snyder ......................518-402-2794/fax: 518-402-9016

    **Air Resources Division**
    Director:
        Steve Flint......................518-402-8452/fax: 518-402-9035
        e-mail: dar.web@dec.ny.gov

    **Climate Change Office**
    Acting Director:
        Lois New.......................518-402-8448/fax: 518-402-9021
        e-mail: climatechange@dec.ny.gov

**Office of Remediation & Materials Management**
Deputy Commissioner:
    Martin Brand .....................518-402-9401/fax: 518-402-9016

    **Environmental Remediation Division**
    Director:
        Robert Schick ..................518-402-9706/fax: 518-402-9020
        e-mail: derweb@dec.ny.gov

    **Materials Management Division**
    Director:
        David Vitale ...................518-402-8652/fax: 518-402-9024
        e-mail: dmm@dec.ny.gov

    **Mineral Resources Division**
    Director:
        Catherine Dickert ...............518-402-8076/fax: 518-402-8060
        e-mail: dmn.info@dec.ny.gov

**General Counsel's Office**
Deputy Commissioner & General Counsel:
    Thomas Berkman...................518-402-8543/fax: 518-402-9018

    **Environmental Justice Office**
    Director:
        Rosa Mendez ....................518-402-8556 or 866-229-0497
        fax: 518-402-9018
        e-mail: justice@dec.ny.gov

**Hearings & Mediation Services Office**
Deputy Commissioner:
    Louis Alexander ..................518-402-8537/fax: 518-402-9016
Chief Administrative Law Judge:
    James McClymonds.................518-402-9003/fax: 518-402-9037
    e-mail: ohms@dec.ny.gov

**Natural Resources Office**
Executive Deputy Commissioner:
    Judy Drabicki.....................518-402-8533/fax: 518-402-9016

    **Fish & Wildlife Division**
    Director:
        Tony Wilkinson.....,............518-402-8924/fax: 518-402-9027
        e-mail: fw.information@dec.ny.gov

    **Lands & Forests Division**
    Director:
        Robert Davies ..................518-402-9405/fax: 518-402-9028
        e-mail: lf.lands@dec.ny.gov

Policy Areas

*Offices and agencies generally appear in alphabetical order, except when specific order is requested by listee.*

**Marine Resources Division**
205 Belle Mead Road, Suite 1, East Setauket, NY 11733
Director:
    Jim Gilmore . . . . . . . . . . . . . . . . . . . .631-444-0430/fax: 631-444-0434
        e-mail: fw.marine@dec.ny.gov

## Water Resources Office
Deputy Commissioner:
    James Tierney . . . . . . . . . . . . . . . . . .518-402-2794/fax: 518-402-8541

**Water Division**
Director:
    Mark Klotz . . . . . . . . . . . . . . . . . .518-402-8233/fax: 518-402-9029
        e-mail: dowinformation@dec.ny.gov

## Office of Administration

**Management & Budget Division**
Director:
    Nancy Lussier . . . . . . . . . . . . . . . . . .518-402-9228/fax: 518-402-9023
        e-mail: mbs.info@dec.ny.gov

**Operations Division**
Director:
    Mark Malinoski . . . . . . . . . . . . . . . . .518-402-9055/fax: 518-402-9053
        e-mail: campinfo@dec.ny.gov

**Public Affairs Division**
Press Operations:
    Erica Ringewald . . . . . . . . . . . . . . . .518-402-8000/fax: 518-402-9016
        e-mail: pressoffice@dec.ny.gov

**Office of Employee Relations**
Director:
    Mark Cadrette . . . . . . . . . . . . . . . . .518-402-9388/fax: 518-486-9957

## Public Information
Press Operations:
    Erica Ringewald . . . . . . . . . . . . . . . . . .518-402-8000/fax: 518-402-9016
        e-mail: pressoffice@dec.ny.gov

## Public Protection & Regional Affairs Office
Deputy Commissioner:
    Steve Smith . . . . . . . . . . . . . . . . . . .518-402-8549/fax: 518-402-9016

**Forest Protection**
Director:
    Eric Lahr . . . . . . . . . . . . . . . . . . . .518-402-8839/fax: 518-402-8840
        e-mail: rangers@dec.ny.gov

**Law Enforcement Division**
Director:
    Joe Schneider . . . . . . . . . . . . . . . . . .518-402-8829/fax: 518-402-8830
        e-mail: central.dispatch@dec.ny.gov

## Regional Offices

**Region 1**
SUNY, 50 Circle Road, Stony Brook, NY 11790
e-mail: r1info@dec.ny.gov
Director:
    Carrie Meek Gallagher . . . . . . . . . . . 631-444-0345/fax: 631-444-0349

**Region 2**
One Hunter's Point Plaza, 47-40 21st Street, Long Island City, NY
    11101-5407
e-mail: r2.info@dec.ny.gov
Director:
    Steven Zahn . . . . . . . . . . . . . . . . . .718-482-4949/fax: 718-482-4026

**Region 3**
21 S Putt Corners Road, New Paltz, NY 12561-1696
e-mail: r3admin@dec.ny.gov
Acting Director:
    Kelly Turturro . . . . . . . . . . . . . . . . . .845-256-3033/fax: 845-255-3042

**Region 4**
1130 N Westcott Road, Schenectady, NY 12306-2014
Director:
    Keith Goertz . . . . . . . . . . . . . . . . . .518-357-2068/fax: 518-357-2398

**Region 5**
1115 NYS Route 86, P.O. Box 296, Ray Brook, NY 12977-0296
e-mail: info.r5@dec.ny.gov
Director:
    Robert Stegemann . . . . . . . . . . . . . . . .518-897-1211/fax: 518-897-1394

**Region 6**
317 Washington Street, Watertown, NY 13601-3787
e-mail: information.r6@dec.ny.gov
Executive Deputy Commissioner:
    Judy Drabicki . . . . . . . . . . . . . . . . . .315-785-2239/fax: 315-785-2242

**Region 7**
615 Erie Boulevard West, Syracuse, NY 13204-2400
e-mail: info.r7@dec.ny.gov
Director:
    Matthew Marko . . . . . . . . . . . . . . . . .315-426-7403/fax: 315-426-7408

**Region 8**
6274 E Avon-Lima Rd, Avon, NY 14414-9519
e-mail: region8@dec.ny.gov
Director:
    Paul D'Amato . . . . . . . . . . . . . . . . . .585-226-5366/fax: 585-226-9485

**Region 9**
270 Michigan Avenue, Buffalo, NY 14203-2915
e-mail: region9@dec.ny.gov
Director:
    Abby Snyder . . . . . . . . . . . . . . . . . .716-851-7200/fax: 716-851-7211

## Special Programs

**Great Lakes Program**
Region 9 NYS DEC, 270 Michigan Avenue, Buffalo, NY 14203
e-mail: greatlakes@dec.ny.gov
Coordinator:
    Donald Zelazny . . . . . . . . . . . . . . . . .716-851-7130/fax: 716-851-7226

**Hudson River Estuary Program**
Region 3 NYS DEC, 21 S Putt Corners Road, New Paltz, NY 12561
Director:
    Vacant . . . . . . . . . . . . . . . . . . . . .845-256-3016/fax: 845-255-3649
        e-mail: hrep@dec.ny.gov

# Health Department
Corning Tower
Empire State Plaza
Albany, NY 12237
518-474-2011 or 518-474-7354
e-mail: dohweb@health.ny.gov
Web site: www.health.ny.gov

Commissioner:
    Howard A Zucker, MD, JD . . . . . . . . . . . . . . . . . . . . . . . .518-474-2011
Executive Deputy Commissioner:
    Lisa J Pino, MA, JD . . . . . . . . . . . . . . . . . . . . . . . . . . . . .518-474-2011
Acting Deputy Commissioner, Administration:
    Marybeth Hefner . . . . . . . . . . . . . . . . . . . . . . . . . . . . . .518-474-8565

## Public Affairs
Assistant Commissioner:
    Gary Holmes . . . . . . . . . . . . . . . . . . . . . . . . . . . . . . . . . .518-474-7354
Deputy Director:
    JP O'Hare . . . . . . . . . . . . . . . . . . . . . . . . . . . . . . . . . . .518-474-7354

## Center for Environmental Health
Administrator:
    Susan Dorward . . . . . . . . . . . . . . . . . . . . . . . . . . . . . . . .518-402-7500

*Offices and agencies generally appear in alphabetical order, except when specific order is requested by listee.*

**Division of Environmental Health Assessment**
Director:
  Elizabeth Lewis-Michl . . . . . . . . . . . . . . . . . . . . . . . . . . .518-402-7500

**Division of Environmental Health Investigation**
Director:
  Vacant. . . . . . . . . . . . . . . . . . . . . . . . . . . . . . . . . . . . . .518-402-7510

**Division of Environmental Health Protection**
Director:
  Vacant. . . . . . . . . . . . . . . . . . . . . . . . . . . . . . . . . . . . . .518-402-7500

## Wadsworth Center
Director:
  Vacant . . . . . . . . . . . . . . . . . . . . . .518-474-3157/fax: 518-474-3439
  e-mail: jill.taylor@health.ny.gov
Deputy Director:
  Victoria Derbyshire. . . . . . . . . . . . . . . . . . . . . . . . . . . . .518-474-7592
  e-mail: victoria.derbyshire@health.ny.gov
Associate Director, Administration:
  Carlene Van Patten . . . . . . . . . . . . . . . . . . . . . . . . . . . . .518-474-7592
  e-mail: carlene.vanpatten@health.ny.gov
Associate Director, Research & Technology:
  Erasmus Schneider . . . . . . . . . . . . . . . . . . . . . . . . . . . . .518-473-4856
  e-mail: erasmus.schneider@health.ny.gov
Associate Director, Medical Affairs:
  Anne Walsh. . . . . . . . . . . . . . . . . . . . . . . . . . . . . . . . . . .518-474-7592
  e-mail: anne.walsh@health.ny.gov

**Environmental Health Sciences**
Director:
  Kenneth Aldous. . . . . . . . . . . . . . . .518-474-7161/fax: 518-473-2895
  e-mail: kenneth.aldous@health.ny.gov
Deputy Director:
  Patrick J Parsons . . . . . . . . . . . . . . .518-473-2938/fax: 518-473-7586
  e-mail: patrick.parsons@health.ny.gov

## Hudson River Valley Greenway
625 Broadway
4th Floor
Albany, NY 12207
518-473-3835
e-mail: hrvg@hudsongreenway.ny.gov
Web site: www.hudsongreenway.ny.gov

**Greenway Conservancy for the Hudson River Valley**
Chairman:
  Kevin M Burke . . . . . . . . . . . . . . . . . . . . . . . . . . . . . . . . .518-473-3835
Executive Director:
  Scott Keller . . . . . . . . . . . . . . . . . . . . . . . . . . . . . . . . . . .518-473-3835

**Hudson River Valley Greenway Communities Council**
Council Chair:
  Barnabas McHenry, Esq. . . . . . . . . . . . . . . . . . . . . . . . . .518-473-3835
Executive Director:
  Scott Keller . . . . . . . . . . . . . . . . . . . . . . . . . . . . . . . . . . .518-473-3835

## Law Department
28 Liberty Street
New York, NY 10005
212-416-8000 or 800-771-7755
Web site: www.ag.ny.gov

State Capitol
Albany, NY 12224-0341
518-776-2000
Fax: 518-650-9401

Attorney General:
  Letitia James. . . . . . . . . . . . . . . . . . . . .212-416-8000 or 518-776-2000

Chief of Staff:
  Brian Mahanna . . . . . . . . . . . . . . . . . . . . . . . . . . . . . . . .212-416-8050
Press Secretary:
  Fernando Aquino. . . . . . . . . . . . . . . . . . .212-416-8060/fax: 212-416-6005
  e-mail: nyag.pressoffice@ag.ny.gov
Bureau Chief, Litigation Bureau:
  Jeffrey Dvorin. . . . . . . . . . . . . . . . . . . . . .518-776-2300 or 212-416-8610

**Social Justice**
Executive Deputy Attorney General:
  Vacant . . . . . . . . . . . . . . . . . . . . . . . . . . .212-416-8450/fax: 212-416-8942

**Environmental Protection Bureau**
Bureau Chief:
  Lemuel Srolovic. . . . . . . . . . . . . . . . .518-776-2400 or 212-416-8448
  fax: 518-416-6007

## Parks, Recreation & Historic Preservation, NYS Office of
625 Broadway
Albany, NY 12207
518-486-0456  Fax: 518-474-4492
Web site: www.parks.ny.gov

Commissioner:
  Rose Harvey . . . . . . . . . . . . . . . . . . . . . . . . . . . . . . . . . .518-474-0443
Executive Deputy Commissioner:
  Tom Alworth
  fax: 518-474-4492
Deputy Commissioner, Finance & Administration:
  Vacant
Deputy Commissioner, Natural Resources:
  Tom Alworth. . . . . . . . . . . . . . . . . . . . . . . . . . . . . . . . . .518-474-0414
General Counsel:
  Paul Laudato . . . . . . . . . . . . . . . . . . . . . . . . . . . . . . . . . .518-474-0414
Public Information Officer:
  Randy Simmons . . . . . . . . . . . . . . . . . . . . . . . . . . . . . . .518-486-1868
Chief Park Police/Director, Law Enforcement:
  Jay Kirschner. . . . . . . . . . . . . . . . . . .518-474-4029/fax: 518-408-1032

**Field Services**
Peebles Island, PO Box 189, Waterford, NY 12118
Deputy Commissioner:
  Vacant. . . . . . . . . . . . . . . . . . . . . . . . . . . . . . . . . . . . . . .518-237-8643

**Historic Sites Bureau**
Peebles Island, Waterford, NY 12188
Acting Director:
  Mark Peckham . . . . . . . . . . . . . . . . . . . . . . . . . . . . . . . .518-237-8643

**Marine & Recreational Vehicles**
Director:
  Brian Kempf . . . . . . . . . . . . . . . . . . . . .518-474-0445/fax: 518-408-1030

**Environmental Management**
Director:
  Pamela Otis . . . . . . . . . . . . . . . . . . . .518-474-0409/fax: 518-474-7013

## State Comptroller, Office of the
110 State Street
15th Floor
Albany, NY 12236
518-474-4044  Fax: 518-473-3004
e-mail: contactus@osc.state.ny.us
Web site: www.osc.state.ny.us

59 Maiden Lane
New York, NY 10038
212-383-1600

State Comptroller:
  Thomas DiNapoli . . . . . . . . . . . . . . . . . .518-474-4040 or 212-681-4469

*Offices and agencies generally appear in alphabetical order, except when specific order is requested by listee.*

## Executive Office
First Deputy Comptroller:
Pete Grannis . . . . . . . . . . . . . . . . . . . . . . . . 518-474-2909 or 212-681-4469
Chief of Staff:
Shawn Thompson . . . . . . . . . . . . . . . . . . . . . . . . . . . . . . . 518-474-4044
General Counsel:
Nancy Groenwegen. . . . . . . . . . . . . . . . . . . . . . . . . . . . . . 518-474-3444

## Oil Spill Fund Office
Executive Director:
Vacant . . . . . . . . . . . . . . . . . . . . . . . . . 518-474-6657/fax: 518-474-9979

## State Department
123 William St
New York, NY 10038-3804
212-417-5800  Fax: 212-417-2383
e-mail: info@dos.ny.gov
Web site: www.dos.ny.gov

One Commerce Plaza
99 Washington Avenue
Albany, NY 12231-0001
518-474-4750
Fax: 518-474-4597

Secretary of State:
Rossana Rosado . . . . . . . . . . . . . . . . . . . . 518-486-9844 or 212-417-5800
First Deputy Secretary of State:
Daniel Shapiro . . . . . . . . . . . . . . . . . . . . . . . . . . . . . . . . . 518-474-4750
Assistant Secretary of State, Communications:
Vacant . . . . . . . . . . . . . . . . . . . . 518-474-4752/fax: 518-474-4597
e-mail: info@dos.state.ny.us
Deputy Secretary of State, Public Affairs:
Vacant . . . . . . . . . . . . . . . . . . . . . . . . . . . . . . . . . . . . . . . 212-417-5800
General Counsel:
Linda Baldwin . . . . . . . . . . . . . . . . . . . . 518-474-6740/fax: 518-473-9211

## Local Government & Community Services
Deputy Secretary of State:
Mark Pattison. . . . . . . . . . . . . . . . . . . . 518-473-3355/fax: 518-474-6572

### Coastal Resources & Waterfront Revitalization Division
Director:
George Stafford. . . . . . . . . . . . . . . 518-474-6000/fax: 518-473-2464
e-mail: coastal@dos.state.ny.us

### Community Services Division
Director:
Veronica Cruz . . . . . . . . . . . . . . . . . . . 518-474-5741/fax: 518-486-4663
e-mail: commserv@dos.state.ny.us

## CORPORATIONS, AUTHORITIES AND COMMISSIONS

## Adirondack Park Agency
1133 NYS Route 86
PO Box 99
Ray Brook, NY 12977
518-891-4050  Fax: 518-891-3938
Web site: www.apa.ny.gov

Chair:
Leilani Ulrich . . . . . . . . . . . . . . . . . . . . . . . . . . . . . . . . . . 518-891-4050
Executive Director:
Terry Martino . . . . . . . . . . . . . . . . . . . . . . . . . . . . . . . . . . 518-891-4050
Counsel:
James Townsend. . . . . . . . . . . . . . . . . . . . . . . . . . . . . . . . 518-891-4050
Public Relations:
Keith McKeever . . . . . . . . . . . . . . . . . . . . . . . . . . . . . . . . 518-891-4050
e-mail: keith.mckeever@apa.ny.gov

## Atlantic States Marine Fisheries Commission
1050 N Highland Street
Ste 200 A-N
Arlington, VA 22201
703-842-0740  Fax: 703-842-0741
e-mail: info@asmfc.org
Web site: www.asmfc.org

Chair (NH):
Douglas E Grout . . . . . . . . . . . . . . . . . . . . . . . . . . . . . . . . 603-868-1095
Vice Chair (NY):
James Gilmore. . . . . . . . . . . . . . . . . . . . . . . . . . . . . . . . . . 516-444-0433
Governor's Appointee, New York:
Emerson C Hasbrouck, Jr . . . . . . . . . . . . . . . . . . . . . . . . . 631-928-1524
Executive Director:
Robert E. Beal. . . . . . . . . . . . . . . . . . . . . . . . . . . . . . . . . . 703-842-0740
e-mail: rbeal@asmfc.org
Director Communications:
Tina Berger . . . . . . . . . . . . . . . . . . . . . . . . . . . . . . . . . . . . 703-842-0740
e-mail: tberger@asmfc.org

## Central Pine Barrens Joint Planning & Policy Commission
624 Old Riverhead Road
Westhampton Beach, NY 11978
631-288-1079  Fax: 631-228-1367
e-mail: info@pb.state.ny.us
Web site: www.pb.state.ny.us

Chair & Governor's Appointee & Region 1 Director DEC:
Peter A Scully . . . . . . . . . . . . . . . . . . . . . . . . . . . . . . . . . . 631-288-1079
Member & Suffolk County Executive:
Steve Bellone . . . . . . . . . . . . . . . . . . . . . . . . . . . . . . . . . . 631-288-1079
Member & Brookhaven Town Supervisor:
Edward P. Romaine . . . . . . . . . . . . . . . . . . . . . . . . . . . . . . 631-288-1079
Member & Riverhead Town Supervisor:
Sean M Walter . . . . . . . . . . . . . . . . . . . . . . . . . . . . . . . . . . 631-288-1079
Member & Southampton Town Supervisor:
Anna E Throne-Holst . . . . . . . . . . . . . . . . . . . . . . . . . . . . . 631-288-1079

## Delaware River Basin Commission
25 State Police Dr
PO Box 7360
West Trenton, NJ 08628-0360
609-883-9500  Fax: 609-883-9522
Web site: www.nj.gov/drbc

New York Member/Vice Chair:
Andrew M. Cuomo . . . . . . . . . . . . . . . . . . . . . . . . . . . . . . 518-474-8390
Executive Director:
Steve Tambini . . . . . . . . . . . . . . . . . . . . . . . . . . . 609-883-9500 x200
e-mail: steve.tambini@drbc.nj.gov
Commission Secretary & Assistant General Counsel:
Pamela Bush . . . . . . . . . . . . . . . . . . . . . . . . . . . . 609-883-9500 x203
e-mail: pamela.bush@drbc.nj.gov
General Counsel:
Kenneth J Warren . . . . . . . . . . . . . . . . . . . . . . . . . . . . . . . 484-383-4834
e-mail: kwarren@warrenenvcounsel.com
Communications Manager:
Clarke Rupert. . . . . . . . . . . . . . . . . . . . . . . . . . . . 609-883-9500 x260

## Great Lakes Commission
2805 S Industrial Hwy
Ste 100
Ann Arbor, MI 48104-6791
734-971-9135  Fax: 734-971-9150
e-mail: teder@glc.org
Web site: www.glc.org

*Offices and agencies generally appear in alphabetical order, except when specific order is requested by listee.*

Chairman:
    Jon W Allan . . . . . . . . . . . . . . . . . . . . . . . . . . . . . .517-284-5035
    e-mail: allanj@michigan.gov
New York State Commissioner:
    Joseph Martens . . . . . . . . . . . . . . . . . . . . . . . . . . . .518-402-8540
    e-mail: joseph.martens@dec.ny.gov
Executive Director:
    Tim A Eder . . . . . . . . . . . . . . . . . . . . . . . . . . . . . . .734-971-9135
    e-mail: teder@glc.org
Deputy Director:
    Thomas R Crane . . . . . . . . . . . . . . . . . . . . . . . . . . .734-971-9135
    e-mail: tcrane@glc.org
CIO:
    Stephen J Cole . . . . . . . . . . . . . . . . . . . . . . . . . . . .734-971-9135
    e-mail: scole@glc.org
Program Director:
    Victoria Pebbles . . . . . . . . . . . . . . . . . . . . . . . . . . .734-971-9135
    e-mail: vpebbles@glc.org
Communications Director:
    Beth Wanamaker. . . . . . . . . . . . . . . . . . . . . . . . . . .734-971-9135
    e-mail: beth@glc.org
Policy Director:
    Matthew Doss . . . . . . . . . . . . . . . . . . . . . . . . . . . . .734-971-9135
    e-mail: mdoss@glc.org

## Hudson River-Black River Regulating District

Hudson River Area Office
350 Northern Blvd, Ste 304
Albany, NY 12204
518-465-3491  Fax: 518-432-2485
e-mail: hrao@hrbrrd.com
Web site: www.hrbrrd.com

Chair:
    Mark M Finkle . . . . . . . . . . . . . . . . . . . . . . . . . . . .518-465-3491
Executive Director (Acting):
    Richard J Ferrara. . . . . . . . . . . . . . . . . . . . . . . . . . .518-465-3491
Chief Engineer:
    Robert S Foltan . . . . . . . . . . . . . . . . . . . . . . . . . . . .518-465-3491
Chief Fiscal Officer:
    Robert J Ferrara. . . . . . . . . . . . . . . . . . . . . . . . . . . .518-465-3491
General Counsel:
    Robert P Leslie . . . . . . . . . . . . . . . . . . . . . . . . . . . .518-465-3491

## Interstate Environmental Commission

2800 Victory Blvd
6S-106
Staten Island, NY 10314
718-982-3792  Fax: 718-698-8472
e-mail: iecmail@iec-nynjct.org
Web site: www.iec-nynjct.org

Chair (CT):
    Patricia Sesto. . . . . . . . . . . . . . . . . . . . . . . . . . . . . .212-967-1414
Vice Chair (NY):
    Judith L Baron . . . . . . . . . . . . . . . . . . . . . . . . . . . .212-967-1414
Vice Chair (NJ):
    John M Scagnelli . . . . . . . . . . . . . . . . . . . . . . . . . . .212-967-1414
Associate Director:
    Evelyn R Powers. . . . . . . . . . . . . . . . . . . . . . . . . . .212-967-1414

## Interstate Oil & Gas Compact Commission

PO Box 53127
900 NE 23rd St
Oklahoma City, OK 73152-3127
405-525-3556  Fax: 405-525-3592
Web site: www.iogcc.ok.gov

Chair:
    Governor Mary Fallin (OK) . . . . . . . . . . . . . . . . . . . .405-525-3556
Vice Chair:
    David Porter . . . . . . . . . . . . . . . . . . . . . . . . . . . . . .405-525-3556
Executive Director:
    Mike Smith . . . . . . . . . . . . . . . . . . . . . . . . . . . . . . .405-525-3556
New York State Official Representative:
    Bradley J Field . . . . . . . . . . . . . . . . . . . . . . . . . . . .518-402-8076
Communications Manager:
    Carol Booth. . . . . . . . . . . . . . . . . . . . . . . . . . . . . . .405-525-3556

## Lake George Park Commission

75 Fort George Rd
PO Box 749
Lake George, NY 12845
518-668-9347  Fax: 518-668-5001
e-mail: info@lgpc.state.ny.us
Web site: www.lgpc.state.ny.us

Chair:
    Bruce E Young . . . . . . . . . . . . . . . . . . . . . . . . . . . .518-668-9347
Executive Director:
    David Wick . . . . . . . . . . . . . . . . . . . . . . . . . . . . . . .518-668-9347
    e-mail: dave@lgpc.state.ny.us
Counsel:
    Eileen Haynes . . . . . . . . . . . . . . . . . . . . . . . . . . . . .518-668-9347
Director of Law Enforcement:
    F. Joe Johns . . . . . . . . . . . . . . . . . . . . . . . . . . . . . .518-668-9347
Director, Operations:
    Keith Fish . . . . . . . . . . . . . . . . . . . . . . . . . . . . . . . .518-668-9347
    e-mail: keith@lgpc.state.ny.us

## New England Interstate Water Pollution Control Commission

Wannalacit Mills
650 Suffolk Street
Suite 410
Lowell, MA 01854
978-323-7929  Fax: 978-323-7919
e-mail: mail@neiwpcc.org
Web site: www.neiwpcc.org

Chair (ME):
    Michael Kuhns . . . . . . . . . . . . . . . . . . . . . . . . . . . .978-323-7929
Vice Chair (MA):
    Douglas Fine . . . . . . . . . . . . . . . . . . . . . . . . . . . . . .978-323-7929
Commissioner, New York State:
    Basil Seggos . . . . . . . . . . . . . . . . . . . . . . . . . . . . . .518-402-8545
Executive Director:
    Ronald F Poltak . . . . . . . . . . . . . . . . . . . . . . . . . . .978-323-7929
    e-mail: rpoltak@neiwpcc.org
Deputy Director:
    Susan Sullivan. . . . . . . . . . . . . . . . . . . . . . . . . . . . .978-323-7929
    e-mail: ssullivan@neiwpcc.org

## New York State Energy Research & Development Authority

17 Columbia Circle
Albany, NY 12203-6399
518-862-1090  Fax: 518-862-1091
e-mail: info@nyserda.ny.gov
Web site: www.nyserda.ny.gov

Chairman:
    Richard L. Kauffman . . . . . . . . . . . . . . . . . . . . . . . . .518-486-9746
President & CEO:
    John B Rhodes. . . . . . . . . . . . . . . . . . . . . . . . . . . .518-862-1090 x3278

*Offices and agencies generally appear in alphabetical order, except when specific order is requested by listee.*

General Counsel:
Noah C Shaw.....................................518-862-1090 x3280
Program Manager, Economic Development & Community Outreach:
Kelly Tyler.........................716-842-1522 x. 3005
e-mail: kelly.tyler@nyserda.ny.gov
Director, Communications:
Kate Muller.................518-862-1090 x3582/fax: 518-862-1091
e-mail: kate.muller@nyserda.ny.gov

## New York State Environmental Facilities Corp
625 Broadway
Albany, NY 12207-2997
518-402-6924 or 800-882-9721  Fax: 518-486-9323
e-mail: press@efc.ny.gov

President/CEO:
Sabrina M Ty .......................................518-402-6951
Legal Division/General Counsel:
James R Levine.....................................518-402-6969
Director, Engineering & Program Management:
Timothy P Burns....................................518-402-7396
Director, Technical Advisory Services:
Vacant..............................................518-402-7461
Director, PIO:
Jon Sorensen.......................................518-402-6924
Controller & Director, Corporate Operations:
Michael Malinoski .................................518-486-9267

## New York State Tug Hill Commission
Dulles State Office Bldg
317 Washington St
Watertown, NY 13601
315-785-2380  Fax: 315-785-2574
e-mail: tughill@tughill.org
Web site: www.tughill.org

Chair:
Jan Bogdanowicz ..................................315-785-2380
Executive Director:
Katie Malinowski...................................315-785-2570
e-mail: katie@tughill.org

## Northeastern Forest Fire Protection Commission
21 Parmenter Terrace
PO Box 6192
China Village, ME 04926
207-968-3782  Fax: 207-968-3782
e-mail: info@nffpc.org
Web site: www.nffpc.org

Executive Committee Chair:
Steven Sinclair ....................................802-241-3680
e-mail: ssinclair@vermont.gov
Executive Director/Center Manager:
Thomas G Parent....................................207-968-3782
e-mail: necompact@fairpoint.net
Operations Committee, Chair:
Rick Vollick .......................................413-770-1235
e-mail: rvollick@gmail.com
New York State Fire Prevention & Education:
Andrew Jacob.......................................518-402-8840
e-mail: atjacob@gw.dec.state.ny.us

## Ohio River Valley Water Sanitation Commission
5735 Kellogg Ave
Cincinnati, OH 45230

513-231-7719  Fax: 513-231-7761
e-mail: info@orsanco.org
Web site: www.orsanco.org

New York State Commissioner:
Douglas E Conroe...................................513-231-7719
New York State Commissioner:
Michael P Wilson...................................513-231-7719
New York State Commissioner:
Basil Seggos ......................................518-402-8545
Executive Director:
Richard Harrison ............................513-231-7719 ext 105
e-mail: rharrison@orsanco.org
Source Water Protection/Emergency Response/External Relations:
Jerry Schulte......................513-231-7719 ext 104
Communications Coordinator:
Lisa Cochran ...............................513-231-7719 ext 102
e-mail: lcochran@orsanco.org

*See Legislative Branch in Section 1 for additional Standing Committee and Subcommittee information.*

## Assembly Standing Committees

### Environmental Conservation
Chair:
Steven Englebright (D)..............................518-455-4804

## Senate Standing Committees

### Environmental Conservation
Chair:
Todd Kaminsky (D) .................................518-455-3401

## Senate/Assembly Legislative Commissions

### Legislative Commission on Rural Resources
Ranking Minority Member:
Pamela Helming (R, C, IP)...........................518-455-2366
Chair:
Frank Skartados (D) ...............518-455-5762/fax: 518-455-5593

## US Commerce Department
Web site: www.commerce.gov

### National Oceanic & Atmospheric Administration

**National Marine Fisheries Svc, Greater Atlantic Regional Office**
55 Great Republic Drive, Gloucester, MA 01930
978-281-9300
Regional Administrator:
John K. Bullard

**National Weather Service, Eastern Region**
630 Johnson Avenue, Suite 202, Bohemia, NY 11716
Web site: www.weather.gov/erh/
Director, Eastern Region:
Jason Tuell, Ph.D...................................631-244-0101
e-mail: jason.tuell@noaa.gov
Deputy Director:
Mickey J Brown ....................................631-244-0100

*Offices and agencies generally appear in alphabetical order, except when specific order is requested by listee.*

Meteorological Services Division Chief:
John Guiney . . . . . . . . . . . . . . . . . . . . . . . . . . . . . .631-244-0121
e-mail: john.guiney@noaa.gov
Scientific Services Division Chief:
Kenneth Johnson . . . . . . . . . . . . . . . . . . . . . . . . . . .631-244-0136
e-mail: kenneth.johnson@noaa.gov

## US Defense Department
Web site: www.defense.gov

### Army Corps of Engineers
Web site: www.usace.army.mil

#### Great Lakes & Ohio River Division (Western NYS)
550 Main Street, Room 10524, Cincinnati, OH 45202-3222
Commander:
BG Richard G. Kaiser. . . . . . . . . . . . . . . . . . . . . . . .513-684-3010
***Buffalo District Office*** . . . . . . . . . . . . . . . . . . . . . . fax: 716-879-4195
1776 Niagara Street, Buffalo, NY 14207
716-879-4104 or 800-833-6390 x3  Fax: 716-879-4195
District Commander:
LTC Karl D. Jansen
Deputy Commander:
MAJ Jared E. Runge

#### North Atlantic Division
302 General Lee Avenue, Brooklyn, NY 11252
Commander & Division Engineer:
BG William H. Graham
Deputy Commander:
Colonel Leon F. Parrott
Director of Programs:
David J. Leach
Director of Business:
Vincent E. Grewatz
Public Affairs Specialist:
Edward Loomis. . . . . . . . . . . . . . . . . . . . . . . . . . . . . .347-370-4550
*Program Directorate*
Director of Programs:
David J. Leach . . . . . . . . . . . . . . . . . . . . . . . . . . .347-370-4550
Chief, Civil Works Integration Division:
Linda Monte
Chief, Military Integration Division:
Thomas Harnedy
Chief, Program Support Division:
Joseph Vietri . . . . . . . . . . . . . . . . . . . . . . . . . . . .718-765-7080
*Regional Business Directorate*
Regional Director of Business:
Vincent E. Grewatz
Chief Financial Officer:
John Primavera
Chief, Business Management Division:
Lawrence Mazzola. . . . . . . . . . . . . . . . . . . . . . . .718-765-7127
Business Technical Division:
Alan Huntley

## US Department of Agriculture

### Forest Service-Northeastern Area State & Private Forestry
11 Campus Blvd, Newtown Square, PA 19073
Area Director:
Tony L. Ferguson . . . . . . . . . . . . . . . . . . . . . . . . . . .610-557-4103
Deputy Area Director:
James S. Barresi . . . . . . . . . . . . . . . . . . . . . . . . . . . .610-557-4103
Asst Director, Forest Health & Economics:
Ralph H. Crawford . . . . . . . . . . . . . . . . . . . . . . . . . .610-557-4158
Fire Management Specialist:
James H. Furman. . . . . . . . . . . . . . . . . . . . . . . . . . . .850-882-8399
Asst Director, Forest Management:
Mark P. Buccowich. . . . . . . . . . . . . . . . . . . . . . . . . .610-557-4029

Deputy Director, WERC:
Edward T. Cesa. . . . . . . . . . . . . . . . . . . . . . . . . . . . .304-285-1530

### Forest Service-Northern Research Station
11 Campus Blvd, Suite 200, Newtown Square, PA 19073
Acting Director:
Tony L. Ferguson . . . . . . . . . . . . . . . . . . . . . . . . . . .610-557-4017
Deputy Director:
Lon M. Yeary . . . . . . . . . . . . . . . . . . . . . . . . . . . . . .608-231-9320

### Forest Service-Region 9
Web site: www.fs.fed.us

#### Green Mountain & Finger Lakes. . . . . . . . . . . . . . . fax: 802-747-6766
231 North Main Street, Rutland, VT 05701
802-747-6700  Fax: 802-747-6766
***Finger Lakes National Forest*** . . . . . . . . . . . . . . . .fax: 607-546-4474
5218 State Route 414, Hector, NY 14841
District Ranger:
Jodie Vanselow

### Natural Resources Conservation Service . . . . . . . . fax: 315-477-6550
441 South Salina Street, Suite 354, Syracuse, NY 13202-2450
Fax: 315-477-6550
Web site: www.nrcs.usda.gov
State Conservationist:
Greg Kist

## US Department of Homeland Security (DHS)

### National Urban Security Technology Laboratory
201 Varick Street, 5th Floor, New York, NY 10014
Director:
Dr. Adam Hutter
e-mail: adam.hutter@dhs.gov

#### Administration
Director:
Alfred Crescenzi

#### Systems Division
Director:
Lawrence Ruth . . . . . . . . . . . . . . . . . . . . . . . . . . . . .212-620-3609
e-mail: lawrence.ruth@dhs.gov

#### Testbeds Division
Acting Director:
Lawrence Ruth

## US Department of the Interior
Web site: www.doi.gov

### Bureau of Land Management
e-mail: woinfo@blm.gov
Web site: www.blm.gov

#### Eastern States Office (includes New York State). . . . fax: 202-912-7710
20 M Street NE, Suite 950, Washington, DC 20003
202-912-7700  Fax: 202-912-7710
Acting State Director:
Ann DeBlasi

### Fish & Wildlife Service . . . . . . . . . . . . . . . . . . . . . . .fax: 413-253-8308
413-253-8200  Fax: 413-253-8308
e-mail: northeast@fws.gov
Web site: www.fws.gov

#### Northeast Region (includes New York State) . . . . . . .fax: 413-253-8308
300 Westgate Center Drive, Hadley, MA 01035-9587
Regional Director:
Wendi Weber

### Geological Survey
Web site: ny.usgs.gov

*Offices and agencies generally appear in alphabetical order, except when specific order is requested by listee.*

**Water Resources Division - New York State District Office**
425 Jordan Road, Troy, NY 12180-8349
Director:
  Robert Breault ................................518-285-5661
  *Coram Sub-District Office* ....................fax: 631-736-4283
    2045 Route 112, Bldg 4, Coram, NY 11727
    Sub-District Chief:
      Stephen A. Terracciano ....................631-736-0783
  *Ithaca Sub-District Office* ....................fax: 607-266-0217
    30 Brown Road, Ithaca, NY 14850-1573
    Sub-District Chief:
      Edward F. Bugliosi ..................607-266-0217 x3005

## National Park Service-Northeast Region
200 Chestnut Street, US Custom House, Philadelphia, PA 19106
Web site: www.nps.gov
Northeast Regional Director:
  Mike Caldwell ...................215-597-7013/fax: 215-597-0815

  **Fire Island National Seashore** ..................fax: 631-289-4898
  120 Laurel Street, Patchogue, NY 11772-3596
  631-687-4750 Fax: 631-289-4898
  Superintendent:
    K. Christopher Soller

## Office of the Secretary, Environmental Policy & Compliance

**Northeast Region (includes New York State)**
15 State Street, Suite 400, Boston, MA 02109
Regional Environmental Officer:
  Andrew L. Raddant .............617-223-8565/fax: 617-223-8569

## Office of the Solicitor

**Northeast Region (includes New York State)** ....... fax: 617-527-6848
One Gateway Center, Suite 612, Newton, MA 02458-2881
Attorney Advisor:
  Peg Romanik............................617-527-3400
Attorney Advisor:
  Martha F. Ansty .........................617-527-3400
Attorney Advisor:
  Mark D. Barash .........................617-527-3400
Attorney:
  Brianna Kenny ..........................617-527-3400
Attorney Advisor:
  Andrew Tittler ...........................617-527-3400

## US Environmental Protection Agency
Web site: www.epa.gov

**Region 2 - New York**...........................fax: 212-637-3526
290 Broadway, New York, NY 10007-1866
212-637-3660 Fax: 212-637-3526
Regional Administrator:
  Judith A. Enck............................212-637-5000
Deputy Regional Administrator:
  Catherine McCabe

  **Caribbean Environmental Protection Division (CEPD)**
  Acting Director:
    Jose Font

  **Clean Air & Sustainability Division (CASD)**
  Acting Director:
    Ariel Iglesias.............................212-637-3315

  **Clean Water Division (CWD)**
  Director:
    Joan Matthews ..........................212-637-3724

  **Division of Enforcement & Compliance Assistance (DECA)**
  Director:
    Dore LaPosta ...........................212-637-4000

  **Division of Environmental Science & Assessment (DESA)**
  2890 Woodbridge Avenue, Edison, NJ 08837-3679
  Director:
    Anahita Williamson

  **Emergency & Remedial Response Division (ERRD)**
  Director:
    Walter Mugdan

  **Policy & Management, Office of**
  Acting Asst Regional Administrator:
    John Filippelli..................................212-637-3736

  **Public Affairs Division (PAD)**
  Director:
    Andre Bowser

  **Regional Counsel, Office of (ORC)**
  Director:
    Eric Schaaf ...................................212-637-3107
    e-mail: schaaf.eric@epa.gov

## U.S. CONGRESS

*See U.S. Congress Chapter for additional Standing Committee and Subcommittee information.*

## House of Representatives Standing Committees

**Agriculture**
Chair:
  K. Michael Conaway (R-TX).........................202-225-3605
Ranking Member:
  Collin C. Peterson (D-MN)..........................202-225-2165

  **Subcommittees**
  *Biotechnology, Horticulture & Research*
  Chair:
    Rodney Davis (R-IL).........................202-225-2371
  Ranking Member:
    Suzan DelBene (D-WA) .....................202-225-6311
  *Conservation & Forestry*
  Chair:
    Glenn Thompson (R-PA).....................202-225-5121
  Ranking Member:
    Michelle Lujan Grisham (D-NM) ..............202-225-6316
  *General Farm Commodities & Risk Management*
  Chair:
    Rick Crawford (R-AR) ......................202-225-4076
  Ranking Member:
    Timothy J. Walz (D-MN) ....................202-225-2472
  *Livestock & Foreign Agriculture*
  Chair:
    David Rouzer (R-NC) .......................202-225-2731
  Ranking Member:
    Jim Costa (D-CA) ..........................202-225-3341
  *Nutrition*
  Chair:
    Jackie Walorski (R-IN) .....................202-225-3915
  Ranking Member:
    Jim McGovern (D-MA).......................202-225-6101

**Energy & Commerce**
Chair:
  Fred Upton (R-MI)................................202-225-3761
Ranking Member:
  Frank Pallone (D-NJ)..............................202-225-4671
New York Delegate:
  Eliot L. Engel (D)................................202-225-2464
New York Delegate:
  Paul Tonko (D).................................202-225-5076

*Offices and agencies generally appear in alphabetical order, except when specific order is requested by listee.*

New York Delegate:
Yvette Clarke (D) . . . . . . . . . . . . . . . . . . . . . . . . . . . . .202-225-6231
New York Delegate:
Chris Collins (R) . . . . . . . . . . . . . . . . . . . . . . . . . . . . . .202-225-5265

**Subcommittees**
*Environment & the Economy*
Chair:
John Shimkus (R-IL) . . . . . . . . . . . . . . . . . . . . .202-225-5271
Ranking Member:
Paul Tonko (D-NY) . . . . . . . . . . . . . . . . . . . . . .202-225-5076

**Natural Resources**
Chair:
Rob Bishop (R-UT) . . . . . . . . . . . . . . . . . . . . . . . . . . .202-225-0453
Ranking Member:
Raul Grijalva (D-AZ) . . . . . . . . . . . . . . . . . . . . . . . . . .202-225-2435

**Science, Space & Technology**
Chair:
Lamar Smith (R-TX) . . . . . . . . . . . . . . . . . . . . . . . . . . .202-225-4236
Ranking Member:
Eddie Bernice Johnson (D-TX) . . . . . . . . . . . . . . . . .202-225-8885
New York Delegate:
Paul Tonko (D) . . . . . . . . . . . . . . . . . . . . . . . . . . . . . .202-225-5076

**Subcommittee**
*Environment*
Chair:
Jim Bridenstine (R-OK) . . . . . . . . . . . . . . . . . . . .202-225-2211
Ranking Member:
Suzanne Bonamici (D-OR) . . . . . . . . . . . . . . . . .202-225-0855

**Transportation & Infrastructure**
Chair:
Bill Shuster (R-PA) . . . . . . . . . . . . . . . . . . . . . . . . . . .202-225-2431
Ranking Member:
Peter A. DeFazio (D-OR) . . . . . . . . . . . . . . . . . . . . . .202-225-6416
New York Delegate:
Richard L. Hanna (R) . . . . . . . . . . . . . . . . . . . . . . . . .202-225-3665
New York Delegate:
John Katko (R) . . . . . . . . . . . . . . . . . . . . . . . . . . . . . .202-225-3701
New York Delegate:
Sean Patrick Maloney (D) . . . . . . . . . . . . . . . . . . . . .202-225-5441
New York Delegate:
Jerrold Nadler (D) . . . . . . . . . . . . . . . . . . . . . . . . . . .202-225-5635

**Subcommittee**
*Water Resources & Environment*
Chair:
Bob Gibbs (R-OH) . . . . . . . . . . . . . . . . . . . . . . .202-225-6265
Ranking Member:
Grace F. Napolitano (D-CA) . . . . . . . . . . . . . . . .202-225-5256
New York Delegate:
Sean Patrick Maloney (D) . . . . . . . . . . . . . . . . .202-225-5441
New York Delegate:
John Katko (R) . . . . . . . . . . . . . . . . . . . . . . . . . .202-225-3701

## Senate Standing Committees

**Agriculture, Nutrition & Forestry**
Chair:
Pat Roberts (R-KS) . . . . . . . . . . . . . . . . . . . . . . . . . . .202-224-4774
Ranking Member:
Debbie Stabenow (D-MI) . . . . . . . . . . . . . . . . . . . . . .202-224-4822

**Subcommittee**
*Conservation, Forestry & Natural Resources*
Chair:
David Perdue (R-GA) . . . . . . . . . . . . . . . . . . . . .202-224-3521
Ranking Member:
Michael Bennet (D-CO) . . . . . . . . . . . . . . . . . . .202-224-5852

**Commerce, Science & Transportation**
Chair:
John Thune (R-SD) . . . . . . . . . . . . . . . . . . . . . . . . . . .202-224-2321
Ranking Member:
Bill Nelson (D-FL) . . . . . . . . . . . . . . . . . . . . . . . . . . .202-224-5274

**Subcommittee**
*Oceans, Atmosphere, Fisheries and Coast Guard*
Chair:
Marco Rubio (R-FL) . . . . . . . . . . . . . . . . . . . . . .202-224-3041
Ranking Member:
Cory Booker (D-NJ) . . . . . . . . . . . . . . . . . . . . . .202-224-3224

**Energy & Natural Resources**
Chair:
Lisa Murkowski (R-AK) . . . . . . . . . . . . . . . . . . . . . . .202-224-6665
Ranking Member:
Maria Cantwell (D-WA) . . . . . . . . . . . . . . . . . . . . . . .202-224-3441

**Environment & Public Works**
Chair:
James M. Inhofe (R-OK) . . . . . . . . . . . . . . . . . . . . . .202-224-4721
Ranking Member:
Barbara Boxer (D-CA) . . . . . . . . . . . . . . . . . . . . . . . .202-224-3553
New York Delegate:
Kirsten Gillibrand (D) . . . . . . . . . . . . . . . . . . . . . . . .202-224-4451

## PRIVATE SECTOR

**Adirondack Council Inc (The)**
103 Hand Avenue, Suite 3, PO Box D-2, Elizabethtown, NY 12932
518-873-2240 or 877-873-2240 Fax: 518-873-6675
e-mail: info@adirondackcouncil.org
Web site: www.adirondackcouncil.org
*Seeks to promote & protect the environmental well-being of Adirondack Park through education, research & advocacy*
William C. Janeway, Executive Director

**AECOM Environmental Services**
100 Park Avenue, New York, NY 10017
212-973-2999 Fax: 212-682-5287
e-mail: info@aecom.com
Web site: www.aecom.com
*Environmental assessment, management, engineering, remediation & related services*
Michael S. Burke, Chief Executive Officer

**American Farmland Trust, New York Office**
112 Spring Street, Suite 207, Saratoga Springs, NY 12866
518-581-0078 Fax: 518-581-0079
e-mail: newyork@farmland.org
Web site: www.farmland.org/newyork
*Advocacy & education to protect farmland & promote environmentally sound farming practices*
David Haight, New York State Director

**American Museum of Natural History**
Central Park West at 79th Street, New York, NY 10024-5192
212-769-5100 Fax: 212-769-5018
Web site: www.amnh.org
*Education, exhibition & scientific research*
Ellen V. Futter, President

**Audubon New York**
2 Third Street, Suite 480, Troy, NY 12180
518-869-9731 Fax: 518-869-0737
*Protecting birds, other wildlife & their habitats*
Erin Crotty, Executive Director

*Offices and agencies generally appear in alphabetical order, except when specific order is requested by listee.*

**Audubon Society of NYS Inc (The) / Audubon International**
120 Defreest Drive, Troy, NY 12180
518-767-9051 or 844-767-9051 Fax: 518-767-9076
e-mail: doug@auduboninternational.org
Web site: www.auduboninternational.org
*Wildlife & water conservation; environmental education; sustainable land management*
Doug Bechtel, Executive Director

**Brooklyn Botanic Garden**
1000 Washington Avenue, Brooklyn, NY 11225-1099
718-623-7200 Fax: 718-857-2430
Web site: www.bbg.org
*Comprehensive study of plant biodiversity in metropolitan New York; home gardener's resource center*
Scot Medbury, President

**Business Council of New York State Inc**
152 Washington Avenue, Albany, NY 12210
518-465-7511 or 800-358-1202 Fax: 518-465-4389
e-mail: heather.briccetti@bcnys.org
Web site: www.bcnys.org
*Taxation, economic development, workers' compensation*
Heather C. Briccetti, President & Chief Executive Officer

**CWM Chemical Services LLC**
1550 Balmer Road, PO Box 200, Model City, NY 14107
716-286-1550
*Hazardous waste treatment, storage & disposal*
Michael Mahar, District Manager

**Cary Institute of Ecosystem Studies**
PO Box AB, Millbrook, NY 12545-0129
845-677-5343 Fax: 845-677-5976
Web site: www.caryinstitute.org
*Ecosystem research; curriculum development & on-site ecology education*
Dr. Joshua R. Ginsberg, President

**Catskill Center for Conservation & Development, The**
43355 State Highway, PO Box 504, Arkville, NY 12406-0504
845-586-2611 Fax: 845-586-3044
e-mail: cccd@catskillcenter.org
Web site: www.catskillcenter.org
*Advocacy for environmental & economic health of the Catskill Mountain region*
Jeff Senterman, Executive Director

**Center for Environmental Information Inc**
700 West Metro Park, Rochester, NY 14623
585-233-6086
Web site: www.geneseeriverwatch.org
*Public information & education on environmental topics*
George Thomas, Executive Director

**Citizens' Environmental Coalition**
33 Central Avenue, 3rd Floor, Albany, NY 12210
518-462-5527 Fax: 518-465-8349
*Organizing & assistance for communities concerned about toxic waste, air & water contamination & pollution prevention*
Barbara Warren, Executive Director

**Colgate University, Department of Geology**
13 Oak Drive, Hamilton, NY 13346
315-228-7201 Fax: 315-228-7187
e-mail: mswong@colgate.edu
*Metamorphic & igneous petrology, Isotope geochemistry*
Martin Wong, Chair, Department of Geology

**Columbia University, MPA in Environmental Science & Policy**
420 West 118th Street, Room 1404, New York, NY 10027
212-851-0261 or 212-854-6216 Fax: 212-864-3748
Web site: mpaenvironment.ei.columbia.edu
*Urban & environmental policy; public management*
Steven Cohen, Program Director

**Cornell Cooperative Extension, Environment & Natural Resources Initiative**
365 Roberts Hall, Cornell University, Ithaca, NY 14853
607-255-2237 Fax: 607-255-0788
e-mail: cce-contact@cornell.edu
Web site: www.cce.cornell.edu/program/environment
*Working to improve the quality & sustainability of human environments & natural resources*
Deb Grantham, Assistant Director

**Cornell University Atkinson Center for a Sustainable Future**
200 Rice Hall, Cornell University, Ithaca, NY 14853-5601
607-255-7535 Fax: 607-255-6714
Web site: www.acsf.cornell.edu
*Environmental research*
Frank DiSalvo, Director

**Dionondehowa Wildlife Sanctuary & School - Not For Profit**
148 Stanton Road, Shushan, NY 12873
518-854-7764
e-mail: dionondehowa@yahoo.com
Web site: www.dionondehowa.org
*Conservation & land use issues, conscious living, nature studies & healing & expressive arts*
Bonnie Hoag, Co-Founder & Director

**Ecology & Environment Inc**
368 Pleasant View Drive, Lancaster, NY 14086-1397
716-684-8060 Fax: 716-684-0844
e-mail: info@ene.com
Web site: www.ene.com
*Environmental scientific & engineering consulting*
Gerard A. Gallagher III, President & Chief Executive Officer

**Empire State Forest Products Association**
47 Van Alstyne Drive, Rensselaer, NY 12144
518-463-1297 Fax: 518-426-9502
Web site: www.esfpa.org
John Bartow, Executive Director

**Environmental Advocates of New York**
353 Hamilton Street, Albany, NY 12210
518-462-5526 Fax: 518-427-0381
e-mail: info@eany.org
Web site: www.eany.org
*Works to protect the environment of NYS by supporting conservation efforts & promoting policies that safeguard natural resources & public health*
Peter Iwanowicz, Executive Director

**Environmental Business Association of NYS Inc**
126 State Street, 3rd Floor, Albany, NY 12207-1637
518-432-6400 x227 Fax: 518-432-1383
*Supports businesses that provide products & services to prevent, monitor, control or remediate pollution or generate, conserve and/or recycle energy & resources*
Suzanne Maloney, Executive Director

**Environmental Defense Fund**
257 Park Avenue South, New York, NY 10010
212-505-2100 Fax: 212-505-2375
Web site: www.edf.org
Fred Krupp, President

*Offices and agencies generally appear in alphabetical order, except when specific order is requested by listee.*

**GreenThumb**
100 Gold Street, Suite 3100, New York, NY 10038
212-602-5300  Fax: 212-602-5334
e-mail: greenthumbinfo@parks.nyc.gov
Web site: www.greenthumbnyc.org
*Development & preservation of community gardens; workshops addressing a variety of topics including gardening, farming & community organizing*
Bill LoSasso, Director

**Greene County Soil & Water Conservation District**
907 Greene County Office Building, Cairo, NY 12413
518-622-3620  Fax: 518-622-0344
e-mail: jeff@gcswcd.com
Web site: www.gcswcd.com
*Natural resource conservation, agriculture & water quality programs, environmental education, stormwater management & wetland mitigation*
Jeff Flack, Executive Director

**Greenmarket/Grow NYC**
100 Gold Street, Suite 3300, New York, NY 10038
212-788-7900  Fax: 212-788-7913
Web site: www.grownyc.org
*Promotes regional sustainable agriculture & improves access to locally grown agricultural products; recycling initiatives & environmental programs*
Marcel Van Ooyen, Executive Director

**Hawk Creek Wildlife Center Inc**
PO Box 662, East Aurora, NY 14052-0662
716-652-8646  Fax: 716-652-8646
Web site: www.hawkcreek.org
*Non-profit organization focused on animal rehabilitation, conservation efforts, environmental education & research*
Loretta C. Jones, President

**Hofstra University, School of Law**
121 Hofstra University, Hempstead, NY 11549
516-463-5858
e-mail: hofstralaw@hofstra.edu
*Land use & environmental law*
Eric Lane, Dean

**Hudson River Environmental Society, Inc**
PO Box 279, Marlboro, NY 12542
e-mail: hudsonriverenvironmental@gmail.com
Web site: www.hres.org
*Facilitates & coordinates research in the physical & biological sciences, environmental engineering & resource management in the Hudson River region*
Lucy Johnson, President

**Hudson River Sloop Clearwater Inc**
724 Wolcott Avenue, Beacon, NY 12508
845-265-8080  Fax: 845-831-2821
e-mail: office@clearwater.org
Web site: www.clearwater.org
*Hudson River water quality, environmental education & advocacy*
Dave Conover, Interim Executive Director

**INFORM Inc**
PO Box 320403, New York, NY 11232
212-361-2400  Fax: 212-361-2412
*Produces educational films about the impact of human activity on natural resources & public health*
Virginia Ramsey, Executive Producer

**Land Trust Alliance Northeast Program**
112 Spring Street, Suite 204, Saratoga Springs, NY 12866
518-587-0774  Fax: 518-587-9586
e-mail: northeast@lta.org
Web site: www.landtrustalliance.org
*Promotes voluntary land conservation; provides leadership, information, skills & resources needed by land trusts*
Kevin Case, Northeast Director

**Messinger Woods Wildlife Care & Education Center Inc**
PO Box 508, Orchard Park, NY 14127
716-345-4239
e-mail: info@messingerwoods.org
Web site: www.messingerwoods.org
*Conservation & wildlife protection efforts through education, community awareness & promotion of quality wildlife rehabilitation & care*
Judy Seiler, President

**Modutank Inc**
41-04 35th Avenue, Long Island City, NY 11101
718-392-1112 or 800-245-6964  Fax: 718-786-1008
e-mail: info@modutank.com
Web site: www.modutank.com
*Manufactures modular storage tanks for potable water, wastewater & liquid chemicals*
Reed Margulis, President

**NY League of Conservation Voters/NY Conservation Education Fund**
30 Broad Street, 30th Floor, New York, NY 10004
212-361-6350  Fax: 212-361-6363
e-mail: info@nylcv.org
Web site: www.nylcv.org
*Endorsement of pro-environmental candidates; environmental advocacy & education statewide*
Marcia Bystryn, President

**NY Sea Grant**
125 Nassau Hall, SUNY at Stony Brook, Stony Brook, NY 11794-5001
631-632-6905  Fax: 631-632-6917
e-mail: nyseagrant@stonybrook.edu
Web site: www.seagrant.sunysb.edu
*Research, education & training related to ocean, coastal & Great Lakes resources*
William Wise, Director

**NYC Community Garden Coalition**
232 East 11th Street, New York, NY 10003
347-699-6099
Web site: www.nyccgc.org
*Works to preserve NYC's community gardens through education & advocacy*
Aziz Dehkan, Executive Director

**NYS Association for Solid Waste Management**
546 East Road, St. Johnsville, NY 13452
518-568-2095
e-mail: jbnysaswm@gmail.com
Web site: www.nysaswm.org
*Represents solid waste professionals in NYS & advocates for environmentally sound waste management practices*
Jeff Bouchard, Executive Director

**NYS Water Resources Institute of Cornell University**
Cornell University, 230 Riley-Robb Hall, Ithaca, NY 14853-5701
607-254-7163  Fax: 607-255-4449
e-mail: nyswri@cornell.edu
Web site: wri.cals.cornell.edu
*Education, research, investigation & technical assistance to agencies & communities concerned with water resources*
M. Todd Walter, Director

*Offices and agencies generally appear in alphabetical order, except when specific order is requested by listee.*

## National Wildlife Federation - Northeast Regional Center
149 State Street, Suite 1, Montpelier, VT 05602
802-229-0650  Fax: 802-229-4532
Web site: www.nwf.org/northeast
*Conservation education, litigation & advocacy for policies to restore &
protect habitat & wildlife*
Curtis Fisher, Regional Executive Director

## Natural Resources Defense Council
40 West 20th Street, 11th Floor, New York, NY 10011
212-727-2700  Fax: 212-727-1773
e-mail: nrdcinfo@nrdc.org
Web site: www.nrdc.org
*Litigation, legislation advocacy & public education to preserve & protect the
environment & public health*
Rhea Suh, President

## Nature Conservancy (The)
195 New Karner Road, Suite 200, Albany, NY 12205
518-690-7850  Fax: 518-869-2332
e-mail: nys@tnc.org
Web site: www.nature.org
*Works to preserve land & water, protect oceans & develop solutions to
climate change & other environmental challenges*
Bill Ulfelder, New York Executive Director

## New York Forest Owners Association Inc
PO Box 541, Lima, NY 14485
800-836-3566
e-mail: president@nyfoa.org
Web site: www.nyfoa.org
*Promote & nurture private woodland stewardship*
Charles Stackhouse, President

## New York Public Interest Research Group
9 Murray Street, Lower Level, New York, NY 10007
212-349-6460  Fax: 212-349-1366
*Environmental preservation, public health, consumer protection &
government reform*
Blair Horner, Executive Director

## New York State Conservation Council, Inc.
8 East Main Street, Ilion, NY 13357-1899
315-894-3302  Fax: 315-894-2893
e-mail: nyscc@nyscc.com
Web site: www.nyscc.com
*Promotes conservation, wise use & management of natural resources*
A. Charles Parker, President

## New York State Woodsmen's Field Days Inc
PO Box 123, 120 Main Street, Boonville, NY 13309
315-942-4593  Fax: 315-942-4452
e-mail: fielddays@aol.com
Web site: www.starinfo.com/woodsmen/
*Promoting the forest products industry*
Phyllis White, Executive Coordinator

## New York Water Environment Association Inc (NYWEA)
525 Plum Street, Suite 102, Syracuse, NY 13204
315-422-7811 or 877-556-9932  Fax: 315-422-3851
e-mail: pcr@nywea.org
Web site: www.nywea.org
*Organization working to protect water resources through education, science
& training*
Patricia Cerro-Reehil, Executive Director

## Northeastern Loggers' Association
3311 State Route 28, PO Box 69, Old Forge, NY 13420
315-369-3078  Fax: 315-369-3736
Web site: www.northernlogger.com
Joseph E. Phaneuf, Executive Director

## Open Space Institute
1350 Broadway, Suite 201, New York, NY 10018-7799
212-290-8200  Fax: 212-244-3441
Web site: www.osiny.org
*Preserves & protects farmland, forests, water & historic landscapes through
land acquisition, research, conservation & environmental education*
Christopher J. Elliman, President & Chief Executive Officer

## Pace University, School of Law Center for Environmental Legal Studies
78 North Broadway, White Plains, NY 10603
914-422-4214  Fax: 914-422-4248
e-mail: nrobinson@law.pace.edu
Web site: www.law.pace.edu
*US & international environmental law*
Nicholas A. Robinson, Co-Director

## Proskauer Rose LLP
Eleven Times Square, New York, NY 10036-8299
212-969-3000  Fax: 212-969-2900
e-mail: info@proskauer.com
Web site: www.proskauer.com
Joseph M. Leccese, Chairman

## Radiac Environmental Services
261 Kent Avenue, Brooklyn, NY 11249
718-963-2233  Fax: 718-388-5107
e-mail: jtekin@radiacenv.com
Web site: www.radiacenv.com
*Radioactive & chemical waste disposal, decontamination & remediation*
John Tekin, Manager

## Radon Testing Corp of America Inc
2 Hayes Street, Elmsford, NY 10523-2502
914-345-3380 or 800-457-2366  Fax: 914-345-8546
e-mail: info@rtca.com
Web site: www.rtca.com
*Radon detection services for health departments, municipalities &
homeowners*
Nancy Bredhoff, President

## Rensselaer Polytechnic Inst, Ecological Economics, Values & Policy Program
Dept of Science & Tech Studies, 110 Eighth Street, Troy, NY 12180
518-276-6000
*Educating leaders for a sustainable future*

## Riverhead Foundation for Marine Research & Preservation (The)
467 East Main Street, Riverhead, NY 11901
631-369-9840  Fax: 631-369-9826
*Marine conservation through education, rehabilitation & research*
Robert A. DiGiovanni, Jr., Executive Director & Senior Biologist

## Riverkeeper Inc
20 Secor Road, Ossining, NY 10562
914-478-4501 or 800-217-4837  Fax: 914-478-4527
e-mail: info@riverkeeper.org
Web site: www.riverkeeper.org
*Nonprofit member-supported environmental organization working to protect
the Hudson River & its tributaries as well as safeguard NYC & Hudson
Valley's drinking water supply*
Paul Gallay, President & Hudson Riverkeeper

## Rural Water Association
PO Box 487, Claverack, NY 12513-0487
518-828-3155  Fax: 518-828-0582
e-mail: nyrwa@nyruralwater.org
Web site: www.nyruralwater.org
*Protects small water & wastewater systems through training & technical
assistance*
Patricia Scalera, Chief Executive Director

*Offices and agencies generally appear in alphabetical order, except when specific order is requested by listee.*

**SCS Engineers PC**
4 Executive Blvd, Suite 303, Suffern, NY 10901
845-357-1510  Fax: 845-357-1049
e-mail: gmccarron@scsengineers.com
Web site: www.scsengineers.com
*Environmental consulting*
Greg McCarron, Vice President

**SUNY at Cortland, Center for Environmental & Outdoor Education**
PO Box 2000, Cortland, NY 13045
607-753-5488  Fax: 607-753-5985
e-mail: robert.rubendall@cortland.edu
Web site: www.cortland.edu
Robert L. Rubendall, Director

**NYS Bar Assn, Environmental Law Section**
**Sahn Ward Coschignano, PLLC**
333 Earle Ovington Blvd, Suite 601, Uniondale, NY 11553
516-228-1300  Fax: 516-228-0038
e-mail: info@swc-law.com
Web site: www.swc-law.com
Miriam E. Villani, Partner

**Scenic Hudson**
1 Civic Center Plaza, Suite 200, Poughkeepsie, NY 12601
845-473-4440  Fax: 845-473-2648
e-mail: info@scenichudson.org
Web site: www.scenichudson.org
*Environmental advocacy, air & water quality, riverfront protection, land/historic preservation, smart growth planning*
Ned Sullivan, President

**Sierra Club, Atlantic Chapter**
744 Broadway, Albany, NY 12207
518-426-9144
e-mail: atlantic.chapter@sierraclub.org
Web site: www.atlantic2.sierraclub.org
*Environmental protection advocacy and education, and outdoor recreation.*
Roger Downs, Conservation Director
Caitlin Ferrante, Conservation & Development Program Manager

**Spectra Environmental Group Inc**
19 British American Blvd West, Latham, NY 12110
518-782-0882  Fax: 518-782-0973
*Environmental & infrastructure engineering, architecture, surveying, air quality, ground penetrating radar & power generation consulting & services*
Robert C. LaFleur, President

**St John's University, School of Law**
8000 Utopia Pkwy, Queens, NY 11439
718-990-6600
*Environmental law*
Jack A. Raisner, Professor

**Sustainable Management LLC**
1370 Broadway, 5th Floor, New York, NY 10018
646-380-1940  Fax: 646-380-1220
*Environmental planning & housing development consulting services*
Ethan Eldon, President

**Syracuse University Press**
621 Skytop Road, Suite 110, Syracuse, NY 13244-5290
315-443-5534  Fax: 315-443-5545
e-mail: supress@syr.edu
Web site: www.syracuseuniversitypress.syr.edu
*Adirondack & regional NYS studies series*
Alice Randel Pfeiffer, Director

**Syracuse University, Maxwell School of Citizenship & Public Affairs**
200 Eggers Hall, Syracuse, NY 13244-1020
315-443-2252
e-mail: whlambri@maxwell.syr.edu
Web site: www.maxwell.syr.edu
*Environment & energy; social & economic policy*
W. Henry Lambright, Professor

**Trees New York**
100 Gold Street, Suite 3100, New York, NY 10038
212-227-1887  Fax: 212-732-5325
e-mail: info@treesny.org
Web site: www.treesny.org
*Planting, preserving & protecting street trees; urban forestry resources, reference materials & programs in NYC*
Nelson Villarrubia, Executive Director

**University of Rochester School of Medicine**
601 Elmwood Avenue, Box EHSC, Rochester, NY 14642
585-275-4203  Fax: 585-256-2591
Web site: www2.envmed.rochester.edu
*Environmental health science & toxicology education & research*
Thomas W. Clarkson, Professor, Department of Environmental Medicine

**Upstate Freshwater Institute**
PO Box 506, Syracuse, NY 13214
315-431-4962  Fax: 315-431-4969
e-mail: uficontact@upstatefreshwater.org
Web site: www.upstatefreshwater.org
*Freshwater water quality research*
Steven W. Effler, Chief Executive Officer & Director of Research

**Waterkeeper Alliance**
180 Maiden Lane, Suite 603, New York, NY 10038
212-747-0622
e-mail: info@waterkeeper.org
Web site: www.waterkeeper.org
*Seeks to protect & restore the quality of the world's waterways*
Marc Yaggi, Executive Director

**Whiteman Osterman & Hanna LLP**
One Commerce Plaza, Albany, NY 12260
518-487-7600  Fax: 518-487-7777
e-mail: druzow@woh.com
Web site: www.woh.com
*Environmental & zoning law*
Daniel A. Ruzow, Partner

**Wildlife Conservation Society**
2300 Southern Blvd, Bronx, NY 10460
718-220-5100
e-mail: jcalvelli@wcs.org
Web site: www.wcs.org
*Biodiversity conservation & education*
John F. Calvelli, Executive Vice President, Public Affairs

*Offices and agencies generally appear in alphabetical order, except when specific order is requested by listee.*

## GOVERNMENT OPERATIONS

### NEW YORK STATE

### GOVERNOR'S OFFICE

**Governor's Office**
Executive Chamber
State Capitol
Albany, NY 12224
518-474-8390 Fax: 518-474-1513
Web site: www.ny.gov

Governor:
  Andrew M Cuomo . . . . . . . . . . . . . . . . . . . . . . . . . . . . . . .518-474-8390
Secretary to the Governor:
  Melissa DeRosa . . . . . . . . . . . . . . . . . . . .518-474-4246 or 212-681-4580
Counsel to the Governor:
  Kumiki Gibson . . . . . . . . . . . . . . . . . . . .518-474-8343 or 212-681-4580
Deputy Director of State Operations:
  Christian Jackstadt . . . . . . . . . . . . . . . . . . . . . . . . . . . . .212-681-4586
Executive Deputy Secretary:
  Joseph Rabito . . . . . . . . . . . . . . . . . . . .518-473-5704 or 212-681-4580
Director of Policy:
  David Yassky . . . . . . . . . . . . . . . . . . . . . . . . . . . . . . . .518-408-2576
Deputy Secretary, Public Safety:
  Jeremy Schockett . . . . . . . . . . . . . . . . . . . . . . . . . . . . .518-474-3522
Chief of Staff:
  Jill DesRosiers . . . . . . . . . . . . . . . . . . .518-474-8390 or 212-681-4580
Director, Communications:
  Peter Ajemian . . . . . . . . . . . . . . . . . . . .518-474-8418 or 212-681-4640

**New York City Office**
  633 Third Ave, 38th Fl, New York, NY 10017

**Washington Office of the Governor**
  444 N Capitol St NW, Washington, DC 20001
Director:
  Alexander Cochran . . . . . . . . . . . . . . . . . . . . . . . . . . . . .202-434-7100

**Lieutenant Governor's Office**
Executive Chamber
State Capitol
Albany, NY 12224
518-402-2292 Fax: 518-474-1513

633 Third Ave
New York, NY 10017
212-681-4575

Lieutenant Governor:
  Kathleen C. Hochul. . . . . . . . . . . . . . . . . . . . . . . . . . . . .581-402-2292

### EXECUTIVE DEPARTMENTS AND RELATED AGENCIES

**Budget, Division of the**
State Capitol
Room 128
Albany, NY 12224-0341
518-474-2300
e-mail: dob.sm.press@budget.ny.gov
Web site: www.budget.ny.gov

Director:
  Robert F. Mujica. . . . . . . . . . . . . . . . . . . . . . . . . . . . . . .518-474-2300

Deputy Director:
  Sandra Beattie . . . . . . . . . . . . . . . . . . . . . . . . . . . . . . . .518-474-2300
Deputy Director:
  Charles Williams. . . . . . . . . . . . . . . . . . . . . . . . . . . . . . .518-474-2300
Press Officer:
  Morris Peters. . . . . . . . . . . . . . . . . . . . . . . . . . . . . . . . .518-473-3885
  e-mail: dob.sm.press@budget.ny.gov

**CIO & Office of Information Technology Services (ITS)**
State Capitol
Empire State Plaza
P.O. Box 2062
Albany, NY 12220-0062
518-402-3899 or 844-891-1786
e-mail: fixit@its.ny.gov
Web site: www.its.ny.gov

Chief Information Officer & Director:
  Robert H. Samson . . . . . . . . . . . . . . . . . . . . . . . . . . . . .518-408-2140
Executive Deputy Chief Information Officer:
  Karen Geduldig. . . . . . . . . . . . . . . . . . . . . . . . . . . . . . .518-473-9450
Chief General Counsel:
  Shoshanah Bewlay . . . . . . . . . . . . . . . . . . . . . . . . . . . . .518-408-2484
Director, Public Information:
  Vacant . . . . . . . . . . . . . . . . . . . . . . . . . . . . . . . . . . . . .518-402-3899
Chief Portfolio Officer:
  Nancy Mulholland . . . . . . . . . . . . . . . . . . . . . . . . . . . . .518-473-9450
Chief Operating Officer:
  Ray Rose . . . . . . . . . . . . . . . . . . . . . . . . . . . . . . . . . . .518-402-7000
Director, Administration:
  Theresa Papa. . . . . . . . . . . . . . . . . . . . . . . . . . . . . . . . .518-408-2484
Chief Technology Officer:
  Rajiv Rao . . . . . . . . . . . . . . . . . . . . . . . . . . . . . . . . . . .518-486-9200
Acting Chief Data Officer:
  John Rager

**Homeland Security & Emergency Services, Division of**
1220 Washington Avenue
Building 7A
Suite 710
Albany, NY 12242
518-242-5000 Fax: 518-322-4978
Web site: www.dhses.ny.gov

633 Third Avenue
32nd Floor
New York, NY 10017
212-867-7060

Commissioner:
  Roger L. Parrino, Sr.. . . . . . . . . . . . . . . . . . . . . . . . . . . .518-242-5103
Program Officer, Office of Counter Terrorism:
  Jennifer Margulies . . . . . . . . . . . . . . . . . . . . . . . . . . . . .518-242-5000
Director, Office of Emergency Management:
  Kevin Wisely . . . . . . . . . . . . . . . . .518-292-2301/fax: 518-322-4978
State Fire Administrator, Office of Fire Prevention and Control:
  Francis J Nerney, Jr . . . . . . . . . . . . . . . . . . . . . . . . . . . .518-474-6746
  e-mail: fire@dhses.ny.gov
Director, Office of Interoperable & Emergency Communications:
  Michael Sprague . . . . . . . . . . . . . . . . . . . . . . . . . . . . . .518-242-8275
  e-mail: dhses.oiec@dhses.ny.gov
Public Information Officer:
  Kristin Devoe . . . . . . . . . . . . . . . . . . . . . . . . . . . . . . . .518-242-5153

**General Services, Office of**
Corning Tower
41st Floor

*Offices and agencies generally appear in alphabetical order, except when specific order is requested by listee.*

Empire State Plaza
Albany, NY 12242
518-474-3899
e-mail: comments@ogs.ny.gov
Web site: www.ogs.ny.gov

Commissioner:
   RoAnn Destito . . . . . . . . . . . . . . . . . . . . 518-474-5991/fax: 518-486-9179
Executive Deputy Commissioner:
   Vacant . . . . . . . . . . . . . . . . . . . . . . . . . . . 518-473-6953
Deputy Commissioner, Legal Services & Counsel:
   Bradley Allen . . . . . . . . . . . . . . . . . . . 518-474-5988/fax: 518-473-4973
Director, Communications:
   Heather Groll . . . . . . . . . . . . . . . . . . . 518-474-5987/fax: 518-486-9179
   e-mail: heather.groll@ogs.ny.gov

## Administration
Deputy Commissioner:
   Eric S McShane . . . . . . . . . . . . . . . . . . . . . . . . 518-474-3199
Chief Financial Officer, Financial Administration:
   Brian C Matthews . . . . . . . . . . . . . . 518-474-4546/fax: 518-486-3651
Director, Financial Administration:
   Robert Curtin . . . . . . . . . . . . . . . . . . . . . . . 518-474-4546
Director, Human Resource Management:
   Matthew Guinane . . . . . . . . . . . . . . . . . . . . 518-474-5995
Director, Personnel:
   Christina Gavin . . . . . . . . . . . . . . . . . . . . . . 518-474-5995
Director, Bureau of Risk, Insurance & Fleet Management:
   Leighann Brown . . . . . . . . . . . . . . . . . . . . . 518-474-4725

### Support Services
Director, Support Services Operations:
   Thomas Osterhout . . . . . . . . . . . . . . . . . . . . 518-402-5557
Printing & Mailing Services:
   Annemarie Pingelski . . . . . . . . . . . . . . . . . . . 518-457-6593
Assistant Director, State & Federal Surplus Property:
   Michael Harris . . . . . . . . . . . . . . . 518-457-6335/fax: 518-457-4641
   e-mail: nysstore@ogs.ny.gov
Director, Food Distribution & Warehousing:
   Annemarie Garceau . . . . . . . . . . . . . 518-474-5122/fax: 518-486-5660
   e-mail: ogsdonatedfoods@ogs.ny.gov
Director, Fleet Management:
   Mike Matthews . . . . . . . . . . . . . . . 518-457-1744/fax: 518-457-7263
   e-mail: fleet.admin@ogs.ny.gov
Director, Mail & Freight Security Services:
   Arthur Hasson . . . . . . . . . . . . . . . 518-474-6707/fax: 518-473-0244
   e-mail: mailfreight@ogs.ny.gov

## Design & Construction
Deputy Commissioner:
   Margaret Larkin . . . . . . . . . . . . . . . . . . . . . 518-474-0337
Director, Construction:
   Marc Prendergast . . . . . . . . . . . . . . . . . . . . 518-474-0331
Director, Design:
   Erik Deyoe, PE . . . . . . . . . . . . . . . . . . . . . . 518-474-0337

## Information Technology & Procurement Services
Deputy Commissioner:
   Vacant . . . . . . . . . . . . . . . . . . . 518-473-3933/fax: 518-486-9166

### Information Resource Management
Assistant Director:
   Eliel Mamousette . . . . . . . . . . . . . . . . . . . . 518-473-4788

### Procurement Services Group
Deputy Chief:
   Susan Filburn . . . . . . . . . . . . . . . 518-474-5294/fax: 518-474-2437
Director:
   Bruce Hallenbeck . . . . . . . . . . . . . . . . . . . . 518-408-1705
Director:
   Kathleen McAuley . . . . . . . . . . . . . . . . . . . . 518-474-1994

Assistant Director:
   Anne Samson . . . . . . . . . . . . . . . . . . . . . . . 518-474-3855

### Real Estate Planning & Development Group
Director:
   James Sproat . . . . . . . . . . . . . . . . . . . . . . . 518-474-4944
Deputy Director, Real Estate Planning & Development:
   Jessica Gabriel . . . . . . . . . . . . . . . . . . . . . . 518-474-4944
Bureau Chief, Land Management:
   Charles Sheifer . . . . . . . . . . . . . . . . . . . . . . 518-474-2195
Bureau Chief, Leasing & Assistant Director, Real Estate Planning:
   Leah Nicholson . . . . . . . . . . . . . . . . . . . . . . 518-486-1484

### Real Property Management Group
Executive Deputy Commissioner:
   Daniel Cunningham . . . . . . . . . . . . . . 518-474-6057/fax: 518-474-1523
Director, Empire State Plaza & Downtown Buildings:
   Carl Olsen . . . . . . . . . . . . . . . . . . . . . . . 518-474-6148
Director, Downstate Regional Buildings:
   Kevin Cahill . . . . . . . . . . . . . . . 212-961-4390/fax: 212-961-4404
Assistant Director, Empire State Plaza & Downtown Buildings:
   Andy Papale . . . . . . . . . . . . . . . . . . . . . . . 518-402-5753
Regional Director, Campus & Upstate Regional Director:
   Louis Salerno . . . . . . . . . . . . . . . 518-457-2290/fax: 518-457-8297
Director, Utilities Management & Statewide Energy:
   Robert Lobdell . . . . . . . . . . . . . . . 518-474-3249/fax: 518-402-5682

### Empire State's Convention & Cultural Events Office
Director:
   Susan Cleary . . . . . . . . . . . . . . . . . . . . . . . 518-474-0549
Manager, Convention Center:
   Vacant . . . . . . . . . . . . . . . . . . . 518-474-0558/fax: 518-473-2190
Director, Curatorial & Tour Services:
   Barbara Maggio . . . . . . . . . . . . . . . 518-473-7521/fax: 518-474-0954
NYS Vietnam Memorial:
   Information . . . . . . . . . . . . . . . . . . 518-474-2418 or 518-473-5546

## Inspector General (NYS), Office of the
Empire State Plaza
Building 2
16th Floor
Albany, NY 12223
518-474-1010 or 800-367-4448 Fax: 518-486-3745
Web site: www.ig.ny.gov

61 Broadway
Suite 2100
New York, NY 10006
212-635-3150
Fax: 212-809-1630

State Inspector General:
   Catharine Leahy Scott . . . . . . . . . . . . . 212-635-3150 or 518-474-1010
   e-mail: inspector.general@ig.ny.gov
Executive Deputy Inspector General:
   Spencer Freedman . . . . . . . . . . . . . . . 212-635-3150 or 518-474-1010
Special Deputy Inspector General:
   Philip Foglia . . . . . . . . . . . . . . . . . . . . . . 212-635-3150
Special Deputy, Communications & External Affairs:
   Vacant . . . . . . . . . . . . . . . . . . . 518-474-1010 or 212-635-3150

## Law Department
28 Liberty Street
New York, NY 10005
212-416-8000 or 800-771-7755
Web site: www.ag.ny.gov

State Capitol
Albany, NY 12224-0341

*Offices and agencies generally appear in alphabetical order, except when specific order is requested by listee.*

518-776-2000
Fax: 518-650-9401

Attorney General:
Letitia James.........................212-416-8000 or 518-776-2000
Chief of Staff:
Ibrahim Khan ............................................212-416-8050
Acting Chief Operating Officer:
Joshua Carr ..............................................212-416-8050
Executive Deputy Attorney General for Criminal Justice:
Vacant .....................................................212-416-8050

## State Comptroller, Office of the
110 State Street
15th Floor
Albany, NY 12236
518-474-4044  Fax: 518-473-3004
e-mail: contactus@osc.state.ny.us
Web site: www.osc.state.ny.us

59 Maiden Lane
New York, NY 10038
212-383-1600

State Comptroller:
Thomas P. DiNapoli................518-474-4044 or 212-383-1600
Deputy Comptroller, Budget & Policy Analysis:
Robert Ward ............................................518-473-4333
Assistant Comptroller, Labor Affairs:
Kathy McCormack ......................................518-473-8409

### Executive Office
First Deputy Comptroller:
Pete Grannis ......................518-474-2909 or 212-681-4469
Chief of Staff:
Shawn Thompson .......................................518-474-4044
Chief Information Officer:
Robert Loomis .........................................518-486-4349
Director, IT Services:
Mary Anne Barry ....................518-474-8089 or 212-681-4840
Director, Communications:
Jennifer Freeman ...................518-474-4015 or 212-383-2501
Assistant Comptroller, Communications & Digital Media:
Ellen Evans........................518-474-4040 or 212-383-7412
Deputy Comptroller, Office of the State Deputy Comptroller for the City of
New York:
Ken Bliewas ...........................................212-383-3905

### Human Resources & Administration
Deputy Comptroller, Human Resources & Administration:
Angela Dixon ..........................................518-474-5512
Assistant Comptroller, Administration:
Larry Appel............................................518-402-3043
Director, Financial Administration:
Brian Matthews ........................................518-474-2709
Assistant Director, Management Services:
Beth Bristol...........................................518-486-7433

### Inspector General
Inspector General, Internal Audit:
Stephen Hamilton ......................................518-408-4906

### Intergovernmental Affairs
Assistant Comptroller, Intergovernmental & Community Affairs:
Carlos Rodriguez...................518-402-3234/fax: 518-408-3852

### Legal Services
General Counsel:
Nancy Groenwegen.......................................518-474-3444
Special Counsel for Ethics:
Barbara Smith..........................................518-408-3855

### Operations
Executive Deputy Comptroller:
John Traylor ..........................................518-402-4103
Deputy Comptroller, Contracts & Expenditures:
Margaret N. Becker.....................................518-486-9544
Deputy Comptroller, Payroll, Accounting & Revenue Services (PARS):
Chris Gorka............................................518-408-4149

### Pension Investment & Cash Management
Assistant Comptroller, Real Estate Investments:
Marjorie Tsang ........................................212-681-2589

### Retirement
Deputy Comptroller:
Kevin Murray ..........................................518-474-2600

### Local Government & School Accountability
Deputy Comptroller:
Steve Hancox ..........................................518-474-4037

### State Government Accountability
Executive Deputy Comptroller:
Andrew San Filippo ....................................518-474-4593
Deputy Comptroller:
Elliot Pagliaccio ....................................518-473-3596
Assistant Comptroller:
Jerry Barber..........................................518-473-0334

## State Department
One Commerce Plaza
99 Washington Ave
Albany, NY 12231-0001
518-474-4750  Fax: 518-474-4597
e-mail: info@dos.ny.gov
Web site: www.dos.ny.gov

123 William St
New York, NY 10038-3804
212-417-5800
Fax: 212-417-2383

Secretary of State:
Rossana Rosado ....................518-486-9844 or 212-417-5800
First Deputy Secretary of State:
Daniel Shapiro .......................................518-474-4750
Deputy Secretary of State, Public Affairs:
Vacant................................................212-417-5800
General Counsel:
Linda Baldwin.....................518-474-6740/fax: 518-473-9211
Assistant Secretary of State, Communications:
Vacant.............................518-474-4752/fax: 518-474-4597
e-mail: info@dos.state.ny.us

### Licensing Services Division
Deputy Secretary of State:
Marcos Vigil ......................518-473-2728/fax: 518-473-2730

#### Administrative Rules Division
Manager, Publications:
Maribeth St. Germain .............518-474-6957/fax: 518-473-9055
e-mail: adminrules@dos.state.ny.us

#### Cemeteries Division
Director:
Richard D Fishman ................518-474-6226 or 212-417-5713
fax: 518-473-0876
e-mail: cemeteries@dos.state.ny.us

*Offices and agencies generally appear in alphabetical order, except when specific order is requested by listee.*

## Corporations, State Records & UCC Division
Director:
Sandra J. Tallman . . . . . . . . . . . . . . . .518-473-2492/fax: 518-474-1418
e-mail: corporations@dos.ny.gov

## Local Government & Community Services
Deputy Secretary of State:
Mark Pattison. . . . . . . . . . . . . . . . . . . . .518-473-3355/fax: 518-474-6572

### Coastal Resources & Waterfront Revitalization Division
Director:
George Stafford . . . . . . . . . . . . . . . . . . . . . . . . . . .518-474-6000
e-mail: coastal@dos.state.ny.us

### Code Enforcement & Administration Division
Director:
Ronald E Piester . . . . . . . . . . . . . . .518-474-4073/fax: 518-486-4487
e-mail: codes@dos.state.ny.us

### Community Services Division
Director:
Veronica Cruz . . . . . . . . . . . . . . . . .518-474-5741/fax: 518-486-4663
e-mail: commserv@dos.state.ny.us

### Local Government Services Division
Deputy Secretary of State:
Mark Pattison . . . . . . . . . . . . . . . . .518-473-3355/fax: 518-474-6572
e-mail: localgov@dos.ny.gov

## Open Government Committee
Executive Director:
Robert J Freeman. . . . . . . . . . . . . . . . .518-474-2518/fax: 518-474-1927
e-mail: opengov@dos.state.ny.us

## Operations
Director, Administration & Management:
Judith E Kenny . . . . . . . . . . . . . . . . . .518-474-4751/fax: 518-474-4765

### Administrative Support Services
Director:
Rebecca Sebesta . . . . . . . . . . . . . . . .518-473-8221/fax: 518-473-7182

### Affirmative Action. . . . . . . . . . . . . . . . . . . . . . . . . .fax: 518-473-3294
Affirmative Action Officer:
Teneka Frost-Amusa . . . . . . . . . . . . . . . . . . . . . . .518-474-6740

### Fiscal Management
Director:
George Lupe . . . . . . . . . . . . . . . . . .518-474-2754/fax: 518-474-4777

### Human Resources Management
Director:
Philip Kelly. . . . . . . . . . . . . . . . . . . .518-474-2752/fax: 518-473-3294

### Internal Audit
Acting Director:
Louis Canter . . . . . . . . . . . . . . . . . . . . . . . . . . . . . . .518-474-1859

### Information Technology Management
Director:
Steven S Lovelett . . . . . . . . . . . . . . .518-474-8512/fax: 518-474-6239

## Regional Services
Assistant Director:
Brian S. Tollisen . . . . . . . . . . . . . . . .518-474-4073/fax: 518-474-5788

### Regional Offices
*Region 9 - Capital District Office* . . . . . . . . . . . . . .fax: 518-477-2369
One Commerce Plaza, 99 Washington Avenue, Albany, NY 12231
518-474-7497  Fax: 518-477-2369
Regional Representative:
Joseph McGrath. . . . . . . . . . . . . . . . . . . . . . . . . .518-477-7497
*Region 4 - Kingston Office* . . . . . . . . . . . . . . . . .fax: 845-334-9373
One Albany Avenue, Suite G-%, Kingston, NY 12401
845-334-9768  Fax: 845-334-9373

Regional Representative:
Dan Nichols . . . . . . . . . . . . . . .845-334-9768/fax: 845-334-9373
*Region 1 - Buffalo Office*. . . . . . . . . . . . . . . . . . . .fax: 716-847-7941
65 Court St, Room 208, Buffalo, NY 14202
716-847-7611 or 716-847-7612  Fax: 716-847-7941
Regional Representative:
Kumar Vijaykumar . . . . . . . . . . . . . . . . . . . . . . . .716-847-7611
Regional Representative:
Andrew Hvisdak . . . . . . . . . . . . . . . . . . . . . . . . . .716-847-7612
*Region 12/13 - Long Island Office* . . . . . . . . . . . . .fax: 631-952-4911
Suffolk State Office Bldg., 250 Veterans Memorial Highway,
Hauppauge, NY 11788
631-952-4915  Fax: 631-952-4911
Regional Representative:
Courtney Nation. . . . . . . . . . . .631-952-4915/fax: 631-952-4911
Regional Representative:
Richard Smith . . . . . . . . . . . . . . . . . . . . . . . . . . . .631-952-4912
*Region 10 - Northern New York Office*
PO Box 341, Lake George, NY 12845
Regional Representative:
Whitney Russell . . . . . . . . . . . .518-441-1895/fax: 518-668-5369
*Region 2 - Peekskill Office*
2 John Walsh Blvd., Suite 206, Peekskill, NY 10566
Regional Representative:
Erika Krieger . . . . . . . . . . . . . .914-734-1347/fax: 914-734-1763
*Region 5 - Syracuse Office*
St Ofc Bldg, 333 E Washington St, Rm 514, Syracuse, NY 13202
Regional Representative:
James King . . . . . . . . . . . . . . . .315-428-4434/fax: 578-428-4655
*Region 6 - Utica Office*
State Office Bldg, 207 Genesee St, Utica, NY 13501
Regional Representative:
Thomas Romanowski. . . . . . . . .315-793-2526/fax: 315-793-2569
*Region 7/8 - Western New York Office*
PO Box 141, Conesus, NY 14435
585-402-3017
Regional Representative:
Deborah Babbitt. . . . . . . . . . . . . . . . . . . . . . . . . . .585-402-3017

## State Athletic Commission
123 William St, 2nd Fl, New York, NY 10038
Chair:
Tom Hoover. . . . . . . . . . . . . . . . . . . . .212-417-5700/fax: 212-417-4987
e-mail: athletic@dos.ny.gov

## Welfare Inspector General, Office of NYS
Empire State Plaza
Agency Bldg 2
16th Floor
Albany, NY 12223
518-474-1010 or 800-367-4448  Fax: 518-486-3745
e-mail: inspector.general@ig.ny.gov
Web site: www.owig.state.ny.us

Welfare Inspector General:
Letizia Tagliafierro. . . . . . . . . . . . . . . .518-474-1010 or 212-635-3150
Chief Investigator:
Joseph Bucci. . . . . . . . . . . . . . . . . . . .718-923-4290 or 518-474-1010
Confidential Assistant/Office Manager:
Joy Quiles. . . . . . . . . . . . . . . . . . . . . .718-923-4290 or 518-474-1010
fax: 718-923-4310

## CORPORATIONS, AUTHORITIES AND COMMISSIONS

## Legislative Bill Drafting Commission
Capitol, Rm 308
Albany, NY 12224
518-455-7500  Fax: 518-455-7598

*Offices and agencies generally appear in alphabetical order, except when specific order is requested by listee.*

Commissioner:
  Randall G Bluth . . . . . . . . . . . . . . . . . . . . . . . . . . . . . .518-455-7506
  e-mail: bluth@lbdc.state.ny.us

**Legislative Retrieval System** . . . . . . . . . . . . . . . . . .fax: 518-455-7679
  1450 Western Ave, Albany, NY 12203
  800-356-6566  Fax: 518-455-7679
Director:
  Burleigh McCutcheon. . . . . . . . . . . . . . . . . . . . . . . . . . .518-455-7672
  e-mail: mccutcheon@lbdc.state.ny.us

## New York State Athletic Commission
123 William St
2nd Fl
New York, NY 10038
212-417-5700  Fax: 212-417-4987
e-mail: info@dos.ny.gov
Web site: www.dos.ny.gov/athletic

Chair:
  Tom Hoover . . . . . . . . . . . . . . . . . . . . . . . . . . . . . . . . . .212-417-5700

## New York State Commission on the Restoration of the Capitol
Corning Tower, 31st Fl
Empire State Plaza
Albany, NY 12242
518-473-0341  Fax: 518-486-5720

Executive Director:
  Andrea J Lazarski. . . . . . . . . . . . . . . . . . . . . . . . . . . . . .518-473-0341
  e-mail: andrea.lazarski@ogs.ny.gov

## New York State Disaster Preparedness Commission
Building 7A, Suite 710
1220 Washington Ave
Albany, NY 12242
518-242-5000
Web site: www.dhses.ny.gov/oem/disaster-prep

NYS Div. of Homeland Sec./Emerg. Serv.
633 Third Ave.
32nd Fl.
New York, NY 10017
212-867-7060

Chairman:
  Roger L. Parrino, Sr.

## New York State Dormitory Authority
515 Broadway
Albany, NY 12207-2964
518-257-3000  Fax: 518-257-3100
e-mail: dabonds@dasny.org
Web site: www.dasny.org

One Penn Plaza
52nd Fl
New York, NY 10119-0098
212-273-5000
Fax: 212-273-5121

539 Franklin St
Buffalo, NY 14202-1109
716-884-9780
Fax: 716-884-9787

Chair:
  Alfonso L Carney Jr . . . . . . . . . . . .518-257-3000/fax: 518-257-3100
President/CEO:
  Paul T Williams Jr. . . . . . . . . . . . . . .518-257-3180/fax: 518-257-3183
Vice President:
  Michael T Corrigan . . . . . . . . . . . . .518-257-3192/fax: 518-257-3183
Chief Financial Officer:
  Linda H Button . . . . . . . . . . . . . . . . .518-257-3562/fax: 518-257-3100
General Counsel:
  Michael Cusack . . . . . . . . . . . . . . . . .518-257-3120/fax: 518-257-3101
Managing Director, Construction:
  Stephen D Curro, PE . . . . . . . . . . . . .518-257-3271/fax: 518-257-3100
  e-mail: scurro@dasny.org
Managing Director, Public Finance & Portfolio Monitoring:
  Portia Lee. . . . . . . . . . . . . . . . . . .518-257-3362/fax: 518-257-3100
  e-mail: plee@dasny.org
Public Information Officer:
  John Chirlin. . . . . . . . . . . . . . . . . . . . . . . . . . . . . . . . . .518-257-3380
  e-mail: jchirlin@dasny.org

## Joint Commission on Public Ethics (JCOPE)
540 Broadway
Albany, NY 12207
518-408-3976  Fax: 518-408-3975
e-mail: jcope@jcope.ny.gov
Web site: www.jcope.ny.gov

Executive Director:
  Seth Agata. . . . . . . . . . . . . . . . . . . . . . . . . . . . . . . . . . . .518-408-3976
Chair:
  Daniel J Horwitz. . . . . . . . . . . . . . . . . . . . . . . . . . . . . . .518-408-3976
General Counsel:
  Monica Stamm . . . . . . . . . . . . . . . . . . . . . . . . . . . . . . . .518-408-3976
Chief of Staff:
  Kevin T Gagan . . . . . . . . . . . . . . . . . . . . . . . . . . . . . . . .518-408-3976

## New York State Financial Control Board
123 William St
23rd Fl
New York, NY 10038-3804
212-417-5046  Fax: 212-417-5055
e-mail: nysfcb@fcb.state.ny.us
Web site: www.fcb.state.ny.us

Acting Executive Director:
  Jeffrey Sommer. . . . . . . . . . . . . . . . . . . . . . . . . . . . . . . .212-417-5066
Deputy Director, Expenditure & Covered Organization Analysis:
  Dennis DeLisle . . . . . . . . . . . . . . . . . . . . . . . . . . . . . . . .212-417-5069
Acting Deputy Director, Economic & Revenue Analysis:
  Martin Fischman. . . . . . . . . . . . . . . . . . . . . . . . . . . . . . .212-417-5068
Associate Director, Administration:
  Mattie W Taylor . . . . . . . . . . . . . . . . . . . . . . . . . . . . . . .212-417-5053

## New York State Law Reporting Bureau
17 Lodge Street
Albany, NY 12207
518-453-6900  Fax: 518-426-1640
Web site: www.courts.state.ny.us/reporter

State Reporter:
  William J Hooks. . . . . . . . . . . . . . . . . . . . . . . . . . . . . . .518-453-6900
Deputy State Reporter:
  Katherine D LaBoda, Esq. . . . . . . . . . . . . . . . . . . . . . . .518-453-6900
  e-mail: Reporter@courts.state.ny.us
Assistant State Reporter:
  Cara J Broussea, Esq. . . . . . . . . . . . . . . . . . . . . . . . . . . .518-453-6900
  e-mail: Reporter@courts.state.ny.us

*Offices and agencies generally appear in alphabetical order, except when specific order is requested by listee.*

## Uniform State Laws Commission

c/o Coughlin & Gerhart LLP,
99 Corporate Drive
PO Box 2089
Binghamton, NY 13902-2039
607-723-9511  Fax: 607-723-1530

Chair:
Richard B Long . . . . . . . . . . . . . . . . . . . . . . . . . . . . .607-821-2202
e-mail: rlong@cglawoffices.com
Member:
Sandra Stern . . . . . . . . . . . . . . . . . . . . . . . . . . . . .212-207-8150
Member:
Norman L. Greene . . . . . . . . . . . . . . . . . . . . . . . . .212-661-5030
Member:
Justin L. Vigdor . . . . . . . . . . . . . . . . . . . . .585-232-5300 ext 228
Member:
Mark F Glaser . . . . . . . . . . . . . . . . . . . . . . . . . . . .518-689-1413

## United Nations Development Corporation

Two United Nations Plaza
27th Fl
New York, NY 10017
212-888-1618  Fax: 212-588-0758
e-mail: info@undc.org
Web site: www.undc.org

Chair, Board of Directors:
George Klein . . . . . . . . . . . . . . . . . . . . . . . . . . . . .212-888-1618
Sr VP & General Counsel/Secretary:
Robert Cole . . . . . . . . . . . . . . . . . . . . . . . . . . . . . .212-888-1618
Controller/Treasurer:
Jorge Ortiz . . . . . . . . . . . . . . . . . . . . . . . . . . . . . . .212-888-1618
Vice President:
Kenneth Coopersmith . . . . . . . . . . . . . . . . . . . . . . .212-888-1618

## NEW YORK STATE LEGISLATURE

*See Legislative Branch in Section 1 for additional Standing Committee and Subcommittee information.*

## Assembly Standing Committees

### Consumer Affairs & Protection
Chair:
Nily Rozic (D, WF) . . . . . . . . . . . . . . . . . . . . . . . . .518-455-4545

### Corporations, Authorities & Commissions
Chair:
Amy Paulin (D) . . . . . . . . . . . . . . . . . . . . . . . . . . . .518-455-5585

### Ethics & Guidance
Chair:
Vacant . . . . . . . . . . . . . . . . . . . . . . . . . . . . . . . . . .518-455-5014

### Governmental Operations
Chair:
Michele R. Titus (D) . . . . . . . . . . . . . . . . . . . . . . . .518-455-5668

### Oversight, Analysis & Investigation

### Rules
Chair:
Carl E Heastie (D) . . . . . . . . . . . . . . .518-455-3791/fax: 518-455-4812

### Ways & Means
Chair:
Helene E Weinstein (D) . . . . . . . . . . . . . . . . . . . . . .518-455-5462

## Assembly Task Forces & Caucus

### State-Federal Relations Task Force
Chair:
Vacant . . . . . . . . . . . . . . . . . . . . . . . . . . . . . . . . . .518-455-5172
Program Manager:
Robert Stern . . . . . . . . . . . . . . . . . . . . . . . . . . . . . .518-455-3632

## Senate Standing Committees

### Civil Service & Pensions
Chair:
Andrew Gounardes (D) . . . . . . . . . . . . . . . . . . . . . . .518-455-3270

### Consumer Protection
Chair:
Kevin Thomas (D) . . . . . . . . . . . . . . . . . . . . . . . . . .518-455-3260
Minority Member:
James Tedisco (R, C) . . . . . . . . . . . . . . . . . . . . . . . .518-455-2181

### Corporations, Authorities & Commissions
Chair:
Leroy Comrie (D) . . . . . . . . . . . . . . . . . . . . . . . . . .518-455-2701

### Ethics
Chair:
Alessandra Biaggi (D, WF) . . . . . . . . . . . . . . . . . . . .518-455-3595
Ranking Minority Member:
Catharine Young (R, C, IP) . . . . . . . . . . . . . . . . . . . .518-455-3563

### Finance
Chair:
Liz Krueger (D, WF) . . . . . . . . . . . . . . . . . . . . . . . . .518-455-2297
Ranking Minority Member:
Thomas F O'Mara (R, C, IP)

### Investigations & Government Operations
Chair:
James Skoufis (D) . . . . . . . . . . . . . . . . . . . . . . . . . .518-455-3290

### Rules
Chair:
Andrea Stewart-Cousins (D/IP/WF) . . . . . . . . . . . . . . .518-455-2585
Ranking Minority Leader:
Robert G Ortt (R, C, IP)

## Senate/Assembly Legislative Commissions

### Government Administration, Legislative Commission on
Assembly Chair:
Brian Kavanagh (D, WF) . . . . . . . . . . . . . . . . . . . . .518-455-5506
Senate Vice Chair:
Vacant . . . . . . . . . . . . . . . . . . . . . . . . . . . . . . . . . .518-455-0000

## AMERICAN INDIAN TRIBES

## Cayuga Nation of New York

2540 SR-89
PO Box 803
Seneca Falls, NY 13148
315-568-0750  Fax: 315-568-0752
Web site: www.cayuganation-nsn.gov

Federal Representative:
Clint Halftown

## Oneida Indian Nation

2037 Dream Catcher Plaza
Oneida, NY 13421

*Offices and agencies generally appear in alphabetical order, except when specific order is requested by listee.*

315-829-8900 or 800-685-6115  Fax: 315-829-8958
e-mail: info@oneida-nation.org
Web site: www.oneidaindiannation.com

Nation Repesentative:
  Ray Halbritter

## Onondaga Nation
3951 Route 11
Nedrow, NY 13120
315-492-1922  Fax: 315-469-4717
Web site: www.onondaganation.org

Chief:
  Sidney Hill

## Seneca Nation of Indians
William Seneca Building
12837 Route 438
Irving, NY 14081
716-532-4900
e-mail: sni@sni.org
Web site: www.sni.org

President:
  Maurice A John, Sr

## Shinnecock Indian Nation
PO Box 5006
Southampton, NY 11969-5006
631-283-6143 or 631-287-3752  Fax: 631-283-0751
e-mail: sination@optonline.net

Chairperson:
  Daniel Collins, Sr.
Director of Communications:
  Beverly Jensen
  e-mail: nationsvoice@shinnecock.org

## Saint Regis Mohawk Tribe
71 Margaret Terrace Memorial Way
Akwesasne, NY 13655
518-358-2272  Fax: 518-358-3203
Web site: www.srmt-nsn.gov

Tribal Chief:
  Beverly Cook . . . . . . . . . . . . . . . . . . . . . . . . . . . .518-358-2272
Tribal Chief:
  Eric Thompson . . . . . . . . . . . . . . . . . . . . . . . . . . .518-258-2272
Tribal Chief:
  Michael Conners. . . . . . . . . . . . . . . . . . . . . . . . . .518-258-2272

## Unkechaug Nation
Poospatuck Reservation
PO Box 86
Mastic, NY 11950
631-281-6464 or 631-281-4143  Fax: 631-281-2125
e-mail: hwal1@aol.com
Web site: http://unkechaug.wordpress.com/

Chief:
  Harry Wallace

## U.S. GOVERNMENT

### EXECUTIVE DEPARTMENTS AND RELATED AGENCIES

**New York Regional Office** . . . . . . . . . . . . . . . . . . . . .fax: 212-352-5441
  201 Varick Street, Suite 1025, New York, NY 10014
  855-855-1961 or 212-352-5440  Fax: 212-352-5441
  e-mail: nyinfo@peacecorps.gov
  Web site: www.peacecorps.gov
Regional Recruitment Supervisor:
  Anthony Trujillo . . . . . . . . . . . . . . . . . . . . . . . . . . .212-352-5440
Public Affairs Specialist:
  Elizabeth Chamberlain . . . . . . . . . . . . . . . . . . . . . . . .774-330-9200
  e-mail: echamberlain@peacecorps.gov

## US Department of Homeland Security (DHS)
Web site: www.dhs.gov

### Bureau of Immigration & Customs Enforcement (ICE)
500 12th St  SW, Washington, DC 20536
Web site: www.ice.gov

**New York District Office** . . . . . . . . . . . . . . . . . . . . . .fax: 646-230-3255
  601 West 26th Street, 7th Floor, New York, NY 10001
  646-230-3200  Fax: 646-230-3255
  Special Agent-in-Charge:
  Raymond R. Parmer Jr.
  ***Buffalo Office*** . . . . . . . . . . . . . . . . . . . . . . . . . . .fax: 716-565-9509
    1780 Wehrle Drive, Suite D, Williamsville, NY 14221
    716-565-2039  Fax: 716-565-9509
    Special Agent-in-Charge:
    James C. Spero

### Customs & Border Protection (CBP)
202-325-8000 or 877-227-5511
Web site: www.cbp.gov

**Agriculture Inspections (AI)**
  ***Buffalo, Port of***
    726 Exchange Street, Suite 400, Buffalo, NY 14210
    Supervisory CBP Officer:
      Gary Friedman . . . . . . . . . . . . . . . . . . . . . . . . . . .716-843-8300
  ***Champlain, Port of*** . . . . . . . . . . . . . . . . . . . . . . .fax: 518-298-8395
    237 West Service Road, Champlain, NY 12919
    518-298-8311  Fax: 518-298-8395
    Port Director:
      Paul Mongillo . . . . . . . . . . . . . .518-298-8311/fax: 518-298-8395
  ***JFK International Airport Area Office*** . . . . . . . . . . .fax: 718-487-5191
    JFK International Airport, Building 77, 2nd Floor, Jamaica, NY
    11430
    718-487-5164  Fax: 718-487-5191
    Public Affairs Officer:
      Anthony Bucci . . . . . . . . . . . . . . . . . . . . . . . . . . .646-733-3275

**Buffalo Field Office**
300 Airborne Parkway, Suite 300, Buffalo, NY 14225
716-626-0400
Acting Director:
  Rose Hilmey . . . . . . . . . . . . . . . . . . . . . . . . . . . . .716-626-0400
  ***Albany, Port of*** . . . . . . . . . . . . . . . . . . . . . . . . . .fax: 518-431-0203
    445 Broadway, Room 216, Albany, NY 12207
    518-431-0200  Fax: 518-431-0203
    Port Director:
      Andrew Wescott
  ***Alexandria Bay, Port of*** . . . . . . . . . . . . . . . . . . . .fax: 315-482-5304
    46735 Interstate Route 81, Alexandria Bay, NY 13607
    315-482-2065  Fax: 315-482-5304
    Supervisory CBP Officer:
      Darren Erwin . . . . . . . . . . . . . . . . . . . . . . . . . . .315-482-2681
  ***Binghamton, Port of***
    2534 Airport Road, Box 4, Johnson City, NY 13790

*Offices and agencies generally appear in alphabetical order, except when specific order is requested by listee.*

607-763-4294
***Buffalo, Port of***
726 Exchange Street, Suite 400, Buffalo, NY 14210
716-843-8300
Supervisory CBP Officer:
Gary Friedman . . . . . . . . . . . . . . . . . . . . . . . . . . . . .716-843-8300
***Champlain, Port of*** . . . . . . . . . . . . . . . . . . . . . . .fax: 518-298-8395
237 West Service Road, Champlain, NY 12919
518-298-8311  Fax: 518-298-8395
Area Port Director:
Paul Mongillo . . . . . . . . . . . . . . . . . . . . . . . . . . .518-298-8311
***Massena, Port of***
30M Seaway International Bridge, Rooseveltown, NY 13683
315-769-3091
Tribal Liaison Officer:
Tracey S. Casey . . . . . . . . . . . . . . . . . . . . . . . . . . .315-769-3091
***Ogdensburg, Port of***
104 Bridge Approach Road, Ogdensburg, NY 13669
Port Director:
Wade Davis . . . . . . . . . . . . . . . . . . . . . . . . . . . . .313-393-1390
***Rochester, Port of*** . . . . . . . . . . . . . . . . . . . . . .fax: 585-263-5828
1200 Brooks Avenue, Rochester, NY 14624
585-263-6293  Fax: 585-263-5828
Port Director:
Ronald Menz . . . . . . . . . . . . . . . . . . . . . . . . . . . . .585-263-6293
***Rome, Port of***
650 Hanger Road, Rome, NY 13441
315-356-4731
***Syracuse, Port of***
152 Air Cargo Road, Suite 201, Syracuse, NY 13212
315-455-8446
Port Director:
David Harris. . . . . . . . . . . . . . . . . . . . . . . . . . . . . .315-455-8446
***Trout River, Port of*** . . . . . . . . . . . . . . . . . . . . .fax: 518-483-3717
17013 State Route 30, Constable, NY 12926
518-483-0821  Fax: 518-483-3717

**New York Field Office**. . . . . . . . . . . . . . . . . . . . . . .fax: 646-733-3245
1 World Trade Center, Suite 50.200, New York, NY 10007
646-733-3100  Fax: 646-733-3245
Director, Field Operations:
Robert E. Perez
Public Affairs Specialist:
Anthony Bucci . . . . . . . . . . . . . . . . . . . . . . . . . . . . .646-733-3275
***Field Counsel - New York***
Deputy Associate Chief Counsel:
Colleen Piccone
***Laboratory Division***
Director:
Laura W. Goldstein . . . . . . . . . . . . . . . . . . . . . . . .973-368-1900

**National Urban Security Technology Laboratory**
201 Varick Street, 5th Floor, New York, NY 10014
Director:
Dr. Adam Hutter

**Administration**
Director:
Alfred Crescenzi

**Systems Division**
Director:
Lawrence Ruth . . . . . . . . . . . . . . . . . . . . . . . . . . . . .212-620-3609
e-mail: lawrence.ruth@dhs.gov

**Testbeds Division**
Acting Director:
Lawrence Ruth

**Federal Emergency Management Agency (FEMA)**
TTY: 800-462-7585 or 202-646-2500
Web site: www.fema.gov

**New York Regional Office**
26 Federal Plaza, New York, NY 10278-0002
212-680-3600
Regional Administrator:
Jerome Hatfield

**Federal Protective Service (The)**
26 Federal Plaza, Room 17-130, New York, NY 10278
Director:
L. Eric Patterson

**Plum Island Animal Disease Center**
PO Box 848, Greenport, NY 11944
Director:
Larry Barrett

**Transportation Security Administration (TSA)**
75-20 Astoria Blvd, Suite 300, East Elmhurst, NY 11370
718-426-1350
Regional Spokesperson:
Lisa Farbstein

**US Citizenship & Immigration Services (USCIS)**
TTY: 800-767-1833 or 800-375-5283
Web site: www.uscis.gov

**Buffalo District Office**. . . . . . . . . . . . . . . . . . . . . .fax: 716-551-3131
Federal Center, 306 Delaware Avenue, Buffalo, NY 14202
District Director:
Edward A. Newman . . . . . . . . . . . . . . . . . . . . . . . .716-843-7900
***Albany Field Office***
1086 Troy-Schenectady Road, Latham, NY 12110
Field Office Director:
Gwynne Dinolfo

**CIS Asylum Offices**
***New York Asylum Office***
1065 Stewart Avenue, Suite 200, Bethpage, NY 11714
516-261-0000
Director:
Patricia Menges . . . . . . . . . . . . . . . . . . . . . . . . . .516-261-0000
Deputy Director:
Ashley Caudill-Mirillo
***Newark Asylum Office-Including NYS not served by New York City***
1200 Wall Street West, 4th Floor, Lyndhurst, NJ 07071
201-508-6100
Director:
Susan Raufer . . . . . . . . . . . . . . . . . . . . . . . . . . . .201-531-0555
Deputy Director:
Sunil R. Varghese

**New York City District Office**
Jacob K. Javits Federal Building, 26 Federal Plaza, Room 3-120, New
York, NY 10278
District Director:
Phyllis Coven
***Long Island Field Office***
30 Barretts Avenue, Holtsville, NY 11742
Field Office Director:
Elizabeth Miller
***Queens Field Office***
26 Federal Plaza, Room 8-100, New York, NY 10278
Field Office Director:
Bryan P. Christian

**US General Services Administration**
1800 F Street NW
Washington, DC 20405
Web site: www.gsa.gov

*Offices and agencies generally appear in alphabetical order, except when specific order is requested by listee.*

## Region 2—New York

1 World Trade Center, 55th Floor, Room 55W09, New York, NY 10007-0089
212-264-3305
e-mail: r2contact@gsa.gov
Regional Administrator:
  Denise L. Pease...................................212-264-2600
    e-mail: denise.pease@gsa.gov
Special Assistant to the Regional Administrator:
  Dawne Troupe....................................212-264-2041
Human Resources Officer:
  Maureen Gannon.................................215-446-4963
    e-mail: maureen.gannon@gsa.gov
Regional Counsel:
  Carol Latterman ................................212-264-8308
    e-mail: carol.latterman@gsa.gov

### Federal Acquisition Service

FAS Regional Commissioner:
  Gregory Hammond...............................212-264-3590
Director, Supply & Acquisition Center:
  Peter Han ........................................212-264-6949
    e-mail: peter.han@gsa.gov
Director, Fleet Management Services Division:
  Brian Smith......................................212-264-3930
    e-mail: brian.smith@gsa.gov
Director, Customer Accounts & Research Division:
  Frank Mayer.....................................212-264-1179
    e-mail: frank.mayer@gsa.gov
Director, Personal Property Division:
  Christina Shaw ..................................215-446-5083
    e-mail: christina.shaw@gsa.gov
Acting Director, Network Services Division:
  Theresa Ramos ..................................212-264-2690
    e-mail: theresa.ramos@gsa.gov
Director, Assisted Acquisition Services Division:
  Joann Lee ........................................212-264-1885
    e-mail: joann.lee@gsa.gov

### Inspector General's Office

Regional Director, Audit:
  Steve Jurysta....................................212-264-8620

### Public Buildings Service

PBS Regional Commissioner:
  Frank Santella...................................212-264-4282
    e-mail: frank.santella@gsa.gov
Director, Project Management Division:
  Ken Chin.........................................212-264-0802
    e-mail: ken.chin@gsa.gov
Director, Leasing Division:
  Warren Hall......................................212-264-4241
    e-mail: warren.hall@gsa.gov
Director, Facilities Management & Services Program Division:
  David Segermeister .............................212-264-4273
    e-mail: david.segermeister@gsa.gov
Director, Portfolio Management Division:
  Vincent Scalcione...............................212-264-1547
    e-mail: vincent.scalcione@gsa.gov

## US Government Printing Office

e-mail: infonewyork@gpo.gov
Web site: www.gpo.gov

### Region 2-I (New York)

Printing Procurement Office ................... fax: 212-264-2413
26 Federal Plaza, Room 2930, New York, NY 10278
212-264-2252  Fax: 212-264-2413
Manager:
  Debra Rozdzielski

## US Postal Service

Web site: www.usps.com

### NORTHEAST AREA (Includes part of New York State)

6 Griffin Road North, Windsor, CT 06006-7070
800-275-8777
Vice President, Delivery Operations:
  Edward F. Phelan Jr.

## US State Department

Web site: www.state.gov

### Bureau of Educational & Cultural Affairs-NY Pgm Branch

666 Fifth Avenue, Suite 603, New York, NY 10103
212-399-5750
Director:
  Donna F. Shirreffs...............................212-399-5750

## US Mission to the United Nations

799 UN Plaza, New York, NY 10017
US Permanent Representative to the United Nations:
  Samantha Power
US Deputy Permanent Representative to the United Nations:
  Michele J. Sison
Alternate Representative for Special Political Affairs to the United Nations:
  David Pressman
US Representative on the Economic & Social Council at the United Nations:
  Sarah Mendelson
US Representative to the United Nations for UN Management & Reform:
  Isobel Coleman

## U.S. CONGRESS

*See U.S. Congress Chapter for additional Standing Committee and Subcommittee information.*

## House of Representatives Standing Committees

### Oversight & Government Reform

Chair:
  Jason Chaffetz (R-UT) ..........................202-225-7751
Ranking Member:
  Elijah Cummings (D-MD) ......................202-225-4741
New York Delegate:
  Carolyn B. Maloney (D)..........................202-225-7944

### Homeland Security

Chair:
  Michael McCaul (R-TX) .........................202-225-2401
Ranking Member:
  Bennie G. Thompson (D-MS) ...................202-225-5876
New York Delegate:
  Brian Higgins (D) ...............................202-225-3306
New York Delegate:
  Kathleen M. Rice (D) ............................202-225-5516
New York Delegate:
  Peter T. King (R)................................202-225-7896
New York Delegate:
  John Katko (R) ..................................202-225-3701
New York Delegate:
  Dan Donovan (R) ...............................202-225-3371

#### Subcommittees

*Emergency Preparedness, Response and Communications*
  Chair:
    Dan Donovan (R-NY) .......................202-225-3371
  Ranking Member:
    Donald M. Payne (D-NJ)....................202-225-3436

*Offices and agencies generally appear in alphabetical order, except when specific order is requested by listee.*

*Cybersecurity, Infrastructure Protection, and Security Technologies*
Chair:
John Ratcliffe (R-TX) . . . . . . . . . . . . . . . . . . . . . . .202-225-6673
Ranking Member:
Cedric L. Richmond (D-LA) . . . . . . . . . . . . . . . .202-225-6636
*Counterterrorism & Intelligence*
Chair:
Peter T. King (R-NY) . . . . . . . . . . . . . . . . . . . . .202-225-7896
Ranking Member:
Brian Higgins (D-NY) . . . . . . . . . . . . . . . . . . . . .202-225-3306
*Oversight & Management Efficiency*
Chair:
Scott Perry (R-PA) . . . . . . . . . . . . . . . . . . . . . . . .202-225-5836
Ranking Member:
Bonnie Watson Coleman (D-NJ) . . . . . . . . . . . . .202-225-5801
*Transportation Security*
Chair:
John Katko (R-NY) . . . . . . . . . . . . . . . . . . . . . . .202-225-3701
Ranking Member:
Kathleen M. Rice (D-NY) . . . . . . . . . . . . . . . . . .202-225-5516

## Intelligence, Permanent Select Committee on
Chair:
Devin Nunes (R-CA) . . . . . . . . . . . . . . . . . . . . . .202-225-2523
Ranking Member:
Adam Schiff (D-CA) . . . . . . . . . . . . . . . . . . . . . .202-225-4176

### Subcommittee
*Emerging Threats*
Chair:
Tom Rooney (R-FL) . . . . . . . . . . . . . . . . . . . . . .202-225-5792
Ranking Member:
Mike Quigley (D-IL) . . . . . . . . . . . . . . . . . . . . . .202-225-4061

## Ethics
Chair:
Charles W. Dent (R-PA) . . . . . . . . . . . . . . . . . . .202-225-6411
Ranking Member:
Linda T. Sanchez (D-CA) . . . . . . . . . . . . . . . . . .202-225-6676

# Senate Standing Committees

## Ethics, Select Committee on
Chair:
Johnny Isakson (R-GA) . . . . . . . . . . . . . . . . . . . .202-224-3643
Vice Chair:
Barbara Boxer (D-CA) . . . . . . . . . . . . . . . . . . . .202-224-3553

## Homeland Security & Governmental Affairs
Chair:
Ron Johnson (R-WI) . . . . . . . . . . . . . . . . . . . . . .202-224-5323
Ranking Member:
Thomas R. Carper (D-DE) . . . . . . . . . . . . . . . . .202-224-2441

## Indian Affairs, Committee on
Chair:
John Barrasso (R-WY) . . . . . . . . . . . . . . . . . . . .202-224-6441
Vice Chair:
Jon Tester (D-MT) . . . . . . . . . . . . . . . . . . . . . . .202-224-2644

## Intelligence, Select Committee on
Chair:
Richard Burr (R-NC) . . . . . . . . . . . . . . . . . . . . .202-224-3154
Vice Chair:
Dianne Feinstein (D-CA) . . . . . . . . . . . . . . . . . .202-224-3841

## Judiciary
Chair:
Chuck Grassley (R-IA) . . . . . . . . . . . . . . . . . . . .202-224-3744
Ranking Member:
Patrick Leahy (D-VT) . . . . . . . . . . . . . . . . . . . . .202-224-4242

New York Delegate:
Charles E. Schumer (D) . . . . . . . . . . . . . . . . . . . .202-224-6542
**Subcommittees**
*Crime & Terrorism*
Chair:
Lindsey Graham (R-SC) . . . . . . . . . . . . . . . . . . .202-224-5972
Ranking Member:
Sheldon Whitehouse (D-RI) . . . . . . . . . . . . . . . .202-224-2921
*Immigration and The National Interest*
Chair:
Jeff Sessions (R-AL) . . . . . . . . . . . . . . . . . . . . . .202-224-4124
Ranking Member:
Charles E. Schumer (D-NY) . . . . . . . . . . . . . . . .202-224-6542

## PRIVATE SECTOR

### Academy of Political Science
475 Riverside Drive, Suite 1274, New York, NY 10115-1274
212-870-2500  Fax: 212-870-2202
e-mail: aps@psqonline.org
Web site: www.psqonline.org
*Analysis of government, economic & social issues*
Demetrios James Caraley, President

### Albany Law School, Government Law Center
80 New Scotland Avenue, Albany, NY 12208-3494
518-445-2311
e-mail: rbres@albanylaw.edu
Web site: www.albanylaw.edu
*Legal aspects of public policy reform*
Ray Brescia, Director, Government Law Center & Associate Professor of
Law

### Association of Government Accountants, NY Capital Chapter
PO Box 1923, Albany, NY 12201
Web site: www.aganycap.org
*Education for the government financial management community*
Jamie Cote, Chapter President

### Center for Governmental Research Inc (CGR)
1 South Washington Street, Suite 400, Rochester, NY 14614-1135
585-325-6360  Fax: 888-388-8521
e-mail: info@cgr.org
Web site: www.cgr.org
*Nonprofit institution devoted to providing policy analysis in the areas of
government, education, economics, public finance, health & human services*
Dr. Joseph Stefko, President & Chief Executive Officer

### Center for Technology in Government, University at Albany, SUNY
187 Wolf Road, Suite 301, Albany, NY 12205-1138
518-442-3892  Fax: 518-442-3886
e-mail: info@ctg.albany.edu
Web site: www.ctg.albany.edu
*Works to enhance the quality of government & public services through
research, partnership projects & the development of innovative strategies in
technology, policy & management*
Theresa Pardo, Director

### Citizens Union of the City of New York
299 Broadway, Suite 700, New York, NY 10007-1978
212-227-0342  Fax: 212-227-0345
e-mail: citizens@citizensunion.org
Web site: www.citizensunion.org
*Government watchdog organization; city & state public policy issues;
political & government reform*
Dick Dadey, Executive Director

*Offices and agencies generally appear in alphabetical order, except when specific order is requested by listee.*

## Coalition of Fathers & Families NY, PAC
PO Box 252, Stillwater, NY 12170
518-288-6755
e-mail: info@fafny.org
Web site: www.fafny.org
*Political action for fathers & families in New York*
Jack Frost, President

## Columbia University, Exec Graduate Pgm in Public Policy & Administration
420 West 118th Street, Room 1408, New York, NY 10027
212-854-4445  Fax: 212-864-3748
e-mail: sc32@columbia.edu
Web site: www.sipa.columbia.edu
*Urban & environmental policy; public management*
Steven Cohen, Director, Program in Environmental Science & Policy

## Common Cause/NY
80 Broad Street, New York, NY 10004
212-691-6421  Fax: 212-807-1809
e-mail: nyoffice@commoncause.org
Web site: www.commoncause.org/states/new-york/
*Campaign finance reform, ballot access, political gift disclosure & public interest lobbying*
Susan Lerner, Executive Director

## NYS Bar Assn, Task Force to Review Terrorism Legislation Cmte
## Connors LLP
1000 Liberty Building, 424 Main Street, Buffalo, NY 14202-3510
716-852-5533  Fax: 716-852-5649
Web site: www.connorsllp.com
Vincent E. Doyle, III, Partner

## Council of State Governments, Eastern Conference
22 Cortlandt Street, 22nd Floor, New York, NY 10007
212-482-2320  Fax: 212-482-2344
e-mail: info_erc@csg.org
Web site: www.csg-erc.org
*Training, research & information sharing for state government officials*
Wendell Hannaford, Regional Director

## Crane & Parente, PLLC
48 Howard Street, Albany, NY 12207
518-432-8000
*Governmental relations, banking & financial services, corporate law, construction law, energy, utilities, communications, land use, environmental & wireless telecommunications law*
James B. Crane, II, Managing Member

## DeGraff, Foy & Kunz, LLP
41 State Street, Albany, NY 12207
518-462-5300  Fax: 518-436-0210
e-mail: inquiry@dfklawfirm.com
Web site: www.degraff-foy.com
*Government relations, administrative law & tax exempt/municipal financing, education, energy, transportation, public authorities & the environment*
David F. Kunz, Managing Partner

## Fiscal Policy Institute
1 Lear Jet Lane, Latham, NY 12110
518-786-3156  Fax: 518-786-3146
e-mail: deutsch@fiscalpolicy.org
Web site: www.fiscalpolicy.org
*Nonpartisan research & education; tax, budget, economic & related public policy issues that affect quality of life & economic well-being*
Ron Deutsch, Executive Director
Kendra Moses, Operations Manager
David Kallick, Deputy Director & Director of Immigration Research

## Fordham University, Department of Political Science
441 East Fordham Road, Bronx, NY 10458
718-817-3964
e-mail: rhume@fordham.edu
Web site: www.fordham.edu
*American politics & political theory; importance of gender in understanding modes of governance; campaign management*
Dr. Robert J. Hume, Department Chair

## Geto & de Milly Inc
276 Fifth Avenue, Suite 806, New York, NY 10001
212-686-4551  Fax: 212-213-6850
e-mail: pr@getodemilly.com
Web site: www.getodemilly.com
*Public & government relations*
Ethan Geto, President

## NYS Bar Assn, Legislative Policy Cmte
## Greenberg Traurig, LLP
54 State Street, 6th Floor, Albany, NY 12207
518-689-1400  Fax: 518-689-1499
e-mail: info@gtlaw.com
Web site: www.gtlaw.com
Henry M. Greenberg, Partner

## Institute of Public Administration/NYU Wagner
295 Lafayette Street, 2nd Floor, New York, NY 10012-9604
212-998-7400
e-mail: wagner.officeofthedean@nyu.edu
*Public policy & public service research, consulting & educational institute*
Sherry Glied, Dean & Professor of Public Service

## KPMG LLP
515 Broadway, Albany, NY 12207-2974
518-427-4600  Fax: 518-689-4717
e-mail: us-mktwebmaster@kpmg.com
Web site: www.kpmg.com
*State & local government audit & advisory service*
Nancy Valley, Managing Partner

## League of Women Voters of New York State
62 Grand Street, Albany, NY 12207-2712
518-465-4162  Fax: 518-465-0812
e-mail: laura@lwvny.org
Web site: www.lwvny.org
*Public policy issues forum; good government advocacy*
Laura Ladd Bierman, Executive Director

## Manhattan Institute for Policy Research
52 Vanderbilt Avenue, 2nd Floor, New York, NY 10017
212-599-7000  Fax: 212-599-3494
e-mail: communications@manhattan-institute.org
Web site: www.manhattan-institute.org
*Produces & promotes research on taxes, welfare, education & other public policy issues*
Lawrence J. Mone, President

## NYS Bar Assn, Court Structure & Judicial Selection Cmte
## McMahon & Grow
301 North Washington Street, PO Box 4350, Rome, NY 13442-4350
315-336-4700  Fax: 315-336-5851
e-mail: rsimons@mgglaw.com
Web site: www.mgglaw.com
*Retired Judge-NYS Court of Appeals*
Hon Richard D. Simons, Chair

---

*Offices and agencies generally appear in alphabetical order, except when specific order is requested by listee.*

**NYS Bar Assn, Federal Constitution & Legislation Cmte**
**Mulholland & Knapp, LLP**
110 East 42nd Street, Suite 1302, New York, NY 10017
212-702-9027  Fax: 212-702-9092
e-mail: admin@mklex.com
Web site: www.mklex.com
Robert P. Knapp, III, Chair

**NY Coalition of 100 Black Women - Not For Profit**
PO Box 2555, Grand Central Station, New York, NY 10163
212-517-5700
*Leadership by example; advocates & agents for change; improving the quality of life by focusing resources in education, health & community services*
Avalyn Simon, President

**NY StateWatch Inc**
126 State Street, 4th Floor, Albany, NY 12207
518-449-7425
e-mail: mikep@statewatch.com
Web site: www.nystatewatch.net
*Legislative information service; bill tracking*
Michael Poulopoulos, Director

**NYS Association of Counties**
540 Broadway, 5th Floor, Albany, NY 12207
518-465-1473  Fax: 518-465-0506
Web site: www.nysac.org
*Lobbying, research & training services*
Stephen J. Acquario, Executive Director

**NYS Bar Assn, Mass Disaster Response Committee**
**NYS Grievance Committee**
Renaissance Plaza, 335 Adams Street, Suite 2400, Brooklyn, NY 11201-3745
718-923-6300  Fax: 718-624-2978

**NYS Bar Assn, Law Youth & Citizenship Committee**
**NYS Supreme Court**
92 Franklin Street, 2nd Floor, Buffalo, NY 14202
716-845-9327  Fax: 716-851-5163
Oliver C. Young, Principal Court Attorney

**Nelson A Rockefeller Institute of Government**
411 State Street, Albany, NY 12203-1003
518-443-5522  Fax: 518-443-5788
e-mail: info@rockinst.suny.edu
Web site: www.rockinst.org
*Management & finance, welfare, social services, health, education, homeland security & public safety at state & local levels of government*
Thomas L. Gais, Director

**New York Public Interest Research Group**
9 Murray Street, Lower Level, New York, NY 10007
212-349-6460  Fax: 212-349-1366
*Environmental preservation, public health, consumer protection & government reform*
Blair Horner, Executive Director

**New York State Directory**
4919 Route 22, PO Box 56, Amenia, NY 12501
518-789-8700 or 800-562-2139  Fax: 518-789-0556
e-mail: books@greyhouse.com
Web site: www.greyhouse.com
*State government public policy directory*
Leslie Mackenzie, Publisher

**Pioneer Savings Bank**
21 Second Street, Troy, NY 12180
518-687-5400  Fax: 518-274-1060
Web site: www.pioneerbanking.com
Thomas L. Amell, President & Chief Executive Officer

**PricewaterhouseCoopers LLP**
726 Exchange Street, Suite 1010, Buffalo, NY 14210-1484
716-856-4650  Fax: 716-856-1208
Web site: www.pwc.com
Mark Ross, Managing Partner

**Spec Cmte on Collateral Consequence of Criminal Proceedings**
**Proskauer Rose LLP**
11 Times Square, New York, NY 10036
212-969-3000  Fax: 212-969-2900
e-mail: info@proskauer.com
Web site: www.proskauer.com
Peter J.W. Sherwin, Partner

**Public Agenda**
6 East 39th Street, 9th Floor, New York, NY 10016
212-686-6610  Fax: 212-889-3461
e-mail: info@publicagenda.org
Web site: www.publicagenda.org
*Nonpartisan, nonprofit organization dedicated to conducting unbiased public opinion research & producing fair-minded citizen education materials*
Will Friedman, President

**SUNY at Albany, Center for Women in Government & Civil Society**
135 Western Avenue, Draper Hall, Room 302, Albany, NY 12222
518-442-3900  Fax: 518-442-3877
e-mail: cwgcs@albany.edu
Web site: www.cwig.albany.edu
*Works to strengthen women's public policy leadership & advance equality in government, nonprofit & business sectors through education, research, leadership development & advocacy for equitable policies & practices*
Dina Refki, Executive Director

**SUNY at Albany, Rockefeller College**
135 Western Avenue, Albany, NY 12222
518-442-5244  Fax: 518-442-5298
e-mail: hildreth@albany.edu
Web site: www.albany.edu/rockefeller
*Intergovernmental relations; NY state & local government; ethics in government; election systems & voting*
Anne Hildreth, Associate Professor

**SUNY at New Paltz, College of Liberal Arts & Sciences**
1 Hawk Drive, New Paltz, NY 12561-2499
845-257-7869 or 877-696-7411
e-mail: barrettl@newpaltz.edu
Web site: www.newpaltz.edu
*Local & state government process & structure; regionalism; politics & election law*
Laura Barrett, Dean

**SUNY at New Paltz, Department of History**
600 Hawk Drive, New Paltz, NY 12561-2440
845-257-3545  Fax: 845-257-2735
Web site: www.newpaltz.edu/history/
*Historical studies of legal systems, economic & business institutions, technology, cultures & societies*
Andrew Evans, Chair

**Syracuse University, Maxwell School of Citizenship & Public Affairs**
200 Eggers Hall, Syracuse, NY 13244-1020
315-443-2252
e-mail: info@maxwell.syr.edu
Web site: www.maxwell.syr.edu
*Education, healthcare, entrpreneurship policies, social welfare, income distribution & comparative social policies*
James B. Steinberg, Dean

*Offices and agencies generally appear in alphabetical order, except when specific order is requested by listee.*

# HEALTH

## NEW YORK STATE

### GOVERNOR'S OFFICE

## Governor's Office
Executive Chamber
State Capitol
Albany, NY 12224
518-474-8390  Fax: 518-474-1513
Web site: www.ny.gov

Governor:
    Andrew M Cuomo . . . . . . . . . . . . . . . . . . . . . . . . . . . . . . 518-474-8390
Secretary to the Governor:
    Melissa DeRosa . . . . . . . . . . . . . . . . . . . . 518-474-4246 or 212-681-4580
Counsel to the Governor:
    Kumiki Gibson . . . . . . . . . . . . . . . . 518-474-8343 or 212-681-4580
Deputy Secretary, Health & Human Services:
    Richard Beker . . . . . . . . . . . . . . . . . . . 518-408-2500 or 212-681-4580
Chief of Staff:
    Jill DesRosiers . . . . . . . . . . . . . . . . . . . . 518-474-8390 or 212-681-4580
Director, Communications:
    Peter Ajemian . . . . . . . . . . . . . . . . . . . . 518-474-8418 or 212-681-4640

### EXECUTIVE DEPARTMENTS AND RELATED AGENCIES

## Alcoholism & Substance Abuse Services, Office of
1450 Western Avenue
Albany, NY 12203-3526
518-473-3460
e-mail: communications@oasas.ny.gov
Web site: www.oasas.ny.gov

501 7th Avenue
8th Floor
New York, NY 10018-5903
646-728-4533

Commissioner:
    Arlene González-Sánchez. . . . . . . . . . . . . . . . . . . . . . . 518-457-2061
Executive Deputy Commissioner:
    Sean M Byrne . . . . . . . . . . . . . . . . . . . . . . . . . . . . . . . 518-485-2337

### Office of Public Information & Communications
Director:
    Edison Alban

### Office of Counsel & Internal Controls
Chief Counsel, Office of Counsel & Internal Controls:
    Robert Kent. . . . . . . . . . . . . . . . . . . . . . . . . . . . . . . 518-485-2312
Office of Audit Services:
    Steven Shrager . . . . . . . . . . . . . . . . . . . . . . . . . . . . . 518-485-2053
Internal Control Unit:
    Sandra Scleicher. . . . . . . . . . . . . . . . . . . . . . . . . . . . 518-485-1109
Associate Commissioner, Division of Prevention & Problem Gambling
    Services:
    Patricia Zuber-Wilson. . . . . . . . . . . . . . . . . . . . . . . . 518-485-1484
Chief Operating Officer:
    Ramon Rodriguez. . . . . . . . . . . . . . . . . . . . . . . . . . . 646-728-4720
Director:
    Manuel Mosquera. . . . . . . . . . . . . . . . . . . . . . . . . . . 646-728-4720
Affirmative Action Unit Officer:
    Loretta Poole. . . . . . . . . . . . . . . . . . . . . . . . . . . . . . 646-728-4530

## Office of the Medical Director
Director, Office of the Medical Director:
    Vacant. . . . . . . . . . . . . . . . . . . . . . . . . . . . . . . . . . 845-359-8500
Director, Health Initiatives:
    Peggy Bonneau . . . . . . . . . . . . . . . . . . . . . . . . . . . . 518-457-5989

## Fiscal Administration Division
Associate Commissioner:
    Vittoria Parry . . . . . . . . . . . . . . . . . . . . . . . . . . . . . 518-457-5312

### Bureau of Budget Management
Director:
    Tara Gabriel . . . . . . . . . . . . . . . . . . . . . . . . . . . . . . 518-485-2193

### Bureau of Capital Management
Director:
    Jeff Emad . . . . . . . . . . . . . . . . . . . . . . . . . . . . . . . 518-457-2545

### Bureau of Financial Management
Director:
    Kevin Doherty . . . . . . . . . . . . . . . . . . . . . . . . . . . . 518-457-3562

### Bureau of Health Care Financing & 3rd Party Reimbursement
Director:
    Laurie Felter. . . . . . . . . . . . . . . . . . . . . . . . . . . . . . 518-457-5312

## Outcome Management & System Information Division
Associate Commissioner:
    William F. Hogan . . . . . . . . . . . . . . . . . . . . . . . . . . 518-485-2322

### Bureau of State/Local Planning
Director:
    Vacant. . . . . . . . . . . . . . . . . . . . . . . . . . . . . . . . . 518-485-2322

### Bureau of Data Analysis, Data Quality & Evaluation
Director:
    Vacant. . . . . . . . . . . . . . . . . . . . . . . . . . . . . . . . . 518-485-7189

### Bureau of Research, Epidemiology & Practice Improvement
Director:
    Vacant. . . . . . . . . . . . . . . . . . . . . . . . . . . . . . . . . 518-485-5989

## Office of Statewide Field Operations
Director:
    Sean Byrne . . . . . . . . . . . . . . . . . . . . . . . . . . . . . . 518-485-2337

## Prevention, Housing & Management Services Division
Director, Division of Prevention:
    Scott Brady . . . . . . . . . . . . . . . . . . . . . . . . . . . . . . 518-485-6022

### Bureau of Housing
Director:
    Henri Williams. . . . . . . . . . . . . . . . . . . . . . . . . . . . 518-485-0496

### Bureau of Prevention Services
Director:
    Scott Brady. . . . . . . . . . . . . . . . . . . . . . . . . . . . . . 518-485-6022

### Bureau of Management Services
Director:
    Vacant. . . . . . . . . . . . . . . . . . . . . . . . . . . . . . . . . 518-485-6689

### Information Technology Services
Director:
    Laura Frost . . . . . . . . . . . . . . . . . . . . . . . . . . . . . . 518-485-2351

## Quality Assurance & Performance Improvement Division
Associate Commissioner:
    Keith McCarthy . . . . . . . . . . . . . . . . . . . . . . . . . . . 518-485-2257

### Bureau of Certification & Systems Management
Director:
    Janet Paloski. . . . . . . . . . . . . . . . . . . . . . . . . . . . . 518-485-2250

*Offices and agencies generally appear in alphabetical order, except when specific order is requested by listee.*

**Bureau of Standards Compliance**
Director:
  Vacant.....................................518-485-2255

**Bureau of Talent Management & Credentializing**
Director:
  Julia Fesko...................................518-485-2033

## Treatment & Practice Innovation Division
Associate Commissioner:
  Steve Hanson ................................518-457-7077

**Bureau of Addiction Treatment Centers**
Assistant Director:
  Paula Bradwell...................518-457-7077 or 585-461-0410

## Education Department
State Education Building
89 Washington Avenue
Albany, NY 12234
518-474-3852
Web site: www.nysed.gov

Interim Commissioner & University President:
  Betty A Rosa..................................518-474-5844
Executive Deputy Commissioner:
  Vacant.......................................518-473-8381
Acting Counsel & Deputy Commissioner, Legal Affairs:
  Aaron Baldwin...............................518-474-6400
  e-mail: legal@nysed.gov
Assistant Commissioner, Office of Innovation and School Reform:
  Cheryl Atkinson .............................518-473-8852

## Office of the Professions.....................fax: 518-474-1449
  89 Washington Ave, Education Building, 2nd Floor, West Mezzanine,
    Albany, NY 12234
  Fax: 518-474-1449
  e-mail: op4info@nysed.gov
  Web site: www.op.nysed.gov
Deputy Commissioner:
  Sarah Benson ................................518-486-1765

**Office of Professional Discipline**

**Registration Unit**
Assistant Director:
  Vacant ................518-474-3817 x410/fax: 518-474-3004
  e-mail: opregfee@nysed.gov

**Professional Licensing Services**
Director:
  Susan Naccarato...........518-474-3817 x340/fax: 518-402-5265
  e-mail: opdpls@nysed.gov

## Health Department
Corning Tower
Empire State Plaza
Albany, NY 12237
518-474-2011 or 518-474-7354
e-mail: dohweb@health.ny.gov
Web site: www.health.ny.gov

## Office of the Commissioner
Commissioner:
  Howard A Zucker, MD, JD ...................518-474-2011
Executive Deputy Commissioner:
  Lisa J Pino, MA, JD ..........................518-474-2011

## Division of Administration
Acting Deputy Commissioner, Administration:
  Marybeth Hefner.............................518-474-8565

## AIDS Institute
Director:
  Johanne Morne, E, MS..............212-417-5500 or 518-474-6399
Deputy Director, HIV Health Care, Grant & Data Management:
  Mona Scully .................................518-474-8404
Deputy Director, Office of Medicaid Policy & Programs:
  Ira Feldman..................................518-486-1383
Deputy Director, Surveillance, Prevention, Drug User Health & Administration:
  Valerie White................................518-474-5577
Director, DEER:
  James Tesoriero .............................518-473-3379
Assistant Director, NYC Office:
  Joan Edwards................................212-417-4508
Medical Director, Office of the Medical Director:
  Bruce D Agins ...............................212-417-4536
Deputy Director, Office of the Medical Director:
  Lyn Stevens..................................518-473-8815

## Center for Community Health
Director:
  Vacant.......................................518-473-4371
Associate Director:
  Adrienne Mazeau..................518-473-4371/fax: 518-473-8389

**Chronic Disease Prevention & Adult Health Division**
Director:
  Barbara Wallace .................518-474-0512/fax: 518-474-5396
Associate Director:
  Rachel Iverson...................518-474-0512/fax: 518-474-5396

**Epidemiology Division**
Director:
  Debra Blog, M.D..................518-473-4464/fax: 518-473-2301
Associate Director:
  Stephanie Ostrowski ..............518-473-4465/fax: 518-473-2301

**Family Health Division**
Director:
  Lauren Tobias................................518-474-6968
Associate Director:
  Wendy Shaw..................................518-474-6968
Medical Director:
  Marilyn Kacica...............................518-473-9883
Associate Medical Director:
  Christopher A Kus ...........................518-473-9883

**Information Technology & Project Management**
Director:
  Linh Le ........................518-473-1809/fax: 518-486-1632
Assistant Director:
  Audra McDonald .............................518-408-1121

**Minority Health**
Director:
  Yvonne Graham ..................518-474-2180/fax: 518-474-4695

**Nutrition Division**
Director:
  Loretta Santilli...................518-402-7090/fax: 518-402-1149
Associate Director:
  Patricia Race ....................518-402-7090/fax: 518-402-1149
Associate Director:
  Jill Dunkel......................518-402-7090/fax: 518-402-1149

## Center for Environmental Health
Director:
  Dr. Nathan Graber.............................518-402-7500

**Division of Environmental Health Assessment**
Director:
  Kevin Gleason ...............................518-402-7511

*Offices and agencies generally appear in alphabetical order, except when specific order is requested by listee.*

**Division of Environmental Health Investigation**
Director:
    Vacant.................................................518-402-7510

**Division of Environmental Health Protection**
Director:
    Michael Cambridge .............................518-402-7500

## Executive Offices

**Office of Governmental & External Affairs**
Assistant Commissioner:
    Estibaliz Alonso ................................518-473-1124
    *Division of Council Operations*
    Deputy Director:
        Kelly Seebald.................................518-474-8009
    *Division of External Affairs*
    Deputy Director:
        Angie Corsi ...................................518-473-8007
    *Division of Governmental Affairs*
    Deputy Director:
        Esti Alonso...................................518-473-1124

**Office of Health Insurance Programs**
Deputy Commissioner & NYS Health Executive Director:
    Donna Frescatore ..............................518-474-3018
Deputy Director:
    Elizabeth Misa.................518-474-8646/fax: 518-486-1346
Medical Director:
    Alda Osinaga, MD ............................518-486-1042
Medical Director:
    Douglas Fish, MD .............................518-473-0919
Director, Division of Eligibility & Marketplace Integration:
    Judith Arnold ................................518-474-0180
Director, Division of OHIP Operations Systems:
    Anton Venter .................................518-433-3453
Director, Division of OHIP Operations:
    Jonathan Bick .................................518-474-8161
Director, Division of Health Plan Contracting & Oversight:
    Vallencia Lloyd ...............................518-474-5737
Director, Division of Program Development & Mngmnt:
    Gregory Allen.................................518-473-0919
Director & CFO, Division of Finance & Rate Setting:
    John Ulberg ...................................518-474-6350
Director, Division of Long Term Care:
    Mark Kissinger................................518-402-5673
Director, Division of Employee & Program Support:
    Ralph Bielefeldt ..............................518-486-5386

**Office of Quality & Patient Safety**
Director:
    Patrick Roohan................................518-473-2941
Deputy Director:
    Joseph Anarella ...............................518-486-9012
Medical Director:
    Foster Gesten, MD, FACP .....................518-486-6865

**Office of Public Health**
Deputy Commissioner:
    Vacant.......................................518-473-0771
Deputy Director:
    Ellen Anderson................................518-473-0771
Director, Office of Public Health Practice:
    Sylvia Pirani..................................518-473-4223
Director, Health Emergency Preparedness:
    Michael J Primeau ............................518-474-2893

**School of Public Health, SUNY at Albany** .........fax: 518-402-0329
One University Place, Rensselaer, NY 12144
518-402-0283 Fax: 518-402-0329
Dean:
    Philip C Nasca PhD..............518-402-0281/fax: 518-402-0329

Assistant Dean, Administration:
    Deb Oriola ...................................518-402-0281

**Health Facilities Management**
Director:
    David J Hernandez ................518-474-2772/fax: 518-474-0611

**Helen Hayes Hospital**
Rte 9W, West Haverstraw, NY 10993-1195
845-786-4000
e-mail: info@helenhayeshospital.org
Web site: www.helenhayeshospital.org
CEO:
    Edmund Coletti..................845-786-4202/fax: 845-947-0036
COO:
    Kathleen Martucci .............................845-786-4201

**New York State Veterans' Home at Batavia**
220 Richmond Ave, Batavia, NY 14020
585-345-2000
Web site: www.nysvets.org
Administrator:
    Joanne I Hernick .................585-345-2076/fax: 585-345-9030
Acting Medical Director:
    Margaret Mitchell, MD .........................585-345-2042
Director, Nursing:
    Stephanie Sulyma ..........................585-345-2000 x2041

**New York State Veterans' Home at Montrose**......fax: 914-788-6100
2090 Albany Post Rd, Montrose, NY 10548
Fax: 914-788-6100
Web site: www.nysvets.org
Administrator:
    Nancy Baa-Danso..............................914-788-6003
Acting Medical Director:
    George Gorich, MD ............................914-788-6025
Director, Nursing:
    Christene St Paul Joseph .......................914-788-6021

**New York State Veterans' Home at Oxford**
4211 State Highway 220, Oxford, NY 13830
607-843-3100
Web site: www.nysvets.org
Administrator:
    James Wyzykowski..............607-843-3129/fax: 607-843-3199
Medical Director:
    Donna Hussman, MD...........................607-843-3140

**New York State Veterans' Home at St Albans**
178-50 Linden Blvd, Jamaica, NY 11434-1467
718-990-0300
Administrator:
    Neville Goldson ...............................718-990-0329
Medical Director:
    Thomas Bizarro MD............................718-990-0328
Director, Nursing:
    Elmina Wilson-Hew............................718-990-0316

**Health Research Inc**
Riverview Center, 150 Broadway, Ste 560, Menands, NY 12204-2719
Web site: www.healthresearch.org
Executive Director:
    Cheryl Mattox.................................518-431-1204

**Office of Primary Care & Health Systems Management**
Deputy Commissioner:
    Daniel B. Sheppard.............................518-474-1686
Deputy Director & Director, Office of Professional Medical Conduct:
    Keith W Servis ................................518-408-1828
Director, Planning & Performance Group (PPG):
    Paul Ambrose ................................518-486-9177
Director, Administrative Mgmnt Services Group (AMS):
    Karyn Andrade ...............................518-486-9177

*Offices and agencies generally appear in alphabetical order, except when specific order is requested by listee.*

Director, Data Management, Analysis & Research Group (DAR):
 Ying Wang . . . . . . . . . . . . . . . . . . . . . . . . . . . . . . . . . . . . . . . . 518-473-7019
Assistant Director, Center for Health Care Provider Services & Oversight (PSO):
 Mark Hennessey . . . . . . . . . . . . . . . . . . . . . . . . . . . . . . . . . . . 518-485-9914
Director, Division of Adult Care Facilities & Assisted Living Surveillance:
 Valerie Deetz . . . . . . . . . . . . . . . . . . . . . . . . . . . . . . . . . . . . . . 518-408-1133
Deputy Director, Division of Adult Care Facilities & Assisted Living Surveillance:
 Timothy Perry-Coon. . . . . . . . . . . . . . . . . . . . . . . . . . . . . . . . . 518-408-1133
Director, Bureau of Emergency Medical Services:
 Lee Burns . . . . . . . . . . . . . . . . . . . . . . . . . . . . . . . . . . . . . . . . . 518-402-0997
Deputy Director, Office of Professional Medical Conduct (OPMC):
 Paula M Breen. . . . . . . . . . . . . . . . . . . . . . . . . . . . . . . . . . . . . . 518-402-0855
Director, Division of Nursing Homes & Intermediate Care Facilities:
 Shelly Glock . . . . . . . . . . . . . . . . . . . . . . . . . . . . . . . . . . . . . . . 518-408-1267

## Human Resources Management Group
Director:
 Joyce M Neznek . . . . . . . . . . . . . . . . . 518-473-3394/fax: 518-486-7374

### Operations Management Group
Director:
 John Reith . . . . . . . . . . . . . . . . . . . . . 518-474-6936/fax: 518-474-8163

## Office of Information Technology Services (ITS) Health Cluster
Health Cluster CIO:
 John P McInnes . . . . . . . . . . . . . . . . . . 518-474-8373/fax: 518-474-2288
Deputy Health Cluster CIO:
 Linh Le

## Legal Affairs
General Counsel:
 Richard J Zahnleuter. . . . . . . . . . . . . . . . . . . . . . . . . . . . . . . . 518-474-7553
Deputy General Counsel:
 Elsie Chun . . . . . . . . . . . . . . . . . . . . . 518-474-7553/fax: 518-473-2802
Director, Bureau of Adjudication:
 James Horan . . . . . . . . . . . . . . . . . . . . 518-402-0748/fax: 518-402-0751
Director, Bureau of Administrative Hearings:
 Mark Fleischer. . . . . . . . . . . . . . . . . . . 518-473-1707/fax: 518-486-1858
Director, Bureau of House Counsel:
 Justin Pfeiffer . . . . . . . . . . . . . . . . . . . 518-473-3233/fax: 518-473-2019
Director, Bureau of Litigation:
 Michael Bass . . . . . . . . . . . . . . . . . . . . 518-473-4631/fax: 518-473-2802
Director, Bureau of Health Insurance Programs:
 Daniel Tarantino . . . . . . . . . . . . . . . . . 518-408-1495/fax: 518-486-4834
Director, Bureau of Health Facility Planning & Development:
 Mark Furnish . . . . . . . . . . . . . . . . . . . . 518-473-3303/fax: 518-473-2019
Chief Counsel, Professional Medical Conduct Unit:
 Henry Weintraub . . . . . . . . . . . . . . . . . 518-474-8266/fax: 518-473-2430
Acting Records Access Officer:
 Danielle Levine. . . . . . . . . . . . . . . . . . . . . . . . . . . . . . . . . . . . . 518-474-8734

### Task Force On Life & The Law
90 Church St, New York, NY 10007
Executive Director:
 Stuart C Sherman . . . . . . . . . . . . . . . . . . . . . . . . . . . . . . . . . . 212-417-5444

## Public Affairs
Director:
 James Plastiras. . . . . . . . . . . . . . . . . . 518-474-6540/fax: 518-473-3456
Deputy Director:
 Vacant . . . . . . . . . . . . . . . . . . . . . . . . . . . . . . . . . . . . 518-474-7354 x1

## Regional Offices

### Central New York Regional Office
217 S Salina St, 3rd Fl, Syracuse, NY 13202
315-477-8100
Director:
 David C. Brittain, MD . . . . . . . . . . . . . . . . . . . . . . . . . . . 315-477-8100
Deputy Director:
 Maria MacPherson . . . . . . . . . . . . . . . . . . . . . . . . . . . . . . . . . 315-477-8100

### Metropolitan Area/Regional Office
90 Church St, New York, NY 10007
Regional Director:
 Celeste M Johnson . . . . . . . . . . . . . . . . . . . . . . . . . . . . . . . 212-417-5550
Deputy Regional Director:
 Ellen Poliski . . . . . . . . . . . . . . . . . . . . . . . . . . . . . . . . . . . . . . 212-417-5550

### Western Regional Office
584 Delaware Ave, Buffalo, NY 14202-1295
716-847-4500
Acting Associate Commissioner:
 Gregory Young. . . . . . . . . . . . . . . . . . . . . . . . . . . . . . . . . . . . . 716-847-4505

## Roswell Park Cancer Institute Corporation
Elm & Carlton Streets, Buffalo, NY 14263-0999
716-845-2300
Web site: www.roswellpark.org
President/CEO:
 Candace S Johnson, PhD. . . . . . . . . . . . 716-845-5772/fax: 716-845-8261
Executive Director:
 Vacant . . . . . . . . . . . . . . . . . . . . . . . . . . . . . . . . . . . . . . . . . . . 716-845-3385
Chief Medical Officer:
 Boris Kuvshinoff, MD . . . . . . . . . . . . . . . . . . . . . . . . . . . . . 716-845-7724
Legal Counsel:
 Michael Sexton . . . . . . . . . . . . . . . . . . . . . . . . . . . . . . . . . . . 716-845-8717
VP, Government Affairs:
 Lisa Damiani. . . . . . . . . . . . . . . . . . . . . . . . . . . . . . . . . . . . . . 716-845-3079
 e-mail: lisa.damiani@roswellpark.org

## Wadsworth Center
Director:
 Vacant . . . . . . . . . . . . . . . . . . . . . . . . 518-474-3157/fax: 518-474-3439
 e-mail: jill.taylor@health.ny.gov
Deputy Director:
 Vicky Derbyshire . . . . . . . . . . . . . . . . . . . . . . . . . . . . . . . . . 518-474-7592
Associate Director, Administration:
 Carlene Van Patten . . . . . . . . . . . . . . . . . . . . . . . . . . . . . . . 518-474-7592
Associate Director, Research & Technology:
 Erasmus Schneider . . . . . . . . . . . . . . . . . . . . . . . . . . . . . . . 518-473-4856
Associate Director, Laboratory Operations:
 Elizabeth Mahoney . . . . . . . . . . . . . . . . . . . . . . . . . . . . . . . 518-474-1002
Associate Director, Medical Affairs:
 Anne Walsh. . . . . . . . . . . . . . . . . . . . . . . . . . . . . . . . . . . . . . . 518-474-7592

### Environmental Health Sciences
Director:
 Ken Aldous . . . . . . . . . . . . . . . . . . . . 518-474-7161/fax: 518-473-2895
Deputy Director:
 Patrick Parsons . . . . . . . . . . . . . . . . . . . . . . . . . . . . . . . . . . . 518-474-7161

### Genetics
Director:
 Keith Derbyshire . . . . . . . . . . . . . . . . . . . . . . . . . . . . . . . . . 518-473-6079
Deputy Director:
 Michele Caggana . . . . . . . . . . . . . . . . . . . . . . . . . . . . . . . . . 518-473-3854

### Herbert W Dickerman Library . . . . . . . . . . . . . . . . . . fax: 518-474-3933
518-474-6172 Fax: 518-474-3933

### Infectious Disease
Director:
 Ron Limberger . . . . . . . . . . . . . . . . . . . . . . . . . . . . . . . . . . . 518-474-8660
Deputy Director:
 Kathleen McDonough . . . . . . . . . . . . . . . . . . . . . . . . . . . . 518-486-4253

### Laboratory Quality Certification
Director:
 Michael Ryan . . . . . . . . . . . . . . . . . . . . . . . . . . . . . . . . . . . . . 518-473-3424

### Translational Medicine
Director:
 Michael Koonce . . . . . . . . . . . . . . . . . . . . . . . . . . . . . . . . . . 518-486-1490

*Offices and agencies generally appear in alphabetical order, except when specific order is requested by listee.*

**173**

Deputy Director:
Rajendra Agrawal............................518-486-5797

## Financial Services Department
One State Street
New York, NY 10004-1511
212-480-6400 or 800-342-3736
e-mail: public-affairs@dfs.ny.gov
Web site: www.dfs.ny.gov

One Commerce Plaza
Albany, NY 12257
Fax:

Walter Mahoney Office Building
65 Court Street, Room 7
Buffalo, NY 14202
Fax:

Superintendent:
Maria T. Vullo ...............................212-709-3500
Chief Administrative Officer:
Cheryl Aini .................................518-473-6160
Director, Communications:
David Neustadt .............212-480-5265/fax: 212-480-6077
Assistant Director, Administration & Operations:
Lori Fraser...................................518-486-4737

### Health Bureau
Chief:
Vacant ....................518-486-2970/fax: 518-474-3397

### Life Bureau
Chief Examiner:
Gail Keren .................212-480-5030/fax: 212-480-5329

## Labor Department
W.A. Harriman Campus
Building 12
Albany, NY 12240
518-457-9000 or 888-469-7365  Fax: 518-457-6908
e-mail: nysdol@labor.ny.gov
Web site: www.labor.ny.gov

Commissioner:
Roberta Reardon...............................518-457-9000
Associate Commissioner, Communications:
Peter Brancato.................................518-457-5519

### Worker Protection
Acting Deputy Commissioner, Worker Protection:
Milan Bhatt

#### Safety & Health Division
Deputy Commissioner:
Eileen Franko................................518-457-3518
*Asbestos Control Bureau*
Program Manager:
Robert Perez.............518-457-1255/fax: 518-485-8054
*Industry Inspection Unit*
Program Manager, License & Certification:
Martha Waldman..........................518-457-2375
*On-Site Consultation Unit*
Program Manager:
James Rush..............518-457-2238/fax: 518-457-3454
*Public Employees Safety & Health (PESH) Unit*
Program Manager:
Normand Labbe ...........518-457-1263/fax: 518-457-5545

## Law Department
28 Liberty Street
New York, NY 10005
212-416-8000 or 800-771-7755
Web site: www.ag.ny.gov

State Capitol
Albany, NY 12224-0341
518-776-2000
Fax: 518-650-9401

Attorney General:
Letitia James.....................212-416-8000 or 518-776-2000
Chief of Staff:
Brian Mahanna ...............................212-416-8050
Director, Public Information:
Shawn Morris .................518-776-2357/fax: 518-650-9401
Press Secretary:
Fernando Aquino.................212-416-8060/fax: 212-416-6005
e-mail: nyag.pressoffice@ag.ny.gov

### Criminal Justice
Executive Deputy Attorney General:
Vacant......................................212-416-8050

#### Medicaid Fraud Control Unit
Deputy Attorney General in Charge & Director:
Amy Held ....................212-417-5250/fax: 212-417-4284
First Asst Attorney General, Legal Affrs:
Monica Hickey-Martin ...........212-417-5339/fax: 212-417-4284
First Asst Attorney General, Operations:
Florence L Finkle .............................212-417-5850
Deputy Regional Director, Buffalo:
Gary A Baldauf..............716-853-8507/fax: 716-852-8525
Regional Director, Long Island:
Jane Turkin ..............631-952-6400/fax: 631-952-6382
Regional Director, Rochester:
Catherine Wagner ..............716-262-2860/fax: 716-262-2866
Regional Director, Syracuse:
Ralph Tortora, III ...............315-423-1104/fax: 315-423-1120
Deputy Regional Director, Pearl River:
Anne S Jardine ................845-732-7525/fax: 845-732-7555

### Social Justice
Executive Deputy Attorney General:
Vacant .......................212-416-8450/fax: 212-416-8942

#### Healthcare Bureau
Bureau Chief:
Lisa Landau ....................518-776-2477 or 212-416-6305
fax: 518-650-9365

### State Counsel

#### Claims Bureau
Bureau Chief:
Katharine Brooks .................518-776-2300 or 212-416-8500

#### Litigation Bureau
Bureau Chief:
Jeffrey Dvorin .................518-776-2300 or 212-416-8610

## CORPORATIONS, AUTHORITIES AND COMMISSIONS

## New York State Dormitory Authority
515 Broadway
Albany, NY 12207-2964
518-257-3000  Fax: 518-257-3100
e-mail: dabonds@dasny.org
Web site: www.dasny.org

*Offices and agencies generally appear in alphabetical order, except when specific order is requested by listee.*

One Penn Plaza
52nd Fl
New York, NY 10119-0098
212-273-5000
Fax: 212-273-5121

539 Franklin St
Buffalo, NY 14202-1109
716-884-9780
Fax: 716-884-9787

Chair:
   Alfonso L Carney Jr . . . . . . . . . . . . . . .518-257-3000/fax: 518-257-3100
President/CEO:
   Paul T Williams Jr. . . . . . . . . . . . . . . .518-257-3180/fax: 518-257-3183
Vice President:
   Michael T Corrigan . . . . . . . . . . . . . . .518-257-3192/fax: 518-257-3183
Chief Financial Officer:
   Linda H Button . . . . . . . . . . . . . . . . . .518-257-3562/fax: 518-257-3100
General Counsel:
   Michael Cusack . . . . . . . . . . . . . . . . . .518-257-3120/fax: 518-257-3101
Managing Director, Construction:
   Stephen D Curro, PE . . . . . . . . . . . . . .518-257-3271/fax: 518-257-3100
   e-mail: scurro@dasny.org
Managing Director, Public Finance & Portfolio Monitoring:
   Portia Lee. . . . . . . . . . . . . . . . . . . . . . .518-257-3362/fax: 518-257-3100
   e-mail: plee@dasny.org
Public Information Officer:
   John Chirlin. . . . . . . . . . . . . . . . . . . . . . . . . . . . . . . .518-257-3380
   e-mail: jchirlin@dasny.org

## NEW YORK STATE LEGISLATURE

*See Legislative Branch in Section 1 for additional Standing Committee and Subcommittee information.*

## Assembly Standing Committees

### Aging
Chair:
   Ron Kim (D) . . . . . . . . . . . . . . . . . . . . . . . . . . . .518-455-4527

### Alcoholism & Drug Abuse
Chair:
   Phil Steck . . . . . . . . . . . . . . . . . . . . . . . . . . . . . .518-455-5802

### Children & Families
Chair:
   Andrew Hevesi . . . . . . . . . . . . . . . . . . . . . . . . . . .518-455-5118

### Consumer Affairs & Protection
Chair:
   Nily Rozic (D, WF). . . . . . . . . . . . . . . . . . . . . . . . .518-455-4545

### Health
Chair:
   Richard N Gottfried (D) . . . . . . . . . . .518-455-4941/fax: 518-455-5939

## Senate Standing Committees

### Aging
Chair:
   Rachel May (D, WF). . . . . . . . . . . . . . . . . . . . . . . .518-455-2838
Ranking Minority Member:
   Sue Serino (R, C, IP) . . . . . . . . . . . . . . . . . . . . . . .518-455-2945

### Children & Families

### Consumer Protection
Chair:
   Kevin Thomas (D) . . . . . . . . . . . . . . . . . . . . . . . . .518-455-3260
Minority Member:
   James Tedisco (R, C) . . . . . . . . . . . . . . . . . . . . . . .518-455-2181

### Health
Chair:
   Gustavo Rivera (D, WF). . . . . . . . . . . . . . . . . . . . . .518-455-3395
Ranking Minority Member:
   Patrick M Gallivan (R, C, IP). . . . . . . . . . . . . . . . . . .518-455-3471

### Social Services
Chair:
   Roxanne J Persaud (D). . . . . . . . . . . . . . . . . . . . . . .518-455-2788
Minority Member:
   Sue Serino (R, C, IP) . . . . . . . . . . . . . . . . . . . . . . .518-455-2945

## U.S. GOVERNMENT

## EXECUTIVE DEPARTMENTS AND RELATED AGENCIES

### US Department of Agriculture
Web site: www.usda.gov

#### Food & Nutrition Service

**Northeast Regional Office**
10 Causeway Street, Room 501, Boston, MA 02222-1069
Acting Regional Administrator:
   Kurt Messner

**New York City Field Office**
201 Varick Street, Room 609, New York, NY 10014
212-620-6307
Section Chief:
   Denise Thomas . . . . . . . . . . . . . . . . . . . . . . . . . . .212-620-6338

#### Food Safety & Inspection Service
Web site: www.fsis.usda.gov

**Field Operations-Philadelphia District Office (includes New York)** fax: 215-597-4217
701 Market Street, Suite 4100A, Philadelphia, PA 19106
215-597-4219  Fax: 215-597-4217
District Manager:
   Susan Scarcia . . . . . . . . . . . . . . . . . . . . . . . . . . .215-430-6302

### US Department of Health & Human Services
Web site: www.hhs.gov

**Administration for Children & Families** . . . . . . . . fax: 212-264-4881
26 Federal Plaza, Room 4114, New York, NY 10278
212-264-2890  Fax: 212-264-4881
Web site: www.acf.hhs.gov
Regional Administrator:
Joyce A. Thomas

**Administration on Aging** . . . . . . . . . . . . . . . . . . . fax: 212-264-0114
26 Federal Plaza, Room 38-102, New York, NY 10278
212-264-2976  Fax: 212-264-0114
Web site: www.aoa.gov
Regional Administrator:
Kathleen Otte
e-mail: kathleen.otte@acl.hhs.gov

**Centers for Disease Control & Prevention**
Web site: www.cdc.gov

*Offices and agencies generally appear in alphabetical order, except when specific order is requested by listee.*

**Agency for Toxic Substances & Disease Registry-EPA Region 2**
290 Broadway North, 20th Floor, New York, NY 10007
Web site: www.atsdr.cdc.gov
Regional Director:
  Leah Graziano, RS ................................212-637-4306

**New York Quarantine Station** ..................fax: 718-553-1524
JFK International Airport, Terminal 4, Room 219.016, 2nd Floor, East
  Concourse, Jamaica, NY 11430-1081
718-553-1685  Fax: 718-553-1524
Officer-in-Charge:
  Donald Spatz

## Centers for Medicare & Medicaid Services
26 Federal Plaza, Room 3811, New York, NY 10278-0063
Web site: www.cms.gov
Regional Administrator:
  Raymond Hurd ................................617-565-1188
  e-mail: robosora@cms.hhs.gov
Deputy Regional Administrator:
  Dr. Gilbert Kunken ..............212-616-2205/fax: 212-264-6189

### Medicaid and Children's Health Operations
Associate Regional Administrator:
  Michael Melendez .............................212-616-2430
  e-mail: ronydmch@cms.hhs.gov

### Medicare Financial Management & Fee for Service Operations
Associate Regional Administrator:
  Victoria Abril ...............................212-616-2505

### Medicare Quality Improvement and Survey & Certification Operations
Associate Regional Administrator:
  William R. Taylor.............................617-565-1323
  e-mail: robosdqi@cms.hhs.gov

## Food & Drug Administration
888-463-6332
Web site: www.fda.gov

### Northeast Region
158-15 Liberty Avenue, Jamaica, NY 11433
Deputy Regional Director:
  W. Charles Becoat
  *New York District Office*
    District Director:
      Ronald Pace
  *Northeast Regional Laboratory*
    158-15 Liberty Avenue, Jamaica, NY 11433
    Director:
      Vacant

## Health Resources & Svcs Admin-Region 2
26 Federal Plaza, Room 3337, New York, NY 10278
212-264-4498
Regional Administrator:
  Ronald Moss...................................212-264-2664
Deputy Regional Administrator:
  Cheryl Donald.................................212-264-4498
  e-mail: cheryl.donald@hrsa.hhs.gov
Senior Public Health Analyst:
  George Pourakis ..............................212-264-4498

## Indian Health Services-Area Office
5600 Fishers Lane, Rockville, MD 20857
301-443-3593
Principal Deputy Director:
  Mary L. Smith................................301-443-3593

## Office of Assistant Secretary for Preparedness & Response
Web site: www.phe.gov

**National Disaster Medical System**
200 Independence Avenue SW, Room 638G, Washington, DC 20201
Acting Director:
  Ron Miller

**Office of Secretary's Regional Representative-Region 2-NY**..fax: 212-264-3620
26 Federal Plaza, Suite 3835, New York, NY 10278
212-264-4600  Fax: 212-264-3620
Regional Director:
  Jackie Cornell-Bechelli

**Office for Civil Rights**.........................fax: 202-619-3818
26 Federal Plaza, Suite 3312, New York, NY 10278
Fax: 202-619-3818
Web site: www.hhs.gov/ocr
Regional Manager:
  Linda Colon ................................212-264-3313

**Office of General Counsel**
26 Federal Plaza, Room 3908, New York, NY 10278
Chief Counsel:
  Joel Lerner .................................212-264-6373

**Office of Inspector General**
Regional Inspector General, Audit:
  James P. Edert.............................212-264-4620
Regional Special Agent in Charge of Investigations:
  Scott J. Lampert
Regional Inspector General, Evaluations & Inspections:
  Jodi Nudelman

**Office of the Assistant Secretary for Health (ASH)**
26 Federal Plaza, Suite 3835, New York, NY 10278
Regional Health Administrator:
  Michelle S. Davis...........................212-264-2560
Regional Public Affairs Specialist:
  Karina Aguilar ............................212-264-2535
Regional Family Planning Consultant:
  Delores Stewart ...........................212-264-3935
Regional Minority Health Consultant:
  Marline Vignier ...........................212-264-2560
Regional Women's Health Coordinator:
  Sandra Bennett-Pagan ......................212-264-4628

---

# US Department of Homeland Security (DHS)
Web site: www.dhs.gov

## Federal Emergency Management Agency (FEMA)
TTY: 800-462-7585 or 202-646-2500

### New York Regional Office
26 Federal Plaza, New York, NY 10278-0002
212-680-3600
Regional Administrator:
  Jerome Hatfield

---

# US Labor Department
Web site: www.dol.gov

## Occupational Safety & Health Adminstration (OSHA).......fax: 212-337-2371
201 Varick Street, Room 670, New York, NY 10014
212-337-2378  Fax: 212-337-2371
Web site: www.osha.gov
Regional Administrator:
  Robert D. Kulick

### Albany Area Office
401 New Karner Road, Suite 300, Albany, NY 12205-3809
Area Director:
  Kim Castillon ...............518-464-4338/fax: 518-464-4337

*Offices and agencies generally appear in alphabetical order, except when specific order is requested by listee.*

**Buffalo Area Office**
130 South Elmwood Avenue, Suite 500, Buffalo, NY 14202-2465
Area Director:
Michael Scime . . . . . . . . . . . . . . . . . 716-551-3053/fax: 716-551-3126

**Long Island Area Office**
1400 Old Country Road, Suite 208, Westbury, NY 11590
Area Director:
Anthony Ciuffo . . . . . . . . . . . . . . . . 516-334-3344/fax: 516-334-3326

**Manhattan Area Office**
201 Varick Street, Room 908, New York, NY 10014
Area Director:
Kay Gee . . . . . . . . . . . . . . . . . . . . 212-620-3200/fax: 212-620-4121

**Syracuse Area Office**
3300 Vickery Road, North Syracuse, NY 13212
Area Director:
Christopher Adams . . . . . . . . . . . . . 315-451-0808/fax: 315-451-1351

**Tarrytown Area Office**
660 White Plains Road, 4th Floor, Tarrytown, NY 10591-5107
Area Director:
Diana Cortez . . . . . . . . . . . . . . . . . 914-524-7510/fax: 914-524-7515

## U.S. CONGRESS

*See U.S. Congress Chapter for additional Standing Committee and Subcommittee information.*

## House of Representatives Standing Committees

### Agriculture
Chair:
K. Michael Conaway (R-TX) . . . . . . . . . . . . . . . . . 202-225-3605
Ranking Member:
Collin C. Peterson (D-MN) . . . . . . . . . . . . . . . . . 202-225-2165

**Subcommittee**
*Nutrition*
Chair:
Jackie Walorski (R-IN) . . . . . . . . . . . . . . . 202-225-3915
Ranking Member:
Jim McGovern (D-MA) . . . . . . . . . . . . . . . 202-225-6101

### Energy & Commerce
Chair:
Fred Upton (R-MI) . . . . . . . . . . . . . . . . . 202-225-3761
Ranking Member:
Frank Pallone (D-NJ) . . . . . . . . . . . . . . . . 202-225-4671
New York Delegate:
Eliot L. Engel (D) . . . . . . . . . . . . . . . . . 202-225-2464
New York Delegate:
Paul Tonko (D) . . . . . . . . . . . . . . . . . . 202-225-5076
New York Delegate:
Yvette Clarke (D) . . . . . . . . . . . . . . . . . 202-225-6231
New York Delegate:
Chris Collins (R) . . . . . . . . . . . . . . . . . 202-225-5265

**Subcommittee**
*Health*
Chair:
Joseph Pitts (R-PA) . . . . . . . . . . . . . . . 202-225-2411
Ranking Member:
Gene Green (D-TX) . . . . . . . . . . . . . . . 202-225-1688
New York Delegate:
Eliot L. Engel (D) . . . . . . . . . . . . . . . 202-225-2464

### Ways & Means
Chair:
Kevin Brady (R-TX) . . . . . . . . . . . . . . . . . 202-225-4901

Ranking Member:
Sander Levin (D-MI) . . . . . . . . . . . . . . . . . 888-810-3880
New York Delegate:
Charles B. Rangel (D) . . . . . . . . . . . . . . . . 202-225-4365
New York Delegate:
Joseph Crowley (D) . . . . . . . . . . . . . . . . 202-225-3965
New York Delegate:
Tom Reed (R) . . . . . . . . . . . . . . . . . . 202-225-3161

**Subcommittee**
*Health*
Chair:
Pat Tiberi (R-OH) . . . . . . . . . . . . . . . 202-225-5355
Ranking Member:
Jim McDermott (D-WA) . . . . . . . . . . . . . 202-225-3106

## Senate Standing Committees

### Aging, Special Committee on
Chair:
Susan M. Collins (R-ME) . . . . . . . . . . . . . . . 202-224-2523
Ranking Member:
Claire McCaskill (D-MO) . . . . . . . . . . . . . . . 202-224-6154

### Agriculture, Nutrition & Forestry
Chair:
Pat Roberts (R-KS) . . . . . . . . . . . . . . . . . 202-224-4774
Ranking Member:
Debbie Stabenow (D-MI) . . . . . . . . . . . . . . . 202-224-4822

### Health, Education, Labor & Pensions
Chair:
Lamar Alexander (R-TN) . . . . . . . . . . . . . . . 202-224-4944
Ranking Member:
Patty Murray (D-WA) . . . . . . . . . . . . . . . . 202-224-2621

**Subcommittees**
*Primary Health & Retirement Security*
Chair:
Michael B. Enzi (R-WY) . . . . . . . . . . . . . 202-224-3424
Ranking Member:
Bernie Sanders (D-VT) . . . . . . . . . . . . . 202-224-5141

## PRIVATE SECTOR

**Adelphi NY Statewide Breast Cancer Hotline & Support Program**
Adelphi University, Social Work Building, 1 South Avenue, PO Box 701, Garden City, NY 11530-0701
800-877-8077 or 516-877-4320  Fax: 516-877-4336
e-mail: breastcancerhotline@adelphi.edu
Web site: breast-cancer.adelphi.edu
*Breast cancer support, information & referral hotline for all of New York State; community education, support groups, counseling & advocacy*
Hillary Rutter, Executive Director

**Alliance for Positive Health**
927 Broadway, Albany, NY 12207-1306
518-434-4686 or 800-201-2437  Fax: 518-427-8184
Web site: www.allianceforpositivehealth.org
*Provides HIV/AIDS education & testing to at-risk individuals; offers assistance & care coordination to persons with chronic diseases; advocacy for better access to quality health services*
William F. Faragon, Executive Director

*Offices and agencies generally appear in alphabetical order, except when specific order is requested by listee.*

**Alzheimer's Association, Northeastern NY**
4 Pine West Plaza, Suite 405, Albany, NY 12205
518-867-4999 or 800-272-3900  Fax: 518-867-4997
e-mail: infoneny@alz.org
Web site: www.alz.org/northeasternny
*Research & support for individuals affected by Alzheimer's disease*
Elizabeth Smith Boivin, Executive Director & Chief Executive Officer

**American Cancer Society-Capital NY Region**
1 Penny Lane, Latham, NY 12110
518-220-6901 or 800-227-2345
Web site: www.cancer.org
Kathryn Ozimek, Director, Human Resources

**American College of Nurse-Midwives, NYC Chapter**
426 13th Street, Brooklyn, NY 11215
Web site: www.nycmidwives.org
*Midwifery/women's health*
Gina Eichenbaum-Pikser, Co-Chair

**American College of Physicians, New York Chapter**
744 Broadway, Albany, NY 12207
518-427-0366  Fax: 518-427-1991
e-mail: info@nyacp.org
Web site: www.nyacp.org
*Develops & advocates for policies on health issues*
Linda A. Lambert, Executive Director

**American Congress of Obstetricians & Gynecologists/NYS**
100 Great Oaks Blvd, Suite 109, Albany, NY 12203
518-436-3461  Fax: 518-426-4728
e-mail: info@ny.acog.org
Web site: www.acogny.org
*Women's health care & physician education*
Christa R. Christakis, Executive Director

**American Heart Association Founders Affiliate**
122 East 42nd Street, 18th Floor, New York, NY 10168
212-878-5900
Web site: www.heart.org
*Research, education & community service to reduce disability & death from heart disease & stroke*
Heather Kinder, Executive Vice President

**American Liver Foundation, Greater NY Chapter**
39 Broadway, Suite 2700, New York, NY 10006
212-943-1059  Fax: 212-943-1314
Web site: www.liverfoundation.org
*Disease research, public education & patient support*
Paul Bolter, Community Outreach & Education Manager

**American Lung Association of NYS Inc**
418 Broadway, 1st Floor, Albany, NY 12207
518-465-2013
e-mail: info@lungne.org
Web site: www.lung.org
*Education, research & advocacy for lung health & lung disease prevention*
Michael Seilback, Vice President, Public Policy & Communications

**AMSUS-The Society of Federal Health Professionals**
9320 Old Georgetown Road, Bethesda, MD 20814
301-897-8800  Fax: 301-530-5446
Web site: www.amsus.org
*Works to improve federal healthcare service & represent military, federal & international health care professionals*
VADM Mike Cowan, Executive Director

**Associated Medical Schools of New York**
1270 Avenue of the Americas, Suite 606, New York, NY 10020
212-218-4610  Fax: 212-218-4278
e-mail: info@amsny.org
Web site: www.amsny.org
*A consortium of the sixteen medical schools in New York State; advocacy, resources & educational development programs*
Jo Wiederhorn, President & Chief Executive Officer

**Bausch & Lomb Inc**
1400 North Goodman Street, Rochester, NY 14609
800-553-5340  Fax: 585-338-6896
Web site: www.bausch.com
*Development, manufacture & marketing of contact lenses & lens care products, opthalmic surgical & pharmaceutical products*
RJ Crawford, Procurement Manager

**New York University School of Medicine Bellevue Hospital Center, Department of Emergency Medicine**
462 First Avenue, Room A345, New York, NY 10016
212-562-6561  Fax: 212-562-3001
e-mail: robert.femia@nyumc.org
Web site: www.med.nyu.edu
*Emergency medicine; medical toxicology*
Robert J. Femia, Chair

**Brain Injury Association of NYS (BIANYS)**
10 Colvin Avenue, Albany, NY 12206
518-459-7911 or 800-228-8201  Fax: 518-482-5285
e-mail: info@bianys.org
Web site: www.bianys.org
*Public education & advocacy for individuals & families affected by brain injuries*
Eileen Reardon, Executive Director

**Bristol-Myers Squibb Co**
345 Park Avenue, New York, NY 10154
212-546-4000 or 800-332-2056
Web site: www.bms.com
*Develops & markets pharmaceuticals*
Giovanni Caforio, Chief Executive Officer

**Bronx-Lebanon Hospital Center**
1276 Fulton Avenue, Bronx, NY 10456
718-590-1800 or 718-326-4591  Fax: 718-299-5447
e-mail: ecsvp@erols.com
Web site: www.bronxcare.org
Dr. Sridhar Chilimuri, Chairman, Department of Medicine

**Center for Hearing and Communication**
50 Broadway, 6th Floor, New York, NY 10004-1607
917-305-7700 or TTY: 917-305-7999  Fax: 917-305-7888
e-mail: postmaster@chchearing.org
Web site: www.chchearing.org
*Rehabilitation & other services for deaf & hard of hearing individuals*
Laurie Hanin, Executive Director

**Cerebral Palsy Associations of New York State**
330 West 34th Street, 15th Floor, New York, NY 10001-2488
212-947-5770  Fax: 212-594-4538
e-mail: information@cpofnys.org
Web site: www.cpofnys.org
*Serves individuals with cerebral palsy & other significant disabilities as well as their families through advocacy, technical assistance, publications & networking events*
Susan Constantino, President & Chief Executive Officer

*Offices and agencies generally appear in alphabetical order, except when specific order is requested by listee.*

**Coalition of Fathers & Families NY**
PO Box 252, Stillwater, NY 12170
518-288-6755
e-mail: info@fafny.org
Web site: www.fafny.org
*Political action, education & advocacy for fathers & families in NY*
Jack Frost, President

**Columbia University, Mailman School of Public Health**
722 West 168th Street, New York, NY 10032
212-854-1754  Fax: 212-305-9342
e-mail: lpfried@columbia.edu
Web site: www.mailman.columbia.edu
*Theory, analysis & development of policy & programs supporting public health & human rights*
Linda P Fried, Dean

**Commissioned Officers Assn of the US Public Health Svc Inc (COA)**
8201 Corporate Drive, Suite 200, Landover, MD 20785
301-731-9080  Fax: 301-731-9084
e-mail: jcurrie@coausphs.org
Web site: www.coausphs.org
*Committed to improving the public health of the US; supports the interests of corps officers & advocates through leadership, training, education & communication*
Jim Currie, Executive Director

**Committee of Methadone Program Administrators Inc of NYS (COMPA)**
911 Central Avenue, Suite 322, Albany, NY 12206
e-mail: info@compa-ny.org
Web site: www.compa-ny.org
*Substance abuse treatment through pharmacotherapy; advocacy, community education, standards & regulatory review & policy development*
Allegra Schorr, President

**Commonwealth Fund**
1 East 75th Street, New York, NY 10021-2692
212-606-3800  Fax: 212-606-3500
e-mail: info@cmwf.org
Web site: www.commonwealthfund.org
*Supports independent research on health access, coverage & quality issues affecting minorities, women, children, elderly & low-income individuals*
David Blumenthal, President

**Community Health Care Association of NYS**
111 Broadway, Suite 1402, New York, NY 10006
212-279-9686  Fax: 212-279-3851
e-mail: info@chcanys.org
Web site: www.chcanys.org
*Advocacy, education & services for the medically underserved throughout NYS*
Elizabeth H. Swain, President & Chief Executive Officer

**Community Healthcare Network**
60 Madison Avenue, 5th Floor, New York, NY 10010
212-545-2400 or 866-246-8259
Web site: www.chnnyc.org
*Health & social services for low-income, ethnically diverse, medically underserved neighborhoods of NYC*
Robert Hayes, President & Chief Executive Officer

**Outreach & Extension**
**Cornell Cooperative Extension, College of Human Ecology, Nutrition, Food Safety & Security**
249 Martha Van Rensselaer Hall, Cornell University, Ithaca, NY 14853
607-254-6517  Fax: 607-255-4071
e-mail: kak33@cornell.edu
Web site: www.cce.cornell.edu
*Promoting nutritional well-being; safe preparation & storage of food; reducing food insecurity; improving access to health services*
Kim Kopko, Assistant Director, Human Ecology

**County Nursing Facilities of New York Inc**
c/o NYSAC, 540 Broadway, 5th Floor, Albany, NY 12207
518-465-1473  Fax: 518-465-0506
Web site: www.nysac.org
Edmond Marchi, President

**Dental Hygienists' Association of the State of New York Inc**
PO Box 16041, Albany, NY 12212
518-477-0343
e-mail: info@dhasny.org
Web site: www.dhasny.org
*Professional association representing registered dental hygienists; working to improve the oral health of New Yorkers*
Beth Krueger, Executive Director

**Doctors Without Borders USA**
333 7th Avenue, 2nd Floor, New York, NY 10001-5004
212-679-6800  Fax: 212-679-7016
Web site: www.doctorswithoutborders.org
*International medical assistance for victims of natural or man-made disasters & armed conflict*
Jason Cone, Executive Director

**Empire Blue Cross & Blue Shield**
1 Liberty Plaza, New York, NY 10006
212-476-1000  Fax: 212-476-1281
Web site: www.empireblue.com
*Health insurance*
Lawrence Schreiber, President

**Empire State Association of Assisted Living**
646 Plank Road, Suite 207, Clifton Park, NY 12065
518-371-2573  Fax: 518-371-3774
e-mail: lnewcomb@esaal.org
Web site: www.esaal.org
*Trade association representing NYS assisted living providers*
Lisa Newcomb, Executive Director

**Epilepsy Coalition of New York State Inc**
450 West Nyack Road, West Nyack, NY 10980
845-627-0627
Web site: www.epilepsyny.org
*Epilepsy awareness & advocacy for improved services for people with epilepsy*
Janice W. Gay, President

**Excellus BCBS**
165 Court Street, Rochester, NY 14647
585-454-1700  Fax: 585-238-4233
Web site: www.excellusbcbs.com
*Health insurance*
Dorothy Coleman, Executive Vice President

**Eye-Bank for Sight Restoration Inc (The)**
120 Wall Street, New York, NY 10005-3902
212-742-9000  Fax: 212-269-3139
e-mail: info@ebsr.org
Web site: www.eyedonation.org
*Cornea & scleral transplants, eye donations*
Patricia Dahl, Executive Director & Chief Executive Officer

*Offices and agencies generally appear in alphabetical order, except when specific order is requested by listee.*

**Family Planning Advocates of New York State**
194 Washington Avenue, Suite 620, Albany, NY 12210
518-436-8408  Fax: 518-436-0004
e-mail: info@familyplanningadvocates.org
Web site: www.familyplanningadvocates.org
*Reproductive rights*
Kim Atkins, Chair

**Generic Pharmaceutical Association**
777 Sixth Street NW, Suite 510, Washington, DC 20001
202-249-7100  Fax: 202-249-7105
e-mail: media@gphaonline.org
*Association for manufacturers & suppliers of prescription drugs &
pharmaceuticals; works to improve access to affordable generic medicines*
Chester Davis, President & Chief Executive Officer

**Gertrude H Sergievsky Center (The)**
630 West 168th Street, New York, NY 10032
212-305-2515  Fax: 212-305-2426
e-mail: rpm2@columbia.edu
Web site: www.cumc.columbia.edu
*Neurological disease research correlating epidemiological techniques with
genetic analysis & clinical investigation*
Richard Mayeux, Director

**Greater New York Hospital Association**
555 West 57th Street, 15th Floor, New York, NY 10019
212-246-7100  Fax: 212-262-6350
e-mail: info@gnyha.org
Web site: www.gnyha.org
*Trade association representing the interests of more than 160 hospitals &
health systems*
Kenneth E. Raske, President

**Group Health Inc**
PO Box 3000, New York, NY 10116-3000
212-501-4444 or 800-624-2414
Web site: www.emblemhealth.com
*Health insurance*

**Healthcare Association of New York State**
1 Empire Drive, Rensselaer, NY 12144
518-431-7600  Fax: 518-431-7915
Web site: www.hanys.org
*Representing New York's not-for-profit & public hospitals, health systems &
continuing care providers*
Dennis Whalen, President

**Home Care Association of New York State Inc**
388 Broadway, 4th Floor, Albany, NY 12207
518-426-8764  Fax: 518-426-8788
e-mail: info@hcanys.org
Web site: www.hca-nys.org
*Advocacy for home health care & related health services*
Joanne Cunningham, President

**Hospice & Palliative Care Association of NYS Inc**
2 Computer Drive West, Suite 105, Albany, NY 12205
518-446-1483  Fax: 518-446-1484
e-mail: info@hpcanys.org
Web site: www.hpcanys.org
*Hospice & palliative care information & referral service; educational
programs; clinical, psychosocial & bereavement issues*
Timothy D. Nichols, President & Chief Executive Officer

**INFORM Inc**
PO Box 320403, Brooklyn, NY 11232
212-361-2400  Fax: 212-361-2412
e-mail: ramsey@informinc.org
*Produces educational films about the impact of human activity on natural
resources & public health*
Virginia Ramsey, Executive Producer

**Institute for Family Health (The)**
2006 Madison Avenue, New York, NY 10035
212-633-0800  Fax: 212-691-4610
Web site: www.institute.org
*Family practice healthcare for NYC's underserved; health professions
training; research & advocacy*
Neil S. Calman, President & Chief Executive Officer

**Iroquois Healthcare Alliance**
15 Executive Park Drive, Clifton Park, NY 12065
518-383-5060  Fax: 518-383-2616
e-mail: gfitzgerald@iroquois.org
Web site: www.iroquois.org
*Represents healthcare providers in upstate New York*
Gary Fitzgerald, President

**LeadingAge New York**
13 British American Blvd, Suite 2, Latham, NY 12110-1431
518-867-8383  Fax: 518-867-8384
e-mail: info@leadingageny.org
Web site: www.leadingageny.org
*Represents continuing care providers*
James W. Clyne Jr., President

**Lighthouse Guild**
15 West 65th Street, New York, NY 10023
800-284-4422
Web site: www.lighthouseguild.org
*Vision rehabilitation, research, education & awareness*
Alan R. Morse, President & Chief Executive Officer

**Marion S Whelan School of Practical Nursing**
Geneva General Hospital, 196 North Street, Geneva, NY 14456
315-787-4005  Fax: 315-787-4770
Web site: www.flhealth.org
*Health education; clinical training*
Victoria Record, EdD, RN, CNE, Director

**Medical Society of the State of NY, Governmental Affairs
Division**
1 Commerce Plaza, 99 Washington Avenue, Suite 408, Albany, NY 12210
518-465-8085  Fax: 518-465-0976
e-mail: mssny@mssny.org
Web site: www.mssny.org
*Healthcare legislation & advocacy*
Elizabeth Dears, Senior VP

**Memorial Sloan-Kettering Cancer Center**
1275 York Avenue, New York, NY 10065
212-639-2000  Fax: 212-639-3576
Web site: www.mskcc.org
*National Cancer Institute designated comprehensive cancer center; research,
education & patient care*
Avice Meehan, Senior VP & Chief Communications Officer

**Montefiore Health System, Albert Einstein College of Medicine,
OB/GYN & Women's Health**
1300 Morris Park Avenue, Belfer Educational Center, Room 501, Bronx, NY
10461
718-430-2000 or 718-430-3581  Fax: 718-430-8739
Web site: www.einstein.yu.edu
Avalon Lance, Unified Administrator

**Mount Sinai Health System**
One Gustave L. Levy Plaza, New York, NY 10029-6574
212-241-6500 or 212-590-3300
Web site: www.mountsinai.org
Kenneth L. Davis, MD, President & Chief Executive Officer

*Offices and agencies generally appear in alphabetical order, except when specific order is requested by listee.*

**NY Health Information Management Association Inc**
1450 Western Avenue, Suite 101, Albany, NY 12203
518-435-0422 Fax: 518-463-8656
e-mail: nyhima@caphill.com
Web site: www.nyhima.org
Michele B. Bohley, President & Chair

**NY Physical Therapy Association**
971 Albany Shaker Road, Latham, NY 12110
518-459-4499 Fax: 518-459-8953
e-mail: kgarceau@nypta.org
Web site: www.nypta.org
Kelly Garceau, Executive Director

**NY State Society of Physician Assistants**
100 North 20th Street, Suite 400, Philadelphia, PA 19103
877-769-7722 Fax: 215-564-2175
Web site: www.nysspa.org
Kyle Fernley, Executive Director

**NYS Academy of Family Physicians**
260 Osborne Road, Albany, NY 12211-1822
518-489-8945 or 800-822-0700 Fax: 518-489-8961
e-mail: fp@nysafp.org
Web site: www.nysafp.org
Vito F. Grasso, Executive Vice President

**NYS Association of County Health Officials**
One United Way, Pine West Plaza, Albany, NY 12205
518-456-7905 Fax: 518-452-5435
e-mail: linda@nysacho.org
Web site: www.nysacho.org
Linda Wagner, Executive Director

**NYS Association of Health Care Providers**
20 Corporate Woods Blvd, 2nd Floor, Albany, NY 12211
518-463-1118 Fax: 518-463-1606
e-mail: hcp@nyshcp.org
Web site: www.nyshcp.org
*Home health care; health care services for the aging*
Claudia Hammar, President

**NYS Association of Nurse Anesthetists (NYSANA)**
c/o McKenna Management, 6 Boston Road, Suite 202, Chelmsford, MA 01824
978-674-6214 Fax: 978-250-1117
e-mail: admin@nysana.com
Web site: www.nysana.com
Joanne Woersching, President

**NYS Dental Association**
20 Corporate Woods Blvd, Suite 602, Albany, NY 12211
518-465-0044 Fax: 518-465-3219
e-mail: info@nysdental.org
Web site: www.nysdental.org
Mark J. Feldman, D.M.D., Executive Director

**NYS Federation of Physicians & Dentists**
521 5th Avenue, Suite 1700, New York, NY 10175-0003
212-986-3859
Larry Nathan, Executive Director

**NYS Optometric Association Inc**
119 Washington Avenue, 2nd Floor, Albany, NY 12210
518-449-7300 or 800-342-9836 Fax: 518-432-5902
e-mail: nysoa2020@gmail.com
Web site: www.nysoa.org
Jan Dorman, Executive Director

**NYS Public Health Association**
PO Box 38127, Albany, NY 12203
518-427-5835
e-mail: info@nyspha.org
Web site: www.nyspha.org
*Advocates for policies to protect public health & enhance health equity in NYS*
Michael Seserman, President

**National Amputation Foundation Inc**
40 Church Street, Malverne, NY 11565
516-887-3600 Fax: 516-887-3667
e-mail: amps76@aol.com
Web site: www.nationalamputation.org
*Provides services designed to help amputees, including AMP-to-AMP & medical giveaway programs, information, resources, hospital visits & support group & amputee organization referrals*
Paul Bernacchio, President

**National League for Nursing (NLN)**
61 Broadway, New York, NY 10006
212-363-5555
Web site: www.nln.org
*Promotes superior nursing education & the nursing profession; provides research grants, networking opportunities & professional development programs*
Dr. Beverly Malone, Chief Executive Officer

**National Marfan Foundation**
22 Manhasset Avenue, Port Washington, NY 11050
516-883-8712 Fax: 516-883-8040
e-mail: staff@marfan.org
Web site: www.marfan.org
*Marfan syndrome research, education & support*
Michael Weamer, President & Chief Executive Officer

**New Jewish Home (The)**
120 West 106th Street, New York, NY 10025
212-870-5000 or 212-870-4715
e-mail: aweiner@jewishhome.org
Web site: www.jewishhome.org
*Long term care & rehabilitation*
Audrey Weiner, President & Chief Executive Officer

**New School University, Milano School of International Affairs, Management & Urban Policy**
72 Fifth Avenue, 3rd Floor, New York, NY 10011
212-229-5150 Fax: 212-627-2695
Web site: www.newschool.edu
Michelle J. DePass, Dean

**New York AIDS Coalition**
231 W 29th St, New York, NY 10001
212-629-3075 Fax: 212-629-8409
*HIV/AIDS-related public policy & education*
James Darden, Office Manager

**New York Health Care Alliance**
39 Broadway, Suite 1710, New York, NY 10006
212-425-5050 or 877-446-9422 Fax: 212-968-7710
e-mail: info@nyhca.com
Web site: www.nyhca.com
*Nursing facilities affiliation focused on disseminating information, addressing health plans & facilities issues & providing patient placement services*
Neil J. Heyman, Chief Executive Officer

*Offices and agencies generally appear in alphabetical order, except when specific order is requested by listee.*

**New York Health Plan Association**
90 State Street, Suite 825, Albany, NY 12207-1717
518-462-2293  Fax: 518-462-2150
e-mail: info@nyhpa.org
Web site: www.nyhpa.org
*Promotes managed care & health service plans*
Andrew Fogarty, Director, Government Affairs

**New York Medical College**
40 Sunshine Cottage Road, Valhalla, NY 10595
914-594-4000
Web site: www.nymc.edu
*Cardiovascular physiology, graduate education*
Edward C Halperin, M.D., M.A., Chancellor & Chief Executive Officer

**New York Medical College, Department of Medicine**
19 Skyline, Valhalla, NY 10595
914-594-2080  Fax: 914-493-7506
Web site: www.nymc.edu
*Research, education & clinical training*
Maryanne Pratt, Department Administrator

**New York Medical College, School of Health Sciences and Practice**
School of Health Science & Practice Bldg, 30 Plaza West, Valhalla, NY 10595
914-594-4510 or 888-336-NYMC  Fax: 914-594-3961
Web site: www.nymc.edu/shsp
*Public health education & research*
Pamela Suett, Director of Recruitment

**New York Presbyterian Hospital**
525 East 68th Street, New York, NY 10065
212-746-5454
Web site: www.nyp.org; www.weill.cornell.edu
Steven J. Corwin, MD, President & Chief Executive Officer

**New York State Association of Ambulatory Surgery Centers**
C/N Group Inc., Center for Ambulatory Surgery, LLC, 550 Orchard Park Road, B101, West Seneca, NY 14224
716-997-9474 or 716-896-3815
e-mail: nysaasc@gmail.com
Web site: www.nysaasc.org
*Promotes superior ambulatory surgical care in NYS*
Thomas Faith, President

**New York State Health Facilities Association Inc**
33 Elk Street, Suite 300, Albany, NY 12207-1010
518-462-4800  Fax: 518-426-4051
e-mail: info@nyshfa.org
Web site: www.nyshfa.org
*Association for long term care providers*
Richard J. Herrick, President & Chief Executive Officer

**New York State Nurses Association**
131 West 33rd Street, 4th Floor, New York, NY 10001
212-785-0157
e-mail: info@nysna.org
Web site: www.nysna.org
*Labor union & professional association for registered nurses*
Jill Furillo, Executive Director

**New York State Ophthalmological Society**
408 Kenwood Avenue, Delmar, NY 12054
518-439-2020  Fax: 518-439-2040
e-mail: admin@nysos.com
Web site: www.nysos.com
Robin M. Pellegrino, Executive Director

**New York State Osteopathic Medical Society**
1855 Broadway, New York, NY 10023
212-261-1784 or 800-841-4131  Fax: 212-261-1786
e-mail: info@nysoms.org
Web site: www.nysoms.org
*Represents the interests of osteopathic physicians through information dissemination, advocacy, continuing medical education programs & other membership services*
Steven I. Sherman, President

**New York State Podiatric Medical Association**
555 Eighth Avenue, Suite 1902, New York, NY 10018
212-996-4400  Fax: 646-672-9344
e-mail: info@nyspma.org
Web site: www.nyspma.org
*Association working to promote the interests of the podiatric community through advocacy, information & continuing medical education*
Michael Borden, Executive Director

**New York State Radiological Society Inc**
585 Stewart Avenue, Suite 412, Garden City, NY 11530
516-222-1150  Fax: 516-222-1204
e-mail: nysrad@aol.com
Web site: www.nysrs.org
Richard A. Schiffer, Executive Director

**New York University, Robert F Wagner Graduate School of Public Service**
295 Lafayette Street, Room 3040A, New York, NY 10012-9604
212-998-7400 or 212-998-7455
e-mail: john.billings@nyu.edu
*Health policy & management education*
John Billings, Director, Health Policy & Management Program

**Next Wave Inc**
24 Madison Avenue Extension, Albany, NY 12203
518-452-3351  Fax: 518-452-3358
Web site: www.nextwave.info
*Health services research, evaluation & management consulting*
John D. Shaw, President

**Northeast Business Group on Health Inc**
61 Broadway, Suite 2705, New York, NY 10006
212-252-7440  Fax: 212-252-7448
e-mail: laurel@nebgh.org
Web site: www.nebgh.org
*Business employers addressing healthcare cost & quality; non-profit coalition of health systems & organizations*
Laurel Pickering, President & Chief Executive Officer

**Nurse Practitioner Association NYS (The)**
12 Corporate Drive, Clifton Park, NY 12065
518-348-0719  Fax: 518-348-0720
e-mail: info@thenpa.org
Web site: www.thenpa.org
*Representation, communication & advocacy*
Stephen Ferrara, Executive Director

**Path2Parenthood**
315 Madison Avenue, Suite 901, New York, NY 10017
888-917-3777
e-mail: info@path2parenthood.org
Web site: www.path2parenthood.org
*Education, support, advocacy, resources & outreach programs centered on infertility, reproductive health & adoption*
Ken Mosesian, Executive Director

*Offices and agencies generally appear in alphabetical order, except when specific order is requested by listee.*

**Pharmacists Society of the State of New York**
210 Washington Avenue Extension, Albany, NY 12203
518-869-6595 or 800-632-8822 Fax: 518-464-0618
e-mail: kathy.febraio@pssny.org
Web site: www.pssny.org
*Continuing education, public information, health advocacy*
Kathy Febraio, Executive Director

**Premier Senior Living LLC**
299 Park Avenue, 6th Floor, New York, NY 10171
800-380-8908
Web site: www.pslgroupllc.com
*Assisted living, memory & personal care services*
Robert P. Borsody, Co-Founder & Managing Member

**Radon Testing Corp of America Inc**
2 Hayes Street, Elmsford, NY 10523-2502
914-345-3380 or 800-457-2366 Fax: 914-345-8546
e-mail: info@rtca.com
Web site: www.rtca.com
*Radon detection services for health departments, municipalities & homeowners*
Nancy Bredhoff, President

**Regeneron Pharmaceuticals Inc**
777 Old Saw Mill River Road, Tarrytown, NY 10591-6707
914-847-7000
Web site: www.regeneron.com
*Biopharmaceutical company focused on the development of therapeutic drugs for serious medical conditions, including rheumatoid arthritis, cancer, asthma & obesity*
Leonard S. Schleifer, President & Chief Executive Officer

**SUNY at Albany, School of Public Health, Center for Public Health Preparedness**
One University Place, Rensselaer, NY 12144-3456
518-402-0344 Fax: 518-402-4656
e-mail: cphp@uamail.albany.edu
Web site: www.ualbanycphp.org
Edward Waltz, Director

**The Bachmann-Strauss Dystonia & Parkinson Foundation Inc**
PO Box 38016, Albany, NY 12203
212-509-0995 x331
Web site: www.dystonia-parkinsons.org
*Funds research & creates public awareness of dystonia & Parkinson's disease*
Bonnie Strauss, President & Founder

**True, Walsh & Sokoni, LLP**
950 Danby Road, Suite 310, Ithaca, NY 14850
607-273-2301 Fax: 607-272-1901
e-mail: info@truewalshlaw.com
Web site: www.truewalshlaw.com
*Health care, corporate law & estate planning/administration*
Sally T. True, Partner

**United Hospital Fund of New York**
1411 Broadway, 12th Floor, New York, NY 10018
212-494-0700 Fax: 212-494-0800
e-mail: jtallon@uhfnyc.org
Web site: www.uhfnyc.org
*Health services research, public policy analysis & program development*
James R. Tallon, Jr., President

**United New York Ambulance Network (UNYAN)**
1450 Western Avenue, Suite 101, Albany, NY 12203
518-694-4420
Web site: www.unyan.net
*Membership corporation for emergency medical transportation professionals*
Lester Freemantle, Chair

**We Move**
204 W 84th St, New York, NY 10024
800-437-6682 Fax: 212-875-8389
Web site: www.wemove.org
*Education & information about movement disorders for both healthcare providers & patients*
Susan B Bressman, President

**NYS Bar Assn, Health Law Section**
**Wilson Elser Moskowitz Edelman & Dicker**
677 Broadway, Albany, NY 12207
518-449-8893 Fax: 518-449-8927
Web site: www.wilsonelser.com
Jonathan L. Bing, Partner

**Winthrop University Hospital**
259 First Street, Mineola, NY 11501
516-663-0333 or 516-663-2200
Web site: www.winthrop.org
John F. Collins, President & Chief Executive Officer

*Offices and agencies generally appear in alphabetical order, except when specific order is requested by listee.*

## HOUSING & COMMUNITY DEVELOPMENT

### NEW YORK STATE

### GOVERNOR'S OFFICE

**Governor's Office**
Executive Chamber
State Capitol
Albany, NY 12224
518-474-8390  Fax: 518-474-1513
Web site: www.ny.gov

Governor:
  Andrew M Cuomo . . . . . . . . . . . . . . . . . . . . . . . . . . . .518-474-8390
Secretary to the Governor:
  Melissa DeRosa . . . . . . . . . . . . . . . . . . .518-474-4246 or 212-681-4580
Counsel to the Governor:
  Kumiki Gibson . . . . . . . . . . . . . . . . . . . .518-474-8343 or 212-681-4580
Chief of Staff:
  Jill DesRosiers . . . . . . . . . . . . . . . . . . . .518-474-8390 or 212-681-4580
Director, Communications:
  Peter Ajemian . . . . . . . . . . . . . . . . . . . . .518-474-8418 or 212-681-4640
Deputy Secretary for Civil Rights:
  Vacant . . . . . . . . . . . . . . . . . . . . . . . . .212-681-4580 or 518-486-1214

### EXECUTIVE DEPARTMENTS AND RELATED AGENCIES

**Housing & Community Renewal, Division of**
Hampton Plaza
38-40 State Street
Albany, NY 12207
866-ASK-DHCR or 212-480-6700  Fax: 866-275-3427
e-mail: hcrinfo@nyshcr.org
Web site: www.nyshcr.org

641 Lexington Avenue
New York, NY 10022
866-275-3427

535 Washington Street
Electric Tower
Suite 105
Buffalo, NY 14203
Fax:

Commissioner/CEO:
  RuthAnne Visnauskas
President, Office of Housing Preservation:
  Mark Colon . . . . . . . . . . . . . . . . . . . . . . . . . . . . . . . . . . .866-275-3427
FOIL Officer:
  Valerie Molinaro
  e-mail: hcrfoil@nyshcr.org

**Administration**
Commissioner/CEO:
  RuthAnne Visnauskas . . . . . . . . . . . . . . . . . . . . . . . . . . . .866-275-3427

  **Housing Information Systems**
  Director:
    Vacant

**Community Development**
President, Office of Housing Preservation:
  Mark Colon . . . . . . . . . . . . . . . . . . . . . . . . . . . . . . . . . . .866-275-3427

Acting President, Office of Community Renewal:
  Chris Leo
  e-mail: OCRinfo@nyshcr.org
General Counsel:
  Linda Manley

  **Energy Rehabilitation Services**
  Director:
    Vacant . . . . . . . . . . . . . . . . . . . . . . . .518-474-5700/fax: 518-474-9907

  **Environmental Analysis Unit**
  Environmental Analyst:
    John Leahy . . . . . . . . . . . . . . . . . . . . . .518-474-6677 or 518-473-0457

  **Housing Trust Fund Program**
  Executive Deputy Commissioner & Chief Operating Officer:
    Betsy Mallow . . . . . . . . . . . . . . . . . . . . . . . . . . . . . . . .866-275-3427

  **Regional Offices**
  *Finger Lakes, Western NY, Southern Tier*
    535 Washington Street, Suite 105, Electric Tower, Buffalo, NY 14203
    Regional Director:
      Leonard Skrill . . . . . . . . . . . . . . . . . . . . . . . . . . . .716-847-7955
  *New York City, Long Island, Hudson Valley*
    641 Lexington Avenue, New York, NY 10022
    Regional Director:
      Vacant . . . . . . . . . . . . . . . . . . . . . . . . . . . . . . .212-688-4000

**Fair & Equitable Housing**
Assistant Commissioner & Director, Fair & Equitable Housing:
  Lorraine Collins

**Office of Housing Preservation**
President:
  Mark Colon . . . . . . . . . . . . . . . . . . . . . . . . . . . . .212-480-7343
Assistant Commissioner, Section 8:
  Alan L Smith . . . . . . . . . . . . . . . . . . . . . . . . . . . . .212-480-7221
FSS & Homeownership Coordinator:
  Deborah A Moore . . . . . . . . . . . . . . . . . . . . . . . . . . .518-486-5147

  **Office of Housing Management**
  Director:
    Vacant . . . . . . . . . . . . . . . . . . . . . . . . . . . . . . . .212-480-6266

  **Subsidy Services Bureau**
  25 Beaver Street, Room 673, New York, NY 10004
  Director:
    Vacant . . . . . . . . . . . . . . . . . . .212-480-6672/fax: 212-480-6677

**Legal Affairs**
General Counsel:
  Linda Manley . . . . . . . . . . . . . . . . . . . . . . . . . . . . .212-480-6707

**Policy & Intergovernmental Relations**
Director, Intergovernmental Affairs:
  Amy Fraioli . . . . . . . . . . . . . . . . . . . . . . . . . . . . . .518-473-2080
Legislative Liaison:
  Vacant . . . . . . . . . . . . . . . . . . . . . . .518-473-2519/fax: 518-474-5752

**Office of Rent Administration**
Deputy Commissioner:
  Woody Pascal . . . . . . . . . . . . . . . . . .718-262-4822/fax: 718-262-4008

  **Luxury Decontrol/Overcharge**
  Bureau Chief:
    John Lance . . . . . . . . . . . . . . . . . . . . . . . . . . . . . .718-262-4081

  **Property Management**
  Bureau Chief:
    Paul Fuller . . . . . . . . . . . . . . . . . . .718-262-4768/fax: 718-262-7938

  **Rent Control/ETPA**
  Bureau Chief:
    Vacant . . . . . . . . . . . . . . . . . . . . .718-262-4713/fax: 718-262-4008

*Offices and agencies generally appear in alphabetical order, except when specific order is requested by listee.*

**Tenant Protection Unit**
Deputy Commissioner:
   Richard White.....................................718-739-6400

**Law Department**
28 Liberty Street
New York, NY 10005
212-416-8000 or 800-771-7755
Web site: www.ag.ny.gov

State Capitol
Albany, NY 12224-0341
518-776-2000
Fax: 518-650-9401

Attorney General:
   Letitia James.....................212-416-8000 or 518-776-2000
Chief of Staff:
   Brian Mahanna .....................................212-416-8050
Press Secretary:
   Fernando Aquino..................212-416-8060/fax: 212-416-6005
   e-mail: nyag.pressoffice@ag.ny.gov

**Social Justice**
Executive Deputy Attorney General:
   Vacant .........................212-416-8075/fax: 212-416-8942

**Civil Rights Bureau**
Bureau Chief:
   Lourdes Rosado.................212-416-8250/fax: 212-416-8074

**Economic Justice**
Executive Deputy Attorney General:
   Siobhan Kennedy ...................................212-416-8050

**Consumer Frauds & Protection Bureau**
Bureau Chief:
   Jane Azia.......................212-416-8300/fax: 212-416-6003

**State Counsel**
Executive Deputy Attorney General, State Counsel:
   Vacant...........................................212-416-8050

**Litigation Bureau**
Bureau Chief:
   Jeffrey Dvorin ...................518-776-2300 or 212-416-8610

**Real Property Bureau**
Bureau Chief:
   Alison Crocker .................518-776-2700/fax: 518-474-0862

## CORPORATIONS, AUTHORITIES AND COMMISSIONS

**Capital District Regional Planning Commission**
One Park Place
Suite 102
Albany, NY 12205
518-453-0850  Fax: 518-453-0856
e-mail: cdrpc@cdrpc.org
Web site: www.cdrpc.org

Executive Director:
   Rocco A Ferraro ...................................518-453-0850
   e-mail: rocky@cdrpc.org
Financial Officer:
   Tim Canty.........................................518-453-0850

**Development Authority of the North Country**
317 Washington Street
Watertown, NY 13601

315-661-3200
e-mail: info@danc.org
Web site: www.danc.org

Chair:
   Gary Turck .......................................315-661-3200
Executive Director:
   James Wright .....................................315-661-3200
Deputy Executive Director:
   Thomas R Sauter...................................315-661-3200
Director, Engineering:
   Carrie Tuttle .....................................315-661-3210
Telecom Division Manager:
   David Wolf........................................315-661-3200
   e-mail: oatn@danc.org
Landfill Superintendent:
   Steve McElwain ...................................315-661-3230
Director, Regional Development:
   Michelle Capone ..................................315-661-3200

**Empire State Development Corporation**
633 Third Avenue
Floor 37
New York, NY 10017
212-803-3100  Fax: 212-803-3131
Web site: www.esd.ny.gov

625 Broadway
Albany, NY 12245
518-292-5100

95 Perry Street
Suite 500
Buffalo, NY 14203
716-846-8200
Fax: 716-846-8260

President & CEO, Commissioner:
   Howard Zemsky.....................212-803-3700 or 518-292-5100
   e-mail: president@esd.ny.gov
Chief Operating Officer & Deputy Commissioner:
   Kevin Younis .....................................212-803-3100
Executive Vice President, Administration:
   Ed Hamilton.......................................212-803-3700
Chief Financial Officer:
   Elaine Kloss
Chief of Staff:
   Lindsay Boylan.....................212-803-3700 or 518-292-5100

**New York City Housing Development Corporation**
110 William St
10th Fl
New York, NY 10038
212-227-5500  Fax: 212-227-6865
e-mail: info@nychdc.com
Web site: www.nychdc.com

Chairman:
   Vicki Been .......................................212-863-6100
President:
   Gary D Rodney.....................................212-227-3600
Executive VP/COO & General Counsel:
   Richard Froehlich ................................212-227-7435
Executive VP, Real Estate:
   Paula R Carethers ................................212-227-6846
Senior Vice President, Portfolio Management:
   Teresa Gigliello..................................212-227-9133

*Offices and agencies generally appear in alphabetical order, except when specific order is requested by listee.*

Policy Areas

Vice President, Loan Servicing:
  Karen Santiago . . . . . . . . . . . . . . . . . . . . . . . . . . . . . . . . .212-227-7494
Chief Credit Officer:
  Mary Horn. . . . . . . . . . . . . . . . . . . . . . . . . . . . . . . . . . . . . .212-227-9724
Communications/Press Office:
  Vacant . . . . . . . . . . . . . . . . . . . . . . . . . . . . . . . . . . . . . . . .212-227-2644

**New York City Residential Mortgage Insurance Corporation**
Chair:
  Vicki Been . . . . . . . . . . . . . . . . . . . . . . . . . . . . . . . . . . . . .212-863-6100
President:
  Gary D Rodney. . . . . . . . . . . . . . . . . . . . . . . . . . . . . . . . . .212-227-3600

## Roosevelt Island Operating Corporation (RIOC)
591 Main St
Roosevelt Island, NY 10044
212-832-4540  Fax: 212-832-4582
e-mail: information@rioc.ny.gov
Web site: www.rioc.ny.gov

President/CEO:
  Charlene M Indelicato . . . . . . . . . . . . . . . . . . . . . . . . .212-832-4540 x319
Director Island Operations:
  Cyril Opperman . . . . . . . . . . . . . . . . . . . . . . . . . . . . .212-832-4583
  e-mail: cyril.opperman@rioc.ny.gov
VP/General Counsel:
  Donald D. Lewis . . . . . . . . . . . . . . . . . . . . . . . . . . . .212-832-4540 x319
  e-mail: donald.lewis@rioc.ny.gov
VP/Chief Financial Officer:
  Frances Walton . . . . . . . . . . . . . . . . . . . . . . . . . . . . .212-832-4540 x350
Director Public Safety:
  Captain Estrella Suarez. . . . . . . . . . . . . . . . . . . . . . . .212-832-4545
  e-mail: keith.guerra@rioc.ny.gov

## State of New York Mortgage Agency (SONYMA)
641 Lexington Ave
4th Floor
New York, NY 10022
212-688-4000  Fax: 212-872-0789
Web site: www.nyshcr.org

Commissioner & CEO:
  Darryl C. Towns . . . . . . . . . . . . . . . . . . . . . . . . . . . .212-688-4000
President, Finance & Development:
  Vacant . . . . . . . . . . . . . . . . . . . . . . . . . . . . . . . . . . . . .212-688-4000
Director, Fair Housing & Equal Opportunity:
  Wanda Graham. . . . . . . . . . . . . . . . . . . . . . . . . . . . . .212-688-4000
Director, Public Information:
  Charni Sochet . . . . . . . . . . . . . . . . . . . . . . . . . . . . . . .212-872-0338

NEW YORK STATE LEGISLATURE

*See Legislative Branch in Section 1 for additional Standing Commit-
tee and Subcommittee information.*

## Assembly Standing Committees

**Housing**
Chair:
  Steven Cymbrowitz (D) . . . . . . . . . . . . . . . . . . . . . . .518-455-5214

**Local Governments**
Chair:
  Fred W Thiele Jr (I, D, WF). . . . . . . . . . . . . . . . . . . . .518-455-4826

## Senate Standing Committees

**Housing, Construction & Community Development**
Chair:
  Brian Kavanagh (D, WF) . . . . . . . . . . . . . . . . . . . . . . .518-455-2625

**Local Government**
Chair:
  James Gaughran (D) . . . . . . . . . . . . . . . . . . . . . . . . . .518-455-3250

## U.S. GOVERNMENT

### EXECUTIVE DEPARTMENTS AND RELATED AGENCIES

## US Department of Agriculture

**Rural Development**
  Web site: www.rd.usda.gov/ny

**New York State Office**. . . . . . . . . . . . . . . . . . . . . . . . . .fax: 315-477-8540
The Galleries of Syracuse, 441 South Salina Street, Suite 357, Syracuse,
NY 13202
TTY: 315-477-6447 or 315-477-6400  Fax: 315-477-8540
Acting State Director:
  Scott Collins . . . . . . . . . . . . . . . . . . . . . . . . . . . . . . . .215-477-6400
Special Projects Coordinator:
  Christopher Stewart
Eastern Region Area Director:
  Ronda Falkena. . . . . . . . . . . . . . . . . . . . . . . . . . . . . .845-343-1872 x4
Northern Region Area Director:
  Brian Murray. . . . . . . . . . . . . . . . . . . . . . . . . . . . . . .315-386-2401 x4
Western Region Area Director:
  Jim Walfrand. . . . . . . . . . . . . . . . . . . . . . . . . . . . . . .585-343-9167 x4

## US Housing & Urban Development Department
Web site: www.hud.gov

**New York State Office** . . . . . . . . . . . . . . . . . . . . . . . .fax: 212-264-0246
  26 Federal Plaza, Suite 3541, New York, NY 10278-0068
  212-264-8000  Fax: 212-264-0246
Regional Administrator:
  Holly M. Leicht. . . . . . . . . . . . . . . . . . . . . . . . . . . . . .212-542-7109
  e-mail: holly.m.leicht@hud.gov
Deputy Regional Administrator:
  Mirza Orriols. . . . . . . . . . . . . . . . . . . . . . . . . . . . . . . .212-542-7109
  e-mail: mirza.orriols@hud.gov
Public Affairs Officer:
  Charles McNally. . . . . . . . . . . . . . . . . . . . . . . . . . . . . .212-542-7647
  e-mail: charles.e.mcnally@hud.gov

  **Administration**
  Deputy Director, Field Support Services:
    Lisa Surplus . . . . . . . . . . . . . . . . . . . . . . . . . . . . . . .212-542-7331

  **Community Planning & Development**
  Director:
    Vincent Hom. . . . . . . . . . . . . . . . . . . . . . . . . . . . . . .212-542-7401
    e-mail: vincent.hom@hud.gov

  **Fair Housing & Equal Opportunity Office**
  Regional Director:
    Jay Golden . . . . . . . . . . . . . . . . . . . . . . . . . . . . . . . .212-542-7507

  **Field Offices**
  *Albany Area Office & Financial Operations Center* fax: 518-464-4300
    52 Corporate Circle, Albany, NY 12203-5121
    518-862-2800  Fax: 518 464-4300
    Field Office Director:
      Jaime Forero

*Offices and agencies generally appear in alphabetical order, except when specific order is requested by listee.*

*Buffalo Area Office* .........................fax: 716-551-5752
   465 Main Street, Lafayette Court, 2nd Floor, Buffalo, NY
   14203-1780
   Field Office Director:
     Joan Spilman ..............................716-551-5755

**General Counsel**
Regional Counsel:
   John Cahill ....................................212-542-7200

**Housing**
Director, Oversight & Accountability Division:
   Phyllis Ford ...................................212-542-7171

**Inspector General**
Assistant Special Agent-in-Charge:
   Heather Yannello
Assistant Regional Inspector General, Audit:
   Karen A. Campbell

**Public Housing**
Director:
   Luigi D'Ancona ...............................212-542-7649

## U.S. CONGRESS

*See U.S. Congress Chapter for additional Standing Committee and
Subcommittee information.*

### House of Representatives Standing Committees

#### Financial Services
Chair:
   Jeb Hensarling (R-TX) ............................202-225-3484
Ranking Member:
   Maxine Waters (D-CA) ...........................202-225-2201
Vice Chairman:
   Patrick T. McHenry (R-NC).......................202-225-2576
New York Delegate:
   Peter T. King (R)................................202-225-7896
New York Delegate:
   Carolyn B. Maloney (D)..........................202-225-7944
New York Delegate:
   Gregory W. Meeks (D)...........................202-225-3461
New York Delegate:
   Nydia M. Velazquez (D)..........................202-225-2361

   **Subcommittee**
   *Housing & Insurance*
     Chair:
      Blaine Luetkemeyer (R-MO)..................202-225-2956
     Ranking Member:
      Emanuel Cleaver (D-MO) ....................202-225-4535
     Vice Chairman:
      Lynn A. Westmoreland (R-GA) ...............202-225-5901
     New York Delegate:
      Nydia M. Velazquez (D) ....................202-225-2361

#### Transportation & Infrastructure
Chair:
   Bill Shuster (R-PA)..............................202-225-2431
Ranking Member:
   Peter A. DeFazio (D-OR).........................202-225-6416
New York Delegate:
   Sean Patrick Maloney (D).........................202-225-5441
New York Delegate:
   Richard L. Hanna (R) ...........................202-225-3665
New York Delegate:
   John Katko (R) .................................202-225-3701
New York Delegate:
   Jerrold Nadler (D)...............................202-225-5635

   **Subcommittee**
   *Economic Development, Public Buildings & Emergency Management*
     Chair:
      Lou Barletta (R-PA).........................202-225-6511
     Ranking Member:
      Andre Carson (D-IN)........................202-225-4011

### Senate Standing Committees

#### Banking, Housing & Urban Affairs
Chair:
   Richard Shelby (R-AL)...........................202-224-5744
Ranking Member:
   Sherrod Brown (D-OH) ..........................202-224-2315
New York Delegate:
   Charles E. Schumer (D) .........................202-224-6542

## PRIVATE SECTOR

**Albany County Rural Housing Alliance Inc**
PO Box 407, 24 Martin Road, Voorheesville, NY 12186
518-765-2425  Fax: 518-765-9014
e-mail: jeisgruber@acrha.org
Web site: www.acrha.org
*Development & management of low income housing; home repair programs;
housing counseling & education*
Judith Eisgruber, Executive Director

**American Institute of Architects (AIA) New York State Inc**
50 State Street, 5th Floor, Albany, NY 12207
518-449-3334  Fax: 518-426-8176
e-mail: aianys@aianys.org
Web site: www.aianys.org
*Architectural regulations, state policy, smart growth & affordable housing*
Georgi Ann Bailey, Executive Director

**Association for Community Living**
28 Corporate Drive, Suite 102, Clifton Park, NY 12065
518-688-1682  Fax: 518-688-1686
e-mail: admin@aclnys.org
Web site: www.aclnys.org
*Membership organization comprised of agencies that provide housing &
rehabilitation services to individuals with mental illness*
Antonia M. Lasicki, Executive Director

**Association for Neighborhood & Housing Development**
50 Broad Street, Suite 1402, New York, NY 10004-2699
212-747-1117  Fax: 212-747-1114
e-mail: benjamin.d@anhd.org
Web site: www.anhd.org
*Umbrella organization providing assistance to NYC nonprofits advocating
for affordable housing & neighborhood preservation*
Benjamin Dulchin, Executive Director

**Association for a Better New York**
355 Lexington Avenue, 8th Floor, New York, NY 10017
212-370-5800  Fax: 212-661-5877
Web site: www.abny.org
*Networking & advocacy for the development of businesses & communities in
New York*
Angela Pinsky, Executive Director

**Brooklyn Housing & Family Services Inc**
415 Albemarle Road, Brooklyn, NY 11218
718-435-7585  Fax: 718-435-7605
e-mail: ljayson@brooklynhousing.org
*Homelessness prevention, landlord/tenant dispute resolution & advocacy,
immigration services & assistance for victims of mortgage foreclosure*
Larry Jayson, Executive Director

*Offices and agencies generally appear in alphabetical order, except when specific order is requested by listee.*

Policy Areas

**CUNY Hunter College, Urban Affairs & Planning Department**
695 Park Avenue, West Building, Room 1611, New York, NY 10065
212-772-5518  Fax: 212-772-5593
e-mail: urban@hunter.cuny.edu
Web site: www.hunterurban.org
*Urban planning & public policy education, theory & research*
Stanley Moses, Chair

**Center for an Urban Future**
120 Wall Street, 20th Floor, New York, NY 10005
212-479-3344  Fax: 212-479-3338
e-mail: cuf@nycfuture.org
Web site: www.nycfuture.org
*Policy institute dedicated to addressing the critical problems facing cities through research reports, forums & events*
Jonathan Bowles, Executive Director

**Citizens Housing & Planning Council of New York**
42 Broadway, Suite 2010, New York, NY 10004
212-286-9211  Fax: 212-286-9214
e-mail: info@chpcny.org
Web site: www.chpcny.org
Jerilyn Perine, Executive Director

**Community Housing Improvement Program (CHIP)**
5 Hanover Square, Suite 1605, New York, NY 10004
212-838-7442  Fax: 212-838-7456
e-mail: info@chipnyc.org
Web site: www.chipnyc.org
*Representing NYC apartment building owners*
Patrick J. Siconolfi, Executive Director

**Community Preservation Corporation (The)**
28 East 28th Street, 9th Floor, New York, NY 10016-7943
212-869-5300  Fax: 212-683-0694
Web site: www.communityp.com
*Multifamily housing rehabilitation financing for NYC & NJ neighborhoods*
Rafael E. Cestero, President & Chief Executive Officer

**Community Service Society of New York**
633 Third Avenue, 10th Floor, New York, NY 10017
212-254-8900 or 212-614-5538
e-mail: info@cssny.org
Web site: www.cssny.org
*Research & advocacy for public policies & programs that improve housing conditions & opportunities for low-income NYC residents & communities*
David R. Jones, President & Chief Executive Officer

**Cornell Cooperative Extension, Community & Economic Vitality Program**
356 Roberts Hall, Cornell University, Ithaca, NY 14853
607-255-8546
Web site: www.cce.cornell.edu
*Work with community leaders, extension educators & elected officials to strengthen the vitality of New York's communities*
Christopher Watkins, Director, Cornell Cooperative Extension

**Federal Home Loan Bank of New York**
101 Park Avenue, New York, NY 10178-0599
212-681-6000  Fax: 212-441-6890
Web site: www.fhlbny.com
Jose R. Gonzalez, President & Chief Executive Officer

**Grow NYC**
100 Gold Street, Suite 3300, New York, NY 10038
212-788-7900  Fax: 212-788-7913
Web site: www.grownyc.org
*Material & technical assistance for housing groups to create & maintain open community gardens & other public open spaces in NYC*
Marcel Van Ooyen, Executive Director

**Hofstra University, School of Law**
121 Hofstra University, Hempstead, NY 11549
516-463-5858
e-mail: hofstralaw@hofstra.edu
*Land use & environmental law*
Eric Lane, Dean

**Housing Action Council Inc - Not For Profit**
55 South Broadway, 2nd Floor, Tarrytown, NY 10591
914-332-4144  Fax: 914-332-4147
e-mail: hac@affordablehomes.org
Web site: www.housingactioncouncil.org
*Financial feasibility, land use & zoning & affordable housing*
Rosemarie Noonan, Executive Director

**Housing Works Inc**
57 Willoughby Street, 2nd Floor, Brooklyn, NY 11201
347-473-7400 or TTY: 212-925-9560
e-mail: info@housingworks.org
Web site: www.housingworks.org
*Housing, health care, advocacy, job training & support services for homeless NY residents with HIV/AIDS*
Charles King, President & Chief Executive Officer

**Hudson Valley Pattern for Progress**
3 Washington Center, Newburgh, NY 12550
845-565-4900  Fax: 845-565-4918
e-mail: jdrapkin@pfprogress.org
Web site: www.pattern-for-progress.org
*Regional planning, research & policy development*
Jonathan Drapkin, President & Chief Executive Officer

**Local Initiatives Support Corporation**
501 Seventh Avenue, New York, NY 10018
212-455-9800  Fax: 212-682-5929
Web site: www.lisc.org
*Supports the development of local leadership & the creation of affordable housing, commercial, industrial & community facilities, businesses & jobs*
Michael Rubinger, President & Chief Executive Officer

**NY Housing Association Inc**
634 Watervliet Shaker Road, Latham, NY 12110
518-867-3242 or 800-721-4663
e-mail: info@nyhousing.org
Web site: www.nyhousing.org
*Manufactured, factory built, modular & mobile housing*
Nancy P. Geer, Executive Director

**Tenants & Neighbors**
236 West 27th Street, 4th Floor, New York, NY 10001
212-608-4320  Fax: 212-619-7476
Web site: www.tandn.org
*Organizing support, training, technical assistance & advocacy around tenants' rights & the preservation of affordable housing*
Katie Goldstein, Executive Director

**National Trust for Historic Preservation**
2600 Virginia Avenue NW, Suite 1100, Washington, DC 20037
202-588-6000 or 800-944-6847  Fax: 202-588-6038
e-mail: info@savingplaces.org
Web site: www.savingplaces.org
*Provides leadership, education, advocacy & resources to preserve America's historic places & revitalize communities*
Stephanie K. Meeks, President & Chief Executive Officer

**Neighborhood Preservation Coalition of NYS Inc**
126 State Street, Suite 302, Albany, NY 12207
518-432-6757  Fax: 518-432-6758
e-mail: p.gilbert@npcnys.org
Web site: www.npcnys.org
*Community organizations united to preserve & revitalize neighborhoods*
Paula Gilbert, Executive Director

*Offices and agencies generally appear in alphabetical order, except when specific order is requested by listee.*

**Nelson A Rockefeller Inst of Govt, Urban & Metro Studies**
411 State Street, Albany, NY 12203-1003
518-443-5522  Fax: 518-443-5788
Web site: www.rockinst.org
*Research on community capacity building, impacts of welfare reform on community development corporations, empowerment zone/enterprise communities & neighborhood preservation*
Patricia Cadrette, Project Administrative Officer

**New School University, Milano School of International Affairs, Management & Urban Policy**
72 Fifth Avenue, 3rd Floor, New York, NY 10011
212-229-5150  Fax: 212-627-2695
Web site: www.newschool.edu
*Research, policy analysis & evaluation on community development & urban poverty*
Michelle DePass, Dean

**New York Building Congress**
44 West 28th Street, 12th Floor, New York, NY 10001-4212
212-481-9230  Fax: 212-447-6037
e-mail: info@buildingcongress.com
Web site: www.buildingcongress.com
*Coalition of design, construction & real estate organizations*
Richard T. Anderson, President

**New York Community Bank**
615 Merrick Avenue, Westbury, NY 11590
877-786-6560
Web site: www.mynycb.com
Joseph R. Ficalora, President & Chief Executive Officer

**New York Landmarks Conservancy**
1 Whitehall Street, New York, NY 10004
212-995-5260  Fax: 212-995-5268
e-mail: info@nylandmarks.org
Web site: www.nylandmarks.org
*Technical & financial assistance for preservation & reuse of landmark buildings*
Peg Breen, President

**New York Lawyers for the Public Interest**
151 West 30th Street, 11th Floor, New York, NY 10001-4017
212-244-4664  Fax: 212-244-4570
Web site: www.nylpi.org
*Disability rights law; access to health care; environmental justice & community development; Pro Bono Clearinghouse services*
McGregor Smyth, Executive Director

**New York State Community Action Association**
2 Charles Blvd, Guilderland, NY 12084
518-690-0491  Fax: 518-690-0498
*Assists with the growth of community action agencies dedicated to improving the quality of life for low-income New Yorkers through education, technical assistance, training & advocacy*
Karla Digirolamo, Chief Executive Officer

**New York State Rural Advocates**
PO Box 104, Blue Mountain Lake, NY 12812
518-352-7787
*Advocacy & education for affordable housing for rural New Yorkers*
Nancy Berkowitz, Coordinator

**New York State Rural Housing Coalition Inc**
79 N Pearl Street, Albany, NY 12207
518-458-8696  Fax: 518-458-8896
e-mail: colin@ruralhousing.org
Web site: www.ruralhousing.org
*Affordable rural & small city housing; community & economic development*
Colin McKnight, Acting Deputy Director

**New York University, Wagner Graduate School**
295 Lafayette Street, 2nd Floor, New York, NY 10012
212-998-7400
e-mail: mitchell.moss@nyu.edu
*Urban planning research; urban challenges, economic growth, housing, environmental planning & community development*
Mitchell L. Moss, Professor of Urban Policy & Planning

**Park Resident Homeowners' Association Inc**
PO Box 68, Ontario, NY 14519
315-524-6703  Fax: 315-524-6703
*Protecting the rights of homeowners living in mobile/manufactured park communities in NYS*
George R Miles, President

**Parodneck Foundation (The)**
121 6th Avenue, Suite 501, New York, NY 10013
212-431-9700  Fax: 212-431-9783
e-mail: kwray@parodneckfoundation.org
Web site: www.parodneckfoundation.org
*Resident-controlled housing; community development*
Ken Wray, Executive Director

**PathStone Corporation**
400 East Avenue, Rochester, NY 14607-1910
585-340-3300 or 800-888-6770
Web site: www.pathstone.org
*Housing assistance & rehabilitation, property management, real estate development & community revitalization services*
Stuart J Mitchell, President & Chief Executive Officer

**Pratt Center for Community Development**
200 Willoughby Avenue, 3rd Floor East, Brooklyn, NY 11205
718-636-3486
e-mail: afriedman@prattcenter.net
Web site: www.prattcenter.net
*Training, technical assistance & advocacy in community economic development & sustainability*
Adam Friedman, Executive Director

**Project for Public Spaces**
419 Lafayette Street, 7th Floor, New York, NY 10003
212-620-5660  Fax: 212-620-3821
e-mail: info@pps.org
Web site: www.pps.org
*Nonprofit organization providing community planning, design & development services*
Fred Kent, President

**Regional Plan Association**
4 Irving Place, 7th Floor, New York, NY 10003
212-253-2727  Fax: 212-253-5666
e-mail: twright@rpa.org
Web site: www.rpa.org
*Association seeking to enhance economic development & quality of life in the New York metropolitan region through advocacy & research*
Thomas K. Wright, President

**Rent Stabilization Assn of NYC Inc**
123 William Street, 14th Floor, New York, NY 10038
212-214-9200  Fax: 212-732-7519
Web site: www.rsanyc.net
*NYC property owners organization*
Joseph Strasburg, President

**Settlement Housing Fund Inc**
247 West 37th Street, 4th Floor, New York, NY 10018
212-265-6530  Fax: 212-757-0571
Web site: www.settlementhousingfund.org
*Low & moderate income housing development, leasing, community development*
Alexa Sewell, President

*Offices and agencies generally appear in alphabetical order, except when specific order is requested by listee.*

**Urban Homesteading Assistance Board**
120 Wall Street, 20th Floor, New York, NY 10005
212-479-3300  Fax: 212-344-6457
e-mail: help@uhab.org
Web site: www.uhab.org
*Training, technical assistance & services for development & preservation of low income cooperative housing*
Andrew Reicher, Executive Director

**Women's Housing & Economic Development Corporation (WHEDCO)**
50 East 168th Street, Bronx, NY 10452
718-839-1100  Fax: 718-839-1170
e-mail: communications@whedco.org
Web site: www.whedco.org
*Non-profit organization dedicated to the development of communities & affordable housing*
Nancy Biberman, President

# HUMAN RIGHTS

## NEW YORK STATE

### GOVERNOR'S OFFICE

**Governor's Office**
Executive Chamber
State Capitol
Albany, NY 12224
518-474-8390  Fax: 518-474-1513
Web site: www.ny.gov

Governor:
  Andrew M Cuomo . . . . . . . . . . . . . . . . . . . . . . . . . . .518-474-8390
Secretary to the Governor:
  Melissa DeRosa . . . . . . . . . . . . . . . . .518-474-4246 or 212-681-4580
Counsel to the Governor:
  Kumiki Gibson . . . . . . . . . . . . . . . . . . .518-474-8343 or 212-681-4580
Deputy Secretary for Civil Rights:
  Vacant. . . . . . . . . . . . . . . . . . . . . . . .212-681-4580 or 518-486-1214
Chief of Staff:
  Jill DesRosiers . . . . . . . . . . . . . . . . . . .518-474-8390 or 212-681-4580
Director, Communications:
  Peter Ajemian. . . . . . . . . . . . . . . . . . . .518-474-8418 or 212-681-4640

### EXECUTIVE DEPARTMENTS AND RELATED AGENCIES

**Civil Service Department**
Empire State Plaza, Agency Building One
9th Floor
Albany, NY 12239
518-457-2487 or 877-697-5627
e-mail: pio@cs.ny.gov
Web site: www.cs.ny.gov

Commissioner:
  Vacant. . . . . . . . . . . . . . . . . . . . . . . . . . . . . . . . . .518-457-3701
Assistant Commissioner, Strategic Planning and Management:
  Vacant. . . . . . . . . . . . . . . . . . . . . . . . . . . . . . . . . .518-457-2487
Deputy Commissioner, Operations:
  Rebecca Corso . . . . . . . . . . . . . . . . . . . . . . . . . . . . .518-473-9539
Deputy Commissioner, Administration:
  Daquetta Jones
Director, Communications:
  Jian Paolucci. . . . . . . . . . . . . . . . . . . . . . . . . . . . . .518-457-9375
  e-mail: pio@cs.state.ny.us

#### Classification & Compensation Division
Director:
  Patricia A. Itite. . . . . . . . . . . . . . . . . .518-474-1011/fax: 518-474-0787

**Developmental Disabilities Planning Council**
99 Washington Avenue
Suite 1230
Albany, NY 12210
518-486-7505 or 800-395-3372
e-mail: information@ddpc.ny.gov
Web site: www.ddpc.ny.gov

Chairperson:
  Vacant. . . . . . . . . . . . . . . . . . . . . . . . . . . . . . . . . .800-395-3372
Vice Chairperson:
  Vacant. . . . . . . . . . . . . . . . . . . . . . . . . . . . . . . . . .800-395-3372

Executive Director:
  Sheila M Carey . . . . . . . . . . . . . . . . . . . . . . . . . . . .518-486-7505
  e-mail: sheila.carey@ddpc.ny.gov

**Human Rights, State Division of**
1 Fordham Plaza
4th Floor
Bronx, NY 10458
718-741-8400 or 888-392-3644  Fax: 718-741-8318
e-mail: infobronx@dhr.ny.gov
Web site: www.dhr.ny.gov

Commissioner:
  Helen Diane Foster . . . . . . . . . . . . . . . . . . . . . . . . . .718-741-8326
Chief Administrative Law Judge:
  Lilliana Estrella-Castillo. . . . . . . . . . . . . . . . . . . . . . .718-741-8342
Deputy Commissioner, Regional Affairs & Federal Programs:
  Gina N Martinez . . . . . . . . . . . . . . . . . . . . . . . . . . . .718-741-8324
Deputy Commissioner, Enforcement:
  Melissa Franco . . . . . . . . . . . . . . . . . . . . . . . . . . . . .718-741-8326
General Counsel:
  Caroline Downey . . . . . . . . . . . . . . . . . . . . . . . . . . . .718-741-8398
Director, Office of Equal Opportunity & Diversity:
  Rockwell J Chin . . . . . . . . . . . . . . . . . . . . . . . . . . . .718-741-8309
Director, Disability Rights:
  John Herrion . . . . . . . . . . . . . . . . . . . . . . . . . . . . . .718-741-8332

#### Regional Offices

**Albany**
Empire State Plaza, Agency Building One, 2nd Floor, Albany, NY 12220
Regional Director:
  Victor DeAmelia. . . . . . . . . . . . . . .518-474-2705/fax: 518-473-3422
  e-mail: infoalbany@dhr.ny.gov

**Binghamton**
44 Hawley Street, Room 603, Binghamton, NY 13901
Regional Director:
  Victor DeAmelia. . . . . . . . . . . . . . .607-721-8467/fax: 607-721-8470
  e-mail: infobinghamton@dhr.ny.gov

**Brooklyn**
55 Hanson Place, Rm 1084, Brooklyn, NY 11217
Regional Director:
  William Lamot . . . . . . . . . . . . . . . . . . . . . . . . . . . . .718-722-2385
  e-mail: infobrooklyn@dhr.ny.gov

**Buffalo**
W J Mahoney State Office Building, 65 Court Street, Suite 506, Buffalo, NY 14202
e-mail: infobuffalo@dhr.ny.gov
Regional Director:
  Vacant. . . . . . . . . . . . . . . . . . . . . .716-847-7632/fax: 716-847-7625

**Manhattan (Upper)**
Adam Clayton State Office Building, 163 W 125th Street, 4th Floor, New York, NY 10027
Regional Director:
  David Powell. . . . . . . . . . . . . . . . . .212-961-8650/fax: 212-961-4425

**Nassau County**
175 Fulton Avenue, Suite 404, Hempstead, NY 11550
e-mail: infolongisland@dhr.ny.gov
Regional Director:
  Froebel Chungata . . . . . . . . . . . . . . . . . . . . . . . . . . .516-539-6848

**Queens County**
55 Hanson Place, Room 900, Brooklyn, NY 11217
Regional Director:
  Joyce Yearwood-Drury . . . . . . . . . . . . . . . . . . . . . . .718-722-2060

*Offices and agencies generally appear in alphabetical order, except when specific order is requested by listee.*

**Rochester**
One Monroe Square, 259 Monroe Avenue, Suite 308, Rochester, NY 14607
Regional Director:
    Julia Day . . . . . . . . . . . . . . . . . . . . . 585-238-8250/fax: 585-238-8259
    e-mail: inforochester@dhr.ny.gov

**Suffolk County**
State Office Building, 250 Veterans Memorial Highway, Suite 2B-49, Hauppauge, NY 11788
Regional Director:
    Froebel Chungata . . . . . . . . . . . . . . 631-952-6434/fax: 631-952-6436
    e-mail: infolongisland@dhr.ny.gov

**Syracuse**
333 E Washington Street, Room 543, Syracuse, NY 13202
Regional Director:
    Julia Day . . . . . . . . . . . . . . . . . . . . . 315-428-4633/fax: 315-428-4638
    e-mail: infosyracuse@dhr.ny.gov

**White Plains**
7-11 South Broadway, Suite 314, White Plains, NY 10601
Regional Director:
    Linda Fenstermaker . . . . . . . . . . . . . . . . . . . . . . . . . . . 914-989-3120
    e-mail: infopeekskill@dhr.ny.gov

## Law Department

28 Liberty Street
New York, NY 10005
212-416-8000 or 800-771-7755
Web site: www.ag.ny.gov

State Capitol
Albany, NY 12224-0341
518-776-2000
Fax: 518-650-9401

Attorney General:
    Letitia James . . . . . . . . . . . . . . . . . . . . 212-416-8000 or 518-776-2000
Chief of Staff:
    Brian Mahanna . . . . . . . . . . . . . . . . . . . . . . . . . . . . . . . 212-416-8050
Press Secretary:
    Fernando Aquino . . . . . . . . . . . . . . . . . 212-416-8060/fax: 212-416-6005
    e-mail: nyag.pressoffice@ag.ny.gov

### Social Justice
Executive Deputy Attorney General:
    Vacant . . . . . . . . . . . . . . . . . . . . . . . . 212-416-8450/fax: 212-416-8942

#### Civil Rights Bureau
Bureau Chief:
    Lourdes Rosado . . . . . . . . . . . . . . . . . 212-416-8250/fax: 212-416-8074

## Temporary & Disability Assistance, Office of

40 North Pearl Street
Albany, NY 12243
518-473-1090 or 518-474-9516  Fax: 518-486-6255
e-mail: nyspio@otda.ny.gov
Web site: www.otda.ny.gov

Commissioner:
    Samuel D Roberts . . . . . . . . . . . . . . . . 518-474-4152/fax: 518-486-6255
Director, Intergovernmental Affairs:
    Judi West . . . . . . . . . . . . . . . . . . . . . . . . . . . . . . . . . . . . . 518-474-7420
Director, Public Information:
    Tim Ruffinen . . . . . . . . . . . . . . . . . . . . 518-474-9516/fax: 518-486-6935
    e-mail: nyspio@otda.ny.gov

### Integrated Family Assistance Programs Division
Deputy Commissioner:
    Barabara Guinn . . . . . . . . . . . . . . . . . . 518-486-6156 or 212-416-6358

Deputy Commissioner, Child Support Services:
    Eileen Stack . . . . . . . . . . . . . . . . . . . . . . . . . . . . . . . . . 518-474-1078
Assistant Deputy Commissioner, Employment & Income Support Programs:
    Jeff Gaskell . . . . . . . . . . . . . . . . . . . . . . . . . . . . . . . . . . 518-486-7694
Deputy Commissioner, Housing Refugee Services & Disability Determinations:
    Linda Glassman . . . . . . . . . . . . . . . . . . . . . . . . . . . . . . 518-402-3096

### Administrative Services Division
Deputy Commissioner:
    Eric Schwenzfeier . . . . . . . . . . . . . . . . . . . . . . . . . . . . . 518-473-3912

## NEW YORK STATE LEGISLATURE

*See Legislative Branch in Section 1 for additional Standing Committee and Subcommittee information.*

## Assembly Standing Committees

**Aging**
Chair:
    Ron Kim (D) . . . . . . . . . . . . . . . . . . . . . . . . . . . . . . . . . . 518-455-4527

**Correction**
Chair:
    David I Weprin (D) . . . . . . . . . . . . . . . . . . . . . . . . . . . . 518-455-5806

**Labor**
Chair:
    Michele R Titus (D) . . . . . . . . . . . . . . . . . . . . . . . . . . . 518-455-5668

**Mental Health**
Chair:
    Aileen M Gunther (D) . . . . . . . . . . . . . . . . . . . . . . . . . . 518-455-5355

## Assembly Task Forces

**Puerto Rican/Hispanic Task Force**
Chair:
    Maritza Davila (D) . . . . . . . . . . . . . . . . . . . . . . . . . . . . 518-455-5514
Executive Director:
    Guillermo Martinez . . . . . . . . . . . . . . . . . . . . . . . . . . . . 518-455-3608

**Women's Issues, Task Force on**
Chair:
    Rebecca A Seawright . . . . . . . . . . . . . . . . . . . . . . . . . . . 518-455-4466

## Senate Standing Committees

**Aging**
Chair:
    Rachel May (D, WF) . . . . . . . . . . . . . . . . . . . . . . . . . . . 518-455-2838
Ranking Minority Member:
    Sue Serino (R, C, IP) . . . . . . . . . . . . . . . . . . . . . . . . . . . 518-455-2945

**Crime Victims, Crime & Correction**
Ranking Minority Member:
    Fred Akshar (R, C, IP, RFM) . . . . . . . . . . . . . . . . . . . . . 518-455-2677

**Labor**
Chair:
    Jessica Ramos (D, WF) . . . . . . . . . . . . . . . . . . . . . . . . . 518-455-2529
Ranking Minority Member:
    Andrew J Lanza (R, C, IP, RFM) . . . . . . . . . . . . . . . . . . 518-455-3215

*Offices and agencies generally appear in alphabetical order, except when specific order is requested by listee.*

**Mental Health & Developmental Disabilities**

## U.S. GOVERNMENT

### EXECUTIVE DEPARTMENTS AND RELATED AGENCIES

## Equal Employment Opportunity Commission
Web site: www.eeoc.gov

**New York District** . . . . . . . . . . . . . . . . . . . . . . . . . . .fax: 212-336-3790
33 Whitehall Street, 5th Floor, New York, NY 10004
800-669-4000 or TTY: 800-669-6820  Fax: 212-336-3790
Director:
Kevin J. Berry. . . . . . . . . . . . . . . .800-669-4000 or TTY: 800-669-6820
fax: 212-336-3790

**Buffalo Local** . . . . . . . . . . . . . . . . . . . . . . . . . . . . . .fax: 716-551-4387
6 Fountain Plaza, Suite 350, Buffalo, NY 14202
800-669-4000 or TTY: 800-669-6820  Fax: 716-551-4387
Director:
John E. Thompson Jr. . . . . . . . . . . . .800-669-4000/fax: 716-551-4387

## US Commerce Department
Web site: www.commerce.gov

**Minority Business Development Agency**
Web site: www.mbda.gov

**New York Region**
26 Federal Plaza, New York, NY 10278
212-264-3262

**New York Business Center**
535 Fifth Avenue, 16th Floor, New York, NY 10017
648-821-4008
Project Director:
Paul Sawyer

**South Bronx Business Center**
555 Bergen Avenue, 3rd Floor, Bronx, NY 10455
718-732-7540
Project Director:
Sharon Higgins

**Williamsburg Business Center**
12 Heyward Street, 2nd Floor, Brooklyn, NY 11211
718-522-5620
Contact:
Yehuda Turner

## US Commission on Civil Rights
Web site: www.usccr.gov

**EASTERN REGION (includes New York State)**
624 9th Street NW, Suite 500, Washington, DC 20425
Regional Director:
Ivy L. Davis. . . . . . . . . . . . . . . . . . . . .202-376-7533/fax: 202-376-7548

## US Department of Health & Human Services
Web site: www.hhs.gov

**Office of Secretary's Regional Representative-Region 2-NY** . . fax: 212-264-3620
26 Federal Plaza, Suite 3835, New York, NY 10278
Regional Director:
Jackie Cornell-Bechelli. . . . . . . . . . . . . . . . . . . . . . . .212-264-4600

**Office for Civil Rights** . . . . . . . . . . . . . . . . . . . . . . .fax: 202-619-3818
26 Federal Plaza, Suite 3312, New York, NY 10278
Fax: 202-619-3818
Web site: www.hhs.gov/ocr

Regional Manager:
Linda Colon . . . . . . . . . . . . . . . . . . . . . . . . . . . . . . . . .212-264-3313

## US Department of Homeland Security (DHS)
Web site: www.dhs.gov

## US Citizenship & Immigration Services (USCIS)
TTY: 800-767-1833 or 800-375-5283
Web site: www.uscis.gov

**Buffalo District Office** . . . . . . . . . . . . . . . . . . . . . .fax: 716-551-3131
306 Delaware Avenue, Buffalo, NY 14202
District Director:
Edward A. Newman. . . . . . . . . . . . . . . . . . . . . . . . . . .716-843-7900
*Albany Sub Office*
1086 Troy-Schenectady Road, Latham, NY 12110
Director:
Gwynne Dinolfo . . . . . . . . . . . . . . . . . . . . . . . . . . .518-786-3210

**CIS Asylum Offices**
*New York Asylum Office*
1065 Stewart Avenue, Suite 200, Bethpage, NY 11714
516-261-0000
Director:
Patricia Menges . . . . . . . . . . . . . . . . . . . . . . . . . . .516-261-0000
Deputy Director:
Ashley Caudill-Mirillo. . . . . . . . . . . . . . . . . . . . . .516-261-0000
*Newark Asylum Office-Including NYS not served by New York City*
1200 Wall Street West, 4th Floor, Lyndhurst, NJ 07071
201-508-6100
Director:
Susan Raufer . . . . . . . . . . . . . . . . . . . . . . . . . . . . .201-531-0555
Deputy Director:
Sunil R. Varghese

**New York City District Office**
26 Federal Plaza, 3rd Floor, Room 3-120, New York, NY 10278
District Director:
Phyllis Coven
*Long Island Field Office*
30 Barretts Avenue, Holtsville, NY 11742
Field Office Director:
Elizabeth Miller

### U.S. CONGRESS

*See U.S. Congress Chapter for additional Standing Committee and Subcommittee information.*

## House of Representatives Standing Committees

**Education & the Workforce**
Chair:
John Kline (R-MN). . . . . . . . . . . . . . . . . . . . . . . . . . . . . .202-225-2271
Ranking Member:
Robert C. Scott (D-VA) . . . . . . . . . . . . . . . . . . . . . . . . . .202-225-8351
New York Delegate:
Hakeem S. Jeffries (D) . . . . . . . . . . . . . . . . . . . . . . . . . .202-225-5936
New York Delegate:
Elise Stefanik (R) . . . . . . . . . . . . . . . . . . . . . . . . . . . . . .202-225-4611

**Foreign Affairs**
Chair:
Edward R. Royce (R-CA). . . . . . . . . . . . . . . . . . . . . . . . .202-225-4111
Ranking Member:
Eliot L. Engel (D-NY) . . . . . . . . . . . . . . . . . . . . . . . . . . .202-225-2464
New York Delegate:
Brian Higgins (D) . . . . . . . . . . . . . . . . . . . . . . . . . . . . . .202-225-3306
New York Delegate:
Grace Meng (D) . . . . . . . . . . . . . . . . . . . . . . . . . . . . . . .202-225-2601

*Offices and agencies generally appear in alphabetical order, except when specific order is requested by listee.*

New York Delegate:
Gregory W. Meeks (D)..............................202-225-3461
New York Delegate:
Daniel Donovan (R) ................................202-225-3371
New York Delegate:
Lee M. Zeldin (R)...................................202-225-3826

**Subcommittee**
*Terrorism, Nonproliferation and Trade*
Chair:
Ted Poe (R-TX).............................202-225-6565
Ranking Member:
William Keating (D-MA) ....................202-225-3111
New York Delegate:
Brian Higgins (D) .........................202-225-3306

## Senate Standing Committees

### Indian Affairs, Committee on
Chair:
John Barrasso (R-WY) ............................202-224-6441
Vice Chair:
Jon Tester (D-MT) ...............................202-224-2644

## PRIVATE SECTOR

### American Jewish Committee
165 East 56th Street, New York, NY 10022-2709
212-751-4000  Fax: 212-891-1450
Web site: www.ajc.org
*Promoting tolerance, mutual respect & understanding among diverse ethnic, racial & religious groups; advocacy, communications & global diplomacy*
David Harris, Chief Executive Officer

### Amnesty International USA
5 Penn Plaza, 16th Floor, New York, NY 10001
212-807-8400  Fax: 212-627-1451
e-mail: aimember@aiusa.org
Web site: www.amnestyusa.org
*Worldwide campaigning movement working to promote internationally recognized human rights*
Margaret Huang, Interim Executive Director

### Anti-Defamation League
605 Third Avenue, New York, NY 10158
212-885-7700 or 866-386-3235
e-mail: adlmedia@adl.org
Web site: www.adl.org
*Fighting anti-Semitism worldwide*
Jonathan Greenblatt, National Director

### Asian American Legal Defense and Education Fund
99 Hudson Street, 12th Floor, New York, NY 10013-2815
212-966-5932 or 800-966-5946  Fax: 212-966-4303
e-mail: info@aaldef.org
Web site: www.aaldef.org
*Defends civil rights of Asian Americans through litigation, advocacy, education & community organizing*
Margaret Fung, Executive Director

### Bond Schoeneck & King PLLC
One Lincoln Center, 110 West Fayette Street, Syracuse, NY 13202-1355
315-218-8000  Fax: 315-218-8100
Web site: www.bsk.com
*Serves clients across a range of practice areas, including energy, natural resources, health care & higher education*
Kevin M. Bernstein, Chair, Management Committee

### CIDNY - Queens
80-02 Kew Gardens Road, Suite 107, Kew Gardens, NY 11415
646-442-1520 or TTY: 718-886-0427  Fax: 347-561-4883
Web site: www.cidny.org
*Rights & advocacy for disabled individuals*
Susan Dooha, Executive Director
Cyrus Kazi, Director of Administration

### Cardozo School of Law
55 Fifth Avenue, New York, NY 10003
212-790-0200  Fax: 212-790-0205
e-mail: mrosnfld@yu.edu
Web site: www.cardozo.yu.edu
*Law & theory of human rights*
Michel Rosenfeld, Justice Sidney L Robins Professor of Human Rights

### Center for Constitutional Rights
666 Broadway, 7th Floor, New York, NY 10012
212-614-6464  Fax: 212-614-6499
e-mail: info@ccrjustice.org
Web site: www.ccrjustice.org
*Dedicated to protecting human rights & driving social change through litigation, communications, education & advocacy*
Vincent Warren, Executive Director

### Center for Independence of the Disabled in NY (CIDNY)
841 Broadway, Suite 301, New York, NY 10003
212-674-2300 or TTY: 212-674-5619  Fax: 212-254-5953
Web site: www.cidny.org
*Rights & advocacy for disabled individuals*
Susan Dooha, Executive Director

### Center for Migration Studies of New York Inc
307 East 60th Street, 4th Floor, New York, NY 10022
212-337-3080
e-mail: cms@cmsny.org
Web site: www.cmsny.org
*Facilitates the study of international migration & promotes public policies that protect the rights of migrants & refugees*
Donald M. Kerwin, Jr., Executive Director

### Children's Rights Inc
330 Seventh Avenue, 4th Floor, New York, NY 10001
212-683-2210 or 888-283-2210  Fax: 212-683-4015
e-mail: info@childrensrights.org
Web site: www.childrensrights.org
*Advocacy & litigation on behalf of abused & neglected children*
Sandy Santana, Executive Director

### Citizens' Committee for Children of New York Inc
14 Wall Street, Suite 4E, New York, NY 10005-2173
212-673-1800  Fax: 212-979-5063
e-mail: info@cccnewyork.org
Web site: www.cccnewyork.org
*Public policy research, education & advocacy for children's rights & services*
Jennifer March, Executive Director

### Columbia University, Mailman School of Public Health
722 West 168th Street, New York, NY 10032
212-305-3927  Fax: 212-305-9342
e-mail: ph-admit@columbia.edu
Web site: www.mailman.columbia.edu
*Theory, analysis & development of policy & programs supporting public health & human rights*
Linda P Fried, Dean

*Offices and agencies generally appear in alphabetical order, except when specific order is requested by listee.*

**Cornell University, School of Industrial & Labor Relations**
309 Ives Hall, Cornell University, Ithaca, NY 14853
607-255-2762  Fax: 607-255-2185
e-mail: hallock@cornell.edu
Web site: www.ilr.cornell.edu
*Inequality, discrimination, workplace ethics; occupational segregation*
Kevin Hallock, Dean

**Drum Major Institute for Public Policy - Not For Profit**
3041 Broadway, 4th Floor, Auburn Hall, New York, NY 10027
212-203-9219
Web site: www.drummajorinst.org
*Think tank dedicated to facilitating dialogue on social issues & promoting public policies to drive economic justice & social change*
PJ Kim, Executive Director

**NYS Bar Assn, Diversity and Inclusion Cmte**
**Epstein Becker & Green, PC**
250 Park Avenue, New York, NY 10177
212-351-4500  Fax: 212-878-8600
e-mail: kstandard@ebglaw.com
Web site: www.ebglaw.com
Kenneth G. Standard, Co-Chair

**Family Planning Advocates of New York State**
194 Washington Avenue, Suite 620, Albany, NY 12210
518-436-8408  Fax: 518-436-0004
e-mail: info@familyplanningadvocates.org
*Reproductive rights*
Kim Atkins, Chair

**Filipino American Human Services Inc (FAHSI)**
18514 Hillside Avenue, Jamaica, NY 11432
718-883-1295  Fax: 718-523-9606
e-mail: fahsi@fahsi.org
Web site: www.fahsi.org
*FAHSI is a community-based, non-profit organization committed to serving NYC's Filipino & Filipino-American communities through education, advocacy, referrals, counseling services & support programs*
Zultan Bermudez, Chair

**NYS Bar Assn, Disability Rights Cmte**
**Girvin & Ferlazzo, PC**
20 Corporate Woods Blvd, Albany, NY 12211
518-462-0300  Fax: 518-462-5037
Tara Lynn Moffett, Chair

**Human Rights First**
75 Broad Street, 31st Floor, New York, NY 10004
212-845-5200  Fax: 212-845-5299
Web site: www.humanrightsfirst.org
*Advocacy for the promotion & protection of fundamental human rights worldwide*
Elisa Massimino, President & Chief Executive Officer

**Human Rights Watch**
350 Fifth Avenue, 34th Floor, New York, NY 10118-3299
212-290-4700  Fax: 212-736-1300
e-mail: hrwnyc@hrw.org
Web site: www.hrw.org
*Working with victims & activists to prevent discrimination, defend human rights & uphold political freedom across the world through research, reporting & advocacy*
Kenneth Roth, Executive Director

**International Institute of Buffalo, NY, Inc**
864 Delaware Avenue, Buffalo, NY 14209
716-883-1900  Fax: 716-883-9529
e-mail: iib@iibuff.org
Web site: www.iibuff.org
*Assists newly arrived refugees & immigrants with critical needs, medical care & employment training/placement; legal immigration service, translation & interpretation services, school advocacy*
Eva Hassett, Executive Director

**Jewish Community Relations Council of NY Inc**
225 West 34th Street, Suite 1607, New York, NY 10122
212-983-4800  Fax: 212-983-4084
Web site: www.jcrcny.org
*Serves as coordinating body for more than 60 Jewish organizations in metropolitan NY; promotes & protects the rights of NY's Jewish community*
Michael S. Miller, Executive Vice President & Chief Executive Officer

**Lambda Legal**
120 Wall Street, 19th Floor, New York, NY 10005-3919
212-809-8585  Fax: 212-809-0055
Web site: www.lambdalegal.org
*Protects the rights of gay, lesbian, bisexual & transgender people as well as individuals with HIV*
Kevin M. Cathcart, Executive Director

**LatinoJustice PRLDEF**
99 Hudson Street, 14th Floor, New York, NY 10013-2815
212-219-3360 or 800-328-2322  Fax: 212-431-4276
Web site: www.latinojustice.org
*Secures, promotes & protects the civil & human rights of the Latino community through litigation, policy analysis, education & advocacy*
Juan Cartagena, President & General Counsel

**Lesbian, Gay, Bisexual & Transgender Community Center - Not For Profit**
208 West 13th Street, New York, NY 10011-7702
212-620-7310  Fax: 212-924-2657
e-mail: info@gaycenter.org
Web site: www.gaycenter.org
*Mental health counseling, substance abuse treatment & counseling, after-school youth services, HIV/AIDS services, advocacy, cultural programs, affordable meeting & conference services, community-building*
Glennda Testone, Executive Director

**National Council of Jewish Women**
475 Riverside Drive, Suite 1901, New York, NY 10115
212-645-4048  Fax: 212-645-7466
e-mail: action@ncjw.org
Web site: www.ncjw.org
*Human rights & social service advocacy & education*
Nancy K. Kaufman, Chief Executive Officer

**National Organization for Women, NYS**
150 West 28th Street, Suite 304, New York, NY 10001
212-627-9895  Fax: 212-627-9861
e-mail: nownewyorkstate@gmail.com
Web site: www.nownys.org
*Legislative lobbying on issues affecting women*
Sonia Ossorio, President

**New School for Social Research, Department of Politics**
6 East 16th Street, Room 711A, New York, NY 10003
212-229-5747 x3090  Fax: 212-229-5473
e-mail: kalyvasa@newschool.edu
Web site: www.newschool.edu
*Comparative politics, human rights, nationalism & ethnicity*
Andreas Kalyvas, Chair

---

*Offices and agencies generally appear in alphabetical order, except when specific order is requested by listee.*

**New School for Social Research, Zolberg Institute on Migration & Mobility**
6 East 16th Street, 10th Floor, New York, NY 10003
e-mail: migration@newschool.edu
Web site: www.newschool.edu
*International migrations, refugees*
Alexandra Delano, Director

**New York Civil Liberties Union**
125 Broad Street, 19th Floor, New York, NY 10004
212-607-3300  Fax: 212-607-3318
Web site: www.nyclu.org
*Civil rights & civil liberties*
Donna Lieberman, Executive Director

**New York Civil Rights Coalition**
424 West 33rd Street, Suite 350, New York, NY 10001
212-563-5636  Fax: 212-563-9757
e-mail: contact@nycivilrights.org
Web site: www.nycivilrights.org
*Advocacy of racial equality & multiracial cooperation in advancing social progress through the protection & enforcement of civil rights & the unlearning of stereotypes*
Michael Meyers, President & Executive Director

**New York Immigration Coalition (The)**
131 West 33rd Street, Suite 610, New York, NY 10001
212-627-2227  Fax: 212-627-9314
Web site: www.thenyic.org
*Nonprofit umbrella advocacy organization for groups assisting immigrants & refugees in NYS*
Steven Choi, Executive Director

**New York Lawyers for the Public Interest**
151 West 30th Street, 11th Floor, New York, NY 10001-4017
212-244-4664  Fax: 212-244-4570
Web site: www.nylpi.org
*Disability rights law; access to health care; environmental justice & community development; Pro Bono Clearinghouse services*
McGregor Smyth, Executive Director

**New York State Council of Churches**
1580 Central Avenue, Albany, NY 12205
518-436-9319  Fax: 518-427-6705
e-mail: office@nyscoc.org
Web site: www.nyscoc.org
*Organization of Protestant Christian churches in NYS working to address social justice issues & protect Christian communities through education & worship.*
Rev. Peter M. Cook, Executive Director
Karen Lapierre, Office Manager

**Open Society Foundations**
224 West 57th Street, New York, NY 10019
212-548-0600  Fax: 212-548-4600
Web site: www.opensocietyfoundations.org
*Works to build inclusive societies through the promotion of equitable public policies & the development of initiatives for justice, education & public health advancement*
Christopher Stone, President

**Resource Center for Independent Living (RCIL)**
409 Columbia Street, PO Box 210, Utica, NY 13503-0210
315-797-4642 or TTY: 315-797-5837  Fax: 315-797-4747
Web site: www.rcil.com
*Services & advocacy for disabled people; public information, community education & awareness*
Zvia McCormick, Chief Executive Officer

**SUNY Buffalo Human Rights Center**
SUNY Buffalo Law School, 710 O'Brian Hall, Buffalo, NY 14260
716-645-2257
e-mail: buffalohrc@gmail.com
Web site: www.law.buffalo.edu
*Supports, promotes & fosters the study & practice of human rights law through student internships & human rights conferences & events*
Tara J. Melish, Director & Associate Professor

**Schuyler Center for Analysis & Advocacy (SCAA)**
540 Broadway, Albany, NY 12207
518-463-1896  Fax: 518-463-3364
e-mail: kbreslin@scaany.org
Web site: www.scaany.org
*Advocacy & policy analysis on education, child welfare, health, economic security, mental health, revenue & taxation issues*
Kate Breslin, President & Chief Executive Officer

**Self Advocacy Association of NYS**
500 Balltown Road, Building 12, Schenectady, NY 12304
518-382-1454  Fax: 518-382-1594
Web site: www.sanys.org
*Advocacy for & by persons with developmental disabilities to ensure civil rights & opportunities*
Steve Holmes, Administrative Director

**Simon Wiesenthal Center, Museum of Tolerance NY**
226 East 42nd Street, New York, NY 10017
212-697-1180
e-mail: motny@wiesenthal.com
Web site: www.wiesenthal.com
*Preserves the memory of the Holocaust & invites individuals to consider issues of prejudice & tolerance through workshops, exhibits, training programs & educational outreach*
Stacey Eliuk, Program Manager

**Tanenbaum Center for Interreligious Understanding**
254 West 31st Street, 7th Floor, New York, NY 10001
212-967-7707  Fax: 212-967-9001
e-mail: info@tanenbaum.org
Web site: www.tanenbaum.org
*Puts interreligious understanding into practice; reduces and prevents prejudice & violence done in the name of religion*
Joyce S. Dubensky, Chief Executive Officer

**The Legal Aid Society**
199 Water Street, New York, NY 10038
212-577-3300  Fax: 212-509-8761
Web site: www.legal-aid.org
Seymour W. James, Jr., Attorney-in-Chief

**Whiteman Osterman & Hanna LLP**
One Commerce Plaza, Albany, NY 12260
518-487-7600  Fax: 518-487-7777
Web site: www.woh.com
William S. Nolan, Partner

**Women's Refugee Commission**
122 East 42nd Street, New York, NY 10168-1289
212-551-3115  Fax: 212-551-3180
e-mail: info@wrcommission.org
*Advocacy on behalf of refugee women & children worldwide*
Sarah Costa, Executive Director

*Offices and agencies generally appear in alphabetical order, except when specific order is requested by listee.*

# INSURANCE

## NEW YORK STATE

### GOVERNOR'S OFFICE

**Governor's Office**
Executive Chamber
State Capitol
Albany, NY 12224
518-474-8390  Fax: 518-474-1513
Web site: www.ny.gov

Governor:
  Andrew M Cuomo .................................518-474-8390
Secretary to the Governor:
  Melissa DeRosa ....................518-474-4246 or 212-681-4580
Counsel to the Governor:
  Kumiki Gibson......................518-474-8343 or 212-681-4580
Chief of Staff:
  Jill DesRosiers .....................518-474-8390 or 212-681-4580
Director, Communications:
  Peter Ajemian.......................518-474-8418 or 212-681-4640

### EXECUTIVE DEPARTMENTS AND RELATED AGENCIES

**Financial Services Department**
One State Street
New York, NY 10004-1511
212-480-6400 or 800-342-3736
e-mail: public-affairs@dfs.ny.gov
Web site: www.dfs.ny.gov

One Commerce Plaza
Albany, NY 12257
Fax:

Walter Mahoney Office Building
65 Court Street, Room 7
Buffalo, NY 14202
Fax:

Superintendent:
  Maria T. Vullo ......................................212-709-3500
Assistant Director, Administration & Operations:
  Lori Fraser..........................................518-486-4737
Director, Criminal Investigations Bureau:
  Ricardo Velez.......................................212-709-3500
Chief Information Officer:
  Vacant ..............................................212-709-5420
Senior Public Information Specialist:
  Ronald Klug.......................212-480-2285/fax: 212-480-6077
Consumer Representative, State Charter Advisory Board:
  Vacant..............................................212-709-3500

**Banking Division**
Deputy Superintendent:
  Vacant...............................................212-709-1690

**Insurance Division**
Chief, Life Insurance Bureau:
  Gail Keren..........................................212-480-5030
Chief, Health Insurance Bureau:
  Vacant.........................518-486-2970/fax: 518-474-3397
Insurance Examiner 3:
  Michael Maffei .....................................212-480-5023

**Financial Frauds & Consumer Protection Division**
Director, Frauds:
  Frank Orlando .....................212-480-6074/fax: 212-480-3555
Assistant Director, Frauds:
  Angelo Carbone ....................................212-480-5688

**Capital Markets Division**
Director, Capital Markets:
  Vacant .............................212-480-5071/fax: 212-480-6085
Deputy Superintendent, Mortgage Banking:
  Rhonda Ricketts ....................................212-480-5540

---

**Insurance Fund (NYS)**
One Watervliet Avenue Ext
Albany, NY 12206-1629
518-437-6400
Web site: www.nysif.com

199 Church Street
New York, NY 10007-1100
212-587-5435

Executive Director & CEO:
  Eric Madoff.........................................518-437-5220
Deputy Executive Director & Chief of Staff:
  Shirley Stark .......................................518-437-6400
Chief Fiscal Officer:
  Susan D Sharp.......................................518-437-6168
General Attorney:
  Tanisha Edwards, Esq
Chief Financial Officer:
  William Gratrix

**Administration**
Director:
  Joseph Mullen.......................................518-437-5220

**Claims & Medical Operations**
Director:
  Edward Hiller ......................................212-312-7880

**Confidential Investigations**
Director:
  George T Tidona.....................................631-756-4007

**Field Services**
Director:
  Armin Holdorf ......................................212-587-5225

**Information Technology Service**
Chief Information Officer:
  Sean O'Brien........................................518-437-4361
Director, ITS:
  Laurie Endries......................................518-437-3130

**Insurance Fund Board of Commissioners**
Chair:
  Kenneth R Theobalds.................518-437-5220 or 518-437-6400
Vice Chair:
  Barry Swidler ......................518-437-5220 or 518-437-6400
Secretary to the Board:
  Francine James .....................................212-312-7408
Member (ex-officio)/Commissioner, NYS Dept of Labor:
  Peter M. Rivera.....................................518-437-5220
Member:
  Roberta Reardon....................518-437-5220 or 518-437-6400
Member:
  Joseph Canovas.....................................518-437-5220
Member:
  David E Ourlicht....................................518-437-5220

*Offices and agencies generally appear in alphabetical order, except when specific order is requested by listee.*

## Investments

Director:
  Miriam Martinez.....................................212-587-6550

## NYSIF District Offices

### Albany
1 Watervliet Ave Ext, Albany, NY 12206
Business Manager:
  Augusto Bortoloni...............518-437-6401/fax: 518-437-8021

### Buffalo
225 Oak St, Buffalo, NY 14203
Business Manager:
  Ronald Reed ....................716-851-2004/fax: 716-851-2131

### Binghamton
Glendale Technology Park, 2001 E Perimeter Rd, Endicott, NY 13760
Business Manager:
  Thomas Racko..................607-741-6023/fax: 607-741-5029

### Nassau County, Long Island
8 Corporate Center Dr, 2nd Fl, Melville, NY 11747
Business Manager:
  Cliff Meister ...................631-756-4003/fax: 631-756-4030

### Rochester
100 Chestnut St, Ste 1000, Rochester, NY 14604
Business Manager:
  Lisa Ellsworth.................585-258-2100/fax: 585-258-2065

### Suffolk County, Long Island
8 Corporate Center Dr, 3rd Fl, Melville, NY 11747
Business Manager:
  Catherine Carillo...............631-756-4330/fax: 631-756-4260

### Syracuse
1045 Seventh North St, Liverpool, NY 13088
Business Manager:
  Patricia Albert..................315-453-8300/fax: 315-453-8313

### White Plains
105 Corporate Park Dr, Ste 200, White Plains, NY 10604
Business Manager:
  Carl Heitner....................914-701-6292/fax: 914-701-2181

## Premium Audit

Director:
  Glenn Cunningham...............................212-587-7470

## Underwriting

Director:
  John Massetti ....................................212-312-7012

## Labor Department

W.A. Harriman Campus
Building 12
Albany, NY 12240
518-457-9000 or 888-469-7365 Fax: 518-457-6908
e-mail: nysdol@labor.ny.gov
Web site: www.labor.ny.gov

Commissioner:
  Roberta Reardon....................................518-457-9000
Executive Deputy Commissioner:
  Nathaalie Carey....................................518-457-4318
Associate Commissioner, Communications:
  Peter Brancato.....................................518-457-5519

## Hazard Abatement Board

Chair:
  Katherine D. Schrier................................518-457-7629

## Employment Relations Board

Chair:
  Jerome Lefkowitz...................................518-457-2664
  e-mail: perbinfo@perb.ny.gov

## Industrial Board of Appeals

Chair:
  Anne P Stevason...................................518-474-4785

## Unemployment Insurance Appeal Board

Chair:
  Leonard Polletta...................................518-402-0205
Executive Director:
  Susan Borenstein...................................518-402-0205

## State Workforce Investment Board

Chair:
  Vacant .........................518-457-8312/fax: 518-485-8604

## Law Department

28 Liberty Street
New York, NY 10005
212-416-8000 or 800-771-7755
Web site: www.ag.ny.gov

State Capitol
Albany, NY 12224-0341
518-776-2000
Fax: 518-650-9401

Attorney General:
  Letitia James........................212-416-8000 or 518-776-2000
Chief of Staff:
  Brian Mahanna .....................................212-416-8050
Press Secretary:
  Fernando Aquino..................212-416-8060/fax: 212-416-6005
  e-mail: nyag.pressoffice@ag.ny.gov

## State Counsel

Executive Deputy Attorney General, State Counsel:
  Vacant...........................................212-416-8050

### Civil Recoveries Bureau
Bureau Chief:
  John Cremo....................518-776-2173/fax: 518-915-7731

### Claims Bureau
Bureau Chief:
  Katharine Brooks..................518-776-2300 or 212-416-8500

### Litigation Bureau
Bureau Chief:
  Jeffrey Dvorin ...................518-776-2300 or 212-416-8610
  fax: 518-473-1572

### Real Property Bureau
Bureau Chief:
  Alison Crocker ....................................518-776-2700

## Workers' Compensation Board

328 State Street
Schenectady, NY 12305-2318
518-408-0469 or 877-632-4996 Fax: 518-473-1415
e-mail: general_information@wcb.ny.gov
Web site: www.wcb.ny.gov

Executive Director:
  MaryBeth Woods...................................518-408-0469
Chair, Board of Commissioners:
  Clarissa M Rodriguez ..............518-408-0469/fax: 518-473-1415

*Offices and agencies generally appear in alphabetical order, except when specific order is requested by listee.*

Vice Chair:
  Freida Foster . . . . . . . . . . . . . . . . . . . . . . 518-408-0469/fax: 518-473-1415
General Counsel:
  David Wertheim . . . . . . . . . . . . . . . . . . 518-486-9564/fax: 518-402-0113
  e-mail: officeofgeneralcounsel@wcb.ny.gov
Director, Public Information:
  Melissa Stewart . . . . . . . . . . . . . . . . . . . 518-408-0469/fax: 518-473-1415
  e-mail: publicinfo@wcb.ny.gov
Fraud Inspector General:
  Vacant. . . . . . . . . . . . . . . . . . . . . . . . . . . . . . . . . . . . . . .800-367-4448
Advocate for Injured Workers:
  Edwin Ruff . . . . . . . . . . . . . . . . . . . . . . .800-580-6665 or 518-471-8182
  fax: 518-486-7510
  e-mail: advinjwkr@wcb.ny.gov

## Administration
Facilities Management:
  Michael DeBarr. . . . . . . . . . . . . . . . . . . . . . . . . . . . . . . .518-486-9597
Chief, Security:
  Sylvio Mantello . . . . . . . . . . . . . . . . . . .518-486-0373/fax: 518-402-6100
Director, Human Resources:
  Gilda Hernandez . . . . . . . . . . . . . . . . . .518-486-3348/fax: 518-486-6364
Affirmative Action Officer:
  Jaime Benitez. . . . . . . . . . . . . . . . . . . . .518-486-5128/fax: 518-486-6364

## Information Management Systems
Director:
  Vacant . . . . . . . . . . . . . . . . . . . . . . . . .518-474-6557/fax: 518-474-9367
Director, Continuous Improvement/MIS:
  Thomas Wegener . . . . . . . . . . . . . . . . . . . . . . . . . . . . . . .518-486-5143

## Operations
Director, Bureau of Compliance:
  Vacant . . . . . . . . . . . . . . . . . . . . . . . . .518-474-9598/fax: 518-402-6201

### District Offices
*Albany*
  100 Broadway-Menands, Albany, NY 12241
  District Manager:
    Laurie Hart . . . . . . . . . . . . . . . . .866-750-5157/fax: 518-473-9166
*Binghamton*
  State Office Bldg, 44 Hawley St, Binghamton, NY 13901
  District Manager:
    David Gardiner. . . . . . . . . . . . .866-802-3604/fax: 607-721-8464
*Brooklyn*
  111 Livingston St, 22nd Fl, Brooklyn, NY 11201
  District Manager:
    Tom Agostino. . . . . . . . . . . . . .800-877-1373/fax: 718-802-6642
*Buffalo*
  Ellicott Sq Building, 295 Main Street Ste 400, Buffalo, NY 14203
  District Manager:
    Michelle Hirsch . . . . . . . . . . . .866-211-0645/fax: 716-842-2171
*Long Island*
  220 Rabro Drive, Ste 100, Hauppauge, NY 11788-4230
  District Manager:
    Bryan Pile. . . . . . . . . . . . . . . . .866-681-5354/fax: 631-952-7966
*Manhattan*
  215 W 125th St, New York, NY 10027
  District Manager:
    Sherri Cunningham. . . . . . . . . .800-877-1373/fax: 212-864-7204
*Peekskill*
  41 N Division St, Peekskill, NY 10566
  District Manager:
    Vacant. . . . . . . . . . . . . . . . . . . .866-746-0552/fax: 914-788-5809
*Queens*
  168-46 91st Ave, 3rd Fl, Jamaica, NY 11432
  District Manager:
    Bryan Pile. . . . . . . . . . . . . . . . . . . . . . . . . . . . . . . . .800-877-1373
*Rochester*
  130 Main St West, Rochester, NY 14614
  District Manager:
    Matthew Bligh . . . . . . . . . . . . .866-211-0644/fax: 585-238-8351

*Syracuse*
  935 James Street, Syracuse, NY 13203
  District Manager:
    Marc Johnson . . . . . . . . . . . . . .866-802-3730/fax: 315-423-2938

## Workers' Compensation Board of Commissioners
Chair, Board of Commissioners:
  Clarissa M Rodriguez. . . . . . . . . . . . . . . . . . . . . . . . . . . . .518-408-0469
Vice Chair:
  Freida Foster . . . . . . . . . . . . . . . . . . . . . . . . . . . . . . . . . .518-408-0469
Commissioner:
  Frederik M Ausili . . . . . . . . . . . . . . . . . . . . . . . . . . . . . . .518-408-0469
Commissioner:
  Margaret Barbaris . . . . . . . . . . . . . . . . . . . . . . . . . . . . . . .518-408-0469
Commissioner:
  Steven A Crain . . . . . . . . . . . . . . . . . . . . . . . . . . . . . . . . . .518-408-0469
Commissioner:
  Mark Higgins . . . . . . . . . . . . . . . . . . . . . . . . . . . . . . . . . . .518-408-0469
Commissioner:
  Linda Hull. . . . . . . . . . . . . . . . . . . . . . . . . . . . . . . . . . . . . .518-408-0469
Commissioner:
  Ursula Levelt. . . . . . . . . . . . . . . . . . . . . . . . , . . . . . . . . . . .518-408-0469
Commissioner:
  Loren Lobban . . . . . . . . . . . . . . . . . . . . . . . . . . . . . . . . . . .518-408-0469
Commissioner:
  Ellen O Paprocki . . . . . . . . . . . . . . . . . . . . . . . . . . . . . . . .518-408-0469
Chair:
  Clarissa M Rodriguez. . . . . . . . . . . . . . . . . . . . . . . . . . . . .518-408-0469
Commissioner:
  Mark R Stasko . . . . . . . . . . . . . . . . . . . . . . . . . . . . . . . . . .518-408-0469
Commissioner:
  Samuel G Williams. . . . . . . . . . . . . . . . . . . . . . . . . . . . . . .518-408-0469
Secretary to the Board:
  Kim McCarroll . . . . . . . . . . . . . . . . . . . . . . . . . . . . . . . . . .518-402-6070

## NEW YORK STATE LEGISLATURE

*See Legislative Branch in Section 1 for additional Standing Committee and Subcommittee information.*

## Assembly Standing Committees

### Insurance
Chair:
  Kevin A. Cahill (D) . . . . . . . . . . . . . . . . . . . . . . . . . . . . . .518-455-4436

### Labor
Chair:
  Michele R Titus (D) . . . . . . . . . . . . . . . . . . . . . . . . . . . . . .518-455-5668

## Senate Standing Committees

### Insurance
Chair:
  Neil D Breslin (D, IP, WF). . . . . . . . . . . . . . . . . . . . . . . . .518-455-2225

### Labor
Chair:
  Jessica Ramos (D, WF). . . . . . . . . . . . . . . . . . . . . . . . . . . .518-455-2529
Ranking Minority Member:
  Andrew J Lanza (R, C, IP, RFM). . . . . . . . . . . . . . . . . . . . .518-455-3215

## U.S. GOVERNMENT

## U.S. CONGRESS

*See U.S. Congress Chapter for additional Standing Committee and Subcommittee information.*

---

*Offices and agencies generally appear in alphabetical order, except when specific order is requested by listee.*

## House of Representatives Standing Committees

### Financial Services
Chair:
Jeb Hensarling (R-TX) . . . . . . . . . . . . . . . . . . . . . . . . . . . . .202-225-3484
Ranking Member:
Maxine Waters (D-CA) . . . . . . . . . . . . . . . . . . . . . . . . .202-225-2201
Vice Chairman:
Patrick T. McHenry (R-NC). . . . . . . . . . . . . . . . . . . . .202-225-2576
New York Delegate:
Peter T. King (R). . . . . . . . . . . . . . . . . . . . . . . . . . . . . .202-225-7896
New York Delegate:
Carolyn B. Maloney (D). . . . . . . . . . . . . . . . . . . . . . . . .202-225-7944
New York Delegate:
Gregory W. Meeks (D) . . . . . . . . . . . . . . . . . . . . . . . . . .202-225-3461
New York Delegate:
Nydia M. Velazquez (D) . . . . . . . . . . . . . . . . . . . . . . . . .202-225-2361

#### Subcommittee
*Capital Markets & Government Sponsored Enterprises*
Chair:
Scott Garrett (R-NJ) . . . . . . . . . . . . . . . . . . . . . .202-225-4465
Ranking Member:
Carolyn B. Maloney (D-NY) . . . . . . . . . . . . . . .202-225-7944
New York Delegate:
Gregory W. Meeks (D) . . . . . . . . . . . . . . . . . . . .202-225-3461
New York Delegate:
Peter T. King (R) . . . . . . . . . . . . . . . . . . . . . . . . .202-225-7896

## Senate Standing Committees

### Finance
Chair:
Orrin G. Hatch (R-UT) . . . . . . . . . . . . . . . . . . . . . . . . .202-224-5251
Ranking Member:
Ron Wyden (D-OR) . . . . . . . . . . . . . . . . . . . . . . . . . . . .202-224-5244

#### Subcommittees
*Health Care*
Chair:
Patrick J. Toomey (R-PA) . . . . . . . . . . . . . . . . . . .202-224-4254
Ranking Member:
Debbie Stabenow (D-MI) . . . . . . . . . . . . . . . . . .202-224-4822
*Social Security, Pensions and Family Policy*
Chair:
Dean Heller (R-NV) . . . . . . . . . . . . . . . . . . . . . . .202-224-6244
Ranking Member:
Sherrod Brown (D-OH) . . . . . . . . . . . . . . . . . . . .202-224-2315

## PRIVATE SECTOR

### American International Group Inc
175 Water Street, New York, NY 10038
212-770-7000
Web site: www.aig.com
*International business, government & financial services*
Victor Aviles, Director, Corporate Communications

### Aon Service Corporation
199 Water St, 35th Fl, New York, NY 10038
212-441-1150  Fax: 212-441-1929
e-mail: ellen_perle@aon.com
Web site: www.aon.com
*Regulatory Law Licensing*
Ellen Perle, Chief General Counsel/Regulatory Law Licensing

### Associated Risk Managers of New York Inc
4 Airline Drive, Suite 205, Albany, NY 12205
518-690-2072 or 800-735-5441  Fax: 518-690-2074
Web site: www.armnortheast.com
John McLaughlin, Executive Director

### Connors & Corcoran PLLC
Times Square Bldg, 45 Exchange St, Ste 250, Rochester, NY 14614
585-232-5885  Fax: 585-546-3631
e-mail: ebuholtz@connorscorcoran.com
Web site: www.connorscorcoran.com
Eileen E Buholtz, Member

### DeGraff, Foy, & Kunz, LLP
90 State Street, Albany, NY 12207
518-462-5300  Fax: 518-436-0210
e-mail: firm@degraff-foy.com
Web site: www.degraff-foy.com
*Tax law & procedure, administrative law*
David Kunz, Managing Partner

### Dupee & Monroe, PC
211 Main Street, Box 470, Goshen, NY 10924
845-294-8900  Fax: 845-294-3619
Web site: www.dupeelaw.com
*Litigation, personal injury law, medical malpractice, product liability, civil rights, discrimination, sexual harassment*
James E Monroe, Managing Partner

### Empire Blue Cross & Blue Shield
1 Liberty Plaza, New York, NY 10006
212-476-1000  Fax: 212-476-1281
Web site: www.empireblue.com
*Health insurance*
Lawrence Schreiber, President

### Equitable Life Assurance Society of the US
1290 Ave of the Americas, New York, NY 10104
212-314-3828  Fax: 212-707-1890
Web site: www.axa-financial.com  '
*Life insurance regulation*
Wendy E Cooper, Senior Vice President & Associate General Counsel, Government Relations

### Excellus Health Plan Inc
165 Court Street, Rochester, NY 14647
585-327-7581  Fax: 585-327-7585
e-mail: stephen.sloan@excellus.com
*Health insurance*
Stephen R Sloan, Senior Vice President & Chief Administrative Officer, General Counsel

### Excess Line Association of New York
One Exchange Plz, 55 Broadway, 29th Fl, New York, NY 10006
646-292-5555  Fax: 626-292-5505
e-mail: dmaher@elany.org
Web site: www.elany.org
*Industry advisory association; facilitate & encourage compliance with the excess line law*
Daniel F Maher, Executive Director

### Group Health Inc
441 9th Ave, 8th Fl, New York, NY 10001
212-615-0891  Fax: 212-563-8561
Web site: www.ghi.com
*Affordable, quality health insurance for working individuals & families*
Jeffrey Goodwin, Director, Governmental Relations

---

*Offices and agencies generally appear in alphabetical order, except when specific order is requested by listee.*

**Insurance Brokers' Association of the State of New York**
136 Everett Road, Albany, NY 12205
212-509-1592  Fax: 518-935-9448
e-mail: info@ibany.org
Web site: www.ibany.org
*IBANY provides a platform for education, professional development, and networking, serving all generations of the insurance industry, including top-level executives, experienced professionals, and emerging leaders.*
Paul Rovelli, President

**Life Insurance Council of New York, Inc**
551 Fifth Ave, 29th Floor, New York, NY 10176
212-986-6181  Fax: 212-986-6549
e-mail: tworkman@licony.org
Web site: www.licony.org
*Promote a legislative, regulatory & judicial environment that encourages members to conduct & grow their business*
Thomas E Workman, President & Chief Executive Officer

**Marsh & McLennan Companies**
1166 6th Ave, New York, NY 10036-2774
212-345-5000
e-mail: barbara.perlmutter@mmc.com
Web site: www.mmc.com
*Risk & insurance services; investment management; consulting*
Barbara S Perlmutter, Senior Vice President, Public Affairs

**Medical Society of the State of New York, Div of Socio-Medical Economics**
856 Merrick Avenue, Westbury, NY 11590
516-488-6100
e-mail: rmcnally@mssny.org
Web site: www.mssny.org
*Workers compensations; health insurance programs*
Regina McNally, Vice President

**MetLife**
27-01 Queens Plaza North, Long Island City, NY 11101
212-578-3968  Fax: 212-578-8869
e-mail: jfdonnellan@metlife.com
Web site: www.metlife.com
*MetLife, Inc is a leading provider of insurance and financial services.*
James F Donnellan, Vice President Government & Industry Relations

**NY Life Insurance Co**
51 Madison Ave, Suite 1111, New York, NY 10010
212-576-7000  Fax: 212-576-4473
e-mail: gayle_yeomans@newyorklife.com
Web site: www.newyorklife.com
*Insurance products & financial services*
Gayle A Yeomans, Vice President Government Affairs

**NY Property Insurance Underwriting Association**
100 William St, New York, NY 10038
212-208-9700  Fax: 212-344-9676
Web site: www.nypiua.com
Joseph Calvo, President

**NYMAGIC Inc**
919 3rd Ave, 10th Fl, New York, NY 10022-3919
212-551-0600  Fax: 212-551-0724
*Marine insurance & excess & surplus lines*
A George Kallop, President & CEO

**New York Insurance Association Inc**
130 Washington Ave, Albany, NY 12210
518-432-4227  Fax: 518-432-4220
Web site: www.nyia.org
*Property & casualty insurance*
Ellen Melchionni, President

**New York Long-Term Care Brokers Ltd**
11 Halfmoon Executive Park, Clifton Park, NY 12065
518-371-5522 x116  Fax: 518-371-6131
e-mail: kjohnson@nyltcb.com
Web site: www.nyltcb.com
*Long-term care, life & disability insurance; consulting & sales to individual consumers & financial service industry professionals*
Kevin Johnson, President & CEO

**New York Municipal Insurance Reciprocal (NYMIR)**
150 State Street, Albany, NY 12207
518-465-7552  Fax: 518-465-0724
Web site: www.nymir.org
*Property and casualty insurance services for municipalities*
Kevin Crawford, Executive Director

**New York Schools Insurance Reciprocal (NYSIR)**
333 Earle Ovington Blvd, Suite 1030, Uniondale, NY 11553
516-393-2329 or 800-476-9747  Fax: 516-227-2352
Web site: www.nysir.org
*Insurance & risk management services for public school districts*
Joseph Goncalves, Executive Director

**NAIFA - New York State**
17 Elk Street, Suite 3, Albany, NY 12207
518-915-1661  Fax: 518-977-3370
e-mail: info@naifanys.org
Web site: www.naifanys.org
*Association of individuals engaged in the sale of life, health & property/casualty insurance & related financial services*
Greg Serio, Executive Director

**Professional Insurance Agents of New York State**
25 Chamberlain St, PO Box 997, Glenmont, NY 12077-0997
800-424-4244  Fax: 888-225-6935
e-mail: kenb@piaonline.org
Web site: www.piany.org
Ken Bessette, President/Chief Executive Officer

**SBLI USA Mutual Life Insurance Company Inc**
460 W 34th St, Suite 800, New York, NY 10001-2320
212-356-0327  Fax: 212-624-0700
e-mail: dklugman@sbliusa.com
*Corporate insurance regulatory law & government affairs*
Vikki Pryor, President & Chief Executive Officer

**St John's University-Peter J Tobin College of Business, School of Risk Mgmt**
8000 Utopia Pkwy, Queens, NY 11439
718-990-6800
Web site: www.stjohns.edu
Victoria Shoaf, Dean

**Stroock & Stroock & Lavan LLP**
180 Maiden Lane, New York, NY 10038-4982
212-806-5541  Fax: 212-806-2541
e-mail: dgabay@stroock.com
*Insurance, reinsurance, corporate & regulatory law*
Donald D Gabay, Attorney

**Support Services Alliance Inc**
107 Prospect St, PO Box 130, Schoharie, NY 12157
800-322-3920 or 518-295-7966  Fax: 518-295-8556
e-mail: info@ssamembers.com
Web site: www.smallbizgrowth.com
*Small business support services & insurance*
Steven Cole, President

**Unity Mutual Life Insurance Co**
507 Plum St, PO Box 5000, Syracuse, NY 13250-5000
315-448-7000  Fax: 315-448-7100
Jay Wason, Jr, General Counsel

*Offices and agencies generally appear in alphabetical order, except when specific order is requested by listee.*

**Utica Mutual Insurance Co**
PO Box 530, Utica, NY 13503-0530
1-800-274-1914  Fax: 315-734-2662
Web site: www.uticanational.com
*Property, casualty insurance*
Richard Creedon, Executive Vice President, Claims & General Counsel

# JUDICIAL & LEGAL SYSTEMS

## NEW YORK STATE

### GOVERNOR'S OFFICE

**Governor's Office**
Executive Chamber
State Capitol
Albany, NY 12224
518-474-8390  Fax: 518-474-1513
Web site: www.ny.gov

Governor:
 Andrew M Cuomo . . . . . . . . . . . . . . . . . . . . . . . . . . . .518-474-8390
Secretary to the Governor:
 Melissa DeRosa . . . . . . . . . . . . . . . . . . . .518-474-4246 or 212-681-4580
Counsel to the Governor:
 Kumiki Gibson . . . . . . . . . . . . . . . . . . . . .518-474-8343 or 212-681-4580
Chief of Staff:
 Jill DesRosiers . . . . . . . . . . . . . . . . . . . . .518-474-8390 or 212-681-4580
Director, Communications:
 Peter Ajemian . . . . . . . . . . . . . . . . . . . . .518-474-8418 or 212-681-4640
Director, State Operations and Infrastructure:
 Kelly Cummings . . . . . . . . . . . . . . . . . . . . . . . . . . . . .518-486-9871
Deputy Director of State Operations:
 Christian Jackstadt . . . . . . . . . . . . . . . . . . . . . . . . . . .212-681-4586
First Assistant Counsel:
 R Nadine Fontaine . . . . . . . . . . . . . . . . . . . . . . . . . . .518-474-8434

### EXECUTIVE DEPARTMENTS AND RELATED AGENCIES

**Criminal Justice Services, Division of**
80 South Swan Street
Albany, NY 12210
518-457-5837 or 800-262-3257  Fax: 518-457-3089
e-mail: InfoDCJS@dcjs.ny.gov
Web site: www.criminaljustice.ny.gov

Executive Deputy Commissioner:
 Michael C Green . . . . . . . . . . . . . . . . . . . . . . . . . . . . .518-457-1260
Director, Workforce Diversity & Equity Program Unit:
 Wanda Troche . . . . . . . . . . . . . . . . . . . . . . . . . . . . . .518-485-7962
Director, Public Information:
 Janine Kava . . . . . . . . . . . . . . . . . . . . . . . . . . . . . . .518-457-8828
 e-mail: janine.kava@dcjs.ny.gov

 **Human Resources Management**
 Director:
  Karen Davis . . . . . . . . . . . . . . . . . . . . . . . . . . . . . .518-485-1704

 **State Finance & Budget**
 Director, Finance:
  Brad Stevens . . . . . . . . . . . . . . . . . . . . . . . . . . . . .518-457-6105

**Office of Legal Services**
Deputy Commissioner & Counsel:
 John Czajka . . . . . . . . . . . . . . . . . . . . . . . . . . . . . . .518-457-4181

**Commission on Forensic Science**

 **Office of Forensic Services**
 Director:
  Brian J Gestring . . . . . . . . . . . . . . . . . . . . . . . . . . .518-457-4181

**Office of Criminal Justice Operations**
Deputy Commissioner:
 Joe Morrissey . . . . . . . . . . . . . . . . . . . . . . . . . . . . . .518-485-2995

**Office of Internal Audit and Compliance**

**Office of Justice Research & Performance**
Deputy Commissioner:
 Terry Salo . . . . . . . . . . . . . . . . . . . . . . . . . . . . . . . .518-457-7301

**Office of Public Safety**
Deputy Commissioner:
 Michael Wood 518-457-6985

 **Highway Safety Technology Unit**
 518-402-0689

 **Law Enforcement Accreditation Program**

 **Police & Peace Officer Registry & Training**

 **Missing Persons Clearinghouse**

 **Security Guard Training**

**Office of Program Development & Funding**
Deputy Commissioner:
 Vacant . . . . . . . . . . . . . . . . . . . . . . . . . . . . . . . . .518-457-8462
 e-mail: funding@dcjs.ny.gov

**Office of Sex Offender Management**

**Law Department**
28 Liberty Street
New York, NY 10005
212-416-8000 or 800-771-7755
Web site: www.ag.ny.gov

State Capitol
Albany, NY 12224-0341
518-776-2000
Fax: 518-650-9401

**Gun Involved Violence Elimination (GIVE) Initiative**
Director:
 Vacant . . . . . . . . . . . . . . . . . . . . . . . . . . . . . . . . .518-485-7923
Attorney General:
 Letitia James . . . . . . . . . . . . . . . . . . . .212-416-8000 or 518-776-2000

**Administration**
 Agency Bldg 4, Empire State Plaza, Albany, NY 12224-0341
Acting Chief Operating Officer:
 Joshua Carr . . . . . . . . . . . . . . . . . . . . . . . . . . . . . . .212-416-8050

 **Budget & Fiscal Management**
 Director (Acting):
  Peter O'Neil . . . . . . . . . . . . . . . . . . .518-776-2110/fax: 518-915-7751

 **Human Resources Management**
 Director:
  Robert Pablo . . . . . . . . . . . . . . . . . . . . . . . . . . . . .518-776-2500

 **Legal Recruitment**
 Asst Attorney General in Charge:
  Sandra J Grannum . . . . . . . . . . . . . . .212-416-8080/fax: 212-416-8264

**Appeals & Opinions Division**
Solicitor General:
 Vacant . . . . . . . . . . . . . . . . . . . . . . .212-416-8016 or 518-776-2002
Deputy Counsel:
 John Amodeo . . . . . . . . . . . . . . . . . . . . . . . . . . . . . .518-776-2000

 **Law Library**
 Chief, Library Services:
  Patricia Partello . . . . . . . . . . . . . . . .518-776-2566/fax: 518-915-7737
 Legal Support Analyst:
  Vacant . . . . . . . . . . . . . . . . . . . . . .212-416-8012/fax: 212-416-6130

*Offices and agencies generally appear in alphabetical order, except when specific order is requested by listee.*

## Criminal Justice

Chief Deputy Attorney General, Criminal Justice:
José Maldonado ....................................212-416-8050

### Criminal Enforcement & Financial Crimes Bureau
Bureau Chief:
Gary Fishman.....................518-776-2370 or 212-416-8750

### Medicaid Fraud Control Unit
120 Broadway, 13th Fl, New York, NY 10271-0007
Deputy Attorney General in Charge & Director:
Amy Held .......................212-417-5250/fax: 212-417-4284
Asst Deputy Attorney General:
Paul J Mahoney .....................................212-417-5254
Deputy Regional Director, Buffalo:
Gary A Baldauf.................716-853-8507/fax: 716-852-8525
Regional Director, Long Island:
Jane Turkin .....................631-952-6400/fax: 631-952-6382
Regional Director, Albany:
Kathleen Boland ...............518-533-6011/fax: 518-533-6012
Regional Director, Rochester:
Catherine Wagner.............585-262-2860/fax: 585-262-2866
Regional Director, Syracuse:
Ralph Tortora, III ..............315-423-1104/fax: 315-423-1120
Deputy Regional Director, Pearl River:
Anne S Jardine .................845-732-7525/fax: 845-732-7555

## Economic Justice

Executive Deputy Attorney General:
Siobhan Kennedy ...................................212-416-8050

### Antitrust Bureau
Bureau Chief:
Eric J Stock ....................212-416-8282/fax: 212-416-6015

### Consumer Frauds & Protection Bureau
Bureau Chief:
Jane Azia.......................212-416-8300/fax: 212-416-6003

### Internet Bureau
Bureau Chief:
Kathleen McGee ................212-416-8433/fax: 212-416-8369

### Investor Protection Bureau
Bureau Chief:
Chad Johnson ..................212-416-8225/fax: 212-416-8816

## Intergovernmental Relations

Deputy Director, Intergovernmental Affairs:
Lilliam Perez........................................212-416-6044
Director, Intergovernmental Affairs:
Michael Meade .....................................212-416-8985

## Office of the Attorney General

Chief of Staff:
Brian Mahanna.....................................212-416-8050
Senior Advisor/Director, Operations:
Christina Harvey.....................................212-416-8095
Deputy Counsel:
John Amodeo .......................................518-776-2000
Legislative Policy Advisor:
Kate M Powers ..................518-776-2444/fax: 518-650-9401
Press Secretary:
Fernando Aquino................212-416-8060/fax: 212-416-6005
e-mail: nyag.pressoffice@ag.ny.gov
Director, Correspondence:
Jennifer Ticknor ....................................518-776-2356
Director, Public Information:
Shawn Morris ...................518-776-2357/fax: 518-650-9401

## Investigations

Chief, Investigations:
Dominick Zarrella .................212-416-6328/fax: 212-416-8773

Assistant Chief Investigator - Downstate:
John McManus .....................................212-416-8786
First Deputy Chief Investigator:
John Reidy .........................................212-416-6394

## Social Justice

Chief Deputy Attorney General, Social Justice:
Jennifer Levy ......................................212-416-8450

### Charities Bureau
Bureau Chief:
James G Sheehan.............212-416-8410/fax: 212-416-8393

### Civil Rights Bureau
Bureau Chief:
Lourdes Rosado.................212-416-8250/fax: 212-416-8074

### Environmental Protection Bureau
Bureau Chief:
Lemuel Srolovic.................518-776-2400 or 212-416-8448

### Healthcare Bureau
Bureau Chief:
Lisa Landau .....................518-776-2477 or 212-416-6305
fax: 518-650-9365

## Regional Offices Division

Executive Deputy Attorney General, Regional Offices:
Vacant..............................................716-853-8451

### Binghamton
State Office Bldg, 44 Hawley St, 17th Fl, Binghamton, NY 13901-4433
Asst Attorney General in Charge:
James E. Shoemaker ..............607-721-8771/fax: 607-721-8787

### Brooklyn
55 Hanson Place, Ste 1080, Brooklyn, NY 11217
Asst Attorney General in Charge (Acting):
Matthew Eubank ................718-722-3949/fax: 718-722-3951

### Buffalo
Main Place Tower, Ste 300A, 350 Main St, Buffalo, NY 14202
Asst Attorney General in Charge:
J. Michael Russo .................716-853-8400/fax: 716-853-8571

### Harlem
163 West 125th St, Ste 1324, New York, NY 10027
Asst Attorney General in Charge:
Roberto Lebron .................212-364-6010/fax: 646-356-3000

### Nassau
200 Old Country Rd, Ste 460, Mineola, NY 11501-4241
Asst Attorney General in Charge:
Valerie Singleton.................516-248-3302/fax: 516-747-6432

### Plattsburgh
43 Durkee St, Ste 700, Plattsburgh, NY 12901
Asst Attorney General in Charge:
Glen Michaels...................518-562-3288/fax: 518-562-3293

### Poughkeepsie
One Civic Ctr Plaza, Suite 401, Poughkeepsie, NY 12601
Asst Attorney General in Charge:
Jill Faber .......................845-485-3900/fax: 845-452-3303

### Rochester
144 Exchange Blvd, 2nd Fl, Rochester, NY 14614-2176
Asst Attorney General in Charge:
Ted O'Brien .....................585-327-3220/fax: 585-546-7514

### Suffolk
300 Motor Pkwy, Ste 230, Hauppauge, NY 11788
Asst Attorney General in Charge:
Kimberly Kinirons ..............631-231-2424/fax: 631-435-4757

*Offices and agencies generally appear in alphabetical order, except when specific order is requested by listee.*

**Syracuse**
615 Erie Blvd West, Suite 102, Syracuse, NY 13204
Asst Attorney General in Charge:
Ed Thompson . . . . . . . . . . . . . . . . . . 315-448-4800/fax: 315-448-4853

**Utica**
207 Genesee St, Room 508, Utica, NY 13501
Asst Attorney General in Charge:
James Williams . . . . . . . . . . . . . . . . . 315-793-2225/fax: 315-793-2228

**Watertown**
Dulles St Ofc Bldg, 317 Washington St, Watertown, NY 13601
Asst Attorney General in Charge:
Deanna Nelson . . . . . . . . . . . . . . . . . 315-785-2444/fax: 315-785-2294

**Westchester**
44 S Broadway, White Plains, NY 10601
Asst Attorney General in Charge:
Gary S Brown . . . . . . . . . . . . . . . . . . 914-422-8755/fax: 914-422-8706

## State Counsel

Executive Deputy Attorney General, State Counsel:
Vacant . . . . . . . . . . . . . . . . . . . . . . . . . . . . . . .212-416-8050

**Civil Recoveries Bureau**
Bureau Chief:
John Cremo . . . . . . . . . . . . . . . . . . . . 518-776-2173/fax: 518-915-7731

**Claims Bureau**
Bureau Chief:
Katharine Brooks . . . . . . . . . . . . . . . . 518-776-2300 or 212-416-8500

**Litigation Bureau**
Bureau Chief:
Jeffrey Dvorin . . . . . . . . . . . . . . . . . . 518-776-2300 or 212-416-8610

**Real Property Bureau**
Bureau Chief:
Alison Crocker . . . . . . . . . . . . . . . . . . . . . . . . . . . . 518-776-2700

## JUDICIAL SYSTEM AND RELATED AGENCIES

## Attorney Grievance Committee

**1st Judicial Dept, Judicial Dist 1, 12**
61 Broadway, 2nd Fl, New York, NY 10006
Chief Counsel:
Jorge Dopico . . . . . . . . . . . . . . . . . . .212-401-0800/fax: 212-287-1045

**2nd Judicial Dept, Judicial Dist 2, 9, 10, 11, 13**

**Judicial Dist 2, 11, 13**
Renaissance Plz, 335 Adams St, Ste 2400, Brooklyn, NY 11201-3745
Chief Counsel:
Diana M Kearse. . . . . . . . . . . . . . . . . 718-923-6300/fax: 718-624-2978

**Judicial Dist 9**
399 Knollwood Rd, Ste 200, White Plains, NY 10603
Chief Counsel:
Gary L Casella. . . . . . . . . . . . . . . . . . 914-824-5070/fax: 914-949-0997

**Judicial Dist 10**
150 Motor Pkwy, Ste 102, Hauppauge, NY 11788
Chief Counsel:
Robert A. Green . . . . . . . . . . . . . . . . 631-231-3775/fax: 516-364-7355

**3rd Judicial Dept, Judicial Dist 3, 4, 6**
Committee on Professional Standards, 286 Washington Ave Ext, Ste 200,
Albany, NY 12203
518-285-8350
Chief Counsel:
Monica A. Duffy . . . . . . . . . . . . . . . . 518-285-8350/fax: 518-453-4643
e-mail: AD3COPS@nycourts.gov

Deputy Chief Counsel:
Michael G Gaynor . . . . . . . . . . . . . . . . 518-285-8350/fax: 518-453-4643
e-mail: AD3COPS@nycourts.gov

**4th Judicial Dept, Dist 5, 7, 8**

**Judicial Dist 5**. . . . . . . . . . . . . . . . . . . . . . . . . .fax: 315-401-3339
224 Harrison St, Ste 408, Syracuse, NY 13202-3066
Chief Counsel:
Gregory J Huether . . . . . . . . . . . . . . . . . . . . . . . . . . .315-401-3344
Principal Counsel:
Anthony J Gigliotti. . . . . . . . . . . . . . . . . . . . . . . . . . .315-401-3344

**Judicial Dist 7**. . . . . . . . . . . . . . . . . . . . . . . . . .fax: 585-530-3191
50 East Ave, Ste 404, Rochester, NY 14604-2206
Chief Counsel:
Gregory J Huether . . . . . . . . . . . . . . . . . . . . . . . . . .585-530-3180
Principal Counsel:
Daniel A Drake. . . . . . . . . . . . . . . . . . . . . . . . . . . . .585-530-3180

**Judicial Dist 8**. . . . . . . . . . . . . . . . . . . . . . . . . .fax: 716-856-2701
438 Main St, Ste 800, Buffalo, NY 14202
Chief Counsel:
Gregory J Huether . . . . . . . . . . . . . . . . . . . . . . . . . .716-845-3630
Principal Counsel:
Roderick Quebral . . . . . . . . . . . . . . . . . . . . . . . . . . .716-845-3630

## Law Guardian Program

**3rd Judicial Dept** . . . . . . . . . . . . . . . . . . . . . . .fax: 518-471-4757
PO Box 7288, Capital Station, Albany, NY 12224-0288
Fax: 518-471-4757
Web site: www.nycourts.gov/ad3/OAC/index.html
Director:
Betsy R Ruslander . . . . . . . . . . . . . . . . . . . . . . . . . .518-471-4825
e-mail: ad3oac@nycourts.gov

**4th Judicial Dept** . . . . . . . . . . . . . . . . . . . . . . .fax: 585-530-3175
50 East Ave, Ste 304, Rochester, NY 14604
Director:
Tracy M Hamilton . . . . . . . . . . . . . . . . 585-530-3170 or 585-530-3176
e-mail: thamilto@nycourts.gov
Assistant Program Director:
Christine Constantine . . . . . . . . . . . . . . . . . . . . . . . . .585-530-3178
e-mail: cconstan@nycourts.gov

## Mental Hygiene Legal Service

**1st Judicial Dept**
41 Madison Ave, 26th Fl, New York, NY 10010
Director:
Marvin Bernstein. . . . . . . . . . . . . . . . . 646-386-5891/fax: 212-779-7899
Deputy Director:
Stephen Harkavy. . . . . . . . . . . . . . . . . . . . . . . . . . . .646-386-5891

**2nd Judicial Dept**
170 Old Country Rd, Rm 500, Mineola, NY 11501
Director:
Michael D Neville . . . . . . . . . . . . . . . . 516-493-3976/fax: 646-963-6640
e-mail: mneville@nycourts.gov
Deputy Director:
Dennis Feld. . . . . . . . . . . . . . . . . . . . . . . . . . . . . . .516-493-3975
e-mail: mneville@nycourts.gov

**3rd Judicial Dept**
40 Steuben St, Ste 501, Albany, NY 12207
Web site: www.nycourts.gov/ad3/mhls/index.html
Director:
Sheila E Shea. . . . . . . . . . . . . . . . . . 518-451-8710/fax: 518-453-6915
Deputy Director:
Shannon Stockwell . . . . . . . . . . . . . . . . . . . . . . . . . .518-451-8710

*Offices and agencies generally appear in alphabetical order, except when specific order is requested by listee.*

## 4th Judicial Dept
50 East Ave, Ste 402, Rochester, NY 14604
Web site: www.nycourts.gov/ad4
Director:
Emmett J Creahan . . . . . . . . . . . . . . . . . . . . . . . . . . . . . . . . . . .585-530-3050
Deputy Director:
Kevin Wilson . . . . . . . . . . . . . . . . . . . . .585-530-3050/fax: 585-530-3079

## Unified Court System
25 Beaver St
Room 852
New York, NY 10004
212-428-2700  Fax: 212-428-2508
e-mail: questions@nycourts.gov
Web site: www.nycourts.gov

Agency Bldg 4, 20th Fl
Empire State Plaza
Albany, NY 12223
518-474-3828
Fax: 518-473-5514

### Administrative Board of the Courts

#### Appellate Division
*1st Judicial Department*
  Courthouse, 27 Madison Ave, New York, NY 10010
  Presiding Justice:
    Luis A. Gonzalez . . . . . . . . . . . . . . . . . . . . . . . . . . .212-340-0400
*2nd Judicial Department*
  45 Monroe Place, Brooklyn, NY 11201
  Presiding Justice:
    Randall T. Eng . . . . . . . . . . . . . . . . . . . . . . . . . . . .718-875-1300
*3rd Judicial Department*
  Capitol Station, ESP, PO Box 7288, Albany, NY 12224
  Presiding Justice:
    Karen K. Peters . . . . . . . . . . . . . . . . . . . . . . . . .518-471-4777
*4th Judicial Department*
  50 East Ave, Rochester, NY 14604
  Presiding Justice:
    Henry Scudder . . . . . . . . . . . . . . . . . . . . . . . . . . . .585-530-3100

#### Court of Appeals
230 Park Ave, Suite 826, New York, NY 10169
Chief Judge:
  Jonathan Lippman . . . . . . . . . . . . . . . .212-661-6787/fax: 212-682-2778

### Court Administration
Chief Administrative Judge:
  A. Gail Prudenti . . . . . . . . . . . . . . . . . . . . . . . . . . . . . . .212-428-2120
Administrative Director, Office of Court Admin:
  Lawrence K Marks . . . . . . . . . . . . . . . . . . . . . . . . . . . . . .212-428-2884
Deputy Chief Administrative Judge, Courts in NYC:
  Fern A. Fisher . . . . . . . . . . . . . . . . . . . . . . . . . . . . . . . . .646-386-4200
Deputy Chief Administrative Judge, Courts outside NYC:
  Michael V. Coccoma . . . . . . . . . . . . . . . . . . . . . . . . . . . .518-474-3828
Chief, Policy & Planning:
  Judy Harris Kluger . . . . . . . . . . . . . . . . . . . . . . . . . . . . .212-428-2130
Executive Assistant to Deputy Chief Admin Judge, Courts in NYC:
  Maria Logus . . . . . . . . . . . . . . . . . . . . . . . . . . . . . . . . . .646-386-4201
Executive Assistant to Deputy Chief Admin Judge, Courts outside NYC:
  Peter J. Ryan . . . . . . . . . . . . . . . . . . . . . . . . . . . . . . . . .518-474-3828
Chief of Staff:
  Paul Lewis . . . . . . . . . . . . . . . . . . . . . . . . . . . . . . . . . . . .212-428-2120
Executive Director:
  Ron Younkins . . . . . . . . . . . . . . . . . . . . . . . . . . . . . . . . .212-428-2126

**Administrative Judge to the Court of Claims (NYS)**. fax: 866-413-1069
Justice Bldg, Capitol Station, PO Box 7344, Albany, NY 12224

Presiding Judge:
  Richard E Sise . . . . . . . . . . . . . . . . . . . . . . . . . . . . . .518-432-3435

### Administrative Judges to the Courts in New York City
*1st Judicial District (Judicial Department 1)*
  Administrative Judge, Civil Term:
    Sherry Klein-Heitler . . . . . . . . . . . . . . . . . . . . . .646-386-3211
  Administrative Judge, Criminal Term:
    Michael Obus . . . . . . . . . . . . . . . . . . . . . . . . . . .646-386-4051
*2nd Judicial District (Judicial Department 2)*
  320 Jay St, Brooklyn, NY 11201
  Administrative Judge:
    Barry Kamins . . . . . . . . . . . . . . . . . . . . . . . . . . . . .347-296-1200
*Civil Court*
  111 Centre St, New York, NY 10013
  Administrative Judge:
    Lawrence Knipel . . . . . . . . . . . .646-386-5400/fax: 212-374-5709
*Criminal Court*
  100 Centre St, Rm 549A, New York, NY 10013
  Administrative Judge:
    Barry Kamins . . . . . . . . . . . . . . .646-386-4700 or 347-296-1000
    fax: 212-374-3004
*Family Court*
  60 Lafayette St, 11th Floor, New York, NY 10013
  Administrative Judge:
    Edwina Richardson-Mendelson . 646-386-5190/fax: 212-374-2127

### Administrative Judges to the Courts outside New York City
*3rd Judicial District (Judicial Department 3)*
  Courthouse, 80 Second St, Troy, NY 12180
  Acting Administrative Judge:
    Thomas Mercure. . . . . . . . . . . .518-285-6152/fax: 518-270-3788
*4th Judicial District (Judicial Department 3)*
  612 State St, Schenectady, NY 12305
  Administrative Judge:
    Vito Caruso. . . . . . . . . . . . . . . .518-285-8415/fax: 518-347-1972
*5th Judicial District (Judicial Department 4)*
  Onondaga County Court House, 401 Montgomery St, Syracuse, NY 13202
  Administrative Judge:
    James C Tormey. . . . . . . . . . . .315-671-2111/fax: 315-671-1183
*6th Judicial District (Judicial Department 3)*
  320 North Tioga Street, Ithaca, NY 14850
  Administrative Judge:
    Robert Mulvey . . . . . . . . . . . . . . . . . . . . . . . . . . . .607-272-0466
*7th Judicial District (Judicial Department 4)*
  Hall of Justice, Civic Center Plz, 99 Exchange Blvd, Rochester, NY 14614
  Administrative Judge:
    Craig J. Doran . . . . . . . . . . . . . . . . . . . . . . . . . . . .585-396-4239
*8th Judicial District (Judicial Department 4)*
  Erie County Hall, 92 Franklin St, Buffalo, NY 14202
  Administrative Judge:
    Paula L. Feroleto . . . . . . . . . . .716-845-9438/fax: 716-855-1611
*9th Judicial District (Judicial Department 2)*
  County Court House, 111 Dr Martin Luther King Blvd, White Plains, NY 10601
  Administrative Judge:
    Alan Scheinkman . . . . . . . . . . .914-824-5100/fax: 914-995-4111
*10th Judicial District (Judicial Department 2)*
  Administrative Judge, Nassau County:
    Thomas Adams. . . . . . . . . . .516-571-2684/fax: 516-571-3713
  Administrative Judge, Suffolk County:
    C.ÆRandall Hinrichs . . . . . . . .631-853-5368/fax: 631-853-7741
*11th Judicial District (Judicial Department 2)*
  88-11 Sutphin Blvd, Jamaica, NY 11435
  Administrative Judge, Civil:
    Jeremy Weinstein . . . . . . . . . . .718-298-1100/fax: 718-520-2499
  Administrative Judge, Criminal:
    Joseph Zayas

*Offices and agencies generally appear in alphabetical order, except when specific order is requested by listee.*

## 12th Judicial District (Judicial Department 1)
851 Grand Concourse, Bronx, NY 10451
Administrative Judge (Civil & Criminal):
    Douglas E. McKeon............................718-618-1441
Deputy Administrative Judge (Criminal):
    Robert Torres................................718-618-3700
13th Judicial District Administrative Judge:
    Judith N. McMahon...........................718-618-3700

### Counsel's Office
Counsel:
    Vacant.........................212-428-2160/fax: 212-428-2155

### Management Support
**Administrative Services Office**
Director:
    Laura Weigley Ross..........212-428-2860/fax: 212-428-2819
Deputy Director:
    Vacant......................212-428-2812/fax: 212-428-2819
**Court Operations**
Director:
    Nancy M Mangold............212-428-2761/fax: 518-428-2768
Coordinator, Alternative Dispute Resolution Program:
    Daniel M Weitz..............212-428-2892/fax: 212-428-2696
    e-mail: dweitz@nycourts.gov
Director, Court Research & Technology:
    Chester Mount...............212-428-2990/fax: 212-428-2987
Chief of Court Security Services:
    Howard Metzdorff...........212-428-2766/fax: 212-428-2768
    e-mail: ops1@nycourts.gov
Director, Internal Controls Office:
    Dennis Donnelly.............518-238-4303/fax: 518-238-2086
Inspector General:
    Sherrill Spatz.................646-386-3500 or 212-514-7158
    e-mail: sspatz@courts.state.ny.us
Deputy Inspector General:
    Carol Hamm
    e-mail: chamm@courts.state.ny.us
Chief Law Librarian, Legal Info & Records Mgmt:
    Ellen Robinson..............518-238-4373/fax: 518-238-2894
Managing Inspector General, Bias Matters:
    Kay-Ann Porter Campbell....................877-263-2427
    e-mail: ieporter@courts.state.ny.us
Managing Inspector General, Fiduciary Appointments:
    Elizabeth Candreva.........................646-386-3514
    e-mail: ecandreva@courts.state.ny.us
**Financial Management & Audit Services**
Empire State Plaza, Bldg 4, Ste 2001, Albany, NY 12223-1450
Director:
    Charles Hughes.............................518-473-5511
**Workforce Diversity**
Director:
    S. Anthony Walters..........212-428-2540/fax: 212-428-2545
    e-mail: twalters@nycourts.gov
Management Analyst:
    Michael J. Moore...........212-428-2683/fax: 212-428-2545
    e-mail: mmoore@nycourts.gov
Court Analyst:
    Doretha L. Jackson........................212-428-2540
    e-mail: dljackson@nycourts.gov
Deputy Director, Staffing & Security Services:
    Gregory J. Salerno..........646-386-3400/fax: 212-295-4876
Chief of Training/Commanding Officer - NYS Court Officers Academy:
    Chief Joseph Bacceilieri......646-386-5660/fax: 212-406-4533
**Public Affairs Office**
Director:
    Gregory Murray............212-428-2116/fax: 212-428-2117
    e-mail: opaoutreach@courts.state.ny.us

Director, Communications:
    David Bookstaver...........212-428-2500/fax: 212-428-2507
    e-mail: dbooksta@courts.state.ny.us
Assistant Director, Communications Specialist:
    Arlene Hackel..............................212-428-2116
    e-mail: ahackel@courts.state.ny.us
Officer:
    Gary Spencer...............................518-455-7711
    e-mail: gspencer@courts.state.ny.us

## CORPORATIONS, AUTHORITIES AND COMMISSIONS

### Interest on Lawyer Account (IOLA) Fund of the State of NY
11 East 44th St
Ste 1406
New York, NY 10017
646-865-1541 or 800-222-4652  Fax: 646-865-1545
e-mail: iolaf@iola.org
Web site: www.iola.org

Chair:
    Mary Rothwell Davis........................646-865-1541
Executive Director:
    Christopher O'Malley........................646-865-1541
General Counsel:
    Christine M Fecko..........................646-865-1541
Director of Administration:
    Michele D Agard...........................646-865-1541

### Lawyers' Fund for Client Protection
119 Washington Ave
Albany, NY 12210
518-434-1935 or 800-442-FUND  Fax: 518-434-5641
e-mail: info@nylawfund.org
Web site: www.nylawfund.org

Chair:
    Eric A Seiff...............................518-434-1935
Vice Chair:
    Nancy Burner..............................518-434-1935
Executive Director & Counsel:
    Timothy O'Sullivan........................518-434-1935

### New York State Board of Law Examiners
Corporate Plaza Bldg 3
254 Washington Ave Ext
Albany, NY 12203-5195
518-453-5990  Fax: 518-452-5729
Web site: www.nybarexam.org

Chair:
    Diane F Bosse.............................518-453-5990
Executive Director:
    John J McAlary............................518-453-5990

### New York State Commission on Judicial Nomination
c/o Greenberg Traurig LLP
54 State Street
Albany, NY 12207
518-689-1400  Fax: 518-689-1499
Web site: www.nysegov.com/cjn/

Chair:
    Vacant
Counsel:
    Henry Greenberg...........................518-689-1400
    e-mail: greenbergh@gtlaw.com

*Offices and agencies generally appear in alphabetical order, except when specific order is requested by listee.*

## New York State Judicial Conduct Commission

61 Broadway
12th Fl
New York, NY 10006
646-386-4800  Fax: 646-458-0037
e-mail: cjc@cjc.ny.gov
Web site: www.cjc.ny.gov

Corning Tower
Suite 2301
Empire State Plaza
Albany, NY 12223
518-453-4600
Fax: 518-486-1850

Chair:
   Joseph W Belluck . . . . . . . . . . . . . . . . . . . . . . . . . . . . . . .646-386-4800
Vice Chair:
   Paul B Harding . . . . . . . . . . . . . . . . . . . . . . . . . . .646-386-4800
Administrator & Counsel:
   Robert H Tembeckjian . . . . . . . . . . . . . . . . . . . . . . . . . .646-386-4800
Deputy Administrator in Charge, Albany Office:
   Cathleen Cenci . . . . . . . . . . . . . . . . . . . . . . . . . . . .518-453-4600
Deputy Administrator in Charge, Rochester Office:
   John J Postel . . . . . . . . . . . . . . . . . . . . . . . . . . . . .585-232-5756
Deputy Administrator in Charge, New York City Office:
   Mark Levine . . . . . . . . . . . . . . . . . . . . . . . . . . . . .646-386-4800
Deputy Administrator, Litigation:
   Edward Lindner . . . . . . . . . . . . . . . . . . . . . . . . . . .518-474-5617
Clerk:
   Jean M Savanyu, Esq . . . . . . . . . . . . . . . . . . . . . . . .646-386-4800

## New York State Law Reporting Bureau

17 Lodge Street
Albany, NY 12207
518-453-6900  Fax: 518-426-1640
Web site: www.courts.state.ny.us/reporter

State Reporter:
   William J Hooks . . . . . . . . . . . . . . . . . . . . . . . . . . . .518-453-6900
Deputy State Reporter:
   Katherine D LaBoda . . . . . . . . . . . . . . . . . . . . . . . . .518-453-6900
   e-mail: Reporter@courts.state.ny.us
Assistant State Reporter:
   Cara J Broussea, Esq. . . . . . . . . . . . . . . . . . . . . . . . .518-453-6900
   e-mail: Reporter@courts.state.ny.us

## New York State Law Revision Commission

80 New Scotland Ave
Albany, NY 12208
518-472-5858  Fax: 518-445-2303
e-mail: nylrc@albanylaw.edu
Web site: www.lawrevision.state.ny.us

Chairman:
   Peter J. Kiernan . . . . . . . . . . . . . . . . . . . . . . . . . . . .518-408-2051
Executive Director:
   Rose Mary Bailly . . . . . . . . . . . . . . . . . . . . . . . . . . .518-472-5858

## Uniform State Laws Commission

c/o Coughlin & Gerhart LLP
99 Corporate Drive
PO Box 2039
Binghamton, NY 13902-2039
607-723-9511  Fax: 607-723-1530

Chair:
   Richard B Long . . . . . . . . . . . . . . . . . . . . . . . . . . . . . . .607-821-2202
   e-mail: rlong@cglawoffices.com
Member:
   Sandra Stern . . . . . . . . . . . . . . . . . . . . . . . . . . . . .212-207-8150
Member:
   Norman L. Greene . . . . . . . . . . . . . . . . . . . . . . . . . .212-661-5030
Member:
   Justin L. Vigdor . . . . . . . . . . . . . . . . . . . . . . . . .585-232-5300 ext 228
Member:
   Mark F Glaser . . . . . . . . . . . . . . . . . . . . . . . . . . . .518-689-1413

## NEW YORK STATE LEGISLATURE

*See Legislative Branch in Section 1 for additional Standing Committee and Subcommittee information.*

### Assembly Standing Committees

#### Codes
Chair:
   Jeffrey Dinowitz (D) . . . . . . . . . . . . . . . . . . . . . . . . . .518-455-4477

#### Judiciary
Chair:
   Charles D Lavine . . . . . . . . . . . . . . . . .518-455-5965/fax: 518-455-4437

### Senate Standing Committees

#### Codes
Chair:
   Jamaal T Bailey (D) . . . . . . . . . . . . . . . . . . . . . . . . .518-455-2061
Ranking Minority Member:
   Andrew J Lanza (R, C, IP, RFM) . . . . . . . . . . . . . . . . . . . .518-455-3215

#### Judiciary
Chair:
   Brad Hoylman (D, WF) . . . . . . . . . . . . . . . . . . . . . . . .518-455-2451
Minority Member:
   Thomas F O'Mara (R, C, IP) . . . . . . . . . . . . . . . . . . . . .518-455-2091

## U.S. GOVERNMENT

### EXECUTIVE DEPARTMENTS AND FEDERAL COURTS

## US Federal Courts

### US Bankruptcy Court - New York

#### Eastern District
271-C Cadman Plaza East, Suite 1595, Brooklyn, NY 11201-1800
347-394-1700
Web site: www.nyeb.uscourts.gov
Chief Judge:
   Carla E. Craig . . . . . . . . . . . . . . . . . . . . . . . . . . . .347-394-1700
Clerk of the Court:
   Robert A. Gavin Jr. . . . . . . . . . . . . . . . . . . . . . . . . .347-394-1700

#### Northern District
James T. Foley Courthouse, 445 Broadway, Suite 330, Albany, NY 12207
518-257-1661
Web site: www.nynb.uscourts.gov
Chief Bankruptcy Judge:
   Margaret Cangilos-Ruiz . . . . . . . . . . . . . . . . . . . . . . .518-257-1661
Clerk of the Court:
   Kim F. Lefebvre . . . . . . . . . . . . . . . . . . . . . . . . . . .518-257-1661

#### Southern District
1 Bowling Green, New York, NY 10004-1408

*Offices and agencies generally appear in alphabetical order, except when specific order is requested by listee.*

212-668-2870
Web site: www.nysb.uscourts.gov
Chief Judge:
  Cecelia G. Morris . . . . . . . . . . . . . . . . . . . . . . . . . . . .212-668-2870
Clerk of the Court:
  Vito Genna . . . . . . . . . . . . . . . . . . . . . . . . . . . . . . . . .212-668-2870

**Western District**
300 Pearl Street, Suite 250, Buffalo, NY 14202
Web site: www.nywb.uscourts.gov
Chief Judge:
  Carl L. Bucki . . . . . . . . . . . . . . . . . . . . . . . . . . . . . . .716-362-3200
Clerk of the Court:
  Lisa Bertino Beaser . . . . . . . . . . . . . . . . . . . . . . . . . .716-362-3281

## US Court of Appeals for the Second Circuit
Thurgood Marshall U.S. Courthouse, 40 Foley Square, New York, NY
  10007
212-857-8500
Web site: www.ca2.uscourts.gov
Circuit Executive:
  Karen Greve Milton. . . . . . . . . . . . . . .212-857-8700/fax: 212-857-8680
Clerk of the Court:
  Catherine O'Hagan Wolfe . . . . . . . . . . . . . . . . . . . . . .212-857-8500

## US Court of International Trade . . . . . . . . . . . . . . . fax: 212-264-1085
One Federal Plaza, New York, NY 10278-0001
212-264-2800  Fax: 212-264-1085
Web site: www.cit.uscourts.gov
Chief Judge:
  Timothy C. Stanceu . . . . . . . . . . . . . . . . . . . . . . . . . . .212-264-2923
Clerk of the Court:
  Tina Potuto Kimble. . . . . . . . . . . . . . . . . . . . . . . . . . . .212-264-2814
  e-mail: clerk@cit.uscourts.gov

## US DISTRICT COURT - NEW YORK (part of the Second Circuit)
225 Cadman Plaza East, Brooklyn, NY 11201
Web site: www.nyed.uscourts.gov

**Eastern District**
718-613-2600
Chief District Judge:
  Dora L. Irizarry
Clerk of the Court:
  Douglas C. Palmer
Chief Magistrate Judge:
  Roanne L. Mann
District Executive:
  Eugene J. Corcoran
Chief Probation Officer:
  Edward Kanaley

**Northern District**
100 South Clinton Street, PO Box 7367, Syracuse, NY 13261-7367
315-234-8500
Web site: www.nynd.uscourts.gov
Chief District Judge:
  Glenn T. Suddaby
Chief Magistrate Judge:
  David E. Peebles
Clerk of the Court:
  Lawrence K. Baerman . . . . . . . . . . . . . . . . . . . . . . . .315-234-8500
Chief Probation Officer:
  Matt Brown

**Southern District**
300 Quarropas Street, White Plains, NY 10601-4150
914-390-4100
Web site: www.nysd.uscourts.gov
Chief District Judge:
  Loretta A. Preska . . . . . . . . . . . . . . . . . . . . . . . . . . . .212-805-0240

Chief Magistrate Judge:
  Debra Freeman . . . . . . . . . . . . . . . . . . . . . . . . . . . . . .212-805-4250
District Executive:
  Edward Friedland
Clerk of the Court:
  Ruby J. Krajick
Deputy in Charge:
  Robert Rogers

**Western District**
2 Niagara Square, Buffalo, NY 14202-3350
716-551-1700
Web site: www.nywd.uscourts.gov
Chief District Judge:
  Frank P. Geraci, Jr.
Clerk of the Court:
  Mary C. Loewenguth
Magistrate Judge:
  Hugh B. Scott

## US Tax Court
Web site: www.ustaxcourt.gov
Chief Judge:
  Michael B. Thornton. . . . . . . . . . . . . . . . . . . . . . . . . . .202-521-0777
Clerk of the Court:
  Stephanie A. Servoss . . . . . . . . . . . . . . . . . . . . . . . . . .202-521-0700

## US Justice Department
Web site: www.justice.gov

### Antitrust Division—New York Field Office
26 Federal Plaza, Room 3630, New York, NY 10278-0004
Chief:
  Jeffrey Martino . . . . . . . . . . . . . . . . . . . .212-335-8019/fax: 212-335-8021
Assistant Chief:
  Stephen J. McCahey . . . . . . . . . . . . . . . . . . . . . . . . . . .212-335-8026

### Civil Division - Commercial Litigation Branch
26 Federal Plaza, Room 346, New York, NY 10278
Attorney-in-Charge:
  Barbara S. Williams . . . . . . . . . . . . . . . . . . . . . . . . . . .212-264-9240

### Community Relations Service - Northeast & Caribbean Region
26 Federal Plaza, Suite 36-118, New York, NY 10278
Regional Director:
  Reinaldo Rivera, Jr. . . . . . . . . . . . . . . . . . .212-264-0700/fax: 212-264-2143

### OFFICE OF INSPECTOR GENERAL (including New York State)

**Audit Division**
701 Market Street, Suite 201, Philadelphia, PA 19106
Regional Audit Manager:
  Thomas O. Puerzer . . . . . . . . . . . . . . .215-580-2111/fax: 215-597-1348

**Investigations Division**
1 Battery Park Plaza, 29th Floor, New York, NY 10004
Special Agent-in-Charge:
  Ronald G. Gardella

### US Attorney's Office - New York

**Eastern District** . . . . . . . . . . . . . . . . . . . . . . . . . . . . .fax: 718-254-7508
271 Cadman Plaza East, Brooklyn, NY 11201
718-254-7000  Fax: 718-254-7508
US Attorney:
  Robert L. Capers . . . . . . . . . . . . . . . . .718-254-7000/fax: 718-254-7508
Assistant US Attorney:
  James R. Cho. . . . . . . . . . . . . . . . . . . .718-254-6519/fax: 718-254-7508
Assistant US Attorney:
  Joseph Anthony Marutollo . . . . . . . . .718-254-6288/fax: 718-254-7508
Assistant US Attorney:
  Elliot M. Schachner. . . . . . . . . . . . . .718-254-6053/fax: 718-254-7508

*Offices and agencies generally appear in alphabetical order, except when specific order is requested by listee.*

Executive Assistant US Attorney:
William J. Muller ...............718-254-7000/fax: 718-254-7508
Assistant US Attorney, Criminal Division:
Zainab Ahmad
Deputy Chief, Civil Division:
Gail Matthews
Chief of Affirmative Civil Enforcement, Civil Division:
John Vagelatos

**Northern District**
*Albany* .....................................fax: 518-431-0249
445 Broadway, Room 218, Albany, NY 12207-2924
518-431-0247  Fax: 518-431-0249
Assistant US Attorney:
Thomas Spina Jr.
*Binghamton* ..................................fax: 607-773-2901
319 Federal Building, 15 Henry Street, Binghamton, NY 13901
607-773-2887  Fax: 607-773-2901
Assistant US Attorney:
Miro Lovric
*Plattsburgh* ..................................fax: 518-314-7811
14 Durkee Street, Suite 340, Plattsburgh, NY 12901
518-314-7800  Fax: 518-314-7811
Assistant US Attorney:
Elizabeth Horsman
*Syracuse* ....................................fax: 315-448-0689
100 South Clinton Street, PO Box 7198, Syracuse, NY 13261-7198
315-448-0672  Fax: 315-448-0689
US Attorney:
Richard S. Hartunian ......................315-448-0672
Assistant US Attorney:
Tamara B. Thomson........................315-448-0672
Assistant US Attorney, Chief Civil Division:
Thomas Spina Jr.
Assistant US Attorney, Chief Criminal Division:
Elizabeth C. Coombe

**Southern District**
*New York City*
1 Saint Andrews Plaza, New York, NY 10007
212-637-2200
US Attorney:
Preet Bharara
Deputy US Attorney:
Joon H. Kim.............................212-637-2200
Chief, Criminal Division:
Daniel Stein
Chief, Civil Division:
Sara L. Shudofsky
*White Plains*
300 Quarropas Street, White Plains, NY 10601-4150
914-993-1900 or 914-993-1916
Assistant US Attorney, White Plains Co-Chief:
Perry Carbone ..........................914-993-1900

**Western District**
*Buffalo*
138 Delaware Avenue, Buffalo, NY 14202
716-843-5700
US Attorney:
William J. Hochul, Jr.
Chief of Appellate Division:
Joseph J. Karaszewski
Assistant US Attorney, Civil Division Chief:
Mary Pat Fleming ........................716-843-5867
Chief, Criminal Division:
Joseph M. Guerra, III.....................716-843-5824
Assistant US Attorney, National Security Coordinator:
Anthony M. Bruce
Chief, General Crimes Section:
Michael DiGiacomo

Administrative Officer:
Amy L. Smith
*Rochester* ...................................fax: 585-263-6226
100 State Street, Suite 500, Rochester, NY 14614
585-263-6760  Fax: 585-263-6226
Assistant US Attorney-in-Charge:
Richard A. Resnick .........................585-263-6760

**US Marshals' Service - New York**

**Eastern District**
*Brooklyn*
225 Cadman Plaza, Brooklyn, NY 11201
US Marshal:
Charles Dunne .............................718-260-0400
*Central Islip*
100 Federal Plaza, Central Islip, NY 11722
US Marshal:
Charles Dunne .............................631-712-6000

**Northern District**
*Albany*
James T. Foley Courthouse, 445 Broadway, Albany, NY 12201
US Marshal:
David McNulty .............................518-472-5401
*Binghamton*
US Courthouse & Federal Building, 15 Henry Street, Binghamton, NY 13902
US Marshal:
David McNulty .............................607-773-2723
*Syracuse*
US District Courthouse, 100 South Clinton Street, Syracuse, NY 13261
US Marshal:
David McNulty .............................315-473-7601
*Utica*
Alexander Pirnie Federal Building, 10 Broad Street, Room 213, Utica, NY 13501
US Marshal:
David McNulty .............................315-793-8109

**Southern District**
500 Pearl Street, New York, NY 10007
US Marshal:
Michael Greco...................212-331-7200/fax: 212-637-6130

**Western District**
*Buffalo*
2 Niagara Square, Buffalo, NY 14202
US Marshal:
Charles Salina .............................716-348-5300
*Rochester*
US Courthouse, 100 State Street, Room 2240, Rochester, NY 14614
US Marshal:
Charles Salina .............................585-263-5787

**US Trustee - Bankruptcy, Region 2**
201 Varick Street, Suite 1006, New York, NY 10014
US Trustee:
William K. Harrington...........212-510-0500/fax: 212-668-2256

## U.S. CONGRESS

*See U.S. Congress Chapter for additional Standing Committee and Subcommittee information.*

### House of Representatives Standing Committees

**Judiciary**
Chair:
Bob Goodlatte (R-VA) .............................202-225-5431

*Offices and agencies generally appear in alphabetical order, except when specific order is requested by listee.*

Ranking Member:
   John Conyers, Jr. (D-MI) ..........................202-225-5126
New York Delegate:
   Hakeem Jeffries (D) ..............................202-225-5936
New York Delegate:
   Jerrold Nadler (D)................................202-225-5635

## Senate Standing Committees

### Judiciary
Chair:
   Chuck Grassley (R-IA)............................202-224-3744
Ranking Member:
   Patrick Leahy (D-VT).............................202-224-4242
New York Delegate:
   Charles E. Schumer (D) ..........................202-224-6542

## PRIVATE SECTOR

**NYS Bar Assn, International Law & Practice Section**
**Alston & Bird LLP**
90 Park Ave, 15th Fl, New York, NY 10016-1387
212-210-9540  Fax: 212-210-9444
e-mail: pmfrank@alston.com
Jamie Hutchinson, Chair

**NYS Bar Assn, Lawyer Referral Service Cmte**
**Amdursky Pelky Fennell & Wallen**
26 E Oneida St, Oswego, NY 13126-2695
315-343-6363  Fax: 315-343-0134
Web site: www.apfwlaw.com
Timothy J Fennell, Chair

**Asian American Legal Defense and Education Fund**
99 Hudson St, 12th Fl, New York, NY 10013-2815
212-966-5932 or 800-966-5946  Fax: 212-966-4303
e-mail: info@aaldef.org
Web site: www.aaldef.org
*Defend civil rights of Asian Americans through litigation, legal advocacy & community education*
Margaret Fung, Executive Director

**Association of the Bar of the City of New York**
42 W 44th St, New York, NY 10036-6689
212-382-6655  Fax: 212-768-8630
e-mail: jbigelsen@nycbar.org
Web site: www.nycbar.org
Jayne Bigelsen, Director, Communications/Legislative Affrs

**NYS Bar Assn, Review the Code of Judicial Conduct Cmte**
**Securities Industry & Financial Markets Association (SIFMA)**
360 Madison Ave, 18th Fl, New York, NY 10017-7111
646-637-9200  Fax: 646-637-9126
Web site: www.sifma.org
Herbert H McDade III, Chair

**NYS Bar Assn, President's Cmte on Access to Justice**
**Boylan Brown**
2400 Chase Sq, Rochester, NY 14604
585-232-5300 x256  Fax: 585-232-3528
Web site: www.boylanbrown.com
C Bruce Lawrence, Secretary New York State Bar Association

**NYS Bar Assn, Tort System Cmte**
**Bracken Margolin Besunder LLP**
1050 Old Nichols Road, Suite 200, Islandia, NY 11749
631-234-8585  Fax: 631-234-8702
John P Bracken, Judicial Screening

**Brooklyn Law School**
250 Joralemon St, Brooklyn, NY 11201
718-780-7900  Fax: 718-780-0393
e-mail: joan.wexler@brooklaw.edu
Web site: www.brooklaw.edu
*18 legal clincs include immigration, new media, the arts, criminal defense and prosecution, bankruptcy, real estate, health, and securities arbitration.*
Joan G Wexler, Dean

**NYS Bar Assn, Cyberspace Law Cmte**
**Thelen Reid Brown Raysman & Steiner**
875 Third Ave, New York, NY 10022
212-603-2196  Fax: 212-603-2001
Jeffrey D Neuburger, Chair

**CASA: Advocates for Children of NYS (CASANYS)**
911 Central Avenue, Suite 117, Albany, NY 12206
315-246-3558
e-mail: mail@casanys.org
Web site: www.casanys.org
*Volunteer advocates appointed by family court judges to represent abused & neglected children in court*
Barbara Benedict, Executive Director

**CPR, The International Institute for Conflict Prevention & Resolution**
575 Lexington Ave, 21st Fl, New York, NY 10022
212-949-6490  Fax: 212-949-8859
e-mail: info@cpradr.org
Web site: www.cpradr.org
*Alternative dispute resolution*
Kathleen A Bryan, President & Chief Executive Officer

**Center for Court Innovation**
520 8th Ave, New York, NY 10018
212-397-3050  Fax: 212-397-0985
e-mail: info@courtinnovation.org
Web site: www.courtinnovation.org
*Foster innovation within NYS courts addressing quality-of-life crime, substance abuse, child neglect, domestic violence & landlord-tenant disputes*
Greg Berman, Director

**Center for Judicial Accountability Inc (CJA)**
283 Soundview Avenue, White Plains, NY 10606-3821
914-421-1200  Fax: 914-684-6554
e-mail: mail@judgewatch.org
Web site: www.judgewatch.org
*National, nonpartisan, non-profit citizens' organization documentingthe politicization & corruption of the judicial selection & discipline processes*
Doris L Sassower, President

**Center for Law & Justice**
Pine West Plaza, Bldg 2, Washington Ave Ext, Albany, NY 12205
518-427-8361  Fax: 518-427-8362
e-mail: cflj@verizon.net
*Advocacy for fair treatment of poor people & communities of color by the justice system; referral, workshops, community lawyering & education*
Alice P Green, Executive Director

**Coalition of Fathers & Families NY, PAC**
P.O. Box 252, Clifton Park, NY 12170
518-288-6755
e-mail: info@fafny.org
Web site: www.fafny.org
*Political Action for fathers and families in New York*
James Hays, Treasurer

*Offices and agencies generally appear in alphabetical order, except when specific order is requested by listee.*

**NYS Bar Assn, Trial Lawyers Section**
**Connors & Connors, PC**
766 Castleton Ave, Staten Island, NY 10310
718-442-1700  Fax: 718-442-1717
e-mail: jconnorsjr@connorslaw.com
Web site: www.connorslaw.com
John P Connors Jr, Chair

**NYS Bar Assn, Torts, Insurance & Compensation Law Section**
**Connors & Corcoran LLP**
Times Square Bldg, 45 Exchange St, Ste 250, Rochester, NY 14614
585-232-5885  Fax: 585-546-3631
e-mail: law@connorscorcoran.com
Web site: www.connorscorcoran.com
Eileen E Buholtz, Partner

**Cornell Law School, Legal Information Institute**
Myron Taylor Hall, Ithaca, NY 14853
607-255-1221  Fax: 607-255-7193
Web site: www.law.cornell.edu
*Distributes legal documents via the web & electronic mail*
Thomas R Bruce, Director

**NYS Bar Assn, Judicial Section**
**Court of Claims**
140 Grand St, Ste 507, White Plains, NY 10601
914-289-2310  Fax: 914-289-2313
e-mail: truderma@courts.state.ny.us
Hon Terry Jane Ruderman, Judge

**NYS Bar Assn, Federal Constitution & Legislation Cmte**
**Day Pitney LLP**
7 Times Square, New York, NY 10036-7311
973-966-8180  Fax: 973-966-1015
e-mail: jmaloney@daypitney.com
Web site: www.daypitney.com
*One Jefferson Road, Parsippany, New Jersey 07054*
John C Maloney Jr, Partner

**NYS Bar Assn, Trusts & Estates Law Section**
**Day Pitney LLP**
7 Times Square, 41st & 42nd St, New York, NY 10036
212-297-5800 or 212-297-2468  Fax: 212-916-2940
e-mail: gwwhitaker@daypitney.com
Web site: www.daypitney.com
*Domestic and international trusts and estates.*
G Warren Whitaker,

**NYS Bar Assn, Public Trust & Confidence in the Legal System**
**Debevoise & Plimpton LLP**
919 Third Ave, New York, NY 10022
212-909-6000  Fax: 212-909-6836
Web site: www.debevoise.com
Ellen Lieberman,

**NYS Bar Assn, Alternative Dispute Resolution Cmte**
**Elayne E Greenberg, MS, Esq**
25 Potters Lane, Great Neck, NY 11024
516-829-5521  Fax: 516-466-8130
Elayne E Greenberg, Chair

**Empire Justice Center**
119 Washington Ave, Albany, NY 12210
518-462-6831  Fax: 518-462-6687
e-mail: aerickson@empirejustice.org
Web site: www.empirejustice.org
*Policy analysis and research in issues impacting civil legal matters for low-income residents*
Anne Erickson, President & CEO

**NYS Bar Assn, Review Judicial Nominations Cmte**
**Englert, Coffey, McHugh & Fantauzzi LLP**
224 State St, PO Box 1092, Schenectady, NY 12305
518-370-4645  Fax: 518-374-5422
e-mail: pcoffey@ecmlaw.com
Peter V Coffey, Chair

**NYS Bar Assn, Cmte on the Jury System**
**FitzGerald Morris et al**
One Broad St Plz, PO Box 2017, Glens Falls, NY 12801-4360
518-745-1400  Fax: 518-745-1576
e-mail: pdf@fmbf-law.com
Peter D FitzGerald, Chair

**Fund for Modern Courts (The)**
205 East 42nd Street, 16th Floor, New York, NY 10017
212-541-6741  Fax: 212-541-7301
e-mail: justice@moderncourts.org
Web site: www.moderncourts.org
*Improve the administration & quality of justice in NYS courts*
Dennis R Hawkins, Executive Director

**NYS Bar Assn, Court Operations Cmte**
**Getnick, Livingston, Atkinson, Gigliotti & Priore LLP**
258 Genesee St, Ste 401, Utica, NY 13502-4642
315-797-9261  Fax: 315-732-0755
Linda A Juteau, Office Manager

**NYS Bar Assn, Labor & Employment Law Section**
**Goodman & Zuchlewski LLP**
500 5th Ave, Ste 5100, New York, NY 10110-5197
212-869-4646  Fax: 212-869-4648
e-mail: pz@kzlaw.net
Pearl Zuchlewski, Chair

**Harris Beach LLP**
99 Garnsey Rd, Pittsford, NY 14534
585-419-8800  Fax: 585-419-8801
e-mail: vbuzard@harrisbeach.com

**NYS Bar Assn, Intellectual Property Law Section**
**Hartman & Winnicki, PC**
115 W Century Rd, Paramus, NJ 7654
201-967-8040  Fax: 201-967-0590
e-mail: rick@ravin.com
Web site: www.hartmanwinnicki.com
*Internet and Computer Law, Intellectual Property Law, and Debtors & Creditors Rights.*
Richard L Ravin, Chair

**NYS Bar Assn, Fiduciary Appointments Cmte**
**Harvey B Besunder PC**
One Suffolk Sq, Ste 315, Islandia, NY 11749
631-234-9240  Fax: 631-234-9278
e-mail: hbb@besunderlaw.com
Harvey Besunder, Owner

**NYS Bar Assn, Procedures for Judicial Discipline Cmte**
**Hollyer Brady et al**
380 Madison Avenue, 22nd Fl, New York, NY 10017
212-818-1110  Fax: 212-818-0494
A Rene Hollyer, Chair

**JAMS**
620 Eighth Ave, 34th Floor, New York, NY 10018
212-607-2763  Fax: 212-751-4099
e-mail: mshaw@jamsadr.com
Web site: www.jamsadr.com
*Mediation of civil, commercial & employment disputes; training & systems design*
Margaret L Shaw, Mediator & Arburator

*Offices and agencies generally appear in alphabetical order, except when specific order is requested by listee.*

**NYS Bar Assn, Real Property Section**
**Law Office of Anne Reynolds Copps**
126 State St, 6th Fl, Albany, NY 12207
518-436-4170  Fax: 518-436-1456
e-mail: arcopps@nycap.rr.com
Anne Reynolds Copps, Partner/Owner

**NYS Bar Assn, General Practice Section**
**Law Offices of Frank G. D'Angelo & Associates**
901 Stewart Avenue, Suite 230, Garden City, NY 11530
516-742-7601 or 516-222-1122  Fax: 516-742-6070
e-mail: fgdangeloesq@aol.com
*Queens Village Office- 224-44 Braddock Ave, Queens Village, NY 11428*
*Phone; 718-776-7475*
Frank G D'Angelo, Elder Law Attorney

**Legal Action Center**
225 Varick Street, 4th Floor, New York, NY 10014
212-243-1313  Fax: 212-675-0286
e-mail: lacinfo@lac.org
Web site: www.lac.org
*Legal & policy issues, alcohol/drug abuse, AIDS & criminal justice*
Paul N Samuels, President & Director

**Legal Aid Society**
199 Water Street, New York, NY 10038
212-577-3277  Fax: 212-809-1574
Web site: www.legal-aid.org
*Civil & criminal defense, appeals, juvenile rights, civil legal services*
Steven Banks, Attorney-In-Chief

**NYS Bar Assn, Legal Aid Cmte/Funding for Civil Legal Svcs Cmte**
**Legal Services of the Hudson Valley**
90 Maple Avenue, White Plains, NY 10601
914-949-1305 x136  Fax: 914-949-6213
e-mail: bfinkelstein@lshv.org
Web site: www.lshv.org
*Established to provide free legal representation in civil matters to low-income people. Legal assistance is provided in the following areas; Westchester, Putnam, Dutchess, Orange, Sullivan and Ulster Counties.*
Barbara D Finkelstein, Executive Director

**Levene, Gouldin & Thompson LLP**
PO Box F-1706, 450 Plaza Drive, Binghamton, NY 13902
607-584-5706  Fax: 607-763-9212
e-mail: jpollock@binghamtonlaw.com
Web site: www.binghamtonlaw.com
*Commercial and personal injury litigation*
John J. Pollock, Managing Partner

**NYS Bar Assn, Elder Law Section**
**Littman Krooks LLP**
655 Third Avenue, 20th Floor, New York, NY 10017
212-490-2020  Fax: 212-490-2990
e-mail: bkrooks@littmankrooks.com
*Littman Krooks LLP provides sophisticated legal advice and a high level of expertise in areas such as elder law, estate planning, special needs planning, special education advocacy, and corporate and securities.*
Bernard A Krooks, Esq., Managing Partner

**NYS Bar Assn, Unlawful Practice of Law Cmte**
**Schlather, Geldenhuys, Stumbar & Salk**
200 E Buffalo St, PO Box 353, Ithaca, NY 14851
607-273-2202  Fax: 607-273-4436
Web site: www.ithacalaw.com
Mark J Solomon, Chair

**NYS Bar Assn, Court Structure & Judicial Selection Cmte**
**McMahon & Grow**
301 N Washington St, PO Box 4350, Rome, NY 13442-4350
315-336-4700  Fax: 315-336-5851
Web site: www.mgglaw.com
Hon Richard D Simons,

**NYS Bar Assn, Resolutions Committee**
**Meyer Suozzi English & Klein, PC**
990 Stewart Ave, Garden City, NY 11530-9194
516-592-5704  Fax: 516-741-6706
A Thomas Levin, Chair

**NYS Bar Assn, Commercial & Federal Litigation Section**
**Montclare & Wachtler**
67 Wall St, 22nd Fl, New York, NY 10005
212-509-3900  Fax: 212-509-7239
Lauren J Wachtler, Chair

**NY County Lawyers' Association**
14 Vessey St, New York, NY 10007
212-267-6646  Fax: 212-406-9252
Web site: www.nycla.org
Stewart D Aaron, President

**NYS Association of Criminal Defense Lawyers**
245 Fifth Ave, 19th Fl, New York, NY 10016
212-532-4434  Fax: 212-532-4668
e-mail: nysacdl@aol.com
Web site: www.nysacdl.org
*Criminal law*
Patricia Marcus, Executive Director

**NYS Bar Assn, Cmte on Diversity & Leadership Development**
1 Elk St, Albany, NY 12207
518-487-5555 or 212-351-4670  Fax: 212-878-8641
e-mail: kstandard@ebglaw.com
Kenneth G Standard, Co-Chair

**NYS Council of Probation Administrators**
Box 2 272 Broadway, Albany, NY 12204
518-434-9194  Fax: 518-434-0392
Web site: www.nyscopa.org
*Provide supervision & investigation services to courts*
Patricia Aikens, President

**NYS Court Clerks Association**
170 Duane St, New York, NY 10013
212-941-5700  Fax: 212-941-5705
Kevin E Scanlon, Sr, President

**NYS Defenders Association**
194 Washington Ave, Ste 500, Albany, NY 12210-2314
518-465-3524  Fax: 518-465-3249
e-mail: info@nysda.org
Web site: www.nysda.org
*Criminal defense*
Jonathan E Gradess, Executive Director

**NYS Dispute Resolution Association**
255 River St, #4, Troy, NY 12180
518-687-2240  Fax: 518-687-2245
Web site: www.nysdra.org
*Dispute resolution-mediation, arbitration, facilitation*
Lisa U Hicks, Executive Director

**NYS Magistrates Association**
750 Delaware Ave, Delmar, NY 12054-1124
518-439-1087  Fax: 518-439-1204
*Association of town & village justices*
Tanja Sirago, Executive Director

Policy Areas

*Offices and agencies generally appear in alphabetical order, except when specific order is requested by listee.*

**NYS Bar Assn, Civil Practice Law & Rules Committee**
**NYS Supreme Court**
50 Delaware Ave, Buffalo, NY 14202
716-845-9478  Fax: 716-851-3265
Sharon Stern Gerstman, Chair

**National Academy of Forensic Engineers**
174 Brady Ave, Hawthorne, NY 10532
914-741-0633  Fax: 914-747-2988
e-mail: nafe@nafe.org
Web site: www.nafe.org
*Engineering consultants to legal professionals & expert witnesses in court,
arbitration & administrative adjudication proceedings*
Marvin M Specter, P.E., L.S, Executive Director

**NYS Bar Assn, Public Utility Law Committee**
**National Fuel Gas Distribution**
455 Main St, Buffalo, NY 14203
716-686-6123
Web site: www.natfuel.com
Michael W Reville, Chair

**NYS Bar Assn, Municipal Law Section**
**New York State Court of Claims**
500 Court Exchange Bldg, 144 Exchange Blvd, Rochester, NY 14614
585-987-4212  Fax: 585-262-3019
Web site: www.nyscourtofclaims.courts.state.ny.us/
Hon Renee Forgensi Minarik,

**New York State Law Enforcement Council**
One Hogan Place, New York, NY 10013
212-335-8927  Fax: 212-335-3808
*Founded in 1982 as a legislative advocate for NY's law enforcement
community. The members represent leading law enforcement professionals
throughout the state. An active voice and participant in improving the quality
of justice and a safer NY.*
Leroy Frazer, Jr, Coordinator

**New York State Supreme Court Officers Association**
80 Broad Street, Suite 1200, New York, NY 10004
212-406-4292 or 212-406-4276  Fax: 212-791-8420
Web site: www.nysscoa.org
*Supreme Court Officers Union*
Patrick Cullen, President

**New York State Trial Lawyers**
132 Nassau St, 2nd Fl, New York, NY 10038-2486
212-349-5890  Fax: 212-608-2310
e-mail: info@nystla.org
Web site: www.nystla.org
Lawrence Park, Executive Director

**New York University School of Law**
40 Washington Square South, New York, NY 10012
212-998-6100
e-mail: trevor.morrison@nyu.edu
Web site: www.law.nyu.edu
*Judicial education & research*
Trevor W. Morrison, Dean

**NYS Bar Assn, Media Law Committee**
**New Yorker**
1 World Trade Center, New York, NY 10007
800-444-7570
e-mail: fabio.bertoni@newyorker.com
Web site: www.newyorker.com
Fabio Bertoni, Member

**NYS Bar Assn, Courts of Appellate Jurisdiction Cmte**
**Norman A Olch, Esq**
233 Broadway, Suite 705, New York, NY 10279
212-964-6171  Fax: 212-964-7634
e-mail: norman@nolch.com
Norman A Olch, Chair

**NYS Bar Assn, Judicial Campaign Monitoring Cmte**
**Ostertag O'Leary & Barrett**
17 Collegeview Ave, Poughkeepsie, NY 12603
845-486-4300  Fax: 845-486-4080
e-mail: r.ostertag@verizon.net
Robert L Ostertag, Chair

**Pace University, School of Law, John Jay Legal Services Inc**
80 N Broadway, White Plains, NY 10603-3711
914-422-4333  Fax: 914-422-4391
e-mail: jjls@law.pace.edu
Web site: www.law.pace.edu
*Law school clinical program with programs in the areas of health law,
poverty law, domestic violence, immigration, criminal justice, and investor
rights.*
Margaret M Flint, Executive Director

**Prisoners' Legal Services of New York**
114 Prospect St, Ithaca, NY 14850-5616
607-273-2283  Fax: 607-272-9122
Susan Johnson, Executive Director

**Pro Bono Net**
151 West 30th St, 10th Fl, New York, NY 10001
212-760-2554  Fax: 212-760-2557
e-mail: info@probono.net
Web site: www.probono.net; www.lawhelp.org
*Connects & organizes the public interest legal community in an online
environment; a lawyer-to-lawyer network*
Mark O'Brien, Executive Director

**NYS Bar Assn, Multi-jurisdictional Practice Cmte**
**Proskauer Rose LLP**
1585 Broadway, New York, NY 10036-8299
212-969-3000  Fax: 212-969-2900
e-mail: keppler@proskauer.com
Web site: www.proskauer.com
*Business Law, Securities*
Klaus Eppler, Partner

**Puerto Rican Legal Defense & Education Fund Inc (PRLDEF)**
99 Hudson St, 14th Fl, New York, NY 10013-2815
212-219-3360 or 800-328-2322  Fax: 212-431-4276
Web site: www.prldef.org
*Secure, promote & protect the civil & human rights of the Puerto Rican &
wider Latino community through litigation, policy analysis & education*
Cesar A Perales, President & General Counsel

**NYS Bar Assn, Judicial Campaign Conduct Cmte**
**Supreme Court**
401 Montgomery St, Rm 401, Syracuse, NY 13202-2127
315-671-1100  Fax: 315-671-1183
e-mail: maklein@courts.state.ny.us
Michael A Klein, Chair

**Vera Institute of Justice**
233 Broadway, 12th Fl, New York, NY 10279-1299
212-334-1300  Fax: 212-941-9407
e-mail: contactvera@vera.org
Web site: www.vera.org
*Research, design & implementation of demonstration projects in criminal
justice & social equity in partnership with government & nonprofit
organizations. Involved in child-welfare, cost-benefit analysis, substance
abuse and mental health.*
Michael Jacobson, Director

---

*Offices and agencies generally appear in alphabetical order, except when specific order is requested by listee.*

**NYS Bar Assn, Family Law Section**
**Vincent F Stempel, Jr Esq**
1205 Franklin Ave, Ste 280, Garden City, NY 11530
516-742-8620  Fax: 516-742-6859
e-mail: vstempel@yahoo.com
Vincent F Stempel, Jr, Chair

**Volunteers of Legal Service, Inc**
281 Park Avenue South, New York, NY 10010
212-966-4400  Fax: 212-219-8943
e-mail: blienhard@volsprobono.org
*Providing pro bono civil legal services to poor people in New York City.*
Bill Lienhard, Executive Director

**NYS Bar Assn, Health Law Section**
**Wilson Elser Moskowitz Edelman & Dicker**
677 Broadway, Albany, NY 12207
518-449-8893  Fax: 518-449-4292
Philip Rosenberg,

**Women's Bar Association of the State of New York**
PO Box 936, Planetarium Station, New York, NY 10024-0546
212-362-4445  Fax: 212-721-1620
e-mail: info@wbasny.org
Web site: www.wbasny.org
Linda A Chiaverini, Executive Director

Policy Areas

*Offices and agencies generally appear in alphabetical order, except when specific order is requested by listee.*

## LABOR & EMPLOYMENT PRACTICES

### NEW YORK STATE

### GOVERNOR'S OFFICE

## Governor's Office
Executive Chamber
State Capitol
Albany, NY 12224
518-474-8390  Fax: 518-474-1513
Web site: www.ny.gov

Governor:
   Andrew M Cuomo . . . . . . . . . . . . . . . . . . . . . . . . . . . . . . . . 518-474-8390
Secretary to the Governor:
   Melissa DeRosa . . . . . . . . . . . . . . . . . . . . 518-474-4246 or 212-681-4580
Counsel to the Governor:
   Kumiki Gibson . . . . . . . . . . . . . . . . . 518-474-8343 or 212-681-4580
Deputy Secretary, Labour:
   Vacant. . . . . . . . . . . . . . . . . . . . . . . . . 212-681-4584 or 518-486-1214
Chief of Staff:
   Jill DesRosiers . . . . . . . . . . . . . . . . . . 518-474-8390 or 212-681-4580
Director, Communications:
   Peter Ajemian. . . . . . . . . . . . . . . . . . . 518-474-8418 or 212-681-4640

### EXECUTIVE DEPARTMENTS AND RELATED AGENCIES

## Insurance Fund (NYS)
One Watervliet Ave Ext
Albany, NY 12206-1629
518-437-6400
Web site: www.nysif.com

199 Church Street
New York, NY 10007-1100
212-587-5435

Executive Director & CEO:
   Eric Madoff. . . . . . . . . . . . . . . . . . . . . . . . . . . . . . . . . 518-437-5220
Deputy Executive Director & Chief of Staff:
   Shirley Stark . . . . . . . . . . . . . . . . . . . . . . . . . . . . . . . . 518-437-6400
Chief Fiscal Officer:
   Susan D Sharp. . . . . . . . . . . . . . . . . . . . . . . . . . . . . . . 518-437-6168
General Attorney:
   Tanisha Edwards, Esq
Chief Financial Officer:
   William Gratrix

## Administration
Director:
   Joseph Mullen. . . . . . . . . . . . . . . . . . . . . . . . . . . . . . . 518-437-5220

## Claims & Medical Operations
Director:
   Edward Hiller . . . . . . . . . . . . . . . . . . . . . . . . . . . . . . . 212-312-7880

## Confidential Investigations
Director:
   George Tidona . . . . . . . . . . . . . . . . . . . . . . . . . . . . . . . 631-756-4007

## Field Services
Director:
   Armin Holdorf . . . . . . . . . . . . . . . . . . . . . . . . . . . . . . . 212-587-5225

## Information Technology Service
Chief Information Officer:
   Sean O'Brien. . . . . . . . . . . . . . . . . . . . . . . . . . . . . . . . 518-437-4361

Director, ITS:
   Laurie Endries. . . . . . . . . . . . . . . . . . . . . . . . . . . . . . . 518-437-3130

## Insurance Fund Board of Commissioners
Chair:
   Kenneth R Theobalds . . . . . . . . . . . . . . . 518-437-5220 or 518-437-6400
Vice Chair:
   Barry Swidler . . . . . . . . . . . . . . . . . . . . 518-437-5220 or 518-437-6400
Secretary to the Board:
   Michael Miliano . . . . . . . . . . . . . . . . . . . . . . . . . . . . . 212-312-7408
Member(ex-offico)/Commissioner, NYS Dept of Labor:
   Peter M. Rivera. . . . . . . . . . . . . . . . . . . . . . . . . . . . . . 518-437-5220
Member:
   Roberta Reardon. . . . . . . . . . . . . . . . . . 518-437-5220 or 518-437-6400
Member:
   Joseph Canovas. . . . . . . . . . . . . . . . . . . . . . . . . . . . . . 518-437-5220
Member:
   David E Ourlicht. . . . . . . . . . . . . . . . . . . . . . . . . . . . . . 518-437-5220

## Investments
Director:
   Miriam Martinez. . . . . . . . . . . . . . . . . . . . . . . . . . . . . . 212-587-6550

## NYSIF District Offices

**Albany**
1 Watervliet Ave Ext, Albany, NY 12206
Business Manager:
   Augusto Bortoloni. . . . . . . . . . . . . . . . 518-437-6401/fax: 518-437-8021

**Buffalo**
225 Oak St, Buffalo, NY 14203
Business Manager:
   Ronald Reed . . . . . . . . . . . . . . . . . . . . 716-851-2004/fax: 716-851-2131

**Binghamton**
Glendale Technology Park, 2001 E Perimeter Rd, Endicott, NY 13760
Business Manager:
   Thomas Racko. . . . . . . . . . . . . . . . . . . 607-741-6023/fax: 607-741-5029

**Nassau County, Long Island**
8 Corporate Center Dr, 2nd Fl, Melville, NY 11747
Business Manager:
   Cliff Meister . . . . . . . . . . . . . . . . . . . . 631-756-4003/fax: 631-756-4030

**Rochester**
100 Chestnut St, Ste 1000, Rochester, NY 14604
Business Manager:
   Lisa Ellsworth . . . . . . . . . . . . . . . . . . . 585-258-2100/fax: 585-258-2065

**Suffolk County, Long Island**
8 Corporate Center Dr, 3rd Fl, Melville, NY 11747
Business Manager:
   Catherine Carillo. . . . . . . . . . . . . . . . . 631-756-4330/fax: 631-756-4260

**Syracuse**
1045 Seventh North St, Liverpool, NY 13088
Business Manager:
   Patricia Albert. . . . . . . . . . . . . . . . . . . 315-453-8300/fax: 315-453-8313

**White Plains**
105 Corporate Park Dr, Ste 200, White Plains, NY 10604
Business Manager:
   Carl Heitner. . . . . . . . . . . . . . . . . . . . . 914-701-6292/fax: 914-701-2181

## Premium Audit
Director:
   Glenn Cunningham. . . . . . . . . . . . . . . . . . . . . . . . . . . . 212-587-7470

## Underwriting
Director:
   John Massetti . . . . . . . . . . . . . . . . . . . . . . . . . . . . . . . 212-312-7012

*Offices and agencies generally appear in alphabetical order, except when specific order is requested by listee.*

## Labor Department

W.A. Harriman Campus
Building 12
Albany, NY 12240
518-457-9000 or 888-469-7365  Fax: 518-457-6908
e-mail: nysdol@labor.ny.gov
Web site: www.labor.ny.gov

Commissioner:
Roberta Reardon . . . . . . . . . . . . . . . . . . . . . . . . . . . . .518-457-9000
Executive Deputy Commissioner:
Nathaalie Carey . . . . . . . . . . . . . . . . . . . . . . . . . . . . . .518-457-4318

### Hazard Abatement Board
Chair:
Katherine D. Schrier . . . . . . . . . . . . . . . . . . . . . . . . . . .518-457-7629

### Employment Relations Board
Chair:
Jerome Lefkowitz . . . . . . . . . . . . . . . . . . . . . . . . . . . . .518-457-2664
e-mail: perbinfo@perb.ny.gov

### Industrial Board of Appeals
Chair:
Anne P Stevason . . . . . . . . . . . . . . . . . . . . . . . . . . . . . .518-474-4785

### Unemployment Insurance Appeal Board
Chair:
Leonard Polletta . . . . . . . . . . . . . . . . . . . . . . . . . . . . . .518-402-0205
Executive Director:
Susan Borenstein . . . . . . . . . . . . . . . . . . . . . . . . . . . . . .518-402-0205

## Administration & Public Affairs
Director:
Roger Bailie . . . . . . . . . . . . . . . . . . . . . . . . . . . . . . . . .518-457-2647
Associate Commissioner, Communications:
Peter Brancato . . . . . . . . . . . . . . . . . . . . . . . . . . . . . . .518-457-5519
Director, Personnel:
Carol Owsiany . . . . . . . . . . . . . . . . . . . . . . . . . . . . . . .518-457-1020
Acting Director, Staff & Organization Development:
Sherry Edwards . . . . . . . . . . . . . . . . . . . . . . . . . . . . . .518-457-7442
Director, Equal Opportunity Development:
Omoye Cooper . . . . . . . . . . . . . . . . . . . . . . . . . . . . . . .518-457-1984

## Counsel's Office
Acting Counsel:
Jill Archambault

## Federal Programs
Deputy Commissioner, Federal Programs:
Bruce Herman . . . . . . . . . . . . . . . . . . . . . . . . . . . . . . .518-485-6410

### Employment Services Division
Director:
Vacant . . . . . . . . . . . . . . . . . . . . . . . . . . . . . . . . . . . . .518-457-3584
Assistant Director:
Russell Oliver . . . . . . . . . . . . . . . . . . . . . . . . . . . . . . . .518-457-3584

### Unemployment Insurance Division
Director:
Richard Marino . . . . . . . . . . . . . . . .518-457-2878/fax: 518-485-8604

### Workforce Development & Training Division
Deputy Commissioner:
Karen Coleman . . . . . . . . . . . . . . . . . . . . . . . . . . . . . . .518-457-4317
*Employability Development/Apprentice Training*
Acting Director:
Yue Yee . . . . . . . . . . . . . . . . . . . . . . . . . . . . . . . . . . . .518-457-6820

## Labor Planning & Technology
Director, Enterprise Architecture:
David A. Palmisano . . . . . . . . . . . . . . . . . . . . . . . . . . . .518-485-7395

## Research & Statistics Division
Chief:
Bohdan Wynnyk . . . . . . . . . . . . . . . . . . . . . . . . . . . . . .518-485-7990
Chief of Labor Market Information:
Norman Steele . . . . . . . . . . . . . . . . . . . . . . . . . . . . . . .518-457-6638
Statewide Labor Market Analyst:
Kevin Jack . . . . . . . . . . . . . . . . . . . . . . . . . . . . . . . . . .518-457-2919
e-mail: kevin.jack@labor.ny.gov

## Special Investigations
Acting Deputy Commissioner, Administration:
Jack Dougherty
Director, Internal Audit:
Timothy Burleski . . . . . . . . . . . . . . . . . . . . . . . . . . . . .518-457-7012

## Veterans Services
Program Coordinator:
Vacant . . . . . . . . . . . . . . . . . . . . . . . . . . . . . . . . . . . . .518-457-1343

### Employer Services
Director:
Vacant . . . . . . . . . . . . . . . . . . . . . . . . . . . . . . . . . . . . .518-457-6821
Rural Labor Services:
Valerie Sewell . . . . . . . . . . . . . . . . . . . . . . . . . . . . . . . .518-485-8539

### Regional Offices
*Central/Mohawk Valley* . . . . . . . . . . . . . . . . . . . . . .fax: 315-793-2342
207 Genesee St, Ste 712, Utica, NY 13501
*Finger Lakes Region* . . . . . . . . . . . . . . . . . . . . . . . .fax: 585-258-8859
276 Waring Road, Rochester, NY 14607
*Greater Capital District* . . . . . . . . . . . . . . . . . . . . .fax: 518-462-2777
175 Central Ave, Albany, NY 12206-2902
*Hudson Valley* . . . . . . . . . . . . . . . . . . . . . . . . . . . . .fax: 914-287-2058
120 Bloomingdale Rd, White Plains, NY 10605
*Long Island Region* . . . . . . . . . . . . . . . . . . . . . . . .fax: 516-934-8553
303 W Old County Rd, Hicksville, NY 11801
*New York City* . . . . . . . . . . . . . . . . . . . . . . . . . . . . .fax: 212-621-0730
247 West 54th St, New York, NY 10019
*Southern Tier* . . . . . . . . . . . . . . . . . . . . . . . . . . . . .fax: 607-741-4516
2001 Perimeter Rd East, Ste 3, Endicott, NY 13760
*Western Region* . . . . . . . . . . . . . . . . . . . . . . . . . . .fax: 716-851-2792
284 Main St, Buffalo, NY 14202

## Worker Protection
Acting Deputy Commissioner:
Milan Bhatt

### Labor Standards Division
Director:
Carmine Ruberto . . . . . . . . . . . . . . . . . . . . . . . . . . . .518-457-4256

### Public Work Bureau
Director:
Chris Alund . . . . . . . . . . . . . . . . . . . . . . . . . . . . . . . . .518-485-5696

### Safety & Health Division
Deputy Commissioner:
Eileen Franko . . . . . . . . . . . . . . . . . . . . . . . . . . . . . . . .518-457-3518
*Asbestos Control Bureau*
Program Manager:
Robert Perez . . . . . . . . . . . . . . .518-457-1255/fax: 518-485-8054
*Industry Inspection Unit*
Program Manage, License & Certification:
Martha Waldman . . . . . . . . . . . . . . . . . . . . . . . . . . .518-457-2735
*On-site Consultation Unit*
Program Manager:
James Rush . . . . . . . . . . . . . . . .518-457-2238/fax: 518-457-3454
*Public Employees Safety & Health (PESH) Unit*
Program Manager:
Normand Labbe . . . . . . . . . . . .518-457-1263/fax: 518-457-5545

*Offices and agencies generally appear in alphabetical order, except when specific order is requested by listee.*

Policy Areas

## Law Department
28 Liberty Street
New York, NY 10005
212-416-8000 or 800-771-7755
Web site: www.ag.ny.gov

State Capitol
Albany, NY 12224-0341
518-776-2000
Fax: 518-650-9401

Attorney General:
  Letitia James.........................212-416-8000 or 518-776-2000
Chief of Staff:
  Brian Mahanna..........................................212-416-8050
Press Secretary:
  Fernando Aquino...................212-416-8060/fax: 212-416-6005
  e-mail: nyag.pressoffice@ag.ny.gov

## Social Justice
Executive Deputy Attorney General:
  Vacant...................................................212-416-8450

### Civil Rights Bureau
Bureau Chief:
  Lourdes Rosado.................212-416-8250/fax: 212-416-8074

## State Counsel
Chief Deputy Attorney General & Counsel:
  Harlan Levy..............................................212-416-8525
Executive Deputy Attorney General, State Counsel:
  Vacant...................................................212-416-8050

### Civil Recoveries Bureau
Bureau Chief:
  John Cremo.....................518-776-2173/fax: 518-915-7731

## Workers' Compensation Board
328 State Street
Schenectady, NY 12305-2318
518-408-0469 or 877-632-4996  Fax: 518-473-1415
e-mail: general_information@wcb.ny.gov
Web site: www.wcb.ny.gov

Executive Director:
  MaryBeth Woods ...............................518-408-0469
Chair, Board of Commissioners:
  Clarissa M Rodriguez ...............518-408-0469/fax: 518-473-1415
Vice Chair:
  Freida Foster ......................518-408-0469/fax: 518-473-1415
General Counsel:
  David Wertheim ..................518-486-9564/fax: 518-402-0113
  e-mail: officeofgeneralcounsel@wcb.ny.gov
Director, Public Information:
  Melissa Stewart ...................518-408-0469/fax: 518-473-1415
  e-mail: publicinfo@wcb.ny.gov
Fraud Inspector General:
  Vacant..................................................800-367-4448

## Administration
Director, Facilities Management:
  Michael DeBarr....................................518-486-9597
Chief, Security:
  Sylvio Mantello.................518-486-0373/fax: 518-402-6100
Director, Human Resources:
  Gilda Hernandez...............518-486-3348/fax: 518-486-6364
Affirmative Action Officer:
  Jaime Benitez....................518-486-5128/fax: 518-486-6364

## Information Management Systems
Director:
  Vacant
Director, Continuous Improvement/MIS:
  Thomas Wegener .................................518-486-5143

## Operations
Director, Bureau of Compliance:
  Vacant.........................518-474-9598/fax: 518-402-6201

### District Offices
*Albany*
  100 Broadway-Menands, Albany, NY 12241
  District Manager:
    Laurie Hart ................866-750-5157/fax: 518-473-9166
*Binghamton*
  State Office Bldg, 44 Hawley St, Binghamton, NY 13901
  District Manager:
    David Gardiner.............866-802-3604/fax: 607-721-8464
*Brooklyn*
  111 Livingston St, 22nd Fl, Brooklyn, NY 11201
  District Manager:
    Tom Agostino..............800-877-1373/fax: 718-802-6642
*Buffalo*
  Ellicott Sq Building, 295 Main Street Ste 400, Buffalo, NY 14203
  District Manager:
    Michelle Hirsch .............866-211-0645/fax: 716-842-2171
*Long Island*
  220 Rabro Drive, Ste 100, Hauppauge, NY 11788-4230
  District Manager:
    Bryan Pile................866-681-5354/fax: 631-952-7966
*Manhattan*
  215 W 125th St, New York, NY 10027
  District Manager:
    Sherri Cunningham...........800-877-1373/fax: 212-864-7204
*Peekskill*
  41 N Division St, Peekskill, NY 10566
  District Manager:
    Luis A Torres ...............866-746-0552/fax: 914-788-5809
*Queens*
  168-46 91st Ave, 3rd Fl, Jamaica, NY 11432
  District Administrator:
    Bryan Pile..................800-877-1373/fax: 718-291-7248
*Rochester*
  130 Main St West, Rochester, NY 14614
  District Manager:
    Matthew Bligh ..............866-211-0644/fax: 585-238-8351
*Syracuse*
  935 James Street, Syracuse, NY 13203
  District Manager:
    Marc Johnson ..............866-802-3730/fax: 315-423-2938

## Workers' Compensation Board of Commissioners
Chair:
  Clarissa M Rodriguez............................518-408-0469
Vice Chair:
  Freida Foster......................................518-408-0469
Commissioner:
  Frederick M Ausili ................................518-408-0469
Commissioner:
  Margaret A Barberis ..............................518-408-0469
Commissioner:
  Steven A Crain ...................................518-408-0469
Commissioner:
  Mark Higgins .....................................518-408-0469
Commissioner:
  Linda Hull........................................518-408-0469
Commissioner:
  Ursula Levelt......................................518-408-0469
Commissioner:
  Loren Lobban .....................................518-408-0469

*Offices and agencies generally appear in alphabetical order, except when specific order is requested by listee.*

Commissioner:
Ellen O Paprocki...................................518-408-0469
Chair:
Clarissa M Rodriguez............................518-408-0469
Commissioner:
Mark R Stasko ....................................518-408-0469
Commissioner:
Samuel G Williams...............................518-408-0469
Secretary to the Board:
Kim McCarroll ....................................518-402-6070

## CORPORATIONS, AUTHORITIES AND COMMISSIONS

### Waterfront Commission of New York Harbor
39 Broadway
4th Fl
New York, NY 10006
212-742-9280  Fax: 212-480-0587
Web site: www.wcnyh.org

Commissioner, New York:
Ronald Goldstock.................................212-742-9280
Commissioner, New Jersey:
Michael Murphy...................................212-742-9280
Executive Director:
Walter M Arsenault ..............................212-905-9201

## NEW YORK STATE LEGISLATURE

*See Legislative Branch in Section 1 for additional Standing Committee and Subcommittee information.*

### Assembly Standing Committees

#### Labor
Chair:
Michele R Titus (D) ..............................518-455-5668

### Assembly Task Forces

#### Puerto Rican/Hispanic Task Force
Chair:
Maritza Davila (D) ...............................518-455-5514
Executive Director:
Guillermo Martinez...............................518-455-3608

#### Skills Development & Career Education, Legislative Commission on
Assembly Chair:
Vacant.............................................518-455-4527

#### Women's Issues, Task Force on
Chair:
Rebecca A Seawright .............................518-455-4466

### Senate Standing Committees

#### Labor
Chair:
Jessica Ramos (D, WF)...........................518-455-2529
Ranking Minority Member:
Andrew J Lanza (R, C, IP, RFM)..................518-455-3215

## U.S. GOVERNMENT

### EXECUTIVE DEPARTMENTS AND RELATED AGENCIES

### Equal Employment Opportunity Commission
Web site: www.eeoc.gov

**New York District**
33 Whitehall St, 5th Fl, New York, NY 10004
District Director:
Kevin J. Berry...................800-669-4000 or 800-669-6820 tty
fax: 212-336-3790

**Buffalo Local**
6 Fountain Plaza, Ste 350, Buffalo, NY 14202
Director:
John E Thompson Jr.............800-669-4000 or 800-669-3820 tty
fax: 716-551-4387

### Federal Labor Relations Authority
Web site: www.flra.gov

**Boston Regional Office**.........................fax: 617-565-6262
O'Neill Federal Bldg, 10 Causeway St, Ste 472, Boston, MA 02222
617-565-5100  Fax: 617-565-6262
Regional Director:
Phillip T. Roberts .................617-424-5730/fax: 312-886-5997

### Federal Mediation & Conciliation Service
Web site: www.fmcs.gov

**Northeastern Region**...........................fax: 973-297-4860
1 Newark Center, 16th Floor, Newark, NJ 07102
732-726-3120  Fax: 973-297-4860
Regional Director:
Ken Kowalski.....................................973-645-2000
Director, Mediation Services:
Jack Sweeny ......................................973-645-2200
e-mail: jsweeny@fmcs.gov

### National Labor Relations Board
Web site: www.nlrb.gov

**Region 2 - New York City Metro Area** ..........fax: 212-264-2450
26 Federal Plaza, Rm 3614, New York, NY 10278-0104
212-264-0300  Fax: 212-264-2450
Regional Director:
Karen P. Fernbach.................212-264-0300/fax: 212-264-2450

**Region 29 - Brooklyn Area** .....................fax: 718-330-7579
Two MetroTech Center, 100 Myrtle Ave, 5th Fl, Brooklyn, NY
11201-4201
718-330-7713  Fax: 718-330-7579
Regional Director:
James G. Paulsen..................718-330-7713/fax: 718-330-7579

**Region 3 - Buffalo Area** .......................fax: 716-551-4972
Niagara Center Building, 130 South Elmwood Ave, Ste 630, Buffalo, NY
14202-2387
716-551-4931  Fax: 716-551-4972
Regional Director:
Rhonda P. Ley.....................716-551-4931/fax: 716-551-4972

**Albany Resident Office** ........................fax: 518-431-4157
Leo W O'Brien Fed Bldg, Rm 342, Clinton Ave and N Pearl St, Albany,
NY 12207-2350
518-431-4155  Fax: 518-431-4157
Resident Officer:
Jon Mackle .......................518-431-4155/fax: 518-431-4157

*Offices and agencies generally appear in alphabetical order, except when specific order is requested by listee.*

## US Labor Department
Web site: www.dol.gov

### Bureau of Labor Statistics (BLS)
201 Varick St, Rm 808, New York, NY 10014
Web site: www.bls.gov
Regional Commissioner (NY & Boston):
Deborah A. Brown . . . . . . . . . . . . . . . . . . . . . . . . . . . . . .617-565-2331
Reg Comm (NY):
Vacant

### Employee Benefits Security Administration (EBSA)
33 Whitehall St, Ste 1200, New York, NY 10004
Regional Director:
Jonathan Kay . . . . . . . . . . . . . . . . . . . . .212-607-8600/fax: 212-607-8681

### Employment & Training Administration (ETA)
JFK Federal Bldg, Rm E/350, 25 New Sudbury Street, Boston, MA 02203
Regional Administrator:
Holly O'Brien . . . . . . . . . . . . . . . . . . .617-788-0170/fax: 617-788-0101

### Employment Standards Administration

#### Federal Contract Compliance Programs Office (OFCCP)
26 Federal Plaza, Rm. 36-116, New York, NY 10278
Regional Director:
Eduardo Fountaine . . . . . . . . . . . . . . 646-264-3170/fax: 646-264-3009

#### Labor-Management Standards Office (OLMS)
Web site: www.olms.dol.gov
##### Buffalo District Office
130 South Elmwood Street, Suite 510, Buffalo, NY 14202
District Director:
Joseph Wasik . . . . . . . . . . . . . . 716-842-2900/fax: 716-842-2901
##### New York District Office
201 Varick St, Rm 878, New York, NY 10014
District Director:
Adrianna Vamuateas . . . . . . . . . 646-264-3190/fax: 646-264-3191

#### Wage-Hour Division (WHD)-Northeast Regional Office
170 So Independence Mall, Ste 850 West, Philadelphia, PA 19106
Regional Admin:
Corlis L Sellers . . . . . . . . . . . . . . . . .215-861-5800/fax: 215-861-5840
##### Albany District Office
Leo W O'Brien Fed Bldg, Rm 822, Albany, NY 12207
District Director:
Jay Rosenblum. . . . . . . . . . . . . . . . . . . . . . . .518-431-6460
##### Long Island District Office
1400 Old Country Rd, Ste 410, Westbury, NY 11590
District Director:
Irv Miljoner . . . . . . . . . . . . . . .516-338-1890/fax: 516-338-8901
##### New York City District Office
26 Federal Plz, Rm 3700, New York, NY 10278
District Director:
Maria Rosado . . . . . . . . . . . . . 212-264-8185/fax: 212-264-9548

#### Workers' Compensation Programs (OWCP)
201 Varick St, Rm 740, New York, NY 10014
Regional Director:
Zev Sapir. . . . . . . . . . . . . . . . . . . . . . . . . . . . . . .212-868-0844

### Inspector General

#### Inspector General's Office for Audit (OIG-A)
201 Varick St, Rm 871, New York, NY 10014
Audit Director:
Mark Schwartz . . . . . . . . . . . . . . . . . . . . . . . . . . . . . .646-264-3511

### Occupational Safety & Health Administration (OSHA)
201 Varick St, Rm 670, New York, NY 10014
212-337-2378
Web site: www.osha.gov

Regional Administrator:
Robert Kulick . . . . . . . . . . . . . . . . . . . . . . . . . . . . . .212-337-2378

#### Albany Area Office
401 New Karner Rd, Ste 300, Albany, NY 12205-3809
Area Director:
Kimberly Castillion. . . . . . . . . . . . . .518-464-4338/fax: 518-464-4337

#### Buffalo Area Office
130 Elmwood Avenue, Suite 500, Buffalo, NY 14026
Area Director:
Arthur Dube . . . . . . . . . . . . . . . . . .716-551-3053/fax: 716-551-3126

#### Manhattan Area Office
201 Varick St, Rm 908, New York, NY 10014
Area Director:
Richard Mendelson . . . . . . . . . . . . . .212-620-3200/fax: 212-620-4121

#### Queens Area Office
45-17 Marathon Parkway, Little Neck, NY 11362
Assistant Area Director:
Kay Gee. . . . . . . . . . . . . . . . . . . . . .718-279-9060/fax: 718-279-9057

#### Syracuse Area Office
3300 Vickery Rd, North Syracuse, NY 13212
Area Director:
Christopher Adams . . . . . . . . . . . . . . .315-451-0808/fax: 315-451-1351

#### Tarrytown Area Office
660 White Plains Rd, 4th Floor, Tarrytown, NY 10591-5107
Area Director:
Diana Cortez . . . . . . . . . . . . . . . . . . .914-524-7510/fax: 914-524-7515

### Office of Asst Secretary for Administration & Mgmt (OASAM)
201 Varick St, Rm 815, New York, NY 10014
Regional Administrator (NY & Boston):
Mark D. Falk. . . . . . . . . . . . . . . . . . . . . . . . . . . . . . . . .646-264-5018

### Office of the Solicitor . . . . . . . . . . . . . . . . . . . . . . . . .fax: 646-246-3660
201 Varick St, Rm 983, New York, NY 10014
646-264-3650  Fax: 646-246-3660
Reg Solicitor:
Patricia M Rodenhausen . . . . . . . . . . . . .212-337-2078/fax: 212-337-2112

### Region 2 - New York Office of Secretary's Representative
201 Varick St, Rm 605-B, New York, NY 10014
Secretary's Regional Representative (SRR):
Angelica O Tang . . . . . . . . . . . . . . . . . .212-337-2317/fax: 212-337-2586

#### Jobs Corps (JC)
JFK Fed Bldg, Room E350, Boston, NY 02203
Regional Director:
Joseph A Semansky . . . . . . . . . . . . . .617-788-0197/fax: 617-788-0184

#### Office of Public Affairs (OPA) (serving New York State)
JFK Federal Bldg, Rm E120, Boston, MA 2203
Regional Director, Public Affairs:
John Chavez . . . . . . . . . . . . . . . . . . .617-565-2072/fax: 617-565-2076

### Region 2 New York - Women's Bureau (WB) . . . fax: 646-264-3794
201 Varick St, Rm 602, New York, NY 10014-4811
646-264-3789  Fax: 646-264-3794
Regional Administrator:
Grace Protos . . . . . . . . . . . . . . . . . . . . . . . . . . . . . . . . . .646-264-3789

## US Merit Systems Protection Board
Web site: www.mspb.gov

### New York Field Office
26 Federal Plaza, Room 3137A, New York, NY 10278
Chief Administrative Judge:
Arthur S. Joseph . . . . . . . . . . . . . . . . .212-264-9372/fax: 212-264-1417

*Offices and agencies generally appear in alphabetical order, except when specific order is requested by listee.*

## US Office of Personnel Management

### PHILADELPHIA SERVICE CENTER (serving New York)
William J Green Fed Bldg, Rm 3256, 600 Arch St, Philadelphia, PA 19106
Director:
    Joseph D Stix......................215-861-3031/fax: 215-861-3030
    e-mail: philadelphia@opm.gov

## US Railroad Retirement Board

### New York District Offices

**Albany**..........................................fax: 518-431-4000
11A Clinton Avenue, Suite 264, Albany, NY 12207-2399
877-772-5772  Fax: 518-431-4000
District Manager:
    Daniel M Layton, Jr ..............877-772-5772/fax: 518-431-4000
    e-mail: albany@rrb.gov

**Buffalo**..........................................fax: 716-551-3802
186 Exchange Streeet, Suite 110, Buffalo, NY 14204-2085
877-772-5772  Fax: 716-551-3802
District Manager:
    Philip C Dissek ..................877-772-5772/fax: 716-551-3802
    e-mail: buffalo@rrb.gov

**New York** .......................................fax: 212-264-1687
26 Federal Plaza, Rm 3404, New York, NY 10278
877-772-5772  Fax: 212-264-1687
District Manager:
    Rose I Jonas.....................877-772-5772/fax: 212-264-1687
    e-mail: newyork@rrb.gov

**Westbury** .......................................fax: 516-334-4763
1400 Old Country Rd, Ste 202, Westbury, NY 11590
877-772-5772 or 716-835-7808  Fax: 516-334-4763
District Manager:
    Marie Baran.....................877-772-5772/fax: 516-334-4763

## U.S. CONGRESS

*See U.S. Congress Chapter for additional Standing Committee and Subcommittee information.*

## House of Representatives Standing Committees

### Education & Labor
Chair:
    John Kline (R-MN)................................202-225-2271
Ranking Member:
    George Miller (D-CA) .............................202-225-2095
New York Delegate:
    Timothy H Bishop (D) .............................202-225-3826
New York Delegate:
    Carolyn McCarthy (D) ............................202-225-5516
New York Delegate:
    Paul Tonko (D) ..................................202-225-5076

### Small Business
Chair:
    Sam Graves (R-MO)..............................202-225-7041
Ranking Member:
    Nydia Velazquez (D-NY)..........................202-225-2361
New York Delegate:
    Grace Meng (D) .................................202-225-2601

#### Subcommittees
*Contracting and Workforce*
Chair:
    Richard L. Hanna (R-NY) .....................202-225-3665

Ranking Member:
    Grace Meng (D-NY) .........................202-225-2601
Chair:
    David Schweikert (R-AZ) .....................202-225-2190
Ranking Member:
    Yvette Clarke (D-NY) .........................202-225-6231

## Senate Standing Committees

### Health, Education, Labor & Pensions
Chair:
    Tom Harkin (D-IA)...............................202-224-3254
Ranking Member:
    Lamar Alexander (R-TN)...........................202-224-4944

### Small Business & Entrepreneurship
Chair:
    Mary L. Landrieu (D-LA)..........................202-224-5824
Ranking Member:
    James E. Risch (R-ID) ...........................202-224-2752

## PRIVATE SECTOR

### 1199 SEIU United Healthcare Workers East
310 W 43rd St, New York, NY 10036
212-261-2222  Fax: 212-956-5140
Web site: www.1199seiuonline.org
*Representing New York State healthcare workers*
George Gresham, President

### Abilities Inc, Abilities!
201 IU Willets Rd, Albertson, NY 11507-1599
516-465-1400 or 516-747-5355 (TTY)  Fax: 516-465-3757
e-mail: jswiesky@abilitiesinc.org
*Provides comprehensive services to help individuals with disabilities reach their employment goals; provides support services & technical assistance to employers who hire persons with disabilities*
Alice Muterspaw, Consumer Services/Provider Relations Director

### American Federation of Teachers
555 New Jersey Ave NW, Washington, DC 20001
800-238-1133  Fax: 202-393-7479
e-mail: emcelroy@aft.org
Web site: www.aft.org
Edward J McElroy, President

### Associated Builders & Contractors, Construction Training Center of NYS
6369 Collamer Drive, East Syracuse, NY 13057-1115
315-463-7539 or 800-477-7743  Fax: 315-463-7621
e-mail: info@abc.org
*Merit shop construction trades apprenticeship program*
Thomas Schlueter, Vice President of Education Programs

### Blitman & King LLP
443 N Franklin St, Ste 300, Syracuse, NY 13204
315-422-7111  Fax: 315-471-2623
e-mail: btking@bklawyers.com
Web site: www.bklawyers.com
*Labor & employee benefits*
Bernard T King, Attorney/Senior Partner

### Center for an Urban Future
120 Wall St, 20th Fl, New York, NY 10005
212-479-3319  Fax: 212-479-3338
e-mail: cuf@nycfuture.org
Web site: www.nycfuture.org
*A New York City-based think tank that publishes studies about economic development, workforce development and other critical issues facing New York.*
Jonathan Bowles, Director

*Offices and agencies generally appear in alphabetical order, except when specific order is requested by listee.*

**Civil Service Employees Union (CSEA), Local 1000, AFSCME, AFL-CIO**
143 Washington Ave, Capitol Station Box 7125, Albany, NY 12210-0125
518-257-1000 or 800-342-4146  Fax: 518-462-3639
*Public/private employees union*
Danny Donohue, President

**Communications Workers of America, District 1**
80 Pine St, 37th Floor, New York, NY 10005
212-344-2515  Fax: 212-425-2947
Web site: www.cwa-union.org
Christopher Shelton, Vice President

**Cornell University, Institute on Conflict Resolution**
412 Dolgen Hall, Ithaca, NY 14853-3901
607-255-5378  Fax: 607-255-6974
e-mail: dbl4@cornell.edu
Web site: www.ilr.cornell.edu
*Collective bargaining; dispute resolution, negotiation*
David Lipsky, Director

**Cornell University, Sch of Industr & Labor Relations Institute for Workplace Studies**
16 E 34th Street, 4th Fl, New York, NY 10016
212-340-2850  Fax: 212-340-2893
e-mail: sb22@cornell.edu
Web site: www.ilr.cornell.edu/iws
*Substance abuse in the workplace; power & bargaining in organizations*
Samuel B Bacharach, McKelvey-Grant Professor & Director

**Cornell University, School of Industrial & Labor Relations**
Ives Hall, Ithaca, NY 14853-3901
607-255-4375 or 607-255-2223  Fax: 607-255-1836
e-mail: vmb2@cornell.edu
Web site: www.ilr.cornell.edu
*Immigration policy; labor market trends & analysis*
Vernon Briggs, Professor

**Cullen & Dykman LLP**
100 Quentin Roosevelt Blvd, Garden City Ctr, Garden City, NY 11530-4850
516-357-3703  Fax: 516-357-3792
e-mail: gfishberg@cullenanddykman.com
Web site: www.cullenanddykman.com
*Municipal & labor law*
Gerard Fishberg, Partner

**Empire State Regional Council of Carpenters**
1284 Central Avenue, Ste 1, Albany, NY 12205
518-459-7182  Fax: 518-459-7798
Michael Conroy, Political Director

**JAMS**
620 Eighth Avenue, 34th Floor, New York, NY 10018
212-751-2700  Fax: 212-751-4099
Web site: www.jamsadr.com
*Mediation of civil, commercial & employment disputes: training & systems design*
Carol Wittenberg, Arbitrator/Mediator

**Kaye Scholer LLP**
250 West 55th Street, New York, NY 10019-9710
212-836-8000  Fax: 212-836-8689
e-mail: william.wallace@kayescholer.com
Web site: www.kayescholer.com
*Chair, Labor & Employment Law Group (representing employers)*
William E. Wallace, Jr., Partner

**NYS Bar Assn, Labor & Employment Law Section Kraus & Zuchlewski LLP**
500 Fifth Ave, Ste 5100, New York, NY 10110
212-869-4646  Fax: 212-869-4648
e-mail: pz@kzlaw.net
Pearl Zuchlewski, Chair

**Lancer Insurance Co/Lancer Compliance Services**
370 West Park Ave, Long Beach, NY 11561-3245
516-432-5000  Fax: 516-431-0926
e-mail: bcrescenzo@lancer-ins.com
*Substance abuse management & testing services for the transportation industry*
Bob Crescenzo, Vice President

**MDRC**
16 East 34th St, 19th Floor, New York, NY 10016-5936
212-532-3200  Fax: 212-684-0832
e-mail: information@mdrc.org
Web site: www.mdrc.org
*Nonprofit research & field testing of education & employment programs for disadvantaged adults & youth*
Gordon Berlin, President

**Manhattan-Bronx Minority Business Enterprise Center**
225 W 34th St, Ste 2007, New York, NY 10122
212-947-5351 or 212-947-4900  Fax: 212-947-1506
*Information & advocacy for local employment & business & contract opportunities*
Lorraine Kelsey, Executive Director

**NY Association of Training & Employment Professionals (NYATEP)**
540 Broadway, 5th Floor, Albany, NY 12207
518-433-1200  Fax: 518-433-7424
Web site: www.nyatep.org
*Represent local workforce development partnerships*
John Twomey, Executive Director

**NYS Building & Construction Trades Council**
50 State Street, 3rd Floor, Albany, NY 12207
518-435-9108  Fax: 518-435-9204
e-mail: nybuildingtrades@me.com
Web site: www.nybuildingtrades.com
James Cahill, President

**NYS Industries for the Disabled (NYSID) Inc**
11 Columbia Circle Dr., Albany, NY 12203
518-463-9706 or 800-221-5994  Fax: 518-463-9708
e-mail: administrator@nysid.org
Web site: www.nysid.org
*Business development through 'preferred source' purchasing to increase employment opportunities for people with disabilities*
Lawrence L Barker, Jr, President & Chief Executive Officer

**National Federation of Independent Business**
100 State Street, Suite 440, Albany, NY 12207
518-434-1262  Fax: 518-426-8799
e-mail: mike.durant@nfib.org
Web site: www.nfib.com/new-york/
*Small business advocacy; supporting pro-small business candidates at the state & federal levels*
Michael P. Durant, State Director

**National Writers Union**
113 University Pl, 6th Fl, New York, NY 10003
212-254-0279  Fax: 212-254-0673
e-mail: nwu@nwu.org
Web site: www.nwu.org
Gerard Colby, President

*Offices and agencies generally appear in alphabetical order, except when specific order is requested by listee.*

**New York Committee for Occupational Safety & Health**
61 Broadway, Suite 1710, New York, NY 10006
212-227-6440  Fax: 212-227-9854
e-mail: nycosh@nycosh.org
Web site: www.nycosh.org
*Provide occupational safety & health training & technical assistance*
Joel Shufro, Executive Director

**New York State Nurses Association**
11 Cornell Rd, Latham, NY 12110
518-782-9400 x279  Fax: 518-783-5207
e-mail: executive@nysna.org
Web site: www.nysna.org
*Labor union & professional association for registered nurses*

**New York University, Graduate School of Journalism**
20 Cooper Square, 6th Floor, New York, NY 10003
212-998-7980  Fax: 212-995-4148
Web site: www.journalism.nyu.edu
*Labor issues & reporting*
Perri Klass, Director

**Osborne Association**
809 Westchester Avenue, Bronx, NY 10455
718-707-2600  Fax: 718-707-3102
e-mail: info@osborneny.org
Web site: www.osborneny.org
*Career/educational counseling, job referrals & training for recently released prisoners, substance abuse treatment, case management, HIV/AIDS counseling & prevention, family services, parenting education, re-entry services, housing placement assistan*
Tanya L Phillips, Director of Employment & Training

**Public/Private Ventures**
The Chanin Building, 122 East 42nd St, 42nd Fl, New York, NY 10168
212-822-2400  Fax: 212-949-0439
*A national nonprofit, nonpartisan organization that tackles critical challenges facing low-income communities by seeking out and designing innovative programs, rigorously testing them, and promoting the solutions proven to work.*
Sheila Maguire, VP, Labor Market Initiatives

**Realty Advisory Board on Labor Relations**
292 Madison Ave, New York, NY 10017
212-889-4100  Fax: 212-889-4105
e-mail: jberg@rabolr.com
Web site: www.rabolr.com
*Labor negotiations for realtors & realty firms*
James Berg, President

**Transport Workers Union of America, AFL-CIO**
1700 Broadway, 2nd Fl, New York, NY 10019
212-259-4900  Fax: 212-265-5704
Web site: www.twu.com
*Bus, train, railroad & airline workers' union*
James C Little, International President

**UNITE HERE**
275 7th Ave, Fl 11, New York, NY 10001-6708
212-265-7000  Fax: 212-765-7751
Web site: www.uniteunion.org
Bruce Raynor, General President

**United Food & Commercial Workers Local 1**
5911 Airport Road, Oriskany, NY 13424
315-797-9600 or 800-697-8329  Fax: 315-793-1182
e-mail: organize@ufcwone.org
Web site: www.ufcwone.org
Frank C DeRiso, President

**Vedder Price PC**
1633 Broadway, New York, NY 10019
212-407-7750 or 917-214-6441  Fax: 212-407-7799
Web site: www.vedderprice.com
*Representing Management*
Alan M Koral, Shareholder

**Vladeck, Waldman, Elias & Engelhard PC**
1501 Broadway, Suite 800, New York, NY 10036
212-403-7300  Fax: 212-221-3172
e-mail: jvladeck@vladeck.com
*Employment law, including discrimination cases*
Judith Vladeck, Senior Law Partner

Policy Areas

*Offices and agencies generally appear in alphabetical order, except when specific order is requested by listee.*

## MENTAL HYGIENE

## NEW YORK STATE

### GOVERNOR'S OFFICE

### Governor's Office
Executive Chamber
State Capitol
Albany, NY 12224
518-474-8390  Fax: 518-474-1513
Web site: www.ny.gov

Governor:
　Andrew M Cuomo . . . . . . . . . . . . . . . . . . . . . . . . . . . . . .518-474-8390
Secretary to the Governor:
　Melissa DeRosa . . . . . . . . . . . . . . . . . .518-474-4246 or 212-681-4580
Counsel to the Governor:
　Kumiki Gibson . . . . . . . . . . . . . . . . . .518-474-8343 or 212-681-4580
Deputy Secretary, Health & Human Services:
　Richard Beker. . . . . . . . . . . . . . . . . . . . .518-408-2500 or 212-681-4580
Chief of Staff:
　Jill DesRosiers . . . . . . . . . . . . . . . . . . . .518-474-8390 or 212-681-4580
Director, Communications:
　Peter Ajemian. . . . . . . . . . . . . . . . . . . . .518-474-8418 or 212-681-4640

### EXECUTIVE DEPARTMENTS AND RELATED AGENCIES

### Alcoholism & Substance Abuse Services, Office of
1450 Western Avenue
Albany, NY 12203-3526
518-473-3460
e-mail: communications@oasas.ny.gov
Web site: www.oasas.ny.gov

501 7th Avenue
8th Floor
New York, NY 10018-5903
646-728-4533

Commissioner:
　Arlene González-Sánchez. . . . . . . . . . . . . . . . . . . . . . . .518-457-2061
Executive Deputy Commissioner:
　Sean M Byrne . . . . . . . . . . . . . . . . . . . . . . . . . . . . . . . . . .518-485-2337
Director, Office of Public Information & Communications:
　Edison Alban
Director, Office of the Medical Director:
　Vacant. . . . . . . . . . . . . . . . . . . . . . . . . . . . . . . . . . . . . . . .845-359-8500
Director, Internal Audit:
　Steven Shrager . . . . . . . . . . . . . . . . . . . . . . . . . . . . . . . .518-485-2255
Affirmative Action Officer:
　Loretta Poole. . . . . . . . . . . . . . . . . . . . . . . . . . . . . . . . . .646-728-4530
Director, Office of Statewide Field Operations:
　Kathleen Caggiano-Siino . . . . . . . . . . . . . . . . . . . . . . . .518-457-1758

### Fiscal Administration Division
Associate Commissioner:
　Vittoria Parry . . . . . . . . . . . . . . . . . . . . . . . . . . . . . . . . .518-457-5312
Director, Facility Evaluation & Inspection Unit:
　John Van Horn . . . . . . . . . . . . . . . . . . . . . . . . . . . . . . . .518-485-2246
Director, Bureau of Capital Management:
　Jeff Emad . . . . . . . . . . . . . . . . . . . . . . . . . . . . . . . . . . . . .518-457-2545
Director, Budget Management:
　Tara Gabriel . . . . . . . . . . . . . . . . . . . . . . . . . . . . . . . . . .518-485-2193
Director, Bureau of Health Care Financing & 3rd Party Reimbursement:
　Laurie Felter . . . . . . . . . . . . . . . . . . . . . . . . . . . . . . . . .518-457-2545

### Quality Assurance & Performance Improvement Division
Associate Commissioner:
　Keith McCarthy . . . . . . . . . . . . . . . . . . . . . . . . . . . . . . .518-485-2257
Director, Bureau of Standards Compliance:
　William Lachanski . . . . . . . . . . . . . . . . . . . . . . . . . . . . . .518-485-2255

### Prevention, Housing & Management Services Division
Director, Division of Prevention:
　Scott Brady . . . . . . . . . . . . . . . . . . . . . . . . . . . . . . . . . .518-485-6022
Director, Management Services:
　Vacant. . . . . . . . . . . . . . . . . . . . . . . . . . . . . . . . . . . . . . .518-485-6689

### Outcome Management & System Information Division
Associate Commissioner:
　William F. Hogan . . . . . . . . . . . . . . . . . . . . . . . . . . . . . .518-485-2322
Director, Bureau of State/Local Planning & Outcome Mgmt:
　Vacant. . . . . . . . . . . . . . . . . . . . . . . . . . . . . . . . . . . . . . .518-485-2322
Director, Bureau of Research, Epidemiology & Practice Improvement:
　Vacant. . . . . . . . . . . . . . . . . . . . . . . . . . . . . . . . . . . . . . .518-485-5989

### Developmental Disabilities Planning Council
99 Washington Avenue
Suite 1230
Albany, NY 12210
518-486-7505 or 800-395-3372
e-mail: information@ddpc.ny.gov
Web site: www.ddpc.ny.gov

Chairperson:
　Vacant. . . . . . . . . . . . . . . . . . . . . . . . . . . . . . . . . . . . . . .800-395-3372
Vice Chairperson:
　Vacant. . . . . . . . . . . . . . . . . . . . . . . . . . . . . . . . . . . . . . .800-395-3372
Executive Director:
　Sheila M Carey. . . . . . . . . . . . . . . . . . . . . . . . . . . . . . . .518-486-7505
　e-mail: sheila.carey@ddpc.ny.gov

### Education Department
State Education Building
89 Washington Avenue
Albany, NY 12234
518-474-3852
Web site: www.nysed.gov

Interim Commissioner & University President:
　Betty A Rosa. . . . . . . . . . . . . . . . . . . . . . . . . . . . . . . . . .518-474-5844
Executive Deputy Commissioner:
　Vacant. . . . . . . . . . . . . . . . . . . . . . . . . . . . . . . . . . . . . . .518-473-8381
Acting Counsel & Deputy Commissioner, Legal Affairs:
　Aaron Baldwin . . . . . . . . . . . . . . . . . . . . . . . . . . . . . . . .518-474-6400
　e-mail: legal@nysed.gov
Assistant Commissioner, Office of Innovation and School Reform:
　Cheryl Atkinson . . . . . . . . . . . . . . . . . . . . . . . . . . . . . . .518-473-8852

### Office of the Professions. . . . . . . . . . . . . . . . . . . .fax: 518-474-3863
　89 Washington Avenue, EB 2nd Floor, West Mezzanine, Albany, NY
　　12234
　Fax: 518-474-3863
　Web site: www.op.nysed.gov
Deputy Commissioner:
　Sarah Benson . . . . . . . . . . . . . . . . . . . . . . . . . . . . . . . . .518-486-1765

#### Office of Professional Discipline

#### Registration Unit

#### Professional Licensing Services
Director:
　Susan Naccarato . . . . . . . . . . . . . . . . . . . . . . . . . .518-474-3817 x340
　e-mail: opdpls@nysed.gov

*Offices and agencies generally appear in alphabetical order, except when specific order is requested by listee.*

## Office of Adult Career & Continuing Education Services (ACCES) ....................................fax: 518-474-8802

89 Washington Avenue, Room 460 EBA, Albany, NY 12234
Fax: 518-474-8802
Web site: www.acces.nysed.gov
Deputy Commissioner:
Kevin Smith ........................................518-474-2714
Assistant Commissioner:
Deborah Brown-Johnson............518-402-3955/fax: 518-473-6073
e-mail: accesadm@nysed.gov

### Fiscal & Administrative Services
Coordinator:
Vacant.........................................518-486-4038

### Quality Assurance Monitoring
Administrative Support:
Tim Dworakowski ..............................800-222-5627

### Vocational Rehabilitation Operations
Assistant Commsioner:
Debora Brown-Jackson...........518-402-3955/fax: 518-473-6073

# Mental Health, Office of
44 Holland Avenue
Albany, NY 12229
518-474-4403 or 800-597-8481
Web site: www.omh.ny.gov

Commissioner:
Ann Marie T Sullivan, MD...........................518-474-4403
Executive Deputy Commissioner:
Christopher Tavella, PhD ...........518-474-7056/fax: 518-473-4690
Medical Director:
Lloyd I. Sederer, MD .........................212-330-1650 x 360
Deputy Commissioner & General Counsel:
Mark Noordsy.....................................518-474-1331

## Division of Adult Services
Senior Deputy Commissioner & Division Director:
Robert Myers, PhD .................518-486-4327/fax: 518-473-4690
State Operated Children's & Adult Svcs: Associate Commissioner/Deputy Director:
May Lum......................518-474-0121/fax: 518-473-7926

## Division of Integrated Community Services for Children & Families
Associate Commissioner:
Donna Bradbury ..................518-473-6328/fax: 518-473-4690

## Center for Human Resource Management
Director:
J Lynn Heath ....................518-474-0171/fax: 518-474-7536

## Center for Information Technology
Deputy Commissioner & CIO:
John Norton......................518-474-7359/fax: 518-473-2778

## Division of Forensic Services
Associate Commissioner:
Donna Hall, PhD ..................518-549-5000/fax: 518-549-5090

## Facilities

### NYC Children's Center-Bronx Campus
1000 Waters Place, Bronx, NY 10461-2799
Interim Acting Executive Director:
Marcia Alkins ..................718-239-3600/fax: 929-348-4044

### Bronx Psychiatric Center
1500 Waters Place, Bronx, NY 10461-2796
Acting Executive Director:
Anita Daniels....................718-862-3300/fax: 718-826-4858

### NYC Children's Center - Brooklyn Campus
1819 Bergen Street, Brooklyn, NY 11233
Interim Acting Executive Director:
Marcia Alkins ...................718-613-3100/fax: 718-771-0086

### Buffalo Psychiatric Center
400 Forest Avenue, Buffalo, NY 14213-1298
Executive Director:
Celia Spacone, PhD.............716-816-2001/fax: 716-885-0710

### Capital District Psychiatric Center
75 New Scotland Avenue, Albany, NY 12208-3474
Executive Director:
William Dickson.................518-549-6000/fax: 518-549-6804

### Central New York Psychiatric Center
P.O. Box 300, Marcy, NY 13404-0300
Executive Director:
Deborah McCulloch ..............315-765-3620/fax: 315-765-3629

### Creedmoor Psychiatric Center
79-25 Winchester Boulevard, Queens Village, NY 11427-2199
Executive Director:
Ann Marie Barbarotta ...........718-264-3600/fax: 718-264-3635

### Elmira Psychiatric Center
100 Washington Street, Elmira, NY 14902-1527
Executive Director:
David Peppel...................607-737-4738/fax: 607-737-9080

### Greater Binghamton Health Center
425 Robinson Street, Binghamton, NY 13904-1775
Executive Director:
David Peppel...................607-773-4082/fax: 607-773-4387

### Hutchings Psychiatric Center
620 Madison Street, Syracuse, NY 13210-2319
Executive Director:
Mark Cattalani...................315-426-3632/fax: 315-426-3603

### Kingsboro Psychiatric Center
681 Clarkson Avenue, Brooklyn, NY 11203-2199
Executive Director:
Deborah Parchment..............718-221-7395/fax: 718-221-7206

### Kirby Forensic Psychiatric Center
600 East 125th Street, New York, NY 10035
Executive Director:
Vincent Miccoli.................646-672-5858/fax: 646-672-6446

### Manhattan Psychiatric Center
600 East 125th Street, Ward's Island Complex, New York, NY 10035
Executive Director:
Vincent Miccoli.................646-672-6767/fax: 646-672-6446

### Mid-Hudson Forensic Psychiatric Center
2834 Route 17-M, New Hampton, NY 10958
Executive Director:
Joseph Freebern.................845-374-8700/fax: 845-738-8860

### Mohawk Valley Psychiatric Center
1400 Noyes Street at York, Utica, NY 13502-3082
Acting Executive Director:
Mark Cattalani...................315-738-4404/fax: 315-738-4414

### Nathan S Kline Institute for Psychiatric Research
140 Old Orangeburg Road, Orangeburg, NY 10952-1197
Director:
Donald C Goff, MD .............845-398-5500/fax: 845-398-5510

### New York Psychiatric Institute
1051 Riverside Drive, New York, NY 10032-2695
Director:
Jeffrey A Lieberman, MD.........646-774-5300/fax: 646-774-5316

*Offices and agencies generally appear in alphabetical order, except when specific order is requested by listee.*

Policy Areas

**Pilgrim Psychiatric Center**
998 Crooked Hill Road, West Brentwood, NY 11717-1087
Executive Director:
  Kathy O'Keefe . . . . . . . . . . . . . . . .631-761-3500/fax: 631-761-2600

**NYC Children's Center - Queens Campus**
74-03 Commonwealth Boulevard, Bellerose, NY 11426-1890
Interim Acting Executive Director:
  Marcia Alkins . . . . . . . . . . . . . . . .718-264-4500 or 718-692-2543
  fax: 718-740-0968

**Rochester Psychiatric Center**
1111 Elmwood Avenue, Rochester, NY 14620-3972
Executive Director:
  Philip Griffin . . . . . . . . . . . . . . . . .585-241-1594/fax: 585-241-1424

**Rockland Children's Psychiatric Center**
2 First Avenue, Orangeburg, NY 10962-1199
Executive Director:
  Janet J Monroe . . . . . . . . . . . . . .845-359-7400/fax: 845-680-8900

**Rockland Psychiatric Center**
140 Old Orangeburg Road, Orangeburg, NY 10962-1196
Executive Director:
  Janet J Monroe . . . . . . . . . . . . . .845-359-1000/fax: 845-680-5580

**Sagamore Children's Psychiatric Center**
197 Half Hollow Road, Dix Hills, NY 11746
Acting Executive Director:
  Kathy O'Keefe . . . . . . . . . . . . . . .631-370-1700/fax: 631-370-1714

**South Beach Psychiatric Center**
777 Seaview Avenue, Staten Island, NY 10305-3499
Acting Executive Director:
  Doreen Piazza . . . . . . . . . . . . . . . .718-667-2709/fax: 718-667-2344

**St Lawrence Psychiatric Center**
1 Chimney Point Drive, Ogdensburg, NY 13669-2291
Executive Director:
  Tim Farrell . . . . . . . . . . . . . . . . . .315-541-2112/fax: 315-541-2041

**Western New York Children's Psychiatric Center**
1010 East & West Road, West Seneca, NY 14224-3699
Acting Executive Director:
  David Privett, LCSW . . . . . . . . . . .716-677-7000/fax: 716-675-6455

## Office of Consumer Affairs
Director:
  John Allen . . . . . . . . . . . . . . . . . .518-473-6579/fax: 518-474-8998

## Office of Financial Management
Deputy Commissioner & Chief Fiscal Officer:
  Emil Slane . . . . . . . . . . . . . . . . . . . . . . . . . . . . . .518-474-3631

## Office of Public Affairs
Director:
  James Plastiras . . . . . . . . . . . . . . .518-474-6540/fax: 518-473-3456

## Division of Quality Management
Deputy Commissioner:
  Suzanne Feeney . . . . . . . . . . . . . . . . . . . . . . . . .518-474-6587

## NYS Office for People with Developmental Disabilities
44 Holland Ave
Albany, NY 12229
866-946-9733 or TTY: 866-933-4889  Fax: 518-474-1335
Web site: www.opwdd.ny.gov

Acting Commissioner:
  Kerry Delaney . . . . . . . . . . . . . . . . . . . . . . . . . .518-473-1997
Director, Advocacy Services:
  Deborah Franchini . . . . . . . . . . . . . . . . . . . . . . .518-473-1997
Executive Deputy Commissioner:
  Roger Bearden . . . . . . . . . . . . . . . . . . . . . . . . . .518-473-1873

Deputy Commissioner, Enterprise Solutions:
  Kevin Valenchis . . . . . . . . . . . . . . . . . . . . . . . . .518-473-9697
Director, Legislative & Intergovernmental Affairs:
  Greg Roberts . . . . . . . . . . . . . . . . . . . . . . . . . . .518-473-8084
Affirmative Action/Equal Opportunity:
  Keith Gilmore . . . . . . . . . . . . . . . . . . . . . . . . . . .518-473-8084
Director, Audit Services:
  James Nellegar . . . . . . . . . . . . . . . . . . . . . . . . . .518-474-4376

## New York City Regional Office
75 Morton St, New York, NY 10014
Director:
  Donna Limiti . . . . . . . . . . . . . . . .212-229-3231/fax: 212-229-3234

## Information Support Services
Balltown & Consaul Roads, Schenectady, NY 12304
Director:
  Dianne Henk . . . . . . . . . . . . . . . . . . . . . . . . . . .518-473-1997

## Developmental Disabilities Services Offices - State Operations

**Bernard Fineson Developmental Disabilities Services Office**
Hillside Complex Bldg 12, 80-45 Winchester Blvd, Queens Vlg, NY 11427
Director:
  Jan Williamson . . . . . . . . . . . . . . . . . . . . . . . . . .718-217-5890

**Brooklyn Developmental Disabilities Services Office**
888 Fountain Ave, Brooklyn, NY 11208
Director:
  Sheryl Minter-Brooks . . . . . . . . . . . .718-642-6000/fax: 718-642-6282

**Broome Developmental Disabilities Services Office**
249 Glenwood Rd, Binghamton, NY 13905
Director:
  Jim Skrzeckowski . . . . . . . . . . . . . .607-770-0211/fax: 607-770-8037

**Capital District Developmental Disabilities Services Office**
Balltown & Consaul Rds, Schenectady, NY 12304
Acting Director:
  Stephanie Dunham . . . . . . . . . . . . . .518-370-7331/fax: 518-370-7401

**Central New York Developmental Disabilities Services Office**
101 W Liberty St, Box 550, Rome, NY 13442
Deputy Director:
  Lynette O'Brien . . . . . . . . . . . . . . . .315-336-2300 or 315-473-2949
  fax: 315-339-5456

**Finger Lakes Developmental Disabilities Services Office**
620 Westfall Rd, Rochester, NY 14620
Director:
  Michael Feeney . . . . . . . . . . . . . . . .585-461-8500/fax: 585-461-8764

**Hudson Valley Developmental Disabilities Services Office**
Admin Bldg, 2 Ridge Rd, PO Box 470, Thiells, NY 10984
Director:
  Catherine Varano . . . . . . . . . . . . . . .845-947-6000/fax: 845-947-6004

**Long Island Developmental Disabilities Services Office**
45 Mall Dr, Ste 1, Commack, NY 11725
Deputy Director:
  Barry Ockner . . . . . . . . . . . . . . . . .631-493-1701/fax: 631-493-1803

**Metro New York Developmental Disabilities Services Office**
75 Morton St, New York, NY 10014
Deputy Director:
  Joyce White . . . . . . . . . . . . . . . . . . . . . . . . . . .646-766-3471

**Staten Island Developmental Disabilities Services Office**
1150 Forest Hill Rd, Staten Island, NY 10314
Director:
  Sheryl Minter-Brooks . . . . . . . . . . . .718-983-5321/fax: 718-983-9768

**Sunmount Developmental Disabilities Services Office**
2445 State Rte 30, Tupper Lake, NY 12986-2502

*Offices and agencies generally appear in alphabetical order, except when specific order is requested by listee.*

Acting Director:
Stephanie Dunham . . . . . . . . . . . . . .518-359-3311/fax: 518-359-2276

**Taconic Developmental Disabilities Services Office**
26 Center Circle, Wassaic, NY 12592
Deputy Director:
Jackie DeVille. . . . . . . . . . . . . . . . .845-877-6821/fax: 845-877-9177

**Western New York Developmental Disabilities Services Office**
1200 East & West Rd, West Seneca, NY 14224
Director:
Kirk Maurer. . . . . . . . . . . . . . . . . .716-674-6310/fax: 716-674-7488

**Institute for Basic Research in Developmental Disabilities**
1050 Forest Hill Rd, Staten Island, NY 10314
Director:
Donna Limiti. . . . . . . . . . . . . . . . . . . . . . . . . . . . . .718-983-5233

## JUDICIAL SYSTEM AND RELATED AGENCIES

### Mental Hygiene Legal Service

#### 1st Judicial Dept
41 Madison Ave, 26th Fl, New York, NY 10010
Director:
Marvin Bernstein. . . . . . . . . . . . . . . . . .212-779-1734/fax: 212-779-7899

#### 2nd Judicial Dept
170 Old Country Rd, Rm 500, Mineola, NY 11501
Director:
Michael D Neville . . . . . . . . . . . . . . . . .516-493-3976/fax: 646-963-6640

#### 3rd Judicial Dept
40 Steuben St, Ste 501, Albany, NY 12207-2109
Web site: www.nycourts.gov/ad3/mhls/index.html
Director:
Sheila E Shea. . . . . . . . . . . . . . . . . . . . .518-451-8710/fax: 518-453-6915

#### 4th Judicial Dept
50 East Ave, Ste 402, Rochester, NY 14604
Director:
Emmett J Creahan. . . . . . . . . . . . . . . . . . . . . . . . . . . . .585-530-3050
Deputy Director:
Kevin Wilson. . . . . . . . . . . . . . . . . . . .585-530-3050/fax: 585-530-3079

## NEW YORK STATE LEGISLATURE

*See Legislative Branch in Section 1 for additional Standing Committee and Subcommittee information.*

### Assembly Standing Committees

#### Alcoholism & Drug Abuse
Chair:
Phil Steck . . . . . . . . . . . . . . . . . . . . . . . . . . . . . . . . . .518-455-5802

#### Mental Health
Chair:
Aileen M Gunther (D). . . . . . . . . . . . . . . . . . . . . . . . .518-455-5355

### Senate Standing Committees

#### Mental Health & Developmental Disabilities

## PRIVATE SECTOR

**AIM Services Inc**
4227 Route 9, Saratoga Springs, NY 12866
518-587-3208 Fax: 518-587-7236
Web site: www.aimservicesinc.org
*Residential & home-based services for individuals with developmental disabilities & traumatic brain injuries*
June MacClelland, Executive Director

**Albert Einstein College of Medicine - Division of Substance Abuse**
260 E 161 Street, Track Level, Bronx, NY 10451
718-993-3397 Fax: 718-993-2460
e-mail: schurch@dosa.aecom.yu.edu
Sarah Church, PhD, Director

**AMAC, Association for Metroarea Autistic Children**
25 W 17th St, New York, NY 10011
212-645-5005 Fax: 212-645-0170
*Providing lifelong services to austistic & special needs children & adults; specializing in applied behavior analysis (ABA) methodology; serving ages 2 years to adults, schools, camps, group homes*
Frederica Blausten, Executive Director

**Association for Addiction Professionals of New York**
PO Box 4053, Albany, NY 12204
877-862-2769 Fax: 585-394-1111
*Alcohol & chemical dependency counselor organization; addiction treatment & prevention*
Ferd Haverly, President

**Association for Community Living**
28 Corporate Drive, Suite 102, Clifton Park, NY 12065
518-688-1682 Fax: 518-688-1686
e-mail: admin@aclnys.org
Web site: www.aclnys.org
*Membership organization for agencies that provide housing & rehab services to individuals diagnosed with serious mental illness*
Antonia Lasicki, Director

**Association for Eating Disorders - Capital Region**
PO Box 3123, Saratoga Springs, NY 12866
518-464-9043
e-mail: CRAEDOffice@GMail.com
*Support & referral services, wellness programs & education for recovering individuals, parents & health professionals*
William Friske, Treasurer

**AHRC New York City**
83 Maiden Lane, New York, NY 10038
212-780-2500 or 212-780-2692 Fax: 212-780-2353
e-mail: webmaster@ahrcnyc.org
Web site: www.ahrcnyc.org
*Also known as the NYS Chapter of NYSARC, Inc. Social services, education, medical services, advocacy & public information on developmental disabilities*
Michael Goldfarb, Executive Director

**Brain Injury Association of NYS (BIANYS)**
10 Colvin Ave, Albany, NY 12206
518-459-7911 or 800-444-6443 Fax: 518-482-5285
e-mail: info@bianys.org
Web site: www.bianys.org
*Public education & advocacy for persons with brain injury & their families*
Judith I Avner, Executive Director

*Offices and agencies generally appear in alphabetical order, except when specific order is requested by listee.*

Policy Areas

**Cerebral Palsy Associations of New York State**
330 West 34th Street, 15th Floor, New York, NY 10001-2488
212-947-5770  Fax: 212-594-4538
e-mail: information@cpofnys.org
Web site: www.cpofnys.org
*Serves individuals with cerebral palsy & other significant disabilities as well as their families through advocacy, technical assistance, publications & networking events*
Susan Constantino, President & Chief Executive Officer

**Children's Village (The)**
Echo Hills, Dobbs Ferry, NY 10522
914-693-0600 x1201  Fax: 914-674-9208
e-mail: jkohomban@childrensvillage.org
Web site: www.childrensvillage.org
*Residential school, located 20 minutes outside of NYC. Treatment & prevention of behavioral problems for youth; residential & community-based services; mental health, education, employment & runaway shelter services*
Jeremy Kohomban, PhD, President & Chief Executive Officer

**Coalition of Behavioral Health Agencies, Inc (The)**
90 Broad St, New York, NY 10004-2205
212-742-1600 x115  Fax: 212-742-2080
e-mail: mailbox@coalitionny.org
Web site: www.coalitionny.org
*Advocacy organization representing over 100 nonprofit, community-based mental health and addictions services agencies in NYC.*
Phillip A Saperia, Executive Director

**Committee of Methadone Program Administrators Inc of NYS (COMPA)**
1 Columbus Place, 4th Fl, Albany, NY 12207
518-689-0457  Fax: 518-426-1046
e-mail: compahb@hotmail.com
Web site: www.compa-ny.org
*Methadone treatment & substance abuse coalition building; advocacy, community education, standards & regulatory review & policy development*
Henry Bartlett, Executive Director

**Families Together in NYS Inc**
737 Madison Avenue, Albany, NY 12208
518-432-0333 x20 or 888-326-8644 (referr  Fax: 518-434-6478
e-mail: info@ftnys.org
Web site: www.ftnys.org
*Advocacy for families with children having special social, emotional & behavioral needs; working to improve services & support for children & families*
Paige Pierce, Executive Director

**Federation Employment & Guidance Service (FEGS) Inc**
315 Hudson St, 9th Fl, New York, NY 10013
212-366-8400  Fax: 212-366-8441
e-mail: info@fegs.org
Web site: www.fegs.org
*Diversified health & human services system to help individuals achieve their potential at work, at home, at school and in the community*
Jonas Waizer, PhD, Chief Operating Officer

**Federation of Organizations Inc**
One Farmingdale Road, Route 109, West Babylon, NY 11704-6207
631-669-5355  Fax: 631-669-1114
e-mail: bfaron@fedoforg.org
Web site: www.fedoforg.org
*Social welfare agency with programs in mental health & aging*
Barbara Faron, CEO

**InterAgency Council of Mental Retardatn & Developmental Disabilities**
150 W 30th Street, 15th Floor, New York, NY 10001
212-645-6360 or 917-750-1497  Fax: 212-627-8847
e-mail: mames@iacny.org
Web site: www.iacny.org
*A membership association representing non-profit providers of services to individuals with developmental disabilities in the metropolitan NYC area.*
Margery E Ames, Executive Director

**Jewish Board of Family & Children's Services**
120 W 57th St, New York, NY 10019
212-582-9100 or 888-523-2769  Fax: 212-956-5676
e-mail: asiskind@jbfcs.org
Web site: www.jbfcs.org
*Mental health services/human services*
Alan B Siskind, PhD, Executive Vice President & Chief Executive Officer

**Lesbian, Gay, Bisexual & Transgender Community Ctr - Not For Profit**
208 W 13th St, New York, NY 10011-7702
212-620-7310  Fax: 212-924-2657
Web site: www.gaycenter.org
*Mental health counseling, out-patient chemical dependency treatment center, after-school youth services, HIV/AIDS services, advocacy, culutral programs, affordable meeting and conference services, and community-building.*
Miriam Yeung, Director, Public Policy

**Lifespire**
1 Whitehall Street, 9th Floor, New York, NY 10004
212-741-0100  Fax: 212-463-9814
e-mail: info@lifespire.org
Web site: www.lifespire.org
*Services for adults with developmental disabilites throughout the five boroughs of New York City*
Mark van Voorst, President & Chief Executive Officer

**Mental Health Association of NYC Inc**
666 Broadway, Ste 200, New York, NY 10012
212-254-0333 x307  Fax: 212-529-1959
e-mail: helpdesk@mhaofnyc.org
Web site: www.mhaofnyc.org
*Advocacy, public education, community-based services*
Giselle Stolper, Executive Director

**Mental Health Association of NYS Inc**
194 Washington Ave, Ste 415, Albany, NY 12210
518-434-0439  Fax: 518-427-8676
e-mail: info@mhanys.org
Web site: www.mhanys.org
*Technical assistance, advocacy, training & resource clearinghouse*
Glen Liebman, Chief Executive Officer

**NAMI-NYS**
260 Washington Ave, Albany, NY 12210
518-462-2000  Fax: 518-462-3811
e-mail: info@naminys.org
Web site: www.naminys.org
*Family and consumer advocates for those with mental illness.*
Donald P Capone, Executive Director

**NY Council on Problem Gambling**
100 Great Oaks Boulevard, Suite 126, Albany, NY 12203
518-867-4084  Fax: 518-867-4087
e-mail: jmaney@nyproblemgambling.org
Web site: www.nyproblemgambling.org
*Statewide helpline, public information, referral svcs, advocacy for treatment & support svcs, in-service training & workshops*
James Maney, Executive Director

*Offices and agencies generally appear in alphabetical order, except when specific order is requested by listee.*

## NY Counseling Association Inc
PO Box 12636, Albany, NY 12212-2636
518-235-2026  Fax: 518-235-0910
e-mail: nycaoffice@nycounseling.org
Web site: www.nycounseling.org
*Counseling professionals in education, mental health, career, employment, rehabilitation & adult development*
Donald Newell, Executive Manager

## NYS Association of Community & Residential Agencies
99 Pine St, Ste C-110, Albany, NY 12207
518-449-7551  Fax: 518-449-1509
Web site: www.nysacra.org
*Advocating for agencies that serve individuals with developmental disabilities*
Ann M Hardiman, Executive Director

## NYS Conference of Local Mental Hygiene Directors
41 State Street, Suite 505, Albany, NY 12207
518-462-9422  Fax: 518-465-2695
e-mail: ds@clmhd.org
Web site: www.clmhd.org
Kelly A Hansen, Executive Director

## NYS Council for Community Behavioral Healthcare
911 Central Avenue, Suite 152, Albany, NY 12206-1350
518-461-8200
e-mail: nyscouncil@albany.twcbc.com
Web site: www.nyscouncil.org
*Statewide membership organization representing community mental health centers*
Lauri Cole, Executive Director

## NYS Psychological Association
3 Pine West Plaza, Suite 308, Albany, NY 12205
518-437-1040  Fax: 518-437-0177
e-mail: nyspa@nyspa.org
Web site: www.nyspa.org
*Promote & advance profession of psychology; referral service*
Deborah Martinez, Executive Director
Rosemary E Aguirre, Manager, Membership
Sara Wheeler, Manager, Communication
Lori Cote, Office Manager

## NYSARC Inc
29 British American Boulevard, 2nd Floor, Latham, NY 12110
518-439-8311  Fax: 518-439-1893
e-mail: info@nysarc.org
Web site: www.nysarc.org
*Developmental disabilities programs, services & advocacy*
Steven Kroll, Executive Director

## New York Association of Psychiatric Rehabilitation Services (NYAPRS)
194 Washington Avenue, Suite 400, Albany, NY 12210
518-436-0008  Fax: 518-436-0044
*Promoting the recovery, rehabilitation & rights of New Yorkers with psychiatric disabilities*
Harvey Rosenthal, Executive Director

## New York Presbyterian Hospital, Department of Psychiatry
180 Fort Washington Ave, Room 270, New York, NY 10032
212-305-9249  Fax: 212-305-4724
*Psychotherapy & public policy*
Herbert J Schlesinger, PhD, Director, Clinical Psychology

## New York State Rehabilitation Association
155 Washington Ave, Suite 410, Albany, NY 12210
518-449-2976  Fax: 518-426-4329
e-mail: nysra@nyrehab.org
Web site: www.nyrehab.org
*Political advocacy, education, communications, networking & referral services for people with disabilities*
Jeff Wise, JD, Vice President

## Postgrad Center for Mental Health, Child, Adolescent & Family-Couples
138 E 26th St, Fl 4, New York, NY 10010-1843
212-576-4190  Fax: 212-576-4129
*Psychotherapy & assessment services for children, adolescents & families*
Diana Daimwood, Director

## Postgraduate Center for Mental Health
344 W 36th St, New York, NY 10018
212-560-6757  Fax: 212-244-2034
e-mail: mholman@pgcmh.org
Web site: www.pgcmh.org
*Community-based rehabilitation & employment services for adults with mental illness*
Marcia Holman, CSW/Vice President, Clinical Services

## Research Foundation for Mental Hygiene Inc
Riverview Center, 150 Broadway, Suite 301, Menands, NY 12204
518-474-5661  Fax: 518-474-6995
*Not-for-profit responsible for administering grants & sponsored research contracts for the NYS Department of Mental Health & its agencies*
Robert E Burke, Managing Director

## SUNY at Albany, Professional Development Program, NE States Addiction
Rockefeller College, 1400 Washington Ave, Room 412A, Albany, NY 12222
518-956-7800  Fax: 518-956-7865
Web site: www.pdp.albany.edu
*Dissemination of current research & best clinical practice information; coursework & programs for professionals in the field of addictions*
Eugene J Monaco, Director

## Samaritan Village Inc
138-02 Queens Blvd, Briarwood, NY 11435
718-206-2000  Fax: 718-657-6982
Web site: www.samaritanvillage.org
*Substance abuse treatment; residential & outpatient therapeutic community*
Ron Solarz, Executive Director

## Schuyler Center for Analysis & Advocacy (SCAA)
540 Broadway, Albany, NY 12207
518-463-1896  Fax: 518-463-3364
e-mail: kbreslin@scaany.org
Web site: www.scaany.org
*Advocacy, analysis & forums on mental health issues.*
Kate Breslin, President & Chief Executive Officer

## Self Advocacy Association of NYS
Capital District DSO, 500 Balltown Rd, Schenectady, NY 12304
518-382-1454  Fax: 518-382-1594
*Advocacy for & by persons with developmental disabilities to ensure civil rights & opportunities*
Steve Holmes, Adminstrative Director

## Springbrook
2705 State Hwy 28, Oneonta, NY 13820
607-286-7171  Fax: 607-286-7166
Web site: www.springbrookny.org
*Education/mental hygiene*
Patricia E Kennedy, Executive Director

Policy Areas

*Offices and agencies generally appear in alphabetical order, except when specific order is requested by listee.*

**St Joseph's Rehabilitation Center Inc**
PO Box 470, Saranac Lake, NY 12983
518-891-3950 or 518-891-3801  Fax: 518-891-3986
Web site: www.sjrcrehab.org
*Inpatient & outpatient alcohol & substance abuse treatment*
Robert A Ross, CEO

**Statewide Black & Puerto Rican/Latino Substance Abuse Task Force**
2730 Atlantic Ave, Brooklyn, NY 11207-2820
718-647-8275  Fax: 718-647-7889
*Substance abuse, HIV/AIDS & HepC prevention & treatment*
Ralph Gonzalez, Executive Director

**University at Buffalo, Research Institute on Addictions**
1021 Main St, Buffalo, NY 14203-1016
716-887-2566  Fax: 716-887-2252
e-mail: connors@ria.buffalo.edu
*Alcohol & substance abuse prevention, treatment & policy research*
Gerard Connors, Director

**YAI/National Institute for People with Disabilities**
460 W 34th St, New York, NY 10001-2382
212-273-6110 or 866-2-YAI-LINK  Fax: 212-947-7524
Web site: www.yai.org
*Programs, services & advocacy for people with autism, mental retardation & other developmental disabilities as well as learning disabilities of all ages & their families; special education & early learning programs*
Joel M Levy, Chief Executive Officer

**Yeshiva University, A Einstein Clg of Med, Div of Subs Abuse**
1510 Waters Place, Bronx, NY 10461
718-409-9450 x312  Fax: 718-892-7115
*Screening, assessment, diagnosis, treatment, support services, research & teaching & training related to chemical dependency & substance abuse*
Sarah Church, PhD, Executive Director

*Offices and agencies generally appear in alphabetical order, except when specific order is requested by listee.*

## MUNICIPAL & LOCAL GOVERNMENTS

### NEW YORK STATE

### GOVERNOR'S OFFICE

**Governor's Office**
Executive Chamber
State Capitol
Albany, NY 12224
518-474-8390  Fax: 518-474-1513
Web site: www.ny.gov

Governor:
   Andrew M Cuomo ....................................518-474-8390
Secretary to the Governor:
   Melissa DeRosa ...................518-474-4246 or 212-681-4580
Counsel to the Governor:
   Kumiki Gibson.......................518-474-8343 or 212-681-4580
Chief of Staff:
   Jill DesRosiers ....................518-474-8390 or 212-681-4580
Director, Communications:
   Peter Ajemian.......................518-474-8418 or 212-681-4640
Director, State Operations Infrastructure:
   Kelly Cummings....................................518-486-9871

**New York City Office**
633 Third Ave, New York, NY 10017

### EXECUTIVE DEPARTMENTS AND RELATED AGENCIES

**Budget, Division of the**
State Capitol
Room 128
Albany, NY 12224-0341
518-474-2300
e-mail: dob.sm.press@budget.ny.gov
Web site: www.budget.ny.gov

Director:
   Robert F. Mujica....................................518-474-2300
Deputy Director:
   Sandra Beattie.......................................518-474-2300
Deputy Director:
   Charles Williams....................................518-474-2300
Press Officer:
   Morris Peters.......................................518-473-3885
   e-mail: dob.sm.press@budget.ny.gov

**Civil Service Department**
Empire State Plaza, Agency Building One
9th Floor
Albany, NY 12239
518-457-2487 or 877-697-5627
e-mail: pio@cs.ny.gov
Web site: www.cs.ny.gov

Commissioner:
   Lola W Brabham....................................518-457-2487
Assistant Commissioner, Strategic Planning and Management:
   Vacant..............................................518-457-2487
Deputy Commissioner, Operations:
   Rebecca Corso .....................................518-473-9539
Deputy Commissioner, Administration:
   Daquetta Jones

Special Counsel:
   Marc Hannibal .....................................518-473-2624
Director, Financial Administration:
   Dominique Choute ..................................518-473-2269
Director, Human Resources & Administrative Planning:
   Vacant..............................................518-473-4306
Director, Communications:
   Jian Paolucci ......................................518-457-9375
   e-mail: pio@cs.state.ny.us

**Divisions**

**Classification & Compensation Division**
Director:
   Patricia A. Itite .................518-474-1011/fax: 518-474-0787

**Employee Benefits Division**
Director:
   James DeWan.......................................518-473-1977
Director, Employee Insurance Programs:
   Mary B Frye ....................518-457-1771/fax: 518-473-3292
Asst Director, Financial Management & Accounting:
   David Boland .......................................518-402-4264

**Employee Health Services Division**
Administrator, EHS:
   Maria C Steinbach................518-233-3112/fax: 518-233-3133
Director, Health Services Nursing:
   Mary M McSweeney ...............................518-233-3112

**Information Resource Management**
Director:
   Frank Slade........................................518-473-7516

**Commission Operations & Municipal Assistance Division**
Director:
   Nancy B. Kiyonaga ................................518-473-5022
Local Examinations:
   Will Martin.........................................518-473-5055

**Staffing Services Division**
Director:
   Blaine Ryan-Lynch.................................518-473-6437
Asst Director:
   Richard Papa.......................................518-473-6436

**Testing Services Division**
Director:
   Marcia Dudden.....................................518-474-2105
Assistant Director:
   Debbi Parrington ..................................518-486-4590

**Civil Service Commission**
   Web site: www.cs.ny.gov/commission
President:
   Lola W Brabham....................................518-457-3701
Commissioner:
   Vacant..............................................518-473-6326
Commissioner:
   Vacant..............................................518-473-9539

**Criminal Justice Services, Division of**
80 South Swan Street
Albany, NY 12210
518-457-5837 or 800-262-3257  Fax: 518-457-3089
e-mail: InfoDCJS@dcjs.ny.gov
Web site: www.criminaljustice.ny.gov

Executive Deputy Commissioner:
   Michael C Green....................................518-457-1260
Director, Workforce Diversity & Equity Program Unit:
   Wanda Troche.......................................518-485-7962

*Offices and agencies generally appear in alphabetical order, except when specific order is requested by listee.*

Policy Areas

Director, Public Information:
Janine Kava.........................................518-457-8828
e-mail: janine.kava@dcjs.ny.gov

**Human Resources Management**
Director:
Karen Davis ....................................518-485-1704

**State Finance & Budget**
Director, Finance:
Brad Stevens.....................................518-457-6105

## Office of Legal Services
Deputy Commissioner & Counsel:
John Czajka......................................518-457-4181

## Office of Forensic Services
Director:
Brian J Gestring ................................518-457-4181

## Office of Criminal Justice Operations
Deputy Commissioner:
Joe Morrissey ...................................518-485-2995

## Office of Internal Audit and Compliance
Deputy Commissioner:
Terry Salo .......................................518-457-7301

## Office of Program Development & Funding
Deputy Commissioner:
Vacant...........................................518-457-8462
e-mail: funding@dcjs.ny.gov

## Office of Public Safety
Deputy Commissioner:
Michael Wood518-457-6985

**Law Enforcement Accreditation Program**

**Highway Safety Technology Unit**

**Missing Persons Clearinghouse**

**Municipal Police Training Council**
Chair:
Sheriff Ronald G Spike

**Police & Peace Officer Registry & Training**

**Security Guard Training**

## Office of Sex Offender Management

---

## Homeland Security & Emergency Services, Division of
1220 Washington Avenue
Building 7A
Suite 710
Albany, NY 12242
518-242-5000  Fax: 518-322-4978
Web site: www.dhses.ny.gov

633 Third Avenue
32nd Floor
New York, NY 10017
212-867-7060

Commissioner:
Roger L. Parrino, Sr..............................518-242-5103
Program Officer, Office of Counterterrorism:
Jennifer Margulies ..............................518-242-5000
State Fire Administrator, Office of Fire Prevention and Control:
Francis J Nerney, Jr .............................518-474-6746
e-mail: fire@dhses.ny.gov

Director, Office of Interoperable & Emergency Communications:
Michael Sprague................................518-242-8275
e-mail: dhses.oiec@dhses.ny.gov
Public Information Officer:
Kristin Devoe ...................................518-242-5153

---

## Real Property Tax Services, Office of
NYS Dept of Tax & Finance
WA Harriman State Campus
Building 8A
Albany, NY 12227
518-4757-7377 or 518-591-5232
Web site: www.tax.ny.gov/about/orpts/albany.htm

Director:
Tim Maher ....................518-530-4081 or 518-474-2982
Secretary of the Board & Assistant Deputy Commissioner:
Vacant
State Board Member (Chair):
Matthew Rand...................................518-474-3793
State Board Member:
Scott C Becker ................518-474-3793 or 518-591-5232
State Board Member:
Samuel J Casella.................518-474-3793 or 518-591-5232

**Albany (Northern Region)**
WA Harriman State Campus, Bldg. 8A, Albany, NY 12227
Regional Director:
Tim Maher......................518-486-4403/fax: 518-435-8593
e-mail: orpts.northern@tax.ny.gov

**Batavia (Western Region)**
Genesee County Bldg 2, 3837 W Main Street, Batavia, NY 14020
Regional Director:
Christine Bannister ...............585-343-4363/fax: 585-435-8598
e-mail: orpts.western@tax.ny.gov

**Long Island Satellite Office**
250 Veterans Memorial Hgwy, Rm 4A-6, Hauppauge, NY 11788
Manager:
Steve Hartnett ...................631-595-4071/fax: 518-435-8572
e-mail: orpts.southern@tax.ny.gov

**Ray Brook Satellite Office**
884 NYS Rte 86, PO Box 309, Ray Brook, NY 12977
Regional Director:
Tim Maher......................518-891-1780/fax: 518-435-8593
e-mail: orpts.raybrook@tax.ny.gov

**Syracuse (Central Region)**
333 E. Washington St, Syracuse, NY 13202
Regional Director:
Christine Bannister ...............315-471-2347/fax: 315-435-8583
e-mail: orpts.central@tax.ny.gov

**White Plains (South Region)**
44 South Broadway, 6th Floor, White Plains, NY 10601
Regional Director:
John Wolham ...................914-215-6300/fax: 518-435-8498
e-mail: orpts.southern@tax.ny.gov

---

## State Comptroller, Office of the
110 State Street
15th Floor
Albany, NY 12236
518-474-4044  Fax: 518-473-3004
e-mail: contactus@osc.state.ny.us
Web site: www.osc.state.ny.us

---

*Offices and agencies generally appear in alphabetical order, except when specific order is requested by listee.*

59 Maiden Lane
New York, NY 10038
212-383-1600

State Comptroller:
Thomas P. DiNapoli . . . . . . . . . . . . . . . . . 518-474-4044 or 212-383-1600
Deputy Comptroller, Budget & Policy Analysis:
Robert Ward . . . . . . . . . . . . . . . . . . . . . . . . . . . . . . . .518-473-4333
Assistant Comptroller, Labor Affairs:
Kathy McCormack . . . . . . . . . . . . . . . . . . . . . . . . . . . . . .518-473-8409

## Executive Office
First Deputy Comptroller:
Pete Grannis . . . . . . . . . . . . . . . . . . . . . . .518-474-2909 or 212-681-4469
Chief of Staff:
Shawn Thompson . . . . . . . . . . . . . . . . . . . . . . . . . . . . . .518-474-4044
Chief Information Officer:
Robert Loomis . . . . . . . . . . . . . . . . . . . . . . . . . . . . . . .518-486-4349
Director, IT Services:
Mary Anne Barry . . . . . . . . . . . . . . . . . .518-474-8089 or 212-681-4840
Director, Communications:
Jennifer Freeman . . . . . . . . . . . . . . . . . .518-474-4015 or 212-383-2501
Assistant Comptroller, Communications & Digital Media:
Ellen Evans. . . . . . . . . . . . . . . . . . . . . . .518-474-4040 or 212-383-7412
Deputy Comptroller, City of New York:
Ken Bleiwas . . . . . . . . . . . . . . . . . . . . . . . . . . . . . . . . .212-383-3900

## Human Resources & Administration
Deputy Comptroller, Human Resources & Administration:
Angela Dixon . . . . . . . . . . . . . . . . . . . . . . . . . . . . . . . .518-474-5512
Assistant Comptroller, Administration:
Larry Appel . . . . . . . . . . . . . . . . . . . . . . . . . . . . . . . . .518-402-3043
Director, Financial Administration:
Brian Matthews. . . . . . . . . . . . . . . . . . . . . . . . . . . . . . . .518-474-2709
Director, Management Services:
Beth Bristol . . . . . . . . . . . . . . . . . . . . . . . . . . . . . . . . .518-486-7433

## Inspector General
Inspector General, Internal Audit:
Stephen Hamilton . . . . . . . . . . . . . . . . . . . . . . . . . . . . . .518-408-4906

## Intergovernmental Affairs
Assistant Comptroller, Intergovernmental Affairs:
Carlos Rodriguez. . . . . . . . . . . . . . . . . .518-402-3234/fax: 518-408-3852

## Legal Services
General Counsel:
Nancy Groenwegen. . . . . . . . . . . . . . . . . . . . . . . . . . . . . .518-474-3444
Special Counsel for Ethics:
Barbara Smith . . . . . . . . . . . . . . . . . . . . . . . . . . . . . . . .518-408-3855

## Operations
Executive Deputy Comptroller:
John Traylor . . . . . . . . . . . . . . . . . . . . . . . . . . . . . . . . .518-408-4103
Deputy Director, Payroll, Accounting and Revenue Services (PARS):
Chris Gorka. . . . . . . . . . . . . . . . . . . . . . . . . . . . . . . . . .518-408-4149

## Retirement
Deputy Comptroller:
Kevin Murray . . . . . . . . . . . . . . . . . . . . . . . . . . . . . . . . .518-474-2600

## State Government Accountability
Executive Deputy Comptroller:
Andrew SanFilippo. . . . . . . . . . . . . . . . . . . . . . . . . . . . . .518-474-4593
Deputy Comptroller:
Elliot Pagliaccio . . . . . . . . . . . . . . . . . . . . . . . . . . . . . .518-473-3596
Assistant Comptroller:
Jerry Barber. . . . . . . . . . . . . . . . . . . . . . . . . . . . . . . . . .518-473-0334

### Local Government and School Accountability
Deputy Comptroller:
Steve Hancox . . . . . . . . . . . . . . . . . . . . . . . . . . . . . . . . .518-474-4037

Executive Deputy Comptroller:
John Traylor . . . . . . . . . . . . . . . . . . . . . . . . . . . . . . . . .518-474-4037

## State Department
One Commerce Plaza
99 Washington Avenue
Albany, NY 12231-0001
518-474-4750  Fax: 518-474-4597
e-mail: info@dos.ny.gov
Web site: www.dos.ny.gov

123 William St
New York, NY 10038-3804
212-417-5800
Fax: 212-417-2383

Secretary of State:
Rossana Rosado . . . . . . . . . . . . . . . . . .518-486-9844 or 212-417-5800
First Deputy Secretary of State:
Daniel Shapiro . . . . . . . . . . . . . . . . . . . . . . . . . . . . . . . .518-474-4750
Deputy Secretary of State, Public Affairs:
Vacant . . . . . . . . . . . . . . . . . . . . . . . . . . . . . . . . . . . . .212-417-5800
General Counsel:
Linda Baldwin . . . . . . . . . . . . . . . . . .518-474-6740/fax: 518-473-9211
Assistant Secretary of State, Communications:
Vacant . . . . . . . . . . . . . . . . . . . . . . . .518-474-4752/fax: 518-474-4597
e-mail: info@dos.state.ny.us

## Local Government & Community Services
Deputy Secretary of State:
Mark Pattison. . . . . . . . . . . . . . . . . . .518-473-3355/fax: 518-474-6572

### Coastal Resources & Waterfront Revitalization Division
Director:
George Stafford . . . . . . . . . . . . . . . . . . . . . . . . . . . . . . .518-474-6000
e-mail: coastal@dos.state.ny.us

### Code Enforcement & Administration Division
Director:
Ronald E Piester . . . . . . . . . . . . . . . .518-474-4073/fax: 518-486-4487
e-mail: codes@dos.state.ny.us

### Community Services Division
Director:
Veronica Cruz . . . . . . . . . . . . . . . . . .518-474-5741/fax: 518-486-4663
e-mail: commserv@dos.state.ny.us

### Local Government Services Division
Deputy Secretary of State:
Mark Pattison . . . . . . . . . . . . . . . . . .518-473-3355/fax: 518-474-6572
e-mail: localgov@dos.ny.gov

## Open Government Committee
Executive Director:
Robert J Freeman. . . . . . . . . . . . . . . . .518-474-2518/fax: 518-474-1927
e-mail: opengov@dos.state.ny.us

## CORPORATIONS, AUTHORITIES AND COMMISSIONS

## New York State Assn of Fire Districts
PO Box 1419
Massapequa, NY 11758
631-947-2079 or 800-520-9594  Fax: 631-207-1655
Web site: www.firedistnys.com

President:
Anthony J Gallino. . . . . . . . . . . . . . . . . . . . . . . . . . . . . . .631-831-6875
e-mail: president@afdsny.org

*Offices and agencies generally appear in alphabetical order, except when specific order is requested by listee.*

First Vice President:
  Thomas Rinaldi.....................................518-664-6538
    e-mail: 1vp.president@afdsny.org
Second Vice President:
  Frederick Senti Jr ................................516-486-3023
    e-mail: 2vp.president@afdsny.org
Secretary & Treasurer:
  Joseph P DeStefano ................631-947-2079 or 800-520-9594
    fax: 516-799-2516
    e-mail: dacomish@aol.com
Counsel:
  William N Young ..................800-349-2904 or 518-456-6767
    fax: 518-456-4644
    e-mail: byoung@yfkblaw.com

## New York State Disaster Preparedness Commission

Building 7A, Suite 710
1220 Washington Ave
Albany, NY 12242
518-242-5000
Web site: www.dhses.ny.gov/oem/disaster-prep

NYS Div. of Homeland Sec./Emerg. Serv.
633 Third Ave.
32nd Fl.
New York, NY 10017
212-867-7060

Chairman:
  Roger L. Parrino, Sr.

## NEW YORK STATE LEGISLATURE

*See Legislative Branch in Section 1 for additional Standing Committee and Subcommittee information.*

## Assembly Legislative Commissions

### State Federal Relations, Task Force on
Assembly Chair:
  Matthew Titone (D) ..............................518-455-4677
Program Manager:
  Robert Stern .......................................518-455-3632

## Assembly Standing Committees

### Cities
Chair:
  Edward C Braunstein (D)..........................518-455-5425

### Economic Development, Job Creation, Commerce & Industry
Chair:
  Harry B Bronson (D) .............................518-455-4767

### Housing
Chair:
  Steven Cymbrowitz (D) ..........................518-455-5214

### Local Governments
Chair:
  Fred W Thiele Jr (I, D, WF).......................518-455-4826

### Transportation
Chair:
  William B Magnarelli (D)..........................518-455-5606

### Ways & Means
Chair:
  Helene E Weinstein (D) ..........................518-455-5462

## Senate Standing Committees

### Cities
Chair:
  Robert Jackson (D, WF)...........................518-455-2041
Ranking Minority Member:
  Andrew J Lanza (R, C, IP, RFM)...................518-455-3215

### Commerce, Economic Development & Small Business
Chair:
  Anna M Kaplan (D, IP, WF)........................518-455-2170
Minority Member:
  Pamela Helming (R, C, IP)........................518-455-2366

### Finance
Chair:
  Liz Kreuger (D, WF)..............................518-455-2297
Ranking Minority Member:
  Thomas F O'Mara (R, C, IP)

### Housing, Construction & Community Development
Chair:
  Brian Kavanagh (D, WF)..........................518-455-2625

### Local Government
Chair:
  James Gaughran (D)..............................518-455-3250

### Transportation
Chair:
  Timothy M Kennedy (D, IP, WF)...................518-455-2426

## PRIVATE SECTOR

### Association of Fire Districts of the State of NY Inc
948 North Bay Avenue, North Massapequa, NY 11758-2581
516-799-8575 or 800-520-9594  Fax: 516-799-2516
e-mail: FNOC@aol.com
Web site: www.firedistnys.com
*Obtain greater economy in the administration of fire district affairs*
Frank A Nocerino, Secretary-Treasurer

### Association of Towns of the State of New York
150 State St, Albany, NY 12207
518-465-7933  Fax: 518-465-0724
Web site: www.nytowns.org
*Advocacy, education for local government*
G Jeffrey Haber, Executive Director

### Citizens Budget Commission
One Penn Plaza, Ste 640, New York, NY 10119
212-279-2605  Fax: 212-868-4745
Web site: www.cbcny.org
*Nonpartisan, nonprofit civic organization devoted to influencing constructive change in the finances and services of New York City and New York State government*
Charles Brecher, Executive VP & Director, Research

### Citizens Union of the City of New York
299 Broadway, Rm 700, New York, NY 10007-1978
212-227-0342  Fax: 212-227-0345
e-mail: citizens@citizensunion.org
Web site: www.citizensunion.org
*Government watchdog organization; city & state public policy issues; political and government reform*
Dick Dadey, Executive Director

---

*Offices and agencies generally appear in alphabetical order, except when specific order is requested by listee.*

**Columbia Law School, Legislative Drafting Research Fund**
435 W 116th St, New York, NY 10027-7297
212-854-2640 or 212-854-2638  Fax: 212-854-7946
e-mail: rb34@columbia.edu
Web site: www.law.columbia.edu
*State & local government law, property law & election law*
Richard Briffault, Vice Dean & Executive Director

**Council of State Governments, Eastern Conference**
100 Wall St, 20th Fl, New York, NY 10005
212-482-2320  Fax: 212-482-2344
Web site: www.csgeast.org
*Training, research & information sharing for state government officials*
Alan V Sokolow, Regional Director

**Cullen & Dykman LLP**
100 Quentin Roosevelt Blvd, Garden City Ctr, Garden City, NY 11530-4850
516-357-3703  Fax: 516-396-9155
e-mail: gfishberg@cullenanddykman.com
Web site: www.cullenanddykman.com
*Municipal & labor law*
Gerard Fishberg, Partner

**Fordham University, Department of Political Science**
441 East Fordham Road, Bronx, NY 10458
718-817-3960  Fax: 718-817-3972
e-mail: kantor@fordham.edu
*Urban politics, urban economic development and the social condition of American cities.*
Paul Kantor, Professor of Political Science

**Fund for the City of New York**
121 Ave of the Americas, 6th Fl, New York, NY 10013
212-925-6675  Fax: 212-925-5675
e-mail: mmccormick@fcny.org
Web site: www.fcny.org
*Innovations in policy, programs, practice & technology to advance the functioning of government & nonprofit organizations in NYC & beyond*
Mary McCormick, President

**Genesee Transportation Council**
50 West Main Street, Suite 8112, Rochester, NY 14614-1227
585-232-6240  Fax: 585-262-3106
e-mail: rperrin@gtcmpo.org
Web site: www.gtcmpo.org
*Nine-county metropolitan planning organization*
Richard Perrin, Executive Director

**Hawkins Delafield & Wood LLP**
One Chase Manhattan Plaza, 42nd Fl, New York, NY 10005
212-820-9300  Fax: 212-820-9391
e-mail: hzucker@hawkins.com
Web site: www.hawkins.com
*Transportation, municipal & local government law*
Howard Zucker, Partner

**Housing Action Council Inc - Not For Profit**
55 S Broadway, Tarrytown, NY 10591
914-332-4144  Fax: 914-332-4147
e-mail: rnoonan@affordablehomes.org
*Financial feasibility, land use & zoning & affordable housing*
Rosemarie Noonan, Executive Director

**Institute of Public Administration/NYU Wagner**
295 Lafayette St, 2nd Floor, New York, NY 10012-9604
212-998-7400
e-mail: wagner@nyu.edu
*Non-profit research, consulting & educational institute*
David Mammen, President

**KPMG LLP**
345 Park Avenue, New York, NY 10154-0102
212-758-9700  Fax: 212-758-9819
Web site: www.kpmg.com
*Accounting*
Lynne Doughtie, Chairman & Chief Executive Officer

**League of Women Voters of New York State**
62 Grand St, Albany, NY 12207-2712
518-465-4162  Fax: 518-465-0812
e-mail: lwvny@lwvny.org
Web site: www.lwvny.org
*Public policy issues forum; good government advocacy*
Kristen Hansen, Executive Director

**MBIA Insurance Corporation**
113 King St, Armonk, NY 10504
914-273-4545  Fax: 914-765-3555
Web site: www.mbia.com
*Insure municipal bonds & structured transactions*
Ethel Z Geisinger, Vice President, Government Relations

**Manhattan Institute, Center for Civic Innovation**
52 Vanderbilt Ave, 2nd Fl, New York, NY 10017
212-599-7000  Fax: 212-599-3494
Web site: www.manhattan-institute.org
*Urban policy, reinventing government, civil society*
Lindsay Young, Executive Director, Communications

**Moody's Investors Service, Public Finance Group**
99 Church St, New York, NY 10007
212-553-7780  Fax: 212-298-7113
Web site: www.moodys.com
*Municipal debt ratings & analysis*
Dennis M Farrell, Group Managing Director

**NY State Association of Town Superintendents of Highways Inc**
119 Washington Avenue, Suite 300, Albany, NY 12210
518-694-9313  Fax: 518-694-9314
Web site: www.nystownhwys.org
Michael K Thompson, Communications Director

**NYS Association of Counties**
540 Broadway, 5th Floor, Albany, NY 12207
518-465-1473  Fax: 518-465-0506
e-mail: info@NYSAC.org
Web site: www.nysac.org
*Lobbying, research & training services*
Stephen J Acquario, Executive Director

**NYS Conference of Mayors & Municipal Officials**
119 Washington Ave, Albany, NY 12210
518-463-1185  Fax: 518-463-1190
e-mail: info@nycom.org
Web site: www.nycom.org
*Legislative advocacy for NYS cities & villages*
Peter A Baynes, Executive Director

**NYS Magistrates Association**
750 Delaware Ave, Delmar, NY 12054-1124
518-439-1087  Fax: 518-439-1204
Web site: www.nysma.net
*Association of town & village justices*
Tanja Sirago, Executive Director

**New York Municipal Insurance Reciprocal (NYMIR)**
150 State Street, Albany, NY 12207
518-465-7552  Fax: 518-465-0724
Web site: www.nymir.org
*Property and casualty insurance services for municipalities*
Kevin Crawford, Executive Director

*Policy Areas*

*Offices and agencies generally appear in alphabetical order, except when specific order is requested by listee.*

**New York State Government Finance Officers Association Inc**
126 State St, 5th Fl, Albany, NY 12207
518-465-1512  Fax: 518-434-4640
Web site: www.nysgfoa.org
*Membership organization dedicated to the professional management of governmental resources*
Maura K Ryan, Executive Director

**New York University, Wagner Graduate School**
295 Lafayette Street, 2nd Floor, New York, NY 10012
212-998-7400
e-mail: mitchell.moss@nyu.edu
*Research on urban planning & development, with special emphasis on technology & the future of cities*
Mitchell L. Moss, Professor of Urban Policy & Planning

**Syracuse University, Maxwell School of Citizenship & Public Affairs**
215 Eggers Hall, Syracuse, NY 13244-1090
315-443-4000  Fax: 315-443-9721
e-mail: sibretsc@maxwell.syr.edu
*Capital financing & debt management; public employee pensions; financial management*
Stuart Bretschneider, Associate Dean & Chair, Professor of Public
    Administration

**Urbanomics**
115 Fifth Ave, 3rd Fl, New York, NY 10003
212-353-7464  Fax: 212-353-7494
e-mail: r.armstrong@urbanomics.org
Web site: www.urbanomics.org
*Economic development planning studies, market studies, tax policy analyses, program evaluations, economic & demographic forecasts*
Regina B Armstrong, Principal

**Whiteman Osterman & Hanna LLP**
One Commerce Plaza, Albany, NY 12260
518-487-7600  Fax: 518-487-7777
e-mail: rsweeney@woh.com
Web site: www.woh.com
Robert L Sweeney, Partner

*Offices and agencies generally appear in alphabetical order, except when specific order is requested by listee.*

# PUBLIC EMPLOYEES

## NEW YORK STATE

### GOVERNOR'S OFFICE

## Governor's Office

Executive Chamber
State Capitol
Albany, NY 12224
518-474-8390  Fax: 518-474-1513
Web site: www.ny.gov

Governor:
    Andrew M Cuomo . . . . . . . . . . . . . . . . . . . . . . . . . . . . .518-474-8390
Secretary to the Governor:
    Melissa DeRosa . . . . . . . . . . . . . . . . .518-474-4246 or 212-681-4580
Counsel to the Governor:
    Kumiki Gibson . . . . . . . . . . . . . . . . . . . . .518-474-8343 or 212-681-4580
Deputy Secretary, Public Safety:
    Jeremy Schockett . . . . . . . . . . . . . . . . . . . . . . . . . . . . .518-474-3522
Chief of Staff:
    Jill DesRosiers . . . . . . . . . . . . . . . . . . . . .518-474-8390 or 212-681-4580
Director, Communications:
    Peter Ajemian . . . . . . . . . . . . . . . . . . . . . .518-474-8418 or 212-681-4640
First Assistant Counsel:
    R Nadine Fontaine . . . . . . . . . . . . . . . . . . . . . . . . . .518-474-8434

### EXECUTIVE DEPARTMENTS AND RELATED AGENCIES

## Civil Service Department

Empire State Plaza, Agency Building One
9th Floor
Albany, NY 12239
518-457-2487 or 877-697-5627
e-mail: pio@cs.ny.gov
Web site: www.cs.ny.gov

Commissioner:
    Lola W Brabham. . . . . . . . . . . . . . . . . . . . . . . . . . . . . .518-457-2487
Assistant Commissioner, Strategic Planning and Management:
    Vacant . . . . . . . . . . . . . . . . . . . . . . . . . . . . . . . . . . .518-457-2487
Deputy Commissioner, Operations:
    Rebecca Corso . . . . . . . . . . . . . . . . . . . . . . . . . . . .518-473-9539
Deputy Commissioner, Administration:
    Daquetta Jones
Special Counsel:
    Marc Hannibal . . . . . . . . . . . . . . . . . . . . . . . . . . . . .518-473-2624
Director, Financial Administration:
    Dominique Choute . . . . . . . . . . . . . . . . . . . . . . . . . . .518-473-2269
Director, Human Resources & Administrative Planning:
    Valerie Morrison. . . . . . . . . . . . . . . . . . . . . . . . . . . . . .518-473-4306
Director, Communications:
    Jian Paolucci. . . . . . . . . . . . . . . . . . . . . . . . . . . . . . . .518-457-9375
    e-mail: pio@cs.state.ny.us

## Divisions

### Classification & Compensation Division
Director:
    Patricia A. Itite . . . . . . . . . . . . . . . . .518-474-1011/fax: 518-474-0787

### Employee Benefits Division
Director:
    James DeWan. . . . . . . . . . . . . . . . . . . . . . . . . . . . . .518-473-1977
Director, Employee Insurance Programs:
    Mary B Frye . . . . . . . . . . . . . . . . . . .518-457-1771/fax: 518-473-3292

Asst Director, Financial Management & Accounting:
    David Boland . . . . . . . . . . . . . . . . . . . . . . . . . . . . . . . .518-402-4264

### Employee Health Services Division
Administrator, EHS:
    Maria C Steinbach. . . . . . . . . . . . . . .518-233-3112/fax: 518-233-3133
Director, Health Services Nursing:
    Mary M McSweeney . . . . . . . . . . . . . . . . . . . . . . . . . . .518-233-3112

### Information Resource Management
Director:
    Frank Slade. . . . . . . . . . . . . . . . . . . . . . . . . . . . . . . . .518-473-7516

### Commission Operations & Municipal Assistance Division
Director:
    Nancy B. Kiyonaya . . . . . . . . . . . . . . . . . . . . . . . . . . .518-473-5022
Local Examinations:
    Will Martin . . . . . . . . . . . . . . . . . . . . . . . . . . . . . . . . . .518-473-5055

### Staffing Services Division
Director:
    Blaine Ryan-Lynch. . . . . . . . . . . . . . . . . . . . . . . . . . . .518-473-6437
Asst Director:
    Richard Papa. . . . . . . . . . . . . . . . . . . . . . . . . . . . . . . .518-473-6436

### Testing Services Division
Director:
    Marcia Dudden. . . . . . . . . . . . . . . . . . . . . . . . . . . . . .518-474-2105
Director:
    Debbi Parrington . . . . . . . . . . . . . . . . . . . . . . . . . . . . .518-486-4590

## Civil Service Commission
Web site: www.cs.ny.gov/commission
President:
    Lola W Brabham. . . . . . . . . . . . . . . . . . . . . . . . . . . . . .518-457-3701
Commissioner:
    Vacant. . . . . . . . . . . . . . . . . . . . . . . . . . . . . . . . . . . . .518-473-9539
Commissioner:
    Vacant. . . . . . . . . . . . . . . . . . . . . . . . . . . . . . . . . . . . .518-473-6326

## Employee Relations, Governor's Office of

2 Empire State Plaza
Albany, NY 12223
518-473-3130  Fax: 518-486-7304
e-mail: info@goer.ny.gov
Web site: www.goer.ny.gov

Director:
    Michael N Volforte . . . . . . . . . . . . . . . .518-474-6988/fax: 518-486-7304
Deputy Director, Contract Negotiations & Administration:
    Vacant . . . . . . . . . . . . . . . . . . . . . . . .518-473-3130/fax: 518-486-7304
Deputy Counsel:
    Amy Petragnani. . . . . . . . . . . . . . . . . .518-474-4090/fax: 518-486-7304
Administrative Officer:
    Dawn M LaPointe . . . . . . . . . . . . . . . .518-473-3467/fax: 518-473-6725
Director, Employee Benefits Unit:
    Darryl Decker . . . . . . . . . . . . . . . . . . .518-473-6211/fax: 518-473-6294
Payroll Benefits Administrator:
    Kelly J. Catman. . . . . . . . . . . . . . . . . .518-473-3466/fax: 518-486-5602

### Labor/Management Committees

#### Family Benefits Committee
10B Airline Drive, Albany, NY 12235
e-mail: worklife@goer.ny.gov

#### NYS/CSEA Partnership for Education & Training  . fax: 518-473-0056
240 Washington Ave Extension, Suite 502, Albany, NY 12203
800-253-4332 or 518-486-7814  Fax: 518-473-0056
e-mail: learning@nyscseapartnership.org
Web site: www.nyscseapartnership.org
Co-Director:
    Jeannine Morell . . . . . . . . . . . . . . . . . . . . . . . . . . . . . .518-486-7814

*Offices and agencies generally appear in alphabetical order, except when specific order is requested by listee.*

Policy Areas

Co-Director:
Peter Trolio...........................518-486-7814

**NYS/SSU Joint Labor-Management Committee** .... fax: 518-457-9445
Employee Program Assistant:
Vacant...................................518-457-9420

**NYS/UUP Labor-Management Committee** ........ fax: 518-486-9220
Two Empire State Plaza, 13th Floor, Albany, NY 12223
Fax: 518-486-9220
e-mail: nysuuplmc@goer.ny.gov
Web site: www.nysuup.lmc.ny.gov
Director:
Tina Kaplan ............................518-486-4666
e-mail: tina.kaplan@goer.ny.gov

**Work-Life Services/Employee Assistance Programs**
10B Airline Drive, Albany, NY 12210-2316
800-822-0244
Web site: worklife.ny.gov
EAP Coordinator:
Lou Ann Evans...........................518-473-1395

## Public Employment Relations Board
Empire State Plaza
Agency Bldg 2, 18th & 20th Floors
PO Box 2074
Albany, NY 12220-0074
518-457-2578  Fax: 518-457-2664
e-mail: perbinfo@perb.ny.gov
Web site: www.perb.ny.gov

55 Hanson Place
Suite 700
Brooklyn, NY 11217
718-722-4545

The Electric Tower
535 Washington Street
Suite 302
Buffalo, NY 14203
716-847-3449

Chair:
John Wirenius...........................518-457-2578
Member:
Robert Hite.............................518-457-2578
Executive Director, Office of Administration:
Jonathan O'Rourke.......................518-457-2676
General Counsel:
David P Quinn...........................518-457-2678

### Administration Section
Executive Director:
Jonathan O'Rourke.......................518-457-2676

### Conciliation Office
Director:
Kevin B Flanigan .......................518-457-2690

### District Offices

**Buffalo**
Electric Tower, 535 Washington Street, Suite 302, Buffalo, NY 14203
Chief Regional Mediator & Director:
Gregory Poland............716-847-3449/fax: 716-847-3690

**Brooklyn**
55 Hanson Place, Suite 700, Brooklyn, NY 11217
Mediator:
Karen R. Kenney..........718-722-4545/fax: 718-722-4550

### Employment Practices & Representation Office
Director:
Melanie Wlasuk .........................518-457-5973
Assistant Director:
Nancy L Burritt.........................518-457-5973

### Legal Section
General Counsel:
David P Quinn ..........................518-457-2678

## State Comptroller, Office of the
110 State Street
15th Floor
Albany, NY 12236
518-474-4044  Fax: 518-473-3004
e-mail: contactus@osc.state.ny.us
Web site: www.osc.state.ny.us

59 Maiden Lane
New York, NY 10038
212-383-1600

State Comptroller:
Thomas P. DiNapoli...........518-474-4044 or 212-383-1600

### Operations
Executive Deputy Comptroller, Operations:
John Traylor ...........................518-402-4103

**Payroll & Revenue Services Division**
Deputy Comptroller:
Daniel Berry............................518-408-4149
Director, Unclaimed Funds:
Lawrence Schantz........................518-473-6438
Director, State Payroll Services:
Robin R Rabii...........................518-474-3400

### Executive Office
First Deputy Comptroller:
Pete Grannis ...............518-474-2909 or 212-681-4469
Chief of Staff:
Shawn Thompson..........................518-474-4044
Chief Information Officer:
Robert Loomis ..........................518-486-4349

### Retirement Services
Deputy Comptroller:
Kevin Murray ...........................518-474-2600
Asst Comptroller:
Nancy Burton ...........................518-474-4600

**Accounting Bureau**
Director:
Michelle Camuglia.......................518-474-3670

**Actuarial Bureau**
Actuary:
Teri Landin.............................518-474-4537

**Benefit Calculations & Disbursements**
Director:
James Normile ..........................518-474-5556

**Disability Processing/Hearing Administration**
Director:
Kathy Nowak ............................518-473-1347

**Member & Employee Services**
Director:
Ginger Dame.............................518-474-1101

*Offices and agencies generally appear in alphabetical order, except when specific order is requested by listee.*

**Retirement Communications**
Director:
Paul Kentoffio . . . . . . . . . . . . . . . . . . . . . . . . . . . . . . . .518-474-7096

## CORPORATIONS, AUTHORITIES AND COMMISSIONS

### New York State Teachers' Retirement System
10 Corporate Woods Dr
Albany, NY 12211-2395
518-447-2900 or 800-348-7298  Fax: 518-447-2695
Web site: www.nystrs.org

Executive Director:
Thomas K Lee. . . . . . . . . . . . . . . . . . . . . . . . . . . . . . . . .518-447-2726
General Counsel:
Joseph J. Indelicato, Jr. . . . . . . . . . . . . . . . . . . . . . . . . . .518-447-2722
Actuary:
Richard Young . . . . . . . . . . . . . . . . . . . . . . . . . . . . . . . .518-447-2692
Managing Director Operations:
Kevin Schaefer . . . . . . . . . . . . . . . . . . . . . . . . . . . . . . . .518-447-2730
Director, Member Relations:
Sheila Gardella . . . . . . . . . . . . . . . . . . . . . . . . . . . . . . . .518-447-2684
Manager, Public Information:
John Cardillo . . . . . . . . . . . . . . . . . .518-447-4743/fax: 518-447-2875
Managing Director Real Estate:
David C. Gillian . . . . . . . . . . . . . . . . . . . . . . . . . . . . . . .518-447-2751
Managing Director, Private Equity:
John W. Virtanen

## NEW YORK STATE LEGISLATURE

*See Legislative Branch in Section 1 for additional Standing Committee and Subcommittee information.*

### Assembly Standing Committees

#### Governmental Employees
Chair:
Peter J Abbate, Jr (D) . . . . . . . . . . . . . . . . . . . . . . . . . . .518-455-3053

#### Labor
Chair:
Michele R Titus (D) . . . . . . . . . . . . . . . . . . . . . . . . . . . . .518-455-5668

### Senate Standing Committees

#### Civil Service & Pensions
Chair:
Andrew Gounardes (D). . . . . . . . . . . . . . . . . . . . . . . . . . .518-455-3270

#### Labor
Chair:
Jessica Ramos (D, WF). . . . . . . . . . . . . . . . . . . . . . . . . . .518-455-2529
Ranking Minority Member:
Andrew J Lanza (R, C, IP, RFM). . . . . . . . . . . . . . . . . . . . .518-455-3215

### Senate/Assembly Legislative Commissions

#### Government Administration, Legislative Commission on
Assembly Chair:
Brian P. Kavanagh (D, WF) . . . . . . . . . . . . . . . . . . . . . . . .518-455-5506
Senate Vice Chair:
Vacant . . . . . . . . . . . . . . . . . . . . . . . . . . . . . . . . . . . . . . .518-455-0000

## EXECUTIVE DEPARTMENTS AND RELATED AGENCIES

### US Merit Systems Protection Board
Web site: www.mspb.gov

**New York Field Office**
26 Federal Plaza, Room 3137A, New York, NY 10278-0022
Chief Administrative Judge:
Arthur S. Joseph . . . . . . . . . . . . . . . . . .212-264-9372/fax: 212-264-1417

### US Office of Personnel Management

**PHILADELPHIA SERVICE CENTER (serving New York)**
William J Green Fed Bldg, Rm 3400, 600 Arch St, Philadelphia, PA 19106
Director:
Joseph D Stix. . . . . . . . . . . . . . . . . . . . . .215-861-3031/fax: 215-861-3030
e-mail: philadelphia@opm.gov

## U.S. CONGRESS

*See U.S. Congress Chapter for additional Standing Committee and Subcommittee information.*

### House of Representatives Standing Committees

#### Oversight and Government Reform
Chair:
Darrell E. Issa (R-CA) . . . . . . . . . . . . . . . . . . . . . . . . . . .202-225-3906
Ranking Member:
Elijah Cummings (D-MD) . . . . . . . . . . . . . . . . . . . . . . . . .202-225-4741
New York Delegate:
Carolyn B Maloney (D) . . . . . . . . . . . . . . . . . . . . . . . . . .202-225-7944

##### Subcommittee
*Federal Workforce, Postal Service and the District of Columbia*
Chair:
Blake Farenthold (R-TX). . . . . . . . . . . . . . . . . . . . .202-225-7742
Ranking Member:
Stephen F. Lynch (D-MA). . . . . . . . . . . . . . . . . . . . .202-225-8273

### Senate Standing Committees

#### Homeland Security & Governmental Affairs
Chair:
Thomas R. Carper (D-DE) . . . . . . . . . . . . . . . . . . . . . . . .202-224-2441
Ranking Member:
Tom Coburn (R-OK) . . . . . . . . . . . . . . . . . . . . . . . . . . . .202-224-5754

## PRIVATE SECTOR

### AFSCME District Council 37
150 State St, Albany, NY 12207
518-436-0665 or 212-815-1550  Fax: 518-436-1066
*NYC employees union*
Wanda Williams, Director

### American Federation of State, County and Municipal Employees (AFSCME)
212 Great Oaks Blvd, Albany, NY 12203
518-869-2245  Fax: 518-869-8649
e-mail: bmcdonnell@afscme.org
Web site: www.afscme.org
*Union representing public service & healthcare workers; American Federation of State, County & Municipal Employees*
Brian McDonnell, Legislative & Political Director

*Offices and agencies generally appear in alphabetical order, except when specific order is requested by listee.*

**Civil Service Employees Assn of NY (CSEA), Local 1000, AFSCME, AFL-CIO**
143 Washington Ave, Albany, NY 12210
518-257-1000 or 800-342-4146 Fax: 518-462-3639
*Public/private employees union*
Danny Donohue, President

**Cornell University, School of Industrial & Labor Relations**
356 ILR Research Bldg, Ithaca, NY 14853-3901
607-255-7581 Fax: 607-255-0245
e-mail: klb23@cornell.edu
Web site: www.ilr.cornell.edu
*Public sector organizations; leadership; temporary & contract workers; union organizing; & collective bargaining*
Kate Bronfenbrenner, Director, Labor Education Research

**District Council 37, AFSCME, AFL-CIO**
125 Barclay St, New York, NY 10007
212-815-1000 Fax: 212-815-1402
e-mail: dsullivan@dc37.net
Web site: www.dc37.net
*NYC employees union*
Dennis Sullivan, Director, Research & Negotiations

**NYC Board of Education Employees, Local 372/AFSCME, AFL-CIO**
125 Barclay Street, 6th Floor, New York, NY 10007
212-815-1372 Fax: 212-815-1347
Web site: www.local372.com
Veronica Montgomery-Costa, President - District Council 37/372

**NYS Association of Chiefs of Police Inc**
2697 Hamburg Street, Schenectady, NY 12303-3783
518-355-3371 Fax: 518-356-5767
Web site: www.nychiefs.org
Joseph S Dominelli, Executive Director

**NYS Association of Fire Chiefs**
1670 Columbia Turnpike, Box 328, East Schodack, NY 12063-0328
518-477-2631 Fax: 518-477-4430
Web site: www.nysfirechiefs.com
Thomas LaBelle, Executive Director

**NYS Correctional Officers & Police Benevolent Association Inc**
102 Hackett Blvd, Albany, NY 12209
518-427-1551 or 888-484-7279 Fax: 518-426-1635
e-mail: nyscopba@nyscopba.org
Web site: www.nyscopba.org
Mary Gulino,

**NYS Court Clerks Association**
170 Duane St, New York, NY 10013
212-941-5700 Fax: 212-941-5705
Kevin E Scanlon, Sr, President

**NYS Deputies Association Inc**
61 Laredo Dr, Rochester, NY 14624
585-247-9322 Fax: 585-247-6661
e-mail: tross1@rochester.rr.com
Web site: www.nysdeputy.org
Thomas H Ross, Executive Director

**NYS Bar Assn, Attorneys in Public Service Cmte**
**NYS Health Department**
Corning Tower, Empire State Plaza, Albany, NY 12237
518-474-2011
Web site: www.health.ny.gov
*Advancing the interests of NY governmental & not-for-profit attorneys*
Hon James F Horan, Administrative Law Judge

**NYS Law Enforcement Officers Union, Council 82, AFSCME, AFL-CIO**
Hollis V Chase Bldg, 63 Colvin Ave, Albany, NY 12206
518-489-8424 Fax: 518-489-8430
e-mail: c82@council82.org
Web site: www.council82.org
Daniel J Valente, Legislative Director

**NYS Parole Officers Association**
PO Box 5821, Albany, NY 12205-0821
518-393-6541 Fax: 518-393-6541
e-mail: hsj195@localnet.com
*Professional association representing NYS parole officers*
H Susan Jeffords, President

**NYS Sheriffs' Association**
27 Elk St, Albany, NY 12207
518-434-9091 Fax: 518-434-9093
e-mail: pkehoe@nysheriffs.org
Web site: www.nysheriffs.org
Peter R Kehoe, Executive Director

**New York State Law Enforcement Council**
One Hogan Place, New York, NY 10013
212-335-8927 Fax: 212-335-3808
*Founded in 1982 as a legislative advocate for NY's law enforcement community. The members represent leading law enforcement professionals throughout the state. An active voice and participant in improving the quality of justice and a safer NY.*
Leroy Frazer, Jr, Coordinator

**New York State Public Employees Federation (PEF)**
1168-70 Troy-Schenectady Rd, PO Box 12414, Albany, NY 12212
518-785-1900 x211 Fax: 518-783-1117
e-mail: kbrynien@pef.org
*Professional, scientific & technical employees union*
Kenneth D Brynien, President

**New York State Supreme Court Officers Association**
80 Broad Street, Suite 1200, New York, NY 10004
212-406-4292 or 212-406-4276 Fax: 212-791-8420
Web site: www.nysscoa.org
*Supreme Court Officers Union*
Patrick Cullen, President

**New York State United Teachers/AFT, AFL-CIO**
800 Troy-Schenectady Road, Latham, NY 12110-2455
518-213-6000 or 800-342-9810
Web site: www.nysut.org
Richard Iannuzzi, President

**Organization of NYS Management Confidential Employees**
5 Pine West Plaza, Suite 513, Albany, NY 12205
518-456-5241 or 800-828-6623 Fax: 518-456-3838
e-mail: nysomce@gmail.com
Web site: www.nysomce.com
*Professional organization of state management & confidential employees*
Barbara Zaron, President

**Patrolmen's Benevolent Association**
40 Fulton St, 17th Fl, New York, NY 10038
212-233-5531 Fax: 212-233-3952
Web site: www.nycpba.org
*NYC patrolmen's union*
Patrick Lynch, President

*Offices and agencies generally appear in alphabetical order, except when specific order is requested by listee.*

**Police Conference of NY Inc (PCNY)**
112 State St, Ste 1120, Albany, NY 12207
518-463-3283  Fax: 518-463-2488
e-mail: pcnyinfo@pcny.org
Web site: www.pcny.org
*Advocacy for law enforcement officers*
Richard Wells, President

**Professional Fire Fighters Association Inc (NYS)**
174 Washington Avenue, Albany, NY 12210
518-436-8827  Fax: 518-436-8830
e-mail: profire@nyspffa.org
Web site: www.nyspffa.org
*Union representing city, village & town firefighters*
Michael McManus, President

**Retired Public Employees Association**
435 New Karner Road, Albany, NY 12205-3833
518-869-2542  Fax: 518-869-0631
e-mail: mail@rpea.org
Web site: www.rpea.org
*Advocacy for retired public employees & their families*
Alan Dorn, Executive Director
Anthony Cantore, Legislative Representative

**State Employees Federal Credit Union**
1239 Washington Avenue, Albany, NY 12206-1067
518-452-8234  Fax: 518-464-5227
Web site: www.sefcu.com
John Gallagher, Director, Internal Audit

**Syracuse University, Maxwell School of Citizenship & Public Affairs**
215 Eggers Hall, Syracuse, NY 13244-1090
315-443-4000  Fax: 315-443-9721
e-mail: sibretsc@maxwell.syr.edu
*Capital financing & debt management; public employee pensions; financial management*
Stuart Bretschneider, Associate Dean & Chair, Professor of Public
  Administration

**Trooper Foundation-State of New York Inc**
3 Airport Park Blvd, Latham, NY 12110-1441
518-785-1002  Fax: 518-785-1003
e-mail: rmincher@nystf.org
Web site: www.nystrooperfoundation.org
*Supports programs & services of the NYS Police*
Rachael L Mincher, Foundation Administrator

**Uniformed Fire Officers Association**
225 Broadway, Suite 401, New York, NY 10007
212-293-9300  Fax: 212-292-1560
e-mail: administrator@ufoa.org
Web site: www.ufoa.org
*NYC fire officers' union*
John J McDonnell, President

**United Transportation Union**
35 Fuller Road, Suite 205, Albany, NY 12205
518-438-8403  Fax: 518-438-8404
e-mail: sjnasca@aol.com
Web site: www.utu.org
*Federal government railroad, bus & airline employees; public employees*
Samuel Nasca, Legislative Director

**United University Professions**
PO Box 15143, Albany, NY 12212-5143
518-640-6600  Fax: 518-640-6698
Web site: www.uupinfo.org
*SUNY labor union of academic & other professional faculty*
William E Scheuerman, President

Policy Areas

*Offices and agencies generally appear in alphabetical order, except when specific order is requested by listee.*

# REAL PROPERTY

## NEW YORK STATE

### GOVERNOR'S OFFICE

**Governor's Office**
Executive Chamber
State Capitol
Albany, NY 12224
518-474-8390  Fax: 518-474-1513
Web site: www.ny.gov

Governor:
    Andrew M Cuomo . . . . . . . . . . . . . . . . . . . . . . . . . . . . . . .518-474-8390
Secretary to the Governor:
    Melissa DeRosa . . . . . . . . . . . . . . . . . . . .518-474-4246 or 212-681-4580
Counsel to the Governor:
    Kumiki Gibson . . . . . . . . . . . . . . . . . . . .518-474-8343 or 212-681-4580
Chief of Staff:
    Jill DesRosiers . . . . . . . . . . . . . . . . . . .518-474-8390 or 212-681-4580
Director, Communications:
    Peter Ajemian . . . . . . . . . . . . . . . . . . . .518-474-8418 or 212-681-4640
First Assistant Counsel:
    R Nadine Fontaine . . . . . . . . . . . . . . . . . . . . . . . . . . . . . .518-474-8434

### EXECUTIVE DEPARTMENTS AND RELATED AGENCIES

**General Services, Office of**
Corning Tower
41st Floor
Empire State Plaza
Albany, NY 12242
518-474-3899
e-mail: comments@ogs.ny.gov
Web site: www.ogs.ny.gov

Commissioner:
    RoAnn Destito . . . . . . . . . . . . . . . . . . . . .518-474-5991/fax: 518-486-9179
Executive Deputy Commissioner:
    Vacant . . . . . . . . . . . . . . . . . . . . . . . . . . . . . . . . . . . . . .518-473-6953
Director, Communications:
    Heather Groll . . . . . . . . . . . . . . . . . . . . .518-474-5987/fax: 518-486-9179
    e-mail: heather.groll@ogs.ny.gov

**Real Estate Planning & Development Group**
Director:
    James Sproat . . . . . . . . . . . . . . . . . . . . . . . . . . . . . . . . . .518-474-4944
Deputy Director, Real Estate Planning & Development:
    Jessica Gabriel . . . . . . . . . . . . . . . . . . . . . . . . . . . . . . . . .518-474-4944
Bureau Chief, Land Management & Assistant Director, Real Estate &
    Planning Development:
    Charles Sheifer . . . . . . . . . . . . . . . . . . . . . . . . . . . . . . . . .518-474-2195
Bureau Chief, Leasing & Assistant Director, Real Estate Planning:
    Leah Nicholson . . . . . . . . . . . . . . . . . . . . . . . . . . . . . . . . .518-486-1484

**Real Property Management Group**
Executive Deputy Commissioner:
    Daniel Cunningham . . . . . . . . . . . . . . . .518-474-6057/fax: 518-474-1523
Director, Downstate Regional Buildings:
    Kevin Cahill . . . . . . . . . . . . . . . . . . . . .212-961-4390/fax: 212-961-4404
Assistant Director, Empire State Plaza & Downtown Buildings:
    Andy Papale . . . . . . . . . . . . . . . . . . . . . . . . . . . . . . . . . . .518-402-5753
Regional Director, Campus & Upstate Regional Director:
    Louis Salerno . . . . . . . . . . . . . . . . . . . .518-457-2290/fax: 518-457-8297
Director, Utilities Management & Statewide Energy:
    Robert Lobdell . . . . . . . . . . . . . . . . . . . .518-474-3249/fax: 518-402-5682

**Law Department**
28 Liberty Street
New York, NY 10005
212-416-8000 or 800-771-7755
Web site: www.ag.ny.gov

State Capitol
Albany, NY 12224-0341
518-776-2000
Fax: 518-650-9401

Attorney General:
    Letitia James . . . . . . . . . . . . . . . . . . . . . . .212-416-8000 or 518-776-2000

**Social Justice**
Executive Deputy Attorney General:
    Vacant . . . . . . . . . . . . . . . . . . . . . . . . . .212-416-8450/fax: 212-416-8942

    **Civil Rights Bureau**
    Bureau Chief:
        Lourdes Rosado . . . . . . . . . . . . . . . . .212-416-8250/fax: 212-416-8074

    **Investor Protection Bureau**
    Bureau Chief:
        Chad Johnson . . . . . . . . . . . . . . . . . .212-416-8225/fax: 212-416-8816

**State Counsel**

    **Claims Bureau**
    Bureau Chief:
        Katharine Brooks . . . . . . . . . . . . . . . .518-776-2300 or 212-416-8500

    **Real Property Bureau**
    Bureau Chief:
        Alison Crocker . . . . . . . . . . . . . . . . . . . . . . . . . . . . . . .518-776-2700

**Real Property Tax Services, Office of**
NYS Dept of Tax & Finance
WA Harriman State Campus
Building 8A
Albany, NY 12227
518-457-7377 or 518-591-5232
Web site: www.tax.ny.gov/about/orpts/albany.htm

State Board Member (Chair):
    Matthew Rand . . . . . . . . . . . . . . . . . . . . . . . . . . . . . . . . . .518-474-3793
State Board Member:
    John M. Bacheller . . . . . . . . . . . . . . . . . . . . . . . . . . . . . . .518-474-3793
State Board Member:
    Edgar A. King . . . . . . . . . . . . . . . . . . . . . . . . . . . . . . . . . .518-474-3793
Director:
    Tim Maher . . . . . . . . . . . . . . . . . . . . . . .518-530-4081 or 518-474-2982

**Research, Information & Policy Development**
Director:
    James Dunne . . . . . . . . . . . . . . . . . . . . . . . . . . . . . . . . . . .518-473-4532
    e-mail: jim.dunne@orps.state.ny.us
Director:
    David Williams . . . . . . . . . . . . . . . . . . . . . . . . . . . . . . . . .518-473-8743
Secretary of Board & Assistant Deputy Commissioner:
    Vacant

    **Albany (Northern Region)**
    WA Harriman State Campus, Bldg 8A, Albany, NY 12227
    Regional Director:
        Robert Aiken . . . . . . . . . . . . . . . . . . .518-486-4403/fax: 518-435-8573
        e-mail: orpts.northern@tax.ny.gov

    **Batavia (Western Region)**
    Genesee County Bldg 2, 3837 W Main Rd, Batavia, NY 14020

*Offices and agencies generally appear in alphabetical order, except when specific order is requested by listee.*

Regional Director:
    Christine Bannister . . . . . . . . . . . . . .585-343-4363/fax: 518-435-8598
    e-mail: orpts.western@tax.ny.gov

**Long Island Satellite Office**
250 Veterans Memorial Hgwy, Rm 4A-6, Hauppauge, NY 11788
Manager:
    Steve Hartnett . . . . . . . . . . . . . . . . . .631-595-4071/fax: 518-435-8572
    e-mail: orpts.southern@tax.ny.gov

**Newburgh (South)**
263 Route 17K, Ste 2001, Newburgh, NY 12550
Regional Director:
    John Wolham . . . . . . . . . . . . . . . . .845-567-2648/fax: 518-435-8498
    e-mail: orpts.southern@tax.ny.gov

**Ray Brook Satellite Office**
884 NYS Rte 86, PO Box 309, Ray Brook, NY 12977
Regional Director:
    Robert Aiken . . . . . . . . . . . . . . . . . .518-891-1780/fax: 518-435-8593
    e-mail: orpts.raybrook@tax.ny.gov

**Syracuse (Central Region)** . . . . . . . . . . . . . . . . . . . . fax: 315-471-3634
401 South Salina St, 5th Floor, Syracuse, NY 13202
Regional Director:
    Teresa Frank . . . . . . . . . . . . . . . . . .315-471-2347/fax: 518-435-8583

## Transportation Department
50 Wolf Road
Albany, NY 12232
518-457-6195  Fax: 518-457-5583
Web site: www.dot.ny.gov

Acting Commissioner:
    Paul A Karas . . . . . . . . . . . . . . . . . . . . . . . . . . . . . . . . .518-457-4422
Assistant Commissioner, Operations & Asset Management:
    Sam Zhou . . . . . . . . . . . . . . . . . . . . . . . . . . . . . . . . . . .518-457-9684

### Engineering Division
Chief Engineer:
    Nicolas Choubah . . . . . . . . . . . . . . . . . . . . . . . . . . . . . .518-457-4430
Office of Design:
    Richard Lee . . . . . . . . . . . . . . . . . . . . . . . . . . . . . . . . . .518-457-6452
Office of Structures:
    Richard Marchione . . . . . . . . . . . . . . . . . . . . . . . . . . . .518-457-6827
Office of Environment:
    Dan Hitt . . . . . . . . . . . . . . . . . . . . . . . . . . . . . . . . . . . .518-457-5672
Office of Major Projects:
    Nicolas Choubah . . . . . . . . . . . . . . . . . . . . . . . . . . . . . .518-457-4430
Office of Technical Services:
    Robert Sack, PE . . . . . . . . . . . . . . . . . . . . . . . . . . . . . .518-457-4445
Office of Construction:
    Brian DeWald, PE . . . . . . . . . . . . . . . . . . . . . . . . . . . . .518-457-6472
Office of Construction:
    Jose Rivera, PE . . . . . . . . . . . . . . . . . . . . . . . . . . . . . . .518-457-6472

## NEW YORK STATE LEGISLATURE

*See Legislative Branch in Section 1 for additional Standing Committee and Subcommittee information.*

## Assembly Standing Committees

### Economic Development, Job Creation, Commerce & Industry
Chair:
    Harry B Bronson (D) . . . . . . . . . . . . . . . . . . . . . . . . . . .518-455-4767

### Housing
Chair:
    Steven Cymbrowitz (D) . . . . . . . . . . . . . . . . . . . . . . . . .518-455-5214

### Real Property Taxation
Chair:
    Sandy Galef (D) . . . . . . . . . . . . . . . . . . . . . . . . . . . . . . .518-455-5348

## Senate Standing Committees

### Commerce, Economic Development & Small Business
Chair:
    Anna M Kaplan (D, IP, WF) . . . . . . . . . . . . . . . . . . . . . .518-455-2170
Minority Member:
    Pamela Helming (R, C, IP) . . . . . . . . . . . . . . . . . . . . . . .518-455-2366

### Housing Construction & Community Development

## U.S. GOVERNMENT

## EXECUTIVE DEPARTMENTS AND RELATED AGENCIES

## US Department of Agriculture

### Rural Development
Web site: www.rurdev.usda.gov/ny

**New York State Office** . . . . . . . . . . . . . . . . . . . . . . . . .fax: 315-477-6438
The Galleries of Syracuse, 441 S Salina St, Ste 357, Syracuse, NY
    13202-2441
315-477-6400  Fax: 315-477-6438
State Director:
    Stanley Telega . . . . . . . . . . . . . . . . . . . . . . . . . . . . . . .315-477-6437

## US General Services Administration
Web site: www.gsa.gov

### Region 2—New York
1 World Trade Center, 55th Floor, Room 55W09, New York, NY
    10007-0089
212-264-3305
Acting Regional Administrator:
    Frank Santella . . . . . . . . . . . . . . . . . . . . . . . . . . . . . . .212-264-2600
    e-mail: frank.santella@gsa.gov
Program Specialist to the Regional Administrator:
    Yolonda Jones . . . . . . . . . . . . . . . . . . . . . . . . . . . . . . .212-264-2600
    e-mail: yolonda.jones@gsa.gov

#### Administration
Human Resources Officer:
    Maureen Gannon . . . . . . . . . . . . . . . . . . . . . . . . . . . . .215-446-4963
    e-mail: maureen.gannon@gsa.gov

#### Federal Supply Service
Acting Asst Regional Administrator:
    Charles B Weill . . . . . . . . . . . . . . . .212-264-3590/fax: 212-264-9759

#### Federal Technology Service
Asst Regional Administrator (Acting):
    Steve Ruggiero . . . . . . . . . . . . . . . . . . . . . . . . . . . . . . .212-264-3590

#### Inspector General's Office
Asst Regional Inspector, Investigations:
    Daniel Walsh . . . . . . . . . . . . . . . . . .212-264-7300/fax: 212-264-7154
Regional Director, Audit:
    Joseph Mastropietro . . . . . . . . . . . . . . . . . . . . . . . . . . .212-264-8620

#### Public Buildings Service
Regional Commissioner:
    Frank Santella . . . . . . . . . . . . . . . . . . . . . . . . . . . . . . .212-264-4282
    e-mail: frank.santella@gsa.gov
Deputy Asst Regional Administrator:
    Vacant . . . . . . . . . . . . . . . . . . . . . . . . . . . . . . . . . . . . .212-264-4285
Program Management Officer:
    David Segermeister . . . . . . . . . . . . .212-264-4273/fax: 212-264-2746

*Offices and agencies generally appear in alphabetical order, except when specific order is requested by listee.*

Regional Program Manager:
Jason Cahill . . . . . . . . . . . . . . . . . . . . 212-264-0083/fax: 212-264-2650

## PRIVATE SECTOR

**Appraisal Education Network School & Merrell Institute**
1461 Lakeland Ave, Bohemia, NY 11716
631-563-7720 Fax: 631-563-7719
e-mail: bcm@doctor.com
Web site: www.merrellinstitute.com
*Real estate sales, broker, appraiser, mortgage & property management education courses, paralegal, continuing education, home inspection*
Bill C Merrell, Director

**Brookfield Properties Corporation**
Three World Financial Center, 200 Vesey Street, 11th Floor, New York, NY 10281
212-417-7000 Fax: 212-417-7214
e-mail: kkane@brookfieldproperties.com
Web site: www.brookfieldproperties.com
*Commercial real estate*
Kathleen G Kane, General Counsel

**Building & Realty Institute**
80 Business Park Dr, Armonk, NY 10504
914-273-0730 Fax: 914-273-7051
e-mail: aaaa@buildersinstitute.org
Web site: www.buildersinstitute.org
*Building, realty & construction industry membership organization*
Albert A Annunziata, Executive Director

**NYS Bar Assn, Real Property Law Section**
**D H Ferguson, Attorney, PLLC**
141 Sully's Trail, Suite 12, Pittsford, NY 14534
585-586-0459 or 585-586-0450 Fax: 585-586-2297
e-mail: dhferguson@frontiernet.net
Dorothy H Ferguson, Chair

**DTZ/Cushman & Wakefield**
277 Park Avenue, New York, NY 10172
212-758-0800 Fax: 212-758-6192
*Commercial real estate & property management services*
Peter Hennessy, President, New York Tri-State Region

**Ernst & Young**
5 Times Square, New York, NY 10036-6350
212-773-4500 Fax: 212-773-4986
Web site: www.ey.com
Dale Anne Reiss, Global & Americas Director Real Estate

**FirstService Williams**
380 Madison Ave, 3rd Floor, New York, NY 10017
212-716-3760 Fax: 212-716-3710
*Real estate brokerage, ownership, sales, leasing, management & consulting*
Joseph J Caridi, Executive Managing Director

**Fisher Brothers**
299 Park Ave, New York, NY 10171
212-752-5000 Fax: 212-940-6879
*Real estate investment & development*
Arnold Fisher, Partner

**Glenwood Management Corporation**
1200 Union Turnpike, New Hyde Park, NY 11040
718-343-6400 Fax: 718-343-0009
Web site: www.glenwoodmanagement.com
*Property management*
Leonard Litwin, President

**Greater Rochester Association of Realtors Inc**
930 East Avenue, Rochester, NY 14607
585-292-5000 Fax: 585-292-5008
Web site: www.homesteadnet.com
Karen Wingender, Chief Executive Officer

**Greater Syracuse Association of Realtors Inc**
5958 East Taft Road, North Syracuse, NY 13212
315-457-5979 Fax: 315-457-5884
Web site: www.cnyrealtor.com
Lynnore Fetyko, Chief Executive Officer

**H J Kalikow & Co LLC**
101 Park Ave, 25th Fl, New York, NY 10178
212-808-7000 Fax: 212-573-6380
Web site: www.hjkalikow.com
*Real estate development*
Peter S Kalikow, President

**J J Higgins Properties Inc**
20 North Main St, Pittsford, NY 14534
585-381-6030 Fax: 585-381-0571
e-mail: jjhigginsproperties@frontiernet.net
*Residental properties, relocation, commercial properties, home sales & listings, buyer agency*
John J Higgins, President

**Landauer Realty Group Inc**
1177 Avenue of the Americas, New York, NY 10036
212-759-9700 or 212-326-4752 Fax: 212-326-4802
Web site: www.landauer.com
*Commercial real estate appraisers, analysts & transaction consultants*
David Arena, President

**MJ Peterson Corporation**
501 Audubon Pkwy, Amherst, NY 14228
716-688-1234 Fax: 716-688-5463
Web site: www.mjpeterson.com
*Residential, commercial, property management, development and new homes*
Victor L Peterson, Jr, President

**Mancuso Business Development Group**
56 Harvester Ave, Batavia, NY 14020
585-343-2800 Fax: 585-343-7096
e-mail: tom@mancusogroup.com
Web site: www.mancusogroup.com
*Improve operating performances of multi tenant industrial and office and business incubator properties*
Tom Mancuso, President

**Metro/Colvin Realty Inc**
2211 Sheridan Dr, Kenmore, NY 14223
716-874-0110 Fax: 716-874-9015
e-mail: metrocolvin1@aol.com
*Residential & commercial property*
John Riordan, President

**Metro/Horohoe-Leimbach**
3199 Delaware Ave, Kenmore, NY 14217
716-873-5404 Fax: 716-873-8901
e-mail: whorohoe@aol.com
*Residential real estate*
William Horohoe, President

**NY Commercial Association of Realtors**
130 Washington Ave, Albany, NY 12210
518-463-0300 Fax: 518-462-5474
Web site: www.nyscarxchange.com
*Commercial real estate*
Maureen D Wilson, President

*Offices and agencies generally appear in alphabetical order, except when specific order is requested by listee.*

**NYS Association of Realtors**
130 Washington Ave, Albany, NY 12210-2298
518-463-0300  Fax: 518-462-5474
e-mail: admin@nysar.com
Web site: www.nysar.com
Duncan R MacKenzie, Chief Executive Officer

**NYS Land Title Association**
65 Broadway, Suite 501, New York, NY 10006-2544
212-964-3701  Fax: 212-964-7185
e-mail: rgt@nyslta.org
Web site: www.nyslta.org
*Trade association for title insurance industry*
Robert Treuber, Executive Director

**NYS Society of Real Estate Appraisers**
130 Washington Ave, Albany, NY 12210-2298
518-463-0300  Fax: 518-462-5474
Web site: www.nyrealestateappraisers.com
*Real estate appraisal*
Wayne Feinberg, President

**Community Bankers Assn of NY State, Mortgages & Real Estate Cmte**
**New York Community Bank**
615 Merrick Ave, Westbury, NY 11590
516-683-4100  Fax: 516-683-8344
Web site: www.mynycb.com
James O'Donovan, Chair

**New York Landmarks Conservancy**
1 Whitehall St, 21 Fl, New York, NY 10004
212-995-5260  Fax: 212-995-5268
e-mail: nylandmarks@nylandmarks.org
Web site: www.nylandmarks.org
*Technical & financial assistance for preservation & reuse of landmark buildings*
Peg Breen, President

**New York State Assessors' Association**
P.O. Box 5586, Cortland, NY 13045
315-706-3424  Fax: 315-410-5660
e-mail: admin@nyassessor.com
Web site: www.nyassessor.com
*Real property tax issues*
David W Briggs, FIAO, Executive Director

**Pomeroy Appraisal Associates Inc**
Pomeroy Pl, 225 W Jefferson St, Syracuse, NY 13202
315-422-7106  Fax: 315-476-1011
*Real estate appraisal & consultation*
Donald A Fisher, MAI, ARA

**R W Bronstein Corporation**
3666 Main St, Buffalo, NY 14226
716-835-7400 or 800-642-2500  Fax: 716-835-7419
e-mail: value@bronstein.net
Web site: www.bronstein.net
*Real estate, appraisals & auctions; valuation & marketing of all types of realty and chattels*
Richard W Bronstein, President

**Real Estate Board of New York Inc**
570 Lexington Ave, New York, NY 10022
212-532-3120  Fax: 212-481-0122
e-mail: stevenspinola@rebny.com
Web site: www.rebny.com
*Representing real estate professionals & firms in New York City*
Steven Spinola, President

**Realty Advisory Board on Labor Relations**
292 Madison Ave, New York, NY 10017
212-889-4100  Fax: 212-889-4105
e-mail: jberg@rabolr.com
Web site: www.rabolr.com
*Labor negotiations for realtors & realty firms*
James Berg, President

**Realty USA**
6505 E Quaker Rd, Orchard Park, NY 14127
716-662-2000  Fax: 716-662-3385
e-mail: mwhitehead@realtyusa.com
Web site: www.realtyusa.com
*Residential real estate*
Merle Whitehead, President & Chief Executive Officer

**Red Barn Properties**
Six Schoen Pl, Pittsford, NY 14534
585-381-2222 x11  Fax: 585-381-1854
Web site: www.redbarnproperties.com
*Specializing in local, national & global residential relocation*
Estelle O'Connell, Relocation Director

**Related Companies LP**
60 Columbus Circle, 19th Fl, New York, NY 10023
212-421-5333  Fax: 212-801-1036
e-mail: bbeal@related.com
Web site: www.related.com
*Residential & commercial real estate*
Bruce A Beal, Jr, Executive Vice President, NY Development Group

**Robert Schalkenbach Foundation**
90 John Street, Suite 501, New York, NY 10038
212-683-6424  Fax: 212-683-6454
e-mail: msullivan@schalkenbach.org
Web site: www.schalkenbach.org
*Land value taxation, real property & economic publications*
Mark A Sullivan, Administrative Director

**Roohan Realty**
519 Broadway, Saratoga Springs, NY 12866-2208
518-587-4500  Fax: 518-587-4509
e-mail: troohan@roohanrealty.com
Web site: www.roohanrealty.com
*Commercial & residential property*
J Thomas Roohan, President

**Silverstein Properties Inc**
7 World Trade Center, 250 Greenwich Street, 38th Floor, New York, NY 10036
212-490-0666  Fax: 212-687-0067
*NYC commercial real estate*
Larry A Silverstein, President, Chief Executive Officer

**Sonnenblick-Goldman Company**
712 Fifth Ave, New York, NY 10019
212-841-9200  Fax: 212-262-4224
e-mail: asonnenblick@sonngold.com
*Real estate investment banking*
Arthur I Sonnenblick, Senior Managing Director

**Tishman Speyer Properties**
Rockefeller Center, 45 Rockefeller Plaza, New York, NY 10111
212-715-0300  Fax: 212-319-1745
e-mail: jspeyer@tishmanspeyer.com
Web site: www.tishmanspeyer.com
*Owners/builders*
Jerry I Speyer, President

*Policy Areas*

*Offices and agencies generally appear in alphabetical order, except when specific order is requested by listee.*

**UJA-Federation of New York**
130 E 59th St, New York, NY 10022
212-980-1000  Fax: 212-836-1653
e-mail: flynnc@ujafedny.org
Web site: www.ujafedny.org
*Real property portfolio management*
John S Ruskay, Executive Vice President & Chief Executive Officer

## SOCIAL SERVICES

### NEW YORK STATE

### GOVERNOR'S OFFICE

## Governor's Office
Executive Chamber
State Capitol
Albany, NY 12224
518-474-8390  Fax: 518-474-1513
Web site: www.ny.gov

Governor:
Andrew M Cuomo . . . . . . . . . . . . . . . . . . . . . . . . . . . . . . .518-474-8390
Secretary to the Governor:
Melissa DeRosa . . . . . . . . . . . . . . . . . . . .518-474-4246 or 212-681-4580
Counsel to the Governor:
Kumiki Gibson . . . . . . . . . . . . . . . . . . . .518-474-8343 or 212-681-4580
Deputy Secretary, Health & Human Services:
Richard Beker. . . . . . . . . . . . . . . . . . . . .518-408-2500 or 212-681-4580
Chief of Staff:
Jill DesRosiers . . . . . . . . . . . . . . . . . . . .518-474-8390 or 212-681-4580
Director, Communications:
Peter Ajemian. . . . . . . . . . . . . . . . . . . . .518-474-8418 or 212-681-4640
Executive Deputy Secretary:
Joseph Rabito . . . . . . . . . . . . . . . . . . . . .518-473-5704 or 212-681-4580
Director, State Operations and Infrastructure:
Kelly Cummings. . . . . . . . . . . . . . . . . . . . . . . . . . . . . . . .518-486-9871

### EXECUTIVE DEPARTMENTS AND RELATED AGENCIES

## Aging, Office for the
2 Empire State Plaza
Albany, NY 12223-1251
844-697-6321 or 800-342-9871
e-mail: nysofa@aging.ny.gov
Web site: www.aging.ny.gov

Director:
Vacant
Director:
Greg Olsen . . . . . . . . . . . . . . . . . . . . . . . . . . . . . . . . . . .518-474-7012
Counsel:
Vacant. . . . . . . . . . . . . . . . . . . . . . . . . . . . . . . . . . . . . . .518-474-0388
Public Information Officer:
Reza Mizbani . . . . . . . . . . . . . . . . . . . . . . . . . . . . . . . . .518-474-7181
e-mail: reza.mizbani@aging.ny.gov
Deputy Director, Agency Operations:
John Cochran . . . . . . . . . . . . . . . . . . . . . . . . . . . . . . . . .518-474-7012
Deputy Director, Division of Policy, Planning, Program & Outcomes:
Laurie Pferr. . . . . . . . . . . . . . . . . . . . . . . . . . . . . . . . . . .518-474-7012

### Federal Relations
Staff Liaison:
Keri O'Connell . . . . . . . . . . . . . . . . . . . . . . . . . . . . . . . .518-474-5041
Deputy Director:
John J Lynch. . . . . . . . . . . . . . . . . . . . . . . . . . . . . . . . . .518-473-4808

### Aging Projects
Director of Aging Projects:
Kelly Mateja. . . . . . . . . . . . . . . . . . . . . . . . . . . . . . . . . .518-473-7424

## Agriculture & Markets Department
10B Airline Drive
Albany, NY 12235

518-457-4188 or 800-554-4501  Fax: 518-457-3087
e-mail: info@agriculture.ny.gov
Web site: www.agriculture.ny.gov

Commissioner:
Richard Ball . . . . . . . . . . . . . . . . . . . . . .518-457-8876 or 518-457-4188
First Deputy Commissioner:
Steve McGrattan. . . . . . . . . . . . . . . . . . . . . . . . . . . . . . .518-457-2771
Public Information Officer:
Jola Szubielski . . . . . . . . . . . . . . . . . .518-485-7728 or 518-457-3136
fax: 518-457-3087
e-mail: jola.szubielski@agriculture.ny.gov

### Agricultural Development Division
Director:
Steve McGrattan . . . . . . . . . . . . . . . . . . . . . . . . . . . . . . .518-457-7076

## Alcoholism & Substance Abuse Services, Office of
1450 Western Avenue
Albany, NY 12203-3526
518-473-3460
e-mail: communications@oasas.ny.gov
Web site: www.oasas.ny.gov

501 7th Avenue
8th Floor
New York, NY 10018-5903
646-728-4533

Commissioner:
Arlene González-Sánchez. . . . . . . . . . . . . . . . . . . . . . .518-457-2061
Executive Deputy Commissioner:
Sean M Byrne . . . . . . . . . . . . . . . . . . . . . . . . . . . . . . . . .518-485-2337
Director, Office of the Medical Director:
Vacant. . . . . . . . . . . . . . . . . . . . . . . . . . . . . . . . . . . . . . .845-359-8500
General Counsel:
Trisha Schell-Guy. . . . . . . . . . . . . . . . . . . . . . . . . . . . . .518-485-2312
Associate Commissioner, Division of Prevention & Problem Gambling
Services:
Patricia Zuber-Wilson. . . . . . . . . . . . . . . . . . . . . . . . . . .518-485-1484
Director, Office of NYC Operations, Affirmative Action and Bureau of
Statewide Field Operations:
Manuel Mosquera . . . . . . . . . . . . . . . . . . . . . . . . . . . . . .646-728-4720

### Office of Public Information & Communications
Director:
Edison Alban

### Fiscal Administration Division
Associate Commissioner:
Vittoria Parry . . . . . . . . . . . . . . . . . . . . . . . . . . . . . . . . .518-457-5312
Director, Bureau of Budget Management:
Tara Gabriel . . . . . . . . . . . . . . . . . . . . . . . . . . . . . . . . . .518-485-2193
Director, Bureau of Capital Management:
Jeff Emad . . . . . . . . . . . . . . . . . . . . . . . . . . . . . . . . . . . .518-457-2545
Director, Bureau of Health Care Financing & Performance Improvement:
Laurie Felter . . . . . . . . . . . . . . . . . . . . . . . . . . . . . . . . . .518-457-2545

### Outcome Management & System Information Division
Associate Commissioner:
William F. Hogan . . . . . . . . . . . . . . . . . . . . . . . . . . . . . .518-485-2322

### Prevention, Housing & Management Services Division
Director, Division of Prevention:
Scott Brady . . . . . . . . . . . . . . . . . . . . . . . . . . . . . . . . . . .518-485-6022
Director, Bureau of Housing & Employment:
Henri Williams . . . . . . . . . . . . . . . . . . . . . . . . . . . . . . . .518-485-0498
Director, Division of Prevention:
Scott Brady . . . . . . . . . . . . . . . . . . . . . . . . . . . . . . . . . . .518-485-6022
Director, Management Services:
Vacant. . . . . . . . . . . . . . . . . . . . . . . . . . . . . . . . . . . . . . .518-485-6689

*Offices and agencies generally appear in alphabetical order, except when specific order is requested by listee.*

Director, Bureau of Recovery Services:
  Susan Brandau . . . . . . . . . . . . . . . . . . . . . . . . . . . . .518-485-2107

**Quality Assurance & Performance Improvement Division**
Associate Commissioner:
  Keith McCarthy . . . . . . . . . . . . . . . . . . . . . . . . . . . . .518-485-2257
Director, Bureau of Certification:
  Janet Paloski . . . . . . . . . . . . . . . . . . . . . . . . . . . . . . .518-485-2250
Director, Bureau of Standards Compliance:
  William Lanchanski . . . . . . . . . . . . . . . . . . . . . . . . . . .518-485-2255
Director, Bureau of Workforce Developement & Fiscal Evaluation:
  Douglas Rosenberry . . . . . . . . . . . . . . . . . . . . . . . . . .518-485-2033

**Treatment & Practice Innovation Division**
Associate Commissioner:
  Steve Hanson . . . . . . . . . . . . . . . . . . . . . . . . . . . . . . .518-457-7077
Assistant Director, Bureau of Addiction Treatment Centers:
  Paula Bradwell . . . . . . . . . . . . . . . .518-457-7077 or 585-461-0410

## Children & Family Services, Office of
52 Washington Street
Rensselaer, NY 12144-2834
518-473-7793  Fax: 518-486-7550
e-mail: info@ocfs.ny.gov
Web site: ocfs.ny.gov

Commissioner:
  Sheila Poole . . . . . . . . . . . . . . . . . . . . . . . . . . . . . . .518-473-8437
  e-mail: info@ocfs.ny.gov
Ombudsman:
  Viola I Abbitt . . . . . . . . . . . . . . . . . . . . . . . . . . . . . .518-486-7082
Executive Secretary:
  Nancy Degree . . . . . . . . . . . . . . . . . . . . . . . . . . . . . .518-402-3108

**Administration, Division of**
Associate Commissioner:
  Mary Carli. . . . . . . . . . . . . . . . .518-486-6942 or 518-402-3211
  Contract Management:
    Richard DiMezza . . . . . . . . . . . . . . . . . . . . . . . . . .518-486-7224

  **Financial Management, Office of**
  Associate Commissioner:
    Derek Holtzclaw. . . . . . . . . . . . . . . . . . . . . . . . . . .518-486-7218
  Director, Budget Management Bureau:
    Gabrielle Ares. . . . . . . . . . . . . . . . . . . . . . . . . . . . .518-474-1361
  Director, Financial Operations:
    Susan A Costello . . . . . . . . . . . . . . . . . . . . . . . . . . .518-486-3848

**Commission for the Blind & Visually Handicapped (CBVH)**
Associate Commissioner:
  Brian Daniels . . . . . . . . . . . . . . . . . . . . . . . . . . . . . .518-474-7812
Director, Bureau of Program Evaluation,Support & Business Svcs:
  Roger Gray . . . . . . . . . . . . . . . . . . . . . . . . . . . . . . . .518-474-7812
Director, Bureau of Field Operations & Implementation:
  Janice O'Connor . . . . . . . . . . . . . . . . . . . . . . . . . . . .518-473-9685

**Child Welfare and Community Services, Division of (CWCS)**
Deputy Commissioner:
  Lisa Ghartey Ogundimu . . . . . . . . . . . . . . . . . . . . . . .518-474-3377

  **Special Populations, Office of**
  Assistant Commissioner:
    Lisa Ghartey Ogundimu. . . . . . . . . . . . . . . . . . . . . .518-473-9447
    *State Central Registry*
    Director:
      Linda A. Joyce. . . . . . . . . . . . . . . . . . . . . . . . . . .518-474-9607
    *Native American Services*
    Affairs Specialist:
      Vacant . . . . . . . . . . . . . . . . . . . . . . . . . . . . . . . .716-847-3123

**Prevention, Permanency & Program Support, Office of**
Associate Commissioner:
  Renee Hallock . . . . . . . . . . . . . . . . . . . . . . . . . . . . . .518-402-3181
  *Adult Protective Services*
  Director:
    Alan Lawitz. . . . . . . . . . . . . . . . . . . . . . . . . . . . . . .518-402-6782
  *Adoption Services*
  Director:
    Brenda Rivers . . . . . . . . . . . . . . . . . . . . . . . . . . . .518-473-1901

**Child Care Services, Division of (DCCS)**
Deputy Commissioner:
  Janice Molnar. . . . . . . . . . . . . . . . . . . . . . . . . . . . . .518-486-6247

**Information Technology, Division of**
40 N Pearl Street, Albany, NY 12243
Business Solutions Director:
  John Birtwistle . . . . . . . . . . . . . . . . . . . . . . . . . . . . .518-408-3046

**Legal Affairs, Division of**
Acting Deputy Commissioner & General Counsel:
  Lee Prochera . . . . . . . . . . . . . . . . . . . . . . . . . . . . . . .518-473-8418

**Communications, Office of**
Assistant Commissioner:
  Monica Mahaffey . . . . . . . . . . . . . . . . . . . . . . . . . . . .518-473-7793
  e-mail: info@ocfs.ny.gov

**Juvenile Justice & Opportunities for Youth, Division of (DJJOY)**
Deputy Commissioner:
  Felicia Reid. . . . . . . . . . . . . . . . . . . . . . . . . . . . . . . .518-473-1786

**Facility Management, Office of**
Associate Commissioner:
  Vacant. . . . . . . . . . . . . . . . . . . . . . . . . . . . . . . . . . .518-473-4411
Facility Coordinator:
  Wendy Phillips . . . . . . . . . . . . . . . . . . . . . . . . . . . . .212-961-4121
Facility Coordinator:
  Dan Comins . . . . . . . . . . . . . . . . . . . . . . . . . . . . . . .607-538-1401
ACA Accreditation Coordinator:
  Kurt Pfisterer. . . . . . . . . . . . . . . . . . . . . . . . . . . . . . .518-408-3825
Supervisor, Facilities Fire Safety:
  Scott Hecox. . . . . . . . . . . . . . . . . . . . . . . . . . . . . . . .518-473-5325
DOJ Settlement Coordinator:
  Edgardo Lopez . . . . . . . . . . . . . . . . . . . . . . . . . . . . .315-479-8356
Director, Management & Program Supprot, Bureau of:
  Merle Brandwene . . . . . . . . . . . . . . . . . . . . . . . . . . .518-486-7029

**Community Partnerships, Office of**
Associate Commissioner:
  Tim Roche. . . . . . . . . . . . . . . . . . . . . . . . . . . . . . . . .518-486-7170
Director, Upstate/Long Island:
  Daniel Maxwell. . . . . . . . . . . . . . . . . . . . . . . . . . . . .518-486-4018
Downstate Area Manager:
  Robert Ellis . . . . . . . . . . . . . . . . . . . . . . . . . . . . . . . .212-961-4112
Director, Technical Support, IT, Office of:
  Jeff Evans . . . . . . . . . . . . . . . . . . . . . . . . . . . . . . . . .518-486-4335

**Special Investigations Unit**
Chief of Investigations:
  Lisa Thorne. . . . . . . . . . . . . . . . . . . . . . . . . . . . . . . .518-474-9478

**Strategic Planning & Policy Development, Office of**
Director:
  Vacant . . . . . . . . . . . . . . . . . . . . . . . . . . . . . . . . . . .518-473-1776
Bureau of Policy Analysis:
  Rayana Gonzales. . . . . . . . . . . . . . . . . . . . . . . . . . . .518-473-6237
Bureau of Research, Evaluation & Performance Analytics:
  Rebecca Colman . . . . . . . . . . . . . . . . . . . . . . . . . . . .518-474-9426
Director, Special Projects, Bureau of:
  Greg Owens . . . . . . . . . . . . . . . . . . . . . . . . . . . . . . .518-473-3990

*Offices and agencies generally appear in alphabetical order, except when specific order is requested by listee.*

**Native American Services** ......................fax: 716-847-3812
716-847-3123  Fax: 716-847-3812
Director:
Vacant..........................................716-847-3123

**Youth Development, Office of** .................fax: 518-473-6692
52 Washington Avenue, Room 1155, Rensselaer, NY 12144
Director:
Matt Beck ......................................518-402-3296

**Council on Children & Families (CCF)** .........fax: 518-473-2570
52 Washington St, West Building, Suite 99, Rensselaer, NY 12144
518-474-5522 or 518-473-3652  Fax: 518-473-2570
e-mail: council@ccf.ny.gov
Web site: www.ccf.ny.gov
Executive Director:
Deborah Benson ..................518-473-3652/fax: 518-473-2570
e-mail: debbie.benson@ccf.ny.gov
Deputy Director & Counsel:
Elana Marton....................518-473-3652/fax: 518-473-2570
e-mail: elana.marton@ccf.ny.gov

**Bureau of Policy, Research & Planning**
Project Director, Head Start Collaboration:
Patricia Persell ...................................518-474-9352
e-mail: patricia.persell@ccf.ny.gov

**Bureau of Interagency Coordination & Case Resolution**
Policy Analyst & Kids Count Director:
Cate Teuten Bohn

## Victim Services, Office of
AE Smith Building
80 S Swan Street
2nd Floor
Albany, NY 12210
518-457-8727 or 800-247-8035  Fax: 518-457-8658
Web site: www.ovs.ny.gov

55 Hanson Place
10th Floor
Brooklyn, NY 11217
718-923-4325
Fax: 718-923-4347

Director:
Elizabeth Cronin, Esq..............................518-485-5719
General Counsel/Legal Unit:
John Watson ....................518-457-8066/fax: 518-457-8658
Deputy Director, Administration:
Virginia Miller ...................................518-457-8003
Deputy Director, Claims:
Maureen Fahy.....................................518-457-8050
Brooklyn Investigations Unit, Crime Compensation:
Claudette Christian Bullock ......................718-923-4348
Director, Compensation:
Noreen Fyvie......................................518-457-8727

## Developmental Disabilities Planning Council
99 Washington Avenue
Suite 1230
Albany, NY 12210
518-486-7505 or 800-395-3372
e-mail: information@ddpc.ny.gov
Web site: www.ddpc.ny.gov

Chairperson:
Vacant..........................................800-395-3372
Vice Chairperson:
Vacant..........................................800-395-3372

Executive Director:
Sheila M Carey...................................518-486-7505
e-mail: sheila.carey@ddpc.ny.gov

## Education Department
State Education Building
89 Washington Avenue
Albany, NY 12234
518-474-3852
Web site: www.nysed.gov

Interim Commissioner & University President:
Betty A Rosa......................................518-474-5844
Executive Deputy Commissioner:
Vacant..........................................518-474-8381
Chief Financial Officer:
Phyllis Morris ....................................518-474-7751
Assistant Commissioner, Public Affairs:
Emily DeSantis....................................518-474-1201

**Office of the Professions**.....................fax: 518-474-1449
89 Washington Avenue, 2nd Floor, West Mezzanine, Albany, NY 12234
Fax: 518-474-1449
Web site: www.op.nysed.gov
Deputy Commissioner:
Sarah Benson .....................................518-486-1765

**Office of Adult Career & Continuing Education Services
(ACCES)** .....................................fax: 518-474-8802
89 Washington Avenue, Room 460 EBA, Albany, NY 12234
Fax: 518-474-8802
Web site: www.acces.nysed.gov
Deputy Commissioner:
Kevin Smith ......................................518-474-2714

**Vocational Rehabilitation Administration**
Statewide Coordinator, Workforce Development & Business Relations:
Joseph Tedesco................................518-473-6829
e-mail: joseph.tedesco@nysed.gov

## Labor Department
W.A. Harriman Campus
Building 12
Albany, NY 12240
518-457-9000 or 888-469-7365  Fax: 518-457-6908
e-mail: nysdol@labor.ny.gov
Web site: www.labor.ny.gov

Commissioner:
Roberta Reardon...................................518-457-9000
Executive Deputy Commissioner:
Nathaalie Carey...................................518-457-4318
Acting Counsel:
Jill Archambault
Acting Deputy Commissioner, Administration:
Jack Dougherty
Associate Commissioner, Communications:
Peter Brancato....................................518-457-5519

## Federal Programs
Deputy Commissioner, Federal Programs:
Bruce Herman.....................................518-485-6410

**Employment Services Division**
Director:
Vacant..........................................518-457-3584

**Unemployment Insurance Division**
Director:
Richard Marino ................518-457-2878/fax: 518-485-8604

*Offices and agencies generally appear in alphabetical order, except when specific order is requested by listee.*

Policy Areas

**Workforce Development & Training Division**
Deputy Commissioner:
  Karen Coleman.....................................518-457-4317

**Veterans Services**
Program Coordinator:
  Vacant............................................518-457-1343

**Worker Protection**
Acting Deputy Commissioner:
  Milan Bhatt

  **Labor Standards Division**
  Director:
    Carmine Ruberto ...........................518-457-4256

  **Safety & Health Division**
  Deputy Commissioner:
    Eileen Franko .............................518-457-3518

## Prevention of Domestic Violence, Office for the
80 South Swan Street
11th Floor, Room 1157
Albany, NY 12210
518-457-5800  Fax: 518-457-5810
e-mail: opdvpublicinfo@opdv.ny.gov
Web site: www.opdv.ny.gov

90 Church Street
13th Floor
New York, NY 10007
212-417-4477
Fax: 212-417-4972

Executive Director:
  Gwen Wright ...................518-457-5800 or 518-457-5916
Director, NYC Program:
  Sujata Warrier ...................212-417-4477/fax: 518-417-4972
Counsel:
  Ellen Schell....................................518-457-5757
Director, Bureau of Public Awareness & Prevention:
  Suzanne Cecala...............................518-457-5744
  e-mail: suzanne.cecala@opdv.ny.gov

## Temporary & Disability Assistance, Office of
40 North Pearl Street
Albany, NY 12243
518-473-1090 or 518-474-9516  Fax: 518-486-6255
e-mail: nyspio@otda.ny.gov
Web site: www.otda.ny.gov

Commissioner:
  Samuel D Roberts ................518-474-4152/fax: 518-486-6255

**Budget, Finance & Data Management**
Director:
  Nancy Maney .................................518-474-0183

**Child Support Services**
Deputy Commissioner:
  Eileen Stack ...................................518-474-1078

**Employment and Income Support Programs**
Assistant Deputy Commissioner:
  Jeff Gaskell....................................518-486-7694

**Specialized Services**
Deputy Commissioner:
  Linda Glassman ...............................518-402-3096

**Information Technology Services**
Acting Chief Information Officer:
  Rick Ryan .....................................518-486-1012

**Legal Affairs Division**
General Counsel:
  Krista Rock....................................518-474-9502

**Administrative Services Division**
Deputy Commissioner:
  Eric Schwenzfeier..............................518-473-3912

**Public Information**
Director:
  Tim Ruffinen...................518-474-9516/fax: 518-486-6935
  e-mail: nyspio@otda.ny.gov

## Welfare Inspector General, Office of NYS
Empire State Plaza
Agency Bldg 2
16th Floor
Albany, NY 12223
518-474-1010 or 800-367-4448  Fax: 518-486-3745
e-mail: inspector.general@ig.ny.gov
Web site: www.owig.ny.gov

Welfare Inspector General:
  Letizia Tagliafierro..................518-474-1010 or 212-635-3150
Chief Investigator:
  Joseph Bucci......................718-923-4290 or 518-474-1010
Confidential Assistant/Office Manager:
  Joy Quiles........................718-923-4290 or 518-474-1010
  fax: 718-923-4310

## NEW YORK STATE LEGISLATURE

*See Legislative Branch in Section 1 for additional Standing Committee and Subcommittee information.*

## Assembly Standing Committees

**Aging**
Chair:
  Ron Kim (D)...................................518-455-4527

**Alcoholism & Drug Abuse**
Chair:
  Phil Steck .....................................518-455-5802

**Children & Families**
Chair:
  Andrew Hevesi.................................518-455-5118

**Social Services**
Chair:
  Linda B Rosenthal (D, WF).......................518-455-4926

## Assembly Task Forces

**Puerto Rican/Hispanic Task Force**
Chair:
  Maritza Davila (D)..............................518-455-5514
Executive Director:
  Guillermo Martinez.............................518-455-3608

**Women's Issues, Task Force on**
Chair:
  Rebecca A Seawright ...........................518-455-4466

*Offices and agencies generally appear in alphabetical order, except when specific order is requested by listee.*

## Senate Standing Committees

### Aging
Chair:
    Rachel May (D, WF)...............................518-455-2838
Ranking Minority Member:
    Sue Serino (R, C, IP) ...........................518-455-2945

### Children & Families

### Social Services
Chair:
    Roxanne J Persaud (D)...........................518-455-2788
Minority Member:
    Sue Serino (R, C, IP) ...........................518-455-2945

## U.S. GOVERNMENT

### EXECUTIVE DEPARTMENTS AND RELATED AGENCIES

## Corporation for National & Community Service

**New York Program Office**
52 Washington Street, Room 228, North Building, Rensselaer, NY
    12144-2796
Executive Director:
    Mark J. Walter....................518-473-8882/fax: 518-402-3817

## Social Security Administration
Web site: www.socialsecurity.gov

**Region 2—New York** ......................fax: 212-264-6372
26 Federal Plz, Rm 3904, New York, NY 10278
Regional Commissioner:
    Beatrice M Disman................................212-264-3915
Deputy Regional Commissioner:
    Paul M Doersam..................................212-264-3915
Employer Services Liaison Officer:
    Tyrone S. Benefield .............................212-264-1117
Executive Officer:
    Bernie Bowles....................................212-264-4007

**Office of Hearings & Appeals**
Regional Chief Administrative Law Judge:
    G Stephen Wright................................212-264-4036

**Office of Quality Assurance**
Director:
    Susan Pike ......................................212-264-2827

**Office of the General Counsel**
Chief Counsel:
    Lewis Spivak ....................................212-264-3650

**Program Operations Center**
Director:
    Janet Mullarkey .................................212-264-4004

**Public Affairs**
Public Affairs Director:
    John E Shallman ................212-264-2500/fax: 212-264-1444

## US Department of Health & Human Services
Web site: www.os.dhhs.gov; www.hhs.gov/region2/

**Administration for Children & Families** ........fax: 212-264-4881
26 Federal Plaza, Rm 4114, New York, NY 10278
212-264-2890  Fax: 212-264-4881
Web site: www.acf.hhs.gov
Regional Administrator:
    Joyce A. Thomas.................................212-264-2890

**Administration on Aging** ......................fax: 212-264-0114
26 Federal Plaza, Rm 38-102, New York, NY 10278
212-264-2976  Fax: 212-264-0114
Web site: www.aoa.gov
Regional Administrator:
    Kathleen Otte ...................................212-264-2976
e-mail: kathleen.otte@aoa.hhs.gov

**Centers for Disease Control & Prevention**
Web site: www.cdc.gov

**Agency for Toxic Substances & Disease Registry-EPA Region 2**
290 Broadway, 20th Fl, New York, NY 10007
Web site: www.atsdr.cdc.gov
Director:
    Leah Graziano, RS ..............212-637-4306/fax: 212-637-3253

**New York Quarantine Station** ...................fax: 718-553-1524
Terminal 4E, Rm 219 016, JFK Airport, 2nd Floor, East Concourse,
    Jamaica, NY 11430-1081
718-553-1685  Fax: 718-553-1524
Officer-in-Charge:
    Margaret A Becker ..............718-553-1685/fax: 718-553-1524

**Centers for Medicare & Medicaid Services**
26 Federal Plaza, Rm 3811, New York, NY 10278
Web site: www.cms.hhs.gov
Consortium Administrator:
    James T. Kerr.....................212-616-2205/fax: 212-264-6189
Regional Administrator:
    Jay Weisman, MD.................................212-616-2500

**Medicaid and Children's Health (DMCH)**
Associate Regional Administrator:
    Michael Melendez

**Medicare Financial Management (DMFM)**
Associate Regional Administrator:
    Vacant

**Medicare Operations Division (DMO)**
Associate Regional Administrator:
    Reginald Slaten.................................212-616-2300

## Food & Drug Administration
888-463-6332
Web site: www.fda.gov

**Northeast Region**
158-15 Liberty Ave, Jamaica, NY 11433
Regional Director:
    Elizabeth O'Malley..............718-340-7000/fax: 718-662-5434
    *New York District Office*
    District Director:
        Ronald Pace ...............718-662-5447/fax: 718-662-5665
    *Northeast Regional Laboratory*
    158-15 Liberty Ave, Queens, NY 11433
    Director:
        Michael J Palmieri ..........718-662-5450/fax: 718-662-5439

**Health Resources & Svcs Admin Office of Performance
Review** .......................................fax: 212-264-2673
26 Federal Plaza, Rm 3337, New York, NY 10278
Regional Division Director:
    Ron Moss .......................................212-264-2664
Operations Director:
    Margaret Lee.....................................212-264-2571
Director, Ofc of Engineering Services:
    Emilio Pucillo...................................212-264-3600

**Indian Health Services-Area Office** .............fax: 615-467-1501
711 Stewarts Ferry Pike, Nashville, TN 37214-2634
Director:
    Martha Ketcher, MBA/HCM .........................615-467-1500

*Offices and agencies generally appear in alphabetical order, except when specific order is requested by listee.*

Policy Areas

**Office of Secretary's Regional Representative-Region 2-NY** . . fax: 212-264-3620
26 Federal Plaza, Rm 3835, New York, NY 10278
Regional Director:
    Deborah Konopko . . . . . . . . . . . . . . . . . . . . . . . . . . . . . . . . 212-264-4600
Sr Intergovernmental Affairs Specialist:
    Dennis Gonzalez . . . . . . . . . . . . . . . . . . . . . . . . . . . . . . . . 212-264-4600
    e-mail: dennis.gonzalez@hhs.gov
Intergovernmental Affairs Specialist:
    Katherine Williams . . . . . . . . . . . . . . . . . . . . . . . . . . . . . . 212-264-4600

**Office for Civil Rights** . . . . . . . . . . . . . . . . . . . . . . . fax: 212-264-3039
26 Federal Plaza, Rm 3312, New York, NY 10278
Fax: 212-264-3039
Web site: www.hhs.gov/ocr
Regional Manager:
    Michael Carter . . . . . . . . . . . . . . . . 212-264-3313/fax: 212-264-3039
Deputy Regional Manager:
    Linda Colon . . . . . . . . . . . . . . . . . . . . . . . . . . . . . . . . . 212-264-3313

**Office of General Counsel**
26 Federal Plaza, Rm 3908, New York, NY 10278
Chief Counsel:
    Joel Lerner . . . . . . . . . . . . . . . . . . . . . . . . . . . . . . . . . . 212-264-6373

**Office of Inspector General**
Regional Inspector General, Audit:
    James P Edert . . . . . . . . . . . . . . . . . . . . . . . . . . . . . . . . . 212-264-4620
Regional Inspector General & Regional Coordinator, Investigations:
    Gary Heuer . . . . . . . . . . . . . . . . . . . . . . . . . . . . . . . . . . 212-264-1691
Regional Inspector General, Evaluations & Inspections:
    Jodi Nudelman . . . . . . . . . . . . . . . . . . . . . . . . . . . . . . . . 212-264-1998

**Office of Public Health & Science**
26 Federal Plaza, Rm 3835, New York, NY 10278
Acting Regional Health Administrator:
    Robert Davidson . . . . . . . . . . . . . . . . . . . . . . . . . . . . . . . 212-264-2560
Deputy Regional Health Administrator:
    Robert L Davidson . . . . . . . . . . . . . . . . . . . . . . . . . . . . . 212-264-2560
Regional Family Planning Consultant:
    Robin Lane . . . . . . . . . . . . . . . . . . . . . . . . . . . . . . . . . . 212-264-3935
Regional Minority Health Consultant:
    Claude Colimon . . . . . . . . . . . . . . . . . . . . . . . . . . . . . . . 212-264-2560
Regional Women's Health Coordinator:
    Sandra Estepa . . . . . . . . . . . . . . . . . . . . . . . . . . . . . . . . 212-264-2560

## U.S. CONGRESS

*See U.S. Congress Chapter for additional Standing Committee and Subcommittee information.*

### House of Representatives Standing Committees

**Ways & Means**
Chair:
    Dave Kamp (R-MI) . . . . . . . . . . . . . . . . . . . . . . . . . . . . . 202-225-3561
New York Delegate:
    Charles B. Rangel (D) . . . . . . . . . . . . . . . . . . . . . . . . . . . 202-225-4365
New York Delegate:
    Joseph Crowley (D) . . . . . . . . . . . . . . . . . . . . . . . . . . . . 202-225-3965
New York Delegate:
    Tom Reed (R) . . . . . . . . . . . . . . . . . . . . . . . . . . . . . . . . . 202-225-3106

    **Subcommittee**
    *Social Security*
        Chair:
            Sam Johnson (R-TX) . . . . . . . . . . . . . . . . . . . . . 202 225 4201
        Ranking Member:
            Xavier Becerra (D-CA) . . . . . . . . . . . . . . . . . . . 202-225-6325

### Senate Standing Committees

**Health, Education, Labor & Pensions**
Chair:
    Tom Harkin (D-IA) . . . . . . . . . . . . . . . . . . . . . . . . . . . . 202-224-3254
Ranking Member:
    Lamar Alexander (R-TN) . . . . . . . . . . . . . . . . . . . . . . . . 202-224-4944

**Aging, Special Committee on**
Chair:
    Bill Nelson (D-FL) . . . . . . . . . . . . . . . . . . . . . . . . . . . . . 202-224-5274
Ranking Member:
    Susan Collins (R-ME) . . . . . . . . . . . . . . . . . . . . . . . . . . . 202-224-2523

## PRIVATE SECTOR

**AARP**
750 Third Avenue, 31st Floor, New York, NY 10017-
866-227-7442  Fax: 212-644-6390
Web site: www.aarp.org
*AARP*
Lois Aronstein, NY State Director

**Abilities Inc, at Abilities!**
201 IU Willets Rd, Albertson, NY 11507-1599
516-465-1490 or 516-747-5355 (TTY)  Fax: 516-405-3757
e-mail: amuterspaw@abilitiesinc.org
*Provides comprehensive services to help individuals with disabilities reach their employment goals; provides support services & technical assistance to employers who hire persons with disabilities.*
Alice Muterspaw, Director of Consumer Services & Provider Relations

**Action for a Better Community Inc**
550 E Main St, Rochester, NY 14604
585-325-5116 or 585-295-1726  Fax: 585-325-9108
Web site: www.abcinfo.org
*Advocacy for programs enabling the low-income to become self-sufficient; social services for the needy*
Freddie Caldwell, Deputy Director

**American Red Cross in NYS**
33 Everett Rd, Albany, NY 12205-1437
518-458-8111 x5113  Fax: 518-459-8262
e-mail: elizabeth.briand@redcross.org
Elizabeth H Briand, Director, State Government Relations

**Asian American Federation**
120 Wall St, 9th Floor, New York, NY 10005
212-344-5878  Fax: 212-344-5636
e-mail: info@aafederation.org
Web site: www.aafederation.org
*Nonprofit leadership organization for member health & human services agencies serving the Asian American community*
Cao K. O, Executive Director

**Asian Americans for Equality**
108 Norfolk Street, New York, NY 10002
212-979-8381  Fax: 212-979-8386
Web site: www.aafe.org
*Equal opportunities for minorities; affordable housing development, homeownership counseling, immigration services, housing rights*
Christopher Kui, Executive Director

**Berkshire Farm Center & Services for Youth**
13640 Route 22, Canaan, NY 12029
518-781-4567 ext2211  Fax: 518-781-4577
e-mail: dharrington@berkshirefarm.org
Web site: www.berkshirefarm.org
*Multi-function agency for troubled youth & families*
Harith Flagg, Chief Executive Officer

*Offices and agencies generally appear in alphabetical order, except when specific order is requested by listee.*

**Big Brothers Big Sisters of NYC**
223 East 30th St, New York, NY 10016
212-686-2042 Fax: 212-779-1221
e-mail: help@bigsnyc.org
Web site: www.bigsnyc.org
*Providing disadvantaged youth with one-to-one, long-term relationships with a trained volunteer*
Hector Batista, Executive Director

**CIDNY - Queens**
137-02A Northern Blvd, Flushing, NY 11354
646-442-1520 or TTY 718-886-0427 Fax: 718-886-0428
Web site: www.cidny.org
*Rights & advocacy for the disabled*
Susan Dooha, Executive Director

**CASA: Advocates for Children of NYS (CASANYS)**
911 Central Avenue, Suite 117, Albany, NY 12206
315-246-3558
e-mail: mail@casanys.org
Web site: www.casanys.org
*Volunteer advocates appointed by family court judges to represent abused & neglected children in court*
Barbara Benedict, Executive Director

**Camp Venture Inc**
25 Smith Street, Suite 510, Nanuet, NY 10954
845-624-3860 Fax: 845-624-7064
Web site: www.campventure.org
*Services for the developmentally disabled*
Daniel Lukens, Executive Director

**Catholic Charities of Onondaga County**
1654 W Onondaga St, Syracuse, NY 13204
315-424-1800 Fax: 315-424-8262
Web site: www.ccoc.us
Eleanor Carr, Director, Elder Abuse Prevention Program

**Center for Anti-Violence Education Inc**
327 7th St, 2nd Fl, Brooklyn, NY 11215
718-788-1775 Fax: 718-499-2284
e-mail: info@caeny.org
Web site: www.caeny.org
*Self-defense & violence prevention education for children, youth, women & LGBT people*
Tracy Hobson, Executive Director

**Center for Family & Youth (The)**
135 Ontario Street, PO Box 6240, Albany, NY 12206
518-462-4585 or 518-462-5366 Fax: 518-427-1465
*Child welfare services, Project STRIVE*
David A Bosworth, Executive Director

**Center for Independence of the Disabled in NY (CIDNY)**
841 Broadway, Ste 301, New York, NY 10003
212-674-2300 or TTY: 212-674-5619 Fax: 212-254-5953
Web site: www.cidny.org
*Rights & advocacy for the disabled*
Susan Dooha, Executive Director

**Center for Urban Community Services**
198 E 121st Street, New York, NY 10035
212-801-3300 Fax: 212-635-2191
e-mail: cucsinfo@cucs.org
Web site: www.cucs.org
*Services to the homeless & low-income individuals, training & technical assistance to not-for-profit organizations*
Anthony Hannigan, Executive Director

**Center for Disability Services**
314 S Manning Blvd, Albany, NY 12208
518-437-5700 Fax: 518-437-5705
Web site: www.cfdsny.org
*Medical & dental services; education, adult & residential services & service coordination*
Alan Krafchin, President & Chief Executive Officer

**Cerebral Palsy Associations of New York State**
330 West 34th Street, 15th Floor, New York, NY 10001-2488
212-947-5770 Fax: 212-594-4538
e-mail: information@cpofnys.org
Web site: www.cpofnys.org
*Serves individuals with cerebral palsy & other significant disabilities as well as their families through advocacy, technical assistance, publications & networking events*
Susan Constantino, President & Chief Executive Officer

**Children's Aid Society (The)**
105 E 22nd St, New York, NY 10010
212-949-4921 Fax: 212-460-5941
e-mail: pmoses@childrensaidsociety.org
Web site: www.childrensaidsociety.org
*Child welfare, health, foster care/adoption, preventive services, community centers & public schools, camps*
C Warren Moses, Chief Executive Officer

**Children's Rights Inc**
330 Seventh Ave, 4th Floor, New York, NY 10001
212-683-2210 Fax: 212-683-4015
e-mail: info@childrensrights.org
Web site: www.childrensrights.org
*Advocacy & class action lawsuits on behalf of abused & neglected children*
Marcia Robinson Lowry, Executive Director

**Children's Village (The)**
Echo Hills, Dobbs Ferry, NY 10522
914-693-0600 x1201 Fax: 914-674-9208
e-mail: jkohomban@childrensvillage.org
Web site: www.childrensvillage.org
*Residential school, located 20 minutes outside of NYC. Treatment & prevention of behavioral problems for youth; residential & community-based services; mental health, education, employment & runaway shelter services*
Jeremy Kohomban, PhD, President & Chief Executive Officer

**Citizens' Committee for Children of New York Inc**
14 Wall Street, Suite 4E, New York, NY 10005-2173
212-673-1800 Fax: 212-979-5063
e-mail: info@cccnewyork.org
Web site: www.cccnewyork.org
*Public policy advocacy for children's rights & services; promoting improved quality of life for NYC children & families in need*
Jennifer March, Executive Director

**Coalition Against Domestic Violence, NYS**
350 New Scotland Ave, Albany, NY 12208
518-482-5465 Fax: 518-482-3807
e-mail: vasquez@nyscadv.org
Web site: www.nyscadv.org
Jessica Vasquez, Executive Director

**Coalition for Asian American Children & Families**
50 Broad St, Rm 1701, New York, NY 10004
212-809-4675 Fax: 212-785-4601
e-mail: cacf@cacf.org
Web site: www.cacf.org
*Advocacy for programs & policies supporting Asian American children & families; training & resources for service providers*
Wayne H Ho, Executive Director

*Offices and agencies generally appear in alphabetical order, except when specific order is requested by listee.*

**Coalition for the Homeless**
129 Fulton St, 1st Flr, New York, NY 10038
212-776-2000  Fax: 212-964-1303
e-mail: info@cfthomeless.org
Web site: www.coalitionforthehomeless.org
*Food, shelter, clothing assistance program, services for homeless New Yorkers*
Mary Brosnahan Sullivan, Executive Director

**Coalition of Animal Care Societies (The)**
437 Old Albany Post Rd, Garrison, NY 10524
845-788-5070  Fax: 845-788-5071
e-mail: tzaleski@sprynet.com
*Association of humane societies & animal welfare groups in NYS*
Terence M Zaleski, Special Counsel

**Coalition of Fathers & Families NY**
P.O. Box 252, Stillwater, NY 12170
518-383-8202
e-mail: info@fafny.org
*Working to keep fathers & families together*
Jack Frost, President

**Commission on Economic Opportunity for the Greater Capital Region**
2331 Fifth Ave, Troy, NY 12180
518-272-6012  Fax: 518-272-0658
Web site: www.ceo-cap.org
*Preserve & advance the self-sufficiency, well-being & growth of individuals & families through education, guidance & resources*
Karen E Gordon, Executive Director

**Community Healthcare Network**
79 Madison Avenue, Fl 6, New York, NY 10016-7802
212-366-4500  Fax: 212-463-8411
e-mail: cabate@chnnyc.org
Web site: www.chnnyc.org
*Health & social services for low-income, ethnically diverse, medically underserved neighborhoods of NYC*
Catherine Abate, President & Chief Executive Officer

**Cornell Cooperative Extension, College of Human Ecology, Nutrition, Health**
186 Martha Van Rensselaer Hall, Cornell University, Ithaca, NY 14853-4401
607-255-2247  Fax: 607-254-4403
e-mail: jas56@cornell.edu
Web site: www.cce.cornell.edu
*Children, youth & family economic & social well-being*
Josephine Swanson, Associate Director, Assistant Dean

**Council of Community Services of NYS Inc**
272 Broadway, Albany, NY 12204
518-434-9194 x103  Fax: 518-434-0392
Web site: www.ccsnys.org
*Build healthy, caring communities & human care delivery systems through a strong charitable nonprofit sector & quality community-based planning*
Doug Sauer, Executive Director

**Council of Family & Child Caring Agencies**
254 West 31st Street, 5th Floor, New York, NY 10001
212-929-2626  Fax: 212-929-0870
e-mail: jpurcell@cofcca.org
Web site: www.cofcca.org
*Child welfare services membership organization*
Jim Purcell, Chief Executive Officer

**EPIC-Every Person Influences Children Inc**
1000 Main St, Buffalo, NY 14202
716-332-4100  Fax: 716-332-4101
Web site: www.epicforchildren.org
*Uniting parents, teachers & community members to prevent child abuse & neglect, school dropout, juvenile crime, substance abuse & teenage pregnancy*
Vito J Borrello, President

**Early Care & Learning Council**
230 Washington Ave Ext, Albany, NY 12203-5390
518-690-4217  Fax: 518-690-2887
e-mail: mbasloe@earlycareandlearning.org
Web site: www.earlycareandlearning.org
*Advocacy & education for the development of accessible and affordable, quality child care services*
Marsha Basloe, Executive Director

**Education & Assistance Corp Inc**
50 Clinton St, Ste 107, Hempstead, NY 11550
516-539-0150  Fax: 516-539-0160
e-mail: lelder@eacinc.org
Web site: www.eacinc.org
*Rehabilitation for nonviolent offenders; advocacy, education & counseling programs for youth, elderly & families*
Lance W Elder, President & Chief Executive Officer

**Empire Justice Center**
119 Washington Ave, Albany, NY 12210
518-462-6831  Fax: 518-462-6687
Web site: www.empirejustice.org
*Empire Justice protects and strengthens the legal rights of people in New York State who are poor, disabled or disenfranchised.*
Anne Erickson, President & Chief Executive Officer

**Family Planning Advocates of New York State**
17 Elk St, Albany, NY 12207
518-436-8408  Fax: 518-436-0004
e-mail: info@fpaofnys.org
Web site: www.fpaofnys.org
*Reproductive rights*
JoAnn M Smith, President/Chief Executive Officer

**Federation Employment & Guidance Service (FEGS) Inc**
315 Hudson St, 9th Fl, New York, NY 10013
212-366-8400  Fax: 212-366-8441
e-mail: info@fegs.org
Web site: www.fegs.org
*Diversified health & human services system to help individuals achieve their potential at work, at home, at school and in the community*
Gail Magaliff, Chief Executive Officer

**Federation of Protestant Welfare Agencies Inc**
281 Park Ave South, New York, NY 10010
212-777-4800 x322  Fax: 212-673-4085
e-mail: fgoldman@fpwa.org
Web site: www.fpwa.org
*Childcare & child welfare, HIV/AIDS, elderly, income security*
Fatima Goldman, Executive Director

**Filipino American Human Services Inc (FAHSI)**
185-14 Hillside Ave, Jamaica, NY 11432
718-883-1295  Fax: 718-523-9606
e-mail: admin@fahsi.org
Web site: www.fahsi.org
*FAHSI is a community-based, non-profit organization dedicated to serving the Filipino and Filipino American community of New York City, particularly, marginalized sections such as youth, women, recent immigrants, and the elderly.*
Johanna Martinez LMSW, Executive Director

*Offices and agencies generally appear in alphabetical order, except when specific order is requested by listee.*

**Fordham University, Graduate School of Social Service**
113 West 60th Street, Lincoln Center, New York, NY 10023
212-636-6616  Fax: 212-636-7876
e-mail: vaughan@fordham.edu
Web site: www.fordham.edu
*Social work education, clinical social work, administration, client centered management*
Debra M McPhee, Dean

**Friends & Relatives of Institutionalized Aged Inc (FRIA)**
18 John St, Suite 905, New York, NY 10038
212-732-5667 or 212-732-4455  Fax: 212-732-6945
Web site: www.fria.org
*Free bilingual telephone helpline for information assistance and complaints about nursing homes, assisted living and other long-term care issues.*
Betti Weimersheimer, Executive Director

**Green Chimneys School-Green Chimneys Children's Services Inc**
400 Doansburg Rd, Box 719, Brewster, NY 10509
845-279-2995 x119  Fax: 845-279-3077
Web site: www.greenchimneys.org
*Residential treatment programs for emotionally troubled children & youths; therapeutic/educational Farm & Wildlife Conservation Center programs; therapeutic day school program*
Joseph A Whalen, Executive Director

**Guide Dog Foundation for the Blind Inc**
371 East Jericho Turnpike, Smithtown, NY 11787-2976
631-930-9000 or 800-548-4337  Fax: 631-930-9009
e-mail: info@guidedog.org
Web site: www.guidedog.org
*Provide guide dogs without charge to sight-impaired persons seeking enhanced mobility & independence*
Wells B Jones, Chief Executive Officer

**HeartShare Human Services of New York, Roman Catholic Diocese of Brooklyn**
12 MetroTech Center, 29th Floor, Brooklyn, NY 11201
718-422-HEART  Fax: 718-522-4506
e-mail: info@heartshare.org
Web site: www.heartshare.org
*Service for the developmentally disabled children & family services & programs for people with HIV/AIDS*
William R Guarinello, President & Chief Executive Officer

**Helen Keller Services for the Blind**
57 Willoughby Street, Brooklyn, NY 11201
718-522-2122  Fax: 718-935-9463
e-mail: info@helenkeller.org
Web site: www.helenkeller.org
*Preschool, rehabilitation, employment & senior services, low vision & braille library services*
Deborah Rodriguez-Samuelson, Director of Communications & Development

**Hispanic Federation**
55 Exchange Place, 5th Floor, New York, NY 10005
212-233-8955  Fax: 212-233-8996
Web site: www.hispanicfederation.org
*Technical assistance, capacity building, grantmaking & advocacy for Latino nonprofit service providers*
Lillian Rodriguez Lopez, President

**Hispanic Outreach Services**
40 North Main Ave, 5th Floor, Albany, NY 12010
518-453-6655  Fax: 518-641-6830
*Social service, youth guidance, language translation & immigration assistance programs*
Elaine Escobales, Executive Director

**Hospice & Palliative Care Association of NYS Inc**
2 Computer Drive West, Suite 105, Albany, NY 12205
518-446-1483  Fax: 518-446-1484
e-mail: info@hpcanys.org
Web site: www.hpcanys.org
*Hospice & palliative care information & referral service; educational programs; clinical, psychosocial & bereavement issues*
Kathy A McMahon, President & Chief Executive Officer

**Housing Works Inc**
57 Willoughby Street, Brooklyn, NY 11201
347-473-7400  Fax: 347-473-7464
Web site: www.housingworks.org
*Housing, health care, advocacy, job training & support services for homeless NY residents with HIV or AIDS*
Michael Kink, Statewide Advocacy Coordinator & Legislative Counsel

**Humane Society of the United States, New York State**
200 West 57th Street, Suite 705, New York, NY 10019
917-331-7187
Web site: www.humanesociety.org
*Promotes humane treatment of animals; abuse & violence prevention; animal rescue & disaster preparedness*
Brian Shapiro, State Director

**Hunger Action Network of NYS (HANNYS)**
275 State St, Albany, NY 12210
518-434-7371  Fax: 518-434-7390
e-mail: bhpham@hungeractionnys.org
Web site: www.hungeractionnys.org
*Developing unified efforts to address the root causes of hunger & promote social justice*
Bich Ha Pham, Executive Director

**Hunter College, Brookdale Center for Healthy Aging and Longevity**
425 E 25th St, New York, NY 10010
212-481-5420 or 212-481-4595  Fax: 212-481-3791
Web site: www.brookdale.org
*Policy research & development, training, publications & resources for institutions & community agencies*
Marianne Fahs, Executive Director

**Institute for Socio-Economic Studies**
10 New King St, White Plains, NY 10604
914-686-7112  Fax: 914-686-0581
*Welfare reform, socioeconomic incentives, tax & healthcare reform*
Leonard M Greene, President

**Japanese American Social Services Inc**
100 Gold St, Lower Level, New York, NY 10038
212-442-1541  Fax: 212-442-8627
e-mail: info@jassi.org
Web site: www.jassi.org
*Bilingual/bicultural programs; assistance with government benefits, housing, immigration & legal rights*
Margaret Fung, Executive Director

**Korean Community Services of Metropolitan NY**
149 West 24th St, 6th Fl, New York, NY 10011
212-463-9685  Fax: 212-463-8347
Web site: www.kcsny.org
*Develop & deliver social services to support & assist members of the Korean & neighboring communities*
Shin Son, Executive Director

**NYS Bar Assn, Children & the Law Committee**
**Law Office of Anne Reynolds Copps**
126 State St, 6th Fl, Albany, NY 12207
518-436-4170  Fax: 518-436-1456
e-mail: arcopps@nycap.rr.com
Anne Reynolds Copps, Chair

*Offices and agencies generally appear in alphabetical order, except when specific order is requested by listee.*

## Lesbian, Gay, Bisexual & Transgender Community Ctr - Not For Profit
208 W 13th Street, New York, NY 10011-7702
212-620-7310  Fax: 212-924-2657
Web site: www.gaycenter.org
*Mental health counseling, out-patient chemical dependency treatment center, after-school youth services, HIV/AIDS services, advocacy, cultural programs, affordable meeting and conference services, and community-building.*
Glennda Testone, Executive Director
Rob Wheeler, Director of Operations

## Little Flower Children & Family Services
186 Joralemon St, Brooklyn, NY 11201-4326
718-875-3500 ext3650 or 631-929-6200 ext1123  Fax: 718-260-8863
Web site: www.littleflowerny.org
*Foster care, adoption, child welfare, residential treatment services and residences for the developmentally disabled & day care; union free school district; corporate eldercare counseling services.*
Hon. Herbert W. Stupp, Chief Executive Officer

## Littman Krooks LLP
655 Third Ave, 20th Floor, New York, NY 10017
212-490-2020  Fax: 212-490-2990
e-mail: bkrooks@littmankrooks.com
Web site: www.littmankrooks.com
*Elder law and special needs planning*
Bernard A Krooks, Esq., Managing Partner
Nicole Garcia, Executive Assistant/Special Education Case Manager

## March of Dimes Birth Defects Foundation
1275 Mamaroneck Ave, White Plains, NY 10605
914-997-4641  Fax: 914-997-4662
e-mail: dstaples@marchofdimes.com
Web site: www.marchofdimes.com

## New York Association for New Americans, Inc (NYANA)
2 Washington St, 9th Fl, New York, NY 10004-1102
212-425-2900  Fax: 212-344-1621
*Social service referrals for immigrants*
Joseph Lazar, CEO

## NY Counseling Association Inc
PO Box 12636, Albany, NY 12212-2636
518-235-2026  Fax: 518-235-0910
Web site: www.nycounseling.org
*Counseling professionals in education, mental health, career, employment, rehabilitation & adult development*
Donald Newell, Executive Manager

## NY Foundation for Senior Citizens Inc
11 Park Place, 14th Fl, New York, NY 10007-2801
212-962-7559  Fax: 212-227-2952
e-mail: nyfscinc@aol.com
Web site: www.nyfsc.org
*Social services for seniors in New York City*
Linda Hoffman, President

## NYC Coalition Against Hunger
16 Beaver St, 3rd Fl, New York, NY 10004
212-825-0028  Fax: 212-825-0267
e-mail: jberg@nyccah.org
Web site: www.nyccah.org
Joel Berg, Executive Director

## NYS Association of Area Agencies on Aging
272 Broadway, Albany, NY 12204-2717
518-449-7080  Fax: 518-449-7055
*Agencies working to enhance effectiveness of programs for older persons*
Laura A Cameron, Executive Director

## NYS Corps Collaboration
24 Century Hill Drive, Ste 200, Latham, NY 12110
518-470-4995  Fax: 518-783-3577
*Statewide youth service & conservation corps addressing society's unmet needs & buiding self-esteem, a sense of civic responsibility & leadership skills*
Linda J Cohen, Executive Director

## NYS Industries for the Disabled (NYSID) Inc
11 Columbia Circle Drive, Albany, NY 12203
518-463-9706 or 800-221-5994  Fax: 518-463-9708
e-mail: administrator@nysid.org
Web site: www.nysid.org
*Business development through 'preferred source' purchasing to increase employment opportunities for people with disabilities*
Ronald P Romano, President & Chief Executive Officer

## National Association of Social Workers, NYS Chapter
188 Washington Ave, Albany, NY 12210-2304
518-463-4741 or 800-724-6279  Fax: 518-463-6446
Web site: www.naswnys.org
*Professional development & specialized training for professional social workers; standards for social work practice; advocacy for policies, services & programs that promote social justice*
Jacqueline Melecio, Assistant Executive Director

## National Council of Jewish Women
53 W 23rd St, 6th Fl, New York, NY 10010
212-645-4048  Fax: 212-645-7466
e-mail: action@ncjw.org
Web site: www.ncjw.org
*Human rights & social service advocacy & education*
Phyllis Snyder, President

## National Urban League Inc (The)
120 Wall St, New York, NY 10005
212-558-5300  Fax: 212-344-5332
e-mail: info@nul.org
Web site: www.nul.org
*Community-based movement devoted to empowering African Americans to enter the economic & social mainstream*
Michele M Moore, Senior Vice President Communications & Marketing

## Nelson A Rockefeller Inst of Govt, Federalism Research Grp
411 State St, Albany, NY 12203-1003
518-443-5522  Fax: 518-443-5788
e-mail: gaist@rockinst.org
Web site: www.rockinst.org
*State management systems for social service programs*
Thomas L Gais, Co-Director

## New York Association of Homes & Services for the Aging
150 State St, Ste 301, Albany, NY 12207-1698
518-449-2707  Fax: 518-455-8908
e-mail: cyoung@nyahsa.org
*Long term care*
Carl Young, President

## New York Community Trust (The)
909 Third Avenue, 22nd Fl, New York, NY 10022
212-686-0010  Fax: 212-532-8528
Web site: www.nycommunitytrust.org
*Administrators of philanthropic funds*
Lorie A Slutsky, President/Director

---

*Offices and agencies generally appear in alphabetical order, except when specific order is requested by listee.*

**New York Public Welfare Association**
130 Washington Ave, Albany, NY 12210
518-465-9305  Fax: 518-465-5633
e-mail: nypwa@nycap.rr.com
Web site: www.nypwa.com
*Partnership of local social services districts dedicated to improve the quality & effectiveness of social welfare policy*
Sheila Harrigan, Executive Director

**New York Society for the Deaf**
161 William St, 11th Fl, New York, NY 10038
646-278-8172 or TTY: 646-278-8171  Fax: 212-777-5740
*Ensure full & equal access to appropriate, comprehensive clinical, residential & support services for deaf & deaf-blind persons*
Kathleen Cox, Executive Director

**New York State Association of Family Service Agencies Inc**
29 North Hamilton Street, Suite 112, Poughkeepsie, NY 12601
845-790-5900  Fax: 845-790-5922
e-mail: info@nysafsa.org
Web site: www.nysafsa.org
*Provides a forum for the exchange of information on issues relevant to children and families.*
Allan Thomas, Executive Director

**New York State Catholic Conference**
465 State St, Albany, NY 12203-1004
518-434-6195  Fax: 518-434-9796
e-mail: info@nyscatholic.org
Web site: www.nyscatholic.org
*Identify, formulate & implement public policy objectives of the NYS Bishops in health, education, welfare, human & civil rights*
Richard E Barnes, Executive Director

**New York State Citizens' Coalition for Children Inc**
410 East Upland Road, Ithaca, NY 14850-2551
607-272-0034  Fax: 607-272-0035
Web site: www.nysccc.org
*Adoption & foster care advocacy*
Judith Ashton, Executive Director

**New York State Community Action Association**
2 Charles Blvd, Guilderland, NY 12084
518-690-0491  Fax: 518-690-0498
*Dedicated to the growth & education of community action agencies in NYS to sustain their efforts in advocating & improving the lives of low-income New Yorkers*
Daniel Maskin, Chief Executive Officer

**New York State Rehabilitation Association**
155 Washington Ave, Suite 410, Albany, NY 12210
518-449-2976  Fax: 518-426-4329
Web site: www.nyrehab.org
*Political advocacy, education, communications, networking & referral services for people with disabilities*
Jeff Wise, JD, President

**New York Urban League**
204 W 136th St, New York, NY 10030
212-926-8000  Fax: 212-283-2736
Web site: www.nyul.org
*Social services, job training, education & advocacy*
Darwin M Davis, President & Chief Executive Officer

**Nonprofit Coordinating Committee of New York**
1350 Broadway, Rm 1801, New York, NY 10018-7802
212-502-4191  Fax: 212-502-4189
Web site: www.npccny.org
*Advocacy & government activities monitoring for NYC nonprofits*
Michael Clark, Executive Director/President

**North Shore Animal League America**
25 Lewyt Street, Port Washington, NY 11050
516-883-7900 x257  Fax: 516-944-5732
e-mail: webmaster@nsalamerica.org
Web site: www.nsalamerica.org
*Rescue, care & adoption services for orphaned companion animals*
Perry Fina, Director, Marketing

**Planned Parenthood of NYC, Inc**
26 Bleecker St, New York, NY 10012
212-274-7292  Fax: 212-274-7276
e-mail: carla.goldstein@ppnyc.org
Web site: www.ppnyc.org
Carla Goldstein, Vice President, Public Affairs

**Prevent Child Abuse New York**
33 Elk Street, 2nd Floor, Albany, NY 12207
518-445-1273 or 800-CHILDREN  Fax: 518-436-5889
e-mail: info@preventchildabuseny.org
Web site: www.preventchildabuseny.org
*Child abuse prevention advocacy, education, technical assistance*
Christine Deyss, Executive Director

**ProLiteracy Worldwide**
1320 Jamesville Ave, Syracuse, NY 13210-4224
315-422-9121  Fax: 315-422-6369
e-mail: info@proliteracy.org
Web site: www.proliteracy.org
*Sponsors educational programs & services to empower adults & families through the acquisition of literacy skills & practices*
Rochelle A Cassella, Director, Corporate Communications

**Public/Private Ventures**
The Chanin Building, 122 East 42nd St, 42nd Fl, New York, NY 10168
212-822-2400  Fax: 212-949-0439
*A national nonprofit, nonpartisan organization that tackles critical challenges facing low-income communities by seeking out and designing innovatove programs, rigorously testing them, and promoting the solutions proven to work.*
Sheila Maguire, VP, Labor Market Initiatives

**Resource Center for Independent Living (RCIL)**
401-409 Columbia St, PO Box 210, Utica, NY 13503-0210
315-797-4642 or TTY 315-797-5837  Fax: 315-797-4747
Web site: www.rcil.com
*Services & advocacy for the disabled; public information & community education and awareness.*
Burt Danovitz, Executive Director

**Roman Catholic Diocese of Albany, Catholic Charities**
40 N Main Ave, Albany, NY 12203
518-453-6650  Fax: 518-453-6792
Web site: www.ccrcda.org
*Social & human services assistance: housing, shelters, day care, counseling, transportation, health & emergency*
Sister Maureen Joyce, Chief Executive Officer

**Rural & Migrant Ministry Inc**
PO Box 4757, Poughkeepsie, NY 12602
845-485-8627  Fax: 845-485-1963
e-mail: hope@ruralmigrantministry.org
Web site: www.ruralmigrantministry.org
*Working to end poverty & increase self-determination, education & economic resources for migrant farmworkers & the rural poor*
Richard Witt, Executive Director

**PathStone Corporation**
400 East Ave, Rochester, NY 14607
585-340-3300 or 800-888-6770
Web site: www.pathstone.org
*Advance self-sufficiency of farm workers, low-income & other disenfranchised people & communities through advocacy & programs*

*Offices and agencies generally appear in alphabetical order, except when specific order is requested by listee.*

*including training & employment, housing child development, health & safety, & home ownership*
Jeffrey Lewis, Sr Vice President of Direct Services

### Salvation Army, Empire State Division
PO Box 148, Syracuse, NY 13206-0148
315-434-1300 x310  Fax: 315-434-1399
Web site: www.salvationarmy.org
Donald Lance, Divisional Commander

### Springbrook NY, Inc
2705 State Highway 28, Oneonta, NY 13820
607-286-7171  Fax: 607-286-7166
Web site: www.springbrookny.org
Patricia E Kennedy, Executive Director

### Center for Policy Research
### Syracuse University, Maxwell School of Citizenship & Public Affairs
200 Eggers Hall, Syracuse, NY 13244-1020
315-443-3114  Fax: 315-443-1081
e-mail: ctrpol@syr.edu
Web site: www.maxwell.syr.edu
*Education, healthcare, entrepreneurship policies, social welfare, income distribution & comparative social policies*
Christine L Himes, Professor of Sociology, Director

### United Jewish Appeal-Federation of Jewish Philanthropies of NY
130 East 59th Street, New York, NY 10022
212-980-1000  Fax: 518-463-1266
e-mail: contact@ujafedny.org
Web site: www.ujafedny.org
*Cares for those in need, rescues those in harm's way, and renews and strengthens the Jewish people in New York, in Israel , and around the world.*
Jerry Levin, President

### United Neighborhood Houses - Not For Profit
70 W 36th St, 5th Fl, New York, NY 10018
212-967-0322  Fax: 212-967-0792
e-mail: nwackstein@unhny.org
Web site: www.unhny.org
*Federation of NYC settlement houses that provides issue advocacy & management assistance for member agencies' social, educational & cultural programs*
Nancy Wackstein, Executive Director

### United Way of Central New York
518 James St, PO Box 2129, Syracuse, NY 13220-2227
315-428-2216
e-mail: ccollie@unitedway-cny.org
Web site: www.unitedway-cny.org
*Fundraising & support to human & social services organizations*
Craig E Collie, Vice President, Volunteer Resource Development

### United Way of New York City
2 Park Ave, New York, NY 10016
212-251-2500  Fax: 212-696-1220
Web site: www.unitedwaynyc.org
*Works with partners from all sectors to create, support, & execute strategic initiatives that seek to achieve measurable improvement in the lives of the city's most valuable residents and communities*
Lawrence Mandell, President & Chief Executive Officer

### Upstate Homes for Children & Adults Inc
2705 State Hwy 28, Oneonta, NY 13820
607-286-7171  Fax: 607-286-7166
*Education/mental hygiene*
Patricia E Kennedy, Executive Director

### Welfare Research Inc
112 State St, Suite 1340, Albany, NY 12207
518-432-2563  Fax: 518-432-2564
Web site: www.welfareresearch.org
*Contract research in social service & related policy areas*
Virginia Hayes Sibbison, Executive Director

### World Hunger Year Inc
505 Eighth Ave, Suite 2100, New York, NY 10018-6582
212-629-8850  Fax: 212-465-9274
Web site: www.worldhungeryear.org
*Addresses root causes of hunger & poverty by promoting effective & innovative community-based solutions*
Bill Ayres, Executive Director

### YAI/National Institute for People with Disabilities
460 W 34th St, New York, NY 10001-2382
212-273-6110 or 866-2-YAI-LINK  Fax: 212-947-7524
Web site: www.yai.org
*Programs, services & advocacy for people with autism, mental retardation & other developmental disabilities of all ages, and their families; special education & early learning programs*
Joel M Levy, Chief Executive Officer

*Offices and agencies generally appear in alphabetical order, except when specific order is requested by listee.*

# TAXATION & REVENUE

## NEW YORK STATE

## GOVERNOR'S OFFICE

### Governor's Office
Executive Chamber
State Capitol
Albany, NY 12224
518-474-8390  Fax: 518-474-1513
Web site: www.ny.gov

Governor:
   Andrew M Cuomo . . . . . . . . . . . . . . . . . . . . . . . . . . . . . .518-474-8390
Secretary to the Governor:
   Melissa DeRosa . . . . . . . . . . . . . . . . . . .518-474-4246 or 212-681-4580
Counsel to the Governor:
   Kumiki Gibson . . . . . . . . . . . . . . . . . . . . .518-474-8343 or 212-681-4580
Chief of Staff:
   Jill DesRosiers . . . . . . . . . . . . . . . . . . . . .518-474-8390 or 212-681-4580
Director, Communications:
   Peter Ajemian . . . . . . . . . . . . . . . . . . . . . .518-474-8418 or 212-681-4640

## EXECUTIVE DEPARTMENTS AND RELATED AGENCIES

### New York State Liquor Authority (Division of Alcoholic Beverage Control)
80 South Swan Street
Suite 900
Albany, NY 12210-8002
518-474-3114
Web site: www.sla.ny.gov

317 Lenox Avenue
New York, NY 10027
Fax:

535 Washington Street
Suite 303
Buffalo, NY 14203
518-474-3114
Fax: 716-847-3435

Chairman:
   Vincent G Bradley . . . . . . . . . . . . . . . . . .212-961-8300 or 518-474-3114
Commissioner:
   Greeley T Ford . . . . . . . . . . . . . . . . . . . . .212-961-8300 or 518-474-3114
Counsel to the Authority:
   Vacant . . . . . . . . . . . . . . . . . . . . . . . . . . . . . . . . . . . .518-474-3114

### Administration
Secretary to the Authority:
   Thomas Donohue . . . . . . . . . . . . . . . . . . . . . . . . . . . .518-474-3114
   e-mail: Thomas.Donohue@sla.ny.gov
Deputy Commissioner, Administration:
   Chad Loshbaugh . . . . . . . . . . . . . . . . . . . . . . . . . . . . .518-473-0365
Director, Public Affairs:
   William Crowley . . . . . . . . . . . . .518-474-3114 or 518-474-4875
   fax: 518-473-9565
   e-mail: William.Crowley@sla.ny.gov

### Licensing & Enforcement

#### Albany (Zone II)
80 S Swan St, Ste 900, Albany, NY 12210-8002

Director, Enforcement:
   Joseph Finelli . . . . . . . . . . . . . . . . . . . . . . . . . . . . .518-474-3114
   e-mail: Joseph.Finelli@sla.ny.gov
Deputy Counsel:
   Lisa Ogden . . . . . . . . . . . . . . . . . . . . . . . . . . . . . . . .518-474-3114
   e-mail: Lisa.Ogden@sla.ny.gov

#### Buffalo (Zone III)
Iskalo Electric Tower, 535 Washington St, Ste 303, Buffalo, NY 14203
716-847-3035
Deputy Commissioner, Licensing:
   David L Edmunds Jr . . . . . . . . . . . . . . . . . . . . . . . . . . .716-847-3001
Supervising Beverage Control Investigator:
   Gary Bartikofsky . . . . . . . . . . . . . . . . . . . . . . . . . . . .716-847-3035

#### New York City (Zone I)
317 Lenox Avenue, New York, NY 10027
212-961-8385
Supervising Beverage Control Investigator:
   Franklin Englander . . . . . . . . . . . . . . . . . . . . . . . . . . .212-961-8376
Deputy Chief Executive Officer:
   Michael Jones . . . . . . . . . . . . . . . . . . . . . . . . . . . . . . .212-961-8300

### Budget, Division of the
State Capitol
Room 128
Albany, NY 12224-0341
518-474-2300
e-mail: dob.sm.press@budget.ny.gov
Web site: www.budget.ny.gov

Director:
   Robert F. Mujica . . . . . . . . . . . . . . . . . . . . . . . . . . . . .518-474-2300
Deputy Director:
   Sandra Beattie . . . . . . . . . . . . . . . . . . . . . . . . . . . . . . .518-474-2300
Deputy Director:
   Charles Williams . . . . . . . . . . . . . . . . . . . . . . . . . . . . .518-474-2300
Press Officer:
   Morris Peters . . . . . . . . . . . . . . . . . . . . . . . . . . . . . . . .518-473-3885
   e-mail: dob.sm.press@budget.ny.gov

### Law Department
28 Liberty Street
New York, NY 10005
212-416-8000 or 800-771-7755
Web site: www.ag.ny.gov

State Capitol
Albany, NY 12224-0341
518-776-2000
Fax: 518-650-9401

Attorney General:
   Letitia James . . . . . . . . . . . . . . . . . . . . . . .212-416-8000 or 518-776-2000

### Social Justice
Executive Deputy Attorney General:
   Vacant . . . . . . . . . . . . . . . . . . . . . . . . . .212-416-8075/fax: 212-416-8942

#### Charities Bureau
Bureau Chief:
   James G Sheehan . . . . . . . . . . . . . . . . . . . . . . . . . . . .212-416-8410

### Economic Justice
Executive Deputy Attorney General:
   Siobhan Kennedy . . . . . . . . . . . . . . . . . . . . . . . . . . . .212-416-8050

#### Internet Bureau
Bureau Chief:
   Kathleen McGee . . . . . . . . . . . . . . . .212-416-8433/fax: 212-416-8369

Policy Areas

*Offices and agencies generally appear in alphabetical order, except when specific order is requested by listee.*

**Investor Protection Bureau**
Bureau Chief:
Chad Johnson ...................212-416-8225/fax: 212-416-8816

## State Counsel

**Civil Recoveries Bureau**
Bureau Chief:
John Cremo.....................518-776-2173/fax: 518-915-7731

**Litigation Bureau**
Bureau Chief:
Jeffrey Dvorin ..................518-776-2300 or 212-416-8610

## New York State Gaming Commission

1 Broadway Center
P.O. Box 7500
Schenectady, NY 12301-7500
518-388-3300
e-mail: info@gaming.ny.gov
Web site: www.gaming.ny.gov

Executive Director:
Robert Williams ...............................518-388-3400
General Counsel:
Edmund Burns ................................518-388-3408
Director, Lottery Division:
Gweneth Dean................................518-388-3352
Director, Communications:
Brad Maione ..................................518-388-3415
Director, Marketing:
Daniel J Martin ...................518-388-3430/fax: 518-388-3433

## Regional Offices

**Eastern Region**
One Broadway Center, Suite 700, Schenectady, NY 12301
Contact:
Fred Chick.....................518-388-3428/fax: 518-388-3437

**Central/Finger Lakes Regions**
*Rochester Office*
First Federal Plaza Bldg, 28 E Main St, Rochester, NY 14614
Contact:
Vacant.....................585-246-4200/fax: 585-246-4201
*Syracuse Office*
Deys Centennial Bldg, 401 S Salina St, Syracuse, NY 13202
Contact:
Robin Sywulski .............315-448-4300/fax: 315-448-4313

**Hudson Valley Region**
18 Westage Drive, Ste 6, Fishkill, NY 12524
Contact:
Georgene Perlman...............845-897-2412/fax: 845-897-3528

**Long Island Region**
1000 Zeckendorf Blvd, Garden City, NY 11530
Contact:
Jim Benoit.....................516-222-8260/fax: 516-222-8279

**New York City Region**
15 Beaver St, New York, NY 10004
Contact:
Thomas Breig .................646-486-6100/fax: 646-486-6177

**Western Region**
165 Genesse St, Buffalo, NY 14203
Contact:
Doug Bautz.....................716-847-3469/fax: 716-847-3479

**Gaming Commission**
Executive Director:
Robert Williams................................518-388-3400

Director, Communications:
Brad Maione .................................518-388-3415

## Real Property Tax Services, Office of

NYS Dept of Tax & Finance
WA Harriman State Campus
Building 8A
Albany, NY 12227
518-457-7377 or 518-591-5232
Web site; www.tax.ny.gov/about/orpts/albany.htm

Director:
Tim Maher ......................518-530-4081 or 518-474-2982
Secretary of the Board & Assistant Deputy Commissioner:
Vacant
State Board Member (Chair):
Matthew Rand....................................518-474-3793
State Board Member:
Scott C Becker ................518-474-3793 or 518-591-5232
State Board Member:
Samuel J Casella...................518-474-3793 or 518-591-5232

**Albany (Northern Region)**
WA Harriman State Campus, Bldg. 8A, Albany, NY 12227
Regional Director:
Tim Maher...................518-486-4403/fax: 518-435-8593
e-mail: orpts.northern@tax.ny.gov

**Batavia (Western Region)**
Genesee County Bldg 2, 3837 W Main Street, Batavia, NY 14020
Regional Director:
Christine Bannister ...........585-343-4363/fax: 585-435-8598
e-mail: orpts.western@tax.ny.gov

**Long Island Satellite Office**
250 Veterans Memorial Hgwy, Rm 4A-6, Hauppauge, NY 11788
Manager:
Steve Hartnett ...................631-595-4071/fax: 518-435-8572
e-mail: orpts.southern@tax.ny.gov

**South Region (White Plains)**
44 S. Broadway, 6th Floor, White Plains, NY 10601
Regional Director:
John Wolham ..................914-215-6300/fax: 518-435-8498
e-mail: orpts.southern@tax.ny.gov

**Ray Brook Satellite Office**
884 NYS Rte 86, PO Box 309, Ray Brook, NY 12977
Regional Director:
Tim Maher.....................518-891-1780/fax: 518-435-8593
e-mail: orpts.raybrook@tax.ny.gov

**Syracuse (Central Region)**
333 E. Washington Street, Syracuse, NY 13202
Regional Director:
Christine Bannister ..............315-471-2347/fax: 518-435-8583
e-mail: orpts.central@tax.ny.gov

## Tax Appeals, Division of

Agency Building 1
Empire State Plaza
Albany, NY 12223
518-266-3000 Fax: 518-271-0886
e-mail: dta@dta.ny.gov
Web site: www.dta.ny.gov

**Tax Appeals Tribunal**
President & Commissioner:
Roberta Moseley Nero ............................518-266-3050
Commissioner:
Anthony Giardina ................................518-266-3050

*Offices and agencies generally appear in alphabetical order, except when specific order is requested by listee.*

Commissioner:
  Deirdre K Scozzafava.............................518-266-3050
Counsel:
  Timothy J Alston.................................518-266-3052
Secretary to the Tribunal:
  Jean A McDonnell ...............................518-266-3036

## Administrative Law Judges & Officers
Supervising Administrative Law Judge:
  Herbert M Friedman, Jr..........................518-266-3000
Presiding Officer:
  Vacant..........................................518-266-3000

## Taxation & Finance Department
W.A. Harriman Campus
Building 9
Albany, NY 12227
518-457-4242 or 518-457-2244  Fax: 518-457-2486
Web site: www.tax.ny.gov

Commissioner:
  Vacant..........................................518-457-2244
Executive Deputy Commissioner:
  Nonie Manion...............518-530-4444 or 518-530-5000
Deputy Commissioner & Counsel:
  Amanda Hiller.............518-457-3746 or 518-530-5300
  fax: 518-457-8247
Director, Conciliation & Mediation Services:
  Robert Farrelly ................................518-485-8063
Director, Executive Correspondence & Legislative Affairs:
  Maryann Tucker ................................518-457-2398
Director, Public Information:
  Geoffrey Gloak .................................518-457-7377

## Office of Processing & Taxpayer Services (OPTS)
Deputy Commissioner:
  Edward Chaszczewski ...........................518-530-5320

### Human Resources Management
Director:
  Valerie DeBerry ................................518-457-2786

## Office of Budget & Management Analysis
Chief Fiscal Officer:
  Eric Mostert ...............518-485-5080 or 518-530-4000
  Chief Fiscal Officer:
  Eric Mostert ...............518-485-5080 or 518-530-4000

### Planning & Management Analysis Bureau
Director:
  Mary Ellen Nagengast ..........................518-457-8660

## Office of Processing & Taxpayer Services
Director:
  Edward Chaszczewski ...........................518-530-5320

## Office of State Treasury
Deputy Commissioner & State Treasurer:
  Christopher Curtis ................518-474-4250/fax: 518-402-4118

## Office of Criminal Enforcement
Deputy Commissioner:
  Argi O'Leary...................................518-599-6517

### Audit Division
Director:
  Joe Carzo ......................................518-451-8910

### Collections & Civil Enforcement
Deputy Commissioner:
  Argi O'Leary ..................................518-591-1980

## Office of Tax Policy Analysis
Deputy Commissioner:
  Robert D Plattner ..................518-457-4357 or 518-530-5344

## CORPORATIONS, AUTHORITIES AND COMMISSIONS

### New York State Financial Control Board
123 William St
23rd Fl
New York, NY 10038-3804
212-417-5046  Fax: 212-417-5055
e-mail: nysfcb@fcb.state.ny.us
Web site: www.fcb.state.ny.us

Acting Executive Director:
  Jeffrey Sommer.................................212-417-5066
Deputy Director, Expenditure & Covered Organization Analysis:
  Dennis DeLisle.................................212-417-5069
Deputy Director, Finance & Capital Analysis:
  Jewel A. Douglas
Acting Deputy Director, Economic & Revenue Analysis:
  Martin Fischman ...............................212-417-5068
Associate Director, Administration:
  Mattie W Taylor ...............................212-417-5053

## NEW YORK STATE LEGISLATURE

*See Legislative Branch in Section 1 for additional Standing Committee and Subcommittee information.*

## Assembly Standing Committees

### Racing & Wagering
Chair:
  J Gary Pretlow (D)..............518-455-5291/fax: 518-455-5447

### Real Property Taxation
Chair:
  Sandy Galef (D) ................................518-455-5348

### Ways & Means
Chair:
  Helene E Weinstein (D) .........................518-455-5462

## Senate Standing Committees

### Finance
Chair:
  Liz Krueger (D, WF)............................518-455-2297
Ranking Minority Member:
  Thomas F O'Mara (R, C, IP)

### Racing, Gaming & Wagering
Chair:
  Joseph P Addabbo, Jr (D).......................518-455-2322
Ranking Minority Member:
  Daphne Jordan (R, C, IP, RFM)..................518-455-2381

## U.S. GOVERNMENT

## EXECUTIVE DEPARTMENTS AND RELATED AGENCIES

### US Department of Homeland Security (DHS)
Web site: www.dhs.gov

### Bureau of Immigration & Customs Enforcement (ICE)
Web site: www.ice.gov

*Offices and agencies generally appear in alphabetical order, except when specific order is requested by listee.*

## New York District Office
601 W 26th St, Ste 700, New York, NY 10001
Special Agent-in-Charge:
Andrew M. McLees . . . . . . . . . . . . . . . . . . . . . . . . . . 646-230-3200
### Albany Sub Office
1 Clinton Avenue, #746, Albany, NY 12207-2354
Group Supervisor:
LeRoy Tario . . . . . . . . . . . . . . . . . . . . . . . . . . . 518-220-2100
Resident Agent-in-Charge:
Jack McQuade . . . . . . . . . . . . . . . . . . . . . . . . . . 518-220-2100

## Customs & Border Protection (CBP)
202-354-1000
Web site: www.cbp.gov

### Buffalo Field Office
300 Airborne Parkway, Suite 300, Buffalo, NY 14225
716-626-0400
Director:
James T. Engelman . . . . . . . . . . 716-626-0400 x201/fax: 716-626-9281
#### Albany, Port of
445 Broadway, Room 216, Albany, NY 12207
518-431-0200
Port Director:
Drew Wescott . . . . . . . . . . . . . . 518-431-0200/fax: 518-431-0203
#### Buffalo, Port of
Larkin at Exchange, 726 Exchange, Suite 400, Buffalo, NY 14210
716-843-8300
Area Port Director:
Joseph Wilson . . . . . . . . . . . . . . . . . . . . . . . . . . 716-843-8300
#### Champlain, Port of . . . . . . . . . . . . . . . . . . . . . . . . fax: 518-298-8395
237 W Service Rd, Champlain, NY 12919
518-298-8311 Fax: 518-298-8395
Area Port Director:
Christopher Perry . . . . . . . . . . . 518-298-8347/fax: 518-298-8314
#### Ogdensburg, Port of
104 Bridge Approach Rd, Ogdensburg, NY 13669
Port Director:
William Mitchell . . . . . . . . . . . 315-393-1390/fax: 315-393-7472

### New York Field Office . . . . . . . . . . . . . . . . . . . . . . fax: 646-733-3245
1 Penn Plaza, 11th Fl, New York, NY 10119
646-733-3100 Fax: 646-733-3245
Director, Field Operations:
Susan T Mitchell . . . . . . . . . . . . . . . . . . . . . . . . . . 646-733-3100
Public Affairs Liaison:
John Saleh . . . . . . . . . . . . . . . . . . . . . . . . . . . . . . . 646-733-3215
#### Field Counsel - New York
Director, New York Field Operations:
Robert Perez . . . . . . . . . . . . . . . . . . . . . . . . . . . . 646-733-3200
#### Laboratory Division
Director:
Tom Governo . . . . . . . . . . . . . . . . . . . . . . . . . . . . 973-368-1901

## US Justice Department
Web site: www.usdoj.gov

## Bureau of Alcohol, Tobacco, Firearms & Explosives
Web site: www.atf.gov

### New York Field Division . . . . . . . . . . . . . . . . . . . . . fax: 646-335-9061
Financial Square, 32 Old Slip, Suite 3500, New York, NY 10005
646-335-9060 Fax: 646-335-9061
Special Agent-in-Charge:
Delano Reid . . . . . . . . . . . . . . . . . . . . . . . . . . . . . 646-335-9060
Public Information Officer:
Charles Mulham . . . . . . . . . . . . . . . . . . . . . . . . . . 646-335-9000

## US Treasury Department
Web site: www.treasury.gov

## Internal Revenue Service
Web site: www.irs.gov

### Appeals Unit - Office of Directors
290 Broadway, 13th Fl, New York, NY 10007
Director, Appeals, Area 1 (Large Business & Specialty):
Richard Guevara . . . . . . . . . . . . . 212-298-2270/fax: 212-298-2282
Director, Appeals, Area 1 (General):
Raymond Wolff . . . . . . . . . . . . . . . 212-298-2400/fax: 212-298-2648

### Criminal Investigation Unit - New York Field Office
Spec Agent-in-Chg:
Toni Weirauch

### Large & Mid-Size Business Division (LMSB)
290 Broadway, 12th Fl, New York, NY 10007
Director, Financial Services:
Rosemary Sereti . . . . . . . . . . . . . 212-298-2130/fax: 212-298-2124
#### Office of Chief Counsel LMSB Area 1 . . . . . . . . . . fax: 917-421-3937
33 Maiden Ln, 12th Fl, New York, NY 10038
Area Counsel:
Roland Barral . . . . . . . . . . . . . . . . . . . . . . . . . . 917-421-4667
Deputy Area Counsel:
Peter J Graziano . . . . . . . . . . . . . . . . . . . . . . . . 917-421-4632

### Management Information Technology Services - Northeast Area
290 Broadway, 12th Fl, New York, NY 10007
Director, Information Technology:
Vacant . . . . . . . . . . . . . . . . . . . . . . . 212-298-2050/fax: 212-298-2595

### Office of Chief Counsel
33 Maiden Ln, 14th Fl, New York, NY 10038
Area Counsel for SBSE & W & I:
Frances Regan . . . . . . . . . . . . . . . . . . 917-421-4737/fax: 917-421-3944
Associate Area Counsel for SBSE & W & I:
Janet F Appel . . . . . . . . . . . . . . . . . . . . . . . . . . . . . 516-688-1707

### Small Business & Self-Employed Division (SBSE)
#### New York SBSE Compliance Services
290 Broadway, 14th Fl, New York, NY 10007
Program Manager, Compliance Centers Document Matching
Programs:
Shirley Greene . . . . . . . . . . . . . 212-298-2001/fax: 212-298-2062
#### SBSE-Compliance Area 2/New York
290 Broadway, 7th Fl, New York, NY 10007
Director, Compliance Area 2:
Michael Donovan . . . . . . . . . . . 212-436-1886/fax: 212-436-1046
#### SBSE-Taxpayer Education & Communication (TEC)
10 Metro Tech Center, 625 Fulton St, 6th Fl, Brooklyn, NY 11201
Area Director:
Ellen Murphy . . . . . . . . . . . . . . 718-488-2000/fax: 718-488-2077

### Tax Exempt & Government Entities Div (TEGE)-Northeast Area
10 Metro Tech Center, 625 Fulton St, PO Box 029162, Brooklyn, NY 11201
Area Manager, Employee Plans:
Robert Henn . . . . . . . . . . . . . . . . . . . . . . . . . . . . . . 718-488-2014
#### TEGE Area Counsel's Office
1600 Stewart Ave, Ste 601, Westbury, NY 11590
Area Counsel:
Laurence Ziegler . . . . . . . . . . . . 516-688-1701/fax: 516-688-1750

### Taxpayer Advocate Service (TAS)
#### Andover Campus Service Center
310 Lowell St, Stop 120, Andover, MA 1812
Taxpayer Advocate for Upstate NY:
Vicki L Coss . . . . . . . . . . . . . . . 973-474-5549/fax: 978-247-9034
#### Brookhaven Campus Service Center
1040 Waverly Ave, Stop 02, Holtsville, NY 11742
Taxpayer Advocate for Downstate NY:
Ed Safrey . . . . . . . . . . . . . . . . . 631-654-6686/fax: 631-447-4879

*Offices and agencies generally appear in alphabetical order, except when specific order is requested by listee.*

*Brooklyn Office*
2 Metro Tech Center, 100 Myrtle Avenue, 7th Floor, Brooklyn, NY 11201
Taxpayer Advocate:
Anita Kitson . . . . . . . . . . . . . . 718-834-2200/fax: 718-834-6545
*Manhattan Office*
290 Broadway, 5th Fl, New York, NY 10007
Taxpayer Advocate:
Peter L Gorga, Jr. . . . . . . . . . . . 212-436-1011/fax: 212-436-1900
*Office of Director, Area 1 (New York State & New England)*
290 Broadway, 14th Fl, New York, NY 10007
Area Director:
Mary Ann Silvaggio . . . . . . . . . 212-298-2015/fax: 212-298-2016
*Upstate New York Office*
Leo O'Brien Federal Bldg, Rm 354, 1 Clinton Sq, Albany, NY 12207
Taxpayer Advocate:
Georgeann Smith . . . . . . . . . . . 518-427-5413/fax: 518-427-5494
*Western New York State Office*
201 Como Park Blvd, Buffalo, NY 14227-1416
Taxpayer Advocate:
William Wirth . . . . . . . . . . . . . . 716-686-4850/fax: 716-686-4851

**Wage & Investmnt Div-Stakehldr Partnership Ed & Comm (SPEC)**
*Albany Territory*
1 Clinton Ave, Rm 600, Albany, NY 12207
Territory Manager:
Amy Albee . . . . . . . . . . . . . . . . . . . . . . . . . . . . 518-427-5424
*Area 1 Director's Office*
135 High St, Hartford, CT 06103
Area Director:
Robert Nadeau . . . . . . . . . . . . . . . . . . . . . . . . . 860-756-4566
*Buffalo Territory*
201 Como Park Blvd, Cheektowaga, NY 14227
Territory Manager:
Rick Pearl . . . . . . . . . . . . . . . . . . . . . . . . . . . . . 716-961-5123
*New York Territory*
290 Broadway, 7th Fl, New York, NY 10007
Territory Mgr:
Susan Quackenbush . . . . . . . . . . . . . . . . . . . . . 212-436-1517

**US Mint** . . . . . . . . . . . . . . . . . . . . . . . . . . . . . fax: 845-446-6258
Rte 218, PO Box 37, West Point, NY 10996
Fax: 845-446-6258
Web site: www.usmint.gov
Plant Manager:
David Motl . . . . . . . . . . . . . . . . . . . . . . . . . . . . . 800-872-6468

## U.S. CONGRESS

*See U.S. Congress Chapter for additional Standing Committee and Subcommittee information.*

## House of Representatives Standing Committees

### Appropriations
Chair:
Harold Rogers (R-KY) . . . . . . . . . . . . . . . . . . . . . 202-225-4601
Ranking Member:
Nita M. Lowey (D-NY) . . . . . . . . . . . . . . . . . . . . . 202-225-6506
New York Delegate:
Bill Owens (D) . . . . . . . . . . . . . . . . . . . . . . . . . . 202-225-4611
New York Delegate:
Jose E Serrano (D) . . . . . . . . . . . . . . . . . . . . . . . 202-225-4361

### Budget
Chair:
Paul Ryan (R-WI) . . . . . . . . . . . . . . . . . . . . . . . . 202-225-4601
Ranking Member:
Chris Van Hollen (D-MD) . . . . . . . . . . . . . . . . . . 202-225-5341

New York Delegate:
Hakeem Jeffries (D) . . . . . . . . . . . . . . . . . . . . . . 202-225-5936

### Ways & Means
Chair:
Dave Camp (R-MI) . . . . . . . . . . . . . . . . . . . . . . . 202-225-3561
Ranking Member:
Sander Levin (D-MI) . . . . . . . . . . . . . . . . . . . . . . 202-225-3880
New York Delegate:
Joseph Crowley (D) . . . . . . . . . . . . . . . . . . . . . . 202-225-3965
New York Delegate:
Tom Reed (R) . . . . . . . . . . . . . . . . . . . . . . . . . . 202-225-3161
New York Delegate:
Charles B. Rangel (D). . . . . . . . . . . . . . . . . . . . . 202-225-4365

## Joint Senate & House Standing Committees

### Joint Committee on Taxation
Chair:
Dave Camp (R-MI) . . . . . . . . . . . . . . . . . . . . . . . 202-224-3561
Vice Chair:
Max Baucus (D-MT) . . . . . . . . . . . . . . . . . . . . . . 202-225-2651

## Senate Standing Committees

### Appropriations
Chair:
Barbara A. Mikulski (D-MD) . . . . . . . . . . . . . . . . . 202-224-4654
Vice Chair:
Richard C. Shelby (R-AL) . . . . . . . . . . . . . . . . . . 202-224-5744

### Budget
Chair:
Patty Murray (D-WA) . . . . . . . . . . . . . . . . . . . . . . 202-224-2621
Ranking Member:
Jeff Sessions (R-AL). . . . . . . . . . . . . . . . . . . . . . 202-224-4124

### Finance
Chair:
Max Baucus (R-MT) . . . . . . . . . . . . . . . . . . . . . . 202-224-2651
Ranking Member:
Orrin G. Hatch (R-UT) . . . . . . . . . . . . . . . . . . . . . 202-224-5251

#### Subcommittee
*Taxation & IRS Oversight*
Chair:
Michael F. Bennet (D-CO) . . . . . . . . . . . . . . . . 202-224-5852
Ranking Member:
Michael B. Enzi (R-WY) . . . . . . . . . . . . . . . . . . 202-224-3424

### Homeland Security & Governmental Affairs
Chair:
Thomas R. Carper (D-DE) . . . . . . . . . . . . . . . . . . 202-224-2441
Ranking Member:
Tom Coburn (R-OK) . . . . . . . . . . . . . . . . . . . . . . 202-224-5754

## PRIVATE SECTOR

**NYS Bar Assn, Pension Simplification Cmte**
**Alvin D Lurie PC**
13 Country Club Drive, Larchmont, NY 10538
914-834-6725  Fax: 914-834-6725
e-mail: allurie@optonline.net
*First recipient of Lifetime Employee Benefits Achievement Award of American Bar Association's Employee Benefits Committee of the Tax Section. 1st appointee of Assistant Commissioner in the Internal Revenue Service.*
Alvin D Lurie, President

Policy Areas

## Association of Towns of the State of New York
150 State St, Albany, NY 12207
518-465-7933  Fax: 518-465-0724
Web site: www.nytowns.org
*Advocacy, education for local government*
G Jeffrey Haber, Executive Director

## Citizens Budget Commission
Two Penn Plaza, Fifth Floor, New York, NY 10121
212-279-2605  Fax: 212-868-4745
e-mail: cmb2@nyu.edu
Web site: www.cbcny.org
*Nonpartisan, nonprofit civic organization devoted to influencing constructive change in the finances and services of New York City and New York State government*
Charles Brecher, Consulting Research Director

## Council of State Governments, Eastern Conference
100 Wall St, 20th Fl, New York, NY 10005
212-482-2320  Fax: 212-482-2344
Web site: www.csgeast.org
*Economic & fiscal programs*
Alan V Sokolow, Regional Director

## NYS Bar Assn, Tax Section
## Sullivan & Cromwell LLP
125 Broad Street, New York, NY 10004
212-558-4000  Fax: 212-558-3588
Web site: www.sullcrom.com
David P Hariton, Partner

## NYS Bar Assn, Trusts & Estates Law Section
## Day Pitney LLP
7 Times Square, 41st & 42nd St, New York, NY 10036
212-297-5800 or 212-297-2468  Fax: 212-916-2940
e-mail: gwwhitaker@daypitney.com
Web site: www.daypitney.com
*Domestic and international trusts and estates.*
G Warren Whitaker,

## Fiscal Policy Institute
1 Lear Jet Lane, Latham, NY 12110
518-786-3156  Fax: 518-786-3146
e-mail: deutsch@fiscalpolicy.org
Web site: www.fiscalpolicy.org
*Nonpartisan research & education; tax, budget, economic & related public policy issues*
Ron Deutsch, Executive Director
Kendra Moses, Operations Manager
David Kallick, Deputy Director & Director of Immigration Research

## Community Bankers Assn of NY State, Accounting & Taxation Cmte
## North Fork Bank
275 Broadhollow Road, Melville, NY 11747
631-844-1004
Aurelie Campbell, Co-Chair

## Hawkins Delafield & Wood LLP
One Chase Manhattan Plaza, 43rd Floor, New York, NY 10005
212-820-9434  Fax: 212-820-9666
e-mail: jprogers@hawkins.com
Web site: www.hawkins.com
*Tax law; public finance & municipal contracts*
Joseph P Rogers, Jr, Counsel

## Manhattan Institute, Center for Civic Innovation
52 Vanderbilt Ave, 2nd Fl, New York, NY 10017
212-599-7000  Fax: 212-599-3494
Web site: www.manhattan-institute.org
*NY city & state tax, fiscal policy*
Lindsay Young, Executive Director, Communications

## Moody's Investors Service, Public Finance Group
99 Church St, New York, NY 10007
212-553-7780  Fax: 212-298-7113
Web site: www.moodys.com
*Municipal debt ratings & analysis*
Dennis M Farrell, Group Managing Director

## NYS Conference of Mayors & Municipal Officials
119 Washington Ave, Albany, NY 12210
518-463-1185  Fax: 518-463-1190
e-mail: info@nycom.org
Web site: www.nycom.org
*Legislative advocacy for NYS cities & villages*
Peter A Baynes, Executive Director

## National Federation of Independent Business
100 State Street, Suite 440, Albany, NY 12207
518-434-1262  Fax: 518-426-8799
e-mail: mike.durant@nfib.org
Web site: www.nfib.com/new-york/
*Small business advocacy; supporting pro-small business candidates at the state & federal levels*
Michael P. Durant, State Director

## Nelson A Rockefeller Institute of Government
411 State St, Albany, NY 12203-1003
518-443-5522  Fax: 518-443-5788
Web site: www.rockinst.org
*Management & finance of welfare, health & employment of state & local governments nationally & especially in NY*
Richard P Nathan, Director

## New York State Assessors' Association
P.O. Box 5586, Cortland, NY 13045
315-706-3424  Fax: 315-410-5660
e-mail: admin@nyassessor.com
Web site: www.nyassessor.com
*Real property tax issues*
David W Briggs, FIAO, Executive Director

## New York State Government Finance Officers Association Inc
126 State St, 5th Fl, Albany, NY 12207
518-465-1512  Fax: 518-434-4640
Web site: www.nysgfoa.org
*Membership organization dedicated to the professional management of governmental resources*
Brian Roulin CPA, President

## New York State Society of Certified Public Accountants
3 Park Avenue, 18th Floor, New York, NY 10016-5991
212-719-8418  Fax: 212-719-3364
e-mail: doleary@nysscpa.org
Web site: www.nysscpa.org
Dennis O'Leary, Director, Government Relations

## New York State Society of Enrolled Agents
## Office of David J Silverman
866 UN Plaza, #415, New York, NY 10017
212-752-6983  Fax: 212-758-5478
e-mail: taxproblm@aol.com
Web site: www.nyssea.org
David J Silverman, Chair, Legislative/Government Relations Committee

## Robert Schalkenbach Foundation
90 John Street, Suite 501, New York, NY 10038
212-683-6424  Fax: 212-683-6454
Web site: www.schalkenbach.org
*Land value taxation, real property & economic publications*
Mark A Sullivan, Administrative Director

---

*Offices and agencies generally appear in alphabetical order, except when specific order is requested by listee.*

**Urbanomics**
115 Fifth Ave, 3rd Fl, New York, NY 10003
212-353-7462  Fax: 212-353-7494
e-mail: r.armstrong@urbanomics.org
Web site: www.urbanomics.org
*Economic development planning studies, market studies, tax policy analyses,*
*program evaluations, economic & demographic forecasts*
Regina B Armstrong, Principal

**Wachtell, Lipton, Rosen & Katz**
51 W 52nd St, New York, NY 10019
212-403-1241  Fax: 212-403-2241
e-mail: pccanellos@wlrk.com
Web site: www.wlrk.com
*Tax law*
Peter C Canellos, Office of Counsel

Policy Areas

# TOURISM, ARTS & SPORTS

## NEW YORK STATE

### GOVERNOR'S OFFICE

**Governor's Office**
Executive Chamber
State Capitol
Albany, NY 12224
518-474-8390 Fax: 518-474-1513
Web site: www.ny.gov

Governor:
Andrew M Cuomo . . . . . . . . . . . . . . . . . . . . . . . . . . . . .518-474-8390
Secretary to the Governor:
Melissa DeRosa . . . . . . . . . . . . . . . . . . . .518-474-4246 or 212-681-4580
Counsel to the Governor:
Kumiki Gibson. . . . . . . . . . . . . . . . . . . .518-474-8343 or 212-681-4580
Director of Policy:
David Yassky . . . . . . . . . . . . . . . . . . . . . . . . . . . . .518-408-2576
Chief of Staff:
Jill DesRosiers . . . . . . . . . . . . . . . . . .518-474-8390 or 212-681-4580
Director, Communications:
Peter Ajemian. . . . . . . . . . . . . . . . . . . .518-474-8418 or 212-681-4640
First Assistant Counsel:
R Nadine Fontaine . . . . . . . . . . . . . . . . . . . . . . . . . . . .518-474-8434

### EXECUTIVE DEPARTMENTS AND RELATED AGENCIES

**Council on the Arts**
300 Park Avenue South
10th Floor
New York, NY 10010
212-459-8800
e-mail: info@arts.ny.gov
Web site: www.arts.ny.gov

Chair:
Katherine Nicholls
Executive Director:
Mara Manus . . . . . . . . . . . . . . . . . . . . . . . . . . . . . .212-459-8808
e-mail: mara.manus@arts.ny.gov
Deputy Director, Programs:
Megan White. . . . . . . . . . . . . . . . . . . . . . . . . . . . . .212-459-8806
e-mail: megan.white@arts.ny.gov
Director, Agency Operations/HR Liaison:
Brenda K Brown. . . . . . . . . . . . . . . . . . . . . . . . . . . .212-459-8827
e-mail: brenda.brown@arts.ny.gov
Deputy Director, Operations & General Counsel:
Abigail Young. . . . . . . . . . . . . . . . . . . . . . . . . . . . .212-459-8832
e-mail: Abigail.Young@arts.ny.gov

**Administrative Services**
Director:
Tracy Hamilton. . . . . . . . . . . . . . . . . . . . . . . . . . . . .212-459-8822
e-mail: tracy.hamilton@arts.ny.gov
Purchasing:
Judy Evans . . . . . . . . . . . . . . . . . . . . . . . . . . . . . .212-459-8817
e-mail: judy.evans@arts.ny.gov

**Fiscal Management**
Associate Auditor:
Edward Leung. . . . . . . . . . . . . . . . . . . . . . . . . . . . .212-459-8813
e-mail: edward.leung@arts.ny.gov

**Information Technology**
Manager:
Lenn Savoca Ditman. . . . . . . . . . . . . . . . . . . . . . . . . .212-459-8810
e-mail: lenn.ditman@arts.ny.gov

**Program Staff**

**Architecture & Design/Museum**
Director:
Kristin Herron. . . . . . . . . . . . . . . . . . . . . . . . . . . . .212-459-8825
e-mail: kristin.herron@arts.ny.gov

**Arts Education/Facilities**
Director:
Christine Leahy . . . . . . . . . . . . . . . . . . . . . . . . . . . .212-459-8818
e-mail: christine.leahy@arts.ny.gov

**Dance/State & Local Partnerships/Decentralization**
Director:
Leanne Tintori Wells . . . . . . . . . . . . . . . . . . . . . . . . .212-459-8816
e-mail: leanne.wells@arts.ny.gov

**Electronic Media & Film/Visual Arts**
Director:
Karen Helmerson . . . . . . . . . . . . . . . . . . . . . . . . . . .212-459-8824
e-mail: karen.helmerson@arts.ny.gov

**Folk Arts/Music**
Director:
Robert Baron . . . . . . . . . . . . . . . . . . . . . . . . . . . . .212-459-8821
e-mail: robert.baron@arts.ny.gov
Director:
Arian Blanco. . . . . . . . . . . . . . . . . . . . . . . . . . . . . .212-459-8815
e-mail: arian.blanco@arts.ny.gov

**Literature/Theatre**
Director:
Kathleen Masterson . . . . . . . . . . . . . . . . . . . . . . . . . .212-459-8826
e-mail: kathleen.masterson@arts.ny.gov

**Presenting/Special Arts Services**
Director:
Susan Peirez . . . . . . . . . . . . . . . . . . . . . . . . . . . . . .212-459-8829
e-mail: susan.peirez@arts.ny.gov

## Education Department
State Education Building
89 Washington Avenue
Albany, NY 12234
518-474-3852
Web site: www.nysed.gov

Interim Commissioner & University President:
Betty A Rosa. . . . . . . . . . . . . . . . . . . . . . . . . . . . . .518-474-5844
Executive Deputy Commissioner:
Vacant. . . . . . . . . . . . . . . . . . . . . . . . . . . . . . . . .518-473-8381
Acting Counsel & Deputy Commissioner, Legal Affairs:
Aaron Baldwin . . . . . . . . . . . . . . . . . . . . . . . . . . . . .518-474-6400
e-mail: legal@nysed.gov

**Cultural Education Office**
Cultural Education Center, 222 Madison Avenue, Albany, NY 12230
e-mail: archinfo@nysed.gov
Web site: www.oce.nysed.gov
Deputy Commissioner:
Mark Schaming. . . . . . . . . . . . . . . . . . . . . . . . . . . . .518-474-5976

**State Museum Office**
Web site: www.nysm.nysed.gov
Director:
Mark A Schaming. . . . . . . . . . . . . . . . . . . . . . . . . . . .518-474-5812
e-mail: nysmweb@nysed.gov

*Offices and agencies generally appear in alphabetical order, except when specific order is requested by listee.*

Coordinator, Public Programs:
    Nicole LaFountain . . . . . . . . . . . . . . . . . . . . . . . . . . . . .518-474-0575
    e-mail: nicole.lafountain@nysed.gov
State Historian:
    Devin R. Lander . . . . . . . . . . . . . . . . . . . . . . . . . . . . .518-474-0206
    e-mail: devin.lander@nysed.gov
Director, Research & Collections:
    Dr. John P. Hart . . . . . . . . . . . . . . . . . . . . . . . . . . . .518-474-5816
    e-mail: john.hart@nysed.gov
Chief Curator of History:
    Dr. Jennifer Lemak . . . . . . . . . . . . . . . . . . . . . . . . . . . .518-474-5842
    e-mail: jennifer.lemak@nysed.gov

## Empire State Development Corporation

633 Third Avenue
Floor 37
New York, NY 10017
212-803-3100  Fax: 212-803-3131
Web site: www.esd.ny.gov

625 Broadway
Albany, NY 12245
518-292-5100

95 Perry Street
Suite 500
Buffalo, NY 14203
716-846-8200
Fax: 716-846-8260

President & CEO, Commissioner:
    Howard Zemsky . . . . . . . . . . . . . . . . . . . .212-803-3700 or 518-292-5100
    e-mail: president@esd.ny.gov
Chief Operating Officer & Deputy Commissioner:
    Kevin Younis . . . . . . . . . . . . . . . . . . . . . . . . . . . . . . .212-803-3100
Chief Financial Officer:
    Elaine Kloss

## General Services, Office of

Corning Tower
41st Floor
Empire State Plaza
Albany, NY 12242
518-474-3899
e-mail: comments@ogs.ny.gov
Web site: www.ogs.ny.gov

Commissioner:
    RoAnn Destito . . . . . . . . . . . . . . . . . . .518-474-5991/fax: 518-486-9179
Executive Deputy Commissioner:
    Vacant . . . . . . . . . . . . . . . . . . . . . . . . . . . . . . .518-473-6953
Director, Communications:
    Heather Groll . . . . . . . . . . . . . . . . . . . .518-474-5987/fax: 518-486-9179
    e-mail: heather.groll@ogs.ny.gov

### Empire State's Convention & Cultural Events Office
Director:
    Susan Cleary . . . . . . . . . . . . . . . . . . . . . . . . . . . . . .518-474-0549
Manager, Convention Center:
    Vacant . . . . . . . . . . . . . . . . . . . . . .518-474-0558/fax: 518-473-0558
    e-mail: convention.center@ogs.ny.gov
Director, Marketing:
    Michael J Snyder . . . . . . . . . . . . . . . . . . . . . . . . . .518-486-1873
    e-mail: michael.snyder@ogs.ny.gov
Director, Curatorial & Tour Services:
    Barbara Maggio . . . . . . . . . . . . . . . . . .518-473-7521/fax: 518-474-0954

## Hudson River Valley Greenway

625 Broadway
4th Floor
Albany, NY 12207
518-473-3835
e-mail: hrvg@hudsongreenway.ny.gov
Web site: www.hudsongreenway.ny.gov

### Greenway Conservancy for the Hudson River Valley
Chairman:
    Kevin M Burke . . . . . . . . . . . . . . . . . . . . . . . . . . .518-473-3835
Executive Director:
    Scott Keller . . . . . . . . . . . . . . . . . . . . . . . . . . . . . .518-473-3835

### Hudson River Valley Greenway Communities Council
Council Chair:
    Barnabas McHenry, Esq. . . . . . . . . . . . . . . . . . . . . . .518-473-3835
Executive Director:
    Scott Keller . . . . . . . . . . . . . . . . . . . . . . . . . . . . . .518-473-3835

## Parks, Recreation & Historic Preservation, NYS Office of

625 Broadway
Albany, NY 12207
518-486-0456  Fax: 518-474-4492
Web site: www.parks.ny.gov

Commissioner:
    Rose Harvey . . . . . . . . . . . . . . . . . . . . . . . . . . . . .518-474-0443
Executive Deputy Commissioner:
    Tom Alworth
    fax: 518-474-4492
Deputy Commissioner, Finance & Administration:
    Vacant
Deputy Commissioner, Historic Preservation:
    Vacant . . . . . . . . . . . . . . . . . . . . . . . .518-237-8643 x3269
Secretary:
    Virginia Davis . . . . . . . . . . . . . . . . . . . . . . . . . . . . .518-474-0443
General Counsel:
    Paul Laudato . . . . . . . . . . . . . . . . . . . . . . . . . . . . .518-474-0414
Deputy Commissioner, Natural Resources:
    Tom Alworth . . . . . . . . . . . . . . . . . . . . . . . . . . . . .518-474-0414
Park Police/Director, Law Enforcement:
    Jay Kirschner . . . . . . . . . . . . . . . . . . .518-474-4029/fax: 518-408-1032
Public Information Officer:
    Dan Keefe . . . . . . . . . . . . . . . . . . . . . . . . . . . . . . .518-486-1868
Chief Public Information Officer:
    Randy Simon . . . . . . . . . . . . . . . . . . . . . . . . . . . . .518-486-1868

### Concession Management
Director:
    Harold Hagemann . . . . . . . . . . . . . . . . .518-486-2932/fax: 518-486-2372

### Historic Preservation

#### Field Services
Peebles Island, PO Box 189, Waterford, NY 12118
Deputy Commissioner:
    Vacant . . . . . . . . . . . . . . . . . . . . . . . . . . . . . . . .518-237-8643

#### Historic Sites Bureau
Peebles Island, Waterford, NY 12188
Acting Director:
    Mark Peckham . . . . . . . . . . . . . . . . . . . . . . . . . . . .518-237-8643

### Marine & Recreational Vehicles
Director:
    Brian Kempf . . . . . . . . . . . . . . . . . . . .518-474-0445/fax: 518-408-1030

### Regional Offices
Director, Regional Programs & Services:
    Debra Keville . . . . . . . . . . . . . . . . . . . . . . . . . . . . .518-474-8081

*Offices and agencies generally appear in alphabetical order, except when specific order is requested by listee.*

**Central Region** . . . . . . . . . . . . . . . . . . . . . . . . . . . . . . . . . . fax: 315-492-3277
6105 E Seneca Turnpike, Jamesville, NY 13078-9516
315-492-1756  Fax: 315-492-3277
Regional Director:
    Robert Hiltbrand . . . . . . . . . . . . . . . . . . . . . . . . . . . . . . .315-492-1756

**Finger Lakes Region** . . . . . . . . . . . . . . . . . . . . . . . . . . . fax: 607-387-3390
2221 Taughannock Park Rd, Box 1055, Trumansburg, NY 14886
607-387-7041  Fax: 607-387-3390
Regional Director:
    Tim Joseph . . . . . . . . . . . . . . . . . . . . . . . . . . . . . . . . . . .607-387-7041

**Long Island Region** . . . . . . . . . . . . . . . . . . . . . . . . . . . . . fax: 631-422-0638
625 Belmont Ave, Box 247, West Babylon, NY 11702-0247
631-669-1000  Fax: 631-422-0638
Acting Regional Director:
    George Gorman . . . . . . . . . . . . . . . . . . . . . . . . . . . . . . . .631-321-3403

**Palisades Region** . . . . . . . . . . . . . . . . . . . . . . . . . . . . . . . fax: 845-786-2776
Administration Headquarters, Bear Mountain, NY 10911
Executive Director:
    Jim Hall . . . . . . . . . . . . . . . . . . . . . . . . . . . . . . . . . . . . . . .845-786-2701

**Saratoga/Capital District Region** . . . . . . . . . . . . . . . . fax: 518-584-5694
19 Roosevelt Drive, Saratoga Springs, NY 12866
518-584-2000  Fax: 518-584-5694
Regional Director:
    Alane Ball Chinian . . . . . . . . . . . . . . . . . . . . . . . . . . . . .518-584-2000

**Thousand Islands Region** . . . . . . . . . . . . . . . . . . . . . . . fax: 315-482-9413
Keewaydin State Park, 45165 NYS Rte 12, Alexandria Bay, NY 13607
315-482-2593  Fax: 315-482-9413
Regional Director:
    Kevin Kieff . . . . . . . . . . . . . . . . . . . . . . . . . . . . . . . . . . . .315-482-2593

## Regional Offices-Downstate District

**New York City Region** . . . . . . . . . . . . . . . . . . . . . . . . . fax: 212-961-4382
A C Powell State Ofc Bldg, 163 W 125th St, New York, NY 10027
212-866-3100  Fax: 212-961-4382
Regional Director:
    Karen Phillips . . . . . . . . . . . . . . . . . . . . . . . . . . . . . . . . .212-866-3100

**Taconic Region** . . . . . . . . . . . . . . . . . . . . . . . . . . . . . . . . fax: 845-889-8217
9 Old Post Road, PO Box 308, Staatsburg, NY 12580
845-889-4100  Fax: 845-889-8217
Regional Director:
    Linda Cooper . . . . . . . . . . . . . . . . . . . . . . . . . . . . . . . . . .845-889-4100

## Regional Offices-Western District

**Allegany Region** . . . . . . . . . . . . . . . . . . . . . . . . . . . . . . . .fax: 716-354-6725
2373 Allegany State Park, Suite 3, Salamanca, NY 14779
716-354-9101  Fax: 716-354-6725
Acting Regional Director:
    Mark Whitecomb . . . . . . . . . . . . . . . . . . . . . . . . . . . . . . .716-354-9101

**Genesee Region** . . . . . . . . . . . . . . . . . . . . . . . . . . . . . . . .fax: 585-493-5272
One Letchworth State Park, Castile, NY 14427-1124
585-493-3600  Fax: 585-493-5272
Regional Director:
    Richard Parker . . . . . . . . . . . . . . . . . . . . . . . . . . . . . . . .585-493-3600

**Niagara Region & Western District Office** . . . . . . . . fax: 716-278-1725
Niagara Frontier Park Region, Prospect P, PO Box 1132, Niagara Falls,
    NY 14303-0132
716-278-1770  Fax: 716-278-1725
Regional Director:
    Mark Thomas . . . . . . . . . . . . . . . . . . . . . . . . . . . . . . . . . .716-278-1770

## Environmental Management
Director:
    Pamela Otis . . . . . . . . . . . . . . . . . . . . .518-474-0409/fax: 518-474-7013

## New York State Gaming Commission
1 Broadway Center
P.O. Box 7500
Schenectady, NY 12301-7500
518-388-3300
e-mail: info@gaming.ny.gov
Web site: www.gaming.ny.gov

Gaming Commissioner:
    Peter J Moschetti, Jr . . . . . . . . . . . . . . . . . . . . . . . . . . .518-388-3400
Gaming Commissioner:
    Todd R. Snyder . . . . . . . . . . . . . . . . . . . . . . . . . . . . . . .518-388-3400
Gaming Commissioner & Chair:
    Barry Sample . . . . . . . . . . . . . . . . . . . . . . . . . . . . . . . . .518-388-3400
Gaming Commissioner:
    John J Poklemba . . . . . . . . . . . . . . . . . . . . . . . . . . . . . .518-388-3400
Gaming Commissioner:
    John A Crotty . . . . . . . . . . . . . . . . . . . . . . . . . . . . . . . . .518-388-3400
Executive Director:
    Robert Williams . . . . . . . . . . . . . . . . . . . . . . . . . . . . . . .518-388-3400
Director, Communications:
    Brad Maione . . . . . . . . . . . . . . . . . . . . . . . . . . . . . . . . .518-388-3415

## CORPORATIONS, AUTHORITIES AND COMMISSIONS

### Adirondack Park Agency
1133 NYS Route 86
PO Box 99
Ray Brook, NY 12977
518-891-4050  Fax: 518-891-3938
Web site: www.apa.ny.gov

Chair:
    Leilani Ulrich . . . . . . . . . . . . . . . . . . . . . . . . . . . . . . . . .518-891-4050
Executive Director:
    Terry Martino . . . . . . . . . . . . . . . . . . . . . . . . . . . . . . . . .518-891-4050
Counsel:
    James Townsend . . . . . . . . . . . . . . . . . . . . . . . . . . . . . .518-891-4050
Public Relations:
    Keith McKeever . . . . . . . . . . . . . . . . . . . . . . . . . . . . . . .518-891-4050
    e-mail: keith.mckeever@apa.ny.gov

### Agriculture & NYS Horse Breeding Development Fund
1 Broadway Center
Schenectady, NY 12305
518-388-0178  Fax: 518-388-2791
e-mail: info@nysirestakes.com
Web site: www.nysirestakes.com

Executive Director:
    M. Kelly Young

### Battery Park City Authority (Hugh L Carey)
One World Financial Center, 24th Fl
200 Liberty Street
New York, NY 10281
212-417-2000  Fax: 212-417-2001
e-mail: info.bpc@bpca.ny.gov
Web site: www.bpca.ny.gov

Chair & Chief Operating Officer:
    Dennis Mehiel . . . . . . . . . . . . . . . . . . . . . . . . . . . . . . . .212-417-2000
President & Chief Operating Officer:
    Shari Hyman . . . . . . . . . . . . . . . . . . .212-417-4205/fax: 212-417-4153
Vice Chair:
    Donald Cappocia . . . . . . . . . . . . . . . . . . . . . . . . . . . . . .212-417-2000
Member:
    Hector Batista . . . . . . . . . . . . . . . . . . . . . . . . . . . . . . . .212-417-2000

*Offices and agencies generally appear in alphabetical order, except when specific order is requested by listee.*

Member:
    Lester Petracca . . . . . . . . . . . . . . . . . . . . . . . . . . . . . . . . .212-417-2000
Member:
    Martha J Gallo. . . . . . . . . . . . . . . . . . . . . . . . . . . . . . . . . .212-417-2000
VP External Relations:
    Robin Forst . . . . . . . . . . . . . . . . . . . . . .212-417-2276/fax: 212-417-2279
    e-mail: robin.forst@bpca.ny.gov

## Capital District Regional Off-Track Betting Corporation
510 Smith St
Schenectady, NY 12305
518-344-5266 or 800-292-2387  Fax: 518-370-5460
e-mail: customerservice@capitalotb.com
Web site: www.capitalotb.com

Chair:
    Marcel Webb. . . . . . . . . . . . . . . . . . . . . . . . . . . . . . . . . .518-344-5225
Board Secretary & Director:
    F James Mumpton. . . . . . . . . . . . . . . . . . . . . . . . . . . . . . .518-344-5225
President & Chief Executive Officer:
    John F Signor . . . . . . . . . . . . . . . . . . . . . . . . . . . . . . . . .518-344-5225
VP, Corporate Operations:
    Tod Grenci . . . . . . . . . . . . . . . . . . . . . . . . . . . . . . . . . . .518-344-5408
VP, Legal Affairs/General Counsel:
    Robert Hemsworth . . . . . . . . . . . . . . . . . . . . . . . . . . . . . .518-344-5298
VP, Finance/Comptroller:
    Nancy Priputen-Madrian . . . . . . . . . . . . . . . . . . . . . . . . . .518-344-5233
VP, Human Resources:
    Robert Dantz. . . . . . . . . . . . . . . . . . . . . . . . . . . . . . . . . .518-344-5301

## Catskill Off-Track Betting Corporation
Park Place
Box 3000
Pomona, NY 10970
845-362-0407  Fax: 845-362-0419
e-mail: otb@interbets.com
Web site: www.interbets.com

President:
    Donald J Groth . . . . . . . . . . . . . . . . . . . . . . . . . . . . . . . .845-362-0400

## Nassau Regional Off-Track Betting Corporation
139 Liberty Ave
Mineola, NY 11501
516-572-2800  Fax: 516-572-2840
e-mail: webmaster@nassauotb.com
Web site: www.nassauotb.com

President:
    Joseph G Cairo, Jr. . . . . . . . . . . . . . . . . . . . . . . . . . . . . .516-572-2800
Director, Facilities Development:
    John J Sparacio . . . . . . . . . . . . . . . . . . . . . . . . . . . . . . . .516-572-2800

## New York Convention Center Operating Corporation
655 W 34th St
New York, NY 10001-1188
212-216-2000  Fax: 212-216-2588
e-mail: moreinfo@javitscenter.com
Web site: www.javitscenter.com

Chair:
    Henry Silverman. . . . . . . . . . . . . . . . . . . . . . . . . . . . . . . .212-216-2130
President & Chief Operating Officer:
    Alan Steel . . . . . . . . . . . . . . . . . . . . . . . . . . . . . . . . . . .212-216-2000
Senior Vice President & Chief Financial Officer:
    John Menapace . . . . . . . . . . . . . . . . . . . . . . . . . . . . . . . .212-216-2369
Senior Vice President & General Counsel:
    Bradley Siciliano. . . . . . . . . . . . . . . . . . . . . . . . . . . . . . .212-216-2125

Senior Vice President, Sales & Marketing:
    Doreen Guerin. . . . . . . . . . . . . . . . . . . . . . . . . . . . . . . . .212-216-2335

## New York State Athletic Commission
123 William St
2nd Fl
New York, NY 10038
212-417-5700  Fax: 212-417-4987
e-mail: info@dos.ny.gov
Web site: www.dos.ny.gov/athletic

Chair:
    Tom Hoover . . . . . . . . . . . . . . . . . . . . . . . . . . . . . . . . . .212-417-5700

## New York State Commission on the Restoration of the Capitol
Corning Tower, 31st Fl
Empire State Plaza
Albany, NY 12242
518-473-0341  Fax: 518-486-5720

Executive Director:
    Andrea J Lazarski. . . . . . . . . . . . . . . . . . . . . . . . . . . . . . .518-473-0341
    e-mail: andrea.lazarski@ogs.ny.gov

## New York State Olympic Regional Development Authority
Olympic Center
2634 Main St
Lake Placid, NY 12946
518-523-1655  Fax: 518-523-9275
e-mail: info@orda.org
Web site: www.orda.org/corporate

President & CEO:
    Ted Blazer . . . . . . . . . . . . . . . . . . . . . . . . . . . . . . . .518-523-1655 x201
    e-mail: blazer@orda.org
Vice President:
    Jeffrey Byrne . . . . . . . . . . . . . . . . . . . . . . . . . . . . . . .518-523-1655 x203
    e-mail: byrne@orda.org
Olympic Center Manager:
    Dennis Allen . . . . . . . . . . . . . . . . . . . . . . . . . . . . . . .518-523-1655 x222
    e-mail: allen@orda.org
Director, Corporate Development:
    Jeff Potter . . . . . . . . . . . . . . . . . . . . . . . . . . . . . . . . . . .518-523-1655
    e-mail: jpotter@orda.org
Director, Events:
    Katie Million . . . . . . . . . . . . . . . . . . . . . . . . . . . . . .518-523-1655 x212
    e-mail: kmillion@orda.org
Director, Finance:
    Padraig Power . . . . . . . . . . . . . . . . . . . . . . . . . . . . . .518-523-1655 x217
    e-mail: ppower@orda.org
Communications Manager:
    Jon Lundin . . . . . . . . . . . . . . . . . . . . . . . . . . . . . . . . . .518-523-1655
    e-mail: jlundin@orda.org

## New York State Thoroughbred Breeding & Development Fund Corporation
One Broadway Center
Suite 601
Schenectady, NY 12305
518-388-0174  Fax: 518-344-1235
e-mail: nybreds@nybreds.com
Web site: www.nybreds.com

Executive Director:
    Tracy Egan . . . . . . . . . . . . . . . . . . . . . . . . . . . . . . . . . .518-388-0174

*Offices and agencies generally appear in alphabetical order, except when specific order is requested by listee.*

## New York State Thruway Authority

200 Southern Blvd
PO Box 189
Albany, NY 12201
518-436-2700  Fax: 518-436-2899
Web site: www.thruway.ny.gov

Chair:
  Joanne M Mahoney . . . . . . . . . . . . . . . . . . . . . . . . . . . . . . 518-436-3000
Interim Executive Director:
  Maria Lehman . . . . . . . . . . . . . . . . . . . . . . . . . . . . . . . . 518-436-2900
General Counsel:
  Gordon Cuffy . . . . . . . . . . . . . . . . . . . . . . . . . . . . . . . . 518-436-2840
Director, Media Relations & Communications:
  Jennifer Givner . . . . . . . . . . . . . . . . . . . . . . . . . . . . . . . 518-471-5300
CFO:
  Matt Howard . . . . . . . . . . . . . . . . . . . . . . . . . . . . . . . . . 518-436-2840
Director, Administrative Services:
  John F. Barr . . . . . . . . . . . . . . . . . . . . . . . . . . . . . . . . . 518-436-2700

## New York State Canal Corporation

  Web site: www.canals.ny.gov
Interim Executive Director:
  Maria Lehman . . . . . . . . . . . . . . . 518-436-3055/fax: 518-471-5023

## Roosevelt Island Operating Corporation (RIOC)

591 Main St
Roosevelt Island, NY 10044
212-832-4540  Fax: 212-832-4582
e-mail: information@rioc.ny.gov
Web site: www.rioc.ny.gov

President/CEO:
  Charlene M Indelicato . . . . . . . . . . . . . . . . . . . . . . . 212-832-4540 x319
Director Island Operations:
  Cyril Opperman . . . . . . . . . . . . . . . . . . . . . . . . . . . . . 212-832-4583
  e-mail: cyril.opperman@rioc.ny.gov
VP/General Counsel:
  Donald D. Lewis . . . . . . . . . . . . . . . . . . . . . . . . 212-832-4540 x311
  e-mail: donald.lewis@rioc.ny.gov
VP/Chief Financial Officer:
  Frances Walton . . . . . . . . . . . . . . . . . . . . . . . . . 212-832-4540 x350
Interim Director Public Safety:
  Captain Estrella Suarez . . . . . . . . . . . . . . . . . . . . . . 212-832-4545
  e-mail: keith.guerra@rioc.ny.gov

## Suffolk Regional Off-Track Betting Corporation

425 Oser Ave
Ste 2
Hauppauge, NY 11788
631-853-1000  Fax: 631-853-1086
e-mail: customerservice@suffolkotb.com
Web site: www.suffolkotb.com

President/CEO:
  Philip C. Nolan . . . . . . . . . . . . . . . . . . . . . . . . . . . . . . 631-853-1000
Vice President:
  Anthony Pancella . . . . . . . . . . . . . . . . . . . . . . . . . . . . . 631-853-1000
General Counsel:
  James McManmon . . . . . . . . . . . . . . . . . . . . . . . . . . . . . 631-853-1000
Director Governmental & Public Affairs:
  Debbie Pfeiffer . . . . . . . . . . . . . . . . . . . . . . . . . . . . . . 631-853-1000

## Western Regional Off-Track Betting Corp

8315 Park Road
Batavia, NY 14020

585-343-3750  Fax: 585-343-6873
e-mail: info@westernotb.com
Web site: www.westernotb.com

Chair:
  Richard D Bianchi . . . . . . . . . . . . . . . . . . . . . . . . . . . . . 585-343-3750
President & Chief Executive Officer:
  Michael D Kane . . . . . . . . . . . . . . . . . . . . . . . . . . . . . . . 585-343-3750
General Counsel:
  Henry Wojtaszek . . . . . . . . . . . . . . . . . . . . . . . . . . . . . . 585-343-3750
Director, Video Gaming:
  Mark Wolf . . . . . . . . . . . . . . . . . . . . . . . . . . . . . . . . . . . 585-343-3750
Communications/Mutuels Manager:
  James Haas . . . . . . . . . . . . . . . . . . . . . . . . . . . . . . . . . . 585-343-3750
Manager, Branch Operations:
  Edward Merriman . . . . . . . . . . . . . . . . . . . . . . . . . . . . . 585-343-3750
VP-Administration:
  William R White . . . . . . . . . . . . . . . . . . . . . . . . . . . . . . 585-343-3750

## CONVENTION & VISITORS BUREAUS

## Convention Centers & Visitors Bureaus

**Albany County Convention & Visitors Bureau** . . fax: 518-434-0887
  25 Quackenbush Sq, Albany, NY 12207
  800-258-3582 or 518-434-1217  Fax: 518-434-0887
  Web site: www.albany.org
President & CEO:
  Michele Vennard . . . . . . . . . . . . . 518-434-1217 x300/fax: 518-434-0887
  e-mail: mvennard@albany.org

**Greater Binghamton New York Convention and Visitors Bureau**
  49 Court St, 2nd Floor, PO Box 995, Binghamton, NY 13902
  800-836-6740 or 607-772-8860
  Web site: www.binghamtoncvb.com; www.visitbinghamton.org
President:
  Lou Santoni
  e-mail: lou@visitbinghamton.org

**Buffalo Niagara Convention & Visitors Bureau**
  617 Main St, Ste 200, Buffalo, NY 14203
  800-283-3256
  e-mail: info@visitbuffaloniagara.com
  Web site: www.visitbuffaloniagara.com
President & CEO:
  Patrick Kaler . . . . . . . . . . . . . . . . . . . . . . . . . . . . . . . . 716-961-0200
  e-mail: kaler@visitbuffaloniagara.com

**Chautauqua County Visitors Bureau**
  Chautauqua Main Gate, Route 394, PO Box 1441, Chautauqua, NY 14722
  866-908-4569
  e-mail: info@tourchautauqua.com
  Web site: www.tourchautauqua.com
Executive Director:
  Andrew Nixon . . . . . . . . . . . . . . . . . . . . 716-357-4569/fax: 716-357-2284
  e-mail: nixon@tourchautauqua.com

**Greater Rochester Visitors Association**
  Visit Rochester, 45 East Ave, Ste 400, Rochester, NY 14604-2294
  800-677-7282
  Web site: www.visitrochester.com
Director:
  Michael Hardy . . . . . . . . . . . . . . . . . . . . . . . . . . . . . . . . 585-279-8303
  e-mail: michaelh@visitrochester.com

**Ithaca/Tompkins County Convention & Visitors Bureau**
  904 E Shore Dr, Ithaca, NY 14850
  800-28-ITHACA
  e-mail: info@visitithaca.com
  Web site: www.visitithaca.com

*Offices and agencies generally appear in alphabetical order, except when specific order is requested by listee.*

Director:
Fred Bonn . . . . . . . . . . . . . . . . . . . . . . .607-272-1313/fax: 607-272-7617

**Lake Placid/Essex County Convention & Visitors Bureau**
2608 Main St, Lake Placid, NY 12946
800-447-5224
Web site: www.lakeplacid.com
CEO:
James McKenna. . . . . . . . . . . . . . . . . . .518-523-2445/fax: 518-523-2605
e-mail: james@lakeplacid.com

**Long Island Convention & Visitors Bureau & Sports Commission**
330 Motor Pkwy, Ste 203, Hauppauge, NY 11788
877-386-6654
e-mail: tourism@discoverlongisland.com
Web site: www.discoverlongisland.com
President:
R Moke McGowan. . . . . . . . . . . . 631-951-3900 x305/fax: 631-951-3439
e-mail: mmcgowan@discoverlongisland.com

**NYC & Company/Convention & Visitors Bureau** fax: 212-245-5943
810 Seventh Ave, 3 Fl, New York, NY 10019
212-484-1200  Fax: 212-245-5943
e-mail: visitorinfo@nycgo.com
Web site: www.nycgo.com
CEO:
George Fertitta. . . . . . . . . . . . . . . . . . .212-484-1265/fax: 212-245-5943

**Oneida County Convention & Visitors Bureau**
Oneida Cty Welcome Ctr, PO Box 551, dba: Oneida County Tourism,
    Utica, NY 13503-0551
800-426-3132 or 888-999-6560
President:
Kelly Blazosky . . . . . . . . . . . . . . . . . .315-724-7221/fax: 315-724-7335
e-mail: kelly@oneidacountytourism.com

**Ontario County/Finger Lakes Visitors Connection**
25 Gorham St, Canandaigua, NY 14424
877-386-4669
e-mail: info@visitfingerlakes.com
Web site: www.visitfingerlakes.com
President:
Valerie Knoblauch. . . . . . . . . . . . . . . . .585-394-3915/fax: 585-394-4067

**Saratoga Convention & Tourism Bureau**
60 Railroad Pl, Ste 100, Saratoga Springs, NY 12866
855-424-6073
Web site: www.discoversaratoga.org
President:
Todd Garofano . . . . . . . . . . . . . . . 518-584-1531 x106/fax: 518-584-2969
e-mail: todd@discoversaratoga.org

**Steuben County Conference & Visitors Bureau**
1 West Market St, Corning, NY 14830
866-946-3386
e-mail: sccvb@corningfingerlakes.com
Web site: www.corningfingerlakes.com
President:
Peggy Coleman . . . . . . . . . . . . . . . . . . .607-936-6544/fax: 607-936-6575

**Sullivan County Visitors Association**
100 Sullivan Avenue, Suite 2, PO Box 248, Ferndale, NY 12734
800-882-2287
Web site: www.scva.net
President & CEO:
Roberta Byron Lockwood . . . . . . . . . . .845-747-4449/fax: 845-747-4468

**Syracuse Convention & Vistors Bureau**
572 S Salina St, Syracuse, NY 13202
800-234-4797
Web site: www.visitsyracuse.org

President:
David Holder . . . . . . . . . . . . . . . . . . . . .315-470-1911/fax: 315-471-8545

**Tourism Bureau of the Thousand Islands Region**
Box 400, Alexandria Bay, NY 13607
800-847-5263
Web site: www.visit1000islands.com
Director of Tourism:
Gary DeYoung. . . . . . . . . . . . . . . . . . . .315-482-2520/fax: 315-482-5906
e-mail: gary@visit1000islands.com

**Westchester County Tourism & Film**
148 Martine Ave, Ste 104, White Plains, NY 10601
800-833-9282
e-mail: tourism@westchestergov.com
Director of Tourism:
Natasha Caputo. . . . . . . . . . . . . . . . . . . . . . . . . . . . . . .914-995-8502
e-mail: ncaputo@visitwestchesterny.com

## NEW YORK STATE LEGISLATURE

*See Legislative Branch in Section 1 for additional Standing Committee and Subcommittee information.*

### Assembly Standing Committees

**Racing & Wagering**
Chair:
J Gary Pretlow (D). . . . . . . . . . . . . . . . .518-455-5291/fax: 518-455-5447

**Tourism, Parks, Arts & Sports Development**
Chair:
Daniel J O'Donnell (D). . . . . . . . . . . . . . . . . . . . . . . . . . . .518-455-4755

### Senate Standing Committees

**Cultural Affairs, Tourism, Parks & Recreation**
Chair:
Jose M Serrano (D, WF). . . . . . . . . . . . . . . . . . . . . . . . . . .518-455-2795

**Racing, Gaming & Wagering**
Chair:
Joseph P Addabbo, Jr (D) . . . . . . . . . . . . . . . . . . . . . . . . . .518-455-2322
Ranking Minority Member:
Daphne Jordan (R, C, IP, RFM). . . . . . . . . . . . . . . . . . . . . .518-455-2381

## U.S. GOVERNMENT

### EXECUTIVE DEPARTMENTS AND RELATED AGENCIES

### National Archives & Records Administration

**Franklin D Roosevelt Presidential Library & Museum**
4079 Albany Post Rd, Hyde Park, NY 12538
845-486-7770
Web site: www.fdrlibrary.marist.edu
Director:
Lynn A. Bassanese . . . . . . . . . . . . . . . . . . . . . . . . . . . . . .845-486-7741

### Smithsonian Institution

**Cooper-Hewitt National Design Museum**
2 East 91st St, New York, NY 10128
212-849-8400
Web site: www.cooperhewitt.org
Director:
Caroline Bauman . . . . . . . . . . . . . . . . . . . . . . . . . . . . . .212-849-8400

*Offices and agencies generally appear in alphabetical order, except when specific order is requested by listee.*

**National Museum of the American Indian-George Gustav Heye Center**
US Custom House, One Bowling Green, New York, NY 10004
212-514-3700
Web site: www.nmai.si.edu
GGHC Director:
Kevin Gouer . . . . . . . . . . . . . . . . . . . . . . . . . . . . . . . . . . . 212-514-3700

## US Department of the Interior
202-208-3100
e-mail: webteam@ios.doi.gov
Web site: www.doi.gov

**Fish & Wildlife Service-Northeast Region** . . . . . . fax: 413-253-8308
300 Westgate Center Dr, Hadley, MA 01035-9589
413-253-8200  Fax: 413-253-8308
e-mail: northeast@fws.gov
Regional Director:
Wendi Weber . . . . . . . . . . . . . . . . . . . . . . . . . . . . . . . . 413-253-8300

**National Park Service-Northeast Region**
200 Chestnut St, US Custom House, 5th Floor, Philadelphia, PA 19106
Web site: www.nps.gov
Northeast Regional Director:
Dennis R. Reidenbach . . . . . . . . . . . . . . . . . . . . . . . . . . 215-597-5823
National Heritage Area Program Director:
Peter Samuel

**Fire Island National Seashore** . . . . . . . . . . . . . . . . . fax: 631-289-3010
120 Laurel St, Patchogue, NY 11772-3596
631-289-4750  Fax: 631-289-3010
Web site: www.nps.gov/fiis/
Superintendent:
Chris Soller . . . . . . . . . . . . . . . . . . . . 631-289-4750/fax: 631-289-3010

**Fort Stanwix National Monument** . . . . . . . . . . . . . . . . fax: 315-334-5051
112 E Park St, Rome, NY 13440
315-338-7730  Fax: 315-334-5051
Web site: www.nps.gov/fost/
Superintendent:
Deborah Conway. . . . . . . . . . . . . . . . . 315-338-7730/fax: 315-334-5051

**Gateway National Recreation Area**
210 New York Ave, Staten Island, NY 10305
Web site: www.nps.gov/gate
General Superintendent:
Linda Canzanelli . . . . . . . . . . . . . . . . . 718-354-4606/fax: 718-354-4764
*Jamaica Bay Unit*
Coordinator:
Dave Taft . . . . . . . . . . . . . . . . . . . . . . . . . . . . . . . . . 718-338-3379
*Sandy Hook Unit*
Coordinator:
Pete McCarthy . . . . . . . . . . . . . . . . . . . . . . . . . . . . 732-872-5970
*Staten Island Unit*
Coordinator:
Brian Feeney . . . . . . . . . . . . . . . . . . . . . . . . . . . . . . 718-354-6970

**Manhattan Sites**
26 Wall St, New York, NY 10005
212-668-5180
Web site: www.nps.gov/masi
Commissioner:
Maria Burtes . . . . . . . . . . . . . . . . . . . . . . . . . . . . . . . . . 212-668-2322

**Martin Van Buren National Historic Site** . . . . . . . . . . fax: 518-758-6986
1013 Old Post Rd, Kinderhook, NY 12106
518-758-9689  Fax: 518-758-6986
Web site: www.nps.gov/mava
Superintendent:
Daniel J Dattilio . . . . . . . . . . . . . . . . 518-758-9689/fax: 518-758-6986

**Roosevelt-Vanderbilt National Historic Sites**
4097 Albany Post Rd, Hyde Park, NY 12538
845-229-9115 x. 2010
Web site: www.nps.gov/hofr
Superintendent:
Sarah Olson . . . . . . . . . . . . . . . . . . . . . 845-229-9115/fax: 845-229-0739

**Sagamore Hill National Historic Site** . . . . . . . . . . . . fax: 516-922-4792
20 Sagamore Hill Road, Oyster Bay, NY 11771
516-922-4788  Fax: 516-922-4792
Web site: www.nps.gov/sahi
Superintendent:
Tom Ross. . . . . . . . . . . . . . . . . . . . . 516-922-4788/fax: 516-922-4792

**Saratoga National Historical Park**. . . . . . . . . . . . . . . . fax: 518-664-3349
648 Rt 32, Stillwater, NY 12170
518-664-9821 X224  Fax: 518-664-3349
Web site: www.nps.gov/sara
Superintendent:
Joe Finan . . . . . . . . . . . . . . 518-664-9821 ext 224/fax: 518-664-3349

**Statue of Liberty National Monument & Ellis Island**
Liberty Island, New York, NY 10004
TTY: 212-363-3211 or 212-363-3200
Web site: www.nps.gov/stli/
Superintendent:
David Luchsinger . . . . . . . . . . . . . . . . . . . . . . . . . . . . 212-363-3200

**Theodore Roosevelt Inaugural National Historic Site** fax: 716-884-0330
641 Delaware Ave, Buffalo, NY 14202
716-884-0095  Fax: 716-884-0330
Web site: www.nps.gov/thri/
Superintendent:
Molly Quackenbush . . . . . . . . . . . . . 716-884-0095/fax: 716-884-0330

**Women's Rights National Historical Park** . . . . . . . . . fax: 315-568-2141
136 Fall St, Seneca Falls, NY 13148
315-568-2991  Fax: 315-568-2141
Web site: www.nps.gov/wori
Superintendent:
Tammy Duchesne . . . . . . . . . . . . . . . 315-568-2991/fax: 315-568-2141

## U.S. CONGRESS

*See U.S. Congress Chapter for additional Standing Committee and Subcommittee information.*

## House of Representatives Standing Committees

### Natural Resources
Chair:
Doc Hastings (R-WA) . . . . . . . . . . . . . . . . . . . . . . . . . . . 202-225-5816
Ranking Minority Member:
Edward J. Markey (D-MA). . . . . . . . . . . . . . . . . . . . . . . 202-225-2836

**Subcommittee**
*Public Lands & Environmental Regulations*
Chair:
Rob Bishop (R-UT) . . . . . . . . . . . . . . . . . . . . . . . . . 202-225-0453
Ranking Minority Member:
Raul M. Grijalva (D-AZ). . . . . . . . . . . . . . . . . . . . . 202-225-2435

## Senate Standing Committees

### Energy & Natural Resources
Chair:
Ron Wyden (D-OR) . . . . . . . . . . . . . . . . . . . . . . . . . . . . 202-224-5244
Ranking Minority Member:
Lisa Murkowski (R-AK). . . . . . . . . . . . . . . . . . . . . . . . . 202-224-6665

*Offices and agencies generally appear in alphabetical order, except when specific order is requested by listee.*

**Subcommittees**

*National Parks*
Chair:
    Mark Udall (D-CO) . . . . . . . . . . . . . . . . . . . . . . . .202-224-4971
*Public Lands, Forests & Mining*
Chair:
    Joe Manchin (D-WV) . . . . . . . . . . . . . . . . . . . . . .202-224-3954
Ranking Minority Member:
    John Barrasso (R-WY) . . . . . . . . . . . . . . . . . . . . .202-224-6441

## PRIVATE SECTOR

**AAA Northway**
1626 Union St, Schenectady, NY 12309
518-374-4575  Fax: 518-374-3140
*Capital region membership, travel & touring sales & services*
Eric Stigberg, Marketing, Public & Government Affairs Manager

**AAA Western and Central NY**
100 International Dr, Buffalo, NY 14221
716-626-3225  Fax: 716-631-5925
Web site: www.AAA.com
Wallace Smith, Vice President

**Adirondack Lakes Center for the Arts**
Rte 28, PO Box 205, Blue Mountain Lake, NY 12812-0205
518-352-7715  Fax: 518-352-7333
e-mail: alca@frontiernet.net
*Multi/Arts Center*
Stephen Svoboda, Executive Director

**Adirondack/Pine Hill/NY Trailways**
499 Hurley Ave, Hurley, NY 12443-5119
845-339-4230  Fax: 845-853-7035
e-mail: info@trailwaysny.com
Web site: www.trailwaysny.com
*Tour & charter service*
Eugene J Berardi, Jr, President

**Alliance for the Arts**
330 W 42nd St, Ste 1701, New York, NY 10036
212-947-6340  Fax: 212-947-6416
e-mail: info@allianceforarts.org
Web site: www.allianceforarts.org
*Advocacy, promotion, research, information, referrals & publications*
Randall Bourscheidt, President

**Alliance of Resident Theatres/New York (ART/New York)**
520 Eighth Ave, Ste 319, New York, NY 10018
212-244-6667  Fax: 212-714-1918
Web site: www.art-newyork.org
*Services & advocacy for New York City's not-for-profit theatre community*
Virginia P Louloudes, Executive Director

**American Museum of Natural History**
Central Park West at 79th St, New York, NY 10024-5192
212-769-5100  Fax: 212-769-5018
Web site: www.amnh.org
*Education, exhibition & scientific research*
Ellen V Futter, President

**Art & Science Collaborations Inc**
130 East End Ave 1A, New York, NY 10028
505-988-2994
e-mail: asci@asci.org
Web site: www.asci.org
*Raising public awareness of art & artists using science & technology to explore new forms of creative expression*
Cynthia Pannucci, Director

**ArtsConnection Inc (The)**
520 8th Ave, #321, New York, NY 10018
212-302-7433  Fax: 212-302-1132
e-mail: artsconnection@artsconnection.org
Web site: www.artsconnection.org
*Arts-in-education programming & training for children, teachers & artists*
Steven Tennen, Executive Director

**Associated Musicians of Greater New York, Local 802 AFM, AFL-CIO**
322 West 48th St, 5th Fl, New York, NY 10036
212-245-4802  Fax: 212-245-6255
Web site: www.local802afm.org
Paul Molloy, Political/Public Relations Director

**Association of Independent Video & Filmmakers (AIVF), (The)**
304 Hudson St, 6th Fl, New York, NY 10013
212-807-1400  Fax: 212-463-8519
Web site: www.aivf.org
*Membership service organization for independent producers & filmmakers*
Beni Matias, Executive Director

**Automobile Club of New York**
1415 Kellum Place, Garden City, NY 11530
516-873-2252  Fax: 516-873-2375
Dennis J Crossley, President

**Brooklyn Botanic Garden**
1000 Washington Ave, Brooklyn, NY 11225-1009
718-623-7200  Fax: 718-857-2430
Web site: www.bbg.org
*Comprehensive study of plant biodiversity in metropolitan New York; home gardener's resource center*
Scot Medbury, President & CEO

**Brooklyn Museum of Art**
200 Eastern Pkwy, Brooklyn, NY 11238
718-638-5000  Fax: 718-501-6136
Web site: www.brooklynmuseum.org
Schawannah Wright, Manager, Community Involvement

**Buffalo Bills**
One Bills Drive, Orchard Park, NY 14127
716-648-1800 x8701  Fax: 716-648-3202
Web site: www.buffalobills.com
Scott Berchtold, Vice President-Communications

**Buffalo Sabres**
One Seymour H Knox III Plz, Buffalo, NY 14203
716-855-4100 x526  Fax: 716-855-4110
e-mail: michael.gilbert@sabres.com
Web site: www.sabres.com
Michael Gilbert, Director Public Relations

**Buffalo Trotting Association Inc**
5600 McKinley Parkway, Hamburg, NY 14075
716-649-1280  Fax: 716-649-0033
e-mail: mangoj@buffaloraceway.com
Web site: www.buffaloraceway.com
*Harness horse racing*
James Mango, General Manager

**CUNY New York City College of Technology, Hospitality Mgmt**
300 Jay St, Room 220, Brooklyn, NY 11201-2983
718-260 5630  Fax: 718-260-5997
*Hospitality & food service management; tourism*
Jerry Van Loon, Professor & Chair

*Offices and agencies generally appear in alphabetical order, except when specific order is requested by listee.*

**Campground Owners of New York**
1 Grove Street, Suite 200, Pittsford, NY 14534
585-586-4360  Fax: 585-586-4360
e-mail: cony@frontiernet.net
Web site: www.nycampgrounds.com
Donald G Bennett Jr, Executive Administrator

**Coalition of Living Museums**
1000 Washington Ave, Brooklyn, NY 11225
718-623-7225 or 718-623-7373  Fax: 718-857-2430
Web site: www.livingmuseums.org
*Advocacy organization for living museums (zoos, botanical gardens, aquaria, arboreta & nature centers) in NYS*
Lois Carswell, Chair, Steering Committee

**Cold Spring Harbor Fish Hatchery & Aquarium**
1660 Route 25A, Cold Spring Harbor, NY 11724
516-692-6768  Fax: 516-692-6769
Web site: www.cshfha.org
*Largest living collection of NYS freshwater fish, amphibians & turtles*
Norman Soule, Director

**Columbia University, School of the Arts**
305 Dodge Hall, 2960 Broadway, MC 1803, New York, NY 10027
212-854-2875  Fax: 212-854-7733
Web site: arts.columbia.edu
Carol Becker, Dean

**Culinary Institute of America**
1946 Campus Drive, Hyde Park, NY 12538-1499
845-452-9600
e-mail: N_Harvin@culinary.edu
Web site: www.ciachef.edu
*Four-year regionally accredited college offering Associate and Occupational Studies and Bachelor of Professional Studies in culinary and baking/pastry arts management. Campuses in Hyde Park, New York, and St Helena, California.*
Victor A.L. Gielisse, Vice President for Advancement & Business Development

**Darien Lake Theme Park Resort**
9993 Allegheny Rd, PO Box 91, Darien Center, NY 14040
585-599-4641  Fax: 585-599-4053
Web site: www.darienlake.com
*Darien Lake Theme Park Resort is New York State's largest theme park and resort, located between Buffalo and Rochester, NY and just a short drive from Niagara Falls.*
Christopher Thorpe, Vice President & General Manager

**Egg (The), Center for the Performing Arts**
Empire State Plaza, PO Box 2065, Albany, NY 12220
518-473-1061 or 518-473-1845  Fax: 518-473-1848
e-mail: info@theegg.org
Web site: www.theegg.org
*Dance, theatre, family entertainment, music, special events*
Peter Lesser, Executive Director

**NYS Bar Assn, Entertainment, Arts & Sports Law Section**
**Elissa D Hecker, Esq**
90 Quail Close, Irvington, NY 10533
914-478-0457
e-mail: eheckeresq@yahoo.com
Elissa D Hecker, Chair

**Empire State Restaurant & Tavern Association Inc**
12 Sheridan Avenue, Albany, NY 12207
518-436-8121  Fax: 518-436-7287
e-mail: esrta@verizon.net
Web site: www.esrta.org
Scott Wexler, Executive Director

**Entertainment Software Association**
317 Madison Ave, 22nd Fl, New York, NY 10017
917-522-3250  Fax: 917-522-3258
Web site: www.theesa.com
Michael D Gallagher, President/CEO

**Exhibition Alliance Inc (The)**
Route 12B South, PO Box 345, Hamilton, NY 13346
315-824-2510  Fax: 315-824-1683
e-mail: donnao@exhibitionalliance.org
*Exhibit-related services for museums in NYS & the surrounding region*
Donna Ostraszewski Anderson, Executive Director

**Farmer's Museum (The)**
PO Box 30, Cooperstown, NY 13326
607-547-1400  Fax: 607-547-1404
Web site: www.farmersmuseum.org
*Historical & cultural exhibition, preservation and education*
D Stephen Elliott, President

**Film/Video Arts**
270 W 96th St, New York, NY 10025
212-941-8787
Web site: www.fva.com
*Low cost training, postproduction suites, fiscal sponsorship, mentorship, internships*
Chloe Kurabi, Programs Director, Fiscal Sponsorship and Filmmaker

**Finger Lakes Racing Association**
PO Box 25250, Farmington, NY 14425
585-924-3232  Fax: 585-924-3239
Web site: www.fingerlakesracetrack.com
*Horse racing & video lottery gaming*
Christian Riegle, General Manager

**Finger Lakes Tourism Alliance**
309 Lake St, Penn Yan, NY 14527
315-536-7488  Fax: 315-536-1237
e-mail: info@fingerlakes.org
Web site: www.fingerlakes.org
*Regional tourism promotion*
Cynthia Kimble, President

**Gertrude Stein Repertory Theatre (The)**
15 West 26th St, 2nd Fl, New York, NY 10010
212-725-0436  Fax: 212-725-7267
e-mail: info@gerstein.org
Web site: www.gerstein.org
*Avant garde theater emphasizing international collaboration in experimental works incorporating new technologies*
Liz Dreyer, General Manager

**Great Escape Theme Park LLC (The)**
PO Box 511, Lake George, NY 12845
518-792-3500  Fax: 518-792-3404
John Collins, General Manager

**Harvestworks**
596 Broadway, Suite 602, New York, NY 10012
212-431-1130  Fax: 212-431-8473
Web site: www.harvestworks.org
*Nonprofit arts organization providing computer education & production studios for the digital media arts*
Carol Parkinson, Director

**Historic Hudson Valley**
150 White Plains Rd, Tarrytown, NY 10591
914-631-8200  Fax: 914-631-0089
e-mail: mail@hudsonvalley.org
Web site: www.hudsonvalley.org
*Tourism promotion*
Waddell Stillman, President

*Offices and agencies generally appear in alphabetical order, except when specific order is requested by listee.*

**Hotel Association of New York City Inc**
320 Park Ave, 22nd Fl, New York, NY 10022-6838
212-754-6700  Fax: 212-688-2838
e-mail: jspinnato@hanyc.org
Web site: www.hanyc.org
Joseph E Spinnato, President

**Hudson River Cruises**
Rondout Landing, 1 East Strand Street, Kingston, NY 12401-3605
845-340-4700 or 800-843-7472  Fax: 845-340-4702
Web site: www.hudsonrivercruises.com
*Sightseeing, music & dinner cruises and Private Charters*
Sandra Henne, President

**Hunter Mountain Ski Bowl**
PO Box 295, Hunter, NY 12442
888-486-8376 or 518-263-4223  Fax: 518-263-3704
Web site: www.huntermtn.com
*Skiing, snowshoeing, snowboarding & snowtubing; coaching & race camps;
summer & fall festivals; Kaatskill Mountain Club/Hotel, Loftside Village
Condominiums, and other Four Season Mountain Resort activities.*
Orville A Slutzky, General Manager

**Jewish Museum (The)**
1109 Fifth Ave, New York, NY 10128-0117
212-423-3200  Fax: 212-423-3232
e-mail: info@thejm.org
Web site: www.thejewishmuseum.org
*Museum of art and Jewish culture*
Anne Scher, Senior Director, Communications

**Lincoln Center for the Performing Arts Inc**
70 Lincoln Center Plaza, New York, NY 10023-6583
212-875-5319  Fax: 212-875-5456
Web site: www.lincolncenter.org
*Guided tours of Lincoln Center; Meet-the-Artist programs*
Jennifer Berry, Director, Visitor Services

**Lower Manhattan Cultural Council**
125 Maiden Lane, 2nd Floor, New York, NY 10038
212-219-9401  Fax: 212-219-2058
e-mail: info@lmcc.net
Web site: www.lmcc.net
*Supporting Manhattan arts organizations through funding assistance,
support for creation & presentation of work & audience development*
Mark Vevle, Director, Marketing & Communications

**Madison Square Garden Corp**
Two Penn Plaza, Madison Square Garden, New York, NY 10121
212-465-6000  Fax: 212-465-4423
Web site: www.thegarden.com
*NY Knicks, NY Rangers,NY Liberty concerts, special events*
Barry Watkins, Senior Vice President, Communications

**Major League Baseball**
245 Park Ave, New York, NY 10167
212-931-7800  Fax: 212-949-5654
Web site: www.mlb.com
Rich Levin, Senior Vice President, Public Relations

**Metropolitan Museum of Art (The)**
1000 Fifth Ave, New York, NY 10028
212-535-7710  Fax: 212-650-2102
Web site: www.metmuseum.org
Philippe de Montebello, Director;, Harold Holzer, Senior Vice President for
    External Affairs

**Monticello Gaming & Raceway**
204 Rte 17-B, PO Box 5013, Monticello, NY 12701
845-794-4100  Fax: 845-791-1402
Web site: www.monticelloraceway.com
*Horse racing and video gaming machines.*
Clifford Ehrlich, Senior Vice President/General Manager

**Museum Association of New York**
265 River St, Troy, NY 12180
518-273-3400  Fax: 518-273-3416
e-mail: info@manyonline.org
Web site: www.manyonline.org
*An information and advocacy resource for the state's museum community.*
Anne Ackerson, Director

**NY Film Academy**
100 East 17th St, New York, NY 10003-2160
212-674-4300  Fax: 212-477-1414
e-mail: film@nyfa.com
*Film making and acting for film.*
Jerry Sherlock, President & Founder

**NY State Historical Association/Fenimore Art Museum**
PO Box 800, Cooperstown, NY 13326-0800
607-547-1400  Fax: 607-547-1404
Web site: www.nysha.org; www.farmersmuseum.org
*Historical & cultural exhibition, preservation & education*
Paul S D'Ambroso, PhD, President/Chief Executive Officer

**NYC Arts Coalition**
351 West 54th St, New York, NY 10019
212-246-3788  Fax: 212-246-3366
*Develops public policy analysis, provides reports on arts policy & funding
issues & acts as an advocacy vehicle for a united voice for the nonprofit arts
sector*
Norma P Munn, Chair

**NYS Alliance for Arts Education**
PO Box 2217, Albany, NY 12220-0217
800-ARTS-N-ED or 518-473-0823  Fax: 518-486-7329
Web site: www.nysaae.org
*Advocacy, professional development, technical assistance & information for
educators, organizations, artists, parents, policymakers*
Jeremy Johannesen, Executive Director

**NYS Arts**
PO Box 96, Mattituck, NY 11952-0096
631-298-1234  Fax: 631-298-1101
*Technical assistance, professional development & advocacy services*
Angela Lipfert, Office Manager

**NYS Outdoor Guides Association**
1936 Saranac Ave, Suite 2 PO Box 150, Lake Placid, NY 12946-1402
866-469-7642 or 518-359-8194  Fax: 518-359-8194
e-mail: info@nysoga.org
Web site: www.nysoga.org
*Provides information about member guide services & the profession of
guiding through distribution of printed/electronic material and educational
programs. Provides NYS licensed guides with support services,
representation and sense of community*
Sonny Young, President

**NYS Passenger Vessel Association**
PO Box 98, Brightwaters, NY 11718
631-321-9005
Web site: www.cruisenewyork.com
*Promote cruises on NYS's waterways*
Mike Eagan, Treasurer

*Offices and agencies generally appear in alphabetical order, except when specific order is requested by listee.*

**NYS Theatre Institute**
37 First St, 1218 O, Troy, NY 12180
518-274-3200  Fax: 518-274-3815
Web site: www.nysti.org
*Professional theater productions for family and school audiences; training &
education, internships, community/school outreach & cultural exchange
programs*
Patricia Di Benedetto Snyder, Producing Artistic Director

**NYS Turfgrass Association**
PO Box 612, Latham, NY 12110
518-783-1229 or 800-873-8873  Fax: 518-783-1258
e-mail: nysta@nysta.org
Web site: www.nysta.org
*Provides education & research for individuals in the turfgrass & grounds
industry*
Beth Seme, Executive Director

**National Basketball Association**
645 5th Ave, New York, NY 10022
212-407-8000  Fax: 212-826-0579
Web site: www.nba.com
Brian McIntyre, Senior Vice President, Communications

**National Football League**
280 Park Ave, New York, NY 10017
212-450-2000  Fax: 212-681-7599
Web site: www.nfl.com
Greg Aiello, Vice President, Public Relations

**National Hockey League**
15, 1185 Avenue of the Americas, New York, NY 10036
212-789-2000  Fax: 212-789-2020
e-mail: fbrown@nhl.com
Web site: www.nhl.com
Frank Brown, Vice President, Media Relations

**National Women's Hall of Fame**
PO Box 335, 76 Fall Street, Seneca Falls, NY 13148
315-568-8060  Fax: 315-568-2976
Web site: www.greatwomen.org
*The hall celebrates outstanding American women & their achievements*
Billie Luisi-Potts, Executive Director

**New School University, Department of Sociology**
65 Fifth Ave, New York, NY 10003
212-229-5782 or 212-229-5737  Fax: 212-229-5595
e-mail: zolbergv@newschool.edu
*Sociology of the arts; censorship; collective memory; outsider art*
Vera Zolberg, Professor, Sociology & Liberal Studies

**New York Academy of Art Inc**
111 Franklin St, New York, NY 10013-2911
212-966-0300  Fax: 212-966-3217
e-mail: info@nyaa.edu
Web site: www.nyaa.edu
Wayne A Linker, Executive Director

**New York Aquarium**
Surf Ave at West 8th St, Brooklyn, NY 11224
718-265-3428 or 718-265-FISH  Fax: 718-265-3400
e-mail: fhackett@wcs.org
Web site: www.nyaquarium.com
*Conservation, education & research*
Fran Hackett, Communications

**New York Artists Equity Association Inc**
498 Broome St, New York, NY 10013
212-941-0130  Fax: 212-941-0138
e-mail: reginas@tiac.net
Web site: www.anny.org
*Web based advocacy for visual arts & cultural organizations; Call first to
send fax*
Regina Stewart, Executive Director

**New York City Opera**
20 Lincoln Center, New York, NY 10023
212-870-5600  Fax: 212-724-1120
Web site: www.nycopera.com
Susan Woelzl, Director, Press & Public Relations

**New York Foundation for the Arts**
155 Ave of the Americas, 14th Floor, New York, NY 10013-1507
212-366-6900  Fax: 212-366-1778
Web site: www.nyfa.org
*Advocacy, leadership, financial & resource support & collaborative
relationships with those committed to the arts*
Theodore S Berger, Executive Director

**New York Giants**
Giants Stadium, East Rutherford, NJ 07073
201-935-8111  Fax: 201-935-8493
Web site: www.giants.com
Pat Hanlon, Vice President, Communications

**New York Hall of Science**
4701 111th Street, Queens, NY 11368
718-699-0005 x323  Fax: 718-699-1341
Web site: www.nysci.org
*Hands-on science exhibits & education program*
Mary Record, Director, Communications

**New York Islanders**
1535 Old Country Rd, Plainview, NY 11803
516-501-6700  Fax: 516-501-6762
e-mail: customerservice@newyorkislanders.com
Web site: www.newyorkislanders.com
Chris Botta, Vice President, Communications

**New York Jets**
1000 Fulton Ave, Hempstead, NY 11550
516-560-8100  Fax: 516-560-8197
Web site: www.newyorkjets.com
Bruce Speight, Public Relations

**New York Marine Trades Association**
194 Park Ave, Suite B, Amityville, NY 11701
631-691-7050  Fax: 631-691-2724
e-mail: csqueri@aol.com
Web site: www.nymta.com
*Promote & protect the marine & boating industry; own & operate two boat
shows; monitor local, state & federal marine legislation*
Christopher Squeri, Executive Director

**New York Mets**
Shea Stadium, 123-01 Roosevelt Ave, Flushing, NY 11368
718-507-6387  Fax: 718-639-3619
Web site: www.mets.com
Fred Wilpon, Chairman & Chief Executive Officer

**New York Racing Association**
PO Box 90, Jamaica, NY 11417
718-641-4700  Fax: 718-843-7673
Web site: www.nyra.com
*Horse racing at Aqueduct, Belmont Park, and Saratoga.*
Francis LaBelle, Jr, Director, Communications

*Offices and agencies generally appear in alphabetical order, except when specific order is requested by listee.*

**New York State Hospitality & Tourism Association**
80 Wolf Rd, Albany, NY 12205
800-642-5313 x13 or 518-465-2300  Fax: 518-465-4025
Web site: www.nyshta.org
*Hotels, motels, amusement parks & attractions*
Daniel C Murphy, President

**New York State Restaurant Association**
409 New Karner Rd, Albany, NY 12205
518-452-4222  Fax: 518-452-4497
e-mail: ricks@nysra.org
Web site: www.nysra.org
Rick J Sampson, President & Chief Executive Officer

**New York State School Music Association (NYSSMA)**
718 The Plain Rd, Westbury, NY 11590-5931
516-997-7200  Fax: 516-997-1700
e-mail: executive@nyssma.org
Web site: www.nyssma.org
*Advocacy for a quality school music education for every student*
Steven Schopp, Executive Director

**New York State Snowmobile Association**
PO Box 612, Long Lake, NY 12847
518-624-3849  Fax: 518-624-2441
Web site: www.nyssnowassoc.org
*Working to preserve & enhance snowmobiling & improve trails, facilities & services for participants*
Jim Jennings, Executive Director

**New York State Theatre Education Association**
63 Hecla St, Buffalo, NY 14216
716-837-9434  Fax: 716-626-8207
e-mail: rogersouth@aol.com
Web site: www.nystea.org
*Working to preserve & enhance drama & theater education & opportunities in NY schools & communities*
Roger Paolini, President

**New York State Travel & Vacation Association**
PO Box 285, Akron, NY 14001
888-698-2970 or 716-542-1586  Fax: 716-542-1404
Web site: www.nystva.org
*The NYSTVA is the tourism industry's leader in communication, legislative awareness, professional development, and promotion.*
Dawn L Borchert, Executive Director

**New York University, Tisch School of the Arts**
721 Broadway, New York, NY 10003
212-998-1800
Web site: www.tisch.nyu.edu
Allyson Green, Dean, Tisch School of the Arts

**New York Wine & Grape Foundation**
800 S Main St, Ste 200, Canandaigua, NY 14424
585-394-3620  Fax: 585-394-3649
e-mail: info@newyorkwines.org
Web site: www.newyorkwines.org
*Promotion of wine & grape products of New York; research for wine & grape related products & issues*
James Trezise, President

**New York Yankees**
800 Ruppert Place, Bronx, NY 10451
718-293-4300  Fax: 718-293-8431
Web site: www.yankees.com
Randy Levine, President

**Resources for Artists with Disabilities Inc**
77 7th Avenue, Suite PHH, New York, NY 10011-6644
212-691-5490  Fax: 212-691-5490
*Organizes & promotes exhibition opportunities for visual artists with physical disabilities*
Dr Lois Kaggen, President & Founder

**Saratoga Gaming & Raceway**
PO Box 356, Saratoga Springs, NY 12866
518-584-2110 or 518-581-5748  Fax: 518-583-1269
*Horse racing*
John R Matarazzo, Director of Racing Operations

**Seaway Trail Inc**
401 West Main Street, Ray & West Main Streets, PO Box 660, Sackets Harbor, NY 13685
315-646-1000 or 800-SEAWAY-T  Fax: 315-646-1004
Web site: www.seawaytrail.com
*Promotes coastal recreation, economic development, resource management & heritage, cultural, agricultural & culinary tourism along a 454 mile NYS highway system*
Teresa Mitchell, President

**Ski Areas of New York Inc**
PO Box 928, Tupper Lake, NY 12986
518-796-3601 or 315-696-6550  Fax: 315-696-6567
e-mail: scottbrandi@iskiny.com
Web site: www.iskiny.com
*Promote skiing in NYS*
Scott Brandi, President

**Solomon R Guggenheim Foundation**
1071 5th Ave, New York, NY 10128
212-423-3680
e-mail: directorsoffice@guggenheim.org
Web site: www.guggenheim.org
Thomas Krens, Director

**Special Olympics New York, Inc**
504 Balltown Road, Schenectady, NY 12304-2290
518-388-0790  Fax: 518-388-0795
Web site: www.nyso.org
*Not-for-profit organization provides year-round sports training & competition in Olympic-style sports for athletes with intellectual disabilities.*
Neal J Johnson, President & Chief Executive Officer

**Sports & Arts in Schools Foundation**
58-12 Queens Blvd, Suite 1 - 59th Entrance, Woodside, NY 11377
718-786-7110  Fax: 718-786-7635
Web site: www.sasfny.org
*After-school, summer camps & clinics, winter-break festival*
James R O'Neill, Executive Director

**Staten Island Zoo**
614 Broadway, Staten Island, NY 10310
718-442-3101  Fax: 718-981-8711
e-mail: kmithcell@statenislandzoo.org
Web site: www.statenislandzoo.org
Kenneth C. Mitchell, Interim Executive Director

**Tribeca Film Institute**
32 Avenue of the Americas, 27 FL, New York, NY 10013
212-274-8080  Fax: 212-274-8081
Web site: www.tribecafilminstitute.org
Anna Ponder, Executive Director

Policy Areas

*Offices and agencies generally appear in alphabetical order, except when specific order is requested by listee.*

**USA Track & Field, Adirondack Association Inc**
233 Fourth St, Troy, NY 12180
518-273-5552  Fax: 518-273-0647
Web site: www.usatfadir.org
*Leadership & opportunities for athletes pursuing excellence in running, race walking & track & field*
George Regan, President

**Vernon Downs/Gaming-Racing-Entertainment**
4229 Stuhlman Rd, PO Box 1040, Vernon Downs, NY 13476
315-829-2201  Fax: 315-829-3787
e-mail: vernonevents@vernondowns.com
Web site: www.vernondowns.com
*Horse racing, concerts, motorcross, motorcycle, craft fairs & other entertainment*
Ursula Hardin, President

**Willow Mixed Media Inc**
PO Box 194, Glenford, NY 12433
845-657-2914
e-mail: video@hvc.rr.com
Web site: www.willowmixedmedia.org
*Not-for-profit specializing in documentary video & arts projects addressing social concerns*
Tobe Carey, President

**Yonkers Raceway**
810 Central Park Ave, Yonkers, NY 10704
914-968-4200  Fax: 914-968-4479
*Horse racing and video gaming entertainment*
Timothy Rooney, President

*Offices and agencies generally appear in alphabetical order, except when specific order is requested by listee.*

# TRANSPORTATION

## NEW YORK STATE

### GOVERNOR'S OFFICE

**Governor's Office**
Executive Chamber
State Capitol
Albany, NY 12224
518-474-8390  Fax: 518-474-1513
Web site: www.ny.gov

Governor:
  Andrew M Cuomo ................................518-474-8390
Secretary to the Governor:
  Melissa DeRosa ............518-474-4246 or 212-681-4580
Counsel to the Governor:
  Kumiki Gibson ............518-474-8343 or 212-681-4580
Chief of Staff:
  Jill DesRosiers ............518-474-8390 or 212-681-4580
Director, Communications:
  Peter Ajemian............518-474-8418 or 212-681-4640
Deputy Secretary, Transportation:
  Christopher O'Brien ............................518-473-6745
Deputy Secretary, Public Safety:
  Jeremy Schockett ...............................518-474-3522

### EXECUTIVE DEPARTMENTS AND RELATED AGENCIES

**Motor Vehicles Department**
6 Empire State Plaza
Albany, NY 12228
518-486-9786
Web site: dmv.ny.gov/

Executive Deputy Commissioner:
  Theresa L Egan ..................518-474-0846/fax: 518-474-0712
Assistant Commissioner, Communications & Marketing:
  Lisa Koumjian....................518-473-7000/fax: 518-473-1930

**Administration, Office for**
Deputy Commissioner:
  Gregory J Kline..................518-474-6876/fax: 518-474-0712
Director, Audit Services:
  Jannette Potera ...................................518-474-0881
Director, Fiscal Management:
  Paul Gauthier ....................................518-474-7602
Director, Human Resources:
  Vacant.............................................518-474-7602
Director, Agency Program Services:
  Ann Scott .........................................518-474-8328
Labor Relations:
  Nancy Spenziero....................................518-474-2902
Director, Program Analysis:
  Mary Bidell.......................................518-474-0623

**Governor's Traffic Safety Committee**
  Web site: www.safeny.ny.gov
Assistant Commissioner:
  Chuck DeWeese ...................................518-474-0972
Director, Traffic Safety Committee:
  Jim Allen..........................................518-474-5777

**Legal Affairs, Office for**
Deputy Commissioner, Legal Affairs:
  Neal Schoen.....................518-473-1965/fax: 518-474-0712

Director, Legal:
  Ida Traschen .....................................518-474-0871
Appeals Board:
  Deborah Dugan....................................518-474-0645

**Operations & Customer Service, Office for**
Deputy Commissioner & Counsel:
  Timothy B Lennon ................518-473-1965/fax: 518-474-0712
Legislative Liaison:
  Meg Murray ......................................518-474-7726
Director, Field Operations:
  Cheryl Wasley.....................................518-486-7400
Director, Operations:
  Joseph Crisafulli .................................518-473-7254
Director, Central Office Operations:
  Roseanne Kitchner ...............................518-402-4746

**Safety, Consumer Protection & Clean Air, Office for**
Deputy Commissioner:
  Heriberto Barbot .................518-474-0846/fax: 518-474-0712
Director, Driver/Vehicle Safety:
  Jean Rosenthal ...................................518-473-3347
Director, Field Investigation:
  Owen McShane....................................518-474-8805
Director, Driver Safety Programs:
  Gerald Clark ......................................518-473-7197
Vehicle Safety & Clean Air:
  Steve Cooper......................................518-474-3785

**Transportation Department**
50 Wolf Road
Albany, NY 12232
518-457-6195  Fax: 518-457-5583
Web site: www.dot.ny.gov

Acting Commissioner:
  Paul A Karas......................................518-457-4422
Executive Deputy Commissioner:
  Phil Eng...........................................518-457-4422
Chief Counsel, Legal Affairs Division:
  Jan McLachlan ...................................518-457-2411
Assistant Commissioner, Operations & Asset Management:
  Sam Zhou .........................................518-457-9684
Executive Deputy Commissioner, Policy & Planning Division:
  Ron Epstein.......................................518-457-2320
Chief Engineer, Engineering Division:
  Nicolas Choubah..................................518-457-4430
Director, Audit:
  Theresa Vottis.....................................518-457-1590
Director, Communications Office:
  Joseph Morrissey .................................518-457-6400

**Administrative Services Division**
Director:
  Grace Boss........................................518-457-6300
Director, Contract Management Bureau:
  Bill Howe .........................................518-457-2600
Director, Communications Office:
  Joseph Morrissey .................................518-457-6400
Director, Facilities Management:
  Colleen Schnorr ..................................518-457-6445
Director, Purchase Unit:
  Matthew Haas.....................................518-457-4401

**Engineering Division**
Chief Engineer:
  Nicolas Choubah..................................518-457-4430
Office of Design:
  Richard Lee.......................................518-457-6452
Office of Structures:
  Richard Marchione ...............................518-457-6827

*Offices and agencies generally appear in alphabetical order, except when specific order is requested by listee.*

279

Office of Environment:
Dan Hitt . . . . . . . . . . . . . . . . . . . . . . . . . . . .518-457-5672
Office of Major Projects:
Nicolas Choubah . . . . . . . . . . . . . . . . . . . . .518-457-4430
Office of Technical Services:
Robert Sack, PE . . . . . . . . . . . . . . . . . . . . . .518-457-4445
Office of Construction:
Brian DeWald, PE. . . . . . . . . . . . . . . . . . . . .518-457-6472
Office of Construction:
Jose Rivera, PE . . . . . . . . . . . . . . . . . . . . . . .518-457-6472

## Legal Affairs Division
Chief Counsel:
Jan McLachlan . . . . . . . . . . . . . . . . . . . . . . . .518-457-2411

## Operations & Asset Management Division
Assistant Commissioner:
Sam Zhou . . . . . . . . . . . . . . . . . . . . . . . . . . .518-457-9684
Modal Safety & Security Office:
William Leonard . . . . . . . . . . . . . . . . . . . . . .518-457-6512
Fleet Administration & Support Office:
Shane Gilchrest . . . . . . . . . . . . . . . . . . . . . . .518-457-2875
Transportation Maintenance Office:
Bob Winans . . . . . . . . . . . . . . . . . . . . . . . . . .518-457-6435
Traffic Safety & Mobility Office (Acting):
Rob Limoges . . . . . . . . . . . . . . . . . . . . . . . . .518-457-0271
Employee Health & Safety:
Brian Gibney . . . . . . . . . . . . . . . . . . . . . . . . .518-457-2420

## Policy & Planning Division
Executive Deputy Commissioner:
Ron Epstein . . . . . . . . . . . . . . . . . . . . . . . . . .518-457-2320
Executive Deputy Commissioner:
Ron Epstein . . . . . . . . . . . . . . . . . . . . . . . . . .518-457-2320
Policy, Planning & Performance Office:
Lynn Weiskopf . . . . . . . . . . . . . . . . . . . . . . .518-457-2320
Integrated Modal Services:
Diane Kenneally . . . . . . . . . . . . . . . . . . . . . .518-457-2320
Regional Planning & Program Coordination:
Dave Rettig . . . . . . . . . . . . . . . . . . . . . . . . . .518-457-2320

## Audit & Civil Rights Division
Director, Audit:
Theresa Vottis . . . . . . . . . . . . . . . . . . . . . . . .518-457-1590
Office of Civil Rights:
Sondra Little . . . . . . . . . . . . . . . . . . . . . . . . .518-457-1129
Contracts Management Bureau:
William Howe . . . . . . . . . . . . . . . . . . . . . . . .518-457-2600
Investigations Bureau:
Robert Keihm . . . . . . . . . . . . . . . . . . . . . . . . .518-457-2411

## Office of Regional Affairs
Director:
Matt Bomirski . . . . . . . . . . . . . . . . . . . . . . . .518-485-0822

### Regional Offices
*Region 1*
50 Wolf Road, Albany, NY 12232
Director:
Sam Zhou. . . . . . . . . . . . . . . . . . . . . . . . . .518-451-3522
*Region 2*
Utica State Ofc Bldg, 207 Genesee St, Utica, NY 13501
Director:
Nicolas Choubah . . . . . . . . . . . . . . . . . . .315-793-2447
*Region 3*
State Ofc Bldg, 333 E Washington St, Syracuse, NY 13202
Director:
David Smith . . . . . . . . . . . . .315-428-4351/fax: 315-428-4834
*Region 4*
1530 Jefferson Rd, Rochester, NY 14623
Director:
Kevin Bush. . . . . . . . . . . . . .585-272-3310/fax: 585-427-8480

*Region 5*
100 Seneca Street, Buffalo, NY 14203
Director:
Frank Cirillo . . . . . . . . . . . . . . .716-847-3238/fax: 716-847-3961
*Region 6*
107 Broadway, Hornell, NY 14843
Director:
Brian Kelly . . . . . . . . . . . . . . .607-324-8404/fax: 607-324-0790
*Region 7*
Dulles State Ofc Bldg, 317 Washington St, Watertown, NY 13601
Director:
Steve Kokkoris . . . . . . . . . . . . .315-785-2333/fax: 315-785-2507
*Region 8*
Eleanor Roosevelt State Ofc Bldg, 4 Burnett Blvd, Poughkeepsie, NY 12603
Director:
Todd Westhuis . . . . . . . . . . . . .845-431-5750/fax: 845-431-5703
*Region 9*
44 Hawley St, Binghamton, NY 13901
Director:
Jack Williams . . . . . . . . . . . . .607-721-8116/fax: 607-721-8119
*Region 10*
State Ofc Bldg, 250 Veterans Memorial Hwy, Hauppauge, NY 11788
Director:
Joseph Brown . . . . . . . . . . . . .631-952-6632/fax: 631-952-6311
*Region 11*
One Hunters Point Plaza, 47-40 21st St, Long Island City, NY 11101
Director:
Sonia Pichardo . . . . . . . . . . . . .718-482-4526/fax: 718-482-4525

## CORPORATIONS, AUTHORITIES AND COMMISSIONS

## Albany County Airport Authority
Albany International Airport
Administration Building
Second Floor
Albany, NY 12211
518-242-2222 x1 Fax: 518-242-2641
e-mail: info@albanyairport.com
Web site: www.albanyairport.com

Chief Executive Officer:
John A O'Donnell PE . . . . . . . . . . . . . . . . . . . . . . . . . . .518-242-2222 x1
Chief Financial Officer:
William O'Reilly . . . . . . . . . . . . . . . . . . . . . . . . . . .518-242-2222 x1
Director, Public Affairs:
Douglas I. Myers . . . . . . . . . . . . . . . . . . . . . . . . . . .518-242-2222 x1
Counsel:
Peter F Stuto . . . . . . . . . . . . . . . . . . . . . . . . . . .518-242-2222 x1
Airport Planner:
Stephen A Iachetta . . . . . . . . . . . . . . . . . . . . . . . . . . .518-242-2222 x1
Administrative Services:
Liz Charland . . . . . . . . . . . . . . . . . . . . . . . . . . .518-242-2222 x1

## Albany Port District Commission
106 Smith Blvd, Admin Bldg
Port of Albany
Albany, NY 12202
518-463-8763 Fax: 518-463-8767
e-mail: portofalbany@portofalbany.us
Web site: www.portofalbany.us

Chair:
Georgette Steffens. . . . . . . . . . . . . . . . . . . . . . . . . . .518-463-8763
General Manager:
Richard Hendrick . . . . . . . . . . . . . . . . . . . . . . . . . . .518-463-8763
e-mail: rhendrick@portofalbany.us
Counsel:
Thomas Owens . . . . . . . . . . . . . . . . . . . . . . . . . . .518-694-0910

*Offices and agencies generally appear in alphabetical order, except when specific order is requested by listee.*

## Buffalo & Fort Erie Public Bridge Authority (Peace Bridge Authority)

One Peace Bridge Plaza
Buffalo, NY 14213-2494
716-884-6744  Fax: 716-884-2089
Web site: www.peacebridge.com

Chair (US):
William Hoyt . . . . . . . . . . . . . . . . . . . . . 716-884-6744/fax: 716-883-7246
Vice Chair (Canada):
Anthony M Annunziata . . . . . . . . . . . . . . 716-884-6744/fax: 716-883-7246
General Manager:
Ron Rienas . . . . . . . . . . . . . . . . . . . . . . . . . . . . . . . . . . . . 716-884-6744

## Capital District Transportation Authority

110 Watervliet Ave
Albany, NY 12206
518-437-8300 or 518-482-8822  Fax: 518-437-8318
Web site: www.cdta.org

Chair:
David M Stackrow . . . . . . . . . . . . . . . . . . . . . . . . . . 518-437-8311
Vice Chair:
Georgeanna Nugent Lussier . . . . . . . . . . . . . . . . . . . . . 518-437-8311
CEO:
Carm Basile . . . . . . . . . . . . . . . . . . . 518-437-6840/fax: 518-437-8349
e-mail: carmb@cdta.org
General Counsel:
Amanda A Avery. . . . . . . . . . . . . . . . . 518-437-8315/fax: 518-473-8318
e-mail: amandaa@cdta.org
VP, Finance & Administration:
Michael P Collins . . . . . . . . . . . . . . . 518-437-8330/fax: 518-437-8347
e-mail: mikec@cdta.org
Director of Transportation:
Frederick C Gilliam. . . . . . . . . . . . . . . 518-437-8372/fax: 518-437-8328
e-mail: fredg@cdta.org
VP, Planning & Infrastructure:
Christopher G Desany . . . . . . . . . . . . . 518-437-8320/fax: 518-437-8328
e-mail: chrisd@cdta.org

## Central New York Regional Transportation Authority

200 Cortland Ave
PO Box 820
Syracuse, NY 13205-0820
315-442-3400  Fax: 315-442-3337

Chair, Board of Directors:
Brian M Schultz . . . . . . . . . . . . . . . . . . . . . . . . . . . . . . 315-442-3300
CEO:
Richard Lee. . . . . . . . . . . . . . . . . . . . . . . . . . . . . . . . . . 315-442-3360
VP, Finance:
Christine LoCurto . . . . . . . . . . . . . . . . . . . . . . . . . . . . . 315-442-3355
Counsel:
Barry Shulman . . . . . . . . . . . . . . . . . . . . . . . . . . . . . . . 315-442-3400

## MTA Bridges & Tunnels

2 Broadway
22nd Floor
New York, NY 10004-2801
646-252-7000  Fax: 646-252-7408
Web site: www.mta.info/bandt

President:
Donald Spero . . . . . . . . . . . . . . . . . . . . . . . . . . . . . . . 212-360-3100
Chief Engineer:
Joseph Keane . . . . . . . . . . . . . . . . . . . . . . . . . . . . . . . 212-878-7200
Vice President, Administration:
Sharon Gallo-Kotcher. . . . . . . . . . . . . . . . . . . . . . . . . 212-360-3015

Vice President, Operations:
Patrick Parisi. . . . . . . . . . . . . . . . . . . . . . . . . . . . . . . . 212-878-7200
Chief Procurement Officer:
Gavin Masterson . . . . . . . . . . . . . . . . . . . . . . . . . . . . . 646-252-7084
Vice President, Staff Services & Chief of Staff:
Albert Rivera. . . . . . . . . . . . . . . . . . . . . . . . . . . . . . . . 646-252-7421
Chief Financial Officer (Acting):
Mildred Chua . . . . . . . . . . . . . . . . . . . . . . . . . . . . . . . 646-252-7132
General Counsel:
M. Margaret Terry . . . . . . . . . . . . . . . . . . . . . . . . . . . 212-878-7200
Manager, Public Affairs:
Judith Glave . . . . . . . . . . . . . . . . . . . . . . . . . . . . . . . . 646-252-7276

## MTA Bus Company

2 Broadway
New York, NY 10004
212-878-7174  Fax: 2512-878-0205
Web site: www.mta.info/busco

President:
Daryl Irick. . . . . . . . . . . . . . . . . . . . . . . . . . . . . . . . . . 212-878-7174

## MTA Capital Construction

2 Broadway
8th Fl
New York, NY 10002
646-252-4575
Web site: www.mta.info/capital

President:
Dr Michael Horodniceanu . . . . . . . . . . . . . . . . . . . . . . 646-252-4277
Chief of Staff:
Ayala Malinovitz . . . . . . . . . . . . . . . . . . . . . . . . . . . . . 646-252-4011
Senior Director, Government & Community Affairs:
Richard Mulieri. . . . . . . . . . . . . . . . . . . . . . . . . . . . . . 646-252-4197
Executive Vice President:
William Goldstein. . . . . . . . . . . . . . . . . . . . . . . . . . . . 646-252-4277
Senior Vice President & General Counsel:
Evan Eisland . . . . . . . . . . . . . . . . . . . . . . . . . . . . . . . . 646-252-4274
Senior Director & Chief Procurement Officer:
David Cannon . . . . . . . . . . . . . . . . . . . . . . . . . . . . . . . 646-252-2321
Vice President & Chief Engineer:
Mike Kyriacou . . . . . . . . . . . . . . . . . . . . . . . . . . . . . . 646-252-4500
Senior Vice President & Program Executive, East Side Access:
Alan Paskoff. . . . . . . . . . . . . . . . . . . . . . . . . . . . . . . . 212-967-0118
Senior Vice President & Program Executive, 2nd Ave Subway:
William Goodrich . . . . . . . . . . . . . . . . . . . . . . . . . . . . 212-510-2661
VP & Program Executive, #7 Subway Line Extension:
Mark Schiffman . . . . . . . . . . . . . . . . . . . . . . . . . . . . . 646-252-3723
Director, System Safety & Security:
Eric Osnes. . . . . . . . . . . . . . . . . . . . . . . . . . . . . . . . . . 646-252-4556
Vice President, Program Controls & Quality Safety:
Raymond Schaeffer. . . . . . . . . . . . . . . . . . . . . . . . . . . 646-252-5393
Vice President, Planning, Development & External Relations:
Joseph Petrocelli. . . . . . . . . . . . . . . . . . . . . . . . . . . . . 646-252-3813

## MTA Long Island Rail Road

Jamaica Station
Jamaica, NY 11435
718-558-7400  Fax: 718-558-8212
Web site: www.mta.info/lirr

President:
Patrick A Nowakowski. . . . . . . . . . . . . . . . . . . . . . . . . 718-558-8252
Executive Vice President:
Albert Cosenza . . . . . . . . . . . . . . . . . . . . . . . . . . . . . . 718-558-7993
e-mail: accosen@lirr.org
Chief Information Officer:
Scott Dieterich . . . . . . . . . . . . . . . . . . . . . . . . . . . . . . 718-588-8166

Policy Areas

*Offices and agencies generally appear in alphabetical order, except when specific order is requested by listee.*

Vice President, General Counsel & Secretary:
 Richard Gans.....................................718-558-8264
Chief Engineer:
 Kevin Tomlinson .................................718-558-7400
Vice President, Labor Relations:
 Michael Chirillo ..................................718-558-7405
Vice President, Market Development & Public Affairs:
 Joseph Calderone ................................718-558-7301
Vice President, ESA/Special Projects:
 John Coulter .....................................718-558-7363
 e-mail: jwcoult@lirr.org
Director, Safety System:
 Frank Lo Presti ..................................718-588-7711
General Manager, Public Affairs:
 Susan McGowan ..................................718-558-7400

## MTA Metro-North Railroad
347 Madison Ave
New York, NY 10017
212-340-2677  Fax: 212-340-4995
Web site: www.mta.info/mnr

President:
 Joseph Giulietti .................................212-340-2677
General Counsel:
 Seth Cummins....................................212-340-4933
VP, Finanace & Informational Systems:
 D. Kim Porcelain .................................212-340-2636
Senior VP, Operations:
 Robert Lieblong ..................................212-499-4300
Senior Director, Capital Planning & Program:
 John Kennard .....................................212-340-2500
Chief of Staff & Operations:
 David Treasure ...................................212-340-2677
Chief Safety & Security Officer:
 Anne Kirsch ......................................212-340-4913
Senior Director, Capital Programs:
 Timothy McCartney...............................212-499-4403
Vice President, Business Operations:
 Thomas Tendy ....................................212-672-1251
Senior Director, Corporate & Public Affairs:
 Mark Mannix .....................................212-340-2142

## MTA New York City Transit
2 Broadway
New York, NY 10004
718-330-3000  Fax: 718-596-2146
Web site: www.mta.info/nyct

President:
 Veronique Hakim .................................646-252-5800
Chief Transportation Officer:
 Herbert Lambert ..................................718-330-3000
Vice President, Labor Relations:
 Christopher Johnson ..............................718-330-3000
Vice President, Corporate Communications:
 Paul Fleuranges...................................646-252-5873
Vice President, Technology & Information Services:
 Sidney Gellineau..................................718-330-3000
Vice President & General Counsel:
 Martin Schnabel ..................................718-694-3900
Director, Labor Relations:
 Andrew Paul .....................................646-252-5880
Chief Officer, Staten Island Railway:
 John Gaul ........................................718-876-8239

## MTA (Metropolitan Transportation Authority)
347 Madison Ave
New York, NY 10017

212-878-7000  Fax: 212-878-7264
Web site: www.mta.info

Chairman/CEO:
 Thomas F. Prendergast............................212-878-7200
Director of Security:
 Raymond Diaz ....................................212-878-7155
Deputy Executive Director, Government & Community Affairs:
 Justin Bernbach...................................212-878-7160
Senior Director, Human Resources/Retirement:
 Margaret M. Connor
CAO/Employee Relations:
 Anita Miller......................................212-878-7438
Auditor General:
 Michael J Fucilli .................................212-878-7236
Chief Financial Officer:
 Robert E Foran ...................................212-878-7278
Chief Financial Officer:
 Robert E. Foran
General Counsel:
 Jerome F Page ....................212-878-7313/fax: 212-878-7050
Chief of Staff:
 Donna Evans......................................212-878-1001
Director, External Communications:
 Adam Lisberg .....................................212-878-7440

## MTA Office of the Inspector General
2 Penn Plaza, 5th Fl
New York, NY 10121
212-878-0000 or 800-682-4448  Fax: 212-878-0003
Web site: www.mtaig.state.ny.us

Inspector General:
 Barry L Kluger ...................................212-878-0000

## New York Metropolitan Transportation Council
25 Beaver Street
Ste 201
New York, NY 10004
212-383-7200  Fax: 212-383-2418
e-mail: nymtc-web@dot.ny.gov
Web site: www.nymtc.org

Interim Executive Director:
 Lisa Daglian .....................................212-383-7200
Acting Director, Administration:
 Nina Del Senno...................................212-383-2402
 e-mail: nina.delsenno@dot.ny.gov
Director, Planning:
 Gerard J Bogacz ..................................212-383-7260
 e-mail: gerry.bogacz@dot.ny.gov
PIO:
 Stacy Graham-Hunt ...............................212-383-7203
 e-mail: stacy.graham-hunt@dot.ny.gov

## New York State Bridge Authority
Mid-Hudson Bridge Plaza
PO Box 1010
Highland, NY 12528
845-691-7245  Fax: 845-691-3560
e-mail: info@nysba.ny.gov
Web site: www.nysba.ny.gov

Chair:
 Richard A. Gerentine .............................845-691-7245
Vice Chair:
 Joseph Ramaglia ..................................845-691-7245
Executive Director:
 Joseph Ruggiero ..................................845-691-7245

*Offices and agencies generally appear in alphabetical order, except when specific order is requested by listee.*

Director, IT:
Gregory J Herd . . . . . . . . . . . . . . . . . . . . . . . . . . . . . .518-828-4107
Director, Toll Collections & Operations:
Wayne V Ferguson . . . . . . . . . . . . . . . . . . . . . . . . . . . .845-691-7245

## New York State Thruway Authority
200 Southern Blvd
PO Box 189
Albany, NY 12201
518-436-2700  Fax: 518-436-2899
Web site: www.thruway.ny.gov

Chair:
Joanne M Mahoney . . . . . . . . . . . . . . . . . . . . . . . . . . . .518-436-3000
Interim Executive Director:
Maria Lehman . . . . . . . . . . . . . . . . . . . . . . . . . . . . . . . .518-436-2900
General Counsel:
Gordon Cuffy . . . . . . . . . . . . . . . . . . . . . . . . . . . . . . . . .518-436-2840
CFO:
Matt Howard . . . . . . . . . . . . . . . . . . . . . . . . . . . . . . . . .518-436-2840
Director, Media Relations & Communications:
Jennifer Givner . . . . . . . . . . . . . . . . . . . . . . . . . . . . . . .518-471-5300
e-mail: publicinfo@thruway.ny.gov
Director, Administrative Services:
John F. Barr
e-mail: publicinfo@thruway.ny.gov

## New York State Canal Corporation
Web site: www.canals.ny.gov
Interim Executive Director:
Maria Lehman . . . . . . . . . . . . . . . . . . .518-436-3055/fax: 518-471-5023

## Niagara Falls Bridge Commission
5365 Military Rd
Lewiston, NY 14092
716-285-6322 or 905-354-5641  Fax: 716-282-3292
e-mail: general_inquiries@niagarafallsbridges.com
Web site: www.niagarafallsbridges.com

Chair:
Linda L McAusland . . . . . . . . . . . . . . . . . . . . . . . . . . . .716-285-6322
Vice Chair:
Russell G Quarantello . . . . . . . . . . . . . . . . . . . . . . . . . .716-285-6322
Treasurer:
Harry R Palladino . . . . . . . . . . . . . . . . . . . . . . . . . . . . .716-285-6322
Secretary:
John Lopinski . . . . . . . . . . . . . . . . . . . . . . . . . . . . . . . .716-285-6322

## Niagara Frontier Transportation Authority
181 Ellicott St
Buffalo, NY 14203
716-855-7300 or 800-622-1220  Fax: 716-855-6655
Web site: www.nfta.com

Chair:
Sister Denise A. Roche
Executive Director:
Kimberley A Minkel . . . . . . . . . . . . . . . . . . . . . . . . . . . .716-855-7470
Chief Financial Officer:
John Cox . . . . . . . . . . . . . . . . . . . . . . . . . . . . . . . . . . . .716-855-7300
General Counsel:
David J State . . . . . . . . . . . . . . . . . . . . . . . . . . . . . . . . .716-855-7686
Director, Aviation:
William Vanecek . . . . . . . . . . . . . . . . . . . . . . . . . . . . . .716-630-6030
Director, Human Resources:
Karen Novo . . . . . . . . . . . . . . . . . . . . . . . . . . . . . . . . . .716-855-7343
Director, Public Transit:
Thomas George . . . . . . . . . . . . . . . . . . . . . . . . . . . . . . .716-855-7390
Director, Engineering:
Michael Bykowski . . . . . . . . . . . . . . . . . . . . . . . . . . . . .716-855-7389

Director, Public Affairs:
C Douglas Hartmayer . . . . . . . . . . . . . . . . . . . . . . . . . .716-855-7420
Chief, NFTA Police:
George W. Gast. . . . . . . . . . . . . . . . . . . . . . . . . . . . . . . .716-855-7666

## Ogdensburg Bridge & Port Authority
One Bridge Plaza
Ogdensburg, NY 13669
315-393-4080  Fax: 315-393-7068
e-mail: obpa@ogdensport.com
Web site: www.ogdensport.com

Chair:
Samuel J LaMacchia . . . . . . . . . . . . . . . . . . . . . . . . . . .315-393-4080
Deputy Executive Director:
Wade A Davis . . . . . . . . . . . . . . . . . . . . . . . . . . . . . . . .315-393-4080
e-mail: wadavis@ogdensport.com

## Port Authority of New York & New Jersey
4 World Trade Center
150 Greenwich Street
New York, NY 10007
212-435-7000  Fax: 212-435-4032
Web site: www.panynj.gov

Chair, New Jersey:
John J Degnan . . . . . . . . . . . . . . . . . . . . . . . . . . . . . . . .212-435-7000
Vice Chair, New York:
Scott H Rechler . . . . . . . . . . . . . . . . . . . . . . . . . . . . . . .212-435-7000
Executive Director:
Patrick Foye . . . . . . . . . . . . . . . . . . . . . . . . . . . . . . . . . .212-435-7271
Director World Trade Center Operations:
Hugh P McCann . . . . . . . . . . . . . . . . . . . . . . . . . . . . . . .212-435-7887
Director Government & Community Affairs - NY (Acting):
Ian R Van Praagh . . . . . . . . . . . . . . . . . . . . . . . . . . . . . .212-435-6903
Assistant General Counsel:
Carlene V McIntyre . . . . . . . . . . . . . . . . . . . . . . . . . . . .212-435-3515
Chief Financial Officer:
Elizabeth McCarthy . . . . . . . . . . . . . . . . . . . . . . . . . . . .212-435-7738
Director Media Relations:
Ron Marsico . . . . . . . . . . . . . . . . . . . . . .212-435-7777/fax: 212-435-4032
Director, Public Safety/Superintendent of Police:
Michael A Fedorko . . . . . . . . . . . . . . . . . . . . . . . . . . . . .212-435-7000
Chief Engineer:
James A Starace . . . . . . . . . . . . . . . . . . . . . . . . . . . . . . .212-435-7449

## Port of Oswego Authority
1 East Second St
Oswego, NY 13126
315-343-4503  Fax: 315-343-5498
e-mail: shipping@portoswego.com
Web site: www.portoswego.com

Chair:
Terrence Hammill . . . . . . . . . . . . . . . . . . . . . . . . . . . . . .315-343-4503
Executive Director & CEO:
Zelko N. Kirincich . . . . . . . . . . . . . . . . . . . . . . . . . . .315-343-4503 x111
Manager, Administrative Services/Facility Security Officer:
William Scriber . . . . . . . . . . . . . . . . . . . . . . . . . . . . .315-343-4503 x108
e-mail: wscriber@portoswego.com
Supervisor of Marina Operations:
Bernie Bacon. . . . . . . . . . . . . . . . . . . . . . . . . . . . . . . . . .315-343-1967
e-mail: oswegomarina@yahoo.com

*Offices and agencies generally appear in alphabetical order, except when specific order is requested by listee.*

## Rochester-Genesee Regional Transportation Authority-RTS
1372 E Main St
PO Box 90629
Rochester, NY 14609
585-654-0200  Fax: 585-654-0224
Web site: www.myrts.com

Chief Executive Officer:
  Bill Carpenter . . . . . . . . . . . . . . . . . . . . . .585-654-0200
Chief Operating Officer:
  Miguel A Velazquez. . . . . . . . . . . . . . . . . . . .585-654-0200
Chief Financial Officer:
  Scott Adair . . . . . . . . . . . . . . . . . . . . . . .585-654-0200
General Counsel/CAO:
  Daniel DeLaus . . . . . . . . . . . . . . . . . . . . . .585-654-0200
Public Information Officer:
  Tom Brede. . . . . . . . . . . . . . . . . . . . . . . . .585-654-0730

## Thousand Islands Bridge Authority
PO Box 428, Collins Landing
43530 Interstate 81
Alexandria Bay, NY 13607
315-482-2501 or 315-658-2281  Fax: 315-482-5925
e-mail: info@tibridge.com
Web site: www.tibridge.com

Chair:
  Robert Barnard . . . . . . . . . . . . . . . . . . . . .315-482-2501
Executive Director:
  Robert G Horr, III. . . . . . . . . . . . . . . . . . . .315-482-2501
  e-mail: roberthorr@tibridge.com
Legal Counsel:
  Dennis Whelpley. . . . . . . . . . . . . . . . . . . . .315-482-2501

## Waterfront Commission of New York Harbor
39 Broadway
4th Fl
New York, NY 10006
212-742-9280  Fax: 212-480-0587
Web site: www.wcnyh.org

Commissioner, New York:
  Ronald Goldstock . . . . . . . . . . . . . . . . . . . .212-742-9280
Commissioner, New Jersey:
  Michael Murphy . . . . . . . . . . . . . . . . . . . . .212-742-9280
Executive Director:
  Walter M Arsenault . . . . . . . . . . . . . . . . . . .212-905-9201

### NEW YORK STATE LEGISLATURE

*See Legislative Branch in Section 1 for additional Standing Committee and Subcommittee information.*

## Assembly Standing Committees

### Corporations, Authorities & Commissions
Chair:
  Amy Paulin (D). . . . . . . . . . . . . . . . . . . . . .518-455-5585

### Economic Development, Job Creation, Commerce & Industry
Chair:
  Harry B Bronson (D) . . . . . . . . . . . . . . . . . . .518-455-4767

### Transportation
Chair:
  William B Magnarelli (D). . . . . . . . . . . . . . . . .518-455-5606

## Senate Standing Committees

### Commerce, Economic Development & Small Business
Chair:
  Anna M Kaplan (D, IP, WF). . . . . . . . . . . . . . . .518-455-2170
Minority Member:
  Pamela Helming (R, C, IP). . . . . . . . . . . . . . . .518-455-2366

### Corporations, Authorities & Commissions
Chair:
  Leroy Comrie (D) . . . . . . . . . . . . . . . . . . . .518-455-2701

### Transportation
Chair:
  Timothy M Kennedy (D, IP, WF). . . . . . . . . . . . . .518-455-2426

### U.S. GOVERNMENT

### EXECUTIVE DEPARTMENTS AND RELATED AGENCIES

## Federal Maritime Commission
Web site: www.fmc.gov

**New York Area Office**
  Bldg 75, Rm 205B, JFK Intl Airport, Jamaica, NY 11430
Area Rep:
  Emanuel J Mingione . . . . . . . . . . . . . .718-553-2228/fax: 718-553-2229

## National Transportation Safety Board
Web site: www.ntsb.gov

**Aviation Division, Northeast Regional Office**
  2001 Route 46, Ste 203, Parsippany, NJ 07054
Regional Director:
  David Muzio

**Office of Administrative Law Judges**
  490 L'Enfant Plaza, ESW, Washington, DC 20594
Chief Judge:
  Alfonso J. Montano . . . . . . . . . . . . . .202-314-6151/fax: 202-314-8758

## US Department of Homeland Security (DHS)
Web site: www.dhs.gov

**Transportation Security Administration (TSA)**
  201 Varick St, Rm 1101, New York, NY 10014
Regional Spokesperson:
  Lisa Farbstein . . . . . . . . . . . . . . . . . . . . .212-620-3608

## US Transportation Department
Web site: www.dot.gov

**Federal Aviation Administration-Eastern Region**
  One Aviation Plaza, Jamaica, NY 11434-4809
  718-553-3001
  Web site: www.faa.gov
Regional Administrator:
  Carmine Gallo. . . . . . . . . . . . . . . . . . . . . .718-553-3001
Deputy Regional Administrator:
  Diane Crean . . . . . . . . . . . . . . . . . . . . . . .718-553-3001

  **Accounting Division**
  Manager:
    Fred Glassberg . . . . . . . . . . . . . . . . . . . .718-553-4190

  **Aerospace Medicine Division**
  Regional Flight Surgeon:
    Harriet Lester . . . . . . . . . . . . . . . . . . . .718-553-3300

*Offices and agencies generally appear in alphabetical order, except when specific order is requested by listee.*

**Air Traffic Division**
Acting Area Director:
 John G McCartney . . . . . . . . . . . . . . . . . . . . . . . . . .718-553-4500

**Airports Division**
Manager:
 Steve Urlass . . . . . . . . . . . . . . . . . . . . . . . . . . . . . .516-227-3803

**Aviation Information & Services Division**
Manager:
 Alan Siperstein . . . . . . . . . . . . . . . . . . . . . . . . . . . .718-553-3358

**Engineering Services**
Manager:
 Selin Haber . . . . . . . . . . . . . . . . . . . . . . . . . . . . . . .718-553-3400

**Flight Standards Division**
Manager:
 John M. Krepp . . . . . . . . . . . . . . . . . . . . . . .516-228-8029 x. 200

**Human Resource Management Division**
Manager:
 Gloria Quay . . . . . . . . . . . . . . . . . . . . . . . . . . . . . .718-553-3132

**Logistics Division**
Manager:
 Vacant . . . . . . . . . . . . . . . . . . . . . . . . . . . . . . . . . . .718-553-3050

**Military Liaison Officers to the Federal Aviation Admin (NYS)**
12 New England Executive Park, Burlington, MA 1803
 *Air Force Regional Representatives*
 Representative:
  Vacant . . . . . . . . . . . . . . . . . .781-238-7901/fax: 781-238-7903
 Transportation Specialist:
  Cheryl W Carpenter . . . . . . . . . . . . . . . . . . . . . .781-238-7910
 *Army Regional Representatives*
 Liaison Officer:
  LTC Bill Walsh . . . . . . . . . . . . . . . . . . . . . . . . . . .781-238-7906
 Liaison Officer:
  MSGT Jason Williams . . . . . . . . . . . . . . . . . . . . . .781-238-7905
 *Navy Regional Representatives*
 Liaison Officer:
  CDR Rick Perez . . . . . . . . . . . . . . . . . . . . . . . . . . .781-238-7907
 Liaison Officer:
  ACCS Mark Moon . . . . . . . . . .781-238-7908/fax: 781-238-7902

**Runway Safety Manager**
Manager:
 Bill DeGraaff . . . . . . . . . . . . . . . . . . . . . . . . . . . . .718-553-3326

**Federal Highway Administration-New York Division** . . . . . . . .fax:
518-431-4121
 Leo W O'Brien Federal Bldg, Rm 719 Clinton Ave & N Pearl St, Albany,
 NY 12207
 518-431-4125 Fax: 518-431-4121
 Web site: www.fhwa.dot.gov
Division Administrator:
 John M. McDade . . . . . . . . . . . . . . . . . . . . . . . . . . .518-431-8897
Acting Chief Operating Officer:
 Robert Clark . . . . . . . . . . . . . . . . . . . . . . . . . . . . . .518-431-8879
 e-mail: robert.clark@dot.gov
NYC Federal Aid Liaison:
 John Formosa . . . . . . . . . . . . . . . . . . . . . . . . . . . . .212-668-2205
 e-mail: john.formosa@dot.gov
Engineer Coordinator:
 Joan P. Walters . . . . . . . . . . . . . . . . . . . . . . . . . . . .518-431-8868
 e-mail: joan.walters@dot.gov

**Federal Motor Carrier Safety Admin-New York Division** . . . .fax:
518-431-4140
 Leo O'Brien Federal Bldg, Rm 815, Clinton Avenue & North Pearl Street,
 Albany, NY 12207
 518-431-4145 Fax: 518-431-4140
 Web site: www.fmcsa.dot.gov

Division Administrator:
 Brian Temperine . . . . . . . . . . . . . . . . . . . . . . . .518-431-4145 x311
Field Office Supervisor, Upstate:
 Pamela Noyes . . . . . . . . . . . . . . . . . . . . . . . . . .518-431-4145 x316
State Program Specialist:
 Vacant
Manager, Intelligent Transportation Systems Commercial Vehicle Operati:
 Carolyn Temperine . . . . . . . . . . . . . . . . . . . . . .518-431-4145 x270

**Federal Railroad Administration-Field Offices**
 Web site: www.fra.dot.gov

 **Hazardous Material**
 1 Aviation Plaza, Jamaica, NY 11434-4089
 Inspector:
  Steven Joseph . . . . . . . . . . . . . . . . . . . . . . . . . . . . .718-553-2596

 **Highway-Rail Grade Crossing**
 PO Box 2144, Ballston Spa, NY 12020
 Program Manager:
  Randall L Dickinson . . . . . . . . . . . . .518-899-5372/fax: 518-899-5372

**Federal Transit Administration, Region II-New York**
 One Bowling Green, Rm 429, New York, NY 10004-1415
 Web site: www.fta.dot.gov
Regional Admin:
 Marilyn G. Shazor . . . . . . . . . . . . . . . . .212-668-2170/fax: 212-668-2136

**Maritime Administration**
 Web site: www.marad.dot.gov

 **Great Lakes Region (includes part of New York State)**
 500 West Madison Street, Suite 1110, Chicago, IL 60661
 312-353-1032
 Regional Director:
  Floyd Miras . . . . . . . . . . . . . . . . . . . .312-353-1032/fax: 312-353-1036

 **North Atlantic Region**
 One Bowling Green, Rm 418, New York, NY 10004
 Regional Director:
  Jeffrey Flumignan . . . . . . . . . . . . . . . . . . . . . . . . . . .212-668-3330

 **US Merchant Marine Academy**
 300 Steamboat Rd, Kings Point, NY 11024-1699
 516-726-5800
 Web site: www.usmma.edu
 Superintendent:
  RADM James A. Helis . . . . . . . . . . . . . . . . . . . . . . . .516-726-5800

**National Highway Traffic Safety Administration, Reg II-NY**
 222 Mamaroneck Ave, Suite 204, White Plains, NY 10605
 Web site: www.nhtsa.dot.gov
Team Leader:
 Richard Simon . . . . . . . . . . . . . . . . . . . .914-682-6162/fax: 914-682-6239
 e-mail: region2@dot.gov

**Office of Inspector General, Region II-New York**
 80 Madison Lane, New York, NY 10038
 Web site: www.oig.dot.gov
Inspector General:
 Debra Herlica . . . . . . . . . . . . . . . . . . . .212-825-2413/fax: 212-825-3238
 e-mail: dherlica@doi.nyc.gov

**Saint Lawrence Seaway Development Corporation**
 180 Andrews St, Massena, NY 13662
 Web site: www.greatlakes-seaway.com
Assoc Administrator:
 Salvatore Pisani . . . . . . . . . . . . . . . . . . .315-764-3209/fax: 315-764-3235

## U.S. CONGRESS

*See U.S. Congress Chapter for additional Standing Committee and Subcommittee information.*

*Offices and agencies generally appear in alphabetical order, except when specific order is requested by listee.*

## House of Representatives Standing Committees

### Transportation & Infrastructure
Chair:
  Bill Shuster (R-PA)......................................202-225-2431
Ranking Minority Member:
  Nick J. Rahall II (D-WV)............................202-225-3452
New York Delegate:
  Sean Patrick Maloney (D).........................202-225-5441
New York Delegate:
  Timothy H Bishop (D) ............................202-225-3826
New York Delegate:
  Richard L. Hanna ...................................202-225-3665
New York Delegate:
  Jerrold Nadler (D).....................................202-225-5635

## Senate Standing Committees

### Commerce, Science & Transportation
Chair:
  John D Rockefeller IV (D-WV) ......................202-224-6472
Vice Chair:
  John Thune (R-SD)................................202-224-2321

### Environment & Public Works
Chair:
  Barbara Boxer (D-CA)..............................202-224-8832
Ranking Minority Member:
  David Vitter (R-LA)...................................202-224-4623
New York Delegate:
  Kirsten Gillibrand (D)................................202-224-4451

  #### Subcommittee
  *Transportation & Infrastructure*
    Chair:
      Max Baucus (D-MT)........................202-224-2651
    Ranking Minority Member:
      John Barrasso (R-WY) ....................202-224-6441

## PRIVATE SECTOR

### ALSTOM Transportation Inc
1 Transit Dr, Hornell, NY 14843
607-281-2487  Fax: 607-324-2641
Web site: www.transport.alstom.com
*High-speed trains, rapid transit vehicles, commuter cars, AC propulsion & signaling, passenger locomotives*
Wallace Smith, Vice President
Chuck Wochele, Vice President Business Development

### A&W Architects and Engineers
### Ammann & Whitney Consulting Engineers
96 Morton St, New York, NY 10014
212-462-8500  Fax: 212-929-5356
e-mail: nivanoff@ammann-whitney.com
Web site: www.ammann-whitney.com
*Planning, engineering & construction mgmt for airport, transit, gov't, recreation & commercial facilities; highways; bridges*
Nick Ivanoff, President & Chief Executive Officer

### Automobile Club of New York
1415 Kellum Place, Garden City, NY 11530
516-873-2259  Fax: 516-873-2355
John Corlett, Director Government Affairs

### Automotive Technology & Energy Group of Western NY
2568 Walden Avenue, Suite 103, Cheektowaga, NY 14225
716-651-4645  Fax: 716-651-4662
*Garage & service station owners*
Robert Gliss, Executive Director

### British Airways PLC
75-20 Astoria Blvd, Jackson Heights, NY 11370
347-418-4729  Fax: 347-418-4204
e-mail: john.lampl@ba.com
Web site: www.ba.com
John Lampl, Vice President, Corporate Communications-Americas

### CP Rail System
200 Clifton Corporate Parkway, PO Box 8002, Clifton Park, NY 12065
518-383-7200  Fax: 518-383-7222
*Freight transport*
Brent Szafron, Service Area Manager

### DKI Engineering & Consulting USA, PC, Corporate World Headquarters
632 Plank Rd, Ste 208, Clifton Park, NY 12065
518-373-4999  Fax: 518-373-8989
e-mail: dki123@aol.com
*Design, engineering, planning, construction management & program management oversight for airports, bridges, highways, railroads, transit, tunnels, water & wastewater facilities*
D K Gupta, President & Chief Executive Officer

### Empire State Passengers Association
PO Box 434, Syracuse, NY 13209
716-741-6384  Fax: 716-632-3044
Web site: www.esparail.org
*Advocacy for improvement of rail passenger service*
Bruce Becker, President

### Gandhi Engineering Inc
111 John St, 3rd Fl, New York, NY 10038-3002
212-349-2900  Fax: 212-285-0205
e-mail: gandhi@gandhieng.com
Web site: www.gandhieng.com
*Consulting architects & engineers; infrastructure projects & transportation facilities*
Kirti Gandhi, President

### General Contractors Association of NY
60 East 42nd St, Rm 3510, New York, NY 10165
212-687-3131  Fax: 212-808-5267
*Heavy construction, transportation*
Felice Farber, Director, External Affairs

### Jacobs Engineering
260 Madison Ave, 12th Floor, Suite 1200, New York, NY 10016
212-268-1500  Fax: 212-481-9484
Web site: www.jacobs.com
*Multi-modal surface transportation planning, design, engineering, construction & inspection services*
Vincent Mangieri, Vice President

### Komanoff Energy Associates
636 Broadway, Rm 602, New York, NY 10012-2623
212-260-5237
e-mail: kea@igc.org
*Energy, utilities & transportation consulting*
Charles Komanoff, Director

### Konheim & Ketcham Inc
175 Pacific St, Brooklyn, NY 11201
718-330-0550  Fax: 718-330-0582
e-mail: csk@konheimketcham.com
*Environmental impact analysis, traffic engineering, transportation planning & technical assistance to community groups*
Carolyn Konheim, President

---

*Offices and agencies generally appear in alphabetical order, except when specific order is requested by listee.*

**Kriss, Kriss & Brignola, LLP**
350 Northern Blvd, Suite 306, Albany, NY 12204
518-449-2037 Fax: 518-449-7875
e-mail: office@krisslaw.com
Web site: www.krisslawoffice.com
*Advocates for highway & auto safety*
Mark C Kriss, Partner

**Long Island Rail Road Commuter's Council**
347 Madison Ave, 8th Fl, New York, NY 10017
212-878-7087 Fax: 212-878-7461
Web site: www.lirrcc.org
*Represent interest of LIRR riders*
Mark Epstein, Chair

**Metro-North Railroad Commuter Council**
347 Madison Ave, New York, NY 10017
212-878-7077 or 212-878-7087 Fax: 212-878-7461
e-mail: mail@pcac.org
Web site: www.pcac.org
*Represent interests of MNR riders*
William Henderson, Chair

**NY Airport Service**
15 Second Ave, Brooklyn, NY 11215
718-875-8200 Fax: 718-875-7056
Web site: www.nyairportservice.com
*Airport shuttle bus services*
Mark Marmurstein, Vice President

**NY State Association of Town Superintendents of Highways Inc**
119 Washington Avenue, Suite 300, Albany, NY 12210
518-694-9313 Fax: 518-694-9314
Web site: www.nystownhwys.org
Michael K Thompson, Communications Director

**NYS Association of Service Stations & Repair Shops**
6 Walker Way, Albany, NY 12205-4946
518-452-4367 Fax: 518-452-1955
e-mail: nysassn@together.net
Web site: www.nysassrs.com
*Protect the interests of independent service stations & repair shops & the motoring public*
Ralph Bombardiere, Executive Director

**NYS County Hwy Super Assn / NY Aviation Mgt Assn / NY Public Transit Assn**
119 Washington Ave, Ste 100, Albany, NY 12210
518-465-1694 Fax: 518-465-1942
Web site: www.countyhwys.org; www.nyama.com; www.nytransit.org
*County highways & bridges in NYS; aviation industry in NYS; public transit industry in NYS*
Kathleen A Van De Loo, Communications Director

**National Economic Research Associates**
308 N Cayuga St, Ithaca, NY 14850
607-277-3007 Fax: 607-277-1581
e-mail: alfred.kahn@nera.com
Web site: www.nera.com
*Utility & transportation regulation, deregulation & antitrust*
Alfred E Kahn, Professor Emeritus & Special Consultant

**New England Steamship Agents Inc**
730 Downing St, Niskayuna, NY 12309
518-463-5749 Fax: 518-463-5751
e-mail: nesa0025@aol.com
*Domestic transportation, vessel agency/husbandry, customs brokerage & vessel brokerage*
Diane Delory, President

**New York & Atlantic Railway (NYA)**
68-01 Otto Rd, Glendale, NY 11385
7189497-3023 Fax: 718-497-3364
Web site: www.anacostia.com
*Freight transport*
Paul Victor, President

**New York Public Interest Research Group Straphangers Campaign**
9 Murray Street, Lower Level, New York, NY 10007
212-349-6460 Fax: 212-349-1366
e-mail: grussian@nypirg.org
Web site: www.straphangers.org
*Mass transit & government reform*
Gene Russianoff, Senior Staff Attorney

**New York Roadway Improvement Coalition (NYRIC)**
629 Old White Plains Road, Tarrytown, NY 10591
914-631-6070 Fax: 914-631-5172
*Heavy highway & bridge construction*
Ross Pepe, President

**New York Shipping Association Inc**
100 Wood Ave South, Ste 304, Iselin, NJ 08830-2716
732-452-7800 Fax: 732-452-6312
e-mail: jcobb@nysanet.org
Web site: www.nysanet.org
*Maximizing the efficiency, cost competitiveness, safety & quality of marine cargo operations in the Port of New York & New Jersey*
James H Cobb, Jr, Director, Governmental Affairs

**New York State Auto Dealers Association**
37 Elk St, Albany, NY 12207
518-463-1148 x204 Fax: 518-432-1309
e-mail: bob@nysada.com
Web site: www.nysada.com
Robert Vancavage, President

**Trucking Association of New York**
7 Corporate Drive, Clifton Park, NY 12065
518-458-9696 Fax: 518-458-2525
e-mail: khems@nytrucks.org
Web site: www.nytrucks.org
*Safety & regulatory compliance*
Kendra Hems, President
Karin White, Deputy Director

**New York State Transportation Engineering Alliance (NYSTEA)**
99 Pine St, Ste 207, Albany, NY 12207
518-436-0786 Fax: 518-427-0452
e-mail: sdm@fwc-law.com
*Transportation & infrastructure*
Stephen D Morgan, Secretary

**New York, Susquehanna & Western Railway Corporation, The**
1 Railroad Ave, Cooperstown, NY 13326-1110
607-547-2555 Fax: 607-547-9834
e-mail: nfenno@nysw.com
Web site: www.nysw.com
*Subsidiaries operate freight railroad systems*
Nathan R Fenno, President

**Parsons Brinckerhoff**
One Penn Plaza, New York, NY 10119
212-465-5000 Fax: 212-465-5096
*Engineering, planning, construction management & consulting for transit & transportation, power & telecom projects*
Joel H Bennett, Senior Vice President

*Offices and agencies generally appear in alphabetical order, except when specific order is requested by listee.*

**Regional Plan Association**
4 Irving Place, 7th Fl, New York, NY 10003
212-253-2727  Fax: 212-253-5666
e-mail: jeff@rpa.org
Web site: www.rpa.org
*Regional transportation planning & development issues*
Jeffrey M Zupan, Senior Fellow, Transportation

**Seneca Flight Operations**
2262 Airport Dr, Penn Yan, NY 14527
315-536-4471  Fax: 315-536-4558
e-mail: rleppert@senecafoods.com
Web site: www.senecafoods.com
*Executive air transportation*
Richard Leppert, General Manager

**Simmons-Boardman Publishing Corp**
345 Hudson St, 12th Fl, New York, NY 10014-4590
212-620-7200  Fax: 212-633-1863
Web site: www.railwayage.com or www.rtands.com or www.railjournal.com
*Publisher of: Railway Age, International Railway Journal & Rapid Transit Review, Railway Track & Structures*
Robert DeMarco, Publisher

**Systra Consulting Inc**
470 Seventh Ave, 10th Floor, New York, NY 10018
212-494-9111  Fax: 212-494-9112
*Engineering consultants specializing in urban rail & transit systems, passenger & freight railroads & high speed rail*
Peter Allibone, Executive Vice President

**Transport Workers Union of America, AFL-CIO**
1700 Broadway, 2nd Fl, New York, NY 10019
212-259-4900  Fax: 212-265-5704
Web site: www.twu.com
*Bus, train, railroad & airline workers' union*
James C Little, International President

**Transportation Alternatives**
111 John Street, Suite 260, New York, NY 10038
212-629-8080  Fax: 212-629-8334
e-mail: info@transalt.org
Web site: www.transalt.org
*NYC commute alternatives, traffic calming, pedestrian safety issues, bicycling, public space*
Paul Steely White, Executive Director

**Tri-State Transportation Campaign**
350 W 31st St, Room 802, New York, NY 10001-2726
212-268-7474  Fax: 212-268-7333
e-mail: tstc@tstc.org
Web site: www.tstc.org
*Public interest, transit advocacy, planning & environmental organizations working to reform transportation policies*
Kate Slevin, Executive Director

**United Transportation Union**
35 Fuller Road, Suite 205, Albany, NY 12205
518-438-8403  Fax: 518-438-8404
e-mail: sjnasca@aol.com
Web site: www.utu.org
*Federal government railroad, bus & airline employees; public employees*
Samuel Nasca, Legislative Director

**Urbitran Group**
71 West 23rd St, 11th Fl, New York, NY 10010
212-366-6200  Fax: 212-366-6214
Web site: www.urbitran.com
*Engineering, architecture & planning*
Michael Horodniceaenu, President & Chief Executive Officer

# VETERANS AND MILITARY

## NEW YORK STATE

### GOVERNOR'S OFFICE

**Governor's Office**
Executive Chamber
State Capitol
Albany, NY 12224
518-474-8390  Fax: 518-474-1513
Web site: www.ny.gov

Governor:
  Andrew M Cuomo .................................518-474-8390
Secretary to the Governor:
  Melissa DeRosa ...................518-474-4246 or 212-681-4580
Counsel to the Governor:
  Kumiki Gibson.....................518-474-8343 or 212-681-4580
Chief of Staff:
  Jill DesRosiers....................518-474-8390 or 212-681-4580
Director, Communications:
  Peter Ajemian.....................518-474-8418 or 212-681-4640

### EXECUTIVE DEPARTMENTS AND RELATED AGENCIES

**Health Department**
Corning Tower
Empire State Plaza
Albany, NY 12237
518-474-2011 or 518-474-7354
e-mail: dohweb@health.ny.gov
Web site: www.health.ny.gov

**Health Facilities Management**
Director:
  David J Hernandez ................518-474-2772/fax: 518-474-0611

**Helen Hayes Hospital**
Rte 9W, West Haverstraw, NY 10993-1195
845-786-4000
e-mail: info@helenhayeshospital.org
Web site: www.helenhayeshospital.org
CEO:
  Edmund Coletti.................845-786-4202/fax: 845-947-0036
Chief Operating Officer:
  Kathleen Martucci ...............................845-786-4201

**New York State Veterans' Home at Batavia**
220 Richmond Ave, Batavia, NY 14020
585-345-2000
Web site: www.nysvets.org
Administrator:
  Joanne I Hernick ................585-345-2076/fax: 585-345-9030
Acting Medical Director:
  Margaret Mitchell, MD ...........................585-345-2042
Director, Nursing:
  Stephanie Sulyma .........................585-345-2000 x2041

**New York State Veterans' Home at Montrose**......fax: 914-788-6100
2090 Albany Post Rd, Montrose, NY 10548
Fax: 914-788-6100
Web site: www.nysvets.org
Administrator:
  Nancy Baa-Danso.............................914-788-6003
Medical Director:
  George Gorich, MD ...........................914-788-6025

Director, Nursing:
  Christene St Paul Joseph .........................914-788-6021

**New York State Veterans' Home at Oxford**
4211 State Highway 220, Oxford, NY 13830
607-843-3100
Web site: www.nysvets.org
Administrator:
  James Wyzykowski..............607-843-3129/fax: 607-843-3199
Acting Medical Director:
  Donna Hussman, MD............................607-843-3140
Director, Nursing:
  Linda Winston ................................607-843-3165

**New York State Veterans' Home at St Albans**
178-50 Linden Blvd, Jamaica, NY 11434-1467
718-990-0300
Web site: www.nysvets.org
Administrator:
  Neville Goldson ...............................718-990-0329
Medical Director:
  Thomas Bizarro MD.............................718-990-0328
Director, Nursing:
  Elmina Wilson-Hew.............................718-990-0316

**Labor Department**
W.A. Harriman Campus
Building 12
Albany, NY 12240
518-457-9000 or 888-469-7365  Fax: 518-457-6908
e-mail: nysdol@labor.ny.gov
Web site: www.labor.ny.gov

Commissioner:
  Roberta Reardon...............................518-457-9000
Executive Deputy Commissioner:
  Nathaalie Carey................................518-457-4318

**Federal Programs**
Deputy Commissioner, Federal Programs:
  Bruce Herman..................................518-485-6410

**Employment Services Division**
Director:
  Vacant......................................518-457-3584
Assistant Director:
  Russell Oliver................................518-457-3584

**Veterans Services**
Program Coordinator:
  Vacant......................................518-457-1343

**Employer Services**
Director:
  Vacant......................................518-457-6821
Rural Labor Services:
  Valerie Sewell................................518-457-8539

**Military & Naval Affairs, Division of**
330 Old Niskayuna Rd
Latham, NY 12110-3514
518-786-4781 or 518-489-6188  Fax: 518-786-4649
e-mail: ng.ny.nyarng.list.dmnawm@mail.mil
Web site: www.dmna.ny.gov

Adjutant General:
  Major Gen Anthony P German......................518-786-4502
Adjutant General - Air:
  Anthony P. German .............................518-786-4317
Executive Officer:
  Donald McKnight...............................518-786-4388

*Offices and agencies generally appear in alphabetical order, except when specific order is requested by listee.*

Policy Areas

Legal Counsel:
Robert G Conway, Jr ..............................518-786-4541
Director, Budget & Finance:
Robert A Martin ..................................518-786-4514
Director, Governmental & Community Affairs:
James M Huelle...................................518-786-4580
Director, Public Affairs:
Eric Durr ....................518-786-4581/fax: 518-786-4649

## Veterans' Affairs, Division of
2 Empire State Plaza
17th Floor
Albany, NY 12223
518-474-6114 or 888-838-7697  Fax: 518-473-0379
e-mail: dvainfo@veterans.ny.gov
Web site: www.veterans.ny.gov

Director:
Vacant...........................................518-474-6114
Executive Deputy Director:
Joel Evans ......................................518-474-6114
Secretary to the Director:
Mary Quay ......................................518-474-6114
e-mail: m.quay@veterans.ny.gov
Deputy Director, VA Programs:
Benjamin Pomerance .............................518-474-6114
Counsel:
Jonathan Fishbein ...............................518-474-6114

### Bureau of Veterans Education
Bureau Chief:
James Bombard...................................518-474-5322
Supervisor:
Craig Farley ....................................518-474-7606

### Counseling & Claims Service
State Veteran Counselor:
Sue Doan........................................315-428-4046
State Veteran Counselor:
Lloyd Collins ...................................315-428-4046
State Veteran Counselor:
Mark Tamkus ...................................315-785-2468

#### Eastern Region
55 Hanson Place, Brooklyn, NY 11217
Deputy Director:
Andrew Roberts ................................718-722-2584

#### Western Region
65 Court St, ste 310, Buffalo, NY 14202-3406
Deputy Director:
Vacant......................716-847-3414/fax: 716-847-3410

## Veterans' Service Organizations

### Albany Housing Coalition Inc .................fax: 518-465-6499
278 Clinton Ave, Albany, NY 12210
Fax: 518-465-6499
e-mail: admin@ahcvets.org
Web site: www.ahcvets.org
Executive Director:
Joseph Sluszka.................................518-465-5251
e-mail: jsluszka@ahcvets.org
Director, Veterans Svcs:
Lee Vartigan ...................................518-465-5251
e-mail: l.vartigan@ahcvets.org

### COPIN HOUSE (Homeless Veterans)...........fax: 716-283-5712
5622 Buffalo Ave, Niagara Falls, NY 14304
Executive Director:
Sharon McGrath .................................716-283-5622

## Continuum of Care for Homeless Veterans in New York City

### 30th Street Shelter
400-430 East 30th St, New York, NY 10016
Director:
Yvonne Ballard..................................212-481-4730

### Project TORCH, Veterans Health Care Center
40 Flatbush Ave Ext, 8th Fl, Brooklyn, NY 11201
Program Coordinator:
Julie Irwin .....................718-439-4345/fax: 718-439-4356

### Hicksville Counseling Center, Veterans' Resource Center ... fax: 516-935-2717
385 West John St, Hicksville, NY 11801
Director, Substance Abuse Program & Veterans Resource Center:
Geryl Pecora ...................................516-935-6858

### Saratoga Cnty Rural Preservation Co (Homeless Veterans)
36 Church Ave, Ballston Spa, NY 12020
Executive Director:
Cheryl Hage-Perez..........518-885-0091/fax: 518-885-0998
e-mail: chp@saratogarpc.org

### Suffolk County United Veterans Halfway House Project Inc
PO Box 598, Patchogue, NY 11772
Executive Director:
John Lynch ...............631-924-8088/fax: 631-924-0160

### Veterans House (The)........................fax: 518-465-6499
180 First St, Albany, NY 12210
House Manager:
John Jacobie ...................................518-449-8430

### Veterans Outreach Center Inc.................fax: 585-546-5234
447 South Ave, Rochester, NY 14620
Fax: 585-546-5234
Web site: www.veteransoutreachcenter.org
SSVF Program Manager:
Sean Sizer .....................................585-295-7801
e-mail: info@veteransoutreachcenter.org

### Veterans Services Center of the Southern Tier .. fax: 607-771-9395
174 Clinton St, Binghamton, NY 13905
Executive Director:
Patricia Gaven..................................607-771-8387

### Veterans' Coalition of the Hudson Valley .......fax: 845-471-6113
9 Vassar St, Poughkeepsie, NY 12601
845-471-6113  Fax: 845-471-6113
Administrator:
Marilyn Wickman................................845-471-6113

## CORPORATIONS, AUTHORITIES AND COMMISSIONS

## Brooklyn Navy Yard Development Corporation
63 Flushing Ave, Unit #300
Bldg 292, 3rd Fl
Brooklyn, NY 11205
718-907-5900  Fax: 718-643-9296
e-mail: info@brooklynnavyyard.org
Web site: www.brooklynnavyyard.org

Chair:
Henry Gutman....................................718-907-5900
President & Chief Executive Officer:
David Ehrenberg.................................718-907-5900
Executive Vice President & Chief Operating Officer:
Elliot S. Matz ..................................718-907-5900
Senior Vice President, External Affairs:
Richard Drucker .................................718-907-5900

*Offices and agencies generally appear in alphabetical order, except when specific order is requested by listee.*

EVP/Chief of Staff:
Clare Newman ....................................718-907-5900
General Counsel:
Paul Kelly .......................................718-907-5900

## NEW YORK STATE LEGISLATURE

*See Legislative Branch in Section 1 for additional Standing Committee and Subcommittee information.*

## Assembly Standing Committees

**Veterans' Affairs**
Chair:
Didi Barrett......................................518-455-4545

## Senate Standing Committees

**Veterans, Homeland Security & Military Affairs**
Chair:
John E Brooks (D) ...............................518-455-2765

## U.S. GOVERNMENT

## EXECUTIVE DEPARTMENTS AND RELATED AGENCIES

## US Defense Department
Web site: www.defenselink.mil

**AIR FORCE-National Media Outreach** ........ fax: 212-784-0149
805 Third Ave, 9th Fl, New York, NY 10022
Director:
Angela Billings...................................212-784-0147
e-mail: big.saf@us.af.mil
Public Relations Director:
Wesley Preston Miller ...........................212-784-0147

### Air National Guard

**Francis S Gabreski Airport, 106th Rescue Wing**.... fax: 631-723-7179
150 Old Riverhead Rd, Westhampton Beach, NY 11978
Commander:
Col. Thomas J. Owens II ........................631-723-7400
Public Affairs Officer:
Tech Sgt. Eric Miller ............................631-723-7470

**Hancock Field, 174th Fighter Wing**
6001 E Molloy Rd, Syracuse, NY 13211
315-454-6146
Commander:
Col. Greg A. Semmel...........................315-454-6146

### Army

**Fort Drum**.....................................fax: 315-772-8295
10012 South Riva Ridge Loop, Fort Drum, NY 13602-5028
315-772-5461  Fax: 315-772-8295
Commander:
Maj. Stephen J. Townsend .......................315-772-8295
Community Relations Officer:
Lori Haney .......................................315-772-8295

**Fort Hamilton** ...............................fax: 718-630-4709
Fort Hamilton, New York, NY 11252
Commander:
Col. Eluyn Gines ...............................718-630-4101

**Watervliet Arsenal**
1 Buffington Street, Watervliet, NY 12189-4050
518-266-5111

Commander:
Mark F. Migaleddi ...............................518-266-5111
Public Affairs Officer:
John Snyder .....................................518-266-5055

## Marine Corps

**1st Marine Corps District**
605 Stewart Ave, Garden City, NY 11530
Commander:
Col. J.J. Dill ....................................516-228-5661
Executive Officer:
Lt. Col. Mark T. Donar..........................516-228-5661

**Public Affairs Office** ...........................fax: 212-784-0169
805 Third Ave, 9th Fl, New York, NY 10022
Director:
Lt. Col. Christopher Perrine ......................347-292-8762

## Navy

**Saratoga Springs Naval Support Unit**
19 JF King Dr, Saratoga Springs, NY 12866-9267
Commander:
CDR Vince D. Garcia............518-886-0200/fax: 518-886-0120

## US Department of Veterans Affairs
Web site: www.va.gov

### National Cemetery Administration
Web site: www.cem.va.gov

**Bath National Cemetery**
San Juan Ave, Bath, NY 14810
Director:
Walter Baroody.................607-664-4853/fax: 607-664-4761

**Calverton National Cemetery**
210 Princeton Blvd, Calverton, NY 11933-1031
Director:
Michael G Picerno ..............................631-727-5410

**Cypress Hills National Cemetery**................fax: 631-694-5422
625 Jamaica Ave, Brooklyn, NY 11208
631-454-4949  Fax: 631-694-5422
Director:
Michael G Picerno ..............631-454-4949/fax: 631-694-5422

**Gerald B.H. Solomon Saratoga National Cemetery**
200 Duell Rd, Schuylerville, NY 12871-1721
Director:
Daniel Cassidy .................518-581-9128/fax: 518-583-6975

**Long Island National Cemetery**..................fax: 631-694-5422
2040 Wellwood Ave, Farmingdale, NY 11735
631-454-4949  Fax: 631-694-5422
Director:
Michael G Picerno ..............631-454-4949/fax: 631-694-5422

**Woodlawn National Cemetery**
1825 Davis St, Elmira, NY 14901
Director:
Walter Baroody.................607-732-5411/fax: 607-742-1769

### VA Regional Office of Public Affairs, Field Operations Svc
245 W Houston St, Ste 315B, New York, NY 10014
Regional Director:
Lawrence M Devine ..............212-807-3429/fax: 212-807-4030
Public Affairs Specialist:
James A Blue ....................................212-807-3429
Public Affairs Specialist:
Leo Marinacci....................................212-807-3429

*Offices and agencies generally appear in alphabetical order, except when specific order is requested by listee.*

Policy Areas

## Veterans Benefits Administration

### Buffalo Regional Office
130 South Elmwood Avenue, Buffalo, NY 14202-2478
800-827-1000
Regional Director:
  Donna Ferrell . . . . . . . . . . . . . . . . . .716-857-3020/fax: 716-551-3072
Assistant Director:
  Lillie Jackson . . . . . . . . . . . . . . . . . . . . . . . . . . . . . . . . . .800-827-1000
Veterans Service Center Manager:
  James Rogers . . . . . . . . . . . . . . . . . . . . . . . . . . . . . . . . . .800-827-1000
Regional Counsel:
  Joseph Moreno . . . . . . . . . . . . . . . . . . . . . . . . . . . . . . . . .800-827-1000
Vocational Rehabilitation & Employment Division:
  Joseph Senulis . . . . . . . . . . . . . . . . . . . . . . . . . . . . . . . . .800-827-1000
Chief, Education Division:
  Robert Quall . . . . . . . . . . . . . . . . . . . . . . . . . . . . . . . . . . .800-827-1000

### New York City Regional Office . . . . . . . . . . . . . . . .fax: 212-807-4024
245 West Houston St, New York, NY 10014-4085
Director:
  Patricia Amberg-Blyskal . . . . . . . . . . . . . . . . . . . . . . . .212-807-3055
Veterans Benefits & Services Officer:
  Joseph Collorafi . . . . . . . . . . . . . . . . . . . . . . . . . . . . . . .212-807-3420
Vocational Rehabilitation & Counseling Division:
  Bernard Finger . . . . . . . . . . . . . . . . . . . . . . . . . . . . . . . .212-807-3030

## Veterans Health Admin Integrated Svc Network (VISN)

### VA Healthcare Network Upstate New York (VISN2)
113 Holland Ave, Bldg 7, Albany, NY 12208
Acting Network Director:
  Michael Finegan . . . . . . . . . . . . . . . . . . . . . . .518-626-7317 x67317
Network Communications Manager:
  Kathleen Hider . . . . . . . . . . . . . . . .585-463-2642/fax: 585-463-2649
  *Albany VA Medical Center*
    113 Holland Ave, Albany, NY 12208
    Director:
      Lisa W. Weiss, MS . . . . . . . . . . . . . . . . . . . . . .518-626-5000
    Patient Advocate:
      Bridgette Qualls . . . . . . . . . . . . . . . . . . . . . . . .518-626-7125
  *Batavia VA Medical Center* . . . . . . . . . . . . . . . .fax: 585-344-3305
    222 Richmond Ave, Batavia, NY 14020
    716-343-7500  Fax: 585-344-3305
    Director:
      Brian G. Stiller. . . . . . . . . . . . . . . . . . . . . . . . . .716-862-8529
    Patient Advocate:
      Tom Bligh . . . . . . . . . . . . . . . . . . . . . . . . . . . . . .585-297-1257
  *Bath VA Medical Center*
    76 Veterans Ave, Bath, NY 14810
    Director:
      Michael Swartz . . . . . . . . . . . . . . . . . . . . . . . . . .607-664-4722
    Patient Advocate:
      Cheryl Mills
  *Buffalo VA Medical Center* . . . . . . . . . . . . . . . . . .fax: 716-862-8759
    3495 Bailey Ave, Buffalo, NY 14215
    716-834-9200  Fax: 716-862-8759
    Director:
      Brian G. Stiller. . . . . . . . . . . . . . . . . . . . . . . . . .716-862-8529
    Public Affairs Officer:
      Christine Krupski. . . . . . . . . . . . . . . . . . . . . . . . .716-862-8852
  *Canandaigua VA Medical Center*
    400 Fort Hill Ave, Canandaigua, NY 14424
    Director:
      Michael Swartz . . . . . . . . . . . . . . . . . . . . . . . . . .585-394-2000
    Patient Advocate:
      Laurie Guererri . . . . . . . . . . . . . . . . . . . . . . . . . .585-393-7612
  *Syracuse VA Medical Center & Clinics*
    800 Irving Ave, Syracuse, NY 13210
    Director:
      James Cody . . . . . . . . . . . . . . . . . . . . . . . . . . . . .315-425-4892

Patient Advocate:
  Colleen Lancette . . . . . . . . . . . . . . . . . . . . . . . . . . . .315-425-4345

### VA NY/NJ Veterans Healthcare Network (VISN3)
Bldg 16, 130 W Kingsbridge Rd, Bronx, NY 10468
Network Director:
  Michael A. Sabo . . . . . . . . . . . . . . . .718-741-4143/fax: 718-741-4141
Chief Medical Officer:
  Joan McInerney, MD
  *James J. Peters VA Medical Center* . . . . . . . . . . . .fax: 718-741-4269
    130 W Kingsbridge Rd, Bronx, NY 10468
    Director:
      MaryAnn Musumeci. . . . . . . . . . . . . . . . . .718-584-9000 x6512
    Director of Government/Community Relations:
      Jim Connell
  *Brooklyn Campus of the NY Harbor Healthcare System*
    800 Poly Pl, Brooklyn, NY 11209
    718-836-6600
    Director:
      John J Donnellan, Jr . . . . . . . . .718-630-3521/fax: 718-630-2840
    Associate Director:
      Veronica J Foy. . . . . . . . . . . . . . . . . . . . . . . . . . .718-630-3524
  *Castle Point Campus of the VA Hudson Vly Healthcare System* . . fax:
    845-838-5193
    PO Box 100, 100 Rte 9D, Castle Point, NY 12511
    845-831-2000  Fax: 845-838-5193
    Executive Director:
      Michael A Sabo . . . . . . . . . . . . . . . . . . . . . .845-737-4400 x2460
  *Montrose Campus of the VA Hudson Valley Healthcare System* . . fax:
    914-788-4244
    2094 Albany Post Rd, Montrose, NY 10548
    Director:
      Michael A. Sabo . . . . . . . . . . . . . . . . . . . . . . . . .914-737-4400
    Public Affairs:
      Nancy A Winter . . . . . . . . . . . . . . . . . . . . . .914-737-4400 x2255
  *New York Campus of the NY Harbor Healthcare System*
    423 East 23rd St, New York, NY 10010
    212-686-7500
    Executive Chief of Staff:
      Michael S Simberkoff . . . . . . . . . . . . . . . . . . . . .212-951-3417
    Associate Director:
      Martina A Parauda. . . . . . . . . . . . . . . . . . . . . . . .212-951-3240
  *Northport VA Medical Center* . . . . . . . . . . . . . . . .fax: 631-754-7933
    79 Middleville Rd, Northport, NY 11768
    Director:
      Robert Schuster. . . . . . . . . . . . . . . . . . . . . .631-261-4400 x2747
    Public Affairs Officer:
      Joe Sledge

## US Labor Department
Web site: www.dol.gov/vets/

### Field Offices

#### New York State Field Offices
  *Albany* . . . . . . . . . . . . . . . . . . . . . . . . . . . . . . . . . . . .fax: 518-435-0833
    Harriman State Campus, Bldg 12, Rm 518, Albany, NY 12240-0099
    518-457-7465  Fax: 518-435-0833
    Director:
      Barry Morgan . . . . . . . . . . . . . . .518-457-7465/fax: 518-435-0833
    Veteran's Program Assistant:
      Joan M Cramer. . . . . . . . . . . . . . . . . . . . . . . . . . .518-457-7465
  *Brooklyn*
    9 Bond Street, Room 301/302, Brooklyn, NY 11201
    Assistant Director:
      Daniel A Friedman. . . . . . . . . . . . . . . . . . . . . . . .718-613-3676
    Veteran's Program Specialist:
      Edward L. Diaz . . . . . . . . . . . . . . . . . . . . . . . . . .718-613-3676
      e-mail: diaz.edward.L@dol.gov

---

*Offices and agencies generally appear in alphabetical order, except when specific order is requested by listee.*

## US State Department
Web site: www.state.gov

## US Mission to the United Nations
799 United Nations Plaza, New York, NY 10017
Permanent US Representative to the United Nations:
Ambassador Susan E. Rice
Deputy Permanent US Representative to the United Nations:
Ambassador Rosemary A. DiCarlo
Alternate Representative for Special Political Affairs to the United Nations:
Ambassador Jeffrey DeLaurentis

## U.S. CONGRESS

*See U.S. Congress Chapter for additional Standing Committee and Subcommittee information.*

## House of Representatives Standing Committees

### Armed Services
McKeon (R-CA):
Howard P. Buck"" ..........................Chair or 202-225-1956
Ranking Minority Member:
Adam Smith (D-WA).............................202-225-8901
New York Delegate:
Dan Maffei (D).................................202-225-3701
New York Delegate:
Chris Gibson (R)...............................202-225-5614

### Veterans' Affairs
Chair:
Jeff Miller (R-FL)................................202-225-4136
Ranking Minority Member:
Michael H. Michaud (D-ME).......................202-225-6306

## Senate Standing Committees

### Armed Services
Chair:
Carl Levin (D-MI)................................202-224-6221
Ranking Minority Member:
James M. Inhofe (R-OK) .........................202-224-4721

### Veterans' Affairs
Chair:
Bernard Sanders (D-VT)..........................202-224-5141
Ranking Minority Member:
Richard Burr (R-NC) ............................202-224-3154

## PRIVATE SECTOR

### 369th Veterans Association Inc
PO Box 91, Lincolnton Station, New York, NY 10037
212-281-3308  Fax: 212-281-6308
*Assistance & referrals for all veterans*
Nathaniel James, National President

### Air Force Association (AFA)
1501 Lee Highway, Arlington, VA 22209-1198
703-247-5800  Fax: 703-247-5853
Web site: www.afa.org
*Support & advance the interest & recognition of the US Air Force*
Donald L Peterson, Executive Director

### Air Force Sergeants Association (AFSA), Division 1
557 Sixth St, Dover, NH 3820
603-742-4844
Web site: www.afsahq.org
*Protect rights & benefits of enlisted personnel-active, retired, National Guard, reserve & their families*
Alfred B Caldwell, President Division 1

### Air Force Women Officers Associated (AFWOA)
PO Box 780155, San Antonio, TX 78278
210-481-6383
*Represent interests of active duty, retired & former women officers of the Air Force; preserve the history & promote recognition of the role of military women*
Col Patricia M Murphy, USAF Retired, President

### Albany Housing Coalition Inc
278 Clinton Ave, Albany, NY 12210
518-465-5251  Fax: 518-465-6499
e-mail: admin@ahcvets.org
Web site: www.ahcvets.org
*Providing a continuum of affordable housing for veterans & their families; rental housing referrals*
Bryon Koshgarian, Phd, Director, Veterans Services

### American Legion, Department of New York
112 State St, Suite 1300, Albany, NY 12207
518-463-2215  Fax: 518-427-8443
e-mail: info@nylegion.org
Web site: www.ny.legion.org
*Advocate for veterans; entitlements for wartime veterans, their families & service to the community, children & youth of our nation*
Richard M Pedro, New York State Adjutant

### American Military Retirees Association Inc
5436 Peru St, Ste 1, Plattsburgh, NY 12901
800-424-2969 or 518-563-9479  Fax: 518-324-5204
Web site: www.amra1973.org
*Works on behalf of military retirees aand their families to protect their rights and benefits under the law and to lobby on their behalf in Washington D.C. and elsewhere.*
Peg Bergeron, Executive Director

### Army Aviation Association of America (AAAA)
755 Main St, Ste 4D, Monroe, CT 06468-2830
203-268-2450  Fax: 203-268-5870
*Advance the cause & recognition of US Army aviation; benefit all personnel, current, retired, families & survivors*
William R Harris, Executive Director

### Army Aviation Association of America (AAAA), Empire Chapter
3 Glendale Dr, Clifton Park, NY 12065
518-786-4397  Fax: 518-786-4393
e-mail: mark.f.burke@us.army.mil
*Advance the cause & recognition of US Army aviation; benefit all Army aviation personnel, current, retired, families & survivors*
COL Mark F Burke, Chapter President

### Association of Military Surgeons of the US (AMSUS), NY Chapter
105 Franklin Ave, Malverne, NY 11565-1926
516-542-0025  Fax: 516-593-3114
e-mail: amsusny@aol.com
*Improve federal healthcare service; support & represent military & other health care professionals*
Col John J Hassett, USAR, President NY Chapter

*Offices and agencies generally appear in alphabetical order, except when specific order is requested by listee.*

Policy Areas

## Association of the US Army (AUSA)
2425 Wilson Blvd, Arlington, VA 22201
703-841-4300 x639 or 800-336-4570  Fax: 703-525-9039
Web site: www.ausa.org
*Champion the cause & objectives of the US Army by public relations, communications & legislative action*
William Loper, Director Government Affairs

## Black Veterans for Social Justice Inc
665 Willoughby Street, Brooklyn, NY 11221
718-852-6004  Fax: 718-852-4805
Web site: www.bvsj.org
*Assist all veterans in obtaining benefits, entitlements, employment & housing*
Job Mashariki, President & Chief Executive Officer

## Blinded Veterans Association New York Inc
245 W Houston St, 2nd Fl, Rm 208, New York, NY 10014
212-807-3173  Fax: 212-807-4022
Web site: www.bva.org
Jack Shapiro, Director

## Catholic War Veterans of the United States of America
346 Broadway, Suite 812, New York, NY 10013
212-962-0988  Fax: 212-894-0517
e-mail: nyscwv@aol.com
*Veterans & auxiliary of the Roman Catholic faith; assisting all veterans & their families*
Richard Dogal, MA, State Commander

## Commissioned Officers Assn of the US Public Health Svc Inc (COA)
8201 Corporate Dr, Ste 200, Landover, MD 20785
301-731-9080  Fax: 301-731-9084
e-mail: gfarrell@coausphs.org
Web site: www.coausphs.org
*Committed to improving the public health of the US; supports corps officers & advocates for their interests through leadership, education & communication*
Jerry Farrell, Executive Director

## Disabled American Veterans, Department of New York
162 Atlantic Ave, Lynbrook, NY 11563-3597
516-887-7100  Fax: 516-887-7175
e-mail: davny@optonline.net
Web site: www.davny.org
*Service, support & enhance healthcare & benefits for wartime disabled veterans*
Sidney Siller, Adjutant

## Fleet Reserve Association (FRA)
125 North West St, Alexandria, VA 22314
703-683-1400  Fax: 703-549-6610
Web site: www.fra.org
*Serving the interests of active duty, retired & reserve enlisted members of the US Navy, Marine Corps & Coast Guard*
Joseph L Barnes, National Executive Secretary & Chief Lobbyist

## Fleet Reserve Association (FRA), NE Region (NJ, NY, PA)
1118 West Jefferson Street, Philadelphia, PA 19122-3442
215-235-7796  Fax: 215-765-2671
e-mail: charleserainey@post.com
Web site: www.fra.org
*Serving the interests of active duty, retired & reserve enlisted members of the US Navy, Marine Corps & Coast Guard*
Charles Rainey, Regional President

## Gold Star Wives of America Inc
24 Clayton Blvd, Baldwin, NY 10505
914-305-2322
*National nonprofit working to advance issues important to military service widows*
Mary Dwyer, President

## Jewish War Veterans of the USA
1811 R St NW, Washington, DC 20009
202-265-6280  Fax: 202-234-5662
e-mail: jwv@jwv.org
Web site: www.jwv.org
*Honoring & supporting all Jewish war veterans, their benefits & rights; fight bigotry & discrimination; patriotic voice of American Jewry*
Steve Zeitz, National Commander

## Jewish War Veterans of the USA, State of NY
346 Broadway, Rm 817, New York, NY 10013
212-349-6640  Fax: 212-577-2575
Web site: www.jwv.org
*Honoring & supporting Jewish war veterans*
Saul Rosenberg, Department Commander

## Korean War Veterans
54 Lyncrest Drive, Rochester, NY 14616-5238
518-865-0145
e-mail: kwvfn@aol.com
Web site: www.kwva.org
*Ensuring that Korean war vets are remembered*
Frank Nicalozzo, President

## Marine Corps League
PO Box 505, White Plains, NY 10602
914-941-2118  Fax: 914-864-7129
Web site: www.mclwestchester.org
*Marine Corps fraternal/veterans association*
Lu Caldara, Coordinator

## Marine Corps League (MCL)
PO Box 3070, Merrifield, VA 22116
703-207-9588 or 800-625-1775  Fax: 703-207-0047
e-mail: mcl@mcleague.org
*Support & promote the interests, history & tradition of the Marine Corps & all Marines*
Michael Blum, Executive Director

## Marine Corps League (MCL), Department of NY
46 Marine Corp Blvd, Staten Island, NY 10301
718-447-2306  Fax: 718-556-0590
*Support & promote the interests, history & tradition of the Marine Corps & all Marines*
Bob Powell, Commandant, Department of NY

## Military Chaplains Association of the USA (MCA)
PO Box 7056, Arlington, VA 22207
703-533-5890
e-mail: chaplains@mca-usa.org
*Promotes the recognition & interests of military, Civil Air Patrol & VA chaplains; develops & encourages candidates through national institutes, scholarships & outreach*
David White, Executive Director

## Military Officers Association of America
201 N Washington St, Alexandria, VA 22314-2539
703-549-2311 or 800-234-6622  Fax: 703-838-8173
Web site: www.moaa.org
*Preserve earned entitlements of members of the uniformed services, their families & survivors; support of strong national defense; scholarship & support to members' families*
Col Steve Strobridge, USAF Retired, Director Government Relations

## Military Officers Association of America (MOAA), NYS Council
258 Randwood Dr, Williamsville, NY 14221
716-689-6295  Fax: 716-847-6405
e-mail: patc258@aol.com
*Benefit members of uniformed services, active & retired, family & survivors; promote strong national defense*
Col Patrick Cunningham, USA Retired, President, NYS Council of Chapters

*Offices and agencies generally appear in alphabetical order, except when specific order is requested by listee.*

## Military Order of the Purple Heart
Syracuse Veterans Administration Medical, 800 Irving Ave, Room A176, Syracuse, NY 13210-2796
315-425-4685
*Veterans' benefits & rehabilitation*
Catherine Alexander, National Service Officer

## Military Order of the Purple Heart (MOPH)
5413B Backlick Rd, Springfield, VA 22151
703-642-5360  Fax: 703-642-1841
e-mail: goberh@aol.com
Web site: www.purpleheart.org
*Congressionally chartered organization representing the interests of America's combat-wounded veterans*
Hershel Gober, National Legislative Director

## Montford Point Marine Association
346 Broadway St, New York, NY 10013
212-267-3318  Fax: 212-566-4903
Web site: www.montfordpointmarines.com
James Maillard, Financial Secretary

## National Amputation Foundation Inc
40 Church St, Malverne, NY 11565
516-887-3600  Fax: 516-887-3667
e-mail: amps76@aol.com
Web site: www.nationalamputation.org
*Programs & services geared to help the amputee; donated medical equipment give-away program. Items must be picked up at the office-for anyone in need. Scholarship program for students with major limb amputation attending college full-time.*
Paul Bernacchio, President

## National Guard Association of the US (NGAUS)
One Massachusetts Ave NW, Washington, DC 20001
202-408-5882
e-mail: ngaus@ngaus.org
Web site: www.ngaus.org
*Promote the interests of the Army National Guard through legislative action;*
Bill Goss, Director, Legislative Affairs

## National Military Family Association (NMFA)
2500 North Van Dorn St, Ste 102, Alexandria, VA 22302-1601
703-931-6632 or 800-260-0218  Fax: 703-931-4600
Web site: www.nmfa.org
*Service to the families of active duty, retirees, reserve & National Guard uniformed personnel*
Joyce Raezer, Director Government Relations

## Naval Enlisted Reserve Association (NERA)
6703 Farragut Ave, Falls Church, VA 22042-2189
703-534-1329 or 800-776-9020
e-mail: members@nera.org
Web site: www.nera.org
*Ensuring strong & well-trained Naval, Coast Guard & Marine Corps Reserves; improving reserve equipment, promotion, pay & retirement benefits through legislative action*
Stephen R Sandy, Executive Director

## Naval Reserve Association (NRA)
1619 King St, Alexandria, VA 22314-3647
703-548-5800 or 866-672-4968  Fax: 866-683-3647
*Premier education & professional organization for Naval Reserve officers & the association voice of the Naval Reserve*
Ike Puzon, USNR Retired, Director of Legislation

## Navy League of the US (NLUS)
2300 Wilson Blvd, Arlington, VA 22201-3308
703-528-1775 or 800-356-5760  Fax: 703-528-2333
e-mail: jfleet@navyleague.org
Web site: www.navyleague.org
*Citizens in support of the Sea Services*
John Fleet, Director for Legislative Affairs

## Navy League of the US (NLUS), New York Council
c/o US Coast Guard, Battery Park Bldg, 1 South St, Rm 318, New York, NY 10004
212-825-7333  Fax: 212-668-2138
Web site: www.nynavyleague.org
*Represent citizens in support of the Sea Services*
J Robert Lunney, President

## New Era Veterans, Inc
1150 Commonwealth Avenue, Bronx, NY 10472
718-904-7036  Fax: 718-904-7024
*Housing and services for homeless veterans.*
Jason Ortiz, Program Director

## New York State Air Force Association
PO Box 539, Merrick, NY 11566-0539
516-623-5714
*Support & advance the interest & recognition of the US Air Force*
Robert Braverman, Vice President Government Relations

## North Country Vietnam Veterans Association, Post 1
PO Box 1161, 27 Town Line Rd, Plattsburgh, NY 12901
518-563-3426
e-mail: kenhynes@charter.net
Web site: www.ncvva.org
*Peer counseling & referral*
Ken Hynes, Contact

## Reserve Officers Association (ROA)
One Constitution Ave, NE, Washington, DC 20002
202-479-2200 or 800-809-9448  Fax: 202-547-1641
Web site: www.roa.org
*Advance the cause of reserve officers through legislative action; promote the interests & recognition of ROTC & military academy students*
Susan Lukas, Legislative Director

## Office of Chief, Army Reserves
3 Wildwood Rd, Congers, NY 10920
845-638-5215 or 845-596-3494  Fax: 845-638-5035
e-mail: robert.j.winzinger@us.army.mil
*Advance the cause of reserve officers of the US Armed Forces; promote the interests & recognition of ROTC & military academy students*
Robert Winzinger, Army Reserve Ambassador - New York

## United Spinal Association
75-20 Astoria Blvd, Jackson Heights, NY 11370
718-803-3782  Fax: 718-803-0414
e-mail: info@unitedspinal.org
Web site: www.unitedspinal.org
*Managed & long-term care, disability assistance & benefits, advocacy & legislation*
Linda Gutmann, Advocacy

## Veterans of Foreign Wars
1044 Broadway, Albany, NY 12204
518-463-7427  Fax: 518-426-8904
Art Koch III, State Adjutant

Policy Areas

**Veterans of Foreign Wars (VFW)**
200 Maryland Ave, NE, Washington, DC 20002
202-543-2239  Fax: 202-543-0961
Web site: www.vfw.org
*Legislative action, community service & volunteerism in support of the*
*nation's veterans, their families & survivors*
Dennis Cullinan, Director National Legislative Affairs

**Veterans' Widows International Network Inc (VWIN)**
3657 E South Laredo, Aurora, CO 80013
303-693-4745
e-mail: vwin95@aol.com
*Outreach to American veterans' survivors; assist with obtaining benefits;*
*provide local contacts & support*

**Vietnam Veterans of America, NYS Council**
8 Queen Dian Lane, Queensbury, NY 12804
518-293-7801
e-mail: nedvva@adelphia.net
Ned D Foote, President

**Women Marines Association**
59 Sawyer Ave, Dorchester, MA 02125-2040
617-265-1572
e-mail: sgtkwm@aol.com
Web site: www.womenmarines.org
Catherine Carpenter, Area 1 Director

# Section 3:
# STATE & LOCAL GOVERNMENT PUBLIC INFORMATION

# PUBLIC INFORMATION OFFICES

*This chapter includes state public information contacts with telephone and fax numbers as well as e-mail and Web site addresses, if available. For additional information, please refer to the related policy area or the indexes.*

## NEW YORK STATE

### GOVERNOR'S OFFICE

#### Governor's Office
Web site: www.governor.ny.gov; www.ny.gov

Director, Communications:
Peter Ajemian . . . . . . . . . . . . . . . . . . . . . . .518-474-8418 or 212-681-4640

#### Washington Office of the Governor
Director:
Alexander Cochran . . . . . . . . . . . . . . . . . . . . . . . . . . . . . .202-434-7100

#### Lieutenant Governor's Office
Chief of Staff:
Jeffrey Lewis. . . . . . . . . . . . . . . . . . . . . . . . . . . . . . . . .518-402-2292

### EXECUTIVE & ADMINISTRATIVE DEPARTMENTS & AGENCIES

#### Aging, Office for the
Web site: www.aging.ny.gov

Public Information Officer:
Reza Mizbani . . . . . . . . . . . . . . . . . . . . . . . . . . . . . . . .518-474-7181
e-mail: reza.mizbani@aging.ny.gov

#### Agriculture & Markets Department
Web site: www.agriculture.ny.gov

Public Information Officer:
Jola Szubielski . . . . . . . . . . . . . . . . . . . . .518-485-7728 or 518-457-3136
fax: 518-457-3087
e-mail: jola.szubielski@agriculture.ny.gov

#### New York State Liquor Authority (Division of Alcoholic Beverage Control)
Web site: www.sla.ny.gov

Director, Public Affairs:
William Crowley . . . . . . . . . . . . . . . . . . .518-474-3114 or 518-474-4875
fax: 518-473-9565
e-mail: William.Crowley@sla.ny.gov

#### Alcoholism & Substance Abuse Services, Office of
e-mail: communications@oasas.ny.gov
Web site: www.oasas.ny.gov

Director, Office of Public Information & Communications:
Edison Alban

#### Financial Services Department
e-mail: public-affairs@dfs.ny.gov
Web site: www.dfs.ny.gov

Chief Information Officer:
Vacant

#### Budget, Division of the
518-473-3885
e-mail: dob.sm.press@budget.ny.gov
Web site: www.budget.ny.gov

Press Officer:
Freeman Klopott . . . . . . . . . . . . . . . . . . . . . . . . . . . . . .518-473-3885
e-mail: dob.sm.press@budget.ny.gov

#### CIO & Office of Information Technology Services (ITS)
518-402-3899 or 844-891-1786
e-mail: fixit@its.ny.gov
Web site: www.its.ny.gov

Chief Information Officer/Director of Information Technology Services:
Angelo Riddick . . . . . . . . . . . . . . . . . . . . . . . . . . . . . . .518-408-2140

#### Children & Family Services, Office of
518-473-7793  Fax: 518-486-7550
e-mail: info@ocfs.ny.gov
Web site: ocfs.ny.gov

Council on Children & Families . . . . . . . . . . . . . . . .fax: 518-473-2570
518-474-5522 or 518-473-3652  Fax: 518-473-2570
e-mail: council@ccf.ny.gov
Web site: www.ccf.ny.gov
Executive Director:
Renée L Rider . . . . . . . . . . . . . . . . . . . . .518-473-3652/fax: 518-473-2570

#### Civil Service Department
518-457-2487 or 877-697-5627
e-mail: pio@cs.ny.gov
Web site: www.cs.ny.gov

Director, Communications:
Jian Paolucci . . . . . . . . . . . . . . . . . . . . . . . . . . . . . . . .518-457-9375
e-mail: pio@cs.state.ny.us

#### Consumer Protection, Division of
e-mail: info@dos.ny.gov
Web site: www.dos.ny.gov/consumerprotection/

Executive Deputy Director:
Aiesha Battle. . . . . . . . . . . . . . . . . . . . . . . . . . . . . . . . .518-474-2363

#### Corrections & Community Supervision Department
Web site: www.doccs.ny.gov

Public Information Officer:
Thomas Mailey . . . . . . . . . . . . . . . . . . . . . . . . . . . . . . .518-457-8182
e-mail: thomas.mailey@doccs.ny.gov

#### Council on the Arts
e-mail: info@arts.ny.gov
Web site: www.arts.ny.gov

Director, Public Information:
Ronni Reich . . . . . . . . . . . . . . . . . . . . . . . . . . . . . . . . .212-459-8859
e-mail: ronni.reich@arts.ny.gov

#### Victim Services, Office of
Web site: www.ovs.ny.gov

Director, Public Information:
Janine Kava. . . . . . . . . . . . . . . . . . . . . . . . . . . . . . . . . .518-457-8828
e-mail: janine.kava@dcjs.ny.gov

*Offices and agencies generally appear in alphabetical order, except when specific order is requested by listee.*

## Criminal Justice Services, Division of
e-mail: InfoDCJS@dcjs.ny.gov
Web site: www.criminaljustice.ny.gov

Director, Public Information:
    Janine Kava......................................518-457-8828
    e-mail: janine.kava@dcjs.ny.gov

## Developmental Disabilities Planning Council
e-mail: information@ddpc.ny.gov
Web site: www.ddpc.ny.gov

## Education Department
Web site: www.nysed.gov

Secretary to the Board of Regents:
    Anthony Lofrumento ...............................518-474-5889
Chief, External Affairs:
    Vacant.......................518-474-1201/fax: 518-473-2977
Assistant Commissioner, Public Affairs:
    Emily DeSantis....................................518-474-1201

## Elections, State Board of
e-mail: info@elections.ny.gov
Web site: www.elections.ny.gov

Director, Public Information:
    John W Conklin...................518-474-1953/fax: 518-473-8315
    e-mail: info@elections.ny.gov

## Homeland Security & Emergency Services, Division of
Web site: www.dhses.ny.gov

Public Information Officer:
    Kristin Devoe ....................................518-242-5153

## Empire State Development Corporation
Web site: www.esd.ny.gov

Executive Vice President, Public Affairs & Communications:
    Vacant...........................................800-260-7313

## Employee Relations, Governor's Office of
e-mail: info@goer.ny.gov
Web site: www.goer.ny.gov

Public Information Officer:
    Vacant...........................................518-457-9375

## Environmental Conservation Department
e-mail: contact@dec.ny.gov
Web site: www.dec.ny.gov

Deputy Commissioner, Public Affairs:
    Erica Ringewald...............518-402-8000/fax: 518-402-9016
    e-mail: pressoffice@dec.ny.gov
Press Operations:
    Erica Ringewald .................518-402-8000/fax: 518-402-9016

## General Services, Office of
e-mail: comments@ogs.ny.gov
Web site: www.ogs.ny.gov

Director, Communications:
    Heather Groll.................518-474-5987/fax: 518-486-9179
    e-mail: heather.groll@ogs.ny.gov

## Health Department
e-mail: dohweb@health.ny.gov
Web site: www.health.ny.gov

Director, Public Information:
    Jonah Bruno......................518-474-7354/fax: 518-473-3456
Assistant Commissioner, Public Affairs:
    Gary Holmes......................................518-474-7354
Deputy Director, Governmental Affairs:
    Michelle Newman ............................518-474-7354 x1

## Housing & Community Renewal, Division of
e-mail: hcrinfo@nyshcr.org
Web site: www.nyshcr.org

FOIL Officer:
    Valerie Molinaro
    e-mail: hcrfoil@nyshcr.org

## Hudson River Valley Greenway
e-mail: hrvg@hudsongreenway.ny.gov
Web site: www.hudsongreenway.ny.gov

Executive Director:
    Scott Keller......................................518-473-3835

## Human Rights, State Division of
e-mail: infobronx@dhr.ny.gov
Web site: www.dhr.ny.gov

Director, External Relations:
    Vacant...........................................718-741-8400

## Inspector General (NYS), Office of the
Web site: www.ig.ny.gov

Special Deputy, Communications & External Affairs:
    Vacant.........................518-474-1010 or 212-635-3150

## Insurance Fund (NYS)
Web site: www.nysif.com

## Labor Department
e-mail: nysdol@labor.ny.gov
Web site: www.labor.ny.gov

Associate Commissioner, Communications:
    Peter Brancato....................................518-457-5519

## Law Department
Web site: www.ag.ny.gov

Director, Public Affairs & Press Secretary:
    Fernando Aquino...................212-416-8060/fax: 212-416-6005
    e-mail: nyag.pressoffice@ag.ny.gov

## New York State Gaming Commission
e-mail: info@gaming.ny.gov
Web site: www.gaming.ny.gov

Director, Communications:
    Brad Maione .....................................518-388-3415
Public Information Officer:
    Vacant...........................................518-388-3415

## Mental Health, Office of
Web site: www.omh.ny.gov

Director, Public Information:
    James Plastiras...................518-474-6540/fax: 518-473-3456

*Offices and agencies generally appear in alphabetical order, except when specific order is requested by listee.*

## NYS Office for People with Developmental Disabilities
e-mail: communications.office@opwdd.ny.gov
Web site: www.opwdd.ny.gov

Director, Communications & Public Affairs:
    Vacant . . . . . . . . . . . . . . . . . . . . . . 518-474-6601/fax: 518-473-1271
Director Public Information:
    Vacant . . . . . . . . . . . . . . . . . . . . . . . . . . . . . . . . . . . 518-473-1997

## Military & Naval Affairs, Division of
Web site: www.dmna.ny.gov

Director, Public Affairs:
    Eric Durr . . . . . . . . . . . . . . . . . . . . . 518-786-4581/fax: 518-786-4649

## Motor Vehicles Department
Web site: dmv.ny.gov/

Assistant Commissioner, Communications & Marketing:
    Lisa Koumjian . . . . . . . . . . . . . . . . . . . 518-473-7000/fax: 518-473-1930

## NYSTAR - Division of Science, Technology & Innovation
Web site: www.esd.ny.gov/nystar

Executive Vice President, Public Affairs & Strategic Initiatives:
    Kay Wright . . . . . . . . . . . . . . . . . . . . . 518-292-5700/fax: 518-292-5798

## Parks, Recreation & Historic Preservation, NYS Office of
Web site: www.parks.ny.gov

Deputy Public Information Officer:
    Brian Nearing . . . . . . . . . . . . . . . . . . . . . . . . . . . . 518-486-1868
Public Information Officer:
    Dan Keefe . . . . . . . . . . . . . . . . . . . . . . . . . . . . . . . 518-486-1868

## Parole Board, The
Web site: www.parole.ny.gov; doccs.ny.gov

Director, Public Information:
    Thomas Mailey . . . . . . . . . . . . . . . . . . . . . . . . . . . 518-457-8182

## Prevention of Domestic Violence, Office for the
Web site: www.opdv.ny.gov

Director, Bureau of Public Awareness & Prevention:
    Suzanne Cecala . . . . . . . . . . . . . . . . . . 518-457-5744/fax: 518-457-5810
    e-mail: suzanne.cecala@opdv.ny.gov

## Public Employment Relations Board
e-mail: perbinfo@perb.ny.gov
Web site: www.perb.ny.gov

Executive Director, Office of Administration:
    Jonathan O'Rourke . . . . . . . . . . . . . . . . . . . . . . . . . 518-457-2676

## Public Service Commission
Web site: www.dps.ny.gov

Director, Public Affairs:
    James Denn . . . . . . . . . . . . . . . . . . . 518-474-7080/fax: 518-473-2838
    e-mail: james.denn@dps.ny.gov

## Real Property Tax Services, Office of
Director, Public Information:
    Vacant . . . . . . . . . . . . . . . . . . . . . . 518-486-3418/fax: 518-474-9276

## State Comptroller, Office of the
e-mail: contactus@osc.state.ny.us
Web site: www.osc.state.ny.us

Director, Communications:
    Jennifer Freeman . . . . . . . . . . . . . . . . . . . 518-474-4015 or 212-383-2501
    fax: 518-473-8940

## State Department
e-mail: info@dos.ny.gov

Deputy Secretary, Public Affairs:
    Vacant . . . . . . . . . . . . . . . . . . . . . . 518-474-4752/fax: 518-474-4597
    e-mail: info@dos.state.ny.us

## State Police, Division of
e-mail: nyspmail@troopers.ny.gov
Web site: www.troopers.ny.gov

Director, Public Information:
    Beau Duffy . . . . . . . . . . . . . . . . . . . 518-457-2180/fax: 518-485-7818
    e-mail: pio@troopers.ny.gov

## Tax Appeals, Division of
e-mail: dta@dta.ny.gov
Web site: www.dta.ny.gov

Secretary to the Tribunal:
    Jean A McDonnell . . . . . . . . . . . . . . . . . . . . . . . . . 518-266-3036

## Taxation & Finance Department
Web site: www.tax.ny.gov

Director, Public Information:
    Geoffrey Gloak . . . . . . . . . . . . . . . . . . 518-457-4242 or 518-457-7377
    fax: 518-457-2486

## Temporary & Disability Assistance, Office of
e-mail: nyspio@otda.ny.gov
Web site: www.otda.ny.gov

Director, Public Information:
    Anthony Farmer . . . . . . . . . . . . . . . . . . 518-474-9516/fax: 518-486-6935
    e-mail: nyspio@otda.ny.gov

## Transportation Department
Web site: www.dot.ny.gov

Director, Communications Office:
    Joseph Morrissey . . . . . . . . . . . . . . . . . . . . . . . . . . 518-457-6400

## Veterans' Affairs, Division of
e-mail: dvainfo@veterans.ny.gov
Web site: www.veterans.ny.gov

Counsel:
    Jonathan Fishbein . . . . . . . . . . . . . . . . . . . . . . . . . 518-474-6114

## Welfare Inspector General, Office of NYS
e-mail: inspector.general@ig.ny.gov
Web site: www.owig.ny.gov

Confidential Assistant/Office Manager:
    Joy Quiles . . . . . . . . . . . . . . . . . . . . 718-923-4290 or 518-474-1010
    fax: 718-923-4310

## Workers' Compensation Board
e-mail: general_information@wcb.ny.gov
Web site: www.wcb.ny.gov

Director, Public Information:
    Melissa Stewart . . . . . . . . . . . . . . . . . . 518-408-0469/fax: 518-473-1415
    e-mail: publicinfo@wcb.ny.gov

*Offices and agencies generally appear in alphabetical order, except when specific order is requested by listee.*

State & Local Government Public Information

## JUDICIAL SYSTEM AND RELATED AGENCIES

### Unified Court System
Web site: www.nycourts.gov

Director, Public Affairs:
Mary C Kornman . . . . . . . . . . . . . . . . . . 212-428-2116/fax: 212-428-2117
Director, Communications:
David Bookstaver . . . . . . . . . . . . . . . . 212-428-2500/fax: 212-428-2507
e-mail: dbooksta@courts.state.ny.us
Chief Law Librarian:
Vacant . . . . . . . . . . . . . . . . . . . . . . . . . 518-238-4373/fax: 518-238-2894

## LEGISLATIVE BRANCH

### Assembly
Press Secretary to the Speaker:
Mike Whyland . . . . . . . . . . . . . . . . . . . . 518-455-3791/fax: 518-455-4812
Director, Minority Communications:
Michael Fraser . . . . . . . . . . . . . . . . . . . 518-455-3751/fax: 518-455-3750
e-mail: fraserm@assembly.state.ny.us
Public Information Officer:
Robin Marilla. . . . . . . . . . . . . . . . . . . 518-455-4218/fax: 518-455-5175
Director, Communications:
Morgan E Weinberg . . . . . . . . . . . . . . . . . . . . . . . . . . 518-455-5767
Director, Information Services:
Vacant . . . . . . . . . . . . . . . . . . . . . . . . 518-455-5767/fax: 518-455-4963

### Legislative Library
Legislative Librarian:
Kate Balassie . . . . . . . . . . . . . . . . . . . . 518-455-2468/fax: 518-426-6901
Legislative Librarian:
James Giliberto . . . . . . . . . . . . . . . . . . . . . . . . . . . . . . 518-455-2468

### Senate
Director, Minority Communications:
Candice Giove. . . . . . . . . . . . . . . . . . . . . . . . . . . . . . . 518-455-3545
Majority Press Secretary:
Vacant . . . . . . . . . . . . . . . . . . . . . . . . 518-455-3191/fax: 518-455-2448
Director, Minority Communications:
Vacant . . . . . . . . . . . . . . . . . . . . . . . . 518-455-2415/fax: 518-426-6933
Minority Press Secretary:
Vacant . . . . . . . . . . . . . . . . . . . . . . . . 518-455-2415/fax: 518-426-6955
Director, Student Programs Office:
Krista Ketterer . . . . . . . . . . . . . . . . . . . 518-455-2611/fax: 518-432-5470

## CORPORATIONS, AUTHORITIES AND COMMISSIONS

### Adirondack Park Agency
Web site: www.apa.ny.gov

Public Relations:
Keith McKeever . . . . . . . . . . . . . . . . . 518-891-4050/fax: 518-891-3938
e-mail: keith.mckeever@apa.ny.gov

### Agriculture & NYS Horse Breeding Development Fund
Web site: www.nysirestakes.com

Executive Director:
M Kelly Young. . . . . . . . . . . . . . . . . . . . . . . . . . . . . . . 518-388-0178

### Albany County Airport Authority
Web site: www.albanyairport.com

Director, Public Affairs:
Vacant. . . . . . . . . . . . . . . . . . . . . . . 518-242-2222 x1/fax: 518-242-2641
e-mail: info@albanyairport.com

### Albany Port District Commission
Web site: www.portofalbany.us

Chief Executive Officer:
Richard J Hendrick . . . . . . . . . . . . . . . 518-463-8763/fax: 518-463-8767
e-mail: rhendrick@portofalbany.us

### Atlantic States Marine Fisheries Commission
Web site: www.asmfc.org

Director Communications:
Tina Berger . . . . . . . . . . . . . . . . . . . . 703-842-0740/fax: 703-842-0741
e-mail: tberger@asmfc.org

### Battery Park City Authority (Hugh L Carey)
Web site: www.bpca.ny.gov

VP External Relations:
Vacant . . . . . . . . . . . . . . . . . . . . . . . . 212-417-2276/fax: 212-417-2279

### Brooklyn Navy Yard Development Corporation
e-mail: info@brooklynnavyyard.org
Web site: www.brooklynnavyyard.org

Senior Vice President, External Affairs:
Tiffany Townsend . . . . . . . . . . . . . . . . . 718-907-5900/fax: 718-643-9296

### Buffalo & Fort Erie Public Bridge Authority (Peace Bridge Authority)
Web site: www.peacebridge.com

General Manager:
Ron Rienas. . . . . . . . . . . . . . . . . . . . . 716-884-6744/fax: 716-884-2089

### Capital District Regional Off-Track Betting Corporation
e-mail: customerservice@capitalotb.com
Web site: www.capitalotb.com

Secretary & Director:
Vacant . . . . . . . . . . . . . . . . . . . . . . . . 518-344-5225/fax: 518-370-5460

### Capital District Regional Planning Commission
e-mail: cdrpc@cdrpc.org
Web site: www.cdrpc.org

Financial Officer:
Tim Canty . . . . . . . . . . . . . . . . . . . . . 518-453-0850/fax: 518-453-0856

### Capital District Transportation Authority
Web site: www.cdta.org

VP, Planning & Infrastructure:
Christopher G Desany . . . . . . . . . . . . . . 518-437-8320/fax: 518-437-8328
e-mail: chrisd@cdta.org

### Catskill Off-Track Betting Corporation
Web site: www.interbets.com

President:
Donald J Groth . . . . . . . . . . . . . . . . . . 845-362-0400/fax: 845-362-0419
e-mail: otb@interbets.com

### Central New York Regional Market Authority
Web site: www.cnyregionalmarket.com

Commissioner's Representative:
Christina Nowak . . . . . . . . . . . . . . . . . . 315-422-8647/fax: 315-442-6897

### Central New York Regional Transportation Authority
Web site: www.centro.org

*Offices and agencies generally appear in alphabetical order, except when specific order is requested by listee.*

CEO:
    Richard Lee . . . . . . . . . . . . . . . . . . . . . . . .315-442-3360/fax: 315-422-3337

## Central Pine Barrens Joint Planning & Policy Commission
e-mail: info@pb.state.ny.us
Web site: www.pb.state.ny.us

Executive Director:
    John W Pavacic . . . . . . . . . . . . . . . . . . . . . . . . . . . . . . . . . . . .631-288-1079

## City University Construction Fund
Counsel:
    Frederick Schaffer . . . . . . . . . . . . . . . . . . . . . . . . . . . . . . .646-664-9210
    e-mail: frederick.schaffer@mail.cuny.edu

## Delaware River Basin Commission
Web site: www.nj.gov/drbc

Communications Manager:
    Kate Schmidt . . . . . . . . . . . . . . . . . . . . . . . . . . . . . . . .609-883-9500 x205

## Development Authority of the North Country
Web site: www.danc.org

Executive Director:
    James W Wright . . . . . . . . . . . . . . . . . . . . . . . . . . . . . . . . . . .315-661-3200

## Empire State Development Corporation
Web site: www.esd.ny.gov

Executive Vice President, Public Affairs & Communications:
    Matthew Gorton . . . . . . . . . . . . . . . . . . . . . . . . . . . . . . . . .800-260-7313

## Great Lakes Commission
Web site: www.glc.org

Communications Director:
    Beth Wanamaker . . . . . . . . . . . . . . . . . . .734-971-9135/fax: 734-971-9150
    e-mail: beth@glc.org

## Hudson River-Black River Regulating District
Web site: www.hrbrrd.com

Executive Director:
    John C Callaghan . . . . . . . . . . . . . . . . . . .518-465-3491/fax: 518-432-2485

## Interest on Lawyer Account (IOLA) Fund of the State of NY
Web site: www.iola.org

Executive Director:
    Christopher O'Malley . . . . . . . . . . . . . . .646-865-1541/fax: 646-865-1545

## Interstate Environmental Commission
Web site: www.iec-nynjct.org

Senior Manager:
    Evelyn R Powers . . . . . . . . . . . . . . . . . .212-967-1414/fax: 212-967-1430
    e-mail: iecmail@iec-nynjct.org

## Interstate Oil & Gas Compact Commission
Executive Director:
    Lori Wrotenbery . . . . . . . . . . . . . . . . . . . . . . . . . . . . . . . . . .405-522-8380

## Lake George Park Commission
Web site: www.lgpc.state.ny.us

Executive Director:
    David Wick . . . . . . . . . . . . . . . . . . . . . . .518-668-9347/fax: 518-668-5001
    e-mail: info@lgpc.state.ny.us

## Lawyers' Fund for Client Protection
Web site: www.nylawfund.org

Executive Director & Counsel:
    Michael Knight . . . . . . . . . . . . . . . . . . .518-434-1935/fax: 518-434-5641
    e-mail: info@nylawfund.org

## Legislative Bill Drafting Commission
Commissioner:
    Randall G Bluth . . . . . . . . . . . . . . . . . . .518-455-7506/fax: 518-455-7598

## MTA (Metropolitan Transportation Authority)
Web site: www.mta.info

Chief Executive Officer:
    Patrick J Foye . . . . . . . . . . . . . . . . . . . . . . . . . . . . . . . . . . . .212-878-7440

## MTA Bridges & Tunnels
Web site: www.mta.info/bandt

Manager, Public Affairs:
    Vacant . . . . . . . . . . . . . . . . . . . . . . . . . . . . . . . . . . . . . . . . . .646-252-7276

## MTA Bus Company
Web site: www.mta.info/busco

Media Relations:
    Vacant . . . . . . . . . . . . . . . . . . . . . . . . .212-878-7440/fax: 212-878-7030

## MTA Capital Construction
Senior Director/Chief Procurement Officer:
    David Cannon . . . . . . . . . . . . . . . . . . . . . . . . . . . . . . . . . . .646-252-2678

## MTA Long Island Rail Road
Web site: www.mta.info/lirr

General Manager, Public Affairs:
    Susan McGowan . . . . . . . . . . . . . . . . . . .718-558-7301/fax: 718-558-8212

## MTA Metro-North Railroad
Web site: www.mta.info/mnr

Senior Director, Corporate & Public Affairs:
    Mark Mannix . . . . . . . . . . . . . . . . . . . . .212-340-2142/fax: 212-340-3460
Vice President, Business Operations:
    Vacant . . . . . . . . . . . . . . . . . . . . . . . . . . . . . . . . . . . . . . . . . .212-672-1251

## MTA New York City Transit
Web site: www.mta.info/nyct

Corporate Communications:
    Vacant . . . . . . . . . . . . . . . . . . . . . . . . . . . . . . . . . . . . . . . . . .646-252-5873

## MTA Office of the Inspector General
Web site: www.mtaig.state.ny.us

Inspector General:
    Carolyn Pokorny . . . . . . . . . . . . . . . . . .212-878-0000/fax: 212-878-0003

## Nassau Regional Off-Track Betting Corporation
Web site: www.nassauotb.com

Director, Public Affairs:
    Vacant . . . . . . . . . . . . . . . . . . . . . . . . .516-572-2800 x124/fax: 516-572-2840

State & Local
Government
Public Information

*Offices and agencies generally appear in alphabetical order, except when specific order is requested by listee.*

## New England Interstate Water Pollution Control Commission
Web site: www.neiwpcc.org

Director of Communications:
Adam Auster......................................978-349-2507
e-mail: aauster@neiwpcc.org

## New York City Housing Development Corporation
e-mail: info@nychdc.com
Web site: www.nychdc.com

Communications/Press Office:
Vacant.........................212-227-2644/fax: B12-227-8580

## New York City School Construction Authority
Web site: www.nycsca.org

Manager, Communications & External Affairs:
Kevin Ortiz
e-mail: KORTIZ2@nycsca.org

## New York Convention Center Operating Corporation
Web site: www.javitscenter.com

SVP/Chief Communications Officer:
Tony Sclafani........................................212-216-2325
e-mail: tsclafani@javitscenter.com

## New York Metropolitan Transportation Council
Web site: www.nymtc.org

Public Information Officer:
Vacant.........................212-383-7203/fax: 212-383-2418

## New York Power Authority
Web site: www.nypa.gov

SVP/Chief Information Officer:
Robert Piascik......................................914-390-8171

## New York State Assn of Fire Districts
Web site: www.firedistnys.com

Counsel:
Joseph F Frank, Esq ..................800-349-2904 or 518-456-6767
fax: 518-456-4644
e-mail: sapfrankjff@optonline.net

## New York State Athletic Commission
Web site: www.dos.ny.gov/athletic

Executive Director:
Kim Sumbler......................212-417-5700/fax: 212-417-4987
e-mail: info@dos.ny.gov

## New York State Board of Law Examiners
Web site: www.nybarexam.org

Executive Director:
John J McAlary....................518-453-5990/fax: 518-452-5729

## New York State Bridge Authority
e-mail: info@nysba.ny.gov
Web site: www.nysba.ny.gov

Director, Toll Collections & Bridge Operations:
Frank Pavlin ......................................845-691-7245

## New York State Commission of Correction
Web site: www.scoc.ny.gov

Deputy Director Public Information:
Peter Thorne .....................518-485-2346/fax: 518-485-2467
e-mail: infoscoc@scoc.ny.gov

## New York State Commission on Judicial Nomination
Web site: www.nysegov.com/cjn/

Counsel:
Henry Greenberg..................518-689-1400/fax: 518-689-1499
e-mail: greenbergh@gtlaw.com

## New York State Commission on the Restoration of the Capitol
Executive Director:
Andrea J Lazarski .................518-473-0341/fax: 518-486-5720
e-mail: andrea.lazarski@ogs.ny.gov

## New York State Disaster Preparedness Commission
Web site: www.dhses.ny.gov/oem/disaster-prep

Chairman/Director:
Jerome M Hauer ...................518-292-2301/fax: 518-322-4978

## New York State Dormitory Authority
Web site: www.dasny.org

Chief of Staff:
Caroline V Griffin .................518-257-3380/fax: 518-257-3387

## New York State Energy Research & Development Authority
e-mail: info@nyserda.ny.gov
Web site: www.nyserda.ny.gov

Counsel & Secretary to the Authority:
Peter Costello......................518-862-1090/fax: 518-862-1091

## New York State Environmental Facilities Corp
Web site: www.efc.ny.gov/environmental-facilities-corporation

Chief Information Officer:
Franklin W Hsia ...................518-402-6924/fax: 518-486-9323

## Joint Commission on Public Ethics (JCOPE)
Web site: www.jcope.ny.gov

Director, External Affairs:
Walter J McClure .................518-408-3976/fax: 518-408-3975
Chief of Staff:
Vacant ..............................518-408-3976/fax: 518-408-3975

## New York State Financial Control Board
Web site: www.fcb.state.ny.us

Executive Director:
Jeffrey Sommer....................212-417-5066/fax: 212-417-5055

## New York State Higher Education Services Corp (NYSHESC)
e-mail: hescpublicaffairsoffice@hesc.ny.gov
Web site: www.hesc.ny.gov

Communications Division:
Vacant..............................518-474-5592 or 518-474-5775
fax: 518-474-5593

*Offices and agencies generally appear in alphabetical order, except when specific order is requested by listee.*

## New York State Judicial Conduct Commission
Web site: www.cjc.ny.gov

Administrator & Counsel:
Robert H Tembeckjian . . . . . . . . . . . . . . . . . . . . . . . . . . . . .646-386-4800
   e-mail: cjc@cjc.ny.gov
Information Officer:
Amy Carpinello. . . . . . . . . . . . . . . . . . . . . . . . . . . . . . . . . .646-386-4800

## New York State Law Reporting Bureau
Web site: www.courts.state.ny.us/reporter

State Reporter:
Cara J Brousseau. . . . . . . . . . . . . . . . . . . . . . . . . . . . . . . . .518-453-6900
Deputy State Reporter:
Katherine G Breitenbach. . . . . . . . . . . .518-453-6900/fax: 518-426-1640
   e-mail: Reporter@courts.state.ny.us

## New York State Law Revision Commission
Web site: www.lawrevision.state.ny.us

Executive Director:
Rose Mary Bailly. . . . . . . . . . . . . . . . . . .518-472-5858/fax: 518-445-2303

## New York State Liquor Authority (Division of Alcoholic Beverage Control)
Web site: www.sla.ny.gov

Director, Public Affairs:
William Crowley . . . . . . . . . . . . . . . . . .518-474-3114 or 518-474-4875
   fax: 518-473-9565
   e-mail: William.Crowley@sla.ny.gov

## New York State Olympic Regional Development Authority
Web site: www.orda.org/corporate

Communications Manager:
Jon Lundin. . . . . . . . . . . . . . . . . . . . . . .518-523-1655/fax: 518-523-9275
   e-mail: jlundin@orda.org

## New York State Teachers' Retirement System
Web site: www.nystrs.org

Manager, Public Information:
John Cardillo . . . . . . . . . . . . . . . . . . . . .518-447-4743/fax: 518-447-2875
   e-mail: john.cardillo@nystrs.org

## New York State Thoroughbred Breeding & Development Fund Corporation
Web site: www.nybreds.com

Executive Director:
Tracy Egan. . . . . . . . . . . . . . . . . . . . . . .518-388-0174/fax: 518-344-1235

## New York State Thruway Authority
Web site: www.thruway.ny.gov

Chief Information Officer:
Kim McKinney. . . . . . . . . . . . . . . . . . . . . . . . . . . . . . . . . .518-471-5300

## New York State Tug Hill Commission
Web site: www.tughill.org

Executive Director:
Katie Malinowski . . . . . . . . . . . . . . . . .315-785-2570/fax: 315-785-2574
   e-mail: katie@tughill.org

## Niagara Falls Bridge Commission
Web site: www.niagarafallsbridges.com

General Manager:
Kenneth Bieger . . . . . . . . . . . . 716-285-6322 ext4151/fax: 716-282-3292

## Niagara Frontier Transportation Authority
Web site: www.nfta.com

Director, Public Affairs:
Helen Tederous . . . . . . . . . . . . . . . . . . .716-855-7420/fax: 716-855-6655

## Northeastern Forest Fire Protection Commission
Web site: www.nffpc.org

Executive Director/Center Manager:
Thomas G Parent. . . . . . . . . . . . . . . . . .207-968-3782/fax: 207-968-3782
   e-mail: necompact@fairpoint.net

## Ogdensburg Bridge & Port Authority
Web site: www.ogdensport.com

Executive Director:
Vacant . . . . . . . . . . . . . . . . . . . . . . . . . .315-393-4080/fax: 315-393-7068

## Ohio River Valley Water Sanitation Commission
Web site: www.orsanco.org

Communications Coordinator:
Lisa Cochran. . . . . . . . . . . . . . .513-231-7719 ext 102/fax: 513-231-7761
   e-mail: lcochran@orsanco.org
Public Information:
Melissa Mann . . . . . . . . . . . . . .513-231-7719 ext 101/fax: 513-231-7761
   e-mail: mmann@orsanco.org

## Port Authority of New York & New Jersey
Web site: www.panynj.gov

Director, Corporate Communications:
Lindsay Kryzak . . . . . . . . . . . . . . . . . . .212-435-7777/fax: 212-435-4032
   e-mail: press@panynj.gov

## Port of Oswego Authority
Web site: www.portoswego.com

Executive Director:
William Scriber . . . . . . . . . . . . . . .315-343-4503 x109/fax: 315-343-5498
   e-mail: wscriber@portoswego.com

## Rochester-Genesee Regional Transportation Authority-RTS
Web site: www.myrts.com

Public Information Officer:
Tom Brede. . . . . . . . . . . . . . . . . . . . . . . .585-654-0730/fax: 585-654-0224

## Roosevelt Island Operating Corporation (RIOC)
Web site: www.rioc.ny.gov

Manager, Community Relations/Director, Community Affairs:
Erica Spencer-El. . . . . . . . . . . . . .212-832-4540 x349/fax: 212-832-4582
   e-mail: erica.spencer-el@rioc.ny.gov

## State University Construction Fund
Web site: www.sucf.suny.edu

Deputy General Manager:
William E Held . . . . . . . . . . . . . . . . . . .518-320-1630/fax: 518-443-1008

## State of New York Mortgage Agency (SONYMA)
Web site: https://hcr.ny.gov

*Offices and agencies generally appear in alphabetical order, except when specific order is requested by listee.*

Director, Public Information:
Charni Sochet . . . . . . . . . . . . . . . . . . . . . . . . . . .212-872-0338
e-mail: plentz@nyhomes.org

**State of New York Municipal Bond Bank Agency (MBBA)**
Director of Communications:
Vacant . . . . . . . . . . . . . . . . . . . . . .212-872-0679/fax: 212-872-0789

**Suffolk Regional Off-Track Betting Corporation**
Web site: www.suffolkotb.com

Director, Governmental & Public Affairs:
Debbie Pfieffer . . . . . . . . . . . . . . . . . . .631-853-1000/fax: 631-853-1086
e-mail: customerservice@suffolkotb.com

**Thousand Islands Bridge Authority**
Web site: www.tibridge.com

Executive Director:
Robert G Horr, III . . . . . . . . . . . . . . . . .315-482-2501/fax: 315-482-6064
e-mail: roberthorr@tibridge.com

**Uniform State Laws Commission**
Chair:
Richard B Long . . . . . . . . . . . . . . . . .607-821-2202/fax: 607-723-1530
e-mail: rlong@cglawoffices.com

**United Nations Development Corporation**
Web site: www.undc.org

Vice President:
Kenneth Coopersmith . . . . . . . . . . . . . .212-888-1618/fax: 212-588-0758

**Waterfront Commission of New York Harbor**
Web site: www.wcnyh.org

Executive Director:
Walter M Arsenault . . . . . . . . . . . . . . . . .212-905-9201/fax: 212-480-0587

**Western Regional Off-Track Betting Corp**
Web site: www.westernotb.com

Telecommunications Manager:
James Haas . . . . . . . . . . . . . . . . . . . . . .585-343-3750/fax: 585-344-6188

*Offices and agencies generally appear in alphabetical order, except when specific order is requested by listee.*

# U.S. CONGRESS

## U.S. SENATE: NEW YORK DELEGATION

*Internet access, including e-mail addresses, is available at: www.senate.gov. Biographies of Senate Members appear in a separate section in the back of the book.*

**Kirsten E Gillibrand (D)** . . . . . . . . . . (202) 224-4451/fax: 202-228-0282
478 Russell Senate Office Building, Washington, DC 20510
*Committees:* Foreign Relations;Agriculture; Environment and Public Works; Special Committee on Aging; Senate Armed Services

**Charles E Schumer (D)** . . . . . . . . . . . . 202-224-6542/fax: 202-228-3027
313 Hart Senate Office Building, Washington, DC 20510
*Committees:* Senate Finance; Joint Economic; Judiciary; Rules and Administration; Banking, Housing, and Urban Affairs

## U.S. HOUSE OF REPRESENTATIVES: NEW YORK DELEGATION

*Internet access, including e-mail addresses, is available at: www.house.gov. Biographies of House Members appear in a separate section in the back of the book.*

**Gary L Ackerman (D)** . . . . . . . . . . . . . . 202-225-2601/fax: 202-225-1589
2243 Rayburn House Office Bldg, Washington, DC 20515
*Congressional District:* 5
*Committees:* Foreign Affairs; Financial Services

**Timothy H Bishop (D)** . . . . . . . . . . . . . . 202-225-3826/fax: 202-225-3143
306 Canon House Office Building, Washington, DC 20515
*Congressional District:* 1
*Committees:* Education and Labor; Transportation and Infrastructure; Budget

**Ann Marie Buerkle (D)** . . . . . . . . . . . . . . . . . . . . . . . . . . 315-423-5657
1630 Longworth House Office Building, Washington, DC 20515
*Congressional District:* 25
*Committees:* Foreign Affairs; Oversight and Government Reform; Veterans Affairs

**Yvette D Clarke (D)** . . . . . . . . . . . . . . . 202-225-6231/fax: 202-226-0112
1029 Longworth House Office Building, Washington, DC 20515
*Congressional District:* 11
*Committees:* Homeland Security; Small Business

**Joseph Crowley (D)** . . . . . . . . . . . . . . . . . . . . . . . . . . . 202-225-3965
2404 Rayburn House Office Building, Washington, DC 20515
*Congressional District:* 7
*Committees:* Ways and Means; Foreign Affairs

**Eliot L Engel (D)** . . . . . . . . . . . . . . . . . 202-225-2464/fax: 202-225-5513
2161 Rayburn House Office Building, Washington, DC 20515
*Congressional District:* 17
*Committees:* Energy and Commerce; Foreign Affairs

**Chris Gibson (R)** . . . . . . . . . . . . . . . . . 202-225-5614/fax: 202-225-1168
120 Cannon HOB, Washington, DC 20515
*Congressional District:* 20
*Committees:* Agriculture; Armed Services

**Michael Grimm (R)** . . . . . . . . . . . . . . . . 202-225-3371/fax: 202-226-1272
323 Cannon House Office Building, Washington, DC 20515
*Congressional District:* 13
*Committees:* Financial Services

**Richard Hanna (R)** . . . . . . . . . . . . . . . . . . . . . . . . . . . . 607-756-2470
127 Cannon House Office Building, Washington, DC 20515
*Congressional District:* 24
*Committees:* Transportation and Infrastructure; Education and the Workforce

**Nan Hayworth (R)** . . . . . . . . . . . . . . . . 202-225-5441/fax: 202-225-3289
1217 Longworth House Office Building, Washington, DC 20515
*Congressional District:* 19
*Committees:* Financial Services

**Brian Higgins (D)** . . . . . . . . . . . . . . . . . 202-225-3306/fax: 202-226-0347
431 Cannon House Office Building, Washington, DC 20515
*Congressional District:* 27
*Committees:* Foreign Affairs; Homeland Security

**Maurice D Hinchey (D)** . . . . . . . . . . . . . 202-225-6335/fax: 202-226-0774
2431 Rayburn House Office Building, Washington, DC 20515
*Congressional District:* 22
*Committees:* Appropriations

**Steve Israel (D)** . . . . . . . . . . . . . . . . . . . 202-225-3335/fax: 202-225-4669
2457 Rayburn House Office Building, Washington, DC 20515
*Congressional District:*
*Committees:* Appropriations

**Pete King (R)** . . . . . . . . . . . . . . . . . . . . . . . . . . . . . . . . . 202-225-7896
339 Cannon House Office Building, Washington, DC 20515
*Congressional District:* 3
*Committees:* Homeland Security; Financial Services

**Nita M Lowey (D)** . . . . . . . . . . . . . . . . . 202-225-6506/fax: 202-225-0546
2329 Rayburn House Office Building, Washington, DC 20515
*Congressional District:* 18
*Committees:* House Appropriations; Homeland Security

**Carolyn B Maloney (D)** . . . . . . . . . . . . . 202-225-7944/fax: 202-225-4709
2332 Rayburn House Office Building, Washington, DC 20515
*Congressional District:* 14
*Committees:* Financial Services; Oversight and Government Reform

**Carolyn McCarthy (D)** . . . . . . . . . . . . . 202-225-5516/fax: 202-225-5758
2346 Rayburn House Office Building, Washington, DC 20515
*Congressional District:* 4
*Committees:* Education and Labor; Financial Services

**Gregory W Meeks (D)** . . . . . . . . . . . . . . 202-225-3461/fax: 202-226-4169
2342 Rayburn House Office Building, Washington, DC 20515
*Congressional District:* 6
*Committees:* Financial Services; Foreign Affairs

**Jerrold Nadler (D)** . . . . . . . . . . . . . . . . . . . . . . . . . . . . . 202-225-5635
2334 Rayburn House Office Building, Washington, DC 20515
*Congressional District:* 8
*Committees:* Judiciary; Transportation and Infrastructure

**Bill Owens (R)** . . . . . . . . . . . . . . . . . . . . 202-225-4611/fax: 202-226-0621
2366 Rayburn House Office Building, Washington, DC 20515-3223
*Congressional District:* 23
*Committees:* Agriculture; Armed Services; Small Business

**Charles B Rangel (D)** . . . . . . . . . . . . . . 202-225-4365/fax: 202-225-0816
2354 Rayburn House Office Building, Washington, DC 20515
*Congressional District:* 15
*Committees:* Ways and Means; Taxation

**Tom Reed (R)** . . . . . . . . . . . . . . . . . . . . 202-225-3161/fax: 202-226-6599
1208 Longworth House Office Building, Washington, DC 20515
*Congressional District:* 29
*Committees:* Rules

**Jose E Serrano (D)** . . . . . . . . . . . . . . . . . 202-225-4361/fax: 202-225-6001
2227 Rayburn House Office Building, Washington, DC 20515
*Congressional District:* 16
*Committees:* Appropriations

**Louise M Slaughter (D)** . . . . . . . . . . . . 202-225-3615/fax: 202-225-7822
2469 Rayburn House Office Building, Washington, DC 20515
*Congressional District:* 28
*Committees:* Rules

*Offices and agencies generally appear in alphabetical order, except when specific order is requested by listee.*

**Paul D Tonko (D)**....................202-225-5076/fax: 202-225-5077
128 Cannon House Office Building, Washington, DC 20515
*Congressional District:* 21
*Committees:* Budget; Science and Technology

**Edolphus Towns (D)** ..............202-225-5936/fax: 202-225-1018
2232 Rayburn House Office Building, Washington, DC 20515
*Congressional District:* 10
*Committees:* Energy and Commerce; Oversight and Government

**Nydia M Velazquez (D)**..............202-225-2361/fax: 202-226-0327
2466 Rayburn House Office Building, Washington, DC 20515
*Congressional District:* 12
*Committees:* Small Business; Financial Services

**Anthony D Weiner (D)**............................202-225-6616
2104 Rayburn House Office Building, Washington, DC 20515
*Congressional District:* 9
*Committees:* Homeland Security; Judiciary

## U.S. SENATE STANDING COMMITTEES

### Agriculture, Nutrition & Forestry
328A Senate Russell Office Building
Washington, DC 20510
202-224-2035
Web site: www.agriculture.senate.gov

Chair:
   Tom Harkin (D-IA).................................202-224-3254
Ranking Republican Member:
   Saxby Chambliss (R-GA)...........................202-224-3521

**Subcommittees**

#### Domestic and Foreign Marketing, Inspection and Plant & Animal Health
Chair:
   Max Baucus (D-MT) ................................202-224-2651
Ranking Member:
   Vacant

#### Energy, Science and Technology
Chair:
   Kent Conrad (D-ND) ...............................202-224-2043
Ranking Member:
   John Thune (R-SD) ................................202-224-2321

#### Nutrition & Food Assistance, Sustainable & Organic Agriculture & Gen Legis
Chair:
   Patrick J Leahy (D-VT) ...........................202-224-4242
Ranking Member:
   Norm Coleman (R-MN)..........................202-224-5641

#### Production, Income Protection and Price Support
Chair:
   Blanche L Lincoln (D-AR).........................202-224-4843
Ranking Member:
   Pat Roberts (R-KS)................................202-224-4774

#### Rural Revitalization, Conservation, Forestry and Credit
Chair:
   Debbie Stabenow (D-MI)..........................202-224-4822
Ranking Member:
   Mike Crapo (R-ID)................................202-224-6142

### Appropriations
The Capitol
S-128
Washington, DC 20510
202-224-7363
Web site: www.appropriations.senate.gov

Chair:
   Daniel K Inouye (D-HI) ...........................202-224-3934
Vice Chair:
   Thad Cochran (R-MS) ............................202-224-5054

**Subcommittees**

#### Agriculture, Rural Development, FDA, and Related Agencies
Chair:
   Herb Kohl (D-WI) ...............................202-224-5653
Ranking Member:
   Sam Brownback (R-KS)...........................202-224-6521

#### Commerce, Justice, Science and Related Agencies
Chair:
   Barbara Mikulski (D-MD) .........................202-224-4645
Ranking Member:
   Richard Shelby (R-AL) ...........................202-224-5744

#### Defense
Chair:
   Daniel Inouye (D-HI)..............................202-224-3934
Ranking Member:
   Thad Cochran (R-MS) ............................202-224-5054

#### Energy and Water Development
Chair:
   Byron Dorgan (D-ND) ............................202-224-2551
Ranking Member:
   Robert Bennett (R-UT)............................202-224-5444

#### Financial Services and General Government
Chair:
   Richard Durbin (D-IL).............................202-224-2152
Ranking Member:
   Susan M Collins (R-ME) ..........................202-224-2523

#### Homeland Security
Chair:
   Robert C Byrd (D-WV) ...........................202-224-3954
Ranking Member:
   George V Voinovich (R-OH).......................202-224-3353

#### Interior, Environment and Related Agencies
Chair:
   Dianne Feinstein (D-CA)..........................202-224-3841
Ranking Member:
   Lamar Alexander (R-TN)..........................202-224-4944

#### Labor, Health and Human Services, Education and Related Agencies
Chair:
   Tom Harkin (D-IA) ..............................202-224-3254
Ranking Member:
   Arlen Specter (R-PA).............................202-224-4254

#### Legislative Branch
Chair:
   Ben Nelson (D-NE) ..............................202-224-6551
Ranking Member:
   Barbara Mikulsi (R-MD) ..........................202-224-4645

#### Military Construction, Veterans Affairs and Related Agencies
Chair:
   Tim Johnson (D-SD) .............................202-224-5842
Ranking Member:
   Kay Bailey Hutchison (R-TX) ......................202-224-5922

#### State, Foreign Operations and Related Programs
Chair:
   Patrick Leahy (D-VT).............................202-224-4242
Ranking Member:
   Judd Gregg (D-NH) ..............................202-224-3324

*Offices and agencies generally appear in alphabetical order, except when specific order is requested by listee.*

**Transportation, Housing and Urban Development, and Related Agencies**
Chair:
Patty Murray (D-WA) .............................202-224-2621
Ranking Member:
Christopher Bond (R-MO).......................202-224-5721

## Armed Services
Russell Senate Office Building
Room SR-228
Washington, DC 20510
202-224-3871
Web site: www.armed-services.senate.gov

Chair:
Carl Levin (D-MI)..................................202-224-6221
Ranking Member:
John McCain (R-AZ) ..............................202-224-2235

### Subcommittees

**Airland**
Chair:
Joseph I Liberman (D-CT)........................202-224-4041
Ranking Member:
John Thune (R-SD) ...............................202-224-2321

**Emerging Threats & Capabilities**
Chair:
Jack Reed (D-RI) ..................................202-224-4642
Ranking Member:
Roger F Wicker (R-MS)...........................202-224-6253

**Personnel**
Chair:
Ben Nelson (D-FL)..................................202-224-5274
Ranking Member:
Lindsey O Graham (R-SC).........................202-224-5972

**Readiness & Management Support**
Chair:
Evan Bayh (D-IN) ..................................202-224-5623
Ranking Member:
Richard Burr (R-NC) ..............................202-224-3154

**SeaPower**
Chair:
Edward M Kennedy (D-MA)........................202-224-4543
Ranking Member:
Mel Martinez (R-FL) ...............................202-224-3041

**Strategic Forces**
Chair:
Bill Nelson (D-FL) .................................202-224-5274
Ranking Member:
Jeff Sessions (R-AL) ...............................202-224-4124

## Banking, Housing & Urban Affairs
534 Dirksen Seanate Office Building
Washington, DC 20510
202-224-7391
Web site: www.banking.senate.gov

Chair:
Christopher J Dodd (D-CT).........................202-224-2823
Ranking Member:
Richard C Shelby (R-AL)...........................202-224-5744

### Subcommittees

**Economic Policy**
Chair:
Sherrod Brown (D-OH) ...........................202-224-2315

Ranking Member:
Jim DeMint (R-SC) ................................202-224-6121

**Financial Institutions**
Chair:
Tim Johnson (D-SD) ..............................202-224-5842
Ranking Member:
Mike Crapo (R-ID)................................202-224-6142

**Housing, Transportation and Community Development**
Chair:
Robert Menendez (D-NJ).........................202-224-4744
Ranking Member:
David Vitter (R-LA ...............................202-224-4623

**Securities, Insurance and Investment**
Chair:
Jack Reed (D-RI) .................................202-224-4642
Ranking Member:
Jim Bunning (R-KY)..............................202-224-4343

**Security and International Trade and Finance**
Chair:
Evan Bayh (D-IN) ................................202-224-5623
Ranking Member:
Bob Corker (R-TN) ..............................202-224-3344

## Budget
624 Dirksen Senate Office Building
Washington, DC 20510
202-224-0642
Web site: www.budget.senate.gov

Chair:
Kent Conrad (D-ND) .............................202-224-0642
Ranking Member:
Judd Gregg (R-NH) ..............................202-224-0642

## Commerce, Science & Transportation
508 Dirksen Building
Washington, DC 20510
202-224-5115
Web site: www.commerce.senate.gov

Chair:
John D Rockefeller, IV (D-WV) ..................202-224-6472
Ranking Member:
Kay Bailey Hutchison (R-TX) ....................202-224-5922

### Subcommittees

**Aviation Operations, Safety & Security**
Chair:
Byron L Dorgan (D-ND) .........................202-224-9000
Ranking Member:
Jim DeMint (R-SC) ..............................202-224-5184

**Communications, Technology, & the Internet**
Chair:
John Kerry (D-MA) ..............................202-224-0415
Ranking Member:
John Ensign (R-NV)..............................202-224-4852
Chair:
Amy Klobuchar (R-MN) .........................202-224-1270
Ranking Member:
Mel Martinez (R-FL).............................202-224-5183

**Consumer Protection, Product Safety, & Insurance**
Chair:
Mark Pryor (D-AR) ..............................202-224-1270
Ranking Member:
Roger F Wicker (R-MS)..........................202-224-5183

*Offices and agencies generally appear in alphabetical order, except when specific order is requested by listee.*

**Oceans, Atmosphere, Fisheries and Coast Guard**
Chair:
    Maria Cantwell (D-WA)..........................202-224-4912
Ranking Member:
    Olympia J Snowe (R-ME)......................202-224-8172

**Science and Space**
Chair:
    Bill Nelson (D-FL)...............................202-224-0415
Ranking Member:
    David Vitter (R-LA)..............................202-224-4852

**Surface Transportation & Merchant Marine Infrastructure, Safety & Security**
Chair:
    Frank R Lautneberg (D-NJ)....................202-224-9000
Ranking Member:
    John Thune (R-SD)..............................202-224-4852

## Energy & Natural Resources
304 Dirksen Senate Building
Washington, DC 20510
202-224-4971
Web site: energy.senate.gov

Chair:
    Jeff Bingaman (D-NM)..........................202-224-5521
Ranking Member:
    Lisa Murkowski (R-AK)........................202-224-6665

### Subcommittees

**Energy**
Chair:
    Maria Cantwell (D-WA)........................202-224-4971
Ranking Member:
    James E Risch (R-ID)............................202-224-0541

**National Parks**
Chair:
    Mark Udall (D-CO)..............................202-224-4971
Ranking Member:
    Richard Burr (R-NC)............................202-224-0539

**Public Lands & Forests**
Chair:
    Ron Wyden (D-OR)..............................202-224-4971
Ranking Member:
    John Barrasso (R-WY)..........................202-224-7970

**Water & Power**
Chair:
    Debbie Stabenow (D-MI)........................202-224-4971
Ranking Member:
    Sam Brownback (R-KS)..........................202-224-7970

## Environment & Public Works
410 Dirksen Senate Building
Washington, DC 20510
202-224-8832
Web site: http://epw.senate.gov

Chair:
    Barbara Boxer (D-CA)...........................202-224-8832
Ranking Minority Member:
    James M Inhofe (R-OK).........................202-224-6176
New York Delegate:
    Kisrten Gillibrand (D)...........................202-224-4451

### Subcommittees

**Children's Health**
Chair:
    Amy Klobuchar (D-MN).........................202-224-3244
Ranking Member:
    Lamar Alexander (R-TN)........................202-224-4944

**Clean Air and Nuclear Safety**
Chair:
    Thomas R Carper (D-DE)........................202-224-2441
Ranking Member:
    David Vitter (R-LA)..............................202-224-4623

**Green Jobs and the New Economy**
Chair:
    Bernard Sanders (D-VT).........................202-224-5141
Ranking Member:
    Christopher S Bond (R-MO)....................202-224-5721

**Oversight**
Chair:
    Sheldon Whitehouse (D-RI)....................202-224-2921
Ranking Member:
    John Barrasso (R-WY)..........................202-224-6441

**Superfund, Toxics and Environmental Health**
Chair:
    Frank R Lautenberg (D-NJ)....................202-224-3224
Ranking Member:
    Arlen Specter (R-PA)............................202-224-4254

**Transportation & Infrastructure**
Chair:
    Max Baucus (D-MT).............................202-224-2651
Ranking Member:
    Johnny Isakson (R-GA).........................202-224-3643

**Water & Wildlife**
Chair:
    Benjamin L Cardin (D-MD).....................202-224-4524
Ranking Member:
    Mike Crapo (R-ID)..............................202-224-6142

## Finance
219 Dirksen Senate Building
Washington, DC 20510
202-224-4515
Web site: www.finance.senate.gov

Chair:
    Max Baucus (D-MT)............................202-224-2651
Ranking Member:
    Chuck Grassley (R-IA).........................202-224-3744

### Subcommittees

**Energy, Natural Resources and Infrastructure**
Chair:
    Jeff Bingaman (D-NM)..........................202-224-5521
Ranking Member:
    Jim Bunning (R-KY)............................202-224-4343

**Health Care**
Chair:
    John D Rockefeller, IV (D-WV)...............202-224-6472
Ranking Member:
    Orrin G Hatch (R-UT)..........................202-224-5251

**International Trade, and Global Competitiveness**
Chair:
    Ron Wyden (D-OR).............................202-224-5244
Ranking Member:
    Mike Crapo (R-ID)..............................202-224-6142

*Offices and agencies generally appear in alphabetical order, except when specific order is requested by listee.*

**Social Security, Pensions, and Family Policy**
Chair:
Blanche L Lincoln (D-AR)..............202-224-1371
Ranking Member:
Pat Roberts (R-KS)..............202-224-4774

**Taxation, IRS Oversight and Long-Term Growth**
Chair:
Kent Conrad (D-ND)..............202-224-2043
Ranking Member:
Jon Kyl (R-AZ)..............202-224-4521

## Foreign Relations
Dirksen Senate Building
Washington, DC 20510
202-224-4651
Web site: www.foreign.senate.gov

Chair:
John F Kerry (D-MA)..............202-224-2742
Ranking Member:
Richard G Lugar (R-IN)..............202-224-0360

### Subcommittees

**African Affairs**
Chair:
Russell D Feingold (D-WI)..............202-224-5323
Ranking Minority Member:
Johnny Isakson (R-GA)..............202-224-3643

**East Asian & Pacific Affairs**
Chair:
Jim Webb (D-VA)..............202-224-4024
Ranking Member:
Republican Leader Designee

**European Affairs**
Chair:
Jeanne Shaheen (D-NH)..............202-224-2841
Ranking Member:
Jim DeMint (R-SC)..............202-224-6121

**International Development, Foreign Assist, Economic Affairs & Environment**
Chair:
Robert Menendez (D-NJ)..............202-224-4744
Ranking Member:
Bob Corker (R-TN)..............202-224-3344

**International Ops & Orgs, Human Rights, Democracy & Global Women's Issues**
Chair:
Barbara Boxer (D-CA)..............202-224-3553
Ranking Member:
Roger F Wicker (R-MS)..............202-224-6253

**Near Eastern and South and Central Asian Affairs**
Chair:
Robert P Casey, Jr (D-PA)..............202-224-6324
Ranking Member:
James E Risch (R-ID)..............202-224-2752

**Western Hemisphere, Peace Corps & Narcotics Affairs**
Chair:
Christopher J Dodd (D-CT)..............202-224-2823
Ranking Member:
John Barrasso (R-WY)..............202-224-6441

## Health, Education, Labor, & Pensions
428 Dirksen Senate Building
Washington, DC 20510
Web site: www.help.senate.gov

Chair:
Edward M Kennedy (D-MA)..............202-224-4543
Ranking Member:
Michael B Enzi (R-WY)..............202-224-3424
New York Delegate:
Hillary Rodham Clinton (D)..............202-224-4451

### Subcommittees

**Children and Families**
Chair:
Christopher J Dodd (D-CT)..............202-224-2823
Ranking Member:
Lamar Alexander (R-TN)..............202-224-4944

**Employment & Workplace Safety**
Chair:
Patty Murray (D-WA)..............202-224-2621
Ranking Member:
Johnny Isakson (R-GA)..............202-224-3643

**Retirement and Aging**
Chair:
Barbara Mikulski (D-MD)..............202-224-4654
Ranking Member:
Richard Burr (R-NC)..............202-224-3154
New York Delegate:
Hillary Rodham Clinton (D-NY)..............202-224-4451

## Homeland Security & Governmental Affairs
340 Dirksen Senate Building
Washington, DC 20510
202-224-2627
Web site: www.hsgac.senate.gov

Chair:
Joseph I Lieberman (D-CT)..............202-224-4041
Ranking Member:
Susan Collins (R-ME)..............202-224-2523

### Subcommittees

**Disaster Recovery**
Chair:
Mary L Landrieu (D-LA)..............202-224-5824
Ranking Member:
Lindsey O Graham (R-SC)..............202-224-4751

**Federal Financial Mgt, Govt Info, Federal Svcs, & International Security**
Chair:
Thomas R Carper (D-DE)..............202-224-2441
Ranking Member:
John Coburn (R-AZ)..............202-224-2235

**Oversight of Government Management, Federal Workforce & District of Columbia**
Chair:
Daniel K Akaka (D-HI)..............202-224-6361
Ranking Member:
George V Voinovich (R-OH)..............202-224-3353

**Permanent Subcommittee on Investigations**
Chair:
Carl Levin (D-MI)..............202-224-6221
Ranking Member:
Tom Coburn (R-OK)..............202-224-5754

**State, Local, and Private Sector Preparedness and Integration**
Chair:
Mark L Pryor (D-AR)..............202-224-2353
Ranking Member:
John Ensign (R-NV)..............202-224-6244

*Offices and agencies generally appear in alphabetical order, except when specific order is requested by listee.*

## Judiciary
226 Dirksen Senate Building
Washington, DC 20510
Web site: www.judiciary.senate.gov

Chair:
    Patrick J Leahy (D-VT) . . . . . . . . . . . . . . . . . . . . . . . . . 202-224-4242
Ranking Member:
    Arlen Specter (R-PA) . . . . . . . . . . . . . . . . . . . . . . . . . . 202-224-4254

### Subcommittees

#### Administrative Oversight & the Courts
Chair:
    Sheldon Whitehead (D-RI) . . . . . . . . . . . . . . . . . . . . . . 202-224-2921
Ranking Member:
    Jeff Sessions (R-AL) . . . . . . . . . . . . . . . . . . . . . . . . . . 202-224-4124

#### Antitrust, Competition Policy & Consumer Rights
Chair:
    Herb Kohl (D-WI) . . . . . . . . . . . . . . . . . . . . . . . . . . . . . 202-224-5653
Ranking Member:
    Orrin G Hatch (R-UT) . . . . . . . . . . . . . . . . . . . . . . . . . 202-224-5251

#### Constitution, The
Chair:
    Russell D Feingold (D-WI) . . . . . . . . . . . . . . . . . . . . . 202-224-5323
Ranking Member:
    Tom Coburn (R-OK) . . . . . . . . . . . . . . . . . . . . . . . . . . . 202-224-5754

#### Crime & Drugs
Chair:
    Richard J Durbin (D-IL) . . . . . . . . . . . . . . . . . . . . . . . 202-224-2152
Ranking Member:
    Lindsey O Graham (R-SC) . . . . . . . . . . . . . . . . . . . . . 202-224-5972

#### Immigration, Refugees and Border Security
Chair:
    Charles E Schumer (D-NY) . . . . . . . . . . . . . . . . . . . . . 202-224-6542
Ranking Member:
    John Cornyn (R-TX) . . . . . . . . . . . . . . . . . . . . . . . . . . 202-224-2934
Chair:
    Benjamin L Cardin (D-MD) . . . . . . . . . . . . . . . . . . . . 202-224-4524
Ranking Member:
    Jon Kyl (R-AZ) . . . . . . . . . . . . . . . . . . . . . . . . . . . . . . . 202-224-4521

## Rules & Administration
305 Russell Senate Building
Washington, DC 20510
202-224-6352
Web site: www.rules.senate.gov

Chair:
    Charles E Schumer (D-NY) . . . . . . . . . . . . . . . . . . . . . 202-224-6542
Ranking Member:
    Bob Bennett (R-UT) . . . . . . . . . . . . . . . . . . . . . . . . . . . 202-224-5444

## Small Business & Entrepreneurship
428A Russell Senate Building
Washington, DC 20510
202-224-5175
Web site: www.sbc.senate.gov

Chair:
    Mary L Landrieu (D-LA) . . . . . . . . . . . . . . . . . . . . . . . 202-224-5824
Ranking Member:
    Olympia J Snowe (R-ME) . . . . . . . . . . . . . . . . . . . . . . 202-224-5344

## Veterans' Affairs
412 Russell Senate Building
Washington, DC 20510

202-224-9126
Web site: www.veterans.senate.gov

Chair:
    Daniel Akaka (D-HI) . . . . . . . . . . . . . . . . . . . . . . . . . . 202-224-6361
Ranking Member:
    Richard Burr (R-NC) . . . . . . . . . . . . . . . . . . . . . . . . . . 202-224-3154

## OTHER, SELECT & SPECIAL COMMITTEES

### Aging, Special Committee on
G31 Dirksen Senate Building
Washington, DC 20510
202-224-5364
Web site: www.aging.senate.gov

Chair:
    Herb Kohl (D-WI) . . . . . . . . . . . . . . . . . . . . . . . . . . . . . 202-224-5653
Vice Chair:
    Gordon Smith (R-OR) . . . . . . . . . . . . . . . . . . . . . . . . . 202-224-3753

### Ethics, Select Committee on
220 Hart Building
Washington, DC 20510
202-224-2981
Web site: www.ethics.senate.gov

Chair:
    Barbara Boxer (D-CA) . . . . . . . . . . . . . . . . . . . . . . . . . 202-224-3553
Vice Chair:
    Johnny Isakson (R-GA) . . . . . . . . . . . . . . . . . . . . . . . 202-224-3643

### Indian Affairs, Committee on
838 Hart Office Building
Washington, DC 20510
202-224-2251
Web site: indian.senate.gov

Chair:
    Byron L Dorgan (D-ND) . . . . . . . . . . . . . . . . . . . . . . . 202-224-2251
Vice Chair:
    John Barrasso (R-WY) . . . . . . . . . . . . . . . . . . . . . . . . 202-224-6641

### Intelligence, Select Committee on
211 Hart Senate Building
Washington, DC 20510
202-224-1700
Web site: www.intelligence.senate.gov

Chair:
    Dianne Feinstein (D-CA) . . . . . . . . . . . . . . . . . . . . . . . 202-224-3841
Vice Chair:
    Christopher S Bond (R-MO) . . . . . . . . . . . . . . . . . . . 202-224-5721

## U.S. HOUSE OF REPRESENTATIVES STANDING COMMITTEES

### Agriculture
1301 Longworth House Office Building
Washington, DC 20515
202-225-2171
Web site: agriculture.house.gov

Chair:
    Collin C Peterson (D-MN) . . . . . . . . . . . . . . . . . . . . . . 202-225-2165
Ranking Member:
    Frank D Lucas (R-OK) . . . . . . . . . . . . . . . . . . . . . . . . 202-225-5565

*Offices and agencies generally appear in alphabetical order, except when specific order is requested by listee.*

**Subcommittees**

### Conservation, Credit, Energy, and Research
Chair:
Tim Holden (D-PA) . . . . . . . . . . . . . . . . . . . . . . . . . .202-225-5546
Ranking Member:
Bob Goodlatte (D-VA) . . . . . . . . . . . . . . . . . . . . . . .202-225-5431

### Department Operations, Oversight, Nutrition, & Forestry
Chair:
Joe Baca (D-CA) . . . . . . . . . . . . . . . . . . . . . . . . . . . . .202-225-6161
Ranking Member:
Jeff Fortenberry (R-NE . . . . . . . . . . . . . . . . . . . . . . .202-225-4806

### General Farm Commodities & Risk Management
Chair:
Leonard L Boswell (D-IA) . . . . . . . . . . . . . . . . . . . . .202-225-3806
Ranking Member:
Jerry Moran (R-KS) . . . . . . . . . . . . . . . . . . . . . . . . . .202-225-2715

### Horticulture and Organic Agriculture
Chair:
Dennis A Cardoza (D-CA) . . . . . . . . . . . . . . . . . . . . .202-225-6131
Ranking Member:
Jean Schmidt (R-OH) . . . . . . . . . . . . . . . . . . . . . . . . .202-225-3164

### Livestock, Dairy, and Poultry
Chair:
David Scott (D-GA) . . . . . . . . . . . . . . . . . . . . . . . . . .202-225-2939
Ranking Member:
Randy Neugebauer (R-TX) . . . . . . . . . . . . . . . . . . . .202-225-4005

### Specialty Crops, Rural Development and Foreign Agriculture
Chair:
Mike McIntyre (D-NC) . . . . . . . . . . . . . . . . . . . . . . .202-225-2731
Ranking Member:
K Michael Conaway (R-TX) . . . . . . . . . . . . . . . . . . .202-225-3605

## Appropriations
H-218 US Capitol
Washington, DC 20515
202-225-2771
Web site: appropriations.house.gov

Chair:
David R Obey (D-WI) . . . . . . . . . . . . . . . . . . . . . . . . .202-225-3365
Ranking Member:
Jerry Lewis (R-CA). . . . . . . . . . . . . . . . . . . . . . . . . . .202-225-5861
New York Delegate:
Maurice D Hinchey (D) . . . . . . . . . . . . . . . . . . . . . . .202-225-6335
New York Delegate:
Steve Israel (D) . . . . . . . . . . . . . . . . . . . . . . . . . . . . . .202-225-3335
New York Delegate:
Nita M Lowey (D) . . . . . . . . . . . . . . . . . . . . . . . . . . . .202-225-6506
New York Delegate:
Jose E Serrano (D) . . . . . . . . . . . . . . . . . . . . . . . . . . .202-225-4361

**Subcommittees**

### Agriculture, Rural Development, FDA & Related Agencies
Chair:
Rosa DeLauro (D-CT) . . . . . . . . . . . . . . . . . . . . . . . .202-225-3661
Ranking Member:
Jack Kingston (R-GA) . . . . . . . . . . . . . . . . . . . . . . . .202-225-5831

### Commerce, Justice, Science and Related Agencies
Chair:
Alan B Mollohan (D-WV) . . . . . . . . . . . . . . . . . . . . .202-225-4172
Ranking Member:
Frank R Wolf (R-VA) . . . . . . . . . . . . . . . . . . . . . . . .202-225-5136

### Defense
Chair:
John P Murtha (D-PA) . . . . . . . . . . . . . . . . . . . . . . . .202-225-2847
Ranking Member:
C W Bill Young (R-FL) . . . . . . . . . . . . . . . . . . . . . . .202-225-5961

### Energy and Water Development
Chair:
Peter J Visclosky (D-IN) . . . . . . . . . . . . . . . . . . . . . .202-225-2461
Ranking Member:
Rodney P Frelinghuysen (R-NJ) . . . . . . . . . . . . . . . .202-225-5034

### Financial Services and General Government
Chair:
Jose Serrano (D-NY) . . . . . . . . . . . . . . . . . . . . . . . . .202-225-4361
Ranking Member:
Jo Ann Emerson (R-MO). . . . . . . . . . . . . . . . . . . . . .202-225-4404

### Homeland Security
Chair:
David E Price (D-NC) . . . . . . . . . . . . . . . . . . . . . . . .202-225-1784
Ranking Member:
Harold Rogers (R-KY). . . . . . . . . . . . . . . . . . . . . . . .202-225-4601

### Interior, Environment and Related Agencies
Chair:
Norman D Dicks (D-WA) . . . . . . . . . . . . . . . . . . . . .202-225-5916
Ranking Member:
Michael K Simpson (R-ID) . . . . . . . . . . . . . . . . . . . .202-225-5531

### Labor, Health & Human Services, Education and Related Agencies
Chair:
David R Obey (D-WI) . . . . . . . . . . . . . . . . . . . . . . . . .202-225-3365
Ranking Member:
Todd Tiahrt (R-KS) . . . . . . . . . . . . . . . . . . . . . . . . . .202-225-6216

### Legislative Branch
Chair:
Debbie Wasserman Schultz (D-FL) . . . . . . . . . . . . . . .202-225-7931
Ranking Member:
Robert B Aderholt (R-AL) . . . . . . . . . . . . . . . . . . . . .202-225-4876

### Military Construction, Veterans Affairs and Related Agencies
Chair:
Chet Edwards (D-TX) . . . . . . . . . . . . . . . . . . . . . . . .202-225-6105
Ranking Member:
Zach Wamp (R-TN) . . . . . . . . . . . . . . . . . . . . . . . . . .202-225-3271

### State, Foreign Operations and Related Programs
Chair:
Nita M Lowey (D-NY). . . . . . . . . . . . . . . . . . . . . . . .202-225-6506
Ranking Member:
Kay Granger (R-TX) . . . . . . . . . . . . . . . . . . . . . . . . .202-225-5071

### Transportation, Housing and Urban Development, and Related Agencies
Chair:
John W Olver (D-MA) . . . . . . . . . . . . . . . . . . . . . . . .202-225-5335
Ranking Member:
Tom Latham (R-IA) . . . . . . . . . . . . . . . . . . . . . . . . . .202-225-5476

## Armed Services
2120 Rayburn House Building
Washington, DC 20515
202-225-9077  Fax: 202-225-4151

Chair:
Ike Skelton (D-MO) . . . . . . . . . . . . . . . . . . . . . . . . . .202-225-2876
Ranking Member:
John M McHugh (R-NY) . . . . . . . . . . . . . . . . . . . . . .202-225-4611
New York Delegate:
Eric JJ Massa (D) . . . . . . . . . . . . . . . . . . . . . . . . . . . .202-225-3161

*Offices and agencies generally appear in alphabetical order, except when specific order is requested by listee.*

New York Delegate:
Scott Murphy (D) . . . . . . . . . . . . . . . . . . . . . .202-225-5614

## Subcommittees

### Air and Land Forces
Chair:
Neil Abercrombie (D-HI). . . . . . . . . . . . . . . . . .202-225-2726
Ranking Member:
Roscoe G Bartlett (R-MD) . . . . . . . . . . . . . . . . .202-225-2721

### Military Personnel
Chair:
Susan A Davis (D-CA). . . . . . . . . . . . . . . . . . . .202-225-2040
Ranking Member:
Joe Wilson (R-SC) . . . . . . . . . . . . . . . . . . . . . .202-225-2452

### Oversight and Investigations
Chair:
Vic Snyder (D-AR). . . . . . . . . . . . . . . . . . . . . .202-225-2506
Ranking Member:
Rob Wittman (R-VA). . . . . . . . . . . . . . . . . . . . .202-225-4261

### Readiness
Chair:
Solomon P Ortiz (D-TX) . . . . . . . . . . . . . . . . . .202-225-7742
Ranking Member:
J Randy Forbes (R-VA) . . . . . . . . . . . . . . . . . . .202-225-6365

### Seapower and Expeditionary Forces
Chair:
Gene Taylor (D-MS) . . . . . . . . . . . . . . . . . . . . .202-225-5772
Ranking Member:
W Todd Akin (R-MO) . . . . . . . . . . . . . . . . . . . .202-225-2561

### Strategic Forces
Chair:
Ellen O Tauscher (D-CA). . . . . . . . . . . . . . . . . .202-225-1880
Ranking Member:
Michael Turner (R-OH) . . . . . . . . . . . . . . . . . . .202-225-6465

### Terrorism, Unconventional Threats and Capabilities
Chair:
Adam Smith (D-WA). . . . . . . . . . . . . . . . . . . . .202-225-8901
Ranking Member:
Jeff Miller (R-TX) . . . . . . . . . . . . . . . . . . . . . .202-225-4136

## Budget
207 Cannon House Building
Washington, DC 20515
202-226-7200  Fax: 202-225-9905
Web site: http://budget.house.gov

Chair:
John M Spratt, Jr (D-SC) . . . . . . . . . . . . . . . . . .202-225-5501
Ranking Member:
Paul Ryan (R-WI). . . . . . . . . . . . . . . . . . . . . . .202-225-3031
New York Delegate:
Tim Bishop (D) . . . . . . . . . . . . . . . . . . . . . . . .202-225-3826

## Education & Labor
2181 Rayburn House Building
Washington, DC 20515
202-225-3725
Web site: http://edworkforce.house.gov

Chair:
George Miller (D-CA) . . . . . . . . . . . . . . . . . . . .202-225-2095
Ranking Member:
Howard P (Buck) McKeon (R-CA) . . . . . . . . . . .202-225-1956
New York Delegate:
Timothy H Bishop (D) . . . . . . . . . . . . . . . . . . . .202-225-3826

New York Delegate:
Yvette Clarke (D) . . . . . . . . . . . . . . . . . . . . . . .202-225-6231
New York Delegate:
Carolyn McCarthy (D) . . . . . . . . . . . . . . . . . . . .202-225-5516
New York Delegate:
Paul Tonko (D) . . . . . . . . . . . . . . . . . . . . . . . . .202-225-5076

## Subcommittees

### Early Childhood, Elementary and Secondary Education
Chair:
Dale E Kildee (D-MI). . . . . . . . . . . . . . . . . . . . .202-225-3611
Ranking Member:
Michael N Castle (R-DE). . . . . . . . . . . . . . . . . .202-225-4165

### Healthy Families and Communities
Chair:
Carolyn McCarthy (D-NY) . . . . . . . . . . . . . . . . .202-225-5516
Ranking Member:
Todd (Russell) Platts (R-PA) . . . . . . . . . . . . . . .202-225-5836

### Higher Education, Lifelong Learning, and Competitiveness
Chair:
Rubén Hinojosa (D-TX) . . . . . . . . . . . . . . . . . . .202-225-2531
Ranking Member:
Brett Guthrie (R-KY) . . . . . . . . . . . . . . . . . . . .202-225-3501

### Health, Employment, Labor and Pensions
Chair:
Robert Andrews (D-NJ) . . . . . . . . . . . . . . . . . . .202-225-6501
Ranking Member:
John Kline (R-MN). . . . . . . . . . . . . . . . . . . . . .202-225-2271

### Workforce Protections
Chair:
Lynn C Woolsey (D-CA) . . . . . . . . . . . . . . . . . .202-225-5161
Ranking Member:
Tom Price (R-GA) . . . . . . . . . . . . . . . . . . . . . . .202-225-4501

## Energy & Commerce
2125 Rayburn House Building
Washington, DC 20515
202-225-2927
Web site: energycommerce.house.gov

Chair:
Henry A Waxman (D-CA) . . . . . . . . . . . . . . . . . .202-225-3976
Ranking Member:
Joe Barton (R-TX) . . . . . . . . . . . . . . . . . . . . . .202-225-2002
New York Delegate:
Eliot L Engel (D) . . . . . . . . . . . . . . . . . . . . . . .202-225-2464
New York Delegate:
Anthony D Weiner (D). . . . . . . . . . . . . . . . . . . .202-225-6616

## Subcommittees

### Commerce, Trade & Consumer Protection
Chair:
Bobby L Rush (D-IL). . . . . . . . . . . . . . . . . . . . .202-225-4372
Ranking Member:
George Radanovich (R-CA). . . . . . . . . . . . . . . . .202-225-4540

### Communications, Technology & the Internet
Chair:
Rick Boucher (D-VA) . . . . . . . . . . . . . . . . . . . .202-225-3861
Ranking Member:
Cliff Stearns (R-FL) . . . . . . . . . . . . . . . . . . . . .202-225-5744

### Energy & the Environment
Chair:
Edward J Markey (D-MA). . . . . . . . . . . . . . . . . .202-225-2836
Ranking Member:
Fred Upton (R-MI) . . . . . . . . . . . . . . . . . . . . . .202-225-3761

*Offices and agencies generally appear in alphabetical order, except when specific order is requested by listee.*

**Health**
Chair:
    Frank J Pallone, Jr (D-NJ) . . . . . . . . . . . . . . . . . . . . .202-225-4671
Ranking Member:
    Nathan Deal (R-GA). . . . . . . . . . . . . . . . . . . . . . . . . .202-225-5211

**Oversight & Investigations**
Chair:
    Bart Stupak (D-MI) . . . . . . . . . . . . . . . . . . . . . . . . . .202-225-4735
Ranking Member:
    Greg Walden (R-OR) . . . . . . . . . . . . . . . . . . . . . . . . .202-225-6730

# Financial Services
2129 Rayburn House Building
Washington, DC 20515
202-225-4247  Fax: 202-225-6952
Web site: http://financialservices.house.gov

Chair:
    Barney Frank (D-MA) . . . . . . . . . . . . . . . . . . . . . . . . .202-225-5931
Ranking Member:
    Spencer Bachus (R-AL) . . . . . . . . . . . . . . . . . . . . . . .202-225-4921
New York Delegate:
    Gary L Ackerman (D). . . . . . . . . . . . . . . . . . . . . . . . .202-225-2601
New York Delegate:
    Peter T King (R) . . . . . . . . . . . . . . . . . . . . . . . . . . . .202-225-7896
New York Delegate:
    Christopher Lee (R) . . . . . . . . . . . . . . . . . . . . . . . . .202-225-5265
New York Delegate:
    Dan Maffei (D) . . . . . . . . . . . . . . . . . . . . . . . . . . . . .202-225-3701
New York Delegate:
    Carolyn B Maloney (D) . . . . . . . . . . . . . . . . . . . . . . .202-225-7944
New York Delegate:
    Carolyn McCarthy (D) . . . . . . . . . . . . . . . . . . . . . . .202-225-5516
New York Delegate:
    Gregory W Meeks (D) . . . . . . . . . . . . . . . . . . . . . . . .202-225-3461
New York Delegate:
    Nydia M Velazquez (D) . . . . . . . . . . . . . . . . . . . . . . .202-225-2361

## Subcommittees

### Capital Markets, Insurance & Government Sponsored Enterprises
Chair:
    Paul E Kanjorski (D-PA) . . . . . . . . . . . . . . . . . . . . .202-225-6511
Ranking Member:
    Scott Garrett (R-NJ) . . . . . . . . . . . . . . . . . . . . . . . .202-225-4465
New York Delegate:
    Gary L Ackerman (D). . . . . . . . . . . . . . . . . . . . . . . . .202-225-2601
New York Delegate:
    Peter T King (R). . . . . . . . . . . . . . . . . . . . . . . . . . . .202-225-7896
New York Delegate:
    Carolyn McCarthy (D) . . . . . . . . . . . . . . . . . . . . . . .202-225-5516
New York Delegate:
    Carolyn B Maloney (D) . . . . . . . . . . . . . . . . . . . . . . .202-225-7944
New York Delegate:
    Nydia M Velazquez (D) . . . . . . . . . . . . . . . . . . . . . . .202-225-2361

### Domestic Monetary Policy & Technology
Chair:
    Melvin L Watt (D-NC). . . . . . . . . . . . . . . . . . . . . . . .202-225-1510
Ranking Member:
    Ron Paul (R-TX) . . . . . . . . . . . . . . . . . . . . . . . . . . .202-225-2831
New York Delegate:
    Carolyn B Maloney (D) . . . . . . . . . . . . . . . . . . . . . . .202-225-7944
New York Delegate:
    Gregory W Meeks (D) . . . . . . . . . . . . . . . . . . . . . . . .202-225-3461

### Financial Institutions & Consumer Credit
Chair:
    Luis V Gutierrez (D-IL). . . . . . . . . . . . . . . . . . . . . . .202-225-8203
Ranking Member:
    Jeb Hensarling (R-TX). . . . . . . . . . . . . . . . . . . . . . . .202-225-3484

New York Delegate:
    Gary L Ackerman (D). . . . . . . . . . . . . . . . . . . . . . . . .202-225-2601
New York Delegate:
    Peter King (R). . . . . . . . . . . . . . . . . . . . . . . . . . . . . .202-225-7896
New York Delegate:
    Christopher Lee (R) . . . . . . . . . . . . . . . . . . . . . . . . .202-225-5265
New York Delegate:
    Carolyn B Maloney (D) . . . . . . . . . . . . . . . . . . . . . . .202-225-7944
New York Delegate:
    Carolyn McCarthy (D) . . . . . . . . . . . . . . . . . . . . . . .202-225-5516
New York Delegate:
    Gregory W Meeks (D) . . . . . . . . . . . . . . . . . . . . . . . .202-225-3461

### Housing & Community Opportunity
Chair:
    Maxine Waters (D-CA) . . . . . . . . . . . . . . . . . . . . . . .202-225-2201
Ranking Member:
    Shelley Moore Capito (R-WV) . . . . . . . . . . . . . . . . .202-225-2711
New York Delegate:
    Dan Maffei (D) . . . . . . . . . . . . . . . . . . . . . . . . . . . . .202-225-3701
New York Delegate:
    Nydia M Velazquez (D) . . . . . . . . . . . . . . . . . . . . . . .202-225-2361

### International Monetary Policy & Trade
Chair:
    Gregory W Meeks (D-NY). . . . . . . . . . . . . . . . . . . . .202-225-3461
Ranking Member:
    Gary Miller (R-CA) . . . . . . . . . . . . . . . . . . . . . . . . .202-225-3201
New York Delegate:
    Dan Maffei (D) . . . . . . . . . . . . . . . . . . . . . . . . . . . . .202-225-3701

### Oversight & Investigations
Chair:
    Dennis Moore (D-KS) . . . . . . . . . . . . . . . . . . . . . . .202-225-2865
Ranking Member:
    Judy Biggert (R-IL) . . . . . . . . . . . . . . . . . . . . . . . . .202-225-3515
New York Delegate:
    Christopher Lee (R) . . . . . . . . . . . . . . . . . . . . . . . . .202-225-5265

# Foreign Affairs
2170 Rayburn House Building
Washington, DC 20515
202-225-5021
Web site: foreignaffairs.house.gov

Chair:
    Howard L Berman (D-CA). . . . . . . . . . . . . . . . . . . . .202-225-3531
Ranking Member:
    Ileana Ros- Lehtinen (R-FL) . . . . . . . . . . . . . . . . . .202-225-3931
New York Delegate:
    Gary Ackerman (D) . . . . . . . . . . . . . . . . . . . . . . . . .202-225-2601
New York Delegate:
    Joseph Crowley (D) . . . . . . . . . . . . . . . . . . . . . . . . .202-225-3965
New York Delegate:
    Eliot L Engel (D) . . . . . . . . . . . . . . . . . . . . . . . . . . .202-225-2464
New York Delegate:
    Michael E McMahon (D) . . . . . . . . . . . . . . . . . . . . .202-225-3371
New York Delegate:
    Gregory W Meeks (D) . . . . . . . . . . . . . . . . . . . . . . . .202-225-3461

## Subcommittees

### Africa & Global Health
Chair:
    Donald M Payne (D-NJ). . . . . . . . . . . . . . . . . . . . . .202-225-3436
Ranking Member:
    Christopher H Smith (R-NJ). . . . . . . . . . . . . . . . . . .202-225-3765
New York Delegate:
    Gregory W Meeks (D) . . . . . . . . . . . . . . . . . . . . . . . .202-225-3461

*Offices and agencies generally appear in alphabetical order, except when specific order is requested by listee.*

### Asia, the Pacific and the Global Environment
Chair:
Eni F H Faleomavaega (D-AS) .....................202-225-8577
Ranking Member:
Donald A Manzullo (R-IL).........................202-225-5676
New York Delegate:
Gary L Ackerman (D)..............................202-225-2601
New York Delegate:
Eliot L Engel (D) ................................202-225-2464
New York Delegate:
Gregory W Meeks (D) .............................202-225-3461

### Europe
Chair:
Robert Wexler (D-FL) ............................202-225-3001
Ranking Member:
Elton Gallegly (R-CA)............................202-225-5811
New York Delegate:
Michael E McMahon (D)............................202-225-3371

### International Organizations, Human Rights and Oversight
Chair:
Bill Delahunt (D-MA) ............................202-225-3111
Ranking Member:
Dana Rohrabacher (R-CA)..........................202-225-2415

### Middle East and South Asia
Chair:
Gary Ackerman (D-NY).............................202-225-2601
Ranking Member:
Dan Burton (R-IN) ...............................202-225-2276
New York Delegate:
Joseph Crowley (D) ..............................202-225-3965
New York Delegate:
Eliot L Engel (D) ...............................202-225-2464
New York Delegate:
Michael E McMahon (D)............................202-225-3371

### Terrorism, Nonproliferation and Trade
Chair:
Brad Sherman (D-CA)..............................202-225-5911
Ranking Member:
Edward R Royce (R-CA) ...........................202-225-4111

### Western Hemisphere
Chair:
Eliot Engel (D-NY) ..............................202-225-2464
Ranking Member:
Connie Mack (R-FL) ..............................202-225-2536
New York Delegate:
Joseph Crowley (D) ..............................202-225-3965
New York Delegate:
Gregory W Meeks (D) .............................202-225-3461

## Homeland Security
176 Ford House Building
Washington, DC 20515
202-226-2616  Fax: 202-226-4499

Chair:
Bennie G Thompson (D-MS).........................202-225-5876
Ranking Member:
Peter T King (R-NY) .............................202-225-7896
New York Delegate:
Yvette D Clarke (D)..............................202-225-6231
New York Delegate:
Eric JJ Massa (D) ...............................202-225-3161

### Subcommittees

#### Border, Maritime and Global Counterterrorism
Chair:
Loretta Sanchez (D-CA)...........................202-225-2965

Ranking Member:
Mark Souder (R-IN)...............................202-225-4436

### Emergency Communications, Preparedness and Response
Chair:
Henry Cuellar (D-TX) ............................202-225-1640
Ranking Member:
Mark Rogers (R-AL) ..............................202-225-3261

### Emerging Threats, Cybersecurity and Science and Technology
Chair:
Yvette D Clark (D-NY)............................202-225-6231
Ranking Member:
Dan Lundgren (R-CA)..............................202-225-5716

### Intelligence, Information Sharing and Terrorism Risk Assessment
Chair:
Jane Harman (D-CA)...............................202-225-8220
Ranking Member:
Michael McCall (R-TX)............................202-225-2401

### Management, Investigations and Oversight
Chair:
Christopher P Carney (D-PA)......................202-225-3731
Ranking Member:
Gus Bilirakis (R-FL)............................202-225-5755

### Transportation Security and Infrastructure Protection
Chair:
Sheila Jackson- Lee (D-TX).......................202-225-3816
Ranking Member:
Charlie Dent (R-PA).............................202-225-6411

## House Administration
1309 Longworth Building
Washington, DC 20515
202-225-2061  Fax: 202-226-2774
Web site: http://cha.house.gov

Chair:
Robert A Brady (D-PA) ...........................202-225-4731
Ranking Member:
Dan Lundgren (R-CA) .............................202-225-5671

## Judiciary
2138 Rayburn House Building
Washington, DC 20515
Chair:
John Conyers, Jr (D-MI)..........................202-225-5126
Ranking Member:
Lamar S Smith (R-TX).............................202-225-4236
New York Delegate:
Dan Maffei (D)...................................202-225-3701
New York Delegate:
Jerrold Nadler (D)...............................202-225-5635
New York Delegate:
Anthony D Weiner (D).............................202-225-6616

### Subcommittees

#### Commercial & Administrative Law
Chair:
Steve Cohen (D-TN)...............................202-225-3265
Ranking Member:
Trent Franks (R-AZ).............................202-225-4576

#### Constitution, Civil Rights and Civil Liberties
Chair:
Jerrold Nadler (D-NY)...........................202-225-5635
Ranking Member:
F James Sensenbrenner, Jr (R-WI)................202-225-5101

*Offices and agencies generally appear in alphabetical order, except when specific order is requested by listee.*

**Courts & Competition Policy**
Chair:
    Hank Johnson (D-GA) . . . . . . . . . . . . . . . . . . . . . . .202-225-1605
Ranking Member:
    Howard Coble (R-NC) . . . . . . . . . . . . . . . . . . . . . . .202-225-3065

**Crime, Terrorism and Homeland Security**
Chair:
    Robert C Scott (D-VA). . . . . . . . . . . . . . . . . . . . . . .202-225-8351
Ranking Member:
    Louie Gohmert (R-TX). . . . . . . . . . . . . . . . . . . . . . .202-225-3035

**Immigration, Citizenship, Refugees, Border Security and International Law**
Chair:
    Zoe Lofgren (D-CA). . . . . . . . . . . . . . . . . . . . . . . .202-225-3072
Ranking Member:
    Steve King (R-IA) . . . . . . . . . . . . . . . . . . . . . . . . .202-225-4426

## Natural Resources
1324 Longworth Building
Washington, DC 20515
202-225-6065  Fax: 202-225-1931

New York Delegate:
    Maurice D Hinchey (D) . . . . . . . . . . . . . . . . . . . . . .202-225-6335
Chair:
    Nick J Rahall, II (D-WV) . . . . . . . . . . . . . . . . . . . .202-225-3452
Ranking Member:
    Doc Hastings (R-WA) . . . . . . . . . . . . . . . . . . . . . . .202-225-5816

### Office of Indian Affairs

### Subcommittees

**Energy & Mineral Resources**
Chair:
    Jim Costa (D-CA). . . . . . . . . . . . . . . . . . . . . . . . .202-225-3341
Ranking Member:
    Doug Lamborn (R-CO) . . . . . . . . . . . . . . . . . . . . . .202-225-4422

**Insular Affairs, Oceans & Wildlife**
Chair:
    Madelaine Z Bordallo (D-Guam). . . . . . . . . . . . . . . .202-225-1188
Ranking Member:
    Henry E Brown, Jr (R-SC) . . . . . . . . . . . . . . . . . . .202-225-3176

**National Parks, Forests and Public Lands**
Chair:
    Raul M Grijalva (R-AZ). . . . . . . . . . . . . . . . . . . . .202-225-2435
Ranking Member:
    Rob Bishop (R-UT) . . . . . . . . . . . . . . . . . . . . . . . .202-225-0453

**Water & Power**
Chair:
    Grace F Napolitano (D-CA). . . . . . . . . . . . . . . . . . .202-225-5256
Ranking Member:
    Cathy McMorris Rodgers (R-WA) . . . . . . . . . . . . . .202-225-2006

## Oversight and Government Reform
2157 Rayburn House Building
Washington, DC 20515
202-225-5051
Web site: oversight.house.gov

Chair:
    Edolphus Towns (D-NY) . . . . . . . . . . . . . . . . . . . .202-225-5936
Ranking Member:
    Darrell E Issa (R-CA). . . . . . . . . . . . . . . . . . . . . .202-225-3906
New York Delegate:
    Carolyn B Maloney (D) . . . . . . . . . . . . . . . . . . . . .202-225-7944
New York Delegate:
    John M McHugh (R). . . . . . . . . . . . . . . . . . . . . . . .202-225-4611

### Subcommittees

**Domestic Policy**
Chair:
    Dennis J Kucinich (D-OH). . . . . . . . . . . . . . . . . . .202-225-5871
Ranking Member:
    Jim Jordan (R-OH) . . . . . . . . . . . . . . . . . . . . . . . .202-225-2676

**Federal Workforce, Postal Service and the District of Columbia**
Chair:
    Stephen F Lynch (D-MA) . . . . . . . . . . . . . . . . . . . .202-225-8273
Ranking Member:
    Jason Chaffetz (R-UT) . . . . . . . . . . . . . . . . . . . . .202-225-7751
New York Delegate:
    Carolyn D Maloney (D) . . . . . . . . . . . . . . . . . . . . .202-225-7944

**Government Management, Organization and Procurement**
Chair:
    Diane E Watson (D-CA) . . . . . . . . . . . . . . . . . . . .202-225-7084
Ranking Member:
    Brian Bilbray (R-CA). . . . . . . . . . . . . . . . . . . . . .202-225-0508

**Information Policy, Census and National Archives**
Chair:
    William Lacy Clay (D-MO). . . . . . . . . . . . . . . . . . .202-225-2406
Ranking Member:
    Patrick McHenry (R-NC) . . . . . . . . . . . . . . . . . . . .202-225-2576
New York Delegate:
    Carolyn B Maloney (D) . . . . . . . . . . . . . . . . . . . . .202-225-7944

**National Security and Foreign Affairs**
Chair:
    John F Tierney (D-MA) . . . . . . . . . . . . . . . . . . . . .202-225-8020
Ranking Member:
    Jeff Flake (R-AZ). . . . . . . . . . . . . . . . . . . . . . . . .202-225-2635
New York Delegate:
    Carolyn B Maloney (D) . . . . . . . . . . . . . . . . . . . . .202-225-7944

## Rules
H-312 The Capitol
Washington, DC 20515
202-225-9091

Chair:
    Louise McIntosh Slaughter (D-NY). . . . . . . . . . . . .202-225-3615
Ranking Member:
    David Dreier (R-CA) . . . . . . . . . . . . . . . . . . . . . .202-225-2305

### Subcommittees

**Legislative & Budget Process**
Chair:
    Alcee L Hastings (D-FL) . . . . . . . . . . . . . . . . . . . .202-225-1313
Ranking Member:
    Lincoln Diaz-Balart (R-FL) . . . . . . . . . . . . . . . . . .202-225-4211

**Rules & Organization of the House**
Chair:
    James F McGovern (D-MA) . . . . . . . . . . . . . . . . . .202-225-6101
Ranking Member:
    Pete Sessions (R-TX) . . . . . . . . . . . . . . . . . . . . . .202-225-2231

## Science & Technology
2321 Rayburn Building
Washington, DC 20515
202-225-6375  Fax: 202-225-3895

Chair:
    Bart Gordon (D-TN). . . . . . . . . . . . . . . . . . . . . . .202-225-4231
Ranking Member:
    Ralph M Hall (R-TX) . . . . . . . . . . . . . . . . . . . . . .202-225-6673
New York Delegate:
    Paul D Tonko (D) . . . . . . . . . . . . . . . . . . . . . . . .202-225-5076

*Offices and agencies generally appear in alphabetical order, except when specific order is requested by listee.*

## Subcommittees

### Energy & Environment
Chair:
Brian Baird (D-WA)...................................202-225-3536
Ranking Member:
Bob Inglis (R-SC)....................................202-225-6030

### Investigations and Oversights
Chair:
Brad Miller (D-NC)..................................202-225-3032
Ranking Member:
Paul C Brown (R-GA)................................202-225-4101

### Research and Science Education
Chair:
Daniel Lipinski (D-IL)..............................202-225-5701
Ranking Member:
Vernon J Ehlers (R-MI).............................202-225-3831

### Space and Aeronautics
Chair:
Gabrielle Giffords (D-AZ).........................202-225-2542
Ranking Member:
Pete Olson (R-TX)..................................202-225-5951

### Technology and Innovation
Chair:
David Wu (D-OR)...................................202-225-0855
Ranking Member:
Adrian Smith (R-NE)..............................202-225-6435

## Small Business
2361 Rayburn House Building
Washington, DC 20515
202-225-4038  Fax: 202-226-5276

Chair:
Nydia Velazquez (D-NY)...........................202-225-2361
Ranking Member:
Sam Graves (R-MO)...............................202-225-7041
New York Delegate:
Yvette D Clark (D).................................202-225-6231

## Subcommittees

### Contracting and Technology
Chair:
Glenn C Nye III (D-IA)............................202-225-4215
Ranking Member:
Aaron Schock (R-IL)...............................202-225-6201

### Finance and Tax
Chair:
Kurt Schrader (D-OR).............................202-225-5711
Ranking Member:
Vern Buchanan (R-FL)............................202-225-5015

### Investigations and Oversight
Chair:
Jason Altmire (D-PA)..............................202-225-2565
Ranking Member:
Mary Fallin (R-OK)................................202-225-2132

### Regulations and Health Care
Chair:
Kathy Dahlkemper (D-PA).........................202-225-5406
Ranking Member:
Lynn Westmoreland (R-GA)........................202-225-5901

### Rural and Urban Entrepreneurship
Chair:
Heath Shuler (D-NC)..............................202-225-6401

Ranking Member:
Blaine Luetkemeyer (R-MO).......................202-225-2956

## Standards of Official Conduct
HT-2, The Capitol
Washington, DC 20515
202-225-7103  Fax: 202-225-7392
Web site: ethics.house.gov

Chair:
Zoe Lofgren (D-CA)................................202-225-3072
Ranking Member:
Jo Bonner (R-AL)..................................202-225-4931

## Transportation & Infrastructure
2165 Rayburn House Building
Washington, DC 20515
202-225-4472  Fax: 202-226-1270

Chair:
James L Oberstar (D-MN)...........................202-225-4472
Ranking Member:
John L Mica (R-FL)................................202-225-4035
New York Delegate:
Michael A Arcuri (D)..............................202-225-3665
New York Delegate:
Timothy H Bishop (D)..............................202-225-3826
New York Delegate:
John J Hall (D)...................................202-225-5441
New York Delegate:
Michael E McMahon (D).............................202-225-3371
New York Delegate:
Jerrold Nadler (D)................................202-225-5635

## Subcommittees

### Aviation
Chair:
Jerry F Costello (D-IL)...........................202-225-5661
Ranking Member:
Thomas E Petri (R-WI).............................202-225-2476
New York Delegate:
John J Hall (D)...................................202-225-5441
New York Delegate:
Michael E McMahon (D).............................202-225-3371

### Coast Guard & Maritime Transportation
Chair:
Elijah E Cummings (D-MD)..........................202-225-4741
Ranking Member:
Frank LoBiondo (R-NJ).............................202-225-6572
New York Delegate:
Timothy H Bishop (D)..............................202-225-3826
New York Delegate:
Michael E McMahon (D).............................202-225-3371

### Economic Development, Public Buildings & Emergency Management
Chair:
Eleanor Holmes Norton (D-DC).....................202-225-9961
Ranking Member:
Mario Diaz-Balart (R-FL)..........................202-225-4211
New York Delegate:
Michael A Arcuri (D)..............................202-225-3665

### Highway and Transit
Chair:
Peter A DeFazio (D-OR)............................202-225-9989
Ranking Minority Member:
John J Duncan, Jr (R-TN)..........................202-225-5435
New York Delegate:
Michael A Arcuri (D)..............................202-225-3665

*Offices and agencies generally appear in alphabetical order, except when specific order is requested by listee.*

New York Delegate:
Timothy H Bishop (D) . . . . . . . . . . . . . . . . . . . . . . . . . . .202-225-3826
New York Delegate:
John J Hall (D) . . . . . . . . . . . . . . . . . . . . . . . . . . . . .202-225-5441
New York Delegate:
Jerrold Nadler (D). . . . . . . . . . . . . . . . . . . . . . . . . . . .202-225-5635

**Railroads, Pipelines and Hazardous Materials**
Chair:
Corrine Brown (D-FL) . . . . . . . . . . . . . . . . . . . . . . . . .202-225-3274
Ranking Member:
Bill Schuster (PA). . . . . . . . . . . . . . . . . . . . . . . . . . .202-225-2431
New York Delegate:
Michael A Arcuri (D) . . . . . . . . . . . . . . . . . . . . . . . . .202-225-3665
New York Delegate:
Michael E McMahon (D) . . . . . . . . . . . . . . . . . . . . . .202-225-3371
New York Delegate:
Jerrold Nadler (D). . . . . . . . . . . . . . . . . . . . . . . . . . . .202-225-5635

**Water Resources & Environment**
Chair:
Eddie Bernice Johnson (D-TX) . . . . . . . . . . . . . . . . .202-225-0060
Ranking Member:
John Boozman (R-AR). . . . . . . . . . . . . . . . . . . . . . . .202-225-4301
New York Delegate:
Timothy H Bishop (D) . . . . . . . . . . . . . . . . . . . . . . . .202-225-3826
New York Delegate:
John J Hall (D) . . . . . . . . . . . . . . . . . . . . . . . . . . . . .202-225-5441

## Veterans' Affairs
335 Cannon House Building
Washington, DC 20515
202-225-9756

Chair:
Bob Filner (D-CA) . . . . . . . . . . . . . . . . . . . . . . . . . . .202-225-8045
Ranking Member:
Steve Buyer (D-IN). . . . . . . . . . . . . . . . . . . . . . . . . . .202-225-5037
New York Delegate:
John J Hall (D) . . . . . . . . . . . . . . . . . . . . . . . . . . . . .202-225-5441

### Subcommittees

**Disability Assistance & Memorial Affairs**
Chair:
John Hall (D-NY). . . . . . . . . . . . . . . . . . . . . . . . . . . .202-225-5441
Ranking Member:
Doug Lamborn (R-CO) . . . . . . . . . . . . . . . . . . . . . . .202-225-4422

**Economic Opportunity**
Chair:
Stephanie Herseth Sandlin (D-SD) . . . . . . . . . . . . . .202-225-2801
Ranking Member:
John Boozman (R-AR). . . . . . . . . . . . . . . . . . . . . . . .202-225-4301

**Health**
Chair:
Mike Michaud (D-ME). . . . . . . . . . . . . . . . . . . . . . . .202-225-6306
Ranking Member:
Henry E Brown, Jr (R-SC) . . . . . . . . . . . . . . . . . . . .202-225-3176

**Oversight & Investigations**
Chair:
Harry E Mitchell (D-AZ) . . . . . . . . . . . . . . . . . . . . .202-225-2190
Ranking Member:
Phil Roe (R-TN) . . . . . . . . . . . . . . . . . . . . . . . . . . . .202-225-6356

## Ways & Means
1102 Longworth House Building
Washington, DC 20515
202-225-3625 Fax: 202-225-2610
Web site: waysandmeans.house.gov

Chair:
Charles B Rangel (D-NY) . . . . . . . . . . . . . . . . . . . . .202-225-4365
Ranking Member:
Dave Camp (R-MI). . . . . . . . . . . . . . . . . . . . . . . . . .202-225-3561
New York Delegate:
Joseph Crowley (D) . . . . . . . . . . . . . . . . . . . . . . . . . .202-225-3965
New York Delegate:
Brian Higgins (D) . . . . . . . . . . . . . . . . . . . . . . . . . . .202-225-3306

### Subcommittees

**Health**
Chair:
Fortney Pete Stark (D-CA). . . . . . . . . . . . . . . . . . . .202-225-5065
Ranking Member:
Wally Herger (D-CA). . . . . . . . . . . . . . . . . . . . . . . .202-225-3076

**Income Security and Family Support**
Chair:
Jim McDermott (D-WA) . . . . . . . . . . . . . . . . . . . . .202-225-3106
Ranking Member:
John Linder (R-GA) . . . . . . . . . . . . . . . . . . . . . . . . .202-225-

**Oversight**
Chair:
John Lewis (D-GA) . . . . . . . . . . . . . . . . . . . . . . . . .202-225-3801
Ranking Member:
Charles W Boustany, Jr (R-LA). . . . . . . . . . . . . . . .202-225-2031
New York Delegate:
Brian Higgins (D). . . . . . . . . . . . . . . . . . . . . . . . . . .202-225-3306

**Select Revenue Measures**
Chair:
Richard E Neal (D-MA). . . . . . . . . . . . . . . . . . . . . .202-225-5601
Ranking Member:
Pat Tiberi (R-OH). . . . . . . . . . . . . . . . . . . . . . . . . . .202-225-5355
New York Delegate:
Joseph Crowley (D) . . . . . . . . . . . . . . . . . . . . . . . . .202-225-3965

**Social Security**
Chair:
John S Tanner (D-TN) . . . . . . . . . . . . . . . . . . . . . . .202-225-4714
Ranking Member:
Sam Johnson (R-TX) . . . . . . . . . . . . . . . . . . . . . . . .202-225-4201
New York Delegate:
Joseph Crowley (D) . . . . . . . . . . . . . . . . . . . . . . . . .202-225-3965

**Trade**
Chair:
Sander M Levin (MI) . . . . . . . . . . . . . . . . . . . . . . . .202-225-4961
Ranking Member:
Kevin Brady (R-TX). . . . . . . . . . . . . . . . . . . . . . . . .202-225-4901

## OTHER, SELECT & SPECIAL COMMITTEES

### Energy Independence & Global Warming, House Select Committee on
B243 Longworth House Building
Washington, DC 20515
202-225-4012 Fax: 202-225-4092

Chair:
Ed Markey (D-MA) . . . . . . . . . . . . . . . . . . . . . . . . .202-225-2836
Ranking Member:
James F Sensenbrenner, Jr (R-WI). . . . . . . . . . . . . .202-225-5101

### Intelligence, House Permanent Select Committee on
Web site: intelligence.house.gov

Chair:
Silvestre Reyes (D-TX) . . . . . . . . . . . . . . . . . . . . . .202-225-4831

*Offices and agencies generally appear in alphabetical order, except when specific order is requested by listee.*

Ranking Member:
  Peter Hoekstra (R-MI) ............................... 202-225-4401

**Subcommittees**

**Intelligence Community Management**
Chair:
  Anna G Eshoo (D-CA) .......................... 202-225-8104
Ranking Member:
  Sue Myrick (R-NC) ............................... 202-225-1976

**Oversight and Investigations**
Chair:
  Jan Schakowsky (D-AL) ........................ 202-225-2111
Ranking Member:
  Jeff Miller (R-FL) ................................ 202-225-4136

**Technical and Tactical Intelligence**
Chair:
  C A Dutch Ruppersberger (D-MD) ................. 202-225-3061
Ranking Member:
  Mack Thornberry (R-TX) ....................... 202-225-3706

**Terrorism/HUMIT, Analysis and Counterintelligence**
Chair:
  Mike Thompson (D-CA) .......................... 202-225-3311
Ranking Member:
  Mike Rogers (R-MI) ............................. 202-225-4872

## JOINT SENATE AND HOUSE COMMITTEES

## Economic Committee, Joint
Chair, House:
  Carolyn B Maloney (D-NY) ...................... 202-224-7944

Vice Chair, Senate:
  Charles E Schumer (D-NY) ...................... 202-224-6542
Ranking Member, House:
  Kevin Brady (R-TX) ............................. 202-225-4901
Ranking Member, Senate:
  Sam Brownback (R-KS) .......................... 202-225-6521
New York Delegate:
  Maurice D Hinchey (D) .......................... 202-224-6335

## Library, Joint Committee on the
Chair:
  Charles E Schumer (D-NY) ...................... 202-224-6542
Ranking Member:
  Robert Bennett (R-UT) .......................... 202-224-5444

## Printing, Joint Committee on
Chair:
  Charles E Schumer (D-NY ....................... 202-224-6542
Vice Chair:
  Robert F Bennett (R-UT) ........................ 202-224-5444

## Taxation, Joint Committee on
1015 Longworth House Building
Washington, DC 20515
202-225-3621

Chair:
  Charles B Rangel (D-NY) ........................ 202-225-4365
Vice Chair:
  Max Baucus (D-MT) ............................. 202-224-2651

*Offices and agencies generally appear in alphabetical order, except when specific order is requested by listee.*

## COUNTY GOVERNMENT

*This section identifies senior government officials in all New York counties.*

## COUNTY GOVERNMENT

### Albany County
112 State Street
Albany, NY 12207
518-447-7040  Fax: 518-447-5589
Web site: www.albanycounty.com

Chairman, County Legislature (D):
Shawn M. Morse . . . . . . . . . . . . . . . . . 518-447-7168/fax: 518-447-5695
e-mail: shawn.morse@albanycounty.com
County Executive:
Daniel P. McCoy . . . . . . . . . . . . . . . . . 518-447-7040/fax: 518-447-5589
e-mail: county_executive@albanycounty.com
County Clerk:
Thomas G Clingan . . . . . . . . . . . . . . . . 518-487-5100/fax: 518-487-5099
e-mail: countyclerk@albanycounty.com
County Attorney:
Thomas Marcelle . . . . . . . . . . . . . . . . . 518-447-7110/fax: 518-447-5564
District Attorney:
P David Soares . . . . . . . . . . . . . . . . . 518-487-5460/fax: 518-487-5093
Sheriff:
Craig D. Apple, Sr. . . . . . . . . . . . . . . . 518-487-5400/fax: 518-487-5037
Comptroller:
Michael F Conners, II . . . . . . . . . . . . . . 518-447-7130/fax: 518-433-1554
e-mail: mconners@albanycounty.com
General Services Commissioner:
John T. Evers . . . . . . . . . . . . . . . . . . 518-447-7210/fax: 518-447-7747
Commissioner, Management & Budget:
David Friedfel . . . . . . . . . . . . . . . . . 518-447-5525/fax: 518-447-5589
e-mail: budget@albanycounty.com

### Allegany County
County Office Bldg, 7 Court St
Belmont, NY 14813
585-268-9222  Fax: 585-268-9446
Web site: www.alleganyco.com

Chairman, Board of Legislators (R):
Curtis W Crandall . . . . . . . . . . . . . . . . . . . . . . . . . . . . . 585-268-9222
Majority Leader (R):
Theodore L Hopkins . . . . . . . . . . . . . . . . . . . . . . . . . . . . 585-268-9222
Minority Leader (D):
Vacant . . . . . . . . . . . . . . . . . . . . . . . . . . . . . . . . . . 585-268-9222
Clerk, Board of Legislators:
Brenda A Rigby Riehle . . . . . . . . . . . . 585-268-9222/fax: 585-268-9446
e-mail: rigbyba@alleganyco.com
County Administrator:
John E Margeson . . . . . . . . . . . . . . . . 585-268-9217/fax: 585-268-9623
e-mail: margesj@alleganyco.com
County Clerk:
Robert L Christman . . . . . . . . . . . . . . . 585-268-9270/fax: 585-268-9659
e-mail: christr@alleganyco.com
District Attorney (Acting):
Keith Slep . . . . . . . . . . . . . . . . . . . . 585-268-9225/fax: 585-268-9727
e-mail: slepka@alleganyco.com
Public Defender:
Barbara J Kelley . . . . . . . . . . . . . . . . 585-268-9246/fax: 585-268-5888
e-mail: kelleybj@alleganyco.com
Sheriff:
Rick Whitney . . . . . . . . . . . . . . . . . . 585-268-9200/fax: 585-268-9484
e-mail: whitneyrl@alleganyco.com

Treasurer:
Terri L Ross . . . . . . . . . . . . . . . . . . . 585-268-9289/fax: 585-268-7506
e-mail: rosstl@alleganyco.com
County Attorney:
Thomas A Miner . . . . . . . . . . . . . . . . . 585-268-9410/fax: 585-268-9651
e-mail: minerta@alleganyco.com
Director, Emergency Management & Fire:
Jeff Luckey . . . . . . . . . . . . . . . . . . . . . . . . . . . . . . . . . 585-268-5290
e-mail: luckeyj@alleganyco.com
Superintendent, Public Works:
Guy James . . . . . . . . . . . . . . . . . . . . 585-268-9230/fax: 585-268-9648
e-mail: roeskeds@alleganyco.com
Fire Coordinator:
Paul W Gallmann . . . . . . . . . . . . . . . . 585-268-5290/fax: 585-268-9695
e-mail: gallmapw@alleganyco.com
County Historian:
Craig R Braack . . . . . . . . . . . . . . . . . . . . . . . . . . . . . . . 585-268-9293
e-mail: historian@alleganyco.com

### Bronx County (NYC Borough of the Bronx)
851 Grand Concourse
Room 118
Bronx, NY 10451
866-797-7214  Fax: 718-590-8122

Borough President:
Ruben Diaz Jr . . . . . . . . . . . . . . . . . . 718-590-3557/fax: 718-590-3537
Deputy Borough President:
Aurelia Greene . . . . . . . . . . . . . . . . . . . . . . . . . . . . . . . 718-590-4036
County Clerk:
Luis M. Diaz . . . . . . . . . . . . . . . . . . 866-797-7214/fax: 718-590-8122
e-mail: hdiaz@courts.state.ny.us
District Attorney:
Robert T Johnson . . . . . . . . . . . . . . . . 718-590-2000/fax: 718-590-2198

### Broome County
County Office Bldg
60 Hawley St
PO Box 1766
Binghamton, NY 13902-1766
607-778-2109  Fax: 607-778-2044
e-mail: legclerk@co.broome.ny.us
Web site: www.gobroomecounty.com

Chairman, County Legislature (D):
Jerry F Marinich . . . . . . . . . . . . . . . . 607-778-2131/fax: 607-778-8869
e-mail: jmarinich@co.broome.ny.us
Majority Leader (D):
Wayne Howard . . . . . . . . . . . . . . . . . 607-778-2131/fax: 607-778-8869
Minority Leader (R):
Mark R Whalen . . . . . . . . . . . . . . . . . 607-778-2131/fax: 607-778-8869
County Executive:
Debra A. Preston . . . . . . . . . . . . . . . . 607-778-2109/fax: 607-778-2044
County Clerk:
Richard R Blythe . . . . . . . . . . . . . . . . 607-778-2255/fax: 607-778-2243
e-mail: clerkinfo@co.broome.ny.us
District Attorney:
Gerald F Mollen . . . . . . . . . . . . . . . . 607-778-2423/fax: 607-778-8870
e-mail: gmollen@co.broome.ny.us
Public Defender:
Jay L Wilber . . . . . . . . . . . . . . . . . . 607-778-2403/fax: 607-778-2432
e-mail: jwilber@co.broome.ny.us
Sheriff:
David E Harder . . . . . . . . . . . . . . . . . 607-778-1911/fax: 607-778-2100
e-mail: bcsheriff@co.broome.ny.us
Director, Emergency Services:
Brett B Chellis . . . . . . . . . . . . . . . . . 607-778-2170/fax: 607-778-1150
e-mail: bchellis@co.broome.ny.us

*Offices and agencies generally appear in alphabetical order, except when specific order is requested by listee.*

Office of Management & Budget:
Marie F. Kalka.................607-778-2467/fax: 607-778-2044
e-mail: jknebel@co.broome.ny.us
County Historian:
Gerald R Smith ..................607-778-2076/fax: 607-778-6249
e-mail: gsmith@co.broome.ny.us

## Cattaraugus County
County Center
303 Court St
Little Valley, NY 14755
716-938-2577  Fax: 716-938-2760
Web site: www.cattco.org

Chair, County Legislature (R):
Norman L. Marsh ................716-938-6620/fax: 716-938-9698
Vice Chairman (R):
Michael T O'Brien..........................716-938-9111 x2386
Majority Leader (R):
James J Snyder...........................716-938-9111 x2333
Minority Leader (D):
Linda Witte .............................716-938-9111 x2397
County Administrator & Clerk, Legislature:
Jack Searles .................716-938-9111 x2577/fax: 716-938-9306
County Clerk:
James Griffith ...............716-938-2297/fax: 716-938-6009
County Attorney:
Thomas C. Brady.................716-938-2931/fax: 716-938-2763
District Attorney:
Lori Pettit Rieman ...............716-938-2220/fax: 716-938-2763
Sheriff:
Dennis B John ..............716-938-9111 x2204/fax: 716-938-6420
Treasurer:
Joseph Keller......................716-373-2290/fax: 716-938-2762
Public Defender:
Mark S Williams...............716-373-0004 x11/fax: 716-373-3462
County Historian:
Sharon Fellows ..........................716-353-8200 x4721

## Cayuga County
160 Genesee St
Auburn, NY 13021
315-253-1525  Fax: 315-253-1586
Web site: www.cayugacounty.us

Chairman, County Legislature (R):
Peter A Tortorici....................................315-253-1273
Clerk, Legislature:
Sheila Smith ......................................315-253-1498
County Manager:
Wayne D Allen.....................................315-253-1525
County Clerk:
Susan M Dwyer......................................315-253-1271
e-mail: sdwyer@cayugacounty.us
County Attorney:
Fredrick Westphal..................................315-253-1274
e-mail: coatty@cayugacounty.us
District Attorney:
Jon E Budelmann ...................................315-253-1391
e-mail: cayugada@cayugacounty.us
Director, Planning & Economic Development:
Steve Lynch ......................................315-253-1276
Emergency Management Director:
Brian P Dahl .....................................315-255-1161
e-mail: ccoes@cayugacounty.us
Sheriff:
David S Gould ....................................315-253-1222
e-mail: sheriff@cayugacounty.us
Treasurer:
Jim H Orman.......................................315-253-1211

County Historian:
Linda Frank.......................................315-253-1300

## Chautauqua County
3 N Erie St
Mayville, NY 14757-1007
716-753-4241  Fax: 716-753-4756
Web site: www.co.chautauqua.ny.us

Majority Leader (D):
Maria Kindberg.....................................716-753-4215
e-mail: chuckcornell@hotmail.com
Chairman, City Legislature:
Frank (Jay) Gould, III..............................716-753-4215
Clerk, Legislature:
Janet M. Jankowski.................................716-753-4215
e-mail: cafliscj@co.chautauqua.ny.us
County Executive:
Gregory J Edwards..................................716-753-4211
e-mail: edwardsg@co.chautauqua.ny.us
County Clerk:
Sandra K Sopak...............716-753-4331/fax: 716-753-4293
District Attorney:
David Foley........................................716-753-4241
Public Defender:
Nathaniel L. Barone, II.............................716-753-4376
Director, Emergency Services:
Julius Leone ......................................716-753-4341
Sheriff:
Joseph A Gerace....................................716-753-2131
Finance Director:
Susan Marsh .......................................716-753-4223

## Chemung County
John H Hazlett Bldg, 203 Lake St
PO Box 588
Elmira, NY 14902-0588
607-737-2912  Fax: 607-737-0351
Web site: www.chemungcounty.com

Chairman, County Legislature (R):
Donna Draxler....................607-737-2066/fax: 607-737-2851
Majority Leader (R):
Sidney S Graubard.................607-737-2066/fax: 607-737-2851
Minority Leader (D):
Theodore A Bennett ...............607-737-2066/fax: 607-737-2851
e-mail: ted.benn@verizon.net
Clerk, Legislature:
Linda D Palmer ...................607-737-2066/fax: 607-737-2851
e-mail: lpalmer@co.chemung.ny.us
County Executive:
Thomas J Santulli .................607-737-2912/fax: 607-737-0351
County Clerk:
Catherine K Hughes.................607-737-2920/fax: 607-737-2897
e-mail: chughes@co.chemung.ny.us
District Attorney:
Weeden A Wetmore .................607-737-2944/fax: 607-737-2965
e-mail: wwetmore@co.chemung.ny.us
Public Defender:
Scott N Fierro ...................607-737-2969/fax: 607-737-2853
Sheriff:
Christopher J Moss ...............607-737-2987/fax: 607-737-2930
e-mail: cmoss@co.chemung.ny.us

## Chenango County
County Office Bldg
5 Court St
Norwich, NY 13815

*Offices and agencies generally appear in alphabetical order, except when specific order is requested by listee.*

607-337-1700  Fax: 607-334-8768
Web site: www.co.chenango.ny.us

Chairman, Board of Supervisors (R):
  Lawrence N Wilcox . . . . . . . . . . . . . . . . . . . . . . . . . . . . . .607-337-1401
Clerk, Board of Supervisors:
  R C Woodford. . . . . . . . . . . . . . . . . . . . . . . . . . . . . . . . . . .607-337-1430
County Clerk:
  Mary C Weidman . . . . . . . . . . . . . . . . . . . . . . . . . . . . . . . .607-337-1450
Sheriff:
  Ernest R Cutting Jr . . . . . . . . . . . . . . . . . . . . . . . . . . . . . . .607-334-2000
Treasurer:
  William E Evans . . . . . . . . . . . . . . . . . . . . . . . . . . . . . . . . .607-337-1414
Director, Public Works:
  Shawn Fry P.E., L.S.. . . . . . . . . . . . . . . . . . . . . . . . . . . . . . .607-337-1710
County Historian:
  Patricia E. Evans. . . . . . . . . . . . . . . . . . . . . . . . . . . . . . . . .607-337-1845

## Clinton County
County Government Ctr
137 Margaret St, Ste 208
Plattsburgh, NY 12901
518-565-4600  Fax: 518-565-4616
Web site: www.clintoncountygov.com

Chairman (R):
  James R Langley, Jr. . . . . . . . . . . . . . . .518-643-9052/fax: 518-643-6640
  e-mail: langleyins@charter.net
Majority Leader (R):
  Samuel J Trombley . . . . . . . . . . . . . . . .518-597-7742/fax: 518-594-7742
  e-mail: trombleyma@aol.com
Minority Leader (D):
  Dr John Gallagher. . . . . . . . . . . . . . . . . . . . . . . . . . . . .518-561-0484
  e-mail: vze3gnnn@verizon.net
Clerk, Board of Legislators & County Administrator:
  Michael E Zurlo. . . . . . . . . . . . . . . . . . .518-565-4600/fax: 518-565-4616
County Clerk:
  John H Zurlo . . . . . . . . . . . . . . . . . . . . .518-565-4700/fax: 518-565-4718
County Attorney:
  William Favreau . . . . . . . . . . . . . . . . . .518-561-4400/fax: 518-561-4848
District Attorney:
  Andrew J Wylie. . . . . . . . . . . . . . . . . . .518-565-4770/fax: 518-565-4777
Director, Emergency Services:
  Eric Day. . . . . . . . . . . . . . . . . . . . . . . . .518-565-4791/fax: 518-566-1202
Sheriff:
  David N Favro. . . . . . . . . . . . . . . . . . . .518-565-4300/fax: 518-565-4333
Treasurer:
  Joseph W Giroux. . . . . . . . . . . . . . . . . .518-565-4730/fax: 518-565-4516

## Columbia County
401 State St
Hudson, NY 12534
518-828-1527  Fax: 518-822-0684
Web site: www.columbiacountyny.com

Chairman, Board of Supervisors (R):
  Patrick M Gratton . . . . . . . . . . . . . . . .518-828-1527/fax: 518-828-0684
County Clerk:
  Holly C Tanner . . . . . . . . . . . . . . . . . . .518-828-3339/fax: 518-828-5299
  e-mail: htanner@govt.co.columbia.ny.us
County Attorney:
  Robert J Fitzsimmons . . . . . . . . . . . . . .518-828-3303/fax: 518-828-9535
District Attorney:
  Paul Czajka. . . . . . . . . . . . . . . . . . . . . . . . . . . . . . . . . . . .518-828-3414
Public Defender:
  Robert W. Linville. . . . . . . . . . . . . . . . .518-828-3410/fax: 518-828-4076
Sheriff:
  David W Harrison Jr . . . . . . . . . . . . . . .518-828-0601/fax: 518-828-9088
Fire Coordinator:
  John Howe. . . . . . . . . . . . . . . . . . . . . . .518-822-8610/fax: 518-828-1279

Director, Emergency Management:
  William Black . . . . . . . . . . . . . . . . . . . .518-828-1212/fax: 518-828-1279
Treasurer:
  PJ Keeler . . . . . . . . . . . . . . . . . . . . . . . .518-828-0513/fax: 518-822-1110
County Historian:
  Mary Howell . . . . . . . . . . . . . . . . . . . . .518-828-3442/fax: 518-828-2969

## Cortland County
County Office Bldg
60 Central Ave
Cortland, NY 13045
607-753-5048  Fax: 607-756-3492

Chairperson, County Legislature (D):
  Mike Park . . . . . . . . . . . . . . . . . . . . . . . . . . . . . . . . . . . . .607-753-5048
Clerk, Legislature:
  Jeremy Boylan. . . . . . . . . . . . . . . . . . . .607-753-5049/fax: 607-756-3492
  e-mail: jboylan@cortland-co.org
County Clerk:
  Elizabeth P Larkin . . . . . . . . . . . . . . . . . . . . . . . . . . . . . .607-753-5021
  e-mail: elarkin@cortland-co.org
County Attorney:
  Edward Purser. . . . . . . . . . . . . . . . . . . . . . . . . . . . . . . . . .607-753-5095
District Attorney:
  Mark Suben. . . . . . . . . . . . . . . . . . . . . . . . . . . . . . . . . . . .607-753-5008
Public Defender:
  Edward Goehler. . . . . . . . . . . . . . . . . . .607-753-5046/fax: 607-753-0781
  e-mail: publicdefender@cortland-co.org
Sheriff:
  Lee A Price . . . . . . . . . . . . . . . . . . . . . . . . . . . . . . . . . . . .607-753-5006
Fire/Emergency Management Coordinator:
  Scott Roman . . . . . . . . . . . . . . . . . . . . .607-753-5064/fax: 607-756-8457
Treasurer:
  Cynthia Monroe. . . . . . . . . . . . . . . . . . .607-753-5070/fax: 607-758-5512
County Historian:
  Jeremy Boylan . . . . . . . . . . . . . . . . . . . .607-753-5360
  e-mail: jboylan@cortland-co.org

## Delaware County
County Office Bldg
111 Main St
Delhi, NY 13753
607-746-2603  Fax: 607-746-7012
Web site: www.co.delaware.ny.us

Chairman, Board of Supervisors (R):
  James E Eisel, Sr. . . . . . . . . . . . . . . . . . . . . . . . . . . . . . . .607-652-4350
Vice Chairman, Board of Supervisors (R):
  Tina Mole . . . . . . . . . . . . . . . . . . . . . . . . . . . . . . . . . . . . .607-832-4312
Clerk, Board of Supervisors:
  Christa M Schafer . . . . . . . . . . . . . . . . .607-832-5110/fax: 607-832-5111
  e-mail: cob@co.delaware.ny.us
County Clerk:
  Sharon O'Dell. . . . . . . . . . . . . . . . . . . . . . . . . . . . . . . . . .607-746-2123
County Attorney:
  Richard B Spinney. . . . . . . . . . . . . . . . .607-652-3443/fax: 607-652-3334
District Attorney:
  Richard D Northrup, Jr . . . . . . . . . . . . .607-746-3557/fax: 607-746-2297
Sheriff:
  Thomas E Mills. . . . . . . . . . . . . . . . . . .607-746-2336/fax: 607-746-8151
County Treasurer:
  Beverly J Shields. . . . . . . . . . . . . . . . . .607-832-5070/fax: 607-832-5077
  e-mail: treas@co.delaware.ny.us
Director, Emergency Services:
  Richard Bell . . . . . . . . . . . . . . . . . . . . . . . . . . . . . . . . . . .607-746-9600
Commissioner, Public Works:
  Wayne Reynolds. . . . . . . . . . . . . . . . . . . . . . . . . . . . . . . .607-746-2128
County Historian:
  Gabrielle Price . . . . . . . . . . . . . . . . . . . . . . . . . . . . . . . . .607-746-8660
  e-mail: hist@co.delaware.ny.us

*Offices and agencies generally appear in alphabetical order, except when specific order is requested by listee.*

## Dutchess County
County Office Bldg
22 Market St, 6th Fl
Poughkeepsie, NY 12601
845-486-2100  Fax: 845-486-2113
e-mail: internetsupport1@co.dutchess.ny.us
Web site: www.dutchessny.gov

Chairman, County Legislature (R):
  Robert Rolison . . . . . . . . . . . . . . . . . . 845-486-2100/fax: 845-486-2113
Majority Leader (D):
  Sandra Goldberg . . . . . . . . . . . . . . . . . . . . . . . . . . . . . . 845-297-76770
Minority Leader (R):
  Gary Cooper . . . . . . . . . . . . . . . . . . 845-297-8757/fax: 845-486-2113
County Executive:
  Marcus J. Molinaro . . . . . . . . . . . . . . 845-486-2000/fax: 845-486-2021
  e-mail: countyexec@co.dutchess.ny.us
Clerk, Legislature:
  Carolyn Morris . . . . . . . . . . . . . . . . 845-486-2100/fax: 845-486-2113
  e-mail: countylegislature@co.dutchess.ny.us
County Clerk:
  Bradford Kendall . . . . . . . . . . . . . . . . 845-486-2120/fax: 845-486-2138
County Attorney:
  James M Fedorchak . . . . . . . . . . . . . . 845-486-2110/fax: 845-486-2002
  e-mail: countyattorney@co.dutchess.ny.us
District Attorney:
  William V Grady . . . . . . . . . . . . . . . . 845-486-2300/fax: 845-486-2324
Public Defender (Acting):
  Thomas Angell . . . . . . . . . . . . . . . . 845-486-2280/fax: 845-486-2266
  e-mail: publicdefender@co.dutchess.ny.us
Sheriff:
  Adrian H Anderson . . . . . . . . . . . . . . . . . . . . . . . . . . 845-486-3800
  e-mail: sheriff@co.dutchess.ny.us
Comptroller:
  Jim Coughlan . . . . . . . . . . . . . . . . . . 845-486-2050/fax: 845-486-2055
  e-mail: comptroller@co.dutchess.ny.us
Finance Commissioner:
  Pamela Barrack . . . . . . . . . . . . . . . . 845-486-2025/fax: 845-486-2198
Emergency Response Coordinator:
  Dana Smith . . . . . . . . . . . . . . . . . . 845-486-2080/fax: 845-486-3998
County Historian:
  William P. Tatum, III . . . . . . . . . . . . . . . . . . . . . . . . . 845-486-2381

## Erie County
County Office Bldg
95 Franklin St
16th Fl
Buffalo, NY 14202
716-858-7500  Fax: 716-858-8895
e-mail: public_feedback@erie.gov
Web site: www2.erie.gov

Chair, County Legislature (D):
  Betty Jean Grant . . . . . . . . . . . . . . . . 716-894-0914/fax: 716-896-1463
  e-mail: bjg@erie.gov
Majority Leader, County Legislature (D):
  Thomas J. Mazur . . . . . . . . . . . . . . . . 716-893-4385/fax: 716-894-4539
  e-mail: mazurt@erie.gov
Minority Leader, County Legislature (R):
  John J Mills . . . . . . . . . . . . . . . . . . 716-858-8850/fax: 716-858-8818
  e-mail: jmills13@erie.gov
Clerk, Legislature:
  Robert M Graber . . . . . . . . . . . . . . . . 716-858-7500/fax: 716-858-8895
County Executive:
  Mark C Poloncarz . . . . . . . . . . . . . . . . . . . . . . . . . . . 716-858-8500
County Clerk:
  Christopher L Jacobs . . . . . . . . . . . . . . 716-858-8785/fax: 716-858-6550
  e-mail: eriecountyclerk@erie.gov

District Attorney:
  Frank A Sedita III . . . . . . . . . . . . . . . . 716-858-2400/fax: 716-858-7425
Sheriff:
  Timothy B Howard . . . . . . . . . . . . . . . . . . . . . . . . . . . 716-585-7618
Civil Defense/Disaster Preparedness Deputy Commissioner:
  Dean Messing . . . . . . . . . . . . . . . . 716-858-8477/fax: 716-858-7937
  e-mail: messingd@erie.gov
Comptroller:
  Stefan I. Mychajliw . . . . . . . . . . . . . . 716-858-8400/fax: 716-858-8507

## Essex County
County Government Ctr
7551 Court St
PO Box 217
Elizabethtown, NY 12932
518-873-3350  Fax: 518-873-3356
Web site: www.co.essex.ny.us

Chairman, Board of Supervisors (D):
  Randall T Douglas
Vice Chairman, Board of Supervisors (R):
  Robert T Politi
  e-mail: super@northelba.org
Clerk, Board of Supervisors:
  Judith A. Garrison . . . . . . . . . . . . . . . . 518-873-3353/fax: 518-873-3356
  e-mail: dpalmer@co.essex.ny.us
County Manager:
  Daniel Palmer . . . . . . . . . . . . . . . . 518-873-3333/fax: 518-873-3339
  e-mail: danp@co.essex.ny.us
County Clerk:
  Joseph A Provoncha . . . . . . . . . . . . . . 518-873-3601/fax: 518-873-3548
  e-mail: jprovon@co.essex.ny.us
County Attorney:
  Daniel Manning III . . . . . . . . . . . . . . 518-873-3380/fax: 518-873-3894
  e-mail: dmanning@co.essex.ny.us
District Attorney:
  Kristy Sprague . . . . . . . . . . . . . . . . 518-873-3335/fax: 518-873-3788
  e-mail: ksprague@co.essex.ny.us
Public Defender:
  Brandon E Boutelle . . . . . . . . . . . . . . 518-873-3880/fax: 518-873-3888
Sheriff:
  Richard C Cutting . . . . . . . . . . . . . . . . 518-873-6902/fax: 518-873-6949
Director, Emergency Services:
  Donald Jaquish . . . . . . . . . . . . . . . . 518-873-3900/fax: 518-873-3963
  e-mail: wwade@co.essex.ny.us
Treasurer:
  Michael G Diskin . . . . . . . . . . . . . . . . 518-873-3317/fax: 518-873-3318
  e-mail: mdiskin@co.essex.ny.us

## Franklin County
Courthouse
355 W Main St
Malone, NY 12953
518-481-1641 or 800-397-8686  Fax: 518-483-0141
Web site: www.franklincony.org

Chairman, County Legislature (D):
  D. Billy Jones . . . . . . . . . . . . . . . . 518-353-1204/fax: 518-481-1639
Vice Chairman, County Legislature (D):
  Gordan Crossman . . . . . . . . . . . . . . . . 518-483-5634/fax: 518-481-1639
Majority Leader, County Legislature (D):
  Guy Smith . . . . . . . . . . . . . . . . . . 518-358-2592/fax: 518-481-1639
Minority Leader, County Legislature (R):
  Paul A Maroun . . . . . . . . . . . . . . . . 518-359-3066/fax: 518-481-1639
  e-mail: wawbeck@aol.com
Clerk, Legislature:
  Gloria Valone . . . . . . . . . . . . . . . . 518-481-1640/fax: 518-481-1639
County Manager:
  Thomas Leitz . . . . . . . . . . . . . . . . . . . . . . . . . . . . . . 518-481-1693

*Offices and agencies generally appear in alphabetical order, except when specific order is requested by listee.*

County Clerk:
Wanda D Murtagh.................518-481-1681/fax: 518-483-9143
County Attorney:
Jonathan J Miller...................518-483-8400/fax: 518-483-2054
District Attorney:
Derek P Champagne ..............518-481-1544/fax: 518-481-1545
e-mail: da@co.franklin.ny.us
Public Defender:
Thomas G Soucia ................................518-481-1624
Sheriff:
Kevin Mulverhill..................................518-483-3304
Director, Emergency Services:
Ricky Provost .....................................518-483-2580
e-mail: rprovost@co.franklin.ny.us
Treasurer:
Byron A Varin..................518-481-1513/fax: 518-483-2326
e-mail: bvarin@co.franklin.ny.us
Conflict Defender:
Lorellei Miller....................................518-481-1593
Assigned Counsel Coordinator:
Jill Dyer..........................................518-481-1423

## Fulton County
County Office Bldg
223 W Main St
Johnstown, NY 12095
518-736-5540  Fax: 518-762-0224
e-mail: fultbos@co.fulton.ny.us
Web site: www.fultoncountyny.gov

Chairman, Board of Supervisors:
WIlliam H. Waldron.............................518-736-5540
County Clerk:
William E Eschler..................518-736-5555/fax: 518-762-9214
District Attorney:
Louise K. Sira.....................518-736-5511/fax: 518-762-2042
Public Defender:
J Gerard McAuliffe, Jr..............518-736-5820/fax: 518-762-0122
Sheriff:
Thomas J Lorey....................518-736-2100/fax: 518-736-2126
Treasurer:
Edgar T Blodgett...................518-736-5580/fax: 518-736-1794
Fire Coordinator & Director, Civil Defense:
Allan Polmateer....................518-736-5858/fax: 518-762-4938
County Historian:
Peter Betz .........................................518-736-5667

## Genesee County
Old Courthouse, 7 Main Street
Batavia, NY 14020
585-344-2550  Fax: 585-344-8582
e-mail: legis@co.genesee.ny.us
Web site: www.co.genesee.ny.us

County Manager:
Jay Gsell....................585-344-2550 x2204/fax: 585-344-8582
e-mail: comanager@co.genesee.ny.us
District Attorney:
Lawrence Friedman ..........585-344-2550 x2250/fax: 585-344-8544
Public Defender:
Gary Horton ................585-344-2550 x2280/fax: 716-344-8553
e-mail: publicdefender@co.genesee.ny.us
Sheriff:
Gary T Maha.......................................585-345-3000
e-mail: sheriff@co.genesee.ny.us
Treasurer:
Scott D German .........................585-344-2550 x2210
e-mail: treas@co.genesee.ny.us

County Historian:
Susan L Conklin ...........................585-344-2550 x2613
e-mail: history@co.genesee.ny.us

## Greene County
411 Main St, 4th Fl
PO Box 467
Catskill, NY 12414
518-719-3270  Fax: 518-719-3793
e-mail: countyadministrator@discovergreene.com
Web site: www.greenegovernment.com

Chairman, County Legislature (R):
Wayne Speenburgh ................518-929-1200/fax: 518-719-3793
County Administrator (Acting):
Shaun S Groden....................518-719-3270/fax: 518-719-3793
e-mail: countyadministrator@discovergreene.com
County Clerk:
Michael Flynn .....................518-719-3255/fax: 518-719-3284
e-mail: countyclerk@discovergreene.com
County Attorney:
Carol D Stevens.....................518-719-3540/fax: 518-719-3790
District Attorney:
Terry J Wilhelm....................518-719-3590/fax: 518-719-3792
e-mail: twilhelm@discovergreene.com
Public Defender:
Angelo F. Scaturro .................518-719-3220/fax: 518-719-3785
e-mail: publicdefender@discovergreene.com
Sheriff:
Gregory R Seeley ..................518-943-3300/fax: 518-943-6832
e-mail: sheriff@discovergreene.com
Director, Emergency Services:
John P Farrell Jr....................518-622-3643/fax: 518-622-0572
e-mail: emergency@discovergreene.com
Treasurer:
Peter Markov.......................................518-719-3530

## Hamilton County
County Courthouse, Rte 8
PO Box 205
Lake Pleasant, NY 12108
518-548-6651  Fax: 518-548-7608
e-mail: hamcosup@klink.net
Web site: www.hamiltoncounty.com

Chairman, Board of Supervisors (R):
William G Farber ...............................518-548-6385
e-mail: chairman@hamiltoncountyny.gov
Deputy Chairman, Board of Supervisors:
Brian Towers....................................518-548-6385
Clerk, Board of Supervisors:
Laura A Abrams ..................518-548-6651/fax: 518-548-7608
e-mail: clerkofboard@hamiltoncountyny.gov
County Clerk:
Jane S. Zarecki....................518-548-7111/fax: 518-548-9740
County Attorney:
Charles Getty Jr....................315-336-3900/fax: 315-336-3902
e-mail: cgetty@gettylaw.com
District Attorney:
Marsha Purdue.....................518-648-5113/fax: 518-648-5724
e-mail: districtattorney@hamiltoncountyny.gov
Sheriff:
Karl G Abrams.....................518-548-3113/fax: 518-548-5704
e-mail: sheriff@hamiltoncountyny.gov
Treasurer:
Beth Hunt.........................518-548-7911/fax: 518-548-4519
e-mail: treasurer@hamiltoncountyny.gov

*Offices and agencies generally appear in alphabetical order, except when specific order is requested by listee.*

## Herkimer County
109 Mary St, Ste 1204
Herkimer, NY 13350
315-867-1108  Fax: 315-867-1109
e-mail: hclegislature@herkimercounty.org
Web site: herkimercounty.org

Chairman, County Legislature (R):
  Vincent Bono.....................315-867-1108/fax: 315-867-1109
Majority Leader (R):
  Patrick E Russell...................315-867-1108/fax: 315-867-1109
Minority Leader (D):
  John L Brezinski...................315-867-1108/fax: 315-867-1109
Clerk, Legislature:
  Carole L LaLonde.................315-867-1108/fax: 315-867-1109
County Administrator:
  James W Wallace, Jr.............315-867-1112/fax: 315-867-1109
County Clerk:
  Sylvia M Rowan.....................................315-867-1129
District Attorney:
  John H Crandall.........315-867-1155/fax: 315-867-1348
Sheriff:
  Christopher P Farber.............315-867-1167/fax: 315-867-1354
Director, Emergency Management:
  Robert Vandawalker...............315-867-1212/fax: 315-867-5873
Treasurer:
  Kim Enea........................315-867-1145/fax: 315-867-1315
  e-mail: kenea@herkimercounty.org

## Jefferson County
County Office Bldg
175 Arsenal St
Watertown, NY 13601
315-785-3075  Fax: 315-785-5070
Web site: www.co.jefferson.ny.us

Chairwoman, Board of Legislators (R):
  Carolyn D Fitzpatrick................................315-785-3075
County Administrator/Budget Officer & Clerk, Board:
  Robert F Hagemann, III..............315-785-3075/fax: 315-785-5070
Deputy County Administrator:
  Michael E Kaskan...................315-785-3075/fax: 315-785-5070
County Clerk:
  Cheryl D Lane....................315-785-3081/fax: 315-785-5145
County Attorney:
  David J Paulsen....................315-785-3088/fax: 315-785-5178
District Attorney:
  Cindy Intschert ...................315-785-3053/fax: 315-785-3371
Public Defender:
  Julie Hutchins ...................315-785-3152/fax: 315-785-5060
Sheriff:
  John P Burns
Director, Fire & Emergency Management (Acting):
  Joseph D Plummer ................................315-786-2654
Treasurer:
  Karen Christie ...................315-785-3055/fax: 315-785-7589

## Kings County (NYC Borough of Brooklyn)
209 Joralemon St
Brooklyn, NY 11201
718-802-3700
Web site: www.brooklyn-usa.org

Borough President (D):
  Marty Markowitz ...............................718-802-3700
  e-mail: askmarty@brooklynbp.nyc.gov
Deputy Borough President:
  Sandra Chapman...............................718-802-3884
  e-mail: ygraham@brooklynbp.nyc.gov

County Clerk:
  Nancy T Sunshine................................347-404-9772
District Attorney:
  Charles J Hynes ................................718-250-2000

## Lewis County
Courthouse
7660 N State St
Lowville, NY 13367
315-377-2000  Fax: 315-376-5445
Web site: www.lewiscountyny.org

Clerk, Board of Legislature:
  Terry Clark ..............315-376-5355/fax: 315-376-5445
County Clerk:
  Douglas P Hanno...................315-376-5333/fax: 315-376-3768
County Attorney:
  Richard Graham..................315-376-5282/fax: 315-376-3857
District Attorney:
  Leanne Moser .....................315-376-5390/fax: 315-376-5873
Public Defender:
  Lewis Defenders PLLC...........315-376-7543/fax: 315-376-8766
Sheriff:
  Michael Carpinelli..................315-376-3511/fax: 315-376-5232
Treasurer:
  Patricia O'Brien....................315-376-5325/fax: 315-376-8552
County Manager:
  David Pendergast..................315-376-5354/fax: 315-376-5445
Fire & Emergency Management:
  James Martin ..............315-376-5305/fax: 315-376-5293
County Historian:
  Lewis County Historical Society ....................315-376-2825

## Livingston County
Government Center
6 Court St, Rm 302
Geneseo, NY 14454
585-243-7030  Fax: 585-335-1701
Web site: www.co.livingston.state.ny.us

Chairman, Board of Supervisors (R):
  James C Merrick...................................585-243-7030
Vice Chairman, Board of Supervisors (R):
  Gary D Moore......................................585-243-7030
Clerk, Board of Supervisors:
  Virginia O Amico....................................585-243-7030
County Administrator:
  Ian M Coyle.........................................585-243-7040
  e-mail: icoyle@co.livingston.ny.us
County Clerk:
  James A Culbertson ................................585-243-7010
County Attorney:
  David J Morris .....................................585-243-7033
District Attorney:
  Gregory J. McCaffrey...............................585-243-7020
Public Defender:
  Marcea Clark Tetamore.............585-243-7028/fax: 585-243-7193
  e-mail: lcpd@co.livingston.ny.us
Emergency Management Services:
  Kevin Niedermaier ..............................585-243-7160
  e-mail: kniedermaier@co.livingston.ny.us
Sheriff:
  John M York ..............585-243-7120/fax: 585-243-7104
  e-mail: lcso@co.livingston.ny.us
Treasurer:
  Carolyn D Taylor................585-243-7050/fax: 585-243-7597
Historian:
  Amie Alden .....................585-243-7955/fax: 585-243-7956
  e-mail: historian@co.livingston.ny.us

*Offices and agencies generally appear in alphabetical order, except when specific order is requested by listee.*

## Madison County

County Office Bldg
138 N Court St
PO Box 635
Wampsville, NY 13163
315-366-2201  Fax: 315-366-2502

Chairman, Board of Supervisors (R):
    John M Becker.....................315-366-2201/fax: 315-366-2502
Clerk, Board of Supervisors:
    Cindy Urtz........................315-366-2201/fax: 315-366-2502
County Clerk:
    Kenneth J Kunkel Jr ..............................315-366-2261
County Attorney:
    S John Campanie...................315-366-2203/fax: 315-366-2502
District Attorney:
    William G Gabor...................315-366-2236/fax: 315-366-2503
Public Defender Director:
    Paul H Hadley ....................315-366-2585/fax: 315-366-2583
Fire Coordinator/Emergency Preparedness:
    Joe DeFrancisco...................315-366-2258/fax: 315-366-2452
Sheriff:
    Allen Riley.......................315-366-2318/fax: 315-366-2286
Treasurer:
    Cindy Edick.......................315-366-2371/fax: 315-366-2705
Public Information Officer:
    Sharon A Driscoll .................................315-366-2788

## Monroe County

County Office Bldg
39 W Main St
Rochester, NY 14614
585-753-1950  Fax: 585-753-1932
Web site: www.monroecounty.gov

President, County Legislature (R):
    Jeffrey R Adair ...................585-753-1950/fax: 585-753-1932
Majority Leader (R):
    William W. Napier ................585-753-1922/fax: 585-753-1960
Minority Leader (D):
    Joe Rittler.......................585-753-1941/fax: 585-753-1946
Clerk, Legislature:
    Cheryl Rozzi......................................585-753-1950
County Executive:
    Maggie Brooks ....................585-753-1000/fax: 585-753-1014
    e-mail: countyexecutive@monroecounty.gov
County Clerk:
    Cheryl Dinolfo....................585-753-1600/fax: 585-753-1624
    e-mail: mcclerk@monroecounty.gov
District Attorney:
    Sandra Doorley ...................585-753-4500/fax: 585-753-4576
    e-mail: districtattorney@monroecounty.gov
Sheriff:
    Patrick M O'Flynn.................585-753-4178/fax: 585-753-4524
Public Defender:
    Tim Donaher ......................585-753-4210/fax: 585-753-4234
    e-mail: mcpublicdefender@monroecounty.gov
Chief Financial Officer:
    Robert Franklin ..................585-753-1157/fax: 585-753-1133
    e-mail: mcfinance@monroecounty.gov
Director, Communications:
    Justin Feasel.....................585-753-1080/fax: 585 753-1068
    e-mail: communications@monroecounty.gov
County Historian:
    Carolyn Vacca.....................585-385-8244/fax: 585-428-8353

## Montgomery County

County Annex Bldg
PO Box 1500
Fonda, NY 12068-1500
518-853-4304  Fax: 518-853-8220
Web site: www.co.montgomery.ny.us

Chairman, Board of Supervisors:
    John W. Thayer....................518-853-4304/fax: 518-853-8220
Clerk, Board of Supervisors:
    Robin Loske.......................518-853-4304/fax: 518-853-8220
County Clerk:
    Helen A Bartone ..................518-853-8111/fax: 518-853-8171
County Attorney:
    Douglas E Landon..................518-843-1300/fax: 518-842-5331
District Attorney:
    James E Conboy ...................518-853-8250/fax: 518-853-8212
Public Defender:
    William Martuscello ..............518-853-8305/fax: 518-853-8308
Sheriff:
    Michael J Amato ..................518-853-5500/fax: 518-853-4096
Director, Emergency Management/Fire Coordinator:
    Adam Schwabrow ...................518-853-4011/fax: 518-853-4714
Treasurer:
    Shawn J Bowerman..................518-853-8175/fax: 518-853-8344
County Historian:
    Kelly A. Farquhar .................518-853-8187/fax: 518-853-8392

## Nassau County

1550 Franklin Avenue
Mineola, NY 11501
516-571-3000 or 516-571-6200  Fax: 516-739-2636
Web site: www.nassaucountyny.gov

Presiding Officer of the Legislature (D):
    Peter J Schmitt ..................................516-571-6212
Deputy Presiding Officer of the Legislature (R):
    John J Ciotti ....................................516-571-6203
Minority Leader (R):
    Diane Yatauro ....................516-571-6218/fax: 516-571-6158
Clerk, Legislature:
    William J Muller..................................516-571-4252
County Executive:
    Edward P Mangano..................................516-571-3131
County Clerk:
    Maureen O'Connell ................................516-571-2664
County Attorney:
    John Ciampoli.....................................516-571-3056
District Attorney:
    Kathleen M Rice...................................516-571-3800
    e-mail: nassauda@nassauda.org
Emergency Management Commissioner:
    James J Callahan II...............................516-573-0636
Police Commissioner:
    Thomas V. Dale ...................................516-573-8800
Comptroller:
    George Maragos ...................................516-571-2386
    e-mail: nccomptroller@nassaucountyny.gov
Treasurer:
    John A Mastromarino...............................516-571-2090

## New York County (NYC Borough of Manhattan)

Municipal Bldg
One Centre St, 19th Fl
New York, NY 10007
212-669-8300  Fax: 212-669-4305
Web site: www.mbpo.org

*Offices and agencies generally appear in alphabetical order, except when specific order is requested by listee.*

Borough President:
Scott M Stringer ............................212-669-8300
e-mail: bp@manhattanbp.org
County Clerk:
Norman Goodman..............................646-386-5955
District Attorney:
Cyrus Vance, Jr. ...........................212-335-9000
Public Advocate:
Betsy Gotbaum ..................212-669-7200/fax: 212-669-4091

## Niagara County
County Courthouse
175 Hawley Street
1st Floor
Lockport, NY 14094
716-439-7000  Fax: 716-439-7124
Web site: www.niagaracounty.com

Chairman, County Legislature (R):
William L Ross...............................716-731-5949
e-mail: william.ross@niagaracounty.com
Majority Leader (R):
Richard Updegrove............................716-434-2140
e-mail: richard.updegrove@niagaracounty.com
Minority Leader (D):
Dennis F Virtuoso............................716-284-1582
e-mail: dennis.virtuoso@niagaracounty.com
Clerk, Legislature:
Mary Jo Tamburlin ...............716-439-7177/fax: 716-439-7124
County Manager:
Jeffrey M Glatz ................716-439-7006/fax: 716-439-7212
e-mail: jeff.glatz@niagaracounty.com
County Clerk:
Wayne F Jagow ..................716-439-7022/fax: 716-439-7035
e-mail: niagaracountyclerk@niagaracounty.com
County Attorney:
Claude A Joerg ................716-439-7105/fax: 716-439-7114
e-mail: claude.joerg@niagaracounty.com
District Attorney:
Michael J Violante............716-439-7085/fax: 716-439-7102
e-mail: ncda@niagaracounty.com
Public Defender:
David J Farrugia ...........................716-439-7071
Sheriff:
James R Voutour ...............716-438-3393/fax: 716-438-3357
Emergency Services, Acting Director:
John F Cecula III
fax: 716-438-3173
Treasurer:
Kyle R Andrews .................716-439-7018/fax: 716-439-7021

## Oneida County
County Office Bldg
800 Park Ave
Utica, NY 13501
315-798-5900  Fax: 315-798-5924
Web site: www.co.oneida.ny.us or www.ocgov.net

Chairman, County Legislature (R):
Gerald J Fiorini............................315-798-5900
e-mail: gfiorini@ocgov.net
Majority Leader (R):
David J Wood...............................315-337-1989
e-mail: dwood@ocgov.net
Minority Leader (D):
Patricia A Hudak...........................315-339-9960
e-mail: phudak@ocgov.net
County Executive:
Anthony J Picente Jr .............315-798-5800/fax: 315-798-2390
e-mail: ce@ocgov.net

County Clerk:
Sandra J DePerno ...........................315-798-5794
e-mail: countyclerk@ocgov.net
County Attorney:
Gregory J. Amoroso, Esq............315-798-5910/fax: 315-798-5603
e-mail: countyattorney@ocgov.net
District Attorney:
Scott D McNamara...............315-798-5766/fax: 315-798-5582
e-mail: smcnamara@ocgov.net
Public Defender-Criminal Division:
Frank J Nebush Jr ..............315-798-5870/fax: 315-734-0364
e-mail: pubdef@ocgov.net
Public Defender-Civil Division:
Frank J Furno..................315-266-6100/fax: 315-266-6105
e-mail: pdcivil@ocgov.net
Sheriff:
Rob M. Maciol.................315-738-7804/fax: 315-765-2205
Finance Commissioner:
Anthony R Carvelli..........................315-798-5750

## Onondaga County
401 Montgomery Street
Room 407
Syracuse, NY 13202
315-435-2070  Fax: 315-435-8434
Web site: www.ongov.net

Chairman, County Legislature (R):
J. Ryan McMahon II ...............315-435-2070/fax: 315-435-8434
County Executive:
Joanne M Mahoney.................315-435-3516/fax: 315-435-8582
Clerk, Legislature:
Deborah L Maturo.................315-435-2070/fax: 315-435-8434
e-mail: debbiematuro@ongov.net
County Clerk:
Sandra A. Schepp ................315-435-2227/fax: 315-435-2229
County Attorney:
Gordon J Cuffy
District Attorney:
William J Fitzpatrick.......................315-435-2470
Emergency Management Director:
Peter P Alberti ...............315-435-2525/fax: 315-435-3309
e-mail: emweb01@ongov.net
Sheriff:
Kevin E Walsh .............................315-435-3044
Commissioner:
Kevin Wisely .............................315-435-3044
Comptroller:
Robert E Antonacci ...............315-435-2130/fax: 315-435-2250
e-mail: bobantonacci@ongov.net
Chief Fiscal Officer:
Steven Morgan...................315-435-2426/fax: 315-435-2421

## Ontario County
Ontario Co Municipal Bldg
20 Ontario St
1st Fl Mezzanine
Canandaigua, NY 14424
585-396-4447  Fax: 585-396-8818
e-mail: bos@co.ontario.ny.us
Web site: www.co.ontario.ny.us

Chairman, Board of Supervisors (R):
Theodore Fafinski .................585-396-4447/fax: 585-396-8818
Vice Chairman, Board of Supervisors (R):
Wayne F Houseman ...........................585-396-4447
Clerk, Board of Supervisors:
Karen R DeMay....................585-396-4447/fax: 585-396-8818
e-mail: karen.demay@co.ontario.ny.us

*Offices and agencies generally appear in alphabetical order, except when specific order is requested by listee.*

County Administrator:
John E. Garvey . . . . . . . . . . . . . . . . . . . . . . . . . . . . . .585-396-4400
e-mail: county.administrator@co.ontario.ny.us
County Clerk:
Matthew J. Hoose . . . . . . . . . . . . . . . . . . . . . . . . . . . . .585-396-4200
Human Resources Director:
Mary A. Krause . . . . . . . . . . . . . . . . . . . .585-396-4465 or 315-719-0321
District Attorney:
R Michael Tantillo. . . . . . . . . . . . . . . . .585-396-4010/fax: 585-396-4860
e-mail: michael.tantillo@co.ontario.ny.us
Emergency Management Director:
Jeffrey R Harloff . . . . . . . . . . . . . . . . . . .585-396-4310/fax: 585-396-4583
Public Works Commissioner:
Bill Wright. . . . . . . . . . . . . . . . . . . . . . .585-396-4000/fax: 585-396-4283

## Orange County
County Government Center
255 Main St
Goshen, NY 10924
845-291-4800
e-mail: legislature@co.orange.ny.us
Web site: www.co.orange.ny.us

Chairman, County Legislature (R):
Michael R Pillmeier . . . . . . . . . . . . . . . . . . . . . . . . . .845-651-7415
Majority Leader (R):
Melissa Bonacic . . . . . . . . . . . . . . . . . . . . . . . . . . . . .845-858-2546
Minority Leader (D):
Jeffrey D Berkman . . . . . . . . . . . . . . . . . . . . . . . . . . .845-342-6813
County Executive:
Edward A Diana . . . . . . . . . . . . . . . . . .845-291-2700/fax: 845-291-2724
County Clerk:
Donna L Benson . . . . . . . . . . . . . . . . .845-291-2690/fax: 845-291-2691
County Attorney:
David L Darwin . . . . . . . . . . . . . . . . . . . . . . . . . . . . . .845-291-3150
District Attorney:
Francis D Phillips . . . . . . . . . . . . . . . . . . . . . . . . . . . .845-291-2050
Emergency Services Commissioner:
Walter C Koury. . . . . . . . . . . . . . . . . . . . . . . . . . . . . .845-615-0400
Sheriff:
Carl E DuBois . . . . . . . . . . . . . . . . . . .845-291-4033/fax: 845-294-1590
Finance Commissioner:
Joel Kleiman . . . . . . . . . . . . . . . . . . . .845-291-2485/fax: 845-291-2516
Historian:
Cornelia W. Bush . . . . . . . . . . . . . . . .845-291-2388/fax: 845-291-2027

## Orleans County
Courthouse Sq
3 South Main St
Albion, NY 14411-1495
585-589-7053  Fax: 585-589-1618
Web site: www.orleansny.com

Chairman, County Legislature (R):
David Callard . . . . . . . . . . . . . . . . . . . . . . . . . . . . . .585-589-7053
Vice Chairman (R):
George Bower. . . . . . . . . . . . . . . . . . . . . . . . . . . . . . .585-589-7053
Clerk, Legislature:
Nadine P Hanlon . . . . . . . . . . . . . . . . .585-589-7053/fax: 585-589-1618
e-mail: hanlonn@orleansny.com
Chief Administrative Officer:
Charles II Nesbitt Jr . . . . . . . . . . . . . . .585-589-7053/fax: 585-589-1618
e-mail: cnesbitt@orleansny.com
County Clerk:
Karen Lake-Maynard. . . . . . . . . . . . . . .585-589-5334/fax: 585-589-0181
e-mail: lakemaynardk@orleansny.com
County Attorney:
David C Schubel . . . . . . . . . . . . . . . . . .585-798-2250/fax: 585-798-0776
e-mail: occoa@orleansny.com

District Attorney:
Joseph V Cardone . . . . . . . . . . . . . . . . .585-590-4130/fax: 585-590-4129
e-mail: da@orleansny.com
Public Defender:
Sanford A Church . . . . . . . . . . . . . . . . .585-589-7335/fax: 585-589-2592
Emergency Management Director:
Paul Wagner . . . . . . . . . . . . . . . . . . . .585-589-4414/fax: 585-589-7671
e-mail: pwagner@orleansny.com
Sheriff:
Scott D Hess . . . . . . . . . . . . . . . . . . . .585-590-4142/fax: 585-590-4178
e-mail: ocsher@orleansny.com
Treasurer:
Susan M Heard . . . . . . . . . . . . . . . . . . .585-589-5353/fax: 585-589-9220
e-mail: sheard@orleansny.com
County Historian:
C W Lattin. . . . . . . . . . . . . . . . . . . . . . . . . . . . . . . . . .585-589-4174

## Oswego County
46 E Bridge St
Oswego, NY 13126
315-349-8230  Fax: 315-349-8237
Web site: www.co.oswego.ny.us

Chairman, County Legislature (R):
Fred Beardsley. . . . . . . . . . . . . . . . . . . .315-349-8230/fax: 315-349-8237
Majority Leader (R):
James Oldenburg . . . . . . . . . . . . . . . . . .315-343-3744/fax: 315-668-3638
Minority Leader (D):
Michael Kunzwiler . . . . . . . . . . . . . . . . . . . . . . . . . . .315-343-8358
e-mail: mikekunzwiler@twcny.rr.com
Clerk, Legislature:
Wendy Falls. . . . . . . . . . . . . . . . . . . . .315-349-8230/fax: 315-349-8237
County Administrator:
Philip R Church. . . . . . . . . . . . . . . . . . .315-349-8235/fax: 315-349-8237
e-mail: pchurch@oswegocounty.com
County Clerk:
Michael C. Backus . . . . . . . . . . . . . . . . .315-349-8621/fax: 315-349-8383
County Attorney:
Richard C Mitchell . . . . . . . . . . . . . . . . . . . . . . . . . . .315-349-8296
e-mail: rich@oswegocounty.com
District Attorney/Coroner:
Gregory S. Oakes. . . . . . . . . . . . . . . . . .315-349-3200/fax: 315-349-3212
Treasurer:
Fred Beardsley. . . . . . . . . . . . . . . . . . . .315-349-8393/fax: 315-349-8255
Sheriff:
Reuel A Todd . . . . . . . . . . . . . . . . . . . .315-349-3302/fax: 315-349-3303
e-mail: mtodd@oswegocounty.com
Vice Chairman:
Kevin Gardner . . . . . . . . . . . . . . . . . . . .315-349-8230/fax: 315-349-8237
e-mail: mtodd@oswegocounty.com

## Otsego County
County Office Bldg
197 Main St
Cooperstown, NY 13326-1129
607-547-4202  Fax: 607-547-4260
Web site: www.otsegocounty.com

Chairman, Board of Representatives (R):
Kathleen Clark . . . . . . . . . . . . . . . . . . . . . . . . . . . . . .607-988-7844
Vice Chairman, Board of Representatives (R):
James V Johnson. . . . . . . . . . . . . . . . . . . . . . . . . . . . .607-547-2095
e-mail: johnsonjv@otsegocounty.com
Clerk, Board of Representatives:
Carol McGovern . . . . . . . . . . . . . . . . . .607-547-4202/fax: 607-547-4260
e-mail: mcgovern@otsegocounty.com
County Clerk:
Kathy Sinnott Gardner. . . . . . . . . . . . . .607-547-4276/fax: 607-547-7544
e-mail: gardnerk@otsegocounty.com

*Offices and agencies generally appear in alphabetical order, except when specific order is requested by listee.*

State & Local
Government
Public Information

County Attorney:
  Ellen Coccoma.....................607-547-4208/fax: 607-547-7572
  e-mail: coccomae@otsegocounty.com
District Attorney:
  John M Muehl....................607-547-4249/fax: 607-547-4373
Public Defender:
  Richard A Rothermel........................607-432-7410
Sheriff:
  Richard Devlin Jr..............607-547-4271 or 607-547-4273
  fax: 607-547-6413
  e-mail: sheriff@otsegocounty.com
Coordinator, Emergency Services:
  Kevin N. Ritton.................................607-547-4227
Treasurer:
  Dan Crowell.....................607-547-4235/fax: 607-547-7579
  e-mail: crowelld@otsegocounty.com
County Historian:
  Vacant.......................................607-397-9705

## Putnam County
40 Gleneida Avenue
Carmel, NY 10512
845-225-8690 Fax: 845-225-0715
e-mail: putcoleg@putnamcountyny.com
Web site: www.putnamcountyny.com

Chairman, County Legislature (R):
  Richard T. Othmer, Jr...............845-808-1020/fax: 845-225-0715
Deputy Chair, County Legislature (R):
  Anthony DiCarlo...................845-808-1020/fax: 845-225-0715
Clerk, Legislature:
  Diane Schonfeld..................845-808-1020/fax: 845-808-1933
Legislative Counsel:
  Clement Van Ross..................845-808-1020/fax: 845-808-1933
County Executive:
  Mary Ellen Odell.................845-808-1001/fax: 845-808-1901
County Clerk:
  Dennis J Sant...............................845-808-1142
County Attorney:
  Jennifer S Bumgarner.......................845-228-0480
District Attorney:
  Adam Levy...................................845-808-1050
Emergency Services Bureau Commissioner:
  Adam B. Stiebeling.............845-808-4000/fax: 845-808-4010
Sheriff:
  Donald Blaine Smith..............845-225-4300/fax: 845-225-4399
Finance Commissioner:
  William J Carlin, Jr...............845-808-1075 or 845-808-1910
  fax: 845-225-8290
County Historian:
  Vacant.....................845-808-1420/fax: 845-278-4865

## Queens County (NYC Borough of Queens)
120-55 Queens Blvd
Kew Gardens, NY 11424
718-286-3000 Fax: 718-286-2876
e-mail: info@queensbp.org
Web site: www.queensbp.org

Borough President:
  Helen M Marshall..................718-286-3000/fax: 718-286-2876
Director of Community Boards:
  Barry Grodenchik.........................718-286-2900
Public Information Officer/Press Office:
  Daniel Andrews..........................718-286-2640
County Clerk:
  Gloria D'Amico.............718-298-0605 or 718-520-3137
District Attorney:
  Richard A Brown...........................718-286-6000

Communications Director:
  Kevin R Ryan
Public Administrator:
  Lois M Rosenblatt.................718-526-5037 or 718-520-3710
  fax: 718-526-5043
  e-mail: mail@queenscountypa.com
Counsel:
  Gerard J Sweeney.................718-459-9000/fax: 718-459-3163

## Rensselaer County
Ned Pattison Government Center
1600 Seventh Avenue
Troy, NY 12180
518-270-2880 Fax: 518-270-2983
Web site: www.rensco.com or www.rensselaercounty.org

Chairperson, County Legislature (R):
  Martin T Reid.....................518-270-2880/fax: 518-270-2983
Vice Chairman (R):
  Stan Brownell.....................518-270-2880/fax: 518-270-2983
Vice Chairman-Finance (R):
  Philip Danaher....................518-270-2880/fax: 518-270-2983
Majority Leader (C):
  Kenneth H Herrington..............518-270-2880/fax: 518-270-2983
  e-mail: kherrington@rensco.com
Minority Leader (D):
  Peter Grimm.......................518-270-2890/fax: 518-270-2975
Clerk, Legislature:
  Janèt Marra
County Executive:
  Kathleen M Jimino.................518-270-2900/fax: 518-270-2961
County Clerk:
  Frank Merola......................518-270-4080/fax: 518-271-7998
County Attorney:
  Stephen A Pechenik.................518-270-2950/fax: 518-270-2954
District Attorney:
  Richard J McNally Jr..........................518-270-4040
Public Defender:
  Jerome K Frost...............................518-270-4030
Sheriff:
  Jack Mahar........................518-266-1900/fax: 518-270-5447
Chief Fiscal Officer:
  Michael J Slawson.................518-270-2750/fax: 518-270-2728

## Richmond County (NYC Borough of Staten Island)
Borough Hall
120 Borough Hall
Staten Island, NY 10301
718-816-2000 Fax: 718-876-2026
Web site: www.statenislandusa.com

Borough President:
  James P Molinaro...........................718-816-2000
County Clerk:
  Stephen J Fiala............................718-675-7700
District Attorney:
  Daniel M Donovan Jr.......................718-876-6300
  e-mail: info@rcda.nyc.gov

## Rockland County
County Office Bldg
11 New Hempstead Rd
New City, NY 10956
845-638-5100 Fax: 845-638-5675
Web site: rocklandgov.com

Chairwoman, County Legislature (D):
  Harriet D Cornell..................................845-638-5269
  e-mail: cornellh@co.rockland.ny.us

*Offices and agencies generally appear in alphabetical order, except when specific order is requested by listee.*

Majority Leader (D):
Jay Hood, Jr. . . . . . . . . . . . . . . . . . . . . . . . . .845-638-5751
Minority Leader (R):
Christopher J. Carey . . . . . . . . . . . . . . . . . . . . . . .845-638-5100
Clerk, Legislature:
Laurence O Toole . . . . . . . . . . . . . . . .845-638-5100/fax: 845-638-5675
e-mail: toolel@co.rockland.ny.us
County Executive:
C Scott Vanderhoef. . . . . . . . . . . . . . . . . . . . . . . .845-638-5122
County Clerk:
Paul Piperato . . . . . . . . . . . . . . . . .845-638-5070/fax: 845-638-5647
e-mail: rocklandcountyclerk@co.rockland.ny.us
Director Veterans Services:
Gerald Donnellan . . . . . . . . . . . . . .845-638-5244/fax: 845-638-5730
District Attorney:
Thomas P Zugibe. . . . . . . . . . . . . . .845-638-5001/fax: 845-638-5298
Public Defender:
James D Licata . . . . . . . . . . . . . . . . . . . . . . . . . .845-638-5660
e-mail: licataj@co.rockland.ny.us
Sheriff:
Louis Falco, III . . . . . . . . . . . . . . . .845-638-5400/fax: 845-638-5035
Finance/Budget Commissioner:
Stephen F. DeGroat. . . . . . . . . . . . . . . . . . . . . . . .845-638-5131
e-mail: kopfc@co.rockland.ny.us

## Saratoga County
County Municipal Center
40 McMaster St
Ballston Spa, NY 12020
518-884-4742  Fax: 518-884-4723
Web site: www.saratogacountyny.gov

Chairman, Board of Supervisors (R):
Alan Grattidge
County Administrator:
Spencer P Hellwig. . . . . . . . . . . . . .518-884-4742/fax: 518-884-4723
Clerk, Board of Supervisors:
Pamela A Hargrave . . . . . . . . . . . . .518-885-2240/fax: 518-884-4771
Deputy County Clerk:
Charles Foehser, II. . . . . . . . . . . . . .518-885-2213/fax: 518-884-4726
County Attorney:
Stephen M Dorsey. . . . . . . . . . . . . .518-884-4770/fax: 518-884-4720
District Attorney:
James A Murphy, III . . . . . . . . . . . . .518-885-2263/fax: 518-884-8627
Public Defender:
John H Ciulla Jr. . . . . . . . . . . . . . . .518-884-4795/fax: 518-884-4789
Veterans Services:
Felipe Moon. . . . . . . . . . . . . . . . . .518-884-4115/fax: 518-884-4290
County Treasurer:
Sam Pitcheralle . . . . . . . . . . . . . . . .518-884-4724/fax: 518-884-4775

## Schenectady County
County Legislature
620 State St
Schenectady, NY 12305
518-388-4280  Fax: 518-388-4591
Web site: www.schenectadycounty.com

Chairperson, County Legislature (D):
Judith Dagostino . . . . . . . . . . . . . .518-388-4280/fax: 518-388-4591
Majority Leader (D):
Gary Hughes . . . . . . . . . . . . . . . . .518-388-4280/fax: 518-388-4591
Minority Leader (R):
James Buhrmaster . . . . . . . . . . . . . .518-388-4280/fax: 518-388-4591
Clerk, Legislature:
Goeffrey T Hall . . . . . . . . . . . . . . . .518-388-4280/fax: 518-388-4591
County Clerk:
John J Woodward . . . . . . . . . . . . . .518-388-4220/fax: 518-388-4224
District Attorney:
Robert M Carney . . . . . . . . . . . . . . . . . . . . . . . .518-388-4364

Public Defender:
Mark J Caruso. . . . . . . . . . . . . . . . . . . . . . . . . .518-386-2266
Sheriff:
Dominic A. D'Agostino . . . . . . . . . . .518-388-4300/fax: 518-388-4593
Director, Emergency Management:
Mark LaViolette . . . . . . . . . . . . . . . . . . . .518-370-3113 ext. 1
Deputy Director, Emergency Management:
Kyle Rudolph . . . . . . . . . . . . . . . . . . . . . .518-370-3113 ext. 5

## Schoharie County
Cty Office Bldg
284 Main Street, Rm 365
PO Box 429
Schoharie, NY 12157
518-295-8347  Fax: 518-295-8482
Web site: www.schohariecounty-ny.gov

Chairman, Board of Supervisors (R):
Philip Skowfoe, Jr. . . . . . . . . . . . . .518-827-4896/fax: 518-827-7972
Clerk, Board of Supervisors:
Sheryl Largeteau . . . . . . . . . . . . . .518-295-8421/fax: 518-295-8482
e-mail: millerk@co.schoharie.ny.us
County Clerk:
M Indica Jaycox . . . . . . . . . . . . . . .518-295-8316/fax: 518-295-8338
County Attorney:
Michael West. . . . . . . . . . . . . . . . .518-296-8844/fax: 518-296-8855
District Attorney:
James L Sacket . . . . . . . . . . . . . . . .518-295-2272/fax: 518-295-2273
Sheriff:
Anthony F Desmond . . . . . . . . . . . .518-295-2266/fax: 518-295-2267
Director, Emergency Management:
Kevin Neary. . . . . . . . . . . . . . . . . .518-295-2276/fax: 518-296-8632
Treasurer:
William E Cherry. . . . . . . . . . . . . . .518-295-8386/fax: 518-295-8364
Administrator Legal Defense:
Raynor B Duncombe. . . . . . . . . . . . .518-295-7515/fax: 518-295-7519

## Schuyler County
County Bldg
105 Ninth St, Unit 6
Watkins Glen, NY 14891
607-535-8100  Fax: 607-535-8109
e-mail: legislature@co.schuyler.ny.us
Web site: www.schuylercounty.us

Chairman, County Legislature (R):
Dennis A Fagan . . . . . . . . . . . . . . . . . . . . . . . .607-535-8100
Clerk, Legislature:
Stacey B Husted . . . . . . . . . . . . . . . . . . . . . . . .607-535-8100
County Clerk:
Linda M Compton . . . . . . . . . . . . . .607-535-8133/fax: 607-535-8130
e-mail: lcompton@co.schuyler.ny.us
County Administrator:
Timothy M O'Hearn . . . . . . . . . . . . .607-535-8106/fax: 607-535-8108
e-mail: tohearn@co.schuyler.ny.us
District Attorney:
Joseph G Fazzary. . . . . . . . . . . . . . .607-535-8383/fax: 607-535-8385
Public Defender:
Wesley A. Rose, Esq. . . . . . . . . . . . .607-535-6400/fax: 607-535-6404
Sheriff:
William E Yessman Jr. . . . . . . . . . . . .607-535-8222/fax: 607-535-8216
e-mail: wyessman@co.schuyler.ny.us
Treasurer:
Gary Whyman . . . . . . . . . . . . . . . .607-535-8181/fax: 607-535-8187
County Historian:
Marion M. Boyce . . . . . . . . . . . . . . . . . . . . . . . .607-535-4730

*Offices and agencies generally appear in alphabetical order, except when specific order is requested by listee.*

## Seneca County

County Office Bldg
1 DiPronio Dr
Waterloo, NY 13165
315-539-1700  Fax: 315-539-0207
Web site: www.co.seneca.ny.us

Chairman, Board of Supervisors (R):
  Robert W Hayssen..................315-539-1700/fax: 315-539-0207
Majority Leader (R):
  Robert Shipley.....................315-539-1700/fax: 315-539-0207
  e-mail: rshipley@co.seneca.ny.us
Minority Leader (D):
  Cindy Garlick Lorenzetti............315-539-1700/fax: 315-539-0207
  e-mail: cindyl@rochester.rr.com
Clerk, Board of Supervisors:
  Margaret E Li.....................315-539-1700/fax: 315-539-0207
County Clerk:
  Christina L Lotz ...........................315-539-1771
  e-mail: clotz@co.seneca.ny.us
County Manager:
  C. Mitchell Rowe...............315-539-1701/fax: 315-539-0207
County Attorney:
  Frank R Fisher.................315-539-1989/fax: 315-539-1657
  e-mail: ffisher@co.seneca.ny.us
District Attorney:
  Barry Porsch .....................315-539-1300/fax: 315-539-0531
Sheriff:
  Jack S Stenberg ..................315-220-3200/fax: 315-220-3478
Public Defender:
  Michael J Mirras............................315-568-4975
Treasurer:
  Nicholas A Sciotti .................315-539-1735/fax: 315-539-1731
  e-mail: nsciotti@co.seneca.ny.us
County Historian:
  Walter Gable.................................315-539-1785
  e-mail: wgable@co.seneca.ny.us

## St Lawrence County

County Courthouse
48 Court St
Canton, NY 13617
315-379-2276  Fax: 315-379-2463
Web site: www.co.st-lawrence.ny.us

Chair, Board of Legislators (D):
  Jonathan S. Putney ................315-379-2276/fax: 315-379-2463
  e-mail: jputney@stlawco.org
Vice Chair, Board of Legislators (R):
  Donald Peck.....................315-379-2276/fax: 315-379-2463
  e-mail: peck_donald@yahoo.com
County Administrator:
  Karen St Hilaire...................315-379-2276/fax: 315-379-2463
  e-mail: ksth@co.st-lawrence.ny.us
County Clerk:
  MaryLou Rupp ....................315-379-2237/fax: 315-379-2302
Dept Head, County Attorney:
  Michael Crowe·...................315-379-2269/fax: 315-379-2254
District Attorney:
  Nicole M Duve ...................315-379-2225/fax: 315-379-2301
Public Defender:
  Stephen D. Button .................315-379-2115/fax: 315-386-8241
Emergency Services, Dept Head:
  Joseph M. Gilbert ................315-379-2240/fax: 315-379-0681
  e-mail: thowie@co.st-lawrence.ny.us
Sheriff (Department Head):
  Kevin M Wells ...................315-379-2222/fax: 315-379-0335
  e-mail: kwells@stlawco.org

Treasurer:
  Kevin Felt .....................315-386-2234/fax: 315-379-5274
  e-mail: kfelt@co.st-lawrence.ny.us

## Steuben County

County Office Bldg
3 East Pulteney Square
Bath, NY 14810
607-776-9631  Fax: 607-776-6926
Web site: www.steubencony.org

Chairman, County Legislature (R):
  Joseph J Hauryski........................607-664-2247
Vice Chair, County Legislature (R):
  Patrick McAllister.......................607-664-2247
Clerk, County Legislature:
  Brenda Mori...............607-664-2247/fax: 607-664-2282
County Administrator:
  Mark R Alger...............607-664-2245/fax: 607-664-2282
County Clerk:
  Judith M Hunter ........................607-664-2563
District Attorney:
  Brooks Baker ...........................607-664-2270
Public Defender:
  Philip J. Roche, Esq. ..............607-664-2413/fax: 607-664-2410
Acting Director:
  Timothy D. Marshall.......................607-664-2700
Sheriff:
  David V. Cole.................607-622-3901 or 800-724-7777
Treasurer:
  Patrick F Donnelly................607-664-2488/fax: 607-664-2188
  e-mail: treasurer@co.steuben.ny.us
Historian:
  Twila O'Dell ...........................607-664-2199
  e-mail: historian@co.steuben.ny.us

## Suffolk County

William H Rogers Building
725 Veterans Memorial Hwy
North County Complex
Smithtown, NY 11787
631-853-4070  Fax: 631-853-4899
Web site: www.suffolkcountyny.gov

Presiding Officer, County Legislature (D):
  DuWayne Gregory.................631-854-1111/fax: 631-854-1114
  e-mail: duwayne.gregory@suffolkcountyny.gov
Deputy Presiding Officer, County Legislature (D):
  Rob Calarco.......................631-854-1400/fax: 631-854-1403
Majority Leader (D):
  Kara Hahn ......................631-854-1650/fax: 631-854-1653
Minority Leader (R):
  Kevin McCaffrey..................631-854-1100/fax: 631-854-1103
  e-mail: kevin.mccaffrey@suffolkcountyny.gov
Clerk, County Legislature:
  Jason Richberg ..................631-853-4070/fax: 631-853-4899
  e-mail: jason.richberg@suffolkcountyny.gov
County Executive:
  Steven Bellone ...........................631-853-4000
  e-mail: county.executive@suffolkcountyny.gov
County Clerk:
  Judith A Pascale ...........................631-852-2000
  e-mail: countyclerk@suffolkcountyny.gov
County Attorney:
  Dennis M Brown ..................631-853-4049/fax: 631-853-5169
District Attorney:
  Thomas J Spota...........................631-853-4161
  e-mail: infoda@suffolkcountyny.gov

---

*Offices and agencies generally appear in alphabetical order, except when specific order is requested by listee.*

Director, Emergency Management:
 Edward C Schneyer . . . . . . . . . . . . . . . . .631-852-4900/fax: 631-852-4922
  e-mail: scdfres@suffolkcountyny.gov
Sheriff:
 Vincent F DeMarco . . . . . . . . . . . . . . . . . . . . . . . . . . . . .631-852-2200
  e-mail: suffolk_sheriff@suffolkcountyny.gov
Comptroller:
 John M Kennedy Jr . . . . . . . . . . . . . . . . . . . . . . . . . . . . .631-853-5040
  e-mail: comptroller@suffolkcountyny.gov
Treasurer:
 Barry S Paul . . . . . . . . . . . . . . . . . . . . .631-852-1500/fax: 631-852-1507
  e-mail: treasurer@suffolkcountyny.gov

## Sullivan County
County Gov't Center
100 North St
PO Box 5012
Monticello, NY 12701
845-807-0435  Fax: 845-807-0447
e-mail: info@co.sullivan.ny.us
Web site: www.co.sullivan.ny.us

Chairman (D):
 Scott B Samuelson . . . . . . . . . . . . . . . . . . . . . . . . . . . . .845-807-0443
  e-mail: scott.samuelson@co.sullivan.ny.us
Vice-Chairman (D):
 Eugene L. Benson. . . . . . . . . . . . . . . . . . . . . . . . . . . . . .845-807-0439
  e-mail: gene.benson@co.sullivan.ny.us
Majority Leader (D):
 Kathleen LaBuda . . . . . . . . . . . . . . . . . . . . . . . . . . . . . .845-807-0442
  e-mail: kathy.labuda@co.sullivan.ny.us
Minority Leader (R):
 Alan J. Sorenson . . . . . . . . . . . . . . . . . . . . . . . . . . . . . .845-807-0444
  e-mail: alan.sorensen@co.sullivan.ny.us
Acting County Manager:
 Joshua Potosek . . . . . . . . . . . . . . . . .845-807-0450/fax: 845-807-0460
County Clerk:
 Daniel Briggs. . . . . . . . . . . . . . . . . . . .845-807-0411/fax: 845-807-0434
County Attorney:
 Sam Yasgur . . . . . . . . . . . . . . . . . . . . .845-807-0560/fax: 845-807-0574
District Attorney:
 James R Farrell . . . . . . . . . . . . . . . . . .845-794-3344/fax: 845-794-3646
Public Safety Commissioner:
 Richard A Martinkovic. . . . . . . . . . . . . . . . . . . . . . . . . . .845-807-0512
Sheriff:
 Michael A Schiff. . . . . . . . . . . . . . . . . .845-794-7100/fax: 845-794-7100
County Treasurer:
 Ira J Cohen. . . . . . . . . . . . . . . . . . . . . .845-807-0200/fax: 845-807-0220
  e-mail: ira.cohen@co.sullivan.ny.us

## Tioga County
56 Main St
Owego, NY 13827
607-687-8200 or 607-687-8240  Fax: 607-687-8232
Web site: www.tiogacountyny.com

Chair, County Legislature (R):
 Martha Sauerbrey . . . . . . . . . . . . . . . .607-687-2911/fax: 607-687-8232
  e-mail: sauerbreym@co.tioga.ny.us
Clerk, County Legislature:
 Maureen L Dougherty . . . . . . . . . . . . . .607-687-8235/fax: 607-687-8232
  e-mail: doughertym@co.tioga.ny.us
County Clerk:
 Andrea Klett . . . . . . . . . . . . . . . . . . . . .607-687-8660/fax: 607-687-8686
County Attorney:
 Judith M Quigley. . . . . . . . . . . . . . . . . .607-687-8253/fax: 607-223-7003
  e-mail: quigleyj@co.tioga.ny.us
District Attorney:
 Kirk Martin . . . . . . . . . . . . . . . . . . . . . . . . . . . . . . . . . . .607-687-8650

Public Defender:
 George C Awad Jr. . . . . . . . . . . . . . . . . . . . . . . . . . . . . . .607-687-1000
Director, Emergency Management:
 Richard LeCount. . . . . . . . . . . . . . . . . . . . . . . . . . . . . . . .607-687-2023
Sheriff:
 Gary W Howard . . . . . . . . . . . . . . . . . . . . . . . . . . . . . . . .607-687-1010
Treasurer:
 James P McFadden . . . . . . . . . . . . . . .607-687-8670/fax: 607-223-7035
  e-mail: mcfaddenj@co.tioga.ny.us

## Tompkins County
125 E Court St
Ithaca, NY 14850
607-274-5551  Fax: 607-274-5558

Chairman, County Legislature (D):
 Martha Robertson . . . . . . . . . . . . . . . .607-274-5434/fax: 607-274-5430
  e-mail: mrobertson@tompkins-co.org
County Administrator:
 Joe Mareane. . . . . . . . . . . . . . . . . . . . .607-274-5551/fax: 607-274-5558
County Clerk:
 Aurora R Valenti . . . . . . . . . . . . . . . . . .607-274-5431/fax: 607-274-5445
  e-mail: countyclerkmail@tompkins-co.org
County Attorney:
 Jonathan Wood . . . . . . . . . . . . . . . . . .607-274-5546/fax: 607-274-5547
  e-mail: countyattorney@tompkins-co.org
District Attorney:
 Gwen Wilkinson . . . . . . . . . . . . . . . . . .607-274-5461/fax: 607-274-5429
Sheriff:
 Kenneth W Lansing. . . . . . . . . . . . . . . .607-257-1345/fax: 607-266-5436
Finance Director:
 David Squires . . . . . . . . . . . . . . . . . . . . . . . . . . . . . . . . .607-274-5545
  e-mail: finance@tompkins-co.org
Historian:
 Vacant. . . . . . . . . . . . . . . . . . . . . . . . . . . . . . . . . . . . . . .607-274-5434
  e-mail: historian@tompkins-co.org

## Ulster County
County Office Building
244 Fair Street
6th Floor
Kingston, NY 12401
845-340-3800  Fax: 845-334-5724
e-mail: exec@co.ulster.ny.us
Web site: www.ulstercountyny.gov

Chairman, County Legislature (D):
 Terry L Bernardo. . . . . . . . . . . . . . . . . .845-340-3900/fax: 845-340-3651
Majority Leader (D):
 Kenneth J. Ronk, Jr. . . . . . . . . . . . . . . . . . . . . . . . . . . . . .845-340-3900
Minority Leader (R):
 David B. Donaldson . . . . . . . . . . . . . . . . . . . . . . . . . . . . .845-340-3900
Clerk of the County Legislature:
 Victoria Fabella. . . . . . . . . . . . . . . . . . .845-340-3900/fax: 845-340-3651
County Executive:
 Michael P Hein . . . . . . . . . . . . . . . . . . .845-340-3800/fax: 845-334-5724
  e-mail: exec@co.ulster.ny.us
County Clerk:
 Nina Postupack . . . . . . . . . . . . . . . . . . .845-340-3288/fax: 845-340-3299
  e-mail: countyclerk@co.ulster.ny.us
County Attorney:
 Beatrice Havranek. . . . . . . . . . . . . . . . .845-340-3685/fax: 845-340-3691
  e-mail: bhav@co.ulster.ny.us
District Attorney:
 D Holley Carnright . . . . . . . . . . . . . . . . .845-340-3280/fax: 845-340-3185
Public Defender:
 Andrew Kossover . . . . . . . . . . . . . . . . .845-340-3232/fax: 845-340-3744
  e-mail: akos@co.ulster.ny.us

State & Local
Government
Public Information

*Offices and agencies generally appear in alphabetical order, except when specific order is requested by listee.*

**333**

Director, Emergency Management:
  Arthur R Snyder ...................845-331-7000/fax: 845-331-1738
  e-mail: asny@co.ulster.ny.us
Sheriff:
  PJ Van Blarcum....................845-338-3640/fax: 845-331-2810
  e-mail: sheriff@co.ulster.ny.us
Commissioner of Finance:
  Burt Gulnick, Jr. .................845-340-3460/fax: 845-340-3430
  e-mail: bgul@co.ulster.ny.us
Historian:
  Anne M Gordon ......................................845-331-7380
  e-mail: pasaran@msn.com

## Warren County
Municipal Center
1340 State Rte 9
Lake George, NY 12845
800-958-4748 x143 Fax: 518-761-6368
Web site: www.warrencountyny.gov

Chairman, Board of Supervisors (R):
  Kevin B. Geraghty ...................................518-761-6536
Clerk, Board of Supervisors:
  Joan Sady ...........................................518-761-6563
Commissioner, Administrative & Fiscal Services:
  JoAnn McKinstry .....................................518-761-7655
County Clerk:
  Pamela J Vogel ..............518-761-6427/fax: 518-761-6551
County Attorney:
  Martin D. Auffredov ...........518-761-6463/fax: 518-761-6377
District Attorney:
  Kathleen B Hogan.............518-761-6405/fax: 518-761-6254
Public Defender:
  John P M Wappett...............518-761-6207/fax: 518-761-6208
Treasurer:
  Michael R. Swan .............518-761-6379/fax: 518-761-6470
Historian:
  Ann McCann ......................518-761-6544/fax: 518-761-6551

## Washington County
383 Broadway
Fort Edward, NY 12828
518-746-2100 Fax: 518-746-2108
Web site: www.co.washington.ny.us

Chairman, Board of Supervisors:
  John A. Rymph ......................................518-746-2210
Clerk, Board of Supervisors:
  Debbie Prehoda......................................518-746-2210
County Administrator:
  Kevin G Hayes .......................................518-746-2590
County Clerk:
  Dona Crandall ..............518-746-2170/fax: 518-746-2177
County Attorney:
  Roger A Wickes .....................................518-746-2216
District Attorney:
  Kevin C Kortright...................................518-746-2525
Public Defender:
  Vacant...............................................518-747-2403
Sheriff:
  Jeff Murphy.........................................518-746-2475
Fire Coordinator:
  Raymond Rathbun .....................................518-746-2255
Treasurer:
  Albert Nolette ......................................518-746-2220

## Wayne County
Wayne County Courthouse
26 Church St
Lyons, NY 14489
315-946-5400 Fax: 315-946-5407

Chairman, Board of Supervisors (R):
  James Hoffman ...............315-946-5400/fax: 315-946-5407
County Administrator:
  James Marquette ..............315-946-5480/fax: 315-946-5407
County Clerk:
  Michael Jankowski ...........315-946-7470/fax: 315-946-5978
County Attorney:
  Daniel Connors......................................315-946-7442
District Attorney:
  Richard Healy ...............315-946-5905/fax: 315-946-5911
Public Defender:
  Ronald C Valentine..................................315-946-7472
Director, Emergency Management:
  George Bastedo...............315-946-5663/fax: 315-946-9721
Sheriff:
  Barry Virts.................315-946-9711/fax: 315-946-5811
Treasurer:
  Thomas A Warnick ............315-946-7441/fax: 315-946-5949
County Historian:
  Peter Evans .........................................315-946-5470

## Westchester County
**Board of Legislators**
800 Michaelian Office Bldg
148 Martine Ave, 8th Fl
White Plains, NY 10601
914-995-2800 Fax: 914-995-3884
Web site: www.westchesterlegislators.com

Chair, Board of Legislators (D):
  Kenneth W Jenkins...................................914-995-2829
Majority Leader (D):
  Peter Harckham......................................914-995-2810
  e-mail: rogowsky@westchesterlegislators.com
Minority Leader (R):
  James Maisano .......................................914-995-2826
Clerk, Board of Legislature & Chief of Staff:
  Tina Seckerson ......................................914-995-2823
  e-mail: tinas@westchesterlegislators.com

## Westchester County
**Administration**
900 Michaelian Office Building
148 Martine Ave
White Plains, NY 10601
914-995-2900
Web site: www3.westchestergov.com

County Executive:
  Robert P. Astorino .................................914-995-2900
  e-mail: ce@westchestergov.com
Deputy County Executive:
  Kevin J. Plunkett ...........914-995-2909/fax: 914-995-3372
County Clerk:
  Timothy C Idoni .............914-995-3080/fax: 914-995-4030
County Attorney:
  Robert Meehan.......................................914-995-2690
  e-mail: rfm5@westchestergov.com
District Attorney:
  Janet Difiore ......................................915-995-3414
Sheriff/Public Safety Commissioner:
  George Longworth ...................................914-864-7710
  e-mail: gnl1@westchestergov.com

*Offices and agencies generally appear in alphabetical order, except when specific order is requested by listee.*

Finance Commissioner:
    Ann Marie Berg . . . . . . . . . . . . . . . . . . . . 914-995-2757/fax: 914-995-3230
Public Works Acting Commissioner:
    Jay T. Pisco . . . . . . . . . . . . . . . . . . . . . . . 914-995-2546/fax: 914-995-4479
    e-mail: jtp2@westchestergov.com
Emergency Management Office:
    John M. Cullen . . . . . . . . . . . . . . . . . . . 914-231-1851/fax: 914-231-1622
    e-mail: jmc5@westchestergov.com

## Wyoming County
Gov't Center, 143 N Main St
Warsaw, NY 14569
585-786-8800  Fax: 585-786-8802
e-mail: CKetchum@wyomingco.net
Web site: www.wyomingco.net

Chairman, Board of Supervisors (R):
    A Berwanger . . . . . . . . . . . . . . . . . . . . . 585-786-8800/fax: 585-786-8802
    e-mail: abberwanger@wyomingco.net
Vice Chairman, Board of Supervisors (R):
    Douglas Patti . . . . . . . . . . . . . . . . . . . . . . . . . . . . . . . . . . . . 585-786-8800
Clerk, Board of Supervisors:
    Cheryl J Ketchum . . . . . . . . . . . . . . . . . 585-786-8800/fax: 585-786-8802
    e-mail: cketchum@wyomingco.net
County Clerk:
    Rhonda Pierce . . . . . . . . . . . . . . . . 585-786-8810/fax: 585-786-3703
    e-mail: county.clerk@wyomingco.net
County Attorney:
    James Wvjcik. . . . . . . . . . . . . . . . . . . . 585-591-1724/fax: 585-591-1722
District Attorney:
    Donald G O'Geen . . . . . . . . . . . . . . . . . 585-786-8822/fax: 585-786-8842
    e-mail: dogeen@wyomingco.net
Public Defender:
    Norman P Effman . . . . . . . . . . . . . . . . . 585-756-8450/fax: 585-786-8478
    e-mail: attlegal@yahoo.com
Director, Fire & Emergency Management:
    Anthony Santoro . . . . . . . . . . . . . . . . 585-786-8867/fax: 585-786-8961
    e-mail: asantoro@wyomingco.net
Sheriff:
    Farris H Heimann . . . . . . . . . . . . . . . . 585-786-2255/fax: 585-786-8961
    e-mail: fheimann@wyomingco.net

Treasurer:
    Cheryl Mayer. . . . . . . . . . . . . . . . . . . . 585-786-8812/fax: 585-786-0466
    e-mail: cdmayer@wyomingco.net
County Historian:
    Doris Bannister . . . . . . . . . . . . . . . . . . . . . . . . . . . . . . . . . . 585-786-8818

## Yates County
417 Liberty St
Penn Yan, NY 14527
315-536-5150  Fax: 315-536-5166
Web site: www.yatescounty.org

Chairman, County Legislature (R):
    H Taylor Fitch . . . . . . . . . . . . . . . . . . . 315-536-5150/fax: 315-536-5166
    e-mail: legislature@yatescounty.org
County Administrator:
    Sarah Purdy . . . . . . . . . . . . . . . . . . . . . 315-536-5509/fax: 315-536-5118
    e-mail: ycadministrator@yatescounty.org
Clerk, County Legislature:
    Connie C Hayes. . . . . . . . . . . . . . . . . . . 315-536-5150/fax: 315-536-5166
    e-mail: legislature@yatescounty.org
County Clerk:
    Julie D Betts . . . . . . . . . . . . . . . . . . . . 315-536-5120/fax: 315-536-5545
    e-mail: countyclerk@yatescounty.org
County Attorney:
    Scott P. Falvey. . . . . . . . . . . . . . . . . . . 315-531-3233/fax: 315-531-3234
District Attorney:
    Jason Cook. . . . . . . . . . . . . . . . . . . . . . . 315-536-5550/fax: 315-536-5556
Public Defender:
    Edward J Brockman . . . . . . . . . . . . . . . 585-374-6439 or 315-536-0352
Sheriff:
    Ronald G Spike . . . . . . . . . . . . . . . . . . . 315-536-4438/fax: 315-536-5191
    e-mail: sheriff@yatescounty.org
Treasurer:
    Winona B. Flynn. . . . . . . . . . . . . . . . . . . . . . . . . . . . . . . . . 315-536-5192
    e-mail: treasurer@yatescounty.org
Emergency Management Director:
    Vacant . . . . . . . . . . . . . . . . . . . . . . . . . 315-536-3000/fax: 315-536-5106
    e-mail: emergencymanagement@yatescounty.org
Historian:
    Frances Dumas . . . . . . . . . . . . . . . . . . . 315-536-5147/fax: 315-531-3226
    e-mail: history@yatescounty.org

State & Local
Government
Public Information

*Offices and agencies generally appear in alphabetical order, except when specific order is requested by listee.*

## MUNICIPAL GOVERNMENT

This section identifies senior public officials for cities, towns and villages in New York State with populations greater than 20,000. New York City departments are included in the city listing.

## MUNICIPAL GOVERNMENT

### Albany, City of
City Hall
24 Eagle St
Albany, NY 12207
518-434-5175
e-mail: webmaster@ci.albany.ny.us
Web site: www.albanyny.gov

Mayor:
   Gerald D Jennings . . . . . . . . . . . . . . . . . .518-434-5100/fax: 518-434-5013
   e-mail: mayor@ci.albany.ny.us
Deputy Mayor:
   Philip F Calderone. . . . . . . . . . . . . . . . . .518-434-5077/fax: 518-434-5074
President, Common Council:
   Carolyn McLaughlin. . . . . . . . . . . . . . . . . . . . . . . . . .518-462-1458
   e-mail: onlybelv@aol.com
City Clerk:
   Nala Woodward. . . . . . . . . . . . . . . . . .518-434-5090/fax: 518-434-5081
Corporation Counsel:
   John Reilly. . . . . . . . . . . . . . . . . .518-434-5050/fax: 518-434-5070
City Deputy Auditor:
   Debra Perks. . . . . . . . . . . . . . . . . . . . . . . . . . . .518-434-5023
City Treasurer:
   Kathy Sheehan. . . . . . . . . . . . . . . . .518-434-5036/fax: 518-434-5041
Commissioner, General Services:
   Nicolas J D'Antonio . . . . . . . . . . . . . .518-432-1144/fax: 518-427-7499
   e-mail: generalservices@ci.albany.ny.us
Commissioner, Assessment & Taxation:
   Keith McDonald . . . . . . . . . . . . . . . . .518-434-5155/fax: 518-434-5013
Police Chief:
   Steven Krokoff . . . . . . . . . . . . . . . . . . . . . . . . . . .518-462-8013
Fire Chief/Emergency Services:
   Robert Forezzi Sr. . . . . . . . . . . .518-447-7877/fax: 518-434-8675
Director, Community Development:
   Faye Andrews. . . . . . . . . . . . . . . . . . . . . . . . . . . .518-434-5265
Director, Building & Codes:
   Jeffrey Jamison . . . . . . . . . . . . . . . .518-434-5165/fax: 518-434-6015

### Amherst, Town of
5583 Main St
Williamsville, NY 14221
716-631-7000  Fax: 716-631-7146
Web site: www.amherst.ny.us

Town Supervisor:
   Barry A Weinstein . . . . . . . . . . . . . . . . . . . . . . . . . . . .716-631-7032
Town Clerk:
   Marjory Jaeger . . . . . . . . . . . . .716-631-7021 x7010/fax: 716-631-7152
Town Attorney:
   E Thomas Jones . . . . . . . . . . . . . . . . . . . . . . . . . . . .716-631-7164
Comptroller:
   Darlene Carroll . . . . . . . . . . . . . . . . . . . . . . . . . . . .716-631-7008
Director Emergency Services & Safety:
   James J Zymanek . . . . . . . . . . . . . . . . . . . . . . . . . . .716-839-6707
Police Chief:
   John C Askey. . . . . . . . . . . . . . . . .716-689-1311/fax: 716-689-1310

### Auburn, City of
Memorial City Hall
24 South Street
Auburn, NY 13021
315-255-4104  Fax: 315-253-8345

Mayor:
   Michael Quill. . . . . . . . . . . . . . . . . . . . .315-255-4104/fax: 315-253-8345
City Manager:
   Doug Selby . . . . . . . . . . . . . . . . .315-255-4146/fax: 315-255-4735
City Clerk:
   Debra A McCormick. . . . . . . . . . . . . . . .315-255-4100/fax: 315-255-4181
Corporation Counsel:
   John Rossi . . . . . . . . . . . . . . . . . . . .315-255-4176/fax: 315-255-4735
Planning & Economic Development Director:
   Jennifer Haines . . . . . . . . . . . . . . . . .315-255-4115/fax: 315-253-0282
Comptroller:
   Lauren Poehlman. . . . . . . . . . . . . . . . . .315-255-4138/fax: 315-255-4727
Treasurer:
   Robert Gauthier . . . . . . . . . . . . . . . . . .315-255-4143/fax: 315-255-4727
Police Chief:
   Brian Neagle . . . . . . . . . . . . . . . . .315-253-3235/fax: 315-255-2601
Fire Chief:
   Jeff Dygert. . . . . . . . . . . . . . . . . . .315-253-4031/fax: 315-252-0318

### Babylon, Town of
200 E Sunrise Highway
Lindenhurst, NY 11757-2598
631-957-3000  Fax: 631-957-7440
e-mail: info@townofbabylon.com
Web site: www.townofbabylon.com

Town Supervisor:
   Rich Schaffer. . . . . . . . . . . . . . . . . .631-957-3072/fax: 631-957-7440
Town Clerk:
   Carol Quirk. . . . . . . . . . . . . . . . . . . . . . . . . . . .631-957-4291
Town Attorney:
   Joseph Wilson. . . . . . . . . . . . . . . . . . . . . . . . . . . .631-957-3029
Comptroller:
   Victoria Marotta . . . . . . . . . . . . . . . . . . . . . . . . . . .631-957-3179
Commissioner, Public Works:
   Tom Stay. . . . . . . . . . . . . . . . . . . . . . . . . . . .631-957-3161
Deputy Commissioner, Public Safety:
   Patrick Farrell . . . . . . . . . . . . . . . . .631-422-7600/fax: 631-893-1031
Commissioner, General Services:
   Theresa Sabatino. . . . . . . . . . . . . . . . . . . . . . . . . . . .631-957-3025

### Bethlehem, Town of
445 Delaware Ave
Delmar, NY 12054
518-439-4955  Fax: 518-439-1699
e-mail: djacon@townofbethlehem.org
Web site: www.townofbethlehem.org

Town Supervisor:
   John Clarkson . . . . . . . . . . . . . . . . . . . . . .518-439-4955 x1164
   e-mail: jclarkson@townofbethlehem.org
Town Clerk:
   Nanci Moquin. . . . . . . . . . . .518-439-4955 x1183/fax: 518-439-1699
   e-mail: nmoquin@townofbethlehem.org
Town Attorney:
   James Potter. . . . . . . . . . . . . . . . . . . . . . . .518-439-4955 x1164
   e-mail: jpotter@townofbethlehem.org
Comptroller:
   Michael E. Cohen . . . . . . . . . . . . . . . . . . . .518-439-4955 x1123
   e-mail: mcohen@townofbethlehem.org
Police Chief:
   Louis G Corsi . . . . . . . . . . . . . . . . . .518-439-9973/fax: 518-439-6965

*Offices and agencies generally appear in alphabetical order, except when specific order is requested by listee.*

Emergency Management Director:
John E Brennan .........................518-439-4955 x1166
e-mail: jbrennan@townofbethlehem.org
Historian:
Susan E Leath .............................518-439-4955 x1160
e-mail: sleath@townofbethlehem.org

## Binghamton, City of
City Hall
38 Hawley St
Binghamton, NY 13901
607-772-7005 Fax: 607-772-0508
Web site: www.cityofbinghamton.com

Mayor:
Matthew T Ryan ...................607-772-7001/fax: 607-772-7079
e-mail: mayor@cityofbinghamton.com
Executive Assistant to the Mayor:
Andrew Block .....................607-772-7001/fax: 607-772-7079
e-mail: awblock@cityofbinghamton.com
City Clerk:
Angela Holmes ...................607-772-7005/fax: 607-772-7155
e-mail: clerk@cityofbinghamton.com
Corporation Counsel:
Kenneth Frank.....................................607-772-7013
City Treasurer:
Pauline Penrose ...................607-772-7027/fax: 607-772-7015
e-mail: treasurer@cityofbinghamton.com
City Assessor:
Scott Snyder......................607-772-7002/fax: 607-772-7106
e-mail: assessor@cityofbinghamton.com
Commissioner, Public Works:
Luke Day .........................607-772-7021/fax: 607-772-7023
e-mail: dpw@cityofbinghamton.com
Police Chief:
Joseph Zikuski....................607-772-7090/fax: 607-772-7996
e-mail: police@cityofbinghamton.com
Acting Administrator, Civil Service:
Judith Robb ......................607-772-7008/fax: 607-772-7066
e-mail: cs@cityofbinghamton.com
Acting Director, Finance/Comptroller:
Charles Pearsall ..................607-772-7011/fax: 607-772-7106
e-mail: finance@cityofbinghamton.com
Director, Planning/Housing/Community Development:
Tarik Abdelazim ..................607-772-7028/fax: 607-772-7063
e-mail: tabdelazim@cityofbinghamton.com
Director, Economic Development:
Merry Harris ......................607-772-7161/fax: 607-772-7244
e-mail: maharris@cityofbinghamton.com

## Brighton, Town of
2300 Elmwood Ave
Rochester, NY 14618
585-784-5250 Fax: 585-784-5373
Web site: www.townofbrighton.org

Town Supervisor:
William W Moehle..............................585-784-5252
Town Clerk:
Dan Aman .......................585-784-5240/fax: 585-784-5374
Director, Finance:
Suzanne Zaso.....................585-784-5210/fax: 585-784-5396
e-mail: suzanne.zaso@townofbrighton.org
Police Chief:
Mark Henderson ..................585-784-5150/fax: 585-784-5151
Fire Marshal:
Christopher Roth ..................585-784-5220/fax: 585-785-5207
e-mail: christopher.roth@townofbrighton.org
Town Attorney:
Kenneth W. Gordon ..............585-244-1070/fax: 585-244-1085

Commissioner, Public Works:
Tim Keef .....................585-784-5250/fax: 585-784-5223
Director, Communications:
Douglas Clapp...................................585-784-5253

## Brookhaven, Town of
One Independence Hill
Farmingville, NY 11738
631-451-6655 Fax: 631-451-6677
Web site: www.brookhaven.org

Town Supervisor:
Edward P. Romaine.................631-451-8696/fax: 631-451-6447
Town Clerk/Registrar:
Patricia Eddington ................631-451-9101/fax: 631-451-9264
Commissioner of Finance:
Tamara Wright.....................631-451-6680/fax: 631-451-6692
e-mail: finance@brookhaven.org
Commissioner, Public Safety:
Peter O'Leary ....................631-451-6291/fax: 631-451-6908

## Buffalo, City of
City Hall
65 Niagara Square
Buffalo, NY 14202
716-851-4200 Fax: 716-851-4360
Web site: www.ci.buffalo.ny.us

Mayor:
Byron W Brown
e-mail: mayor@city-buffalo.com
Council President:
Richard A. Fontana ................716-851-5151/fax: 716-851-5141
e-mail: rfontana@city-buffalo.com
City Clerk:
Gerald Chwalinski..................716-851-5431/fax: 716-851-4845
e-mail: gchwalinski@city-buffalo.com
Comptroller:
Mark JF Schroeder ................716-851-5255/fax: 716-851-4031
Commissioner, Administration, Finance & Urban Affairs:
Donna Estrich .....................................716-851-5922
e-mail: destrich@city-buffalo.com
Police Commissioner:
Daniel Derenda.....................716-851-4444 or 716-851-4571
Fire Commissioner:
Garnell W Whitfield Jr .............................716-851-5333
e-mail: gwhitfield@bfdny.org
Director Emergency Management:
Garnell W. Whitfield, Jr..............716-851-5333/fax: 716-851-5341

## Camillus, Town of
4600 W Genesee Street
Syracuse, NY 13219
315-488-1335 Fax: 315-488-8768
Web site: www.townofcamillus.com

Town Supervisor:
Mary Ann Coogan..................315-488-1335/fax: 315-488-8768
e-mail: macoogan@townofcamillus.com
Town Clerk:
Martha Dickson-McMahon ..........315-488-1234/fax: 315-488-8983
e-mail: mdickson@townofcamillus.com
Comptroller:
Catherine Albunio .................315-488-2266/fax: 315-468-4179
e-mail: calbunio@townofcamillus.com
Police Chief:
Thomas Winn .....................315-487-0102/fax: 315-487-5572
e-mail: twinn@townofcamillus.com

*Offices and agencies generally appear in alphabetical order, except when specific order is requested by listee.*

337

## Carmel, Town of
Town Hall
60 McAlpin Ave
Mahopac, NY 10541
845-628-1500  Fax: 845-628-7434

Town Supervisor:
  Kenneth Schmitt . . . . . . . . . . . . . . . . . .845-628-1500/fax: 845-628-6836
Town Clerk:
  Ann Spofford. . . . . . . . . . . . . . . . . . . . .845-628-1500/fax: 845-628-7434
Town Counsel:
  Gregory Folchetti. . . . . . . . . . . . . . . . . .845-225-1900/fax: 845-228-4228
Police Chief:
  Michael R Johnson . . . . . . . . . . . . . . . .845-628-1300/fax: 845-628-2597

## Cheektowaga, Town of
Town Hall
3301 Broadway
Cheektowaga, NY 14227
716-686-3400  Fax: 716-686-3515
Web site: www.tocny.org

Town Supervisor:
  Mary F Holtz . . . . . . . . . . . . . . . . . . . .716-686-3465/fax: 716-686-3551
Town Clerk:
  Alice Magierski . . . . . . . . . . . . . . . . . .716-686-3434/fax: 716-686-3515
  e-mail: townclerkwebmail@tocny.org
Town Attorney:
  Kevin Schenk. . . . . . . . . . . . . . . . . . . .716-686-3457/fax: 716-686-3997
  e-mail: lawweb@tocny.org
Emergency Services Manager:
  Earl Loder . . . . . . . . . . . . . . . . . . . . . .716-893-0847/fax: 716-893-0835
  e-mail: eloder@tocny.org
Police Chief:
  David Zack . . . . . . . . . . . . . . . . . . . . .716-686-3500/fax: 716-685-1239

## Chili, Town of
3235 Chili Avenue
Rochester, NY 14624
585-889-3550  Fax: 585-889-8710
e-mail: info@townofchili.org
Web site: www.townofchili.org

Town Supervisor:
  David Dunning . . . . . . . . . . . . . . . . . . . . . . . . . . . . . . .585-889-6111
Town Clerk:
  Richard J Brongo . . . . . . . . . . . . . . . . . . . . . . . . . . . . .585-889-6122
  e-mail: rbrongo@townofchili.org
Director of Finance:
  Dianne O'Meara . . . . . . . . . . . . . . . . . . . . . . . . . . . . . .585-889-6120
Town Historian:
  Bonnie Moore . . . . . . . . . . . . . . . . . . . . . . . . . . . . . . . .585-889-6123

## Cicero, Town of
Town Hall
8236 S Main St
PO Box 1517
Cicero, NY 13039
315-699-1414  Fax: 315-699-0039
Web site: www.ciceronewyork.net

Town Supervisor:
  Jim Corl. . . . . . . . . . . . . . . . . . . . . . . . . . . . . . . . . . . .315-699-1414
Town Clerk:
  Tracy M Cosilmon. . . . . . . . . . . . . . . .315-699-8109/fax. 315-699-0039
  e-mail: clerk@ciceronewyork.net
Comptroller:
  Shirlie Stuart . . . . . . . . . . . . . . . . . . .315-699-2759/fax: 315-698-0851
  e-mail: sstuart@ciceronewyork.net

Receiver of Taxes:
  Sharon Edick . . . . . . . . . . . . . . . . . . .315-699-2756/fax: 315-699-9562
Police Chief:
  Joseph F Snell Jr . . . . . . . . . . . . . . . . .315-699-3677/fax: 315-699-8128

## Clarence, Town of
1 Town Place
Clarence, NY 14031
716-741-8930  Fax: 716-741-4715
Web site: www.clarence.ny.us

Town Supervisor:
  David C. Hartzell, Jr. . . . . . . . . . . . . . .716-741-8930/fax: 716-741-4715
Town Clerk:
  Nancy C Metzger. . . . . . . . . . . . . . . . .716-741-8938/fax: 716-407-2190
Town Attorney:
  Lawrence M. Meckler . . . . . . . . . . . . .716-741-8935/fax: 716-741-4715
Chief Security Officer:
  Joseph D Meacham. . . . . . . . . . . . . . . . . . . . . . . . . . . . .716-406-8928

## Clarkstown, Town of
10 Maple Ave
New City, NY 10956
845-639-2050  Fax: 845-639-2008
Web site: www.town.clarkstown.ny.us

Town Supervisor:
  Alexander J Gromack . . . . . . . . . . . . . .845-639-2050/fax: 845-634-5456
Deputy Supervisor:
  Councilman Shirley Lasker . . . . . . . . . .845-639-2050/fax: 845-634-5456
Town Clerk:
  Justin Sweet . . . . . . . . . . . . . . . . . . . .845-639-2010/fax: 845-639-2008
  e-mail: clerk@clarkstown.org
Town Attorney:
  Amy Mele . . . . . . . . . . . . . . . . . . . . . .845-639-2060/fax: 845-639-2189

## Clay, Town of
4401 State Route 31
Clay, NY 13041
315-652-3800  Fax: 315-622-7259
Web site: www.townofclay.org

Town Supervisor:
  Damian M Ulatowski . . . . . . . . . . .315-652-3800 x114/fax: 315-622-7259
  e-mail: supervisor@townofclay.org
Town Clerk:
  Jill Hageman-Clark. . . . . . . . . .315-652-3800 ext 145/fax: 315-622-7259
  e-mail: townclerk@townofclay.org
Town Attorney:
  Robert M Germain . . . . . . . . . . . .315-652-3800 x151/fax: 315-622-7259
  e-mail: legal@townofclay.org
Commissioner of Finance:
  John Shehadi . . . . . . . . . . . . . . . . . . . . . . . . . . .315-652-3800 x121
Commissioner, Public Safety:
  Mark Territo . . . . . . . . . . . . . . . . . . . . . . . . . . . . . .315-622-7259
  e-mail: planning@townofclay.org
Fire Chief:
  Daniel L Ford . . . . . . . . . . . . . . . . . . . . . . . . . . . . . . .315-625-4242

## Clifton Park, Town of
1 Town Hall Plaza
Clifton Park, NY 12065
518-371-6651  Fax: 518-371-1136
e-mail: info@cliftonpark.org
Web site: www.cliftonpark.org

Town Supervisor:
  Philip Barrett . . . . . . . . . . . . . . . . . . .518-371-6651/fax: 518-371-1136

*Offices and agencies generally appear in alphabetical order, except when specific order is requested by listee.*

Town Administrator:
Michael Shahen. . . . . . . . . . . . . . . . . . . . . . . . . . . . .518-371-6651 ext243
Town Clerk:
Patricia O'Donnell. . . . . . . . . . . . . . . .518-371-6681/fax: 518-383-5088
Comptroller:
Mark Heggen. . . . . . . . . . . . . . . . . . . .518-371-6651/fax: 518-371-1136
Historian:
John Scherer . . . . . . . . . . . . . . . . . . . .518-371-2691/fax: 518-383-2668

## Colonie, Town of

Memorial Town Hall
534 Loudon Rd
Newtonville, NY 12128
518-783-2700  Fax: 518-782-2360
e-mail: colonie@colonie.org
Web site: www.colonie.org

Town Supervisor:
Paula A Mahan . . . . . . . . . . . . . . . . . . . . . . . . . . . . . . .518-783-2700
Town Clerk:
Elizabeth A DelTorto . . . . . . . . . . . . . .518-783-2734/fax: 518-783-3409
e-mail: deltortoe@colonie.org
Town Attorney:
Michael C Magguilli. . . . . . . . . . . . . . .518-783-2704/fax: 518-786-7324
e-mail: attorney@colonie.org
Comptroller:
Craig Blair . . . . . . . . . . . . . . . . . . . . . .518-783-2708/fax: 518-783-2877
e-mail: blairc@colonie.org
Emergency Management & Planning:
Michael Rayball . . . . . . . . . . . . . . . . . . . . . . . . . . . . . .518-782-2609
e-mail: Rayballm@colonie.org
Police Chief:
Steven H Heider . . . . . . . . . . . . . . . . . .518-783-2744/fax: 518-786-7326
e-mail: heiders@colonie.org
Public Works Commissioner:
John H Cunningham . . . . . . . . . . . . . . .518-783-6292/fax: 518-785-3529
e-mail: infodpw@colonie.org
Town Historian:
Kevin Franklin . . . . . . . . . . . . . . . . . . . . . . . . . . . . . . .518-782-2601
e-mail: historian@colonie.org

## Cortlandt, Town of

1 Heady St
Cortlandt Manor, NY 10567-1224
914-734-1002  Fax: 914-734-1025
e-mail: townhall@townofcortlandt.com
Web site: www.townofcortlandt.com

Town Supervisor:
Linda D Puglisi . . . . . . . . . . . . . . . . . .914-734-1002/fax: 914-734-1003
e-mail: lindap@townofcortlandt.com
Town Clerk:
Joann Dyckman . . . . . . . . . . . . . . . . . .914-734-1020/fax: 914-734-1102
Town Attorney:
Thomas F Wood . . . . . . . . . . . . . . . . . .914-736-0930/fax: 914-736-9082
Comptroller:
Glenn Cestaro . . . . . . . . . . . . . . . . . . .914-734-1071/fax: 914-734-1077
e-mail: glennc@townofcortlandt.com
DES/Director:
Jeff Coleman . . . . . . . . . . . . . . . . . . . .914-737-0100/fax: 914-862-3376
e-mail: jefft@townofcortlandt.com
Homeland Security:
Linda Puglisi. . . . . . . . . . . . . . . . . . . . . . . . . . . . . . . . .914-734-1001
e-mail: jefft@townofcortlandt.com

## DeWitt, Town of

5400 Butternut Drive
East Syracuse, NY 13057-8509

315-446-3910  Fax: 315-449-2065
Web site: www.townofdewitt.com

Town Supervisor:
Edward M Michalenko . . . . . . . . . .315-446-3910 ext5/fax: 315-449-0620
e-mail: supervisor@townofdewitt.com
Town Clerk:
Barbara K Klim . . . . . . . . . . . . . .315-446-3910 ext 2/fax: 315-449-2065
e-mail: clerk@townofdewitt.com
Police Chief:
Eugene J Conway . . . . . . . . . . . . . . . .315-449-3640/fax: 315-449-3644
e-mail: police@townofdewitt.com
Comptroller:
Timothy Redmond . . . . . . . . . . . . .315-446-3392 ext 6/fax: 315-449-2065
e-mail: comptroller@townofdewitt.com

## East Fishkill, Town of

Town Hall
330 Route 376
Hopewell Junction, NY 12533
845-221-9191
Web site: www.eastfishkillny.org

Town Supervisor:
John L Hickman Jr . . . . . . . . . . . . . . . . . . . . . . . . . . . .845-221-4303
Town Clerk:
Carol Hurray . . . . . . . . . . . . . . . . . . . . . . . . . . . . . . . .845-221-9191
Police Chief:
Brian C Nichols . . . . . . . . . . . . . . . . . . . . . . . . . . . . . .845-221-2111
Fire Inspector:
William Stuart. . . . . . . . . . . . . . . . . . . . . . . . . . . . . . . .845-221-0378

## East Hampton, Town of

159 Pantigo Rd
East Hampton, NY 11937
631-324-4140  Fax: 631-324-2789

Town Supervisor:
William J Wilkinson . . . . . . . . . . . . . . .631-324-4140/fax: 631-324-2789
Town Clerk:
Fred Overton . . . . . . . . . . . . . . . . . . . .631-324-4142/fax: 631-324-4128
Division of Finance/ Budget Officer:
Len Bernard. . . . . . . . . . . . . . . . . . . . .631-324-4141/fax: 631-324-2789
Town Attorney:
John Jilnicki. . . . . . . . . . . . . . . . . . . . .631-324-8787/fax: 631-329-5371
Police Chief:
Edward V Ecker Jr. . . . . . . . . . . . . . . .631-537-7575/fax: 631-537-6833
Emergency Services:
Bruce Bates. . . . . . . . . . . . . . . . . . . . . . . . . . . . . . . . . .631-324-1736
Chief Fire Marshall:
David Browne . . . . . . . . . . . . . . . . . . .631-329-3473/fax: 631-329-9403

## Eastchester, Town of

Town Hall
40 Mill Rd
Eastchester, NY 10709
914-771-3300  Fax: 914-771-3366
Web site: www.eastchester.org

Town Supervisor:
Anthony S Colavita. . . . . . . . . . . . . . . .914-771-3301/fax: 914-793-2168
e-mail: supervisor@eastchester.org
Town Clerk:
Linda Doherty . . . . . . . . . . . . . . . . . . .914-771-3351/fax: 914-771-3366
e-mail: townclerk@eastchester.org
Town Attorney:
Louis J. Reda. . . . . . . . . . . . . . . . . . . .914-771-3325/fax: 914-771-3367
e-mail: legal@eastchester.org

*Offices and agencies generally appear in alphabetical order, except when specific order is requested by listee.*

Comptroller:
  Dawn T Donovan . . . . . . . . . . . . . . . .914-771-3330/fax: 914-771-9409
  e-mail: comptroller@eastchester.org

## Elmira, City of
City Hall
317 E Church St
Elmira, NY 14901
607-737-5644  Fax: 607-737-5824
Web site: www.cityofelmira.net

Mayor:
  Susan J. Skidmore. . . . . . . . . . . . . . . . . . . . . . . . . . . . .607-737-5644
City Manager:
  John J Burin . . . . . . . . . . . . . . . . . . . . . . . . . . . . . . . . .607-737-5644
City Clerk:
  Angela J Williams . . . . . . . . . . . . . . 607-737-5672/fax: 607-737-5783
Chamberlain:
  David Vandermark . . . . . . . . . . . 607-737-5661/fax: 607-737-5783
Director, Public Works:
  Brian Beasley . . . . . . . . . . . . . . . . . . . . . . . . . . . . . . . .607-737-5679
Police Chief:
  Michael Robertson . . . . . . . . . . . . . . . . . . . . . . . . . . .607-737-5811
Fire Chief:
  Patrick Bermingham . . . . . . . . . . . . . . . . . . . . . . . . . . .607-737-5700

## Fishkill, Town of
807 Route 52
Fishkill, NY 12524
845-831-7800  Fax: 845-831-6040
e-mail: tof@fishkill-ny.gov
Web site: www.fishkill-ny.gov

Town Supervisor:
  Robert LaColla. . . . . . . . . . . . . . . . . . . . . . .845-831-7800 x. 3309
Town Clerk:
  Darlene Bellis . . . . . . . . . . . . . . . . . . . . . . .845-831-7800 x. 3329
  e-mail: dbellis@fishkill-ny.gov
Comptroller:
  Dawn H. Kertesz-Lee . . . . . . . . . . . . . . . . . . . .845-831-7800 x3339
  e-mail: rwheeling@fishkill-ny.gov

## Freeport, Village of
46 North Ocean Ave
Freeport, NY 11520
516-377-2200  Fax: 516-377-2323
e-mail: freeportmail1@freeportny.gov
Web site: www.freeportny.com

Village Mayor:
  Robert T. Kennedy . . . . . . . . . . . . . . .516-377-2252/fax: 516-377-2323
  e-mail: mayor@freeportny.gov
Village Clerk:
  Pamela Walsh Boening . . . . . . . . . . . . .516-377-2300/fax: 516-771-4127
Village Attorney:
  Howard E Colton. . . . . . . . . . . . . . . .516-377-2249/fax: 516-377-2366
  e-mail: hcolton@freeportny.gov
Treasurer:
  Ismaela Hernandez . . . . . . . . . . . . . .516-377-2212/fax: 516-377-2255
  e-mail: vmontes@freeportny.gov
Superintendent, Public Works:
  Robert R. Fisenne, P.E.. . . . . . . . . . . . . . . . . . . . . .516-377-2289
  e-mail: srichardson@freeportny.gov
Emergency Management Director:
  Richard E Holdener . . . . . . . . . . . . . . . . . . . . . . .516-377-2188
  e-mail: rholdener@freeportny.gov
Police Chief:
  Miguel Bermudez . . . . . . . . . . . . . . .516-377-2411/fax: 516-377-2432
  e-mail: mwoodword@freeportny.gov

Secretary to Fire Chief:
  Raymond Maguire . . . . . . . . . . . . . . . . . . . . . . . . . . .516-377-2190
  e-mail: rmaguire@freeportny.gov
Chief of the Fire Department:
  Stanley Kistela . . . . . . . . . . . . . . . . . . . . . . . . . . . . .516-377-2190
  e-mail: rmaguire@freeportny.gov

## Garden City, Village of
351 Stewart Ave
Garden City, NY 11530
516-465-4000  Fax: 516-742-5223
Web site: www.gardencityny.net

Mayor:
  John J. Watras. . . . . . . . . . . . . . . . . . . . . . . . . . . . .516-465-4051
  e-mail: mayor@gardencityny.net
Administrator:
  Robert L Schoelle, Jr . . . . . . . . . . . . . . . . . . . . . . . . .516-465-4051
Fire Chief:
  William J Castoro . . . . . . . . . . . . . . . . . . . . . . . . . . .516-746-4130
  e-mail: wcastoro@gardencityny.net
Director, Public Works:
  Robert J Mangan. . . . . . . . . . . . . . . . . . . . . . . . . . . .516-465-4004
  e-mail: rmangan@gardencityny.net

## Gates, Town of
1605 Buffalo Rd
Gates, NY 14624
585-247-6100  Fax: 585-247-0017
e-mail: admin@townofgates.org
Web site: www.townofgates.org

Town Supervisor:
  Mark W Assini . . . . . . . . . . . . . . . . . . . . . . . . . . . . .585-247-6100
Town Clerk:
  Richard A Warner. . . . . . . . . . . . . . . . . . . . . . . . . . . .585-247-6100
Finance Director:
  Art Plewa . . . . . . . . . . . . . . . . . . . . . . . . . . . . . . . . .585-247-6100
Police Chief:
  David R DiCaro . . . . . . . . . . . . . . . . . . . . . . . . . . . . .585-247-2262
Director, Building & Public Works:
  John Lathrop . . . . . . . . . . . . . . . . . . . . . . . . .585-247-6100 x241
Town Historian:
  Judy DeRooy. . . . . . . . . . . . . . . . . . . . . . . . . . . . . . .585-247-6100

## Glen Cove, City of
9 Glen St
Glen Cove, NY 11542
516-676-2000  Fax: 516-676-0108
Web site: www.glencove-li.com

Mayor:
  Ralph V Suozzi . . . . . . . . . . . . . . . .516-676-2004/fax: 516-676-0108
City Clerk:
  Tina Pemberton. . . . . . . . . . . . . . . .516-676-3345 or 516-676-3357
City Attorney:
  Vincent Taranto . . . . . . . . . . . . . . . . . . . . . . . . . . . . .516-759-1111
Controller:
  Sal Lombardi. . . . . . . . . . . . . . . . . . . . . . . . . . . . . . .516-676-2789
Director, Public Works:
  William Archambault . . . . . . . . . . . . . . . . . . . . . . . . . .516-676-4402
Police Chief:
  William Whitton. . . . . . . . . . . . . . . . . . . . . . . . . . . . .516-676-1000

## Glenville, Town of
18 Glenridge Rd
Glenville, NY 12302
518-688-1200  Fax: 518-384-0140

*Offices and agencies generally appear in alphabetical order, except when specific order is requested by listee.*

Town Supervisor:
  Christopher A Koetzle . . . . . . . . . . . . . . 518-688-1202/fax: 518-384-0140
  e-mail: ckoetzle@townofglenville.org
Town Clerk:
  Linda Neals . . . . . . . . . . . . . . . . . . 518-688-1200x402/fax: 518-384-0140
  e-mail: lneals@townofglenville.org
Town Attorney:
  Michael R Cuevas . . . . . . . . . . . . . . . . 518-688-1200/fax: 518-384-0140
Town Planner:
  Kevin Corcoran . . . . . . . . . . . . . . . 518-688-1200x407/fax: 518-384-0140
  e-mail: kcorcoran@townofglenville.org
Comptroller:
  Jason Cuthbert . . . . . . . . . . . . . . 518-688-1200 ext306/fax: 518-384-0140
  e-mail: gphillips@townofglenville.org
Highway Superintendent & Commissioner, Public Works:
  Thomas Coppola . . . . . . . . . . . . . . . . 518-382-1406/fax: 518-382-3015
  e-mail: tcoppola@townofglenville.org
Historian:
  Joan Szablewski . . . . . . . . . . . . . . . . 518-982-0643/fax: 518-384-0140
Police Chief:
  Michael Ranalli . . . . . . . . . . . . . . . . . 518-384-3444/fax: 518-384-0141
  e-mail: mranalli@townofglenville.org

## Grand Island, Town of
Grand Island Town Hall
2255 Baseline Road
Grand Island, NY 14072
716-773-9618  Fax: 716-773-9618
Web site: www.gigov.com

Town Supervisor:
  Mary Cooke . . . . . . . . . . . . . . . . . . . 716-773-9600/fax: 716-773-9618
  e-mail: supervisor@grand-island.ny.us
Assistant/Deputy Supervisor:
  Elizabeth Wilbert . . . . . . . . . . . . . . . . 716-773-9600/fax: 716-773-9618
  e-mail: lwilbert@grand-island.ny.us
Town Clerk:
  Pattie Frentzel . . . . . . . . . . . . . . . . . . 716-773-9600/fax: 716-773-9618
  e-mail: pfrentzel@grand-island.ny.us
Town Attorney:
  Peter Godfrey . . . . . . . . . . . . . . . . . . 716-773-9600/fax: 716-773-9618
Town Accountant:
  Pamela Barton . . . . . . . . . . . . . . . . . . 716-773-9600/fax: 716-773-9618
  e-mail: pbarton@grand-island.ny.us
Town Assessor:
  Judy M Tafelski . . . . . . . . . . . . . . . . . 716-773-9600/fax: 716-773-9618
  e-mail: assessor@grand-island.ny.us

## Greece, Town of
1 Vince Tofany Blvd
Greece, NY 14612
585-225-2000  Fax: 585-225-1915
Web site: greeceny.gov

Town Supervisor:
  John T Auberger . . . . . . . . . . . . . . . . . . . . . . . . . . . . . .585-723-2311
Deputy Town Supervisor:
  Jeffery McCann . . . . . . . . . . . . . . . . . . . . . . . . . . . . . .585-723-2000
Director, Constituent Services:
  Kathryn J Firkins . . . . . . . . . . . . . . . . . . . . . . . . . . . .585-723-2000
Town Clerk:
  Patricia Anthony . . . . . . . . . . . . . . . . . 585-723-2341/fax: 585-723-2459
Town Attorney:
  Jeffery McCann . . . . . . . . . . . . . . . . . 585-225-2000/fax: 585-225-1915
Director, Finance:
  Rick Pellegrino . . . . . . . . . . . . . . . . . . . . . . . . . . . . .585-723-2335
Police Chief:
  Todd Baxter . . . . . . . . . . . . . . . . . . . . . . . . . . . . . . . .585-865-9200
Town Assessor:
  Leo Carroll . . . . . . . . . . . . . . . . . . . . . . . . . . . . . . . . .585-723-2308

## Greenburgh, Town of
177 Hillside Avenue
Greenburgh, NY 10607
914-993-1500  Fax: 914-993-1626
Web site: www.greenburghny.com

Town Supervisor:
  Paul J Feiner . . . . . . . . . . . . . . . . . . . . 914-993-1540/fax: 914-993-1541
  e-mail: pfeiner@greenburghny.com
Town Clerk:
  Judith A Beville . . . . . . . . . . . . . . . . . . 914-993-1500/fax: 914-993-1626
  e-mail: townclerk@greenburghny.com
Historian:
  Frank Jazzo . . . . . . . . . . . . . . . . . . . . . 914-993-1641/fax: 914-993-1626
Chief of Police:
  Joseph DiCarlo . . . . . . . . . . . . . . . . . . . 914-682-5300/fax: 914-683-5342

## Guilderland, Town of
Town Hall
5209 Western Turnpike
PO Box 339
Guilderland, NY 12084
518-356-1980  Fax: 518-356-3955
Web site: www.townofguilderland.org

Town Supervisor:
  Kenneth Runion . . . . . . . . . . . . . 518-356-1980 x1022/fax: 518-356-5514
  e-mail: runionk@townofguilderland.org
Town Clerk:
  Rosemary Centi . . . . . . . . . . . . . . . . . . 518-356-1980/fax: 518-356-3955
Police Chief:
  Carol Lawlor . . . . . . . . . . . . . . . . . . . . 518-356-1980/fax: 518-356-4668
  e-mail: lawlorc@guilderlandpd.org
Town Historian:
  Alice Begley . . . . . . . . . . . . . . . . 518-356-1980 x1050/fax: 518-356-3955

## Hamburg, Town of
6100 South Park Ave
Hamburg, NY 14075
716-649-6111  Fax: 716-649-4087
Web site: www.townofhamburgny.com

Town Supervisor:
  Steven J Walters . . . . . . . . . . . . . . . . . . . . . . . . .716-649-6111 x2381
  e-mail: supervisor@townofhamburgny.com
Town Clerk:
  Catherine A Rybczynski . . . . . . . 716-649-6111 x2360/fax: 716-646-1384
  e-mail: townclerk@townofhamburgny.com
Senior Public Safety Dispatcher:
  Thomas E Taylor . . . . . . . . . . . . . . . . . . . . . . . . .716-649-6111 x2412
Town Historian:
  James Baker . . . . . . . . . . . . . . . . . . . . . . . . . . . .716-649-6111 x. 2400

## Harrison, Town/Village of
11 Heineman Place
Harrison, NY 10528
914-670-3000  Fax: 914-835-8067

Supervisor/Mayor:
  Ron Belmont . . . . . . . . . . . . . . . . . . . . . 914-670-3005/fax: 914-835-8067
  e-mail: jwalsh@harrison-ny.gov
Town Clerk:
  Jacqueline Greer . . . . . . . . . . . . . . . . . . 914-670-3030/fax: 914-835-2009
  e-mail: jgreer@harrison-ny.gov
Comptroller/Treasurer:
  Maureen MacKenzie . . . . . . . . . . . . . . 914-670-3080/fax: 914-835-2759
  e-mail: comptroller@harrison-ny.gov
Police Chief:
  Anthony Marraccini . . . . . . . . . . . . . . . . . . . . . . . . . . . .914-967-5110

Commissioner, Public Works:
  Anthony P Robinson . . . . . . . . . . . . . . . . 914-670-3229/fax: 914-835-2387
  e-mail: arobinson@harrison-ny.gov
Fire Marshal/Fire Prevention Dept:
  Robert Fitzsimmons. . . . . . . . . . . . . . . . 914-670-3051/fax: 914-670-3170

## Haverstraw, Town of
1 Rosman Rd
Garnerville, NY 10923
845-429-2200  Fax: 845-429-4701
Web site: www.townofhaverstraw.us

Town Supervisor:
  Howard T Phillips, Jr. . . . . . . . . . . . . . 845-429-2200/fax: 845-429-4701
Town Clerk:
  Karen L. Bulley . . . . . . . . . . . 845-942-3727 or 845-942-3728
  fax: 845-942-4964
Town Attorney:
  William Stein . . . . . . . . . . . . . . . . . . . . . . . . . . . . . . 845-429-2200
Finance Director:
  Michael J Gamboli . . . . . . . . . . . . . . . . . . . . . . . . . . 845-429-2200

## Hempstead, Town of
Town Hall Plaza
1 Washington St
Hempstead, NY 11550
516-489-5000  Fax: 516-538-2908
Web site: www.townofhempstead.org; www.toh.li

Town Supervisor:
  Kate Murray. . . . . . . . . . . . . . . . . . . . . . . . . . . 516-489-6000 x3260
Town Clerk:
  Mark A Bonilla . . . . . . . . . . . . . . . . . . . . . . . . . 516-489-5000 x3046

## Hempstead, Village of
99 Nichols Court
Hempstead, NY 11550
516-489-3400  Fax: 516-489-4285
Web site: www.villageofhempstead.org

Mayor:
  Wayne J Hall Sr . . . . . . . . . . . . . . . . . . . . . . . . . . . . 516-478-6200
Village Clerk:
  Patricia Perez . . . . . . . . . . . . . . . . . . . . . . . . . . . . . 516-478-6202
  e-mail: clerksoffice@villageofhempsteadny.gov
Public Works Director:
  Frank Germinaro . . . . . . . . . . . . . . . . . . . . . . . 516-489-3400 x270
Chief of Police:
  Michael McGown . . . . . . . . . . . . . . . . . . . . . . . . . . . 516-483-6200

## Henrietta, Town of
475 Calkins Rd
Henrietta, NY 14467
585-334-7700  Fax: 585-334-9667
Web site: www.henrietta.org

Town Supervisor:
  Michael B Yudelson . . . . . . . . . . . . . . . 585-359-7001/fax: 585-334-9667
Town Clerk:
  Leann Case . . . . . . . . . . . . . . . . . . . 585-334-7700/fax: 585-334-9667
Sewer, Drainage, & Sidewalks Foreman:
  Michael Catalano. . . . . . . . . . . . . . . . . 585-444-2211/fax: 585-359-7029

## Huntington, Town of
100 Main St
Huntington, NY 11743
631-351-3000  Fax: 631-424-7856
Web site: http://huntingtonny.gov

Town Supervisor:
  Frank P Petrone . . . . . . . . . . . . . . . . . . . 631-351-3030/fax: 631-424-7856
Town Clerk:
  Jo-Ann Raia. . . . . . . . . . . . . . . . . . . . 631-351-3206/fax: 631-351-3205
Town Attorney:
  Cindy Elan-Mangano . . . . . . . . . . . . . . 631-351-3042/fax: 631-351-3032
Public Safety Director:
  Vacant . . . . . . . . . . . . . . . . . . . . . . . 631-351-3167/fax: 631-351-3169
Director, General Services:
  Thomas J Boccard . . . . . . . . . . . . . . . . . 631-351-3365/fax: 631-351-3337
Historian:
  Robert C Hughes . . . . . . . . . . . . . . . . . . 631-351-3244/fax: 631-351-3245
  e-mail: huntingtonhistorial@verizon.net

## Hyde Park, Town of
4383 Albany Post Rd
Hyde Park, NY 12538
845-229-5111  Fax: 845-229-0831
Web site: www.hydeparkny.us

Town Supervisor:
  Aileen Rohr . . . . . . . . . . . . . . . . . . . 845-229-5111 x8/fax: 845-229-0831
  e-mail: supervisor@hydeparkny.us
Town Clerk:
  Donna McGrogan. . . . . . . . . . . . . . . 845-229-5111 x5/fax: 845-229-7583
Police Chief:
  Eric Paolilli . . . . . . . . . . . . . . . . . . . 845-229-9340/fax: 845-229-6953
Town Historian:
  Carey Rhinevault . . . . . . . . . . . . . . . . . . . . . . . . . . . 845-229-8225

## Irondequoit, Town of
Town Hall
1280 Titus Ave
Rochester, NY 14617
585-467-8840  Fax: 585-467-7294
e-mail: feedback@irondequoit.org
Web site: www.irondequoit.org

Town Supervisor:
  Mary Joyce D'Aurizio . . . . . . . . . . . . . . . . . . . . . . . . 585-336-6034
Town Clerk/Receiver of Taxes:
  Barbara Genier . . . . . . . . . . . . . . . . . . . . . . . . . . . . . 585-336-6045
  e-mail: bgenier@irondequoit.org
Comptroller:
  Annie C Sealy. . . . . . . . . . . . . . . . . . . . . . . . . . . . . . 585-336-6010
  e-mail: asealy@irondequoit.org
Fire Marshal:
  Greg Merrick. . . . . . . . . . . . . . . . . . . . . . . . . . . . . . . 585-336-6097
  e-mail: firemarshal@irondequoit.org
Town Historian:
  Patricia Wayne . . . . . . . . . . . . . . . . . . . . . . . . . . . . . 585-336-7269
  e-mail: pwayne@irondequoit.org

## Islip, Town of
Town Hall
655 Main St
Islip, NY 11751
631-224-5500 or 631-224-5691  Fax: 631-581-8424
Web site: www.townofislip-ny.gov

Town Supervisor:
  Tom Croci. . . . . . . . . . . . . . . . . . . . . . . . . . . . . . . . . 631-224-5500
  e-mail: supervisorsoffice@townofislip-ny.gov
Town Clerk:
  Olga H. Murray . . . . . . . . . . . . . . . . . 631-224-5490/fax: 631 224-5574
  e-mail: townclerk@townofislip-ny.gov
Town Attorney:
  Robert L. Cicale. . . . . . . . . . . . . . . . . . 631-224-5550/fax: 631-224-5573
  e-mail: townattorney@townofislip-ny.gov

*Offices and agencies generally appear in alphabetical order, except when specific order is requested by listee.*

Comptroller:
  Joseph Ludwig.....................631-595-3840/fax: 631-224-5701
  e-mail: comptroller@townofislip-ny.gov
Receiver of Taxes:
  Alexis Weik ......................................631-224-5580
  e-mail: vallen@townofislip-ny.gov
Commissioner, Public Works:
  Thomas Owens ..............................631-224-5600
  e-mail: commissioner-dpw@townofislip-ny.gov
Harbor Police Chief:
  Robert Sgroi ....................................631-224-5656
  e-mail: harborpolice@townofislip-ny.gov

## Ithaca, City of
City Hall
108 E Green St
Ithaca, NY 14850
607-274-6570  Fax: 307-274-6432
Web site: www.cityofithaca.org

Mayor:
  Svante Myrick ....................607-274-6501/fax: 607-274-6526
  e-mail: asherman@cityofithaca.org
City Clerk:
  Julie Conley Holcomb..............607-274-6570/fax: 607-274-6432
  e-mail: julieh@cityofithaca.org
City Chamberlain:
  Debra Parsons....................607-274-6580/fax: 607-272-7348
  e-mail: debrap@cityofithaca.org
City Attorney:
  Aaron O. Lavine ..................607-274-6504/fax: 607-274-6507
  e-mail: attorney@cityofithaca.org
Controller:
  Steven P Thayer...................607-274-6576/fax: 607-274-6415
  e-mail: dredsicker@cityofithaca.org
Police Chief (Acting):
  John R. Barber ..................................607-272-9973
  e-mail: edv@cityofithaca.org

## Ithaca, Town of
Town Hall
215 North Tioga Street
Ithaca, NY 14850
607-273-1721
Web site: www.town.ithaca.ny.us

Town Supervisor:
  Herb Engman................................607-273-1721 x125
  e-mail: Hengman@town.ithaca.ny.us
Town Clerk:
  Paulette Terwilliger........................607-273-1721 x110
  e-mail: pterwilliger@town.ithaca.ny.us
Town Budget Officer:
  Al Carvill..................................607-273-1721 x113
  e-mail: acarvill@town.ithaca.ny.us
Town Historian:
  Laura Johnson-Kelly
  e-mail: lwjl@town.ithaca.ny.us

## Jamestown, City of
Municipal Bldg
200 E Third St
Jamestown, NY 14701
716-483-7612  Fax: 716-483-7502
Web site: www.jamestownny.net

Mayor:
  Samuel Teresi ...................716-483-7600/fax: 716-483-7591

City Clerk:
  James Olson.......................716-483-7612/fax: 716-483-7502
Corporation Counsel:
  Marilyn Fiore-Lehman ..............716-483-7540/fax: 716-483-7591
Comptroller:
  Joseph A Bellitto.................716-483-7538/fax: 716-483-7771
Director Financial Services:
  James Olson.......................716-483-7512/fax: 716-483-7502
Police Chief/Director Public Safety:
  Harry Snellings ...................716-483-7536/fax: 716-483-7722

## Kingston, City of
420 Broadway
Kingston, NY 12401
845-331-0080  Fax: 845-334-3904
Web site: www.ci.kingston.ny.us

Mayor:
  Shayne R Gallo ...................845-334-3902/fax: 845-334-3904
  e-mail: mayor@kingston-ny.gov
City Clerk:
  Carly Williams....................845-334-3915/fax: 845-334-3918
  e-mail: cwilliams@kingston-ny.gov
Corporation Counsel:
  Andrew Zweben ...................845-334-3947/fax: 845-334-3959
  e-mail: corpcounsel@kingston-ny.gov
Comptroller:
  John Tuey ........................845-334-3935/fax: 845-334-3944
  e-mail: comptroller@kingston-ny.gov
Executive Director, Community Development:
  Michael Murphy ...................845-334-3924/fax: 845-334-3932
  e-mail: mmurphy@kingston-ny.gov
Chief of Police/Commissioner:
  Egidio F. Tinti .....................845-331-1671 or 845-943-5720
  e-mail: gkeller@kingston-ny.gov
Fire Chief:
  John Reinhardt....................845-331-1326/fax: 845-331-3252
  e-mail: fire@kingston-ny.gov

## Lancaster, Town of
21 Central Ave
Lancaster, NY 14086
716-683-1610  Fax: 716-683-0512
e-mail: lookatus@lancasterny.com

Town Supervisor:
  Dino J Fudoli.....................716-683-1610/fax: 716-683-0512
Town Clerk:
  Johanna M Coleman ...............716-683-9028/fax: 716-683-2094
Town Attorney:
  John M Dudziak ..................716-684-3342/fax: 716-681-7475
  e-mail: jdudziak@lancasterny.com
Director, Administration & Finance:
  David J Brown ................................716-683-1610
Police Chief:
  Gerald Gill Jr.....................716-683-2800/fax: 716-681-2352
Emergency Management/Nat'l Disaster Coordinator:
  Robert MacPeek ...................716-684-1232/fax: 716-684-1237
Town Assessor:
  Christine Fusco................716-683-1311 x112/fax: 716-681-7054
  e-mail: assessor@lancasterny.com
Historian:
  Edward Mikula .................................716-683-6529

## LeRay, Town of
8650 LeRay Street
Evans Mill, NY 13637-3191
315-629-4052  Fax: 315-629-4393
Web site: www.townofleray.org

*Offices and agencies generally appear in alphabetical order, except when specific order is requested by listee.*

Town Supervisor:
   Ronald C Taylor . . . . . . . . . . . . . . . . . . .315-629-5532/fax: 315-629-4393
   e-mail: lerayadmin@nnymail.com
Town Clerk/Receiver/Registrar:
   Mary C Smith . . . . . . . . . . . . . . . . . .315-629-4052/fax: 315-629-4393
   e-mail: lerayclerk@nnymail.com

## Lindenhurst, Village of
430 S Wellwood Ave
Lindenhurst, NY 11757
631-957-7500  Fax: 631-957-4605

Village Mayor:
   Thomas A Brennan . . . . . . . . . . . . . . . . . . . . . . . . . . . . .631-957-7500
Deputy Mayor:
   Kevin McCaffey . . . . . . . . . . . . . . . . . . . . . . . . . . . . . . . .631-957-7500
Clerk/Treasurer:
   Shawn Cullinane
Deputy Clerk:
   Doug M Madlon
Fire Marshall:
   Richard Lyman . . . . . . . . . . . . . . . . . . . . . . . . . . . . . . . . .631-957-7514

## Lockport, City of
Lockport Municipal Building
One Locks Plaza
Lockport, NY 14094
716-439-6665  Fax: 716-439-6668
Web site: www.elockport.com

Mayor:
   Michael W Tucker . . . . . . . . . . . . . . . .716-439-6665/fax: 716-439-6668
City Clerk:
   Richelle J. Pasceri . . . . . . . . . . . . . . .716-439-6676/fax: 716-439-6650
Treasurer:
   Michael White . . . . . . . . . . . . . . . . . . .716-439-6744/fax: 716-439-6617
Police Chief:
   Lawrence Eggert . . . . . . . . . . . . . . . . . . . . . . . . . . . . . . .716-439-6689
Fire Department Chief:
   Thomas J Passuite . . . . . . . . . . . . . . . . . . . . . . . . . . . . . .716-439-6724

## Lockport, Town of
6560 Dysinger Rd
Lockport, NY 14094
716-439-9520  Fax: 716-439-0528
Web site: www.elockport.com

Town Supervisor:
   Marc Smith . . . . . . . . . . . . . . . . . . . . .716-439-9520/fax: 716-439-0528
Town Clerk:
   Nancy Brooks . . . . . . . . . . . . . . . . . . .716-439-9524/fax: 716-438-5465
Town Historian:
   Laurence Haseley . . . . . . . . . . . . . . . . . . . . . . . . . . . . . . .716-438-2159

## Long Beach, City of
City Hall
1 West Chester St
Long Beach, NY 11561
516-431-1000  Fax: 516-431-1389
e-mail: info@longbeachny.org
Web site: www.longbeachny.org

City Manager:
   Jack Schnirman . . . . . . . . . . . . . . . . . . . . . . . . . . . . . . . . .516-431-1001
City Clerk:
   David W Fraser . . . . . . . . . . . . . . . . . .516-431-1002/fax: 516-431-2717
Corporation Counsel:
   Corey Klein . . . . . . . . . . . . . . . . . . . . . . . . . . . . . . . . . . . .516-431-1003

Comptroller:
   Jeff Nogid . . . . . . . . . . . . . . . . . . . . . . . . . . . . . . . . . . . . .516-431-1004
Police Commissioner:
   Michael Tangney . . . . . . . . . . . . . . . . . . . . . . . . . . . . . . .516-431-1800
   e-mail: lbpd@longbeachny.org

## Lysander, Town of
Town Hall
8220 Loop Rd
Baldwinsville, NY 13027
315-638-4264  Fax: 315-635-1515
Web site: www.townoflysander.org

Town Supervisor:
   John A Salisbury . . . . . . . . . . . . . . . . . .315-857-0281/fax: 315-635-1515
   e-mail: supervisor@townoflysander.org
Town Clerk:
   Lisa Dell . . . . . . . . . . . . . . . . . . . . . . .315-638-0224/fax: 315-635-1515
   e-mail: townclerk@townoflysander.org
Comptroller:
   David J Rahrle . . . . . . . . . . . . . . . . . . .315-635-1443/fax: 315-635-1515
   e-mail: comptroller@townoflysander.org
Town Historian:
   Bonnie Kisselstein . . . . . . . . . . . . . . . .315-638-0224/fax: 315-635-1515
   e-mail: bkissels@twcny.rr.com

## Mamaroneck, Town of
Town Center
740 W Boston Post Rd
Mamaroneck, NY 10543
914-381-7805  Fax: 914-381-7809
e-mail: townclerk@townofmamaroneck.org
Web site: www.townofmamaroneck.org

Town Supervisor:
   Nancy Seligson
   e-mail: supervisor@townofmamaroneck.org
Town Administrator:
   Stephen Altieri . . . . . . . . . . . . . . . . . . .914-381-7810/fax: 914-381-7809
   e-mail: townadministrator@townofmamaroneck.org
Town Clerk:
   Christina Battalia . . . . . . . . . . . . . . . . . .914-381-7870/fax: 914-381-7813
   e-mail: townclerk@townofmamaroneck.org
Police Chief:
   Richard Rivera . . . . . . . . . . . . . . . . . . . .914-381-6100/fax: 914-381-7897
   e-mail: policechief@townofmamaroneck.org
Emergency Management Coordinator:
   Michael Liverzani . . . . . . . . . . . . . . . . . . . . . . . . . . . . . . .914-381-7838

## Manlius, Town of
301 Brooklea Dr
Fayetteville, NY 13066
315-637-3521  Fax: 315-637-0713
Web site: www.townofmanlius.org

Town Supervisor:
   Edmond J Theobald . . . . . . . . . . . . . . . .315-637-3414/fax: 315-637-0713
   e-mail: etheobald@townofmanlius.org
Town Clerk:
   Allison A Edsall . . . . . . . . . . . . . . . . . .315-637-3521/fax: 315-637-0713
Receiver of Taxes:
   Laura Peschel . . . . . . . . . . . . . . . . . . . .315-637-6481/fax: 315-637-0713
Police Chief:
   Francis Marlowe . . . . . . . . . . . . . . . . . .315-682-2212/fax: 315-682-4527

## Middletown, City of
City Hall
16 James St
Middletown, NY 10940

*Offices and agencies generally appear in alphabetical order, except when specific order is requested by listee.*

845-346-4100  Fax: 845-343-7439
Web site: www.middletown-ny.com

Mayor:
　Joseph M DeStefano . . . . . . . . . . . . . . . 845-346-4100/fax: 845-343-7439
　e-mail: mayor@middletown-ny.com
Common Council President:
　J Miguel Rodrigues . . . . . . . . . . . . . . . . . . . . . . . . . . . . . . . 845-742-8775
　e-mail: mrodrigues@middletown-ny.com
Common Council Clerk/Registrar:
　John Naumchik . . . . . . . . . . . . . . . . . . . 845-346-4168/fax: 845-344-5428
City Attorney:
　Alex Smith . . . . . . . . . . . . . . . . . . . . . . . 845-346-4140/fax: 845-346-4146
Treasurer:
　Donald Paris . . . . . . . . . . . . . . . . . . . . . 845-346-4150/fax: 845-343-1101
Commissioner, Public Works:
　Jacob Tawil . . . . . . . . . . . . . . . . . . . . . . 845-343-3169/fax: 845-343-4014
Chief of Police:
　Ramon Bethencourt . . . . . . . . . . . . . . . . 845-343-3151/fax: 845-343-2660
　e-mail: rbethencourt@middletown-ny.com
Fire Chief:
　Tom Amodio . . . . . . . . . . . . . . . . . . . . . 845-344-5003/fax: 845-344-5031
　e-mail: info@middletownfiredept.com

## Monroe, Town of
11 Stage Road
Monroe, NY 10950
845-783-1900  Fax: 845-782-5597
Web site: www.monroeny.org

Town Supervisor:
　Sandy Leonard . . . . . . . . . . . . . . . 845-783-1900 x227/fax: 845-782-5597
Town Clerk:
　Mary Ellen Beams . . . . . . . . . . . . 845-783-1900 x221/fax: 845-782-5597
　e-mail: maryellen@monroeny.org
Tax Collector:
　Mary Ellen Beams . . . . . . . . . . . . 845-783-1990 x221/fax: 845-782-5597
Historian:
　James Nelson . . . . . . . . . . . . . . . . . . . . . . . . . . . . . . . . . . 845-783-3406
　e-mail: nelsonja@fastmail.fm

## Montgomery, Town of
110 Bracken Rd
Montgomery, NY 12549
845-457-2660  Fax: 845-457-2613
Web site: www.townofmontgomery.com

Town Supervisor:
　Michael Hayes . . . . . . . . . . . . . . . . . . . . . . . . . . . . . . . . . 845-457-2600
Town Clerk:
　Tara Stickles . . . . . . . . . . . . . . . . . . . 845-457-2660/fax: 845-457-2613
Town Attorney:
　Charles T Bazydlo . . . . . . . . . . . . . . . . . . . . . . . . . . . . . . 845-361-3668
Receiver of Taxes:
　Janice A Cocks . . . . . . . . . . . . . . . . . . 845-457-2630/fax: 845-457-2613
　e-mail: tomtax@frontiernet.net
Police Chief:
　Arnold Amthor . . . . . . . . . . . . . . . . . . . . . . . . . . . . . . . . . 845-457-9211
　e-mail: TMPDChief@frontiernet.net
Town Historian:
　Suzanne Isaksen . . . . . . . . . . . . . . . . . . . . . . . . . . . . . . . 845-457-9098
　e-mail: tomhistorian@frontiernet.net

## Mount Pleasant, Town of
One Town Hall Plaza
Valhalla, NY 10595
914-742-2360  Fax: 914-769-3155

Town Supervisor:
　Joan A Maybury . . . . . . . . . . . . . . . . . . 914-742-2301/fax: 914-769-3155
　e-mail: jmaybury@mtpleasantny.com
Town Clerk:
　Patricia June Scova . . . . . . . . . . . . . . . . 914-742-2312/fax: 914-747-6172
　e-mail: pscova@mtpleasantny.com
Deputy Town Attorney:
　Christopher W. McClure . . . . . . . . . . . . 914-742-2357/fax: 914-769-3155
Comptroller:
　Tina Peretti . . . . . . . . . . . . . . . . . . . . . . . . . . . . . . . . . . . 914-742-2360
Police Chief:
　Louis Alagno . . . . . . . . . . . . . . . . . . . . . 914-769-1941/fax: 914-769-7199
　e-mail: lalagno@mtpleasantny.com

## Mount Vernon, City of
City Hall
1 Roosevelt Square
Mount Vernon, NY 10550
914-665-2300  Fax: 914-665-2496
Web site: cmvny.com

Mayor:
　Ernest D. Davis . . . . . . . . . . . . . . . . . . . . . . . . . . . . . . . . . 914-665-2360
　e-mail: mayor@cmvny.com
City Clerk/Registrar:
　George Brown . . . . . . . . . . . . . . . . . . . . . . . . . . . . . . . . . . 914-665-2348
Comptroller:
　Maureen Walker . . . . . . . . . . . . . . . . . . . . . . . . . . . . . . . . 914-665-2312
Police Commissioner:
　John Roland . . . . . . . . . . . . . . . . . . . . . . . . . . . . . . . . . . . 914-665-2500
Police Chief:
　James Dumser . . . . . . . . . . . . . . . . . . . . . . . . . . . . . . . . . 914-665-2500
Fire Chief:
　Edward Stephenson . . . . . . . . . . . . . . . . . . . . . . . . . . . . . 914-665-2626
Deputy Public Works Commissioner:
　Curtis J Woods . . . . . . . . . . . . . . . . . . . . . . . . . . . . . . . . . 914-665-2334

## New Hartford, Town of
Butler Hall
48 Genesee Street
New Hartford, NY 13413
315-733-7500
Web site: www.newhartfordtown.com

Town Supervisor:
　Patrick M Tyksinski . . . . . . . . . . . . . . . . . . . . . . . . . 315-733-7500 x2332
　e-mail: nhsupervisor@town.new-hartford.ny.us
Town Clerk:
　Gail Wolanin Young . . . . . . . . . . 315-733-7500 x2322/fax: 315-797-9986
　e-mail: gyoung@town.new-hartford.ny.us
Receiver of Taxes:
　Gail Wolanin Young . . . . . . . . . . 315-733-7500 x2324/fax: 315-797-9986
Police Chief:
　Michael Inserra . . . . . . . . . . . . . . . . . . . 315-724-7111/fax: 315-724-8618

## New Rochelle, City of
City Hall
515 North Ave
New Rochelle, NY 10801
914-654-2000  Fax: 914-654-2174
Web site: www.newrochelleny.com

Mayor:
　Noam Bramson . . . . . . . . . . . . . . . . . . . 914-654-2150/fax: 914-654-2357
　e-mail: nbramson@newrochelleny.com
City Manager:
　Charles B Strome III . . . . . . . . . . . . . . . 914-654-2140/fax: 914-654-2174
　e-mail: cstrome@newrochelleny.com

State & Local
Government
Public Information

*Offices and agencies generally appear in alphabetical order, except when specific order is requested by listee.*

City Clerk:
  Bennie F Giles......................914-654-2159/fax: 914-654-2158
Corporation Counsel:
  Kathleen Gill......................914-654-2120/fax: 914-654-2345
Finance Commissioner:
  Howard Rattner....................914-654-2062/fax: 914-654-2344
Public Works Commissioner:
  Alexander Tergis..................914-654-2129/fax: 914-654-2195
Police Commissioner:
  Patrick J Carroll.................................914-654-2228
Fire Chief:
  Louis DeMeglio....................914-654-2212/fax: 914-632-2907
  e-mail: rkiernan@newrochelleny.com

## New Windsor, Town of
555 Union Avenue
New Windsor, NY 12553
845-565-8800  Fax: 845-563-4693
e-mail: info@town.new-windsor.ny.us
Web site: http://town.new-windsor.ny.us

Town Supervisor/Chief Fiscal Officer:
  George A Green....................845-563-4610/fax: 845-563-4610
Town Clerk:
  Deborah Green.....................845-563-4611/fax: 845-563-4611
  e-mail: dgreen@town.new-windsor.ny.us
Town Attorney:
  Michael Blythe....................845-563-4630/fax: 845-563-4630
  e-mail: mblythe@town.new-windsor.ny.us
Comptroller:
  Jack Finnegan.....................845-563-4623/fax: 845-563-4623
Police Chief:
  Michael C Biasotti................845-565-7000/fax: 845-563-4694
  e-mail: pdadmin@town.new-windsor.ny.us
Fire Inspector & Department Head:
  Jennifer Gallagher................845-563-4618/fax: 845-563-4618
Town Historian:
  Glenn Marshall
  e-mail: historynw@aol.com

## New York City
City Hall
New York, NY 10007
212-788-3000  Fax: 212-788-3247
Web site: www.nyc.gov

Mayor:
  Bill de Blasio................212-788-3000 or 212-639-9675
  fax: 212-312-0700
First Deputy Mayor:
  Dean Fuleihan.....................212-788-3000/fax: 212-312-0700
Deputy Mayor, Strategic Policy Initiatives:
  Richard Buery.....................212-788-3000/fax: 212-312-0700
Deputy Mayor, Housing & Economic Development:
  Alicia Glen.......................212-788-3000/fax: 212-312-0700
Deputy Mayor, Health & Human Services:
  Herminia Palacio..................212-788-3000/fax: 212-312-0700
Director, Communications:
  Michael Casca.................................212-788-3000
Senior Advisor to Mayor, Strategic Planning:
  Andrea Hagelgans..................212-788-3000/fax: 212-312-0700
Press Secretary:
  Eric Phillips.....................212-788-3000/fax: 212-788-2460

**Aging, Dept for the, NYC**....................fax: 212-442-1095
  2 Lafayette St, New York, NY 10007
  212-442-1322  Fax: 212-442-1095
  Web site: www.nyc.gov/aging

Commissioner:
  Lilliam Barrios-Paoli
  e-mail: emendez@aging.nyc.gov
First Deputy Commissioner:
  Sally Renfro
  e-mail: srenfro@aging.nyc.gov
General Counsel:
  Steven Foo.................................212-442-3159
  e-mail: mamurphy@aging.nyc.gov
Deputy Commissioner, External Affairs:
  Caryn Resnick..............................212-442-1277
  e-mail: cresnick@aging.nyc.gov
Executive Director, Aging in NY Fund:
  Ali Hodin-Baier............................212-442-1375
Director, Public Affairs:
  Christopher Miller
  e-mail: cmiller@aging.nyc.gov

**Public Design Commission, NYC**..............fax: 212-788-3086
  City Hall, 3rd Fl, New York, NY 10007
  212-788-3071  Fax: 212-788-3086
  Web site: www.nyc.gov/artcommission
Executive Director:
  Jackie Snyder.....................212-788-3071/fax: 212-788-3086
  e-mail: jsnyder@cityhall.nyc.gov
President:
  Signe Nielsen.....................212-788-3071/fax: 212-788-3086
Project Manager:
  Rivka Weinstock...................212-788-3071/fax: 212-788-3086
Special Projects Manager:
  Julianna Monjeau..................212-788-3071/fax: 212-788-3086
Sculptor:
  Maria Elena-Gonzalez..............212-788-3071/fax: 212-788-3086
Painter:
  Byron Kim.........................212-788-3071/fax: 212-788-3086
Architect:
  James Stewart Polshek..............212-788-3071/fax: 212-788-3086
Director, Tour Programs:
  Joan H Bright.....................212-788-3071/fax: 212-788-3086

**Buildings, Department of, NYC**...............fax: 212-566-3784
  280 Broadway, 7th Fl, New York, NY 10007-1801
  212-566-5000 or TTY: 212-566-4769  Fax: 212-566-3784
  Web site: www.nyc.gov/buildings
Commissioner:
  Robert D LiMandri..............................212-566-0011
First Deputy Cmsr, Operations:
  Thomas Fariello, R.A.
Deputy Commissioner, Technology & Analysis:
  Marilyn King-Festa................212-566-4225/fax: 212-566-3865
Deputy Commissioner, Technical Affairs:
  Fatma Amer
General Counsel:
  Mona Sehgal.......................212-566-3291/fax: 212-566-3843

**Campaign Finance Board, NYC**.................fax: 212-306-7143
  40 Rector St, 7th Fl, New York, NY 10006
  212-306-7100  Fax: 212-306-7143
  e-mail: info@nyccfb.info
  Web site: www.nyccfb.info
Chair:
  Joseph P Parkes
Executive Director:
  Amy M Loprest
Chief of Administrative Services:
  Elizabeth Bauer
Director of External Affairs:
  Eric Friedman

**City Council, NYC**..........................fax: 212-788-7093
  250 Broadway, 18th Fl, New York, NY 10007

*Offices and agencies generally appear in alphabetical order, except when specific order is requested by listee.*

212-788-7084  Fax: 212-788-7093
Web site: council.nyc.gov
Speaker:
Corey Johnson
e-mail: SpeakerJohnson@council.nyc.gov
Majority Leader:
Laurie Cumbo . . . . . . . . . . . . . . . . . . . . . .718-260-9191/fax: 718-398-2808
e-mail: LCumbo@council.nyc.gov
Minority Leader:
Steven Matteo . . . . . . . . . . . . . . . . . . . . .718-980-1017/fax: 718-980-1051
e-mail: SMatteo@council.nyc.gov

**City Planning, Department of, NYC** . . . . . . . . . . . .fax: 212-720-3219
22 Reade St, New York, NY 10007-1216
212-720-3300  Fax: 212-720-3219
Web site: www.nyc.gov
Chair:
Amanda M Burden
Executive Director:
Richard Barth
Director, Operations:
David J Zagor . . . . . . . . . . . . . . . . . . . . . . . . . . . . . . . . . .212-720-3650
Director, Public Affairs:
Rachaele Raynoff . . . . . . . . . . . . . . . . . . . . . . . . . . . . . . .212-720-3471
General Counsel:
David Karnovsky . . . . . . . . . . . . . . . . . . . . . . . . . . . . . . .212-720-3400

**Citywide Administrative Services, Department of, NYC** . . . . .fax:
212-669-8992
One Centre St, 17th Fl S, New York, NY 10007
212-669-7000  Fax: 212-669-8992
Web site: www.nyc.gov/dcas
Commissioner:
Edna Wells Handy
Chief Communication Officer:
Julianne Cho . . . . . . . . . . . . . . . . . . . . . . . . . . . . . . . . . .212-669-7140

**Civil Service Commission, NYC**
212-669-2609
Web site: www.cs.ny.gov/commission
Chairwoman:
Nancy G. Chaffetz
Acting Director & General Counsel:
Norma I Lopez . . . . . . . . . . . . . . . . . . . . . . . . . . . . . . . .212-669-2609
Office Manager:
Evelyn Horowitz . . . . . . . . . . . . . . . . . . . . . . . . . . . . . . .212-669-2608

**Collective Bargaining, Office of, NYC** . . . . . . . . . . .fax: 212-306-7167
40 Rector St, 7th Fl, New York, NY 10006
212-306-7160  Fax: 212-306-7167
e-mail: nyc-ocb@ocb.nyc.gov
Web site: www.ocb-nyc.org
Director:
Marlene A Gold
Deputy Chair, Dispute Resolution:
Susan Panepento
General Counsel:
Philip Maier

**Comptroller, NYC** . . . . . . . . . . . . . . . . . . . . . . . . . . .fax: 212-669-2707
Municipal Bldg, One Centre St, Rm 530, New York, NY 10007
212-669-3500  Fax: 212-669-2707
Web site: www.comptroller.nyc.gov
Comptroller:
John C Liu
First Deputy Comptroller:
Ricardo E. Morales
Deputy Comptroller/General Counsel:
Valerie Budzik
Deputy Comptroller, Public Finance:
Carol Kostik

Deputy Comptroller, Budget and Public Affairs:
Ari Hoffnung

**Conflicts of Interest Board, NYC** . . . . . . . . . . . . . .fax: 212-442-1407
2 Lafayette St, Ste 1010, New York, NY 10007
212-442-1400  Fax: 212-442-1407
Web site: www.nyc.gov/ethics
Executive Director:
Mark Davies . . . . . . . . . . . . . . . . . . . . . . . . . . . . . . . . . .212-442-1424
e-mail: davies@coib.nyc.gov
Deputy Exec Director/General Counsel:
Wayne G Hawley . . . . . . . . . . . . . . . . . . . . . . . . . . . . . . .212-442-1415
e-mail: hawley@coib.nyc.gov
Director, Enforcement:
Carolyn Lisa Miller. . . . . . . . . . . . . . . . . . . . . . . . . . . . . .212-442-1419
e-mail: miller@coib.nyc.gov
Director, Administration:
Ute O'Malley . . . . . . . . . . . . . . . . . . . . . . . . . . . . . . . . . .212-442-1427
e-mail: omalley@coib.nyc.gov
Director, Information Technology:
Derick Yu . . . . . . . . . . . . . . . . . . . . . . . . . . . . . . . . . . . . .212-442-1605
e-mail: yu@coib.nyc.gov
Director, Training/Education Unit:
Alexander Kipp. . . . . . . . . . . . . . . . . . . . . . . . . . . . . . . . .212-442-1421
e-mail: kipp@coib.nyc.gov
Director, Financial Disclosure/Special Counsel:
Felicia A. Mennin . . . . . . . . . . . . . . . . . . . . . . . . . . . . . . .212-442-1455
e-mail: mennin@coib.nyc.gov

**Consumer Affairs, Department of, NYC** . . . . . . . .fax: 212-487-4221
42 Broadway, New York, NY 10004
212-487-4401  Fax: 212-487-4221
Web site: www.nyc.gov/html/dca
Commissioner:
Jonathan Mintz
Deputy Director, Communications:
Vacant . . . . . . . . . . . . . . . . . . . . . . . . . . . . . . . . . . . . . . .212-487-4283

**Correction, Board of, NYC** . . . . . . . . . . . . . . . . . . . .fax: 212-788-7860
51 Chambers St, Room 923, New York, NY 10007
212-788-7840  Fax: 212-788-7860
Web site: www.nyc.gov/boc
Chair:
Gerald Harris
Executive Director:
Cathy Porter
Director, Field Operations:
Felix Martinez

**Correction, Department of, NYC** . . . . . . . . . . . . . . .fax: 646-248-1219
60 Hudson St, 6th Fl, New York, NY 10013-4393
212-266-1500  Fax: 646-248-1219
Web site: www.nyc.gov/doc
Commissioner:
Dora B Schriro
Senior Dep Commissioner:
John J Antonelli

**Cultural Affairs, Department of, NYC**
31 Chambers St, New York, NY 10007
212-513-9300
Web site: www.nyc.gov/html/dcla
Commissioner:
Kate D Levin
Deputy Commissioner:
Margaret Morton
Chief of Staff:
Shirley Levy

**Design & Construction, Dept of, NYC** . . . . . . . . . .fax: 718-391-1608
30-30 Thomson Avenue, Long Island City, NY 11101

718-391-1000  Fax: 718-391-1608
Web site: www.nyc.gov/html/ddc
Commissioner:
David J Burney.............................718-391-1000
Chief of Staff:
Ana Barrio......................718-391-2300/fax: 718-391-1893
Public Information:
Joe Soldevere..................718-391-1641/fax: 718-391-2600
Chief Contracting Officer:
Carol DiAgostino ...............718-391-1501/fax: 718-391-2600
General Counsel:
David Varoli ...................718-391-1721/fax: 718-391-2600

**Disabilities, Mayor's Office, for People with** ..... fax: 212-341-9843
100 Gold Street, 2nd Floor, New York, NY 10038
212-788-2830 or TTY 212-504-4115  Fax: 212-341-9843
Web site: www.nyc.gov/html/mopd
Commissioner:
Matthew P Sapolin ..............................212-788-2830

**Economic Development Corp, NYC**
110 William Street, New York, NY 10038
212-619-5000 or 888-692-0100
Web site: www.nycedc.com
President:
Seth W Pinsky...............................212-312-3500
Senior VP, Budget:
Tom Jones....................................212-312-3877

**Education, Dept of, NYC** ....................... fax: 212-374-5588
52 Chambers St, New York, NY 10007
718-935-2000  Fax: 212-374-5588
Web site: www.nycenet.edu
Chancellor:
Dennis M Walcott
Deputy Chancellor, Finance/Admin:
Photeine Anagnostopoulos
Deputy Chancellor, Teaching/Learning:
Eric Nadelstern
Director, Strategic Partnerships:
Stephanie Dua
General Counsel & Legal Services Office:
Courtenaye Jackson-Chase
Executive Director, Intergovernmental Affairs:
Lenny Speiller
Communications & Media Relations:
David Cantor

**Elections, Board of, NYC**.......................fax: 212-487-5349
32 Broadway, 7th Fl, New York, NY 10004-1609
212-487-5300 or TDD 212-487-5496  Fax: 212-487-5349
Web site: www.vote.nyc.ny.us
President, Commissioners:
Frederic M. Umane
e-mail: fumane@boe.nyc.ny.us
Executive Director:
Vacant
Deputy Executive Director:
Dawn Sandow
Administrative Manager:
Pamela Perkins
Director, Public Affairs & Communications:
Valerie Vazquez

**Environmental Protection, Department of, NYC**
59-17 Junction Blvd, 13th Fl, Flushing, NY 11373-5108
212-639-6975
Web site: www.nyc.gov/dep
Commissioner:
Carter Strickland...............................718-595-6565
e-mail: cward@dep.nyc.gov

First Dep Commissioner/Exec Dir Water Board:
Steven Lawitts..................................718-595-6576
Chief of Staff:
Kathryn Garcia
General Counsel:
Mark D Hoffer .................................718-595-6528
Director, Public & Intergovernmental Affairs:
Charles G Sturcken..............................718-595-6568

**Equal Employment Practices Commission, NYC** fax: 212-615-8931
253 Broadway, Suite 602, New York, NY 10007
212-615-8939  Fax: 212-615-8931
Web site: www1.nyc.gov/site/eepc/index.page
Executive Director:
Charise L. Terry....................212-615-8933/fax: 212-615-8931
e-mail: cterry@eepc.nyc.gov
Deputy Director/Agency Counsel:
Judith Garcia Quinonez ...........................212-615-8940
e-mail: jquinonez@eepc.nyc.gov
Agency Attorney/Director, Compliance:
Marie E Giraud .................................212-615-8942
e-mail: mgiraud@eepc.nyc.gov

**Film, Theatre & Broadcasting, Mayor's Office of, NYC** ..... fax: 212-307-6237
Ed Sullivan Theatre Bldg, 1697 Broadway, Ste 602, New York, NY 10019
212-489-6710  Fax: 212-307-6237
e-mail: info@film.nyc.gov
Web site: www.nyc.gov/film
Commissioner:
Katherine Oliver
Deputy Commissioner:
John Battista..................................212-489-6710
Director, Production:
Dean McCann...................................212-489-6710

**Finance, Department of, NYC**
One Centre Street, 22nd Floor, New York, NY 10007
212-639-9675
Web site: www.nyc.gov/finance
Commissioner:
David M Frankel
First Deputy Commissioner:
Rochelle Patricof................................212-669-2525
Assistant Commissioner, Communications/Government Affairs:
Sam Miller
Budget Director:
Pat Mattera-Russell
Treasury Deputy Commissioner:
Robert Lee

**Fire Department, NYC**.......................fax: 718-999-2582
9 Metrotech Center, 8th Fl, Brooklyn, NY 11201
718-999-2000  Fax: 718-999-2582
Web site: www.nyc.gov/fdny
Commissioner:
Salvatore J Cassano
First Deputy Commissioner:
Daniel Shacknai
Chief of NYC Fire Department:
Edward Kilduff
Deputy Commissioner, Administration:
Douglas White
Deputy Commissioner, Technology & Support Services:
Joel Golub
Deputy Commissioner, Intergovernmental Affairs:
Daniel Shacknai .................................718-999-2013
Deputy Commissioner, Legal:
Mylan Denerstein ...............................718-999-2016
Deputy Commissioner, Public Information:
Francis X Gribbon

*Offices and agencies generally appear in alphabetical order, except when specific order is requested by listee.*

Chief of Operations:
James Esposito

**Health & Hospitals Corporation, NYC** . . . . . . . . . fax: 212-788-0040
125 Worth St, New York, NY 10013
212-788-3321  Fax: 212-788-0040
Web site: www.nyc.gov/hhc
Presdient/CEO:
Alan D Aviles
Senior VP, Corporate Planning/Community Health/Intergvt Relations:
LaRay Brown
Senior VP, Operations:
Frank J Cirillo
Senior VP/Chief Medical Officer, Medical & Professional Affairs:
Ross Wilson . . . . . . . . . . . . . . . . . . . . . . . . . . . . . . . .212-788-3648
Senior VP, Finance/Capital/CFO:
Marlene Zurack. . . . . . . . . . . . . . . . . . . . . . . . . . . . . .212-788-3494
General Counsel (Senior VP General Counsel):
Salvatore J Russo
Senior VP Corporate Communications & Marketing:
Ana Marengo

**Health & Mental Hygiene, Dept of, NYC** . . . . . . . . fax: 212-964-0472
125 Worth St, New York, NY 10013
212-788-5290 or 212-825-5400  Fax: 212-964-0472
Web site: www.nyc.gov/html/doh
Commissioner:
Thomas Farley . . . . . . . . . . . . . . . . . . . . . . . . . . . . . .212-219-5261
Executive Deputy Commissioner, Mental Hygiene:
Adam Karpati
Chief of Staff:
Emiko Otsubo
Deputy Commissioner, Administration:
Julie Friesen
Deputy Commissioner, Disease Control:
Jay Varma
Deputy Commissioner, Health Care Access/Improvement:
Amanda Parsons
Deputy Commissioner, Epidemiology:
Carolyn Greene
Deputy Commissioner, Environmental Health:
Daniel Kass
Deputy Commissioner, Health Promotion/Disease Prevention:
Andrew Goodman
General Counsel:
Thomas Merrill. . . . . . . . . . . . . . . . . . . . . . . . . . . . . .212-788-5290

**Homeless Services, Department of, NYC** . . . . . . . . fax: 212-361-7950
33 Beaver St, 17th Fl, New York, NY 10004
212-361-8000  Fax: 212-361-7950
Web site: www.nyc.gov/dhs
Commissioner:
Seth Diamond
EEO Officer:
Mark Neal
Deputy Commissioner, Communications/External Affairs:
Barbara Brancaccio
General Counsel:
Michele Ovesey
Deputy Commissioner, Prevention, Policy & Planning:
Ellen Howard-Cooper
Deputy Commissioner, Adult Services:
Douglas C. James
Executive Deputy Commissioner, Family Services:
Anne Heller
Deputy Commissioner, Facility Maint/Development:
Yianna Pavlakos

**Housing Authority, NYC** . . . . . . . . . . . . . . . . . . . . fax: 212-306-8888
250 Broadway, New York, NY 10007
212-306-3000  Fax: 212-306-8888
Web site: www.nyc.gov/nycha

Chairman:
John B Rhea
General Manager:
Cecil House
Acting Executive Vice President, Legal Affairs & General Counsel:
K. MacNeal
Chief of Staff:
H. Morillo
Chief Information Officer & Executive Vice President:
A. Riazi
Deputy General Mgr, Finance:
Felix Lam
Executive Vice President, Operations:
C. Laboy-Diaz
Executive Vice President & Chief, Administration:
N. Rivers
Executive Vice President, Community Programs:
S. Myrie

**Housing Preservation & Development, Dept of, NYC** . . . . . . . . fax: 212-863-6302
100 Gold St, 5th Fl, New York, NY 10038
212-863-6300  Fax: 212-863-6302
Web site: www.nyc.gov/hpd
Commissioner:
Mathew M Wambua
Firsy Deputy Commissioner:
Douglas Apple
Deputy Commissioner/Legal Affairs:
Matthew Shafit
Senior Counsel, State & Legislative Affairs:
Joseph Rosenberg
Assistant Commissioner, Housing Supervision:
J. Walpert
Assistant Commissioner, Preservation Services:
E. Enderlin . . . . . . . . . . . . . . . . . . . . . . . . . . . . . .212-863-7001
Assistant Commissioner, Administration:
J. Cucchiaro
Deputy Commissioner, Community Partnerships:
Kimberly D Hardy. . . . . . . . . . . . . . . . . .212-863-5128/fax: 212-863-8907

**Human Resources Administration, Dept of, NYC** fax: 212-331-8042
150 Greenwich St., 42nd Fl, New York, NY 10007
929-221-7315  Fax: 212-331-8042
e-mail: banksst@hra.nyc.gov
Web site: www.nyc.gov/html/hra
Commissioner:
Robert Doar. . . . . . . . . . . . . . . . . . . . . . . . . . . . . . .212-331-6000
e-mail: egglestonv@hra.nyc.gov
First Deputy Commissioner:
Patricia M Smith. . . . . . . . . . . . . . . . . . . . . . . . . . . .212-331-6230
Senior Exec Dep Commissioner:
Thomas DePippo. . . . . . . . . . . . . . . . . . . . . . . . . . . .212-331-6000
Exec Dep Commissioner, Medical Insur/Community Svcs Administration:
Mary Harper . . . . . . . . . . . . . . . . . . . . . . . . . . . . . .212-273-0001
Executive Deputy Commissioner, Finance Office:
Jill Berry . . . . . . . . . . . . . . . . . . . . . . . . . . . . . . . . .212-331-3980
Agency Chief Contracting Officer:
Vincent Pullo . . . . . . . . . . . . . . . . . . . . . . . . . . . . . .212-331-3434
Executive Deputy Commissioner, Family Independence Administration:
Matt Brune . . . . . . . . . . . . . . . . . . . . . . . . . . . . . . . .212-331-6180
Deputy Commissioner, Data Reporting & Analysis:
Joe DeMartino. . . . . . . . . . . . . . . . . . . . . . . . . . . . . .212-331-6000
Executive Deputy Commissioner, Staff Resources:
Rachel Levine . . . . . . . . . . . . . . . . . . . . . . . . . . . . . .212-331-3333
Executive Deputy Commissioner, Customized Assistance Services:
Frank R Lipton . . . . . . . . . . . . . . . . . . . . . . . . . . . . .212-495-2606
Deputy Commissioner, General Support Services:
Joseph Santino . . . . . . . . . . . . . . . . . . . . . . . . . . . . .212-274-5200
Deputy Commissioner, Constituency Services & Policy Improvement:
Jane Corbett

*Offices and agencies generally appear in alphabetical order, except when specific order is requested by listee.*

Executive Deputy Commissioner, Domestic Violence & Emergency
Intervention Office:
Cecile Noel . . . . . . . . . . . . . . . . . . . . . . . . . . . . . . . . . .212-331-4500
Chief Integrity Officer, Ingestigation, Revenue & Enforcement:
James Sheehan . . . . . . . . . . . . . . . . . . . . . . . . . . . . . .212-274-4740
First Deputy General Counsel, Legal Affairs:
Maureen Walsh. . . . . . . . . . . . . . . . . . . . . . . . . . . . . .212-331-6167
Chief of Staff:
Anne Heller. . . . . . . . . . . . . . . . . . . . . . . . . . . . . . . . .212-331-6225
Deputy Commissioner, Communications & Marketing:
Connie Ress . . . . . . . . . . . . . . . . . . . . . . . . . . . . . . . .212-331-6200

**Human Rights Commission on, NYC** . . . . . . . . . . . fax: 212-306-7658
40 Rector St, 10th Fl, New York, NY 10006
212-306-5070  Fax: 212-306-7658
Web site: www.nyc.gov/cchr
Commissioner:
Patricia L Gatling . . . . . . . . . . . . . . . . . . . . . . . . . . .212-306-7560
Deputy Commissioner/General Counsel:
Cliff Mulqueen . . . . . . . . . . . . . . . . . . . . . . . . . . . . .212-306-7741
Executive Director, Law Enforcement:
Carlos Velez . . . . . . . . . . . . . . . . . . . . . . . . . . . . . . .212-306-7764
Deputy Commissioner, Public Affairs:
Dr Lee Hudson . . . . . . . . . . . . . . . . . . . . . . . . . . . . .212-306-7773
Director, Communications:
Betsy Herzog. . . . . . . . . . . . . . . . . . . . . . . . . . . . . . .212-306-7530
Executive Director, Community Relations:
Alexander Korkhov . . . . . . . . . . . . . . . . . . . . . . . . . .212-306-7423

**Information Technology & Telecommunications, Dept of,
NYC** . . . . . . . . . . . . . . . . . . . . . . . . . . . . . . . . . . . . . .fax: 212-788-8130
75 Park Place, 9th Fl, New York, NY 10007
212-788-6600  Fax: 212-788-8130
Web site: www.nyc.gov/doitt
Commissioner:
Rahul N. Merchant . . . . . . . . . . . . . . . . . . . . . . . . . .212-788-6633
EEO Officer:
Emily Johnson. . . . . . . . . . . . . . . . . . . . . . . . . . . . . .212-788-6624
Chief of Staff/Governance & External Affairs:
Evan Hines . . . . . . . . . . . . . . . . . . . . . . . . . . . . . . . .718-403-8100
Executive Assistant, NYC 3-1-1:
Jessica Diaz. . . . . . . . . . . . . . . . . . . . . . . . . . . . . . . .212-504-4421
General Counsel:
Charles Fraser . . . . . . . . . . . . . . . . . . . . . . . . . . . . . .212-788-6640
Deputy Commissioner, Finance/Admin:
Brett Robinson . . . . . . . . . . . . . . . . . . . . . . . . . . . . .212-788-6616

**Investigation, Department of, NYC** . . . . . . . . . . . . . fax: 212-825-2823
80 Maiden Lane, New York, NY 10038
212-825-5900  Fax: 212-825-2823
Web site: www.nyc.gov/html/doi
Commissioner:
Rose Gill Hearn . . . . . . . . . . . . . . . . . . . . . . . . . . . .212-825-5913
e-mail: rghearn@doi.nyc.gov
Chief of Staff:
Michael Vitiello . . . . . . . . . . . . . . . . . . . . . . . . . . . .212-825-2870
Deputy Commissioner, Investigations:
Kim Berger . . . . . . . . . . . . . . . . . . . . . . . . . . . . . . . .212-825-5979
General Counsel:
Marjorie Landa . . . . . . . . . . . . . . . . . . . . . . . . . . . . .212-825-2404
Public Information Officer:
Diane Struzzi. . . . . . . . . . . . . . . . . . . . . . . . . . . . . . .212-825-3514

**Juvenile Justice, Department of, NYC** . . . . . . . . . . fax: 212-442-8546
110th William St., 14th Floor, New York, NY 10038
212-442-8000 or TTY/TDD:212-442-8578  Fax: 212-442-8546
e-mail: nycdjj@djj.nyc.gov
Web site: www.nyc.gov/html/acs
Commissioner:
Ronald E. Richter . . . . . . . . . . . . . . . . . . . . . . . . . . .212-442-7630
First Deputy Commissioner:
Judith Pincus . . . . . . . . . . . . . . . . .212-442-7510/fax: 212-442-8512

Deputy Commissioner, Operations & Detention:
Jerome Davis . . . . . . . . . . . . . . . . . . . . . .212-442-7245/fax: 212-442-8508
Deputy Commissioner, Administration:
Donald Brosen . . . . . . . . . . . . . . . . . . . . .212-442-7840/fax: 212-442-8512
General Counsel:
Joseph Cardieri . . . . . . . . . . . . . . . . . . . .212-442-7530/fax: 212-442-8517
Deputy Commissioner, Communications and Community Affairs:
Michael Fagan . . . . . . . . . . . . . . . . . . . . .212-442-7534/fax: 718-935-6454

**Labor Relations, Office of, NYC** . . . . . . . . . . . . . . . . fax: 212-306-7202
40 Rector St, 4th Fl, New York, NY 10006
212-306-7200  Fax: 212-306-7202
Web site: www.nyc.gov/html/olr
Commissioner:
James F Hanley. . . . . . . . . . . . . . . . . . . . . . . . . . . . .212-306-7200
Associate Commissioner:
Jean N Brewer
General Counsel:
Mayra Bell. . . . . . . . . . . . . . . . . . . . . .212-306-7230/fax: 212-306-7223
Director, Employee Benefits Program:
Dorothy A Wolfe . . . . . . . . . . . . . . . . . . . . . . . . . . .212-306-7200

**Landmarks Preservation Commission, NYC** . . . . fax: 212-669-7960
One Centre Street, 9th Fl North, New York, NY 10007
212-669-7817  Fax: 212-669-7960
Web site: www.nyc.gov/html/lpc
Chair:
Robert B Tierney . . . . . . . . . . . . . . . . . . . . . . . . . . .212-669-7888

**Law, Department of, NYC** . . . . . . . . . . . . . . . . . . . . .fax: 212-788-0367
100 Church St, New York, NY 10007-2601
212-788-0303  Fax: 212-788-0367
Web site: www.nyc.gov/html/law
Corporation Counsel:
Michael A Cardozo . . . . . . . . . . . . . .212-356-1000/fax: 212-356-1148
e-mail: mcardozo@law.nyc.gov
Managing Attorney:
G Foster Mills . . . . . . . . . . . . . . . . . . .212-356-2200/fax: 212-356-3585
e-mail: gmills@law.nyc.gov
Chief of Operations:
Kenneth J Majerus . . . . . . . . . . . . . . .212-356-4040 or 212-356-4049
Director, Legal Recruitment:
Stuart Smith. . . . . . . . . . . . . . . . . . .212-356-4070/fax: 212-227-6177
Inspector General:
Michael Siller . . . . . . . . . . . . . . . . . . .212-825-0646 or 212-825-2505
e-mail: cmorrick@doi.nyc.gov
Communications Director:
Kate Ahlers. . . . . . . . . . . . . . . . . . . . .212-356-4001 or 212-788-8716
fax: 212-788-8716
e-mail: kahlers@law.nyc.gov

**Legislative Affairs Office, NYC Mayor's City** . . . fax: 212-788-2647
253 Broadway, 14th Fl, New York, NY 10007
212-788-3678  Fax: 212-788-2647
e-mail: citylegislativeaffairs@cityhall.nyc.gov
Web site: www.nyc.gov/html/moiga
Director:
Patrick Wehle . . . . . . . . . . . . . . . . . . .212-788-3678/fax: 212-788-2647

**Legislative Affairs Office, NYC Mayor's State** . . fax: 518-462-5870
119 Washington Ave, 3rd Fl, Albany, NY 12210
518-447-5200  Fax: 518-462-5870
Director:
Joseph N. Garba. . . . . . . . . . . . . . . . .212-278-8820/fax: 212-278-1497

**Library, Brooklyn Public** . . . . . . . . . . . . . . . . . . . . .fax: 718-398-6798
203 Arlington Avenue, Warwick St., Brooklyn, NY 11207
718-277-6105  Fax: 718-398-6798
Web site: www.bklynpubliclibrary.org
President & CEO:
Linda E Johnson . . . . . . . . . . . . . . . . . . . . . . . . . . . .718-230-2403

*Offices and agencies generally appear in alphabetical order, except when specific order is requested by listee.*

Chair, BPL Foundation:
Anthony W Crowell . . . . . . . . . . . . . . . . . . . . . . . . . . . . . . .718-230-2158
Director, Public Affairs:
Antonia Yuille Williams. . . . . . . . . . . . . . . . . . . . . . . . . . . .718-277-6105

**Library, New York Public**. . . . . . . . . . . . . . . . . . . . .fax: 212-930-9299
5th Ave & 42nd St, New York, NY 10018
212-930-0800 or 212-340-0849  Fax: 212-930-9299
Web site: www.nypl.org
President & CEO:
Dr. Anthony W. Marx. . . . . . . . . . . . . . . . . . . . . . . . . . . . .212-930-0736
e-mail: president@nypl.org
Senior VP, External Affairs:
Vacant. . . . . . . . . . . . . . . . . . . . . . . . . . . . . . . . . . . . . . . . .212-930-0611
Chief Operating Officer:
David Offensend. . . . . . . . . . . . . . . . . . . . . . . . . . . . . . . . .212-930-0600
Vice President, Development:
Jennifer Zaslow. . . . . . . . . . . . . . . . . . . . . . . . . . . . . . . . . .212-930-0692
Director, Budget & Planning:
Marjoel Montalbo . . . . . . . . . . . . . . .212-592-7400/fax: 212-592-7440
Vice President, Government & Community Affairs:
George D. Mihaltses. . . . . . . . . . . . . . . . . . . . . . . . . . . . . .212-930-0051
VP, Communications & Marketing:
Ken Weine . . . . . . . . . . . . . . . . . . . . . . . . . . . . . . . . . . . . .212-592-7700

**Library, Queens Borough Public** . . . . . . . . . . . . . .fax: 718-291-8936
89-11 Merrick Blvd, Jamaica, NY 11432
718-990-0700 or TTY 718-990-0809  Fax: 718-291-8936
Web site: www.queenslibrary.org
President & CEO:
Dennis Walcott. . . . . . . . . . . . . . . . . . . . . . . . . . . . . . . . . .718-990-0728
Director, Government Affairs:
Jonathan Chung . . . . . . . . . . . . . . . . . . . . . . . . . . . . . . . . .718-990-0700
Director, Communications:
Joanne King. . . . . . . . . . . . . . . . . . . . .718-990-0704/fax: 718-291-2695

**Loft Board, NYC** . . . . . . . . . . . . . . . . . . . . . . . . . . . . .fax: 212-788-7501
100 Gold St, 2nd Fl, New York, NY 10038
212-788-7610  Fax: 212-788-7501
Web site: www.nyc.gov/html/loft
Chairperson:
Robert D LiMandri. . . . . . . . . . . . . . . . . . . . . . . . . . . . . . .212-788-7610
Executive Director:
Lanny R Alexander. . . . . . . . . . . . . . . . . . . . . . . . . . . . . . .212-788-7619

**Management & Budget, Office of, NYC**. . . . . . . . .fax: 212-788-6300
75 Park Place, 8th Fl, New York, NY 10007
212-788-5800  Fax: 212-788-6300
Web site: www.nyc.gov/omb
Director:
Mark Page. . . . . . . . . . . . . . . . . . . . . . . . . . . . . . . . . . . . . .212-788-5900
First Deputy Director:
Stuart Klein. . . . . . . . . . . . . . . . . . . . . . . . . . . . . . . . . . . . .212-788-5904
Deputy Director/General Counsel:
Marjorie Henning . . . . . . . . . . . . . . . . . . . . . . . . . . . . . . . .212-788-5880
Deputy Director:
P V Anatharam . . . . . . . . . . . . . . . . . . . . . . . . . . . . . . . . . .212-788-5894
Deputy Director:
Michael Dardia . . . . . . . . . . . . . . . . . . . . . . . . . . . . . . . . . .212-788-5891

**Medical Examiner, Office of Chief, NYC**. . . . . . . .fax: 212-447-2716
520 First Ave, New York, NY 10016
212-447-2030  Fax: 212-447-2716
Web site: www.nyc.gov/html/ocme
Acting Chief Medical Examiner:
Barbara A. Sampson. . . . . . . . . . . . . . . . . . . . . . . . . . . . . .212-447-2034
First Deputy Commissioner:
Barbara Sampson . . . . . . . . . . . . . . . . . . . . . . . . . . . . . . . .212-447-2335
Deputy Commissioner, Administration/Finance:
Janice English. . . . . . . . . . . . . . . . . . . . . . . . . . . . . . . . . . .212-447-5351
Director, Medicolegal Investigations:
Barbara Butcher . . . . . . . . . . . . . . . . . . . . . . . . . . . . . . . . .212-447-2036

Director, Public Affairs:
Ellen Borakove . . . . . . . . . . . . . . . . . .212-447-2401/fax: 212-447-2755
General Counsel:
Jody Lipton . . . . . . . . . . . . . . . . . . . . . . . . . . . . . . . . . . . . .212-447-2046

**Parks & Recreation, Department of, NYC** . . . . . .fax: 212-360-1329
The Arsenal, Central Park, 830 Fifth Ave, New York, NY 10065
212-360-8111  Fax: 212-360-1329
e-mail: commissioner@parks.nyc.gov
Commissioner:
Veronica M. White . . . . . . . . . . . . . . . . .212-360-1305/fax: 202-360-1345
First Deputy Commissioner, Operations:
Liam Kavanagh. . . . . . . . . . . . . . . . . . . . . . . . . . . . . . . . . .212-360-1307
Deputy Commissioner, Capital Projects:
Theresa Braddick . . . . . . . . . . . . . . . . . . . . . . . . . . . . . . . .718-760-6602
Assistant Commissioner, Public Programs:
Annika Holder. . . . . . . . . . . . . . . . . . . . . . . . . . . . . . . . . . .212-360-1381
Deputy Commissioner, Management/Budget:
Robert L Garafola . . . . . . . . . . . . . . . . . . . . . . . . . . . . . . . .212-360-1302
Director, Public Affairs:
Vicki Karp. . . . . . . . . . . . . . . . . . . . . . . . . . . . . . . . . . . . . .212-360-1311

**Police Department, NYC** . . . . . . . . . . . . . . . . . . . . . .fax: 646-610-5865
One Police Plaza, New York, NY 10038
646-610-5000  Fax: 646-610-5865
Web site: www.nyc.gov/nypd
Police Commissioner:
Raymond W Kelly . . . . . . . . . . . . . . . . . . . . . . . . . . . . . . . .646-610-5410
First Dep Commissioner:
Rafael Pineiro . . . . . . . . . . . . . . . . . . . . . . . . . . . . . . . . . . .646-610-5420
Deputy Commissioner, Strategic Initiatives:
Michael J Farrell. . . . . . . . . . . . . . . . . . . . . . . . . . . . . . . . .646-610-8534
Deputy Commissioner, Counter Terrorism:
Richard A Daddario . . . . . . . . . . . . . . . . . . . . . . . . . . . . . .646-610-6169
Deputy Commissioner, Intelligence:
David Cohen . . . . . . . . . . . . . . . . . . . . . . . . . . . . . . . . . . . .646-610-5403
Deputy Commissioner, Equal Employment Opportunity:
Neldra M Zeigler. . . . . . . . . . . . . . . . . . . . . . . . . . . . . . . . .646-610-5330
Deputy Commissioner, Labor Relations:
John P Beirne . . . . . . . . . . . . . . . . . . . . . . . . . . . . . . . . . . .646-610-5060
Deputy Commissioner, Trials:
Martin G Karopkin . . . . . . . . . . . . . . . . . . . . . . . . . . . . . . .646-610-5424
Deputy Commissioner, Training:
Dr. James O'Keefe . . . . . . . . . . . . . . . . . . . . . . . . . . . . . . .646-610-4675
Deputy Commissioner, Legal Matters:
Douglas B. Maynard. . . . . . . . . . . . . . . . . . . . . . . . . . . . . .646-610-5336
Deputy Commissioner, Management & Budget:
Vincent Grippo . . . . . . . . . . . . . . . . . . . . . . . . . . . . . . . . . .646-610-6670
Deputy Commissioner, Operations:
John Bilich . . . . . . . . . . . . . . . . . . . . . . . . . . . . . . . . . . . . .646-610-6100
Deputy Commissioner, Technological Development:
V James Onalfo. . . . . . . . . . . . . . . . . . . . . . . . . . . . . . . . . .646-610-6873
Deputy Commissioner, Public Information:
Paul J Browne. . . . . . . . . . . . . . . . . . . . . . . . . . . . . . . . . . .646-610-6700

**Probation, Department of, NYC** . . . . . . . . . . . . . . .fax: 212-361-0686
33 Beaver St, New York, NY 10004
212-361-8973  Fax: 212-361-0686
Web site: www.nyc.gov/html/prob
Commissioner:
Vincent N Schrialdi. . . . . . . . . . . . . . . . .212-361-8977/fax: 212-361-8985
e-mail: mhorn@probation.nyc.gov
Senior Policy Advisor to the Commissioner:
Mark Ferrante . . . . . . . . . . . . . . . . . . . . . . . . . . . . . . . . . . .212-361-8970
e-mail: mferrante@probation.nyc.gov
Director, Press & Public Information:
Ryan Dodge . . . . . . . . . . . . . . . . . . . . . . . . . . . . . . . . . . . .212-232-0684
e-mail: rdodge@probation.nyc.gov
Chief of Staff:
Michael Ognibene. . . . . . . . . . . . . . . . . . . . . . . . . . . . . . . .212-361-8973

*Offices and agencies generally appear in alphabetical order, except when specific order is requested by listee.*

**351**

General Counsel:
Wayne McKenzie . . . . . . . . . . . . . . . . . . . . . . . . . . .212-232-0700
Deputy Commissioner, Administration:
Michael Forte . . . . . . . . . . . . . . . . . . . . . . . . . . . . . .212-361-8965
Deputy Commissioner, Family Court Services:
Patricia Brennan . . . . . . . . . . . . . . . . . . . . . . . . . . . .212-232-0486
Deputy Commssioner, Adult Services:
Clinton Lacey . . . . . . . . . . . . . . . . . . . . . . . . . . . . . .212-361-8982
Chief Information Officer:
Barry Abrams . . . . . . . . . . . . . . . . . . . . . . . . . . . . . .212-232-0455

**Public Advocate, Office of the** . . . . . . . . . . . . . . . . . fax: 212-669-4701
Municipal Bldg, One Centre St, 15th Fl North, New York, NY 10007
212-669-7200  Fax: 212-669-4701
Web site: www.pubadvocate.nyc.gov
Public Advocate:
Bill de Blasio . . . . . . . . . . . . . . . . . . . . . . . . . . . . . .212-669-4102
General Counsel:
Steven Newmark . . . . . . . . . . . . . . . . . . . . . . . . . . . .212-669-4719
Chief of Staff:
Dominick Williams . . . . . . . . . . . . . . . . . . . . . . . . . .212-669-4743
Director, Administration:
Elba Feliciano . . . . . . . . . . . . . . . . . . . . . . . . . . . . . .212-669-2179
Director, Intergovernmental Affairs:
Warren Gardiner . . . . . . . . . . . . . . . . . . . . . . . . . . . .212-669-4388
Executive Assistant:
Jane Schatz . . . . . . . . . . . . . . . . . . . . . . . . . . . . . . . .212-669-4258

**Records & Information Services, Dept of, NYC** . fax: 212-788-8614
31 Chambers St, Rm 305, New York, NY 10007
212-639-9675 or TTY: 212-788-8615  Fax: 212-788-8614
Web site: www.nyc.gov/records
Deputy Commissioner:
Eileen M Flannelly . . . . . . . . . . . . . . . . . . . . . . . . . .212-788-8607
Director, Administration:
Vickie Moore . . . . . . . . . . . . . . . . . . . . . . . . . . . . . .212-788-8622
Director, Municipal Archives:
Leonora Gidlund . . . . . . . . . . . . . . . . . . . . . . . . . . . .212-788-8585
Director, Municipal Records Management Division:
Pearl L Boatswain . . . . . . . . . . . . . . . . . . . . . . . . . . .212-788-8550
Director, City Hall Library:
Paul C Perkus . . . . . . . . . . . . . . . . . . . . . . . . . . . . . .212-788-8596

**Rent Guidelines Board, NYC** . . . . . . . . . . . . . . . . . . fax: 212-385-2554
51 Chambers St, Ste 202, New York, NY 10007
212-385-2934  Fax: 212-385-2554
Web site: www.nycrgb.org
Chair:
Jonathan L Kimmel . . . . . . . . . . . . . . . . . . . . . . . . . .212-385-2934
Executive Director:
Andrew McLaughlin
Public Information Officer:
Charmaine Superville
Senior Research Associate:
Brian Hoberman . . . . . . . . . . . . . . . . . . . . . . . . . . . .212-385-2934

**Sanitation, Department of, NYC**
346 Broadway, 10th Floor, New York, NY 10013
e-mail: comroffc@dsny.nyc.gov
Web site: www.nyc.gov/html/dsny
Commissioner:
John J Doherty . . . . . . . . . . . . . . . . . . . . . . . . . . . . .646-885-5020
First Deputy Commissioner:
Bernard Sullivan . . . . . . . . . . . . . . . . . . . . . . . . . . . .646-885-4727
Deputy Commissioner, of Public Info & Community Affairs:
Vito A Turso . . . . . . . . . . . . . . . . . . .646-885-5020/fax: 212-791-3386

**Small Business Services, Department of, NYC** . . . fax: 212-618-8991
110 William St, 7th Fl, New York, NY 10038
212-513-6300  Fax: 212-618-8991
Web site: www.nyc.gov/html/sbs

Commissioner:
Robert W Walsh . . . . . . . . . . . . . . . . . . . . . . . . . . . .212-513-6350
First Deputy Commissioner, Financial Management/Administration:
Andrew Schwartz . . . . . . . . . . . . . . . . . . . . . . . . . . .212-513-6428
Assistant Commissioner, Business Development & Recruitment:
Katherine Janeski . . . . . . . . . . . . . . . . . . . . . . . . . . .212-618-6710
General Counsel:
Deborah Buyer . . . . . . . . . . . . . . . . . . . . . . . . . . . . .212-442-6432
Assistant Commissioner, Finance & Administration:
Shaazad Ali . . . . . . . . . . . . . . . . . . . . . . . . . . . . . . . .212-618-8735
Chief of Staff:
Sarah Krauss . . . . . . . . . . . . . . . . . . . . . . . . . . . . . . .212-513-6300

**Sports Commission, NYC** . . . . . . . . . . . . . . . . . . . . . fax: 212-788-7514
2 Washington Street, 15th Floor, New York, NY 10004
877-692-7767  Fax: 212-788-7514
Commissioner:
Kenneth J Podziba . . . . . . . . . . . . . . . . . . . . . . . . . . .212-487-5676
e-mail: kpodziba@cityhall.nyc.gov

**Standards & Appeals, Board of, NYC** . . . . . . . . . . . fax: 212-788-8769
40 Rector Street, 9th Floor, New York, NY 10006
212-788-8500  Fax: 212-788-8769
e-mail: ppacific@dcas.nyc.gov
Web site: www.nyc.gov/html/bsa
Chair:
Meenakshi Srinivasan . . . . . . . . . . . . . . . . . . . . . . . .212-788-8547
Vice Chair:
Christopher Collins
Commissioner:
Susan M Hinkson
Executive Director:
Jeff Mulligan . . . . . . . . . . . . . . . . . . . . . . . . . . . . . . .212-788-8805

**Tax Commission, NYC** . . . . . . . . . . . . . . . . . . . . . . . fax: 212-669-8636
Municipal Building, 1 Centre St, Rm 936, New York, NY 10007
212-669-4410  Fax: 212-669-8636
Web site: www.nyc.gov/html/taxcomm
President:
Glenn Newman . . . . . . . . . . . . . . . . . . . . . . . . . . . . .212-669-4401
Director, Operations:
Myrna Hall. . . . . . . . . . . . . . . . .212-669-4420/fax: 212-669-2003
Director, Information Technology:
Iftikhar Ahmad . . . . . . . . . . . . . . . . . . . . . . . . . . . . .212-669-2954
Director, Appraisal & Hearings:
Carlo Silvestri . . . . . . . . . . . . . . . . . . . . . . . . . . . . . .212-669-4402
General Counsel:
Vacant . . . . . . . . . . . . . . . . . . . . . . . . . . . . . . . . . . . .212-669-4407

**Taxi & Limousine Commission, NYC** . . . . . . . . . . . fax: 212-676-1100
40 Rector St, New York, NY 10006
212-639-9675  Fax: 212-676-1100
Web site: www.nyc.gov/taxi
Commissioner/Chair/CEO:
David Yassky . . . . . . . . . . . . . . . . . . . . . . . . . . . . . . .212-676-1003
Chief of Staff:
Ira Goldstein . . . . . . . . . . . . . .212-676-1017/fax: 212-676-2002
First Deputy Commissioner:
Andrew Salkin . . . . . . . . . . . .212-676-1147 or 212-676-1148
Deputy Commissioner, Legal Affairs:
Charles Fraser . . . . . . . . . . . . . . . . . . . . . . . . . . . . . .212-676-1117
Deputy Commissioner, Licensing:
Barbara Schechter . . . . . . . . . . . . . .718-391-5667 or 718-391-5666
Deputy Commissioner, Public Affairs:
Allan J Fromberg . . . . . . . . . . . . . . .212-676-1013/fax: 212-676-1101
Deputy Commissioner of Financial Management & Administration:
Louis Tazzi . . . . . . . . . . . . . . . . . . . . . . . . . . . . . . . . .212-676-1035

**Transportation, Department of, NYC**
55 Water Street, 9th Floor, New York, NY 10041
212-639-9675 or TTY: 212-504-4115
Web site: www.nyc.gov/dot

*Offices and agencies generally appear in alphabetical order, except when specific order is requested by listee.*

Commissioner:
Janette Sadik-Khan . . . . . . . . . . . . . . .212-676-0868/fax: 212-442-7007
First Deputy Commissioner:
Lori Ardito . . . . . . . . . . . . . . . . . . . . . . . . . . . . . .212-839-6403
Deputy Commissioner, External Affairs:
Seth Solomonow. . . . . . . . . . . . . . . . . . . . . . . . . . .212-839-4850
Deputy Commissioner, Sidewalks & Inspection Mgmt Division:
Leon W Heyward . . . . . . . . . . . . . . . . . . . . . . . . . . .212-839-4300

**Veterans' Affairs, Mayor's Office of, NYC** . . . . . . fax: 212-442-4170
346 Broadway, 8 W, New York, NY 10007
212-442-4171  Fax: 212-442-4170
Web site: www.nyc.gov/html/vets
Commissioner:
Terrance Holliday. . . . . . . . . . . . . . . . . . . . . . . . . . .212-442-4171
Deputy Commissioner:
Clarice Joynes. . . . . . . . . . . . . . . . . . . . . . . . . . . . .212-442-4171

**Voter Assistance Commission (VAC), NYC** . . . . . fax: 212-788-2527
100 Gold Street, 2nd Floor, New York, NY 10038
212-788-8384  Fax: 212-788-2527
Web site: www.nyccfb.info
Chairman:
Joseph P. Parkes . . . . . . . . . . . . . . . . . .212-306-7100/fax: 212-306-7143
Vice Chair:
Jane Kalmus . . . . . . . . . . . . . . . . . . . . . . . . . . . . . .212-306-7100
Executive Director/Coordinator:
Amy M. Loprest . . . . . . . . . . . . . . . . . . . . . . . . . . . .212-306-7100

**Water Finance Authority, Municipal, NYC** . . . . . fax: 212-788-9197
75 Park Place, 6th Fl, New York, NY 10007
212-788-5889  Fax: 212-788-9197
Web site: www.nyc.gov/html/nyw
Executive Director:
Thomas G Paolicelli . . . . . . . . . . . . . . . . . . . . . . . . .212-788-5889
e-mail: paolicellit@omb.nyc.gov
Comptroller:
Michele Mark Levine . . . . . . . . . . . . . . . . . . . . . . . . .212-788-5889
e-mail: levinem@omb.nyc.gov

**Youth & Community Development, Department of, NYC**
2 Lafayette Street, 19th Floor, New York, NY 10007
646-343-6800 or 800-246-4646
Web site: www.nyc.gov/dycd
Commissioner:
Bill Chong. . . . . . . . . . . . . . . . . . . . . . . . . . . . . . . .646-343-6800
General Counsel:
Caroline Press . . . . . . . . . . . . . . . . . . . . . . . . . . . . .212-442-5980
Chief of Staff:
Regina Miller . . . . . . . . . . . . . . . . . . . . . . . . . . . . . .212-442-5989
Deputy Commissioner, Administration:
John Cirolia. . . . . . . . . . . . . . . . . . . . . . . . . . . . . . .212-442-8573
Deputy Commissioner, Community Development:
Sandra Gutierrez. . . . . . . . . . . . . . . . . . . . . . . . . . . .212-442-6015

## New York City Boroughs

**Bronx (Bronx County)** . . . . . . . . . . . . . . . . . . . . . .fax: 718-590-3537
Executive Division, 851 Grand Concourse, 3rd Floor, Bronx, NY 10451
718-590-3500  Fax: 718-590-3537
e-mail: webmail@bronxbp.nyc.gov
Borough President:
Rueben Diaz Jr . . . . . . . . . . . . . . . . . . . . . . . . . . . .718-590-3557
Deputy Borough President:
Aurelia Greene . . . . . . . . . . . . . . . . . . . . . . . . . . . .718-590-4036
Director, Communications:
John DeSio . . . . . . . . . . . . . . . . . . . . . . . . . . . . . . .718-590-3543
Counsel:
Al Rodriguez. . . . . . . . . . . . . . . . . . . . . . . . . . . . . .718-590-8555
Press Secretary:
Liseth Perez-Almeida . . . . . . . . . . . . . . . . . . . . . . . . .718-590-2509

**Brooklyn (Kings County)**. . . . . . . . . . . . . . . . . . . . .fax: 718-802-3805
Borough Hall, 209 Joralemon St, Brooklyn, NY 11201
718-802-3700  Fax: 718-802-3805
Web site: www.brooklyn-usa.org
Borough President:
Marty Markowitz . . . . . . . . . . . . . . . . . . . . . . . . . . .718-802-3700
e-mail: askmarty@brooklynbp.nyc.gov
Deputy Borough President:
Sandra Chapman . . . . . . . . . . . . . . . . . . . . . . . . . . .718-802-3884
e-mail: ygraham@brooklynbp.nyc.gov

**Manhattan (New York County)**. . . . . . . . . . . . . . . .fax: 212-669-4305
Municipal Bldg, One Centre St, 19th Fl, New York, NY 10007
212-669-8300  Fax: 212-669-4305
Web site: www.mbpo.org
Borough President:
Scott M Stringer . . . . . . . . . . . . . . . . . . . . . . . . . . .212-669-8155
e-mail: bp@manhattanbp.org
Deputy Borough President:
Rose Pierre-Louis . . . . . . . . . . . . . . . . . . . . . . . . . . .212-669-8137
e-mail: rpierre-louis@manhattanbp.org
Chief of Staff:
Alaina Gilligo . . . . . . . . . . . . . . . . . . . . . . . . . . . . .212-669-2527
e-mail: agilligo@manhattanbp.org
General Counsel:
Jimmy Yan . . . . . . . . . . . . . . . . . . . . . . . . . . . . . . .212-669-8157
e-mail: jyan@manhattanbp.org
Director of Human Resources & Operations:
Lisa Kaufer . . . . . . . . . . . . . . . . . . . . . . . . . . . . . . .212-669-8300
e-mail: lkaufer@manhattanbp.org
Director, Policy & Research:
David Saltonstall . . . . . . . . . . . . . . . . . . . . . . . . . . .212-669-8300
e-mail: dsaltonstall@manhattanbp.org
Director, Communications:
Josh Getlin . . . . . . . . . . . . . . . . . . . . . . . . . . . . . . .212-669-8139
e-mail: jgetlin@manhattanbp.org
Press Secretary:
Audrey Gelman . . . . . . . . . . . . . . . . .212-669-3882/fax: 212-669-3380
e-mail: agelman@manhattanbp.org

**Queens (Queens County)** . . . . . . . . . . . . . . . . . . . .fax: 718-286-2876
Executive Division, 120-55 Queens Blvd, Kew Gardens, NY 11424
718-286-3000  Fax: 718-286-2876
e-mail: info@queensbp.org
Web site: www.queensbp.org
Borough President:
Helen M Marshall . . . . . . . . . . . . . . . . .718-286-3000/fax: 718-286-2876
Deputy Borough President:
Barry Grodenchik . . . . . . . . . . . . . . . . . . . . . . . . . . .718-286-2900
Chief of Staff:
Alexandra Rosa. . . . . . . . . . . . . . . . . . . . . . . . . . . . .718-286-3000
General Counsel:
Hugh Weinberg. . . . . . . . . . . . . . . . . . . . . . . . . . . . .718-286-3000
Director, Management & Budget:
Carol Ricci . . . . . . . . . . . . . . . . . . . . . . . . . . . . . . .718-286-2660
Director, Planning & Development:
Irving Poy . . . . . . . . . . . . . . . . . . . . . . . . . . . . . . . .718-286-2860
Immigrant/Intercultural Affairs:
Susie Tanenbaum . . . . . . . . . . . . . . . . . . . . . . . . . . .718-286-2741
Press Office:
Daniel Andrews . . . . . . . . . . . . . . . . . . . . . . . . . . . .718-286-2640

**Staten Island (Richmond County)** . . . . . . . . . . . . .fax: 718-816-2026
10 Richmond Terrace, Room 120, Staten Island, NY 10301
718-816-2000  Fax: 718-816-2026
Web site: www.statenislandusa.com
Borough President:
James P Molinaro . . . . . . . . . . . . . . . . . . . . . . . . . . .718-816-2200
Deputy Borough President:
Edward Burke. . . . . . . . . . . . . . . . . . . . . . . . . . . . . .718-816-2231

*Offices and agencies generally appear in alphabetical order, except when specific order is requested by listee.*

Chief of Staff:
  Joseph Sciortino . . . . . . . . . . . . . . . . . . . . . . . . . . . . . . . . . . .718-816-2058
Legal Counsel:
  John Zaccone . . . . . . . . . . . . . . . . . . . . . . . . . . . . . . . . . . . . .718-816-2056
Borough Commissioner, DOT:
  Thomas Cocola . . . . . . . . . . . . . . . . . . . . . . . . . . . . . . . . . .718-816-2373

## Newburgh, City of
83 Broadway
Newburgh, NY 12550
845-569-7300  Fax: 845-569-7370

Mayor:
  Judy Kennedy . . . . . . . . . . . . . . . . . . . . . . . . . . . . . . . . . .845-569-7303
City Manager:
  Richard F Herbeck . . . . . . . . . . . . . . . . . . . . . . . . . . . . . .845-569-7301
Acting Director, Planning & Development:
  Ian MacDougall. . . . . . . . . . . . . . . . . . . .845-569-9400/fax: 845-569-9700
City Clerk:
  Lorene Vitek . . . . . . . . . . . . . . . . . . . .845-569-7311/fax: 845-569-7314
Corporation Counsel:
  Michelle Kelson. . . . . . . . . . . . . . . . . . .845-569-7335/fax: 845-569-7338
Chief:
  Michael Ferrara . . . . . . . . . . . . . . . . . .845-561-3131/fax: 845-565-5662
Fire Chief:
  Michael Vatter. . . . . . . . . . . . . . . . . . . .845-569-7415/fax: 845-569-7435
Historian:
  Mary McTamaney. . . . . . . . . . . . . . . . . . . . . . . . . . . . . .845-569-8090
  e-mail: newburghhistory@usa.com

## Newburgh, Town of
1496 Rte 300
Newburgh, NY 12550
845-564-4552  Fax: 845-566-9486
Web site: www.townofnewburgh.org

Town Supervisor:
  Wayne C Booth. . . . . . . . . . . . . . . . . . .845-564-4552/fax: 845-566-9486
Town Clerk:
  Andrew J Zarutskie . . . . . . . . . . . . . . .845-564-4554/fax: 945-564-8589
Accountant:
  Jacqueline Calarco . . . . . . . . . . . . . . . . . . . . . . . . . . . .845-564-5220
Police Chief:
  Michael Clancy . . . . . . . . . . . . . . . . . .845-564-1100/fax: 845-564-1870

## Niagara Falls, City of
City Hall
745 Main St, PO Box 69
Niagara Falls, NY 14302-0069
716-286-4300  Fax: 716-286-4349
Web site: www.niagarafallsusa.org

Mayor:
  Paul Dyster . . . . . . . . . . . . . . . . . . . . .716-286-4310/fax: 716-286-4349
City Administrator:
  Donna D Owens . . . . . . . . . . . . . . . . .716-286-4320/fax: 716-286-4376
City Clerk:
  Carol Antonucci . . . . . . . . . . . . . . . . . . . . . . . . . . . . . . .716-286-4393
Corporate Counsel:
  Craig H Johnson . . . . . . . . . . . . . . . . .716-286-4422/fax: 716-286-4424
Controller:
  Maria C Brown . . . . . . . . . . . . . . . . . . . . . . . . . . . . . . . . .716-286-4340
Police Superintendent:
  John Chella . . . . . . . . . . . . . . . . . . . . . . . . . . . . . . . . . . . .716-286-4545
Director, Public Works & Parks:
  David L Kinney. . . . . . . . . . . . . . . . . . .716-286-4940/fax: 716-286-4877

## Niskayuna, Town of
One Niskayuna Circle
Niskayuna, NY 12309
518-386-4500  Fax: 518-386-4592

Town Supervisor:
  Joe Landry. . . . . . . . . . . . . . . . . . . .518-386-4503/fax: 518-386-4592
  e-mail: supervisor@niskayuna.org
Deputy Town Clerk:
  Barbara Nottke. . . . . . . . . . . . . . . .518-386-4511/fax: 518-386-4509
Comptroller:
  Paul Sebesta. . . . . . . . . . . . . . . . . .518-386-4508/fax: 518-386-4592
Town Attorney:
  Peter Scagnelli. . . . . . . . . . . . . . . .518-386-4503/fax: 518-386-4592
Police Chief:
  John Lubrant . . . . . . . . . . . . . . . . .518-386-4585/fax: 518-386-4594

## North Hempstead, Town of
220 Plandome Rd
Manhasset, NY 11030
516-869-6311  Fax: 516-627-4204
e-mail: feedback@northhempstead.com
Web site: www.northhempstead.com

Town Supervisor:
  Jon Kaiman . . . . . . . . . . . . . . . . . . . . . . . . . . . . . . . . .516-869-6311
  e-mail: kaimanj@northhempstead.com
Town Clerk:
  Leslie Gross . . . . . . . . . . . . . . . . . . . . . . . . . . . . . . . . .516-869-6311
  e-mail: grossl@northhempstead.com
Town Attorney:
  Richard S Finkel. . . . . . . . . . . . . . . . . . . . . . . . . . . . . .516-869-7600
  e-mail: finkelr@northhempstead.com
Director, Public Safety:
  Andrew DeMartin. . . . . . . . . . . . . . . . . . . . . . . . . . . . .516-869-6311
  e-mail: demartin@northhempstead.com
Commissioner, Public Works:
  Paul DiMaria. . . . . . . . . . . . . . . . . . . . . . . . . . . . . . . . .516-739-6710
  e-mail: guineyj@northhempstead.com
Commissioner, Finance:
  JoAnne Taormina . . . . . . . . . . . . . . . . . . . . . . . . . . . . .516-869-6311
  e-mail: taorminaja@northhempstead.com
Comptroller:
  Kathleen Mitterway . . . . . . . . . . . . . . . . . . . . . . . . . . .516-869-7766
  e-mail: mitterwayk@northhempstead.com
Community Services:
  Kimberly Corcoran . . . . . . . . . . . . . . . . . . . . . . . . . . . .516-869-6311
  e-mail: corcorank@northhempstead.com

## North Tonawanda, City of
City Hall
216 Payne Ave
North Tonawanda, NY 14120
716-695-8555  Fax: 716-695-8557
Web site: www.northtonawanda.org

Mayor:
  Robert G Ortt. . . . . . . . . . . . . . . .716-695-8540/fax: 716-695-8541
  e-mail: robertort@northtonawanda.org
Common Council President:
  Richard L. Andres, Jr. . . . . . . . . . . . . . .716-695-8555/fax: 716-695-8557
City Clerk:
  Scott P Kiedrowski . . . . . . . . . . . . . . .716-695-8555/fax: 716-695-8557
  e-mail: scottkie@northtonawanda.org
City Attorney:
  Shawn P Nickerson . . . . . . . . . . . . . .716-695-8590/fax: 716-695-8592
City Engineer:
  Dale W Marshall . . . . . . . . . . . . . . . .716-695-8565/fax: 716-695-8568
  e-mail: dalemar@northtonawanda.org

*Offices and agencies generally appear in alphabetical order, except when specific order is requested by listee.*

Police Chief:
William R. Hall . . . . . . . . . . . . . . . . . . .716-692-4325/fax: 716-692-4321
Fire Chief:
Joseph L Krantz. . . . . . . . . . . . . . . . . . .716-693-2201/fax: 716-693-2216

## Onondaga, Town of
5020 Ball Road
Syracuse, NY 13215
315-469-3888  Fax: 315-498-6129
Web site: www.townofonondagany.com

Town Supervisor:
Thomas Andino . . . . . . . . . . . . . . . . . . .315-469-3888/fax: 315-498-6129
Town Clerk:
Lisa Goodwin . . . . . . . . . . . . . . . . . . . .315-469-1583/fax: 315-469-3461
e-mail: lgoodwin@townofonondaga.com
Tax Receiver:
Michele Kresser. . . . . . . . . . . . . . . . . . .315-469-0483/fax: 315-469-3461
Town Attorney:
Kevin Gilligan . . . . . . . . . . . . . . . . . . . .315-422-1152/fax: 315-422-1139
Town Historian:
Mary Nowyj . . . . . . . . . . . . . . . . . . . . . . . . . . . . . . . . .315-214-2383

## Orangetown, Town of
26 Orangeburg Rd
Orangeburg, NY 10962
845-359-5100  Fax: 845-359-2623
Web site: www.orangetown.com

Town Supervisor:
Andy Stewart . . . . . . . . . . . . . . . . . . . . . . . . . . .845-359-5100 x2261
e-mail: supervisor@orangetown.com
Town Clerk:
Charlotte E Madigan . . . . . . . . . .845-359-5100 x5004/fax: 845-359-5126
e-mail: townclerk@orangetown.com
Town Attorney:
John S Edwards . . . . . . . . . . . . . .845-359-5100 x2215/fax: 845-359-2715
e-mail: townattorney@orangetown.com
Director, Finance:
Jeffrey W. Bencik . . . . . . . . . . . . . . . . . . . . . . . . .845-359-5100 x2204
e-mail: jbencik@orangetown.com
Police Chief:
Kevin A Nulty. . . . . . . . . . . . . . . . . . . . . . . . . . . . . . . .845-359-3700
e-mail: orangetownpd@yahoo.com

## Orchard Park, Town of
4295 S Buffalo Rd
Orchard Park, NY 14127
716-662-6400  Fax: 716-662-6479
Web site: www.orchardparkny.org

Town Supervisor:
Janis Colarusso . . . . . . . . . . . . . . . . . . . . . . . . . . . . . .716-662-6400
Town Clerk:
Carol R Hutton . . . . . . . . . . . . . . . . . . . . . . . . . . . . . .716-662-6410
Receiver of Taxes:
Carol R. Hutton . . . . . . . . . . . . . . . . . .716-662-6405/fax: 716-662-6465

## Ossining, Town of
16 Croton Ave
Ossining, NY 10562
914-762-6000  Fax: 914-762-7710
Web site: www.townofossining.com

Town Supervisor:
Susanne Donnelly . . . . . . . . . . . . . . . .914-762-6001/fax: 914-762-0833
e-mail: sdonnelly@townofossining.com

Town Clerk:
MaryAnn Roberts . . . . . . . . . . . . . . . . .914-762-8428/fax: 914-914-0627
e-mail: townclerk@townofossining.com
Receiver of Taxes:
Gloria Fried . . . . . . . . . . . . . . . . . . . . .914-762-8790/fax: 914-762-0635
Police Chief:
Mark E Busche . . . . . . . . . . . . . . . . . . .914-762-6007/fax: 914-762-6900
e-mail: topd@ossiningtownpolice.com

## Ossining, Village of
16 Croton Ave
Ossining, NY 10562
914-941-3554

Mayor:
William R Hanauer. . . . . . . . . . . . . . . . . . . . . . . . . . . .914-941-3554
Village Manager:
Richard A Leins . . . . . . . . . . . . . . . . . . . . . . . . . . . . .914-941-3554
Village Clerk:
Mary Ann Roberts . . . . . . . . . . . . . . .914-762-8428/fax: 914-762-7710
Corporation Counsel:
Lori Lee Dickson. . . . . . . . . . . . . . . . .914-941-3554/fax: 914-941-5940
Police Chief:
Joseph Burton Jr . . . . . . . . . . . . . . . . . . . . . . . . . . . . .914-941-4099

## Owego, Town of
2354 NYS Route 434
Apalachin, NY 13732
607-687-0123  Fax: 607-687-5191
Web site: www.townofowego.com

Town Supervisor:
Donald Castellucci Jr. . . . . . . . . . . . . . .607-687-0123/fax: 607-687-5191
e-mail: dcastellucci@townofowego.com
Town Clerk/Receiver of Taxes:
Michael E Zimmer. . . . . . . . . . . . . . . . .607-687-0123 or  607-687-6381
e-mail: owegotownclerk@gmail.com
Town Attorney:
Eric Gartenman. . . . . . . . . . . . . . . . . . . . . . . . . . . . . .607-687-0123
Director, Water/Sewer:
Michael Trivisonno. . . . . . . . . . . . . . . . . . . . . . . . . . . .607-625-2197
e-mail: mtrivisonno@townofowego.com
Town Historian:
Vacant . . . . . . . . . . . . . . . . . . . . . . . . . . . . . . . . . . . .607-687-1961

## Oyster Bay, Town of
Town Hall East
54 Audrey Ave
Oyster Bay, NY 11771
516-624-6498  Fax: 516-624-6387
Web site: www.oysterbaytown.com

Town Supervisor:
John Venditto . . . . . . . . . . . . . . . . . . . . . . . . . . . . . . .516-624-6350
Town Clerk:
Steven L Labriola . . . . . . . . . . . . . . . . . . . . . . . . . . . . .516-624-6332
Attorney:
Gregory J Giammalvo. . . . . . . . . . . . . . . . . . . . . . . . . . .516-624-6150
Comptroller:
Robert J McEvoy . . . . . . . . . . . . . . . . . . . . . . . . . . . . .516-624-6440

## Peekskill, City of
City Hall
840 Main Street
Peekskill, NY 10566
914-737-3400
Web site: www.cityofpeekskill.com

*Offices and agencies generally appear in alphabetical order, except when specific order is requested by listee.*

Mayor:
  Mary F Foster . . . . . . . . . . . . . . . . . . . . . . . . . . . . . . . . .914-734-4105
Acting City Manager:
  Brian Havranek . . . . . . . . . . . . . . . . . . . . . . . . . . . . . . . .914-734-4246
  e-mail: rfinn@cityofpeekskill.com
City Clerk:
  Pamela Beach . . . . . . . . . . . . . . . . . . . . . . . . . . . . . . . . .914-737-3400
  e-mail: pbeach@cityofpeekskill.com
Comptroller:
  Charles Emberger . . . . . . . . . . . . . . . . . . . . . . . . . . . . . . .914-734-4118
  e-mail: cemberger@cityofpeekskill.com
Police Chief:
  Eric Johansen
  e-mail: ejohansen@police.com

## Penfield, Town of
3100 Atlantic Ave
Penfield, NY 14526
585-340-8600  Fax: 585-340-8667
Web site: www.penfield.org

Town Supervisor:
  Tony LaFountain . . . . . . . . . . . . . . . . . .585-340-8630/fax: 585-340-8762
  e-mail: supervisor@penfield.org
Town Clerk:
  Amy Steklof. . . . . . . . . . . . . . . . . . . . . .585-340-8629/fax: 585-340-8752
  e-mail: clerk@penfield.org
Fire Marshal:
  Wayne Cichetti . . . . . . . . . . . . . . . . . . .585-340-8643/fax: 585-340-8644
  e-mail: firemarshal@penfield.org
Town Historian:
  Kathy Kanauer. . . . . . . . . . . . . . . . . . . .585-340-8740/fax: 585-340-8748
  e-mail: historian@penfield.org

## Perinton, Town of
1350 Turk Hill Rd
Fairport, NY 14450
585-223-0770  Fax: 585-223-3629
Web site: www.perinton.org

Town Supervisor:
  James E Smith. . . . . . . . . . . . . . . . . . . . . . . . . . . . . . . . . .585-223-0770
Town Clerk:
  Jennifer West . . . . . . . . . . . . . . . . . . . . . . . . . . . . . . . . . .585-223-0770
Public Works:
  Thomas C Beck. . . . . . . . . . . . . . . . . . . . . . . . . . . . . . . . .585-223-5115
Director, Finance:
  Kevin Spacher. . . . . . . . . . . . . . . . . . . . . . . . . . . . . . . . . .585-223-0770
Historian:
  Bill Poray . . . . . . . . . . . . . . . . . . . . . . . . . . . . . . . . . . . . .585-223-0770

## Pittsford, Town of
11 S Main St
Pittsford, NY 14534
585-248-6200  Fax: 585-248-6247

Town Supervisor:
  Sandra F. Zutes . . . . . . . . . . . . . . . . . . .585-248-6220/fax: 585-248-6247
  e-mail: szutes@townofpittsford.org
Town Clerk:
  Pat Chuhta . . . . . . . . . . . . . . . . . . . . . .585-248-6210/fax: 585-248-6440
  e-mail: pchuhta@townofpittsford.org
Town Attorney:
  Richard T Williams II. . . . . . . . . . . . . . . . . . . . . . . . . . . .585-248-6216
  e-mail: rwilliams@townofpittsford.org
Director, Finance:
  Gregory J Duane . . . . . . . . . . . . . . . . . .585-248-6225/fax: 585-248-6247
  e-mail: gduane@townofpittsford.org

Town Historian:
  Audrey M Johnson . . . . . . . . . . . . . . . .585-248-6245/fax: 585-248-6247
  e-mail: ajohnson@townofpittsford.org

## Port Chester, Village of
222 Grace Church St
Port Chester, NY 10573
914-939-5202  Fax: 914-937-3169
Web site: www.portchesterny.com

Mayor:
  Neil J. Pagano. . . . . . . . . . . . . . . . . . . . . . . . . . . . . . . . . .914-939-5201
Village Manager:
  Christopher Steers . . . . . . . . . . . . . . . . .914-939-2200/fax: 914-937-3169
Treasurer:
  Leonie Douglas . . . . . . . . . . . . . . . . . . .914-939-5205/fax: 914-305-2570
Village Attorney:
  Anthony Cerreto . . . . . . . . . . . . . . . . . .914-939-5208/fax: 914-937-3169
Public Works General Foreman:
  Rocky Morabito . . . . . . . . . . . . . . . . . . . . . . . . . . . . . . . . .914-939-5207
Police Chief:
  Joseph Krzeminski. . . . . . . . . . . . . . . . .914-939-1000/fax: 914-939-2303

## Poughkeepsie, City of
62 Civic Center Plaza
Poughkeepsie, NY 12601
845-451-4072
Web site: www.cityofpoughkeepsie.com

Mayor:
  John C Tkazyik . . . . . . . . . . . . . . . . . . .845-451-4073/fax: 845-451-4201
  e-mail: jtkazyik@cityofpoughkeepsie.com
City Administrator:
  Milo Bunyi. . . . . . . . . . . . . . . . . . . . . . .845-451-4072/fax: 845-451-4013
  e-mail: mbunyi@cityofpoughkeepsie.com
City Chamberlain/Clerk:
  Deanne Flynn . . . . . . . . . . . . . . . . . . . .845-451-4276/fax: 845-451-4239
  e-mail: dflynn@cityofpoughkeepsie.com
Acting Finance Commissioner:
  Karen Sorrell . . . . . . . . . . . . . . . . . . . . .845-451-4027/fax: 845-451-4028
  e-mail: ksorrell@cityofpoughkeepsie.com
Police Chief:
  Ronald Knapp . . . . . . . . . . . . . . . . . . . . . . . . . . . . . . . . . .845-451-4132

## Poughkeepsie, Town of
One Overocker Rd
Poughkeepsie, NY 12603
845-485-3600  Fax: 845-485-3701
Web site: www.townofpoughkeepsie.com

Town Supervisor:
  Todd Tancredi . . . . . . . . . . . . . . . . . . . .845-485-3607/fax: 845-485-3701
Town Clerk:
  Susan Miller. . . . . . . . . . . . . . . . . . . . . .845-485-3620/fax: 845-485-8583
Comptroller:
  Jim Wojtowicz. . . . . . . . . . . . . . . . . . . .845-485-3610/fax: 845-485-1130
Police Chief:
  Thomas Mauro. . . . . . . . . . . . . . . . . . . .845-485-3666/fax: 845-485-3756
  e-mail: townpolice@hotmail.com

## Queensbury, Town of
742 Bay Road
Queensbury, NY 12804
518-761-8200  Fax: 518-798-8359
Web site: www.queensbury.net

Town Supervisor:
  Dan Stec. . . . . . . . . . . . . . . . . . . . . . . . .518-761-8229/fax: 518-798-8359
  e-mail: supervisor@queensbury.net

*Offices and agencies generally appear in alphabetical order, except when specific order is requested by listee.*

Town Clerk/Receiver of Taxes:
   Darleen Dougher....................................518-761-8234
   e-mail: townclerk@queensbury.net
Town Counsel, Legal Assistant:
   Pamela Hunsinger .................518-761-8251/fax: 518-745-4408
   e-mail: towncounsel@queensbury.net
Fire Marshal:
   Mike Palmer .....................518-761-8206/fax: 518-745-4437
   e-mail: firemarshal@queensbury.net
Historian:
   Dr Marilyn VanDyke ..............................518-761-8252
   e-mail: historian@queensbury.net

## Ramapo, Town of
Town Hall, 237 Route 59
Suffern, NY 10901
845-357-5100  Fax: 845-357-3877
Web site: www.ramapo.org

Town Supervisor:
   Christopher P St Lawrence .....................845-357-5100 x202
Town Clerk:
   Christian G Sampson ..........845-357-5100 x263/fax: 845-357-8513
   e-mail: townclerk@ramapo.org
Town Attorney:
   Michael L Klein................................845-357-5100 x237
Director, Finance:
   Nathan Oberman ...............................845-357-5100 x247
Director, Public Works:
   Ted Dzurinko..................................845-357-0591 x112
Police Chief:
   Peter Brower ..................................845-357-2400

## Riverhead, Town of
200 Howell Avenue
Riverhead, NY 11901
631-727-3200  Fax: 631-727-6712
Web site: www.townofriverheadny.gov

Town Supervisor:
   Sean Walter ..................................631-727-3200 x251
Town Clerk:
   Diane M Wilhelm.............631-727-3200 x260/fax: 631-208-4034
Fire Marshal:
   Craig Zitek .................631-727-3200 x209/fax: 631-727-3370
Town Attorney:
   Robert Kozakiewicz...........631-727-3200 x216/fax: 631-727-6712

## Rochester, City of
City Hall
30 Church St
Rochester, NY 14614
585-428-5990  Fax: 585-428-6059
e-mail: info@cityofrochester.gov
Web site: www.cityofrochester.gov

Mayor:
   Thomas S Richards..............................585-428-7045
Deputy Mayor:
   Leonard E. Redon ..............................585-428-7163
Council President:
   Lovely A Warren ...............................585-428-7538
City Clerk:
   Daniel B Karin ................................585-428-7421
Corporation Counsel:
   Robert Bergin .................................585-428-6990
City Treasurer:
   Charles A Benincasa............................585-428-6705
   e-mail: charles.benincasa@cityofrochester.gov

Commissioner, Environmental Services:
   Paul Holahan..................................585-428-6855
Police Chief:
   James Sheppard.................................585-428-7033
Fire Chief:
   Salvatore Mitrano, III ........................585-428-7037
Director, Emergency Communications:
   John M Merklinger..............................585-528-2200
Director, Finance:
   Brian L Roulin ................................585-428-7151

## Rockville Centre, Village of
1 College Place
Rockville Centre, NY 11571
516-678-9300  Fax: 516-678-9225
Web site: www.rvcny.us

Village Mayor:
   Francis X Murray ..............................516-678-9260
Deputy Clerk Treasurer/Payroll:
   Mary Schmeling ................................516-678-9263
Village Attorney:
   Vacant........................................516-678-9206
Comptroller:
   Michael Schussheim.............................516-678-9226
Police Commissioner:
   Charles Gennario...............................516-766-1500
Superintendent, Public Works:
   Harry Weed....................................516-678-9293

## Rome, City of
City Hall
Liberty Plaza
198 N Washington St
Rome, NY 13440
315-339-7677  Fax: 315-339-7667
Web site: www.romenewyork.com

Mayor:
   Joseph R Fusco Jr .................315-339-7677/fax: 315-339-7667
Common Council President:
   John J Mazzaferro...............................315-838-1731
City Clerk:
   Louise Glasso ....................315-339-7658/fax: 315-838-1160
   e-mail: jreid@romecitygov.com
Corporation Counsel:
   Timothy Benedict ..................315-339-7668/fax: 315-838-1166
Treasurer:
   David Nolan.......................315-339-7690/fax: 315-838-1165
Public Safety Commissioner:
   Mike Grande ......................315-339-7676/fax: 315-339-7667
Commissioner, Public Works:
   Frank Tallarino ..................315-339-7625/fax: 315-339-1167

## Rotterdam, Town of
John F Kirvin Government Center
1100 Sunrise Blvd
Rotterdam, NY 12306
518-355-7575 x393  Fax: 518-355-7837
Web site: www.rotterdamny.org

Town Supervisor:
   Harry C Buffardi .............................518-355-7575 x393
Town Clerk:
   Diane M. Marco................................518-355-7575 x318
Town Attorney:
   Kate McGuirl .................................518-355-7575
Comptroller:
   Jackie Every.................................518-355-7575 x394

State & Local
Government
Public Information

Police Chief:
  James Hamilton.....................................518-355-7331
  e-mail: jhamilton@rotterdamny.org
Public Works Coordiantor:
  Vince Romano ..............518-355-7575 x395/fax: 518-355-2725

## Rye, Town of
222 Grace Church Street
3rd Floor
Port Chester, NY 10573
914-939-3075  Fax: 914-939-1465
e-mail: DReisner@Townofryeny.com
Web site: www.townofryeny.com

Town Supervisor:
  Gary Zuckerman....................................914-939-3075
Town Clerk:
  Hope B. Vespia....................................914-939-3570
  e-mail: HVespia@Townofryeny.com
Town Attorney:
  Jeffrey M. Binder
Deputy Comptroller:
  Joseph Fazzino ....................................914-967-7303
  e-mail: jfazzino@ryeny.gov
Commissioner:
  Paul Rosenberg....................................914-939-3075

## Salina, Town of
201 School Rd
Liverpool, NY 13088
315-457-6661  Fax: 315-457-4317
Web site: salina.ny.us

Town Supervisor:
  Mark A Nicotra ....................315-457-6661/fax: 315-457-4476
  e-mail: supervisor@salina.ny.us
Town Clerk:
  Jeannie Ventre....................315-457-2710/fax: 315-457-4317
Town Attorney:
  Timothy A. Frateschi ....................................315-475-6661
Comptroller:
  Greg Maxwell....................................315-451-4210

## Saratoga Springs, City of
City Hall
474 Broadway
Saratoga Springs, NY 12866
518-587-3550  Fax: 518-587-1688
e-mail: email@saratoga-springs.org
Web site: www.saratoga-springs.org

Mayor:
  Scott Johnson....................................518-587-3550 x2514
Accounts Commissioner:
  John Franck....................................518-587-3550 x2543
Finance Commissioner:
  Michele Madigan....................................518-587-3550 x2571
Public Safety Commissioner:
  Christian Mathiesen....................................518-587-3550 x2627
Public Works Commissioner:
  Anthony Scirocco ....................................518-587-3550 x2561

## Saugerties, Town of
4 High Street
Saugerties, NY 12477
845-246-2800  Fax: 845-246-0355
Web site: www.saugerties.ny.us

Town Supervisor:
  Kelly Myers .................845-246-2800 x345/fax: 845-247-0355
Town Clerk:
  Lisa Stanley ..................845-246-2800 x343/fax: 845-246-0127
  e-mail: lstanley@saugerties.ny.us
Accounting Office:
  Deborah Martino ..............................845-246-2800 x348

## Schenectady, City of
City Hall
105 Jay St
Schenectady, NY 12305
518-382-5000  Fax: 518-382-5272
Web site: www.cityofschenectady.com

Mayor:
  Gary McCarthy .....................518-382-5000/fax: 518-382-5272
City Council President:
  Margaret King....................................518-370-1885
City Clerk:
  Chuck Thorne ....................................518-382-5199 x5303
Finance Commissioner:
  Deborah W. DeGenova....................................518-382-5010
Public Safety Commissioner:
  Wayne Bennett .....................518-382-5201/fax: 518-382-5299
Historian:
  Don Rittner ....................................518-788-1255
Police Chief:
  Brian Kilcullen .....................518-382-5201/fax: 518-382-5299

## Smithtown, Town of
99 W Main St
PO Box 9090
Smithtown, NY 11787
631-360-7600  Fax: 631-360-7668
Web site: www.smithtownny.gov

Town Supervisor:
  Patrick R Vecchio ..................631-360-7600/fax: 631-360-7668
Town Clerk:
  Vincent Puleo .....................631-360-7620/fax: 631-360-7692
  e-mail: vpuleo@tosgov.com
Town Attorney:
  John B. Zollo......................631-360-7570/fax: 631-360-7719
  e-mail: townattorney@tosgov.com
Comptroller:
  Louis A. Necroto..................631-360-7530/fax: 631-360-7625
Director, Public Safety:
  Chief John Valentine...............631-360-7553/fax: 631-360-7677
  e-mail: publicsafety@tosgov.com

## Southampton, Town of
116 Hampton Rd
Southampton, NY 11968
631-283-6000  Fax: 631-283-5606
Web site: www.southamptontownny.gov

Town Supervisor:
  Anna Throne-Holst .................631-283-6055/fax: 631-287-5708
Town Clerk:
  Hon Sundy A Schermeyer...........631-287-5740/fax: 631-283-5606
Town Attorney:
  Michael C Sordi ....................................631-287-3065
Comptroller:
  Leonard J. Marchese ..............631-702-1887/fax: 631-287-5709
  e-mail: lmarchese@southamptontownny.gov
Commissioner, Public Works/Highway Superintendent:
  Alex  D Gregor ....................631-728-3600/fax: 631-728-3605
  e-mail: agregor@southamptontownny.gov

*Offices and agencies generally appear in alphabetical order, except when specific order is requested by listee.*

Police Chief:
  Robert Pearce . . . . . . . . . . . . . . . . . . . . . . . . . . . . . . . .631-728-5000
Town Historian:
  Henry Moeller. . . . . . . . . . . . . . . . . . . . . . . . . . . . . . . . .631-287-5740

## Southold, Town of
53095 Route 25
PO Box 1179
Southold, NY 11971
631-765-1800  Fax: 631-765-6145

Town Supervisor & Emergency Coordinator:
  Scott A Russell . . . . . . . . . . . . . . . . .631-765-1889/fax: 631-765-1823
  e-mail: supervisor@town.southold.ny.us
Town Clerk/Registrar:
  Elizabeth A Neville . . . . . . . . . . . . . . . .631-765-1800/fax: 631-765-6145
  e-mail: e.neville@town.southold.ny.us
Comptroller:
  John Cushman . . . . . . . . . . . . . . . . . . .631-765-4333/fax: 631-765-1366
  e-mail: accounting@town.southold.ny.us
Town Attorney:
  Martin Finnegan . . . . . . . . . . . . . . . . .631-765-1939/fax: 631-765-6639
Police Chief:
  Martin Flatley . . . . . . . . . . . . . . . . . . .631-765-2600/fax: 631-734-2315
Historian:
  Antonia Booth . . . . . . . . . . . . . . . . . . .631-765-1981/fax: 631-765-1366

## Spring Valley, Village of
200 North Main Street
Spring Valley, NY 10977
845-352-1100  Fax: 845-352-1164
Web site: www.villagespringvalley.org

Mayor:
  Noramie Jasmin. . . . . . . . . . . . . . . . . . . . . . . . . . . . . .845-573-5864
Village Clerk:
  Sherry M Scott. . . . . . . . . . . . . . . . . . . . . . . . . .845-517-1128 x108
Treasurer:
  Kuruvilla Cherian . . . . . . . . . . . . . . . . . . . . . . .845-517-1121 x101
  e-mail: kcherian@villagespringvalley.org
Superintendent:
  Neil Vitiello . . . . . . . . . . . . . . . .845-573-1198 x253/fax: 845-573-5802
Police Chief:
  Paul J. Modica . . . . . . . . . . . . . . . . . . . .845-573-5833 or 845-356-7400
  fax: 845-573-5859

## Syracuse, City of
233 East Washington St
203 City Hall
Syracuse, NY 13202
315-448-8005  Fax: 315-448-8067
e-mail: cityhall@ci.syracuse.ny.us
Web site: www.syracuse.ny.us

Mayor:
  Stephanie A Miner. . . . . . . . . . . . . . . . .315-448-8005/fax: 315-448-8067
  e-mail: cityhall@syrgov.net
Common Council President:
  Hon Van B Robinson . . . . . . . . . . . . .315-448-8466/fax: 315-448-8423
City Clerk:
  John P Copanas . . . . . . . . . . . . . . . . . .315-448-8216/fax: 315-448-8489
Commissioner, Assessment:
  David Clifford . . . . . . . . . . . . . . . . . . .315-448-8280/fax: 315-448-8190
  e-mail: assessment@syrgov.net
Commissioner, Neighborhood & Business Development:
  Paul Driscoll . . . . . . . . . . . . . . . . . . . .315-448-8100/fax: 315-488-8036
  e-mail: cd@ci.syracuse.ny.us

Commissioner, Finance:
  David DelVecchio . . . . . . . . . . . . . . . .315-448-8279/fax: 315-448-8424
  e-mail: finance@ci.syracuse.ny.us
Director, Administration & Budget Management:
  Mary Vossler . . . . . . . . . . . . . . . . . . .315-448-8252 or 315-448-8116
  e-mail: budget@syrgov.net
Police Chief:
  Frank L Fowler . . . . . . . . . . . . . . . . . .315-442-5111/fax: 315-442-5198
Fire Chief:
  Paul Linnertz . . . . . . . . . . . . . . . . . . . .315-473-5525/fax: 315-422-7766

## Tonawanda, Town of
2919 Delaware Ave
Kenmore, NY 14217
716-877-8800  Fax: 716-877-0578
Web site: www.tonawanda.ny.us

Town Supervisor:
  Anthony F Caruana . . . . . . . . . . . . . . .716-877-8804/fax: 716-877-1261
  e-mail: acaruana@tonawanda.ny.us
Town Clerk:
  Marguerite Greco . . . . . . . . . . . . . .716-877-8800 x810/fax: 716-877-0578
  e-mail: mbrinson@tonawanda.ny.us
Town Attorney:
  John J Flynn. . . . . . . . . . . . . . . . . . . .716-875-9947/fax: 716-875-9948
  e-mail: jflynn@tonawanda.ny.us
Comptroller:
  Edward D Mongold. . . . . . . . . . . . . . .716-877-8810/fax: 716-877-8236
  e-mail: emongold@tonawanda.ny.us
Police Chief:
  Anthony J Palombo . . . . . . . . . . . . . . .716-876-6607/fax: 716-876-6644

## Troy, City of
City Hall
1776 Sixth Avenue
Troy, NY 12180
518-270-4401  Fax: 518-270-4609
Web site: www.troyny.gov

Mayor:
  Lou Rosamilia . . . . . . . . . . . . . . . . . . .518-279-7130/fax: 518-270-4609
  e-mail: mayorsoffice@troyny.gov
President, City Council:
  Lynn Kopka. . . . . . . . . . . . . . . . . . . . .518-279-7317/fax: 518-270-4639
  e-mail: citycouncil@troyny.gov
City Clerk:
  William A McInerney. . . . . . . . . . . . . . . . . . . . . . . . . . .518-279-7134
Chief of Police:
  John Tedesco. . . . . . . . . . . . . . . . . . . . . . . . . . . . . . . . .518-270-4421
Fire Chief:
  Thomas O Garrett . . . . . . . . . . . . . . . . . . . . . . . . . . . . . .518-270-4471

## Union, Town of
3111 E Main St
Endwell, NY 13760
607-786-2900  Fax: 607-786-2998
Web site: www.townofunion.com

Town Supervisor:
  Rose Sotak. . . . . . . . . . . . . . . . . . . . . .607-786-2995/fax: 607-786-2998
  e-mail: rsotak@townofunion.com
Town Clerk:
  Gail L Springer . . . . . . . . . . . . . . . . . .607-786-2915/fax: 607-786-2913
  e-mail: townclerk@townofunion.com
Town Attorney:
  Alan J Pope. . . . . . . . . . . . . . . . . . . . . . . . . . . . . . . . . .607-786-2910
  e-mail: attorney@townofunion.com

*Offices and agencies generally appear in alphabetical order, except when specific order is requested by listee.*

Comptroller/Finance:
  Laura Lindsley....................607-786-2930/fax: 607-786-2998
  e-mail: llindsley@townofunion.com
Historian:
  Suzanne Meredith....................607-786-5786
  e-mail: historian@townofunion.com

## Utica, City of
City Hall
One Kennedy Plz
Utica, NY 13502
315-797-5847  Fax: 315-734-9250
Web site: www.cityofutica.com

Mayor:
  Robert Palmieri....................315-792-0100
  e-mail: mayor@cityofutica.com
Common Council President:
  William C Morehouse.............315-792-0113/fax: 315-792-0220
City Clerk:
  Joan M Brenon..................315-792-0113/fax: 315-792-0220
  e-mail: jbrenon@cityofutica.com
First Assistant Corporation Counsel:
  Charles N Brown.................315-792-0171/fax: 315-792-0175
Comptroller:
  Michael T. Cerminaro.............315-792-0133/fax: 315-797-5847
  e-mail: mcerminaro@cityofutica.com
City Assessor:
  David H Williams................315-792-0125/fax: 315-792-9028
Commissioner, Parks & Public Works:
  David Short....................315-738-0172
Deputy City Engineer:
  Goran Smiljic..................315-792-0152/fax: 315-792-0236

## Valley Stream, Village of
123 S Central Ave
Valley Stream, NY 11580
516-825-4200  Fax: 516-825-8316
Web site: www.vsvny.org

Mayor:
  Edwin Fare ....................516-825-4200
Village Clerk/Administrator:
  Robert Barra ....................516-825-4200
Treasurer:
  Michael J. Fox....................516-825-4200

## Vestal, Town of
605 Vestal Parkway West
Vestal, NY 13850
607-748-1514  Fax: 607-786-3631
Web site: www.vestalny.com

Town Supervisor:
  W. John Schaffer....................607-748-1514 x329
Town Clerk:
  Emil Bielecki....................607-748-1514 ext321
  e-mail: ebielecki@vestalny.com
Town Attorney:
  David Berger....................607-748-1514 ext389
Comptroller:
  Laura McKane ....................607-748-1514 ext324
  e-mail: lmckane@vestalny.com
Police Chief:
  John Butler ....................607-754-2386 ext341
  e-mail: jbutler@vestalny.com
Fire Chief:
  Pat McPherson ....................607-748-1514 x383
  e-mail: pmcpherson_vfd@vestalny.com

Historian:
  Margaret Hadsell....................607-754-4243
  e-mail: mhadsell@vestalny.com

## Wallkill, Town of
99 Tower Drive
Building A
Middletown, NY 10941
845-692-7800
Web site: www.townofwallkill.com

Town Supervisor:
  Dan Depew....................845-692-7832/fax: 845-692-2546
  e-mail: supervisor@townofwallkill.com
Town Clerk:
  Louisa Ingrassia....................845-692-7826/fax: 845-692-6051
Chief of Police:
  Robert Hertman....................845-692-7859/fax: 845-692-4166
  e-mail: chiefofpolice@townofwallkill.com

## Wappinger, Town of
20 Middlebush Road
Wappinger Falls, NY 12590
845-297-5771  Fax: 845-298-1478
Web site: www.townofwappinger.us

Town Supervisor:
  Barbara Gutzler....................845-297-2744
Town Clerk:
  Christine Fulton....................845-297-5771/fax: 845-298-1478
Receiver of Taxes:
  Patricia Maupin....................845-297-4342/fax: 845-298-1478
Fire Inspector:
  Mark Liebermann....................845-297-1373
Historian:
  Constance O Smith

## Warwick, Town of
132 Kings Highway
Warwick, NY 10990
845-986-1124
e-mail: townhall@townofwarwick.org
Web site: www.townofwarwick.org

Town Supervisor:
  Michael Sweeton....................845-986-1120 x240
Deputy Supervisor:
  James Gerstner....................845-986-1120 x241
Town Clerk:
  Marjorie Quackenbush....................845-986-1124 x246
Public Works Commissioner:
  Jeffrey Feagles ....................845-986-3358
Police Chief:
  Thomas McGovern Jr....................845-986-3423

## Watertown, City of
245 Washington St, Rm 302
Watertown, NY 13601
315-785-7730  Fax: 315-785-7796
Web site: www.watertown-ny.gov

Mayor:
  Jeffrey E Graham....................315-785-7720/fax: 315-782-9014
City Manager:
  Sharon Addison....................315-785-7730/fax. 315-782-9014
City Clerk:
  Ann Saunders....................315-785-7780/fax: 315-785-7796

*Offices and agencies generally appear in alphabetical order, except when specific order is requested by listee.*

Comptroller:
James Mills . . . . . . . . . . . . . . . . . . . . . .315-785-7754/fax: 315-785-7826
e-mail: jmills@watertown-ny.gov
Fire Chief:
Dale Herman . . . . . . . . . . . . . . . . . . . . .315-785-7800/fax: 315-785-7821

## Webster, Town of
1000 Ridge Rd
Webster, NY 14580
585-872-1000 Fax: 585-872-1352
Web site: www.ci.webster.ny.us

Supervisor:
Ronald Nesbitt . . . . . . . . . . . . . . . . . . . . . . .585-872-1000
e-mail: supervisor@ci.webster.ny.us
Town Clerk:
Barbara Ottenschot . . . . . . . . . . . . . . . . .585-872-1000/fax: 585-872-7058
e-mail: townclerk@ci.webster.ny.us
Director, Finance:
Kathy Tanea. . . . . . . . . . . . . . . . . . . .585-872-7067/fax: 585-872-7008
e-mail: finance@ci.webster.ny.us
Public Works:
Gary Kleist. . . . . . . . . . . . . . . . . . . . .585-872-7025/fax: 585-872-1352
Police:
Gerald Pickering. . . . . . . . . . . . .585-872-1216 x240/fax: 585-872-7010
e-mail: police@ci.webster.ny.us
Historian:
Lynn Barton . . . . . . . . . . . . . . . . . . . . . . . .585-265-3308

## West Seneca, Town of
1250 Union Rd
West Seneca, NY 14224
716-674-5600 Fax: 716-677-4330
Web site: www.westseneca.net

Town Supervisor:
Sheila Meegan . . . . . . . . . . . . . . . . . .716-997-7200 or 716-558-3202
e-mail: smeegan@twsny.org
Town Clerk:
Jacqueline A. Felser . . . . . . . . . . . . . . . . . . . . . . . .716-558-3215
Town Attorney:
Shawn P Martin . . . . . . . . . . . . . . . . . . . . . . . . .716-558-3240
Comptroller:
Robert J Bielecki. . . . . . . . . . . . . . . . . . . . . . .716-558-3205
e-mail: rbielecki@swccpas.com
Police Chief:
Daniel Denz . . . . . . . . . . . . . . . . . . . . . . . . .716-674-2280
e-mail: denz@wspolice.com

## White Plains, City of
City Hall
255 Main St
White Plains, NY 10601
914-422-1200 Fax: 914-422-1395
Web site: www.cityofwhiteplains.com

Mayor:
Thomas M Roach . . . . . . . . . . . . . . . . . . . . . . . . . .914-422-1411
Common Council President:
Beth N. Smayda . . . . . . . . . . . . . . . . . . . . . . . .914-419-6891
Commissioner, Public Works:
Joseph Nicoletti Jr. . . . . . . . . . . . . . . . . . . . . . . . .914-422-1206

Chief of Police:
James Bradley. . . . . . . . . . . . . . . . . . . . . . . . . . . .914-422-6230

## Yonkers, City of
City Hall
40 S Broadway
Yonkers, NY 10701-3700
914-377-6000 Fax: 914-377-6048
Web site: www.cityofyonkers.com

Mayor:
Mike Spano. . . . . . . . . . . . . . . . . . . . . . . . . . . . .914-377-6300
Chief of Staff:
Rachelle Richard. . . . . . . . . . . . . . . . . . . . . . . . .914-377-6300
President, City Council:
Chuck Lesnick . . . . . . . . . . . . . . . . . . . . . . . . . .914-377-6060
Acting City Clerk:
Vincent E. Spano . . . . . . . . . . . . . . . . . . . . . . . .914-377-6020
Corporation Counsel:
MIchael V. Curti. . . . . . . . . . . . . . . . . . . . . . . . .914-377-6250
City Assessor:
Mark Russell. . . . . . . . . . . . . . . . . . . . . . . . . . .914-377-6200
Acting Commissioner, Affordable Housing:
William J. Schneider. . . . . . . . . . . . . . . . . . . . . .914-377-6501
Commissioner, Finance & Mgmt Services:
James LaPerche. . . . . . . . . . . . . . . . . . . . . . . . . .914-377-6100
Commissioner, Parks, Recreation & Conservation:
Yvette E. Hartsfield . . . . . . . . . . . . . . . . . . . . . .914-377-6450
Commissioner, Public Works:
Thomas G. Meier . . . . . . . . . . . . . . . . . . . . . . . .914-377-6270
Acting Commissioner, Planning & Development:
Wilson Kimball. . . . . . . . . . . . . . . . . . . . . . . . . .914-377-6150
Director, Public Affairs & Community Relations:
Richard Halevy . . . . . . . . . . . . . . . . . . . . . . . . . .914-377-6053
Director Economic Development:
Louis C Kirven . . . . . . . . . . . . . . . .914-377-6797/fax: 914-377-6003
Emergency Management Director:
John Donaghy . . . . . . . . . . . . . .914-377-7325/fax: 914-965-8430
Police Commissioner:
Charles Gardner . . . . . . . . . . . . . . . . . . . . . . . .914-377-7900
Fire Commissioner:
Anthony Pagano . . . . . . . . . . . . . . . . . . . . . . . .914-377-7500

## Yorktown, Town of
363 Underhill Avenue
Yorktown Heights, NY 10598
914-962-5722 Fax: 914-962-1731
Web site: www.yorktownny.org

Town Supervisor:
Michael Grace . . . . . . . . . . . . . . .914-962-5722 x271/fax: 914-962-1004
e-mail: supervisor@yorktownny.org
Town Clerk:
Alice Roker. . . . . . . . . . . . . . . . .914-962-5722 x209/fax: 914-962-6591
e-mail: townclerk@yorktownny.org
Comptroller:
Patricia Caporale . . . . . . . . . . . . .914-962-5722 x206/fax: 914-962-1004
Chief of Police:
Daniel McMahon. . . . . . . . . . . . . . .914-962-4141/fax: 914-962-4458
e-mail: info@yorktownpd.org

State & Local
Government
Public Information

# Section 4:
# POLITICAL PARTIES & RELATED ORGANIZATIONS

## NEW YORK POLITICAL PARTIES

### NEW YORK STATE CONSERVATIVE PARTY

**New York State Conservative Party**
486 78th Street
Brooklyn, NY 11209
718-921-2158  Fax: 718-921-5268
e-mail: cpnys@nybiz.rr.com
Web site: www.cpnys.org

Capital District Office
325 Parkview Dr
Schenectady, NY 12303
518-356-7882
Fax: 518-356-3773

**Statewide Party Officials**
State Chairman:
Gerard Kassar . . . . . . . . . . . . . . . . . . . . 718-921-2158/fax: 718-921-5268
486 78th Street, Brooklyn, NY 11209
Executive Vice Chairwoman and Executive Director:
Shaun Marie Levine . . . . . . . . . . . . . . 518-356-7882/fax: 518-356-3773
325 Parkview Dr, Schenectady, NY 12303
Secretary:
Howard Lim, Jr. Esq. . . . . . . . . . . . . . . . . . . . . . . . . . . . . 914-659-5656
83 Valley Terrace, Rye Brook, NY 10573
Treasurer:
Frances Vella-Marrone . . . . . . . . . . . . . . . . . . . . . . . . . . . 347-866-4945
7317 12th Avenue, Brooklyn, NY 11228
State Vice Chairman:
Daniel F. Donovan, Jr. . . . . . . . . . . . . . . . . . . . . . . . . . . . 516-509-9725
State Vice Chairman:
Thomas M. Long. . . . . . . . . . . . . . . . . . . . . . . . . . . . . . . . 718-704-4197
State Vice Chairman:
Ralph C. Lorigo, Esq. . . . . . . . . . . . . . . . . . . . . . . . . . . . . 716-310-9002
State Vice Chairman:
James F. Quinn, Jr. . . . . . . . . . . . . . . . . . . . . . . . . . . . . . . 585-733-6800
State Vice Chairman:
Gregory S. Rigby . . . . . . . . . . . . . . . . . . . . . . . . . . . . . . . 315-729-5023
State Vice Chairman:
Allen H. Roth . . . . . . . . . . . . . . . . . . . . . . . . . . . . . . . . . . 718-318-3654
State Vice Chairman:
Frank A. Tinari . . . . . . . . . . . . . . . . . . . . . . . . . . . . . . . . . 631-827-6033
Regional Vice Chairman, Northern Region:
Henry (Hank) Ford . . . . . . . . . . . . . . . . . . . . . . . . . . . . . . 315-212-6194
Regional Vice Chairman, Hudson Valley Region:
Hugh Fox, Jr. . . . . . . . . . . . . . . . . . . . . . . . . . . . . . . . . . . 914-494-3306
Regional Vice Chairman, Capital District:
Brian Gardner . . . . . . . . . . . . . . . . . . . . . . . . . . . . . . . . . . 518-860-3969
Regional Vice Chairman, Mid-Western Region:
Jason J. McGuire. . . . . . . . . . . . . . . . . . . . . . . . . . . . . . . . 585-734-2199
Regional Vice Chairman, Western Region:
Arthur R. Munger . . . . . . . . . . . . . . . . . . . . . . . . . . . . . . . 585-762-9323
Regional Vice Chairman, North Central Region:
H. Leonard Schick . . . . . . . . . . . . . . . . . . . . . . . . . . . . . . 315-439-7944
Regional Vice Chairman, South Central Region:
James M. Thomas. . . . . . . . . . . . . . . . . . . . . . . . . . . . . . . 607-343-8767

### County Chairs

**Albany**
Thomas J. Spargo . . . . . . . . . . . . . . . . . . . . . . . . . . . . . . 518-390-6377
260 Joslyn School Road, E. Bern, NY 12059

**Bronx**
Patrick McManus . . . . . . . . . . . . . . . . . . . . . . . . . . . . . . . 914-450-0246
839 Wilcox Ave, Bronx, NY 10465

**Broome**
Aaron M. Martin. . . . . . . . . . . . . . . . . . . . . . . . . . . . . . . . 607-343-2761
209 Reese Ave, Vestal, NY 13850

**Cattaraugus**
Jay William Frantz . . . . . . . . . . . . . . . . . . . . . . . . . . . . . . 716-938-9133
207 Court St, Little Valley, NY 14755

**Cayuga**
David Pappert . . . . . . . . . . . . . . . . . . . . . . . . . . . . . . . . . . 315-246-4258
250 E Genesee St, Auburn, NY 13021

**Chautauqua**
Anna M. Wilcox . . . . . . . . . . . . . . . . . . . . . . . . . . . . . . . . 716-672-8595
3105 Cable Road, Freedonia, NY 14063

**Chemung**
Louis F. DeCicco . . . . . . . . . . . . . . . . . . . . . . . . . . . . . . . 607-796-5129
4965 Hillview Road, Millport, NY 14864

**Clinton**
Zachery W. Sirk . . . . . . . . . . . . . . . . . . . . . . . . . . . . . . . . 518-314-1172
2017 St Rt 22B, PO Box 582, Morrisonville, NY 12962

**Columbia**
Brian Gardner . . . . . . . . . . . . . . . . . . . . . . . . . . . . . . . . . . 518-860-3969
29 Firehouse Road, Germantown, NY 12526

**Delaware**
James H. Small . . . . . . . . . . . . . . . . . . . . . . . . . . . . . . . . . 607-746-6629
105 Michae's Path, Delhi, NY 13753

**Dutchess**
Donald F. Minichino. . . . . . . . . . . . . . . . . . . . . . . . . . . . . 845-221-6464
110 Gold Rd, Stormville, NY 12582

**Erie**
Ralph C. Lorigo, Esq. . . . . . . . . . . . . . . . . . . . . . . . . . . . . 716-675-8611
101 Slade Ave, West Seneca, NY 14224

**Essex**
William H. McGahay . . . . . . . . . . . . . . . . . . . . . . . . . . . . . 518-369-3700
83 Algonquin Dr, Lake Placid, NY 12946

**Franklin**
Robert E. White, Esq. . . . . . . . . . . . . . . . . . . . . . . . . . . . . 518-327-3714
559 County Rt 60, Rainbow Lake, NY 12976

**Genesee**
Julie Ann Bolas-Carasone. . . . . . . . . . . . . . . . . . . . . . . . . . 585-993-2831
6608 Main Rd, Stafford, NY 14143

**Greene**
Michael Buttino . . . . . . . . . . . . . . . . . . . . . . . . . . . . . . . . 518-634-7672
229 Surprise Result Rd, Earlton, NY 12058

**Herkimer**
Marilyn R. Williams. . . . . . . . . . . . . . . . . . . . . . . . . . . . . . 315-429-9884
106 South Main Street, Dolgeville, NY 13329-1437

**Jefferson**
Kenneth H. Parks . . . . . . . . . . . . . . . . . . . . . . . . . . . . . . . 315-786-2012
19520 Ball Rd, Black River, NY 13612

**Kings**
Frances T. Vella-Marrone. . . . . . . . . . . . . . . . . . . . . . . . . . 347-866-4945
7521 10th Ave, Brooklyn, NY 11228

**Livingston**
Jason J. McGuire. . . . . . . . . . . . . . . . . . . . . . . . . . . . . . . . 585-734-2199
1851 Livingston St, Lima, NY 14485

**Madison**
Christopher J. Kendall, Esq. . . . . . . . . . . . . . . . . . . . . . . . . 315-247-9791
2051 Spring St, Hamilton, NY 13346

*Offices and agencies generally appear in alphabetical order, except when specific order is requested by listee.*

**Monroe**
Donald S. Mazzullo ..............................585-202-8466
16 West Main St, Rochester, NY 14614

**Montgomery**
Robert J. Phelps ...............................518-842-6457
139 Snooks Corner Rd, Amsterdam, NY 12010

**Nassau**
Daniel M. Donovan...............................516-433-8568
1 Sydney Street, Plainview, NY 11803

**New York**
Stuart J. Avrick ...............................212-912-0022
375 South End Ave, #9E, New York, NY 10280

**Niagara**
William L. Ross ................................716-731-5949
6761 Walmore Rd, Niagara Falls, NY 14304

**Oneida**
Daniel F. Fitzgerald, Jr. ......................315-853-8816
118 Sanford Ave, Clinton, NY 13323

**Onondaga**
Bernard Ment ..................................315-278-8927
149 W. Manlius St. #3, Syracuse, NY 13057

**Ontario**
Reid W. Robbins.................................315-879-1450
77 Field St, Port Gibson, NY 14537

**Orange**
John P. DeLessio................................845-562-4963
7 Hill Street, Newburgh, NY 12550

**Orleans**
Paul Lauricella, Jr. ...........................585-589-3274
12469 Roosevelt Highway, Lydonville, NY 14098

**Oswego**
Ronald K. Greenleaf.............................315-564-6427
879 Cayuga Street, Hannibal, NY 13074

**Otsego**
Paul A. Kennedy.................................607-293-8829
157 Pleasant Valley Road, Mt. Vision, NY 13810

**Putnam**
James M. Maxwell ...............................845-628-7716
117 Vista Terrace South, Mahopac, NY 10541

**Queens**
Thomas M. Long..................................718-474-3826
6 Beach 219th St, Rockaway Point, NY 11697

**Rensselaer**
William T. Fiacco...............................518-892-9273
83 Lape Rd, Rensselear, NY 12144

**Richmond**
David Mario Curcio .............................718-370-3604
100 Colfax Avenue Apt 6J, Staten Island, NY 10306

**Rockland**
Simeon Naemit ..................................845-608-3204
465 North Little Tor Rd., New City, NY 10956

**Saratoga**
Robert D. Zordan ...............................518-233-0121
1 Robin Lane, Waterford, NY 12188

**Schenectady**
James J. Barrett, Jr............................518-779-3059
159 Hilltop Rd, Pattersonville, NY 12137

**Schoharie**
William A. Hanson ..............................607-588-6107
801 State Route 990 V, Gilboa, NY 12076

**Seneca**
William R. White ...............................315-539-2534
105 Brookside Dr, Waterloo, NY 13165

**St Lawrence**
Henry (Hank) Ford ..............................315-262-2824
113 Stowe Bay Rd, Colton, NY 13625

**Suffolk**
Michael E. Torres ..............................631-456-9851
3 Seatuck Cove Circle, Eastport, NY 11941

**Sullivan**
Edward A. Magilton .............................845-252-7232
5088 State Route 97, Narrowsburg, NY 12764

**Ulster**
John J. Hayes ..................................845-594-9367
24 Tinkers Lane, Gardiner, NY 12525

**Warren**
Carol Birkholz..................................518-623-9151
1 Pucker St, Warrensburg, NY 12885

**Washington**
Beverly A. Jakway ..............................518-832-3078
2092 County Road 43, Fort Ann, NY 12827

**Wayne**
Michael Garlock ................................315-203-1710
7079 Sodus Bay Heights Drive, Sodus Point, NY 14555

**Westchester**
Hugh Fox, Jr. ..................................914-494-3306
10 Belmont Terrace, Yonkers, NY 10703

**Yates**
Diane C. Harris.................................585-473-7799
PO Box 23973, Rochester, NY 14692

## NEW YORK STATE DEMOCRATIC PARTY

### New York State Democratic Committee
420 Lexington Ave
New York, NY 10170
212-725-8825  Fax: 212-725-8867
e-mail: nysdc@nydems.org
Web site: www.nydems.org

**Statewide Party Officials**
State Chair:
Byron Brown
Vice Chair:
Christine Quinn
Executive Director:
Geoff Berman

**County Chairs**

**Albany**
Matthew Clyne ..................................518-438-8282
22 Colvin Ave, Albany, NY 12206

**Allegany**
Mike McCormick

**Bronx**
Marcos Crespo...................718-679-9000/fax: 347-281-5984
1640 Eastchester Rd, Bronx, NY 10461

*Offices and agencies generally appear in alphabetical order, except when specific order is requested by listee.*

**Broome**
Jim Testani . . . . . . . . . . . . . . . . . . . . . . . . . . . . . . . . . . .607-773-8369
PO Box 854, Binghamton, NY 13902

**Cattaraugus**
Joyce Melfi . . . . . . . . . . . . . . . . . . . . . . . . . . . . . . . . . . . .716-676-5716

**Cayuga**
Kate Lacey . . . . . . . . . . . . . . . . . . . . . . . . . . . . . . . . . . . .315-252-4981
144 Genesee Street, Auburn, NY 13021

**Chautauqua**
Norman Greene

**Chemung**
Jim Carr. . . . . . . . . . . . . . . . . . . . . . . . . . . . . . . . . . . . . . .607-425-3267
518 West Third Street, Elmira, NY 14901

**Chenango**
Bethany Kosmider
110 Fuller Road, Norwich, NY 13815

**Clinton**
Patrick McNeil
80 Rand Hill Road, Morissonville, NY 12962

**Columbia**
Martin D. Mannix, Jr. . . . . . . . . . . . . . . . . . . . . . . . . . . . .518-966-2583
PO Box 507, Ghent, NY 12075

**Cortland**
Cyndy Hall
129 Port Watson Street, Cortland, NY 13045

**Delaware**
Sandy Price
PO Box 366, New Kingston, NY 12459

**Dutchess**
Tom Schimmerling
488 Freedom Plains Rd., Poughkeepsie, NY 12603

**Erie**
Elisa Sumner
671 Seneca St, Buffalo, NY 14210

**Essex**
Jeremy Zellner
PO Box 737, Elizabethtown, NY 12932

**Franklin**
Kathy M. Fleury

**Fulton**
Ed Jasewicz. . . . . . . . . . . . . . . . . . . . . . . . . . . . . . . . . . . .518-762-7598
2714 State Highway 29, Johnstown, NY 12095-9946

**Genesee**
Lorie J. Longhany. . . . . . . . . . . . . . . . . . . . . . . . . . . . . . .716-769-8377

**Greene**
Doreen Davis
PO Box 590, Palenville, NY 12463

**Hamilton**
Linda M. Mitchell

**Herkimer**
Richard Souza

**Jefferson**
Ronald Cole

**Kings**
Frank R. Seddio
16 Court St, Brooklyn, NY 11241

**Lewis**
Linda Sandri
5510 Jackson St, Lowville, NY 13367

**Livingston**
Judith Hunter

**Madison**
Michael Oot

**Monroe**
Jamie Romeo
1150 University Ave, Rochester, NY 14607

**Montgomery**
Bethany Schumann-McGhee

**Nassau**
Jay S. Jacobs. . . . . . . . . . . . . . . . . . . . . . . . . . . . . . . . . . .516-294-3366
1 Old County Rd, Carle Place, NY 11514

**New York**
Keith Wright. . . . . . . . . . . . . . . . . . . . . . . . . . . . . . . . . . .212-687-6540

**Niagara**
Nick Forster

**Oneida**
Mitch Ford

**Onondaga**
Mark English
615 West Genesee St, Syracuse, NY 13204

**Ontario**
John Hurley

**Orange**
Jonathan Jacobson

**Orleans**
Vacant
488 Freedom Plains Rd, Poughkeepsie, NY 12603

**Oswego**
Gordon Prosser
147 W 5th Street, Oswego, NY 13126

**Otsego**
Richard D. Abbate

**Putnam**
Cathy Croft

**Queens**
Joseph Crowley
72-50 Austin St, Forest Hills, NY 11375

**Rensselaer**
Thomas W. Wade
PO Box 846, Troy, NY 12181

**Richmond**
John P. Gulino
35 New Dorp Plaza, Staten Island, NY 10306

**Rockland**
Kristen Stavisky
106 W Strawtown Road, West Nyack, NY 10994

**Saratoga**
Todd Kerner

**Schenectady**
Brian L. Quail
664 Sacandaga Rd, Glenville, NY 12302

*Offices and agencies generally appear in alphabetical order, except when specific order is requested by listee.*

**Schoharie**
Cliff Hay . . . . . . . . . . . . . . . . . . . . . . . . . . . . . . . . . .518-234-7165

**Schuyler**
Dale Walter

**Seneca**
Theodore H. Young

**St Lawrence**
Mark J. Bellardini

**Steuben**
Shawn D. Hogan . . . . . . . . . . . . . . . . . . . . . . . . . .607-324-7629

**Suffolk**
Richard H. Schaffer
1461 Lakeland Ave, Bohemia, NY 11716

**Sullivan**
Darryl Kaplan

**Tioga**
Patricia Bence

**Tompkins**
Irene W. Stein
PO Box 6798, Ithaca, NY 14851

**Ulster**
Frank Cardinale

**Warren**
Lynne Boecher

**Washington**
Sheila A. Comar

**Wayne**
Mark Alquist

**Westchester**
Reginald A. LaFayette
170 East Post Road, White Plains, NY 10601

**Wyoming**
Harold J. Bush, Jr. . . . . . . . . . . . . . . . . . . . . . . . . .585-786-2782

**Yates**
Carolyn M. Schaeffer

## NEW YORK STATE GREEN PARTY

**New York State Green Party**
Web site: www.gpny.org

**Statewide Party Officials**
Co-Chair:
Gloria Mattera . . . . . . . . . . . . . . . . . . . . . . . . . . . .917-886-4538
Co-Chair:
Peter LaVenia . . . . . . . . . . . . . . . . . . . . . . . . . . . .518-495-8001
Secretary:
Ursula Rozum
Treasurer:
Eric Jones

## NEW YORK STATE INDEPENDENCE PARTY

**New York State Independence Party**
225 Broadway
Suite 2010
New York, NY 10007

212-962-1699
Web site: www.ipnyc.org

**County Chairs**

**Bronx**
Nardo Reyes

**Kings**
Robert Conroy. . . . . . . . . . . . . . . . . . . . . . . . . . . . .718-415-0571
323 Putnam Ave., #4, Brooklyn, NY 11216

**Manhattan**
Cathy L. Stewart . . . . . . . . . . . . . . . . . . . . . . . . . .212-962-1699
225 Broadway, New York, NY 10007

**Queens**
Nancy Hanks

**Richmond**
Sarah D. Lyons . . . . . . . . . . . . . . . . . . . . . . . . . . . .718-447-9689
36 Hamilton Ave., #3N, Staten Island, NY 10301

## NEW YORK STATE REFORM PARTY

**New York State Reform Party**
Web site: www.nyreformparty.com

## NEW YORK STATE REPUBLICAN PARTY

**New York State Republican Party**
315 State St
Albany, NY 12210
518-462-2601 Fax: 518-449-7443
e-mail: frontdesk@nygop.org
Web site: nygop.org

**Statewide Party Officials**
Chairman:
Edward F. Cox . . . . . . . . . . . . . . . . . . . . . . . . . . . .518-462-2601
Executive Director:
Jason Weingartner
1st Vice Chair:
Bill Reilich . . . . . . . . . . . . . . . . . . . . . . . . . . . . . . .585-546-8040
National Committeeman:
Charles P. Joyce
National Committeewoman:
Jennifer Saul Rich

**County Officials**

**Albany**
Christine Benedict

**Allegany**
Mike Healy

**Bronx**
Mike Rendino

**Broome**
Bijoy Datta

**Cattaraugus**
Robert Keis

**Cayuga**
Cherl Heary

**Chautauqua**
Dave Wilfong . . . . . . . . . . . . . . . . . . . . . . . . . . . . .716-488-1499

*Offices and agencies generally appear in alphabetical order, except when specific order is requested by listee.*

**Chemung**
Rodney Strange....................................607-731-1579

**Chenango**
Thomas Morrone

**Clinton**
Clark Currier

**Columbia**
Greg Fingar......................................518-545-4467

**Cortland**
Constance White

**Delaware**
Maria Kelso

**Dutchess**
Mike McCormack..................................845-452-2268

**Erie**
Nick Langworthy..................................716-856-8700

**Essex**
Shaun Gillilland.................................518-963-8668

**Franklin**
Ray Scollin

**Fulton**
Susan McNeil.....................................518-332-9722

**Genesee**
Richard Siebert..................................585-344-8562

**Greene**
Brent Bogardus...................................518-731-9700

**Hamilton**
Bill Murphy

**Herkimer**
Sylvia Rowan

**Jefferson**
Don Coon.........................................315-836-1502

**Kings**
Ted Ghorra

**Lewis**
Michael Young

**Livingston**
Lowell Conrad

**Madison**
Todd A. Rouse

**Monroe**
Bill Reilich.....................................585-546-8040

**Montgomery**
Rosemary Smith

**Nassau**
Joseph Mondello

**New York**
Andrea Catsimatidis..............................212-517-8444

**Niagara**
Scott Kiedrowski

**Oneida**
Peter Sobel......................................315-798-2964

**Onondaga**
Tom Dadey........................................315-449-2000

**Ontario**
Trisha Turner....................................585-261-0737

**Orange**
Courtney C. Greene...............................845-291-2436

**Orleans**
Edward Morgan

**Oswego**
Fred Beardsley...................................315-342-0840

**Otsego**
Vince Casale.....................................607-431-8867

**Putnam**
Anthony G. Scannapieco, Jr.......................845-808-1316

**Queens**
Joann Ariola

**Rensselaer**
John Rustin

**Richmond**
Ron Castorina, Jr................................718-701-3100

**Rockland**
Lawrence A. Garvey...............................914-946-2200

**Saratoga**
Carl Zeilman.....................................518-584-7900

**Schenectady**
Mike Cuevas

**Schoharie**
Chris Tague......................................518-365-1573

**Schuyler**
Lester W. Cady

**Seneca**
Tom Fox..........................................315-270-2004

**St Lawrence**
Tom Jenison......................................315-212-3046

**Steuben**
Joe Sempolinski

**Suffolk**
John Jay LaValle.................................631-320-1900

**Sullivan**
Richard Coombe...................................845-701-3342

**Tioga**
Donald Castellucci, Jr...........................607-768-0816

**Tompkins**
Mike Sigler

**Ulster**
Roger Rascoe

**Warren**
Michael Grasso...................................518-783-8754

**Washington**
Dan Boucher

**Wayne**
Bob Oaks

*Offices and agencies generally appear in alphabetical order, except when specific order is requested by listee.*

**Westchester**
Douglas Colety . . . . . . . . . . . . . . . . . . . . . . . . . . . . . . . . . .914-949-3020

**Wyoming**
James Schlick . . . . . . . . . . . . . . . . . . . . . . . . . . . . . . . . . .585-786-8931

**Yates**
Sandra J. King

## NEW YORK STATE WOMEN'S EQUALITY PARTY

**New York State Women's Equality Party**
Web site: womensequalityparty.org

## NEW YORK STATE WORKING FAMILIES PARTY

**New York State Working Families Party**
1 Metrotech Center North
11th Floor
Brooklyn, NY 11201
718-222-3796  Fax: 718-246-3718
Web site: workingfamilies.org

## POLITICAL ACTION COMMITTEES

**1199/SEIU New York State Political Action Fund**
330 West 42nd Street, 7th Floor, New York, NY 10036
212-603-1737
George K. Gresham, Treasurer

**2013 Committee to Elect Gwen Goodwin**
152 East 100th Street, Suite 5E, New York, NY 10029
Gwen Goodwin, Treasurer

**A Different Approach**
19 East 213th Street, Suite 4C, Bronx, NY 10467
718-600-5054
Joseph Smith, Treasurer

**ACEC New York City PAC**
8 West 38th Street, Suite 1101, New York, 10018
212-682-6336
Raymond Daddazio, Chairman
Hannah O'Grady

**Advertising Development Political Action Committee**
PO Box 2269, New York, NY 10163
917-363-2323
Marty Judge, Chairman/Treasurer

**AECOM US FEDERAL PAC**
201 Wilson Boulevard, Suite 700, Arlington, VA 22201
703-465-5872
Nancy Butler, Chairwoman

**Akiel Taylor For Council**
186 Lefferts Place, Brooklyn, NY 11238
917-620-5725
Joseph N. Taylor, Treasurer

**Albert 2013**
427 Bronx Park Avenue, Bronx, NY 10460
347-427-8822
Luis C. Torres, Treasurer

**Alex For NYC**
10 Bethune Stret, Suite 3A, New York, NY 10014
305-992-6875
Ryan S. Reynolds, Treasurer

**Alicia 4 Council 7**
3333 Broadway, Suite D35A, New York, NY 10031
212-283-2019
Sandra Dawson, Treasurer

**American Insurance Association New York City PAC**
2101 L Street Northwest, Suite 400, Washington, DC 20037
202-828-7100
JS Zielezienski, Chairman

**Andy King 2013**
21 Riverdale Avenue, White Plains, NY 10607
646-644-9414
Katrina P. DeLa Cruz, Treasurer

**AON Corporation Political Action Committee**
200 East Randolph, Chicago, IL 60601
312-381-3352
Paul Hagy, Treasurer

**Ari Kagan For City Council**
330 Ocean Parkway, Suite C3, Brooklyn, NY 11218
347-556-4205
Alyona Badalova, Treasurer

**Arroyo 2013**
694 East 133rd Street, #2, Bronx, NY 10454
347-820-3723
Carmen M. Aquino, Treasurer

**Asbestos Workers Local 12 Political Action Committee**
25-19 43rd Avenue, Long Island City, NY 11101
718-784-3456
Nick Grgas, Chairman

**AT&T PAC - New York**
111 Washington Avenue, Albany, NY 12210
518-463-3092
Marissa J. Shorenstein, Chairwoman

**ATU New York Cope Fund**
5025 Wisconsin Avenue, Northwest, Washington, DC 20016
202-537-1645
Lawrence J. Hanley, Treasurer

**Bank of America New York Political Action Committee**
1100 North King Street, DE5-001-02-07, Wilmington, DE 19884
302-432-0956
Brian P. Grip, Chairman

**Bendetto For Assembly**
3280 Giegerich Place, Bronx, NY 10465
718-931-6675
Michael R. Benedetto, Chairman

**Bill Thompson For Mayor**
16 Court Street, 35th Floor, Brooklyn, NY 11241
718-855-2324
James F. Ross, Treasurer

**Blishteyn For NYC**
175-10 Jewel Avenue, Fresh Meadows, NY 11365
718-757-7389
Ross P. Weiner, Treasurer

**Brab PAC, Inc.**
850 Bronx River Road, Suite 105, Yonkers, NY 10708
914-966-2000
Michael Laub, Treasurer

**Brad Lander 2013**
256 13th Street, Brooklyn, NY 11215
917-822-4584
Margaret R. Barnette, Treasurer

**Bricklayers & Allied Craftworkers Local 1 PAC**
4 Court Square, Long Island City, NY 11108
718-392-0525
Jermiah Sullivan Jr., Chairman
Santo Lantzfamne, Treasurer

**Bristol-Meyers Squibb Company Political Action Committee**
345 Park Avenue, New York, NY 10154
609-252-5352
John E. Celentano, Chairman

**Bryan Block 2013**
120-43 219th Street, Cambria Heights, NY 11411
917-837-6102
Sanu K. Thomas, Treasurer

**Building & Construction Trades Council PAC**
71 West 23rd Street, Suite 501, New York, NY 10010
212-647-0700
Gary LaBarbera, Treasurer

*Offices and agencies generally appear in alphabetical order, except when specific order is requested by listee.*

**Building Industry Association of NYC, Inc.**
3130 Amboy Road, Staten Island, NY 10306
718-720-3070
Frank Naso, Chairman

**Cablevision Systems New York PAC**
1111 Stewart Avenue, Bethpage, NY 11714
516-803-2387
Thomas M. Rutledge, Chairman

**Cabrera For City Council**
2792 Sedgwick Avenue, 4A, Bronx, NY 10468
917-804-9298
Paul Susana, Treasurer

**Captains Endowment Association**
233 Broadway, Suite 1801, New York, NY 10279
212-791-8292
Roy T. Richter, Chairman

**Carlo 2013**
1275 81st Street, Brooklyn, NY 11228
917-622-4063
Camille Arezzo, Treasurer

**Carlos For Council**
215 Terrace Place, #3, Brooklyn, NY 11218
646-305-5224
Aimee Davis, Treasurer

**Carolyn's PAC**
24 East 93rd Street, Suite 1B, New York, NY 10128
212-987-5516
Carolyn B. Maloney, Chairwoman

**Carrion 2013**
1 Stuyvesant Oval, 11D, New York, NY 10009
917-952-1915
Loretta Class, Treasurer

**Catholic Citizens Committee PAC**
106 First Place, Brooklyn, NY 11231
917-685-5264
Martin Cottingham, Chairman

**Central Brooklyn Independent Democrats**
476 Tenth Street, Brooklyn, NY 11215
718-788-8698
Lucy Koteen, Chairwoman

**CIR/SEIU Local 1957 Health Care Advocacy Fund**
520 8th Avenue, Suite 1200, New York, NY 10018
212-356-8100
Eric Scherzer, Treasurer

**CITIGROUP Inc. Political Action Committee - Federal/State**
1101 Pennsylvania Avenue Northwest, #1000, Washington, DC 20004
202-879-6805
S. Colin Dowling, Chairman

**Citizens For Sports & Arts, Inc.**
58-12 Queens Boulevard, Suite 1, Woodside, NY 11377
718-786-7110
Lewis H. Hartman, Chairman

**Civil Service Employees Political Action Fund**
143 Washington Avenue, Albany, NY 12210
518-436-8622
Danny F. Donohue, Chairman

**Cliff Stanton For Council**
3861 Cannon Place, Bronx, NY 10463
917-699-5241
Joseph V. Kullhanek, Treasurer

**Clifton Stanley Diaz For NYC Council**
172-20 133rd Avenue, 2D, Jamaica, NY 11434
917-856-5454
David E. Diaz, Treasurer

**Climate Action PAC**
30 Broad Street, 30th Floor, New York, NY 10004
212-361-6350
Robert Hallman, Chairman

**Cohen For Council**
444 East 86th Street, 17H, New York, NY 10028
212-879-2971
Esther Fink-Sinovsky, Treasurer

**Committee For Effective Leadership**
63 Carriage Place, c/o William J. He, Edison, NJ 08820
732-744-1413
Lewis H. Goldstein, Chairman

**Committee to Elect Abiodun Bello**
PO Box 520843, Bronx, NY 10452
917-603-3553
Shakiru O. Kazeem, Treasurer

**Committee to Elect Andy King**
952 East 218th Street, PH, Bronx, NY 10469
718-515-5464
Winslow Luna, Treasurer

**Committee to Elect Ariel Guerrero**
411 East 118th Street, #35, New York, NY 10035
917-826-9661
Nicholas S. Burke, Treasurer

**Committe to Elect Ceceilia Berkowitz for Mayor**
143 East 30th Street, #402, New York, NY 10016
917-923-5760
Alex Castillo, Treasurer

**Committee to Elect Charles A. Bilal 2010**
121 03 Sutphin Boulevard, Jamaica, NY 11431
718-607-9119
Aziza N. Bilal, Treasurer

**Committee to Elect Christopher Banks**
669 Van Siclen Avenue, PH, Brooklyn, NY 11207
718-257-3050
Claudette Elliott, Treasurer

**Committee to Elect Eric Adams**
593 Vanderbilt Avenue, #305, Brooklyn, NY 11238
Eric Adams, Chairman

**Committee to Elect Philip Marks For Mayor**
1658 Ralph Avenue, 6C, Brooklyn, NY 11236
Philip A. Marks, Treasurer

**Committee to Elect Robert E. Cornegy Jr.**
653 Putnam Avenue, Brooklyn, NY 11221
917-586-7444
Michelle R. Cornegy, Treasurer

**Committee to Elect Robert M. Waterman**
207 Lewis Avenue, Brooklyn, NY 11221
Avis Jones, Treasurer

*Offices and agencies generally appear in alphabetical order, except when specific order is requested by listee.*

**Committee to Elect Stephen S. Jones to City Council**
107-52 139th Street, Jamaica, NY 11435
347-447-8148
Kenneth E. Nelson, Treasurer

**Committee to Re-Elect Lawrence A. Warden**
1103 East Gun Hill Road, Bronx, NY 10469
917-345-6860
Marcia E. McGann, Treasurer

**Committee to Re-Elect Nydia M. Velazquez to Congress**
315 Inspiration Lane, Gaithersburg, MD 20878
301-947-0278
Nydia M. Velazquez, Chairwoman

**Committee to Re-Elect Mathieu Eugene**
40 Argyle Road, C6, Brooklyn, NY 11218
347-725-6725
Delsie L. Lawson, Treasurer

**Communications Workers of America Local 1180**
6 Harrison Street, New York, NY 10013
212-226-6565
Arthur Cheliotes, Chairman

**Community Campaign For Naaimat**
10 Richman Plaza, 1K, Bronx, NY 10453
646-470-3436
Momodou S. Sawaneh, Treasurer

**Community For Lynn Nunes**
115-13 Jamaica Avenue, Richmond Hill, NY 11418
347-242-6600
George Parpas, Treasurer

**Community Mental Health Political Action Committee, Inc.**
52 Dublin Drive, Niskayuna, NY 12309
518-783-1417
Christopher Burke, Chairman

**Comrie For NYC**
115-03 Farmers Boulevard, St. Albans, NY 11412
718-772-3975
Tyrone A. Sellers, Treasurer

**Conrad Tillard For Council**
315 Flatbush Avenue, 521, Brooklyn, NY 11217
347-766-3628
Suedamay A. Monderson, Treasurer

**Conservative Party Campaign Committee**
32 Cunard Place, Staten Island, NY 10304
718-816-2237
Carmine Ragucci, Chairman

**Consolidated Edison, Inc. Employees' Political Action Committee**
4 Irving Place, New York, NY 10003
212-460-4202
Frances Resheske, Chairwoman

**Correy For Council**
777 Sixth Avenue, 6D, New York, NY 10001
917-750-5289
Mathew Bergman, Treasurer

**Correction Captains Association - PAC**
189 Montague Street, Suite 400, Brooklyn, NY 11201
718-243-0222
Patrick W. Ferraiuolo, Chairman

**Correction Officers Benevolent Association**
75 Broad Street, Suite 810, New York, NY 10004
212-274-8000
Norman Seabrook, Chairman

**Council of School Supervisors and Administrators, Local 1 AFSA**
40 Rector Street, 12th Floor, New York, NY 10006
212-823-2020  Fax: 212-962-6130
e-mail: askcsa@csa-nyc.org
Web site: www.csa-nyc.org
Ernest Logan, President

**Cozen O'Connor Empire State PAC**
1900 Market Street, Philadelphia, PA 19103
215-665-2000
Thomas A. Decker, Chairman

**Craig Caruana 2013**
7921 67 Drive, Middle Village, NY 11379
917-648-4787
Lawrence J. Caruana, Treasurer

**Crowley For Congress**
84-56 Grand Avenue, Elmhurst, NY 11373
718-639-7010
Joseph Crowley, Chairman

**CWA District One PAC**
80 Pine Street, 37th Floor, New York, NY 10005
212-344-2515
Christopher M. Shelton, Chairman

**CWA SSF (NY)**
80 Pine Street, 37th Floor, NY 10005
212-344-2515
Christopher M. Shelton, Chairman

**Cynthia For Change**
2375 Marion Avenue, 2C, Bronx, NY 10458
917-292-7015
Luana Malavolta, Treasurer

**D & M P.A.C. LLC**
605 Third Avenue, New York, NJ 10158
212-557-7200
Arthur Goldstein, Treasurer

**David Kayode 2013**
106-23 153rd Street, 1, Jamaica, NY 11433
Omolola Kayode, Treasurer

**Davis 2013**
459 Columbus Avenue, 365, New York, NY 10024
917-716-9236
Adam B. Karl, Treasurer

**DC 37 Local 299**
125 Barclay Street, New York, NY 10007
212-815-1299
Jackie Rowe-Adams, Chairwoman

**DC 37 Political Action Committee**
125 Barclay Street, New York, NY 10007
212-815-1550
Lillian Roberts, Chairwoman

**Democracy For America - NYC**
38 Eastwood Drive, Suite 300, South Burlington, VT 05403
802-651-3200
Arshad Hasan, Chairman

*Offices and agencies generally appear in alphabetical order, except when specific order is requested by listee.*

**Democrat, Republican, Independent Voter Education**
25 Louisiana Avenue Northwest, Washington, DC 20001
202-624-6821
James P. Hoffa, Chairman

**Detectives Endowment Association - COPE**
26 Thomas Street, New York, NY 10007
212-587-1000
Michael J. Palladino, Chairman

**Diallo For Council 2013**
3396 3rd Avenue, Suite 1A, Bronx, NY 10456
347-754-8239
Adama I. Barry, Treasurer

**District Council 1707, AFSCME**
101 Avenue of the Americas, 4th Floor, New York, NY 10013
212-219-0022
Raglan George Jr., Chairman

**District Council No. 9 Political Action Committee**
45 West 14th Street, New York, NY 10011
212-255-2950
Joseph Ramaglia, Chairman

**DLA Piper New York Political Action Committee**
1251 Avenue of the Americas, 29th Floor, New York, NY 10020
202-799-4349
John A. Merrigan, Chairman

**Doctors Council SEIU COPE**
50 Broadway, 11th Floor, Suite 1101, New York, NY 10004
212-532-7690
Barry L. Liebowitz, M.D., Chairman

**Dodge Landesman For State Committee**
4 Lexington Avenue, New York, NY 10010
917-453-1523
Dodge Landesman, Treasurer

**Dromm For NYC**
35-24 78th Street, B28, Jackson Heights, NY 11372
718-457-2928
Andrew P. Ronan, Treasurer

**Duane For New York**
43-07 Westmoreland Street, Little Neck, NY 11363
212-949-6720
Margaret M. McConnell, Treasurer

**Duane Morris LLP Government Committee - New York Fund**
30 South 17th Street, Philadelphia, PA 19103
215-979-1450
Lewis F. Gould Jr., Chairman

**Educational Justice Political Action Committee**
76 East 51st Street, 2F, Brooklyn, NY 11203
718-813-6229
Shelly L. Barrow, Treasurer

**Effective Leadership Committee, Inc.**
165 West End Avenue, 14R, New York, NY 10023
212-799-3312
Raymond Hodell, Chairman

**EFO Jeffrey P. Gardner**
124 Highview Terrace, Hawthorne, NJ 07506
973-951-7081
Jeffrey P. Gardner, Chairman

**EISPAC**
3 Park Avenue, 28th Floor, c/o Robe, New York, NY 10016
212-689-7744
Paul Eisland, Chairman

**Elaine Nunes 2010**
95-16 123rd Street, Richmond Hill, NY 11419
646-430-9067
Jaime Nunes, Treasurer

**Eleanor Roosevelt Legacy Committee**
Greeley Square Station, P.O. Box 20293, New York, NY 10010
646-430-9067
Judith Hope, Chairwoman

**Elect Newsome 2013**
955 Sheridan Avenue, 5B, Bronx, NY 10456
347-913-3694
Chivona R. Newsome, Treasurer

**Elizabeth Crowley 2013**
77-24 83rd Street, Glendale, NY 11385
347-891-3973
Moira McDermott, Treasurer

**Emily's List NY**
1120 Connecticut Avenue Northwest, Suite 1100, Washington, DC 20036
202-326-1400
Amy Dacey, Treasurer

**Empire Dental Political Action Committee**
20 Corporate Woods Boulevard, Suite 602, Albany, NY 12211
518-465-0044
Lawrence E. Volland, Treasurer

**Entergy Corporation Political Action Committee - New York**
440 Hamilton Avenue, White Plains, NY 10601
914-272-3558
Michael Balduzzi, Chairman

**Eric Adams 2013**
PO Box 250-294, Brooklyn, NY 11225
917-327-3804
Emrod Martin, Treasurer

**Eric Ulrich 2013**
101-17 84th Street, Ozone Park, NY 11416
917-951-7251
Ronald Kulick, Treasurer

**Ernst & Young Committee For Good Government**
5 Times Square, New York, NY 10036
212-773-7111
David G. Bonagura, Chairman

**Espinal For City Council**
52 Hale Avenue, Brooklyn, NY 11208
347-967-9896
Wilson Rodriguez, Treasurer

**Evergreen For City Council**
41-34 Frame Place, 5K, Flushing, NY 11355
718-888-7412
Justin Lieu, Treasurer

**Farrell 2012**
31 Bleecker Place, Albany, NY 12202
Herman D. Farrell, Jr., Chairman

**Federal Express New York State Political Action Committee**
942 South Shady Grove Road, 1st Floor, Memphis, TN 38120
901-818-7407
Gina F. Adams, Chairwoman

*Offices and agencies generally appear in alphabetical order, except when specific order is requested by listee.*

**Flowers For NYC**
226-16 139th Avenue, Laurelton, NY 11413
718-928-5511
Raymond Baynard Jr., Treasurer

**Food Industry Political Action Committee - NYC**
130 Washington Avenue, Albany, NY 12210
914-220-8347
Jay M. Peltz, Chairman

**Frank's Friends**
9306 Flatlands Avenue, Suite A, Brooklyn, NY 11236
Jaime Rivas-Williams, Treasurer

**Freelancers Union Political Action Committee**
20 Jay Street, Suite 700, Brooklyn, NY 11201
718-532-1515
Ann Boger, Chairwoman

**Friends For Peter Koo**
133-24A 41st Avenue, Flushing, NY 11355
718-961-2931
Xiao Yun M. Yu, Treasurer

**Friends For Ryan Wright**
3025 Kingsland Avenue, PH, Bronx, NY 10469
Daphne C. Lewis, Treasurer

**Friends of Alfonso Quiroz**
76-10 34th Avenue, 2P, Jackson Heights, NY 11372
212-460-1372
Matthew Baker, Treasurer

**Friends of Angel Molina**
411 East 139th Street, Bronx, NY 10454
718-930-9712
Angel D. Molina, Treasurer

**Friends of Antonio Reynoso**
359 South 2nd Street, 3D, Brooklyn, NY 11211
718-909-3888
Pedro Pena, Treasurer

**Friends of Assembly Speaker Joe Roberts**
PO Box 1326, Bellmawr, NJ 08099
609-575-8893
Joe Roberts, Chairman

**Friends of Assemblyman Jeffrey Dinowitz**
c/o Heidi Schwartz, 3050 Fairfiel, Bronx, NY 10463
718-549-1729
Jeffrey Dinowitz, Chairman

**Friends of Audrey Pheffer**
8800 Shore Front Parkway, 10E, Rockaway Beach, NY 11693
917-501-5489
Stacey G. Amato, Treasurer

**Friends of Austin Shafran**
14-23 209th Street, 2F, Bayside, NY 11360
917-838-2404
Jennifer B. Krinsky, Treasurer

**Friends of Balboni**
9 Legends Circle, Melville, NY 11747
631-242-0548
Michael A. Balboni, Chairman

**Friends of Benjamin Kallos**
535 East 88th Street, 5A, New York, NY 10128
212-600-4960
David Kogelman, Treasurer

**Friends of Bill Suggs**
929 Lincoln Place, Brooklyn, NY 11213
646-596-1527
Elizabeth N. Suggs, Treasurer

**Friends of Bola Omotosho**
146 Morton Place, Bronx, NY 10453
718-644-0108
Anthony K. Adjei, Treasurer

**Friends of Breina Payne**
121-02 Sutphin Boulevard, E103, Jamaica, NY 11434
347-894-1287
Nadja M. Taffe, Treasurer

**Friends of Brodie Enoch 2013**
247 West 145th Street, 6A, New York, NY 10039
347-476-9057
Donna L. Linzy, Treasurer

**Friends of Carl E. Heastie**
PO Box 840, Bronx, NY 10469
718-570-1881
Carl E. Heastie, Chairman

**Friends of Catherine Nolan**
6464 229th Street, Oakland Gardens, NY 11364
718-229-4201
Catherine T. Nolan, Chairwoman

**Friends of Costa Constantinides**
24-60 28th Street, Astoria, NY 11102
917-716-4540
Leah A. Carter, Treasurer

**Friends of Cultural Institutions**
540 Broadway, 7th Floor, Albany, NY 12207
518-426-8111
Richard J. Miller, Treasurer

**Friends of Dara Adams**
171 East 77th Street, 2B, New York, NY 10017
646-543-9166
Marilyn Feuer, Treasurer

**Friends of David Kayode For Council**
106-23 153rd Street, #1, Jamaica, Queens, NY 11433
917-747-0837
Alfred Oyewole, Treasurer

**Friends of DeMeo**
2023 73rd Street, Brooklyn, NY 11204
917-913-9111
Claudio DeMeo, Chairman

**Friends of Donovan Richards 2013**
1526 Central Avenue, Far Rockaway, NY 11691
718-471-1117
Carol Richards, Treasurer

**Friends of Dorothy Phelan**
35-53 82nd Street, 1C, Jackson Heights, NY 11372
718-424-2162
Dorothy A. Phelan, Chairwoman

**Friends of Ed Hartzog**
300 East 75th Street, 12J, New York, NY 10021
917-705-6126
Cabot J. Marks, Treasurer

Political Parties, PACs & Lobbying

*Offices and agencies generally appear in alphabetical order, except when specific order is requested by listee.*

**Friends of Ede Fox**
315 Saint Johns Place, 4E, Brooklyn, NY 11238
347-262-7977
Judith T. Pierce, Treasurer

**Friends of Erick Salgado**
2502 86th Street, 3rd Floor, Brooklyn, NY 11214
718-266-4778
Yury S. Rozel, Treasurer

**Friends of F. Richard Hurley 2013**
150 Crown Street, C4, Brooklyn, NY 11225
917-297-9429
Dwayne A. Nicholson, Treasurer

**Friends of Felipe de Los Santos**
2446 University Avenue, 4A, Bronx, NY 10468
718-825-7037
Carlos J. De La Cruz, Treasurer

**Friends of Gale Brewer - 2013**
29 West 95th Street, New York, NY 10025
917-881-3375
Adele Bartlett, Treasurer

**Friends of Harpreet**
79-19 257th Street, Floral Park, NY 11004
718-343-9146
Manjit King, Treasurer

**Friends of I. Daneek Miller**
1078 Clyde Road, Baldwin, NY 11510
516-369-8735
Mark A. Henry, Treasurer

**Friends of Inez Barron**
744 Bradford Street, 2nd Floor, Brooklyn, NY 11207
917-853-9615
Rosalyn C. McIntosh, Treasurer

**Friends of James Vacca**
PO Box 562, Bronx, NY 10461
646-269-8414
Jonathan D. Conte, Treasurer

**Friends of Jean Similien**
3420 Avenue H, 3C, Brooklyn, NY 11210
347-709-5326
Antoine C. Coq, Treasurer

**Friends of Joe Lazar**
1430 East 24th Street, Brooklyn, NY 11210
917-968-5250
Aaron Biderman, Treasurer

**Friends of Joe Marthone**
116-37 227th Street, Cambria Heights, NY 11411
347-722-1126
Henry Derenoncourt, Treasurer

**Friends of Joel R. Rivera**
209 East 165th Street, 1B, Bronx, NY 10456
646-345-4263
Dion J. Powell, Treasurer

**Friens of John Calvelli**
11 Island View Place, New Rochelle, NY 10801
914-636-4045
John F. Calvelli, Chairman

**Friends of John Lisyanskiy**
155 Bay 20th Street, 2-D, Brooklyn, NY 11214
718-996-4609
Bella Waldman, Treasurer

**Friends of John Liu**
PO Box 520631, Flushing, NY 11352
917-501-6781
Shiang Liu, Treasurer

**Friends of Johnnie Goff**
2952 Laconia Avenue, Bronx, NY 10469
917-797-1771
Deborah Wilkerson, Treasurer

**Friends of Jonathan J. Judge**
345 Webster Avenue, 2N, Brooklyn, NY 11230
718-853-1932
Victoria A. Judge, Treasurer

**Friends of Joseph Nwachukwu**
1416 East Gunhill Road, Bronx, NY 10469
917-705-2478
Henrietta U. Ilomudio, Treasurer

**Friends of Joyce Johnson**
733 Amsterdam Avenue, 28B, New York, NY 10025
646-244-8630
Manuel Casanova, Treasurer

**Friends of JR**
321 West 89th Street, 6, New York, NY 10024
646-337-7700
Darrell L. Paster, Treasurer

**Friends of Julio Pabon**
143 East 150th Street, Bronx, NY 10451
718-402-9310
Blanca Canino-Vigo, Treasurer

**Friends of Kevin P. Coenen Jr. Inc.**
417 East 60th Street, 21, New York, NY 10022
917-603-9330
Kevin P. Coenen Jr., Treasurer

**Friends of Kimberly Council**
102 Etna Street, Brooklyn, NY 11208
347-645-1877
Trevor A. Hyde Jr., Treasurer

**Friends of Kirsten John Foy**
215 East 23rd Street, Brooklyn, NY 11226
James Sanon, Treasurer

**Friends of Larry Hirsch 2010**
321 West 89th Street, 6, New York, NY 10024
646-337-7700
Larry Hirsch, Chairman

**Friends of Luis Tejada**
157-10 Riverside Drive, New York, NY 10032
646-399-6163
Aydee Martinez, Treasurer

**Friends of Manny Caughman Committee**
115-05 179th Street, Saint Albans, NY 11412
718-809-6354
Andrea C. Scarborough, Treasurer

**Friends of Marie Adam-Ovide For Council 31**
121-12 234th Street, Laurelton, NY 11422
718-723-0645
Robinson Ovide, Treasurer

*Offices and agencies generally appear in alphabetical order, except when specific order is requested by listee.*

**Friends of Mark Thompson**
77 West 55th Street, 12B, New York, NY 10019
212-616-5810
Joseph G. Hagelmann III, Treasurer

**Friends of Mark Weprin 2013**
80-15 233rd Street, Queens Village, NY 11427
718-898-8500
Jack M. Friedman, Treasurer

**Friends of Mark Winston Griffith**
1238 Dean Street, Brooklyn, NY 11216
917-837-1587
Sharon M. Griffith, Treasurer

**Friends of Martha Taylor**
175-14 Mayfield Road, Jamaica, NY 11432
718-300-7308
Robert P. Miraglia, Treasurer

**Friends of Martha Taylor Butler**
133-02 133rd Avenue, South Ozone Park, NY 11420
917-364-7097
Martha T. Butler, Treasurer

**Friends of Martin For City Council**
292 Martin Avenue, Staten Island, NY 10314
718-698-1776
Martin S. Krongold, Treasurer

**Friends of Menegon**
31 East 92nd Street, 2B, New York, NY 10128
Karl Seidenwurm, Treasurer

**Friends of Michael A. Alvarez**
6120 North Kirkwood, Chicago, IL 60646
847-791-4105
Michael A. Alvarez, Chairman

**Friends of Michael Duncan 2013**
130-05 235th Street, Rosedale, NY 11422
347-528-4479
Tahisha Salmon, Treasurer

**Friends of Michael Simanowitz**
137-31 71st Avenue, Flushing, NY 11367
646-235-5095
Simon Pelman, Treasurer

**Friends of Mike Gianaris**
17 Canterbury Road South, Harrison, NY 10528
917-322-9212
Michael N Gianaris, Treasurer

**Friends of Mike Treybich**
2925 West 5th Street, 23B, Brooklyn, NY 11224
718-288-3625
Daniel Dugan, Treasurer

**Friends of Nicole Paultre Bell**
129-10 Liberty Avenue, Floor 2, Richmond Hill, NY 11419
347-355-2324
Laura A. Harper, Treasurer

**Friends of Olanike Alabi**
PO Box 380075, Brooklyn, NY 11238
718-398-0750
Olanike T. Alabi, Chairman

**Friends of Osina**
1092 Beach 12th Street, Far Rockaway, NY 11691
718-868-2720
Eli Shapiro, Treasurer

**Friends of Paul Drucker**
PO Box 393, Paoli, PA 19301
480-275-1876
Paul Drucker, Chairman

**Friends of Pedro Alvarez**
1411 Townsend Avenue, A3, Bronx, NY 10452
917-775-9865
Jerson R. Mezquita, Treasurer

**Friends of Randy Credico**
4712 Vernon Boulevard, Long Island City, NY 11101
212-924-6980
Melchior Leone, Treasurer

**Friends of Richard del Rio**
208 East Broadway, J604, New York, NY 10002
646-257-9062
Stephanie D. Curry, Treasurer

**Friends of Ruben Wills**
194-19 115th Drive, St. Albans, NY 11412
516-663-0630
Sharon Carnegie-Hall, Treasurer

**Friends of Sean K. Henry 2013**
659 Ashford Street, 2, Brooklyn, NY 11207
718-216-6188
Sean K. Henry, Treasurer

**Friends of Selvena Brooks**
PO Box 130379, Springfield Gardens, NY 11413
347-564-0730
Nyoka Dada, Treasurer

**Friends of Seymour Lachman**
1207 Avenue N, Brooklyn, NY 11230
718-887-6449
Seymour P. Lachman, Chairman

**Friends of Steve Cohn**
16 Court Street, Brooklyn, NY 11241
718-875-7057
Steven Cohn, Chairman

**Friends of Theresa Scavo**
2626 Homecrest Avenue, 7T, Brooklyn, NY 11235
347-668-4548
Anthony Scavo, Treasurer

**Friends of Todd Dobrin**
4216 Manhattan Avenue, Brooklyn, NY 11224
917-667-2139
Deena L. Venezia-Dobrin, Treasurer

**Friends of Tommy Torres**
401 Morgan Avenue, Brooklyn, NY 11211
718-812-0515
Samuel Rodriguez, Treasurer

**Friends of Torres**
PO Box 670192, Bronx, NY 10467
718-635-2827
Marjorie Velazquez, Treasurer

**Friends of Yetta**
350 Broadway, Suite 701, New York, NY 10013
718-852-3710
Leo Glickman, Treasurer

Political Parties, PACs & Lobbying

*Offices and agencies generally appear in alphabetical order, except when specific order is requested by listee.*

**Garodnick 2013**
132 East 43rd Street, #560, New York, NY 10017
212-210-9362
Andrew J. Ehrlich, Treasurer

**Gay and Lesbian Victory Fund**
1133 15th Street, Northwest, Suite 350, Washington, DC 20005
202-842-8679
Charles A. Wolfe, Chairman

**Gentile For the Future**
8901 Shore Road, 7E, Brooklyn, NY 11209
347-272-9734
Mary Brannan, Treasurer

**Gibson For Assembly**
190 West Burnside Avenue, 2D, Bronx, NY 10453
917-309-7854
Vanessa L. Gibson, Chairwoman

**Gibson For City Council**
21 Riverdale Avenue, White Plains, NY 10607
646-644-9414
Katrina De La Cruz, Treasurer

**Gibson, Dunn & Crutcher LLP PAC**
333 South Grand Avenue, Suite 5208, Los Angeles, CA 90071
213-229-7252
Kenneth M. Doran, Treasurer

**Gonzalez 2013**
349 Bleecker Street, 1, Brooklyn, NY 11237
347-743-8322
Julissa G. Santiago, Treasurer

**Gotlieb For City Council**
2930 West 5th Street, 12G, Brooklyn, NY 11224
718-996-5668
Ira Spodek, Treasurer

**Gramercy Stuyvesant Independent Democrats**
145 East 15th Street, 4U, New York, NY 10003
917-445-3370
Sam Albert, Chairman

**Grassy Sprain PAC**
51 Pondfield Road, Bronxville, NY 10708
914-961-6100
William E. Griffin, Chairman

**Greenberg Traurig PA PAC**
54 State Street, 6th Floor, Albany, NY 12207
518-689-1400
Mark F. Glaser, Chairman

**Greenfield 2010**
1011 East 3rd Avenue, Brooklyn, NY 11230
347-985-1135
Jeffrey Leb, Treasurer

**Grodenchik For Queens 2013**
125-28 Queens Boulevard, 504, Kew Gardens Hill, NY 11415
718-670-0720
Simon Pelman, Treasurer

**Gronowicz For Mayor**
2267 Haviland Avenue, 11, Bronx, NY 10462
347-920-1606
Carl L. Lundgren, Treasurer

**Guerriero For Advocate**
PO Box 20105, New York, NY 10014
347-709-5406
Ray Guerriero, Chairman

**Hakeem Jeffries For Assembly**
28 Sterling Street, Brooklyn, NY 11225
212-239-7323
Hakeem Jeffries, Chairman

**Halloran 2013**
166-06 24th Road, Whitestone, NY 11357
Chrissy Voskerichian, Treasurer

**Harlem Charter School Parents PAC**
PO Box 1930, New York, NY 10025
646-363-9047
Thomas A. Lopez-Pierre, Treasurer

**HCA PAC**
433 Delaware Avenue, Delmar, NY 12054
518-810-0664
Joanne Cunningham, Treasurer

**HDR, Inc. Political Action Committee - NY**
8404 Indian Hills Drive, Omaha, NE 68114
248-371-7268
Bryan Foxx, Treasurer

**He Gin Lee Committee to Elect For Mayor**
34-16 149th Street, 2, Flushing, NY 11354
718-461-2917
Nick Polyzogopouos, Treasurer

**Healthcare Association of New York State PAC**
1 Empire Drive, Rensselaer, NY 12144
518-431-7600
Daniel Sisto, Chairman

**Helal A. Sheikh 2013**
190 Forbell Street, 1, Brooklyn, NY 11208
917-415-5681
Hifzur Rahman, Treasurer

**Helen Rosenthal For City Council**
225 West 83rd Street, 4K, New York, NY 10024
917-923-1019
Patricia Craddick, Treasurer

**HF Responsibility Fund**
2 Park Avenue, New York, NY 10016
212-592-1400
George J. Wolf, Treasurer

**Hill 2013**
509 East 81st Street, 10, New York, NY 10028
917-596-2432
Marianne P. Peterson, Treasurer

**Hoffnung 2013**
646 West 227th Street, Bronx, NY 10463
917-687-6106
Jay Horowitz, Treasurer

**Holland and Knight Committee For Responsible Government**
31 West 52nd Street, New York, NY 10019
212-513-3562
Frank G. Sinatra, Chairman

**Hotel Association of New York City, Inc.**
320 Park Avenue, 22nd Floor, New York, NY 10022
212-754-6700
Joseph E. Spinnato, Chairman

*Offices and agencies generally appear in alphabetical order, except when specific order is requested by listee.*

**Housing New York Political Action Committee**
5 Hanover Square, Suite 1605, New York, NY 10004
212-838-7442
Andrew K. Hoffman, Chairman

**Hoylman For Senate**
80 Eighth Avenue, Suite 1802, New York, NY 10011
212-206-0033
Brad Hoylman, Chairman

**HSBC North America Political Action Committee**
1401 Eye Street Northwest, Suite 520, Washington, DC 20005
202-466-3561
Kevin Fromer, Chairman

**Human Rights Campaign New York PAC**
1640 Rhode Island Avenue, Northwest, Washington, DC 20036
202-628-4160
Susanne Salkind, Chairwoman

**Humberto Soto For New York City Council 2013**
268 Jefferson Street, 2B, Brooklyn, NY 11237
917-651-5595
Humberto Soto Jr., Treasurer

**Hunts Point Produce Redevelopment PAC - Corporate Contribution Account**
464 NYC Terminal Market, Bronx, NY 10474
718-589-4095
Jeffrey Haas, Chairman

**Hunts Point Produce Redevelopment PAC - Personal Contribution Account**
464 NYC Terminal Market, Bronx, NY 10474
718-589-4095
Jeffrey Haas, Chairman

**IAFF FIREPAC New York Non-Federal**
1750 New York Avenue, Washington, DC 20006
202-737-8484
Harold Schaitberger, Chairman

**IBT Joint Council No. 16 PAC**
265 West 14th Street, Suite 1201, New York, NY 10011
212-924-0002
George Miranda, Chairman

**Ignizio 2013**
265 Barbara Street, Staten Island, NY 10306
917-763-0951
Susan LaForgia, Treasurer

**Igor 2013**
2928 West 5th Street, 2R, Brooklyn, NY 11224
718-648-9186
Dan U. Levitt, Treasurer

**Int'l Longshoremen's Ass'n, AFL-CIO Committee on Political Education**
17 Battery Place, Suite 930, New York, NY 10004
212-425-1200
Richard P. Hughes Jr., Chairman

**International Brotherhood of Electrical Workers Political Action Committee**
900 Seventh Street N.W., Washington, DC 20001
202-728-6046
Edwin D. Hill, Chairman

**International Union of Operating Engineers Local 14-14B Voluntary Political Action Committee**
141-57 Northern Boulevard, Flushing, NY 11354
718-939-0600
Edwin L. Christian, Treasurer

**International Union of Operating Engineers Local 15 A B C D**
265 West 14th Street, Room 505, New York, NY 10011
212-929-5327
James T. Callahan, Chairman

**International Union of Painters and Allied Trades Political Action Committee**
7234 Parkway Drive, Hanover, MD 21706
410-564-5880
James Williams, Chairman

**Ironworkers Local 46 PAC**
1322 3rd Avenue, New York, NY 10021
347-461-6300
Terrence Moore, Treasurer

**Ironworkers Political Action League**
1750 New York Avenue, NW, Washington, DC 20006
202-383-4881
Joseph J. Hunt, Chairman

**IUOE Local 15 Political Action Fund**
44-40 11th Street, Long Island City, NY 11101
212-929-5327
Daniel J. Schneider, Chairman

**Iwachiw 4 Mayor**
48-35 41st Street, PH, Sunnyside, NY 11104
347-239-0965
Walter Iwachiw, Treasurer

**Jacques Leandre For New York**
232-06A Merrick Boulevard, Laurelton, NY 11413
347-613-2315
John M. Hogan, Treasurer

**Jennings NYC**
130-35 126th Street, South Ozone Park, NY 11420
718-529-5339
Donovan O. Folkes, Treasurer

**Jesse Hamilton 2013**
910 Lincoln Place, Brooklyn, NY 11213
917-553-7953
Denise F. Mann, Treasurer

**Jim Owles Liberal Democratic Club**
450 West 17th Street, 2405, New York, NY 10011
212-741-3677
Allen Roskoff, Chairman

**Joan Flowers For the 27th District**
173-35 113th Avenue, Addisleigh Park, NY 11433
917-723-5713
Leon P. Hart Esq., Treasurer

**Joe Lhota For Mayor, Inc.**
132 East 43rd Street, New York, NY 10017
212-681-0055
Vincent A. Lapadula, Treasurer

**Joel Bauza For City Council**
PO Box 709, Bronx, NY 10460
917-349-2596
Rafael E. Abreu, Treasurer

Political Parties, PACs & Lobbying

*Offices and agencies generally appear in alphabetical order, except when specific order is requested by listee.*

**John Catsimatidis For Mayor 2013 Committee, Inc.**
823 Eleventh Avenue, New York, NY 10019
Deborah A. Heinichen, Treasurer

**John Quaglione For City Council**
449 81st Street, Brooklyn, NY 11209
347-560-4555
Georgea C. Kontzamanis, Treasurer

**Johnson 2013**
3856 Bronx Boulevard, 7H, Bronx, NY 10467
347-762-8683
Geneva A. Johnson, Treasurer

**Johnson NYC 2013**
1426 Morris Avenue, Bronx, NY 10456
718-930-5030
Geoffrey Longmore, Treasurer

**JPMorgan Chase & Co. PAC**
10 South Dearborn, IL 1-0520, Chicago, IL 60603
312-732-5852
Peter L. Scher, Chairman

**JuanPagan2013**
1225 FDR Drive, 4B, New York, NY 10009
646-730-6037
Lillian Rivera, Treasurer

**Judge Analisa Torres For Supreme Court 2011**
321 West 89th Street, #6, New York, NY 10024
646-337-7700
Analisa Torres, Chairwoman

**Julie Menin 2013**
PO Box 1261, New York, NY 10013
646-415-2050
Michael Connolly, Treasurer

**Julissa 2013**
104-01 Roosevelt Avenue, Suite 1, Corona, NY 11368
800-829-7059
Guiyermo DeJesus, Treasurer

**Jumaane 2013**
PO Box 100323, Brooklyn, NY 11210
Joan M. Alexandre-Bakiriddin, Treasurer

**Keeling Campaign 2013**
3614 Johnson Avenue,
Charles K. LaSister, Treasurer

**Kellner Campaign 2013**
135 East 61st Street, 4C, New York, NY 10065
917-558-3198
Cory A. Evans, Treasurer

**Ken 2013**
54 West 76th Street, 4R, New York, NY 10023
703-593-0608
Andrew W. Kalish, Treasurer

**Kesselly For Council**
353 Beach 57th Street, 2F, Arverne, NY 11692
718-233-2590
Hanif Russell, Treasurer

**Khari Edwards 2013**
463 Lincoln Place, Box 121, Brooklyn, NY 11238
347-915-6362
Tyieast S. Lloyd, Treasurer

**Kings County Conservative Party Campaign Committee**
486 78th Street, Brooklyn, NY 11209
718-921-2158
Gerard Kassar, Chairman

**Lancman 2013**
76-21 172nd Street, Hillcrest, NY 11366
917-363-9004
Stephanie Goldstone, Treasurer

**Landis For New York**
400 Central Park West, 6B, New York, NY 10025
917-338-6415
Audrey J. Isaacs, Treasurer

**Lantigua 2013**
230 West 103rd Street, 6G, New York, NY 10025
914-384-5062
Julio C. Negron, Treasurer

**Laurie Cumbo 2013**
2146 Canarsie Road, Brooklyn, NY 11236
917-518-6610
Shante L. Cozier, Treasurer

**Lee New York Political Action Committee**
1413 K Street, NW, 3rd Floor, Washington, DC 20005
202-552-2400
Mike Buman, Chairman

**Lesbian & Gay Democratic Club of Queens**
PO Box 857, Jackson Heights, NY 11372
Bruce I. Friedman, Chairman

**Letitia James 2013**
371 Utica Avenue, Brooklyn, NY 11213
347-470-8813
Latrice M. Walker, Treasurer

**Levin 2013**
576 Morgan Avenue, 3L, Brooklyn, NY 11222
908-380-7626
William J. Harris, Treasurer

**Levine 2013**
900 West 190th Street, 4K, New York, NY 10040
646-382-8992
Janet A. McDowell, Treasurer

**Liutenants Benevolent Association NY Police Department PAC**
233 Broadway, Suite 850, New York, NY 10279
646-610-8682
Dennis Gannon, Chairman

**Lisa G For NY**
45 Grymes Hill Road, Staten Island, NY 10301
718-448-1600
Michael J. Kuharski, Treasurer

**Local 1182 Political Action Fund**
108-18 Queens Boulevard, 7th Floor, Forest Hills, NY 11375
718-793-7755
James S. Huntley, Chairman

**Local 1407 AFSCME Political Committee**
125 Barclay Street, New York, NY 10007
212-815-1933
Maf M. Uddin, Chairman

**Local 147 Political Action Committee**
4332 Katonah Avenue, Bronx, NY 10470
718-994-6664
Christopher Fitzsimmons, Chairman

*Offices and agencies generally appear in alphabetical order, except when specific order is requested by listee.*

**Local 1500 Political Candidates and Education Fund**
425 Merrick Avenue, Westbury, NY 11590
516-214-1300
Bruce W. Both, Chairman

**Local 1814 ILA AFL-CIO Political Action and Education Fund**
70 20th Street, Brooklyn, NY 11232
718-499-9600
Raul Vasquez Jr., Chairman

**Local 2021 AFSCME Political Action Account**
125 Barclay Street, 7th, New York, NY 10007
212-815-1977
Leonard Allen, Chairman

**Local 23-25 Unite State & Local Campaign Committee**
33 West 14th Street, New York, NY 10011
212-929-2600
Edgar Romney, Chairman

**Local 30 IUOE PAC**
16-16 Whitestone Expressway, Whitestone, NY 11357
718-847-8484
Michael Spillane, Treasurer

**Local 32BJ SEIU NY/NJ American Dream Fund**
101 Avenue of the Americas, New York, NY 10013
212-388-2171
Hector J. Figueroa, Chairman

**Local 372 Political Action**
125 Barclay Street, New York, NY 10007
212-815-1960
Veronica Montgomery-Costa, Chairwoman

**Local 4 Action Fund**
2917 Glennwood Road, Brooklyn, NY 11210
718-252-8777
Lewis Resnick, Chairman

**Local 6 Committee on Political Education**
709 8th Avenue, New York, NY 10036
212-957-8000
Peter Ward, Chairman

**Local 891 IUOE Political Education Committee**
63 Flushing Avenue, Building 292, Suite 401, Brooklyn, NY 11205
718-455-9731
Margaret McMahon, Chairwoman

**Local 891 IUOE State Engineers Political Education Committee**
63 Flushing Avenue, Building 292, Suite 401, Brooklyn, NY 11205
718-455-9731
Margaret McMahon, Chairwoman

**Local 94-94A-94B IUOE Political Action Committee**
331-337 West 44th Street, New York, NY 10036
212-245-7040
Kuba Brown, Chairman

**Lotovsky For City Council 2013**
1318 Gravesend Neck Road, Brooklyn, NY 11229
718-554-1741
Alina G. Krasovskaya, Treasurer

**Lundgren For Council**
290 West 234th Street, Bronx, NY 10463
718-510-4926
John H. Reynolds, Treasurer

**Lynn Sanchez For City Council**
1505 Walton Avenue, 3J, Bronx, NY 10452
646-696-4056
Ronnette Summers, Treasurer

**Mailman For Council**
037 East 44th Street, 1403, New York, NY 10017
718-598-0609
Jessica A. Mailman, Treasurer

**Maisel For Council**
1757 Coleman Street, Brooklyn, NY 11234
Reeves Eisen, Treasurer

**Mancuso For Council**
41 Challenger Drive, Staten Island, NY 10312
718-701-3416
Nick Popolo, Treasurer

**Margaret Chin 2013**
3 Hanover Square, 7H, New York, NY 10004
917-582-1845
Yee S. Shau, Treasurer

**Mark Gjonaj 2012**
970 Morris Park Avenue, Bronx, NY 10462
917-731-6850
Mark Gjonaj, Chairman

**Mark Otto For City Council**
474 West 150 Street, 3D, New York, NY 10031
856-981-3656
Cavol Forbes, Treasurer

**Mark Treyger For Council**
2733 Mill Avenue, Brooklyn, NY 11234
917-434-5684
Elina Gofman, Treasurer

**Mark Weprin For New York PAC**
5 Peter Cooper Road, ME c/o E.A.S., New York, NY 10010
212-475-7389
Mark Weprin, Chairman

**Markowitz/Brooklyn**
15 Waldorf Court, Brooklyn, NY 11230
718-434-8430
Marty Markowitz, Chairman

**Marthone For City Council**
179-18 135th Avenue, Jamaica Avenue, NY 11434
917-504-4687
Joseph R. Marthone, Treasurer

**Mason Tenders District Council of Greater New York Political Action Committee**
266 West 37th Street, 7th Floor, New York, NY 10018
212-452-9552
Robert Bonanza, Chairman

**Mateo 2013**
2817 Fulton Street, Brooklyn, NY 11207
Crystal J. Flores, Treasurer

**Matteo For Council**
256 Wardwell Avenue, Staten Island, NY 10314
917-975-5541
Angela M. Thornton, Treasurer

**Maximus Inc. Political Action Committee**
1891 Metro Center Drive, Reston, VA 20190
703-251-8500
David Casey, Chairman

*Offices and agencies generally appear in alphabetical order, except when specific order is requested by listee.*

Political Parties, PACs & Lobbying

**McDonald 2013**
52 Main Street, c/o Parker, Bedford Hills, NY 10507
914-242-2090
Craig R. Parker, Treasurer

**McKenna Long & Aldridge LLP NY PAC**
303 Peachtree Street, Suite 5300, Atlanta, GA 30308
404-527-8527
Eric Tanenblatt, Chairman

**Mel 2013**
10 West 87th Street, 3B, New York, NY 10024
Ken Coughlin, Treasurer

**Melinda Katz 2013**
220 East 23rd Street, Suite 809, New York, NY 10010
212-231-9753
Jennie Berger, Treasurer

**Meloni NYCC**
21-17 23rd Avenue, Astoria, NY 11105
718-626-9514
Angela A. Meloni, Treasurer

**Mercedes For Council**
105-18 Avenue L, Brooklyn, NY 11236
347-731-5091
Lystra Moore-Besson, Treasurer

**METLIFE, Inc. Employees' Political Participation Fund A**
1095 Avenue of the Americas, New York, NY 10036
212-578-4133
Heather Wingate, Chairwoman

**METRET PAC Inc.**
51 East 42nd Street, 17th Floor, New York, NY 10017
212-682-8383
Thomas R. Zapf, Chairman

**Metropolitan Funeral Directors PAC**
322 8th Avenue, New York, NY 10001
800-763-8332
Peter DeLuca, Treasurer

**Michael 2013**
666 East 233 Street, 1C, Bronx, NY 10466
718-231-8003
Michael Welch, Treasurer

**Middle Village Republican Club**
64-82 83rd Street, Middle Village, NY 11379
718-326-8616
Rosemarie Toomey, Treasurer

**Mike Duvalle 4 City Council**
127-16 Liberty Avenue, Richmond Hill, NY 11419
718-323-1100
Michael Duvalle, Treasurer

**Minerva For City Council**
1755 York Avenue, 17D, New York, NY 10128
917-657-8184
Brian T. Carney, Treasurer

**Molinari Republican Club**
1010 Forest Avenue, Staten Island, NY 10310
718-442-0900
Robert J. Scamardella, Treasurer

**Moore 2013**
PO Box 927, Bronx, NY 10451
347-989-2013
Lynette A. Taylor, Treasurer

**Morris & McVeigh NYS PAC**
19 Dove Street, Albany, NY 12210
518-426-8111
Richard Miller, Jr., Treasurer

**Moustafa For NYC**
34-23 Steinway Street, Astoria, NY 11101
718-679-7959
Foseph E. Botros, Treasurer

**MPAC**
137 Fifth Avenue, 3rd Floor, New York, NY 10010
212-681-1380
Heather Swift, Treasurer

**N.S.A. Inc. Action Fund**
30-50 Whitestone Expressway, Suite 301, Whitestone, NY 11354
718-747-2860
Nelson Eusebio, Chairman

**Nachman Caller Community First**
4309 13th Avenue, Brooklyn, NY 11219
718-513-2055
Pesach Osina, Treasurer

**Nadler For Congress**
PO Box 40, Village Station, NY 10014
212-352-0370
Jerrold L. Nadler, Chairman

**NARAL/NY Multcandidate Political Action Committee**
470 Park Avenue South, 7th Floor South, New York, NY 10016
212-343-0114
Lorna Brett Howard, Chairwoman

**National Grid Voluntary New York State Political Action Committee**
40 Sylvan Road, Waltham, MA 02451
781-907-1764
Marcy L. Reed, Chairwoman

**Ndigo For City Council**
PO Box 820, New York, NY 10027
212-726-2063
Lylburn K. Downing, Treasurer

**Neighborhood Preservation Political Action Fund**
123 William Street, 14th Floor, New York, NY 10038
212-214-9266
Sandra K. Paul, Treasurer

**Neighbors For Kenneth Rice**
1345 East 4th Street, 6F, Brooklyn, NY 11230
516-817-0716
Eileen Flaherty, Treasurer

**Neil Grimaldi For New York City Mayor**
2860 Buhre Avenue, New York, NY 10461
646-229-7974
John Tamburri, Chairman

**New Visions Democratic Club**
PO Box 55, Jackson Heights, NY 11372
Yonel Letellier, Chairman

**New York Bankers Political Action Committee**
99 Park Avenue, 4th Floor, New York, NY 10016
212-297-1635
James J. Landy, Chairman

*Offices and agencies generally appear in alphabetical order, except when specific order is requested by listee.*

**New York Building Congress State PAC**
44 West 28th Street, 12th Floor, New York, NY 10038
212-481-1911
Richard T. Anderson, Treasurer

**New York Check P.A.C., Inc.**
286 Madison Avenue, Suite 907, New York, NY 10017
212-268-1911
Henry F. Shyne, Treasurer

**New York City Central Labor Council Political Committee**
275 7th Avenue, 18th Floor, New York, NY 10001
212-604-9552
Jinella Hinds, Treasurer

**New York City Justice Political Action Committee**
132 Nassau Street, Room 200, New York, NY 10038
212-349-5890
Jeffrey A. Lichtman, Treasurer

**New York City Partnership State PAC**
One Battery Park Plaza, 5th Floor, New York, NY 10004
212-493-7400
Barry M. Gosin, Chairman

**New York County Dental Society Political Action Committee**
6 East 43rd Street, New York, NY 10017
212-573-8500
Elliot Davis, Chairman

**New York Hotel & Motel Trades Council Committee**
707 Eighth Avenue, New York, NY 10036
212-245-8100
Christopher K. Cusack, Chairman

**New York Professional Nurses Union Political Action Committee**
1104 Lexington Avenue, New York, NY 10075
212-988-5565
Maureen McCarthy, Chairwoman

**New York State AFL-CIO COPE**
100 South Swan Street, Albany, NY 12210
518-436-8516
Mario Cilento, Chairman

**New York State Association of PBA's PAC**
23 Reynolds Road, Glen Cove, NY 11542
Thomas Willidigg, Chairman

**New York State Council of Machinists PAC Fund**
652 4th Avenue, Brooklyn, NY 11232
718-422-0090
James Conigliaro, Chairman

**New York State Higher Education - PAC**
3210 Avenue H, 6C, Brooklyn, NY 11210
646-331-4612
Robert Ramos, Chairman

**New York State Laborers' Political Action Committee**
18 Corporate Woods Boulevard, Albany, NY 12211
518-449-1715
George S. Truicko, Chairman

**New York State Nurses Association Political Action Committee**
11 Cornell Road, Latham, NY 12110
518-782-9400
Linda O'Brien, Chairwoman

**New Yorkers For Affordable Housing**
15 Verbena Avenue, Suite 100, Floral Park, NY 11001
516-277-9317
Sol Arker, Treasurer

**New Yorkers For De Blasio**
65 Broadway, 803, New York, NY 10006
917-558-1390
Mark Peters, Treasurer

**New Yorkers For Katz**
219-12 74th Avenue, Bayside, NY 11364
718-465-7839
Melinda R. Katz, Chairwoman

**New Yorkers For Putting Students First**
345 7th Avenue, Suite 501, New York, NY 10001
212-257-4411
Enoch Woodhouse, Treasurer

**New Yorkers For Robert Jackson**
499 Fort Washington Avenue, 3A, New York, NY 10033
917-733-0439
Nan Beer, Treasurer

**Nikki Lucas 2013**
566 Essex Street, 2nd Floor, Brooklyn, NY 11208
347-457-8556
Aysha J. Gourdine, Treasurer

**Nixon Peabody LLP PAC**
1300 Clinton Square, Rochester, NY 14604
585-263-1000
Stephen J. Wallace, Chairman

**Noah E. Gotbaum 2013**
330 West 87th Street, New York, NY 10024
212-799-7291
Jeffrey D. Ravetz, Treasurer

**NY CCR Nonpartisan PAC For Good Government**
1 Coca-Cola Plaza NW, Atlanta, GA 30313
404-676-2121
William Hawkins, Chairman

**NY Region 9A UAW PAC Council**
111 South Road, Farmington, CT 06032
860-674-0143
Julie Kushner, Chairwoman

**NYC District Council of Carpenters PAC**
395 Hudson Street, 9th Floor, New York, NY 10014
212-366-3388
Stephen C. McInnis, Treasurer

**NYC Greenfield**
1011 East 3rd Street, Brooklyn, NY 11230
347-985-1135
Jeffrey Leb, Treasurer

**NYS Democratic Senate Campaign Committee**
1275 Scotch Church Road, Pattersonville, NY 12137
Jeffrey Klein, Chairman

**NYSAFAH PAC**
450 7th Avenue, Suite 2401, New York, NY 10123
646-473-1207
Frank J. Anelante, Jr., Treasurer

**NYSRPA-PVF**
90 South Swan Street, Suite 395, Albany, NY 12210
518-272-2654
Thomas H. King, Chairman

**Oddo For Staten Island**
131 Old Town Road, Staten Island, NY 10304
917-533-8241
Marie Carmody-LaFrancesca, Treasurer

*Offices and agencies generally appear in alphabetical order, except when specific order is requested by listee.*

**Olanike Alabi 2013**
PO Box 380075, Brooklyn, NY 10304
718-398-0750
Sharon J. Pierre, Treasurer

**Organization of Staff Analysts PAC**
220 East 23 Street, Suite 707, New York, NY 10010
212-686-1229
Robert J. Croghan, Chairman

**Otano 2013**
367 South 5th Street, 2B, Brooklyn, NY 11211
917-566-7542
Emily E. Gallagher, Treasurer

**PAC L375 CSTG**
125 Barclay Street, New York, NY 10013
212-815-1375
Claude Fort, Chairman

**PAC of the Patrolmen's Benevolent Association of NYC**
125 Broad Street, 11th Floor, New York, NY 10004
212-233-5531
Joseph A. Alejandro, Chairman

**Palma 2013**
1510 UnionPort Road, 11F, Bronx, NY 10462
347-733-5145
Ricky Pizarro, Treasurer

**Pamela Johnson For NYC Council**
3856 Bronx Boulevard, 7H, Bronx, NY 10467
347-762-8683
Geneva Johnson, Treasurer

**Paul Graziano 2013**
146-24 32nd Avenue, Flushing, NY 11354
718-358-2535
Stephen Garza, Treasurer

**People For Albert Baldeo**
106-11 Liberty Avenue, Ozone Park, NY 11417
718-323-8260
Mandrawattie Singh, Treasurer

**People For Bing**
132 East 43rd Street, New York, NY 10022
646-228-9111
Jonathan L. Bing, Chairman

**People For Brodsky**
2121 Saw Mill River Road, White Plains, NY 10607
914-720-5206
Richard L. Brodsky, Chairman

**People For Carlton Berkley**
4555 Carpenter Avenue, PH, New York, NY 10470
917-468-8461
Alexander Williams, Treasurer

**People For Cheryl**
585 West 214 Street, 4C, New York, NY 10034
646-314-3079
Cheryl A. Pahaham, Treasurer

**People For Debra Cooper**
290 West End Avenue, 9A, New York, NY 10024
212-362-7788
Darrell L. Paster, Treasurer

**People For Diaz**
840 Grand Concourse, 1A, Bronx, NY 10451
718-731-2009
Kalman Yeger, Treasurer

**People For Jelani**
83 Lefferts Place, Brooklyn, NY 11238
718-753-3302
Kuzaliwa Campbell, Treasurer

**People For Jerome Rice**
1505 Metropolitan Avenue, MG, Bronx, NY 10462
347-631-4489
Dawn Jeffrey, Treasurer

**People For John C. Whitehead**
903 Drew Street, 410, Brooklyn, NY 11208
718-216-2169
Leslie A. Murray, Treasurer

**People For Lappin**
333 East 55th Street, New York, NY 10022
718-541-3278
Andrew W. Wuertele, Treasurer

**People For Leroy Gadsen**
87-60 113th, 3C, Richmond Hills, NY 11418
917-297-7824
Candace Prince, Treasurer

**People For Miguel Estrella**
3716 10th Avenue, 13L, New York, NY 10034
347-664-7147
Aria Vargas, Treasurer

**People For Pu-Folkes**
78-27 37th Avenue, Suite 4, Jackson Heights, NY 11372
718-595-2045
Bryan R. Pu-Folkes, Chairman

**People For Ydanis**
475 Atlantic Avenue, 3rd Floor, Brooklyn, NY 11217
917-582-1405
Roberto A. Cruz, Treasurer

**People For Yudelka Tapia**
1941 Mulliner Avenue, Bronx, NY 10462
917-685-7810
Juan Mora, Treasurer

**Peralta 2013**
635 Hicksville Road, Far Rockaway, NY 11691
917-723-2097
Monique Renaud, Treasurer

**Peralta For Senate**
635 Hicksville Road, Far Rockaway, NY 11691
718-471-2475
Jose Peralta, Chairman

**Peterson 2013**
25-10 30th Road, Astoria, NY 11102
David Haywood, Treasurer

**Pfizer Inc. PAC**
235 East 42nd Street, New York, NY 10017
212-573-1265
Sally Susman, Chairman

**Plumbers & Steamfitters Local No. 73 State & Local PAC Fund**
705 East Seneca Street, PO Box 911, Oswego, NY 13126
315-343-4037
Patrick Carroll, Treasurer

*Offices and agencies generally appear in alphabetical order, except when specific order is requested by listee.*

**Plumbers Local Union No. 1 NYC - Political Action Committee**
158-29 George Meany Boulevard, Howard Beach, NY 11414
718-738-7500
John J. Murphy, Treasurer

**Port Authority PBA of NY PAC**
611 Palisade Avenue, Englewood Cliffs, NJ 07632
201-871-2100
Paul Nunziato, Chairman

**Port Authority Police DEA NY PAC**
Po Box 300406, JFK Station, Jamaica, NY 11430
201-216-6549
Patrick McNerney, Chairman

**Powell 2013**
134-35 166th Place, 4B, Jamaica, NY 11434
Dawn P. Martin, Treasurer

**PSC PAC**
61 Broadway, 15th Floor, New York, NY 10006
212-354-1252
Steven London, Chairman

**Queens County Republican Committee**
24-55 Francis Lewis Boulevard, Whitestone, NY 11357
718-690-3737
Phil Ragusa, Chairman

**Quinn For New York**
30 Vesey Street, 1st Floor, New York, NY 10007
917-438-7063
Kenneth T. Monteiro, Treasurer

**Ralina Cardona 2013**
286 Alexander Avenue, Bronx, NY 10454
Wilfred Renta, Treasurer

**Rangel For Congress NY State**
193 Lenox Avenue, Suite 1, New York, NY 10023
212-862-4990
James E. Capel, Chairman

**Raquel Batista 2013**
2104 Clinton Avenue, 2, Bronx, NY 10457
Katiuska M. Lopez, Treasurer

**Re-Elect Eric Ulrich**
101-17 84th Street, Ozone Park, NY 11416
917-951-7251
Ronald Kulick, Treasurer

**Re-Elect Koslowitz 2013**
6940 108th Street, c/o R. Croce, 3A, Forest Hills, NY 11375
718-268-3626
Ronnie Croce, Treasurer

**Re-Elect Mealy**
800 Hancock Street, 2A, Brooklyn, NY 11233
Marjorie Parker, Treasurer

**Recchia For New York**
172 Gravesend Neck Road, Brooklyn, NY 11223
718-336-3441
Marianna Wilen, Treasurer

**Regina Powell 2013**
675 Lincoln Avenue, 16F, Brooklyn, NY 11208
917-285-4894
Barrington Rodney, Treasurer

**Reginald Boddie For Supreme Court**
387 Halsey Street, Brooklyn, NY 11233
917-660-1487
Reginald A. Boddie, Chairman

**Rego Hills Republican Club**
85-32 65th Road, c/o Dolores Maddis, Rego Park, NY 11374
718-275-6005
Thomas Hoar, Chairman

**Republican Majority For Choice NF PAC**
2417 Jericho Turnpike, Suite 303, Garden City Park, NY 11040
516-316-6982
Kellie R. Ferguson, Chairman

**Rescare Inc. Advocacy Fund**
9901 Linn Station Road, Louisville, KY 40223
502-394-2335
Roger LaPoint, Chairman

**Reshma For New York**
240 West 23rd Street, 3C, New York, NY 10011
646-386-6398
Sumana Setty, Treasurer

**Retail Wholesale and Department Store Union C.O.P.E.**
30 East 29th Street, New York, NY 10016
212-684-5300
Stuart Appelbaum, Chairman

**Rhonda F. Joseph 2013**
910 Lenox Road, Brooklyn, NY 11203
917-751-7516
Basil A. Davidson, Treasurer

**Rivera 2013**
601 Pelham Parkway North, 501, Bronx, NY 10467
347-601-1551
Joel Rivera, Treasurer

**Rivera 2013**
1936 Haviland Avenue, Bronx, NY 10472
646-533-5228
Kenneth J. Thomas, Treasurer

**Rosenthal For Assembly**
321 West 89th Street, 6, New York, NY 10024
646-337-7700
Linda B. Rosenthal, Chairwoman

**Rosie Mendez 2013**
52 East 1st Street, c/o Kaplan, 2A, New York, NY 10003
646-229-6127
Lisa M. Kaplan, Treasurer

**RPAC of New York**
130 Washington Avenue, Albany, NY 12210
518-463-0300
Harding Mason, Chairman

**RSA PAC City Account**
123 Williams Street, 14th Floor, New York, NY 10038
212-214-9266
Frank P. Ricci, Treasurer

**Ruben Wills 2013**
194-19 115 Drive, St. Albans, NY 11412
516-663-0630
Sharon Carnegie-Hall, Treasurer

*Offices and agencies generally appear in alphabetical order, except when specific order is requested by listee.*

# POLITICAL ACTION COMMITTEES

**RWDSU Local 338 Political Action Committee**
1505 Kellum Place, Mineola, NY 11501
516-294-1338
John R. Durso, Chairman

**Sal 2013**
957 78th Street, Brooklyn, NY 11228
917-992-1693
John H. O'Donnell, Treasurer

**Sanders For Senate**
1526 Central Avenue, 3rd Floor, Far Rockaway, NY 11691
718-471-7111
Donovan J. Richards, Treasurer

**Sanitation Officers Association Volunteer Political Action COPE Account**
8510 Bay 16th Street, 2nd Floor, Brooklyn, NY 11214
718-837-9832
Joseph Mannion, Chairman

**Santiago NYC 2013**
50 Manhattan Avenue, 4H, Brooklyn, NY 11206
Juan C. Pocasangre, Treasurer

**Santos 2013**
420 East 21st Street, Brooklyn, NY 11226
307-340-1074
Luke L. Frye, Treasurer

**Sarah M. Gonzalez 2013**
512 83rd Street, Brooklyn, NY 11209
307-340-1074
Sonia Rodriguez, Treasurer·

**Sasson For NYC**
43-70 Kissena Boulevard, 14H, Flushing, NY 11355
718-461-9338
Amul Mehta, Treasurer

**Saundra Thomas 2013**
490 Stratford Road, Brooklyn, NY 11218
718-282-5595
Gary M. Singer, Treasurer

**Savino For New York**
481 8th Avenue, Suite 1202, New York, NY 10001
212-239-7323
Diane J Savino, Chairwoman

**SEIU Political Education and State Action Fund**
1800 Massachusetts Avenue, N.W., Washington, DC 20036
202-730-7000
Mary Kay Henry, Chairwoman

**Semper Fi NYS PAC Inc.**
17 Christopher Street, New York, NY 10014
212-269-7308
Christopher Johnson, Chairman

**Sergeants Benevolent Association**
35 Worth Street, New York, NY 10013
212-226-2180
Robert Ganley, Chairman

**Service Corporation International Political Association Committee**
1929 Allen Parkway, Houston, TX 77019
713-525-9062
Caressa F. Hughes, Chairwoman

**Sidique Wai For Public Advocate**
770 Empire Boulevard, 2N, Brooklyn, NY 11213
201-526-1422
Fritzner L. Altidor, Treasurer

**Sierra 2013**
1581 Fulton Avenue, 1B, Bronx, NY 10457
201-526-1422
Jonathan Vizcaino, Treasurer

**Silverstein 2013**
211-40 18th Avenue, 3K, Bayside, NY 11360
718-644-0791
Gary Jacobowitz, Treasurer

**Simcha NY**
475 Atlantic Avenue, 3rd Floor, Brooklyn, NY 11217
718-852-3710
Simcha Felder, Chairman

**Simmons-Oliver For City Council**
4120 Hutchinson River Parkway East, 15A, Bronx, NY 10475
917-596-7251
Rafael Paulino, Treasurer

**SMWIA Local 28 Political Action Committee**
500 Greenwich Street, New York, NY 10013
212-941-7700
Frederick Buckheit, Treasurer

**SMART Political Action League Local 137**
50-02 5th Street, Suite A, Long Island City, NY 11101
718-937-4514  Fax: 718-937-4113
Dante Dano, Jr., President & Business Manager

**Soft Drink and Brewery Workers Political Action Committee**
445 Northern Boulevard, Great Neck, NY 11021
516-303-1455
John O'Neill, Chairman

**Sondra Peeden 2013**
40 Memorial Highway, 33F, New Rochelle, NY 10801
914-355-4197
Katrina De La Cruz, Treasurer

**South Asians United For a Better America PAC**
333 East 30th Street, 2D, New York, NY 10016
571-228-6925
Prince Agarwal, Chairman

**Squadron For New York**
219 West 81st Street, 8D, New York, NY 10024
212-228-5222
Anne S. Squadron, Treasurer

**SSL Political Action Committee**
180 Maiden Lane, 34th Floor, New York, NY 10038
212-806-5851
Leonard S. Boxer, Chairman

**Staten Island PAC**
32 Cunard Place, Staten Island, NY 10304
718-816-2237
James P. Molinaro, Chairman

**Steamfitters Local 638 PAC**
32-32 48th Avenue, Long Island City, NY 11101
718-392-3420
John J. Torpey, Chairman

*Offices and agencies generally appear in alphabetical order, except when specific order is requested by listee.*

**Stringer 2013**
40 Worth Street, Suite 812, New York, NY 10013
212-349-2013
Peter Frank, Treasurer

**STV Engineers Inc. Political Action Committee**
205 West Welsh Drive, Douglassville, PA 19518
610-385-8294
Dominick M. Servedio, Chairman

**Suffolk County Association of Municipal Employees, Inc -
Political Action Committee**
30 Orville Drive, Suite A, Bohemia, NY 11716
631-589-8400
Cheryl A. Felice, Chairwoman

**Sullivan For NYC**
138 71st Street, 9F, Brooklyn, NY 11209
516-522-4033
Maureen J. Daly, Treasurer

**Sunny Hahn For City Council**
137-60 45th Avenue, 4N, Flushing, NY 11355
718-888-9420
Stuart Garmise, Treasurer

**Tamika For City Council 2013**
342 East 119th Street, 5B, New York, NY 10035
516-782-9339
Monisha R. Mapp, Treasurer

**Taxpayers For an Affordable New York Political Action
Committee**
570 Lexington Avenue, 2nd Floor, New York, NY 10022
212-616-5224
Steven Spinola, Chairman

**Team Greenfield**
1011 East 3rd Street, Brooklyn, NY 11230
347-985-1135
Jeffrey Leb, Treasurer

**Teamsters Local 813 PAC**
45-18 Court Square, Suite 600, Long Island City, NY 11101
718-937-7010
Anthony Marino, Chairman

**Tempo 802**
322 West 48th Street, New York, NY 10036
John O'Connor, Chairman

**The Committee to Re-Elect Inez E. Dickens 2013**
2153 Adam Calyton Powell Jr. Boulevard, New York, NY 10027
212-749-3615
Delores Richards, Treasurer

**The Debi Rose Campaign Committee**
1300 Richmond Avenue, 23A, Staten Island, NY 10314
646-675-7617
Emanuel Braxton, Treasurer

**The General Contractors Association of New York PAC**
60 East 42nd Street, New York, NY 10165
212-687-3131
Denise M. Richardson, Chairwoman

**The High-Need Hospital PAC, Inc.**
12 Stuyvesant Oval, 9A, New York, NY 10009
212-674-6122
Mark Pollack, Chairman

**The N.Y. Public Library Guild, Local 1930**
125 Barclay Street, Room 701PAC, New York, NJ 10007
212-815-1930
Valentin Colon, Chairman

**The NYS Economic Growth PAC**
60 Columbus Circle, New York, NY 10023
212-801-1162
Eugene Angelo, Treasurer

**Theatrical Teamsters Local 817 PAC Fund**
127 Cutter Mill Road, Great Neck, NY 11021
516-365-3470
Thomas I. O'Donnell, Chairman

**Thomas Lopez-Pierre For City Council 2013**
927 Columbus Avenue, 5S, New York, NY 10025
646-363-9047
Thomas Lopez-Pierre, Treasurer

**Tile, Marble & Terrazzo BAC Union Local 7 PAC Fund**
45-34 Court Square, Long Island City, NY 11101
718-786-7648
Thomas W. Lane, Chairman

**Toll Bros., Inc. PAC**
250 Gibraltar Road, Horsham, PA 19044
215-938-8000
Zvi Barzilay, Chairman

**Tom Allon 2013**
17 east 17th Street, 4th Floor, New York, NY 10003
347-960-2399
Charles Platkin, Treasurer

**Tom Duane For Senate**
80 8th Avenue, #1802, New York, NY 10011
646-265-7082
Thomas K. Duane, Chairman

**Tony Avella For Queens**
PO Box 570052, Whitestone, NY 11357
718-762-0235
Rocco F. D'Erasmo, Treasurer

**Torodash For Truth**
12325 82nd Avenue, 5T, Kew Gardens, NY 11415
646-318-1426
Meredith Helfenbein, Treasurer

**TPU Local One IATSE NYC**
20 West 46th Street, New York, NY 10036
212-333-2500
James J. Claffey, Jr., Chairman

**Transport Workers Union Local 100**
195 Montague Street, 3rd Floor, Brooklyn, NY 11201
212-873-6000
John Samuelsen, Chairman

**Ullico Inc. Political Action Committee**
1625 Eye Street, NW, Washington, DC 20006
Edward M. Smith, Chairman

**Uniformed Fire Officers 527 Account**
225 Broadway, Suite 401, New York, NY 10007
212-293-9300
Alexander Hagan, Chairman

**Uniformed Firefighters Association State FIREPAC**
204 East 23rd Street, New York, NY 10010
212-683-4832
James Slevin, Chairman

Political Parties,
PACs & Lobbying

*Offices and agencies generally appear in alphabetical order, except when specific order is requested by listee.*

**Unite Here Local 2 PAC**
209 Golden Gate Avenue, San Francisco, CA 94102
415-864-8770
Michael Casey, Treasurer

**Unite Here Local 26 Political Committee**
33 Harrison Avenue, 4th Floor, Boston, MA 02111
617-426-1515
Brian Lang, Chairman

**Unite Here Local 5 PAC Fund**
1516 South King Street, Honolulu, HI 96826
808-941-2141
Godfrey T. Maeshiro, Chairman

**Unite Here Local 54 PAC Committee**
203-205 North Sovereign Avenue, Atlantic City, NJ 08401
609-344-5400
Charles R. McDevitt, Chairman

**Unite Here Tip State and Local Fund**
275 Seventh Avenue, 11th Floor, New York, NY 10001
212-265-7000
Donald Taylor, Chairman

**United Federation of Teachers (UFT) on Political Education**
52 Broadway, New York, NY 10004
212-598-7744
Paul Egan, Chairman

**United Food & Commercial Workers Active Ballot Club**
1775 K Street, NW, Washington, DC 20006
202-223-3111
Joseph T. Hansen, Chairman

**United Neighbors for Neville Mitchell**
888 East 233rd Street, Bronx, NY 10469
347-224-9880
Derrick L. Shippy, Treasurer

**United Parcel Service Inc. Political Action Committee - New York**
55 Glenlake Parkway, NE, Atlanta, GA 30328
404-828-6012
Teri P. McClure, Chairwoman

**UWUA Local 1-2 Non Federal PAC**
5 West 37th Street, New York, NY 10018
212-575-4400
Lucia Pagano, Treasurer

**Vallone For New York**
22-45 31st Street, Suite 6, Astoria, NY 11105
718-274-0007
Albana Haxhia, Treasurer

**Van Bramer 2013**
39-19 46th Street, Sunnyside, NY 11104
718-786-1324
Phillip L. Velez, Treasurer

**Vargas 2013**
105 West 104th Street, 3A, New York, NY 10025
646-330-5411
Ruben Vargas, Sr., Treasurer

**Veras For Council 2013**
141-60 84th Road, 5C, Briarwood, NY 11435
917-589-1459
Zlata Akilova, Treasurer

**Verizon Communications Good Government Club PAC**
140 West Street, Floor 30, New York, NY 10007
212-321-8110
James J. Gerace, Chairman

**Victor Babb For N.Y.C. Council**
106-03 Liberty Avenue, Ozone Park, NY 11417
917-324-8071
Henderson Kinch, Treasurer

**Vince Morgan 2013**
130 Lenox Avenue, 1003, New York, NY 10026
347-602-0908
RD Snyden, Treasurer

**Vish Mahadeo 2010**
130-10 109th Avenue, South Ozone Park, NY 11420
646-918-0334
Videsh A. Persaud, Treasurer

**Vito Lopez For City Council**
1704 Decatur Street, Ridgewood, NY 11385
347-744-8632
Andy J. Marte, Treasurer

**Viverito 2013**
211 East 111th Street, 2, New York, NY 10029
212-426-7552
Randolph Mark, Treasurer

**Vote Vallone 2013**
25-59 Francis Lewis Boulevard, Flushing, NY 11358
718-428-7285
Vito Tautonico, Treasurer

**VoteBhusan2013**
2793 Brighton 8th Street, Brooklyn, NY 11235
646-295-0629
Leonard H. Sturner, Treasurer

**Weiner For Mayor**
254 Park Avenue South, 12A, New York, NY 10010
212-777-7755
Nelson Braff, Treasurer

**Wilson Elser Moskowitz Edelman & Dicker LLP, PAC**
677 Broadway, Albany, NY 12207
518-449-8893
Cynthia D. Shenker, Chairwoman

**Win With Winslow**
162-10 South Road, Jamaica, NY 11433
347-423-4233
Shannell T. Harper, Treasurer

**WM NY PAC**
701 Pennsylvania Avenue, NW, Suite 590, Washington, DC 20004
202-639-1221
Barry Caldwell, Chairman

**Women's Democratic Club of NYC**
100 West 12th Street, 4M, New York, NY 10113
646-657-8040
Patricia S. Rudden, Chairwoman

**Wright 2013**
297 Hancock Street, Brooklyn, NY 11216
718-399-3807
Kimberly B. Berry, Treasurer

*Offices and agencies generally appear in alphabetical order, except when specific order is requested by listee.*

**Zead Ramadan 2013**
5900 Arlington Avenue, 22V, Bronx, NY 10471
212-882-1520
Rasul H. Miller, Treasurer

**ZETEPAC**
PO Box 75021, Washington, DC 20013
202-210-5431
Dan Backer, Chairman

*Offices and agencies generally appear in alphabetical order, except when specific order is requested by listee.*

## Lobbying How-to Guide

## What is Lobbying?

Lobbying is a paid activity in which individuals are hired by third parties to conduct activities aimed at influencing or persuading government officials to enact legislation that is beneficial to their client's interests. Simply, a lobbyist represents you and your interests within the government, and helps: enact legislation that is important to you; remove or block legislation that is not in your best interest; and add items to legislation that it will benefit you. In addition, the National Conference of State Legislatures (NCSL) defines lobbying as a citizen's right to: speak freely; affect decisions; and petition the government, a definition that explains citizen or volunteer lobbying, where there is no money involved. In this regard, people or groups who petition their representatives to vote for issues they care about are acting as lobbyists. The specific definition of what constitutes paid lobbying varies from state to state; be sure to research state rules that apply to you and your state.

## Who are Lobbyists?

While there is no formal training to become a lobbyist, the majority of lobbyists are either lawyers or individuals who worked within the government. A lobbyist should have strong communication skills and a good working knowledge of how the legislative process works. A former government worker has professional experience and a good understanding of how governmental processes work, as well as a network of personal and professional contacts. Remember, anyone who petitions the government or contacts members of Congress in an effort to sway the official's decisions is functioning as a lobbyist. However, only professional lobbyists who get paid for their services must register as a lobbyist, disclose who their client is and what their fee is.

## What do Lobbyists do?

Lobbyists open doors, create opportunities for you, and take specific steps to help advance your interests; for example:
- Help translate your goals into a governmental context;
- Help focus your efforts so that they occur at the right time;
- Help educate you on the governmental process, policies, current legislation, regulations, etc.;
- Help represent you/your organization to the government;
- Help develop relationships with the right people in the government through their own network of contacts;
- Help advertise or market you, your project and/or organization to the appropriate people at advantageous times;
- Help identify potential allies or customers within the government;
- Help support your political interests in new laws enacted by the state, by either helping to inform a representative about things they may need to know in order to draft good legislation, or by writing the law for the government official, with specific language that meets your needs;
- Help seek funding for projects or interests from their contacts within the government that are appropriate for your goals.

## How to Find/Hire a Lobbyist

Finding a lobbyist can take some research. There is no comprehensive official directory for individual lobbyists or lobbyist companies. Legally, all professional lobbyists must resister with the government, and this information is public record, and available on several national and state web sites. In addition, the following web sites are helpful:
- OpenSecrets.org
- Lobbyists.info (by subscription)
- www.cityclerk.nyc.gov includes information about NY lobbying rules and regulations, and a lobbyist directory

Once you've done your research, and have compiled a list of lobbyists you are interested in contacting, here are some helpful questions to ask lobbyists in order to determine whether or not they are right for you. Keep in mind that lobbyists can turn you down, for any number of reasons.
- How many lobbyists currently work for you?
- How many of them work full time?
- How many clients do you have right now?
- Are there any particular agencies/issues that are your strengths?
- What is your background?
- How long have you been a lobbyist?
- Would you be the person managing our project?
- Can you give me an estimate of any fees?

## How to Lobby

If you've decided to act as your own lobbyist, the more time and effort you spend, the more successful you will be. Here are general guidelines with some helpful tips.

1. Choose an Issue:
- Lobbyist meetings usually focus on a specific issue, the issue that you, as the lobbyist, are most interested in advocating for to the government official you are meeting. These meetings usually involve requesting support for a specific piece of legislation, releasing a statement, or signing congressional letters, etc.

2. Schedule a visit:
- Once you have the proper contact information, fax or email the appropriate person well in advance of your desired meeting time; governmental officials have busy schedules.
- Once you have an appointment, follow up several days in advance to confirm.

**Tip:** It's a good idea to recruit other interested parties to join the meeting— community leaders, activists, faith or student leaders who are engaged in the issue—but be careful not to overwhelm the government representative with too many people.

3. Prepare:
- Prepare for your meeting by researching your elected official, reviewing recent news or developments surrounding your issue, preparing material handouts for the official; it's crucial to meet in advance with your lobbying group to plan how to conduct the meeting. Practice communicating the following: defining your issue; why you believe it's important; your efforts and/or actions supporting your issue; and—mostly importantly—why this issue matters to the governmental representative/official.

4. The Visit/Meeting:
- If your research shows that your official/representative has a good record of supporting the issue you are concerned with, start the meeting by thanking them for their support. If they have a history of voting against/not supporting your issue, communicate your disappointment and urge them to reconsider. Be assertive, but respectful. If the meeting has gone well and the official seems responsive, discuss any future plans and/or actions they plan to take regarding your issue.

**Tip:** Your time with the government representative/official may be limited, so make sure to use your time wisely. Prioritize what you think is most important to convey/accomplish. Preparation is key.

# Section 5:
# BUSINESS

# CHAMBERS OF COMMERCE and ECONOMIC & INDUSTRIAL DEVELOPMENT ORGANIZATIONS

*Provides a combined listing of public and private organizations involved in regional economic development.*

**Adirondack Economic Development Corporation**
67 Main St, Ste 300, PO Box 747, Saranac Lake, NY 12983-0747
518-891-5523 or 888-243-2332  Fax: 518-891-9820
Web site: www.aedconline.com

**Adirondack Regional Chambers of Commerce**
136 Glen Street, Ste 3, Glens Falls, NY 12801
518-798-1761  Fax: 518-792-4147
e-mail: paust@adirondackchamber.org
Web site: www.adirondackchamber.org
Peter Aust, President & CEO

**Adirondacks Speculator Region Chamber of Commerce**
PO Box 184, Rts 30 & 8, Speculator, NY 12164
518-548-4521  Fax: 518-548-4905
e-mail: info@speculatorchamber.com
Web site: www.speculatorchamber.com
Cathleen Connolly, President

**African American Chamber of Commerce of Westchester & Rockland Counties**
100 Stevens Ave, Ste 202, Mount Vernon, NY 10550
914-699-9050  Fax: 914-699-6279
Web site: www.aaccnys.org
Robin L Douglas, Founder & CEO & President

**Albany County Industrial Development Agency**
112 State St, Room 825, Albany, NY 12207-2017
518-447-7040  Fax: 518-447-5589
e-mail: county_executive@albanycounty.com
Web site: www.albanycounty.com
Daniel McCoy, County Executive

**Albany-Colonie Regional Chamber of Commerce**
5 Computer Drive South, Albany, NY 12205-1631
518-431-1400  Fax: 518-431-1402
e-mail: info@acchamber.org
Mark Egan, CEO

**Alden Chamber of Commerce**
13500 Broadway, PO Box 149, Alden, NY 14004
716-937-6177  Fax: 716-937-4106
e-mail: secretary@aldenny.org
Web site: www.aldenny.org
Christopher Gust, President

**Alexandria Bay Chamber of Commerce**
7 Market St, Alexandria Bay, NY 13607
315-482-9531 or 800-541-2110  Fax: 315-482-5434
e-mail: info@alexbay.org
Web site: www.visitalexbay.org
Susan Boyer, Executive Director

**Allegany County Office of Development & Industrial Development Agency (IDA)**
Crossroads Commerce Center, 6087 NYS Rte 19 North, Suite 100, Belmont, NY 14813
585-268-5500 or 800-836-1869  Fax: 585-268-7473
e-mail: tourism@alleganyco.com
Web site: www.discoveralleganycounty.com
John E Foels, Director of Development & IDA

**American Indonesian Chamber of Commerce**
317 Madison Ave, Suite 1619, New York, NY 10017
212-687-4505
Web site: www.aiccusa.org
Wayne Forrest, President

**Amherst Chamber of Commerce**
Centerpointe Corporate Park, 350 Essjay Road, Suite 200, Williamsville, NY 14221
716-632-6905  Fax: 716-632-0548
e-mail: cdipirro@amherst.org
Web site: www.amherst.org
Colleen C DiPirro, CEO & President

**Amherst Industrial Development Agency (Town of)**
4287 Main Street, Amherst, NY 14226
716-688-9000  Fax: 716-688-0205
e-mail: jallen@amherstida.com
Web site: www.amherstida.com
James Allen, Executive Director

**Amsterdam Industrial Development Agency**
City Hall, 61 Church St, Amsterdam, NY 12010
518-841-4305  Fax: 518-841-4300
Frank Valiante, Executive Director

**Arcade Area Chamber of Commerce**
684 W. Main St., Arcade, NY 14009
585-492-2114  Fax: 585-492-5103
e-mail: aacc278@verizon.net
Web site: www.arcadechamber.org
Dorie Clinch, Executive Secretary

**Babylon Industrial Development Agency**
47 West Main St, Ste 3, Babylon, NY 11702
631-587-3679  Fax: 631-587-3675
e-mail: info@babylonida.org
Web site: www.babylonida.org
Robert Stricoff, CEO

**Bainbridge Chamber of Commerce**
PO Box 2, Bainbridge, NY 13733
607-967-8700
e-mail: bainbridge.chamber@yahoo.com
Web site: www.bainbridgeny.org
Barb Mulkins, President

**Baldwin Chamber of Commerce**
PO Box 804, Baldwin, NY 11510
516-223-8080
e-mail: info@baldwinchamber.com
Web site: baldwinchamber.com
Eric Mahlar, Co-President; Ralph Rose, Co-President

**Baldwinsville Chamber of Commerce (Greater Baldwinsville)**
27 Marble Street, Baldwinsville, NY 13027
315-638-0550  Fax: 315-720-1450
e-mail: baldwinsvillechamger@gmail.com
Web site: www.baldwinsvillechamber.com
Anthony Saraceni, President

**Bath Area Chamber of Commerce (Greater Bath Area)**
10 Pulteney Square W, Bath, NY 14810
607-776-7122  Fax: 607-776-7122
Web site: www.americantowns.com
Jim Maglione, Co-President
Ed Panian, Co-President

*Offices and agencies generally appear in alphabetical order, except when specific order is requested by listee.*

**Bayshore Chamber of Commerce**
77 East Main St, PO Box 5110, Bayshore, NY 11706
631-665-7003  Fax: 631-665-5204
e-mail: bayshorecofcbid@optonline.net
Web site: www.bayshorecommerce.com
Donna Periconi, President

**Bellmores Chamber of Commerce**
2700 Pettit Avenue, N Bellmore, NY 11710
516-679-1875  Fax: 516-409-0544
e-mail: info@bellmorechamber.com
Web site: www.bellmorechamber.com
Debbie Izzo, President

**Bethlehem Chamber of Commerce**
184 Greenwood Avenue, Delmar, NY 12054
518-439-0512  Fax: 518-475-0910
e-mail: info@bethlehemchamber.com
Web site: www.bethlehemchamber.com
Lorraine Schrameck, Co-President
Lisa Whitmore, Co-President

**Bethlehem Industrial Development Agency (Town of)**
445 Delaware Ave, Delmar, NY 12054
518-439-4955  Fax: 518-439-5808
e-mail: mmorelli@townofbethlehem.org
Web site: www.bethlehemida.com
Michael Morellia, Executive Director & CEO

**Bethpage Chamber of Commerce**
PO Box 636, Bethpage, NY 11714
516-433-0010
Dennis Brady, President/CEO

**Binghamton Chamber of Commerce (Greater Binghamton)**
Five South College Drive, Suite 101, Binghamton, NY 13905
607-772-8860  Fax: 607-722-4513
e-mail: chamber@greaterbinghamtonchamber.com
Web site: www.greaterbinghamtonchamber.com
Jennifer Conway, President & CEO

**Black Lake Chamber of Commerce**
PO Box 12, Hammond, NY 13646
315-375-8640
Web site: www.blacklakeny.com
William Dashnshaw, President
Carole McCann, President

**Blue Mountain Lake Association**
PO Box 724, Indian Lake, NY 12842
518-642-5112  Fax: 518-648-5489
Web site: indian-lake.com
Christine Pouch, President

**Bolton Landing Chamber of Commerce**
4928 Lake Shore Drive, P.O. Box 368, Bolton Landing, NY 12814-0368
518-644-3831
e-mail: mail@boltonchamber.com
Web site: www.boltonchamber.com
Elaine Chiovarou-Brown, Executive Director

**Boonville Area Chamber of Commerce**
122 Main St, PO Box 163, Boonville, NY 13309
315-942-5112  Fax: 315-942-6823
e-mail: info@boonvillechamber.com
Web site: www.boonvillechamber.com
Melinda Wittwer, Executive Secretary

**Brewster Chamber of Commerce**
16 Mount Ebo Road S, Ste 12A, Brewster, NY 10509
845-279-2477  Fax: 845-278-8349
e-mail: info@brewsterchamber.com
Web site: www.brewsterchamber.com
Rose Z. Aglieco, Executive Director

**Brockport Chamber of Commerce (Greater Brockport)**
PO Box 119, Brockport, NY 14420
585-234-1512
Web site: brockportchamber.org
Marie Bell, President

**Bronx Chamber of Commerce**
Hutchinson Metro Center, 1200 Waters Place, Suite 106, Bronx, NY 10461
718-828-3900  Fax: 718-409-3748
Web site: www.bronxchamber.org
Lenny Caro, President

**Bronxville Chamber of Commerce**
81 Pondfield Rd, Suite 7, Bronxville, NY 10708
914-337-6040  Fax: 914-337-6040
e-mail: bronxvillechamber@verizon.net
Web site: www.bronxvillechamber.com
Susan Miele, Executive Director

**Town of Brookhaven Industrial Development Agency**
1 Independence Hill, Farmingville, NY 11738
631-451-6563  Fax: 631-451-6925
e-mail: lmulligan@brookhaven.org
Web site: www.brookhavenida.org
Lisa Mulligan, CEO

**Brooklyn Chamber of Commerce**
25 Elm Place, Suite 200, 2nd Floor, Brooklyn, NY 11201
718-875-1000  Fax: 718-222-0781
e-mail: info@brooklynchamber.com
Web site: www.ibrooklyn.com
Veronica Harris, Director/HR/Administration/Operations

**Brooklyn Economic Development Corporation**
2001 Oriental Blvd, Brooklyn, NY 11235
718-368-6790  Fax: 718-368-6788

**Broome County Industrial Development Agency**
60 Hawley Street, 5th Floor, Binghamton, NY 13901
607-584-9000  Fax: 607-584-9009
e-mail: info@theagency-ny.com
Web site: www.theagency-ny.com
Kevin McLaughlin, Executive Director

**Buffalo Economic Renaissance Corporation**
Office of Strategic Planning, City of Buffalo, 920 City Hall, Buffalo, NY 14202-3309
716-851-5035  Fax: 716-842-6942
Web site: www.berc.org
Timothy E Wanamaker, Interim President

**Buffalo Niagara Partnership**
665 Main Street, Suite 200, Buffalo, NY 14203-1487
716-852-7100  Fax: 716-852-2761
Web site: www.thepartnership.org
Andrew J Rudnick, President & CEO

**Business Council of Westchester, The**
800 Westchester Avenue, Suite S-310, Rye Brook, NY 10573
914-948-2110  Fax: 914-948-0122
e-mail: info@thebcw.org
Web site: www.thebcw.org
Dr Marsha Gordon, President & CEO

*Offices and agencies generally appear in alphabetical order, except when specific order is requested by listee.*

**Canandaigua Area Chamber of Commerce**
113 S Main St, Canandaigua, NY 14424
585-394-4400  Fax: 585-394-4546
e-mail: chamber@canandaiguachamber.com
Web site: www.canandaiguachamber.com
Alison Grems, President & CEO

**Canastota Chamber of Commerce**
222 S Peterboro St, PO Box 206, Canastota, NY 13032
315-697-3677
Rick Stevens, President

**Canton Chamber of Commerce**
PO Box 369, 60 Main Street, Canton, NY 13617
315-386-8255  Fax: 315-386-8255
e-mail: cantoncc@northnet.org
Sally Hill, Executive Director

**Cape Vincent Chamber of Commerce**
PO Box 482, 173 N James Street, Cape Vincent, NY 13618
315-654-2481  Fax: 315-654-4141
e-mail: thecape@tds.net
Web site: www.capevincent.org
*501C (6) organization supported by over 200 mebers including businesses, organizations, and individuals.*
Shelley Higgins, Executive Director

**Capitalize Albany Corporation**
21 Lodge St, Albany, NY 12207
518-434-2532  Fax: 518-434-9846
Web site: www.capitalizealbany.com
Michael Yevoli, CEO

**Carthage Area Chamber of Commerce**
120 S. Mechanic Street, Carthage, NY 13619
315-493-3590  Fax: 315-493-3590
Web site: www.carthageny.com
Lori Borland, Executive Director

**Cattaraugus Empire Zone Corporation**
120 N Union St, Olean, NY 14760
716-373-9260  Fax: 716-372-7912
e-mail: meme@oleanny.com
Web site: www.cattempirezone.org
James Snyder, President

**Cayuga County Chamber of Commerce**
2 State Street, Auburn, NY 13021
315-252-7291  Fax: 315-255-3077
e-mail: admin@cayugacountychamber.com
Web site: www.cayugacountychamber.com
Andrew Fish, Executive Director

**Cazenovia Area Chamber of Commerce (Greater Cazenovia Area)**
59 Albany St, Cazenovia, NY 13035
315-655-9243 or 888-218-6305  Fax: 315-655-9244
e-mail: info@cazenovia.com
Web site: www.cazenoviachamber.com
Gene Gissin, Chairman

**Central Adirondack Association**
PO Box 68, Old Forge, NY 13420
315-369-6983 or 877-653-3674  Fax: 315-369-2676
Web site: www.visitmyadirondacks.com
Laurie Barkauskas, Events Coordinator

**Central Catskills Chamber of Commerce**
PO Box 605, Margaretville, NY 12455
845-586-3300  Fax: 845-586-3161
Web site: www.centralcatskills.com
John Tufillaro, President

**Chamber of Commerce of the Tonawandas**
15 Webster Street, North Tonawanda, NY 14120
716-692-5120  Fax: 716-692-1867
e-mail: chamber@the-tonawandas.com
Web site: www.thetonawandas.com
Joyce M Santiago, Executive Director

**Chaumont-Three Mile Bay Chamber of Commerce**
PO Box 24, Three Mile Bay, NY 13693
315-694-3404
e-mail: chaumontchamber@yahoo.com
Web site: www.chaumontchamber.com
Amanda Miller, President

**Chautauqua County Chamber of Commerce**
512 Falconer St, Jamestown, NY 14701
716-484-1101  Fax: 716-487-0785
e-mail: cccc@chautauquachamber.org
Web site: www.chautauquachamber.org
Todd Tranum, President/CEO

**Chautauqua County Chamber of Commerce, Dunkirk Branch**
10785 Bennett Road, Dunkirk, NY 14048
716-366-6200  Fax: 761-366-4276
e-mail: cccc@chautauquachamber.org
Web site: www.chautauquachamber.org

**Chautauqua County Industrial Development Agency**
200 Harrison St, Jamestown, NY 14701
716-661-8900  Fax: 716-664-4515
e-mail: ccida@ccida.com
Web site: www.ccida.com
William Daly, CEO

**Cheektowaga Chamber of Commerce**
AppleTree Business Park, 2875 Union Road, Ste 50, Cheektowaga, NY 14227
716-684-5838  Fax: 716-684-5571
e-mail: chamber@cheektowaga.org
Web site: www.cheektowaga.org
Debra S Liegl, President & CEO

**Chemung County Chamber of Commerce**
400 E Church St, Elmira, NY 14901-2803
607-734-5137  Fax: 607-734-4490
e-mail: info@chemungchamber.org
Web site: www.chemungchamber.org
Kevin D Keeley, President & CEO

**Chemung County Industrial Development Agency**
400  Church Street, Elmira, NY 14901
607-733-6513  Fax: 607-734-2698
Web site: www.steg.com
George Miner, President

**Commerce Chenango**
15 South Broad Street, Norwich, NY 13815
607-334-1400  Fax: 607-336-6963
e-mail: info@chenangony.org
Web site: www.commercechenango.com
*Commerce Chenango plays a leading role in economic and community development, including training and education programs, business planning, business financing, regional demographic information, labor and workforce statistics and more.*
Steve Craig, President/CEO

**Clarence Chamber of Commerce**
8899 Main Street, Suite 4, Clarence, NY 14031
716-631-3888  Fax: 716-631-3946
e-mail: info@clarence.org
Web site: www.clarencechamber.org
Judy Sirianni, President

*Offices and agencies generally appear in alphabetical order, except when specific order is requested by listee.*

**Clarence Industrial Development Agency (Town of)**
1 Town Place, Clarence, NY 14031
716-741-8930  Fax: 716-741-4715
Web site: www.clarence.ny.us
David Hartzell, Chairman

**Clayton Chamber of Commerce**
517 Riverside Dr, Clayton, NY 13624
315-686-3771 or 800-252-9806  Fax: 315-686-5564
e-mail: info@1000islands-clayton.com
Web site: www.1000islands-clayton.com
Tricia Bannister, Executive Director

**Clifton Springs Area Chamber of Commerce**
2 E Main St, PO Box 86, Clifton Springs, NY 14432
315-462-8200  Fax: 315-548-6429
e-mail: info@cliftonspringschamber.com
Web site: www.cliftonspringschamber.com
Jeff Criblear, President

**Clinton Chamber of Commerce Inc**
PO Box 142, Clinton, NY 13323
315-853-1735  Fax: 315-853-1735
e-mail: info@clintonnychamber.org
Web site: www.clintonnychamber.org
Ferris J Betrus, Executive Vice President

**Clinton County, The Development Corporation**
190 Banker Rd, Suite 500, Plattsburgh, NY 12901
518-563-3100 or 888-699-6757  Fax: 518-562-2232
Web site: www.thedevelopcorp.com
Paul Grasso, President/CEO

**Clyde Chamber of Commerce**
24 Park Street, PO Box 69, Clyde, NY 14433
315-923-4862  Fax: 315-923-9862
Rudolph A DeLisio, President

**Clyde Industrial Development Corporation**
PO Box 92, Clyde, NY 14433
315-923-7238  Fax: 315-923-9863
Kenneth DiSanto, President

**Cohoes Industrial Development Agency (City of)**
97 Mohawk Street, Cohoes, NY 12047
518-233-2117  Fax: 518-233-2168
e-mail: mayor@ci.cohoes.ny.us
Web site: www.cohoesida.org
Adam Hotaling, Chairman

**Colonie Chamber of Commerce**
950 New Loudon Rd, Latham, NY 12110
518-785-6995  Fax: 518-785-7173
e-mail: info@coloniechamber.org
Web site: www.coloniechamber.org
Tom Nolte, President

**Columbia County Chamber of Commerce**
1 North Front Street, Hudson, NY 12534
518-828-4417  Fax: 518-822-9539
e-mail: mail@columbiachamber-ny.com
Web site: www.columbiachamber-ny.com
David B Colby, President

**Columbia Hudson Partnership**
4303 Rte 9, Hudson, NY 12534-2415
518-828-4718  Fax: 518-828-0901
e-mail: kenneth.flood@columbiacountyny.com
Web site: www.chpartnership.com
Kenneth J Flood, Executive Director

**Coney Island Chamber of Commerce**
1015 Surf Ave, Brooklyn, NY 11224
718-266-1234  Fax: 718-714-0379
Norman Kaufman, President

**Cooperstown Chamber of Commerce**
31 Chestnut St, Cooperstown, NY 13326
607-547-9983  Fax: 607-547-6006
Web site: www.cooperstownchamber.org
Susan O'Handley, Executive Director

**Copiague Chamber of Commerce**
PO Box 8, Copiague, NY 11726
631-226-2956
e-mail: info@copiaguechamber.org
Web site: copiaguechamber.org
Sharon Fattoruso, Board President

**Corinth Industrial Development Agency (Town of)**
600 Palmer Ave, Corinth, NY 12822
518-654-9232  Fax: 518-654-7615
e-mail: rlucia@townofcorinthny.com
Web site: www.townofcorinthny.com
Richard B Lucia, Chairman

**Corning Area Chamber of Commerce**
1 West Market Street, Suite 202, Corning, NY 14830
607-936-4686 or 866-463-6264  Fax: 607-936-4685
e-mail: info@corningny.com
Web site: www.corningny.com
Denise Ackley, President

**Cortland County Chamber of Commerce**
37 Church St, Cortland, NY 13045
607-756-2814  Fax: 607-756-4698
Web site: www.cortlandareachamber.com
Bob Haight, Executive Director
Bradley Totman, President
Debbie Thayer, Manager of Member Services

**Coxsackie Area Chamber of Commerce**
PO Box 251, Coxsackie, NY 12051
518-731-7300
Bradley Totman, President

**Cutchogue-New Suffolk Chamber of Commerce**
PO Box 610, Cutchogue, NY 11935
631-734-2335  Fax: 631-734-5050
Richard Noncarrow, President

**Dansville Chamber of Commerce**
126 Main St, PO Box 105, Dansville, NY 14437
585-335-6290 or 800-949-0174  Fax: 585-335-6296
e-mail: dansvillechamber@hotmail.com
Web site: www.dansvilleny.net
William Bacon, President

**Delaware County Chamber of Commerce**
5 1/2 Main Street, Delhi, NY 13753
607-746-2281  Fax: 607-746-3571
e-mail: info@delawarecounty.org
Web site: www.delawarecounty.org
Mary Beth Silano, Executive Director

**Delaware County Planning Department**
PO Box 367, Delhi, NY 13753
607-746-2944  Fax: 607-746-8479
e-mail: pln@co.delaware.ny.us
Nicole Franzese, Director of Planning

*Offices and agencies generally appear in alphabetical order, except when specific order is requested by listee.*

# CHAMBERS OF COMMERCE/ECONOMIC DEVELOPMENT ORGANIZATIONS

**Deposit Chamber of Commerce**
PO Box 222, Deposit, NY 13754
Web site: www.depositchamber.com
Nick Barone, President

**Development Authority of the North Country**
317 Washington Street, Watertown, NY 13601
315-661-3200 or 800-662-1220 Fax: 315-785-2591
e-mail: info@danc.org
Web site: www.danc.org
James Wright, Executive Director

**Dover-Wingdale Chamber of Commerce**
PO Box 643, Dover Plains, NY 12522
845-877-9800
Melanie Ryder, President

**Downtown-Lower Manhattan Association**
120 Broadway, Rm 3340, New York, NY 10271
212-566-6700 Fax: 212-566-6707
e-mail: contactus@downtownny.com
Web site: downtownny.com
Elizabeth Berger, President

**Dutchess County Economic Development Corporation**
3 Neptune Rd, Poughkeepsie, NY 12601
845-463-5400 or 845-463-5407 Fax: 845-463-5401
Web site: http://thinkdutchess.com
Pamela J Balga, Administrative Services Manager

**East Aurora Chamber of Commerce (Greater East Aurora)**
652 Main Street, East Aurora, NY 14052-1783
716-652-8444 Fax: 716-652-8384
e-mail: eanycc@verizon.net
Web site: www.eanycc.com
Gary D Grote, Executive Director

**East Hampton Chamber of Commerce**
42 Gingerbread Lane, East Hampton, NY 11937
631-324-0362 Fax: 631-329-1642
e-mail: info@easthamptonchamber.com
Web site: www.easthamptonchamber.com
Marina Van, Executive Director

**East Islip Chamber of Commerce**
PO Box 88, East Islip, NY 11730
631-859-5000
Tony Fanni, President

**East Meadow Chamber of Commerce**
PO Box 77, East Meadow, NY 11554
516-794-3727 Fax: 516-794-3729
Web site: www.eastmeadowchamber.com
Dolloras Rome, President

**East Northport Chamber of Commerce**
24 Larkfield Road, East Northport, NY 11731
631-261-3573 Fax: 631-261-9885
e-mail: enptcc@aol.com
Web site: www.eastnorthport.com
Brian Valeri, President
Jill Bergman, Vice President

**Eastchester-Tuckahoe Chamber of Commerce**
65 Main Street, Suite 202, Tuckahoe, NY 10707
914-779-7344
e-mail: cetcoc@aol.com
Mariam Janusz, Executive Director

**Ellenville/Wawarsing Chamber of Commerce**
PO Box 227, 124 Canal St, Ellenville, NY 12428
845-647-4620
e-mail: info@ewcoc.com
Web site: ewcoc.com
Dr. Mark Craft, President

**Ellicottville Chamber of Commerce**
9 W Washington St, PO Box 456, Ellicottville, NY 14731
716-699-5046 or 800-349-9099 Fax: 716-699-5636
e-mail: info@ellicottvilleny.com
Web site: www.ellicottvilleny.com
Heather Snyder, Administrative Assistant

**Erie County Industrial Development Agency**
143 Genesee Street, Buffalo, NY 14203
716-858-8500 Fax: 716-858-6679
e-mail: info@ecidany.com
Web site: www.ecidany.com
Mark Poloncarz, County Executive

**Erie County Planning & Economic Development**
95 Franklin St, 10th Floor, Buffalo, NY 14202
716-858-6170 Fax: 716-858-7248
Web site: www.erie.gov
Kathy Konst, Commissioner

**Erwin Industrial Development Agency (Town of)**
Three Rivers Dev Corp Inc, 114 Pine St Suite 201, Corning, NY 14830
607-962-4693 Fax: 607-936-9132
Jack Benjamin, President

**Essex County Industrial Development Agency**
7566 Court Street, PO Box 217, Elizabethtown, NY 12932
518-873-9114 Fax: 518-873-2011
e-mail: info@essexcountyida.com
Web site: www.essexcountyida.com
Carol Calabrese; Jody Olcott, Co-Executive Directors

**Evans-Brant Chamber of Commerce**
70 North Main Street, Angola, NY 14006
716-549-3221 Fax: 716-549-3475
Michelle Parker, President

**Fair Haven Area Chamber of Commerce**
PO Box 13, Fair Haven, NY 13064
315-947-6037
Web site: www.fairhavenny.com
Dan Larson, President

**Farmington Chamber of Commerce**
1000 County Rd, #8, Farmington, NY 14425
585-398-2861 Fax: 315-986-4377
Cal Cobb, President

**Farmingville/Holtsville Chamber of Commerce**
PO Box 66, Holtsville, NY 11742
631-926-8259
James V Marciante, President

*Offices and agencies generally appear in alphabetical order, except when specific order is requested by listee.*

# CHAMBERS OF COMMERCE/ECONOMIC DEVELOPMENT ORGANIZATIONS

**Fayetteville Chamber of Commerce**
PO Box 712, Fayetteville, NY 13066
315-637-5544

**Findley Lake Area Chamber of Commerce**
PO Box 211, Findley Lake, NY 14736
716-769-7609 or 888-769-7609  Fax: 716-769-7609
Web site: www.findleylakeinfo.org

**Fort Brewerton/Greater Oneida Lake Chamber**
PO Box 655, Brewerton, NY 13029
315-668-3408  Fax: 315-668-3408
e-mail: info@oneidalakechamber.com
Web site: www.oneidalakechamber.com
Don Deval, President

**Fort Edward Chamber of Commerce**
PO Box 267, Fort Edward, NY 12828
518-747-3000  Fax: 518-747-0622
Web site: www.fortedwardchamber.com
Larry Moffitt, President

**Franklin County Industrial Development Agency**
10 Elm Street, Suite 2, Malone, NY 12953
518-483-9472  Fax: 518-483-2900
e-mail: admin@franklinida.org
Web site: www.franklinida.org
Paul J. Ellis, Interim CEO

**Franklin Square Chamber of Commerce**
PO Box 11, Franklin Square, NY 11010
516-775-0001  Fax: 516-292-0930
Web site: www.fschamberofcommerce.com
Joseph Ardito, President

**Fredonia Chamber of Commerce**
5 East Main St, Fredonia, NY 14063
716-679-1565  Fax: 716-672-5240
Web site: www.fredoniachamber.org
Mary Beth Fagan, Executive Director

**French-American Chamber of Commerce**
1350 Broadway, Suite 2101, New York, NY 10018
212-867-0123  Fax: 212-867-9050
e-mail: info@faccnyc.org
Web site: www.faccnyc.org
Martin Biscoff, Director

**Fulton County Economic Development Corporation**
55 East Main Street, Suite 110, Johnstown, NY 12095
518-773-8700  Fax: 518-773-8701
Web site: www.sites4u.org
Mike Reese, President/CEO

**Fulton County Industrial Development Agency**
One East Montgomery St, Johnstown, NY 12095
518-736-5660  Fax: 518-762-4597
James Mraz, Director

**Fulton County Reg Chamber of Commerce & Ind**
2 N Main St, Gloversville, NY 12078
518-725-0641 or 800-676-3858  Fax: 518-725-0643
Web site: fultoncountyny.org
Mark Kilmer, President

**Garden City Chamber of Commerce**
230 Seventh Street, Garden City, NY 11530
516-746-7724  Fax: 516-746-7725
e-mail: gcchamber@verizon.net
Web site: www.gardencitychamber.org
Althea Robinson, Executive Director

**Genesee County Chamber of Commerce**
210 E Main St, Batavia, NY 14020
585-343-7440  Fax: 585-343-7487
e-mail: chamber@geneseeny.com
Web site: www.geneseeny.com
Lynn Freeman, President

**Genesee County Economic Development Center**
99 MedTech Drive, Suite 106, Batavia, NY 14020
585-343-4866 or 877-343-4866  Fax: 585-343-0848
e-mail: gcedc@gcedc.com
Web site: www.gcedc.com
Steven G Hyde, CEO

**Geneva Industrial Development Agency (City of)**
47 Castle St, Geneva, NY 14456
315-828-6550  Fax: 315-789-0604
Web site: www.geneva.ny.us
Valerie Bassett, Executive Director

**Glen Cove Chamber of Commerce**
19 Village Square, 2nd Floor, Glen Cove, NY 11542
516-676-6666  Fax: 516-676-5490
Web site: www.glencovechamber.org
Phyllis Gorham, Executive Director

**Gore Mountain Region Chamber of Commerce**
228 Main Street, PO Box 84, North Creek, NY 12853
518-251-2612  Fax: 518-251-5317
Web site: www.gorechamber.com
Ed Milner, President

**Goshen Chamber of Commerce**
223 Main Street, PO Box 506, Goshen, NY 10924
845-294-7741  Fax: 845-294-7746
e-mail: info@goshennychamber.com
Web site: www.goshennychamber.com
Lynn A Cione, Executive Director

**Gouverneur Chamber of Commerce**
214 East Main St, Gouverneur, NY 13642
315-287-0331  Fax: 315-287-3694
Web site: www.gouverneurchamber.net
Donna Lawrence, Executive Director

**Gowanda Area Chamber of Commerce**
, PO Box 45, Gowanda, NY 14070
e-mail: gowandachamber@yahoo.com
Web site: gowandachamber.com
Mary Pankow, President

**Grand Island Chamber of Commerce**
2257 Grand Island Blvd, Grand Island, NY 14072
716-773-3651  Fax: 716-773-3316
e-mail: info@gichamber.org
Web site: www.gichamber.org
Eric Fiebelkorn, President

**Granville Chamber of Commerce**
One Main St, PO Box 13, Granville, NY 12832
518-642-2815  Fax: 518-642-2772
Web site: www.granvillechamber.com
Charles King, President

**Great Neck Chamber of Commerce**
Kiosk Information Center, 1 Middle Neck Road, PO Box 220432, Great Neck, NY 11022
516-487-2000  Fax: 516-829-5472
e-mail: greatneckinfo@gmail.com
Web site: www.greatneckchamber.org
Hooshang Nematzadeh, President

*Offices and agencies generally appear in alphabetical order, except when specific order is requested by listee.*

**Greater Cicero Chamber of Commerce**
5701 East Circle Drive, #302, Cicero, NY 13039
315-699-1358
e-mail: info@cicerochamber.com
Web site: www.cicerochamber.com
John Annable, President

**Greater Jamaica Development Corporation**
90-04 161st Street, Jamaica, NY 11432
718-291-0282  Fax: 718-658-1405
Web site: www.gjdc.org
Carlisle Towery, President

**The Greater Mahopac-Carmel Chamber of Commerce**
953 South Lake Blvd, PO Box-160, Mahopac, NY 10541-0160
845-628-5553  Fax: 845-628-5962
e-mail: info@mahopaccarmelchamber.com
Web site: www.mahopaccarmelonline.com
Laurie Lee Ford, Chairwoman

**The Greater Manlius Chamber of Commerce**
425 E Genesee Street, Fayetteville, NY 13066
315-637-4760  Fax: 315-637-4762
e-mail: greatermanlius@windstream.net
Web site: www.manliuschamber.com
Jennifer Baum, Chamber Administrator

**Greater Massena Chamber of Commerce**
16 Church Street, Massena, NY 13662
315-769-3525  Fax: 315-769-5295
e-mail: info@massenachamber.com
Web site: www.massenachamber.com
Nathan Lashomb, Executive Director

**Greater Mexico Chamber of Commerce**
3236 Main Street, Mexico, NY 13114
315-963-1042
Adam Judware, President

**Greater New York Chamber of Commerce**
20 W 44th Street, 4th Floor, New York, NY 10036
212-686-1772  Fax: 212-686-7232
e-mail: info@ny-chamber.com
Web site: www.ny-chamber.com
Mark Jaffe, President & CEO

**Greater Oneida Chamber of Commerce**
136 Lenox Ave, Oneida, NY 13421
315-363-4300  Fax: 315-361-4558
Web site: www.oneidachamberny.org
Rebecca Halstrom-O'Bierne, President
Tari Timmer, Executive Assistant

**Greater Ossining Chamber of Commerce, The**
2 Church Street, Suite 205, Ossining, NY 10562
914-941-0009 or 914-941-0812
e-mail: info@ossiningchamber.org
Web site: www.ossiningchamber.org
Kay Hawley, Administrator

**Greater Port Jefferson Chamber of Commerce**
118 W Broadway, Port Jefferson, NY 11777-1314
631-473-1414  Fax: 631-474-4540
e-mail: info@portjeffchamber.com
Web site: www.portjeffchamber.com
Suzanne Velazquez, President

**Greece Chamber of Commerce**
2402 West Ridge Rd, Suite 201, Rochester, NY 14626-3053
585-227-7272  Fax: 585-227-7275
e-mail: info@greecechamber.org
Web site: www.greecechamber.org
Jodie Perry, President

**Green Island Industrial Development Agency (Village of)**
20 Clinton St, Green Island, NY 12183
518-273-2201  Fax: 518-273-2235
Web site: www.villageofgreenisland.com
*Local government, Industrial Development Agency*
Kristen Swinton, Chief Executive Officer

**Greene County Department of Planning & Economic Development**
411 Main Street, Catskill, NY 12414
518-719-3290  Fax: 518-719-3789
e-mail: business@discovergreene.com
Warren Hart, AICP Director

**Greene County Tourism Promotion**
700 Rte 23B, Leeds, NY 12451
518-943-3223 or 800-355-CATS  Fax: 518-943-2296
e-mail: tourism@discovergreene.com
Web site: www.greenetourism.com
Warren Hart, Director

**Greenport-Southold Chamber of Commerce**
PO Box 1415, Southold, NY 11971
631-765-3161
e-mail: info@northforkchamber.org
Andy Binkowski, President

**Greenvale Chamber of Commerce**
PO Box 123, Greenvale, NY 11548
516-621-6545
Ken White, Board President

**Greenwich Chamber of Commerce (Greater Greenwich)**
6 Academy St, Greenwich, NY 12834
518-692-7979  Fax: 518-692-7979
e-mail: info@greenwichchamber.org
Web site: www.greenwichchamber.org
Kathy Nichols-Tomkins, Secretary

**Greenwich Village-Chelsea Chamber of Commerce**
129 West 27th Street, 6th Floor, New York, NY 10001
646-470-1773  Fax: 212-924-0714
Web site: www.villagechelsea.com
Lauren Danziger, Executive Director

**Greenwood Lake Chamber of Commerce**
PO Box 36, Greenwood Lake, NY 10925
845-477-0112  Fax: 914-477-2798
Joyce Monti, Contact

**Guilderland Chamber of Commerce**
2050 Western Ave, Guilderland, NY 12084
518-456-6611  Fax: 518-456-6690
e-mail: kburbank@guilderlandchamber.com
Web site: www.guilderlandchamber.com
Kathy Burbank, Executive Director

**Guilderland Industrial Development Agency (Town of)**
Town Hall, PO Box 339, Guilderland, NY 12084
518-356-1980  Fax: 518-356-5514
William N Young, Jr., Chairman

**Hague on Lake George Chamber of Commerce**
PO Box 615, Hague, NY 12836
518-543-6441  Fax: 518-585-9890
e-mail: haguechamberofcommerce@yahoo.com
Web site: www.visithague.com

**Hamburg Chamber of Commerce**
6122 S Park Ave, Hamburg, NY 14075
716-649-7917 or 877-322-6890  Fax: 716-649-6362
Web site: www.hamburg-chamber.org
Cindy Galley, Executive Director

*Offices and agencies generally appear in alphabetical order, except when specific order is requested by listee.*

**Hamburg Industrial Development Agency**
S6100 South Park Avenue, Hamburg, NY 14075
716-648-4145  Fax: 716-648-0151
Web site: www.hamburgida.com
Michael J Bartlett, Executive Director

**Hammondsport Chamber of Commerce**
47 Shethar Street, Hammondsport, NY 14840
607-569-2989
e-mail: info@hammondsport.org
Web site: www.hammondsport.org

**Hampton Bays Chamber of Commerce**
140 West Main St, Hampton Bays, NY 11946
631-728-2211
Web site: www.hamptonbayschamber.com
Stan Glinka, President

**Hancock Area Chamber of Commerce**
Box 525, Hancock, NY 13783-0525
607-637-4756 or 800-668-7624  Fax: 607-637-4756
e-mail: hancockchamber@hancock.net
Web site: www.hancockareachamber.com
Lori Ray, President

**Harlem Chamber of Commerce (Greater Harlem)**
200 A West 136th St, New York, NY 10030
212-862-7200 or 877-427-5364  Fax: 212-862-8745
e-mail: info@harlemdiscover.com
Lloyd Williams, President

**Hastings-on-Hudson Chamber of Commerce**
PO Box 405, Hastings-on-Hudson, NY 10706
914-478-0900  Fax: 914-478-1720
Joseph R LoCascio, Jr, President

**Hempstead Industrial Development Agency (Town of)**
350 Front St, Rm 234-A, Hempstead, NY 11550
516-489-5000 x4200 or 800-593-3870  Fax: 516-489-3179
e-mail: fparola@tohmail.org
Web site: www.tohida.org
Frederick Parola, Executive Director

**Henderson Harbor Area Chamber of Commerce**
PO Box 468, Henderson Harbor, NY 13651
315-938-5568 or 888-938-5568
e-mail: thechambertreasure@gmail.com
Web site: www.hendersonharborny.com

**Herkimer County Chamber of Commerce**
420 East German Street, Herkimer, NY 13350
315-866-7820 or 877-984-4636  Fax: 315-866-7833
e-mail: jscarano@herkimercountychamber.com
Web site: www.herkimercountychamber.com
John Scarano, Executive Director

**Herkimer County Industrial Development Agency**
320 N Prospect Street, PO Box 390, Herkimer, NY 13350
315-867-1373  Fax: 315-867-1515
Web site: www.herkimercountyida.com
Mark Feane, Executive Director

**Hicksville Chamber of Commerce**
10 W Marie St, Hicksville, NY 11801
516-931-7170  Fax: 516-931-8546
Web site: www.hicksvillechamber.com
Lionel Chitty, President

**Holbrook Chamber of Commerce, The**
PO Box 565, Holbrook, NY 11741
631-471-2725  Fax: 631-343-4816
e-mail: info@holbrookchamber.com
Web site: www.4holbrook.com
Rick Ammirati, President

**Hornell Area Chamber of Commerce/Hornell Industrial Development Agency (City of)**
40 Main St, Hornell, NY 14843
607-324-0310 or 877-HORNELL  Fax: 607-324-3776
e-mail: margie@hornellny.com
Web site: www.hornellny.com
James W Griffin, President & Executive Director

**Hudson Valley Gateway Chamber of Commerce**
One S Division St, Peekskill, NY 10566
914-737-3600  Fax: 914-737-0541
e-mail: info@hvgatewaychamber.com
Web site: www.hvgatewaychamber.com
Deborah Milone, Executive Director

**Hunter Chamber of Commerce (Town of)**
PO Box 177, Hunter, NY 12442
518-263-4900  Fax: 518-589-0117
e-mail: chamberinfo@hunterchamber.org
Web site: www.hunterchamber.org
Michael McCrary, President

**Huntington Township Chamber of Commerce**
164 Main St, Huntington, NY 11743
631-423-6100  Fax: 631-351-8276
e-mail: info@huntingtonchamber.com
Web site: www.huntingtonchamber.com
Ellen O' Brien, Executive Director

**Hyde Park Chamber of Commerce**
PO Box 17, Hyde Park, NY 12538
845-229-8612  Fax: 845-229-8638
e-mail: info@hydeparkchamber.org
Web site: www.hydeparkchamber.org
Dave Stewart, President

**Indian Lake Chamber of Commerce**
PO Box 724, Indian Lake, NY 12842
518-648-5112 or 800-328-5253  Fax: 518-648-5489
Web site: www.indian-lake.com
Christine Pouch, President

**Inlet Information Office**
160 State Route 28 at Arrowhead Park, Inlet, NY 13360
315-357-5501 or 866-GOINLET  Fax: 315-357-3570
e-mail: info@inletny.com
Web site: www.inletny.com
Adele Burnett, Director of Information & Tourism

**Irvington-on-Hudson Chamber of Commerce**
PO Box 161, Irvington, NY 10533
914-473-4819
e-mail: bettylaurenson@gmail.com
Web site: www.irvingtonnychamber.com
Eric Spino; Betty Laurenson, Presidents

**Islip Chamber of Commerce**
PO Box 112, Islip, NY 11751-0112
631-581-2720  Fax: 631-581-2720
Web site: www.islipchamberofcommerce.org
Jim Guariglia, President

*Offices and agencies generally appear in alphabetical order, except when specific order is requested by listee.*

**Islip Economic Development Division & Industrial Development Agency (Town of)**
40 Nassau Ave, Islip, NY 11751
631-224-5512  Fax: 631-224-5532
e-mail: ecodev@townofislip-ny.gov
Web site: www.islipida.com
Tom Croci, Supervisor

**Islip Industrial Development Agency (Town of)**
40 Nassau Ave, Islip, NY 11751
631-224-5512  Fax: 631-224-5532
e-mail: ecodev@townofislip-ny.gov
Web site: www.townofislip-ny.gov
Phil Nolan, Chairman

**Jamaica Chamber of Commerce**
157-11 Rockaway Boulevard, Jamaica, NY 11432
718-413-7182  Fax: 718-413-2325
Robert M Richards, President

**Jeffersonville Area Chamber of Commerce, The**
PO Box 463, Jeffersonville, NY 12748
845-482-3652
Web site: www.jeffersonvilleny.com

**Japanese Chamber of Commerce**
145 W 57th St, New York, NY 10019
212-246-8001  Fax: 212-246-8002
e-mail: info@jcciny.org
Web site: www.jcciny.org
Seiei Ono, President

**Katonah Chamber of Commerce**
PO Box 389, Katonah, NY 10536
914-232-2668
e-mail: info@katonahchamber.org
Web site: www.katonahchamber.org
Alan Eifert; Anne Hanley, Co-presidents

**Kenmore-Town of Tonawanda Chamber of Commerce**
3411 Delaware Ave, Kenmore, NY 14217
716-874-1202  Fax: 716-874-3151
e-mail: info@ken-ton.org
Web site: www.ken-ton.org
Tracey M Lukasik, Executive Director

**Kings Park Chamber of Commerce**
3 Main St, PO Box 322, Kings Park, NY 11754
631-269-7678  Fax: 631-269-5575
e-mail: info@kingsparkli.com
Dee Grasso, Executive Director

**Lackawanna Area Chamber of Commerce**
638 Ridge Rd, Lackawanna, NY 14218
716-823-8841  Fax: 716-823-8848
Web site: www.lackawannachamber.com
Michael J Sobaszek, Executive Director

**Lake George Regional Chamber of Commerce**
PO Box 272, Lake George, NY 12845
518-668-5755 or 800-705-0059  Fax: 518-668-4286
e-mail: info@lakegeorgechamber.com
Web site: www.lakegeorgechamber.com
Janice Bartkowski-Fox, President

**Lake Luzerne Chamber of Commerce**
PO Box 222, Lake Luzerne, NY 12846-0222
518-696-3500  Fax: 518-696-6122
Web site: www.lakeluzernechamber.org
George Beagle, President

**Lake Placid Chamber of Commerce**
2608 Main Street, Lake Placid, NY 12946-1592
518-523-2445 or 800-447-5224  Fax: 518-523-2605
Web site: www.lakeplacid.com
James McKenna, CEO

**Lancaster Area Chamber of Commerce**
11 W Main Street, Suite 100, PO Box 284, Lancaster, NY 14086
716-681-9755  Fax: 716-684-3385
Megan Burns-Moran, Executive Director

**Lancaster Industrial Development Agency (Town of)**
21 Central Avenue, Lancaster, NY 14086
716-683-1610  Fax: 716-683-0512
e-mail: lida@lancasterny.com
Web site: www.lancasterny.com
Dino J Fudoli, Chairman

**Lewis County Chamber of Commerce**
7576 South State Street, Lowville, NY 13367
315-376-2213 or 800-724-0242  Fax: 315-376-0326
e-mail: info@lewiscountychamber.org
Web site: www.lewiscountychamber.org
Anne Merrill, Executive Director

**Lewis County Industrial Development Agency**
7642 State St, PO Box 106, Lowville, NY 13367
315-376-3014
Web site: www.lcida.org
Richard Porter, Executive Director

**Lindenhurst Chamber of Commerce**
101 Montauk Hwy, Lindenhurst, NY 11757
631-226-4641
Web site: lindenhurstchamber.org
Jo-Ann Boettcher, President

**Liverpool Chamber of Commerce (Greater Liverpool)**
314 Second St, Liverpool, NY 13088
315-457-3895  Fax: 315-234-3226
e-mail: chamber@liverpoolchamber.com
Web site: www.liverpoolchamber.com
Dennis Hebert, President

**Livingston County Chamber of Commerce**
4635 Millennium Dr, Geneseo, NY 14454-1134
585-243-2222  Fax: 585-243-4824
e-mail: llane@livingstoncountychamber.com
Web site: www.livingstoncountychamber.com
Laura Lane, President

**Livingston County Economic Development Office & Industrial Development Agency**
6 Court St, Room 306, Geneseo, NY 14454-1043
585-243-7124  Fax: 585-243-7126
e-mail: info@build-here.com
Web site: www.build-here.com
Julie Marshall, Executive Director

**Lockport Industrial Development Agency (Town of)**
6560 Dysinger Rd, Lockport, NY 14094
716-439-9535  Fax: 719-439-9715
e-mail: LES@elockport.com
Web site: www.lockporteconomicdevelopment.com
David Kinyon, Administrative Director

**Locust Valley Chamber of Commerce**
PO Box 178, Locust Valley, NY 11560
516-671-1310
Web site: www.locustvalleychamber.com
Len Margolis, President

*Offices and agencies generally appear in alphabetical order, except when specific order is requested by listee.*

**Long Beach Chamber of Commerce**
350 National Blvd, Long Beach, NY 11561-3312
516-432-6000  Fax: 516-432-0273
Web site: www.thelongbeachchamber.com
Michael J Kerr, President

**Long Island Association**
300 Broadhollow Road, Suite 110 W, Melville, NY 11747-4840
631-493-3000  Fax: 631-499-2194
e-mail: perlkamer@hotmail.com
Pearl M Kamer, Chief Economist

**Long Island Council of Dedicated Merchants Chamber of Commerce**
PO Box 512, Miller Place, Long Island, NY 11764
631-821-1313
Dr Tom Ianniello, President

**Long Island Development Corporation**
400 Post Avenue, Suite 201A, Westbury, NY 11590
866-433-5432  Fax: 516-433-5046
Web site: www.lidc.org
Roslyn D Goldmacher, President & CEO

**Lynbrook Chamber of Commerce**
PO Box 624, Lynbrook, NY 11563
516-599-5946
e-mail: info@lynbrookusa.com
Web site: www.lynbrookusa.com
Denise Rogers, President

**Madison County Industrial Development Agency**
3215 Seneca Turnpike, Canastota, NY 13032
315-697-9817  Fax: 315-697-8169
Web site: www.madisoncountyida.com
Kipp Hicks, Director

**Malone Chamber of Commerce**
497 East Main Street, Malone, NY 12953
518-483-3760 or 877-625-6631  Fax: 518-483-3172
Web site: www.visitmalone.com
Dene Savage, President

**Mamaroneck Chamber of Commerce**
430 Center Ave, Mamaroneck, NY 10543
914-698-4400
e-mail: chamber10543@optonline.net
Web site: www.mamaroneckchamberofcommerce.org
Rose Silvestro, President

**Manhasset Chamber of Commerce**
PO Box 754, Manhasset, NY 11030
516-627-8688
Web site: www.manhassetny.org
Les Forrai, President

**Manhattan Chamber of Commerce Inc**
1120 Avenue of the Americas, 4th Floor, New York, NY 10036
212-473-7875  Fax: 212-473-8074
e-mail: info@manhattancc.org
Web site: www.manhattancc.org
Jessica Walker, President & CEO

**Marcy Chamber of Commerce**
PO Box 429, Marcy, NY 13403
315-725-3294  Fax: 315-865-6144
e-mail: marcycofc@gmail.com
Web site: www.marcychamber.com
Lesley Grogan, Board President

**Massapequa Chamber of Commerce**
674 Broadway, Massapequa, NY 11758
516-541-1443  Fax: 516-541-8625
e-mail: masscoc@aol.com
Web site: www.massapequachamber.com
Patricia Orzano, President

**Mastics/Shirley Chamber of Commerce**
PO Box 4, Mastic, NY 11950
631-399-2228
e-mail: admin@masticsshirleychamber.com
Mark Smothergill, President

**Mattituck Chamber of Commerce**
PO Box 1056, Mattituck, NY 11952
631-298-5757
e-mail: info@mattituckchamber.org
Web site: www.mattituckchamber.org
Donielle Cardinale, President

**Mayville/Chautauqua Chamber of Commerce**
PO Box 22, Mayville, NY 14757
716-753-3113  Fax: 716-753-3113
e-mail: maychautcham@yahoo.com
Deborah Marsala, Coordinator

**Mechanicville Area Chamber of Commerce**
312 N 3rd Ave, Mechanicville, NY 12118
518-664-7791  Fax: 518-664-0826
Barbara Corsale, President

**Mechanicville/Stillwater Industrial Development Agency**
City Hall, 36 North Main Street, Mechanicville, NY 12118
518-664-8331
Web site: www.mechanicville-stillwater-ida.org
Barbara Zecca Corsale, Chair

**Merrick Chamber of Commerce**
124 Merrick Ave, PO box 53, Merrick, NY 11566
516-771-1171  Fax: 516-868-6692
e-mail: merrickchamber@aol.com
Web site: www.merrickchamber.org
Randy Shotland, President

**Mid-Hudson Pattern for Progress**
Desmond Campus, 6 Albany Post Rd, Newburgh, NY 12550
845-565-4900  Fax: 845-565-4918
e-mail: jdrapkin@pfprogress.org
Web site: www.pattern-for-progress.org
Jonathan Drapkin, President

**Miller Place/Mt Sinai/Sound Beach/Rocky Point Chamber of Commerce**
5507-10 Nesconet Highway, #410, Mount Sinai, NY 11766
631-821-1313
Dr Tom Ianniello, President

**Mineola Chamber of Commerce**
PO Box 62, Mineola, NY 11501
516-408-3554  Fax: 516-408-3554
Web site: www.mineolachamber.com
Ray Sikorski, President

**Mohawk Valley Chamber of Commerce**
Radisson Hotel, Suite 1, 200 Genessee St, Utica, NY 13502
315-724-3151  Fax: 315-724-3177
Thomas Bashant, President

*Offices and agencies generally appear in alphabetical order, except when specific order is requested by listee.*

**Mohawk Valley Economic Development District**
26 W Main St, PO Box 69, Mohawk, NY 13407-0106
315-866-4671  Fax: 315-866-9862
e-mail: info@mvedd.org
Web site: www.mvedd.org
*Regional Economic Development Activities*
Stephen Smith, Director

**Mohawk Valley Economic Development Growth Enterprises**
584 Phoenix Drive, Rome, NY 13441-4105
315-338-0393 or 800-765-4990  Fax: 315-338-5694
Web site: www.mvedge.org
Laura Casamento, President

**Monroe County Industrial Development Agency (COMIDA)**
CityPlace, 50 W Main St, Suite 8100, Rochester, NY 14614
585-753-2000  Fax: 585-753-2002
Web site: www.growmonroe.org
Theresa Mazzullo, Chairman

**Montauk Chamber of Commerce, The**
742 Montauk Hwy, Montauk, NY 11954-5338
631-668-2428  Fax: 631-668-9363
e-mail: info@montaukchamber.com
Web site: www.montaukchamber.com

**Montgomery County Chamber of Commerce/Montgomery County Partnership**
1166 Riverfront Center, Amsterdam, NY 12010
518-842-8200  Fax: 518-684-0111
Peter Capobianco, President

**Moravia Chamber of Commerce**
PO Box 647, Moravia, NY 13118
315-497-1431  Fax: 315-497-9319
Dennis Bilow, President

**Mount Kisco Chamber of Commerce**
3 N Moger Ave, Mount Kisco, NY 10549
914-666-7525  Fax: 914-666-7663
e-mail: mtkiscochamber@aol.com
Web site: www.mtkiscochamber.com
Phil Bronzi, President

**Mount Vernon Chamber of Commerce**
65 Haven Ave, PO Box 351, Mount Vernon, NY 10550
914-667-7500 or 888-716-2460  Fax: 914-699-0139
Web site: www.mtvernonchamber.org
Frank T Fraley, President

**Mount Vernon Industrial Development Agency (City of)**
City Hall, Roosevelt Square, Mount Vernon, NY 10550
914-665-2300  Fax: 914-665-2496
Web site: www.cmvny.com
Yolanda Robinson, Chief of Staff

**Nassau Council of Chambers**
PO Box 365, Bellmore, NY 11710
516-248-1112  Fax: 516-663-6715
Web site: www.ncchambers.org
Julie Marchesella, President

**Nassau County Industrial Development Agency**
1550 Franklin Avenue, Suite 235, Mineola, NY 11501
516-571-1945  Fax: 516-571-1076
Web site: www.nassauida.com
Colleen Pereira, Administrative Director

**New City Chamber of Commerce**
65 N Main St, New City, NY 10956
845-638-1395  Fax: 845-638-1395
e-mail: info@newcitychamber.com
Gary Oteri, President

**New Hyde Park Chamber of Commerce**
PO Box 247, New Hyde Park, NY 11040
888-400-0311
e-mail: info@nhpchamber.com
Web site: www.nhpchamber.com
Mark Laytin, President

**New Paltz Regional Chamber of Commerce**
257 Main St, New Paltz, NY 12561-1525
845-255-0243  Fax: 845-255-5189
e-mail: info@newpaltzchamber.org
Web site: www.newpaltzchamber.org
Michael Smith, President

**New Rochelle, Chamber of Commerce, Inc**
459 Main St, PO Box 140, New Rochelle, NY 10801-6412
914-632-5700  Fax: 914-632-0708
e-mail: info@newrochellechamber.org
Web site: www.newrochellechamber.org
Rosemary McLaughlin, President

**New York Chamber of Commerce (Greater New York)**
20 West 44th Street, 4th fl, New York, NY 10036
212-686-7220  Fax: 212-686-7232
e-mail: info@chamber.com
Web site: www.ny-chamber.com
Mark S Jaffe, President & CEO

**New York City, Partnership for**
One Battery Park Plaza, 5th Floor, New York, NY 10004
212-493-7400  Fax: 212-344-3344
e-mail: info@pfnyc.org
Web site: www.pfnyc.org
Kathryn S Wylde, President & CEO

**New Yorktown Chamber of Commerce (The)**
PO Box 632, Parkside Corner, Yorktown Heights, NY 10598
914-245-4599  Fax: 914-734-7111
e-mail: info@yorktownchamber.org
Web site: www.yorktownchamber.org
Nancy Stingone, Operations Director

**Newark Chamber of Commerce**
199 Van Buren St, Newark, NY 14513
315-331-2705  Fax: 315-331-2705
Web site: www.newarknychamber.org
Tammra Schiller, President

**Niagara County Center for Economic Development**
6311 Inducon Corporate Dr, Ste 1, Sanborn, NY 14132-9099
716-278-8750  Fax: 716-278-8757
e-mail: info@niagaracountybusiness.com
Samuel M Ferraro, Commissioner

**Niagara Falls Chamber of Commerce**
6311 Inducon Corporate Drive, Sanborn, NY 14132
716-285-9141  Fax: 716-285-0941
Web site: niagarachamber.org
Deanna Alterio Brennen, President/CEO

**Niagara USA Chamber of Commerce**
6311 Inducon Corporate Dr, Sanborn, NY 14132
716-285-9141  Fax: 716-285-0941
Web site: niagarachamber.org
Deanna Alterio Brennen, President

**North Fork Chamber of Commerce**
PO Box 1415, Southold, NY 11971
631-765-3161  Fax: 631-765-3161
e-mail: info@northforkchamber.org
Web site: www.northforkchamber.org
Andy Binkowski, President

Chambers of Commerce

**North Greenbush IDA**
2 Douglas Street, Wynantskill, NY 12198-7561
518-283-5313  Fax: 518-283-5345
e-mail: ashworth@townofng.com
Web site: www.townofng.com
James Flanigan, Chairman

**Northport Chamber of Commerce**
PO Box 33, Northport, NY 11768
631-754-3905
Web site: www.northportny.com

**North Warren Chamber of Commerce**
PO Box 490, 3 Dynamite Hill, Chestertown, NY 12817
518-494-2722  Fax: 518-494-2722
Web site: www.northwarren.com
*Promoting local business Sponsors Tourist Information Center on route 8 in Chestertown.*
Barbara Thomas, President

**Nyack Chamber of Commerce**
PO Box 677, Nyack, NY 10960
845-353-2221  Fax: 845-353-4204
Web site: www.nyackchamber.com
Carlo Pelligrini, President

**Oceanside Chamber of Commerce**
PO Box 1, Oceanside, NY 11572
516-763-9177  Fax: 516-766-4575
Web site: www.oceansidechamber.org
Gail Carlin, President

**Ogdensburg Chamber of Commerce (Greater Ogdensburg)**
1 Bridge Plaza, Ogdensburg, NY 13669
315-393-3620  Fax: 315-393-1380
e-mail: chamber@gisco.net
Web site: www.ogdensburgny.com
Sandra Porter, President

**Olean Area Chamber of Commerce (Greater Olean)**
120 N Union Street, Olean, NY 14760
716-372-4433  Fax: 716-372-7912
e-mail: info@oleanny.com
Web site: www.oleanny.com
Jim Stitt Jr, President

**Oneida Industrial Development Agency (City of)**
584 Phoenix Drive, Rome, NY 13441
315-338-0393 or 800-765-4990  Fax: 315-338-5694
e-mail: info@mvedge.org
David C Grow, Chairman

**Onondaga County Industrial Development Agency**
333 West Washington Street, Suite 130, Syracuse, NY 13202
315-435-3770 or 877-797-8222  Fax: 315-435-3669
Web site: www.syracusecentral.com
Marth Beth Primo, Director of Economic Development

**Ontario Chamber of Commerce**
PO Box 100, Ontario, NY 14519-0100
315-524-5886
Web site: www.ontariotown.org
Donna Burolla, Chamber Board of Directors

**Ontario County Industrial Development Agency & Economic Development**
20 Ontario Street, Suite 106-B, Canandaigua, NY 14424
585-396-4460  Fax: 585-396-4594
Michael J Manikowski, Executive Director

**Orange County Chamber of Commerce Inc**
30 Scott's Corners Drive, Montgomery, NY 12549
845-457-9700  Fax: 845-457-8799
e-mail: info@orangeny.com
Web site: www.orangeny.com
Dr John A D'Ambrosio, President

**Orange County Partnership**
40 Matthews St, Suite 108, Goshen, NY 10924
845-294-2323  Fax: 845-294-8023
e-mail: maureen@ocpartnership.org
Web site: www.ocpartnership.org
Scott Batulis, President & CEO

**Orchard Park Chamber of Commerce**
4211 N Buffalo St, Ste 14, Orchard Park, NY 14127-2401
716-662-3366  Fax: 716-662-5946
e-mail: opcc@orchardparkchamber.com
Web site: www.orchardparkchamber.com
Nancy L Conley, Executive Director

**Orleans County Chamber of Commerce**
102 N Main St, Albion, NY 14411
585-589-7727  Fax: 585-589-7326
e-mail: ckelly@orleanschamber.com
Web site: www.orleanschamber.com
Cindy Robinson, President

**Orleans Economic Development Agency (OEDA)**
121 N Main St, Albion, NY 14411
585-589-7060  Fax: 585-589-5258
e-mail: jwhipple@orleansdevelopment.org
Web site: www.orleansdevelopment.org
James Whipple, CEO & CFO

**Oswego-Fulton Chamber of Commerce**
44 East Bridge Street, Oswego, NY 13126
315-343-7681  Fax: 315-342-0831
e-mail: gofcc@oswegofultonchamber.com
Web site: www.oswegofultonchamber.com
Beth A Hilton, Executive Director

**Oswego County, Operation/Oswego County Industrial Development Agency**
44 West Bridge St, Oswego, NY 13126
315-343-1545  Fax: 315-343-1546
e-mail: ooc@oswegocounty.org
Web site: www.oswegocounty.org
L Michael Treadwell, Executive Director

**Otsego County Chamber (The)**
189 Main Street, Suite 201, Oneonta, NY 13820
607-432-4500 or 877-5-OTSEGO  Fax: 607-432-4506
Barbara Ann Heegan, Executive Director

**Otsego County Economic Development Department & Industrial Development Agency**
242 Main St, Oneonta, NY 13820
607-432-8871  Fax: 607-432-5117
Joseph A Bernier, Chair

**Oyster Bay Chamber of Commerce**
PO Box 21, Oyster Bay, NY 11771
516-922-6464  Fax: 516-624-8082
e-mail: obenchamber@gmail.com
Web site: www.visitoysterbay.com
Dottie Simmons, President

---

*Offices and agencies generally appear in alphabetical order, except when specific order is requested by listee.*

**Painted Post Area Board of Trade**
304 South Hamilton Street, PO Box 128, Painted Post, NY 14870
607-937-6162
e-mail: info@paintedpostny.com
Web site: www.paintedpostny.com
Jean Wise-Wicks, President

**Patchogue Chamber of Commerce (Greater Patchogue)**
15 N Ocean Ave, Patchogue, NY 11772
631-207-1000 or 631-475-0121 Fax: 631-475-1599
e-mail: info@patchoguechamber.com
Web site: www.patchoguechamber.com
Gail Hoag, Executive Director

**Patterson Chamber of Commerce**
PO Box 316, Patterson, NY 12563
845-363-6304 Fax: 845-363-6304
Debra Boccarossa, President

**Peekskill Industrial Development Agency (City of)**
840 Main Street, Room 31, Peekskill, NY 10566-2016
914-737-3400 Fax: 914-737-2688
Brian Havranek, Executive Director

**Perry Area Chamber of Commerce**
102 N Center St, PO Box 35, Perry, NY 14530
585-237-5040
e-mail: joinus@perrychamber.com
Web site: www.perrychamber.com
Lorraine Sturm, Secretary

**Phelps Chamber of Commerce**
PO Box 1, Phelps, NY 14532
315-548-5481
e-mail: chamber@phelpsny.com
Web site: www.phelpsny.com

**Plainview-Old Bethpage Chamber of Commerce**
PO Box 577, Plainview, NY 11803
516-937-5646
e-mail: chamber@pobcoc.com
Web site: www.plainview-oldbethpage.org
Gary Epstein, President

**Plattsburgh-North Country Chamber of Commerce**
7061 Route 9, PO Box 310, Plattsburgh, NY 12901
518-563-1000 Fax: 516-563-1028
Web site: www.northcountrychamber.com
Garry Douglas, CEO & President

**Port Chester-Rye Brook Rye Town Chamber of Commerce**
222 Grace Church Street, Port Chester, NY 10573
914-939-1900 Fax: 914-437-7779
e-mail: pcrbchamber@gmail.com
Ken Manning, Executive Director

**Port Jefferson Chamber of Commerce**
118 W Broadway, Port Jefferson, NY 11777
631-473-1414 Fax: 631-474-4540
e-mail: info@portjeffchamber.com
Web site: www.portjeffchamber.com
Suzanne Velazquez, President

**South Bronx Overall Economic Development Corporation**
555 Bergen Ave, Bronx, NY 10455
718-292-3113 Fax: 718-292-3115
e-mail: info@sobro.org
Web site: www.sobro.org
Phillip Morrow, President/CEO

**Port Washington Chamber of Commerce**
PO Box 121, Port Washington, NY 11050
516-883-6566 Fax: 516-883-6591
e-mail: pwcoc@optonline.net
Web site: pwguide.com
Bobbie Polay, Executive Director

**Potsdam Chamber of Commerce**
One Market Street, Potsdam, NY 13676
315-274-9000 Fax: 315-274-9222
Web site: www.potsdamchamber.com
Marylee Ballou, Executive Director

**Dutchess County Regional Chamber of Commerce**
One Civic Center Plaza, Suite 400, Poughkeepsie, NY 12601
845-454-1700 Fax: 845-454-1702
e-mail: info@dcrcoc.org
Web site: www.dcrcoc.org
Charles S North, President & CEO

**Pulaski-Eastern Shore Chamber of Commerce**
3044 State Route 13, PO Box 34, Pulaski, NY 13142-0034
315-298-2213
Nancy Farrell, President

**Putnam County Economic Development Corporation**
34 Gleneida Ave, Carmel, NY 10512
845-228-8066 Fax: 845-225-0311
e-mail: meghan.taylor@putnamcountyny.gov
Web site: www.putnamedc.org
Kevin Bailey, President

**Queens Chamber of Commerce (Borough of)**
75-20 Astoria Blvd, Suite 140, Jackson Heights, NY 11370
718-898-8500 Fax: 718-898-8599
e-mail: info@queenschamber.org
Web site: www.queenschamber.org
Carol Consiato, President

**Red Hook Area Chamber of Commerce**
PO Box 254, Red Hook, NY 12571-0254
845-758-0824 Fax: 845-758-0824
e-mail: info@redhookchamber.org
Web site: www.redhookchamber.org
Ray Amater, President

**Rensselaer County Regional Chamber of Commerce**
255 River St, Troy, NY 12180
518-274-7020 Fax: 518-272-7729
e-mail: info@renscochamber.com
Web site: www.renscochamber.com
Linda Hillman, President

**Rhinebeck Area Chamber of Commerce**
P.O. Box 42, 23F E Market Street, Rhinebeck, NY 12572
845-876-5904 Fax: 845-876-8624
e-mail: info@rhinebeckchamber.com
Web site: www.rhinebeckchamber.com
Kirsten Bonanza, Executive Director

**Richfield Springs Area Chamber of Commerce**
PO Box 909, Richfield Springs, NY 13439-0909
315-858-7028
e-mail: elbudro@aol.com
Web site: www.richfieldspringschamber.org
E Lawrence Budro, Executive Director

**Riverhead Chamber of Commerce**
542 E Main St, Suite 2, Riverhead, NY 11901
631-727-7600 Fax: 631-727-7946
Web site: www.riverheadchamber.com
Tracy Stark James, President
Mary Hughes, Executive Director

*Offices and agencies generally appear in alphabetical order, except when specific order is requested by listee.*

**Rochester Business Alliance Inc**
150 State St, Ste 400, Rochester, NY 14614-1308
585-244-1800  Fax: 585-263-3679
Web site: www.rochesterbusinessalliance.com
Sandra Parker, President & CEO

**Rochester Downtown Development Corporation**
One HSBC Plaza, 100 Chestnut Street, Suite 1910, Rochester, NY 14604
585-546-6920  Fax: 585-546-4784
e-mail: rddc@rddc.org
Web site: www.rochesterdowntown.com
Heidi N Zimmer-Meyer, President

**Rochester Economic Development Corporation**
30 Church Street, Room 223B, Rochester, NY 14614
585-428-8801  Fax: 585-428-6042
Web site: www.cityofrochester.gov
R Carlos Carballada, President

**Rockaway Development & Revitalization Corporation**
1920 Mott Ave, 2nd Fl, Far Rockaway, NY 11691
718-327-5300  Fax: 718-327-4990
e-mail: info@rdrc.org
Web site: www.rdrc.org
Kevin W Alexander, Executive Director

**Rockaways, Chamber of Commerce, Inc**
253 Beach 116th St, Rockaway Park, NY 11694
718-634-1300  Fax: 718-634-9623
e-mail: rockawaychamberofcommerce@gmail.com
Web site: www.rockawaychamberofcommerce.com

**Rockland Chamber of Commerce**
PO Box 2001, New City, NY 10956
914-634-4646  Fax: 914-353-5533
e-mail: martreal@aol.com
Martin Bernstein, President

**Rockland Economic Development Corporation**
2 Blue Hill Plaza, PO Box 1575, Pearl River, NY 10965-1575
845-735-7040  Fax: 845-735-5736
e-mail: stevenp@redc.org
Web site: www.redc.org
Michael DiTullo, President & CEO

**Rockville Centre Chamber of Commerce**
PO Box 226, Rockville Centre, NY 11571
516-766-0666  Fax: 516-706-1550
Web site: www.rvcchamber.com
Lawrence G Siegel, President

**Rome Area Chamber of Commerce**
139 West Dominick St, Rome, NY 13440-5809
315-337-1700  Fax: 315-337-1715
e-mail: info@romechamber.com
Web site: www.romechamber.com
William K Guglielmo, President

**Rome Industrial Development Corporation**
584 Phoenix Drive, Rome, NY 13441
315-338-0393  Fax: 315-338-5694
e-mail: mkaucher@mvedge.org
Web site: www.romeny.org
Mark Kaucher, Executive Director

**Ronkonkoma Chamber of Commerce**
PO Box 2546, Ronkonkoma, NY 11779
631-963-2796
e-mail: info@ronkonkomachamber.com
Web site: www.ronkonkomachamber.com
Denise Schwartz, President

**Sackets Harbor Chamber of Commerce**
PO Box 17, 301 W Main Street, Sackets Harbor, NY 13685
315-646-1700  Fax: 315-646-2160
e-mail: shvisit@gisco.net
Anita Prather Harvell, President

**Sag Harbor Chamber of Commerce**
PO Box 2810, Sag Harbor, NY 11963
631-725-0011  Fax: 631-919-1662
Web site: www.sagharborchamber.com
Kelly Connaughton, President

**Salamanca Area Chamber of Commerce**
26 Main St, Salamanca, NY 14779
716-945-2034  Fax: 716-945-2034
e-mail: info@salmun.com
Web site: www.salamancachamber.org
Jayne L Fenton, President

**Salamanca Industrial Development Agency**
225 Wildwood Ave, Salamanca, NY 14779-1547
716-945-3230  Fax: 716-945-8289
e-mail: pwelch1@salmun.com
Web site: www.salmun.com
Patrick Welch, Office Manager

**Saranac Lake Area Chamber of Commerce**
193 River St, Saranac Lake, NY 12983
518-891-1990 or 800-347-1992  Fax: 518-891-7042
e-mail: info@saranaclake.com
Web site: www.saranaclake.com
Katy Van Anden, Executive Director

**Saratoga County Chamber of Commerce**
28 Clinton St, Saratoga Springs, NY 12866
518-584-3255  Fax: 518-587-0318
e-mail: info@saratoga.org
Web site: www.saratoga.org
Todd Shimkus, President

**Saratoga County Industrial Development Agency**
50 W High St, Ballston Spa, NY 12020
518-884-4705  Fax: 518-884-4780
Web site: www.saratogacountyida.org
Raymond F Callanan, Chairman

**Saratoga Economic Development Corporation**
28 Clinton St, Saratoga Springs, NY 12866
518-587-0945  Fax: 518-587-5855
Web site: www.saratogaedc.com
Dennis Brobston, President

**Sayville Chamber of Commerce (Greater Sayville)**
Bud Van Wyen Memorial BUilding, PO Box 235, Sayville, NY 11782-0235
631-567-5257  Fax: 631-218-0881
Web site: www.greatersayvillechamber.com
Bill Etts, President

**Scarsdale Chamber of Commerce**
PO Box 635, Scarsdale, NY 10583
914-620-2426
Web site: www.scarsdalechamber.org
Lewis Arlt, President

**Schenectady County Chamber of Commerce**
306 State St, Schenectady, NY 12305-2302
518-372-5656 or 800-962-8007  Fax: 518-370-3217
e-mail: info@schenectadychamber.org
Web site: www.schenectadychamber.org
Charles P Steiner, President

*Offices and agencies generally appear in alphabetical order, except when specific order is requested by listee.*

**Schenectady County Industrial Development Agency/Economic Development Corporation**
Center City Plaza, Schenectady, NY 12305
518-377-1109  Fax: 518-382-2575
Web site: www.schenectadycounty.com
Jayme Lahut, President

**Schoharie County Chamber of Commerce**
143 Caverns Road, Howes Cave, NY 12092
518-296-8820  Fax: 518-296-8825
e-mail: info@schohariechamber.com
Web site: www.schohariechamber.com
Georgia Van Dyke, Interim Executive Director

**Schoharie County Industrial Development Agency**
349 Mineral Springs Rd, Cobleskill, NY 12043
518-234-7604  Fax: 518-234-4346
e-mail: rfscrpc@nycap.rr.com
Web site: www.growscny.com
Ronald Filmer, Director

**Schroon Lake Area Chamber of Commerce**
1075 US Rte 9, PO Box 726, Schroon Lake, NY 12870-0726
518-532-7675 or 888-SCHROON
e-mail: chamber@schroonlakeregion.com
Web site: www.schroonlakechamber.com
Mike Bush, President

**Schuyler County Industrial Development Agency**
2 N Franklin St, Ste 330, Watkins Glen, NY 14891
607-535-4341  Fax: 607-535-7221
Web site: www.scoped.biz
J. Kelsey Jones, Executive Director

**Schuyler County Partnership for Economic Development**
2 N Franklin St, Ste 330, Watkins Glen, NY 14891
607-535-4341  Fax: 607-535-7221
Web site: www.scoped.biz
Brian Williams, Economic & Community Development Specialist

**Seaford Chamber of Commerce**
2479 Jackson Avenue, PO Box 1634, Seaford, NY 11783
516-221-2888  Fax: 516-221-8683
e-mail: likoub@gmail.com
Web site: www.seafordchamberofcommerce.com
Kenneth Jacobsen, President

**Seneca County Chamber of Commerce**
2020 Rtes 5 & 20 West, Seneca Falls, NY 13148
315-568-2906 or 800-732-1848  Fax: 315-568-1730
e-mail: info@senecachamber.org
Web site: www.senecachamber.org
Jeff Shipley, Executive Director

**Seneca County Industrial Development Agency**
One Di Pronio Dr, Waterloo, NY 13165
315-539-1725  Fax: 315-539-4340
Web site: www.senecacountyida.org
Robert J Aronson, Executive Director

**Sidney Chamber of Commerce**
24 River St, PO Box 2295, Sidney, NY 13838
607-561-2642  Fax: 607-561-2644
e-mail: office@sidneychamber.org
Web site: www.sidneychamber.org
Kerri Green, President

**Skaneateles Area Chamber of Commerce**
22 Jordan St., PO Box 199, Skaneateles, NY 13152
315-685-0552  Fax: 315-685-0552
e-mail: info@skaneateles.com
Web site: www.skaneateles.com
Susan Dove, Executive Director

**Sleepy Hollow Chamber of Commerce**
1 Neperan Rd, Tarrytown, NY 10591-3660
914-631-1705  Fax: 914-366-4291
Web site: www.sleepyhollowchamber.com
John Sardy, Executive Director

**Slovak American Chamber of Commerce**
10 E 40th Street, New York, NY 10016
212-532-4920

**Smithtown Chamber of Commerce**
79 E Main Street, Suite E, PO Box 1216, Smithtown, NY 11787
631-979-8069  Fax: 631-979-2206
e-mail: info@smithtownchamber.com
Web site: www.smithtownchamber.com
Barbara Franco, Executive Director

**South Jefferson Chamber of Commerce**
PO Box 73, Adams, NY 13605
315-232-4215 or 888-476-5333  Fax: 315-232-3967
Web site: www.1000islands.com

**Southampton Chamber of Commerce**
76 Main St, Southampton, NY 11968
631-283-0402  Fax: 631-283-8707
e-mail: info@southamptonchamber.com
Web site: www.southamptonchamber.com
Micah Schlendorf, President

**Southeastern New York, Council of Industry of**
6 Albany Post Rd, Newburgh, NY 12550
845-565-1355  Fax: 845-565-1427
e-mail: hking@councilofindustry.org
Web site: www.councilofindustry.org
Robert Miniger, President

**Southern Dutchess Chamber of Commerce (Greater Southern Dutchess)**
Nussbickel Building, 2582 S Ave (Route 9D), Wappingers Falls, NY 12590
845-296-0001  Fax: 845-296-0006
Web site: www.gsdcc.org
Ann M Meagher, President/CEO

**Southern Madison County Chamber of Commerce**
10 Utica Street, 2nd Floor, PO Box 3, Hamilton, NY 13346
315-824-8213 or 315-824-0002  Fax: 315-824-0086
Web site: www.hamiltonny.com

**Chamber of Southern Saratoga County**
58 Clifton Country Road, Suite 102, Clifton Park, NY 12065
518-371-7748  Fax: 518-371-5025
e-mail: digital@southernsaratoga.org
Web site: www.southernsaratoga.org
*Southern Saratoga Countys premier local business advocate with over 1025 members.*
Peter P. Bardunias, President & CEO
Liz Roggenbuck, Vice President, Community & Professional Development

**Southern Tier Economic Growth Inc**
400 Church St, Elmira, NY 14901
607-733-6513  Fax: 607-734-2698
e-mail: info@steg.com
Web site: www.steg.com
George Miner, President

**Southern Ulster County Chamber of Commerce**
3553 Route 9W, PO Box 320, Highland, NY 12528
845-691-6070  Fax: 845-691-9194
Web site: www.southernulsterchamber.org
William Farrell, President

*Offices and agencies generally appear in alphabetical order, except when specific order is requested by listee.*

**Springville Area Chamber of Commerce**
23 N Buffalo St, PO Box 310, Springville, NY 14141-0310
716-592-4746  Fax: 716-592-4746
Web site: www.springvillechamber.com
Duane W Fischer, Executive Director

**St James Chamber of Commerce**
PO Box 286, St James, NY 11780
631-584-8510  Fax: 631-862-9839
e-mail: info@stjameschamber.org
Web site: www.stjameschamber.org
Ryan McKenna, President

**St Lawrence County Chamber of Commerce**
101 Main Street, Canton, NY 13617-1248
315-386-4000 or 877-228-7810  Fax: 315-379-0134
e-mail: pmck123@aol.com
Web site: www.northcountryguide.com
Patricia McKeown, Executive Director

**St Lawrence County Industrial Development Agency**
19 Commerce Lane, Suite 1, Canton, NY 13617-1496
315-379-9806  Fax: 315-386-2573
e-mail: info@slcida.com
Web site: www.slcida.com
Patrick Kelly, Chief Executive Officer

**Staten Island Chamber of Commerce**
130 Bay St, Staten Island, NY 10301
718-727-1900  Fax: 718-727-2295
e-mail: info@sichamber.com
Web site: www.sichamber.com
Linda M Baran, President & CEO

**Staten Island Economic Development Corporation**
900 South Ave, Ste 402, Staten Island, NY 10314
718-477-1400  Fax: 718-477-0681
e-mail: newsinfo@siedc.net
Web site: www.siedc.org
Cesar J Claro, President & CEO

**Steuben County Industrial Development Agency**
7234 Rte 54, PO Box 393, Bath, NY 14810-0390
607-776-3316  Fax: 607-776-5039
e-mail: scida@steubencountyida.com
Web site: www.steubencountyida.com
James Johnson, Executive Director

**Suffern Chamber of Commerce**
PO Box 291, 71 Lafayette Avenue, Suffern, NY 10901
845-357-8424
e-mail: suffernchamberofcommerce@yahoo.com

**Sullivan County Chamber of Commerce**
PO Box 405, Mongaup Valley, NY 12762
845-791-4200  Fax: 845-791-4220
e-mail: chamber@catskills.com
Web site: www.catskills.com
Terri Ward, President & CEO

**Sullivan County Industrial Development Agency**
1 Cablevision Ctr, Ferndale, NY 12734
845-295-2603  Fax: 845-295-2604
Web site: www.sullivanida.com
Jennifer C S Brylinski, Executive Director & COO

**Syracuse & Central NY, Metropolitan Development Association of**
572 South Salina Street, Syracuse, NY 13202
315-422-8284  Fax: 315-471-4503
e-mail: ceo@centerstateceo.com
Web site: www.centerstateceo.com
Robert Simpson, President & CEO

**Syracuse Chamber of Commerce (Greater Syracuse)**
572 S Salina St, Syracuse, NY 13202-3320
315-470-1800  Fax: 315-471-8545
e-mail: ceo@centerstateceo.com
Web site: www.centerstateceo.com
Robert Simpson, President

**Syracuse Economic Development**
333 Washington Street, Suite 130, Syracuse, NY 13202
315-435-3770  Fax: 315-435-3669
Web site: www.syracusecentral.com
Mary Beth Primo, Director of Economic Development

**Syracuse Industrial Development Agency**
City Hall, 233 E Washington St, Syracuse, NY 13202
315-448-8100  Fax: 315-448-8036
Web site: www.syracuse.ny.us
William M Ryan, Chair

**Three Rivers Development Foundation Inc**
114 Pine St, Suite 201, Corning, NY 14830
607-962-4693  Fax: 607-936-9132
Web site: www.3riverscorp.com
Jack Benjamin, President

**Ticonderoga Area Chamber of Commerce**
94 Montcalm Street, Suite 1, Ticonderoga, NY 12883
518-585-6619  Fax: 518-585-9184
e-mail: chamberinfo@ticonderogany.com
Web site: www.ticonderogany.com
Pamela Nolan, Executive Director

**Tioga County Chamber of Commerce**
80 North Avenue, Owego, NY 13827
607-687-2020
e-mail: business@tiogachamber.com
Web site: www.tiogachamber.com
Gwen Kania, President & CEO

**Tioga County Industrial Development Agency**
County Office Bldg, 56 Main Street, Owego, NY 13827
607-687-8259  Fax: 607-687-8282
Web site: www.developtioga.com
Aaron Gowan, Chairman

**Tompkins County Area Development**
401 East State Street, Suite 402B, Ithaca, NY 14850
607-273-0005  Fax: 607-273-8964
e-mail: info@tcad.org
Web site: www.tcad.org
John Rudd, President

**Tompkins County Chamber of Commerce**
904 E Shore Drive, Ithaca, NY 14850
607-273-7080  Fax: 607-272-7617
Web site: www.tompkinschamber.org
Jean McPheeters, President

**Tonawanda (Town Of) Development Corporation**
169 Sheridan Parkside Dr, Tonawanda, NY 14150
716-871-8847  Fax: 716-871-8857
e-mail: ttdc@tonawanda.ny.us
Web site: www.tonawanda.com
James Hartz, Director

**Tonawandas, Chamber of Commerce of the**
15 Webster St, North Tonawanda, NY 14120
716-692-5120  Fax: 716-692-1867
Web site: www.the-tonawandas.com
Joyce M Santiago, President

*Offices and agencies generally appear in alphabetical order, except when specific order is requested by listee.*

**Tri-State Chamber of Commerce**
PO Box 386, Lakeville, CT 06039-0386
860-435-0740
e-mail: info@tristatechamber.com
Web site: www.tristatechamber.com
Susan Dickinson, President
Jean Saliter, Vice President
Cheryl Reynolds, President

**Tupper Lake Chamber of Commerce**
121 Park Street, PO Box 987, Tupper Lake, NY 12986
518-359-3328  Fax: 518-359-2434
David Tomerlin, President

**Ulster County Chamber of Commerce**
214 Fair Street, Kingston, NY 12401
845-338-5100  Fax: 845-338-0968
e-mail: info@ulsterchamber.org
Web site: www.ulsterchamber.org
Ward Todd, President

**Ulster County Development Corporation/Ulster County Industrial Development Agency**
244 Fair Street, PO Box 4265, Kingston, NY 12402-4265
845-340-3556  Fax: 845-334-5373
e-mail: oed@co.ulster.ny.us
Web site: www.ulstercountyny.gov
Michael Horodyski, Chair

**Union Local Development Corporation (Town of)**
3111 E Main St, Endwell, NY 13760
607-786-2900  Fax: 607-786-2998
e-mail: economicdevelopment@townofunion.com
Web site: www.townofunion.com
Joseph M Moody, Director of Economic Development

**Utica Industrial Development Agency (City of)**
One Kennedy Plz, Utica, NY 13501
315-792-0195  Fax: 315-792-9819
e-mail: jspaeth@cityofutica.com
Web site: www.cityofutica.com
Jack N Spaeth, Executive Director

**Valley Stream Chamber of Commerce**
PO Box 1016, Valley Stream, NY 11580-1016
516-825-1741
e-mail: valleystreamcc@gmail.com
Web site: www.valleystreamchamber.org

**Victor Chamber of Commerce**
33 West Main Street, Victor, NY 14564
585-742-1476
e-mail: info@victorchamber.com
Web site: www.victorchamber.com
*The Victor Chamber of Commerce is a premier business organization that promotes connections, provides resources and advocates on behalf of our members.*
Jodell A. Raymond, Executive Director

**Waddington Chamber of Commerce**
PO Box 291, Waddington, NY 13694
315-388-4765 or 315-388-5576
e-mail: waddingtonchamber@gmail.com
Alicia Murphy, President

**Walton Chamber of Commerce**
129 North Street, Walton, NY 13856-1217
607-865-6656
e-mail: waltonchamber@yahoo.com
Web site: www.waltonchamber.com
Maureen Wacha, President

**Wantagh Chamber of Commerce**
Pond Rd, PO Box 660, Wantagh, NY 11793
516-679-0100 or 516-781-6145
e-mail: denise@langweberlaw.com
Web site: www.wcc.li
Denise Langweber, President

**Warren & Washington Industrial Development Agency**
5 Warren St, Suite 210, Glens Falls, NY 12801
518-792-1312  Fax: 518-792-4147
e-mail: info@warren-washingtonida.com
Web site: www.warren-washingtonida.com
Harold Taylor, Chairman

**Warren County Economic Development Corporation**
234 Glen Street, Glens Falls, NY 12801
518-761-6007  Fax: 518-761-9053
e-mail: info@edcwc.org
Web site: www.edcwc.org
Leonard Fosbrook, President

**Warrensburg Chamber of Commerce**
3839 Main Street, Warrensburg, NY 12885
518-623-2161
e-mail: info@warrensburgchamber.com
Web site: www.warrensburgchamber.com
*The Warrensburg Chamber promotes and supports businesses, the community, and provides assistance to locals and visitors of the community.*
Suzanne Tyler, Executive Director

**Warsaw Chamber of Commerce (Greater Warsaw)**
PO Box 221, Warsaw, NY 14569
585-786-3989  Fax: 585-786-3083
e-mail: info@warsawchamber.com
Web site: warsawchamber.com
Becky Ryan, President

**Warwick Valley Chamber of Commerce**
South St, Caboose, PO Box 202, Warwick, NY 10990
845-986-2720  Fax: 914-986-6982
e-mail: info@warwickcc.org
Web site: www.warwickcc.org
Michael Johndrow, Executive Director

**Washington County Local Development Corporation**
383 Broadway, Building A, Fort Edward, NY 12828
518-746-2292  Fax: 518-746-2293
Web site: www.wcldc.org
Tori J.E. Riley, President

**Watertown Empire Zone**
PO Box 3367, Saratoga Springs, NY 12866
315-782-1167  Fax: 518-899-9642
Web site: www.watertownempirezone.com
R Michael N'dolo, Zone Coodinator

**Watertown-North Country Chamber of Commerce (Greater Watertown)**
1241 Coffeen St, Watertown, NY 13601
315-788-4400  Fax: 315-788-3369
e-mail: chamber@watertownny.com
Web site: www.watertownny.com
Lynn Pietroski, President & CEO

**Watkins Glen Area Chamber of Commerce**
214 N Franklin St, St Rte 14, Watkins Glen, NY 14891
607-535-4300 or 800-607-4552  Fax: 607-535-6243
Web site: www.watkinsglenchamber.com
Rebekah LaMoreaux, President/CEO

*Offices and agencies generally appear in alphabetical order, except when specific order is requested by listee.*

**Wayne County Industrial Development Agency & Economic Development**
16 William St, Lyons, NY 14489
315-946-5917 or 888-219-2963  Fax: 315-946-5918
Peg Churchill, Executive Director

**Webster Chamber of Commerce**
1110 Crosspointe Lane, Ste C, Webster, NY 14580-3280
585-265-3960  Fax: 585-265-3702
e-mail: info@websterchamber.com
Web site: www.websterchamber.com
Barry Howard, President/CEO

**Weedsport Area Chamber of Commerce**
PO Box 973, Weedsport, NY 13166
315-834-2280
e-mail: weedsportchamber@yahoo.com
Web site: www.weedsportchamber.org
Penny Fay, President

**Wellsville Area Chamber of Commerce**
114 N Main St, Wellsville, NY 14895
585-593-5080  Fax: 585-593-5088
e-mail: info@wellsvilleareachamber.com
Web site: www.wellsvilleareachamber.com
Steven Havey, Executive Director

**Westbury-Carle Place Chamber of Commerce**
PO Box 474, Westbury, NY 11590
516-997-3966
e-mail: info@wcpchamber.com
Web site: www.wcpchamber.com
Frank Frisone, President

**West Manhattan Chamber of Commerce**
150 W 88 St, PO Box 1028, New York, NY 10024
212-787-1112  Fax: 212-787-1115
e-mail: mail@westmanhattanchamber.org
Andrew Albert, Executive Director

**West Seneca Chamber of Commerce**
950A Union Rd, Suite 5, West Seneca, NY 14224
716-674-4900  Fax: 716-674-5846
e-mail: director@westseneca.org
Web site: www.westseneca.org
Frank Calieri, Executive Director

**Westchester County Association Inc (The)**
1133 Westchester Avenue, Suite S-217, White Plains, NY 10604
914-948-6444  Fax: 914-948-6913
e-mail: info@westchester.org
Web site: www.westchester.org
William M Mooney, Jr, President & Chief Executive Officer

**Westchester County Chamber of Commerce**
108 Corporate Park Dr, Ste 101, White Plains, NY 10604
914-948-2110  Fax: 914-948-0122
e-mail: mpgordon@westchesterny.org
Dr Marsha Gordon, President & CEO

**Westchester County Industrial Development Agency**
Room 903, Michaelian Office Building, 148 Martine Avenue, White Plains, NY 10601
914-995-2963  Fax: 914-995-3044
Web site: www.thinkingwestchester.com
Jim Coleman, Executive Director

**Westfield/Barcelona Chamber of Commerce**
27 East Main St, PO Box 125, Westfield, NY 14787-1319
716-326-4000  Fax: 716-326-2299
Tony Pisicoli, President

**Westhampton Chamber of Commerce (Greater Westhampton)**
PO Box 1228, 7 Glovers Lane, Westhampton Beach, NY 11978
631-288-3337  Fax: 631-288-3322
e-mail: info@whbcc.org
Web site: www.whbcc.org
Dwayne Wagner, President

**Whiteface Mountain Regional Visitor's Bureau**
PO Box 277, Wilmington, NY 12997
518-946-2255 or 888-Whiteface  Fax: 518-946-2683
e-mail: info@whitefaceregion.com
Web site: www.whitefaceregion.com
Diane Buckley, Office Manager

**Whitehall Area Chamber of Commerce**
PO Box 97, Whitehall, NY 12887
518-499-4435
Web site: www.whitehall-chamber.org

**Williamson Chamber of Commerce**
PO Box 907, Williamson, NY 14589
315-589-2020  Fax: 315-589-9682
e-mail: williamsoncofc@aol.com
TBA, President

**Willistons Chamber of Commerce**
PO Box 207, Williston Park, NY 11596
516-739-1943  Fax: 516-294-1444
Bobby Shannon, President

**Woodstock Chamber of Commerce & Arts**
PO Box 36, Woodstock, NY 12498
845-679-6234
e-mail: info@woodstockchamber.com
Web site: www.woodstockchamber.com
Nick Altomare, President

**Wurtsboro Board of Trade**
PO Box 907, Wurtsboro, NY 12790
845-888-4884
Web site: www.wurtsboro.org
James Arnott, President

**Wyoming County Chamber of Commerce**
6470 Route 20A, Suite 2, Perry, NY 14530-9798
585-237-0230 or 800-839-3919  Fax: 585-237-0231
e-mail: info@wycochamber.org
Web site: www.wycochamber.org
Laura Lane, President/CEO

**Yates County Chamber of Commerce**
2375 Rte 14A, Penn Yan, NY 14527
800-868-YATES  Fax: 315-536-3791
e-mail: info@yatesny.com
Web site: www.yatesny.com
Michael Linehan, President/CEO

**Finger Lakes Economic Development Center**
One Keuka Business Park, Penn Yan, NY 14527
315-536-7328  Fax: 315-536-2389
e-mail: info@fingerlakesedc.com
Web site: www.fingerlakesedc.com
Steve Griffin, CEO

**Yonkers Chamber of Commerce**
55 Main Street, Yonkers, NY 10701
914-963-0332  Fax: 914-963-0451
e-mail: info@yonkerschamber.com
Web site: www.yonkerschamber.com
Kevin T Cacace, President

---

*Offices and agencies generally appear in alphabetical order, except when specific order is requested by listee.*

**Yonkers Economic Development/Yonkers Industrial Development Agency (City of)**
470 Nepperhan Ave, Suite 200, Yonkers, NY 10701
914-509-8651  Fax: 914-509-8651
e-mail: info@yonkersida.com
Web site: www.cityofyonkersida.com
Melvina Carter, President/CEO

*Offices and agencies generally appear in alphabetical order, except when specific order is requested by listee.*

# Section 6:
# NEWS MEDIA

# NEWS MEDIA

This chapter identifies key journalists and editorial management for daily and weekly newspapers in New York State, major news services with reporters assigned to cover State government, radio stations with a news format and television stations with news staff.

## NEWSPAPERS

Newspapers included in this chapter employ reporters who cover state and regional news. The newspapers are listed alphabetically by primary city served.

### ALBANY

**Legislative Gazette** *Weekly Circulation: 13,222*

**Legislative Gazette**
Empire State Plaza, Concourse Level, PO Box 7329, Room 106, Albany, NY 12224
518-473-9739 Fax: 518-486-6609
e-mail: editor@legislativegazette.com
Web site: www.legislativegazette.com
Executive Publisher/Project Director . . . . . . . . . . Professor Alan S Chartock
Editor. . . . . . . . . . . . . . . . . . . . . . . . . . . . . . . . . . . . . . . James Gormley
       e-mail: editor@legislativegazette.com
Assistant General Manager / Circulation / Production Manager . . . Beth Rider
       e-mail: ads@legislativegazette.com

**American City Business Journals** *Weekly Circulation: 4,000,000*

**The Business Review**
40 British American Blvd, Latham, NY 12210
518-640-6800 Fax: 518-640-6801
e-mail: albany@bizjournals.com
Web site: www.albany.bizjournals.com
Publisher. . . . . . . . . . . . . . . . . . . . . . . . . . . . . . . .Carolyn M Jones
       e-mail: cmjones@bizjournals.com
Editor-in-Chief . . . . . . . . . . . . . . . . . . . . . . . . .Michael Hendricks
       e-mail: mhendricks@bizjournals.com
Managing Editor . . . . . . . . . . . . . . . . . . . . . . . .Robin E Cooper
       e-mail: rcooper@bizjournals.com

**Times Union** *Weekday Circulation: 96,974*

**Times Union**
645 Albany Shaker Road, Albany, NY 12211
518-454-5694 Fax: 518-454-5628
e-mail: tubusiness@timesunion.com
Web site: www.timesunion.com
Publisher/CEO . . . . . . . . . . . . . . . . . . . . . . . .George R Hearst III
       e-mail: rsmith@timesunion.com
VP/Editor. . . . . . . . . . . . . . . . . . . . . . . . . . . . . . . . . .Rex Smith
       e-mail: rsmith@timesunion.com
Associate Editor. . . . . . . . . . . . . . . . . . . . . . . .Michael V Spain
       e-mail: mspain@timesunion.com
Director of Circulation . . . . . . . . . . . . . . . . . . . . .Mark Vinciguerra
Senior Editor/Features. . . . . . . . . . . . . . . . . . . . . . . .Tracy Ormsbee
       e-mail: tormsbee@timesunion.com
Senior News Editor. . . . . . . . . . . . . . . . . . . . . . . .Teresa Buckley
       e-mail: tbuckley@timesunion.com
Senior News Editor/Information Services . . . . . . . . . . . . . . . . . . Tena Tyler
       e-mail: ttyler@timesunion.com

### AMSTERDAM

**Recorder (The)** *Weekly Circulation: 8,000*

**Recorder (The)**
One Venner Rd, Amsterdam, NY 12010
518-843-1100 or 800-453-6397 Fax: 518-843-6580
e-mail: news@recordernews.com
Web site: www.recordernews.com
Publisher . . . . . . . . . . . . . . . . . . . . . . . . . . . . . . . .Kevin McClary
Associate Publisher . . . . . . . . . . . . . . . . . . . . . . . . . . . . . .Geoff Dylong
Executive Editor . . . . . . . . . . . . . . . . . . . . . . . . . .Kevin Mattison
Advertising/Marketing Director . . . . . . . . . . . . . . . . . . . . . .Brian Krohn
Editor . . . . . . . . . . . . . . . . . . . . . . . . . . . . . . . . . .Charlie Kraebel
Business Manager . . . . . . . . . . . . . . . . . . . . . . . . . . . . . .Bill Brzezicki

### AUBURN

**Citizen (The)** *Circulation: Daily 11,770; Sunday 13,600*

**Auburn Publishers Inc**
25 Dill St, Auburn, NY 13201-3605
315-253-3700 Fax: 315-253-6031
Web site: www.auburnpub.com
Publisher . . . . . . . . . . . . . . . . . . . . . . . . . . . . . . .Michael Rifanburg
Executive Editor . . . . . . . . . . . . . . . . . . . . . . . . . . . .Jeremy Boyer
       e-mail: jeremy.boyer@lee.net
Managing Editor . . . . . . . . . . . . . . . . . . . . . . . . . .Michael Dowd
       e-mail: michael.dowd@lee.net
Advertising Director . . . . . . . . . . . . . . . . . . . . . . . . .Sarah Dunham
Circulation Directory. . . . . . . . . . . . . . . . . . . . . . . . .Todd Ackerman
Asst News Editor . . . . . . . . . . . . . . . . . . . . . . . . . . . .Chris Sciria
       e-mail: chris.sciria@lee.net

### BINGHAMTON

**Press & Sun Bulletin** *Weekday Circulation: 37,915*

**Gannet Co Inc**
33 Lewis Rd, Binghamton, NY 13905-1044
607-798-1234 Fax: 607-352-2645
e-mail: bgm-newsroom@gannett.com
Web site: www.pressconnects.com
Publisher. . . . . . . . . . . . . . . . . . . . . . . . . . . . . .Sherman M Bodner
       e-mail: sbodner@gannett.com
Executive Editor . . . . . . . . . . . . . . . . . . . . . . . . . . .Calvin Stovall
       e-mail: cstovall@binghamt.gannett.com
Assistant Managing Editor . . . . . . . . . . . . . . . . . . . . . . . . . . .Al Vieira
       e-mail: avieira@binghamt.gannett.com
Circulation Director . . . . . . . . . . . . . . . . . . . . . . . .Anthony Rapczynski
       e-mail: arapczyn@binghamt.gannett.com
Advertising Director . . . . . . . . . . . . . . . . . . . . . . . . . . .Jodie Riesbeck
       e-mail: jriesbec@binghamt.gannett.com

### BRONXVILLE-EASTCHESTER

**Review**

**Journal News (The)/Gannett Co Inc**
1133 Westchester Avenue, Suite N110, White Plains, NY 10604
914-694-9300 or 703-854-6000
e-mail: info@gannett.com
Web site: www.lohud.com
Publisher. . . . . . . . . . . . . . . . . . . . . . . . . . . . . . . . . . . . . . .David Tyler
       e-mail: dtyler@eaglenewsonline.com
Editor. . . . . . . . . . . . . . . . . . . . . . . . . . . . . . . . . . . . . . . . .Sarah Hall
       e-mail: editor@eaglestarreview.com

*Offices and agencies generally appear in alphabetical order, except when specific order is requested by listee.*

## BROOKLYN

**Brooklyn Daily Eagle** *Weekly Circulation: 13,000*

**Brooklyn Daily Eagle**
16 Court St, Ste 1208, Brooklyn, NY 11241
718-422-7400
e-mail: jdh@brooklyneagle.com
Web site: www.brooklyneagle.com
Publisher..................................J Dozier Hasty
 e-mail: jdh@brooklyneagle.com

**Canarsie Courier Publications, Inc.** *Weekly Circulation: 10,000*

**Canarsie Courier**
1142 East 92nd Street, Brooklyn, NY 11236
718-257-0600  Fax: 718-272-0870
e-mail: canarsiec@aol.com
Web site: www.canarsiecourier.com
Associate Editor .........................Dara Mormile
 e-mail: canarsiec@aol.com
Publisher................................Donna M Marra
Managing Editor ........................Charles Rogers
Associate Editor ..........................Neil Friedman
Business Manager .......................Catherine Rosa

**New York Daily Challenge (The)** *Weekday Circulation: 81,000*

**New York Daily Challenge (The)**
1195 Atlantic Ave, Brooklyn, NY 11216
718-636-9500  Fax: 718-857-9115
Publisher............................Thomas H Watkins, Jr
Managing Editor ..........................Duwad Philip

## BUFFALO

**Buffalo Business First** *Weekly Circulation: 10,000*

**Buffalo Business First**
465 Main Street, Buffalo, NY 14203-1793
716-854-5822  Fax: 716-854-7960
e-mail: buffalo@bizjournals.com
Web site: www.bizjournals.com/buffalo
Publisher.................................Jack Connors
Editor.....................................Tim O'Shei
Advertising Director ...................Shelley Rohaurer
Circulation Marketing Director.............Karen Schiffmacher

**Buffalo News (The)** *Weekday Circulation: 191,000*

**Buffalo News (The)**
1 News Plaza, Buffalo, NY 14240-0100
716-849-4444  Fax: 716-856-5150
e-mail: citydesk@buffnews.com
Web site: www.buffalonews.com
Editor ..................................Mike Connelly
 e-mail: editor@buffnews.com
Managing Editor ........................Brian Connolly
 e-mail: bconnolly@buffnews.com
Deputy Managing Editor ...................Stan L Evans
 e-mail: sevans@buffnews.com
Assistant Managing Editor ...............Margaret Kenny
 e-mail: mkenny@buffnews.com
Editorial Page Editor ......................John Neville
 e-mail: jneville@buffnews.com
City Editor ...............................William Flynn

## CANANDAIGUA

**Daily Messenger (The)** *Weekly Circulation: 400,000*

**Messenger Post Newspapers**
73 Buffalo St, Canandaigua, NY 14424
585-394-0770  Fax: 585-394-1675
e-mail: messenger@mpnewspapers.com
Web site: www.mpnnow.com
Publisher................................Richard Procida
General Manager/Advertising Director .........Beth Kesel
 e-mail: bkesel@messengerpostmedia.com
Regional Editor ..........................Allison Cooper
Local Editor/Wayne County ................Steve Buchiere
Local Editor/Ontario County...................Nora Hicks

## CATSKILL

**Daily Mail (The)** *Weekday Circulation: 3,524*

**Hudson Valley Newspapers Inc**
414 Main St, PO Box 484, Catskill, NY 12414
518-943-2100  Fax: 518-943-2063
e-mail: editorial@thedailymail.net
Web site: www.thedailymail.net
Publisher..............................Roger F Coleman
 e-mail: rpignone@thedailymail.net
Managing Editor ..........................Ray Pignone
 e-mail: rpignone@thedailymail.net
Executive Editor...........................Theresa Hyland
Advertising Director .......................Pamela Geskie

## CORNING

**Corning Leader (The)** *Weekday Circulation: 13,585*

**GateHouse Media**
34 W Pulteney St, Corning, NY 14830
607-936-4651
Web site: www.the-leader.com
Publisher ..................................Fred Benson
News Editor ..............................Stella Dupree
Circulation Manager .......................Elmer Kuehner

## CORTLAND

**Cortland Standard Printing Co Inc** *Weekday Circulation: 10,500*

**Cortland Standard**
110 Main St, Cortland, NY 13045
607-756-5665  Fax: 607-756-5665
e-mail: news@cortlandstandard.net
Publisher.................................Kevin R Howe
Managing/News Editor ......................Kevin Conlon
Editorial Page Editor .......................Skip Chapman

*Offices and agencies generally appear in alphabetical order, except when specific order is requested by listee.*

## DUNKIRK-FREDONIA

**Observer Today** *Weekday Circulation: 11,648*

**Observer (The)**
10 E Second st, PO Box 391, Dunkirk, NY 14048-0391
716-366-3000  Fax: 716-366-3005
e-mail: editorial@observertoday.com
Web site: www.observertoday.com
Publisher..............................................John D'Agostino
    e-mail: jdagostino@observertoday.com
Managing Editor.......................................Greg Bacon
    e-mail: gbacon@observertoday.com
News Editor..........................................Bill Hammond
    e-mail: bhammond@observertoday.com
City Editor...............................................Gib Snyder

## CHEMUNG

**Star-Gazette** *Weekday Circulation: 73,000*

**Gannett Co Inc**
201 Bladwin Street, Elmira, NY 14901
607-734-5151  Fax: 607-732-3786
e-mail: news@stargazette.com
Web site: www.stargazette.com
Publisher........................................Sherman M Bodner
    e-mail: sbodner@gannett.com
Managing Editor & General Manager................Lois Wilson
    e-mail: lowilson@elmira.gannett.com
Circulation Director.........................Anthony Rapczynski
    e-mail: arapczyn@binghamt.gannett.com

## GENEVA

**Finger Lakes Times** *Circulation: Sunday: 19,102; Daily: 16,185*

**Finger Lakes Printing Co**
218 Genesee St, Geneva, NY 14456
315-789-3333 or 800-388-6652  Fax: 315-789-4077
e-mail: fltimes@fltimes.com
Web site: www.fltimes.com
President/Publisher........................William L McLean III
Executive Editor.................................Michael J. Cutillo
Managing Editor..................................Chuck Schading
News Editor.........................................Alan Brignall

## GLENS FALLS

**Post-Star (The)** *Weekday Circulation: 29,000*

**Lee Enterprises Inc**
76 Lawrence St, Glens Falls, NY 12801
518-792-3131 ext3220 or 800-724-2543  Fax: 518-761-1255
e-mail: obits@poststar.com
Web site: www.poststar.com
Publisher.............................................Rick Emanuel
City Editor............................................Bob Condon
    e-mail: condon@poststar.com
News Editor.........................................Rhonda Triller
Sunday Editor.........................................Todd Kehoe
Online News Editor..........................Lindsey Hollenbaugh
Circulation Director.........................Michelle Giorgianni
    e-mail: giorgianni@poststar.com
Editor..................................................Ken Tingley
    e-mail: tingley@poststar.com
News Editor........................................Mary Serkalow
News Editor...........................................Paul Tackett

## GLOVERSVILLE-JOHNSTOWN

**Leader-Herald (The)** *Weekday Circulation: 11,500*

**William B Collins Co**
8 E Fulton St, PO Box 1280, Gloversville, NY 12078
518-725-8616  Fax: 518-725-7407
e-mail: news@leaderherald.com
Web site: www.leaderherald.com
Publisher............................................Patricia Beck
Managing Editor.......................................Tim Fonda
Sr. News Editor....................................Rodney Minor
Sunday Editor....................................Bill Ackerbauer
Circulation Manager.............................Toni Mosconi

## HERKIMER

**Telegram (The)** *Weekday Circulation: 6,000*

**GateHouse Media Inc.**
111 Green St, Herkimer, NY 13350
315-866-2220  Fax: 315-866-5913
e-mail: news@herkimertelegram.com
Web site: www.herkimertelegram.com
Publisher & Advertising Director.................Beth A Brewer
Features Editor..................................Donna Thompson
Managing Editor......................................Todd Dewan

## HORNELL

**Evening Tribune (The)** *Weekday Circulation: 7,562*

**GateHouse Media Inc.**
85 Canisteo St, Hornell, NY 14843
607-324-1425  Fax: 607-324-2317
Web site: www.eveningtribune.com
Publisher.............................................Tom Connors
Marketing Director................................John Frungillo
Managing Editor..............................Andrew Thompson
Circulation.............................................Gary Shaver

## HUDSON

**Register-Star** *Weekday Circulation: 6,100*

**Johnson Newspaper Corporation**
One Hudson City Centre, Hudson, NY 12534
518-828-1616  Fax: 518-828-3870
e-mail: editorial@registerstar.com
Web site: www.registerstar.com
Publisher.......................................Harold B Johnson II
    e-mail: publisher@registerstar.com
Executive Editor.................................Theresa Hyland
City Editor.........................................Mary Dempsey
    e-mail: mdempsey@registerstar.com
Editor................................................Lori Anander
Editor.................................................Karrie Allen

*Offices and agencies generally appear in alphabetical order, except when specific order is requested by listee.*

## ITHACA

**Ithaca Journal (The)** *Weekday Circulation: 10,371*

**Gannett Co Inc**
123 W State St, Ithaca, NY 14850
607-272-2321  Fax: 607-272-4248
Web site: www.theithacajournal.com
Publisher .................................................Sherman M Bodner
    e-mail: sbodner@gannett.com
Managing Editor/General Manager .......................Bruce Estes
    e-mail: bestes@ithaca.gannett.com
News Editor ...............................................Steve Gattine
    e-mail: sgattine@ithaca.gannett.com
Assistant Managing Editor ............................Dave Bohrer
    e-mail: dbohrer@ithacajournal.com

## JAMESTOWN

**Post-Journal, The** *Weekday Circulation: 20,000*

**Post-Journal, The**
PO Box 3386, Jamestown, NY 14702-3386
716-487-1111 or 866-756-9600  Fax: 716-664-3119
e-mail: editorial@post-journal.com
Web site: www.post-journal.com
Publisher ....................................................Michael Bird
    e-mail: mbird@post-journal.com
Editor..........................................................John Whittaker
    e-mail: jwhittaker@post-journal.com
Editor ........................................................Matt Spielman
    e-mail: mspielman@post-journal.com
News/Wire Editor ........................................Mike Rukavina
    e-mail: mrukavina@post-journal.com
Circulation Director......................................Andrew Gee
    e-mail: agee@post-journal.com

## KINGSTON

**Daily Freeman** *Weekday Circulation: 20,391*

**Digital First Media**
79 Hurley Avenue, Kingston, NY 12401
845-331-5000  Fax: 845-331-3557
Web site: www.dailyfreeman.com
General Manager........................................Bob O'Leary
Managing Editor........................................Tony Adamis
    e-mail: tadamis@freemanonline.com
City Editor..................................................Jeremy Schiffres
    e-mail: jschiffres@freemanonline.com
Circualtion Director ...............................Philip Hudson

## LITTLE FALLS

**Times (The)** *Weekday Circulation: 5,042*

**GateHouse Media Inc.**
347 S 2nd St, Little Falls, NY 13365
315-823-3680  Fax: 315-823-4086
e-mail: news@littlefallstimes.com
Web site: www.littlefallstimes.com
Publisher ..................................................Beth Brewer
Production Manager ....................................Wayne Galt
News Editor................................................Todd Dewan
    e-mail: news@littlefallstimes.com

## LOCKPORT

**Journal-Register, The** *Weekday Circulation: 3,500*

**Greater Niagara Newspapers**
170 East Ave, Medina, NY 14094
585-798-1400  Fax: 585-798-0290
Web site: www.journal-register.com
Publisher .................................................Diane Crowe
Managing Editor .......................................John Hopkins
Circulation Manager...................................Beth Podgers

**Lockport Union-Sun & Journal** *Weekday Circulation: 12,300*

**Greater Niagara Newspapers**
170 East Ave, Lockport, NY 14094
716-439-9222  Fax: 716-439-9249
Web site: www.lockportjournal.com
Publisher .................................................Diane Crowe
Managing Editor .......................................John Hopkins
Night/City Editor........................................Scott Leffler
Circulation Manager..............................Elizabeth Podgers

## LONG ISLAND

**Newsday** *Weekday Circulation: 470,316*

**Newsday Inc**
235 Pinelawn Rd, Melville, NY 11747-4250
631-843-2700 or 800-639-7329  Fax: 631-843-2953
e-mail: web@newsday.com
Web site: www.newsday.com
Publisher ...................................................Fred Groser
    e-mail: publisher@newsday.com
Editor-in-Chief............................................Theresa Mills
    e-mail: editor@newsday.com
Editor ........................................................Howard Schneider
Editor ........................................................Ronald Roel
Editor ........................................................Valerie Kellogg
Circulation Manager...................................Sandy Elder

**Queens Gazette** *Weekly Circulation: 160,000*

**Queens Gazette**
42-16 34th Avenue, Long Island City, NY 11101
718-361-6161  Fax: 718-784-7552
e-mail: qgazette@aol.com
Web site: www.qgazette.com
Publisher/Editor..........................................Tony Barsamian
Associate Editor..........................................Jason D. Antos
Contibuting Editor ......................................Linda Wilson

## MALONE

**Malone Telegram, The** *Weekday Circulation: 6,000*

**Johnson Newspaper Corporation**
469 E Main St, Malone, NY 12953
518-483-2000  Fax: 518-483-8579
e-mail: news@mtelegram.com
Web site: www.mtelegram.com
Publisher ....................................................Russell Webster
Editor .........................................................Doug Buchanan
Managing Editor .....................................Connie Jenkins

*Offices and agencies generally appear in alphabetical order, except when specific order is requested by listee.*

## MASSENA

**Daily Courier-Observer** *Weekday Circulation: 7,800*

**Johnson Newspaper Corporation**
1 Harrowgate Commons, PO Box 300, Massena, NY 13662
315-265-6000 Fax: 315-265-6001
Web site: www.mpcourier.com
Publisher . . . . . . . . . . . . . . . . . . . . . . . . . . . . . . . . . . . . . . . . . . .Charles Kelly
Managing Editor . . . . . . . . . . . . . . . . . . . . . . . . . . . . . . . . . . . . .Ryne Martin
Editor . . . . . . . . . . . . . . . . . . . . . . . . . . . . . . . . . . . . . . . . . . . . .Bob Beckstead
District Circulation Manager . . . . . . . . . . . . . . . . . . . . . . . . . . . . .Cris Pitts

## MEDINA

**Journal-Register, The** *Weekday Circulation: 3,500*

**Greater Niagara Newspapers**
541-543 Main St, Medina, NY 14103
585-798-1400 Fax: 585-798-0290
Web site: www.journal-register.com
Publisher . . . . . . . . . . . . . . . . . . . . . . . . . . . . . . . . . . . . . . . . . . .Diane Crowe
Managing Editor . . . . . . . . . . . . . . . . . . . . . . . . . . . . . . . . . . . . .John Hopkins
Circulation Manager. . . . . . . . . . . . . . . . . . . . . . . . . . . . . . . . . . .Beth Podgers

## MIDDLETOWN

**Times Herald-Record** *Weekday Circulation: 80,000*

**Times Herald-Record**
40 Mulberry St, POÆBox 2046, Middletown, NY 10940-6357
845-343-2181 or 800-620-1700 Fax: 845-343-2170
Web site: www.recordonline.com
Executive Editor . . . . . . . . . . . . . . . . . . . . . . . . . . . . . . . . . . . . .Derek Osenenko
Senior Editor/Local News . . . . . . . . . . . . . . . . . . . . . . . . . . . . . .Adrianne Reilly
Editor/Local News . . . . . . . . . . . . . . . . . . . . . . . . . . . . . . . . . . . .Mike Carey
Editor/Night Publications . . . . . . . . . . . . . . . . . . . . . . . . . . . . . .Robert Berczuk
Editor/Community News . . . . . . . . . . . . . . . . . . . . . . . . . . . . . . . .Eric Stutz

## NEW YORK CITY

**AM Law Daily, The** *Weekday Circulation: 16,000*

**American Lawyer Media**
120 Broadway, 5th Fl, New York, NY 10271
800-888-8300 Fax: 646-822-5146
Web site: www.alm.com
Editor-in-Chief . . . . . . . . . . . . . . . . . . . . . . . . . . . . . . . . . . . . . .Robin Sparkman
VP/Group Publisher . . . . . . . . . . . . . . . . . . . . . . . . . . . . . . . . . . .Scott Pierce
Executive Editor . . . . . . . . . . . . . . . . . . . . . . . . . . . . . . . . . . . . . .Emily Barker
Managing Editor . . . . . . . . . . . . . . . . . . . . . . . . . . . . . . . . . . . . .Maryann Saltser
Editor/New Media . . . . . . . . . . . . . . . . . . . . . . . . . . . . . . . . . . . .Jonathan Hayter

**Journal of Commerce, The** *Weekly Circulation: 10,000*

**Journal of Commerce, The**
2 Penn Plaza East, Newark, NJ 07105
973-776-8660 or 877-675-4761
e-mail: news@joc.com
Web site: www.joc.com
SVP/Strategy. . . . . . . . . . . . . . . . . . . . . . . . . . . . . . . . . . . . .Peter M Tirschwell
 e-mail: ptirschwell@joc.com
Executive Editor . . . . . . . . . . . . . . . . . . . . . . . . . . . . . . . . . . . . .Chris Brooks
 e-mail: jbonney@joc.com
Publisher. . . . . . . . . . . . . . . . . . . . . . . . . . . . . . . . . . . . . . . . . . .Tony Stein
 e-mail: tstein@joc.com
Managing Editor . . . . . . . . . . . . . . . . . . . . . . . . . . . . . . . . . . . . .Barbara Wyker
 e-mail: bwyker@joc.com
Senior Editor . . . . . . . . . . . . . . . . . . . . . . . . . . . . . . . . . . . . . . .Joseph Bonney
 e-mail: jbonney@joc.com

**Wall Street Journal (The)** *Daily Circulation: 2,000,000*

**Dow Jones & Company**
1211 Avenue of the Americas, New York, NY 10036
212-416-2000 or 800-568-7625 Fax: 212-416-2653
e-mail: nywireroom@dowjones.com
Web site: www.wsj.com
Publisher . . . . . . . . . . . . . . . . . . . . . . . . . . . . . . . . . . . . . . . . . . .Lex Fenwick
Managing Editor. . . . . . . . . . . . . . . . . . . . . . . . . . . . . . . . . . . . . .Gerard Baker
Managing Editor/Newswires . . . . . . . . . . . . . . . . . . . . . . . . . . . .Neal Lipschutz
Editor-in-Chief/Dow Jones . . . . . . . . . . . . . . . . . . . . . . . . . . . . .Gerard Baker
Managing Director/Dow Jones . . . . . . . . . . . . . . . . . . . . . . . . . .Kelly E. Leach

**People's World** *Weekly Circulation: 27,000*

**Long View Publishing Co**
235 W 23rd St, New York, NY 10011
212-924-2523 Fax: 212-229-1713
e-mail: ny@peoplesworld.org
Web site: www.peoplesworld.org
Co-editor. . . . . . . . . . . . . . . . . . . . . . . . . . . . . . . . . . . . . . . . . . .Teresa Albano
 e-mail: talbano@peoplesworld.org
Managing Editor . . . . . . . . . . . . . . . . . . . . . . . . . . . . . . . . . . . . .Dan Margolis
 e-mail: dmargolis@peoplesworld.org
Labor Editor. . . . . . . . . . . . . . . . . . . . . . . . . . . . . . . . . . . . . . . .John Wojcik
 e-mail: jwojcik@peoplesworld.org

**New York Post** *Weekday Circulation: 686,207*

**NYP Holdings Inc**
1211 Ave of the Americas, New York, NY 10036-8790
212-930-8000 Fax: 212-930-8005
e-mail: letters@nypost.com
Web site: www.nypost.com
Publisher. . . . . . . . . . . . . . . . . . . . . . . . . . . . . . . . . . . . . . . . . . .Paul Carlucci
Managing Editor . . . . . . . . . . . . . . . . . . . . . . . . . . . . . . . . . . . . .Frank Zini
Editor. . . . . . . . . . . . . . . . . . . . . . . . . . . . . . . . . . . . . . . . . . . . . .Debra Birnbaum
Editor. . . . . . . . . . . . . . . . . . . . . . . . . . . . . . . . . . . . . . . . . . . . . .Muhammad Cohen

**New York Daily News** *Weekday Circulation: 688,584*

**New York Daily News**
4 New York Plaza, New York, NY 10004
212-210-2100 Fax: 212-643-7831
e-mail: news@edit.nydailynews.com
Web site: www.nydailynews.com
Publisher . . . . . . . . . . . . . . . . . . . . . . . . . . . . . . . . . . . . . . . . . . .Mortimer Zuckerman
 e-mail: mzuckerman@edit.nydailynews.com
Editor-in-Chief. . . . . . . . . . . . . . . . . . . . . . . . . . . . . . . . . . . . . . .Kevin R. Coney
News Editor. . . . . . . . . . . . . . . . . . . . . . . . . . . . . . . . . . . . . . . . .John Oswald
Managing Editor . . . . . . . . . . . . . . . . . . . . . . . . . . . . . . . . . . . . .Robert Sapio
Editor. . . . . . . . . . . . . . . . . . . . . . . . . . . . . . . . . . . . . . . . . . . . . .Arthur Browne

**The Independent News** *Weekly Circulation: 50,000*

**The Independent News**
74 Montauk Highway, Suite 16, East Hampton, NY 11937
631-324-2500 Fax: 631-324-2544
e-mail: news@indyeastend.com
Web site: www.indyeastend.com
Editor-in-Chief . . . . . . . . . . . . . . . . . . . . . . . . . . . . . . . . . . . . . .Rick Murphy
 e-mail: rmurphy@indyeastend.com
Publisher . . . . . . . . . . . . . . . . . . . . . . . . . . . . . . . . . . . . . . . . . . .James J. Mackin
 e-mail: jim@indyeastend.com
News Editor. . . . . . . . . . . . . . . . . . . . . . . . . . . . . . . . . . . . . . . . .Kitty Merrill

*Offices and agencies generally appear in alphabetical order, except when specific order is requested by listee.*

**New York Observer (The)**  *Weekday Circulation: 50,000*

**The New York Observer**
321 W. 44th St, 6th Floor, New York, NY 10036
212-755-2400 or 800-542-0420  Fax: 212-980-2087
e-mail: editorial@observer.com
Web site: www.observer.com
Publisher . . . . . . . . . . . . . . . . . . . . . . . . . . . . . . . . .Jared Kushner
Editor-in-Chief. . . . . . . . . . . . . . . . . . . . . . . . . . . . . . .Peter Feld
Editor . . . . . . . . . . . . . . . . . . . . . . . . . . . . . . . . . .Elizabeth Spiers
City Editor . . . . . . . . . . . . . . . . . . . . . . . . . . . . . . . .Terry Golway

**The New York Times**  *Weekday Circulation: 1,121,057*

**The New York Times**
620 Eighth Avenue, New York, NY 10018
212-556-1234  Fax: 212-556-3815
e-mail: letters@nytimes.com
Web site: www.nytimes.com
Publisher . . . . . . . . . . . . . . . . . . . . . . . . . .Arthur O. Sulzberger, Jr
    e-mail: publisher@nytimes.com
Executive Editor . . . . . . . . . . . . . . . . . . . . . . . . . . .Jill Abramson
Editorial Page Editor . . . . . . . . . . . . . . . . . . . . . .Andrew M. Rosenthal

**The Putnam County News and Recorder**  *Weekly Circulation: 4,000*

**The Putnam County News and Recorder**
144 Main Street, Cold Spring, NY 10516
845-265-2468  Fax: 845-265-2144
e-mail: editor@pcnr.com
Web site: www.pcnr.com
Publisher . . . . . . . . . . . . . . . . . . . . . . . . . . . . . . .Elizabeth Ailes
Associate Publisher/Editor-in-Chief. . . . . . . . . . . . .Douglas Cunningham

**Village Voice (The)**  *Weekly Circulation: 250,000*

**Village Voice Media, Inc**
36 Cooper Sq, New York, NY 10003
212-475-3333  Fax: 212-475-8944
Web site: www.villagevoice.com
Editor-in-Chief. . . . . . . . . . . . . . . . . . . . . . . . . . . . .Will Bourne
Deputy Editor . . . . . . . . . . . . . . . . . . . . . . . . . . . . .Jessica Lustig
Senior Associate Editor . . . . . . . . . . . . . . . . . . . . . .Angela Ashman
Senior Associate Editor . . . . . . . . . . . . . . . . . . . . . . . .Araceli Cruz

**Wave Publishing Co.**  *Weekly Circulation: 12,300*

**The Wave**
88-08 Rockaway Beach Blvd, PO Box 930097, Rockaway Beach, NY 11693-0097
718-634-4000  Fax: 718-945-0913
e-mail: editor@rockawave.com
Web site: www.rockawave.com
Publisher . . . . . . . . . . . . . . . . . . . . . . . . . . . . . . . .Susan B. Locke
General Manager . . . . . . . . . . . . . . . . . . . . . . . . .Sanford M. Bernstein
Associate Editor . . . . . . . . . . . . . . . . . . . . . . . . . . . .Dan Guarino
Contributing Editor . . . . . . . . . . . . . . . . . . . . . . . .Miriam Rosenberg
    e-mail: miriamsue18@aol.com

**Niagara Gazette**  *Weekday Circulation: 20,268*

**Greater Niagara Newspapers**
310 Niagara St, PO Box 549, Niagara Falls, NY 14302-0549
716-282-2311  Fax: 716-286-3895
Web site: www.niagara-gazette.com
Publisher. . . . . . . . . . . . . . . . . . . . . . . . . . . . . . . . . .Peter Mio
Managing Editor . . . . . . . . . . . . . . . . . . . . . . . .Matt Winterhalter
    e-mail: matt.winterhalter@niagara-gazette.com
City Editor . . . . . . . . . . . . . . . . . . . . . . . . . . . . . . . .Mark Scheer

**Evening Sun**  *Weekday Circulation: 5,200*

**Snyder Communications Corp**
29 Lackawanna Ave, PO Box 151, Norwich, NY 13815
607-334-3276  Fax: 607-334-8273
e-mail: news@evesun.com
Web site: www.evesun.com
Publisher . . . . . . . . . . . . . . . . . . . . . . . . . . . . . . .Richard Snyder
    e-mail: dsnyder@evesun.com
Managing Editor. . . . . . . . . . . . . . . . . . . . . . . . . . . .Brian Golden
Circulation Manager . . . . . . . . . . . . . . . . . . . . . . .Lori Chmieliowiec

**The Journal**  *Weekday Circulation: 5,200*

**St Lawrence County Newspapers**
308 Isabella St, PO Box 409, Ogdensburg, NY 13669
315-393-1003  Fax: 315-393-5108
Web site: www.ogd.com
City Editor . . . . . . . . . . . . . . . . . . . . . . . . . . . . . . .Elizabeth Lyons
District Circulation Manager . . . . . . . . . . . . . . . . . . . .Michael Eldridge

**Olean Times Herald**  *Weekday Circulation: 15,000*

**Bradford Publications Inc**
639 Norton Dr, Olean, NY 14760
716-372-3121  Fax: 716-373-6397
e-mail: news@oleantimesherald.com
Web site: www.oleantimesherald.com
Publisher/General Manager. . . . . . . . . . . . . . . . . . . .Bill Fitzpatrick
Managing Editor . . . . . . . . . . . . . . . . . . . . . . . . . . .Jim Eckstrom
    e-mail: jeckstrom@oleantimesherald.com
City Editor . . . . . . . . . . . . . . . . . . . . . . . . . . . . . . .Brian Lothridge
    e-mail: blothridge@oleantimesherald.com

**Oneida Daily Dispatch**  *Weekday Circulation: 6,818*

**Digital First Media**
130 Broad Street, Oneida, NY 13421
315-231-5139  Fax: 315-363-9832
e-mail: newsroom@oneidadispatch.com
Web site: www.oneidadispatch.com
Publisher . . . . . . . . . . . . . . . . . . . . . . . . . . . . . . . .Bob O'Leary
News Assistant. . . . . . . . . . . . . . . . . . . . . . . . . . . .Laurie Furman
General Manager . . . . . . . . . . . . . . . . . . . . . . . . . . .Karen Alvord
    e-mail: kalvord@21st-centurymedia.com
Circulation Manager . . . . . . . . . . . . . . . . . . . . . . . .Sabrina Sharkey

**Daily Star (The)**  *Weekday Circulation: 21,000*

**Ottaway Newspapers Inc**
102 Chestnut St, Oneonta, NY 13820
607-432-1000  Fax: 607-432-5847
e-mail: webmaster@thedailystar.com
Web site: www.thedailystar.com
Publisher. . . . . . . . . . . . . . . . . . . . . . . . . . . . . . .Mitchell D. Lynch
Editor . . . . . . . . . . . . . . . . . . . . . . . . . . . . . . . . . .Sam Pollak
Editor . . . . . . . . . . . . . . . . . . . . . . . . . . . . . . . . .Mark Boshnack
News Editor . . . . . . . . . . . . . . . . . . . . . . . . . . . . .Denise Richardson

*Offices and agencies generally appear in alphabetical order, except when specific order is requested by listee.*

## OSWEGO-FULTON

**Palladium-Times (The)** *Weekday Circulation: 8,500*

**The Palladium-Times**
140 W First St, Oswego, NY 13126
315-343-3800  Fax: 315-343-0273
e-mail: editor@palltimes.com
Web site: www.pall-times.com
Publisher . . . . . . . . . . . . . . . . . . . . . . . . . . . . . . . . . . . . . . .Jon Spaulding
    e-mail: jspaulding@palltimes.com
Editor . . . . . . . . . . . . . . . . . . . . . . . . . . . . . . . . . . . . . .Sarah McCrobie
    e-mail: smccrobie@palltimes.com
Advertising Manager . . . . . . . . . . . . . . . . . . . . . . . . . . . . .Kate Percival
Circulation . . . . . . . . . . . . . . . . . . . . . . . . . . . . . . . . .Tom Van Schaack

## PLATTSBURGH

**Press-Republican** *Weekday Circulation: 20,210*

**Press-Republican**
PO Box 459, Plattsburgh, NY 12901
518-565-4131  Fax: 518-561-3362
e-mail: news@pressrepublican.com
Web site: www.pressrepublican.com
Publisher . . . . . . . . . . . . . . . . . . . . . . . . . . . . . . . . . .Robert W. Parks
Editor. . . . . . . . . . . . . . . . . . . . . . . . . . . . . . . . . . .Lois M. Clermont
News Editor . . . . . . . . . . . . . . . . . . . . . . . . . . . . . . .Suzanne Moore
Managing Editor. . . . . . . . . . . . . . . . . . . . . . . . . . . . . .Nathan Ovalle

## POUGHKEEPSIE

**Poughkeepsie Journal** *Weekday Circulation: 40,202*

**Gannett Co Inc**
PO Box 1231, Poughkeepsie, NY 12602
845-437-4800  Fax: 845-437-4921
e-mail: newsroom@poughkee.gannett.com
Web site: www.poughkeepsiejournal.com
Publisher/President . . . . . . . . . . . . . . . . . . . . . . . . . . .Barry Rothfeld
    e-mail: brothfeld@gannett.com
Executive Editor. . . . . . . . . . . . . . . . . . . . . . . . . . . . .Stuart Shinske
Local Editor . . . . . . . . . . . . . . . . . . . . . . . . . . . . . . . .Kevin Lenihan
Circulation Manager. . . . . . . . . . . . . . . . . . . . . . . . . . . . .Bill Farrell
Editorial Page Editor . . . . . . . . . . . . . . . . . . . . . . . . . . .John Penney

## ROCHESTER

**Daily Record (The)** *Weekly Circulation: 4,500*

**The Dolan Company**
16 W Main St, Rochester, NY 14614
585-232-6920  Fax: 585-232-2740
Web site: www.nydailyrecord.com
Publisher . . . . . . . . . . . . . . . . . . . . . . . . . . . . . . . . . . .Kevin Momot
Associate Editor. . . . . . . . . . . . . . . . . . . . . . . . . . . .Kristy O'Malley
News Reporter . . . . . . . . . . . . . . . . . . . . . . . . . . . .Denise Champagne

**Democrat and Chronicle** *Weekday Circulation: 170,000*

**Gannett Co Inc**
55 Exchange Blvd, Rochester, NY 14614
585-232-7100  Fax: 585-258-2237
e-mail: webmaster@democratandchronicle.com
President/Publisher . . . . . . . . . . . . . . . . . . . . . . . . . . . .Michael Kane
    e-mail: mgkane@democratandchronicle.com
Vice President/Editor . . . . . . . . . . . . . . . . . . . . . . . .Karen Magnuson
    e-mail: kmagnuso@democratandchronicle.com
Local Editor . . . . . . . . . . . . . . . . . . . . . . . . . . . . .Catherine Roberts
    e-mail: cathyr@democratandchronicle.com
Editorial Page Editor . . . . . . . . . . . . . . . . . . . . . . . .James Lawrence
    e-mail: jlawrenc@democratandchronicle.com

**Suburban News & Hamlin Clarkson Herald** *Weekly Circulation: 32,000*

**Westside News Inc**
1776 hilton-Parma Corners Road, PO Box 106, Spencerport, NY 14559
585-352-3411  Fax: 585-352-4811
Web site: www.westsidenewsny.com
Publisher . . . . . . . . . . . . . . . . . . . . . . . . . . . . . . . . . . . . .Keith Ryan
Editor . . . . . . . . . . . . . . . . . . . . . . . . . . . . . . . . . . . . . .Evelyn Dow
Circulation Manager . . . . . . . . . . . . . . . . . . . . . . . . . . . .Don Griffin
    e-mail: circulation@westsidenewsny.com

## ROME

**Daily Sentinel** *Weekday Circulation: 16,500*

**Rome Sentinel Co**
333 W Dominick St, Rome, NY 13440-5701
315-337-4000  Fax: 315-337-4704
e-mail: sentinel@rny.com
Web site: www.romesentinel.com
Publisher. . . . . . . . . . . . . . . . . . . . . . . . . . . . . . . . . . .Stephen Waters
Managing Editor . . . . . . . . . . . . . . . . . . . . . . . . . . .David C Swanson
Editor . . . . . . . . . . . . . . . . . . . . . . . . . . . . . . . . . . . . .Thomas Merz
    e-mail: editor@rny.com
News Editor . . . . . . . . . . . . . . . . . . . . . . . . . .Kathleen Twellman Haley
    e-mail: editor@rny.com

## SALAMANCA

**Salamanca Press** *Weekday Circulation: 2,200*

**Bradford Publishing Co**
36 River St, Salamanca, NY 14779
716-945-1644  Fax: 716-945-4285
e-mail: salpressnews@verizon.net
Web site: www.salamancapress.com
Managing Editor . . . . . . . . . . . . . . . . . . . . . . . . . . . . . . . .Rich Place
    e-mail: salpressnews@verizon.net

*Offices and agencies generally appear in alphabetical order, except when specific order is requested by listee.*

## SARANAC LAKE

**Adirondack Daily Enterprise** *Weekday Circulation: 5,000*

**Adirondack Publishing Co Inc**
54 Broadway, PO Box 318, Saranac Lake, NY 12983
518-891-2600  Fax: 518-891-2756
e-mail: adenews@adirondackdailyenterprise.com
Web site: www.adirondackdailyenterprise.com
Publisher . . . . . . . . . . . . . . . . . . . . . . . . . . . . . . . . . . . . . . . . .Catherine Moore
    e-mail: cmoore@adirondackdailyenterprise.com
Managing Editor . . . . . . . . . . . . . . . . . . . . . . . . . . . . . . . . . .Peter Crowley
    e-mail: pcrowley@adirondackdailyenterprise.com
News Editor. . . . . . . . . . . . . . . . . . . . . . . . . . . . . . . . . . . . . .Brittany Proulx
    e-mail: adenews@adirondackdailyenterprise.com
Circulation Manager . . . . . . . . . . . . . . . . . . . . . . . . . . . . . .Trinity Bushey
    e-mail: circulation@adirondackdailyenterprise.com

## SARATOGA SPRINGS

**Saratogian (The)** *Weekday Circulation: 10,000*

**Digital First Media**
20 Lake Avenue, Saratoga Springs, NY 12866
518-584-4242  Fax: 518-587-7750
e-mail: news@saratogian.com
Web site: www.saratogian.com
Publisher . . . . . . . . . . . . . . . . . . . . . . . . . . . . . . . . . . . . . . . . .Bob O'Leary
Managing Editor. . . . . . . . . . . . . . . . . . . . . . . . . . . . . . . . . .Charlie Krabel
Circulation District Manager . . . . . . . . . . . . . . . . . . . . . . .Joe Anderson
    e-mail: janderson@digitalfirstmedia.com

## SCHENECTADY

**Daily Gazette (The)** *Weekday Circulation: 53,800*

**Daily Gazette Co**
2345 Maxon Road Extension, Schenectady, NY 12308
518-374-4141  Fax: 518-395-3089
e-mail: news@dailygazette.com
Web site: www.dailygazette.com
Publisher. . . . . . . . . . . . . . . . . . . . . . . . . . . . . . . . . . . .John E N Hume, III
City Editor . . . . . . . . . . . . . . . . . . . . . . . . . . . . . . . . . . . . . . . . . .Irv Dean
News Editor. . . . . . . . . . . . . . . . . . . . . . . . . . . . . . . . . . . . . .William Finelli
Online Editor . . . . . . . . . . . . . . . . . . . . . . . . . . . . . . . . . . . . .Jeffrey Haff
Day City Editor . . . . . . . . . . . . . . . . . . . . . . . . . . . . . . . . . . . .Miles Reed
Circulation Supervisor. . . . . . . . . . . . . . . . . . . . . . . . . . . . . .Brian Zarelli

## STATEN ISLAND

**Staten Island Advance** *Circulation: Monday, Tuesday, Wednesday, Friday: 59,000; Thursday: 67,000; Sunday: 77,000*

**Advance Publications Inc**
950 Fingerboard Rd, Staten Island, NY 10305
718-981-1234  Fax: 718-981-5679
e-mail: editor@siadvance.com
Web site: www.silive.com
Publisher . . . . . . . . . . . . . . . . . . . . . . . . . . . . .Caroline Diamond Harrison
Circulation Manager. . . . . . . . . . . . . . . . . . . . . . . . . . . . .Richard Salemo
    e-mail: salemo@siadvance.com
Editor . . . . . . . . . . . . . . . . . . . . . . . . . . . . . . . . . . . . . . . .Brian J. Laline
    e-mail: laline@siadvance.com
Managing Editor . . . . . . . . . . . . . . . . . . . . . . . . . . . . . .William A. Huus
Editorial Page Editor. . . . . . . . . . . . . . . . . . . . . . . . . . . . . .Mark Hanley
    e-mail: hanley@siadvance.com
City Editor . . . . . . . . . . . . . . . . . . . . . . . . . . . . . . . . . . . . .Tom Checchi
    e-mail: checchi@siadvance.com
News Editor. . . . . . . . . . . . . . . . . . . . . . . . . . . . . . . . . . . . .Richard Ryan
    e-mail: ryan@siadvance.com

## SYRACUSE

**Post-Standard (The)** *Weekday Circulation: 115,000*

**Syracuse Newspapers Inc**
PO Box 4915, Syracuse, NY 13221
315-470-0011  Fax: 315-470-3081
e-mail: business@syracuse.com
Web site: www.syracusemediagroup.com
Vice President of Content . . . . . . . . . . . . . . . . . . . . . . . .Michael J Connor
    e-mail: mconnor@syracuse.com
Director of Content. . . . . . . . . . . . . . . . . . . . . . . . . . . . . . .John Lammers
    e-mail: jlammers@syracuse.com
Director of Publications . . . . . . . . . . . . . . . . . . . . . . . . . . .Stan Linhorst
    e-mail: slinhorst@syracuse.com
Managing Producer/Editor . . . . . . . . . . . . . . . . . . . . .Steven M. Billmeyer
    e-mail: sbillmeyer@syracuse.com

## TONAWANDA

**Tonawanda News** *Weekday Circulation: 9,000*

**Greater Niagara Newspapers**
435 River Road, PO Box 668, North Tonawanda, NY 14120-6809
716-693-1000  Fax: 716-693-0124
e-mail: newsroom@tonawanda-news.com
Web site: www.tonawanda-news.com
Managing Editor. . . . . . . . . . . . . . . . . . . . . . . . . . . . . . . . . . .Eric DuVall
Circulation Director . . . . . . . . . . . . . . . . . . . . . . . . . . . . . . .Ken Skryp
Advertising Director . . . . . . . . . . . . . . . . . . . . . . . . . . . . . .John Brundo
Publisher. . . . . . . . . . . . . . . . . . . . . . . . . . . . . . . . . . . . . . . . . .Peter Mio

## TROY

**Record (The)** *Weekday Circulation: 16,872*

**Digital First Media**
270 River Triangle, Suite 202B, Troy, NY 12180
518-270-1200  Fax: 518-270-1202
e-mail: letters@troyrecord.com
Web site: www.troyrecord.com
Publisher . . . . . . . . . . . . . . . . . . . . . . . . . . . . . . . . . . . . . . . .Bob O'Leary
Editor . . . . . . . . . . . . . . . . . . . . . . . . . . . . . . . . . . . . . . . . .Charlie Krabel
Chief Content Editor . . . . . . . . . . . . . . . . . . . . . . . . . . . . .Paul Tackett
Circulation District Manager . . . . . . . . . . . . . . . . . . . . . .Joe Anderson
    e-mail: janderson@digitalfirstmedia.com

## UTICA

**Observer-Dispatch** *Weekday Circulation: 45,956*

**GateHouse Media**
221 Oriskany Plz, Utica, NY 13501
315-792-5000  Fax: 315-792-5033
e-mail: news@uticaod.com
Web site: www.uticaod.com
President/Publisher . . . . . . . . . . . . . . . . . . . . . . . . . . . . .Donna Donovan
Editor . . . . . . . . . . . . . . . . . . . . . . . . . . . . . . . . . . . . . . . . . .Kris Worrell
Managing Editor . . . . . . . . . . . . . . . . . . . . . . . . . . . . . . . . . .Ron Johns
    e-mail: rjohns1@uticaod.com
News Editor. . . . . . . . . . . . . . . . . . . . . . . . . . . . . . . . . . . . .Fran Perritano

*Offices and agencies generally appear in alphabetical order, except when specific order is requested by listee.*

## WATERTOWN

**Watertown Daily Times** *Weekday Circulation: 27,020*

### Johnson Newspaper Corp
260 Washington St, Watertown, NY 13601
315-782-1000  Fax: 315-661-2523
e-mail: news@wdt.net
Web site: www.watertowndailytimes.com
Executive Editor . . . . . . . . . . . . . . . . . . . . . . . . . . . . . . . . . . . .Bert Gault
Managing Editor . . . . . . . . . . . . . . . . . . . . . . . . . . . . . .Robert Gorman
Editorial Page Editor. . . . . . . . . . . . . . . . . . . . . . . . . . .Francis Pound
Editor (Sunday) . . . . . . . . . . . . . . . . . . . . . . . . . . . . . . .Mary Kaskan

## WELLSVILLE

**Wellsville Daily Reporter/Spectator** *Weekday Circulation: 4,400*

### Gate House Media
159 N Main St, Wellsville, NY 14895
585-593-5300  Fax: 585-593-5303
e-mail: editor@wellsvilledaily.com
Web site: www.wellsvilledaily.com
Publisher . . . . . . . . . . . . . . . . . . . . . . . . . . . . . . . . . . . . . . .Oak Duke
Editor . . . . . . . . . . . . . . . . . . . . . . . . . . . . . . . . . . . . . .John Anderson
Reporter . . . . . . . . . . . . . . . . . . . . . . . . . . . . . . . . . . . .Kathryn Ross
Sports. . . . . . . . . . . . . . . . . . . . . . . . . . . . . . . . . . . . . .Heather Matta

## NEWS SERVICES/MAGAZINES

### ABC News (New York Bureau)
47 W 66th St, New York, NY 10023
212-456-7777  Fax: 212-456-2795
Web site: www.abcnews.go.com
President & Publisher . . . . . . . . . . . . . . . . . . . . . . . . . . . .Ellen Archer
Bureau Chief . . . . . . . . . . . . . . . . . . . . . . . . . . . . . . .Amy Brenholts
Director/Domestic News. . . . . . . . . . . . . . . . . . . . . . . . .Wendy Fisher

### American Metal Market
225 Park Avenue South, 6th Floor, New York, NY 10003
212-213-6202  Fax: 212-213-6617
e-mail: helpdesk@amm.com
Web site: www.amm.com
President . . . . . . . . . . . . . . . . . . . . . . . . . . . . . . . . . .Raju Daswani
   e-mail: rdaswani@amm.com
Editor. . . . . . . . . . . . . . . . . . . . . . . . . . . . . . .Jo Isenberg-O'Loughlin
   e-mail: jisenberg@amm.com
Senior Vice President . . . . . . . . . . . . . . . . . . . . . . . . . . .David Brooks
   e-mail: dbrooks@amm.com
Deputy Managing Editor . . . . . . . . . . . . . . . . . . . . . .Josephine Mason
   e-mail: jmason@amm.com
Chief Correspondent, Steel . . . . . . . . . . . . . . . . . . . . .Scott Robertson
   e-mail: srobertson@amm.com

### Associated Press (New York/Metro)
450 West 33rd St, New York, NY 10001
212-621-1500 or 212-621-5447  Fax: 212-621-1679
e-mail: info@ap.org
Web site: www.ap.org
Bureau Chief. . . . . . . . . . . . . . . . . . . . . . . . . . . . . .Howard Goldberg
   e-mail: hgoldberg@ap.org
Executive Editor . . . . . . . . . . . . . . . . . . . . . . . . . . .Kathleen Carroll
Editor/West Region . . . . . . . . . . . . . . . . . . . . . . . . . . . . .Traci Carl
Editor/Asia Pacific . . . . . . . . . . . . . . . . . . . . . . . . .Brian Carovillano
Editor/South Region. . . . . . . . . . . . . . . . . . . . . . . . . . . . .Lisa Pane
Editor/Central Region . . . . . . . . . . . . . . . . . . . . . . . . . .David Scott

### BNA (formerly Bureau of National Affairs)
PO Box 7169, Albany, NY 12224
518-399-8414  Fax: 518-399-8403
Web site: www.bna.com
NYS Correspondent. . . . . . . . . . . . . . . . . . . . . . . . . .Gerald Silverman

### Business Review
40 British American Blvd, Latham, NY 12110
518-640-6800  Fax: 518-640-6801
e-mail: albany@bizjournals.com
Web site: www.bizjournals.com/albany
Publisher . . . . . . . . . . . . . . . . . . . . . . . . . . . . . . . . . .Carolyn Jones
   e-mail: cjones@bizjournals.com
Managing Editor. . . . . . . . . . . . . . . . . . . . . . . . . . . . .Neil Springer
   e-mail: nspringer@bizjournals.com

### CBS News (New York)
51 West 52nd St, New York, NY 10019-6188
212-975-4321  Fax: 212-975-9387
Web site: www.cbsnews.com
Editor-in-Chief . . . . . . . . . . . . . . . . . . . . . . . . . . . .Jeremy Murphy
Executive Editor . . . . . . . . . . . . . . . . . . . . . . . . . . . . . .Jack Otter
Executive Story Editor. . . . . . . . . . . . . . . . . . . . . . . .Victoria M. Gordon
Executive News Producer . . . . . . . . . . . . . . . . . . . . . . .Peter Wilgoren
News Planning Editor . . . . . . . . . . . . . . . . . . . . . . . . . .Abby Lawing
News Planning Editor. . . . . . . . . . . . . . . . . . . . . . . . .Gretchen White
News Writer . . . . . . . . . . . . . . . . . . . . . . . . . . . . . . . .Arlene Lebe
News Director. . . . . . . . . . . . . . . . . . . . . . . . . . . . . . .Jeff Hatthorn

### Central New York Business Journal
231 Walton Street, Syracuse, NY 13202
315-472-3104  Fax: 315-472-3644
e-mail: info@cnybj.com
Web site: www.cnybj.com
Publisher. . . . . . . . . . . . . . . . . . . . . . . . . . . . . . . .Norman Poltenson
   e-mail: npoltenson@cnybj.com
Editor-in-Chief . . . . . . . . . . . . . . . . . . . . . . . . . . . . . .Adam Rombel
   e-mail: arombel@cnybj.com

### City Journal (Manhattan Institute for Policy Research)
52 Vanderbilt Ave, 3rd Floor, New York, NY 10017
212-599-7000  Fax: 212-599-0371
Web site: www.city-journal.org
Editor. . . . . . . . . . . . . . . . . . . . . . . . . . . . . . . . .Brian C Anderson
Managing Editor. . . . . . . . . . . . . . . . . . . . . . . . . .Benjamin Plotinsky

### Crain's New York Business
711 Third Ave, New York, NY 10017
212-210-0100  Fax: 212-210-0799
e-mail: ecordova@crainsnewyork.com
Web site: www.crainsnewyork.com
Publisher & Vice President . . . . . . . . . . . . . . . . . . . . . . .Jill Kaplan
   e-mail: jkaplan@crainsnewyork.com
Editor. . . . . . . . . . . . . . . . . . . . . . . . . . . . . . . . . .Glenn Coleman
   e-mail: gcoleman@crainsnewyork.com
Managing Editor . . . . . . . . . . . . . . . . . . . . . . . . . . . .Jeremy Smerd
   e-mail: jsmerd@crainsnewyork.com
Deputy Managing Editor. . . . . . . . . . . . . . . . . . . . . . . .Valerie Block
   e-mail: vblock@crainsnewyork.com
Copy Chief . . . . . . . . . . . . . . . . . . . . . . . . . . . . . .Stephen Noveck
   e-mail: snoveck@crainsnewyork.com

### Cuyler News Service
PO Box 7205, State Capitol, Albany, NY 12224
518-465-1745  Fax: 518-465-6849
e-mail: efmnews@aol.com
Owner . . . . . . . . . . . . . . . . . . . . . . . . . . . . . . . . .Elizabeth G Flood
Contact . . . . . . . . . . . . . . . . . . . . . . . . . . . . . . . . . .Janet Sanders
Contact . . . . . . . . . . . . . . . . . . . . . . . . . . . . . . . . . .Amy Despirito

*Offices and agencies generally appear in alphabetical order, except when specific order is requested by listee.*

News Media

**Dow Jones Newswires (Dow Jones & Company)**
1155 Ave of the Americas, 7th Fl, New York, NY 10036
201-938-5400  Fax: 201-938-5600
Web site: www.dowjonesnews.com
Editor-in-Chief . . . . . . . . . . . . . . . . . . . . . . . . . . . . . . . .Gerard Baker
Managing Editor . . . . . . . . . . . . . . . . . . . . . . . . . .Neal Lipschutz

**Empire State Report (CINN Worldwide Inc)**
PO Box 9001, Mount Vernon, NY 10553
914-966-3180  Fax: 914-966-3264
e-mail: empire@cinn.com
Editor/Publisher . . . . . . . . . . . . . . . . . . . . . . . . . . . . .Steve Acunto
Head of Circulation . . . . . . . . . . . . . . . . . . . . . . . . .Jennifer Jehn

**Gannett News Service**
150 State St, 2nd Fl, Albany, NY 12207
518-436-9781  Fax: 518-436-0130
Web site: www.gannett.com
Bureau Chief . . . . . . . . . . . . . . . . . . . . . . . . . . . . .Joseph Spector
   e-mail: spector@gannett.com
Correspondent . . . . . . . . . . . . . . . . . . . . . . . . . . . .Jon Campbell
Correspondent . . . . . . . . . . . . . . . . . . . . . . . . . . . .Cara Matthews
   e-mail: clmatthe@gannett.com

**Hudson Valley Business Journal**
86 East Main Street, Wappingers Falls, NY 12590
845-298-6236  Fax: 845-298-6238
e-mail: debhvbj@gmail.com
Web site: www.hvbj.com
Publisher . . . . . . . . . . . . . . . . . . . . . . . . . . . .Debbie Kwiatoski
   e-mail: debhvbj@gmail.com

**ITAR-TASS News Agency**
780 Third Ave, 19th Fl, New York, NY 10017
212-245-4250  Fax: 212-245-4258
Web site: www.itar-tass.com
Bureau Chief . . . . . . . . . . . . . . . . . . . . . . . . . . . .Vladimir Kikilo

**Legislative Correspondents Association**
PO Box 7340, State Capitol, 3rd Fl, Albany, NY 12224
518-455-2388
Press Room Supervisor . . . . . . . . . . . . . . . . . . . . . . . . .Jean Gutbtodt
President . . . . . . . . . . . . . . . . . . . . . . . . . . . . . . . . .Brendan Scott

**Long Island Business News**
2150 Smithtown Avenue, Ronkonkoma, NY 11779
631-737-1700  Fax: 631-737-1890
e-mail: editor@libn.com
Web site: www.libn.com
Managing Editor . . . . . . . . . . . . . . . . . . . . . . . . . . . .Andrea Jones
Publisher . . . . . . . . . . . . . . . . . . . . . . . . . . . . . . .John Kominicki

**Mid-Hudson News Network**
42 Marcy Lane, Middletown, NY 10941
845-537-1500 or 845-695-2923  Fax: 845-692-2921
e-mail: news@midhudsonnews.com
Web site: www.midhudsonnews.com
Managing Director/Publisher . . . . . . . . . . . . . . . . . . . . . .Hank Gross
. . . . . . . . . . . . . . . . . . . . . . . . . . . . . . . . . . . . . . . . . . . . . . . . .
President/NBC News . . . . . . . . . . . . . . . . . . . . . . . . . . .Steve Capus
SVP/News Marketing and Communications . . . . . . . . . . . . . .Lauren Kapp

**NY Capitolwire**
172 W State St, Trenton, NJ 08608
717-986-0225
e-mail: info@capitolwire.com
Web site: www.capitolwire.com
President/Publisher . . . . . . . . . . . . . . . . . . . . . . . . . . . .Craig Leach

**New York Magazine (New York Media, LLC)**
75 Varick Street, 4th Floor, New York, NY 10013
212-508-0700  Fax: 212-221-9195
Web site: www.nymag.com
Editor-in-Chief . . . . . . . . . . . . . . . . . . . . . . . . . . . . . . . .Adam Moss
Executive Editor . . . . . . . . . . . . . . . . . . . . . . . . . . . .John Homans
Managing Editor . . . . . . . . . . . . . . . . . . . . . . . . . . . . .Ann Clarke
Publisher . . . . . . . . . . . . . . . . . . . . . . . . . . . .Lawrence Burstein
. . . . . . . . . . . . . . . . . . . . . . . . . . . . . . . . . . . . . . . .Jared Hohlt

**Newsweek/The Daily Beast**
7 Hanover Sq, New York, NY 10004
212-445-4600  Fax: 212-445-4425
Web site: www.newsweek.com
Publisher . . . . . . . . . . . . . . . . . . . . . . . . . . . . .Rhona Murphy
Editor/Newsweek International . . . . . . . . . . . . . . . . . . . . .Fareed Zakaria
Executive Editor . . . . . . . . . . . . . . . . . . . . .Justine A. Rosenthal
Editor-at-Large . . . . . . . . . . . . . . . . . . . . . . . . . . . . .Kyle Pope

**Ottaway News Service (NYS only)**
N State Capitol, 3rd Fl, Albany, NY 12224
518-463-1157  Fax: 518-463-7486
Legislative Correspondent . . . . . . . . . . . . . . . . . . . . . . .John Milgrim

**Reuters (Thomson Reuters Markets LLC)**
3 Times Square, New York, NY 10036
646-223-4000  Fax: 646-223-4001
Web site: www.reuters.com
Bureau Chief . . . . . . . . . . . . . . . . . . . . . . . . . . . . .Matthew Bigg
Editor-in-Chief . . . . . . . . . . . . . . . . . . . . . . . . .Stephen J. Adler
Chief White House Correspondent . . . . . . . . . . . . . . . . .Steve Holland
Correspondent . . . . . . . . . . . . . . . . . . . . . . . . . . . .Scott Malone
Correspondent . . . . . . . . . . . . . . . . . . . . . . . . . . . . .Sam Nelson

**Rochester Business Journal**
45 E Avenue, Suite 500, Rochester, NY 14604
585-546-8303  Fax: 585-546-3398
e-mail: rbj@rbj.net
Web site: www.rbjdaily.com
Editor/Vice President . . . . . . . . . . . . . . . . . . . . . . . . . . .Paul Ericson
Associate Editor . . . . . . . . . . . . . . . . . . . . . . . . . . . .Smriti Jacob
Managing Editor . . . . . . . . . . . . . . . . . . . . . . . .Michael Dickinson
President/Publisher . . . . . . . . . . . . . . . . . . . . . . . . .Susan Holliday

**Scripps Howard News Service**
1090 Vermont Ave NW, Ste 1000, Washington, DC 20005
202-408-1484  Fax: 202-408-2062
Web site: www.shns.com
Desk Editor . . . . . . . . . . . . . . . . . . . . . . . . . . . .Carol Guensburg
Photo Editor . . . . . . . . . . . . . . . . . . . . . . . . . . . . .Sheila Person
   e-mail: persons@shns.com
Content Editor . . . . . . . . . . . . . . . . . . . . . . . . . . . .Carolyn Cerbin
National Correspondent . . . . . . . . . . . . . . . . . . . . .Thomas Hargrove

## RADIO

*Stations included in this chapter produce news and/or public affairs programming and are listed alphabetically by primary service area.*

## ALBANY

**WAMC (90.3 FM)**
WAMC, Northeast Public Radio, PO Box 66600, Albany, NY 12206
518-465-5233 or 800-323-9262  Fax: 518-432-6974
Web site: www.wamc.org
President & CEO . . . . . . . . . . . . . . . . . . . . . . . . . . . .Alan Chartock
Associate News Director . . . . . . . . . . . . . . . . . . . . . . . .Joe Donahue
News Director . . . . . . . . . . . . . . . . . . . . . . . . . . . . . . . .Ian Pickus

---

*Offices and agencies generally appear in alphabetical order, except when specific order is requested by listee.*

## BALDWINSVILLE

**WSEN (92.1 FM)**
8456 Smokey Hollow Road, PO Box 1050, Baldwinsville, NY 13027-1050
315-635-3971  Fax: 315-635-3490
General Manager . . . . . . . . . . . . . . . . . . . . . . . . . . . . . . . . . . . . . Judy Kelly

## BATH

**WCIK (103.1 FM)**
7634 Campbell Creek Rd, PO Box 506, Bath, NY 14810-0506
607-776-4151  Fax: 607-776-6929
e-mail: mail@fln.org
Web site: www.fln.org
President/General Manager . . . . . . . . . . . . . . . . . . . . . . . . . Rick Snavely
Program Director . . . . . . . . . . . . . . . . . . . . . . . . . . . . . . . . . . . John Owens
VP/CFO . . . . . . . . . . . . . . . . . . . . . . . . . . . . . . . . . . . . . . . . . Dick Snavely

## BEACON

**WSPK (104.7 FM)**
715 Rte 52, PO Box 310, Beacon, NY 12508
845-838-6000  Fax: 845-838-2109
Web site: www.k104online.com
General Manager . . . . . . . . . . . . . . . . . . . . . . . . . . . . Jason Finkelberg
Promotions Director . . . . . . . . . . . . . . . . . . . . . . . . . . . . Megan Denaut
News Director . . . . . . . . . . . . . . . . . . . . . . . . . . . . . . . . . Allison Dunne
News Director . . . . . . . . . . . . . . . . . . . . . . . . . . . . . . . . . . . . Brian Jones

## BINGHAMTON

**WINR (680 AM)**
320 N Jensen Road, Vestal, NY 13850
607-584-5800  Fax: 607-584-5900
Web site: www.680winr.com
General Manager . . . . . . . . . . . . . . . . . . . . . . . . . . . . . . . . Tom Barney
News Director . . . . . . . . . . . . . . . . . . . . . . . . . . . . . . . . . . . Dave Lozzi

**WNBF (1290 AM)**
PO Box 414, Binghamton, NY 13902-0414
607-772-8400  Fax: 607-772-9806
Web site: www.wnbf.com
News Director . . . . . . . . . . . . . . . . . . . . . . . . . . . . . . . . Bernie Fionte
Program Director . . . . . . . . . . . . . . . . . . . . . . . . . . . . . . . . Roger Neal
Talk Show Host . . . . . . . . . . . . . . . . . . . . . . . . . . . . . . . . Tony Russell

**WSKG (89.3 FM), WSQX (91.5 FM)**
PO Box 3000, Binghamton, NY 13902
607-729-0100  Fax: 607-729-7328
Web site: www.wskg.com
Program Director . . . . . . . . . . . . . . . . . . . . . . . . . . . . . Ken Campbell
Music Director . . . . . . . . . . . . . . . . . . . . . . . . . . . . . . . . . . Bill Snyder
President . . . . . . . . . . . . . . . . . . . . . . . . . . . . . . . . . . . . . . Brian Sickora

## BRONX

**WFUV (90.7 FM)**
441 East Fordham Road, Fordham University, Bronx, NY 10458-5149
718-817-4550  Fax: 718-365-9815
e-mail: thefolks@wfuv.org
Web site: www.wfuv.org
General Manager . . . . . . . . . . . . . . . . . . . . . . . . . . . Chuck Singleton
    e-mail: chucksingleton@wfuv.org
News & Public Affairs Director . . . . . . . . . . . . . . . . . . George Bodarky
Program Director . . . . . . . . . . . . . . . . . . . . . . . . . . . . . . Rita Houston

## BUFFALO

**WBEN (930 AM/FM)**
800 Corporate Parkway, Suite 200, Buffalo, NY 14226
716-803-0930 or 716-843-0600  Fax: 716-832-3080
Web site: www.wben.com
Operations Manager . . . . . . . . . . . . . . . . . . . . . . . . . . . . . Tim Wenger
Anchor/Reporter/Editor . . . . . . . . . . . . . . . . . . . . . . . . . . Dave Debo
Sales Director . . . . . . . . . . . . . . . . . . . . . . . . . . . . . . . . . . . . Tim Holly

**WBLK (93.7 FM), WJYE (96.1 FM)**
14 Lafayette Sq, Ste 1300, Buffalo, NY 14203
716-852-9393 or 800-828-2191  Fax: 716-852-9390
Web site: www.wjye.com; www.wblk.com
General Manager . . . . . . . . . . . . . . . . . . . . . . . . . . . . . . . . . Jeff Silver
Production & Program Director . . . . . . . . . . . . . . . . . . Chris Reynolds
Production Director . . . . . . . . . . . . . . . . . . . . . . . . . . . . Frank Dawkins
Program Director (WJYE) . . . . . . . . . . . . . . . . . . . . . . . . . . Joe Chille

**WDCX (99.5 FM)**
625 Delaware Avenue, Suite 308, Buffalo, NY 14202
716-883-3010  Fax: 716-883-3606
Web site: www.wdcxfm.com
General Manager . . . . . . . . . . . . . . . . . . . . . . . . . . . . . . . Nev Larson
Writer/Producer . . . . . . . . . . . . . . . . . . . . . . . . . . . . . Keri Cardinale
Chief Engineer . . . . . . . . . . . . . . . . . . . . . . . . . . . . Brian Cunningham

**WHTT (104.1 FM)**
50 James Casey Drive, Buffalo, NY 14206
716-881-4555  Fax: 716-884-2931
Web site: www.whtt.com
Regional President . . . . . . . . . . . . . . . . . . . . . . . . . . . Kevin LeGrett
General Manager . . . . . . . . . . . . . . . . . . . . . . . . . . . Chet Osadchey
Program Director . . . . . . . . . . . . . . . . . . . . . . . . . . . . . Joe Siragusa

**WNED (94.5 FM)**
140 Lower Terr., PO Box 1263, Buffalo, NY 14240-1263
716-845-7000  Fax: 716-845-7043
Web site: www.wned.org
Program Director . . . . . . . . . . . . . . . . . . . . . . . . . . . . . Al Wallack
News Director . . . . . . . . . . . . . . . . . . . . . . . . . . . . . . . . . . Jim Ranney

**WYRK (106.5 FM), WBUF (92.9 FM)**
14 Lafayette Sq., Suite 1200, Buffalo, NY 14203
716-852-9292  Fax: 716-852-9290
General Manager . . . . . . . . . . . . . . . . . . . . . . . . . . . . . . . . . Jeff Silver
Program Director (WYRK) . . . . . . . . . . . . . . . . . . . . . . . . RW Smith
Program Director (WBUF) . . . . . . . . . . . . . . . . . . . . . . . . . Joe Russo
Sales Manager (WYRK) . . . . . . . . . . . . . . . . . . . . . . Mark Plimpton
General Sales Manager (WBUF) . . . . . . . . . . . . . . . . Rose Vecchiarelli

## CHAMPLAIN

**WCHP (760 AM)**
137 Rapids Road, PO Box 888, Champlain, NY 12919
518-298-2800  Fax: 518-298-2604
Web site: www.wchp.com
General Manager . . . . . . . . . . . . . . . . . . . . . . . . . . . . . . . Teri Billiter
Program Director . . . . . . . . . . . . . . . . . . . . . . . . . . . . . Brandi Lloyd
Operations Manager . . . . . . . . . . . . . . . . . . . . . . . . . . . Tonya Billiter

## CORTLAND

**WKRT (920 AM), WIII (99.9 or 100.3 FM)**
277 Tompkins Street, Cortland, NY 13045
607-257-6400  Fax: 607-257-6497
Web site: www.i100rocks.com
General Manager . . . . . . . . . . . . . . . . . . . . . . . . . . . . Susan Johnston
Operations Manager . . . . . . . . . . . . . . . . . . . . . . . . . . . Chris Allinger
Director of Sales . . . . . . . . . . . . . . . . . . . . . . . . . . . . Margaret Tollner

*Offices and agencies generally appear in alphabetical order, except when specific order is requested by listee.*

News Media

## ELMIRA

**WPGI (100.9 FM), WWLZ (820 AM)**
2205 College Avenue, Elmira, NY 14903-1201
607-732-4400  Fax: 607-732-7774
General Manager (WWLZ).............................Kevin White
Program Director (WWLZ)..............................Scott Free
Program Director (WWLZ).........................James Poteat

## HORNELL

**WKPQ (105.3 FM)**
1484 Beech St, PO Box 726, Hornell, NY 14843-9404
607-654-0322  Fax: 877-575-1320
General Manager.....................................Kevin White
Station Manager............................Richard O Stevenson

## HORSEHEADS

**WMTT (94.7 FM)**
734 Chemung Street, Horseheads, NY 14845
607-795-0795  Fax: 607-795-1095
General Manager....................................George Hawras
Opertions Manager..................................Steve Shimer
Station Manager ........................................Bob Smith

## ITHACA

**WHCU (870 AM)**
1751 Hanshaw Road, Ithaca, NY 14850
607-257-6400  Fax: 607-257-6497
General Manager...................................Susan Johnston
BPD/News Director/Program Director......................Geoff Dunn

## JAMESTOWN

**WKZA (106.9 FM)**
106 West 3rd Street, Suite 106, Jamestown, NY 14701
716-487-1106 or 866-367-1069  Fax: 716-488-2169
Web site: www.1069kissfm.com
Sales Manager ...................................Sherrie Brookmire
Program Director .................................Steve Rockford

## LATHAM

**WROW (590 AM)**
6 Johnson Road, Latham, NY 12110-5641
518-786-6600  Fax: 518-786-6695
e-mail: wrownews@albanybroadcasting.com
Web site: www.wrow.com
General Manager.......................................Dan Austin
News Director.........................................Mike Carey
Public Affairs Director .................................Joe Condon
  e-mail: jcondon@albanyradio.net
Program Director ....................................Scott Miller

**WPYX (106.5 FM), WRVE (99.5 FM)**
1203 Troy Schenectady Road, Latham, NY 12110
518-452-4800  Fax: 518-452-4813
e-mail: feedback@pyx106.com
Web site: www.pyx106.com
Operations Manager & Program Director (WPYX)..........John Cooper
  e-mail: johncooper@clearchannel.com
VP/General Manager..............................Kristen Delaney

## NEW ROCHELLE

**WVOX (1460 AM)**
1 Broadcast Forum, New Rochelle, NY 10801-2094
914-636-1460  Fax: 914-636-2900
e-mail: don@wvox.com
Web site: www.wvox.com
Editorial Director/President/CEO...............William O'Shaughnessy
Operations Manager ...................................Don Stevens

## NEW YORK CITY

**WABC (770 AM)**
2 Penn Plaza, 17th Floor, New York, NY 10121
212-613-3800  Fax: 212-613-3823
Web site: www.wabcradio.com
Program Director/News Director..........................Phil Boyce
General Manager.......................................Mitch Dolan
Promotions Director...................................Eric Lemieux
  e-mail: ericlemieux@clearchannel.com
Promotions Director/Public Affairs .......................Russ King
Music Director........................................Eric Wellman
  e-mail: ericwellman@clearchannel.com

**WBBR (1130 AM) Bloomberg News**
499 Park Avenue, New York, NY 10022-1240
212-318-2300 or 800-955-4003  Fax: 917-369-5000
Web site: www.bloomberg.com/radio
Editor-in-Chief......................................Matthew Winkler
Managing Editor....................................Michael Clancy
Press Contact......................................Amanda Cowie

**WCBS (880 AM)**
345 Hudson Street, New York, NY 10014
212-975-4321  Fax: 212-975-4675
e-mail: wcbsamdesk@wcbs880.com
Web site: www.wcbs880.com
General Manager/VP....................................Chad Brown
Director of News & Programming .......................Tim Scheld
  e-mail: tscheld@wcbs880.com

**WINS (1010 AM)**
345 Hudson Street, 10th Floor, New York, NY 10014
212-315-7000  Fax: 212-315-7015
e-mail: mevorach@wins.com
Web site: www.1010wins.com
News Director......................................Ben Mevorach
  e-mail: mevorach@wins.com
News Editor...........................................Ralph Saro
  e-mail: saro@wins.com

**WLTW (106.7 FM)**
32 Avenue of the Americas, New York, NY 10013
212-377-7900  Fax: 212-603-4602
Web site: www.1067litefm.com
Program Director.......................................Jim Ryan
Marketing Director..................................Susan Bacich

**WOR (710 AM)**
32 Avenue of the Americas, New York, NY 10013
212-337-7900
Web site: www.wor710.com
General Manager....................................Jerry Crowley
News Director........................................Joe Bartlett

---

*Offices and agencies generally appear in alphabetical order, except when specific order is requested by listee.*

## OLEAN

**WPIG (95.7 FM), WHDL (1450 AM)**
3163 NYS Route 417, Olean, NY 14760-1853
716-372-0161 or 800-877-9749  Fax: 716-372-0164
Web site: www.wpig.com
General Manager.......................................John Morton
Program Manager ..................................Mark Thompson

## PEEKSKILL

**WHUD (100.7 FM)**
715 Rte 52, Box 310, Beacon, NY 12508
845-838-6000  Fax: 845-838-2109
e-mail: newsroom@pamal.com
Web site: www.whud.com
General Manager ..................................Jason Finkelberg
Program Director....................................Steve Petrone
    e-mail: spetrone@pamal.com
News Director .........................................Brian Jones
    e-mail: newsroom@pamal.com

## MIDDLETOWN

**WRRV (92.7 FM)**
2 Pendell Road, Poughkeepsie, NY 12601
845-471-1500  Fax: 845-454-1204
Web site: www.wrrv.com
Business Manager ..................................Kathy Butsko
    e-mail: kathy.butsko@cumulus.com
Program Directory...................................Andrew Boris
    e-mail: andrew.boris@cumulus.com

## POUGHKEEPSIE

**WPDH (101.5 FM)**
2 Pendell Road, Poughkeepsie, NY 12601
845-471-1500  Fax: 845-454-1204
Web site: www.wpdh.com
Business Manager ..................................Kathy Butsko
Program Director....................................Andrew Boris
Branch Manager ..................................Chuck Benfer
Promotions Manager.............................Anthony Verano

## ROCHESTER

**WHAM (1180 AM)**
1700 HSBC Plaza, 100 Chestnut Street, Rochester, NY 14604-2016
585-454-4884  Fax: 585-454-5081
Web site: www.wham1180.com
Station Manager.....................................Jeff Howlett
Promotions Director ..................................Brian Guck
    e-mail: brianguck@clearchannel.com
News Director .......................................Randy Gorbman

## SCHENECTADY

**WGNA (107.7 FM)**
1241 Kings Road, Suite 4200, Schenectady, NY 12303
518-881-1515 or 800-476-1077  Fax: 518-881-1516
Web site: www.wgna.com
Regional Vice President/General Manager...............Robert Ausfeld
Operations Manager/Program Director ..................Tom Jacobsen
Station Manager......................................John Hirsh
Music Director .......................................Bill Earley

## SYRACUSE

**WNTQ (93.1 FM), WAQX (95.7 FM)**
1064 James St, Syracuse, NY 13203
315-472-0200  Fax: 315-478-5625
Web site: www.93Q.com; www.95x.com
General Manager ....................................Dan Austin
Program Director (WNTQ)..............................Janice Cole
Program Director (WAQX).............................Hunter Scott

**WVOA (103.9 FM)**
7095 Myers Road, East Syracuse, NY 13057-9748
315-656-2231  Fax: 315-656-2259
e-mail: programming@wvoaradio.com
Web site: www.wvoaradio.com
General Manager ....................................Sam Furco
Public Service Coordinator .........................Susan Anderson
Music Director .......................................Allen Elson

**WYYY (94.5 FM)**
500 Plum St, Suite 100, Syracuse, NY 13204
315-472-9797  Fax: 315-472-1904
Web site: www.sybercuse.com
Program Director....................................Kathy Rowe
Operations Manager..................................Rich Lauber
    e-mail: richlauber@clearchannel.com

## UTICA

**WOUR (96.9 FM)**
39 Kellogg Rd, New Hartford, NY 13413
315-797-0803  Fax: 315-738-1073
Web site: www.wour.com
General Manager/Sales Manager .....................Brian Delaney
    e-mail: brianelany@clearchannel.com
Program Director.....................................Tom Starr
    e-mail: tomstarr@clearchannel.com

## WATERTOWN

**WFRY (97.5 FM)**
134 Mullin Street, Watertown, NY 13601
315-788-0790  Fax: 315-788-4379
Web site: www.froggy97.com
General Manager....................................Don Wagner
Program Director....................................Matt Raisman

## TELEVISION

*Stations included in this chapter produce news and/or public affairs programming and are listed alphabetically by primary service area.*

## ALBANY

**WMHT (17) Public Broadcasting-NY Capitol Region**
4 Global View Road, Troy, NY 12180
518-880-3400  Fax: 518-880-3409
e-mail: email@wmht.org
Web site: www.wmht.org
Production Manager ............................Dominick Figliomeni
    e-mail: dfigliomeni@wmht.org
Producer/Director...................................Joanne Durfee
    e-mail: jdurfee@wmht.org
Senior Producer/Director ..............................Dave Povero
    e-mail: dpovero@wmht.org
President/CEO ......................................Robert Altman
    e-mail: raltman@wmht.org
Chief Technology Officer.........................Anthony Tassarotti
    e-mail: atassarotti@wmht.org

*Offices and agencies generally appear in alphabetical order, except when specific order is requested by listee.*

News Media

## WNYT (12)
715 N Pearl Street, PO Box 4035, Albany, NY 12204
518-486-4991 or 518-207-4700  Fax: 518-434-0659
e-mail: comments@wnyt.com
Web site: www.wnyt.com
General Manager . . . . . . . . . . . . . . . . . . . . . . . . . . . Steve Baboulis
    e-mail: sbaboulis@wnyt.com
Director Public Affairs/Programming . . . . . . . . . . . . . . . Maryann Ryan
    e-mail: maryan@wnyt.com
News Director . . . . . . . . . . . . . . . . . . . . . . . . . . . . . . . Paul Lewis
General Sales Manager . . . . . . . . . . . . . . . . . . . . . . . . Tony McManus
Engineering Director . . . . . . . . . . . . . . . . . . . . . . . . . . Richard Klein

## WRGB (6)
1400 Balltown Rd, Schenectady, NY 12309
518-346-6666 or 800-666-3355  Fax: 518-381-3736
e-mail: news@cbs6albany.com
Web site: www.cbs6albany.com
General Manager . . . . . . . . . . . . . . . . . . . . . . . . . . . . Bob Furlong
News Director/Station Manager . . . . . . . . . . . . . . . . . Lisa Jackson
Production Manager . . . . . . . . . . . . . . . . . . . . . . . . . . Bill Brandt
Producer . . . . . . . . . . . . . . . . . . . . . . . . . . . . . . . . . . Jessica Harrison

## WTEN (10)
341 Northern Blvd, Albany, NY 12204
518-436-4822 or 800-888-9836  Fax: 518-462-6065
e-mail: news@news10.com
Web site: www.news10.com
Senior Producer . . . . . . . . . . . . . . . . . . . . . . . . . . . . Jeanne Beatty
Programming Coordinator . . . . . . . . . . . . . . . . . . . . . Chris Terwilliger
President & General Manager . . . . . . . . . . . . . . . . . . . Rene LaSpina

## WXXA (23)
341 Northern Blvd, Albany, NY 12204
518-436-4822  Fax: 518-426-4792
e-mail: news@news10.com
Web site: www.news10.com
General Manager . . . . . . . . . . . . . . . . . . . . . . . . . . . . Ron Romines
News Director . . . . . . . . . . . . . . . . . . . . . . . . . . . . . . Matt Miller
President . . . . . . . . . . . . . . . . . . . . . . . . . . . . . . . . . . Sheldon Galloway
Program Director . . . . . . . . . . . . . . . . . . . . . . . . . . . Paul Pelliccia

## WYPX DT-50
1 Charles Blvd, Guilderland, NY 12084
518-464-0143 or 800-646-7296  Fax: 518-464-0633
Station Manager . . . . . . . . . . . . . . . . . . . . . . . . . . . . Renee Osterlitz
Public Service Director . . . . . . . . . . . . . . . . . . . . . . . Chris Iorio

### BINGHAMTON

## WBNG-TV (7)
560 Columbia Dr, Johnson City, NY 13790
607-729-8812  Fax: 607-797-6211
e-mail: wbng@wbngtv.com
Web site: www.wbng.com
News Director . . . . . . . . . . . . . . . . . . . . . . . . . . . . . . Greg Catlin
President/General Manager . . . . . . . . . . . . . . . . . . . . Matt Rosenfeld

## WICZ (40)
4600 Vestal Pkwy E, Vestal, NY 13850
607-770-4040  Fax: 607-798-7950
e-mail: fox40@wicz.com
Web site: www.wicz.com
General Manager . . . . . . . . . . . . . . . . . . . . . . . . . . . . John Leet
    e-mail: wicztv@aol.com
News Director . . . . . . . . . . . . . . . . . . . . . . . . . . . . . . Suh Neubauer
    e-mail: fox40suh@wicz.com
Program Director . . . . . . . . . . . . . . . . . . . . . . . . . . . Vernon Rowlands
News Director . . . . . . . . . . . . . . . . . . . . . . . . . . . . . . Kent Garrett

## WIVT (34)
203 Ingraham Hill Rd, Binghamton, NY 13903
607-771-3434  Fax: 607-723-1034
Web site: www.newschannel34.com
News Director . . . . . . . . . . . . . . . . . . . . . . . . . . . . . . Jim Ehmke
Promotions Manager . . . . . . . . . . . . . . . . . . . . . . . . . Jim La Vasser

## WSKG (46) Public Broadcasting
601 Gates Road, Vestal, NY 13850
607-729-0100  Fax: 607-729-7328
Web site: www.wskg.org
President/CEO/General Mgr . . . . . . . . . . . . . . . . . . . Brian Sicora
Station Manager . . . . . . . . . . . . . . . . . . . . . . . . . . . . Juan Martinez
Operations Director/General Sales Mgr . . . . . . . . . . . Nancy Christensen

### BUFFALO

## WGRZ (33)
259 Delaware Ave, Buffalo, NY 14202
716-849-2222 or 716-849-2200  Fax: 716-849-7602
e-mail: newsdesk@wgrz.com
Web site: www.wgrz.com
News Director . . . . . . . . . . . . . . . . . . . . . . . . . . . . . . Jeff Woodard
    e-mail: ecrookge@wgrz.gannett.com
Assignment Editor . . . . . . . . . . . . . . . . . . . . . . . . . . . Maria Sisti
General Manager/President . . . . . . . . . . . . . . . . . . . . Jim Toellner

## WIVB-TV (39)
2077 Elmwood Ave, Buffalo, NY 14207
716-874-4410  Fax: 716-879-4896
e-mail: newsroom@wivb.com
Web site: www.wivb.com
News Director . . . . . . . . . . . . . . . . . . . . . . . . . . . . . . Joseph Schlaerth
Senior Producer . . . . . . . . . . . . . . . . . . . . . . . . . . . . Vic Baker
Producer . . . . . . . . . . . . . . . . . . . . . . . . . . . . . . . . . . Mary Czopp
News Producer . . . . . . . . . . . . . . . . . . . . . . . . . . . . . Lynne Donley
Executive Producer . . . . . . . . . . . . . . . . . . . . . . . . . . Jeff Sabato
Producer . . . . . . . . . . . . . . . . . . . . . . . . . . . . . . . . . . Andrew Tamutus

## WKBW-TV (38)
7 Broadcast Plaza, Buffalo, NY 14202
716-845-6100  Fax: 716-842-1855
e-mail: news@wkbw.com
Web site: www.wkbw.com
News Director . . . . . . . . . . . . . . . . . . . . . . . . . . . . . . Glen Horn
Station Manager . . . . . . . . . . . . . . . . . . . . . . . . . . . . Michael Nurse
Senior Producer . . . . . . . . . . . . . . . . . . . . . . . . . . . . Paula D'Amico

## WNED (43) Western NY Public Broadcasting
Horizon's Plaza, 140 Lower Terr., PO Box 1263, Buffalo, NY 14202
716-845-7000  Fax: 716-845-7036
Web site: www.wned.org
Station Manager . . . . . . . . . . . . . . . . . . . . . . . . . . . . Ron Santora
VP TV Production . . . . . . . . . . . . . . . . . . . . . . . . . . . David Rotterman
    e-mail: drotterman@wned.org

## WETM (18)
101 E Water Street, Box 1207, Elmira, NY 14901
607-733-5518  Fax: 607-734-1176
Web site: www.wetmtv.com
General Manager . . . . . . . . . . . . . . . . . . . . . . . . . . . . Randy Reid
News Director . . . . . . . . . . . . . . . . . . . . . . . . . . . . . . Scott Nichols
Chief Managing Editor . . . . . . . . . . . . . . . . . . . . . . . . Jeff Stone

*Offices and agencies generally appear in alphabetical order, except when specific order is requested by listee.*

## HORSEHEADS

**WENY (36)**
474 Old Ithaca Rd, Horseheads, NY 14845
607-739-3636  Fax: 607-739-1418
Web site: www.weny.com
Anchor . . . . . . . . . . . . . . . . . . . . . . . . . . . . . . . . . . . . . . . . .Sarah Sheridan
Executive Producer. . . . . . . . . . . . . . . . . . . . . . . . . . . . . . . . .Renata Stiehl
News Director . . . . . . . . . . . . . . . . . . . . . . . . . . . . . . . . . . . . .Scott Cook
President & CEO. . . . . . . . . . . . . . . . . . . . . . . . . . . . . . . . . . .Kevin Lilly

## KINGSTON

**WRNN (48)**
800 Westchester Avenue, Suite S-640, Rye Brook, NY 10573
914-417-2700  Fax: 914-696-0279
e-mail: comments@rnntv.com
Web site: www.rnntv.com
General Manager. . . . . . . . . . . . . . . . . . . . . . . . . . . . . . . . . . .Richard French
Executive Producer . . . . . . . . . . . . . . . . . . . . . . . . . . . . . . . . .Don Dudley

## LONG ISLAND

**WLIW (21) Public Broadcasting**
Box 21, Plainview, NY 11803
516-367-2100  Fax: 516-692-7629
e-mail: programming@wliw.org
Web site: www.wliw.org
General Manager. . . . . . . . . . . . . . . . . . . . . . . . . . . . . . . . . . .Terrel Cass
        e-mail: terrel_cass@wliw.pbs.org
Executive Producer . . . . . . . . . . . . . . . . . . . . . . . . . . . . . . . . .Tom Casciato
President . . . . . . . . . . . . . . . . . . . . . . . . . . . . . . . . . . . . . . . . .Neal Shapiro

## MELVILLE

**WLNY (47)**
270 S Service Road, Suite 55, Melville, NY 11747
631-777-8855  Fax: 631-777-8180
Web site: www.wlnytv.com
Sales VP . . . . . . . . . . . . . . . . . . . . . . . . . . . . . . . . . . . . . . . . .Elliot Simmons
News Director. . . . . . . . . . . . . . . . . . . . . . . . . . . . . . . . . . . . . .Richard Rose

## NEW YORK CITY

**Bloomberg Television**
499 Park Avenue, New York, NY 10022
212-318-2300  Fax: 917-617-5999
Web site: www.bloomberg.com/tv/
Editor-in-Chief. . . . . . . . . . . . . . . . . . . . . . . . . . . . . . . . . . . . .Matthew Winkler
Managing Editor. . . . . . . . . . . . . . . . . . . . . . . . . . . . . . . . . . . .Michael Clancy
Press Contact. . . . . . . . . . . . . . . . . . . . . . . . . . . . . . . . . . . . . .Amanda Cowie

**Fox News Channel**
1211 Ave of the Americas, 2nd Floor, New York, NY 10036
212-301-3000 or 888-369-4762  Fax: 212-301-8274
e-mail: newsmanager@foxnews.com
Web site: www.foxnews.com
SVP/News Operations. . . . . . . . . . . . . . . . . . . . . . . . . . . . . . . .Sharri Berg
EVP/Executive Editor . . . . . . . . . . . . . . . . . . . . . . . . . . . . . . .John Moody
EVP/News . . . . . . . . . . . . . . . . . . . . . . . . . . . . . . . . . . . . . . . .Michael Clemente

**New York 1 News (1)**
75 Ninth Avenue, New York, NY 10011
212-691-6397  Fax: 212-379-3575
Web site: www.ny1.com
Albany Reporter . . . . . . . . . . . . . . . . . . . . . . . . . . . . . . . . . . . .Erin Billups
Geeral Assignment Reporter . . . . . . . . . . . . . . . . . . . . . . . . . .Roger Clark
Anchor. . . . . . . . . . . . . . . . . . . . . . . . . . . . . . . . . . . . . . . . . . .Lewis Dodley
Politcal Reporter . . . . . . . . . . . . . . . . . . . . . . . . . . . . . . . . . . .Bobby Cuza

**WABC (7)**
7 Lincoln Sq, New York, NY 10023
917-260-7697  Fax: 212-456-2290
Web site: www.7online.com
News Director. . . . . . . . . . . . . . . . . . . . . . . . . . . . . . . . . . . . . .Ken Plotnik
VP of Programming . . . . . . . . . . . . . . . . . . . . . . . . . . . . . . . . .Art Moore
Executive Producer . . . . . . . . . . . . . . . . . . . . . . . . . . . . . . . . .Nancy Kennedy

**WCBS (2)**
524 W 57th St, 8th Fl, New York, NY 10019
212-975-4321  Fax: 212-975-4677
e-mail: cbsnewyork@cbs.com
Web site: www.wcbstv.com
News Director. . . . . . . . . . . . . . . . . . . . . . . . . . . . . . . . . . . . . .David M. Friend
Executive Producer . . . . . . . . . . . . . . . . . . . . . . . . . . . . . . . . .Byron Harmon
        e-mail: bharmon@cbs.com

**WNBC (4)**
30 Rockefeller Plaza, New York, NY 10112
212-664-4444  Fax: 212-664-2994
e-mail: newstips@wnbc.com
Web site: www.wnbc.com
Executive Editor. . . . . . . . . . . . . . . . . . . . . . . . . . . . . . . . . . . .Richard Wolfe
VP/News & Product . . . . . . . . . . . . . . . . . . . . . . . . . . . . . . . . .Gregory Gittrich
Editor. . . . . . . . . . . . . . . . . . . . . . . . . . . . . . . . . . . . . . . . . . . .Erica Tilles
Senior Editor . . . . . . . . . . . . . . . . . . . . . . . . . . . . . . . . . . . . . .John Baiata

**WNYW (44)**
205 E 67th St, New York, NY 10021
212-452-5555  Fax: 212-452-5750
Web site: www.myfoxny.com
Executive Producer . . . . . . . . . . . . . . . . . . . . . . . . . . . . . . . . .Byron Harmon
News Writer . . . . . . . . . . . . . . . . . . . . . . . . . . . . . . . . . . . . . . .Donielle Stanton

**WPIX (11)**
220 East 42nd St, 2nd Fl, New York, NY 10017
212-210-2411  Fax: 212-210-2591
e-mail: news@pix11.com
Web site: www.pix11.com
Executive Producer. . . . . . . . . . . . . . . . . . . . . . . . . . . . . . . . . .Monica Zack
Editor. . . . . . . . . . . . . . . . . . . . . . . . . . . . . . . . . . . . . . . . . . . .Brian Waizel
Editor . . . . . . . . . . . . . . . . . . . . . . . . . . . . . . . . . . . . . . . . . . .Reynaldo Meno
Senior Editor . . . . . . . . . . . . . . . . . . . . . . . . . . . . . . . . . . . . . .Jennifer Tanaka

**WWOR (UPN 9)**
205 E 67th Street, New York, NY 10065-6050
212-852-7000  Fax: 212-852-7145
Web site: www.my9tv.com
President & Editor . . . . . . . . . . . . . . . . . . . . . . . . . . . . . . . . . .Edwin A. Finn, Jr.
Managing Editor . . . . . . . . . . . . . . . . . . . . . . . . . . . . . . . . . . .Richard Rescigno
Senior Deputy Managing Editor . . . . . . . . . . . . . . . . . . . . . . .Jonathan Krim

## PLATTSBURGH

**WPTZ (5) NBC**
5 Television Dr, Plattsburgh, NY 12901
518-561-5555  Fax: 518-561-5940
e-mail: newstips@wptz.com
Web site: www.wptz.com
President/General Manager . . . . . . . . . . . . . . . . . . . . . . . . . . . .Paul Sands
News Director . . . . . . . . . . . . . . . . . . . . . . . . . . . . . . . . . . . . . .Kyle Grimes
Assignment Editor. . . . . . . . . . . . . . . . . . . . . . . . . . . . . . . . . . .Matt Morin

*Offices and agencies generally appear in alphabetical order, except when specific order is requested by listee.*

**News Media**

## ROCHESTER

**WHEC (10)**
191 East Ave, Rochester, NY 14604
585-546-5670  Fax: 585-546-5688
e-mail: news1@whec.com
News Director.........................................Mike Goldrick
Producer ...............................................Carla Hanlon
Executive Producer ...................................Ray Sullivan
   e-mail: news1@whec.com

**WHAM (13)**
4225 W Henrietta Road, Box 20555, Rochester, NY 14623
585-334-8700  Fax: 585-359-1570
e-mail: feedback@13wham.com
General Manager......................................Chuck Samuels
   e-mail: csamuels@13wham.com
TV Community Affairs Director......................Charlotte Clarke
News Director.........................................Matt Malyn
General Manager .....................................Kent Beckwith
   e-mail: kbeckwith@13wham.com
Executive Producer ...................................Brad Smith

**WXXI (16) Public Broadcasting**
280 State St, PO Box 30021, Rochester, NY 14603
585-325-7500  Fax: 585-258-0335
Web site: www.wxxi.org
Executive Producer/Assistant VP ....................Todd Mccammon
   e-mail: wxxi@wxxi.org
Vice President, Television ...........................Elissa Orlando
   e-mail: emarra@wxxi.org
News Director.........................................Peter Iglinksi
   e-mail: newsroom@wxxi.org

## SYRACUSE

**WCNY (25)**
415 W Fayette Street, PO Box 2400, Syracuse, NY 13220-2400
315-453-2424  Fax: 315-451-8824
Web site: www.wcny.org
Program Manager ....................................Dale Wagner
President/CEO ........................................Robert Daino
   e-mail: robert_daino@wcny.org
News/Public Affairs Director .......................Susan Arbetter

**WSYR (17)**
5904 Bridge St, Box 699, East Syracuse, NY 13057
315-446-9999  Fax: 315-446-9283
e-mail: newschannel9@9wsyr.com
Web site: www.9wsyr.com
News Director.........................................Jim Tortora
VP/General Manager..................................Theresa Underwood

**WSTM (24)**
1030 James St, Syracuse, NY 13203
315-477-9400  Fax: 315-474-5082
Web site: www.wstm.com
Anchor................................................Matt Mulcahy
Chief Investigative Reporter .........................Jim Kenyon
   e-mail: pphillip@wstm.com
Chief Engineer ......................................Kevin Tubbs
   e-mail: pphillip@wstm.com
News Director.........................................Peggy Phillip

**WSYT (19)**
1000 James St, Syracuse, NY 13203
315-472-6800  Fax: 315-471-8889
e-mail: info@wsyt68.com
Web site: www.wsyt68.com
Program Coordinator .................................Becky Walsh

**WTVH (47)**
980 James St, Syracuse, NY 13203
315-425-5555  Fax: 315-425-5513
Web site: www.wtvh.com
Executive Producer ...................................Megan Tennyson
General Manager/President............................Matt Rosenfeld
News Director.........................................Frank Kracher

## UTICA

**WKTV (29)**
5936 Smith Hill Rd, PO Box 2, Utica, NY 13503
315-733-0404  Fax: 315-793-3498
e-mail: newslink2@wktv.com
Web site: www.wktv.com
Program Director......................................Tom Coyne
News Director.........................................Steve McMurray
   e-mail: smcmurray@wktv.com
Vice President/General Manager.......................Vic Vetters

## WATERTOWN

**WWNY (7)**
120 Arcade St, Watertown, NY 13601
315-788-3800  Fax: 315-788-3787
e-mail: wwny@wwnytv.net
Web site: www.wwnytv.net
General Manager......................................Cathy Pircsuk
   e-mail: cpircsuk@wwnytv.net
News Director ........................................Scott Atkinson
   e-mail: satkinsn@wwnytv.net
Producer/Assistant News Director ....................Anne Richter

**WWTI (21)**
Box 6250, 1222 Arsenal St, Watertown, NY 13601
315-785-8850  Fax: 315-785-0127
Web site: www.newswatch50.com
General Mgr/Sales Mgr ..............................David J Males
News Director.........................................John Moore
   e-mail: johnmoore@clearchannel.com

*Offices and agencies generally appear in alphabetical order, except when specific order is requested by listee.*

# Section 7:
# EDUCATION

## COLLEGES AND UNIVERSITIES

## STATE UNIVERSITY OF NEW YORK

### SUNY Board of Trustees
State University of New York
State University Plz
353 Broadway
Albany, NY 12246
518-320-1157 or 800-342-3811  Fax: 518-443-5131
e-mail: trustees@suny.edu
Web site: www.suny.edu

Chair:
    H. Carl McCall . . . . . . . . . . . . . . . . . . . . . . . . . . .212-239-2362
Vice Chair:
    Merryl Tisch
Member:
    Joseph Belluck . . . . . . . . . . . . . . . . . . . . . . . . .315-320-1157
Member:
    Courtney Burke . . . . . . . . . . . . . . . . . . . . . . . . .315-320-1157
Member:
    Marc Cohen . . . . . . . . . . . . . . . . . . . . . . . . . . .315-320-1157
Member:
    Eric Corngold . . . . . . . . . . . . . . . . . . . . . . . . . .315-320-1157
Member:
    Robert Duffy . . . . . . . . . . . . . . . . . . . . . . . . . . .315-320-1157
Member:
    Angelo Fatta . . . . . . . . . . . . . . . . . . . . . . . . . . .518-320-1157
Member:
    Gwen Kay . . . . . . . . . . . . . . . . . . . . . . . . . . . . .518-320-1157
Member:
    Eunice A. Lewin . . . . . . . . . . . . . . . . . . . . . . . .518-320-1157
Member:
    Marshall Lichtman . . . . . . . . . . . . . . . . . . . . . . .518-320-1157
Member:
    Stanley Litow . . . . . . . . . . . . . . . . . . . . . . . . . .518-320-1157
Member:
    Richard Socarides . . . . . . . . . . . . . . . . . . . . . . .518-320-1157
Member:
    Carl Spielvogel . . . . . . . . . . . . . . . . . . . . . . . . .212-641-6522
Member:
    Edward Spiro . . . . . . . . . . . . . . . . . . . . . . . . . .518-320-1157
Member:
    Cary Staller . . . . . . . . . . . . . . . . . . . . . . . . . . .518-320-1157
Member:
    Nina Tamrowski . . . . . . . . . . . . . . . . . . . . . . . . .518-320-1157

### SUNY System Administration & Executive Council
State University Plz
353 Broadway
Albany, NY 12246
518-443-5555

Chancellor:
    Kristina Johnson . . . . . . . . . . . . . . . . . . . . . . . .518-320-1355
Chief Officer, Academic Health & Hospitals:
    Ricardo Azziz
Vice Chancellor for Academic Affairs & Vice Provost:
    Elizabeth L. Bringsjord . . . . . . . . . . . . . . . . . . . .518-320-1356
President, Research Foundation of SUNY:
    Jeff Cheek
President, Student Assembly:
    Marc Cohen
Senior Vice Chancellor for Community Colleges & the Education Pipeline:
    Johanna Duncan-Poitier . . . . . . . . . . . . . . . . . . .518-320-1276
Vice Chancellor for Legal Affairs & General Counsel:
    Elizabeth Garvey

Vice Chancellor for Capital Facilities & General Manager/Construction Fund:
    Robert Haelen . . . . . . . . . . . . . . . . . . . . . . . . . .518-320-1502
University Faculty Senate President:
    Gwen Kay
Senior Vice Chancellor for Finance & Chief Financial Officer:
    Eileen McLoughlin
Vice Chancellor & Chief Diversity Officer:
    Carlos Medina . . . . . . . . . . . . . . . . . . . . . . . . . .518-320-1176
Senior Vice Chancellor & Chief Operating Officer:
    Robert Megna
Senior Vice Chancellor for Strategic Initiatives & Chief of Staff:
    Teresa Miller
Senior Advisor for External Affairs & Government Relations:
    Allison Newman
Senior Vice Chancellor for Executive Leadership & Employee Development:
    Joseph Porter
Faculty Council of Community Colleges President:
    Nina Tamrowski
Interim Provost & Vice Chancellor for Research & Economic Development:
    Grace Wang

### Rockefeller Institute of Government . . . . . . . . . . . fax: 518-443-5788
411 State St, Albany, NY 12203-1003
518-443-5522  Fax: 518-443-5788
Web site: www.rockinst.org
President:
    Jim Malatras
Director of Policy & Research:
    Thomas Gais . . . . . . . . . . . . . . . . . . . . . . . . . . .518-443-5238
Deputy Director for Research:
    Patricia Strach
Chief of Staff:
    Heather Trela
Director of Communications:
    Kyle Adams
Assistant Director of Policy & Research; Executive Director, Center for Law & Policy Solutions:
    Katie Zuber
Policy Analyst:
    Young Joo Park
Chief External Relations Officer:
    Stacey Hengsterman
Project Coordinator, Regional Gun Violence Research Consortium:
    Nicholas Simons
Director of Publications:
    Michael Cooper
Staff Assistant for Publications:
    Michelle Charbonneau
Senior Staff Assistant for Finance & Administration:
    Heather Stone
Senior Staff Assistant for Finance & Administration:
    Patricia Cadrette
Research Scholar:
    Urska Klancnik
Administrative Staff Assistant:
    Nicolle Otty
General Mechanic:
    Malvin Lumpkin

### SUNY Center for Student Recruitment . . . . . . . . fax: 518-320-1573
33 W 42nd St (across from Bryant Park), New York, NY 10036
212-364-5821  Fax: 518-320-1573
e-mail: csr@suny.edu
Web site: www.suny.edu/student/mrc.cfm
Director:
    Beryl S. Jeffers
Associate Director for Financial Aid Services:
    Julieta Schiffino
Assistant to the Director for Special Programs:
    Gail Reilly

*Offices and agencies generally appear in alphabetical order, except when specific order is requested by listee.*

Colleges, Universities & School Districts

Admissions Recruitment Advisor:
Cynthia Marino
Admissions Recruitment Advisor:
Beverly Santos

**Small Business Development Center**
10 North Pearl St., Albany, NY 12246
518-944-2840 or 800-732-7232
Web site: www.nyssbdc.org
State Director:
Brian Goldstein

**State University Construction Fund**
353 Broadway, Albany, NY 12246
518-320-3200
Web site: www.sucf.suny.edu
General Manager:
Robert Haelen . . . . . . . . . . . . . . . . . . . . . . . . . . . .518-320-1502

### UNIVERSITY CENTERS

**Binghamton University, State University of New York**
4400 Vestal Parkway East
PO Box 6000
Binghamton, NY 13902-6000
607-777-2000
e-mail: info@binghamton.edu
Web site: www.binghamton.edu

President:
Harvey G. Stenger . . . . . . . . . . . . . . .607-777-2131/fax: 607-777-2533
e-mail: president@binghamton.edu

**College of Agriculture & Life Sciences at Cornell University**
260 Roberts Hall
Ithaca, NY 14853-5905
607-255-5335
e-mail: calsdean@cornell.edu
Web site: www.cals.cornell.edu

Dean:
Kathryn Boor . . . . . . . . . . . . . . . . . . . . . . . . .607-255-2241
e-mail: kjb4@cornell.edu

**College of Human Ecology at Cornell University**
1300 Martha Van Rensselaer Hall
Ithaca, NY 14853-4401
607-255-2247
e-mail: humec_admissions@cornell.edu
Web site: www.human.cornell.edu

Dean:
Alan Mathios. . . . . . . . . . . . . . . . . . . . . . . . . .607-255-2138
e-mail: adm5@cornell.edu

**College of Veterinary Medicine at Cornell University**
S2-005 Schurman Hall
Ithaca, NY 14853-6401
607-253-3000  Fax: 607-253-3701
Web site: www.vet.cornell.edu

Dean:
Lorin D Warnick. . . . . . . . . . . . . . . . . . . . . . . .607-253-3771
e-mail: paj4@cornell.edu

**NYS College of Ceramics at Alfred University**
One Saxon Drive
Alfred, NY 14802
607-871-2137  Fax: 607-871-2339
Web site: www.alfred.edu

Provost:
W Richard Stephens . . . . . . . . . . . . . . . . . . . . .607-871-2137
e-mail: stephens@alfred.edu

**SUNY Downstate Medical Center**
450 Clarkson Ave
Brooklyn, NY 11203
718-270-1000  Fax: 718-270-7592
Web site: www.downstate.edu

President:
Wayne Riley . . . . . . . . . . . . . . . . . . . . . . . . . . .718-270-2611

**SUNY State College of Optometry**
33 West 42nd St
New York, NY 10036-8003
212-938-4000 or 212-938-4001
Web site: www.sunyopt.edu

President:
Dr David A Heath. . . . . . . . . . . . . . . . . . . . . . . .212-938-5650
e-mail: dheath@sunyopt.edu

**SUNY Upstate Medical University**
750 E Adams St
Syracuse, NY 13210-2375
315-464-5540  Fax: 315-464-4838
Web site: www.upstate.edu

President:
Danielle Laraque-Arena . . . . . . . . . . . . . . . . . . . .315-464-5540

**School of Industrial & Labor Relations at Cornell University (ILR School)**
309 Ives Hall
Ithaca, NY 14853
607-255-2762  Fax: 607-255-7774
Web site: www.ilr.cornell.edu

Dean:
Kevin F Hallock . . . . . . . . . . . . . . . . . . . . . . . .607-255-2185
e-mail: hallock@cornell.edu

**State University of New York at Albany**
1400 Washington Ave
Albany, NY 12222
518-442-3300
Web site: www.albany.edu

President:
Havidán Rodríguez. . . . . . . . . . . . . . . . . . . . . . .518-956-8010
e-mail: presmail@albany.edu

**State University of New York College of Environmental Science & Forestry**
One Forestry Dr
Syracuse, NY 13210
315-470-6500 or TDD: 315-470-6966  Fax: 315-470-6933
e-mail: esfinfo@esf.edu
Web site: www.esf.edu

*Offices and agencies generally appear in alphabetical order, except when specific order is requested by listee.*

President:
Quentin D Wheeler . . . . . . . . . . . . . . . .315-470-6681/fax: 315-470-6977
e-mail: qwheeler@esf.edu

## Stony Brook University, SUNY
301 Administration Bldg
Stony Brook, NY 11794-0701
631-632-6000
Web site: www.sunysb.edu

President:
Samuel L Stanley. . . . . . . . . . . . . . . . .631-632-6265/fax: 631-632-6621

## University at Buffalo, State University of New York
501 Capen Hall
Buffalo, NY 14260
716-645-2000
Web site: www.buffalo.edu

President:
Satish K Tripathu. . . . . . . . . . . . . . . . .716-645-2901/fax: 716-645-3728
Interim President:
Bahgat G Sammakia
e-mail: president@sunypoly.edu

### UNIVERSITY COLLEGES

## Buffalo State College
1300 Elmwood Ave
Buffalo, NY 14222-1095
716-878-4000 or TTD 716-878-3182  Fax: 716-878-3039
e-mail: webadmin@buffalostate.edu
Web site: www.buffalostate.edu

President:
Katherine S Conway-Turner . . . . . . . . . .716-878-4101/fax: 716-878-6527
e-mail: president@buffalostate.edu

## College at Brockport
350 New Campus Dr
Brockport, NY 14420
585-395-2211 or 585-395-2796  Fax: 585-395-2401
Web site: www.brockport.edu

President:
Heidi Macpherson. . . . . . . . . . . . . . . . . . . . . . . . . . . .585-395-2361
e-mail: president@brockport.edu

## Purchase College, State University of New York
735 Anderson Hill Rd
Purchase, NY 10577
914-251-6000
Web site: www.purchase.edu

President:
Thomas J Schwarz. . . . . . . . . . . . . . . . .914-251-6010/fax: 914-251-6014
e-mail: thomas.schwarz@purchase.edu

## State University at Old Westbury
223 Store Hill Rd
PO Box 210
Old Westbury, NY 11568-0210
516-876-3000

President:
Calvin O Butts, III . . . . . . . . . . . . . . . .516-876-3160/fax: 516-876-3347
e-mail: buttsc@oldwestbury.edu

## State University at Potsdam
44 Pierrepont Ave
Potsdam, NY 13676
315-267-2000 or 877-768-7326
Web site: www.potsdam.edu

President:
Kristin G Esterberg . . . . . . . . . . . . . . . .315-267-2100/fax: 315-267-2496
e-mail: president@potsdam.edu

## State University College at Cortland
Graham Ave
PO Box 2000
Cortland, NY 13045-0900
607-753-2011  Fax: 607-753-5688
Web site: www.cortland.edu

President:
Erik J Bitterbaum. . . . . . . . . . . . . . . . . .607-753-2201/fax: 607-753-5993
e-mail: president@cortland.edu

## State University College at Geneseo
1 College Circle
Geneseo, NY 14454-1450
585-245-5000  Fax: 585-245-5005
e-mail: web@geneseo.edu
Web site: www.geneseo.edu

President:
Denise A Battles . . . . . . . . . . . . . . . . . .585-245-5501/fax: 585-245-5555
e-mail: president@geneseo.edu

## State University College at New Paltz
1 Hawk Drive
New Paltz, NY 12561
845-257-7869 or 877-696-7411  Fax: 845-257-3009
Web site: www.newpaltz.edu

President:
Donald Christian . . . . . . . . . . . . . . . . . .845-257-3288/fax: 845-257-3389
e-mail: president@newpaltz.edu

## State University Empire State College
Two Union Ave
Saratoga Springs, NY 12866
518-587-2100 or 800-847-3000  Fax: 518-587-3033
Web site: www.esc.edu

Officer in Charge:
Mitchell S Nesler . . . . . . . . . . . .518-587-2100 x2260/fax: 518-587-2886
e-mail: president@esc.edu
President:
Virginia Horvath. . . . . . . . . . . . . . . . . . . . . . . . . . . .716-673-3456
e-mail: horvath@fredonia.edu

## State University of New York at Oneonta
108 Ravine Pkwy
Oneonta, NY 13820
607-436-3500
Web site: www.oneonta.edu

President:
Nancy Kleniewski . . . . . . . . . . . . . . . . .607-436-2500/fax: 607-436-3089
e-mail: klenien@oneonta.edu

*Offices and agencies generally appear in alphabetical order, except when specific order is requested by listee.*

## State University of New York at Oswego
7060 Route 104
706 Culkin Hall
Oswego, NY 13126
315-312-2500 Fax: 315-312-2863
Web site: www.oswego.edu

President:
Deborah F Stanley ................................315-312-2211
e-mail: stanley@oswego.edu

## State University of New York at Plattsburgh
101 Broad St
Plattsburgh, NY 12901
518-564-2000 Fax: 518-564-2094
Web site: www.plattsburgh.edu

President:
John Ettling ....................518-564-2010/fax: 518-564-3932
e-mail: president_office@plattsburgh.edu

### COLLEGES OF TECHNOLOGY

## Alfred State College of Technology
10 Upper College Dr
Alfred, NY 14802
607-587-4215 or 800-425-3733 Fax: 607-587-4299
Web site: www.alfredstate.edu

President:
Skip Sullivan ....................607-587-4010/fax: 607-587-4209
e-mail: sullivid@alfredstate.edu

## Farmingdale State College of Technology
2350 Broadhollow Rd
Farmingdale, NY 11735-1021
631-420-2000 Fax: 631-420-2633
Web site: www.farmingdale.edu

President:
John S Nader ....................631-420-2239/fax: 631-420-2753
e-mail: president@farmingdale.edu

## Morrisville State College
Administration Bldg, South St
PO Box 901
Morrisville, NY 13408
315-684-6000 or 800-258-0111 Fax: 315-684-6116
Web site: www.morrisville.edu

President:
David E Rogers ...................315-684-6044/fax: 315-684-6109

## SUNY College of Agriculture & Technology at Cobleskill
106 Suffolk Circle
Knapp Hall Room 202
Cobleskill, NY 12043
518-255-5011 or 800-295-8988 Fax: 518-255-6769
Web site: www.cobleskill.edu

President:
Marion Terenzio ....................................518-255-5111

## State University College of Technology at Canton
34 Cornell Drive
Canton, NY 13617

315-386-7011 or 800-388-7123 Fax: 315-386-7929
e-mail: admissions@canton.edu
Web site: www.canton.edu

President:
Zvi Szafran .....................315-386-7204/fax: 315-386-7934
e-mail: president@canton.edu

## State University College of Technology at Delhi
454 Delhi Drive
Delhi, NY 13753
607-746-4000 or 800-963-3544 Fax: 607-746-4104
Web site: www.delhi.edu

President:
Michael R Laliberte.................607-746-4090/fax: 607-746-4346

## State University Institute of Technology
Horatio St, Marcy Campus
100 Seymour Road
Utica, NY 13502
315-792-7500 Fax: 315-792-7837
Web site: www.sunyit.edu

Interim President:
Wolf Yeigh .......................315-792-7400/fax: 315-792-7407

## State University of New York Maritime College
6 Pennyfield Ave
Throgs Neck, NY 10465
718-409-7200 or 800-642-1874 Fax: 718-409-7465
Web site: www.sunymaritime.edu

President:
Michael A Alfultis ..................................718-409-7271

### COMMUNITY COLLEGES

## Adirondack Community College
640 Bay Rd
Queensbury, NY 12804
518-743-2200 or 888-789-9235 Fax: 518-745-1433
e-mail: info@sunyacc.edu
Web site: www.sunyacc.edu

President:
Kristine D Duffy ..................518-743-2237/fax: 518-743-2262
e-mail: duffyk@sunyacc.edu

## Broome Community College
PO Box 1017
Binghamton, NY 13902
607-778-5000 Fax: 607-778-5310
Web site: www.sunybroome.edu

President:
Kevin E Drumm ....................................607-778-5100
e-mail: drummke@sunybroome.edu

## Cayuga Community College
197 Franklin St
Auburn, NY 13021
315-255-1743 or 866-598-8883 Fax: 315-255-2117
Web site: www.cayuga-cc.edu

President:
Brian M Durant ...........................315-255-1743 x2207
e-mail: bdurant@cayuga-cc.edu

*Offices and agencies generally appear in alphabetical order, except when specific order is requested by listee.*

## Clinton Community College
136 Clinton Point Dr
Plattsburgh, NY 12901
518-562-4200  Fax: 518-562-4159
Web site: www.clinton.edu

President:
  Ray DiPasquale....................................518-562-4100

## Columbia-Greene Community College
4400 Route 23
Hudson, NY 12534-0327
518-828-4181  Fax: 518-828-8543
e-mail: info@sunycgcc.edu
Web site: www.sunycgcc.edu

President:
  James R Campion .............518-828-4181x3325/fax: 518-822-2006
  e-mail: campion@sunycgcc.edu

## Corning Community College
1 Academic Dr
Corning, NY 14830
607-962-9222 or 800-358-7171  Fax: 607-962-9456
Web site: www.corning-cc.edu

President:
  Katherine P Douglas ...............607-962-9232/fax: 607-962-9485
  e-mail: president@corning-cc.edu

## Dutchess Community College
53 Pendell Rd
Poughkeepsie, NY 12601-1595
845-431-8000  Fax: 845-431-8984
Web site: www.sunydutchess.edu

President:
  Pamela R Edington ...................................845-431-8980

## Erie Community College
121 Ellicott St
Buffalo, NY 14203-2698
716-851-1322
e-mail: info@ecc.edu
Web site: www.ecc.edu

President:
  Dan Hocoy ........................................716-851-1200
  e-mail: hocoy@ecc.edu

## Fashion Institute of Technology
Seventh Avenue at 27 Street
Room C908
New York, NY 10001-5992
212-217-7999
e-mail: fitinfo@fitnyc.edu
Web site: www.fitnyc.edu

President:
  Joyce F Brown...................212-217-4000/fax: 212-217-7639

## Finger Lakes Community College
3325 Marvin Sands Drive
Canandaigua, NY 14424
585-394-3500 or 585-394-3522  Fax: 585-394-5017
e-mail: admissions@flcc.edu
Web site: www.flcc.edu

President:
  Robert Nye........................585-785-1201/fax: 585-394-5017
  e-mail: robert.nye@flcc.edu

## Fulton-Montgomery Community College
2805 State Hwy 67
Johnstown, NY 12095-3790
518-736-3622  Fax: 518-762-4334
e-mail: geninfo@fmcc.suny.edu
Web site: www.fmcc.suny.edu

President:
  Dustin Swanger............................518-762-9651 x 8000

## Genesee Community College
One College Rd
Batavia, NY 14020-9704
585-343-0055  Fax: 585-343-4541
Web site: www.genesee.edu

President:
  James M Sunser............................585-343-0055 x6201
  e-mail: jmsunser@genesee.edu

## Herkimer County Community College
100 Reservoir Rd
Herkimer, NY 13350-9987
315-866-0300 or 844-464-4375  Fax: 315-866-7253
Web site: www.herkimer.edu

President:
  Cathleen C McColgin.........315-866-0300 x8261/fax: 315-866-5539
  e-mail: president@herkimer.edu

## Hudson Valley Community College
80 Vandenburgh Ave
Troy, NY 12180
518-629-4822 or 877-325-4822  Fax: 518-629-8070
e-mail: input@hvcc.edu
Web site: www.hvcc.edu

President:
  Andrew Matonak .................................518-629-4530
  e-mail: a.matonak@hvcc.edu

## Jamestown Community College
525 Falconer St
PO Box 20
Jamestown, NY 14702-0020
716-338-1000 or 800-388-8557  Fax: 716-338-1466
Web site: www.sunyjcc.edu

President:
  Cory L Duckworth ...............................716-338-1060

## Jefferson Community College
1220 Coffeen St
Watertown, NY 13601
315-786-2200 or 888-435-6522  Fax: 315-786-0158
e-mail: webmaster@sunyjefferson.edu
Web site: www.sunyjefferson.edu

President:
  Ty Stone .........................................315-786-2230

## Mohawk Valley Community College
1101 Sherman Dr
Utica, NY 13501-5394

*Offices and agencies generally appear in alphabetical order, except when specific order is requested by listee.*

315-792-5400  Fax: 315-792-5666
Web site: www.mvcc.edu

President:
  Randall S Van Wagoner . . . . . . . . . . . .315-792-5333/fax: 315-792-5678
  e-mail: rvanwagoner@mvcc.edu

## Monroe Community College
1000 E Henrietta Rd
Rochester, NY 14623-5780
585-292-2000  Fax: 585-292-3060
e-mail: collcommrelations@monroecc.edu
Web site: www.monroecc.edu

President:
  Anne M Kress PhD . . . . . . . . . . . . . . .585-292-2100/fax: 585-292-3870
  e-mail: akress@monroecc.edu

## Nassau Community College
1 Education Dr
Garden City, NY 11530-6793
516-572-7501  Fax: 516-572-8118
Web site: www.ncc.edu

President:
  W Hubert Keen . . . . . . . . . . . . . . . . . . . . . . . . . . . .516-572-7205
  e-mail: hubert.keen@ncc.edu

## Niagara County Community College
3111 Saunders Settlement Rd
Sanborn, NY 14132
716-614-6222  Fax: 716-614-6700
Web site: www.niagaracc.suny.edu

Interim President:
  William J Murabito. . . . . . . . . . . . . . . . . . . . . . . . . .716-614-5901
  e-mail: wmurabito@niagaracc.suny.edu

## North Country Community College
23 Santanoni Ave
PO Box 89
Saranac Lake, NY 12983-0089
518-891-2915 or 888-879-6222  Fax: 518-891-6562
e-mail: helpdesk@nccc.edu
Web site: www.nccc.edu

President:
  Steve Tyrell . . . . . . . . . . . . . . .518-891-2915 x1201/fax: 518-891-5029
  e-mail: president@nccc.edu

## Onondaga Community College
4585 West Seneca Turnpike
Syracuse, NY 13215
315-498-2000  Fax: 315-469-4475
e-mail: occinfo@sunyocc.edu
Web site: www.sunyocc.edu

President:
  Casey Crabill . . . . . . . . . . . . . . . . . . . . .315-498-2214/fax: 315-469-4475
  e-mail: president@sunyocc.edu

## Orange County Community College
115 South St
Middletown, NY 10940
845-344-6222  Fax: 845-343-1228
Web site: www.sunyorange.edu

President:
  Kristine M Young . . . . . . . . . . . . . . . . .845-341-4700/fax: 845-341-4998
  e-mail: president@sunyorange.edu

## Rockland Community College
145 College Rd
Suffern, NY 10901
845-574-4000
Web site: www.sunyrockland.edu

President:
  Michael Baston . . . . . . . . . . . . . . . . . . . . . . . . . . . . . .845-574-4214
  e-mail: president@sunyrockland.edu

## Schenectady County Community College
78 Washington Ave
Schenectady, NY 12305
518-381-1200  Fax: 518-346-0379
Web site: www.sunysccc.edu

President:
  Steady H Moono . . . . . . . . . . . . . . . . . .518-381-1304/fax: 518-346-8680
  e-mail: moonosh@sunysccc.edu

## Suffolk County Community College
533 College Rd
Selden, NY 11784
631-451-4000  Fax: 631-451-4090
Web site: www3.sunysuffolk.edu

President:
  Shaun L McKay . . . . . . . . . . . . . . . . . . . . . . . . . . . . .631-451-4736
  e-mail: mckays@sunysuffolk.edu

## Sullivan County Community College
112 College Rd
PO Box 4002
Loch Sheldrake, NY 12759
845-434-5750 or 800-577-5243  Fax: 845-434-4806
Web site: www.sullivan.suny.edu

President:
  Jay Quaintance . . . . . . . . . . . . . .845-434-5750 x4261/fax: 845-434-9308
  e-mail: jquaintance@sunysullivan.edu

## Tompkins Cortland Community College
170 North St
PO Box 139
Dryden, NY 13053
607-844-8211 or 888-567-8211  Fax: 607-844-9665
Web site: www.tompkinscortland.edu

President:
  Orinthia Montague . . . . . . . . . . .607-844-8222 x4368/fax: 607-844-6545
  e-mail: otm@tompkinscortland.edu

## Ulster County Community College
491 Cottekill Rd
Stone Ridge, NY 12484
845-687-5000 or 800-724-0833  Fax: 845-687-5083
Web site: www.sunyulster.edu

President:
  Alan P Roberts. . . . . . . . . . . . . . . . . . .845-687-5050/fax: 845-687-5292
  e-mail: robertsal@sunyulster.edu

*Offices and agencies generally appear in alphabetical order, except when specific order is requested by listee.*

## Westchester Community College

75 Grasslands Rd
Valhalla, NY 10595-1693
914-606-6600  Fax: 914-785-6565
e-mail: info@sunywcc.edu
Web site: www.sunywcc.edu

President:
  Belinda S Miles . . . . . . . . . . . . . . . . . . 914-606-6707/fax: 914-785-6780
  e-mail: belinda.miles@sunywcc.edu

### EDUCATIONAL OPPORTUNITY CENTERS

## Bronx Educational Opportunity Center

1666 Bathgate Ave
Bronx, NY 10457
718-530-7000  Fax: 718-530-7047

Executive Director:
  Stephen H Adolphus . . . . . . . . . . . . . . . . . . . . . . . . . . . . . 718-530-7040

## Brooklyn Educational Opportunity Center

111 Livingston St
Brooklyn, NY 11201
718-802-3300  Fax: 718-802-3381

Executive Director/Dean:
  Lois Blades-Rosado . . . . . . . . . . . . . . . . . . . . . . . . . . . . 718-246-2057
  e-mail: rosadol@bklyn.eoc.cuny.edu

## Buffalo Educational Opportunity Center

465 Washington St
Buffalo, NY 14203
716-849-6727 x500  Fax: 716-849-6738
e-mail: eoc465@buffalo.edu

Director:
  Sherryl D Weems. . . . . . . . . . . . . . . . . . . . . . . . . . . 716-849-6727 x125
  e-mail: weems@buffalo.edu

## Capital District Educational Opportunity Center
**a division of Hudson Valley Community College**

431 River Street
Troy, NY 12180
518-273-1900  Fax: 518-273-1919
e-mail: eocinfo@hvcc.edu
Web site: www.hvcc.edu/eoc

Coordinator of Institutional Advancement:
  Elaine Harwood . . . . . . . . . . . . . . . . . . . . . . . . . . . . 518-273-1900 x2219
  e-mail: e.harwood@hvcc.edu

## Educational Opportunity Center of Westchester

26 S Broadway
Yonkers, NY 10701
914-606-7600  Fax: 914-606-7640

Director/Associate Dean:
  Renee Guy. . . . . . . . . . . . . . . . . . . . . . . . . . . . . . . . .914-606-7612
  e-mail: renee.guy@sunywcc.edu

## Long Island Educational Opportunity Center

269 Fulton Ave
Hempstead, NY 11550
516-489-8705
Web site: www.li.sunyeoc.org

Dean/Executive Director:
  Veronica Henry. . . . . . . . . . . . . . . . . . . . . . . . . . . . . . . . 631-420-2507
  e-mail: henryv@farmingdale.edu

## Manhattan Educational Opportunity Center

163 W 125th St
New York, NY 10027
212-961-4400  Fax: 212-961-4343

Executive Director/Dean:
  Rodney Alexander . . . . . . . . . . . . . . . . . . . . . . . . . . . . 212-961-4320

## North Bronx Career Counseling & Outreach Center

2901 White Plains Road
Bronx, NY 10467
718-547-1001  Fax: 718-547-1973
Web site: www.nbx.sunyeoc.org

Director:
  Mitch Duren. . . . . . . . . . . . . . . . . . . . . . . . . . . 718-547-1001 x204
  e-mail: mmduren@sunyeoc.org

## Queens Educational Opportunity Center

SUNY
158-29 Archer Ave
Jamaica, NY 11433
718-725-3300  Fax: 718-658-5604
Web site: www.qns.eoc.suny.edu

Director:
  Khayriyyah Ali . . . . . . . . . . . . . . . . . . . . . . . . . . . . . 718-725-3403
  e-mail: ali_29@eoc.suny.edu

## Rochester Educational Opportunity Center

305 Andrews St
Rochester, NY 14604
585-232-2730  Fax: 585-546-7824
Web site: www.reoc.brockport.edu

Dean/Executive Director:
  Melva L Brown . . . . . . . . . . . . . . 585-232-2730 x269/fax: 585-232-8154
  e-mail: mebrown@brockport.edu

## SUNY College & Career Counseling Center

120 Emmons St
Schenectady, NY 12304
518-370-2654  Fax: 518-370-2661

Director:
  Lois M Tripp. . . . . . . . . . . . . . . . . . . . . . . . . . . . . . . . . 518-370-2654

## Syracuse Educational Opportunity Center

100 New St
Syracuse, NY 13202
315-472-0130  Fax: 315-472-1241
e-mail: wallam@morrisville.edu
Web site: www.syracuseeoc.com

Vice President:
  Tim Penix . . . . . . . . . . . . . . . . . . . . . 315-472-0130/fax: 315-472-1241

### THE CITY UNIVERSITY OF NEW YORK

## CUNY Board of Trustees

535 E 80th St
New York, NY 10021

*Offices and agencies generally appear in alphabetical order, except when specific order is requested by listee.*

Colleges,
Universities &
School Districts

212-794-5450  Fax: 212-794-5678
Web site: www.cuny.edu

Chair:
  Benno C. Schmidt Jr. . . . . . . . . . . . . . . . . . . . . . . 212-794-5450
Vice Chair:
  Philip Alfonso Berry . . . . . . . . . . . . . . . . . . . . . . . 212-794-5450
Member:
  Valerie Lancaster Beal . . . . . . . . . . . . . . . . . . . . 212-794-5450
Member:
  Wellington Z. Chen. . . . . . . . . . . . . . . . . . . . . . . . 212-794-5450
Member:
  Rita DiMartino . . . . . . . . . . . . . . . . . . . . . . . . . . . 212-794-5450
Member:
  Freida Foster . . . . . . . . . . . . . . . . . . . . . . . . . . . . 212-794-5450
Member:
  Judah Gribetz . . . . . . . . . . . . . . . . . . . . . . . . . . . 212-794-5450
Member:
  Joseph J. Lhota . . . . . . . . . . . . . . . . . . . . . . . . . . 212-794-5450
Member:
  Hugo M. Morales . . . . . . . . . . . . . . . . . . . . . . . . 212-794-5450
Member:
  Brian D. Obergfell . . . . . . . . . . . . . . . . . . . . . . . 212-794-5450
Member:
  Peter S. Pantaleo . . . . . . . . . . . . . . . . . . . . . . . . 212-794-5450
Member:
  Kathleen M. Pesile . . . . . . . . . . . . . . . . . . . . . . . 212-794-5450
Member:
  Carol A. Robles-Roman . . . . . . . . . . . . . . . . . . . 212-794-5450
Member:
  Charles A. Shorter. . . . . . . . . . . . . . . . . . . . . . . . 212-794-5450
Member:
  Jeffrey A. Weisenfeld . . . . . . . . . . . . . . . . . . . . . 212-794-5450
Member:
  Kafui Kouakou . . . . . . . . . . . . . . . . . . . . . . . . . . 212-794-5450
Member:
  Terrence F. Martell . . . . . . . . . . . . . . . . . . . . . . . 212-794-5450

### CUNY Central Administration

205 East 42nd Street
New York, NY 10017
646-664-9100
Web site: www.cuny.edu

Chancellor:
  James B. Milliken . . . . . . . . . . . . . . . 646-664-9100/fax: 646-664-3868
Executive Vice Chancellor & COO:
  Allan H. Dobrin . . . . . . . . . . . . . . . . . . . . . . . 646-664-2888
Executive Vice Chancellor & University Provost:
  Vita C. Rabinowitz . . . . . . . . . . . . . . . . . . . . . 646-664-8075
Senior Vice Chancellor, University Relations & Secretary of the Board:
  Jay Hershenson . . . . . . . . . . . . . . . . . . . . . . . 646-664-9001
Senior Vice Chancellor, Legal Affairs & General Counsel:
  Frederick P. Schaffer . . . . . . . . . . . . . . . . . . . 646-664-9210
Vice Chancellor, Budget & Finance:
  Matthew Sapienza. . . . . . . . . . . . . . . . . . . . . . 646-746-4275
Vice Chancellor for Student Affairs:
  Frank D. Sanchez . . . . . . . . . . . . . . . . . . . . . . 646-664-8759
Vice Chancellor, Labor Relations:
  Pamela S. Silverblatt. . . . . . . . . . . . . . . . . . . . 646-664-2977
Vice Chancellor, Research:
  Gillian Small . . . . . . . . . . . . . . . . . . . . . . . . . . 646-664-8910
Vice Chancellor, Human Resources Management:
  Gloriana Waters . . . . . . . . . . . . . . . . . . . . . . . 646-664-3254
Vice Chancellor, Facilities Planning, Construction & Management:
  Judith Bergtraum. . . . . . . . . . . . . . . . . . . . . . . 646-664-2605
Vice Chancellor & University CIO:
  Brian Cohen . . . . . . . . . . . . . . . . . . . . . . . . . . . 646-664-2365

**City University Construction Fund** . . . . . . . . . . . . . fax: 212-541-0175
  555 W 57th St, 10th Fl, New York, NY 10019

212-541-0171  Fax: 212-541-0175
Acting Chairman:
  Philip Berry. . . . . . . . . . . . . . . . . . . . . . . . . . . . . 212-541-0171
Member:
  Wellington Z. Chen. . . . . . . . . . . . . . . . . . . . . . . 212-541-5315
Member:
  Noel N. Hankin
Executive Director:
  Iris Weinshall . . . . . . . . . . . . . . . . . . . . . . . . . . . 212-794-5315
Counsel:
  Frederick P. Schaffer . . . . . . . . . . . . . . . . . . . . . 212-794-5506
Deputy Executive Director:
  Howard Alschuler. . . . . . . . . . . . . . . . . . . . . . . . 212-541-0999
Administrative Officer:
  Denise Philips . . . . . . . . . . . . . . . . . . . . . . . . . . 212-541-0190
Special Assistant:
  Nancy Nichols. . . . . . . . . . . . . . . . . . . . . . . . . . . 212-541-0442

### Bernard M Baruch College

One Bernard Baruch Way
New York, NY 10010
646-312-1000  Fax: 646-312-1362
Web site: www.baruch.cuny.edu

President:
  Mitchel Wallerstein . . . . . . . . . . . . . . . 646-312-3310/fax: 646-312-3311

### Borough of Manhattan Community College

199 Chambers St
New York, NY 10007
212-220-8000  Fax: 212-220-1244
Web site: www.bmcc.cuny.edu

President:
  Antonio Perez . . . . . . . . . . . . . . . . . . . . . . 212-220-1230 x1234
  e-mail: aperez@bmcc.cuny.edu

### Bronx Community College

2155 University Ave
Bronx, NY 10453
718-289-5100
e-mail: webmaster@bcc.cuny.edu
Web site: www.bcc.cuny.edu

Senior VP:
  Carolyn Williams . . . . . . . . . . . . . . . . . . . . . . . . . 718-289-5151

### Brooklyn College

2900 Bedford Ave
Brooklyn, NY 11210
718-951-5000
Web site: www.brooklyn.cuny.edu

President:
  Karen L Gould. . . . . . . . . . . . . . . . . . . . 718-951-5671/fax: 718-951-4872
  e-mail: klgould@brooklyn.cuny.edu

### City College of New York, The

160 Covent Ave
New York, NY 10031
212-650-7000
Web site: www1.ccny.cuny.edu

Interim President:
  Lisa Staiano-Coico . . . . . . . . . . . . . . . . . . . . . . . . 212-650-7285
  e-mail: president@ccny.cuny.edu

*Offices and agencies generally appear in alphabetical order, except when specific order is requested by listee.*

## College of Staten Island
2800 Victory Blvd
Staten Island, NY 10314
718-982-2000
Web site: www.csi.cuny.edu

President:
    Tomas Morales . . . . . . . . . . . . . . . . . . . . . . . . . . . . .718-982-2000 x2400
    e-mail: president@csi.cuny.edu

## Graduate Center
365 Fifth Ave
New York, NY 10016-4309
212-817-7000 or 877-428-6942
Web site: www.gc.cuny.edu

President:
    William P Kelly. . . . . . . . . . . . . . . . . . .212-817-7100/fax: 212-817-1606
    e-mail: pres@gc.cuny.edu

## Graduate School of Journalism
219 W 40th St
New York, NY 10018
646-758-7800
Web site: www.journalism.cuny.edu

Dean:
    Steve Shepard . . . . . . . . . . . . . . . . . . . .646-758-7816/fax: 646-758-7809
    e-mail: steve.shepard@journalism.cuny.edu

## Hostos Community College
500 Grand Concourse
Bronx, NY 10451
718-518-4444 or 718-518-4100
Web site: www.hostos.cuny.edu

President:
    Felix V Matos Rodriguez . . . . . . . . . . . . . . . . . . . . . . . . .718-518-4300
    e-mail: president@hostos.cuny.edu

## Hunter College
695 Park Ave
New York, NY 10021
212-772-4000
Web site: www.hunter.cuny.edu

President:
    Jennifer J Raab . . . . . . . . . . . . . . . . . . . .212-772-4242/fax: 212-772-4724
    e-mail: jennifer.raab@hunter.cuny.edu

## John Jay College of Criminal Justice
899 Tenth Ave
New York, NY 10019
212-237-8000  Fax: 212-237-8607
Web site: www.jjay.cuny.edu

President:
    Jeremy Travis . . . . . . . . . . . . . . . . . . . . . . . . . . . . . . . . .212-237-8600
    e-mail: jtravis@jjay.cuny.edu

## Kingsborough Community College
2001 Oriental Blvd
Brooklyn, NY 11235-2398
718-265-5343
e-mail: info@kbcc.cuny.edu
Web site: www.kbcc.cuny.edu

President:
    Regina S Peruggi . . . . . . . . . . . . . . . . . . . . . . . . . . . . . . .718-368-5100
    e-mail: president@kingsborough.edu

## LaGuardia Community College
31-10 Thomson Ave
Long Island City, NY 11101
718-482-7200
Web site: www.lagcc.cuny.edu

President:
    Gail O Mellow . . . . . . . . . . . . . . . . . . . . . . . . . . . . . . . . .718-482-5050
    e-mail: gmellow@lagcc.cuny.edu

## Lehman College
250 Bedford Park Blvd West
Bronx, NY 10468
718-960-8000 or 877-534-6261
Web site: www.lehman.edu

President:
    Ricardo R Fernandez . . . . . . . . . . . . . . .718-960-8111/fax: 718-584-1765
    e-mail: president@lehman.cuny.edu

## Medgar Evers College
1650 Bedford St
Brooklyn, NY 11225
718-270-4900
Web site: www.mec.cuny.edu

President:
    William Pollard . . . . . . . . . . . . . . . . . . .718-270-5000/fax: 718-270-5126
    e-mail: wlpollard@mec.cuny.edu

## New York City College of Technology
300 Jay St
Brooklyn, NY 11201
718-260-5000
e-mail: connect@citytech.cuny.edu
Web site: www.citytech.cuny.edu

President:
    Russell K Hotzler . . . . . . . . . . . . . . . . . . . . . . . . . . . . . . .718-260-5400
    e-mail: rhotzler@citytech.cuny.edu

## Queens College
65-30 Kissena Blvd
Flushing, NY 11367-1597
718-997-5000
Web site: www.qc.cuny.edu

President:
    Felix V. Matos Rodriguez. . . . . . . . . . . . . . . . . . . . . . . . . .718-997-5550

## Queensborough Community College
222-05 56th Ave
Bayside, NY 11364-1497
718-631-6262
Web site: www.qcc.cuny.edu

President:
    Diane Call . . . . . . . . . . . . . . . . . . . . . .718-631-6222/fax: 718-281-5588

## School of Law at Queens College
2 Court Square
Long Island City, NY 11101-4356
718-340-4200  Fax: 718-340-4435
Web site: www.law.cuny.edu

*Colleges, Universities & School Districts*

*Offices and agencies generally appear in alphabetical order, except when specific order is requested by listee.*

Dean:
    Michelle J. Anderson . . . . . . . . . . . . . . . . . . . . . . . .718-340-4201
    e-mail: anderson@law.cuny.edu

## School of Professional Studies
101 West 31st St
New York, NY 10001
212-652-2869
Web site: sps.cuny.edu

Dean:
    John Mogulescu . . . . . . . . . . . . . . . . . . . . . . . . . . .212-794-5429
    e-mail: john.mogulescu@mail.cuny.edu

## Sophie Davis School of Biomedical Education
160 Convent Ave
New York, NY 10031
212-650-7000  Fax: 212-650-6696

Dean:
    Eitan Friedman . . . . . . . . . . . . . . . . . .212-650-5275/fax: 212-650-6696
    e-mail: friedman@med.cuny.edu

## York College
94-20 Guy R Brewer Blvd
Jamaica, NY 11451
718-262-2000
Web site: york.cuny.edu

President:
    Marcia Keizs . . . . . . . . . . . . . . . . . . . .718-262-2350/fax: 718-262-2352
    e-mail: president@york.cuny.edu

## INDEPENDENT COLLEGES & UNIVERSITIES

## Adelphi University
1 South Ave
PO Box 701
Garden City, NY 11530
516-877-3050 or 800-233-5744  Fax: 516-877-3090
Web site: www.adelphi.edu

President:
    Robert A Scott . . . . . . . . . . . . . . . . . . .516-877-3838/fax: 516-877-3845

## Albany College of Pharmacy
106 New Scotland Ave
Albany, NY 12208-3492
518-694-7200 or 888-203-8010  Fax: 518-694-7202
e-mail: info@acphs.edu
Web site: www.acphs.edu

President:
    James J Gozzo . . . . . . . . . . . . . . . . . . . . . . . . . . . .518-694-7255

## Albany Law School
80 New Scotland Avenue
Albany, NY 12208-3494
518-445-2311  Fax: 518-445-2315
e-mail: info@albanylaw.edu
Web site: www.albanylaw.edu

President & Dean:
    Alicia Ouellette . . . . . . . . . . . . . . . . . . . . . . . . . . .518-445-3398
    e-mail: aouel@albanylaw.edu

Director, Communications & Marketing:
    David Singer . . . . . . . . . . . . . . . . . . . . . . . . . . . . .518-445-3211
    e-mail: dsing@albanylaw.edu

## Albany Medical College
43 New Scotland Ave
Albany, NY 12208
518-262-3125  Fax: 518-262-6515
e-mail: webmaster@mail.amc.edu
Web site: www.amc.edu

Dean:
    Vincent P Verdile . . . . . . . . . . . . . . . . . . . . . . . . . .518-262-6008
    e-mail: verdilv@mail.amc.edu

## Alfred University
1 Saxon Dr
Alfred, NY 14802-1205
800-541-9229 or 607-871-2175  Fax: 607-871-2339
Web site: www.alfred.edu

President:
    Charles M Edmondson . . . . . . . . . . . . . . . . . . . . . . .607-871-2101
    e-mail: edmondson@alfred.edu

## American Academy McAllister Institute of Funeral Service
619 West 54th St, 2nd Fl
New York, NY 10019
212-757-1190  Fax: 212-765-5923
e-mail: info@funeraleducation.org
Web site: www.funeraleducation.org

President/CEO:
    Meg Dunn . . . . . . . . . . . . . . . . . . . . . . . . . . . . . .212-757-1190

## American Academy of Dramatic Arts
120 Madison Ave
New York, NY 10016-7004
212-686-9244 or 800-463-8990
Web site: www.aada.org

Acting President:
    Susan Zech . . . . . . . . . . . . . . . . . . . . . . . . . . . . . .212-686-9244

## Bank Street College of Education/Graduate School
610 West 112th St
New York, NY 10025-1898
212-875-4400  Fax: 212-875-4678
Web site: www.bankstreet.edu

President:
    Elizabeth D Dickey . . . . . . . . . . . . . . . .212-875-4595/fax: 212-875-4594
Dean, Graduate School:
    Virginia Roach . . . . . . . . . . . . . . . . . . . . . . . . . . .212-875-4466
    e-mail: vroach@bankstreet.edu

## Bard College
PO Box 5000
Annandale-on-Hudson, NY 12504-5000
845-758-6822  Fax: 845-758-5208
Web site: www.bard.edu

President:
    Leon Botstein . . . . . . . . . . . . . . . . . . . . . . . . . . . .845-758-7423
    e-mail: president@bard.edu

*Offices and agencies generally appear in alphabetical order, except when specific order is requested by listee.*

## Barnard College
3009 Broadway
New York, NY 10027
212-854-5262  Fax: 212-854-6220
Web site: www.barnard.edu

President:
  Deborah L Spar . . . . . . . . . . . . . . . . . . . . . . . . . . . . . . .212-854-2021
  e-mail: dspar@barnard.edu

## Boricua College
3755 Broadway
New York, NY 10032
212-694-1000  Fax: 212-694-1015
Web site: www.boricuacollege.edu

President:
  Victor G Alicea . . . . . . . . . . . . . . . . . . . . . . . . . . . . . .212-694-1000
  e-mail: valicea@boricuacollege.edu

## Bramson ORT College
69-30 Austin St
Forest Hills, NY 11375-4239
718-261-5800  Fax: 718-575-5118

Director:
  Ephraim Buhks . . . . . . . . . . . . . . . . . . . . . . . . . . . .718-261-5800 x102
  e-mail: ebuhks@bramsonort.edu

## Brooklyn Law School
250 Joralemon St
Brooklyn, NY 11201-3798
718-625-2200  Fax: 718-780-0393
Web site: www.brooklaw.edu

President:
  Joan G Wexler. . . . . . . . . . . . . . . . . . . . . . . . . . . . . . .718-780-7900
  e-mail: joan.wexler@brooklaw.edu

## Canisius College
2001 Main St
Buffalo, NY 14208-1098
716-883-7000  Fax: 716-888-2525
Web site: www.canisius.edu

President:
  John J Huxley . . . . . . . . . . . . . . . . . . . .716-888-2100/fax: 716-888-3220

## Cazenovia College
22 Sullivan St
Cazenovia, NY 13035
315-655-7000 or 800-654-3210  Fax: 315-655-4143
e-mail: admissions@cazenovia.edu
Web site: www.cazenovia.edu

President:
  Mark John Tierno . . . . . . . . . . . . . . . . . . . . . . . . . . . . .315-655-7116
  e-mail: mtierno@cazenovia.edu

## Christ the King Seminary
**Catholic Diocese of Buffalo**
711 Knox Rd
East Aurora, NY 14052-0607
716-652-8900  Fax: 716-652-8903
e-mail: academicoffice@cks.edu
Web site: www.cks.edu

Registrar:
  Julie Galey . . . . . . . . . . . . . . . . . . . . . . . . . . . . . . . . .716-652-8900
  e-mail: jgaley@cks.edu

## Clarkson University
8 Clarkson Ave
Potsdam, NY 13699
315-268-6400 or 800-527-6577  Fax: 315-268-7993
Web site: www.clarkson.edu

President:
  Anthony G Collins . . . . . . . . . . . . . . . . . . . . . . . . . . . . .315-268-6444
  e-mail: collins@clarkson.edu

## Cochran School of Nursing
St John's Riverside Hospital
967 N Broadway, Andrus Pavilion
Yonkers, NY 10701
914-964-4296  Fax: 914-964-4266
e-mail: admissions@cochranschoolofnursing.us
Web site: www.cochranschoolofnursing.us

Vice President & Dean:
  Kathleen Dirschel . . . . . . . . . . . . . . . . . . . . . . . . . . . . .914-964-4280
Director, Administration:
  David T George . . . . . . . . . . . . . . . . . . . . . . . . . . . . . . .914-964-4296

## Colgate Rochester Crozer Divinity School
1100 S Goodman St
Rochester, NY 14620-2589
585-271-1320  Fax: 585-271-8013
Web site: www.crcds.edu

President:
  Rev. Jack McKelvey. . . . . . . . . . . . . . . . . . . . . . . . . . . . .585-340-9680

## Colgate University
13 Oak Dr
Hamilton, NY 13346
315-228-1000  Fax: 315-228-7798
Web site: www.colgate.edu

President:
  Jeffrey Herbst . . . . . . . . . . . . . . . . . . . .315-228-7444/fax: 315-228-6010

## College of Mount Saint Vincent
6301 Riverdale Ave
Riverdale, NY 10471-1093
800-665-2678 or 718-405-3267
Web site: www.mountsaintvincent.edu

President:
  Charles L Flynn Jr. . . . . . . . . . . . . . . . . . . . . . . . . . . . . .718-405-3233
  e-mail: president@mountsaintvincent.edu

## College of New Rochelle (The)
Brooklyn Campus
29 Castle Pl
New Rochelle, NY 10805-2339
914-654-5000 or 800-211-7077  Fax: 914-654-5833
e-mail: info@cnr.edu
Web site: www.cnr.edu

President:
  Stephen J Sweeny . . . . . . . . . . . . . . . . . . . . . . . . . . . . .914-654-5430
  e-mail: ssweeny@cnr.edu

*Offices and agencies generally appear in alphabetical order, except when specific order is requested by listee.*

**College of Saint Rose (The)**
432 Western Ave
Albany, NY 12203-1490
800-637-8556
Web site: www.strose.edu

President:
R Mark Sullivan . . . . . . . . . . . . . . . . . . . . . . . . . . . . . .518-454-5120

**Columbia University**
116th and Broadway
New York, NY 10027
212-854-1754  Fax: 212-854-9973
Web site: www.columbia.edu

President:
Lee C Bollinger . . . . . . . . . . . . . . . . . . .212-854-9970/fax: 212-854-9973
e-mail: officeofthepresident@columbia.edu

**Concordia College**
171 White Plains Rd
Bronxville, NY 10708
914-337-9300  Fax: 914-395-4500
Web site: www.concordia-ny.edu

President:
Viji D George . . . . . . . . . . . . . . . . . . . . . . . . . . . .914-337-9300 x2111
e-mail: viji.george@concordia-ny.edu

**Cooper Union for the Advancement of Science & Art**
30 Cooper Sq, 8th floor
New York, NY 10003-7120
212-353-4100  Fax: 212-353-4327
e-mail: webmaster@cooper.edu
Web site: www.cooper.edu

President:
Jamshed Bhurucha . . . . . . . . . . . . . . . . . . . . . . . . . . .212-353-4195

**Cornell University**
300 Day Hall
Ithaca, NY 14853
607-254-4636  Fax: 607-254-5175
e-mail: info@cornell.edu
Web site: www.cornell.edu

President:
David J Skorton . . . . . . . . . . . . . . . . . . .607-255-5201/fax: 607-255-9924
e-mail: president@cornell.edu

**Crouse Hospital School of Nursing**
736 Irving Ave
Syracuse, NY 13210
315-470-7481  Fax: 315-470-7232
e-mail: crouseson@crouse.org
Web site: www.crouse.org/nursing

Director:
Ann Sedore . . . . . . . . . . . . . . . . . . . . . . . . . . . . . . . .315-470-7932

**Culinary Institute of America**
1946 Campus Drive
Hyde Park, NY 12538-1499
845-452-9600 or 800-285-4627  Fax: 845-451-1068
e-mail: admissions@culinary.edu
Web site: www.ciachef.edu

President:
Tim Ryan. . . . . . . . . . . . . . . . . . . . . . . . . . . . . . . . . .845-451-1352

**D'Youville College**
320 Porter Ave
Buffalo, NY 14201
716-829-8000 or 800-777-3921  Fax: 716-881-7790
Web site: www.dyc.edu

President:
Sister Denise A Roche . . . . . . . . . . . . . . . . . . . . . . . . . .716-829-7673

**Daemen College**
4380 Main St
Amherst, NY 14226
716-839-3600 or 800-462-7652  Fax: 716-839-8516
Web site: www.daemen.edu

President:
Martin J Anisman . . . . . . . . . . . . . . . . .716-839-8210/fax: 716-839-8279
e-mail: manisman@daemen.edu

**Davis College**
400 Riverside Dr
Johnson City, NY 13790
607-729-1581 or 877-949-3248  Fax: 607-729-2962
e-mail: info@davisny.edu
Web site: www.davisny.edu

President:
Dino Pedrone . . . . . . . . . . . . . . . . .607-729-1581 x316/fax: 607-729-1581
e-mail: president@davisny.edu

**Dominican College**
470 Western Highway
Orangeburg, NY 10962
845-359-7800  Fax: 845-359-2313
Web site: www.dc.edu

President:
Sister Mary Eileen O'Brien. . . . . . . . . . .845-848-7801/fax: 845-359-7988
e-mail: mary.eileen.obrien@dc.edu

**Dorothea Hopfer School of Nursing at Mount Vernon Hospital**
53 Valentine St
Mount Vernon, NY 10550
914-361-6221  Fax: 914-665-7047

Dean of Nursing Education:
Joanna Scalabrini . . . . . . . . . . . . . . . . . . . . . . . . . . . . .914-361-6220

**Ellis Hospital School of Nursing**
1101 Nott St
Schenectady, NY 12308
518-243-4471  Fax: 518-243-4470
Web site: www.ehson.org

Director:
Marilyn Stapleton . . . . . . . . . . . . . . . . . . . . . . . . . . . . .518-243-4471
CEO:
Jim Connolly. . . . . . . . . . . . . . . . . . . . . . . . . . . . . . . .518-243-4000

**Elmira College**
One Park Pl
Elmira, NY 14901

607-735-1800 or 800-935-6472
e-mail: admissions@elmira.edu
Web site: www.elmira.edu

President:
Thomas K Meier...................................607-735-1790

## Excelsior College
7 Columbia Cir
Albany, NY 12203-5159
518-464-8500 or 888-647-2388  Fax: 518-464-8777
Web site: www.excelsior.edu

President:
John F Ebersole..................................518-464-8500

## Fordham University
Rose Hill
441 East Fordham Rd
Bronx, NY 10458
718-817-1000
Web site: www.fordham.edu

President:
Joseph M McShane, SJ ............. 718-817-3000/fax: 718-817-3005

## General Theological Seminary of the Episcopal Church
175 Ninth Ave
Chelsea Sq
New York, NY 10011-4977
212-243-5150  Fax: 212-727-3907
Web site: www.gts.edu

Interim President/Dean:
Lang Lowrey ................................212-243-5150 x302

## Hamilton College
198 College Hill Rd
Clinton, NY 13323
315-859-4421 or 800-843-2655  Fax: 315-859-4457
Web site: www.hamilton.edu

President:
Joan Hinde Stewart................................315-859-4104
e-mail: jstewart@hamilton.edu

## Hartwick College
PO Box 4020
Oneonta, NY 13820-4020
800-427-8942 or 607-431-4000  Fax: 607-431-4102
Web site: www.hartwick.edu

President:
Dr Margaret L Drugovich...........................607-431-4990
e-mail: president@hartwick.edu

## Hebrew Union College - Jewish Institute of Religion
The Brookdale Center
One W 4th St
New York, NY 10012
212-674-5300  Fax: 212-388-1720

President:
David Ellenson ..............800-424-1336 x2201/fax: 212-979-0853
e-mail: presoff@huc.edu

## Helene Fuld College of Nursing North General Hospital
24 East 120th St
New York, NY 10035
212-616-7200
Web site: www.helenefuld.edu

President:
Margaret Wines...................................212-423-2750

## Hilbert College
5200 South Park Ave
Hamburg, NY 14075
716-649-7900  Fax: 716-649-0702
e-mail: info@hilbert.edu
Web site: www.hilbert.edu

President:
Cynthia Zane ..............................716-649-7900 x200
e-mail: czane@hilbert.edu

## Hobart & William Smith Colleges
300 Pulteney Street
Geneva, NY 14456
315-781-3000 or 800-852-2256
Web site: www.hws.edu

President:
Mark D Gearan ...................................315-781-3309
e-mail: gearan@hws.edu

## Hofstra University
100 Fulton Ave
Hempstead, NY 11550
800-463-7872 or 516-463-6600  Fax: 516-463-4867
Web site: www.hofstra.edu

President:
Stuart Rabinowitz .................516-463-6800/fax: 516-463-6096
e-mail: president@hofstra.edu

## Houghton College
1 Willard Avenue
Houghton, NY 14744-0128
800-777-2556  Fax: 585-567-9572
Web site: www.houghton.edu

President:
Shirley Mullen ...................................585-567-9310
e-mail: cindy.lastoria@houghton.edu

## Institute of Design & Construction
141 Willoughby St
Brooklyn, NY 11201
718-855-3661  Fax: 718-852-5889

Executive Director:
Vincent C Battista................................718-855-3661

## Iona College
715 North Ave
New Rochelle, NY 10801
914-633-2000 or 800-231-4662  Fax: 914-633-2018
Web site: www.iona.edu

President:
Joseph Nyre......................................914-633-2203

Colleges,
Universities &
School Districts

*Offices and agencies generally appear in alphabetical order, except when specific order is requested by listee.*

## Ithaca College
953 Danby Rd
Ithaca, NY 14850
607-274-3011  Fax: 607-274-1900
e-mail: thurston@ithaca.edu
Web site: www.ithaca.edu

President:
Thomas R Rochon . . . . . . . . . . . . . . . . . .607-274-3111/fax: 607-274-3064
e-mail: president@ithaca.edu

## Jewish Theological Seminary
3080 Broadway
New York, NY 10027-4649
212-678-8000  Fax: 212-678-8947
Web site: www.jtsa.edu

Chancellor/President of Faculties:
Arnold Eisen . . . . . . . . . . . . . . . . . . . . . . . . . . . . . . . .212-678-8072

## Juilliard School (The)
60 Lincoln Center Plz
New York, NY 10023-6588
212-799-5000  Fax: 212-724-0263
Web site: www.juilliard.edu

President:
Joseph W Polisi . . . . . . . . . . . . . . . . . . . . . . . . .212-799-5000 X207
Dean & Provost:
Ara Guzalimian . . . . . . . . . . . . . . . . . . . . . . . . . .212-799-5000 x204

## Keuka College
141 Central Ave
Keuka Park, NY 14478
315-279-5000 or 800-335-3852  Fax: 315-279-5216
Web site: www.keuka.edu

President:
Joseph Burke . . . . . . . . . . . . . . . . . . . . .315-279-5201/fax: 315-279-5335
e-mail: president@keuka.edu

## King's College (The)
56 Broadway
New York, NY 10004
888-969-7200 or 212-659-7200  Fax: 212-659-7210
Web site: www.tkc.edu

President:
Gregory Alan Thornbury . . . . . . . . . . . . . . . . . . . . . . . . .212-659-7200

## Le Moyne College
1419 Salt Springs Rd
Syracuse, NY 13214-1301
315-445-4100  Fax: 315-445-4540
Web site: www.lemoyne.edu

President:
Dr. Fred Pestello . . . . . . . . . . . . . . . . . . . . . . . . . . . . . .315-445-4120

## Long Island College Hospital School of Nursing
340 Court St
Brooklyn, NY 11231
718-780-1953  Fax: 718-780-1936
Web site: www.futurenurselich.org

Dean:
Nancy Dimauro . . . . . . . . . . . . . . . . . . . . . . . . . . . . . . .718-780-1998

## Long Island University
700 Northern Blvd
Brookville, NY 11548
516-299-2000  Fax: 516-299-2072
Web site: www.liu.edu

President:
David J Steinberg . . . . . . . . . . . . . . . . . .516-299-2501/fax: 516-229-2590
e-mail: president@liu.edu

## Manhattan College
4513 Manhattan College Pkwy
Riverdale, NY 10471
718-862-8000 or 800-622-9235
Web site: www.manhattan.edu

President:
Brother Brennan O'Donnell . . . . . . . . . .718-862-7301/fax: 718-862-8030
e-mail: brennan.odonnell@manhattan.edu

## Manhattan School of Music
120 Claremont Ave
New York, NY 10027
212-749-2802  Fax: 212-749-5471
Web site: www.msmnyc.edu

President:
Robert Sirota . . . . . . . . . . . . . . . . . . . . . . . . . . .212-749-2802 x4477
e-mail: officeofthepresident@msmnyc.edu

## Manhattanville College
2900 Purchase St
Purchase, NY 10577
914-694-2200  Fax: 914-694-2386
Web site: www.manhattanville.edu

President:
Molly E Smith . . . . . . . . . . . . . . . . . . . . .914-323-5230/fax: 914-694-6234
e-mail: president@mville.edu

## Maria College of Albany
700 New Scotland Ave
Albany, NY 12208
518-438-3111  Fax: 518-453-1366
Web site: www.mariacollege.edu

President:
Sister Laureen A Fitzgerald . . . . . . . . . . . . . . . . . . . . .518-438-3111 x213

## Marist College
3399 North Rd
Poughkeepsie, NY 12601
845-575-3000
e-mail: timmian.massie@marist.edu
Web site: www.marist.edu

President:
Dennis J Murray . . . . . . . . . . . . . . . . . . . . . . . . . . . . . .845-575-3600
e-mail: dennis.murray@marist.edu

## Marymount Manhattan College
221 East 71st St
New York, NY 10021
800-627-9668 or 212-517-0400  Fax: 212-517-0567
Web site: www.mmm.edu

---

*Offices and agencies generally appear in alphabetical order, except when specific order is requested by listee.*

President:
   Judson R Shaver . . . . . . . . . . . . . . . . . . . . . . . . . . . . . . . . .212-517-0560
   e-mail: jshaver@mmm.edu

## Medaille College
18 Agassiz Cir
Buffalo, NY 14214
716-880-2000 or 800-292-1582
Web site: www.medaille.edu

President:
   Richard Jurasek . . . . . . . . . . . . . . . . . . . . . . . . . . . . . . . . . .716-880-2201
   e-mail: richard.t.jurasek@medaille.edu

## Memorial Hospital School of Nursing
600 Northern Blvd
Albany, NY 12204
518-471-3221  Fax: 518-447-3559
e-mail: dorseyp@nehealth.com
Web site: www.nehealth.com

Director:
   Mary-Jane Araldi . . . . . . . . . . . . . . . . . . . . . . . . . . . . . . . . .518-471-3260
   e-mail: martinm@nehealth.com

## Mercy College
Main Campus
555 Broadway
Dobbs Ferry, NY 10522
914-674-7600  Fax: 914-674-7382
e-mail: admissions@mercy.edu
Web site: www.mercy.edu

President:
   Timothy L Hall . . . . . . . . . . . . . . . . . . . . . . . . . . . . . . . . . . .914-674-7369
   e-mail: president@mercy.edu

## Metropolitan College of New York
431 Canal St
New York, NY 10013
212-343-1234 or 800-338-4465  Fax: 212-343-7399

President:
   Vinton Thompson . . . . . . . . . . . . . . . . . . . . . . . . . .212-343-1234 x3301
   e-mail: vthompson@metropolitan.edu

## Mid-America Baptist Theological Seminary Northeast Branch
2810 Curry Rd
Schenectady, NY 12303
518-355-4000 or 800-209-3447  Fax: 518-355-8298
e-mail: mjohn@mabtsne.edu
Web site: www.mabts.edu

Director:
   Shawn Buice . . . . . . . . . . . . . . . . . . . . . . . . . . . . . . . . . . . . .518-355-4000
   e-mail: sbuice@mabtsne.edu

## Molloy College
1000 Hempstead Ave
PO Box 5002
Rockville Centre, NY 11571-5002
516-678-5000 or 888-466-5569
Web site: www.molloy.edu

President:
   Drew Bogner . . . . . . . . . . . . . . .516-678-5000 x6200/fax: 516-678-5321
   e-mail: presidentdrew@molloy.edu

## Mount Saint Mary College
330 Powell Ave
Newburgh, NY 12550
845-561-0800  Fax: 845-562-6762
Web site: www.msmc.edu

President:
   Fr Kevin E Mackin OFM . . . . . . . . . . . . . . . . . . . . . . . . . .845-569-3202
   e-mail: mackin@msmc.edu

## Mount Sinai School of Medicine of NYU
One Gustave L Levy Pl
New York, NY 10029-6574
212-241-6500
Web site: www.mssm.edu

President/CEO/Dean:
   Kenneth L Davis . . . . . . . . . . . . . . . . . .212-659-8888/fax: 212-659-9800
   e-mail: kenneth.davis@mssm.edu

## Nazareth College of Rochester
4245 East Ave
Rochester, NY 14618-7390
585-389-2525  Fax: 585-586-2452
Web site: www.naz.edu

President:
   Daan Braveman . . . . . . . . . . . . . . . . . . .585-389-2004/fax: 585-389-2015
   e-mail: dbravem7@naz.edu

## New School University (The)
66 West 12th St
New York, NY 10011
212-229-5600  Fax: 212-229-5937
e-mail: kerreyb@newschool.edu
Web site: www.newschool.edu

President:
   David VanZandt . . . . . . . . . . . . . . . . . . . . . . . . . . . . . . . . . .212-229-5656
Dean:
   Linda Dunne . . . . . . . . . . . . . . . . . . . . . . . . . . . . . . . . . . . . .212-229-5613
   e-mail: dunnel@newschool.edu

## New York Academy of Art Inc
111 Franklin St
New York, NY 10013
212-966-0300  Fax: 212-966-3217
e-mail: info@nyaa.edu
Web site: www.nyaa.edu

President:
   David Kratz . . . . . . . . . . . . . . . . . . . . . . . . . . . . . . . . . . . . . .212-966-0300
Dean:
   Peter Drake . . . . . . . . . . . . . . . . . . . . . . . . . . . . . . . . . . . . . .212-966-0300

## New York Chiropractic College
2360 Route 89
Seneca Falls, NY 13148
315-568-3000 or 800-234-6922  Fax: 315-568-3012
Web site: www.nycc.edu

President:
   Frank J Nicchi . . . . . . . . . . . . . . . . . . . . . . . . . . . . . . . . . . . .315-568-3100
   e-mail: fnicchi@nycc.edu

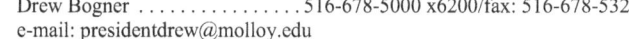

*Offices and agencies generally appear in alphabetical order, except when specific order is requested by listee.*

Colleges, Universities & School Districts

## New York College of Health Professions
6801 Jericho Tpke
Suite 300
Syosset, NY 11791
516-364-0808 or 800-922-7337  Fax: 516-364-0989
e-mail: info@nycollege.edu
Web site: www.nycollege.edu

President:
   Lisa E Pamintuan ..................................516-364-0808

## New York College of Podiatric Medicine
53 East 124th St.
New York, NY 10035-1940
212-410-8000  Fax: 212-722-4918
Web site: www.nycpm.edu

President/CEO:
   Louis L Levine ....................212-410-8024/fax: 212-876-7670
   e-mail: llevine@nycpm.edu

## New York College of Traditional Chinese Medicine
155 First St.
Mineola, NY 11501
516-739-1545
Web site: www.nyctcm.edu

President:
   Yemeng Chen ....................................212-685-0888

## New York Institute of Technology
Northern Blvd
PO Box 8000
Old Westbury, NY 11568-8000
516-686-1000 or 800-345-6948  Fax: 516-686-7613
e-mail: asknyit@nyit.edu
Web site: www.nyit.edu

President:
   Edward Guiliano....................................516-686-7650
   e-mail: nyitop@nyit.edu

## New York Law School
185 W Broadway
New York, NY 10013
212-431-2872 or 212-431-2100  Fax: 212-406-0103
e-mail: alevat@nyls.edu
Web site: www.nyls.edu

President/Dean:
   Richard A Matasar.................212-431-2840/fax: 212-219-3752
   e-mail: ddean@nyls.edu

## New York Medical College
Administration Bldg
40 Sunshine Cottage Rd
Valhalla, NY 10595
914-594-4000
e-mail: vilma_bordonaro@nymc.edu
Web site: www.nymc.edu

President:
   Alan Kadish, M.D. ................................914-594-4900
   e-mail: alan_kasidh@nymc.edu

## New York School of Interior Design
170 East 70th St
New York, NY 10021
212-472-1500 or 800-336-9743  Fax: 212-472-3800
e-mail: info@nysid.edu
Web site: www.nysid.edu

President:
   Christopher Cyphers............212-472-1500 x401/fax: 212-472-1952

## New York Theological Seminary
475 Riverside Dr, Ste 500
New York, NY 10115-0083
212-870-1211  Fax: 212-870-1236
Web site: www.nyts.edu

President:
   Dale T Irvin......................................212-870-1223
   e-mail: dirvin@nyts.edu

## New York University
70 Washington Square South
New York, NY 10012
212-998-1212
Web site: www.nyu.edu

President:
   Andrew Hamilton ..................212-998-2345/fax: 212-995-4790
   e-mail: andrew.hamilton@nyu.edu

## Niagara University
Lewiston Rd
Niagara University, NY 14109
716-285-1212 or 800-778-3450  Fax: 716-286-8710
Web site: www.niagara.edu

President:
   Rev Joseph L Levesque.............716-286-8350/fax: 716-286-8350
   e-mail: jll@niagara.edu

## Northeastern Seminary
2265 Westside Dr
Rochester, NY 14624
585-594-6802 or 800-777-4792  Fax: 585-594-6801
Web site: www.nes.edu

President:
   John A Martin.....................................585-594-6100
   e-mail: martinj@roberts.edu

## Nyack College
1 South Blvd
Nyack, NY 10960-3698
845-358-1710  Fax: 845-358-1751
e-mail: president@nyack.edu
Web site: www.nyack.edu

President:
   Michael Scales................................845-358-1710 x310

## Pace University
1 Pace Plz
New York, NY 10038
212-346-1200 or 800-722-3338  Fax: 212-346-1933
Web site: www.pace.edu

*Offices and agencies generally appear in alphabetical order, except when specific order is requested by listee.*

President:
Stephen J Friedman . . . . . . . . . . . . . . . . .212-346-1097/fax: 212-346-1384
e-mail: sfriedman@pace.edu

## Paul Smith's College
Routes 86 & 30
PO Box 265
Paul Smiths, NY 12970-0265
518-327-6227 or 800-421-2605  Fax: 518-327-6016
e-mail: kaaron@paulsmiths.edu
Web site: www.paulsmiths.edu

President/Acting Provost:
John W Mills . . . . . . . . . . . . . . . . . . . . .518-327-6223/fax: 518-327-6060
e-mail: millsj@paulsmiths.edu

## Phillips Beth Israel School of Nursing
776 Ave of Americas
4th Fl
New York, NY 10001-6354
212-614-6110  Fax: 212-614-6109

Dean:
Janet MacKin . . . . . . . . . . . . . . . . . . . . . . . . . . . . .212-614-6107

## Polytechnic University
Main Campus
6 MetroTech Ctr
Brooklyn, NY 11201-2999
718-260-3600  Fax: 718-260-3136
Web site: www.poly.edu

President:
Jerry MacArthur Hultin . . . . . . . . . . . . .718-260-3500/fax: 718-260-3755

## Pratt Institute
200 Willoughby Ave
Brooklyn, NY 11205
718-636-3600  Fax: 718-636-3785
e-mail: info@pratt.edu
Web site: www.pratt.edu

President:
Thomas F Schutte . . . . . . . . . . . . . . . . . . . . . . . . . . .718-636-3646
e-mail: tschutte@pratt.edu

## Professional Business College
125 Canal St
New York, NY 10002
212-226-7300
Web site: www.pbcny.edu

President:
Leon Y Lee . . . . . . . . . . . . . . . . . . . . . . . . . . . . . . .212-226-7300

## Rensselaer Polytechnic Institute
110 8th St
Troy, NY 12180
518-276-6000
Web site: www.rpi.edu

President:
Shirley Ann Jackson . . . . . . . . . . . . . . .518-276-6211/fax: 518-276-8702
e-mail: president@rpi.edu

## Roberts Wesleyan College
2301 Westside Dr
Rochester, NY 14624-1997

585-594-6000 or 800-777-4792  Fax: 585-594-6371
e-mail: admissions@roberts.edu
Web site: www.roberts.edu

President:
John A Martin . . . . . . . . . . . . . . . . . . . .585-594-6100/fax: 585-594-6780
e-mail: presidentsoffice@roberts.edu

## Rochester Institute of Technology
One Lomb Memorial Dr
Rochester, NY 14623-5603
585-475-2411  Fax: 585-475-5700
Web site: www.rit.edu

President:
William W Destler . . . . . . . . . . . . . . . . . . . . . . . . . . .585-475-2394
e-mail: bill.destler@rit.edu

## Rochester, University of
Wallis Hall
Administration
Rochester, NY 14627
585-275-2121  Fax: 585-275-0359
Web site: www.rochester.edu

President:
Joel Seligman. . . . . . . . . . . . . . . . . . . .585-275-8356/fax: 585-256-2473
e-mail: seligman@rochester.edu

## Rockefeller University
1230 York Ave
New York, NY 10065
212-327-8000  Fax: 212-327-7974
e-mail: pubinfo@rockefeller.edu
Web site: www.rockefeller.edu

President:
Marc Tessier-Lavigne. . . . . . . . . . . . . . . . . . . . . . . . .212-327-8000
e-mail: marc.tessier-lavigne@rockefeller.edu

## Sage Colleges (The)
65 1st Street
Troy, NY 12180
518-244-2000 or 888-837-9724  Fax: 518-244-2470
Web site: www.sage.edu

President:
Susan Scrimshaw . . . . . . . . . . . . . . . . . . . . . . . . . . .518-244-2214
e-mail: scrims@sage.edu

## Salvation Army School for Officer Training
201 Lafayette Ave
Suffern, NY 10901
845-368-7200  Fax: 845-357-6644

Director of Business:
Major Ivan Rock. . . . . . . . . . . . . . . . . . . . . . . . . . . .845-244-2214
e-mail: Ivan.Rock@use.salvationarmy.org

## Samaritan Hospital School of Nursing
2215 Burdett Ave
Troy, NY 12180
518-271-3300  Fax: 518-271-3303
e-mail: dorseyp@nehealth.com
Web site: www.nehealth.com

Director:
Susan Birkhead . . . . . . . . . . . . . . . . . . . . . . . . . . . .518-271-3285

*Offices and agencies generally appear in alphabetical order, except when specific order is requested by listee.*

**451**

## Sarah Lawrence College
1 Mead Way
Bronxville, NY 10708-5999
914-337-0700  Fax: 914-395-2515
e-mail: slcadmit@slc.edu
Web site: www.slc.edu

President:
    Karen Lawrence...................914-395-2201/fax: 914-395-2668
    e-mail: president@sarahlawrence.edu
Dean:
    Jerrilynne Dodds....................................914-395-2303
    e-mail: jdodds@sarahlawrence.edu

## Seminary of the Immaculate Conception
440 West Neck Rd
Huntington, NY 11743
631-423-0483  Fax: 631-423-2346
e-mail: info@icseminary.edu
Web site: www.icseminary.edu

Rector:
    Rev Msgr Peter Vaccari ...........................631-423-0483
    e-mail: pvaccari@icseminary.edu

## Siena College
515 Loudon Rd
Loudonville, NY 12211-1462
518-783-2300 or 888-287-4362  Fax: 518-783-4293
Web site: www.siena.edu

President:
    Fr Kevin Mullen ...................................518-783-2302
    e-mail: kmullen@siena.edu

## Skidmore College
815 N Broadway
Saratoga Springs, NY 12866-1632
518-580-5000  Fax: 518-580-5699
e-mail: info@skidmore.edu
Web site: www.skidmore.edu

President:
    Philip A Glotzbach ................518-580-5700/fax: 518-580-5699
    e-mail: pglotzba@skidmore.edu

## St Bernard's School of Theology & Ministry
120 French Rd
Rochester, NY 14618
585-271-3657  Fax: 585-271-2045
Web site: www.stbernards.edu

President:
    Patricia A Schoelles...........................585-271-3657 x298
    e-mail: pschoelles@stbernards.edu

## St Bonaventure University
3261 W State Rd
St Bonaventure, NY 14778-2284
716-375-2000 or 800-462-5050
Web site: www.sbu.edu

President:
    Sister Margaret Carney...........................716-375-2222
    e-mail: mcarney@sbu.edu

## St Elizabeth College of Nursing
2215 Genesee St
Utica, NY 13501
315-798-8144  Fax: 315-798-8271
Web site: www.secon.edu

Interim President:
    Marian Kovatchitch ...............................315-798-8125

## St Francis College
180 Remsen St
Brooklyn Heights, NY 11201
718-489-5200 or 718-522-2300  Fax: 718-237-8964

President:
    Brendan J Dugan.................................718-489-5416

## St John Fisher College
3690 East Ave
Rochester, NY 14618
585-385-8000  Fax: 585-385-8289
Web site: www.sjfc.edu

President:
    Donald E Bain...................................585-385-8010
    e-mail: dbain@sjfc.edu

## St John's University
Queens Campus
8000 Utopia Pkwy
Queens, NY 11439
718-990-2000 or 888-978-5646  Fax: 718-990-5723
e-mail: admhelp@stjohns.edu
Web site: www.stjohns.edu

President:
    Conrado Gempesaw ..............................718-990-2000

## St Joseph's College
Main Campus
245 Clinton Ave
Brooklyn, NY 11205-3688
718-940-5300  Fax: 718-636-7242
Web site: www.sjcny.edu

President:
    Elizabeth A Hill...................718-940-5989/fax: 718-636-6102

## St Joseph's Seminary Institute of Religious Studies
201 Seminary Ave
Yonkers, NY 10704-1896
914-968-6200  Fax: 914-376-2019
e-mail: vocations@archny.org

Dean:
    Kevin P O'Reilly .................................914-968-6200

## St Lawrence University
23 Romoda Dr
Canton, NY 13617
315-229-5011 or 800-285-1856  Fax: 315-229-7422
Web site: www.stlawu.edu

President:
    William L Fox....................................315-229-5892
    e-mail: wfox@stlawu.edu

*Offices and agencies generally appear in alphabetical order, except when specific order is requested by listee.*

## St Thomas Aquinas College
125 Route 340
Sparkill, NY 10976-1050
845-398-4100
Web site: www.stac.edu

President/CEO:
Margaret M Fitzpatrick . . . . . . . . . . . . . 845-398-4012/fax: 845-359-8136
e-mail: mfitzpat@stac.edu

## St Vladimir's Orthodox Theological Seminary
575 Scarsdale Rd
Yonkers, NY 10707
914-961-8313  Fax: 914-961-4507
e-mail: info@svots.edu
Web site: www.svots.edu

Dean:
Very Rev John Behr . . . . . . . . . . . . . . . . . . . . . . . . 914-961-8313 X326
e-mail: jbehr@svots.edu

## Sunbridge College
285 Hungry Hollow Rd
Chesnut Ridge, NY 10977
845-425-0055  Fax: 845-425-1413
e-mail: info@sunbridge.edu
Web site: www.sunbridge.edu

Executive Director:
Jessica H Ziegler . . . . . . . . . . . . . . . . . . . . . . . . . 845-425-0055 x23
e-mail: jziegler@sunbridge.edu

## Syracuse University
Skytop Office Building
Syracuse, NY 13244-1100
315-443-1870  Fax: 315-443-3503
Web site: www.syr.edu

Chancellor & President:
Nancy Cantor . . . . . . . . . . . . . . . . . . . . . . . . . . . . . . 315-443-2235

## Teachers College, Columbia University
525 W 120th St
New York, NY 10027
212-678-3000
Web site: www.tc.columbia.edu

President:
Dr Susan H Fuhrman . . . . . . . . . . . . . . 212-678-3131/fax: 212-678-3205
e-mail: susanf@exchange.tc.columbia.edu

## Touro College
500 Seventh Avenue
New York, NY 10018
212-463-0400  Fax: 212-627-9144
Web site: www.touro.edu

President:
Alan Kadish . . . . . . . . . . . . . . . . . . . . . . . . . . . . . . 212-463-0400

## Trocaire College
360 Choate Ave
Buffalo, NY 14220-2094
716-826-1200  Fax: 716-828-6109
e-mail: info@trocaire.edu
Web site: www.trocaire.edu

President:
Paul B Hurley, Jr . . . . . . . . . . . . . . . . . . . . . . . . . . . 716-826-1200
e-mail: hurleyp@trocaire.edu

## Unification Theological Seminary
30 Seminary Dr
Barrytown, NY 12507
845-752-3000  Fax: 845-752-3014
e-mail: registrar@uts.edu
Web site: www.uts.edu

President:
Richard Panzer . . . . . . . . . . . . . . . . . . . . . . . . . . 212-563-6647 x110

## Union College
807 Union St
Schenectady, NY 12308-3107
518-388-6000  Fax: 518-388-6006
Web site: www.union.edu

President-Elect:
Stephen C Ainlay . . . . . . . . . . . . . . . . . . . . . . . . . . 518-388-6101
e-mail: ainlays@union.edu
Dean:
Steve Leavitt . . . . . . . . . . . . . . . . . . 518-388-6116/fax: 518-388-6648
e-mail: leavitts@union.edu

## Union Theological Seminary
3041 Broadway at 121st St
New York, NY 10027
212-662-7100  Fax: 212-280-1416
e-mail: contactus@uts.columbia.edu
Web site: www.utsnyc.edu

President:
Serene Jones . . . . . . . . . . . . . . . . . . . . . . . . . . . . . 212-280-1403
e-mail: sjones@uts.columbia.edu

## Utica College
1600 Burrstone Rd
Utica, NY 13502-5159
315-792-3006  Fax: 315-792-3003
Web site: www.utica.edu

President:
Todd S Hutton . . . . . . . . . . . . . . . . . . . . . . . . . . . . . 315-792-3222
e-mail: thutton@utica.edu

## Vassar College
124 Raymond Ave
Box 9
Poughkeepsie, NY 12604
845-437-7400  Fax: 845-437-7187
Web site: www.vassar.edu

President:
Elizabeth Howe Bradley . . . . . . . . . . . . . . . . . . . . . . 845-437-7200

## Vaughn College of Aeronautics & Technology
86-01 23rd Ave
Flushing, NY 11369
718-429-6600 or 866-682-8446  Fax: 718-779-2231
Web site: www.vaughn.edu

President:
John C Fitzpatrick . . . . . . . . . . . . 718-429-6600 x104/fax: 718-429-4020
e-mail: john.fitzpatrick@vaughn.edu

*Offices and agencies generally appear in alphabetical order, except when specific order is requested by listee.*

Colleges, Universities & School Districts

## Villa Maria College of Buffalo
240 Pine Ridge Rd
Buffalo, NY 14225
716-896-0700  Fax: 716-961-1871
e-mail: admissions@villa.edu
Web site: www.villa.edu

President:
Sr Marcella Marie Garus............................716-961-1868
e-mail: smgarus@villa.edu

## Wagner College
1 Campus Rd
Staten Island, NY 10301
718-390-3100 or 800-221-1010  Fax: 718-390-3105
Web site: www.wagner.edu

President:
Richard Guarasci...................718-390-3131/fax: 718-390-3170
e-mail: guarasci@wagner.edu

## Watson School of Biological Sciences at Cold Spring Harbor Laboratory
One Bungtown Rd
Cold Spring Harbor, NY 11724
516-367-8800  Fax: 516-367-6919
e-mail: gradschool@cshl.edu
Web site: www.cshl.edu/gradschool

President/CEO:
Bruce Stillman ....................................516-367-6890

## Webb Institute
298 Crescent Beach Rd
Glen Cove, NY 11542-1398
516-671-2213 or 866-708-9322  Fax: 516-674-9838

President:
Admiral Robert Olsen .........................516-671-2213 x102

## Wells College
170 Main St
Aurora, NY 13026-0500
315-364-3266
Web site: www.wells.edu

President:
Lisa Marsh Ryerson.................315-364-3265/fax: 315-364-3335
e-mail: president@wells.edu

## Yeshiva University
Wilf Campus
500 W 185th St
New York, NY 10033-3201
212-960-5400
Web site: www.yu.edu

President:
Richard M Joel .....................................212-960-5300
e-mail: president@yu.edu

## PROPRIETARY COLLEGES

## ASA Institute of Business & Computer Technology
81 Willoughby St
Brooklyn, NY 11201

877-679-8772
Web site: www.asa.edu

President:
Alex Shchegol.......................................877-679-8772

## Art Institute of New York City (The)
218-232 West 40th Street
New York, NY 10018
212-226-5500 or 800-654-2433  Fax: 212-818-1079
e-mail: ainycadm@aii.edu
Web site: www.artinstitutes.edu/new-york

President:
Jennifer Ramey

## Berkeley College, New York City Campus
3 East 43rd St
New York, NY 10017
212-986-4343 or 800-446-5400  Fax: 212-697-3371
e-mail: info@berkeleycollege.edu
Web site: www.berkeleycollege.edu

President:
Darlo A Cortes.............................973-278-5400 x1102
e-mail: president@berkeleycollege.edu

## Berkeley College, Westchester Campus
99 Church St
White Plains, NY 10601
914-694-1122  Fax: 914-328-9469
e-mail: info@berkeleycollege.edu
Web site: www.berkeleycollege.edu

SVP, Administration:
Cynthia Rubino....................................914-694-1122

## Briarcliffe College-Bethpage
1055 Stewart Ave
Bethpage, NY 11714
516-918-3600 or 88-348-4999  Fax: 516-470-6020
e-mail: info@bcl.edu

President:
George Santiago, Jr..............................516-918-3603
e-mail: gsantiago@bcl.edu

## Briarcliffe College-Patchogue
225 West Main St
Patchogue, NY 11772
631-654-5300
Web site: www.bcpat.com

President:
George Santiago, Jr...............................631-654-5300

## Bryant & Stratton College-Albany Campus
1259 Central Ave
Albany, NY 12205
518-437-1802
e-mail: rpferrell@bryantstratton.edu
Web site: www.bryantstratton.edu

Campus Director:
Michael Gutierrez.................................518-437-1802
e-mail: magutierrez@bryantstratton.edu

*Offices and agencies generally appear in alphabetical order, except when specific order is requested by listee.*

## Bryant & Stratton College-Amherst Campus
3650 Millersport Highway
Getzville, NY 14068
716-625-6300
Web site: www.bryantstratton.edu

Campus Director:
  Michael Mariani . . . . . . . . . . . . . . . . . . . . . . . . . . . . . . . .716-625-6300

## Bryant & Stratton College-Buffalo Campus
465 Main St, Ste 400
Buffalo, NY 14203
716-884-9120
e-mail: buffalo@bryantstratton.edu
Web site: www.bryantstratton.edu

Campus Director:
  Marvel Ross-Jones . . . . . . . . . . . . . . . . . . . . . . . . . . . . . .716-884-9120

## Bryant & Stratton College-Greece Campus
150 Bellwood Dr
Rochester, NY 14606
585-720-0660
Web site: www.bryantstratton.edu

Campus Director:
  Marc Ambrosi. . . . . . . . . . . . . . . . . . . . . . . . . . . . . . . . . . .585-720-0660

## Bryant & Stratton College-Henrietta Campus
1225 Jefferson Rd
Rochester, NY 14623
585-292-5627
e-mail: djprofita@bryantstratton.edu
Web site: www.bryantstratton.edu

Director of Rochester Colleges:
  Jeffrey Moore . . . . . . . . . . . . . . . . . . . . . . . . . . . . . . . . . . .585-292-5627

## Bryant & Stratton College-Southtowns Campus
200 Red Tail
Orchard Park, NY 14127
716-677-9500
e-mail: southtowns@bryantstratton.edu
Web site: www.bryantstratton.edu

Campus Director:
  Paul Bahr. . . . . . . . . . . . . . . . . . . . . . . . . . . . . . . . . . . . . . .716-677-9500

## Bryant & Stratton College-Syracuse Campus
953 James St
Syracuse, NY 13203-2502
315-472-6603
e-mail: syracusedt@bryantstratton.edu
Web site: www.bryantstratton.edu

Campus Director:
  Michael Sattler . . . . . . . . . . . . . . . . . . . . . . . . . . . . . . . . . .315-472-6603

## Bryant & Stratton College-Syracuse North Campus
8687 Carling Rd
Liverpool, NY 13090
315-652-6500
e-mail: sninfo@bryantstratton.edu
Web site: www.bryantstratton.edu

Campus Director:
  Susan Cumoletti . . . . . . . . . . . . . . . . . . . . . . . . . . . . . . . . .315-652-6500

## Business Informatics Center
134 S Central Ave
Valley Stream, NY 11580
516-561-0050  Fax: 516-561-0074

President:
  Constance Brown . . . . . . . . . . . . . . . . . . . . . . . . . . . . . . . . .516-561-0050

## Christie's Education Inc
11 W 42 St
8th Fl
New York, NY 10036
212-355-1501  Fax: 212-355-7370
e-mail: christieseducataion@christies.com

Director of Studies:
  Veronique Chagnon-Burke. . . . . . . . . . . . . . . . . . . . . . . . .212-355-1501
  e-mail: vchagnon-burke@christies.com

## College of Westchester (The)
325 Central Park Ave
PO Box 710
White Plains, NY 10606
914-831-0200 or 800-660-7093  Fax: 914-948-5441
Web site: www.cw.edu

President:
  Karen J Smith . . . . . . . . . . . . . . . . . . . . . . . . . . . . . . . . . . .914-831-0200

## DeVry Institute of Technology, College of New York
180 Madison Av., Suite 900
New York, NY 10016
212-312-4301
Web site: www.ny.devry.edu

Director:
  Newton Myvett. . . . . . . . . . . . . . . . . . . . . . . . . . . . . . . . . . .212-312-4301

## Elmira Business Institute
Langdon Plaza
303 N Main St
Elmira, NY 14901-2731
607-733-7177 or 800-843-1812  Fax: 607-733-7178
e-mail: info@ebi-college.com
Web site: www.ebi-college.com

President:
  Brad C Phillips. . . . . . . . . . . . . . . . . . . . . . . . . . . . . . . . . . .607-733-7177 x202

## Elmira Business Institute-Vestal
Vestal Executive Pk
4100 Vestal Rd
Vestal, NY 13850
607-729-8915 or 866-703-7550  Fax: 607-729-8916
e-mail: info@ebi-college.com
Web site: www.ebi-college.com

Campus Director:
  Bob Williams. . . . . . . . . . . . . . . . . . . . . . . . . . . . . . . . . . . . .607-729-8915 x202

## Everest Institute
1630 Portland Ave
Rochester, NY 14621-3007
585-266-0430 or 888-741-4270  Fax: 585-266-8243
Web site: www.everest.edu

*Offices and agencies generally appear in alphabetical order, except when specific order is requested by listee.*

## Five Towns College
305 N Service Rd
Dix Hills, NY 11746-5871
631-656-2110  Fax: 631-424-7008
Web site: www.ftc.edu

President:
Stanley G Cohen . . . . . . . . . . . . . . . . . .631-424-7000/fax: 631-656-2172

## Globe Institute of Technology
500 7th Ave
New York, NY 10018
212-349-4330  Fax: 212-227-5920

President:
Martin Oliner . . . . . . . . . . . . . . . . . . . . . . . . . . . . . . . .212-349-4330

## ITT Technical Institute
13 Airline Dr
Albany, NY 12205
518-452-9300 or 800-489-1191  Fax: 518-452-9393

Director:
Michael Mariani . . . . . . . . . . . . . . . . . . . . . . . . . . . . .518-452-9300

## Island Drafting & Technical Institute
128 Broadway, Route 110
Amityville, NY 11701-2704
631-691-8733  Fax: 631-691-8738
e-mail: info@idti.edu
Web site: www.idti.edu

President:
James G DiLiberto . . . . . . . . . . . . . . . . . . . . . . . . . . .631-691-8733
e-mail: dilibertoj@idti.edu

## Jamestown Business College
7 Fairmount Ave
Jamestown, NY 14701
716-664-5100  Fax: 716-664-3144

President:
David Conklin. . . . . . . . . . . . . . . . . . . . . . . . . . . . . . . .716-664-5100

## Laboratory Institute of Merchandising
12 E 53 St
New York, NY 10022
212-752-1530 or 800-677-1323  Fax: 212-750-3432
e-mail: info@limcollege.edu
Web site: www.limcollege.edu

President:
Elizabeth S Marcuse. . . . . . . . . . . . . . . . . . . . . . . . . .212-752-1530
e-mail: execs@limcollege.edu

## Long Island Business Institute-Commack
6500 Jericho Tpke
Commack, NY 11725
631-499-7100  Fax: 631-499-7114
e-mail: info@libi.edu
Web site: www.libi.edu

President:
Monica Foote . . . . . . . . . . . . . . . . . . . . . . . . . . . . . . . .631-499-7100

## Long Island Business Institute-Flushing
136-18 39 Ave
Flushing, NY 11354

718-939-5100  Fax: 718-939-9235
Web site: www.libi.edu

President:
Monica Foote . . . . . . . . . . . . . . . . . . . . . . . . . . . . . . . .718-939-5100

## Mandl School
254 W 54th St
New York, NY 10019
212-247-3434
Web site: www.mandlschool.com

## Mildred Elley
855 Central Ave
Albany, NY 12206
518-786-0855 or 800-622-6327  Fax: 518-786-0898
Web site: www.mildred-elley.edu

President:
Faith A Takes . . . . . . . . . . . . . . .518-786-0855 x1213/fax: 518-785-7560
e-mail: faith.takes@mildred-elley.edu

## Monroe College-Bronx
2501 Jerome Ave
Bronx, NY 10468
718-933-6700 or 800-556-6676  Fax: 718-364-3552
Web site: www.monroecollege.edu

President:
Stephen J Jerome . . . . . . . . . . . . . . . . . . . . . . . . . . .718-933-6700 x8252

## Monroe College-New Rochelle
434 Main St
New Rochelle, NY 10801
914-632-5400  Fax: 914-632-5462
Web site: www.monroecollege.edu

President:
Stephen J Jerome

## New York Career Institute
11 Park Place
4th Fl
New York, NY 10007
212-962-0002  Fax: 212-385-7574
e-mail: info@nyci.com
Web site: www.nyci.com

CEO:
Ivan Londa . . . . . . . . . . . . . . . . . . . . . . . . . . . . . . . . .212-962-0002

## Olean Business Institute
301 North Union St
Olean, NY 14760
716-372-7978  Fax: 716-372-2120

President:
Jennifer L Madison . . . . . . . . . . . . . . . . . . . . . . . . . . .716-372-7978

## Pacific College of Oriental Medicine
110 William Street
19th Floor
New York, NY 10038
212-982-3456 or 800-729-3468  Fax: 212-982-6514
Web site: www.pacificcollege.edu

*Offices and agencies generally appear in alphabetical order, except when specific order is requested by listee.*

Dean & Research Director:
Belinda Anderson . . . . . . . . . . . . . . . . . . . . . . . . . . . . . . . . .212-982-3456
e-mail: banderson@pacificcollege.edu

## Plaza College
118-33 Queens Blvd
Forest Hills, NY 11375
718-779-1430  Fax: 718-779-7423
e-mail: info@plazacollege.edu
Web site: www.plazacollege.edu

President:
Charles E Callahan . . . . . . . . . . . . . . . . . . . . . . . . . . . . . .718-779-1430

## School of Visual Arts
209 East 23rd St
New York, NY 10010
212-592-2000 or 888-220-5782  Fax: 212-725-3587
e-mail: admissions@sva.edu

President:
David John Rhodes . . . . . . . . . . . . . . . . . . . . . . . . . . . . . . . .212-592-2350

## Swedish Institute
226 W 26th St
New York, NY 10001
212-924-5900  Fax: 212-924-7600
Web site: www.swedishinstitute.org

President:
William C Ehrhardt

## Technical Career Institutes Inc
320 W 31st St
New York, NY 10001
212-594-4000 or 800-878-8246

President:
James Melville . . . . . . . . . . . . . . . . . . . . . . . . . . . . . . . . . .212-594-4000

## Tri-State College of Acupuncture
80th Ave, Ste 400
New York, NY 10011

212-242-2255  Fax: 212-242-2920

CEO:
Mark D Seem . . . . . . . . . . . . . . . . . . . . . . . . . . . . . . . . . . . .212-496-7514

## US Merchant Marine Academy
300 Steamboat Road
Kings Point, NY 11024
516-773-5000  Fax: 516-773-5774
Web site: www.usmma.edu

Superintendent & Dean:
Phillip Greene, Jr.

## US Military Academy at West Point
626 Swift Road
West Point, NY 10996
845-938-4041 or 800-367-2884  Fax: 845-938-2363
Web site: www.usma.edu

Superintendent:
LTG Franklin L Hagenbeck . . . . . . . . . . . . . . . . . . . . . . . . .845-938-2610

## Utica School of Commerce
201 Bleecker St
Utica, NY 13501
315-733-2300 or 800-321-4872  Fax: 315-733-9281
Web site: www.uscny.edu

President:
Philip M Williams . . . . . . . . . . . . . . . . . . . . . . . . . . . . .315-733-2309 x2214
e-mail: pwilliams@uscny.edu

## Wood Tobe-Coburn
8 E 40th St
New York, NY 10016
212-686-9040 or 800-394-9663  Fax: 212-686-9171
Web site: www.woodtobecoburn.edu

President:
Sandi Gruninger . . . . . . . . . . . . . . . . . . . . . . . . . . . . . . . . .212-686-9040

*Offices and agencies generally appear in alphabetical order, except when specific order is requested by listee.*

## PUBLIC SCHOOL DISTRICTS

### SCHOOL DISTRICT ADMINISTRATORS

#### ALBANY

**Albany City SD**
Academy Park, Albany, NY 12207-1099
518-475-6010  Fax: 518-475-7295
e-mail: rcolucciello@albany.k12.ny.us
Web site: www.albanyschools.org
Raymond Colucciello, Superintendent

**Berne-Knox-Westerlo CSD**
1738 Helderberg Trl, Berne, NY 12023-2926
518-872-1293  Fax: 518-872-0341
Web site: www.bkwcsd.k12.ny.us
Paul Dorward, Superintendent

**Bethlehem CSD**
90 Adams Place, Delmar, NY 12054
518-439-7098  Fax: 518-475-0352
Web site: bcsd.k12.ny.us
Dr Michael D Tebbano, Superintendent

**Cohoes City SD**
7 Bevan Street, Cohoes, NY 12047-3299
518-237-0100  Fax: 518-237-2912
Web site: www.cohoes.org
Robert K Libby, Superintendent

**Green Island UFSD**
171 Hudson Ave, Green Island, NY 12183-1293
518-273-1422  Fax: 518-270-0818
Web site: www.greenisland.org
Michael Mugits, Superintendent

**Guilderland CSD**
6076 State Farm Rd, Guilderland, NY 12084-9533
518-456-6200  Fax: 518-456-1152
Web site: www.guilderlandschools.org
Marie Wiles, Superintendent

**Menands UFSD**
19 Wards Ln, Menands, NY 12204-2197
518-465-4561  Fax: 518-465-4572
Kathleen Meany, Interim Superintendent

**North Colonie CSD**
91 Fiddler's Ln, Latham, NY 12110-5349
518-785-8591  Fax: 518-785-8502
e-mail: dcorr@ncolonie.org
Web site: www.northcolonie.org
Joseph Corr, Superintendent

**Ravena-Coeymans-Selkirk CSD**
26 Thatcher St, Selkirk, NY 12158-0097
518-756-5200  Fax: 518-767-2644
Web site: www.rcscsd.org
Daniel Teplesky, Superintendent

**South Colonie CSD**
102 Loralee Dr, Albany, NY 12205-2298
518-869-3576  Fax: 518-869-6481
Web site: www.southcolonieschools.org
Jonathan Buhner, Superintendent

**Voorheesville CSD**
432 New Salem Rd, Voorheesville, NY 12186-0498
518-765-3313  Fax: 518-765-2751
Teresa T Snyder, Superintendent

**Watervliet City SD**
1245 Hillside Dr, Watervliet, NY 12189
518-629-3200  Fax: 518-629-3265
Web site: www.watervlietcityschools.org
Paul Padalino, Superintendent

#### ALLEGANY

**Alfred-Almond CSD**
6795 Rt 21, Almond, NY 14804-9716
607-276-6500  Fax: 607-276-6304
e-mail: rcalkins@aacs.wnyric.org
Web site: www.aacs.org
Richard Calkins, Superintendent

**Andover CSD**
31-35 Elm St, PO Box G, Andover, NY 14806-0508
607-478-8491 x222  Fax: 607-478-8833
Web site: www.andovercsd.org
William C Berg, Superintendent

**Belfast CSD**
1 King St, Belfast, NY 14711
585-365-9940
e-mail: jmay@belf.wnyric.org
Web site: www.belfast.wnyric.org
Judy May, Superintendent

**Bolivar-Richburg CSD**
100 School St, Bolivar, NY 14715
585-928-2561  Fax: 585-928-1368
Web site: www.brcs.wnyric.org
Marilyn Capawan, Superintendent

**Canaseraga CSD**
4-8 Main St, PO Box 230, Canaseraga, NY 14822-0230
607-545-6421  Fax: 607-545-6265
Web site: www.ccsdny.org
Marie Blum, Superintendent

**Cuba-Rushford CSD**
5476 Rt 305, Cuba, NY 14727-1014
585-968-2650 x4426
Web site: www.crcs.wnyric.org
Kevin Shanley, Superintendent

**Fillmore CSD**
104 W. Main St, Fillmore, NY 14735-0177
585-567-2251
Web site: www.fillmorecsd.org
Martin D Cox, Superintendent

**Friendship CSD**
46 W Main St, Friendship, NY 14739-9702
716-973-3311  Fax: 716-973-2023
Web site: www.friendship.wnyric.org
Maureen Donahue, Superintendent

**Genesee Valley CSD**
1 Jaguar Dr, Belmont, NY 14813-9788
585-268-7900
Web site: www.genvalley.org
Ralph Wilson, Superintendent

**Scio CSD**
3968 Washington St, Scio, NY 14880-9507
716-593-5510  Fax: 716-593-3468
Tracie Preston, Superintendent

*Offices and agencies generally appear in alphabetical order, except when specific order is requested by listee.*

**Wellsville CSD**
126 W State St, Wellsville, NY 14895
585-596-2170  Fax: 585-596-2177
Web site: www.wellsville.wnyric.org
Kimberly Mueller, Superintendent

**Whitesville CSD**
692 Main St, Whitesville, NY 14897
607-356-3301  Fax: 607-356-3598
Web site: www.whitesville.wnyric.org
Douglas H Wyant, Superintendent

## BROOME

**Binghamton City SD**
164 Hawley St, Binghamton, NY 13901-2126
607-762-8100 x318
Web site: www.binghamtonschools.org
Peggy J Wozniak, Superintendent

**Chenango Forks CSD**
One Gordon Dr, Binghamton, NY 13901-5614
607-648-7543  Fax: 607-48-7560
e-mail: bundyr@cforks.org
Web site: www.cforks.org
Robert Bundy, Superintendent

**Chenango Valley CSD**
221 Chenango Bridge Road, Binghamton, NY 13901-1653
607-762-6800  Fax: 607-762-6890
Web site: www.cvcsd.stier.org
Dr Thomas Douglas, Superintendent

**Deposit CSD**
171 Second St, Deposit, NY 13754-1397
607-467-5380  Fax: 607-467-5535
e-mail: bhauber@deposit.stier.org
Web site: www.depositcsd.org
Bonnie Hauber, Superintendent

**Harpursville CSD**
54 Main St, Harpursville, NY 13787-0147
607-693-8101
Web site: www.hcs.stier.org
Kathleen M Wood, Superintendent

**Johnson City CSD**
666 Reynolds Rd, Johnson City, NY 13790-1398
607-763-1230  Fax: 607-729-2767
e-mail: mfrys@jcschools.stier.org
Web site: www.jcschools.com
Mary Kay Frys, Superintendent
Joseph F Stoner, Superintendent

**Susquehanna Valley CSD**
1040 Conklin Rd, Conklin, NY 13748-0200
607-775-0170
Web site: www.svsabers.org
Gerardo Tagliaferri, Acting Superintendent

**Union-Endicott CSD**
1100 E Main St, Endicott, NY 13760-5271
607-757-2103  Fax: 607-757-2809
Web site: www.uek12.org
Suzanne McLeod, Superintendent

**Vestal CSD**
201 Main St, Vestal, NY 13850-1599
607-757-2241
e-mail: mdlaroach@vcs.stier.org
Web site: www.vestal.stier.org
Mark LaRoach, Superintendent

**Whitney Point CSD**
10 Keibel Rd, Whitney Point, NY 13862-0249
607-692-8202  Fax: 607-692-4434
e-mail: mhibbard@wpcsd.org
Web site: www.wpcsd.org
Mary Hibbard, Superintendent

**Windsor CSD**
1191 NY Route 79, Windsor, NY 13865-4134
607-655-8216  Fax: 607-655-3553
e-mail: jandrews@windsor-csd.org
Web site: www.windsor-csd.org
Jason A Andrews, Superintendent

## CATTARAUGUS

**Allegany - Limestone CSD**
3131 Five Mile Rd, Allegany, NY 14706-9627
716-375-6600 x2006
Diane M Munro, Superintendent

**Cattaraugus-Little Valley CSD**
207 Rock City St, Little Valley, NY 14755-1298
716-938-9155 x2210  Fax: 716-938-9367
Web site: www.cattlv.wnyric.org
Jon W Peterson, Superintendent

**Ellicottville CSD**
5873 Route 219, Ellicottville, NY 14731-9719
716-699-2368  Fax: 716-699-6017
Mark Ward, Superintendent

**Franklinville CSD**
31 N Main St, Franklinville, NY 14737-1096
716-676-8029  Fax: 716-676-3779
Michael Spasiano, Superintendent

**Gowanda CSD**
10674 Prospect St, Gowanda, NY 14070
716-532-3325  Fax: 716-995-2156
e-mail: crinaldi@gowcsd.org
Web site: www.gowcsd.org
Charles J Rinaldi, Superintendent

**Hinsdale CSD**
3701 Main St, Hinsdale, NY 14743-0278
716-557-2227 x401
Judy McCarthy, Superintendent

**Olean City SD**
410 W Sullivan St, Olean, NY 14760-2596
716-375-8001
Web site: www.oleanschools.org
Colleen Taggerty, Superintendent

**Yorkshire-Pioneer CSD**
12125 County Line Rd, Yorkshire, NY 14173-0579
716-492-9300  Fax: 716-492-9360
Jeffrey Bowen, Superintendent

**Portville CSD**
500 Elm Street, Portville, NY 14770-9791
716-933-6000  Fax: 716-933-7124
Thomas J Simon, Superintendent

**Randolph Academy UFSD**
336 Main Street ER, Randolph, NY 14772-9696
716-358-6866  Fax: 716-358-9076
Lori DeCarlo, Superintendent

Colleges, Universities & School Districts

*Offices and agencies generally appear in alphabetical order, except when specific order is requested by listee.*

**Randolph CSD**
18 Main St, Randolph, NY 14772-1188
716-358-7005 or 716-358-6161  Fax: 716-358-7072
Web site: www.randolphcsd.org
Kimberly Moritz, Superintendent

**Salamanca City SD**
50 Iroquois Dr, Salamanca, NY 14779-1398
716-945-2403  Fax: 716-945-3964
e-mail: dhay@salamancany.org
Web site: www.salamancany.org
J Douglas Hay, Superintendent

**West Valley CSD**
5359 School St, West Valley, NY 14171
716-942-3293  Fax: 716-942-3440
e-mail: hbowen@wvalley.wnyric.org
Web site: www.wvalley.wnyric.org
Hillary W Bowen, Superintendent

## CAYUGA

**Auburn Enlarged City SD**
78 Thornton Ave, Auburn, NY 13021-4698
315-255-8835
Joseph D Pabis, Superintendent

**Cato-Meridian CSD**
2851 NYS Rt 370, Cato, NY 13033-0100
315-626-3439  Fax: 315-626-2888
W Noel Patterson, Superintendent

**Moravia CSD**
68 S Main St, Moravia, NY 13118-1189
315-497-2670  Fax: 315-497-2260
Michelle Brantner, Superintendent

**Port Byron CSD**
30 Maple Ave, Port Byron, NY 13140-9647
315-776-5728  Fax: 315-776-4050
Neil F O'Brien, Superintendent

**Southern Cayuga CSD**
2384 State Rt 34B, Aurora, NY 13026-9771
315-364-7211  Fax: 315-364-7863
Web site: www.southerncayuga.org
Mary Kay Worth, Superintendent

**Union Springs CSD**
239 Cayuga St, Union Springs, NY 13160
315-889-4101
e-mail: lrice@unionspringscsd.org
Linda Rice, Superintendent

**Weedsport CSD**
2821 E Brutus St, Weedsport, NY 13166-9105
315-834-6637
Shaun A O'Connor, Superintendent

## CHAUTAUQUA

**Bemus Point CSD**
3980 Dutch Hollow Rd, Bemus Point, NY 14712
716-386-2375
Albert D'Attilio, Superintendent

**Brocton CSD**
138 W Main St, Brocton, NY 14716
716-792-2121  Fax: 716-792-7944
Web site: www.broctoncsd.org
John Hertlein, Superintendent

**Cassadaga Valley CSD**
5935 Route 60, PO Box 540, Sinclairville, NY 14782-0540
716-962-5155
John Brown, Superintendent

**Chautauqua Lake CSD**
100 N Erie St, Mayville, NY 14757
716-753-5808  Fax: 716-753-5813
Web site: www.clake.org
Benjamin B Spitzer, Superintendent

**Clymer CSD**
8672 E Main St, Clymer, NY 14724-0580
716-355-4444
Web site: www.clymercsd.org
Scott D Smith, Superintendent

**Dunkirk City SD**
620 Marauder Dr, Dunkirk, NY 14048-1396
716-366-9300
Web site: www.dunkirkcsd.org
Gary Cerne, Superintendent

**Falconer CSD**
2 East Ave N, Falconer, NY 14733
716-665-6624 x4101  Fax: 716-665-9265
Stephen Penhollow, Superintendent

**Forestville CSD**
12 Water St, Forestville, NY 14062-9674
716-965-2742  Fax: 716-965-2265
Web site: www.forestville.com
John O'Connor, Superintendent

**Fredonia CSD**
425 E Main St, Fredonia, NY 14063
716-679-1581
Web site: www.fredonia.wnyric.org
Paul Di Fonzo, Superintendent

**Frewsburg CSD**
26 Institute St, Frewsburg, NY 14738
716-569-9241
Web site: www.frewsburgcsd.org
Stephen Vanstrom, Superintendent

**Jamestown City SD**
197 Martin Road, Jamestown, NY 14701
716-483-4350
Daniel E Kathman, Superintendent

**Panama CSD**
41 North St, Panama, NY 14767-9775
716-782-2455  Fax: 716-782-4674
e-mail: blictus@mx.pancent.org
Web site: www.pancent.org
Bert Lictus, Superintendent

**Pine Valley CSD (South Dayton)**
7755 Rt 83, South Dayton, NY 14138
716-988-3293  Fax: 716-988-3864
Web site: www.pval.org
Peter Morgante, Superintendent

**Ripley CSD**
12 N State St, Ripley, NY 14775
716-736-6201  Fax: 716-736-6226
Karen Krause, Interim Superintendent

*Offices and agencies generally appear in alphabetical order, except when specific order is requested by listee.*

**Sherman CSD**
127 Park St, PO Box 950, Sherman, NY 14781-0950
716-761-6122 x1289  Fax: 716-761-6119
Web site: www.sherman.wnyric.org
Thomas Schmidt, Superintendent

**Silver Creek CSD**
1 Dickinson St, PO Box 270, Silver Creek, NY 14136
716-934-2603  Fax: 716-934-7983
David O'Rourke, Superintendent

**Southwestern CSD at Jamestown**
600 Hunt Rd, Jamestown, NY 14701
716-484-1136
Web site: swcs.wnyric.org
Daniel A George, Superintendent

**Westfield CSD**
203 E Main St, Westfield, NY 14787
716-326-2151
Web site: www.wacs.wnyric.org
Mark Sissel, Superintendent

## CHEMUNG

**Elmira City SD**
951 Hoffman St, Elmira, NY 14905-1715
607-735-3000  Fax: 607-735-3002
Web site: www.elmiracityschools.com
Joseph E Hochreiter, Superintendent

**Elmira Heights CSD**
2083 College Ave, Elmira Heights, NY 14903-1598
607-734-7114  Fax: 607-734-7134
Web site: www.heightsschools.com
Mary Beth Fiore, Superintendent

**Horseheads CSD**
One Raider Ln, Horseheads, NY 14845-2398
607-739-5601 x4200
e-mail: hcsdinfo@horseheadsdistrict.com
Web site: www.horseheadsdistrict.com
Ralph Marino, Superintendent

## CHENANGO

**Afton CSD**
29 Academy St, PO Box 5, Afton, NY 13730-0005
607-639-8229
Web site: www.afton.stier.org
Elizabeth A Briggs, Superintendent

**Bainbridge-Guilford CSD**
18 Juliand St, Bainbridge, NY 13733
607-967-6321  Fax: 607-967-4231
Web site: www.bgcsd.org
Karl Brown, Superintendent

**Greene CSD**
40 S Canal St, Greene, NY 13778
607-656-4161
Web site: www.greenecsd.org
Jonathan R Rietz, Superintendent

**Norwich City SD**
89 Midland Drive, Norwich, NY 13815
607-334-1600 X5523  Fax: 607-336-8652
e-mail: gosulliv@norwich.stier.org
Web site: www.norwichcsd.org
Gerard M O'Sullivan, Superintendent

**Georgetown-South Otselic CSD**
125 County Rd 13A, South Otselic, NY 13155-0161
315-653-7591  Fax: 315-653-7500
Web site: www.ovcs.org
Richard Hughes, Superintendent

**Oxford Academy & CSD**
12 Fort Hill Park, PO Box 192, Oxford, NY 13830-0192
607-843-2025 x4041  Fax: 607-843-3241
Web site: www.oxac.org
Randall Squier, Superintendent

**Sherburne-Earlville CSD**
15 School St, Sherburne, NY 13460-0725
607-674-7300  Fax: 607-674-7386
Web site: www.secsd.org
Gayle H Hellert, Superintendent

**Unadilla Valley CSD**
4238 State Hwy 8, New Berlin, NY 13411
607-847-7500  Fax: 607-847-9194
Web site: www.uvstorm.org
Robert J Mackey, Superintendent

## CLINTON

**Ausable Valley CSD**
1273 Rt 9N, Clintonville, NY 12924-4244
518-834-2845  Fax: 518-834-2843
e-mail: psavage@avcsk12.org
Web site: avcs.org
Paul D Savage, Superintendent

**Beekmantown CSD**
37 Eagle Way, West Chazy, NY 12992-2577
518-563-8250 x5501  Fax: 518-563-8132
Web site: www.bcsdk12.org
Scott A Amo, Superintendent

**Chazy Central RSD**
609 Miner Farm Rd, Chazy, NY 12921-0327
518-846-7135  Fax: 518-846-8322
Web site: www.chazy.org
John Fairchild, Superintendent

**Northeastern Clinton CSD**
103 Route 276, Champlain, NY 12919
518-298-8242  Fax: 518-298-4293
Peter J Turner, Superintendent

**Northern Adirondack CSD**
5572 Rt 11, Ellenburg Depot, NY 12935-0164
518-594-7060
Web site: www.nacs1.org
Laura Marlow, Superintendent

**Peru CSD**
17 School St, PO Box 68, Peru, NY 12972-0068
518-643-6000
Web site: www.perucsd.org
A Paul Scott, Superintendent

**Plattsburgh City SD**
49 Broad St, Plattsburgh, NY 12901-3396
518-957-6002  Fax: 518-957-6026
e-mail: jshort@plattscsd.org
Web site: www.plattscsd.org
James Short, Superintendent

Colleges, Universities & School Districts

*Offices and agencies generally appear in alphabetical order, except when specific order is requested by listee.*

**Saranac CSD**
32 Emmons St, Dannemora, NY 12929
518-565-5600
Web site: www.saranac.org
Kenneth O Cringle, Superintendent

## COLUMBIA

**Berkshire UFSD**
13640 Rt 22, Canaan, NY 12029-0370
518-781-3500 X3545
James G Gaudette, Superintendent

**Chatham CSD**
50 Woodbridge Ave, Chatham, NY 12037-1397
518-392-2400
Web site: www.chathamcentralschools.com
Cheryl Nuciforo, Superintendent

**Germantown CSD**
123 Main St, Germantown, NY 12526
518-537-6280  Fax: 518-537-3284
Patrick Gabriel, Superintendent

**Hudson City SD**
215 Harry Howard Ave, Hudson, NY 12534-4011
518-828-4360 x2101
Web site: www.hudsoncityschooldistrict.com
John F Howe, Superintendent

**Ichabod Crane CSD**
2910 Rt 9, Valatie, NY 12184-0137
518-758-7575 x3002  Fax: 518-758-7579
Web site: www.ichabodcrane.org
Lee Bordick, Superintendent

**New Lebanon CSD**
14665 Route 22, New Lebanon, NY 12125-2307
518-794-9016  Fax: 518-766-5574
Web site: www.newlebanoncsd.org
Karen McGraw, Superintendent

**Taconic Hills CSD**
73 County Rt 11A, PO Box 482, Craryville, NY 12521
518-325-0313  Fax: 518-325-3557
Web site: www.taconichills.k12.ny.us
Mark A Sposato, Superintendent

## CORTLAND

**Cincinnatus CSD**
2809 Cincinnatus Rd, Cincinnatus, NY 13040-9698
607-863-3200  Fax: 607-863-4109
Web site: www.cc.cnyric.org
Steven V Hubbard, Superintendent

**Cortland Enlarged City SD**
1 Valley View Dr, Cortland, NY 13045-3297
607-758-4100  Fax: 607-758-4128
e-mail: superintendent@cortlandschools.org
Web site: www.cortlandschools.org
Larry Spring, Superintendent

**Homer CSD**
Route 281, PO Box 500, Homer, NY 13077-0500
607-749-7241
Web site: www.homercentral.org
Nancy Ruscio, Superintendent

**Marathon CSD**
1 E Main St, PO Box 339, Marathon, NY 13803-0339
607-849-3251  Fax: 607-849-3305
Web site: www.marathonschools.org
Timothy Turecek, Superintendent

**McGraw CSD**
W Academy St, PO Box 556, McGraw, NY 13101-0556
607-836-3636  Fax: 607-836-3635
Web site: www.mcgrawschools.org
Mary Curcio, Superintendent

## DELAWARE

**Andes CSD**
85 Delaware Ave, PO Box 248, Andes, NY 13731-0248
845-676-3167  Fax: 845-676-3181
e-mail: rchakar@andescentralschool.org
Web site: www.andescentralschool.org
Robert Chakar, Superintendent

**Charlotte Valley CSD**
15611 St Hwy 23, Davenport, NY 13750-0202
607-278-5511  Fax: 607-278-5900
Mark R Dupra, Superintendent

**Delhi CSD**
2 Sheldon Dr, Delhi, NY 13753-1276
607-746-1300  Fax: 607-746-6028
Web site: www.delhischools.org
Roger W Adams, Superintendent

**Downsville CSD**
Maple St, Po Box J, Downsville, NY 13755
607-363-2101  Fax: 607-363-2105
Web site: www.dcseagles.org
James F Abrams, Superintendent

**Franklin CSD**
26 Institute St, Franklin, NY 13775-0888
607-829-3551 x309  Fax: 607-829-2101
Web site: www.franklincsd.org
Gordon Daniels, Superintendent

**Hancock CSD**
67 Education Ln, Hancock, NY 13783
607-637-1301
Terrance Dougherty, Superintendent

**Margaretville CSD**
415 Main St, Margaretville, NY 12455-0319
845-586-2647  Fax: 845-586-2949
Web site: www.margaretvillecs.org
Anthony R Albanese, Superintendent

**Roxbury CSD**
53729 NYS Route 30, Roxbury, NY 12474-0207
607-326-4151  Fax: 607-326-4154
Thomas J O'Brien, Superintendent

**Sidney CSD**
95 W Main St, Sidney, NY 13838-1699
607-563-2135  Fax: 607-563-4275
Web site: www.sidneycsd.org
William Christensen, Superintendent

**South Kortright CSD**
58200 State Hwy 10, South Kortright, NY 13842-0113
607-538-9111  Fax: 607-538-9205
Web site: www.skcs.org
Patricia Norton-White, Superintendent

*Offices and agencies generally appear in alphabetical order, except when specific order is requested by listee.*

**Stamford CSD**
1 River St, Stamford, NY 12167-1098
607-652-7301  Fax: 607-652-3446
Web site: www.stamfordcs.org
Tonda Dunbar, Superintendent

**Walton CSD**
47-49 Stockton Ave, Walton, NY 13856
607-865-4116  Fax: 607-865-8568
Web site: www.waltoncsd.org
Thomas P Austin, Superintendent

## DUTCHESS

**Arlington CSD**
696 Dutchess Tpke, Poughkeepsie, NY 12603
845-486-4460
Web site: www.arlingtonschools.org
Geoffrey Hicks, Superintendent

**Beacon City SD**
10 Education Dr, Beacon, NY 12508
845-838-6900 x2010
Web site: www.beaconcityk12.org
Fern Aefsky, Superintendent

**Dover UFSD**
2368 Rt 22, Dover Plains, NY 12522
845-832-4500  Fax: 845-832-4511
e-mail: mike.tierney@doverschools.org
Web site: www.doverschools.org
Michael Tierney, Superintendent

**Hyde Park CSD**
11 Boice Rd, PO Box 2033, Hyde Park, NY 12538-1632
845-229-4000  Fax: 845-229-4056
Greer Fischer, Superintendent

**Millbrook CSD**
PO Box AA-3323 Franklin, Millbrook, NY 12545
845-677-4200 x101
Web site: www.millbrookcsd.org
Lloyd Jaeger, Superintendent

**Pawling CSD**
515 Route 22, Pawling, NY 12564
845-855-4600
Web site: www.pawlingschools.org
Joseph Sciortino, Superintendent

**Pine Plains CSD**
2829 Church St, Pine Plains, NY 12567-5504
518-398-7181  Fax: 518-398-6592
Linda Kaumeyer, Superintendent

**Poughkeepsie City SD**
11 College Ave, Poughkeepsie, NY 12603-3313
845-451-4950  Fax: 845-451-4954
Web site: www.poughkeepsieschools.org
Laval S Wilson, Superintendent

**Red Hook CSD**
7401 South Broadway, Red Hook, NY 12571-9446
845-758-2241  Fax: 845-758-4720
e-mail: pfinch@rhcsd.org
Web site: www.redhookcentralschools.org
Paul Finch, Superintendent

**Rhinebeck CSD**
North Park Rd, Rhinebeck, NY 12572
845-871-5520  Fax: 845-876-4276
e-mail: jphelan@rhinebeckcsd.org
Web site: www.rhinebeckcsd.org
Joseph L Phelan, Superintendent

**Spackenkill UFSD**
15 Croft Rd, Poughkeepsie, NY 12603-5028
845-463-7800  Fax: 845-463-7804
Web site: www.spackenkillschools.org
Lois Powell, Superintendent

**Wappingers CSD**
167 Meyers Corners Rd, Wappingers Falls, NY 12590-3296
845-298-5000
Web site: www.wappingersschools.org
James Parla, Superintendent
David Paciencia, Superintendent

## ERIE

**Akron CSD**
47 Bloomingdale Ave, Akron, NY 14001-1197
716-542-5010  Fax: 716-542-5018
e-mail: rzymroz@akronschools.org
Web site: www.akronschools.org
Robin B Zymroz, Superintendent of Schools

**Alden CSD**
13190 Park St, Alden, NY 14004
716-937-9116
Web site: aldenschools.org
Lynn Marie Fusco, Superintendent

**Amherst CSD**
55 Kings Hwy, Amherst, NY 14226
716-362-3051  Fax: 716-836-2537
Web site: www.amherstschools.org
Laura Chabe, Superintendent

**Buffalo SD**
712 City Hall, Buffalo, NY 14202-3375
716-816-3500  Fax: 716-816-3600
Web site: www.buffaloschools.org
James A Williams, Superintendent

**Cheektowaga CSD**
3600 Union Rd, Cheektowaga, NY 14225-5170
716-686-3606  Fax: 716-681-5232
Web site: www.cheektowagaschools.org
Dennis Kane, Superintendent

**Cheektowaga-Sloan UFSD**
166 Halstead Ave, Sloan, NY 14212
716-891-6402
Web site: www.sloanschools.org
James P Mazgajewski, Superintendent

**Clarence CSD**
9625 Main St, Clarence, NY 14031-2083
716-407-9102
Web site: www.clarenceschools.org
Thomas G Coseo, Superintendent

**Cleveland Hill UFSD**
105 Mapleview Rd, Cheektowaga, NY 14225-1599
716-836-7200
Web site: www.clevehill.wnyric.org
Sharon Huff, Superintendent

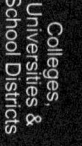

Colleges
Universities &
School Districts

*Offices and agencies generally appear in alphabetical order, except when specific order is requested by listee.*

**Depew UFSD**
591 Terrace Blvd, Depew, NY 14043-4535
716-686-5105  Fax: 716-686-2269
Web site: www.depewschools.org
Jeffrey Rabey, Superintendent

**East Aurora UFSD**
430 Main St, East Aurora, NY 14052
716-687-2302
Brian Russ, Superintendent

**Eden CSD**
3150 Schoolview Rd, Eden, NY 14057
716-992-3629
Ronald Buggs, Superintendent

**Evans-Brant CSD (Lake Shore)**
959 Beach Rd, Angola, NY 14006
716-549-2300 or 716-926-2201  Fax: 716-549-6407
Web site: www.lakeshore.wnyric.org
James Przepasniak, Superintendent

**Frontier CSD**
5120 Orchard Ave, Hamburg, NY 14075-5657
716-926-1700  Fax: 716-926-1776
Web site: www.frontier.wnyric.org
James Bodziak, Superintendent

**Grand Island CSD**
1100 Ransom Rd, Grand Island, NY 14072-1460
716-773-8801
Web site: www.k12.ginet.org
Robert W Christmann, Superintendent

**Hamburg CSD**
5305 Abbott Rd, Hamburg, NY 14075
716-646-3220  Fax: 716-646-3209
Web site: www.hamburgschools.org
Steven Achramovitch, Superintendent

**Holland CSD**
103 Canada St, Holland, NY 14080
716-537-8222
e-mail: djohnson@holland.wnyric.org
Dennis Johnson, Superintendent

**Hopevale UFSD at Hamburg**
3780 Howard Rd, Hamburg, NY 14075-2252
716-648-1930  Fax: 716-648-2361
Cynthia Stachowski, Superintendent

**Iroquois CSD**
2111 Girdle Rd, Elma, NY 14059-0032
716-652-3000
Bruce Fraser, Superintendent

**Kenmore-Tonawanda UFSD**
1500 Colvin Blvd, Buffalo, NY 14223-1196
716-874-8400  Fax: 716-874-8624
Web site: www.kenton.k12.ny.us
Mark P Mondanaro, Superintendent

**Lackawanna City SD**
245 South Shore Blvd, Lackawanna, NY 14218
716-827-6767  Fax: 716-827-6710
Web site: www.lackawannaschools.org
Nicholas Korach, Superintendent

**Lancaster CSD**
177 Central Ave, Lancaster, NY 14086-1897
716-686-3200
Web site: www.lancasterschools.org
Edward Myszka, Interim Superintendent

**Cheektowaga-Maryvale CSD**
1050 Maryvale Dr, Cheektowaga, NY 14225-2386
716-631-0300  Fax: 716-635-4699
Deborah Ziolkowski, Superintendent

**North Collins CSD**
2045 School St, North Collins, NY 14111
716-337-0101
Web site: www.northcollins.com
Benjamin A Halsey, Superintendent

**Orchard Park CSD**
3330 Baker Rd, Orchard Park, NY 14127
716-209-6280  Fax: 716-209-6353
Web site: www.opschools.org
Matthew McGarrity, Superintendent

**Springville-Griffith Inst CSD**
307 Newman St, Springville, NY 14141
716-592-3200 or 716-592-3412
Paul Hashem, Superintendent

**Sweet Home CSD**
1901 Sweet Home Rd, Amherst, NY 14228
716-250-1402  Fax: 716-250-1374
Anthony Day, Superintendent

**Tonawanda City SD**
100 Hinds St, Tonawanda, NY 14150
716-694-7690
Web site: www.tonawandacsd.org
Whitney K Vantine, Superintendent

**West Seneca CSD**
1397 Orchard Park Rd, West Seneca, NY 14224-4098
716-677-3101
Web site: www.wscschools.org
Mark Crawford, Superintendent

**Williamsville CSD**
105 Casey Rd, PO Box 5000, East Amherst, NY 14051-5000
716-626-8005  Fax: 716-626-8089
Web site: www.williamsvillek12.org
Howard S Smith, Superintendent

## ESSEX

**Crown Point CSD**
2758 Main St, Crown Point, NY 12928-0035
518-597-4200  Fax: 518-597-4121
Web site: www.cpcsteam.org
Shari L Brannock, Superintendent

**Elizabethtown-Lewis CSD**
7530 Court St, Elizabethtown, NY 12932-0158
518-873-6371  Fax: 518-873-9552
Gail J Else, Superintendent

**Keene CSD**
33 Market St, PO Box 67, Keene Valley, NY 12943-0067
518-576-4555  Fax: 518-576-4599
e-mail: cfjkcs@yahoo.com
Web site: www.keenecentralschool.org
Cynthia Ford-Johnston, Superintendent

**Lake Placid CSD**
23 Cummings Rd, Lake Placid, NY 12946-1500
518-523-2475
Randy Richards, Superintendent

*Offices and agencies generally appear in alphabetical order, except when specific order is requested by listee.*

**Minerva CSD**
1466 County Rt 29, Olmstedville, NY 12857-0039
518-251-2000  Fax: 518-251-2395
e-mail: farrellt@minervasd.org
Web site: www.minervasd.org
Timothy Farrell, Superintendent

**Moriah CSD**
39 Viking Ln, Port Henry, NY 12974
518-546-3301  Fax: 518-546-7895
Web site: www.moriahk12.org
William Larrow, Superintendent

**Newcomb CSD**
5535 Rt 28 N, Newcomb, NY 12852-0418
518-582-3341  Fax: 518-582-2163
Web site: www.newcombcsd.org
Clark Hults, Superintendent

**Schroon Lake CSD**
1125 US Rt 9, PO Box 338, Schroon Lake, NY 12870-0338
518-532-7164  Fax: 518-532-0284
Web site: www.schroonschool.org
Gerald Blair, Superintendent

**Ticonderoga CSD**
5 Calkins Place, Ticonderoga, NY 12883
518-585-9158
Web site: www.ticonderogak12.org
John C McDonald Jr, Superintendent

**Westport CSD**
25 Sisco St, Westport, NY 12993
518-962-8244  Fax: 518-962-4571
Web site: www.westportcs.org
John W Gallagher, Superintendent

**Willsboro CSD**
29 School Lane, Willsboro, NY 12996-0180
518-963-4456  Fax: 518-963-7577
Web site: www.willsborocsd.org
Stephen Broadwell, Superintendent

## FRANKLIN

**Brushton-Moira CSD**
758 County Rt 7, Brushton, NY 12916
518-529-7342  Fax: 518-529-6062
Web site: www.bmcsd.org
Steven Grenville, Superintendent

**Chateaugay CSD**
42 River St, PO Box 904, Chateaugay, NY 12920-0904
518-497-6611  Fax: 518-497-3170
e-mail: dbreault@mail.fehb.org
Web site: www.chateaugay.org
Dale L Breault, Superintendent

**Malone CSD**
42 Huskie Ln, PO Box 847, Malone, NY 12953-1118
518-483-7800  Fax: 518-483-3071
Wayne C Walbridge, Superintendent

**Salmon River CSD**
637 County Rt 1, Fort Covington, NY 12937-9722
518-358-6600  Fax: 518-358-3492
Web site: www.srk12.org
Jane A Collins, Superintendent

**Saranac Lake CSD**
79 Canaras Ave, Saranac Lake, NY 12983-1500
518-891-5460
Gerald A Goldman, Superintendent

**St Regis Falls CSD**
92 N Main St, PO Box 309, St Regis Falls, NY 12980-0309
518-856-9421
Beverly Ouderkirk, Superintendent

**Tupper Lake CSD**
294 Hosley Ave, Tupper Lake, NY 12986-1899
518-359-3371  Fax: 518-359-7862
Seth McGowan, Superintendent

## FULTON

**Broadalbin-Perth CSD**
20 Pine St, Broadalbin, NY 12025-9997
518-954-2500  Fax: 51-954-2509
Web site: www.bpcsd.org
Stephen M Tomlinson, Superintendent

**Gloversville Enlarged SD**
243 Lincoln St, PO Box 593, Gloversville, NY 12078
518-775-5700  Fax: 518-725-8793
Robert DeLilli, Superintendent

**Greater Johnstown SD**
1 Sir Bills Circle, Ste 101, Johnstown, NY 12095
518-762-4611  Fax: 518-726-6379
Web site: www.johnstownschools.org
Katherine A Sullivan, Superintendent

**Mayfield CSD**
27 School Street, Mayfield, NY 12117-0216
518-661-8207  Fax: 518-661-7666
Web site: www.mayfieldk12.com
Paul G Williamson, Superintendent

**Northville CSD**
131 S Third St, PO Box 608, Northville, NY 12134-0608
518-863-7000 x4121
Web site: northvillecsd.k12.ny.us
Kathy Dougherty, Superintendent

**Oppenheim-Ephratah CSD**
6486 State Hwy 29, St Johnsville, NY 13452-9309
518-568-2014  Fax: 518-568-2941
Dan M Russom, Superintendent

**Wheelerville UFSD**
PO Box 756, Caroga Lake, NY 12032
518-835-2171  Fax: 518-835-3551
David D Carr, Superintendent

## GENESEE

**Alexander CSD**
3314 Buffalo St, Alexander, NY 14005-9769
585-591-1551  Fax: 585-591-2257
Web site: www.alexandercsd.org
Kathleen Maerten, Superintendent

**Batavia City SD**
39 Washington Ave, Batavia, NY 14020
585-343-2480  Fax: 585-344-8204
Web site: www.bataviacsd.org
Margaret L Puzio, Superintendent

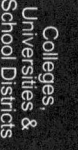

Colleges,
Universities &
School Districts

*Offices and agencies generally appear in alphabetical order, except when specific order is requested by listee.*

**Byron-Bergen CSD**
6917 W Bergen Rd, Bergen, NY 14416
585-494-1220  Fax: 585-494-2613
Web site: www.bbschools.org
Scott G Martzloff, Superintendent

**Elba CSD**
57 S Main St, Elba, NY 14058
585-757-9967 x1034
Web site: www.elbacsd.org
Jerome Piwko Jr, Superintendent

**Le Roy CSD**
2-6 Trigon Park, Le Roy, NY 14482
585-768-8133
Web site: www.leroycsd.org
Kim Cox, Superintendent

**Oakfield-Alabama CSD**
7001 Lewiston Rd, Oakfield, NY 14125
585-948-5211  Fax: 585-948-9362
Web site: www.oacs.k12.ny.us
Christopher Todd, Superintendent

**Pavilion CSD**
7014 Big Tree Rd, Pavilion, NY 14525
585-584-3115
Web site: www.pavilioncsd.org
Kenneth J Ellison, Superintendent

**Pembroke CSD**
Rt 5 & 77, PO Box 308, Corfu, NY 14036
585-599-4525  Fax: 585-762-9993
Gary T Mix Sr, Superintendent

## GREENE

**Cairo-Durham CSD**
424 Main St, Cairo, NY 12413-0780
518-622-8534
Web site: www.cairodurham.org
Sally Sharkey, Superintendent

**Catskill CSD**
343 W Main St, Catskill, NY 12414-1699
518-943-4696  Fax: 518-943-7116
Web site: www.catskillcsd.org
Kathleen Farrell, Superintendent

**Coxsackie-Athens CSD**
24 Sunset Blvd, Coxsackie, NY 12051-1132
518-731-1700  Fax: 518-731-1729
Annemarie Barkman, Interim Superintendent

**Greenville CSD**
4976 Route 81, Greenville, NY 12083-0129
518-966-5070
Web site: www.greenville.k12.ny.us
Cheryl Dudley, Superintendent

**Hunter-Tannersville CSD**
6094 Main St, Tannersville, NY 12485-1018
518-589-5400  Fax: 518-589-5403
e-mail: psweeney@htcsd.org
Web site: www.htcsd.org
Patrick Darfler-Sweeney, Superintendent

**Windham-Ashland-Jewett CSD**
5411 State Route 23, PO Box 429, Windham, NY 12496-0429
518-734-3403  Fax: 518-734-6050
e-mail: jwiktorko@wajcs.org
John Wiktorko, Superintendent

## HAMILTON

**Indian Lake CSD**
28 W Main St, Indian Lake, NY 12842-9716
518-648-5024  Fax: 518-648-6346
Web site: www.ilcsd.org
Mark T Brand, Superintendent

**Inlet Common School**
3002 Rt 28, Old Forge, NY 13420
315-369-3222  Fax: 315-369-6216
Donald Gooley, Superintendent

**Lake Pleasant CSD**
120 Elm Lake Rd, PO Box 140, Speculator, NY 12164-0140
518-548-7571  Fax: 518-548-3230
Ernest D Virgil, Superintendent

**Long Lake CSD**
20 School Lane, PO Box 217, Long Lake, NY 12847-0217
518-624-2221  Fax: 518-624-3896
Web site: www.longlakecsd.org
Mary Jo Dickerson, Acting Superintendent

**Piseco Common SD**
Rt 8, Piseco, NY 12139
518-548-7555  Fax: 518-548-5310
Peter J Hallock, Superintendent

**Raquette Lake UFSD**
PO Box 10, Raquette Lake, NY 13436-0010
315-354-4733
Peter J Hallock, Superintendent

**Wells CSD**
1571 Route 30, PO Box 300, Wells, NY 12190-0300
518-924-6000
John Zeis, Superintendent

## HERKIMER

**Dolgeville CSD**
38 Slawson St, Dolgeville, NY 13329
315-429-3155 x3500  Fax: 315-429-8473
e-mail: creynolds@dolgeville.org
Web site: www.dolgeville.org
Christine Reynolds, Superintendent

**Frankfort-Schuyler CSD**
605 Palmer St, Frankfort, NY 13340
315-894-5083  Fax: 315-895-7011
e-mail: rreina@frankfort-schuyler.org
Web site: www.frankfort-schuyler.org
Robert Reina, Superintendent

**Herkimer CSD**
801 W German St, Herkimer, NY 13350-2199
315-866-2230
Web site: www.herkimercsd.org
Carol Zygo, Superintendent

**Ilion CSD**
1 Golden Bomber Dr, PO Box 480, Ilion, NY 13357-0480
315-894-9934  Fax: 315-894-2716
Cosimo Tangorra, Superintendent

**Little Falls City SD**
15 Petrie St, Little Falls, NY 13365
315-823-1470
Louis J Patrei, Superintendent

*Offices and agencies generally appear in alphabetical order, except when specific order is requested by listee.*

**Mohawk CSD**
28 Grove St, Mohawk, NY 13407-1782
315-867-2904
Joyce M Caputo, Superintendent

**Mount Markham CSD**
500 Fairground Rd, West Winfield, NY 13491-0500
315-822-2800
Web site: www.mmcsd.org
Casey Barduhn, Superintendent

**Poland CSD**
74 Cold Brook St, Poland, NY 13431
315-826-0203  Fax: 315-826-7516
Web site: www.polandcs.com
Laura Dutton, Superintendent

**Town of Webb UFSD**
3002 State Route 28, PO Box 38, Old Forge, NY 13420-0038
315-369-3222  Fax: 315-369-6216
Web site: www.towschool.org
Donald Gooley, Superintendent

**Van Hornesville-Owen D Young CSD**
2316 State Rt 80, PO Box 125, Van Hornesville, NY 13475-0125
315-858-0729  Fax: 315-858-2019
Web site: www.odyoungcsd.org
Virginia Keegan, Superintendent

**West Canada Valley CSD**
5447 State Rt 28, Newport, NY 13416-0360
315-845-6800  Fax: 315-845-8652
Web site: www.westcanada.org
John Banek, Superintendent

## JEFFERSON

**Alexandria CSD**
34 Bolton Ave, Alexandria Bay, NY 13607-1699
315-482-9971
Web site: www.alexandriacentral.org
Robert Wagoner, Superintendent

**Belleville Henderson CSD**
8372 County Rt 75, Belleville, NY 13611-0158
315-846-5826
e-mail: rmoore@bhpanthers.org
Web site: www.bhpanthers.org
Rick T Moore, Superintendent

**Carthage CSD**
25059 County Rt 197, Carthage, NY 13619-9527
315-493-5000
Web site: www.carthagecsd.org
Joseph Catanzaro, Superintendent

**General Brown CSD**
PO Box 500, Dexter, NY 13634
315-639-5100  Fax: 315-639-6916
e-mail: svigliotti@gblions.org
Web site: www.gblions.org
Stephan J Vigliotti Sr, Superintendent

**Indian River CSD**
32735-B County Rt 29, Philadelphia, NY 13673-0308
315-642-3441
Web site: www.ircsd.org
James Kettrick, Superintendent

**La Fargeville CSD**
20414 Sunrise Ave, PO Box 138, La Fargeville, NY 13656
315-658-2241  Fax: 315-658-4223
Web site: www.lafargevillecsd.org
Susan Whitney, Superintendent

**Lyme CSD**
11868 Academy St, PO Box 219, Chaumont, NY 13622-0219
315-649-2417  Fax: 315-649-2663
Web site: www.lymecsd.org
Karen M Donahue, Superintendent

**Sackets Harbor Central School**
215 S Broad St, Sackets Harbor, NY 13685
315-646-3575  Fax: 315-646-1038
Web site: www.sacketspatriots.org
Frederick E Hall, Superintendent

**South Jefferson CSD**
PO Box 10, Adams, NY 13605
315-583-6104
Web site: www.spartanpride.org
Jamie A Moesel, Superintendent

**Thousand Islands CSD**
8483 County Rt 9, PO Box 1000, Clayton, NY 13624-1000
315-686-5594  Fax: 315-686-5511
Joseph Menard, Superintendent

**Watertown City SD**
1351 Washington St, PO Box 586, Watertown, NY 13601
315-785-3700  Fax: 315-785-6855
e-mail: tfralick@watertowncsd.org
Web site: www.watertowncsd.org
Terry N Fralick, Superintendent

## LEWIS

**Beaver River CSD**
9508 Artz Rd, Beaver Falls, NY 13305-0179
315-346-1211  Fax: 315-346-6775
Web site: www.brcsd.org
Leueen Smithing, Interim Superintendent

**Copenhagen CSD**
3020 Mechanic St, Copenhagen, NY 13626-0030
315-688-4411  Fax: 315-688-2001
Web site: www.ccsknights.org
Scott Connell, Superintendent

**Harrisville CSD**
14371 Pirate Lane, PO Box 200, Harrisville, NY 13648
315-543-2707
Web site: www.hcsk12.org
Rolf A Waters, Superintendent

**Lowville Academy & CSD**
7668 State St, Lowville, NY 13367
315-376-9000  Fax: 315-376-1933
Kenneth J McAuliffe, Superintendent

**South Lewis CSD**
PO Box 10, Turin, NY 13473-0010
315-348-2500
Web site: www.southlewis.org
Douglas E Premo, Superintendent

Colleges, Universities & School Districts

*Offices and agencies generally appear in alphabetical order, except when specific order is requested by listee.*

## LIVINGSTON

**Avon CSD**
191 Clinton St, Avon, NY 14414
585-226-2455 x1318  Fax: 585-226-8202
Web site: www.avoncsd.org
Bruce Amey, Superintendent

**Caledonia-Mumford CSD**
99 North St, Caledonia, NY 14423
585-538-3400
Web site: www.cal-mum.org
David V Dinolfo, Superintendent

**Dansville CSD**
284 Main St, Dansville, NY 14437-9798
585-335-4000  Fax: 585-335-4002
Web site: www.dansvillecsd.org
Alioto Paul, Superintendent

**Geneseo CSD**
4050 Avon Rd, Geneseo, NY 14454
585-243-3450  Fax: 585-243-9481
Web site: www.geneseocsd.org
Timothy Hayes, Superintendent

**Dalton-Nunda CSD (Keshequa)**
13 Mill St, Nunda, NY 14517
585-468-2541 x1105  Fax: 585-468-3814
Web site: www.keshequa.org
John Allman, Superintendent

**Livonia CSD**
6 Puppy Lane, PO Box E, Livonia, NY 14487
585-346-4000  Fax: 585-346-6145
Web site: www.livoniacsd.org
Scott Bischoping, Superintendent

**Mt Morris CSD**
30 Bonadonna Ave, Mount Morris, NY 14510
585-658-2568  Fax: 585-658-4814
Web site: www.mtmorriscsd.org
Ed Orman, Superintendent

**York CSD**
2578 Genesee St, PO Box 102, Retsof, NY 14539-0102
585-243-1730 x2223  Fax: 585-243-5269
Web site: www.yorkcsd.org
Daniel Murray, Superintendent

## MADISON

**Brookfield CSD**
1910 Fairground Rd, Brookfield, NY 13314-0060
315-899-3323 x200
Steve Szatko, Interim Superintendent

**Canastota CSD**
120 Roberts St, Canastota, NY 13032-1198
315-697-2025
Web site: www.canastotacsd.org
Frederick J Bragan, Superintendent

**Cazenovia CSD**
31 Emory Ave, Cazenovia, NY 13035-1098
315-655-1317  Fax: 315-655-1375
e-mail: rdubik@caz.cnyric.org
Robert Dubik, Superintendent

**Chittenango CSD**
1732 Fyler Rd, Chittenango, NY 13037-9520
315-687-2840  Fax: 315-687-2841
Web site: www.chittenangoschools.org
Thomas E Marzeski, Superintendent

**De Ruyter CSD**
711 Railroad St, Deruyter, NY 13052-0000
315-852-3410  Fax: 315-852-9600
Web site: www.deruyter.k12.ny.us
Charles W Walters, Superintendent

**Hamilton CSD**
47 W Kendrick Ave, Hamilton, NY 13346-1299
315-824-6310
Diana Bowers, Superintendent

**Madison CSD**
7303 State Route 20, Madison, NY 13402
315-893-1878
Web site: www.madisoncentralny.org
Cynthia DeDominick, Superintendent

**Morrisville-Eaton CSD**
PO Box 990, Morrisville, NY 13408-0990
315-684-9300  Fax: 315-684-9399
Web site: www.m-ecs.org
Michael Drahos, Superintendent

**Oneida City SD**
565 Sayles St, Oneida, NY 13421-0327
315-363-2550
e-mail: rspadafora@oneidacsd.org
Web site: www.oneida.org
Ronald R Spadafora Jr, Superintendent

**Stockbridge Valley CSD**
6011 Williams Rd, Munnsville, NY 13409-0732
315-495-4400  Fax: 315-495-4492
Web site: www.stockbridgevalley.org
Chuck Chafee, Superintendent

## MONROE

**Brighton CSD**
2035 Monroe Ave, Rochester, NY 14618-2027
585-242-5080  Fax: 585-242-5212
Web site: www.bcsd.org
Kevin McGowan, Superintendent

**Brockport CSD**
40 Allen St, Brockport, NY 14420-2296
585-637-1810
Web site: www.brockport.k12.ny.us
Garry Stone, Superintendent

**Churchville-Chili CSD**
139 Fairbanks Rd, Churchville, NY 14428-9797
585-293-1800  Fax: 585-293-1013
Web site: www.cccsd.org
Pam Kissel, Superintendent

**East Irondequoit CSD**
600 Pardee Rd, Rochester, NY 14609
585-339-1210  Fax: 585-288-0713
Susan K Allen, Superintendent

**East Rochester UFSD**
222 Woodbine Ave, East Rochester, NY 14445
585-248-6302  Fax: 585-586-3254
Web site: www.erschools.org
Ray Giamartino, Jr, Superintendent

*Offices and agencies generally appear in alphabetical order, except when specific order is requested by listee.*

**Fairport CSD**
38 W Church St, Fairport, NY 14450-2130
585-421-2004  Fax: 585-421-3421
Web site: www.fairport.org
Jon Hunter, Superintendent

**Gates-Chili CSD**
3 Spartan Way, Rochester, NY 14624
585-247-5050 x1217
Web site: www.gateschili.org
Mark C Davey, Superintendent

**Greece CSD**
PO Box 300, N Greece, NY 14515-0300
585-966-2000  Fax: 585-581-8203
Web site: www.greece.k12.ny.us
John O'Rourke, Interim Superintendent

**Hilton CSD**
225 West Ave, Hilton, NY 14468-1283
585-392-1000  Fax: 585-392-1038
Web site: www.hilton.k12.ny.us
David Dimbleby, Superintendent

**Honeoye Falls-Lima CSD**
20 Church St, Honeoye Falls, NY 14472-1294
585-624-7010
e-mail: michelle_kavanaugh@hflcsd.org
Web site: www.hflcsd.org
Michelle Kavanaugh, Superintendent

**Penfield CSD**
PO Box 900, Penfield, NY 14526-0900
585-249-5700  Fax: 585-248-8412
Web site: penfield.edu
John D Carlevatti, Superintendent

**Pittsford CSD**
75 Barker Road, Pittsford, NY 14534
585-267-1000  Fax: 585-381-2105
Web site: www.pittsfordschools.com
Mary Alice Price, Superintendent

**Rochester City SD**
131 W Broad St, Rochester, NY 14614
585-262-8100
Web site: www.rcsdk12.org
Jean Claude Brizard, Superintendent

**Rush-Henrietta CSD**
2034 Lehigh Station Rd, Henrietta, NY 14467-9692
585-359-5012  Fax: 585-359-5045
Web site: www.rhnet.org
Kenneth Graham, Superintendent

**Spencerport CSD**
71 Lyell Ave, Spencerport, NY 14559-1899
585-349-5000  Fax: 585-349-5011
Web site: www.spencerportschools.org
Bonnie Seaburn, Superintendent

**Webster CSD**
119 South Ave, Webster, NY 14580-3594
585-216-0001  Fax: 585-265-6561
Web site: www.websterschools.org
Adele Bovard, Superintendent

**West Irondequoit CSD**
321 List Ave, Rochester, NY 14617-3125
585-336-2983  Fax: 585-266-1556
Web site: www.westirondequoit.org
Jeffrey B Crane, Superintendent

**Wheatland-Chili CSD**
13 Beckwith Ave, Scottsville, NY 14546
585-889-4500  Fax: 585-889-6284
Web site: www.wheatland.k12.ny.us
Thomas Gallagher, Superintendent

## MONTGOMERY

**Canajoharie CSD**
136 Scholastic Way, Canajoharie, NY 13317
518-673-6302  Fax: 518-673-3177
Web site: www.canajoharieschools.org
Richard Rose, Superintendent

**Fonda-Fultonville CSD**
112 Old Johnstown Rd, Fonda, NY 12068-1501
518-853-4415  Fax: 518-853-4461
e-mail: jhoffman@ffcsd.org
Web site: www.ffcsd.org
James Hoffman, Superintendent

**Fort Plain CSD**
25 High St, Fort Plain, NY 13339-1218
518-993-4000  Fax: 518-993-3393
e-mail: fpcsss@hotmail.com
Web site: www.fortplain.org
Douglas C Burton, Superintendent

**Greater Amsterdam SD**
11 Liberty St, Amsterdam, NY 12010
518-843-3180  Fax: 518-842-0012
Web site: gasd.org
Thomas F Perillo, Superintendent

**St Johnsville CSD**
44 Center St, St Johnsville, NY 13452
518-568-7024  Fax: 518-568-5407
Web site: www.sjcsd.org
Ralph Acquaro, Superintendent

## NASSAU

**Baldwin UFSD**
960 Hastings St, Baldwin, NY 11510
516-377-9200  Fax: 516-377-9421
Web site: www.baldwin.k12.ny.us
James Mapes, Superintendent

**Bellmore UFSD**
580 Winthrop Ave, Bellmore, NY 11710-5099
516-679-2909  Fax: 516-679-3027
Web site: www.bellmore.k12.ny.us
Joseph S Famularo, Superintendent

**Bellmore-Merrick Central HS District**
1260 Meadowbrook Rd, North Merrick, NY 11566
516-992-1000
Web site: www.bellmore-merrick.k12.ny.us
Henry Kiernan, Superintendent

**Bethpage UFSD**
10 Cherry Ave, Bethpage, NY 11714
516-644-4001
Web site: www.bethpagecommunity.com/Schools
Terrence Clark, Superintendent

**Carle Place UFSD**
168 Cherry Ln, Carle Place, NY 11514
516-622-6575
Web site: www.cps.k12.ny.us
David Flatley, Superintendent

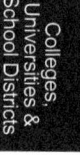

Colleges, Universities & School Districts

*Offices and agencies generally appear in alphabetical order, except when specific order is requested by listee.*

**East Meadow UFSD**
718 The Plain Road, Westbury, NY 11590
516-478-5776
Web site: www.eastmeadow.k12.ny.us
Louis R DeAngelo, Superintendent

**East Rockaway UFSD**
443 Ocean Ave, East Rockaway, NY 11518
516-887-8300
Web site: www.eastrockawayschools.org
Dr. Roseanne Melucci, Superintendent

**East Williston UFSD**
11 Bacon Rd, Old Westbury, NY 11568
516-333-3758  Fax: 516-333-1937
Web site: www.ewsdonline.org
Lorna R Lewis, Superintendent

**Elmont UFSD**
135 Elmont Rd, Elmont, NY 11003-1609
516-326-5500  Fax: 516-326-5574
Web site: www.elmontschools.org
Al Harper, Superintendent

**Farmingdale UFSD**
50 Van Cott Ave, Farmingdale, NY 11735
516-752-6510
Web site: www.farmingdaleschools.org
John Lorentz, Superintendent

**Floral Park-Bellerose UFSD**
One Poppy Pl, Floral Park, NY 11001
516-327-9300  Fax: 516-327-9304
Web site: www.floralpark.k12.ny.us
Lynn Pombonyo, Superintendent

**Franklin Square UFSD**
760 Washington St, Franklin Square, NY 11010
516-481-4100
Web site: franklinsquare.k12.ny.us
Patrick Manley, Superintendent

**Freeport UFSD**
235 N Ocean Ave, Freeport, NY 11520
516-867-5205  Fax: 516-623-4759
e-mail: kkuncham@freeportschools.org
Web site: www.freeportschools.org
Dr. Kishore Kunchan, Superintendent

**Garden City UFSD**
56 Cathedral Ave, PO Box 216, Garden City, NY 11530-0216
516-478-1000
Web site: www.gardencity.k12.ny.us
Robert Feirsen, Superintendent

**Glen Cove City SD**
150 Dosoris Ln, Glen Cove, NY 11542
516-801-7001
Web site: www.glencove.k12.ny.us
Joseph Laria, Superintendent

**Great Neck UFSD**
345 Lakeville Rd, Great Neck, NY 11020
516-441-4001  Fax: 516-773-6685
e-mail: tdolan@greatneck.k12.ny.us
Web site: www.greatneck.k12.ny.us
Dr Thomas P Dolan, Superintendent

**Hempstead UFSD**
185 Peninsula Blvd, Hempstead, NY 11550
516-292-7111 x1001
Web site: www.hempsteadschools.org
Patricia Watkins, Superintendent

**Herricks UFSD**
999 B Herricks Rd, New Hyde Park, NY 11040
516-305-8901
Web site: www.herricks.org
John E Bierwirth, Superintendent

**Hewlett-Woodmere UFSD**
1 Johnson Pl, Woodmere, NY 11598
516-374-8100  Fax: 516-374-8101
Web site: www.hewlett-woodmere.net
Joyce Bisso, Superintendent

**Hicksville UFSD**
200 Division Ave-Adm, Hicksville, NY 11801-4800
516-733-2110
Web site: www.hicksvillepublicschools.org
Maureen K Bright, Superintendent

**Island Park UFSD**
150 Trafalgar Blvd, Island Park, NY 11558
516-431-8100  Fax: 516-431-7550
Web site: www.ips.k12.ny.us
Rosmarie Bovino, Superintendent

**Island Trees UFSD**
74 Farmedge Rd, Levittown, NY 11756
516-520-2100
e-mail: cmurphy@islandtrees.org
Web site: www.islandtrees.org
Charles J Murphy, Superintendent

**Jericho UFSD**
99 Cedar Swamp Rd, Jericho, NY 11753
516-203-3600 x3201
e-mail: hgrishman@jerichoschools.org
Henry L Grishman, Superintendent

**Lawrence UFSD**
195 Broadway, Lawrence, NY 11559
516-295-8000
Web site: www.lawrence.org
John T Fitzsimons, Superintendent

**Levittown UFSD**
150 Abbey Ln, Levittown, NY 11756
516-520-8300  Fax: 516-520-8314
Web site: www.levittownschools.com
Herman A Sirois, Superintendent

**Locust Valley CSD**
22 Horse Hollow Rd, Locust Valley, NY 11560
516-277-5001
Web site: www.lvcsd.k12.ny.us
Anna Hunderfund, Superintendent

**Long Beach City SD**
235 Lido Blvd, Long Beach, NY 11561-5093
516-897-2104
Web site: www.lbeach.org
Robert Greenberg, Superintendent

**Lynbrook UFSD**
111 Atlantic Ave, Lynbrook, NY 11563
516-887-0253
Santo Barbarino, Superintendent

**Malverne UFSD**
301 Wicks Ln, Malverne, NY 11565-2244
516-887-6400
Web site: www.malverne.k12.ny.us
James H Hunderfund, Superintendent

*Offices and agencies generally appear in alphabetical order, except when specific order is requested by listee.*

**Manhasset UFSD**
200 Memorial Pl, Manhasset, NY 11030
516-267-7705  Fax: 516-627-8158
e-mail: ccardillo@manhasset.k12.ny.us
Web site: www.manhasset.k12.ny.us
Charles S Cardillo, Superintendent

**Massapequa UFSD**
4925 Merrick Rd, Massapequa, NY 11758
516-308-5001
Web site: www.msd.k12.ny.us
Charles Sulc, Superintendent

**Merrick UFSD**
21 Babylon Rd, Merrick, NY 11566
516-992-7240
Ranier W Melucci, Superintendent

**Mineola UFSD**
121 Jackson Ave, Mineola, NY 11501
516-237-2001  Fax: 516-237-2008
Web site: www.mineola.k12.ny.us
Michael Nagler, Superintendent

**New Hyde Park-Garden City Park UFSD**
1950 Hillside Ave, New Hyde Park, NY 11040
516-352-6257 x221
Web site: www.nhp-gcp.org
Robert Katulak, Superintendent

**North Bellmore UFSD**
2616 Martin Ave, Bellmore, NY 11710
516-992-3000 x4001
Web site: www.northbellmoreschools.org
Arnold Goldstein, Superintendent

**North Merrick UFSD**
1057 Merrick Ave, Merrick, NY 11566
516-292-3694  Fax: 516-292-3097
Web site: www.nmerrickschools.org
David S Feller, Superintendent

**North Shore CSD**
112 Franklin Ave, Sea Cliff, NY 11579
516-277-7800 or 516-277-7801
Web site: www.northshore.k12.ny.us
Edward K Melnick, Superintendent

**Oceanside UFSD**
145 Merle Ave, Oceanside, NY 11572-2206
516-678-1215
e-mail: hbrown@oceanside.k12.ny.us
Herb R Brown, Superintendent

**Oyster Bay-East Norwich CSD**
1 McCouns Ln, Oyster Bay, NY 11771-3105
516-624-6505
Web site: obenschools.org
Phyllis Harrington, Superintendent

**Plainedge UFSD**
241 Wyngate Dr, PO Box 1669, North Massapequa, NY 11758
516-992-7455  Fax: 516-992-7446
Web site: www.plainedgeschools.org
Christine P'Simer, Superintendent

**Plainview-Old Bethpage CSD**
106 Washington Ave, Plainview, NY 11803-3612
516-937-6301
Gerald W Dempsey, Superintendent

**Port Washington UFSD**
100 Campus Dr, Port Washington, NY 11050
516-767-5005  Fax: 516-767-5007
Web site: www.portnet.k12.ny.us
Geoffrey N Gordon, Superintendent

**Rockville Centre UFSD**
128 Shepherd St, Rockville Centre, NY 11570-2298
516-255-8920
Web site: www.rvcschools.org
William H Johnson, Superintendent

**Roosevelt UFSD**
240 Denton Pl, Roosevelt, NY 11575-1539
516-345-7001  Fax: 516-379-0178

**Roslyn UFSD**
300 Harbor Hill Rd, Roslyn, NY 11576-1531
516-625-6303  Fax: 516-625-6336
e-mail: roslynsd@roslynschools.org
Web site: www.roslynschools.org
Daniel Brenner, Superintendent

**Seaford UFSD**
1600 Washington Ave, Seaford, NY 11783
516-592-4002
e-mail: bconboy@mail.seaford.k12.ny.us
Web site: www.seaford.k12.ny.us
Brian Conboy, Superintendent

**Sewanhaka Central HS District**
77 Landau Ave, Floral Park, NY 11001
516-488-9800  Fax: 516-488-9899
Web site: www.sewanhaka.k12.ny.us
Warren A Meierdiercks, Superintendent

**Syosset CSD**
99 Pell Ln, PO Box 9029, Syosset, NY 11791
516-364-5605
Carole G Hankin, Superintendent

**Uniondale UFSD**
933 Goodrich St, Uniondale, NY 11553-2499
516-560-8824  Fax: 516-292-2659
e-mail: wlloyd@uniondaleschools.org
Web site: district.uniondaleschools.org
William K Lloyd, Superintendent

**Valley Stream 13 UFSD**
585 N Corona Ave, Valley Stream, NY 11580
516-568-6100  Fax: 516-825-2537
Web site: www.valleystream13.com
Elizabeth Lison, Superintendent

**Valley Stream 24 UFSD**
75 Horton Ave, Valley Stream, NY 11581-1420
516-256-0153
Edward M Fale, Superintendent

**Valley Stream 30 UFSD**
175 N Central Ave, Valley Stream, NY 11580-3801
516-285-9881
Web site: www.valleystream30.com
Elaine Kanas, Superintendent

**Valley Stream Central HS District**
One Kent Rd, Valley Stream, NY 11580-3398
516-872-5601  Fax: 516-872-5658
Web site: www.vschsd.org
Richard Marsh, Superintendent

Colleges,
Universities &
School Districts

*Offices and agencies generally appear in alphabetical order, except when specific order is requested by listee.*

**Wantagh UFSD**
3301 Beltagh Ave, Wantagh, NY 11793-3395
516-679-6300
e-mail: wantaghinfo@wantaghschools.org
Web site: www.wantaghschools.org
Lydia Begley, Superintendent

**West Hempstead UFSD**
252 Chestnut St, West Hempstead, NY 11552-2455
516-390-3107  Fax: 516-489-1776
Web site: www.whufsd.com
John J Hogan, Superintendent

**Westbury UFSD**
2 Hitchcock Ln, Old Westbury, NY 11568-1624
516-876-5016  Fax: 516-876-5187
Web site: www.westburyschools.org
Constance R Clark-Snead, Superintendent

### NEW YORK CITY

**NYC Chancellor's Office**
52 Chambers St, New York, NY 10007
212-374-6000  Fax: 212-374-5763
Cathie Black, Chancellor

**NYC Citywide Alternative HS District & Programs**
9027 Sutphin Blvd, Jamaica, NY 11435
718-557-2681
Cami Anderson, Senior Superintendent

**NYC Citywide Special Ed District 75**
400 First Ave, New York, NY 10010
212-802-1500
Gary Hecht, Superintendent

**NYC Region 1**
1 Fordham Plz, Rm 81, Bronx, NY 10458
718-741-7030
Yvonne Torres, Superintendent

**NYC Region 2**
1230 Zerega Ave, Bronx, NY 10462
718-828-2440
Timothy Behr, Superintendent

**NYC Region 3**
30-48 Linden Pl, Flushing, NY 11354
718-281-7575
Anita Saunder, Superintendent

**NYC Region 4**
28-11 Queens Plz N, Long Island City, NY 11101
718-391-8300
Madeline Chan, Superintendent

**NYC Region 5**
82-01 Rockaway Blvd, Queens, NY 11416
718-270-5800 or 718-922-4960
Kathleen M Cashin, Superintendent

**NYC Region 6**
5619 Flatlands Ave, Brooklyn, NY 11234
718-968-6100
Jean Claude Brizard, Superintendent

**NYC Region 7**
715 Ocean Terr, Building 1, Staten Island, NY 10301
718-556-8350
Margaret Schultz, Superintendent

**NYC Region 8**
131 Livingston St, Brooklyn, NY 11201
718-935-3900
Anita Scop, Superintendent

**NYC Region 9**
333 7th Ave & 28th St, Room 712, New York, NY 10001
212-356-7500
Luz Cortazzo, Superintendent

**NYC Region 10**
4360 Broadway, Rm 52, New York, NY 10033
917-521-3700
Gale Reeves, Superintendent

### NIAGARA

**Barker CSD**
1628 Quaker Rd, Barker, NY 14012-0328
716-795-3832
Dr Roger J Klatt, Superintendent

**Lewiston-Porter CSD**
4061 Creek Rd, Youngstown, NY 14174-9799
716-286-7266
e-mail: rappoldd@lew-port.com
Web site: www.lew-port.com
R Christopher Roser, Superintendent

**Lockport City SD**
130 Beattie Ave, Lockport, NY 14094-5099
716-478-4835  Fax: 716-478-4863
Web site: www.lockportschools.wnyric.org
Terry Ann Carbone, Superintendent

**Newfane CSD**
6273 Charlotteville Rd, Newfane, NY 14108
716-778-6850  Fax: 716-778-6852
Web site: www.newfane.wnyric.org
Christine Tibbetts, Superintendent

**Niagara Falls City SD**
630-66th Street, Niagara Falls, NY 14304
716-286-4205  Fax: 716-286-4283
Web site: www.nfschools.net
Cynthia A Bianco, Superintendent

**Niagara-Wheatfield CSD**
6700 Schultz St, Niagara Falls, NY 14304
716-215-3003  Fax: 716-215-3039
Web site: www.nwcsd.k12.ny.us
Carl H Militello, Superintendent

**North Tonawanda City SD**
175 Humphrey St, North Tonawanda, NY 14120-4097
716-807-3500
Web site: www.ntschools.org
Gregory Woytila, Superintendent

**Royalton-Hartland CSD**
54 State St, Middleport, NY 14105-1199
716-735-3031  Fax: 716-735-3660
e-mail: macdonaldk@royhart.org
Web site: www.royhart.org
Kevin MacDonald, Superintendent

**Starpoint CSD**
4363 Mapleton Rd, Lockport, NY 14094
716-210-2342
Web site: www.starpointcsd.org
C Douglas Whelan, Superintendent

*Offices and agencies generally appear in alphabetical order, except when specific order is requested by listee.*

**Wilson CSD**
412 Lake St, Wilson, NY 14172
716-751-9341
Web site: www.wilson.wnyric.org
Michael Wendt, Superintendent

## ONEIDA

**Adirondack CSD**
110 Ford St, Boonville, NY 13309-1200
315-942-9200  Fax: 315-942-5522
Web site: www.adirondackcsd.org
David Hubman, Superintendent

**Camden CSD**
51 Third St, Camden, NY 13316-1114
315-245-4075
Web site: www.camdenschools.org
Dr Jeffrey K Bryant, Superintendent

**Clinton CSD**
75 Chenango Ave, Clinton, NY 13323
315-557-2253  Fax: 315-853-8727
Web site: www.ccs.edu
Matthew Reilly, Superintendent

**Holland Patent CSD**
9601 Main St, Holland Patent, NY 13354-4610
315-865-7221
Web site: www.hpschools.org
Kathleen M Davis, Superintendent

**NY Mills UFSD**
1 Marauder Blvd, New York Mills, NY 13417-1566
315-768-8127  Fax: 315-768-3521
Web site: www.newyorkmills.org
Kathy Houghton, Superintendent

**New Hartford CSD**
33 Oxford Rd, New Hartford, NY 13413
315-624-1218
Web site: www.newhartfordschools.org
Robert J Nole, Superintendent

**Oriskany CSD**
1313 Utica St, Oriskany, NY 13424-0539
315-768-2058  Fax: 315-768-2057
Web site: www.oriskanycsd.org
Gregory Kelahan, Superintendent

**Remsen CSD**
9733 Davis Dr, PO Box 406, Remsen, NY 13438
315-831-3797
Web site: www.remsencsd.org
Joanne Shelmidine, Superintendent

**Rome City SD**
409 Bell Rd, Rome, NY 13440
315-338-6500  Fax: 315-334-7409
Web site: www.romecsd.org
Jeffrey Simons, Superintendent

**Sauquoit Valley CSD**
2601 Oneida St, Sauquoit, NY 13456-1000
315-839-6311
Web site: www.svcsd.org
Ronald J Wheelock, Superintendent

**Sherrill City SD**
5275 State Route 31, PO Box 128, Verona, NY 13478-0128
315-829-2520  Fax: 315-829-4949
Web site: www.vvsschools.org
Norman Reed, Superintendent

**Utica City SD**
106 Memorial Parkway, Utica, NY 13501-3709
315-792-2222
Web site: www.uticaschools.org
James Willis, Superintendent

**Vernon-Verona-Sherrill CSD**
5275 State Rt 31, Verona, NY 13478-0128
315-829-2520  Fax: 315-829-4949
Norman Reed, Superintendent

**Waterville CSD**
381 Madison St, Waterville, NY 13480-1100
315-841-3900
Gary Lonczak, Superintendent

**Westmoreland CSD**
5176 Rt 233, Westmoreland, NY 13490-0430
315-557-2601
Web site: www.westmorelandschool.org
Rocco Migliori, Superintendent

**Whitesboro CSD**
67 Whitesboro St, PO Box 304, Yorkville, NY 13495-0304
315-266-3303  Fax: 315-768-9723
Web site: www.wboro.org
Dave Langone, Superintendent

## ONONDAGA

**Baldwinsville CSD**
29 E Oneida St, Baldwinsville, NY 13027-2480
315-638-6043  Fax: 315-638-6041
Web site: www.bville.org
Jeanne M Dangle, Superintendent

**East Syracuse-Minoa CSD**
407 Fremont Rd, East Syracuse, NY 13057-2631
315-434-3012  Fax: 315-434-3020
e-mail: mvasiloff@esmschools.org
Web site: www.esmschools.org
Dr Donna J DeSiato, Superintendent

**Fabius-Pompey CSD**
1211 Mill St, Fabius, NY 13063-8719
315-683-5301  Fax: 315-683-5827
Web site: www.fabiuspompey.org
Timothy P Ryan, Superintendent

**Fayetteville-Manlius CSD**
8199 E Seneca Tpke, Manlius, NY 13104-2140
315-692-1200  Fax: 315-692-1227
e-mail: ckaiser@fmschools.org
Web site: www.fmschools.org
Corliss Kaiser, Superintendent

**Jamesville-Dewitt CSD**
6845 Edinger Dr, PO Box 606, Dewitt, NY 13214-0606
315-445-8304  Fax: 315-445-8477
e-mail: ckendrick@jd.cnyric.org
Web site: www.jamesvilledewitt.org
Alice Kendrick, Superintendent

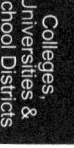

Colleges, Universities & School Districts

**Jordan-Elbridge CSD**
9 N Chappell St, Jordan, NY 13080
315-689-8500 or 315-689-0084
Web site: www.jecsd.org
Lawrence Zacher, Superintendent

**LaFayette CSD**
5955 Rt 20 W, Lafayette, NY 13084-9701
315-677-9728  Fax: 315-677-3372
Web site: www.lafayetteschools.org
Peter A Tigh, Superintendent

**Liverpool CSD**
195 Blackberry Rd, Liverpool, NY 13090
315-622-7125  Fax: 315-622-7115
Web site: www.liverpool.k12.ny.us
Dr Richard N Johns, Superintendent

**Lyncourt UFSD**
2707-2709 Court St, Syracuse, NY 13208
315-455-7571  Fax: 315-455-7573
Michael Schiedo, Superintendent

**Marcellus CSD**
2 Reed Pkwy, Marcellus, NY 13108-1199
315-673-0201  Fax: 315-673-0329
Web site: marcellusschools.org
Craig J Tice, Superintendent

**North Syracuse CSD**
5355 W Taft Rd, North Syracuse, NY 13212-2796
315-218-2151
e-mail: jmelvin@nscsd.org
Web site: www.nscsd.org
Jerome F Melvin, Superintendent

**Onondaga CSD**
4466 S Onondaga Rd, Nedrow, NY 13120-9715
315-552-5000
Web site: www.ocs.cnyric.org
Joseph Rotella, Superintendent

**Skaneateles CSD**
45 E Elizabeth St, Skaneateles, NY 13152
315-685-8361  Fax: 315-685-0347
Web site: www.skanschools.org
Philip D D'Angelo, Superintendent

**Solvay UFSD**
103 3rd St, Solvay, NY 13209-1532
315-468-1111  Fax: 315-468-2755
Web site: www.solvayschools.org
J Francis Manning, Superintendent

**Syracuse City SD**
725 Harrison St, Syracuse, NY 13210
315-435-4161  Fax: 315-435-4015
Web site: www.syracusecityschools.com
Daniel G Lowengard, Superintendent

**Tully CSD**
20 State St, PO Box 628, Tully, NY 13159-0628
315-696-6204
e-mail: kraig@pobox.com
Web site: www.tullyschools.org
Kraig D Pritts, Superintendent

**West Genesee CSD**
300 Sanderson Dr, Camillus, NY 13031-1655
315-487-4562  Fax: 315-487-2999
Web site: www.westgenesee.org
Dr Christopher R Brown, Superintendent

**Westhill CSD**
400 Walberta Rd, Syracuse, NY 13219-2214
315-426-3000  Fax: 315-488-6411
Web site: www.westhillschools.org
Stephen A Bocciolatt, Superintendent

## ONTARIO

**Bloomfield CSD**
45 Maple Ave, Suite A, Bloomfield, NY 14469
585-657-6121
Web site: www.bloomfieldcsd.org
Andy Doell, Superintendent

**Canandaigua City SD**
143 N Pearl St, Canandaigua, NY 14424-1496
585-396-3700
e-mail: rawd@canandaiguaschools.org
Web site: www.canandaiguaschools.org
Ronald Raw Jr, Superintendent

**East Bloomfield CSD**
1 Oakmont Avenue, East Bloomfield, NY 14443
585-657-6121
Web site: www.bloomfieldcsd.org
Michael J Midey, Superintendent

**Geneva City SD**
400 W North St, Geneva, NY 14456
315-781-0400  Fax: 315-781-4128
e-mail: ryoung@genevacsd.org
Web site: www.genevacsd.org
Robert C Young Jr, Superintendent

**Gorham-Middlesex CSD (Marcus Whitman)**
4100 Baldwin Road, Rushville, NY 14544
585-554-4848 X1805
Web site: www.mwcsd.org
Michael Chirco, Superintendent

**Honeoye CSD**
8523 Main St, Honeoye, NY 14471-0170
585-229-4125
Web site: www.honeoye.org
David C Bills, Superintendent

**Manchester-Shortsville CSD**
1506 Rt 21, Shortsville, NY 14548-9502
585-289-3964  Fax: 585-289-6660
Web site: www.redjacket.org
Robert E Leiby, Superintendent

**Marcus Whitman CSD**
4100 Baldwin Rd, Rushville, NY 14544-9799
585-554-4848
e-mail: mchirco@mwcsd.org
Web site: www.mwcsd.org
Michael Chirco, Superintendent

**Naples CSD**
136 N Main St, Naples, NY 14512-9201
585-374-7901
Web site: www.naples.k12.ny.us
Kimberle Ward, Superintendent

**Phelps-Clifton Springs CSD**
1490 Rt 488, Clifton Springs, NY 14432-9334
315-548-6420
Web site: www.midlakes.org
Michael J Ford, Superintendent

*Offices and agencies generally appear in alphabetical order, except when specific order is requested by listee.*

**Victor CSD**
953 High St, Victor, NY 14564-1167
585-924-3252 x1400  Fax: 585-742-7090
Web site: www.victorschools.org
Dawn A Santiago-Marullo, Superintendent

## ORANGE

**Chester UFSD**
64 Hambletonian Ave, Chester, NY 10918
845-469-5052
Sean Michel, Superintendent

**Cornwall CSD**
24 Idlewild Ave, Cornwall on Hudson, NY 12520
845-534-8000  Fax: 845-534-4231
Web site: www.cornwallschools.com
Timothy J Rehm, Superintendent

**Florida UFSD**
51 N Main St, PO Box 7, Florida, NY 10921-0757
845-651-3095
Web site: www.floridaufsd.org
Douglas Burnside, Superintendent

**Goshen CSD**
227 Main St, Goshen, NY 10924
845-615-6720  Fax: 845-615-6725
Web site: www.goshenschoolsny.org
Daniel T Connor, Superintendent of Schools

**Greenwood Lake UFSD**
PO Box 8, Greenwood Lake, NY 10925
845-782-8678
Web site: www.gwlufsd.org
Dr Richard J Brockel, Superintendent

**Highland Falls CSD**
PO Box 287, Highland Falls, NY 10928
845-446-9575  Fax: 845-446-3321
Web site: www.hffmcsd.org
Dr Debra Jackson, Superintendent

**Kiryas Joel Village UFSD**
48 Bakertown Rd- Ste 401, Monroe, NY 10950-0398
845-782-2300
Joel Petlin, Superintendent

**Middletown City SD**
223 Wisner Ave Ext, Middletown, NY 10940-3240
845-326-51158  Fax: 845-343-9938
e-mail: keastwood@ecsdm.org
Web site: middletowncityschools.org
Kenneth Eastwood, Superintendent

**Minisink Valley CSD**
Rt 6, PO Box 217, Slate Hill, NY 10973-0217
845-355-5110
Web site: www.minisink.com
John Latini, Superintendent

**Monroe-Woodbury CSD**
278 Rte 32, Educ Ctr, Central Valley, NY 10917-1001
845-460-6200  Fax: 845-460-6080
Web site: www.mw.k12.ny.us
Edward Mehrhof, Superintendent

**Newburgh Enlarged City SD**
124 Grand St, Newburgh, NY 12550-4600
845-563-3400  Fax: 845-563-3501
Web site: www.newburghschools.org
Ralph A Pizzo, Superintendent

**Pine Bush CSD**
156 State Rt 302, PO Box 700, Pine Bush, NY 12566-0700
845-744-2031
Web site: www.pinebushschools.org
Philip G Steinberg, Superintendent

**Port Jervis City SD**
9 Thompson St, Port Jervis, NY 12771-3058
845-858-3100  Fax: 845-856-1885
Web site: www.pjschools.org
John P Xanthis, Superintendent

**Tuxedo UFSD**
Route 17, Box 2002, Tuxedo Park, NY 10987
845-351-2296  Fax: 845-351-5296
Web site: www.tuxedoschooldistrict.com
Carol Lomascolo, Superintendent

**Valley CSD (Montgomery)**
944 State Rt 17k, Montgomery, NY 12549-2240
845-457-2400
Web site: www.vcsd.k12.ny.us
Richard M Hooley, Superintendent

**Warwick Valley CSD**
PO Box 595, Warwick, NY 10990-0595
845-987-3010
Dr Raymond W Bryant, Superintendent

**Washingtonville CSD**
52 W Main St, Washingtonville, NY 10992-1492
845-497-4000  Fax: 845-496-4031
Roberta Green, Superintendent

## ORLEANS

**Albion CSD**
324 East Ave, Albion, NY 14411
585-589-2056
Web site: www.albionk12.org
Michael Bonnewell, Superintendent

**Holley CSD**
3800 N Main St, Holley, NY 14470-9330
585-638-6316
Web site: www.holleycsd.org
Robert C D'Angelo, Superintendent

**Kendall CSD**
1932 Kendall Rd, Kendall, NY 14476-0777
585-659-2741
e-mail: kcsd@kendallschools.org
Web site: www.kendallschools.org
Julie Christensen, Interim Superintendent

**Lyndonville CSD**
25 Housel Ave, Lyndonville, NY 14098-0540
585-765-2251 x3101
e-mail: bdeane-williams@lyndonville.wnyric.org
Web site: www.lyndonvillecsd.org
Barbara Deane-Williams, Superintendent

**Medina CSD**
One Mustang Dr, Medina, NY 14103-1845
585-798-2700
e-mail: rgalante@medinacsd.org
Web site: www.medinacsd.org
Neal S Miller, Superintendent

*Offices and agencies generally appear in alphabetical order, except when specific order is requested by listee.*

## OSWEGO

**Altmar-Parish-Williamstown CSD**
639 County Rt 22, Parish, NY 13131
315-625-5251
e-mail: dhaab@apw.cnyric.org
Gerry D Hudson, Superintendent

**Central Square CSD**
642 S Main St, Central Square, NY 13036-3511
315-668-4220
Carolyn Costello, Superintendent

**Fulton City SD**
167 S Fourth St, Fulton, NY 13069-1859
315-593-5510
e-mail: blynch@fulton.cnyric.org
William R Lynch, Superintendent

**Hannibal CSD**
928 Cayuga St, Hannibal, NY 13074
315-564-7900
Michael J DiFabio, Superintendent

**Mexico CSD**
40 Academy St, Mexico, NY 13114-3432
315-963-8400
Robert Pritchard, Superintendent

**Oswego City SD**
120 E 1st St, Oswego, NY 13126-2114
315-341-2001
Web site: www.oswego.org
William Crist, Superintendent

**Phoenix CSD**
116 Volney St, Phoenix, NY 13135-9778
315-695-1555
Web site: www.phoenixcsd.org
Judy Belfield, Superintendent

**Pulaski CSD**
2 Hinman Rd, Pulaski, NY 13142-2201
315-298-5188
Marshall Marshall, Superintendent

**Sandy Creek CSD**
124 Salisbury St, Sandy Creek, NY 13145-0248
315-387-3445
Stewart R Amell, Superintendent

## OTSEGO

**Cherry Valley-Springfield CSD**
597 County Hwy 54, Cherry Valley, NY 13320-0485
607-264-3265  Fax: 607-264-3458
e-mail: info@cvscs.org
Web site: www.cvscs.org
Robert Miller, Superintendent

**Cooperstown CSD**
39 Linden Ave, Cooperstown, NY 13326-1496
607-547-5364  Fax: 607-547-1000
Web site: www.cooperstowncs.org
Clifton Hebert, Superintendent

**Edmeston CSD**
11 North St, PO Box 5129, Edmeston, NY 13335-0529
607-965-8931  Fax: 607-965-8942
e-mail: drowley@edmeston.net
David Rowley, Superintendent

**Gilbertsville-Mount Upton CSD**
693 State Hwy 51, Gilbertsville, NY 13776
607-783-2207
e-mail: gmu@gmucsd.org
Web site: www.gmucsd.org
Glenn R Hamilton, Superintendent

**Laurens CSD**
PO Box 301, Laurens, NY 13796-0301
607-432-2050  Fax: 607-432-4388
Romona N Wenck, Superintendent

**Milford CSD**
42 W Main St, Milford, NY 13807-0237
607-286-3341  Fax: 607-286-7879
Peter N Livshin, Superintendent

**Morris CSD**
65 Main St, Morris, NY 13808-0040
607-263-6100  Fax: 607-263-2483
Matthew Sheldon, Superintendent

**Oneonta City SD**
189 Main St, Ste 302, Oneonta, NY 13820-1142
607-433-8232  Fax: 607-433-3641
Web site: www.oneontacsd.org
Michael P Shea, Superintendent

**Otego-Unadilla CSD**
2641 State Hwy 7, Otego, NY 13825
607-988-5038  Fax: 607-988-1039
Web site: www.unatego.org
Charles Molloy, Superintendent

**Richfield Springs CSD**
93 Main St, PO Box 631, Richfield Springs, NY 13439-0631
315-858-0610
Web site: www.richfieldcsd.org
Robert Barraco, Superintendent

**Schenevus CSD**
159 Main St, Schenevus, NY 12155-0008
607-638-5530  Fax: 607-638-5600
Lynda Booknard, Superintendent

**Unatego CSD**
2641 State Hwy 7, Otego, NY 13825
607-988-5000  Fax: 607-988-1039
Web site: www.unatego.org
Charles Molloy, Superintendent

**Worcester CSD**
198 Main St, Worcester, NY 12197
607-397-8785  Fax: 607-397-9454
Gary M Kuch, Superintendent

## PUTNAM

**Brewster CSD**
30 Farm-to-Market Rd, Brewster, NY 10509-9956
845-279-8000
Web site: www.brewsterschools.org
Jane Sandbank, Superintendent

**Carmel CSD**
81 South St, PO Box 296, Patterson, NY 12563-0296
845-878-2094  Fax: 845-878-4337
Web site: www.ccsd.k12.ny.us or www.carmelschools.com
James M Ryan, Superintendent

*Offices and agencies generally appear in alphabetical order, except when specific order is requested by listee.*

**Garrison UFSD**
1100 Rt 9 D, Garrison, NY 10524-0193
845-424-3689  Fax: 845-424-4733
Web site: www.gufs.org
Gloria J Colucci, Superintendent

**Haldane CSD**
15 Craigside Dr, Cold Spring, NY 10516-1899
845-265-9254
Web site: www.haldaneschool.org
Mark Villanti, Superintendent

**Mahopac CSD**
179 East Lake Blvd, Mahopac, NY 10541-1666
845-628-3415 ext 326  Fax: 845-628-5502
Web site: www.mahopac.k12.ny.us
Thomas J Manko, Superintendent

**Putnam Valley CSD**
146 Peekskill Hollow Rd, Putnam Valley, NY 10579-3238
845-528-8143  Fax: 845-528-0274
Web site: www.pvcsd.org
Barbara Fuchs, Superintendent

## RENSSELAER

**Averill Park CSD**
146 Gettle Rd, Averill Park, NY 12018-9798
518-674-7055  Fax: 518-674-3802
Web site: www.averillpark.k12.ny.us
Josephine Moccia, Superintendent

**Berlin CSD**
53 School St, PO Box 259, Berlin, NY 12022-0259
518-658-2690  Fax: 518-658-3822
Web site: www.berlincentral.org
Brian Howard, Acting Superintendent

**Brunswick CSD (Brittonkill)**
3992 NY Rt 2, Troy, NY 12180-9034
518-279-4600 x602  Fax: 518-279-1918
Louis C McIntosh, Superintendent

**East Greenbush CSD**
29 Englewood Ave, East Greenbush, NY 12061
518-207-2500
Web site: www.egcsd.org
Dr Angela M Guptill, Superintendent

**Hoosic Valley CSD**
2 Pleasant Ave, Schaghticoke, NY 12154
518-753-4450
Douglas Kelley, Superintendent

**Hoosick Falls CSD**
21187 NY Rt 22, PO Box 192, Hoosick Falls, NY 12090-0192
518-686-7012  Fax: 518-686-9060
Kenneth A Facin, Superintendent

**Lansingburgh CSD**
576 Fifth Ave, Troy, NY 12182-3295
518-233-6850
George Goodwin, Superintendent

**North Greenbush Common SD (Williams)**
476 N Greenbush Rd, Rensselaer, NY 12144
518-283-6748
Mary Ann Taylor, Superintendent

**Rensselaer City SD**
25 Van Rensselaer Dr, Rensselaer, NY 12144-2694
518-465-7509
Web site: www.rcsd.k12.ny.us
Sally Ann Shields, Superintendent

**Schodack CSD**
1216 Maple Hill Rd, Castleton, NY 12033-1699
518-732-2297  Fax: 518-732-7710
Web site: www.schodack.k12.ny.us
Robert Horan, Superintendent

**Troy City Enlarged SD**
2920 5th Ave, Troy, NY 12180
518-328-5052
Fadhilika Atiba-Weza, Superintendent

**Wynantskill UFSD**
East Ave, PO Box 345, Wynantskill, NY 12198-0345
518-283-4679  Fax: 518-283-3799
Web site: www.wynantskillufsd.org
Christine Hamill, Superintendent

## ROCKLAND

**Clarkstown CSD**
62 Old Middletown Rd, New City, NY 10956
845-639-6419  Fax: 845-639-6488
Web site: www.ccsd.edu
Margaret Keller-Cogan, Superintendent

**East Ramapo CSD (Spring Valley)**
105 S Madison Ave, Spring Valley, NY 10977
845-577-6011
Ira E Oustatcher, Superintendent

**Haverstraw-Stony Point CSD**
65 Chapel Street, Garnerville, NY 10923
845-942-3002
Web site: www.nrcsd.org
Ileana Eckert

**Nanuet UFSD**
101 Church St, Nanuet, NY 10954-3000
845-627-9890
e-mail: mmcneil@nufsd.lhric.org
Mark S McNeill, Superintendent

**North Rockland CSD**
65 Chapel St, Garnerville, NY 10923
845-942-3000  Fax: 845-942-3047
Web site: www.nrcsd.org
Ileana Eckert, Superintendent

**Nyack UFSD**
13A Dickinson Ave, Nyack, NY 10960-2914
845-353-7015  Fax: 845-353-7019
Web site: www.nyackschools.org
Jason Friedman, Acting Superintendent

**Pearl River UFSD**
275 E Central Ave, Pearl River, NY 10965-2799
845-620-3900  Fax: 845-620-3927
Frank V Auriemma, Superintendent

**Ramapo CSD (Suffern)**
45 Mountain Ave, Hillburn, NY 10931-0935
845-357-7783  Fax: 845-357-5707
Robert B MacNaughton, Superintendent

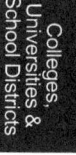

Colleges, Universities & School Districts

*Offices and agencies generally appear in alphabetical order, except when specific order is requested by listee.*

**South Orangetown CSD**
160 Van Wyck Rd, Blauvelt, NY 10913-1299
845-680-1050
Web site: www.socsd.org
Kenneth Mitchell, Superintendent

## SARATOGA

**Ballston Spa CSD**
70 Malta Ave, Ballston Spa, NY 12020-1599
518-884-7195  Fax: 518-885-3201
Web site: www.bscsd.org
Joseph P Dragone, Superintendent

**Burnt Hills-Ballston Lake CSD**
50 Cypress Dr, Glenville, NY 12302
518-399-9141 x5002
Web site: www.bhbl.org
James Schultz, Superintendent

**Corinth CSD**
105 Oak St, Corinth, NY 12822-1295
518-654-2601  Fax: 518-654-6266
Web site: www.corinthcsd.org
Daniel Starr, Superintendent

**Edinburg Common SD**
4 Johnson Rd, Edinburg, NY 12134-5390
518-863-8412
Randy W Teetz, Superintendent

**Galway CSD**
5317 Sacandaga Rd, Galway, NY 12074-0130
518-882-1033  Fax: 518-882-5250
Web site: www.galwaycsd.org
Kimberly Labelle, Superintendent

**Mechanicville City SD**
25 Kniskern Ave, Mechanicville, NY 12118-1995
518-664-5727
Web site: www.mechanicville.org
Michael J McCarthy, Superintendent

**Saratoga Springs City SD**
3 Blue Streak Blvd, Saratoga Springs, NY 12866-5967
518-583-4709
Web site: www.saratogaschools.org
Janice M White, Superintendent

**Schuylerville CSD**
14 Spring St, Schuylerville, NY 12871-1098
518-695-3255  Fax: 518-695-6491
Web site: www.schuylervilleschools.org
Ryan C Sherman, Superintendent

**Shenendehowa CSD**
5 Chelsea Pl, Clifton Park, NY 12065-3240
518-881-0600
e-mail: robioliv@shenet.org
Web site: www.shenet.org
L Oliver Robinson, Superintendent

**South Glens Falls CSD**
6 Bluebird Rd, South Glens Falls, NY 12803-5704
518-793-9617
Web site: www.sgfallssd.org
Gregory J Aidala, Superintendent

**Stillwater CSD**
1068 N Hudson Ave, Stillwater, NY 12170-0490
518-373-6100
Web site: www.scsd.org
Stanley Maziejka, Superintendent

**Waterford-Halfmoon UFSD**
125 Middletown Rd, Waterford, NY 12188-1590
518-237-0800  Fax: 518-237-7335
Web site: www.whufsd.org
Timothy Lange, Superintendent

## SCHENECTADY

**Duanesburg CSD**
133 School Dr, Delanson, NY 12053-0129
518-895-2279  Fax: 518-895-2626
Web site: duanesburg.org
Christine Crowley, Superintendent

**Mohonasen CSD**
2072 Curry Rd, Schenectady, NY 12303-4400
518-356-8200  Fax: 518-356-8247
Web site: www.mohonasen.org
Kathleen A Spring, Superintendent

**Niskayuna CSD**
1239 Van Antwerp Rd, Schenectady, NY 12309-5317
518-377-4666 x206  Fax: 518-377-4074
Web site: www.niskayunaschools.org
Kevin S Baughman, Superintendent

**Rotterdam-Mohonasen CSD**
2072 Curry Road, Schenectady, NY 12303
518-356-8200
Web site: www.mohonasen.org
Kathleen A Spring

**Schalmont CSD**
4 Sabre Dr, Schenectady, NY 12306-1981
518-355-9200  Fax: 518-355-9203
Web site: www.schalmont.org
Valerie Kelsey, Superintendent

**Schenectady City SD**
108 Education Dr, Schenectady, NY 12303-3442
518-370-8100  Fax: 518-370-8173
Web site: www.schenectady.k12.ny.us
John Yagielski, Superintendent

**Scotia-Glenville CSD**
900 Preddice Pkwy, Scotia, NY 12302-1049
518-382-1215  Fax: 518-386-4336
e-mail: sshwartz@sgcsd.net
Susan M Swartz, Superintendent

## SCHOHARIE

**Cobleskill-Richmondville CSD**
155 Washington Ave, Cobleskill, NY 12043-1099
518-234-4032  Fax: 518-234-7721
e-mail: macanl@crcs.k12.ny.us
Web site: www.crcs.k12.ny.us
Lynn Macan, Superintendent

**Gilboa-Conesville CSD**
132 Wyckoff Rd, Gilboa, NY 12076-9703
607-588-7541  Fax: 607-588-6820
Web site: www.gilboa-conesville.k12.ny.us
Ruth Reeve, Superintendent

*Offices and agencies generally appear in alphabetical order, except when specific order is requested by listee.*

**Jefferson CSD**
1332 St Rt 10, Jefferson, NY 12093-0039
607-652-7821  Fax: 607-652-7806
e-mail: c.mummenthey@jeffersoncs.org
Web site: www.jeffersoncs.org
Carl J Mummenthey, Superintendent

**Middleburgh CSD**
168 Main St, Middleburgh, NY 12122
518-827-5567  Fax: 518-827-6632
e-mail: michele.weaver@middleburghcsd.org
Web site: www.middleburghcsd.org
Michele R Weaver, Superintendent

**Schoharie CSD**
136 Academy Drive, PO Box 430, Schoharie, NY 12157-0430
518-295-6679  Fax: 518-295-8178
Web site: www.schoharieschools.org
Brian Sherman, Superintendent

**Sharon Springs CSD**
514 State Rt 20, PO Box 218, Sharon Springs, NY 13459-0218
518-284-2266  Fax: 518-284-9033
e-mail: pgreen@sharonsprings.org
Web site: www.sharonsprings.org
Patterson Green, Superintendent

## SCHUYLER

**Odessa-Montour CSD**
300 College Ave, PO Box 430, Odessa, NY 14869-0430
607-594-3341  Fax: 607-594-3976
e-mail: jframe@gstboces.org
Web site: www.omschools.org
James R Frame, Superintendent

**Watkins Glen CSD**
303 12th St, Watkins Glen, NY 14891-1699
607-535-3219
Web site: www.watkinsglenschools.com
Tom Phillips, Superintendent

## SENECA

**Romulus CSD**
5705 Rt 96, Romulus, NY 14541-9551
866-810-0345 x399
Michael J Hoose, Superintendent

**Seneca Falls CSD**
98 Clinton St, Seneca Falls, NY 13148-1090
315-568-5500  Fax: 315-568-0535
Web site: www.sfcs.k12.ny.us
Robert McKeveny, Superintendent

**South Seneca CSD**
7263 Main St, Ovid, NY 14521-9586
607-869-9636
Web site: www.southseneca.com
Janie L Nusser, Superintendent

**Waterloo CSD**
109 Washington St, Waterloo, NY 13165
315-539-1500
Web site: www.waterloocsd.org
Terry MacNabb, Superintendent

## ST. LAWRENCE

**Brasher Falls CSD**
1039 State Hwy 11C, Brasher Falls, NY 13613-0307
315-389-5131  Fax: 315-389-5245
Web site: www.bfcsd.org
Stephen Putman, Superintendent

**Canton CSD**
99 State St, Canton, NY 13617-1099
315-386-8561
Web site: www.ccsdk12.org
William A Gregory, Superintendent

**Clifton-Fine CSD**
11 Hall Ave, PO Box 75, Star Lake, NY 13690-0075
315-848-3335 x190
Denise Dzikowski, Superintendent

**Colton-Pierrepont CSD**
4921 State Hwy 56, Colton, NY 13625-0005
315-262-2100  Fax: 315-262-2644
Martin Bregg, Superintendent

**Edwards-Knox CSD**
2512 County Hwy 24, PO Box 630, Russell, NY 13684-0630
315-562-8130  Fax: 315-562-2477
Web site: www.ekcsk12.org
Suzanne Kelly, Superintendent

**Gouverneur CSD**
133 E Barney St, Gouverneur, NY 13642-1100
315-287-4870
e-mail: clarose@gcs.neric.org
Christine J Larose, Superintendent

**Hammond CSD**
51 S Main St, PO Box 185, Hammond, NY 13646-0185
315-324-5931 x811
Douglas McQueer, Superintendent

**Hermon-Dekalb CSD**
709 E DeKalb Rd, DeKalb Junction, NY 13630-0213
315-347-3442  Fax: 315-347-3817
Web site: www.hdcsk12.org
Ann M Adams, Superintendent

**Heuvelton CSD**
87 Washington St, PO Box 375, Heuvelton, NY 13654-0375
315-344-2414  Fax: 315-344-2349
Susan E Todd, Superintendent

**Lisbon CSD**
6866 County Rt 10, PO Box 39, Lisbon, NY 13668
315-393-4951  Fax: 315-393-7666
Web site: lisboncs.schoolwires.com
Erin E Woods, Superintendent

**Madrid-Waddington CSD**
2582 State Hwy 345, Madrid, NY 13660-0067
315-322-5746
Web site: www.mwcsk12.org
Lynn Roy, Superintendent

**Massena CSD**
84 Nightengale Ave, Massena, NY 13662-1999
315-764-3700 x3005  Fax: 315-764-3701
Web site: www.mcs.k12.ny.us
Roger B Clough, Superintendent

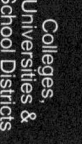

Colleges,
Universities &
School Districts

*Offices and agencies generally appear in alphabetical order, except when specific order is requested by listee.*

**Morristown CSD**
408 Gouverneur St, Morristown, NY 13664-0217
315-375-8814
David J Glover, Superintendent

**Norwood-Norfolk CSD**
PO Box 194, 7852 State Hwy 56, Norwood, NY 13668-0194
315-353-9951
Web site: www.nncsk12.org
Elizabeth Kirnie, Superintendent

**Ogdensburg City SD**
1100 State St, Ogdensburg, NY 13669-3398
315-393-0900  Fax: 315-393-2767
Timothy M Vernsey, Superintendent

**Parishville-Hopkinton CSD**
12 County Rt 47, Parishville, NY 13672-0187
315-265-4642  Fax: 315-268-1309
Web site: phcs.neric.org
Darin P Saiff, Superintendent

**Potsdam CSD**
29 Leroy St, Potsdam, NY 13676-1787
315-265-2000  Fax: 315-265-2048
e-mail: pbrady@potsdam.k12.ny.us
Web site: www.potsdam.k12.ny.us
Patrick Brady, Superintendent

## STEUBEN

**Addison CSD**
7787 State Rt 417, Addison, NY 14801
607-359-2244  Fax: 607-359-2246
Betsey A Stiker, Superintendent

**Arkport CSD**
35 East Ave, PO Box 70, Arkport, NY 14807-0070
607-295-7471  Fax: 607-295-7473
Glenn Niles, Superintendent

**Avoca CSD**
17-29 Oliver St, Avoca, NY 14809-0517
607-566-2221  Fax: 607-566-2398
e-mail: ryochem@avocacsd.org
Richard Yochem, Superintendent

**Bath CSD**
25 Ellas Ave, Bath, NY 14810-1107
607-776-3301  Fax: 607-776-5021
Web site: www.bathcsd.org
Patrick Kelley, Superintendent

**Bradford CSD**
2820 Rt 226, Bradford, NY 14815-9602
607-583-4616  Fax: 607-583-4013
Wendy S Field, Superintendent

**Campbell-Savona CSD**
8455 County Rt 125, Campbell, NY 14821-9518
607-527-9800  Fax: 607-527-8363
e-mail: khagen@cscsd.org
Web site: www.cscsd.org
Kathy Hagenbuch, Superintendent

**Canisteo-Greenwood CSD**
84 Greenwood St, Canisteo, NY 14823-1299
607-698-4225  Fax: 607-698-2833
e-mail: jmatteson@cgcsd.org
Web site: www.cgcsd.org
Jeffrey A Matteson, Superintendent

**Corning-Painted Post Area SD**
165 Charles St, Painted Post, NY 14870-1199
607-936-3704  Fax: 607-654-2735
Michael Ginalski, Superintendent

**Hammondsport CSD**
PO Box 368, Hammondsport, NY 14840-0368
607-569-5200  Fax: 607-569-5212
e-mail: kbower@hport.wnyric.org
Kyle C Bower, Superintendent

**Hornell City SD**
25 Pearl St, Hornell, NY 14843-1504
607-324-1302  Fax: 607-324-4060
e-mail: george.kiley@hornellcsd.org
Web site: www.hornellcityschools.com
George Kiley, Superintendent

**Jasper-Troupsburg CSD**
3769 N Main St, Jasper, NY 14855
607-792-3675  Fax: 607-792-3749
e-mail: chadgroff@jt.wnyric.org
Chad C Groff, Superintendent

**Prattsburgh CSD**
1 Academy St, Prattsburgh, NY 14873-0249
607-522-3795  Fax: 607-522-6221
e-mail: jrumsey@pratts.wnyric.org
Joseph L Rumsey, Superintendent

**Wayland-Cohocton CSD**
2350 Rt 63, Wayland, NY 14572
585-728-2211
e-mail: mwetherbee@wccsk12.org
Web site: www.wccsk12.org
Michael J Wetherbee, Superintendent

## SUFFOLK

**Amagansett UFSD**
320 Main St, PO Box 7062, Amagansett, NY 11930-7062
631-267-3572  Fax: 631-267-7504
Web site: www.amagansettschool.org
Eleanor Tritt, Superintendent

**Amityville UFSD**
150 Park Ave, Amityville, NY 11701-3195
631-598-6520  Fax: 631-598-6516
Web site: www.amityville.k12.ny.us
John R Williams, Superintendent

**Babylon UFSD**
50 Railroad Ave, Babylon, NY 11702-2221
631-893-7925
Web site: www.babylon.k12.ny.us
Ellen Best-Laimit, Superintendent

**Bay Shore UFSD**
75 W Perkal St, Bayshore, NY 11706-6696
631-968-1117  Fax: 631-968-1129
Web site: www.bayshore.k12.ny.us
Evelyn B Holman, Superintendent

**Bayport-Blue Point UFSD**
189 Academy St, Bayport, NY 11705
631-472-7860  Fax: 631-472-7873
Web site: www.bbpschools.org
Anthony J Annunziato, Superintendent

*Offices and agencies generally appear in alphabetical order, except when specific order is requested by listee.*

**Brentwood UFSD**
52 Third Ave, Brentwood, NY 11717-6198
631-434-2325  Fax: 631-434-6575
Web site: www.brentwood.k12.ny.us
Joseph Bond, Superintendent

**Bridgehampton UFSD**
2685 Montauk Hwy, PO Box 3021, Bridgehampton, NY 11932-3021
631-537-0271  Fax: 631-537-1030
Web site: www.bridgehampton.k12.ny.us
Lois Favre, Superintendent

**Brookhaven-Comsewogue UFSD**
290 Norwood Ave, Port Jefferson, NY 11776-2999
631-474-8105  Fax: 631-474-8399
Joseph Rella, Superintendent

**Center Moriches UFSD**
529 Main Street, Center Moriches, NY 11934
631-878-0052  Fax: 631-878-4326
Web site: www.centermoriches.k12.ny.us
Russell Stewart

**Central Islip UFSD**
50 Wheeler Road, Central Islip, NY 11722-9027
631-348-5112  Fax: 631-348-0366
Web site: www.centralislip.k12.ny.us
Craig Carr, Superintendent

**Cold Spring Harbor CSD**
75 Goose Hill Rd, Cold Spring Harbor, NY 11724-9813
631-367-5931
Web site: www.csh.k12.ny.us
Judith A Wilansky, Superintendent

**Commack UFSD**
480 Clay Pitts Rd, East Northport, NY 11731-3828
631-912-2010
e-mail: djames@commack.k12.ny.us
Web site: www.commack.k12.ny.us
Donald James, Superintendent

**Connetquot CSD**
780 Ocean Ave, Bohemia, NY 11716
631-244-2215  Fax: 631-589-0683
Alan B Groveman, Superintendent

**Copiague UFSD**
2650 Great Neck Rd, Copiague, NY 11726-1699
631-842-4015 x501
Web site: www.copiague.k12.ny.us
Charles A Leunig, Superintendent

**Deer Park UFSD**
1881 Deer Park Ave, Deer Park, NY 11729-4326
631-274-4010
Web site: www.deerparkschools.org
Eva J Demyen, Superintendent

**East Hampton UFSD**
4 Long Ln, East Hampton, NY 11937
631-329-4100  Fax: 631-329-0109
Raymond D Gualtieri, Superintendent

**East Islip UFSD**
1 Craig B Gariepy Ave, Islip Terrace, NY 11752
631-224-2000  Fax: 631-581-1617
e-mail: wchu@eischools.org
Web site: www.eischools.org
Wendell Chu, Superintendent

**East Moriches UFSD**
9 Adelaide Ave, East Moriches, NY 11940-1320
631-878-0162  Fax: 631-878-0186
Charles Russo, Superintendent

**East Quogue UFSD**
6 Central Ave, East Quogue, NY 11942
631-653-5210  Fax: 631-653-8644
Les Black, Acting Superintendent

**Eastport-South Manor CSD**
149 Dayton Ave, Manorville, NY 11949
631-874-6720  Fax: 631-878-6308
e-mail: nocero@esmonline.org
Web site: www.esmonline.org
Mark A Nocero, Superintendent

**Elwood UFSD**
100 Kenneth Ave, Greenlawn, NY 11740-2900
631-266-5402
Web site: www.elwood.k12.ny.us
Peter C Scordo, Superintendent

**Fire Island UFSD**
Surf Rd, PO Box 428, Ocean Beach, NY 11770-0428
631-583-5626  Fax: 631-583-5167
Web site: www.fi.k12.ny.us
Loretta Ferraro, Superintendent

**Fishers Island UFSD**
PO Drawer A, Fishers Island, NY 06390
631-788-7444  Fax: 631-788-5532
Web site: www.fischool.com
Charles Meyers, Superintendent

**Greenport UFSD**
720 Front St, Greenport, NY 11944
631-477-1950  Fax: 631-477-2164
Web site: www.greenport.k12.ny.us
Micahel Comanda, Superintendent

**Half Hollow Hills CSD**
525 Half Hollow Rd, Dix Hills, NY 11746-5899
631-592-3008
Web site: www.halfhollowhills.k12.ny.us
Sheldon Karnilow, Superintendent

**Hampton Bays UFSD**
86 E Argonne Rd, Hampton Bays, NY 11946
631-723-2100  Fax: 631-723-2109
Web site: www.hbschools.us
Lars Clemensen, Superintendent

**Harborfields CSD**
2 Oldfield Rd, Greenlawn, NY 11740
631-754-5320 x321
e-mail: carasitif@harborfieldscsd.net
Web site: www.harborfieldscsd.net
Frank J Carasiti, Superintendent

**Hauppauge UFSD**
495 Hoffman Ln, PO Box 6006, Hauppauge, NY 11788
631-761-8208  Fax: 631-265-3649
Web site: www.hauppauge.k12.ny.us
Patricia Sullivan-Kriss, Superintendent

**Huntington UFSD**
50 Tower St, Huntington Station, NY 11746
631-673-2038
e-mail: jfinello@hufsd.edu
Web site: www.hufsd.edu
John J Finello, Superintendent

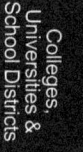

Colleges,
Universities &
School Districts

*Offices and agencies generally appear in alphabetical order, except when specific order is requested by listee.*

**Islip UFSD**
215 Main St, Islip, NY 11751-3435
631-650-8200  Fax: 631-650-8218
Web site: www.islipufsd.org
Susan Schnebel, Superintendent

**Kings Park CSD**
101 Church St, Kings Park, NY 11754-1769
631-269-3310
Web site: www.kpcsd.k12.ny.us
Susan Agruso, Superintendent

**Lindenhurst UFSD**
350 Daniel St, Lindenhurst, NY 11757-0621
631-867-3001
Web site: www.lindenhurstschools.org
Richard Nathan, Superintendent

**Little Flower UFSD**
2460 N Wading River Rd, Wading River, NY 11792
631-929-4300  Fax: 631-929-0303
Web site: www.littleflowerufsd.org
George Grigg, Superintendent

**Longwood CSD**
35 Yaphank-Mid Isl Rd, Middle Island, NY 11953-2369
631-345-2172  Fax: 631-345-2166
Web site: www.longwood.k12.ny.us
Allan Gerstenlauer, Superintendent

**Mattituck-Cutchogue UFSD**
385 Depot Ln, PO Box 1438, Cutchogue, NY 11935
631-298-4242  Fax: 631-298-8520
Web site: www.mufsd.com
James McKenna, Superintendent

**Middle Country CSD**
Eight 43rd St, Centereach, NY 11720-2325
631-285-8005
Web site: www.middlecountry.k12.ny.us
Roberta Gerold, Superintendent

**Miller Place UFSD**
275 Route 25A, Miller Place, NY 11764-2036
631-474-2700  Fax: 631-331-8832
Web site: www.millerplace.k12.ny.us
Susan Hodun, Superintendent

**Montauk UFSD**
50 S Dorset Rd, Montauk, NY 11954
631-668-2474  Fax: 631-668-1107
Web site: www.montaukschool.org
J Philip Perna, Superintendent

**Mt Sinai UFSD**
148 N Country Rd, Mount Sinai, NY 11766-0397
631-870-2554  Fax: 631-473-0905
e-mail: mts@mtsinai.k12.ny.us
Web site: www.mtsinai.k12.ny.us
Dr Anthony J Bonasera, Superintendent

**New Suffolk Common SD**
7605 New Suffolk Rd, PO Box 111, New Suffolk, NY 11956-0111
631-734-6940  Fax: 631-734-6940
Web site: www.newsuffolkschool.com
Robert Feger, Superintendent

**North Babylon UFSD**
5 Jardine Pl, North Babylon, NY 11703-4203
631-321-3226
Web site: www.northbabylonschools.net
Patricia Godek, Superintendent

**Northport-East Northport UFSD**
158 Laurel Ave, Northport, NY 11768-3455
631-262-6604
Web site: www.northport.k12.ny.us
Marylou McDermott, Superintendent

**Oysterponds UFSD**
23405 Main Rd, PO Box 98, Orient, NY 11957
631-323-2410  Fax: 631-323-3713
Web site: www.oysterponds.org
Joan Frisicano, Superintendent

**Patchogue-Medford UFSD**
241 S Ocean Ave, Patchogue, NY 11772-3787
631-687-6380
Web site: www.pmschools.org
Michael Mostow, Superintendent

**Port Jefferson UFSD**
550 Scraggy Hill Rd, Port Jefferson, NY 11777-1969
631-476-4404
Web site: www.portjeff.k12.ny.us
Max Riley, Superintendent

**Quogue UFSD**
10 Edgewood Rd, PO Box 957, Quogue, NY 11959-0957
631-653-4285  Fax: 631-653-4864
Richard J Benson, Superintendent

**Remsenburg-Speonk UFSD**
11 Mill Rd, PO Box 900, Remsenburg, NY 11960-0900
631-325-0203  Fax: 631-325-8439
Ronald Masera, Superintendent

**Riverhead CSD**
700 Osborne Ave, Riverhead, NY 11901
631-369-6717  Fax: 631-369-6718
Web site: www.riverhead.net
Nancy Carney, Superintendent

**Rocky Point UFSD**
170 Rt 25A, Rocky Point, NY 11778-8401
631-744-1600
Web site: www.rockypointschools.org
Michael Ring, Superintendent

**Sachem CSD**
245 Union Ave, Holbrook, NY 11741
631-471-1300  Fax: 631-471-1341
Web site: www.sachem.edu
James Nolan, Superintendent

**Sag Harbor UFSD**
200 Jermain Ave, Sag Harbor, NY 11963-3549
631-725-5300  Fax: 631-725-5330
Web site: www.sagharborschools.org

**Sagaponack Common SD**
Main St, PO Box 1500, Sagaponack, NY 11962-1500
631-537-0651  Fax: 631-537-2342
Lee Ellwood, Superintendent

**Sayville UFSD**
99 Greeley Ave, Sayville, NY 11782
631-244-6510  Fax: 631-244-6504
Walter F Schartner, Superintendent

**Shelter Island UFSD**
33 North Ferry Rd, PO Box 2015, Shelter Island, NY 11964-2015
631-749-0302  Fax: 631-749-1262
Web site: www.shelterisland.k12.ny.us
Robert Parry, Superintendent

*Offices and agencies generally appear in alphabetical order, except when specific order is requested by listee.*

**Shoreham-Wading River CSD**
250B Rt 25A, Shoreham, NY 11786
631-821-8105  Fax: 631-929-3001
Harriet Copel, Superintendent

**Smithtown CSD**
26 New York Ave, Smithtown, NY 11787-3435
631-382-2005  Fax: 631-382-2010
Web site: www.smithtown.k12.ny.us
Edward Ehmann, Superintendent

**South Country CSD**
189 Dunton Ave, East Patchogue, NY 11772
631-730-1510  Fax: 631-286-6394
Web site: www.southcountry.org
Joseph Cipp Jr, Superintendent

**South Huntington UFSD**
60 Weston St, Huntington Station, NY 11746-4098
631-812-3070  Fax: 631-425-5362
Thomas C Shea, Superintendent

**Southampton UFSD**
70 Leland Ln, Southampton, NY 11968
631-591-4510  Fax: 631-287-2870
Richard Boyes, Superintendent

**Southold UFSD**
420 Oaklawn Ave, PO Box 470, Southold, NY 11971-0470
631-765-5400  Fax: 631-765-5086
David A Gamberg, Superintendent

**Springs UFSD**
48 School St, East Hampton, NY 11937
631-324-0144  Fax: 631-324-0269
Michael Hartner, Superintendent

**Three Village CSD**
100 Suffolk Ave, Stony Brook, NY 11790
631-730-4010  Fax: 631-474-7784
e-mail: nlederer@3villagecsd.org
Web site: www.threevillagecsd.org
Neil Lederer, Superintendent

**Tuckahoe Common SD**
468 Magee St, Southampton, NY 11968-3216
631-283-3550  Fax: 631-283-3469
Chris Dyer, Superintendent

**Wainscott Common SD**
PO Box 79, Wainscott, NY 11975-0079
631-537-1080  Fax: 631-537-6977
Stuart Rachlin, Superintendent

**West Babylon UFSD**
10 Farmingdale Rd, West Babylon, NY 11704-6289
631-321-3142  Fax: 631-661-5166
Web site: www.wbschools.org
Anthony Cacciola, Superintendent

**West Islip UFSD**
100 Sherman Ave, West Islip, NY 11795-3237
631-893-3200  Fax: 631-893-3217
Web site: www.wi.k12.ny.us
Richard Simon, Superintendent

**Westhampton Beach UFSD**
340 Mill Rd, Westhampton Beach, NY 11978
631-288-3800  Fax: 631-288-8351
Web site: www.westhamptonbeach.k12.ny.us
Lynn Schwartz, Superintendent

**William Floyd UFSD**
240 Mastic Beach Rd, Mastic Beach, NY 11951
631-874-1201  Fax: 631-281-3047
Web site: www.wfsd.k12.ny.us
Paul Casciano, Superintendent

**Wyandanch UFSD**
1445 MLK Jr Blvd, Wyandanch, NY 11798-3997
631-870-0400  Fax: 631-491-3032
Web site: www.wyandanch.k12.ny.us
Pless Dickerson, Superintendent

## SULLIVAN

**Eldred CSD**
600 Rt 55, Eldred, NY 12732-0249
845-456-1100  Fax: 845-557-3672
Robert Dufour, Superintendent

**Fallsburg CSD**
115 Brickman Rd, PO Box 124, Fallsburg, NY 12733-0124
845-434-5884 x1215
e-mail: ikatz@fallsburgcsd.net
Ivan J Katz, Interim Superintendent

**Liberty CSD**
115 Buckley St, Liberty, NY 12754-1600
845-292-6990  Fax: 845-292-1164
e-mail: vanyomic@libertyk12.org
Web site: www.libertyk12.org
Michael B Vanyo, Superintendent

**Livingston Manor CSD**
19 School St, Livingston Manor, NY 12758-0947
845-439-4400  Fax: 845-439-4717
Web site: lmcs.k12.ny.us
Deborah Fox, Superintendent

**Monticello CSD**
237 Forestburgh Rd, Monticello, NY 12701
845-794-7700  Fax: 845-794-7710
Edward Rhine, Acting Superintendent

**Roscoe CSD**
6 Academy St, Roscoe, NY 12776-0429
607-498-4126
John P Evans, Superintendent

**Sullivan West CSD**
33 Schoolhouse Rd, Jeffersonville, NY 12748
845-482-4610 x3000
Web site: www.swcsd.org
Kenneth H Hilton, Superintendent

**Tri-Valley CSD**
34 Moore Hill Rd, Grahamsville, NY 12740-5609
845-985-2296 x5101
Thomas W Palmer, Superintendent

## TIOGA

**Candor CSD**
1 Academy St, PO Box 145, Candor, NY 13743-0145
607-659-5010
Web site: www.candor.org
Jeffrey J Kisloski, Superintendent

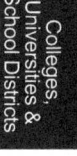

Colleges,
Universities &
School Districts

*Offices and agencies generally appear in alphabetical order, except when specific order is requested by listee.*

**Newark Valley CSD**
79 Whig St, Newark Valley, NY 13811-0547
607-642-3221
Web site: www.nvcs.stier.org
Ryan Dougherty, Superintendent

**Owego-Apalachin CSD**
36 Talcott St, Owego, NY 13827-9965
607-687-6224
Web site: www.oacsd.org
Bill Russell, Superintendent

**Spencer-Van Etten CSD**
16 Dartts Crossroad, PO Box 307, Spencer, NY 14883
607-589-7100  Fax: 607-589-3010
Web site: www.svecsd.org
Joseph Morgan, Superintendent

**Tioga CSD**
27 Fifth Ave, Tioga Center, NY 13845-0241
607-687-8001
Web site: www.tiogacentral.org
Scot Taylor, Superintendent

**Waverly CSD**
15 Frederick St, Waverly, NY 14892-1294
607-565-2841  Fax: 607-565-4997
Web site: www.waverlyschools.com
Michael W McMahon, Superintendent

## TOMPKINS

**Dryden CSD**
118 Freeville Road, PO Box 88, Dryden, NY 13053
607-844-8694 x601
Sandra R Sherwood, Superintendent

**George Junior Republic UFSD**
24 McDonald Rd, Freeville, NY 13068-9699
607-844-6343
J Brad Herman, Superintendent

**Groton CSD**
400 Peru Rd, Groton, NY 13073-1297
607-898-5301  Fax: 607-898-4647
e-mail: jabrams@groton.cnyric.org
Web site: www.grotoncs.org
James Abrams, Superintendent

**Ithaca City SD**
400 Lake St, Ithaca, NY 14851-0549
607-274-2101
Web site: www.icsd.k12.ny.us
Luvelle Brown, Superintendent

**Lansing CSD**
284 Ridge Rd, Lansing, NY 14882
607-533-4294  Fax: 607-533-3602
Web site: www.lcsd.k12.ny.us
Stephen L Grimm, Superintendent

**Newfield CSD**
247 Main St, Newfield, NY 14867-9313
607-564-9955
Web site: www.newfieldschools.org
Cheryl Thomas, Superintendent

**Trumansburg CSD**
100 Whig St, Trumansburg, NY 14886-9179
607-387-7551 x421
Paula Hurley, Superintendent

## ULSTER

**Ellenville CSD**
28 Maple Ave, Ellenville, NY 12428
845-647-0100  Fax: 845-647-0105
Web site: www.ecs.k12.ny.us
Lisa A Wiles, Superintendent

**Highland CSD**
320 Pancake Hollow Rd, Highland, NY 12528-2317
845-691-1012  Fax: 845-691-3904
Web site: www.highland-k12.org
Deborah A Haab, Superintendent

**Kingston City SD**
61 Crown St, Kingston, NY 12401-3833
845-339-3000
Web site: www.kingstoncityschools.org
Gerard M Gretzinger, Superintendent

**Marlboro CSD**
1510 Route 9W, Suite 201, Marlboro, NY 12542
845-236-5804  Fax: 848-236-5817
Web site: marlboroschools.org
Raymond Castellani, Superintendent

**New Paltz CSD**
196 Main St, New Paltz, NY 12561-1200
845-256-4020  Fax: 845-256-4025
Web site: www.newpaltz.k12.ny.us
Maria Rice, Superintendent

**Onteora CSD**
PO Box 300, Boiceville, NY 12412-0300
845-657-6383  Fax: 845-657-9687
e-mail: pmcgill@onteora.k12.ny.us
Phyllis Spiegel McGill, Superintendent

**Rondout Valley CSD**
122 Kyserike Rd, PO Box 9, Accord, NY 12404-0009
845-687-2400  Fax: 845-687-9577
Web site: www.rondout.k12.ny.us
Rosario Agostaro, Superintendent

**Saugerties CSD**
Call Box A, Saugerties, NY 12477
845-247-6500  Fax: 845-246-8364
Seth Turner, Superintendent

**Wallkill CSD**
19 Main St, Wallkill, NY 12589
845-895-7101
Web site: www.wallkillcsd.k12.ny.us
William J Hecht, Superintendent

**West Park UFSD**
2112 Rt 9W, West Park, NY 12493-0010
845-384-6710
Joyce Mucci, Superintendent

## WARREN

**Bolton CSD**
26 Horicon Ave, Bolton Landing, NY 12814-0120
518-644-2400
e-mail: info@boltoncsd.org
Web site: www.boltoncsd.org
Raymond Ciccarelli Jr, Superintendent

*Offices and agencies generally appear in alphabetical order, except when specific order is requested by listee.*

**Glens Falls City SD**
15 Quade St, Glens Falls, NY 12801-2725
518-792-1212
Web site: www.gfsd.org
Thomas F McGowan, Superintendent

**Glens Falls Common SD**
120 Lawrence St, Glens Falls, NY 12801-3758
518-792-3231  Fax: 518-792-2557
Ella W Collins, Superintendent

**Hadley-Luzerne CSD**
273 Lake Ave, Lake Luzerne, NY 12846
518-696-2112 x134
Irwin H Sussman, Superintendent

**Johnsburg CSD**
165 Main St, North Creek, NY 12853-0380
518-251-2921  Fax: 518-251-2562
Web site: www.johnsburgcsd.org
Michael Markwica, Superintendent

**Lake George CSD**
381 Canada St, Lake George, NY 12845-1197
518-668-5456  Fax: 518-668-2285
Web site: www.lkgeorge.org
Patrick Dee, Superintendent

**North Warren CSD**
6110 State Rt 8, Chestertown, NY 12817
518-494-3015
Web site: www.northwarren.k12.ny.us
Joseph R Murphy, Superintendent

**Queensbury UFSD**
429 Aviation Rd, Queensbury, NY 12804-2914
518-824-5602  Fax: 518-793-4476
Web site: www.queensburyschool.org
Douglas W Huntley, Superintendent

**Warrensburg CSD**
103 Schroon River Rd, Warrensburg, NY 12885-4803
518-623-2861
Web site: www.wcsd.org
Timothy D Lawson, Superintendent

## WASHINGTON

**Argyle CSD**
5023 State Rt 40, Argyle, NY 12809-0067
518-638-8243  Fax: 518-638-6373
Web site: www.argylecsd.org
Jan Jehring, Superintendent

**Cambridge CSD**
58 S Park St, Cambridge, NY 12816
518-677-8527  Fax: 518-677-3889
Web site: www.cambridgecsd.org
Vincent Canini, Superintendent

**Fort Ann CSD**
One Catherine St, Fort Ann, NY 12827-5039
518-639-5594  Fax: 518-639-8911
Web site: www.fortannschool.org
Maureen VanBuren, Superintendent

**Fort Edward UFSD**
220 Broadway, Fort Edward, NY 12828-1598
518-747-4594 x100
Web site: www.fortedward.org
Jeffery Ziegler, Superintendent

**Granville CSD**
58 Quaker St, Granville, NY 12832-1596
518-642-1051  Fax: 518-642-2491
Web site: www.granvillecsd.org
Mark Bessen, Superintendent

**Greenwich CSD**
10 Gray Ave, Greenwich, NY 12834-1107
518-692-9542
Web site: www.greenwichcsd.org
Matthias Donnelly, Superintendent

**Hartford CSD**
4704 State Rt 149, Hartford, NY 12838-0079
518-632-5931
Web site: www.hartfordcsd.org
Thomas W Abraham, Administrator

**Hudson Falls CSD**
1153 Burgoyne Ave, Hudson Falls, NY 12839-0710
518-747-2121
Web site: www.hfcsd.org
Mark E Doody, Superintendent

**Putnam CSD**
126 County Rt 2, PO Box 91, Putnam Station, NY 12861
518-547-8266  Fax: 518-547-9567
e-mail: matthew.boucher@putnamcsd.org
Web site: putnamcsd.org
Matthew Boucher, Superintendent

**Salem CSD**
41 E Broadway, Salem, NY 12865-0517
518-854-7855
Kerri Erin Piemme, Superintendent

**Whitehall CSD**
87 Buckley Rd, Whitehall, NY 12887-3633
518-499-1772
e-mail: jwatson@railroaders.net
Web site: www.railroaders.net
James Watson, Superintendent

## WAYNE

**Clyde-Savannah CSD**
215 Glasgow St, Clyde, NY 14433-1222
315-902-3000
Web site: www.clydesavannah.org
Theresa Pulos, Superintendent

**Gananda CSD**
1500 Dayspring Ridge, Walworth, NY 14568
315-986-3521
Web site: www.gananda.org
Shawn Van Scoy, Superintendent

**Lyons CSD**
10 Clyde Rd, Lyons, NY 14489-9371
315-946-2200
Web site: www.lyonscsd.org
Richard Amundson, Superintendent

**Marion CSD**
4034 Warner Rd, Marion, NY 14505-0999
315-926-4228
Web site: www.marioncs.org
Kathryn A Wegman, Superintendent

Colleges,
Universities &
School Districts

*Offices and agencies generally appear in alphabetical order, except when specific order is requested by listee.*

**Newark CSD**
100 E Miller St, Newark, NY 14513-1599
315-332-3217
Web site: www.newark.k12.ny.us
Henry Hann, Acting Superintendent

**North Rose-Wolcott CSD**
11669 Salter-Colvin Rd, Wolcott, NY 14590-9398
315-594-3141 Fax: 315-594-2352
Web site: www.nrwcs.org
John C Walker, Superintendent

**Palmyra-Macedon CSD**
151 Hyde Pkwy, Palmyra, NY 14522-1297
315-597-3401
Robert Ike, Superintendent

**Red Creek CSD**
6815 Church St, PO Box 190, Red Creek, NY 13143-0190
315-754-2010 Fax: 315-754-8169
e-mail: dsholes@rccsd.org
Web site: www.rccsd.org
David G Sholes, Superintendent

**Sodus CSD**
PO Box 220, Sodus, NY 14551-0220
315-483-5201 Fax: 315-483-4755
Web site: www.soduscsd.org
Susan Kay Salvaggio, Superintendent

**Wayne CSD**
6076 Ontario Ctr Rd, Ontario Center, NY 14520-0155
315-524-1001
Web site: www.wayne.k12.ny.us
Renee Garrett, Superintendent

**Williamson CSD**
PO Box 900, Williamson, NY 14589-0900
315-589-9661
Web site: www.williamsoncentral.org
Maria Ehresman, Superintendent

## WESTCHESTER

**Abbott UFSD**
100 N Broadway, Irvington, NY 10533-1254
914-591-7428
Harold A Coles, Superintendent

**Ardsley UFSD**
500 Farm Rd, Ardsley, NY 10502-1410
914-693-6300
Lauren Allan, Superintendent

**Bedford CSD**
Fox Lane Campus, PO Box 180, Mt. Kisco, NY 10549
914-241-6010
Jere Hochman, Superintendent

**Blind Brook-Rye UFSD**
390 North Ridge St, Rye Brook, NY 10573-1105
914-937-3600
Web site: www.blindbrook.org
William J Stark, Superintendent

**Briarcliff Manor UFSD**
45 Ingham Rd, Briarcliff Manor, NY 10510-2221
914-941-8880 x303
Web site: www.briarcliffschools.org
Jerry Cicchelli, Superintendent

**Bronxville UFSD**
177 Pondfield Rd, Bronxville, NY 10708-4829
914-395-0500
Web site: www.bronxville.lhric.org
David Quattrone, Superintendent

**Byram Hills CSD**
10 Tripp Ln, Armonk, NY 10504-2512
914-273-4082
Web site: www.byramhills.org
Jacquelyn Taylor, Superintendent

**Chappaqua CSD**
66 Roaring Brook Rd, Chappaqua, NY 10514-1703
914-238-7200 Fax: 914-238-7231
John Chambers, Superintendent

**Croton-Harmon UFSD**
10 Gerstein St, Croton-on-Hudson, NY 10520-2303
914-271-4793 or 914-271-4713 Fax: 914-271-8685
Web site: www.croton-harmonschools.org
Edward R Fuhrman Jr, Superintendent

**Dobbs Ferry UFSD**
505 Broadway, Dobbs Ferry, NY 10522-1118
914-693-1506 Fax: 914-693-1787
Web site: www.dfsd.org
Debra Kaplan, Superintendent

**Eastchester UFSD**
580 White Plains Rd, Eastchester, NY 10709
914-793-6130 Fax: 914-793-9006
Web site: www.eastchester.k12.ny.us
Marilyn Terranova, Superintendent

**Edgemont UFSD**
300 White Oak Ln, Scarsdale, NY 10583-1725
914-472-7768 Fax: 914-472-6846
Web site: www.edgemont.org
Nancy L Taddiken, Superintendent

**Elmsford UFSD**
98 South Goodwin Ave, Elmsford, NY 10523
914-592-6632
Barbara Peters, Superintendent

**Greenburgh 7 CSD**
475 W Hartsdale Ave, Hartsdale, NY 10530-1398
914-761-6000 x3103
Ronald L Smalls, Superintendent

**Greenburgh Eleven UFSD**
Children's Vlg Campus-W, PO Box 501, Dobbs Ferry, NY 10522-0501
914-693-8500
Sandra G Mallah, Superintendent

**Greenburgh-Graham UFSD**
One S Broadway, Hastings-on-Hudson, NY 10706-3809
914-478-1106
Amy J Goodman, Superintendent

**Greenburgh-North Castle UFSD**
71 S Broadway, Dobbs Ferry, NY 10522-2834
914-693-4309
Edward Placke, Superintendent

**Harrison CSD**
50 Union Ave, Harrison, NY 10528-2032
914-630-3021
Web site: www.harrisoncsd.org
Louis N Wool, Superintendent

*Offices and agencies generally appear in alphabetical order, except when specific order is requested by listee.*

**Hastings-On-Hudson UFSD**
27 Farragut Ave, Hastings-on-Hudson, NY 10706-2395
914-478-6200
Web site: www.hastings.k12.ny.us
Timothy P Connors, Acting Superintendent

**Hawthorne-Cedar Knolls UFSD**
226 Linda Ave, Hawthorne, NY 10532-2099
914-749-2903  Fax: 914-749-2904
Web site: www.hcks.org
Mark K Silverstein, Superintendent

**Hendrick Hudson CSD**
61 Trolley Rd, Montrose, NY 10548-1199
914-257-5100  Fax: 914-257-5101
Web site: www.henhudschools.org
Daniel McCann, Superintendent

**Irvington UFSD**
6 Dows Ln, Irvington, NY 10533-1328
914-591-8501
Web site: www.irvingtonschools.org
Kathleen Matusiak, Superintendent

**Katonah-Lewisboro UFSD**
PO Box 387, Katonah, NY 10536
914-763-7003  Fax: 914-763-7033
Web site: www.klschools.org
Michael Jumper, Superintendent

**Lakeland CSD**
1086 Main St, Shrub Oak, NY 10588-1507
914-245-1700
Web site: www.lakelandschools.org
George Stone, Superintendent

**Mamaroneck UFSD**
1000 W Boston Post Rd, Mamaroneck, NY 10543-3399
914-220-3005
Web site: www.mamkschools.org
Robert Shaps, Superintendent

**Mt Pleasant CSD**
Westlake Drive, Thornwood, NY 10594
914-769-5500  Fax: 914-769-3733
Web site: www.mtplcsd.org
Susan Guiney, Acting Superintendent

**Mt Pleasant-Blythedale UFSD**
95 Bradhurst Ave, Valhalla, NY 10595-1697
914-347-1800  Fax: 914-592-5484
Web site: www.mpbschools.org
Ellen Bergman, Superintendent

**Mt Pleasant-Cottage UFSD**
1075 Broadway, Pleasantville, NY 10570-0008
914-769-0456  Fax: 914-769-7853
Web site: www.mpcsny.org
Norman Freimark, Superintendent

**Mt Vernon City SD**
165 N Columbus Ave, Mount Vernon, NY 10553-1199
914-665-5000
Welton I Sawyer, Superintendent

**New Rochelle City SD**
515 North Ave, New Rochelle, NY 10801-3416
914-576-4200  Fax: 914-632-4144
Web site: www.nred.org
Richard Organisciak, Superintendent

**North Salem CSD**
230 June Rd, North Salem, NY 10560-1211
914-669-5414
Web site: www.northsalemschools.org
Kenneth Freeston, Superintendent

**Ossining UFSD**
190 Croton Ave, Ossining, NY 10562
914-941-7700  Fax: 914-941-2794
Web site: www.ossiningufsd.org
Phyllis Glassman, Superintendent

**Peekskill City SD**
1031 Elm St, Peekskill, NY 10566-3499
914-737-3300  Fax: 914-737-3912
Web site: www.peekskillcsd.org
Lorenzo Licopoli, Superintendent

**Pelham UFSD**
18 Franklin Pl, Pelham, NY 10803
914-738-3434
Web site: www.pelhamschools.org
Dennis Lauro, Superintendent

**Pleasantville UFSD**
60 Romer Ave, Pleasantville, NY 10570-3157
914-741-1400  Fax: 914-741-1499
Web site: www.pleasantvilleschools.com
Mary Fox-Alter, Superintendent

**Pocantico Hills CSD**
599 Bedford Rd, Sleepy Hollow, NY 10591-1215
914-631-2440  Fax: 914-631-3280
Web site: www.pocanticohills.org
Valencia Douglas, Superintendent

**Port Chester SD**
113 Bowman Ave, Port Chester, NY 10573-2851
914-934-7901  Fax: 914-934-0727
Web site: www.portchesterschools.org
Thomas Elliott, Superintendent

**Rye City SD**
411 Theodore Fremd Ave, South Lobby, Rye, NY 10580-3899
914-967-6100  Fax: 914-967-6957
Web site: www.ryeschools.org
Edward J Shine, Superintendent

**Rye Neck UFSD**
310 Hornidge Rd, Mamaroneck, NY 10543-3898
914-777-5200
Web site: www.ryeneck.k12.ny.us
Peter J Mustich, Superintendent

**Scarsdale UFSD**
2 Brewster Rd, Scarsdale, NY 10583-3049
914-721-2410
Web site: www.scarsdaleschools.k12.ny.us
Michael V McGill, Superintendent

**Somers CSD**
334 Route 202, PO Box 620, Somers, NY 10589
914-277-2400
Raymond Blanch, Superintendent

**Tarrytown UFSD**
200 N Broadway, Sleepy Hollow, NY 10591-2696
914-332-6241  Fax: 914-332-4690
Web site: www.tufsd.org
Howard W Smith, Superintendent

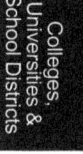

Colleges, Universities & School Districts

*Offices and agencies generally appear in alphabetical order, except when specific order is requested by listee.*

**Tuckahoe UFSD**
29 Elm St, Tuckahoe, NY 10707
914-337-6600
Web site: www.tuckahoeschools.org
Michael Yazurlo, Superintendent

**Valhalla UFSD**
316 Columbus Ave, Valhalla, NY 10595-1300
914-683-5040  Fax: 914-683-5075
Brenda Myers, Superintendent

**White Plains City SD**
5 Homeside Ln, White Plains, NY 10605-4299
914-422-2019 or 914-422-2029  Fax: 914-422-2024
Web site: www.wpcsd.k12.ny.us
Dr Christopher P Clouet, Superintendent

**Yonkers City SD**
1 Larkin Center, Yonkers, NY 10701
914-376-8100
Web site: www.yonkerspublicschools.org
Bernard P Pierorazio, Superintendent

**Yorktown CSD**
2725 Crompond Rd, Yorktown Heights, NY 10598
914-243-8001
Ralph Napolitano, Superintendent

## WYOMING

**Attica CSD**
3338 E Main St, Attica, NY 14011
585-591-2173
Bryce L Thompson, Superintendent

**Letchworth CSD**
5550 School Rd, Gainesville, NY 14066
585-493-5450
Web site: www.letchworth.k12.ny.us
Joseph W Backer, Superintendent

**Perry CSD**
33 Watkins Ave, Perry, NY 14530
585-237-0270 x1000  Fax: 585-237-6172
Web site: www.perry.k12.ny.us
William Stavisky, Superintendent

**Warsaw CSD**
153 W Buffalo St, Warsaw, NY 14569
585-786-8000  Fax: 585-786-8008
Web site: www.warsaw.k12.ny.us
Valerie K Burke, Superintendent

**Wyoming CSD**
Route 19, PO Box 244, Wyoming, NY 14591-0244
585-495-6222  Fax: 585-495-6341
Sandra B Duckworth, Superintendent

## YATES

**Dundee CSD**
55 Water St, Dundee, NY 14837-1099
607-243-5533  Fax: 607-243-7912
Web site: www.dundeecs.org
Kathy Ring, Superintendent

**Penn Yan CSD**
One School Dr, Penn Yan, NY 14527-1099
315-536-3371
Web site: www.pycsd.org
Thomas A Cox, Acting Superintendent

## BOCES DISTRICT SUPERINTENDENTS

**Broome-Delaware-Tioga BOCES**
435 Glenwood Rd, Binghamton, NY 13905-1699
607-766-3802  Fax: 607-763-3691
e-mail: abuyck@btboces.org
Web site: www.btboces.org
Allen D Buyck

**Capital Region (Albany-Schoharie-Schenectady) BOCES**
900 Watervliet-Shaker Rd, Albany, NY 12205-2106
518-862-4901  Fax: 518-862-4903
Web site: www.capregboces.org
Charles Dedrick, District Superintendent

**Cattaraugus-Allegany-Erie-Wyoming BOCES**
Olean Center, 1825 Windfall Rd, Olean, NY 14760-9303
716-376-8246 or 716-376-8200  Fax: 716-376-8452
Web site: www.caboces.org
Tim Cox

**Cayuga-Onondaga BOCES**
1879 West Genesee Street Road, Auburn, NY 13021-9430
315-253-0361  Fax: 315-252-6493
e-mail: bspeck@cayboces.org
Web site: www.cayboces.org
William S Speck

**Champlain Valley Educational Svcs**
**(Clinton-Essex-Warren-Washington)**
1585 Military Tpk, PO Box 455, Plattsburgh, NY 12901-0455
518-536-7340
Web site: www.cves.org
Craig L King

**Delaware-Chenango-Madison-Otsego BOCES**
6678 County Rd #32, Norwich, NY 13815-3554
607-335-1233  Fax: 607-334-9848
Web site: www.dcmoboces.com
Bill Tammaro

**Dutchess BOCES**
5 Boces Rd, Poughkeepsie, NY 12601-6599
845-486-4800  Fax: 845-486-4981
Web site: www.dcboces.org
John C Pennoyer

**Eastern Suffolk BOCES**
James Hines Administration Ctr, 201 Sunrise Hwy, Patchogue, NY 11772-1868
631-687-3006  Fax: 631-289-2529
e-mail: ezero@esboces.org
Web site: www.esboces.org
Edward J Zero

**Erie 1 BOCES**
355 Harlem Rd, West Seneca, NY 14224-1892
716-821-7001  Fax: 716-821-7452
Web site: www.e1b.org
Donald A Ogilvie, District Superintendent

**Erie 2-Chautauqua-Cattaraugus BOCES**
8685 Erie Rd, Angola, NY 14006-9620
716-549-4454 or 800-228-1184  Fax: 716-549-5181
Robert S Guiffreda

**Franklin-Essex-Hamilton BOCES**
23 Huskie Lane, PO Box 28, Malone, NY 12953-0028
518-483-6420  Fax: 518-483-2178
Web site: www.fehb.org
Stephen T Shafer

*Offices and agencies generally appear in alphabetical order, except when specific order is requested by listee.*

**Genesee-Livingston-Steuben-Wyoming BOCES**
80 Munson St, LeRoy, NY 14482-8933
585-658-7903  Fax: 585-344-7903
Web site: www.gvboces.org
Michael A Glover

**Greater Southern Tier BOCES**
**(Schuyler-Chemung-Tioga-Allegany-Steuben)**
9579 Vocational Dr, Painted Post, NY 14870
607-654-2283 or 607-962-3175  Fax: 607-962-1579
Web site: www.gstboces.org
Horst Graefe

**Hamilton-Fulton-Montgomery BOCES**
2755 St Hwy 67, Johnstown, NY 12095
518-736-4300  Fax: 518-736-4301
Web site: www.hfmboces.org
Patrick Michel

**Herkimer-Fulton-Hamilton-Otsego BOCES**
352 Gros Blvd, Herkimer, NY 13350-1499
315-867-2000  Fax: 315-867-2024
Web site: www.herkimer-boces.org
Sandra A Simpson

**Jefferson-Lewis-Hamilton-Herkimer-Oneida BOCES**
20104 State Rte 3, Watertown, NY 13601-5560
315-779-7010  Fax: 315-779-7009
Web site: www.boces.com
Jack J Boak Jr

**Madison-Oneida BOCES**
4937 Spring Rd, PO Box 168, Verona, NY 13478-0168
315-361-5510  Fax: 315-361-5595
e-mail: districtsuperintendent@moboces.org
Web site: www.moboces.org
Jacklin G Starks

**Monroe 1 BOCES**
41 O'Connor Rd, Fairport, NY 14450-1390
585-388-2200  Fax: 585-383-6404
Web site: www.monroe.edu
Frederick A Wille

**Monroe 2-Orleans BOCES**
3599 Big Ridge Rd, Spencerport, NY 14559-1799
585-352-2400  Fax: 585-352-2442
Web site: www.monroe2boces.org
Jo Anne Antonacci

**Nassau BOCES**
71 Clinton Rd, PO Box 9195, Garden City, NY 11530-9196
516-396-2500 or 516-396-2200  Fax: 516-997-8742
Web site: www.nassauboces.org
James D Mapes

**Oneida-Herkimer-Madison BOCES**
PO Box 70, 4747 Middle Settlement Rd, New Hartford, NY 13413-0070
315-793-8561  Fax: 315-793-8541
Web site: www.oneida-boces.org
Thomas Dorr

**Onondaga-Cortland-Madison BOCES**
6820 Thompson Rd, PO Box 4754, Syracuse, NY 13221-4754
315-433-2602  Fax: 315-437-4816
Web site: ocmboces.org
Jessica F Cohen

**Orange-Ulster BOCES**
53 Gibson Rd, Goshen, NY 10924-9777
845-291-0100  Fax: 845-291-0118
Web site: www.ouboces.org
John Pennoyer

**Orleans-Niagara BOCES**
4232 Shelby Basin Rd, Medina, NY 14103-9515
585-344-7903  Fax: 585-798-1317
Web site: www.onboces.org
Clark J Godshall

**Oswego BOCES**
179 County Rte 64, Mexico, NY 13114-4498
315-963-4222  Fax: 315-963-7131
Joseph P Camerino

**Otsego Northern Catskills BOCES**
**(Otsego-Delaware-Schoharie-Greene)**
1914 County Route 35, PO Box 57, Milford, NY 13807
607-286-7715  Fax: 607-652-1215
Web site: www.oncboces.org
Nicholas Savin, District Superintendent

**Putnam-Northern Westchester BOCES**
200 Boces Dr, Yorktown Heights, NY 10598-4399
914-245-2700 or 914-248-2302  Fax: 914-248-2308
Web site: www.pnwboces.org
James T Langlois

**Rensselaer-Columbia-Greene (Questar III) BOCES**
10 Empire State Blvd, 2nd Fl, Castleton, NY 12033-2692
518-477-8771  Fax: 518-477-9833
Web site: www.questar.org
Charles Dedrick

**Rockland BOCES**
65 Parrott Rd, West Nyack, NY 10994-0607
845-627-4700 or 845-627-4702  Fax: 845-624-1764
e-mail: mmarsico@rboces.org
Web site: www.rocklandboces.org
Dr. Mary Jean Marsico, Superintendent

**Southern Westchester BOCES**
17 Berkeley Dr, Rye Brook, NY 10573-1422
914-937-3820 x535  Fax: 914-937-7850
Web site: www.swboces.org
James T Langlois, Superintendent

**St Lawrence-Lewis BOCES**
139 State Street Rd, PO Box 231, Canton, NY 13617
315-386-4504  Fax: 315-386-3395
e-mail: tburns@sllboces.org
Web site: www.sllboces.org
Thomas R Burns

**Sullivan BOCES**
6 Wierk Ave, Liberty, NY 12754-2151
845-295-4000  Fax: 845-292-8694
Web site: www.scboces.org
Lawrence Thomas

**Tompkins-Seneca-Tioga BOCES**
555 Warren Rd, Ithaca, NY 14850-1833
607-257-1551 x201  Fax: 607-257-2825
Web site: www.tstboces.org
Ellen O'Donnell

**Ulster BOCES**
175 Rte 32 North, New Paltz, NY 12561-1034
845-255-1400 or 845-255-3040  Fax: 845-255-7942
Web site: www.ulsterboces.org
Lawrence Thomas

*Offices and agencies generally appear in alphabetical order, except when specific order is requested by listee.*

**Washington-Saratoga-Warren-Hamilton-Essex BOCES**
1153 Burgoyne Ave, Ste 2, Fort Edward, NY 12828-1134
518-746-3310 or 518-581-3310  Fax: 518-746-3319
e-mail: jdexter@wswheboces.org
Web site: www.wswheboces.org
James P Dexter

**Wayne-Finger Lakes BOCES**
131 Drumlin Ct, Newark, NY 14513-1863
315-332-7284  Fax: 315-332-7425
e-mail: cmurray@wflboces.org
Web site: www.wflboces.org
Joseph J Marinelli, District Superintendent

**Western Suffolk BOCES**
507 Deer Park Rd, PO Box 8007, Huntington Station, NY 11746-9007
631-549-4900 x222  Fax: 631-623-4996
e-mail: centraladmin@wsboces.org
Web site: www.wsboces.org
Thomas Rogers, Interim Superintendent

*Offices and agencies generally appear in alphabetical order, except when specific order is requested by listee.*

# Section 8:
# BIOGRAPHIES

# BIOGRAPHIES

## EXECUTIVE BRANCH

### ANDREW M. CUOMO (D)

Andrew M. Cuomo was elected New York's 56th Governor in 2010, and was reelected for a third term in November 2018. Throughout his entire life, Andrew Cuomo has had the same values and the same principles; he has not only believed in those values and principles, but he has developed the skills to fight for them—and to win. As Governor, Andrew Cuomo has fought for social, racial and economic justice for all New Yorkers.

Born on December 6, 1957, Andrew M. Cuomo was the second child of former New York Governor Mario Cuomo and Matilda Raffa Cuomo. Growing up in Queens, Cuomo learned the reality of the middle-class, working family struggle. He graduated from Fordham University in the Bronx in 1979 and received his law degree from Albany Law School in 1982.

After law school, Andrew Cuomo headed the Transition Committee for then Governor-Elect Mario Cuomo and then served as an advisor to the Governor taking a salary of $1 a year. Mario Cuomo instilled in him the belief that government was the vehicle to make change and do justice. Andrew Cuomo's fight for justice focused on helping the neediest and addressing one of the most desperate situations of the time—homelessness. At the age of 28 he founded the Housing Enterprise for the Less Privileged (HELP)—a not-for-profit that set a national model for serving the homeless.

After the 1996 election, President Clinton appointed Andrew Cuomo to serve as HUD Secretary. He worked to transform the agency from a wasteful and inefficient bureaucracy to an effective driver of economic development and housing opportunities. In 2006, Andrew Cuomo was elected New York State Attorney General, and his agenda remained unchanged—to fight for justice: social, racial, and economic justice. He fought discrimination in rental apartments, challenged corporate abuse of the middle class, and took on the big banks that were squandering billions of dollars in bail-out money.

In 2010, Cuomo was elected Governor. Turning toward infrastructure, in 2013 he announced the beginning of formal construction of a replacement for the Tappan Zee Bridge over the Hudson River north of New York City. The renamed Governor Mario M. Cuomo Bridge opened one side for west/northbound traffic in August 2017, with the other direction becoming operational the following year. Not long after winning reelection in 2014, Cuomo took a bold step on a controversial environmental issue: He officially approved the New York Department of Environmental Conservation's call for a ban on hydraulic fracturing, or fracking, which is used to obtain natural gas and oil, making New York became the second state to ban the practice.

Additionally, the Governor unveiled a $4 billion renovation plan for LaGuardia Airport in Queens, holding a groundbreaking ceremony in June 2016. That year Cuomo also enacted legislation to speed up foreclosure of neglected "zombie properties," and published a Consumer Bill of Rights designed to protect homeowners facing foreclosure.

In November 2018, Governor Cuomo was reelected with the largest number of votes of any governor in both the primary and the general elections. In his third term, he continues his fight for justice in the face of a federal government that is threatening the essential American compact of opportunity for all and acceptance of all.

Cuomo surfaced in the national spotlight following the confirmation of the first coronavirus patient in New York on March 1, 2020. Although he pushed New York lawmakers into quickly approving $40 million in emergency funding to contain the virus, the number of confirmed patients exploded in the following weeks, turning New York into the center of the pandemic with more than 25,000 cases by March 24. The Governor requested 30,000 ventilators for hospitals. His request for assistance from the Army Corps of Engineers was heeded, with the Corps quickly transforming the massive Jacob K. Javits Center on Manhattan's west side into a makeshift hospital by the end of March. In mid-April, Cuomo issued an order that required New Yorkers to wear face masks in public places where social distancing was not possible.

Under his leadership, New York passed marriage equality, a $15 minimum wage, the strongest paid family leave program in the nation, the strongest gun safety laws in the nation, equal rights for women, greater protections for immigrants, the largest investment in education in state history, cut taxes for the middle class, implemented a 2 percent property tax cap, put more New Yorkers to work than ever before, and became the first state in the nation to offer free college tuition for middle-class families. He also got the state building again—taking on projects that had been stalled for decades and using union labor every step of the way. Governor Cuomo is the proud father of three girls, Mariah, Cara, and Michaela.

### KATHLEEN C. HOCHUL (D)

Kathleen C. Hochul was elected New York's 77th Lieutenant Governor on November 4, 2014. Hochul is President of the New York State Senate and chairs the Regional Economic Development Councils and the NYS Women's Suffrage 100th Anniversary Commemoration Commission. She co-chairs the NYS Heroin and Opioid Abuse Task Force and Community College Councils. Lieutenant Governor Hochul chairs 10 Regional Economic Development Councils that have transformed the State's economy by building upon regional strengths through long-term strategic plans. The Councils include leaders from academia, business, labor and not-for-profits and, to date, have invested over $6.1 billion into more than 7,300 projects across the State. The Lieutenant Governor also chairs the State Workforce Investment Board, which addresses the number one concern of businesses—the lack of skilled workers.

Hochul spearheaded Governor Cuomo's Enough is Enough campaign to combat sexual assault on college campuses, hosting and attending more than 25 events. As the highest-ranking female elected official in New York State, she continues to be a champion for women and families across the State. In March 2016, she was elected as Chair of the New York State Women's Suffrage 100th Anniversary Commemoration Commission.

Representing Governor Cuomo across the State, Hochul tours main streets, meets with local business owners, visits college campuses, and meets regularly with mayors, supervisors, and other community leaders. The Lieutenant Governor builds support for the Governor's initiatives including the minimum wage increase, paid family leave, ethics reform and infrastructure investment.?

As Lieutenant Governor, Hochul is liaison to New York's federal representatives in Washington, D.C. From 2011 to 2013, she served in the U.S. House representing New York's 26th Congressional District. Then Congresswoman Hochul served on the House Armed Services and Homeland Security Committees, traveling to Afghanistan to confer with military leaders and meet with active duty men and women. Her focus in Congress was job creation and bridging the skills gap by bringing together business and academia, and creating opportunities for returning veterans.

Prior to becoming Lieutenant Governor, she was Group Vice President for Strategic Relationships at M&T Bank, serving as liaison for community matters and significant economic development projects. Lieutenant Governor Hochul served as County Clerk from 2007 to 2011. Before that, Hochul worked for 14 years as a Hamburg Town Councilmember. She served as liaison to the local economic development agency and worked to attract new businesses and create jobs following the loss of the WNY manufacturing base.

The Lieutenant Governor holds a bachelor's degree from Syracuse University and a law degree from Catholic University in Washington, DC. She began her legal career working at a large firm in Washington, DC and later served as Legal Counsel and Legislative Assistant to Congressman John LaFalce and later Senator Daniel Patrick Moynihan. She was instrumental in drafting legislation related to campaign finance reform, immigration reform and combatting drug abuse. In 2006, Hochul joined her mother and aunt in establishing the Kathleen Mary House, a transitional home for victims of domestic violence. She was also cofounder of the Village Action Coalition, and a member of the Board of Trustees at Immaculata Academy in Hamburg.

She is married to William Hochul, the former U.S. Attorney for the Western District of New York, and current general counsel for Delaware North. They reside in Buffalo, New York, and are the parents of a son, William III and a daughter, Caitlin.

## LETITIA JAMES (D)

Letitia James is the 67th Attorney General for the State of New York. With decades of work, she is an experienced attorney and public servant with a long record of accomplishments. She is the first woman of color to hold statewide office in New York and the first woman to be elected Attorney General.

James was elected Public Advocate for the City of New York in 2013. In this office she served as a watchdog over New York City government agencies and as an advocate for the City's most vulnerable communities. She transformed the Public Advocate's office to be a formidable engine for change.

Her office handled over 32,000 constituent complains and passed more legislation than all previous Public Advocates combined, including a groundbreaking law that banned questions about salary history from the employment process to address the gender wage gap. James successfully took on the gun and ammunition retailers. On August 6, 2020, in a televised broadcast, Attorney General Letitia James announced a state civil lawsuit filed in New York Supreme Court against the National Rifle Association (NRA), with four NRA department heads named as codefendants. She also fought in court on behalf of children and families on issues including children in foster care, children with disabilities, and tenant protection. James was elected to a second term in 2017.

Before serving as Public Advocate, James represented the 35th Council District in Brooklyn in the New York City Council for ten years. In the Council, she passed the Safe Housing Act, legislation that forced landlords to improve living conditions for tenants in New York City's worst buildings. She helped uncover the corruption behind the Office of Payroll Administration's CityTime contract, a scheme that cost the City of $600 million. In addition, she pushed through a revolutionary recycling package that included expanding plastic recycling, a new clothing and textile recycling program, and increased access to recycling in public spaces.

Before her election to the City Council, James served as head of Brooklyn Regional Office of the NY State Attorney General's Office. She resolved hundreds of consumer complaints and investigated predatory lenders who preyed on first-time homebuyers. She assisted the Civil Rights Bureau in its investigation of the New York Police Department's stop-and-frisk policy and cracked down on firms engaged in deceptive business practices including violations of human rights, environmental laws, and scams targeting immigrants.

Attorney General James began her career as a public defender at the Legal Aid Society. A proud Brooklynite, she graduated from Lehman College and Howard University School of Law. James lives in the Clinton Hill neighborhood of Brooklyn and is a member of the Emmanuel Baptist Church.[45]

## THOMAS P. DINAPOLI (D)

Thomas P. DiNapoli became New York State's 54th Comptroller in 2007. A lifelong Long Islander, he was raised in a middle-class, union household and saw the value of hard work and stretching every dollar in the example set by his parents.

In 1972, Comptroller DiNapoli won his first election and served as a Trustee on the Mineola Board of Education, becoming the first 18-year-old in New York State to hold public office. He attended Hofstra University, earning a bachelor's degree in history and graduated magna cum laude in 1976. He worked in the telecommunications industry for 10 years, and went to night classes and earned a master's degree from The New School University's Graduate School of Management and Urban Professions.

In 1986, DiNapoli ran for the New York State Assembly and was elected to represent the 16th District in northwestern Nassau County for the next 20 years. He was elected State Comptroller on February 7, 2007, by a bipartisan majority of the State Legislature. DiNapoli was elected Comptroller by New York's voters in 2010, 2014, and 2018. He is known for his integrity, independence, and even-keeled leadership.

As Comptroller, his record of accomplishments include: identified billions in waste, fraud, and cost savings in government; uncovered corruption in State and local governments, leading to dozens of arrests and tens of millions in restitution; provided robust oversight of school district operations and education spending. He has charged his auditors with examining school safety practices, reviewing programs to protect children from harassment and discrimination, monitoring special education providers, and identifying best practices to help schools around the State; developed an early warning system to identify municipalities and school districts showing signs of fiscal stress; managed the third largest public pension fund in the nation through difficult losses during the Great Recession, reformed how it operates and received high praise for industry leading standards; invested nearly $2 billion in private equity and loan programs to benefit New York-based businesses and provide a return to the State pension fund; earned a reputation as one of the leading shareholder voices on many corporate concerns including environmental issues, disability inclusion and corporate political spending; opened up government spending on his transparency website Open Book New York; led the fight for prudent fiscal and procurement reforms to help New York change how it does business and put it on better fiscal footing and Streamlined claims process for individuals to recover lost money. More than $425 million in unclaimed funds are returned to rightful owners each year.

## NEW YORK STATE SENATE

### JOSEPH P. ADDABBO JR. (D)
*15th - Part of Queens County*

159-53 102nd Street, Howard Beach, NY 11414
718-738-1111/addabbo@nysenate.gov

66-85 73rd Place, Middle Village, NY 11379
718-497-1630

88-08 Rockaway Beach Boulevard, Room 311, Rockaway Beach, NY 11693
518-318-0702

188 State Street Room 811, Legislative Office Building, Albany, NY 12247
518-455-2322

Joseph Addabbo Jr. was most recently elected to the New York Senate in 2014, having first been elected in 2008. He carries on the tradition of public service of his father, Congressman Joseph P. Addabbo, Sr. Addabbo's district includes all or part of the following communities: Broad Channel, Elmhurst, Forest Hills, Glendale, Hamilton Beach, Kew Gardens, Kew Gardens Hills, Maspeth, Middle Village, Ozone Park, Rego Park, Richmond Hill, Ridgewood, South Ozone Park, Woodhaven, Woodside, and the Rockaways. Addabbo, a lifelong resident of Queens, is the Ranking Member and Chairman of the Senate Committee on Racing, Gaming and Wagering. He is also a member of the Senate Committees on Aging; Civil Service and Pensions; Children and Families; Domestic Animal Welfare; Education; Labor; Rules; State-Native American Relations; and Veterans, Homeland Security and Military Affairs. As a past Chairman of the Senate Elections Committee, he worked to pass ethics reforms and led the fight to force large corporations to disclose information about money they spend to influence the outcome of elections.

As a member of the Senate, Addabbo is deeply concerned with the welfare of New Yorkers in all stages and walks of life. His legislative record, which includes bills he has introduced and supported, reflects his commitment to fighting on behalf of children, the elderly, families, working people, consumers, and veterans. He has also devoted himself to efforts to protect the environment, create new jobs and economic opportunities for small businesses, provide tax relief for state residents, and improve transparency and accountability in New York's government. As a State Senator, he is well known for organizing and sponsoring dozens of community events for his constituents each year, including job fairs for local residents and veterans, comprehensive recycling events, informational sessions for seniors and consumers, health screenings, Metrocard van visits, and many other free programs.

In addition, he sat on the Senate Bipartisan Task Force on Hurricane Sandy, which impacted his district, to help the community recover from the devastating storm. The Senator's legislative record includes bills reflecting on his commitment to fighting for local youth, the elderly, families, consumers, veterans, fair elections, and employees' rights.

Addabbo practiced law for 10 years at Addabbo and Greenberg. In 2001, he was elected to the New York City Council and served for eight years and secured millions of dollars in funding for improvements in infrastructure, school technology, and senior and youth services. Senator Addabbo has been honored by various organizations including the American Red Cross, the Woodhaven Development Corporation, NYC Department of Parks and Recreation, among others. Joseph Addabbo graduated from St. John's University and Touro Law School. He is married with two daughters.

### FRED AKSHAR (R-C-IP-RFM)
*52nd - Binghamton and the Southern Tier*

44 Hawley Street, Room 1607, Binghamton, NY 13901
607-773-8771/akshar@nysenate.gov

Legislative Office Building, Room 608, Albany, NY 12247
518-455-2677

Fred Akshar was sworn into office as a New York State Senator for the 52nd District on November 3, 2015. As a State Senator, his priorities are strengthening the Southern Tier economy by helping small businesses succeed and create jobs, battling drug addiction and making communities safer, as well as fighting for a fair shake from Albany. He serves as the Ranking Member on the Alcoholism and Substance Abuse; Civil Service and Pensions; and Crime Victims, Crime, and Correction Committees in the Senate and sits on the following Committees: Codes; Commerce, Economic Development and Small Business; Disabilities; Elections; and Labor. He is also a member of the Legislative Commission on Rural Resources.

Akshar's priorities are helping small businesses succeed, creating jobs, battling drug addiction, and making communities safer. Before becoming a state senator, he spent 15 years with local law enforcement, 2 years with the Chenango County Sheriff's Office, and 13 years with the Broome County Sheriff's Office. He is a graduate of the FBI Academy and Broome Community College. Senator Akshar lives in Endwell.

### JAMAAL BAILEY (D)
*36th - Bronx neighborhoods of Norwood, Bedford Park, Williamsbridge, Co-op City, Wakefield and Baychester, Westchester city of Mount Vernon*

959 E. 233rd Street, Bronx, NY 10466-3207
718-547-8854/senatorbailey@nysenate.gov

Legislative Office Building, Room 609, Albany, NY 12247
518-455-2061

3450 Dekalb Avenue, Room 111, Bronx, NY 10467
718-944-3220

Jamaal Bailey grew up in the Bronx, where he attended public schools. After graduating from the Bronx High School of Science, he attended the University at Albany-SUNY and interned with the speaker of the New York State Assembly, Carl Heastie, where he had an impact on the legislative process. He earned his law degree from the CUNY School of Law, where he gained experience in the Community and Economic Development clinic and served as the Social Action Chair for the Black Law Students Association. He briefly practiced law before returning to public service, acting as Speaker Heastie's Community Relations Director. In the State Senate, he is Chair of the Codes Committee and sits on the following Committees: Children and Families; Crime Victims, Crime, and Judiciary; Mental Health; and Rules. Bailey is also a member of the Joint Senate Task Force on Opioids, Addiction & Overdose.

His goals are to promote social and economic justice, including increased access to healthy food and quality health care. He wants to revamp public education to focus on the whole child and the external factors that impact the child rather than "teaching to the test." He promotes funding for such school activities as sports, music, the arts, and the humanities with the goal of fostering a well-rounded person, and he wants to increase opportunities for students to participate in gifted and talented programs. In addition, he promotes criminal justice reform; widespread access to civil legal services; technical skills and job training; income equality; closing the wage gap; and help for people who need to navigate the courts when dealing with family issues and landlord-tenant or property matters. He lives with his wife, Giamara, and daughters in Baychester. He is a member of the Williamsbridge Branch of the NAACP, and he mentors young men at the Butler United Methodist Church.

## BRIAN A. BENJAMIN (D)

163 W. 125th Street, Harlem State Office Building, Suite 912, New York, NY 10027
212-222-7315/bbenjamin@nysenate.gov

188 State Street, Room 917, Legislative Office Building, Albany, NY 12247
518-455-2441

Brian A. Benjamin was first elected to the New York State Senate in 2017. Within the senate, Benjamin has made himself known as a leader in criminal justice reform and affordable housing, while also serving as a Ranking Member of the Civil Service and Pensions Committee and Chair of the Budget and Revenues Committee. Additionally, he sits on the following Committees: Health; Codes; Racing and Gaming; Joint Task Force on Opioids, Addiction & Overdose; and Rules. He also serves as Senior Assistant Majority Leader. His work in the senate also includes sponsoring bills to close Rikers Island and keep rent-controlled apartment affordable, in accordance with his efforts to support affordable housing.

In the New York State Senate, Benjamin has distinguished himself as a leader in criminal justice reform and affordable housing. In 2018, he successfully pushed for the divestment of the state public pension funds from private prisons, and the following year he introduced a bill to forbid state-chartered banks from such investments as well, which helped pressure Bank of America to end their relationship with Geo Group and Core Civic. His proposal to keep rent-controlled apartments affordable was a part of the history-making Tenant Protection Act of 2019, the largest expansion of tenant's rights in decades.

Growing up in Harlem, Benjamin forged a deep bond with his community. In turn, Benjamin uses his position to give back to that community. Prior to being elected to the senate, Benjamin served as Chair of Community Board 10 and the Land Use Committee. He also launched a mentoring program at Harlem's Wadleigh High School in 2013, and serves as an alumni-elected Trustee of Brown University. In addition to his community work, Benjamin also served as a 2012 delegate for President Barack Obama and as a member of President Obama's National Finance Committee. Benjamin holds an undergraduate degree in public policy from Brown University and an MBA from Harvard Business School.

## ALESSANDRA BIAGGI (D-WF)
*34th - Parts of Bronx and Westchester Counties*

3190 Riverdale Avenue, Suite 2, Bronx, NY 10463
718-822-2049/biaggi@nysenate.gov

Legislative Office Building, 188 State Street, Room 905, Albany, NY 12247
518-455-3595

Alessandra Biaggi is the Democratic New York State Senator for District 34. The granddaughter of Italian immigrants who lived in Hunts Point, she is the fourth generation of her family to live in the district. In the Senate, she is Chair of the Committee for Ethics and Internal Governance. She is also a member of the following standing Committees: Aging; Agriculture; Health; Investigation and Government Operations; Judiciary; Rules; and Codes. In addition, she is a member of the Legislative Women's Caucus.

Within her first two months in office, Senator Biaggi chaired the first public hearings in 27 years on sexual harassment in the workplace, and led the charge in New York to pass legislation that strengthens protections for survivors and holds employers accountable for addressing sexual misconduct. In a joint effort with her colleagues in the Democratic conference, the Senator worked to pass transformational legislation including tenant-centered housing reforms, bold climate-change initiatives, unprecedented criminal justice reform, comprehensive workplace protections, and expansive legislation making it easier to vote.

Prior to her election to the Senate, she served in Governor Andrew Cuomo's Counsel's Office focusing on the New York State's women's policy agenda, advocating for passage of the Reproductive Health Act and the Comprehensive Contraceptive Coverage Act. During the historic presidential 2016 election, Biaggi was the Deputy National Operations Director for Hillary Clinton's presidential campaign, overseeing a budget of $500 million, 38 state directors, and 45 associated staff. In addition, she interned for the Kings County District Attorney's Office and the US Attorney's Office for the Southern District of New York, and was a legal fellow for New York State Homes and Community Renewal, working to ensure that families across New York State had access to affordable housing.

Biaggi served as Assistant General Counsel for Governor Cuomo's Office of Storm Recovery, working with small businesses and municipalities to rebuild New York after Hurricane Sandy. She was a 2015 New Leaders Council (NLC) fellow, sat on NLC's Advisory Board, and is a member of the New Agenda's Young Women Leadership Council. Senator Biaggi attended Pelham public schools and holds degrees from New York University and Fordham Law School. She is also a graduate of the Women's Campaign School at Yale University.

## GEORGE M. BORRELLO (R-C-IP-LIBT)
*57th - Allegany, Cattaraugus, and Chautauqua Counties; and parts of Livingston County*

2-6 E. Second Street, Fenton Building, Suite 302, Jamestown, NY 14701
716-664-4603/borrello@nysenate.gov

188 State Street, Legislative Office Building, Room 706, Albany, NY 12247
518-455-3563

700 W. State Street, Westgate Plaza, Olean, NY 14760
716-372-4901

George Borrello was elected New York State Senator for the 57th District in November of 2019 in a special election. The 57th Senate District is one of the state's largest and includes Allegany, Cattaraugus, Chautauqua counties plus eight towns in Livingston County. Borrello is the Ranking Member of the Procurement and Contracts, Agriculture, and Banks Committees and also serves on the following Committees: Aging; Finance; Internet and Technology; and Local Government.

Borrello graduated from Fredonia High School and received his bachelor's degree from Purdue University. He is a successful businessman and entrepreneur, and has been for most of his adult life. He founded his own company, Top-Shelf Marketing, in his early 20s, grew the business into a nationally recognized supplier to the hospitality industry, and after merging it with another company, he spent an additional 20 years in executive management.

Borrello was motivated to enter public service because he wanted to help contribute positive solutions to the challenges his community and the region he loves were struggling with, including: population loss, blighted neighborhoods, an aging infrastructure, and increasing taxes and regulations. He successfully ran for Chautauqua County legislator in 2010, representing the Town of Hanover. During his eight years in office, he pursued projects to promote tourism, improve infrastructure, downsize government, and clean up run-down properties. In 2017, seeking to have an even greater impact, he ran for County Executive, where he prioritized outreach and collaboration in his leadership.

Borrello has spearheaded an innovative project that will vastly improve the region's agricultural sector; created an unprecedented agreement among Chautauqua Lake stakeholders that led to vast improvements in the lake's usability; and crafted county budgets that reduced taxes while making record infrastructure investments. In the Senate, Borrello will set among his priorities: efforts to ease New York's high tax burden to help stem the outflow of jobs and residents from upstate New York; legislation to help the agricultural community, especially small family farms struggling to stay afloat; and workforce development initiatives to ensure young people have access to good-paying jobs and employers have the labor they need to operate and grow their businesses. Borrello will also sponsor the "First Employee Tax Credit Plan," as one of his first in the Senate, which will help ease the disproportionate rise in costs that result from adding just one employee for small businesses.

Borrello and his wife Kelly reside in Sunset Bay and are active in local charity and volunteer organizations. They are also small business owners and operate three businesses in the Town of Hanover.

## PHILIP M. BOYLE (R)
*4th - Part of Suffolk County*

69 W. Main Street Suite B, Bay Shore, NY 11706
631-665-2311/pboyle@nysenate.gov

707 Legislative Office, Building A, Albany, NY 12247
518-455-3411

Philip Boyne was elected to the New York State Senate in 2012. Currently serving his fourth term in the Senate, Boyle serves as the Ranking Minority Member of the Committee on Environmental Conservation and the Ranking Minority Member of the Senate Committee on Corporations, Authorities, and Commissions. He serves as a member of the following Committees: Codes; Commerce, Economic Development, and Small Business; Domestic Animal Welfare; Housing, Construction and Community Development; Rules; Higher Education; Energy and Telecommunications; Ethics and Internal Governance; and Judiciary. In addition, he is a Chair of the Commerce, Economic Development, and Small Business Commission. He is also Co-chair of the New York Legislative Aviation Caucus.

Prior to his election to the Senate, Boyle served in the New York State Assembly from 1994 to 2002, and again starting in 2006. He also served many years as a Senior Congressional Aide in Washington, DC to the late US Representative Frank Horton as Legislative Director, then as Campaign Manager and Chief of Staff to former US Rep. Frank Lazio. Earlier in his legal career he was a founding partner in the law firm of Steinberg & Boyle LLC. He is active in his community, including as a volunteer firefighter for the Great River Fire Department. He holds a BA from the University of North Carolina/Chapel Hill, a JD from Albany Law School, and a MPA from the Rockefeller College of Public Affairs and Policy at the University of Albany. He is married and the stepfather to two.

## NEIL D. BRESLIN (D-IP-WF)
*44th - Parts of Albany and Rensselaer counties*

172 State Street, Room 430C, Capitol, Albany, NY 12247
518-455-2225/breslin@nysenate.gov

Neil Breslin was first elected to the New York State Senate in 1996. He is the Ranking Minority Member and Chair of the Insurance Committee and is Co-chair of the Legislative Ethics Commission. Breslin also serves on the following standing Committees: Banks; Cities 2; Ethics and Internal Governance; Finance; Higher Education; and Rules. In addition, he is a member of the Legislative Commission on Rural Resources.

Breslin has been an associate or partner in law firms, and currently is of counsel to the firm of Barclay Damon LLP. He is an active member of the New York State Bar Association, as well as the National Conference of Insurance Legislators (NCOIL), where he is President of the Executive Committee and former Chair of the State/Federal Relations Committee. His civic involvement includes serving for many years on the board of Arbor House, a women's residence facility, including seven years as its President. In addition, he has been the attorney for St. Anne's Institute in Albany. Senator Breslin has received numerous awards, including the

Distinguished Leadership Award from the Autism Society of the Greater Capital Region in 2014 and the Centennial Medallion from Catholic Charities of the Diocese of Albany in 2017. The Albany native graduated from Fordham University with a BS degree in political science. He received his JD from the University of Toledo in Toledo, Ohio. He is married with three children.

## JABARI BRISPORT (D)
*25th - Part of Kings County*

55 Hanson Place, The Shirley Chisholm State Office Building, Suite 702, Brooklyn, NY 11217
718-643-6140/brisport@nysenate.gov

118 State Street, 915 Legislative Office Building, Albany, NY 12247
518-455-3451

Senator Jabari Brisport Represents New York's 25 State Senate district, which includes Fort Greene, Boerum Hill, Red Hook, Bedford-Stuyvesant, Sunset Park, Gowanus, and Park Slope. In the Senate, he is Chair of the Children and Families Committee and sits on the following Committees: Agriculture, Banks; Codes; Housing Construction and Community Development; Libraries; and New York City Education.

Brisport is a third-generation Caribbean-American resident of Brooklyn who was born in Bed-Stuy and raised in Prospect Heights. He became an activist more than a decade ago when he began organizing efforts in support of a bill to legalize same-sex marriage in New York. The bill was defeated in 2009 but he continued organizing around the issue until same-sex marriage was ultimately legalized in New York two years later. He continued his activism as part of the early Black Lives Matter movement and began organizing rallies and protests, as well as training protesters on what to do if stopped or harassed by the police.

At the time of his election, Senator Brisport was a math teacher at a middle school in Crown Heights and an active member of the United Federation of Teachers (UFT) union. As a teacher, he saw firsthand how the chronic underfunding of our schools and massive increases in policing have created glaring injustices for New York's students, and how those injustices are compounded by lack of access to basic needs like housing and health care.

These experiences shaped his determination to fight for a just state budget that provides funding for the infrastructure and services New Yorkers need to survive and thrive, especially in times of crisis. Brisport is a vocal advocate of raising taxes on the rich, and policies that place the needs of working-class people above corporate profits, including a Green New Deal, the New York Health Act, universal access to housing, and the cancellation of rent and mortgage arrears accumulated during the COVID-19 pandemic. Other legislative priorities include foster care caseload issues, emergency placement of foster care youth, and educator diversity.

## JOHN E. BROOKS (D)
*8th - Long Island, South Shore in Eastern Nassau, Western Suffolk Counties*

5550 Merrick Road, Suite 205, Massapequa, NY 11758
516-882-0630/brooks@nysenate.gov

Legislative Office Building, Room 806, Albany, NY 12247
518-455-2765

John E. Brooks, a lifelong resident of Long Island, is a veteran of the New York Army National Guard. He earned an associate's degree from the SUNY at Farmingdale and a bachelor's degree from the New York Institute of Technology. For more than four decades he has served as a Volunteer Firefighter with the fire departments in Medford and Lindenhurst, as well as in Seaford, where he has also held the position of Chief of the department. For six years he served on the Seaford Board of Education, acting as Vice President from 1997 to 1999. He also chaired the Long Island Hurricane Symposium Programs, working closely with hurricane experts and the National Weather Services to assess storm risk on Long Island. He was an insurance industry executive, and later served as the Director of Risk Management for Nassau County.

In 2016 Brooks was elected to the New York State Senate. Brooks is Chair on the Committee for Veterans, Homeland Security and Military Affairs; He also sits on the following Committees: Agriculture; Education; Mental Health and Developmental Disabilities; Libraries; Local Governments; and Insurance. He has successfully opposed health-insurance rate increases in New York State, resulting in statewide savings of $300 million.

Senator Brooks legislative priorities include tackling government corruption, ensuring that all students receive the highest quality education possible, addressing taxation evaluation, confronting hunger in our communities, protecting Long Island drinking water, combating the opioid epidemic, and making Long Island an affordable place to live and raise a family. One of his priorities is to solve problems having to do with funding assessment tax refunds payable by the county without having to incur the cost of borrowing, and to that end he has developed an Assessment Reform Program. Currently living in Seaford, he has one son and one granddaughter.

## SAMRA G. BROUK (D-WF)
*55th District - Monroe County, Ontario County*

230 Packett's Landing, Fairport, NY 14450
585-223-1800/brouk@nysenate.gov.

188 State Street, Legislative Office Building, Room 615, Albany, NY 12247
518-455-2909

Senator Brouk represents New York's 55th District which includes, portions of Monroe and Ontario counties, including Rush, Mendon, Pittsford, Perinton, Fairport, Penfield, East Rochester, East Irondequoit, Naples, Bloomfield, Victor, and the east side of the City of Rochester. Brouk is Chair of the Mental Committee and is a member of the following Committees: Aging; Alcoholism and Substance Abuse; Education; Elections; Health; and Women's Issues. Her legislative interests also include response units for mental health emergencies; Black youth suicide prevention; and issues related to youth summer camps.

She was born and raised in the City of Rochester and surrounding suburbs, before earning her BA in psychology at Williams College. Senator Brouk has always worked to help provide quality services, greater opportunities, and vital support to those in need. This dedication to public service led her to join the Peace Corps, work with local governments to improve recycling efforts, improve services for seniors aging within their homes, and address inequalities in the public school system. As a leader in nonprofit community development, she has spent a decade building educational, environmental, and senior services initiatives in her own community and across New York State.

## LEROY COMRIE (D)
*14th- Southeast Queens*

113-43 Farmers Boulevard, St. Albans, NY 11412
718-765-6359/Comrie@nysenate.gov

Legislative Office Building, Room 612, Albany, NY 12247
518-455-2701

Leroy Comrie was elected to the New York State Assembly in 2014 to represent a Queens district that includes portions of Jamaica, Cambria Heights, Queens Village, Hollis, St. Albans, Laurelton, Jamaica Estates, Briarwood, Hillcrest, and Kew Gardens. Comrie is Chair of the Committee on Corporations, Authorities, and Commissions. He is a Ranking Minority Member of both the Consumer Protection and Elections

Committees. He also sits on the following Committees: Agriculture; Cities 1; Finance; Procurement and Contracts; and Rules.

Senator Comrie's positive impact in government is evident with his long track record of legislative accomplishments such as increasing tax and property exemptions for seniors, instituting the city's first foreclosure prevention program, curtailing "pay-day" loans, improving the criteria for safety on construction sites, reducing truck traffic emissions, improving electrical and building codes, advocating for the containment of waste transfer stations, and increasing job opportunities by establishing direct-to-work training programs.

Prior to his election, he was Deputy Majority Leader of the New York City Council and Chairman of the Queens Delegation, where his legislative achievements include increasing tax and property exemptions for seniors and instituting the city's first foreclosure prevention program. He was also President of his local Community School Board. The South Queens native attended the University of Bridgeport and is the married father of two.

## JEREMY A. COONEY (D-WF)
*56th - Part of Monroe County*

2300 W. Ridge Road, Rochester, NY 14626
585-225-3650/cooney@nysenate.gov

188 State Street, Legislative Office Building, Room 615, Albany, NY 12247
518-455-2909

Jeremy A. Cooney is Democrat New York State Senator for the 56th District. Adopted from an orphanage in Kolkata, India, Senator Cooney made history as the first Asian elected to state office from upstate New York. He was raised by a single mother in the City of Rochester and is a proud graduate of the Rochester City School District (RCSD). He is the first state senator to have earned an RCSD diploma in decades. Cooney serves as Chair of the Cities 2 Committee and is a member of the following Committees: Codes, Cultural Affairs, Tourism, Parks and Recreation; Higher Education; Insurance; Procurement and Contracts; and Transportation. Additional legislative interests include housing, absentee voting by residents of nursing homes and other long-term care facilities, and Lian's Law.

Senator Cooney began his career working on Capitol Hill for the late U.S. Congresswoman Louise Slaughter. He later served as the Chief of Staff for the City of Rochester under Mayor Lovely Warren. He played a key leadership role in securing the city's federal designation through the competitive Investing in Manufacturing Cities Program (IMCP) under the U.S. Department of Commerce during the Obama Administration. He also helped secure a $1.4M grant from Bloomberg Philanthropies to establish and launch the Mayor's Office of Innovation with a focus on poverty relief initiatives.

Prior to running for public office, Cooney served as the Senior Director for Community Relations with Empire State Development under Governor Andrew M. Cuomo. In that position, he helped lead public affairs for large scale economic development projects.

Senator Cooney is active in the Rochester community. He sits on the President's Advisory Council for Hobart & William Smith Colleges and is a member of the Vestry for Christ Church Rochester. He is a proud Eagle Scout and serves as a vice chair of the Executive Board for the Boy Scouts of America, Seneca Waterways Council. Senator Cooney earned his BA with honors from Hobart College and his JD from Albany Law School. He is married to Dr. Diane Lu, a urologic surgeon with the University of Rochester Medical Center.

## SIMCHA FELDER (D)

*17th - Parts of Brooklyn*

1412 Avenue J, Suite 2E, Brooklyn, NY 11230
718-253-2015

Legislative Office Building, Room 504, Albany, NY 12247
518-455-2754/felder@nysenate.gov

Simcha Felder was first elected to the New York State Senate in 2012. His Brooklyn district includes the neighborhoods of Midwood, Flatbush, Borough Park, Kensington, Sunset Park, Madison and Bensonhurst. He chairs the Administrative Regulations Review Commission. In addition, he is a member of the following Committees: Aging; Mental Health and Developmental Disabilities; Social Services; and New York Education. His legislative achievements include legislation that allows parents of special education children to more easily receive funding for their child's schooling.

Felder has a proven record as a champion of commonsense policies that streamline government and increase accountability to taxpayers. He also passed laws to reduce unfair parking and sanitation tickets, sponsored the five-minute grace period legislation for motorists, and put a stop to the distribution of unwanted circulars and menus. @Bio Text = Professionally, he is a CPA and has been a professor of management at Touro College and CUNY's Brooklyn College. He was Deputy Comptroller for Budget, Accounting, Administration and Information Technology in the New York City Comptroller's Office. He also has worked for the New York State Assembly and as a tax auditor for the New York City Dept. of Finance. He also held previous elective office as a member of the New York City Council, where he chaired two Committees. Felder holds an MBA from Baruch College. He and his family live close to the home where Felder was raised.

## PATRICK M. GALLIVAN (R-C-IP)

*59th - Wyoming, Livingston and Ontario Counties and Part of Erie County*

2721 Transit Road, Suite 116, Elma, NY 14059
716-656-8544/gallivan@nysenate.gov

Legislative Office Building, Room 311, Albany, NY 12247
518-455-3471

Patrick M. Gallivan was elected to the New York State Senate in 2010. He is the Ranking Committee on the Health and Labor Committees; chaired the Crime Victims, Crime, and Correction Committee; and was Vice Chair of the Education Committee. He also sits on the following Committees: Codes; Labor; Crime Victims, Finance; Rules; and Transportation. During his first term in the Senate, Gallivan drafted and introduced more than 20 bills that were signed into law by Governor Andrew Cuomo. Elected on a platform of ensuring the public trust and revitalizing the Western New York Economy, Senator Gallivan has focused on fiscal responsibility, economic development, strengthening the state's vital agriculture industry, and properly representing taxpayers, sportsmen, and small businesses.

He played a central role in landmark accomplishments, including: Enacting a 2 percent cap on local property taxes; limiting state spending to less than 2 percent annually; adopting annual on-time budgets; cutting middle class taxes to their lowest level in 50 years; reducing the manufacturing tax rate to the lowest level since 1917; and cutting corporate taxes to the lowest rate since 1968.

Senator Gallivan also drafted and introduced a transformational piece of Medicaid reform legislation to reform the broken and antiquated cost structure of Medicaid. His proposal would eliminate Medicaid's mandate burden on local governments, protecting vital services, and reducing property taxes on families and business. A portion of this legislation has been adopted and has saved governments over $1.2 billion.

Gallivan has also authored legislation to reform onerous, outdated, duplicative, and unnecessary regulations on private business. He co-chaired a series of forums across the state and helped author a report identifying over two thousand burdensome and unnecessary regulations and why they should be eliminated.

Senator Gallivan was also successful in legalizing the use of crossbows during archery season in New York State and is a strong backer of sportsmen and women. He voted against the NY SAFE Act and continues to support the repeal of the law which he believes infringes on the Second Amendment rights of law-abiding citizens.

Prior to representing the citizens of Western New York in the Senate, Senator Gallivan was twice-elected Sheriff of Erie County, Upstate New York's most populous county. Prior to that, he spent 15 years in the New York State Police, rising to the rank of Captain. He is a former member of the New York State Executive Committee on Counter-terrorism, as well as a member of the New York State Board of Parole. He founded and operates a professional investigation and security firm. He holds an undergraduate degree from Canisius College and a master's degree in criminal justice from SUNY-Albany. He is the married father of two.

## JAMES GAUGHRAN (D)

*5th - Parts of Nassau and Suffolk Counties*

485 Underhill Boulevard, Suite 102, Syosset, NY 11791
516-922-1811
516-922-1811/gaughran@nysenate.gov

Legislative Office Building, Room 848, Albany, NY 12247
518-455-3250

Jim Gaughran is the State Senator for the 5th district, covering the North Shore of Long Island. A practicing attorney, he has decades of experiences as a public official serving the people of Long Island. In the Senate he is Chair of the Local Government Committee and serves on the following standing Committees: Corporations, Authorities, and Commissions; Energy and Telecommunications; Investigations and Government Operations; Racing, Gaming, and Wagering; and Higher Education.

At the age of 26, Gaughran was elected to the Huntington Town Board in 1983, becoming the youngest Councilman in the history of his town. As a member of the Town Board, he wrote one of the State's first ethics laws requiring local officials to disclose all sources of outside income and exposing any possible conflicts of interest.

As Councilman, he ended decades of corrupt garbage collection practices by creating municipal solid waste districts, authored numerous zoning and environmental laws to protect environmentally sensitive areas and, as the lone Democrat, became fiscal watchdog over budgetary issues.

In 1987, Gaughran was elected to the Suffolk County Legislature representing the 17th Legislative District in the town of Huntington. As a legislator, he authored a Charter Amendment taking away the Legislature's ability to amend the Capital Budget anytime they wanted for pet projects. This amendment was received with overwhelming support by the voters in a public referendum, and helped reduce Suffolk's debt for years after.

As chair of the Public Safety Committee, he reformed the Suffolk County Police Department with new community-oriented police policies and he cosponsored the Suffolk Water Protection Act, which led to preserving the Central Pine Barrens and other critical watershed areas in Suffolk County.

From 2008 until his election to the New York State Senate, Gaughran served as both Chair and member of the Suffolk County Water Authority. He implemented smart management practices, which reduced the payroll by 6 percent in 4 years, resulting in the Authority having a high bond rating of AAA issued by Fitch and Standard and Poors.

Senator Gaughran was raised in Dix Hills, where he graduated from Half Hollow Hills High School. He has spent most of his life in Suffolk

County and currently resides with his wife in Northport; they have two children. He has a JD from Hofstra Law School and a bachelor's degree from SUNY at Stony Brook.

## MICHAEL GIANARIS (D)
*12th - Part of Queens County*

31-19 Newtown Avenue, Suite 402, Astoria, NY 11102
718-728-0960/gianaris@nysenate.gov

Capitol Building, Room 427, Albany, NY 12247
518-455-3486

Michael Gianaris was elected to the State Senate in 2010 and is Deputy Majority Leader. He sits on the Ethics and Rules Committees. Prior to being elected to the Senate, he served for ten years in the New York State Assembly. Senator Gianaris is a progressive champion for tenants' rights, better subways, election reforms, a fairer criminal justice system, LGBTQ+ equality, and ending unfair economic development policies. He backed same-sex marriage throughout his public service career, and advocates against dysfunction in state government.

As a first-generation American, Senator Gianaris knows the struggle of immigrant families and leads the fight against harmful federal policies that tear apart families and unfairly discriminate against immigrant communities. He supports and works with community groups, such as Immigrant Families Together, to reunite families separated at the border and wrote legislation barring discrimination based on immigration status. He secured funding for community groups providing legal services to immigrants in need and was one of the first state legislators in the United States to call for abolishing ICE—the Immigration and Customs Enforcement Agency—when it began separating parents from children at the border.

In a city with millions of renters, Senator Gianaris always stands with tenants. Knowing the corrosive impact of real estate money in politics, Senator Gianaris does not accept campaign donations from real estate developers. In 2019, Senator Gianaris passed the most comprehensive tenant protections in New York State history. The new rent reforms, which Senator Gianaris helped author, ended the vacancy bonus, repealed vacancy decontrol, ended increases on preferential rents, and limited landlords abilities to pass capital improvement costs along to tenants. Senator Gianaris also secured funding for tenant legal services for the Ridgewood Tenants Union.

With a strong belief that we must live up to our highest ideals of "justice for all," Senator Gianaris is working hard to transform our criminal justice system. In an effort to end the criminalization of poverty, Senator Gianaris wrote the Bail Elimination Act to end bail in New York and in 2019 passed the most comprehensive bail reform legislation in the United States. He also wrote legislation to create an Innocence Commission to review wrongful convictions and protect juvenile offenders Miranda rights.

Senator Gianaris is a chief critic of the MTA, fighting for transit riders while pushing for improved service and increased accessibility. He understands New York cannot function without reliable mass transit, which is why he helped secure record funding for mass transit and an independent audit of the MTA.

New York has the second-lowest voter turnout in the United States. When more New Yorkers vote, their government is more accountable. Senator Gianaris wrote legislation to register more New Yorkers to vote and sponsored reforms to enact early voting and vote by mail.

Senator Gianais has consistently advocated for education in his community and secured record funding for public schools in the 2019 budget, including tens of thousands of dollars for individual programs at local schools. Our state has many unfunded needs and too many misplaced priorities. Senator Gianaris continues to do battle against wasteful corporate welfare to ensure actual priorities like truly affordable housing, better mass transit and improved schools are fully funded.

Representing the largest public housing development in the United States, Senator Gianaris has fought tirelessly to improve NYCHA on behalf of its residents. Senator Gianaris secured more than $100 million in funds for NYCHA, in addition to funding for job training and violence reduction programming through Urban Upbound and the Jacob Riis Community Center.

Prior to seeking elective office, he was an Aide to Congressman Thomas Manton, Governor Mario Cuomo's Queens County Regional Representative, and Counsel to the Speaker of the Assembly. He has also litigated cases in private practice. He holds an undergraduate degree from Fordham University and a JD from Harvard Law School.

## ANDREW GOUNARDES (D)
*22nd - Part of Kings County*

Legislative Office Building, Room 902, Albany, NY 12247
518-455-3270/gounardes@nysenate.gov

8018 5th Avenue, Brooklyn, NY 11209
718-38-6044

Andrew Gounardes represents New York's 22nd State Senate District, which includes the neighborhoods of Bay Ridge, Dyker Heights, Bensonhurst, Bath Beach, Gravesend, Gerritsen Beach, Manhattan Beach, and Marine Park. He was elected to the State Senate in November 2018. In the Senate he is Chair of the Civil Service and Pensions Committee and sits on the following Committees: Cities 1; Consumer Protection; Insurance; Labor; Judiciary; Higher Education; Codes; and Consumer Protection.

Born and raised in Bay Ridge, Senator Gounardes' passion for public service began as an Aide to former City Councilmember Vincent Gentile and as a Legislative Aide for Investigations in the US Senate. Prior to being elected, he served as Counsel to Brooklyn Borough President Eric Adams and a Trustee of the New York City Employees' Retirement System, one of the largest municipal pension funds in the country.

As an attorney and community advocate, Senator Gounardes' experience taught him that no one can accomplish anything good by themselves: It takes a community willing to unite, organize, and stand together to help our neighborhoods thrive.

Following Superstorm Sandy, Gounardes cofounded Bay Ridge Cares, an organization that prepared 25,000 hot meals for victims after the storm. Today, it still supports community members facing extraordinary need by providing them with emergency assistance. As a member of the Riders Alliance, he organized and formed the Concerned R Train Riders to fight for better service and demand handicapped accessible subway stations in South Brooklyn. Senator Gounardes also worked with Bay Ridge Advocates for Keeping Everyone Safe (BRAKES) and successfully pressured lawmakers to allow speed cameras in school zones. And because he strongly believes in the importance of art and culture in our neighborhoods, Senator Gounardes served as pro bono legal counsel for the Bay Ridge Storefront Art Walk (SAW), and also as past President of the Bay Ridge Historical Society.

In addition to his local and citywide involvement, Gounardes is active at a national level on issues affecting the Greek community. He is a member of the Hellenic American Leadership Council, a network of Greek-American leaders from across the United States that promote civic involvement, human rights, and democratic values in and between the United States and Greece. Additionally, he is a founding member of the St. Andrew's Freedom Forum, an international initiative that raises awareness of the denial of human rights and religious liberties of the Ecumenical Patriarchate of the Eastern Orthodox Church and recognizes human rights and religious freedom defenders throughout the world. Andrew has sat on the Board of Directors of Saint Basil Academy, a licensed resident childcare facility for children who are orphaned or come from broken homes across the United States.

Senator Gounardes earned degrees from Hunter College and George Washington University Law School. He is honored to represent the 22nd District and fight for the issues most important to the constituents of Southern Brooklyn.

## JOSEPH A. GRIFFO (R-C-IP)
*47th - Oneida, Lewis, and St. Lawrence Counties*

207 Genesee Street Room 408, Utica, NY 13501
315-793-9072/griffo@nysenate.gov

Capitol Building, 172 State Street, Room 413C, Albany, NY 12247
518-455-3334

Joseph A. Griffo was elected to the New York State Senate in 2006. Senator Griffo previously served as Deputy Minority Leader and as Chair of the Senate Energy & Telecommunications Committee, He also previously held the title of Deputy Majority Whip and is Co-chair of the New York State Legislative Sportsmen's Caucus. Griffo is Ranking Member of Cities 2 and Transportation Committees and sits on the following standing Committees: Education; Finance; Higher Education; and Rules.

Prior to his election, Griffo held a number of public service positions including Oneida County executive for over three years. In that position, he played a key role in boosting the local economy by over 600 jobs by taking the principal role in efforts to protect US Department of Defense-related jobs at the nearby Griffiss Air Force Base. He also served on the Board of Directors of the New York State Association of Counties. Griffo also served for 11 years as Mayor of his hometown of Rome, New York, an Oneida County legislator, Director of Community Relations for the City of Rome, and as an Administrative Assistant to the Rome Mayor. He holds a BA in political science from the State University of New York at Brockport. He is married and lives in Rome.

## PETER HARCKHAM (D, WF)
*40th - Putnam, Dutchess, and Westchester Counties*

40 Gleneida Avenue, 3rd Floor, Carmel, NY 10512
845-225-3025/harckham@nysenate.gov

1 Park Place, Suite 302, Peekskill, NY 10566
914-241-4600

Legislative Office Building, Room 812, Albany, NY 12247
518-455-2340

Pete Harckham was elected to the New York State Senate in November of 2018. In the Senate, he is Chair of the Alcoholism and Substance Abuse Committee and Co-chair of the Joint Task Force on Opioids, Addiction & Overdose Prevention. Harckham also sits on the following standing Committees: Environmental Conservation; Domestic Animal Welfare; Energy and Telecommunications; Environmental Conservation; Finance; Insurance; Veterans, Homeland Security, and Military Affairs; and Women's Issues.

Prior to his election, Harckham has had a distinguished career in public service, most recently having served in the Administration of Governor Andrew M. Cuomo from 2015 to 2018. In 2015 he was appointed by the Governor as the Assistant Director of the Office of Community Renewal, responsible for the rollout and implementation of a special allotment of $4.3M in CDBG funding for Westchester municipalities. For the past two years he served as the Director of Intergovernmental Affairs for the $3.9B Governor Mario M. Cuomo Bridge project.

Prior to his service to New York State, Harckham served on the Westchester County Board of Legislators from 2008 to 2015. He was first elected in November 2007 representing the 2nd Legislative District, comprising all of northeast Westchester. He was a leading voice for

maintaining vital services; protecting our fragile drinking water supplies the environment; and investing in our families.

In 2010, Harckham was selected by his colleagues to serve as Democratic Majority Leader of the Board of Legislators (BOL). He served as Majority Leader through 2013, honoring his pledge to serve only two terms. During his tenure on the Board, he understood that it is more cost effective to keep people off of expensive social services so he has been a fierce defender of investments that assist the working poor to keep working and to help families on the cusp to stay in their homes. He also passed legislation creating a Westchester County Local Development Corporation to enable nonprofits to obtain low interest financing to expand facilities and create jobs.

In addition, he focused extensive energy into protecting our fragile drinking water supplies. He coauthored groundbreaking legislation to ban the waste from hydrofracking from being treated in any wastewater facility in Westchester and prohibits the brine from hydrofracking from being used on any road in Westchester for deicing or to control dust.

He was at the center of legislative efforts to improve water and air quality, advance human rights, and fair housing law as well as to protect young people from alcohol and drug abuse. He was recognized countywide as a leading advocate for the creation of affordable housing for seniors, emergency first responders, and the working poor.

Before being elected to the BOL, Harckham served as President of the Board of A-HOME from 2004 to 2007, a not-for-profit housing corporation that builds affordable housing in northern Westchester. From 1992 to 2005, Pete served as Vice Chair of the Clarence E. Heller Charitable Foundation, a San Francisco-based foundation that supports the sustainable management of natural resources, the reduction of harmful toxins from the environment, and promotes arts and environmental education to underserved communities.

Harckham has been a communications professional since 1983 when he started his career on Madison Avenue and worked for ten years for major advertising agencies. From 2002 to 2008 he was President of Harckham Media Group, LLC, a strategic partnership of advertising, communications, and production professionals. He also founded K&E Farms, a small horse farm in Katonah, NY, where he donated conservation easements from the farm to the Westchester Land Trust.

Active in his community, Senator Harckham served on the President's Council for the Northern Westchester Hospital, was a board member for the United Way of Westchester and Putnam, the Junior League of Northern Westchester Community Advisory Council, the Livable Communities Council, and for many years was a girls' soccer coach for the Lewisboro Soccer Club.

He is a lifelong resident of the Hudson Valley, having grown up in Rockland County. He lives in South Salem and has two adult daughters, Emma and Kate.

## PAMELA HELMING (R-C-IP)
*54th - Wayne, Ontario, Cayuga, and Seneca Counties*

425 Exchange Street, Geneva, NY 14456
315-568-9816/(fax) 315-789-1946/helming@nysenate.gov

Legislative Office Building, Room 517, Albany, NY 12247
518-455-2366

Senator Helming serves as the Ranking Member of the Commerce, Economic Development, Small Business Committee, the Housing, Construction and Community Development Committee, and the Commission on Rural Resources. She also sits on the following Committees: Agriculture; Cultural Affairs, Tourism, Parks, and Recreation; Racing, Gaming, and Wagering; and Housing, Construction, and Community Development.

Early on in her tenure as Senator, she faced the Lake Ontario flooding that ravaged communities along the lake in Cayuga, Wayne, and Monroe

**501**

Counties. Helming responded with a series of bills aimed at providing relief for the affected municipalities and the people whose homes and businesses were destroyed by the natural disaster. These measures include making emergency funding available immediately to municipalities through the Clean Water Infrastructure Act, setting aside money through New York State Homes and Community Renewal for homeowners impacted by the flooding, and creating a new flood recovery grant program for homeowners, small businesses, and local governments.

A longtime champion for the vast local natural resources in the region, Senator Helming also helped secure $110 million in the New York State budget for projects that will preserve drinking water at its sources by conserving lakes, watersheds, and other buffer areas and protecting against pollutants and invasive species.

With agriculture being the biggest industry in the Finger Lakes Region, Helming aims to work with local farmers and residents to bolster the industry. Throughout the New York State budget process, she successfully advocated for vital investments that support family farming across the state. These efforts include increased funding for agricultural education to build the next generation of farmers, fully restored funding to provide business consulting services and mental health services through New York FarmNet, and support for agricultural research and development through the New York Farm Viability Institute, Cornell University, and other organizations.

Senator Helming supported a package of bills boosting the state economy by training job seekers and existing employees for the job opportunities that are in demand. To help small businesses, she supported measures to save them millions of dollars by reducing their workers' compensation contributions and to boost investment in technology, reduce burdensome regulations, and create significant tax savings to spur job growth.

Helming has continued to work tirelessly to protect the Second Amendment rights of all New Yorkers. She successfully ensured no funding for the SAFE Act was included in the 2017 to 2018 New York State Budget, has worked in conjunction with many of her colleagues on legislation to repeal the SAFE Act in part and as a whole, and has successfully prevented numerous misguided measures from becoming law, such as: requiring gun owners to purchase additional liability insurance, enabling police officers to confiscate legally owned firearms without due process, and further limiting what type of firearms may be sold and owned in New York State.

A 1984 graduate of Hiram College, Pamela Helming began her career by working with developmentally disabled individuals and managing several local group homes. She entered public service as a town board member for Canandaigua, eventually rising to the position of Town Supervisor. As a member of the Canandaigua Lake Watershed Council, she works to enhance water quality and preserve the overall environment in the region. She has also partnered with local farmers and residents to protect hundreds of acres of farmland from nonagriculture development. Additionally, she has served as Vice President of the Board for the Parkside Drive, backed a housing project for veterans, served on the Board of Directors for the Quail Summit Senior Living Center, and is a member of the Canandaigua Lake Watershed Council. Additionally, she has volunteered for the United Way and taken part in fundraising efforts for numerous organizations in the community. She has been honored by the Canandaigua City School District for her support of local youth athletic programs. She and her husband, Gary, have resided in Canandaigua for over thirty years and have raised two children; her daughter, Catherine, is a Physician's Assistant at the Womack Army Medical Center in North Carolina, and her son, Evan, is a graduate of the College of St. Rose.

## MICHELLE HINCHEY (D-WF)
*46th - Montgomery, Ulster, Greene*

721 Broadway, Suite 150, Kingston, NY 12401
845-331-3810

188 State Street, Legislative Office Building, Room 809, Albany, NY 12247
518-455-2350/hinchey@nysenate.gov

Born and raised in Saugerties, Michelle Hinchey brings to the State Senate a much-needed perspective on the unique challenges facing our Upstate communities and is deeply committed to improving the lives of all who call the 46th Senate District home. Senator Hinchey represents all of Greene and Montgomery Counties and parts of Ulster, Schenectady, and Albany Counties, which make up one of the most rural districts in the Democratic Conference with over 1,000 farms that play a vital role in feeding us, preserving our environment, and sustaining our rural economies.

A strong union advocate and champion on energy, environmental protection, and economic development, Hinchey was elected to the New York State Senate in 2020, making history as the youngest woman to represent an Upstate district in the Democratic Majority Conference.

She serves as Chair of the Senate Agriculture Committee and is also a member of the following Committees: Alcoholism and Substance Abuse; Commerce, Economic Development and Small Business; Cultural Affairs; Tourism, Parks and Recreation; Energy and Telecommunications; Environmental Conservation; and Local Government.

Hinchey is a communications veteran of ten years, having worked her way up as an executive in the technology and media fields, managing mission-driven teams, building diverse coalitions, and serving as a central connector across corporate departments. Earlier in her career, Hinchey worked as a grassroots organizer for Environment New York where she successfully campaigned to end the dangerous practice of fracking for the extraction of natural gas in New York. While working in the private sector, she continued her environmental advocacy as a member of the Board of Directors of the Catskill Center for Conservation and Development.

Senator Hinchey graduated in 2009 from the Industrial and Labor Relations School at Cornell University. She studied the history of the American labor movement and the importance of collective action in establishing an equitable labor market and economy.

## BRAD HOYLMAN (D-WF)
*27th - Part of New York County*

322 Eighth Avenue, Suite 1700, New York, NY 10001
212-633-8052/hoylman@nysenate.gov

Legislative Office Building, Room 310, Albany, NY 12247
518-455-2451

Brad Hoylman was elected to the New York State Senate in 2012. His Manhattan district includes Clinton/Hell's Kitchen, Chelsea, Greenwich Village, and parts of the Upper West Side, Midtown/East Midtown, the East Village, and the Lower East Side. Hoylman is Chair of the Judiciary Committee and sits on the following Committees: Cities 1; Cultural Affairs, Tourism, Parks, and Recreation; Disabilities; Finance; Health; and Libraries.

Senator Hoylman champions a wide range of issues, such as housing, transportation, public education, LGBTQ rights, environment and seniors. He has passed over sixty bills in the Senate, including the Child Victims Act, which enabled adult survivors of child sexual abuse to revive legal claims against their abusers; the TRUST Act, which permitted Congress to review the state taxes of elected officials like Donald Trump; Gender Equality Nondiscrimination Act (GENDA), which extended human rights protections to transgender New Yorkers; and banning the practice of sexual orientation change efforts, or so-called "conversion therapy." He was the lead sponsor of legislation to legalize gestational surrogacy for LGBTQ people and individuals struggling with infertility. He led the fight in the State Senate to ban flavored e-cigarettes in New York State and pass legislation that helped eliminate the toxic chemical PFAS from our drinking water. Hoylman has led initiatives to improve traffic safety by requiring the use of backseat seatbelts in taxis and reducing speed limits along the West Side Highway.

Prior to being elected to the Senate, Hoylman was a three-term Chair of Manhattan Community Board 2. In addition, he was a Trustee of the Community Service Society, a board member of the Empire State Pride Agenda, Tenants & Neighborhoods, Class Size Matters, and Citizen Action. He also served as general counsel of the Partnership for New York City, a nonprofit business and civic organization. Hoylman holds an undergraduate degree from West Virginia University, a master's in politics from Oxford University, and a JD from Harvard Law School. He and his husband are parents to one.

## ROBERT JACKSON (D)
*31st - Part of New York County*

5030 Broadway, Suite 701, New York, NY 10034
212-544-0173/jackson@nysenate.gov

Legislative Office Building, 188 State Street, Room 306, Albany, NY 12247
518-455-2041

Robert Jackson is Senator for New York State Senate's 31st District on the west side of Manhattan. His is the first Muslim New York Senator. In the Senate he is Chair of the Cities Committee and serves on the following standing Committees: Education; Labor; Higher Education; Housing, Construction, and Community Development; Civil Service and Pensions; and New York City Education. State Senator also champions public education, workers' rights, climate justice, and gun safety.

In his first elected position as Community School Board President, Robert Jackson filed a lawsuit against the state to fix an inequitable New York State school funding distribution formula that was cheating NYC schools and undermining our children's future. He walked 150 miles to Albany to highlight the cause and won a court judgment that awarded $16 billion for NYC schools. As a result of this landmark decision and "for being a staunch advocate for generations of New York City children, for never giving up on the belief that education is a basic civil right, and for giving millions of city students a fighting chance," NY1 honored Robert as New Yorker of the Year.

In 2001, Jackson was elected to the City Council, and was three times overwhelmingly reelected by the voters of his upper Manhattan district. Because of his experience, commitment, and leadership, he was chosen to Chair the Education Committee and Co-chair the Black, Latino, and Asian Caucus.

On the City Council, Jackson worked to make sure every child had the best education that offered by helping to create more than 4,000 new openings for pre-K, fought to prevent thousands of teacher layoffs, and helped start the Drop-Out Prevention Initiative. He worked to increase jobs and opportunities by sponsoring the landmark NYC Minority- and Women-Owned Business Enterprise (M/WBE) law, the Small Business Survival Act, and helped create a community manpower training program cited as a national model by the Clinton Global Initiative. He passed increased immigrant services, was an earlier advocate for marriage equality, and a leader combatting bullying. He fought for smart budget choices that kept senior centers, libraries, and fire stations open. And he worked to make our neighborhoods safer by getting guns off the street through working with community groups, sponsoring Buy Back Programs and advocating for stronger state and federal legislation.

In 2015, Jackson was elected District Leader and help found the new, progressive grassroots Democratic Club, Uptown Community Democrats. Born and raised in Manhattan, Senator Jackson and his family have lived in Washington Heights since 1975. He attended New York City public schools and graduated from SUNY at New Paltz. He is married and a dedicated father of three daughters.

## DAPHNE JORDAN (R-C-IP-RFM)
*43rd - Columbia County and parts of Rensselaer, Saratoga, and Washington Counties*

1580 Columbia Turnpike, Building 2, Suite 1, Castleton-On-The-Hudson, NY 12033
518-371-2751

Legislative Office Building, 188 State Street, Room 508, Albany, NY 12247
518-455-2381/jordan@nysenate.gov

Daphne Jordan was elected in November of 2018 to serve and represent New York State Senate's 43rd District, which includes parts of Saratoga, Rensselaer, and Washington counties and all of Columbia County. In the Senate, Jordan is Ranking Member of the Racing, Gaming, and Wagering and State-Native American Relations Committees and sits on the following Committees: Agriculture; Procurement and Contracts; Veterans, Homeland Security and Military Affairs; Racing, Gaming and Wagering; Libraries; and Women's Issues. She is also a member of the Legislative Women's Caucus.

Senator Jordan honors our values, keeps her promises and works to deliver real tax relief for hard-working families, support economic development to create better good-paying jobs and grow our economy, cut Albany's wasteful government spending and job-killing red tape, oppose unfunded state mandates that drive up property taxes, support law enforcement/first responders and honor military veterans. She fights every day for a better New York State, one with more affordability, opportunity, and security for everyone. Senator Jordan has been an outspoken voice for protecting innocent life, safeguarding taxpayer dollars, preserving the Second Amendment and upholding the rule of law.

Jordan started and ran two successful small businesses from scratch and employed 14 individuals. She understands the challenges private sector job creators face and will be a true champion for policies to help small businesses that employ over half of all New Yorkers.

Prior to her election to the New York State Senate, Jordan served as a member of the Halfmoon Town Board. Councilwoman Jordan preserved and protected resident's special quality of life, and ensured that the Town remained a great place for families. She helped grow the Town's General Fund balance from $70,000 to almost $4 million, attracted new businesses, expanded recreational trails and open spaces, and was part of the effort to create a Veterans Memorial. In recognition of her many successes and dedicated service, Councilwoman Jordan was overwhelmingly elected to the Halfmoon Town Board in 2014 and was reelected in 2015 with no opposition.

Senator Jordan entered the Senate with a wealth of proven, practical experience. She served as Legislative Director and Senate Local Government Committee Director to former State Senator Kathy Marchione; developed smart public policies that reduced costs for senior citizens and middle-class families; helped and honored military veterans; and addressed the heroin and opioid crisis. She also worked closely with local governments on their home rule legislation and advanced a successful public policy agenda that created 74 new state laws.

Active in her community, Jordan volunteered her time, talents, and expertise by serving as a Trustee, member of the Executive Committee, and as Treasurer for the Clifton Park-Halfmoon Public Library. In these capacities, she oversaw and managed a $3 million operating budget and $15 million construction budget for the new library, which was completed on budget. In addition, she developed the first template for the library's five-year budget plan and served as Liaison to facilitate and procure a $408,000 grant for a Green and LEED Certified Library.

A USA Certified Swim Official, Jordan is a proud swim mom and supporter of the Shenendehowa Men's Swimming and Diving Team and the Clifton Park-Halfmoon Piranhas.

Jordan is a graduate of Penn State Dickinson School of Law where she earned her JD, and also Lehigh University, where she received her BA, graduating with academic honors and recognition. Senator Jordan resides in the Town of Halfmoon with her husband Phil and their sons Lane and James.

## TODD KAMINSKY (D)
*9th - South Shore Long Island*

55 Front Street, Room 1, Rockville Centre, NY 11570-4040
516-766-8383/Kaminsky@nysenate.gov

Legislative Office Building, Room 307, Albany, NY 12247
518-455-3401

Todd Kaminsky represents New York's 20th Assembly District, including Long Beach, Atlantic Beach, East Atlantic Beach, Point Lookout, Lido Beach, Oceanside, Island Park, Lawrence, Cedarhurst, Hewlett, Woodmere, Inwood and portions of East Rockaway.

He is Chair of the Environmental Conservation Committee and is member of the following Senate Committees: Transportation; Health; Codes; Budget and Revenue; Ethics and Internal Governance; Health; and Investigations and Government Operations. Senator Kaminsky's priorities are ethics reform, improving Long Island's commuter rail system; lowering taxes; preserving and protecting Long Island's air, soil, and water; and fighting to expand access to high school diplomas for students with special needs.

As Chair of the Senate Environmental Conservation Committee, Senator Kaminsky is at the forefront of efforts to protect our air, water, and natural resources. He authored the New York Climate Leadership and Community Protection Act—the nation's most aggressive climate change program—putting the State on a path toward carbon neutrality and a green energy economy. He led the fight to regulate carcinogenic contaminants in Long Island's water supply and passed legislation banning products containing these toxic substances. He secured a multibillion-dollar investment in clean water infrastructure received a perfect score from the New York League of Conservation Voters for his collaborative efforts "with colleagues on both sides of the aisle to work on behalf of Long Islanders." Kaminsky also successfully passed legislation to ban toxic toys and mercury flooring in schools.

Senator Kaminsky has led the fight to improve Long Island's commuter rail system. He helped procure billions in the state budget for improved LIRR service, and passed legislation mandating a forensic audit of the MTA. He has held the MTA and LIRR to task at numerous hearings regarding the poor state of infrastructure and service at Penn Station. He has consistently opposed proposed fare hikes and demanded more accountability and better conditions for riders. Newsday called him "the leader of LIRR reform in Albany."

He is a leader on ethics reform, sponsoring legislation to strip pensions from corrupt officials, ban outside income for politicians, create publicly financed elections, strengthen anti-bribery laws, bolster penalties for public corruption and protect taxpayer dollars by increasing oversight of local government contracting. A Long Island native, Kaminsky has been a strong advocate for lower taxes, good jobs and a strong economy. He helped pass the largest middle-class income tax cuts in 70 years, voted more than 250 times against raising taxes and help enact a permanent property tax cap. He also secured tax breaks for Hurricane Sandy victims and has rallied to reform Industrial Development Agencies to protect tax dollars. Each year Kaminsky has been in the Legislature, he has drastically increased aid to local schools, securing nearly $300 million for South Shore schools in this past year's state budget—an increase of nearly $20 million from the year prior.

Prior to his election to the Senate, Kaminsky worked as Acting Deputy Chief of the US Attorney for the Eastern District of New York's Public Integrity Section and served as Assistant District Attorney in the Queens County District Attorney's Office.

Senator Kaminsky has received numerous awards for his work at the Eastern District, including the True American Hero Award from the Federal Drug Agents Foundation. As a community advocate, he has worked vigorously in support of the South Shore. He organized free legal clinics for those affected by Hurricane Sandy, and helped bring tens-of-thousands of dollars in relief funds to local residents. For his efforts, he was awarded the Community Service Award from the United States Attorney's Office for the Eastern District of New York and the Long Beach Martin Luther King Center's Sandy Relief Service Award.

Kaminsky was born and raised in Lido Beach, New York. He graduated from Long Beach High School and attended the University of Michigan, where he graduated summa cum laude. He received his law degree from New York University's School of Law, where he graduated magna cum laude. Senator Kaminsky and his wife, Ellen, live in Long Beach with their son, Rafe.

## ANNA M. KAPLAN (D)
*7th - Part of Nassau County*

Legislative Office Building, Room 805, Albany, NY 12247
518-455-2170/kaplan@nysenate.gov

1 Old Country Road, Suite 270, Carle Place, NY 11514
516-746-5924

Anna Kaplan is a Democratic Senator for the 7th District. She sought the Senate seat for this district in 2018 by calling for: passage of the Reproductive Health Act, sensible gun safety, and economic development in Nassau County.

In the Senate she is Chair of the Economic Development and Small Business Committee and sits on the following standing Committees: Alcoholism and Substance Abuse; Environmental Conservation; Transportation; and Judiciary. Kelles first ran for State Senate in 2018, calling for the passage of the Reproductive Health Act, sensible gun safety legislation, and increased economic development in Nassau County. Her election victory made her the first political refugee and the first Iranian-American elected to the New York State Senate.

Kaplan was born Anna Monahemi in Tabriz, Iran to a Jewish family. When the Islamic Revolution swept the country, her parents made the difficult decision to send her on her own to the United States for safety. Kaplan arrived in Brooklyn as part of an international effort to save Iran's Jewish and was sent to live with a foster family in Chicago, where she learned to speak English and completed high school. She was eventually granted political asylum by the United States government. After her family was finally reunited, they moved to Queens, New York, where she graduated from Yeshiva University Stern College for Women and then Benjamin N. Cardozo School of Law.

Senator Kaplan settled in Great Neck, New York where she and her husband raised two daughters, but felt a strong desire to give back to the country that opened its arms to her as a child in need. After years volunteering at her daughters' public schools and in her community, she decided to run for the Great Neck Library Board, where she served a four-year term. During that time, she was appointed to the Town of North Hempstead Board of Zoning Appeals. In 2011, she was elected Town of North Hempstead Councilwoman for the Fourth District, where she passed groundbreaking legislation such as a townwide ban of gender identity discrimination and Anti-BDS. She advocated and helped secure affordable housing for district seniors and rehabilitated parkland.

## BRIAN KAVANAGH (D-WF)
*26th - The Brooklyn Waterfront & Lower Manhattan*

250 Broadway, Room 2011, New York, NY 10007
212-298-5565/kavanagh@nysenate.gov

Legislative Office Building, Room 512, Albany, NY 12247
518-455-2625

209 Joralemon Street, Suite 300, Brooklyn Borough Hall, Brooklyn, NY 11201
718-857-1517

Brian Kavanagh was first elected to the New York State Senate in 2017, and is Chair of the Housing, Construction and Community Development Committee.. He also sits on the following Committees: Consumer Protection; Energy and Telecommunications; Codes; Environmental Conservation; Elections; and Social Services. His work focuses on promoting affordable housing, preventing gun violence, protecting the environment, creating a more open and equitable political process, and advancing economic and social justice.

As Chair of the Senate Committee on Housing, Construction, and Community Development, Kavanagh has built on his decades of advocating for access to high quality, safe, affordable housing for all New Yorkers. In 2019, he led the Senate effort to enact the Housing Stability and Tenant Protection Act, which gave New York the toughest tenant protections in the nation. The HSTPA dramatically strengthened the rent regulation laws, made them permanent, enabled any locality with a very low vacancy rate to adopt rent regulation, created new protections for residents of mobile and manufactured home parks, and instituted other substantial new rights for all renters statewide.

Under Senator Kavanagh's leadership, the Housing Committee held hearings on enforcement of housing, building, and fire codes and advanced a broad package of legislation that passed the Senate in 2020. Throughout his tenure, he has fought for major improvements in the management, maintenance, and security of public housing. While there have been some successes, including state capital funds allocated in recent years, he continues to advocate for a better response from city, state, and federal government.

In response to thorough reporting by *Newsday* on racial and ethnic discrimination by real estate brokers on Long Island, Kavanagh joined colleagues to investigate the allegations and identify ways to protect all New Yorkers' right to fair access to housing; this work continues in 2020. He also successfully advocated in 2019 and 2020 to restore funding for foreclosure prevention counseling and legal services in every county, and for legislation for a more just foreclosure process.

In his 14 years in the Legislature, Kavanagh has repeatedly taken on the gun industry lobby and won, helping to reduce gun violence in New York and across the country. He is the founder and chair of American State Legislators for Gun Violence Prevention and co-chair of New York Legislators for Gun Violence Prevention. He drafted and passed New York's "red flag" law, enacted in 2019, which empowers families, law enforcement, and schools to obtain Extreme Risk Protection Orders to keep guns away from individuals when evidence shows they are likely to harm themselves or others. In 2013, he helped craft the NY SAFE Act, which requires background checks on all gun sales, and bans military-style assault weapons and high-capacity ammunition magazines. He also advocated successfully for laws requiring safe storage of guns when not in their owner's possession, more support for community-based gun violence intervention, and gun violence prevention research funding. Kavanagh's work earned him the Detective McDonald Law Enforcement Award from New Yorkers Against Gun Violence in 2019.

Kavanagh has also been an environmental leader. He was a proud co-sponsor of the Climate Leadership and Community Protection Act, enacted in 2019, which mandates huge cuts in climate pollution, investment in clean, renewable energy sources, and creation of green jobs to promote environmental justice—the most comprehensive and ambitious climate change law in the United States. He was an early champion of the successful campaign to ban high-volume fracking for fossil fuels, and sponsored legislation to prevent exposure to toxic chemicals and to make producers responsible for recycling or disposing of products at the end of their useful life.

A previous member of the New York State Assembly, Kavanagh introduced well over 200 bills in the Assembly. He was also elected to six

terms on the Democratic and Working Families Party lines to represent Manhattan's East Side, and chaired the Assembly Consumer Affairs and Protection Committee, the Commission on Government Administration, and the Subcommittee on Election Operations and Voter Disenfranchisement and co-chaired the Assembly Workgroup on Legislative Process, Operations, and Public Participation. Kavanagh's legislative successes include legislation to increase New York's commitment to energy efficiency, green energy and alternative to fossil fuels, and ensure equality in civil service laws. Kavanagh's work has led him to receive the League of Conservation Voters Eco-Star Award, top ratings each year from Environmental Advocates of New York, and the City University of New York's Baruch College Legislator of the Year Award, among other awards. Professionally, Kavanagh is admitted to practice law and has served as a Chief of Staff and as an Aide to three New York City Mayors. He holds an undergraduate degree from Princeton University and a JD from New York University Law School. He currently resides in the East Side of Manhattan.

## TIMOTHY M. KENNEDY (D-IP-WF)
*63rd - Part of Erie County*

37 Franklin Street, Suite 550, Buffalo, NY 14202
716-826-2683/kennedy@nysenate.gov

Legislative Office Building, Room 708, Albany, NY 12247
518-455-2426

Timothy M. Kennedy was elected to the New York State Senate in 2010, to a district comprised of Cheektowaga, Lackawanna and most of the city of Buffalo. He is the Assistant Minority Whip and Chair of the State-Native American Relations and Transportation Committees and sits on the following standing Committees: Banks; Cities 2; Rules; Energy and Telecommunications; Finance; and Insurance. In March 2019, three months after being named Chair of the Senate Transportation Committee, Tim delivered an unprecedented $100 million for the Niagara Frontier Transportation Authority (NFTA) to fund a five year capital plan for maintenance and improvements of the Metro Rail. His legislative priorities are: developing a green workforce for emerging clean technology industries; strengthening penalties for repeat child abusers; and securing funding to support workforce training programs to the long-term unemployed. He also played a significant role in helping to strengthen state law against texting while driving.

Since being sworn into office in January 2011, Senator Tim Kennedy has fought to ensure Western New York sees its fair share of funding and state resources. In March 2019, three months after being named Chair of the Senate Transportation Committee, Tim delivered an unprecedented $100 million for the Niagara Frontier Transportation Authority (NFTA) to fund a five-year capital plan for maintenance and improvements of the Metro Rail. In his role as Chair, he has set an aggressive agenda. He sponsored legislation to allow municipalities to install cameras on school buses, in order to more effectively catch drivers who break the law and jeopardize student safety by passing stopped buses. He also spearheaded a package comprehensive limo safety reforms, in order to strengthen the industry standards and better protect New Yorkers who use alternative transportation. Kennedy drafted these reforms alongside the families of victims involved in limo crashes in Schoharie and Cutchogue. Both houses have passed these transportation priorities, and the Governor quickly signed them into law.

Throughout his time in office, Tim has kept a strong focus on protecting the most vulnerable in our community. He spearheaded the passage of Jay-J's law, legislation that stiffens penalties for repeat child abusers. The legislation was inspired by Jay-J Bolvin, a young boy who was brutally abused by his father. Sadly, Jay-J's father received a light sentence due to antiquated sentencing laws, but through Kennedy's advocacy, these penalties were strengthened. He also penned Jackie's Law, which protects victims of domestic violence from GPS stalking, and was signed into law in 2014.

**505**

His prior public service includes service on the Erie County Legislature, Second District, where he chaired the Economic Development Committee and sat on the Board of Directors of the Erie County Industrial Development Agency. He spearheaded a push to include Buffalo Public School No. 84 in the school districts renovation program. As a result, children with the most severe disabilities in Erie County continue to receive good care and education. The licensed occupational therapist has worked with geriatric and pediatric populations. He holds both a bachelor's and a master's degree in occupational therapy from D'Youville College. He is the married father of three.

## LIZ KRUEGER (D-WF)
*28th - Part of New York County, including the Upper East Side*

211 E. 43rd Street, Suite 1201, New York, NY 10017
212-490-9535/lkrueger@nysenate.gov

Capitol Building, 172 State Street, Albany, NY 12247
518-455-2297

First elected to the New York State Senate in a Special Election in February 2002, Senator Krueger is currently the Chair of the Finance Committee. She is also a member of the following Committees: Budget and Revenue; Rules; and the Legislative Women's Caucus. She is also a founding Co-chair of the New York State Bipartisan Legislative Pro-Choice Caucus and has been highly active in the area of women's health. She helped to lead the successful fight to pass the Women's Health and Wellness Act. In addition, she served as Cofacilitator of the New York City Welfare Reform Network. Senator Krueger's legislative initiatives are to expand and protect affordable housing, oppose hydrofracking, and expand access to food stamps and safety net assistance for those in need. Krueger has chaired the New York City Food Stamp Task Force and has sat on the board of the City-Wide Task Force on Housing Court.

Senator Krueger is a strong advocate for tenants' rights, affordable housing, improved access to health care and prescription drug coverage, social services, more equitable funding for public education, and animal welfare. She has made reforming and modernizing New York State's governmental processes, electoral system, and tax policy central goals of her legislative agenda.

Prior to being elected to the Senate, Krueger was Associate Director of the Community Food Resource Center for 15 years. She also was the founding Director of the New York City Food Bank. She holds a BA from Northwestern University and a master's degree from the University of Chicago's Harris Graduate School of Public Policy. She and her husband live on Manhattan's East Side.

## ANDREW J. LANZA (R)
*24th - Part of Richmond County*

3845 Richmond Avenue, Suite 2A, Staten Island, NY 10312
718-984-4073/lanza@nysenate.gov

Legislative Office Building, 188 State Street, Room 606, Albany, NY 12247
518-455-3215

Senator Lanza was elected to the New York State Senate in November 2006. Senator Lanza currently serves as the Ranking Member of the Senate Committees on Codes; Cities; Labor; Ethics and Internal Governance; and New York City Education. He also serves as a member of the following standing Committees: Finance; Rules; Civil Service and Pensions; Education; Investigations and Government Operations; and Judiciary. He is also the Senate Minority Whip.

The former Chair of the Senate Codes Committee, Lanza has a played a major role in shaping criminal justice policy for New York State. He has championed numerous issues to protect women and children from domestic violence, toughen sentences for violent criminals and strengthen the rights of crime victims. His position on the powerful Finance Committee allows him to play a significant role in reviewing the Governor's proposed budget and developing the Senate's priorities for the State Budget. Lanza is also Deputy Majority Leader for Governmental Oversight & Accountability and a Senate Representative of the Metropolitan Transportation Authority Capital Review Board.

Lanza is known for advancing cutting-edge legislation that keeps New York's laws up to date in today's world of constantly evolving technology. He passed a law which makes Internet impersonation a crime and ensured that New York was the first state in the nation to require labels on video games. He also authored legislation which requires that GPS monitoring devices be issued with orders of protection.

In his first year in the Senate, Lanza passed historic legislation which created the 13th Judicial District in the State of New York, comprised solely of Richmond County. The law represented a great victory in Staten Island's decades long quest for its own judicial district. Without the creation of a separate judicial district comprised solely of Richmond County, Staten Island would continue to lack say in the process for selection of Justices to the State's Supreme Court. Lanza hopes that all Staten Islanders recognize June 21, the first day of summer, as Judicial Independence day on Staten Island.

Senator Lanza has brought the fight to reduce high property taxes which hurt families, seniors, and businesses on Staten Island to the Senate. Because higher taxes force families and businesses to leave Staten Island, Lanza voted against the historic tax hikes in the City Council and introduced legislation there to repeal the entire tax increase. He has sponsored tax relief legislation in the Senate and has opposed budget proposals which do not adequately reduce taxes for Staten Island residents. He also authored legislation that would cap property taxes in New York City to provide relief to middle-class taxpayers and seniors living on fixed incomes. Senator Lanza has also stood up to those who seek to cut desperately needed funds from Staten Island's Hospitals and Nursing Homes. Our health care system is vital to the well-being of the people of Staten Island, and Albany must assist, rather than oppose our efforts to improve it.

Other legislative achievements include authoring legislation to create an online database to allow doctors and pharmacists to report and track controlled narcotics in real time, an effort to combat prescription drug abuse; backed efforts to force New York City to restore bus service to Staten Island's 7th and 8th graders; and in 2015, he authored and passed the Trafficking Victims Protection and Justice Act. Prior to being elected to the Senate, Lanza sat on the New York City Council and also served as a Prosecutor. He holds a BS from St. John's University and a JD from Fordham University Law School. He and his wife have three children and reside in Great Kills.

## JOHN LIU (D)
*11th - Part of Nassau County*

38-50 Bell Boulevard, Suite C, Bayside, NY 11361
718-765-6675/liu@nysenate.gov

Legislative Office Building, Room 802, Albany, NY 12247
518-455-2210

John C. Liu is a New York State Senator representing a broad area of northeast Queens.

He is Chairperson of the Senate's committee on New York City Education and also serves on the Committees: Budget and Revenue; Finance; Higher Education; Transportation; and Rules. Liu was Comptroller of the City of New York (2010 to 2013) and a New York City Councilmember (2002 to 2009). In 2013, he was a candidate for Mayor of New York City, in lieu of running for reelection as Comptroller.

As the 43rd Comptroller of New York City, Liu established an impressive record as the Chief Financial Officer for 8.4 million residents and overseeing municipal government with an annual budget of $70 billion. He saved taxpayers $5 billion through rigorous audits of City agencies, detailed scrutiny of contracts with private companies, and refinancing of $20 billion of outstanding City bond debt. During his four-year term of office, he achieved an enviable total investment return, increasing the City's pension asset portfolio to $150 billion. Liu created the nationally acclaimed online application CheckbookNYC.com, providing unprecedented transparency in government spending.

Always emphasizing that "it's not just about numbers, it's about people," Senator Liu championed fairness and equality. An early and staunch opponent of stop-and-frisk tactics, he highlighted the risks to communities and taxpayers alike due to damaged police-community relations. Liu presented daily-updated Minority- and Women-Owned Business Enterprise (M/WBE) Report Cards for City agencies to monitor and encourage greater government contracting opportunities for minority entrepreneurs. He also proposed sound economic policies to create real economic growth and narrow the ever-widening wealth gap, protected wage standards and recouped back wages and fines on behalf of cheated workers from contractors who just don't want to play by the rules, and exposed the billions of dollars in publicly-subsidized corporate welfare doled out by the City that failed to deliver on promised new jobs and fair housing.

Liu's other significant accomplishments as a legislator included exposing financial irregularities at the MTA, enacting legislation like the Equal Access Bill mandating on-demand language services in health and human services agencies, the School Zone Engine Idling Bill limiting engine idling near schools, and the Dignity for All Schools Act requiring the Department of Education to track bullying and harassment in schools. Liu used his office to fight hate and bigotry, and in too many instances denounced violence against immigrant workers such as restaurant delivery workers. His battles with radio shock-jocks and their corporate sponsors successfully brought an end to extreme racist and misogynist broadcasts in the New York market.

Hailed as a trailblazer, John Liu's historic elections—as the first Asian American to win legislative office in New York and then the first to win citywide office—were milestones for Asian Americans in New York and across the nation.

Prior to being elected to office, Liu worked in the private sector for 14 years as a professional Actuary, most recently as a Manager at PricewaterhouseCoopers. He has drawn upon his real-world fiscal expertise to root out waste and mismanagement in government.

Senator Liu emigrated from Taiwan at the age of five. He was educated in New York public schools, including Hunter College High School, Bronx High School of Science, and Binghamton University, attaining a degree in mathematical physics. Currently, he teaches municipal finance and public policy in masters' programs at the CUNY and Columbia University. Liu lives in Flushing with his wife Jenny and their son Joey.

## JOHN W. MANNION (D)
*50th - Part of Syracuse and Onondaga and Cayuga Counties*

333 E. Washington Street, State Office Building, Room 800, Syracuse, NY 13202
315-428-7632/mannion@nysenate.gov

188 State Street, Legislative Office Building, Room 814, Albany, NY 12247
518-455-3511

Senator John Mannion is a lifelong Central New Yorker. The grandchild of Irish immigrants, he grew up on Syracuse's famous Tipperary Hill. He now resides in Geddes with his wife, Jennifer, and his three children Jack, Quinn, and Brady. As a newly elected Senator, Mannion is Chair of the Disabilities Committee and sits on the following standing Committees: Children and Families; Civil Service and Pensions; Education; Environmental Conservation; Housing, Construction and Community Development; and Internet and Technology. His legislative interests in-

clude issues regarding mental health; child support for children over 21 with severe mental and physical disabilities; and housing.

Mannion brings nearly three decades of classroom experience as a teacher in public schools to the Senate. He spent his final twenty-one years as an Advanced Placement Biology teacher at the West Genesee School District. He has also been a strong advocate for teachers and students, serving in the capacity of President for the West Genesee Teachers' Association.

Using his science and education background, he continues to be a strong advocate for environmental protections, to assure a safe and clean environment for future generations of New Yorkers. His community activities include coaching soccer, basketball, and baseball. He and his family enjoy the diverse cultures and historical significance that Central New York offers.

## MIKE MARTUCCI (R-C-IP)
*42nd - Sullivan County and parts of Delaware, Orange, and Ulster Counties*

90 North Street, Suite 205, Middletown, NY 10940
845-344-3311/martucci@nysenate.gov

188 State Street, Legislative Office Building, Room 415, Albany, NY 12247
518-455-2400

Mike Martucci is serving his first term as the Senator for the 42nd NYS Senate District. He has been named the Ranking Member of the Senate Committees on Mental Health and Developmental Disabilities and Small Business, Commerce and Economic Development. He also sits on the following Committees: Children and Families; Cities 1; Corporation, Authorities, and Commissions; and Housing, Construction and Community Development.

Senator Martucci grew up in the Town of Minisink and is a lifelong resident of Orange County. He is a dedicated family man who believes in giving back to his community through volunteerism, teaching, and philanthropy. At the age of 22, Martucci took his life savings and opened a school bus business called Quality Bus Service. With a start-up business loan and his grandmother by his side, he began driving a school bus and providing service to Greenwood Lake Union Free School District in Orange County. Through hard work and with great risk and good fortune, he grew Quality Bus Service to over 550 employees with more than 350 school buses that provided critical services to thousands of local school children each day.

Senator Martucci volunteered to help the school transportation industry improve safety, expand training opportunities, and foster innovation. In 2015, he was elected President of the New York School Bus Contractors Association, becoming a leading state and national voice on school transportation. Martucci worked side by side with parents, school administrators, and unions advocating for stronger school transportation safety laws to protect children, legislation to protect school transportation workers, and smarter laws to help control the cost of school transportation to allow school districts to keep more money in the classroom.

In 2019, he and his wife Erin established the Michael and Erin Martucci Family Foundation and dedicated $250,000 to help support local women and children in need, farmers, job creation, and education. A proud member of the local community and a charity-minded individual, he enjoys volunteering for his church and supporting the Community Foundation of Orange & Sullivan. He is a member of the Board of Directors and Vice President of the SUNY Orange Foundation, which provides scholarships for students seeking a college education. He also chairs the annual SUNY Orange Golfing for Scholarships event to raise money for the college's athletic scholarship fund.

Senator Martucci and his family were directly impacted by the tragic events of 9/11 and because of this, his family established the Michelle

Rene Bratton Foundation to provide college scholarships for children who live in Orange, Sullivan, and Ulster Counties.

He obtained his MBA and his BS degrees at Marist College. Prior to attending Marist College, Martucci graduated with honors from Orange County Community College. Senator Martucci and his wife Erin, a school counselor, are raising their three children, son Mike Jr., and daughters Elizabeth and Catherine in New Hampton-the Town of Wawayanda. He is also a family farmer, and a steward of our environment and understands the importance of preserving open space for future generations.

## MARIO MATTERA (R-C-IP)
*2nd - Part of Suffolk County*

260 Middle Country Road, Suite 102, Smithtown, NY 11787
631-361-2154/mattera@nysenate.gov

Legislative Office Building, Room 604, Albany, NY 12247
518-455-2071

Senator Mario Mattera was elected to the 2nd Senate District of the New York State Senate in November of 2020 and sworn into office of January 5, 2021. He is Ranking Member of the Consumer Protection and Corporations, Authorities and Commissions Committees; he is also a member of the Labor and Transportation Committees.

As someone who has lived and worked in the 2nd Senate District his entire life, Senator Mattera understands the needs of local families and the need to reduce the impact Albany's tax burden is placing on our way of life. As a longtime union leader in the Plumbers Local Union #200, he has cultivated a keen understanding of the needs of our working men and women and how a good economic climate is essential to helping local businesses create much-needed jobs that provide workers with decent pay and benefits.

As a member and leader of the Plumbers Local Union #200 union for over 39 years, he has dedicated himself to working to protect the needs of Long Island's workers and their families. That has led him to oversee the protection of over 1,300 working men and women and manage over $250 million in benefit funds to protect their futures. It has also provided him with the opportunity to help his fellow union brothers and sisters gain access to good paying jobs while ensuring that they have safe work environments where their rights are protected. For his work on behalf of his fellow members, the Senator has been presented with the Order Sons of Italy in America's Golden Lion Award as 2019's Labor Leader of the Year as well as the PBA Columbia's 2012 Labor Leader of the Year. He has also led the way for the younger generation of union employees by serving 25 years as a board member on the apprenticeship program at Plumbers Local Union #200 to improve their opportunities and to ensure that our region has a qualified workforce.

In his community, Mattera has dedicated himself to helping local organizations and has served as a board member on the St. Catherine's Health and Wellness Advisory Board, the Suffolk County Water Authority, Community Association of Greater St. James. and the Smithtown Advisory Board for new construction projects.

His work with the Smithtown Advisory Board was part of their successful effort to work with Senator Flanagan to secure millions in state funding for sewers in the area. This funding will deliver sewers in the Smithtown, Kings Park and St. James business districts to protect the environment while also enhancing business opportunities for local business owners. Additionally, he has joined efforts with the Work Force Housing Committee, Helmets to Hardhats for our returning veterans and the Long Island Housing Partnership where he assisted in their Superstorm Sandy relief program to help people in trying times.

While Senator Mattera has undertaken these efforts for the betterment of his community, he is proud to have been recognized by the Children's Museum at Hallock Farm, St. Catherine of Siena Medical Center, and the Ward Melville Heritage Organization for his efforts. He lives in St. James with his wife Terry and his daughters Jessica and Jayme.

## RACHEL MAY (D)
*53rd - Madison County and parts of Oneida County and Onondaga County, including the city of Syracuse*

333 E. Washington Street, Suite 805, Syracuse, NY 13202
315-478-8745/may@nysenate.gov

Legislative Office Building, 198 State Street, Room 803, Albany, NY 12210
518-455-2838

100 Eaton Street, Morrisville, NY 13408
315-684-3331

Rachel May represents the 53rd District. In the Senate, she is Chair of the Aging and Legislative Commission on Rural Resources Committees and sits on these standing Committees: Agriculture; Banks; Cities 2; Environmental Conservation; Elections; and Health. She is also a member of the Joint Task Force on Opioids, Addiction & Overdose Prevention Committee; the Legislative Women's Caucus; and the State-Native American Relations Committee.

As Chair of the Senate Committee on Aging, she has been a vigorous supporter of home care workforce initiatives, expanded funding for in-home care programs, the Long-Term Care Ombudsman Program, and nursing home accountability. She has sponsored bills to create a Reimagining Long-Term Care Task Force, authorize a family caregiver tax credit, and create a home care jobs innovation fund to support workforce growth.

Senator May has been instrumental in passing transformative legislation, including comprehensive election reforms, tenant-centered housing reforms, unprecedented criminal justice reform, and the nation's most ambitious climate legislation. She has worked hard to bring the people of Central New York into the process of decision-making in Albany, by holding a record number of legislative hearings in and focused on the region, including hearings on the Climate Leadership and Community Preservation Act, rural broadband, farm labor rights, health care for all, and upstate nursing home issues during the COVID-19 crisis. In addition, she has brought her downstate colleagues to Central New York for roundtables on opioid addiction treatment and prevention, minority and women-owned businesses, and childcare and child welfare. She has also sponsored and passed into law a bill to create the first regional STEAM (science, technology, engineering, arts, and mathematics) school for Central New York, which is currently under construction in the City of Syracuse.

She is a lifelong educator who has worked for the last fifteen years in the area of environmental sustainability at Syracuse University and SUNY College of Environmental Science and Forestry.

She has also been deeply involved in the local community, including serving on the Board of the Onondaga County Resource Recovery Agency and the Syracuse Board of Zoning Appeals. In partnership with Native American educators, she secured grants from the EPA and the National Endowment for the Humanities to develop teaching materials and train teachers and students about the extraordinary environmental and human history of Onondaga Lake.

Before moving to Syracuse, May had a successful career as a professor of Russian language and literature, first at Stony Brook and then at Macalester College in St. Paul, Minnesota. She earned a master's degree from Oxford University on a Marshall Scholarship and a PhD in Russian language and literature from Stanford University. In 2001 she and her husband chose to settle in Syracuse, where he is a professor at Le Moyne College; they have one daughter.

## SHELLEY MAYER (D-WF)
*37th - Part of Westchester County*

222 Grace Church Street, Suite 300, Port Chester, NY 10573
914-934-5250/smayer@nysenate.gov

Legislative Office Building, Room 509, Albany, NY 12247
518-455-2031

Shelley Mayer has spent her career as an advocate for New Yorkers. She is an experienced and progressive leader. In an April 2018 Special Election, she was elected to the New York State Senate representing the 37th Senate District, which includes the Cities of Yonkers, White Plains, New Rochelle, and Rye; the Towns of Bedford, Eastchester, Harrison, Mamaroneck, North Castle, and Rye; and the Villages of Bronxville, Larchmont, Mamaroneck, Port Chester, Rye Brook, and Tuckahoe.

In the Senate Mayer is Chair of the Education Committee and sits on the following standing Committees: Environmental Conservation; Corporations, Authorities, and Commissions; Elections; Racing, Gaming, and Wagering; Labor; and Rules. She is also a member of the Legislative Women's Caucus.

Senator Mayer has been a champion for education issues and public schools throughout her time in the State Legislature. From 2013 to 2017, Mayer served as the Chair of the Assembly Education Subcommittee on Students with Special Needs. During this time, she advocated for and ensured that schools which serve the state's most vulnerable students (Special Act, 4201, and 4410 Schools) receive increased funding from the state. While representing the City of Yonkers in the Assembly, she prioritized delivering for the city's 26,000+ public school students. In 2019, after being reelected to the State Senate, Mayer was appointed to serve as the Chair of the State Senate Education Committee. One of her first achievements was the passing of the APPR bill which decoupled teacher evaluations from an undue reliance on state standardized tests. The Senator is also working on a civics package of bills to prepare New York State students for being engaged, active citizens in our democracy. She continues to work with her colleagues to deliver the resources and policies school districts throughout the state need to provide a quality education for every child, regardless of zipcode.

Prior to her election to the Senate she was elected to the New York State Assembly in a special election on March 20, 2012 and subsequently reelected November 2012, 2014, and 2016 from the 90th District (Yonkers). She also served as Chief Counsel to the New York State Senate Democrats, where she helped lead the effort to expel the disgraced Hiram Monserrate and helped draft critical legislation to reform Albany and protect taxpayers.

Before her election to the Assembly, Mayer was a senior counsel at the National State Attorney General Program at Columbia Law School, where she focused on health care and labor law rights. For over seven years, she was Vice President of government and community affairs at Continuum Health Partners, one of New York City's largest teaching hospital systems, working to protect Medicaid and Medicare services and improving the relationship between New York City's diverse communities and the hospital system.

From 1982 to 1994, she was an Assistant Attorney General in the office of New York Attorney General Bob Abrams. She served in the Civil Rights Bureau, as Chief of the Westchester Regional Office, as the Legislative Liaison for the Attorney General and ultimately as a senior advisor to the Attorney General. As an Assistant Attorney General, Mayer fought to protect civil rights for New Yorkers and to broaden laws protecting consumers and tenants.

Senator Mayer has been actively involved in the Yonkers community, serving as a member of the Yonkers NAACP, Yonkers YWCA, Westchester Women's Bar Association, and Westchester Women's Agenda. She is a member of the Yonkers Lawyers Association, New York State Bar Association, and the American Bar Association. She also served on the board of the Jewish Council of Yonkers/Westchester Community Partners and the Yonkers Public Library.

Mayer received a JD from SUNY Buffalo School of Law and a BA from UCLA. She lives in Yonkers with her husband of 36 years, Lee Smith. Shelley and Lee have three adult children—Aaron, Julia, and Arthur.

## ZELLNOR MYRIE (D)
*20th - Part of Kings County*

Legislative Office Building, Room 903, Albany, NY 12247
518-455-2410/myrie@nysenate.gov

1077 Nostrand Avenue, Ground Floor, Brooklyn, NY 11225
718-284-4700

Zellnor Myrie is a Brooklyn native, lawyer, and longtime affordable housing advocate serving the 20th Senate District. In the Senate, he is Chair of the Elections Committee and sits on the following standing Committees: Consumer Protection; Crime Victims, Crime, and Correction; Social Services; Judiciary; Codes; and Housing, Construction, and Community Development.

During his first legislative session, Senator Myrie served in leadership roles on several major legislative victories. Having grown up in a rent-stabilized apartment at the epicenter of the affordable housing crisis, Senator Myrie was honored to colead the Senate's Housing Reform Working Group, which produced New York's strongest affordable housing and tenant protection laws in generations. During the legislature's budget negotiations, Myrie also served on the Senate's Criminal Justice Reform Working Group, resulting in sweeping reforms to cash bail, discovery, and speedy trial laws. As Chair of the Elections Committee, Senator Myrie led hearings on Public Financing of Elections and Automatic Voter Registration, and presided over historic election reforms including Early Voting, closing the LLC loophole, and many other crucial reforms to protect and expand our democracy.

Senator Myrie derives inspiration for his public service from his mother, who moved to Brooklyn 40 years ago from Costa Rica on the promise of a mattress in a friend's apartment and a job at a factory. She raised Myrie in a rent-stabilized apartment in Prospect Lefferts Gardens, allowing him to attend one of the best public schools in the borough.

He is a graduate of Brooklyn Technical High School, earned his BA in communications, and an MA in urban studies from Fordham University. After Fordham, Myrie worked as Legislative Director for City Councilman Fernando Cabrera where, among other bills, he helped draft and pass the Tenant Bill of Rights.

## THOMAS F. O'MARA (R-C-IP)
*58th - Chemung, Schuyler, Steuben, and Yates Counties, and part of Tompkins County including the city and town of Ithaca, and the towns of Enfield, Newfield, and Ulysses*

333 E. Water Street, Suite 301, Elmira, NY 14901
607-735-9671/omara@nysenate.gov

105 E. Steuben Street, Bath, NY 14810
607-776-3201

Legislative Office Building, Room 406, Albany, NY 12247
518-455-2091

Thomas F. O'Mara was elected to the New York State Senate on November 2, 2010. He is a Ranking Member of the Finance and Investigations and Government Operations Committees; former Chair of the Environmental Conservation Committee; and former Vice Chair of the Transportation Committee. O'Mara also sits on the following committees: Codes; Energy and Telecommunications; Finance; Insurance; Investigations and Government Operations; Judiciary; and Rules. He also served as a member of the Task Force on Heroin and Opioid Addiction, the Task Force on Lyme and Tick-borne Diseases, and the Task Force on Workforce Development.

Senator O'Mara has stood as a commonsense, clear, and strong voice in Albany on behalf of his constituents in the Southern Tier and Finger Lakes regions. He has been outspoken in opposition to out-of-control spending in Albany and a strong advocate for cutting waste in government, particularly in the state's $70-billion-plus system of Medicaid where he has championed better ways to manage care, improve disease management and utilize cutting-edge data mining technology to potentially save billions of taxpayer dollars that are being lost to waste, fraud, and abuse.

Throughout his public service, Senator O'Mara has been guided by a longheld belief: Government does not create jobs, business does. That's why he's focused on developing public policies and strategies that allow state government to improve the economic climate for doing business in New York by opposing tax increases, and reducing state spending, mandates, overregulation, and oppressive property taxes. In the Senate, O'Mara has been at the forefront of efforts to revitalize Upstate New York's manufacturing sector.

Prior to his election to the Senate, O'Mara sat in the New York State Assembly for three terms, where he rose to the rank of Assistant Minority Leader Pro Tempore. He is a former Chemung County District Attorney, Chemung County Attorney, and an Assistant District Attorney in both Manhattan and Chemung County. At present, he is a member of the Barclay Damon LLP law firm. He remains active in his community, including as counsel to the Chemung County Industrial Development Agency. He holds a BA from the Catholic University of America and a JD from Syracuse University College of Law. He is married with three children and resides in Big Flats.

## PETER OBERACKER (R-C)
*51st - Clinton, Cortland, Delaware, Herkimer, Otsego Ulster, and Schoharie Counties*

41 S. Main Street, Oneonta, NY 13820
607-432-5524/oberacker@nysenate.gov

4030 West Road, Cortland, NY 13045
607-758-9005

188 State Street, Legislative Office Building, Room 506, Albany, NY 12247
518-455-3131

Senator Peter Oberacker is serving his first term representing the 51st Senate District. Elected in 2020 during a global pandemic, Oberacker is keenly aware of the many critical issues and concerns facing the nine counties he represents. He is a Ranking Member of the Committees on Alcoholism and Substance Abuse, in addition to Internet and Technology; Oberacker also serves as a member on the following Committees: Education; Health; Higher Education; and Judiciary.

Senator Oberacker's leading priorities include: expanding broadband access to meet the needs of the entire state, specifically rural areas that have been left behind; supporting small businesses, ensuring they have the resources needed to increase employment; assisting volunteer EMS squads with training requirements, recruitment, and retention; and improving infrastructure including upstate roads and bridges.

Before his election to the State Senate, he served as a member of the Otsego County Board of Representatives where he chaired the Public Works Committee, served as Vice Chair of the Administration Committee, and was a member of Human Services, Negotiations, and Inter-Governmental Affairs committees. Previously, Oberacker served as Maryland Town Supervisor and as a Town Board member.

Senator Oberacker grew up in a family of sausage makers, working in the family's local market since age eight. He has a long career in product research, development, and implementation in the food industry busi-

ness. In 2007, he created FormTech Solutions and built it into a successful multimillion-dollar business working with major companies around the world to develop and incorporate new and innovative products and then make them applicable in the ever-growing food industry.

In his community, Senator Oberacker is a member of his local fire department and EMS squad and is a member of the Masonic Lodge. He is a graduate of Schenevus High School and SUNY Delhi. Oberacker is married to his high school sweetheart, Shannon, of 34 years and they have two adult children.

## ROBERT ORTT (R-C-IP)
*62nd - Niagara, Orleans, and Monroe Counties*

175 Walnut Street, Suite 6, Lockport, NY 14094
716-434-0680/Ortt@nysenate.gov

Capitol Building, Room 315, Albany, NY 12247
518-455-2024

Robert Ortt was first elected to the New York State Senate in 2014. At the start of the 2019 Legislative session, Senator Ortt became the Ranking Member of the New York State Senate Committee on Agriculture and the Committee on Veterans, Homeland Security, and Military Affairs. In June of 2020, Rob was elected the Minority Leader by his colleagues in the Republican Conference. He chairs the Committee on Mental Health and Developmental Disabilities, and also sits on the following standing Committees: State-Native American Relations and Rules. One of the accomplishments he is most proud of was introducing and expanding the Joseph P. Dwyer Program across Western New York. The program provides peer-to-peer support program for veterans facing the challenges of posttraumatic stress, traumatic brain injuries, and reintegration into civilian life.

He is the former Mayor of North Tonawanda, where he served for four years and developed executive expertise. He was the City Treasurer and Clerk Treasurer from 2007 to 2010. He enlisted in the NY Army National Guard following the 9/11 attacks, and served in Afghanistan as the executive officer/unit movement officer for an infantry company. His awards included the Bronze Star. He is a former independent personal financial analyst and lives in North Tonawanda with his wife.

## ANTHONY H. PALUMBO (R)
*1st - Part of Suffolk County*

28 North Country Road, Suite 203, Mount Sinai, NY 11766
631-473-1461/lavalle@nysenate.gov

Senator Anthony H. Palumbo is the newly elected State Senator for the 1st Senate District. In the Senate, he in Ranking Member of the Codes and Ethics and Internal Governance Committees; he also sits on the following Committees: Environmental Conservation; Investigations and Government Operations; Judiciary; and Mental Health.

Palumbo previously served in the New York State Assembly for several years, first being elected to the 2nd Assembly District in 2013. As an Assemblyman, he was known as being an outspoken advocate for Suffolk County taxpayers and a strong proponent of law enforcement and the area's first responders. As the Ranking Minority Member on the Assembly Judiciary Committee, he led the fight against the dangerous bail reform laws that have made our communities less safe and has been steadfast in his opposition to antipolice rhetoric and policies.

Prior to serving in the State Legislature, Senator Palumbo worked as a Suffolk County Assistant District Attorney, where he prosecuted major crimes and drug traffickers. He has taken that background to Albany, where he's fought to keep our communities safe, hold public officials accountable, and enhance the quality of life that makes Suffolk County unique.

Senator Palumbo has continued to show the drive and vision families on Long Island need and deserve in state government. His very first piece of legislation was a massive tax-cut bill that would save the average Suffolk County resident over $2,500 annually. That same year, he accomplished a rare feat for a freshman GOP Assemblyman by sponsoring and passing major legislation that helped first-time homebuyers and younger residents save thousands and made the dream of homeownership on Long Island more affordable.

In addition to his proven record as a tax reformer, Palumbo hasn't shied away from tackling the tough quality of life and public safety issues Long Island families face. He was a leader of the movement to reform and repeal Common Core; supported and passed a constitutional amendment stripping corrupt politicians of a taxpayer-funded pension; and supported significant investment in improving our water quality and environment. He has also made education a top priority and is a strong advocate in the battle to ensure Long Island taxpayers receive their fair share of school aid and infrastructure funding.

As a Senator, his top priorities are getting our economy back on track postpandemic so our small business can thrive, and repealing the controversial bail and discovery reforms harming our residents and local law enforcement. He will continue to lead and maintain his commitment to defending Suffolk County values and enhancing the quality of life on the East End. As a lifelong resident of Suffolk County, Senator Palumbo will continue to build on his record of protecting and serving the communities he loves.

Senator Palumbo attended Lafayette College in Easton, Pennsylvania on a baseball scholarship and earned a degree in government and law. He received his law degree from St. John's Law School in Jamaica, New York. Today, he and his wife, Tracy, reside in New Suffolk with their two children.

## KEVIN S. PARKER (D-WF)
*21st - Part of Kings County*

3021 Tilden Avenue, 1st Floor and Basement, Brooklyn, NY 11226-5107
718-629-6401/parker@nysenate.gov

Capitol Building, 172 State Street, Room 504C, Albany, NY 12247
518-455-2580

Kevin S. Parker was first elected to the New York State Senate in 2002. He represents an ethnically diverse district that includes Flatbush, East Flatbush, Midwood, Ditmas Park, Kensington, Windsor Terrace, and Park Slope. The Brooklyn-born Parker is currently the Ranking Member and Chair of the Energy and Telecommunications Committee and serves on the following standing Committees: Banks; Finance; Higher Education; Rules; Internet and Technology; Insurance; and Rules. He is former Majority Whip and First Vice Chair of the Association of Black, Puerto Rican & Asian Legislators. He is also Parliamentarian of the NY State Association of Black and Puerto Rican Legislators, Inc.; a member of the New American Task Force; and appointed as the Democratic lead of the Joint Budget Committee on Environment, Agriculture, and Housing.

Before his election to the Senate, Parker was a Special Assistant to former New York State Comptroller H. Carl McCall and managed intergovernmental relations in New York City, and also was liaison between the Comptroller and city, state, and federal elected officials. He was a New York City Urban Fellow and also served as a Special Assistant to former Manhattan Borough President Ruth Messinger; a Legislative Aide to former New York City Councilmember Una Clarke; a Special Assistant to Assemblyman Nick Perry; and a Project Manager with the New York State Urban Development Corporation; and. In addition, he worked on a variety of issues within the financial service industry at UBS PaineWebber in the chairman's office regarding government affairs. Parker previously served as Second Vice Chairman and Chair of Community Board 17's Education Committee and is a member of the Children's Defense Fund's Community Crusade for Children. He has been a

professor of African American studies and political science at Baruch College-CUNY, SUNY Old Westbury, John Jay College, and Brooklyn College. At present, he is an adjunct professor at Brooklyn College's Center for Worker Education. Parker earned a BS from Penn State and an MS from the New School for Social Research Graduate School of Management and Urban Study. He is pursuing a doctorate in political science from CUNY's Graduate School and University Center.

## ROXANNE PERSAUD (D)
*19th - Southeast Brooklyn*

409 Legislative Office Building, Albany, NY 12247
518-455-2788/senatorpersaud@gmail.com

1222 E. 96th Street, Brooklyn, NY 11236
718-649-7653

Roxanne Jacqueline Persaud was elected to the State Senate in November 2015 after serving in the State Assembly. Senator Persaud is Chair of the Social Services Committee and sits on the following standing Committees: Children and Families; Cities 1; Commerce, Economic Development and Small Business; Disabilities; Joint Senate Task Force on Opioids, Addiction & Overdose Presention; Labor; and Transportation. She is also a member of the Legislative Women's Caucus. Her legislative priorities for the District will include safer communities, affordable housing, funding for schools and libraries, supportive services for youth and seniors, and quality healthcare.

Senator Persaud spent many years as a Higher Education Administrator prior to being elected to the State Legislature. In addition, she is a longtime advocate for the community. She served as President of the 69th Precinct Community Council in Canarsie, a member of Community Board 18 and Commissioner on the New York City Districting Commission. She also is a graduate of the NYPD Citizens Police Academy as well as, the New York City Office of Emergency Management-Community Emergency Response Team. Additionally, she was a member of Community Action Board of the New York City Department of Youth and Community Development and Chairperson of the Neighborhood Advisory Board-District 18. She also serves on organizations highlighting domestic violence and cancer awareness among others.

Persaud was born in Guyana, South America and migrated to the United States with her parents and siblings. She is a graduate of Pace University from which she holds a BS and MS in education administration.

## JESSICA RAMOS (D)
*13th - Part of Queens County*

32-37 Junction Boulevard, East Elmhurst, NY 11369
718-205-3881/ramos@nysenate.gov

Legislative Office Building, Room 946, Albany, NY 12247
518-455-2529

Jessica Ramos is Senator for the 13th District. In the Senate, she is Chair of the Labor Committee and sits on the following committees: Agriculture; Commerce, Economic Development and Small Business; Corporation, Authorities, and Commissions; Internet and Technology; New York City Education; and Transportation. She is also a member of the Legislative Women's Caucus.

Ramos has spent her life fighting for working families, advocating for labor, and organizing her local community. Born in Elmhurst to an undocumented seamstress and a printing pressman, she was raised in Astoria, attended Queens public schools, and now lives in Jackson Heights with her two sons.

A strong union advocate, Ramos worked with Build Up NYC to fight for construction, building and hotel maintenance workers in New York City. She also worked with SSEU Local 371 and 32BJ SEIU, where she helped building maintenance workers, office cleaners and public schools cleaners win contracts that protected their rights, wages, and benefits.

Ramos was a member of Queens Community Board 3 and served as Democratic District Leader in the 39th Assembly District. She sat on the boards of the Jackson Heights Beautification Group and Farmspot, and the Jackson Heights' community-supported agriculture (CSA) program. She has received awards for her work with the LGBTQ community and her advocacy on behalf of Women and Minority-Owned Businesses.

As the first American-born in her family, Ramos feels a deep sense of responsibility in bridging the gap between immigrant and nonimmigrant communities. Her mother crossed the Mexican border by herself at 24, and her father was arrested in a workplace immigration raid in the early 1980s and spent days held in a detention center.

Even as a teenager, Ramos was outspoken against poverty and the internal displacement of Colombians. She was elected President of the NYC Colombian Liberal Youth Council in 2002 and subsequently elected President of the NYC Colombian Liberal Party in 2005.

Most recently, Ramos served as Director of Latino Media for the City of New York. As the city's chief Latina spokesperson, she helped keep our city's 1.87 million Spanish-speaking residents, and the community and ethnic media at large, informed about government services and initiatives.

Senator Ramos credits her love for activism and public service to her parents, Colombian immigrants who fought for and won the right to dual citizenship for Colombian-Americans and founded Siempre Colombia, a not-for-profit organization in Jackson Heights.

## EDWARD A. RATH III (R-C-IP)
*61st - Genesee County and Parts of Erie and Monroe Counties*

1961 Wehrle Drive, Suite 9, Williamsville, NY 14221
716-631-8695/rath@nysenate.gov

188 State Street, Legislative Office Building, Room 513, Albany, NY 12247
518-455-3161

Edward A. Rath III was elected to the New York State Senate in 2020. He is a Ranking Member of the Elections and Local Government Committees; In addition, he sits on the following Committees: Budget and Revenue; Cities 2; Health; and Labor. His legislative priorities include small businesses, homeowner property tax stabilization, and safe communities.

Prior to being elected to the Senate, Senator Rath was an Erie County legislator for 13 years. He built a reputation for being a fierce advocate for the community, putting taxpayers first. Rath also advocated for a stronger economy and government transparency and accountability.

As a legislator, his leadership led to the creation of the County's Silver Alert Local Law, an Amber Alert for seniors that has since become a model program statewide. Rath was a longtime member of the Legislature's Public Safety Committee, where he championed first responders and led efforts against cyberbullying.

In addition to his public service, Rath has remained active in the community. He continues to volunteer for organizations that provide assistance throughout the community including the Salvation Army, Meals on Wheels, Rotary International, and the Alzheimer's Foundation.

He received a degree from Syracuse University, with a major in political science and a minor in history. In 2005, he completed the Executive MBA program at Canisius College, graduating magna cum laude. A lifelong Amherst resident, Senator Rath and his wife, Amy have three daughters.

## ELIJAH REICHLIN-MELNICK (D-WF)
*38th - Parts of Rockland and Westchester Counties*

20 S. Main Street, New City, NY 10956
845-623-3627/reichlin@nysenate.gov

2 Church Street, Ossining, NY 10562
914-941-2041

172 State Street, State Capitol Building, Room 514, Albany, NY 12247
518-455-2991

State Senator Elijah Reichlin-Melnick was elected in November, 2020 and is currently serving his first term. He is Chair of the Senate Committee on Contracts and Procurement. Reichlin-Melnick also sits on the following standing Committees: Consumer and Protection; Education; Investigations and Government Operations; Local Government; and Transportation; Veterans, Homeland Security and Military Affairs.

Senator Reichlin-Melnick is a graduate of Nyack High School, Cornell University (BA double major in history and government) and Rutgers University (master's degree in city & regional planning). Prior to his election to the State Senate, he was twice elected as a village Trustee in the Village of Nyack and also served on the staff of several elected officials including State Senator James Skoufis (39th District), former Members of Congress Eliot Engel and Nita Lowey, and former Orangetown Town Supervisor Andy Stewart.

After receiving his master's degree, Senator Reichlin-Melnick spent three years as a senior research planner at Hudson Valley Pattern for Progress, a Newburgh-based nonprofit focused on regional planning and local government issues throughout the Hudson Valley. He began his career as an elementary school teacher at an inner-city public school in New Haven, Connecticut, where he became committed to ensuring that all students can get a great education, no matter where they live.

Senator Reichlin-Melnick's priorities are to ensure that New York state government works for middle-class and working families and protects our quality of life by ensuring safe neighborhoods, affordable healthcare, clean air and water, good roads and mass transit, and well-funded education for our kids. In 2021, he is focused on addressing the public health and economic challenges caused by the COVID-19 pandemic.

Reichlin-Melnick has been an active member of the Nyack Chapter of the NAACP for the past decade. He formerly served as chair of the Nyack Democratic Committee and Vice President of Rockland County Young Democrats. He is an avid hiker and environmentalist who enjoys taking pictures of the beautiful places in the 38th District and throughout the Hudson Valley. Born and raised in Rockland County, he has lived in the 38th District for nearly his whole life and currently resides in Nyack with his wife Shelley.

## PATTY RITCHIE (R-C-IP)
*48th - Oswego, Jefferson and St. Lawrence Counties*

Dulles State Office Building, 317 Washington Street, Room 418, Watertown, NY 13601
315-782-3418/ritchie@nysenate.gov

46 E. Bridge Street, 1st Floor, Oswego, NY 13126
315-342-2057

Legislative Office Building, 188 State Street, Albany, NY 12247
518-455-3438

330 Ford Street (basement of City Hall), Ogdensburg, NY 13669
315-393-3024

Patty Ritchie was elected to the State Senate in 2010. She is Deputy Majority Leader for Senate and Assembly Relations; Secretary of the Senate Minority Conference; Ranking Member of the Energy and Telecommunications and Veterans, Homeland Security and Military Affairs Committees; and Chair of the Agriculture Committee and the Libraries

Committee. Senator Ritchie sits on the following standing Committees: Elections; Environmental Conservation; Finance; and Rules. In addition, she is a member of the Legislative Commission on Rural Resources and Legislative Women's Caucus.

In the Senate, she has authored over 60 new laws that seek to create better opportunity and improve the quality of life for her constituents and citizens of our state, voted to cut taxes to their lowest rates in generations and supported a property tax cap that's saving homeowners millions of dollars each year. She delivered record aid to local schools, to help ensure a quality education for every student and, as a grandmother, has made a priority of issues affecting health care, children and families.

Senator Ritchie recognizes the vital role of agriculture in strengthening and growing the economy of rural Upstate communities and, as the past Chair of the Agriculture Committee, she reversed budget cuts and secured record funding to programs that help strengthen the bottom lines of hardworking farmers. Her "Young Farmers" and "Grown in New York" initiatives are providing millions of dollars to promote innovation and preserve the future of family farming for generations.

As the representative of Fort Drum, the Northeast's largest military installation and Upstate New York's biggest employer, she has championed the cause of service men and women and veterans, and their families, and led community and statewide opposition to federal budget cuts to the post and our strong national defense.

She has also been active in cultivating stronger ties with the government and people of Canada, including those in communities along the longest portion of shared boundary between New York State and the boundaries of the Provinces of Ontario and Quebec, in the 48th Senate District, to promote better economic opportunity and friendship.

Prior to her election to the Senate, Senator Ritchie served as St. Lawrence County Clerk for over a decade. As County Clerk, she made the County Clerk's Office more accessible and user-friendly for residents of her sprawling county; and established four local DMV offices that eliminated long lines, improved efficiency, and increased revenue for the county. She graduated from Mater Dei College and SUNY Potsdam, and lives in Oswegatchie with her husband. They have three children and three grandchildren.

## GUSTAVO RIVERA (D-WF)
*33rd - Part of Bronx County*

2432 Grand Concourse, Suite 506, Bronx, NY 10458
718-933-2034/grivera@nysenate.gov

Capitol Building, 172 State Street, Room 502C, Albany, NY 12247
518-455-3395

In 2010, Gustavo Rivera was elected to the New York State Senate. His district, from Northwest Bronx to parts of the East Bronx, includes Kingsbridge Heights, East Tremont, Crotona Park, Fordham, Belmont, Van Nest, Claremont, Mount Hope, and Morris Park. Rivera is Chair of the Health Committee; Co-chair of the Joint Senate Task Force on Opioids, Addiction & Overdose Prevention; and sits on the following standing Committees: Alcoholism and Substance Abuse; Crime Victims, Crime and Correction; Finance; Higher Education; Housing, Construction and Community Developmet; Mental Health; and State-Native American Relations.

Since taking office, Senator Rivera has focused his efforts on addressing issues of health inequity both legislatively and on the ground. In 2011, he launched the Bronx CAN (Changing Attitudes Now) Health Initiative. The goal of this community-oriented health initiative is not only to encourage Bronx residents to develop healthy behaviors, but to shape policies that will help tear down some of the institutional barriers that stand in the way of Bronxites having a healthier lifestyle.

In 2018, his passion to improve the health of New Yorkers lead Majority Leader Andrea Stewart-Cousins to appoint Senator Rivera as the Chair of the New York State Senate's Health Committee. As the Chair, Senator Rivera's goal is to collaborate with his colleagues, stakeholders, and constituents to improve health outcomes, increase access to coverage, and ensure a financially viable system for the 20 million New Yorkers he proudly serves.

Prior to his appointment to Chair, Senator Rivera served as the Ranking Member of the Senate Health Committee for six years. As a sitting member of the committee, Senator Rivera passed three laws to ban smoking around schools, afterschools, and libraries, and has been a champion of public health and harm reduction policies. In March 2017, he became the main sponsor of the "New York Health Act," an innovative bill to create a single payer health system in New York State.

Previously, Senator Rivera served as the Ranking Member of the Crime Victims, Crime and Corrections Committee. During that time, he introduced and passed legislation to allow charitable organizations throughout the state to post bail bonds for individuals who cannot afford to do so themselves and was able to secure the transfer of the Fulton Correctional Facility to the Osborne Association to be converted into a comprehensive reentry center during the 2013-2014 State Budget.

Senator Rivera has also championed and empowered Latino communities across New York State and the United States. In 2018, the National Association of Latino Elected and Appointed Officials (NALEO) elected Senator Rivera to serve an initial three-year term on the nonpartisan organization's 35-member Board of Directors. NALEO'S mission looks to foster civic engagement in Latino communities, increase the effectiveness of Latino policymakers, and promote policies that advance Latino political engagement. For over a decade, Senator Rivera has also served as a mentor for the annual Model State Senate program, "Somos El Futuro," sponsored by CUNY, SUNY, the NY State Assembly, and the Puerto Rican Hispanic Task Force.

Prior to becoming an elected representative, Gustavo worked as a community organizer for several local and state candidates including Jose Marcos Serrano and Andrea Stewart-Cousins' campaigns for State Senate, as well as Fernando Ferrer's 2001 campaign for Mayor of New York City. In early 2008, SEIU hired him to manage their activities on behalf of then-presidential candidate Barack Obama in several crucial primary states. Rivera traveled to Indiana, Pennsylvania, Virginia, Texas, and his home of Puerto Rico on behalf of Senator Obama. Gustavo was then tapped by Senator Obama to serve as his Constituency Director in the crucial swing state of Florida. He has also been Director of Community Outreach for US Senator Kirsten Gillibrand.

Rivera was an adjunct professor at Pace University and Hunter College, and a former community organizer for candidates running for state senate and the NYC mayor's seats. The Santurce, Puerto Rico-born Rivera graduated from the University of Puerto Rico. He came to New York to attend a doctoral program at the CUNY's Graduate Center. A proud Bronxite, he has lived in Kingsbridge Heights for almost 20 years.

## SEAN M. RYAN (D)
*60th - Parts of Buffalo, Tonawanda, Brant, Evans, Grand Island, Hamburg, Orchard Park, Tonawanda*

60 Lakefront Boulevard, Suite 125, Buffalo, NY 14202
716-854-8705/ryan@nysenate.gov

188 State Street, Legislative Office Building, Room 817, Albany, NY 12247
518-455-3240

Sean M. Ryan was elected to the New York State Senate in 2020, and previously served in the New York State Assembly from 2011 to 2020. In the New York Senate he is Chair of the Libraries Committee; he also serves on the following Committees: Commerce, Economic Development and Small Business; Crime Victims, Crime and Correction; Education; Health; Housing; Construction and Community Development; and Labor.

Ryan grew up in Lackawanna, learning the value of hard work from his firefighter father and teacher mother. Western New York is his home, and Western New York values are a part of who he is. As a kid, he was taught that if you worked hard you will be secure, you will have a place in the economy, and you can live the American dream. During his senior year in high school, that abruptly came to an end as Bethlehem Steel closed down. Thousands lost their jobs, and family, friends, and neighbors were all displaced in the economy. For generations, Western New York struggled to get back on its feet. In the State Assembly, Ryan worked to transform the Western New York economy during his time in office. He learned the lessons of Bethlehem Steel and used those lessons to guide his work to create progress for Buffalo and Western New York.

Senator Ryan is a graduate of SUNY College at Fredonia and Brooklyn Law School and his broad legal experience includes work for Neighborhood Legal Services, a private law practice collaboration with the Learning Disabilities Association of WNY concentrating on the rights of disabled students, and the Legal Aide Bureau of Buffalo. His legal career highlights include a record award for a victim of housing discrimination, a successful challenge to a school district's denial of special education services to children enrolled in parochial schools, and an action to compel enforcement of Buffalo's Living Wage Ordinance.

In 2008, Ryan began working with People United for Sustainable Housing, Inc. to create a nonprofit development entity called the Buffalo Neighborhood Stabilization Company, Inc. (BNSC). He served as the Executive Director and General Counsel of BNSC and worked to create a redevelopment plan for a section of the West Side of Buffalo.

As an Assemblyman, he championed many different issues including creating a fair economy for all, protecting taxpayer dollars, lower taxes for middle-class families and small businesses, increased investment in education, waterfront development, neighborhood redevelopment, and clean air, water, and environmental protection. In the State Senate, Ryan continues his commitment to serve the people of Western New York. Other legislative priorities include broadband and fiber optic services; library and school district petitioning; and prohibiting the exclusion of coverage for damages or losses caused by lead-based paint.

Senator Ryan has served on the Board of Directors and has provided legal representation and guidance to numerous nonprofit organizations including Buffalo Niagara Waterkeeper, Housing Opportunities Made Equal, Autistic Services Inc, Coalition for Economic Justice, and the City of Buffalo's Living Wage Commission. Today, he resides in the City of Buffalo with his wife Catherine Creighton and their two daughters.

## JULIA SALAZAR (D)
*18th - Part of Kings County*

Legislative Office Building, 188 State Street, Room 944, Albany, NY 12247
518-455-2177/salazar@nysenate.gov

212 Evergreen Avenue, Brooklyn, NY 11221
718-573-1726

Julia Salazar represents New York's 18th State Senate District, including the Brooklyn neighborhoods of Bushwick, Cypress Hills, Greenpoint, and Williamsburg, as well as part of Bedford-Stuyvesant, Brownsville, and East New York. Upon her election in 2018, she became the youngest woman to be elected in the history of the New York State Senate. In the Senate, Salazar is Chair of the Crime Victims, Crime and Correction and Women's Issues Committees; she also sits on the following standing Committees: Budget and Revenue; Children and Families; Finance; Health; and Housing, Construction and Community Development. She is also a member of the Legislative Women's Caucus.

Senator Salazar is a strong supporter of tenant rights, criminal justice reform, equal protection for women, and immigration justice. In 2019, Senator Salazar introduced the Comprehensive Contraception Coverage Act

mandating insurance companies' cover all FDA-approved contraceptive drugs, devices, and products for women. Responding to concerns raised by constituents about services provided to victims of domestic violence in the health care system, Senator Salazar introduced bills mandating training for hospital staff regarding domestic violence and guaranteeing victims free and safe transportation home from the hospital. She co-chaired the 2019 NYS Joint Legislative Hearings on Sexual Harassment that led to the enactment of much needed changes to the NYS Human Rights Law.

Salazar is a recognized leader in the fight for tenants' rights and against the power of the New York City real estate lobby. She played a key role in assuring the enactment in 2019 of the strongest legislative protections for tenants in NYS history. This legislation eliminated loopholes making it close to impossible for most working people to afford decent quality housing. Another bill introduced by Senator Salazar, and signed by the Governor provides permanent protections for loft tenants in New York City ending years of uncertainty for thousands previously unprotected by NYS law.

She is committed to ending the harm caused by mass incarceration. In pursuit of this goal, Senator Salazar strongly supported the reforms of pretrial discovery and bail enacted in 2019 and has introduced legislation to decriminalize sex work and to provide judges with greater sentencing discretion. Salazar also cosponsored the historic NYS Dream Act and the "Green Light" bill, granting access to NYS drivers' licenses regardless of immigration status.

Senator Salazar previously worked as a community organizer in the neighborhoods she represents and across New York City. She began her advocacy during her time as a college student at Columbia University, where she advocated for the rights of fellow tenants and service industry workers. She worked for United Auto Workers Local 2110 to support Barnard College adjunct faculty workers in the campaign for their historic first contract. Until her election to the State Senate, Senator Salazar served as a community organizer for Jews for Racial & Economic Justice, working within city- and statewide coalitions to advance criminal legal reform and police accountability legislation.

Salazar is also an active member of the National Association of Latino Elected Officials (NALEO), UAW-NWU Local 1981, and the New York City chapter of the Democratic Socialists of America.

## JAMES SANDERS, JR. (D)
*10th - Parts of Queens County*

142-01 Rockaway Boulevard, South Ozone Park, NY 11436
718-523-3069/sanders@nysenate.gov

1931 Mott Avenue, Suite 305, Far Rockaway, NY 11691
718-327-7017

Legislative Office Building, Room 711, Albany, NY 12247
518-455-3531

James Sanders Jr. was elected to represent the New York State Senate in 2012 to a district that includes South Jamaica, Rochdale Village, Rosedale, Richmond Hill, South Ozone Park, Springfield Gardens and most of the Rockaways. He chairs the Banks Committee, and also sits on the following standing Committees: Civil Service and Pensions; Commerce, Economic Development, and Small Business; Insurance; Procurement and Contracts; Veterans, Home Security, and Military Affairs; Cultural Affairs, Tourism, Parks, and Recreation; and Labor..

In the Senate, Sanders heads the Senate Task Force on Minority and Women-Owned Business Enterprise (MWBE). The Task Force is charged with working to find innovative ways to better encourage and support MWBEs as a valuable part of growing the New York economy. In addition, Sanders is a member of New York City Mayor Bill de Blasio's Advisory Council on MWBEs. The Advisory Council guides policymaking and strategy to aggressively assist the City in reaching its pledge to award more than $16 billion dollars to MWBEs over a 10-year period. It was Sanders, who in his City Council tenure, set the stage as author of MWBE NYC Local Law 1 to help strengthen the MWBE program, and Local Law 129 that established participation goals for MWBEs to help increase the number of certified firms from 700 to over 3,500 program participants, and win over $3 billion dollars in City contracts.

Senator Sanders has been a fierce advocate for working people, families and unions. In his first term in office, he introduced the Fair Wage Act, which would increase the statewide minimum wage to $10.10 per hour, indexed to inflation. The Act would allow municipalities to set their own minimum wage up to $13.13 with the understanding that a one-size-fits-all approach does not work for places like New York City.

Sanders was a key leader in the fight for workers left out of wage increase negotiations to earn higher pay for airport food servers employed by the Port Authority of New York and New Jersey. The Senator was also successful in protecting airport travelers by getting a bill passed to criminalize the use of laser pointers directed toward aircraft. With John F. Kennedy International Airport in the Senator's District, the legislation was critical in ensuring the safety of pilots and passengers, to discourage impairing the visibility of aircraft operators.

Among other several important pieces of legislation he authored and had signed into law include requiring law enforcement agencies to immediately file a report when an adult is reported missing regardless of age, and another requiring the Department of Homeland Security and emergency services to provide recommendations on implementing tornado warning systems in the state.

In addition to his legislative achievements, Senator Sanders provides many services to his constituents including: free legal assistance once a month for veterans, seniors and women; free tax preparation bi-weekly with representatives from the IRS; his Mobile that travels throughout the District to address constituents' questions, concerns, advice and suggestions; Clergy Breakfasts that monthly bring together the faith-based community to learn and receive training on issues important to them and their congregations; grant writing classes to teach local organizations how to obtain funding to start or expand programs that better the District, and employment opportunities including job fairs for residents.

Prior to being elected to the senate, Sanders was a member of the New York City Council for 12 years. He also sat on Queens School Board District 27 for a decade, including seven years as President, having been the first African American who ascended to that post. He also served in the United States Marine Corps for three years, and holds an undergraduate degree from Brooklyn College. Sanders lives in Queens and is the married father of two.

---

## DIANE J. SAVINO (D-IP-WF)
*23rd District - Parts of Kings and Richmond Counties*

36 Richmond Terrace, Suite 112, Staten Island, New York 10301
718-727-9406/Savino@nysenate.gov

2872 W. 15th Street, Brooklyn, NY 11224
718-333-0311

Diane J. Savino was first elected to the New York State Senate in 2004 to represent a district that encompasses the North and East Shore of Staten Island and portions of Southern Brooklyn, including Borough Park, Brighton Beach, Dyker Heights, Gravesend, Coney Island, Bensonhurst, and Sunset Park. She is Chair of the Internet and Technology Committee and has previously served as Chair of the Banks, Labor, Civil Service and Pensions; and Children and Families Committees. Savino is also a member of the following standing Committees: Banks; Civil Service and Pensions; Codes; Finance; Joint Senate Task Force on Opioids, Addiction & Overdose Prevention; Labor; Libraries; and Rules. Senator Savino is a member of the Legislative Women's Caucus and

cofounder of the Independent Democratic Conference and its liaison to the executive branch.

Senator Savino's hard work and influence was evidenced as she championed the Compassionate Care Act through the legislative process despite opposition and a campaign of misinformation. The ACT will allow New Yorkers with serious medical conditions limited access to medical marijuana under the supervision of health care professionals and under strict state regulations.

Savino has authored numerous laws protecting hardworking New Yorkers. Among the laws she has had enacted is the first in the nation Domestic Workers' Bill of Rights, expanding basic worker protection rights to domestic workers; the Prompt Pay Bill, which ensures prompt payment to construction contractors and their employees; Wage Theft Prevention Act, assessing preventative and punitive measures on employers who steal income from their employees; and another national first, the New York State Commercial Goods Transportation Industry Fair Play Act, establishing new standards for determining whether a commercial truck driver is an employee or an independent contractor, helping to further protect workers' rights statewide.

Local initiatives accomplished by Senator Savino include the establishment of a Quiet Zone on the Staten Island Ferry; Access-a-Ride, Railway, Ferry and Express Bus Service Surveys; a Mobile District Office; the annual "Back to School Blasts" to give away free school supplies to students; Veterans' Benefit and Job Fair; Street Games; Soap Box Derbies; Read to Lead literacy programs; Women's Health Events; a series of hearings on the foreclosure and subprime lending crisis; district-wide workshops for seniors on the Medicare prescription drug plan, and statewide hearings on Heroin and Opioid abuse and HPV, the virus and the vaccine. Senator Savino sponsors a wide array of programs in the 23rd District, including the only kosher soup kitchen in New York City, Staten Island's Downtown Drive-In Movies, a mobile mammography unit, as well as a wide variety of programs for at-risk youth and senior citizens.

Professionally, she worked as a caseworker for the New York City's Child Welfare Administration, and she has been active in her local labor union, where she rose through the ranks. She holds a BA from St. John's University and also graduated from Cornell School of Industrial and Labor Relations.

---

## LUIS R. SEPÚLVEDA (D)
*32nd - Part of Bronx County*

900 Roger Place, Bronx, NY 10459
718-991-3161/sepulveda@nysenate.gov

Legislative Office Building, 188 State Street, Room 412, Albany, NY 12247
518-455-2511

Luis R. Sepúlveda was first elected to represent the 32nd Senate District in April 2018. His Bronx district takes in Parkchester, Castle Hill, Soundview, West Farms, Hunts Point, Longwood, Concourse Village, Melrose, Morrisania, Mott Haven, Claremont, East Tremont, Unionport, Westchester Square, Bronx River, and Crotona Park East. In the Senate, he is Chair of the Crime Victims, Crime, and Correction Committee; and sits on the following committees: Banks; Transportation; Mental Health and Development Disabilities; Judiciary; and Investigations and Government Operations. He is also a member of the Latino Caucus, the Black, Puerto Rican, Hispanic, & Asian Legislative Caucus, and the Puerto Rican/Hispanic Task Force.

A staunch advocate for his constituents and the people of the state of New York, Senator Sepúlveda has been a champion of bolstering economic opportunity and social service reforms, especially as they affect middle-class families and the working poor. The Senator has been a leader in criminal justice reform, working to change the culture of distrust between communities of color and the police, and to correct inherent racial biases in the criminal justice system.

As Chair of the Senate Committee on Crimes, Crime Victims, and Corrections, the Senator has been a leader in criminal justice reform, working to change the culture of distrust between communities of color and the police, and to correct inherent racial biases in the justice system. During the 2019 Legislative Session, he oversaw the historic criminal justice reforms in ending cash bail, early discovery, and speedy trial. He continues to lead on legislation supporting rehabilitation and reentry, ending solitary confinement, creating civilian oversight of the state correctional system, and more. Senator Sepúlveda has become a recognized leader in Albany as an advocate for immigrant rights in New York, as the lead sponsor of two of the state's most impactful and historic immigration bills: the NY State Jose Peralta DREAM Act and the Green Light Bill, which respectively expanded access to higher education and driver's licenses for undocumented immigrants.

As a representative of one of lowest income districts in the state and with an unwavering commitment to improving the lives of his constituents, Senator Sepúlveda is deeply engaged in his community and creating opportunities for educational and economic justice. His district office's top priority is to provide reliable, excellent and unrivaled constituent services, on issues including housing, healthcare, immigration, and more. He regularly hosts free workshops, job fairs, and college fairs in the community

Senator Sepúlveda has continuously advocated for increased funding for community health and mental health services. His efforts to raise the visibility among legislators and key opinion leaders of the alarming suicide rate in the Latina teen population proved fruitful most recently when Governor Cuomo announced the formation of the New York State Suicide Prevention Task Force. The Senator also worked closely with Mayor de Blasio in 2014 to secure funding for universal pre-kindergarten in New York City.

He previously served for three terms as the New York State Assemblyman for the 87th Assembly District, covering Parkchester, Castle Hill, West Farms, Van Nest, and Park Stratton. His efforts as Assembly member included sponsoring a bill to create a board to review civilian deaths and near-deaths involving police officers, a bill requiring videotaping of all engagements between uniformed officers and individuals in the community, and advocating for Raise the Age legislation to prevent 16- and 17-year-olds from being charged as adults. He also supported raising penalties for those who commit gun violence against children on school property or at playgrounds, and he backed increased penalties for child sexual abusers.

As a member of the Assembly Corrections Committee, he was honored to serve as Chair of the Subcommittee on Transitional Services, the focal point for legislation to best prepare prison inmates for reentry to the community, prevent recidivism, enhance public safety, and provide the support network and training to help former prisoners become self-sufficient, responsible community members. His legislation signed into law by Governor Andrew Cuomo in October 2015 addressed the critical problem of Friday release dates for parolees, which prevented their all-important next day meetings with parole officers. The new law effectively moves release dates to Thursdays, ensuring, from day one that a parolee be on a steady course when returning to the community.

Sepúlveda has also sought economic justice, including reinstating the New York State Lottery scholarship program, seeking alternatives to financially crippling college student debt; raising the minimum wage to $15 per hour; and providing for paid family leave to help the struggling working class. He has boosted local economic development by hosting a series of workshops for local small business owners, as well as a number of job fairs that drew large numbers of job seekers and employers.

Senator Sepúlveda also supports diversity in the state workforce; fighting gun violence by providing more mental health services and training for teachers; allowing for the recall of public officials; driver's licenses for

immigrants; offering Halal food options during school lunch; expanding voting protections to prevent voting roll purges; and expanding the use of email for important voter information, such as changes in polling sites. As a recognized leader in Albany of efforts to protect privacy, he has introduced legislation to regulate the use of drones by law enforcement agencies and to prevent the unfettered access by government agencies to so-called metadata containing sensitive personal information that should normally be strictly safeguarded.

For his legislative and community service efforts, he has received a number of government, community, and educational awards. Senator Sepúlveda earned his bachelor's from Hofstra University and his law degree from Hofstra's Maurice A. Deane School of Law.

## SUE SERINO (R-C-IP)
*41st - Dutchess County*

117 Town Park Lane, 1st Floor, Putnam Valley, NY 10579
845-528-0417/Serino@nysenate.gov

4254 Albany Post Road, Hyde Park, NY 12538
845-229-0106

Legislative Office Building, 188 State Street, Room 513, Albany, NY 12247
518-455-2945

Susan J. Serino was elected to the New York State Senate in 2014 and is Ranking Member of the Aging and Cultural Affairs, Tourism, Parks and Recreation Committees and she sits on the following standing Committees: Children and Families; Finance; Insurance; Judiciary; Libraries; Social Services; and Transportation. In addition, she is a member of the Legislative Women's Caucus.

Her previous public service was as a member of the Hyde Park Town Board for a year, and then the Dutchess County Legislature where she advocated on behalf of holding the line on taxes and fees. She operates a Hyde Park-based real estate business. She is mother to one.

## JOSÉ M. SERRANO (D-WF)
*29th - Parts of Bronx and New York Counties*

1916 Park Avenue, Suite 202, New York, NY 10037
212-828-5829/serrano@nysenate.gov

Capitol Building, 172 State Street, Room 420C, Albany, NY 12247
518-455-2795

Senator Jose M. Serrano was first elected to the New York State Senate in 2004 and represents the 29th Senate District which includes neighborhoods in the South and West Bronx, East Harlem, Upper Yorkville, Roosevelt Island, Central Park, and the Upper West Side. He is Chair of the Senate Democratic Conference and serves as the Ranking Member of the Committee on Cultural Affairs, Tourism, Parks and Recreation. He also sits on the following Committees: Aging; Environmental Conservation; Social Services; Women's Issues; and Veterans, Homeland Security and Military Affairs.

In Albany, Senator Serrano has introduced a wide variety of bills championing the arts, keeping housing affordable, protecting public health, fostering economic development, defending immigrant rights, closing the income inequality gap and preserving the environment. Among Serrano's legislation passed by the State Senate are: one to mandate the New York State Department of Health to conduct an intensive study on the alarmingly high asthma rates in the Bronx; another requiring the Department of Environmental Conservation to publish a list of areas in the state that are most adversely affected by existing environmental hazards, so that areas that have already been impacted by contamination do not become victims of further environmental damage; and another to incentivize affordable development on vacant properties in Northern Manhattan. During the 2008 to 2009 legislative term, the State Senate passed a Serrano bill making "I Love New York" the official state slogan.

Throughout the 2010 budget negotiations, as Chair of the committee, Senator Serrano led the fight against the closure of New York State Parks and, along with parks advocates, succeeded in keeping State Parks open to the public. Serrano has also been a champion for openness and transparency in government. He led an initiative to improve the tracking of state stimulus funding; launched "Open Legislation," a search engine that allows individuals to search, navigate, share and comment on all Senate Legislation; and in 2009, while in the Senate Majority, he introduced a bill to reform the Legislature's member item system by making it fair, equitable, and transparent.

An avid enthusiast of the great outdoors, Serrano continues to advocate for various initiatives to engage New Yorkers in preserving and beautifying our state and city parks, such as I Love My Park Day and Earth Hour. Earth Hour is a Senate resolution sponsored by Serrano each year to actively encourage all New Yorkers to participate and create awareness for New York State's abundance of natural resources.

As a longtime supporter of the arts, Senator Serrano has consistently called for more arts and music education in our schools, with a firm understanding of the proven beneficial effect of the arts on overall academics. In addition, Serrano is a firm believer that local arts organizations add to our cultural fabric and act as an economic engine for communities throughout New York State.

The Senator is also a vocal defender of immigrant rights, appearing on national television and local media outlets. Serrano, along with many of his colleagues, launched the "East Harlem Against Deportation" coalition. The initiative aimed to stop unjust deportations that destroy families in New York, and developed a comprehensive report with multiple policy recommendations to protect immigrant communities on a City and State level.

Prior to his election to the Senate, Serrano was a member of Community Board 4 in the Bronx, Chairman of the Board for the Institute for Urban Family Health, and, in 2001, he was elected to the New York City Council, where he chaired the Committee on Cultural Affairs. Serrano holds a BA from Manhattan College and lives with his wife and two children in the South Bronx.

## JAMES SKOUFIS (D)
*39th - Parts of Orange, Ulster, and Rockland Counties*

47 Grand Street, Newburgh, NY 12550
845-567-1270
845-567-1270/skoufis@nysenate.gov

Legislative Office Building, 188 State Street, Room 815, Albany, NY 12247
518-455-3290

55 W. Railroad Avenue, Suilgin 24, Suite A2, Garnerville, NY 10923
845-786-6710

James Skoufis was elected in 2018 to represent the 39th District. In the Senate, Skoufis is Chair of the Investigations and Government Operations Committee and is a member of the following standing Committees: Corporations, Authorities, and Commissions; Finance; Judiciary; Labor; and Transportation.

Skoufis and his family moved to the Town of Woodbury from Queens in 1995 for a better quality of life, an education that strives for nothing short of excellence, and a strong, friendly, and caring community.

After graduating from Monroe-Woodbury High School, he went on to become the first in his immediate family to attend college. He earned a bachelor's degree from George Washington University and a master's degree from Columbia University. Along with the fortunate help of

scholarships and student loans, he worked his way through studies, holding a job every semester while in college.

Having spent the first many years of his life in New York City Public Housing and being only one generation removed from food stamps, James knows what it means to struggle. He knows what it means to live paycheck to paycheck or worse.

As a former State Assemblyman for six years, Skoufis fought for the Hudson Valley's working- and middle-classes who are often overlooked by government. He's been a champion of better schools, stronger infrastructure, and leveling the playing field. Prior to his election to the Assembly, Skoufis sat on the Woodbury Town Council, where he led the local relief effort for those impacted by Hurricane Irene. He also worked as a Project Manager for Amerigard Alarm and Security Corporation. Senator Skoufis lives in Cornwall with his wife, Hillary.

## TOBY ANN STAVISKY (D)
*16th - Part of Queens County*

142-29 37th Avenue, Suite 1, Flushing, NY 11354
718-445-0004/stavisky@nysenate.gov.

Legislative Office Building, 188 State Street, Room 913, Albany, NY 12247
518-455-3461

Toby Ann Stavisky was first elected to the Senate in 1999 and is the first woman from Queens County elected to the State Senate and the first woman to chair the Senate Committee on Higher Education. Currently, Stavisky is the Ranking Minority Member and Chair of the Higher Education Committee, and also sits on the following Committees: Education; Ethics and Internal Governance; Finance; Health; Judiciary; and Racing, Gaming and Wagering. She is Leader for Conference Operations; Vice Chair of the Democratic Conference; Treasurer of the Legislative Women's Caucus; and previously served as Assistant Minority Whip. Prior to entering public life, Stavisky worked in the actuarial department of a major insurance company and taught social studies in the New York City high schools, and served as District Manager in Northeast Queens for the US Census.

As a result of her involvement with issues such as better schools, programs for older adults, social justice, opportunities for New Americans, and assisting small business, the Senator has been honored by many organizations. These include the Taiwanese Association, the Korean American Association of Queens and the Forest Hills Volunteer Ambulance Corps. For her "dedicated service to seniors across Queens," Senator Stavisky was presented with the Rose Kryzak Legislative Award from the Queens Interagency Council on the Aging. The New York Branch of the NAACP honored her contributions toward furthering "freedom and human dignity." The Senator is proud to have been honored twice by the Flushing Chinese Business Association and in 2016 by the University Student Senate of CUNY. In June, 2016, at the Queensborough Community College commencement, she was awarded the Presidential Medal for her "exceptional and longstanding commitment to public higher education." She holds an undergraduate degree from Syracuse University, and two MA degrees, one from Hunter College, and one from Queens College. Senator Stavisky lives in Forest Hills.

## DANIEL G. STEC (R)
*45th - Clinton, Essex, Franklin, Warren and parts of St. Lawrence and Washington Counties*

5 Warren Street, Suite 3, Glens Falls, NY 12801
518-743-0968

188 State Street, Legislative Office Building, Room 711B, Albany, NY 12247
518-455-2811

On November 3, 2020, Senator Daniel Stec was elected State Senator. He is a Ranking Member of the Children and Families and Environmental Committees. Stec also serves on the following Senate Committees: Banks; Education; Health; and Libraries.

Senator Stec is a North Country native, Navy veteran, husband, and father. After serving our nation for eight years in the U.S. Navy's nuclear power program, he ran for town council in Queensbury. Stec was then elected Town Supervisor for five terms and chairman of the Warren County Board of Supervisors for two terms.

In 2012, he was elected to the New York State Assembly where he championed a state constitutional amendment to strip corrupt politicians of their public pensions. Stec was also instrumental in the passage of three constitutional amendments important to Adirondack communities.

Senator Stec now puts his passion for public service to work for our families and businesses by fighting for better broadband and cell service, supporting our upstate schools and hospitals, and proposing initiatives to help our economy recover from the pandemic.

### ANDREA STEWART-COUSINS (D-IP-WF)
*35th - Part of Westchester County*

28 Wells Avenue, Building 3, Yonkers, NY 10701
914-423-4031/scousins@nysenate.gov

250 Broadway, Room 1930, New York, NY 10007
212-298-5585

Legislative Office Building, Room 907, Albany, NY 12247
518-455-2585

Andrea Stewart-Cousins was first elected to the New York State Senate in 2006 and her district includes Greenburgh, and parts of White Plains, New Rochelle, Yonkers, and Scarsdale. She is the Leader of the Senate Democratic Conference, becoming the state's first female leader of a legislative conference and Chair of the Rules Committee. Stewart-Cousins is also a member of the Conference of Black Senators and the Legislative Women's Caucus. Majority Leader Stewart-Cousins oversaw the passage of historic and transformative legislation on issues including voting reforms, gun safety, women's rights and health care, immigration and DREAMers, the LGBTQ community, the justice system, and sexual harassment in the workplace. Additionally, the Senate Majority under her leadership passed the most comprehensive and aggressive climate change legislation in the nation, and the strongest tenant protections and affordable housing package in state history.

Her legislative achievements include sponsoring and passing the Government Reorganization and Citizen Empowerment Act, which empowers communities to consolidate local governments, which reduces overlap of municipal services and saves taxpayer dollars. She also sponsored and passed Jimmy Nolan's law in 2009, which extends the time by which 9/11 responders can file compensation claims for injuries sustained from the World Trade Center rescue, recovery or cleanup operations. Finally, she sponsored and passed the Child Health Plus and School Meal Enrollment Coordination Law, the 2010 law that allows families to use their proof of eligibility for Free or Reduced-Price School Meal Programs as proof of income to enroll their child in Medicaid and Child Health Plus.

Stewart-Cousins previously served as Westchester County Legislator, and the first African American Director of Community Affairs for the City of Yonkers. In addition, she developed the Just About Me (JAM) Program in conjunction with the Yonkers Municipal Housing Authority; the Mary J. Blige Center for Women; and Operation SNUG, which is "guns" spelled backwards. This frontline antigun and gang violence prevention efforts helps local law enforcement. Stewart-Cousins has received numerous citations and awards from organization, including the American Cancer Society, the ACLU, and National Association of Social Workers. She holds a BS from Pace University, earned her teach-

ing credentials from Lehman College, and holds a MPA from Pace University. She is the widowed mother of three and grandmother of four.

### JAMES TEDISCO (R-C)
*49th - Parts of Saratoga, Schenectady and Herkimer Counties, Fulton County, Hamilton County*

636 Plank Road, 2nd Floor, Clifton Park, NY 12065-2046
518-885-1829//tedisco@nysenate.gov

Legislative Office Building, Room 515, Albany, NY 12247
518-455-2181/(fax) 518-426-6821

223 W. Main Street, Room B2, Johnstown, NY 12095
@Bio Text = After graduating from Bishop Gibbons High School in 1968, James Tedisco earned a bachelor's degree in psychology from Union College and a graduate degree in special education from the College of Saint Rose. From 1973 to 1982, he worked as an educator, first as a Guidance Counselor, Varsity Basketball Coach, and Athletic Director at Notre Dame-Bishop Gibbons High School in Schenectady, then as a special education teacher, resource room instructor, and varsity basketball coach at Bethlehem Central High School in Delmar. He entered public service in 1977 when, at the age of twenty-seven, he was elected as the youngest city councilman in Schenectady at that time. Before election to the State Senate, he served in the New York State Assembly from 1983 to 2016, where he was minority leader from 2005 to 2009. His focus in the Assembly was reforming state government and the state's budget process, and he sponsored numerous bills designed to make the government more accountable and bring about an on-time, fiscally responsible budget.

Tedisco serves as Ranking Member of the Education and Mental Health Committees. He also sits on the following standing Committees: Banks; Commerce, Economic Development and Small Business; Consumer Protection; Finance; and New York City Education. As the author of the first property tax cap bill, the Property Taxpayers Protection Act, Tedisco ushered in and helped pass the tax cap to finally put a lid on out-of-control property tax hikes. To date, the tax cap has saved New Yorkers $15.3 billion and Senate District 49 taxpayers $344.5 billion.

Realizing that animal cruelty is a bridge crime and those who abuse animals often go on to hurt people, Tedisco was the driving force behind passage of the landmark Buster's Law to protect our pets by making animal cruelty a felony.

Senator Tedisco is a longtime advocate on issues related to missing persons and serves as emcee and legislative sponsor for the annual New York State Missing Persons Day with the Lyall Family and the Center for Hope. As former Chair of the Assembly Minority Task Force on Missing Children, Tedisco authored and passed a landmark noncustodial release law to protect children from being abducted. Tedisco initiated a program to place the pictures of missing children on Thruway toll tickets, enabling New York to become the first state in the nation to use its transportation system to find missing persons. He is the author of a 1996 book, *Missing Children: A Psychological Approach to Understanding the Causes and Consequences of Stranger and Non-Stranger Abduction of Children*. He is a resident of Glenville, where he lives with his wife, Mary, and son Andrew.

### KEVIN THOMAS (D)
*6th - Part of Nassau County*

900 Stewart Avenue, Suite LL45A, Garden City, NY 11530
516-739-1700/thomas@nysenate.gov

Legislative Office Building, Room 947, Albany, NY 12247
518-455-3260

Kevin Thomas represents the 6th District (Mid-Nassau) in the New York State Senate. In the Senate, he is Chair and Ranking Member of the Consumer Protection Committee and sits on the following standing Committees: Aging; Banks; Finance; Health; Internet and Technology; Judiciary and Local Government. As Chairman of the Consumer Protection Committee, Senator Thomas has been the driving force behind several groundbreaking efforts to strengthen consumer protections and safeguards, including the New York Privacy Act, which aims to make New York the national leader in consumer data protection. In the Senate, he has successfully championed legislation to protect consumers' private information from exploitation, expand economic opportunities for Long Island families, and combat the growing student loan debt crisis.

Senator Thomas is a civil rights attorney, who worked on high profile cases in his career before entering politics. He immigrated to the United States at the age of 10. He is now the first Indian American to be elected as State Senator in New York. He lives in Levittown with his wife and daughter.

## ALEXIS WEIK (R-C)
*3rd - Part of Suffolk County*

90-B W. Main Street, Patchogue, NY 11772
631-360-3356/weik@nysenate.gov

188 State Street, Legislative Office Building, Room 413, Albany, NY 12247
518-455-2950

Alexis Weik was elected on November 3, 2020 to represent the 3rd Senate District. She is a Ranking Member of two Committees: Budget and Revenue; and Social Services. In addition, she sits on the following Committees: Civil Service and Pensions; Education; Veterans, Homeland Security and Military Affairs; and Women's Issues.

A lifelong resident of Suffolk County, Alexis was raised in Ronkonkoma and Oakdale, graduated from Connetquot High School, and earned degrees from Dowling College and Farmingdale State College.

Weik served as receiver of taxes for the Town of Islip from 2011 to 2020. As receiver, she made customer service her top priority, embracing a hands-on approach to assist taxpayers, streamline operations, and improve the office's efficiency.

Senator Weik is a member of a law enforcement family—both her husband and oldest son are sworn police officers. She was honored to be supported in her successful campaign for Senate by an unprecedented coalition of law enforcement organizations from across New York State and, as Senator, she has pledged to make public safety a top priority, helping to ensure safe communities where families can thrive.

Weik is a former small business owner who is a strong advocate for small businesses, and will work to find ways to relieve the tax burden on hardworking New Yorkers. Senator Weik lives with her husband in Sayville, on Long Island's South Shore. The couple has three children.

## NEW YORK STATE ASSEMBLY

### PETER J. ABBATE, JR. (D)
*49th - Part of Kings County*

6605 Fort Hamilton Parkway, Brooklyn, NY 11219
718-236-1764/abbatep@nyassembly.gov

Legislative Office Building, Room 839, Albany, NY 12248
518-455-305

Peter Abbate was first elected to the New York State Assembly in 1986. His district includes Dyker Heights, Bath Beach, Bensonhurst, and Borough Park in Brooklyn. He is currently the Chairman of the Assembly Committee on Governmental Employees, a position he was elevated to in 2002 after serving as Chairman of the Committee on Real Property Taxation and the Committee on Cities. Additionally, he is the Chairman of the Subcommittee on Safety in the Workplace, a member of the Assembly Workers' Compensation Task Force and a member of the Distressed Cities Task Force. He is Treasurer of the New York Conference of Italian American State Legislators. His standing Committee assignments are Aging, Banks, Consumer Affairs and Protection and Labor. Abbate has sponsored legislation creating a wide range of laws, including laws to stop unscrupulous prize award schemes by providing for mandatory disclosure, requiring that school bus lights be illuminated while students are being transported, and allowing civil servants union representation during investigation reviews. In addition, he is responsible for a number of laws relating to real taxes, including one to allow a property tax exemption for improvements made to comply with the Americans with Disabilities Act. Representative Abbate worked as a Legislative Assistant to then-Assemblyman Stephen J. Solarz; when Solarz was elected to Congress Abbate became his district representative.

He has been active in community groups such as Heartshare of Brooklyn and Queens; the Civitan Club of Brooklyn, the Boy Scouts of America, the Kiwanis Club of 18th Avenue, the Statewide Homeowners and Tenants Association, and the Guild for Exceptional Children. Abbate has received numerous awards from a range of community groups, including Man of the Year by the Federation of Italian American Organizations of Brooklyn and the Council of Neighborhood Organizations. The lifelong resident of Bensonhurst earned an undergraduate degree in political science from St. John's University.

### THOMAS J. ABINANTI (D)
*92nd - Parts of Westchester and New York Counties*

303 S. Broadway, Suite 229, Tarrytown, NY 10591
914-631-1605/abinanti@nyassembly.gov

Legislative Office Building, Room 731, Albany, NY 12248
518-455-5753

Thomas J. Abinanti was first elected to the New York State Assembly in 2010. His District includes the Towns of Greenburgh and Mount Pleasant. He is Chair of the People with Disabilities Committee, and is a member of the following committees: Codes; Environmental Conservation; Health; and Judiciary. Prior to his election to the Assembly, Abinanti spent ten terms in the Westchester County Legislature where he served three times as Majority Leader. He was instrumental in establishing the Westchester Medical Center as an independent public benefit corporation. In addition, Abinanti sat on the Greenburgh Town Council for two terms. Prior to his election, he worked as Legislative Counsel to Congresswoman Nita Lowey and as Staff Counsel to the New York State Assembly. He served as Prosecuting Attorney for the Villages of Ardsley and Dobbs Ferry, and at Pace Law School and Mercy College of Dobbs Ferry. He also represented the Greenburgh Housing Authority and served as Pro Bono Attorney for the Westchester Coalition for Legal Abortion. Abinanti received a BA from Fordham College and his JD from New York University School of Law. He is married and has two children.

### KHALEEL ANDERSON (D)
*31st - Part of Queens County*

19-31 Mott Avenue, Room 301, Far Rockaway, NY 11691
718-327-845/andersonk@nyassembly.gov

131-17 Rockaway Boulevard, South Ozone Park, NY 11420
718-322-4958

Assembly Member Khaleel Anderson was elected to serve Assembly District 31 in Queens for his first term in November 2020. He represents parts of Arverne, Brookville, Far Rockaway, Hammels, Rosedale, South Ozone Park, South Richmond Hill, Springfield Gardens and John F. Kennedy International Airport. In the Assembly, he is Chair of the Subcommittee on Banking in Underserved Communities and a member of the following Committees: Banks; Children and Families; Energy; Insurance; and People with Disabilities.

Anderson began his young career as a community organizer at the age of 13 and has since been dedicated to leadership, service, and advocacy. In 2011, he was an organizer for a local nonprofit that trains cohorts of youth in civic engagement. He was the youngest member of Queens Community Board 14 and his local Police Precinct Council during his tenure. Anderson's hard work, leadership, and dedication to his community has earned him recognition from Governor Andrew M. Cuomo, Congressman Gregory Meeks, and other state and local elected officials.

Assembly Member Anderson is a leading voice in addressing issues of food insecurity, disaster preparedness, housing, transportation, and healthcare planning in District 31. Prior to his election, he demonstrated his ability to govern while serving as a student activist and a respected community activist. He worked to build a half-acre urban farm that provides fresh produce, workshops, trainings on healthy eating, and employment opportunities for young people. He remains committed to amplifying the unique voices of young people and all his constituents.

Khaleel Anderson was born in Brooklyn and raised in the Rockaways. He graduated Queens College with a BA and is finalizing an MA in urban affairs, with a minor in cities and social medicine. He currently works as a supplemental instructor for the Percy E. Sutton Search for Education, Elevation, and Knowledge (SEEK) Program at Queens College.

As a new member of the legislative body, his priorities include housing and healthcare justice, criminal justice reform, educational equity, transportation equity, and environmental justice. Assembly Member Anderson is the youngest Black Assembly Member in New York State history. He lives in Far Rockaway, New York.

### JOE ANGELINO (R)
*122nd - Parts of Broome, Chenango, Delaware, and Ortega Counties*

Kattelville Road, Suite 1, Binghamton, NY 13901
607-648-6080/angelinoj@nyassembly.gov

Legislative Office Building, Room 549, Albany, NY 12248
518-455-5741

Joseph Angelino was elected to the New York State Assembly on November 3, 2020. His district is comprised of parts of Delaware, Broome, Chenango, and Otsego counties. As an Assemblyman, he works to protect the interests of New York's incredible law enforcement agents, ensure veterans have every opportunity to thrive upon returning from service, and fight for the state's struggling middle class. In the Assembly, he is a member of the following Committees: Banks; Corporation, Authorities and Commissions; Oversight, Analysis and Investigation; People with Disabilities; and Tourism, Parks, Arts and Sports Development.

Angelino is a lifelong resident of Central New York. From a young age, his parents taught him the value of honesty, hard work, and compassion toward others. These traits helped him to become an exceptional police officer, a police sergeant, and ultimately, Chief of Police of the Norwich Police Department for nearly 20 years.

While serving as the Chief of Police, Joseph was tapped to simultaneously act as the city's Fire Chief, thus making him responsible for more than half of the city's budget and personnel from 2006 to 2008. During a leave of absence from the Norwich Police, Angelino enlisted in the United States Marine Corps in 1985. It was in the Marines that his natural leadership abilities catapulted him upward through the ranks. A three-time combat veteran over two wars, he served as a tank commander in Desert Storm and an infantry 1st sergeant during the Iraq Invasion in 2003, and again in 2005, for which he received two Purple Heart medals. Angelino retired from the Marine reserves as a sergeant major, the highest enlisted rank, in 2008.

Angelino is active in a number of other activities outside of his public service. These include serving as Board Member and Past President of the Northeast Classic Car Museum and sitting on the Norwich Housing Authority. In addition to his service medals, he has also been awarded the Chenango County Bar Association Liberty Bell Award and the Distinguished Citizen Award for Chenango County. Assemblyman Angelino is married to Kendall Saber and they reside in Norwich.

## JAKE ASHBY (R-C-I)
*107th - Parts of Rensselaer, Columbia, and Washington Counties*

594 Columbus Turnpike, East Greenbush, NY 10261
518-272-6149/ashbyj@nyassembly.gov

Legislative Office Building, Room 402, Albany, NY 12248
518-455-5777

Jake Ashby was elected to the New York State Assembly on April 24, 2018. His district is comprised of parts of Rensselaer, Columbia, and Washington counties. In the Assembly he sits on the following committees: Aging; Ethics and Guidance; Health; Racing and Wagering; Veterans' Affairs; and Ways and Means.

As an Assemblyman, Ashby fights to roll back the SAFE Act and oppose future infringements of the Second Amendment. As a veteran, he is a strong voice for the men and women who serve our country and identify strategies with local government and businesses that will help provide the best care, support, and opportunities for service members returning home. He believes in the need to improve infrastructure in our communities including water issues. He also is committed to restoring public trust in state government and stimulating economic growth by reducing onerous rules and regulations burdening small businesses.

Ashby served with the US Army Reserves for eight years, rising to the rank of Captain. He completed combat tours in Iraq and Afghanistan, and a humanitarian mission in Africa. During his service career he earned two Bronze Star Medals, the Army Commendation Medal, and the Combat Action Badge. Before his election he worked as an Occupational Therapist and Rehabilitation Director for the last 15 years and started his own community-based practice in 2014. Ashby also previously served as a Rensselaer County Legislator.

He is the past Commander of VFW Post 7337 and is a member of the Nassau Sportsmen's Club. Assemblyman Ashby works as an Instructor at Maria College in the Occupational Therapy Assistant Department and resides in Castleton with his wife, Kristy, and their two children.

## JEFFRION L. AUBRY (D-L)
*35th - Part of Queens County*

98-09 Northern Boulevard, Corona, NY 11368
718-457-3615/AubryJ@nyassembly.gov

Legislative Office Building, Room 646, Albany, NY 12248
518-455-4561

Jeffrion Aubry was first elected to the New York State Assembly in 1992. Assemblyman Aubry is the New York State Speaker Pro Tempore, and is a member of the following Committees: Ways and Means; Rules;

Social Services; and Governmental Employees. In addition he is a member of the Black, Puerto Rican, Hispanic & Asian Legislative Caucus and the Puerto Rican/Hispanic Task Force. Assemblyman Aubry is a member of the Council of State Governments and is a Toll Fellow, a distinguished association of state legislators from across the country. His legislative achievements include backing a 2009 measure that that significantly reformed the Rockefeller Drug Laws in New York State by returning discretion to judges to sentence drug-addicted offenders to treatment as an alternative to prison. He also led the fight to ensure that prisoners suffering from serious mental illness receive needed treatment, and are not confined under inhumane conditions through the enactment of the Special Housing Unit Exclusion Law.

Professionally, Assemblyman Aubrey has been the Director of Economic Development for the Borough President's Office of Queens, Executive Director of Elmcor Youth and Adult Activities, and Director of the North Shore Fair Housing Center; Queens representative to the Economic Development Corporation of the City of New York; and Chairman of the Small Business Development Center's Advisory Board at York College. He has received numerous awards, including Award for Outstanding Legislative Leadership in the Caucus for Justice from the Correctional Association of New York, the Community Leadership Award from the Epilepsy Foundation, the National Alliance on Mental Illness/NYS Legislative Champion Award, and the John R. Dunne Champion of Justice Award from the Prisoner's Legal Services. Aubry holds an undergraduate degree from the College of Santa Fe. He is the married father of five.

## WILLIAM A. BARCLAY (R)
*120th - Parts of Onondaga, Oswego and Jefferson Counties, the cities of Oswego and Fulton*

200 N. Second Street, Fulton, NY 13069
315-598-5185/BarclaW@nyassembly.gov

Legislative Office Building, Room 933, Albany, NY 12248
518-455-3751

William A. Barclay was first elected to the New York State Assembly in 2002. He currently represents the 120th Assembly District, which includes the Oswego County towns of Albion, Amboy, Boylston, Constantia, Granby, Hastings, Mexico, New Haven, Orwell, Palermo, Parish, Redfield, Richland, Sandy Creek, Schroeppel, Scriba, Volney, West Monroe, and Williamstown; the cities of Oswego and Fulton; the Onondaga County town of Lysander; and the Jefferson County town of Ellisburg. He was elected as State Assembly Minority Leader in early 2020 after being the Deputy Minority Leader since 2012. He also sits on the standing Committee on Rules.

He is a partner in the Syracuse law firm of Barclay Damon LLP, specializing in business law, and he serves as a board member of Pathfinder Bank, Countryway Insurance Company, and QMP Enterprises, Inc. Assemblyman Barclay served as a clerk for Judge Roger Miner of the US Court of Appeals, Second Circuit, in Albany and New York City. His civic activity has included membership on the boards of directors for the Friends of the Rosamond Gifford Zoo at Burnet Park, the Everson Museum of Art, and Northern Oswego County Health Services. He is a graduate of St. Lawrence University and Syracuse University College of Law. Assemblyman Barclay represents the eighth generation of his family to live in Pulaski, Oswego County, where he resides with his wife and two sons.

## BRIAN BARNWELL (D)
*30th - Part of Queens County, including Woodside, Maspeth, and parts of Long Island City, Astoria, Sunnyside, and Middle Village*

55-19 69th Street, Maspeth, NY 11378
718-651-3185/BarnwellB@nyassembly.gov

Legislative Office Building, Room 921, Albany, NY 12248
518-455-4755

In the Assembly, Brian Barnwell is Chair on the Commission on State-Local Relations and a member of the following Committees: Aging; Agriculture; Banks; Labor; Real Property Taxation; and Veterans' Affairs; He is also a member of the Asian Pacific American Task Force and the Puerto Rican/Hispanic Task Force.

Assemblyman Barnwell was born in New York City in 1986 to a family of law enforcement officers, nurses, and teachers. An injury prevented him from achieving his first goal, which was to join the armed forces, so instead he attended Arizona State University, where he earned a bachelor's degree in political science, cum laude. Then, as a student at Albany Law School, he worked for two judges, as well as for the Albany County district attorney's office and the Albany Law School Civil Rights and Disabilities Law Clinic. After completing law school, he entered private practice, working as a criminal attorney, before joining the staff of New York City councilman Costa Constantinides, helping organize various community volunteer operations. He continues to organize volunteer groups that work with local churches and with City Harvest to feed the needy. As a legislator he aspires to help seniors and the middle class, as well as veterans, groups that he believes have been taken for granted. Among his specific proposals is a bill that would help struggling seniors remain in their homes by granting a property tax exemption that would increase as the person ages. He also wants to pass bills that would give judges more discretion in sentencing violent criminals and that would prevent New York pet stores from acquiring dogs from puppy mills. Further, he wants to modify the formula used to determine the area median income, or AMI, which is used to peg income requirement for affordable housing in the five boroughs, believing that other counties should be calculated separately. He lives in Woodside in Queens.

## DIDI BARRETT (D-WP)
*106th - Parts of Columbia and Dutchess Counties*

12 Raymond Avenue, Suite 105, Poughkeepsie, NY 12603
845-454-1703/barrettd@nyassembly.gov

751 Warren Street, Hudson, NY 12534
518-828-1961

Legislative Office Building, Room 841, Albany, NY 12248
518-455-5177

Didi Barrett was elected to the New York State Assembly on March 20, 2012. Barrett is Chair of the Committee on Veterans' Affairs and serves as a member on the following committees: Agriculture; Mental Health; Environmental Conservation; and Tourism, Parks, Arts and Sports Development. In addition, she is Chair of the Legislative Women's Caucus and is a member of the Puerto Rican/Hispanic Task Force and the Task Force on Women's Issues.

Barrett has long been active among not-for-profit organizations throughout the Hudson Valley. She helped create and serves on the board of the North East Dutchess Fund (NED) of the Berkshire Taconic Community Foundation, an initiative that focuses on improving life in several towns in northeastern Dutchess County. Additionally, she helped pioneer NED Corps alongside the Dutchess Community Action Partnership and serves on its affiliated Latino Roundtable, working to provide social services to this region's communities that are more rural. She is a member of the board of Sprout Creek Farm, an educational farm, and led the creation of the Dutchess Girls Collaborative to support young women and girls. She is the founding chair of Girls Incorporated of NYC, a former board member of NARAL Pro-Choice New York, and a Trustee Emeritus of the American Folk Art Museum and the Anderson Foundation for Autism. Barrett holds an undergraduate degree in speech communications from UCLA and a MA in folk art studies from NYU. She and her husband have two children.

## CHARLES BARRON (D)
*60 - Part of Kings County*

669 Vermont Street, Brooklyn, NY 11207
718-257-5824/barronc@nyassembly.gov

Legislative Office Building, Room 532, Albany, NY 12248
518-455-5912

Charles Barron was elected to the New York State Assembly in 2014. Assemblyman Barron is Chair of the Subcommittee on Community Integration and sits as a member on the following committees: Aging; Economic Development, Job Creation, Commerce and Industry; Energy; Housing; and Social Services. Barron is also a member of the Black, Puerto Rican, Hispanic & Asian Legislative Caucus. He previously served on the New York City Council for 13 years, where he chaired the Committee on Higher Education and secured funding for parks, schools, and funding for the Black Male Initiative for City University of New York. A community activist for more than 49 years, Assemblyman Barron is a founding member of Operation POWER (People Organizing and Working for Empowerment and Respect), the founding chairperson of the National Black United Front's Harlem Chapter, Chief of Staff to the Chair of the National Black United Front, and Secretary General of African Peoples Christian Organization, operated by Reverend Dr. Herbert Daughtry, Chair of the NBUF. Assemblyman Barron holds an associate's degree from New York Technical College and a BA from Hunter College. He and wife Inez have two adult children and two grandchildren.

## MICHAEL R. BENEDETTO (D)
*82nd - Part of Bronx County*

177 Dreiser Loop, Room 12, Bronx, NY 10475
718-320-2220

3602 E. Tremont Avenue, Suite 201, Bronx, NY 10465
718-892-2235/benedettom@nyassembly.gov

Legislative Office Building, Room 836, Albany, NY 12248
518-455-5296

Michael R. Benedetto was first elected to the New York State Assembly in 2004. He chairs the Committee on Education, and also sits as a member on the following committees: Rules; Labor; and Ways and Means. In addition, Benedetto is a member of the Puerto Rican/Hispanic Task Force; the Subcommittee on Oversight of Minority and Women-Owned Business Enterprises; and the Subcommittee on Retention of Homeownership and Stabilization of Affordable Housing.

As a legislator, Assemblyman Benedetto has focused on educational and child protection issues and has been a strong supporter of union rights. The Bronx native spent 35 years teaching elementary and secondary school students. In 1974, he joined the New York City public school system as a teacher of mentally and physically challenged students; in 1977 he was assigned to PS 160, the Walt Disney School, and in 1988 became coordinator of the special education unit. While with the NYC schools, Assemblyman Benedetto ran the first "very special" Olympics for multiply handicapped children. In addition, he established the Throggs Neck Community Players Community Theater, served as member of Community Planning Board #10, AHEPA, and the Iona College Alumni Board of Directors. Assemblyman Benedetto also started the *Bronx Times Reporter*, which became the largest community paper in the Bronx. He has received numerous awards. He holds an undergraduate degree in history and education from Iona College, and also earned a MA in social studies and education.

## RODNEYSE BICHOTTE HERMELYNN (D)
*42 - Part of King's County*

1312 Flatbush Avenue, Brooklyn, NY 11210
718-940-0428/bichotter@nyassembly.gov

Legislative Office Building, Room 727, Albany, NY 12248
518-455-5385

Rodneyse Bichotte Hermelyn was elected to the New York State Assembly in 2014. She is Chair of the Subcommittee on Oversight of Minority and Women-Owned Business Enterprises and sits as as member on the following Committees: Banks; Education; Government Operations; Health; Higher Education; and Housing. She was elected District Leader in 2010, and in that position has sponsored events in Flatbush such as a Voter's Forum; a mayoral debate; and annual senior luncheons. Professionally, she has been a school teacher, an engineer, and a finance manager. Of Haitian descent, she has traveled the world, including for work. She is also active in her community, including as a member of Community Board 17, Sickle Cell Thalassemia Patient Network, and the National Black MBA Association; and scholarship chair of Chicago Urban League Metroboard Scholarship. Bichotte Hermelyn holds an MBA from Northwestern University's Kellogg School of Management, an MS in electrical engineering from Illinois Institute of Technology, a BS in electrical engineering from SUNY Buffalo, a BS in mathematics in secondary education, and a BS in electrical engineering, both from Buffalo State College. She was born and raised in Brooklyn.

## KEN BLANKENBUSH (R)
*117th - Lewis County, Parts of St. Lawrence, Jefferson and Oswego Counties*

40 Franklin Street, Suite 2, Carthage, NY 13619
315-493-3909/blankenbushk@nyassembly.gov

Legislative Office Building, Room 322, Albany, NY 12248
518-455-5797

Ken Blankenbush was first elected to the New York State Assembly in 2010. His district includes Lewis County and parts of Oneida, Saint Lawrence, and Jefferson counties. He sits on the following committees: Agriculture; Corporations, Authorities, and Commissions; Insurance; Energy; Rules; Ways and Means; and the Commission on Skills Development and Career Education. The longtime Black River resident is a US Air Force veteran of the Vietnam War who was stationed at Plattsburg Air Force Base upon his return. He worked at Metropolitan Life Insurance Company prior to launching BEL Associates, his Watertown-based insurance and financial services business. Blankenbush's public service includes eight years as a councilman in LeRay, and two terms as chair of the Jefferson County Board of Legislators. His memberships include the Association of the United States Army, the Greater Watertown Chamber, Watertown Elks, Black River American Legion, and National Association of Insurance and Financial Advisers. He holds a BS from SUNY Plattsburgh, and also finished two years at Monroe Community College. He is married with two children and six grandchildren.

## KARL A. BRABENEC (R)
*98 - Orange and Rockland Counties*

28 N. Main Street, Suite 2, Florida, NY 10921,
845-544-7551/brabeneck@nyassembly.gov

Legislative Office Building, Room 329, Albany, NY 12248
518-455-5991

Karl Brabenec was elected to the New York State Assembly in 2014 from a district that includes the City of Port Jervis and the towns of Deerpark, Greenville, Minisink, Warwick, Monroe, Tuxedo, and portions of Ramapo. He sits on the following committees: Aging, Election Law, Labor, Rules; Ways and Means; and the Commission on Government Administration. His priorities include alleviating residents' tax burden, and cutting red tape to create jobs and business growth. Prior to his election, he was Deerpark Town Supervisor, an Assistant to the former Orange County Executive, a member of the Deerpark Town Council, and the Deerpark Zoning Board. He is currently a member of the advisory boards for the Orange County Community Development Block Grant

Program and the HOME Program to help county residents to become homeowners. He holds an undergraduate degree from Mount Saint Mary College and an MPA from the John Jay College of Criminal Justice. Brabenec lives in Westbrookville and is the married father of two.

## EDWARD C. BRAUNSTEIN (D)
*26th - Part of Queens County*

213-33 39th Avenue, Suite 238, Bayside, NY 11361
718-357-3588/braunsteine@nyassembly.gov

Legislative Office Building, Room 842, Albany, NY 12248
518-455-5425

Assemblyman Edward C. Braunstein was elected to the New York State Assembly in November, 2010. His Northeast Queens district that includes the neighborhoods of Auburndale, Bay Terrace, Bayside, Bayside Hills, Broadway-Flushing, Douglaston, Floral Park, Glen Oaks, Little Neck, New Hyde Park, North Shore Towers, Oakland Gardens, and Whitestone. Assemblyman Braunstein chairs the Subcommittee on Cities, and is a member of the following committees: Health; Judiciary; Rules; and Ways and Means. His legislative achievements include leading the effort to ban so-called "bath salts," protecting New Yorkers from fraudulent attorneys by making it a felony to practice law without a license, and requiring campuses to notify local law enforcement of on-campus violent crimes and missing persons. Assemblyman Braunstein's professional background includes serving as a Legislative Assistant in Assembly Speaker Sheldon Silver's New York City office. He also served on Community Board 11. He holds a BS in finance from the University at Albany, a law degree from New York Law School, and lives in Whitestone with his wife and two children.

## HARRY B. BRONSON (D)
*138th - Part of Monroe County*

840 University Avenue, Rochester, NY 14607
585-244-5255/bronsonh@nyassembly.gov

Legislative Office Building, Room 847, Albany, NY 12248
518-455-4527

Harry Bronson was first elected to the New York State Assembly in 2010. His district includes parts of the City of Rochester and the towns and villages of Chili and Henrietta. Bronson is Chair of the Committee on Economic Development, Job Creation, Commerce and Industry and he sits on the following standing Committees: Education; Economic Development, Job Creation, Commerce, and Industry; Labor; Transportation; and Ways and means. Bronson has also worked to advance legislation aimed at protecting the quality of life, health, safety, and independence of aging New Yorkers. In addition, he chairs the Commission on Skills Development and Career Education. He is a former law partner at Blitman and King. He currently co-owns Equal=Grounds, a coffeehouse noted as a neighborhood meeting place in the South Wedge neighborhood of the 138th Assembly District. His public service resume includes service as Assistant Minority Leader and Minority Leader of the Monroe County Legislature. He holds an undergraduate degree in public justice from SUNY Oswego and a JD from the University of Buffalo.

## KEITH P. BROWN (R)
*12th - Parts of Suffolk County*

75 Woodbine Avenue, Northport, NY 11768
631-261-4151/brownk@nyassembly.gov

Legislative Office Building, Room 719, Albany, NY 12248
518-455-5952

Keith P. Brown was elected to the New York State Assembly on November 3, 2020. His district is comprised of parts of Suffolk County, including the towns of Huntington, Babylon, and Islip. In the Assembly, he is a member of the following Committees: Alcoholism and Drug Abuse; Environmental Conservation; Housing; Judiciary; and Social Services.

Utilizing his legal expertise and small business background, Brown seeks to provide help to the small business community and boost economic growth for the Long Island region. With multiple family members in the law enforcement community, he has a distinct understanding of the impact of the difficulties associated with New York's latest criminal justice reforms and increased efforts to "defund" the police. In an effort to keep our communities safe, he is seeking to restore greater judicial discretion and repeal bail reform measures. He is also committed to lowering taxes, creating a cleaner Long Island Sound, and seeking greater investment from the state to address water and sewer infrastructure needs.

Assemblyman Brown is a graduate of SUNY Albany, where he interned his final semester for former New York State Senator Norman J. Levy. He graduated from Touro College Law Center in 1990, where he serves on the advisory board for the Institute on Land Use and Sustainable Development Law. Before starting his own law firm, Brown practiced litigation and was appointed to the New York State Office of the Attorney General, where he served as Assistant Attorney General in the Litigation Bureau defending New York in federal and state courts.

Brown is a founding partner of Brown & Altman, LLP, which represents various corporate clients in real estate related matters, including zoning and land-use regulations. He resides in Northport with his wife, Barbara, and their three children.

## CHRIS BURDICK (D)
*93rd - Part of Westchester County*

100 S. Bedford Road, Suite 150, Mount Kisco, NY 10549
914-244-4450/burdickc@nyassembly.gov

Legislative Office Building, Room 331, Albany, NY 12248
518-455-5397

Assembly Member Burdick joined the NYS Assembly in January 2021. In the Assembly he is Chair of the Subcommittee on Employment Opportunities for People with Disabilities and serves as a member on the following Committees: Correction; Environmental Conservation; Housing; and Veterans' Affairs.

Burdick previously served for seven years as Bedford Town Supervisor through December 2020. In that role and working with the Bedford Town Board, he delivered on critical issues for his community, particularly in the areas of combatting the climate crisis, clean water infrastructure, affordable housing, and immigrant protection.

The climate crisis has always been one of Burdick's top priorities. Partnering with Bedford 2020, Bedford reduced greenhouse gas emissions by 44 percent, achieving that goal a year earlier than planned. As one of the first chairs of Sustainable Westchester, he helped launch Community Choice Aggregation to promote renewably sourced electricity for Westchester County.

Burdick also saw the critical need for sewers in certain hamlets of Bedford, as septic failures threatened both water quality and business development. In order to make the expensive sewer project a reality, he secured 95 percent of the necessary funding from New York State, New York City, and Westchester County.

In 2015, he partnered with Bedford's Antioch Baptist Church to convert its vacant former church building into affordable housing. Although told it would be impossible to meet the necessary funding deadline, Burdick recognized the importance of this project and convened 40 morning meetings with his team to get it done.

In 2017, recognizing the moral obligation to protect the immigrant community, Assembly Member Burdick worked with the faith-based community, education leaders, and local law enforcement to craft one of the strongest immigrant protection policies in Westchester County. Since

then, under his leadership, Bedford also passed resolutions against Antisemitism and in support of Black Lives.

Burdick earned his BA in economics and history from the University of California at Berkeley, his MA in international studies from The Johns Hopkins School of International Studies, and his JD from Seton Hall School of Law. Prior to becoming the full-time Supervisor of the Town of Bedford, he had served as senior underwriting counsel for Stewart Title Insurance Company. Burdick was born in New Jersey and moved to Bedford in 1992, where he lives with his wife Illyria. They have three children and a granddaughter.

## KENNY BURGOS (D)
*85th - Part of Bronx County*

1163 Manor Avenue, Store Front #3, Bronx, NY 10472
718-893-0202/burgosk@nyassembly.gov

Legislative Office Building, Room 633, Albany, NY 12248
518-455-5514

Assemblyman Burgos understands the costs of New York's rising income inequality and deep inequities in the lives of Bronx residents because he has lived it. A second-generation Bronxite, he grew up in a split-family home and experienced the realities that face so many members of his community. These experiences inspired him to serve the residents of the 85th Assembly District to address these disparities, racial injustice, and socioeconomic issues.

He attended New York City public schools, graduating from the Bronx High School of Science and received his bachelor's degree in economics from the University at Albany. During his undergraduate studies, his interest in public service was sparked, providing him a firsthand view of the role government has in the lives of its people. A career as a Deputy Chief of Staff and Budget Director on the New York City Council followed after graduation.

Throughout his childhood, Burgos split his time between his parents' two respective neighborhoods in the Bronx, often noticing the impact a zip code can have on an individual's resources, opportunities, and life. In the New York City Council, he worked firsthand with New York City government agencies, nonprofit organizations, and small businesses to solve these disparities and formulate partnerships aimed at improving the communities' local schools, libraries, and playgrounds. He also helped host immigration service events, domestic violence aid, and programs tackling the food insecurity crisis.

The life work of Assembly Member Burgos is to serve, uplift, and empower workers, families, young people, tenants, mom-and-pop small business owners, and all those left behind by an economy that too often serves the top few. In the Assembly, he works to ensure that the Bronx, New York City, and New York State are fairer, more equitable places for all residents. Burgos serves as Chair of the Subcommittee on Transitional Services and is a member of the following Committees: Consumer Affairs and Protection; Correction; Election Law; Labor; and Transportation.

Burgos credits his love for politics, government, and advocacy to his big family. He lives in Soundview with his fiancée and is an amateur bodybuilder.

## PAT BURKE (D)
*142nd - Part of Erie County*

1074 Union Road, West Seneca, NY 14224
716-608-6099/burkep@nyassembly.gov

Legislative Office Building, Room 833, Albany, NY 12248
518-455-4691

Pat Burke was elected to the New York State Assembly in November 2018. His district includes Lackawanna, Buffalo, West Seneca, and Orchard Park. In the Assembly he sits on the following standing Committees: Banks; Children and Families; Economic Development, Job Creation, Commerce and Industry; Environmental Conservation; Local Governments; and Tourism, Parks, Arts, and Sports Development.

From January of 2014 to December of 2018, he served the community as an Erie County Legislator. During Burke's tenure on the legislature, his notable legislative accomplishments included a ban on microbead plastics, a repeal of Sunday Blue Laws, a million-dollar emergency fund created to combat the opioid crisis, and the formation of the Erie County Broadband Committee. He also serves as an Instructor in political science at Buffalo State College.

As a father, protecting the health and well-being of children has been at the forefront of Burke's legislative efforts. He banned smoking in a vehicle with children, wrote the PENCE BILL (Prevention of Emotional Neglect and Child Endangerment) to end harmful gay conversion therapy, and championed a local law implementing a Youth Concussion Protocol to ensure the safety of minors playing contact sports.

Burke also introduced legislation that would make the pharmaceutical industry pay its fair share to keep our local drinking water free of medical waste, and not pass the burden onto taxpayers. And, he introduced the Invest in Erie, Invest in America Act promoting and encouraging local businesses in Erie County.

Assemblyman Burke also serves as an Instructor in political science at Buffalo State College. A Buffalo native, he lives there with his wife and three children.

## MARIANNE BUTTENSCHON (D)
*119th - Part of Oneida County*

207 Genesee Street, Room 401, Utica, NY 13501
315-732-1055/buttenschonm@nyassembly.gov

Legislative Office Building, Room 528, Albany, NY 12248
518-455-5454

Marienne Buttenschon was elected to represent the 199th District in the Assembly. The district is comprised of the suburban and farming communities of Floyd, Marcy, Whitestown, and the Herkimer County Town of Frankfurt. Buttenschon is Chair on the Subcommittee on Export Trades and serves as a member on the following committees: Agriculture; Banks; Economic Development, Job Creation, and Industry; Education; Higher Education; and Veterans' Affairs. She is also a member of the Legislative Women's Caucus and the Task Force on Women's Issues.

Before winning election to the Assembly, she was the Dean of Public Service and Emergency Preparedness at Mohawk Valley Community College. Her 2018 campaign for the Assembly was her first attempt at elected office.

Buttenschon is a career-long educator and a lifelong learner. She earned an AAS from Mohawk Valley Community College, a BA in public justice from SUNY (IT) Polytechnic Institute, an MA in public policy from Binghamton University, and a EdD in education from Northeastern.

Her objectives as a public servant are reflected by her high level of civic and professional engagement. She was Vice President of the Utica Community Food Bank and a member of the League of Women Voters. Buttenschon was also a member of the International Association of Chiefs of Police, the New York State Association of Fire Chiefs, and the Hispanic Association of Colleges and Universities. Based upon her long commitment to public safety and the improvement of New York State's first response capability, Speaker Heastie chose her to be the Assembly's representative on the Interoperable and Emergency Communications Board.

She is married to Don Buttenschon, a retired school psychologist. They have three grown children and one granddaughter. For over 30 years, she

and her husband have operated the Buttenschon Christmas Tree Farm in the Town of Marcy, Oneida County.

## KEVIN M. BYRNE (R-C-I)
*94th - Parts of Westchester and Putnam Counties*

3 Starr Ridge Road, Suite 204, Brewster, NY 10509
845-278-2923/ByrneK@nyassembly.gov

Legislative Office Building, Room 318, Albany, NY 12248
518-455-5783

After graduating from Carmel High School in Putnam County, Kevin M. Byrne attended the University of Scranton. His goal was to serve in the US Army as an ROTC graduate, but he was unable to achieve that goal because of a severe injury he sustained as a wrestler. He earned a bachelor's degree from the university and later graduated from Marist College with a master's of public administration in health care administration. He began a career in public service working as an intern for Congresswoman Sue Kelly, and then served as Deputy District Director for Congresswoman Nan Hayworth. In 2013, he joined the American Heart Association as Regional Director, where he helped individuals and families suffering from cardiovascular disease. Byrne is the chairman of the Assembly Minority Conference Program Committee. Additionally, he serves as Ranking Minority Member on the Health Committee, putting his long years of service in health care to good use. He also sits on the following committees: Governmental Operations; Insurance; Labor; Transportation; and Ways and Means. As a legislator, his goal is to restore ethics and integrity to the state capitol, reduce the tax burden on New Yorkers, attract good jobs back to New York, and support first responders and law enforcement. He supports the repeal of the SAFE Act (the Secure Ammunition and Firearms Enforcement Act of 2013) and the rights of law-abiding gun owners. He joined with other local leaders in opposing the efforts of the Governor and Entergy Corporation to close the Indian Point Nuclear Facility, arguing that the decision was made with no public input and that it demonstrates an unwelcoming climate for business in the state. He is dedicated to serving the community, having volunteered as an Assistant Scoutmaster in the Boy Scouts and as a member of the Putnam Valley planning board. Additionally, he is an active EMT/firefighter for the Kent Volunteer Fire Department and held the position of President for three years. He and his wife, Briana, reside in Mahopac.

## MARJORIE BYRNES (R-C)
*133rd - Parts of Livingston, Monroe, and Steuben Counties*

79 Genesee Street, Avon, NY 14414
528-226-2022/byrnesm@nyassembly.gov

Legislative Office Building, Room 723, Albany, NY 12248
518-455-5662

Marjorie Byrnes was elected to the New York State Assembly on November 6, 2018. Her district is comprised of Livingston County and parts of Monroe and Steuben counties. She sits on the following standing Committees: Children and Families; Ethics and Guidance; Health; Housing; Judiciary; and Small Business. Byrnes is also a member of the Legislative Women's Caucus.

As an Assemblywoman, she advocates for increases to state-funded infrastructure programs such as CHIPS, PAVE-NY, and BRIDGE-NY. She plans to partner with infrastructure and transportation stakeholders to address New York's crumbling infrastructure. She believes the people of New York State are overly burdened by taxes, regulations, and red tape, and fights for economic relief. She strongly supports term limits. Byrnes also pushes for increased school safety, specifically state-funded armed School Resource Officers in schools.

She has been an attorney for 32 years, and for ten years she served as a Rochester City Court Judge. During her time as a judge, she presided over thousands of criminal and civil cases. She was also Court Attorney to Livingston County Court Judge Dennis S. Cohen from 2006-2017. In January of 2017, she retired from the New York State court system and then served as a Caledonia Village Trustee.

Byrnes is a member of the Mt. Morris Sportsmen's Club, the Conesus Lake Sportsmen's Club, Rochester-Brooks Sportsmen's Club, S.C.O.P.E., GOA-NY, and the NRA. She is an avid outdoor enthusiast and a strong advocate for the Second Amendment. She resides in Caledonia.

## KEVIN A. CAHILL (D)
*103rd - Parts of Dutchess and Ulster Counties*

Governor Clinton Building, Suite G-4, 1 Albany Avenue, Kingston, NY 12401
845-338-9610/CahillK@nyassembly.gov

Legislative Office Building, Room 716, Albany, NY 12248
518-45505576

Kevin Cahill was first elected to the New York State Assembly from 1993 to 1995, and was reelected in 1998. He chairs the Committee on Insurance, and also sits on the following committees: Economic Development, Job Creation, Commerce, and Industry; Health; Higher Education; and Ways and Means. He has backed legislation to place a moratorium on fracking. He formerly chaired the Committee on Energy, which allowed him to focus on issues surrounding energy efficiency. Legislation was passed to take proceeds from RGGI, the carbon emission cap and trade program, and direct the funding toward communities and small businesses to create a workforce aimed at improving building energy efficiency. He also helped to increase investments in energy efficiency and renewable power, green the state's facilities and vehicle fleet, and make New York's net-metering law one of the most expansive in the country. In addition, he has backed education, helping to secure $100 million to modernize the campuses of Ulster County Community College and SUNY New Paltz. He formerly served as minority leader of the Ulster County Legislature, and has worked as an attorney and director of a Medicare health plan. Cahill has been effective in securing grants he represents, helping municipalities and nonprofits obtain funding, including the Woodstock Community Center, the Rosendale Theater, the Hudson River Maritime Museum Education Building, among others. He has an undergraduate degree from SUNY New Paltz, a law degree from Albany Law School, is father to two daughters, and is a lifelong resident of Kingston.

## ROBERT C. CARROLL (D)
*44th - Part of Kings County*

416 Seventh Avenue, Brooklyn, NY 11215
718-788-7221/CarrollR@nyassembly.gov

Legislative Office Building, Room 557, Albany, NY 12248
518-455-5377

Assemblyman Carroll is Chair of the Subcommittee on Museums and Cultural Institutions and a member of the following committees: Cities; Corporations, Authorities, and Commissions; Energy; Election Law; Environmental Conservations; and Tourism, Parks, Arts, and Sports Development.

A lifelong Brooklynite, he graduated from Xaverian High School before enrolling at SUNY-Binghamton to study history and theater. He then earned a law degree at New York Law School and entered private practice. He specialized in contract law, election law, trusts and estates, and real estate law. Additionally, he worked with a nonprofit theater as both a writer and actor, and he was the Development Director and fundraiser for an independent theater company in Manhattan. In 2014, a play that he wrote about Brooklyn politics, *The Believers*, was produced on the Upper West Side of Manhattan.

He served on Community Board 7, chairing numerous committees, and is a member of several community organizations, including the Windsor Terrace Food Co-op and the Park Slope Civic Council. He also served as the youngest president of a political reform organization, the Central Brooklyn Independent Democrats. He believes that too often local government has failed to respond to issues of housing affordability and overcrowding of school and public transportation, and to the sense that New York does not fully welcome working families. In schools, he is a proponent of equitable funding and curbing excessive testing, and with regard to election law, his goal is to liberalize ballot access and voting laws. He was born and raised in Windsor Terrace and Kensington and currently resides in a home that belonged to his grandmother on Windsor Place.

## SARAH CLARK (D)
*136th - Part of Monroe County*

1800 Hudson Avenue, Second Floor, Suite 4, Rochester, NY 14617
585-467-0410/ clarks@nyassembly.gov

Legislative Office Building, Room 429, Albany, NY 12248
518-455-5373

A lifelong Rochester resident and SUNY Stony Brook graduate, Assemblywoman Clark has dedicated her career over the last two decades to public service. Prior to running for office, she worked for the U.S. Senate-initially for Senator Hillary Clinton and, for the past eight years, as Senator Kirsten Gillibrand's Deputy State Director. In the Senate, she worked tirelessly on issues impacting her community daily like affordable health care, the high cost of prescription drugs, equitable public education, college affordability, a living wage for all, and protecting seniors from fraud. Clark has also been a longtime advocate on the local and national levels to reform the criminal justice system and identify sustainable solutions to climate change.

In her newly elected position in the Assembly, she is Chair of the Subcommittee on Tuition Assistance Program and sits on the following Committees: Aging; Children and Families; Higher Education; Local Governments; Small Business; and the Task Force on Women's Issues.

For the past seven years, Clark has served as a member of the Community Impact Cabinet and the Women United Steering Committee for the United Way of Greater Rochester. She is also a longtime volunteer at the Summit Federal Credit Union, currently serving as chair of the Nominating Committee.

Clark lives in the Maplewood neighborhood of Rochester with her husband, John, and their three children, Jack, Sean, and Grace. As a working mom and mentor to other moms interested in public office, she utilizes her connections and experience to elevate the needs of children and families in the Assembly.

## WILLIAM COLTON (D-WF)
*47th - Part of Kings County*

155 Kings Highway, Brooklyn, NY 11223
718-236-1598/ColtonW@nyassembly.gov

Legislative Office Building, Room 733, Albany, NY 12248
518-455-5828

William Colton was elected to the New York State Assembly in November 1996 to a district that includes the neighborhoods of Bensonhurst, Gravesend, Bath Beach, Dyker Heights, and Midwood. He is the Assembly's Majority Whip and sits on the following committees: Correction; Environmental Conservation; Government Employees; Labor; Rules; and Ways and Means. In addition, he was a member of the Asian Pacific American Task Force. Prior to running for the Assembly, Colton was cofounder and organizer of the Bensonhurst Tenants Council, and also was the attorney in a successful lawsuit to halt the opening of the Southwest Brooklyn Incinerator. Colton has remained active in his community, including sitting on the Board of Trustees of the Verrazano Lodge of the

Order of the Sons of Italy and the Board of Directors of the Cardinal Stritch Knights Corporation of the Cardinal Stritch Knights of Columbus Council. He has received numerous awards for teaching and for community service. He is a former school teacher, is married with two stepchildren, and holds an undergraduate degree in urban education from St. John's University, an MS in Urban Education from Brooklyn College, and a JD from St. John's School of Law.

## WILLIAM CONRAD (D)
*140th - Parts of Erie and Niagara Counties*

34 Prospect Parkwsy, Tonawanda, NY 14150
716-873-2540/conradw@nyassembly.gov

Legislative Office Building, Room 847, Albany, NY 12248
518-455-4767

William "Bill" Conrad III is a lifelong resident of Town of Tonawanda, where he resides with his wife, Mary Kate, and their four young children, Emma, Liam, Katie, and Molly. As a New York State Assembly Member, he is Chair of the Subcommittee on Volunteer Emergency Services and sits on the following Committees; Education; Energy; Local Government; Science & Technology; and Tourism, Parks, Arts and Sports Development.

Conrad is a proud graduate of the Sweet Home School system, and went on to earn his Bachelor's degree with Honors from Fredonia State College and a master's degree in education from Buffalo State. After graduating, he began his career as a social studies teacher and coach in the Kenmore-Town of Tonawanda public schools, where he worked for 21 years. In that capacity, he served in various leadership roles from department chair to executive board member of the Kenmore Teachers Association. However, his most important role as a teacher was educating and molding his students into our future leaders.

Since 2016, Assembly Member Conrad has had the honor of serving on the Town of Tonawanda Town Board. After winning his 2017 election and securing his seat on the Town Council, he chaired the Water Resources and Youth, Parks and Recreation committees. Over the past five years, as part of a team with community groups, labor and business owners, he has fought for the closure of dangerous polluters, helped develop a state mitigation fund after the closure of the NRG Huntley Plant, and worked to develop a blueprint for our economic future called Tonawanda Tomorrow.

Moreover, he led the Town Committee on NYSERDA Clean Energy Community Designation and the U.S. Department of Energy's award-winning Solarize campaign, which turned a landfill into a "bright-field" with solar panels generating low-cost, clean energy.

As a volunteer, Conrad has been a very active member of the community. He served on the Erie County Youth board and founded the Kenmore Youth Rugby Club. Additionally, he is a member of the Clean Air Coalition, Kenmore-Town of Tonawanda Chamber of Commerce, and is a parishioner of St. John the Baptist Church in Kenmore.

## VIVIAN E. COOK (D)
*32nd - Part of Queens County*

142-15 Rockaway Boulevard, Jamaica, NY 11436
718-322-3975/CookV@nyassembly.gov

Legislative Office Building, Room 939, Albany, NY 12248
518-455-4203

Vivian Cook was elected to the New York State Assembly in 1990. She sits on the following standing Committees: Codes; Corporation, Authorities, and Commissions; Housing; Insurance; Rules; and Ways and Means. Her previous leadership posts include former service as the Assembly's former Majority Whip and chair of the Task Force on Food, Farm and Nutrition Policy. Cook is also a member of the Task Force on

Women's Issues, the Legislative Women's Caucus, the Puerto Rican/Hispanic Task Force, and the Black, Puerto Rican, Hispanic & Asian Legislative Caucus. The Rock Hill, South Carolina native has served as District Leader of Queens County for more than 25 years. She founded the Rockaway Boulevard Local Development Corporation. She has supported community housing programs that provide residents with affordable homes, as well as projects to improve senior services and recreational facilities. She is the recipient of many awards for her community and civic service, including the Brooks Senior Center, the Jamaica Chamber of Commerce, the Congressman Gregory Meeks Congressional Award, and the Angeldocs. She is a graduate of the DeFrans Business Institute.

## CATALINA CRUZ (D)
*39th - Part of Queens County*

41-40 Junction Boulevard, Corona, NY 11368
718-458-5367/cruzc@nyassembly.gov

Legislative Office Building, Room 523, Albany, NY 12248
518-455-4567

Catalina Cruz was elected to serve the residents of the New York State Assembly's 39th District. Assemblywoman Cruz has the privilege of representing one of the most diverse districts in the nation, which encompasses the neighborhoods of Corona, Elmhurst, and Jackson Heights. In the Assembly Cruz is Chair of the Task Force on New Americans and serves as a member on the following committees: Aging; Children and Families; Codes; Ethics and Guidance; Labor; and Small Business. Cruz is also a member of the Black, Puerto Rican, Hispanic & Asian Legislative Caucus, the Puerto Rican/Hispanic Task Force, and the Legislative Women's Caucus.

Cruz was born in Colombia and came to Queens at the age of 9. She grew up as a DREAMer; she lived in the United States for more than 10 years as an undocumented American. She was raised by a single mother, who like many immigrants had to work multiple and menial jobs to provide for her family. As a single mother of four children, she worked long hours during the week as a nanny, cleaned offices at night, and sold tamales and empanadas at the soccer fields on the weekends. Inspired by her mother's perseverance, Cruz has committed her career to fighting for our community and to ensure our workers, neighbors and families not only survive, but thrive.

Cruz is an experienced attorney and a leader for tenant protections, immigration reform, and workers' rights. Prior to becoming Assemblywoman, she most recently served as the Chief of Staff to the New York City Council Finance Chair, Julissa Ferreras. In addition, she worked to help pass key legislation protecting workers, women and small-business owners. She previously served as the Director of the Governor's Exploited Workers Task Force, helping New York become a national leader in the fight against worker exploitation and human trafficking. This first-of-its-kind task force conducted statewide outreach and enforcement within key low-wage industries, including car washes, restaurants and nail salons, where workers are often victims of wage theft and subject to unsafe working conditions, but do not come forward for fear of retaliation.

Assemblywoman Cruz also served as Counsel to the New York City Council's Immigration Committee, where she helped write and implement legislation that led to New York City becoming a Sanctuary City. She worked on projects such as the Detainer Law and IDNYC (municipal identification). Additionally, she served as Counsel to the New York State Department of Labor's Division of Immigrant Policies and Affairs, where she helped this agency become a leader in combating labor trafficking. Cruz began her career as a Staff Attorney, representing low-income, rent-stabilized tenants in New York City housing court, ensuring that they received the full protection of the law under their leases.

527

Cruz lives in Jackson Heights, Queens, with her family. She holds a bachelor's degree from the John Jay College of Criminal Justice and a JD from the City University of New York School of Law.

## MICHAEL J. CUSICK (D)
*63rd - Part of Richmond County*

1911 Richmond Avenue, Staten Island, NY 10314
718-370-1384/CusickM@nyassembly.gov

Legislative Office Building, Room 724, Albany, NY 12248
518-455-5526

Michael Cusick was first elected to the New York State Assembly in 2002. He currently chairs the Energy Committee. Cusick is also a member of the following standing Committees in the Assembly: Governmental Employees; Higher Education; Veterans' Affairs; and Ways and Means. Prior to launching his own elective bid, Cusick was Director of Constituent Services for US Senator Charles E. Schumer, and managed the day-to-day operations for Schumer's New York City office. Prior to that, he was Chief of Staff to former Staten Island Assemblyman Eric N. Vitaliano and Special Assistant to former President of the City Council Andrew J. Stein. Among his legislative achievements since taking office are authoring a law to set a building moratorium that paved the way for the Mid-Island Blue Belt and requiring notice to neighborhood landowners of an application to build on wetland areas. He also created "Total Fitness Challenge" in 2008 to boost youth reading and exercising during summer break. Cusick has sat on the boards of the Staten Island Board of Directors of the Catholic Youth Organization and the Boy Scouts of America. He also chairs the Handicapped Parking Task Force on Staten Island, working with community groups to address parking concerns faced by the disabled. He received his undergraduate degree from Villanova University and is married and lives in his native Staten Island.

## STEVEN H. CYMBROWITZ (D)
*45th - Part of Kings County*

1800 Sheepshead Bay Road, Brooklyn, NY 11235
718-743-4078/CymbroS@nyassembly.gov

Legislative Office Building, Room 943, Albany, NY 12248
518-455-5214

Steven Cymbrowitz was first elected to the New York State Assembly in November 2000. He represents the 45th Assembly District in Brooklyn that includes parts of Sheepshead Bay, Midwood, Manhattan Beach, Gravesend, and Brighton Beach. Cymbrowitz is Chair of the Committee on Housing, and also sits on the following committees: Codes; Environmental Conservation; Health; and Insurance. His was among the districts hard-hit by Hurricane Sandy and has actively worked to help his constituents through the recovery. He also has worked to open the Lena Cymbrowitz Pavilion of the Maimonides Cancer Center in tribute to his late wife, Assemblywoman Lena Cymbrowitz. Before his election to the Assembly, he served as Executive Director of the North Brooklyn Development Corporation, Director of Housing and Community Development for the Metropolitan New York Coordinating Council on Jewish Poverty, Assistant Commissioner of the Division of Homeless Housing Development for the New York City Department of Housing Preservation and Development (HPD), Assistant Commissioner of the Division of Housing Production and Finance for HPD, and Deputy Commissioner of Development at HPD. He also served as the New York City Housing Authority's Director of Intergovernmental Relations. As a child of Holocaust survivors, Assemblyman Cymbrowitz is involved with the international organization World Without Nazism and has been a featured speaker at conferences in Moscow, Berlin, and Riga. He holds a bachelor's degree from C.W. Post College, a master's degree in social work from Adelphi University, and a law degree from Brooklyn Law School.

## TAYLOR DARLING (D)
*18th - Part of Nassau County*

33 Front Street, Suite 104, Hempstead, NY 11550
516-489-6610/darlingt@nyassembly.gov

Legislative Office Building, Room 323, Albany, NY 12248
518-455-5861

Taylor Darling was elected to the New York State Assembly for District 18 on November 6, 2018. In the Assembly, she is Chair of the Subcommittee on Foster Care; and a member of the following Committees: Children and Families; Economic Development, Job Creation, Commerce, and Industry; Local Governments; Small Business; People with Disabilities; and Transportation. She is also a member of the Black, Puerto Rican, Hispanic & Asian Legislative Caucus; the Task Force on Women's Issues; and the Legislative Women's Caucus.

Darling is an American and British citizen who was born in Brooklyn, NY to Raulston and Towana Bertley. During her early childhood, she lived in Europe with her parents. She credits learning the game of chess at an early age with her strategic approach to problem solving, which has served her well.

In an effort to increase the amount of healthy two-parent households in America, Darling has devoted her life to the field of psychology. She attended Spelman College at age 16 and was accepted into a clinical psychology doctoral program at age 19. She eventually transferred to Hofstra University and became an Industrial Organizational Psychologist.

She has worked in several industries creating and implementing systems to increase efficiency, productivity, and profitability. Her holistic and humanistic approach kept her in high demand in the private sector. However, the growing needs of her community began to require her attention.

In the Assembly, Darling is a crusader for inclusion, equity, and economic and social justice. She resides with her family in Long Island, NY.

## MARITZA DAVILA (D)
*53rd - Parts of Kings County*

249 Wilson Avenue, Brooklyn, NY 11237
718-443-1205/DavilaM@nyassembly.gov

Legislative Office Building, Washington, DC 12248
518-455-5789

Maritza Davila was elected to the New York State Assembly on November 5, 2013. She is Chair of the Subcommittee on Retention of Homeownership and Stabilization of Affordable Housing, and also sits on the following committees: Housing; Alcoholism and Drug Abuse; Children and Families; Correction; Economic Development, Job Creation, Commerce and Industry; Rules; and Social Services. She is also Chair of the Puerto Rican/Hispanic Task Force and member of the Black, Puerto Rican, Hispanic & Asian Legislative Caucus; the Legislative Women's Caucus; and the Task Force on Women's Issues. Prior to her election, she served as President of the Community School Board of Education of District 32, and also as the Director of a statewide program to raise awareness for the dangers of lead-based paint. In addition, she advocates for women's rights; as a founding member of the North Brooklyn Coalition Against Domestic Violence she served on its Board for two years. Assemblywoman Davila founded the Northern Brooklyn Residents Association to advocate on behalf of affordable housing and community development. Originally a native of Catano, Puerto Rico, she moved to Bushwick, Brooklyn as a young girl and has lived there ever since. She holds an AA in Political Science from Long Island University and is mother to three children.

## CARMEN N. DE LA ROSA (D)
*72nd - Part of New York County*

210 Sherman Avenue, Suite A & C, New York, NY 10034
212-544-2278/delaRosac@nyassembly.gov

Legislative Office Building, Room 538, Albany, NY 12248
518-455-5807

In the legislature, Assemblywoman De La Rosa is Chair of the Subcommittee on Infrastructure and currently serves on the following committees: Banks; Correction; Corporations, Authorities, and Commissions; Housing; Labor; and Mental Health. She is also a member of the Black, Puerto Rican, Hispanic & Asian Legislative Caucus; the Legislative Women's Caucus; the Task Force on Women's Issues; and the Puerto Rican/Hispanic Task Force. De La Rosa has become known as a fierce advocate for immigrants' rights, criminal justice reform, strengthening rent stabilization laws that protect low-income tenants, women's rights and equality, and mental health services for minority communities.

Carmen De La Rosa, a resident of northern Manhattan, was born in the Dominican Republic and immigrated to the Inwood section of New York City as a young child. She was the first person in her immediate family to graduate from college, receiving a degree in political science and a certification in peace and justice studies from Fordham University. In 2007, she began her career working for State Assembly Member Daniel O'Donnell. She worked with communities on the Upper West Side to improve the quality of life of residents, fight colocations of local public schools (that is, siting traditional public schools and charter schools on the same campus), and preserve affordable housing. After rising through the ranks in state and local government, she was appointed Chief of Staff to New York City Council member Ydanis Rodriguez in 2014, representing the communities of Inwood, Washington Heights, and Marble Hill. In this capacity, she managed the daily operations, strategy, and focus of both the legislative and community offices. She played a role in the passage of nearly a dozen bills related to Mayor Bill de Blasio's Vision Zero initiative. In managing the office's discretionary budget, she worked to support numerous neighborhood institutions-among them senior centers, after-school programs, and social service providers-ensuring that local nonprofits received crucial funding. In May 2016, she completed a program at the Coro New York Leadership Center. A lifelong resident of Inwood, she resides with her husband, Jose, and two-year-old daughter, Mia, on the street she was raised on.

## JOE DESTEFANO (R)
*3rd - Part of Suffolk County*

3245 Route 112, Building 2, Suite 6, Medford, NY 11763
631-207-0073/destefanoj@nyassembly.gov

Legislative Office Building, Room 430, Albany, NY 12248
518-455-4901

Joe DeStefano was elected to the New York State Assembly on November 6, 2018. His district is comprised of parts of Suffolk County, including Medford and Mastic Beach. He sits on the following standing Committees: Aging; Alcoholism and Drug Abuse; Governmental Employees; Labor; and Transportation.

As an Assemblyman, DeStefano fights for safer neighborhoods and stronger communities, to preserve the property tax cap while pushing to curb Albany's spending, and to make college more affordable. He also is an advocate of Angelica's Law, which would make it a felony to drive with five suspensions.

For the last 27 years, DeStefano has served as a Suffolk County Sheriff's Office Public Safety Communication Supervisor, where he managed the day-to-day operations of the dispatchers as well as supervised radio communications and other vital functions. Since 2011, he has served as the Unit President of the Sheriffs/Probation Civilian Unit, representing more than 200 active Suffolk County Association of Municipal Employees members.

Dedicated to making his community a better, safer place, since 1980, he has been an active member of the Medford Fire Department, holding positions including Fire Police Lieutenant, 2nd Lieutenant, Department Recording Secretary, Department Vice President, and Department President.

Additionally, in 1996, he was first elected Commissioner of the Medford Fire District. In 2017, the Suffolk County Fire District Officers' Association named him Commissioner of the Year. Over the years, he has held numerous other roles including Suffolk County Fire District Officers' Association Secretary and Treasurer; Brookhaven Town Fire Districts President; and Regional Director, Secretary, and Treasurer of the New York State Association of Fire Districts.

Assemblyman DeStefano and his wife, Linda, have two children and one grandchild.

## INEZ E. DICKENS (D)
*70th - Part of New York County*

163 W. 125th Street, Suite 911, New York, NY 10027
212-866-5809/Dickensl@nyassembly.gov

Legislative Office Building, Room 734, Albany, NY 12248
518-455-4793

Assemblywoman Dickens is Chair of the Subcommittee on Micro Business and a member of the following committees: Aging, Banks, Education, Libraries and Education Technology, Real Property Taxation, and Small Business. She is also a member of the Black, Puerto Rican, Hispanic & Asian Legislative Caucus; the Legislative Caucus; the Puerto Rican/Hispanic Task Force; and the Task Force on Women's Issues.

Inez E. Dickens is descended from a line of public servants. Her father and mentor was the late Harlem businessman and New York State Assemblyman Lloyd E. Dickens, and her uncle was the late Assemblyman and New York Supreme Court justice Thomas K. Dickens. She studied real estate and land economics at New York University and later studied at Howard University in Washington, DC. She was part owner (with a sister and cousins) of Lloyd E. Dickens & Co., the first wholly-owned African-American Federal Housing Administration-approved mortgage company in the Northeast. She was first elected to office in 1974 as a County Committeewoman, County Judicial Committeewoman, and State Committeewoman. She rose to become the highest-ranking African American woman in the New York State Democratic party, serving as the first Vice Chair of the New York State Democratic Committee. In 2006 she became the council member for the 9th New York City Council district, serving the communities of Central Harlem, Morningside Heights, East Harlem, and parts of the Upper West Side. As a newly elected council member, she was appointed to the leadership positions of Majority Whip and Chair of the Committee on Standards and Ethics. She became the first African American woman in the history of the New York City Council to be appointed to the higher leadership positions of Deputy Majority Leader and Chair of the Subcommittee on Planning, Dispositions, and Concessions. During her tenure in office, she brought millions of dollars in services and resources to her community and to economically distressed communities throughout the city of New York. Throughout her career, her focus has been civil and human rights, social justice, wage equity, inclusion, and diversity. Moreover, she has taken an active role in economic development, supporting small businesses with a focus on minority- and women-owned business enterprises (MWBEs) and strengthening New York's celebrated village of Harlem. She has been a lifelong resident of Harlem.

## ERIC M. DILAN (D)
*54 - Part of King's County*

366 Cornelia Street, Brooklyn, NY 11237
718-386-4576/DilanE@nyassembly.gov

Legislative Office Building, Room 639, Albany, NY 12248
518-455-5821

Erik Dilan was elected to the New York State Assembly in 2014 from a district that includes parts of Bedford Stuyvesant, Bushwick, Cypress-Hills, and East New York. Dilan is Chair on the Committee for the Office of State-Federal Relations and sits on the following committees: Agriculture; Corporations, Authorities, and Commissions; Energy; Housing; and Insurance. He is also a member of the Black, Hispanic & Asian Legislative Caucus and the Puerto Rican/Hispanic Task Force. Prior to his election, Assemblyman Dilan served 12 years on the New York City Council, where his leadership posts included chairing the housing and building committee, the Brooklyn Delegation, and as a member of the budget negotiating team. The lifelong resident of North Brooklyn holds an AS degree in business administration from St. John's University and lives with his wife and two children in Cypress-Hills.

## JEFFREY DINOWITZ (D-L-WF)
*81st - Part of Bronx County*

3107 Kingsbridge Avenue, Bronx, NY 10463
718-796-5345/Dinowij@nyassembly.gov

Legislative Office Building, Room 632, Albany, NY 12248
518-455-5965

Jeffrey Dinowitz was first elected to the New York State Assembly in 1994. The district includes Riverdale, Kingsbridge Heights, Marble Hill, Van Cortlandt Village, Norwood, Woodlawn, and Wakefield. Dinowitz chairs the Codes Committee and serves on the following standing Committees: Election Law, Health, Judicary; and Ways and Means; and Rules. Dinowitz previously chaired the Committee on Aging, the Committee on Alcoholism and Drug Abuse, and the Legislative Commission on Government Administration, as well as others. His legislative interests focus on senior issues, education reform, housing, the environment, and increased education aid for New York City. Assemblyman Dinowitz's professional resume prior to holding elective office includes a decade spent as an Administrative Law Judge for the State of New York for 10 years. In addition, he has served in numerous community organizations, including Vice President of the Riverdale Community Council, member of Bronx Area Policy Board #7, and member of the Boards of Directors for the Bronx High School of Science Foundation and for the Bronx Council for Environmental Quality. His extensive community activity also includes service on the Executive Committee of the Riverdale-Hudson Chapter of B'nai B'rith. In addition, he has been a member of District Council 37 and the Public Employees Federation. The Bronx native is married with two children. He earned a BA from Herbert Lehman College of City University of New York and a JD from Brooklyn Law School.

## DAVID DIPIETRO (R)
*147th - Parts of Erie County and Wyoming County*

411 Main Street, East Aurora, NY 14052
716-655-0951/DiPietroD@nyassembly.gov

Legislative Office Building, Room 546, Albany, NY 12248
518-455-5314

David DiPietro was elected to serve the constituents of the 147th Assembly District on November 6, 2012. His district includes the southern portion of Eric County and all of Wyoming County. He sits on the following committees: Insurance; Labor; Small Business; Transportation; and the Commission on Government Administration. He previously served as Trustee and Mayor of the Village of East Aurora and was recognized at the State of the County of Erie conference as the leader in New York State in mergers and consolidations of government departments and services. As Mayor of East Aurora, DiPietro cut taxes for three consecutive years, and reduced the overall size of the government. His private sector experience includes positions at M&T Bank in Buffalo, Trust Division, and computer and accounting consultant to small businesses in Western New York. Active in his community, he is a member of the East Aurora Moose Lodge 370, American Legion Post 362, East Aurora Rotary Club, Six Towns Youth Court, and the Boys and Girls Club of East Aurora. He received his BS degree in business administration from Wittenberg University. He is married and has three children.

## MICHAEL DURSO (R)
*9th - Parts of Nassau and Suffolk Counties*

512 Park Boulevard, Massapequa Park, NY 11762
16-541-4598/dursom@nyassembly.gov

Legislative Office Building, Room 533, Albany, NY 12248
518-455-505

Michael Durso was elected to the New York State Assembly on November 3, 2020. His district is comprised of parts of both Nassau and Suffolk counties, including South Farmingdale, Massapequa, Massapequa Park, West Babylon, Babylon, West Islip, Brightwaters, and portions of Fire Island and the Great South Bay area. He is a member of the following Committees in the Assembly: Alcoholism and Drug Abuse; Environmental Conservation; Science & Technology; and the Commission on Skills Development and Career Education.

Assembly Member Durso grew up in a blue-collar family in Massapequa Park. At an early age, he learned the importance of hard work while helping his mother make ends meet at her small restaurant. Teaching him the value of starting work early and staying late, his father worked the supermarket deli counter and rose through the ranks to become President of RWDSU Local Union 338 and the Long Island Federation of Labor. With the work ethic of his parents, Durso started his adult career as a sanitation worker riding on the back of a truck.

Before taking office, he served as a Sanitation Supervisor and helped implement environmental policies that increased recycling initiatives. He is a proud member of CSEA Local 881. Like many other struggling families on Long Island, Durso worked second job as a public safety officer at Hofstra University in Hempstead, where his duties included helping protect students on campus. He saw firsthand the dangers students face and knows the importance of strong criminal justice laws. He also served as a member of the Teamsters Local 553 and served on the bargaining unit during their last contract.

As a State Assemblyman, Durso works across the aisle to protect the STAR program, keep property tax rebate checks, and increase funding for local schools. As a graduate of carpentry from BOCES in Levittown, he advocates for additional funding for vocational programs to train our youth and to fill the shortage of skilled labor.

Michael Durso stands shoulder to shoulder with police, firefighters, doctors, nurses, and frontline workers. As a certified first responder, he understands the importance of securing the resources needed to keep our communities safe.

Assemblyman Durso lives Massapequa Park with his wife, Dana, and their two daughters, Nicole and Taylor. Dana serves as Trustee for the Village of Massapequa Park and PTA President for East Lake Elementary School.

## SIMCHA EICHENSTEIN (D)
*48th - Part of Kings County*

1310 48th Street, Unit 204, Brooklyn, NY 11219
718-853-9616/EichensteinS@nyassembly.gov

Legislative Office Building, Room 548, Albany, NY 12248
518-455-5721

Simcha Eichenstein was elected on November 6, 2018, to represent New York's 48th Assembly District, which includes the neighborhoods of Borough Park and Midwood in Brooklyn. He is Chair of the Subcommittee on the Outreach and Oversight of Senior Citizen Program; and sits following standing Committees: Aging; Cities; Governmental Employees; Housing; Real Property Taxation; and Social Services.

Before his election, Eichenstein served on New York City Mayor Bill de Blasio's legislative affairs team in Albany, and as part of the Mayor's Senior Intergovernmental staff at City Hall. During this time, he played a crucial role advocating for budgetary and legislative priorities vital to the City of New York in Albany, and was instrumental in helping craft and pass many pieces of legislation in the state legislature. His City Hall portfolio included the Department of Health and Mental Hygiene (DOHMH), Department for the Aging (DFTA), Department of Homeless Services (DHS), Human Resources Administration (HRA), NYC Health and Hospitals, Administration for Children's Services (ACS), Department of Youth and Community Development (DYCD), Department of Transportation (DOT), Taxi and Limousine Commission (TLC), and ThriveNYC, the nation's most comprehensive approach to mental health.

Before joining the Mayor's team, he served for four years as a Senior Aide to New York State Comptroller Thomas P. DiNapoli, where his responsibilities included working on intergovernmental affairs and a deep involvement with communities across New York State. Eichenstein is proud to have worked with many nonprofit organizations and community groups in helping New Yorkers identify and reclaim funds owed through the state's unclaimed funds program. He also served as the Political Affairs Director at a public relations firm, as a Special Assistant in the New York State legislature, and as a member of Brooklyn's Community Board 12.

Eichenstein is a graduate of New York's yeshiva system and a lifelong resident of Borough Park. He and his wife, Pearl, have four children.

## STEVEN C. ENGLEBRIGHT (D)
*4th - Part of Suffolk County*

149 Main Street, East Setauket, NY 11733
631-751-3094/engles@nyassembly.gov

Legislative Office Building, Room 621, Albany, NY 12248
518-455-4804

Steve Englebright was elected to the New York State Assembly in 1992. His north shore, Long Island district includes Port Jefferson Station and sections of Coram, Centereach, Selden and Lake Grove as well as the historic maritime communities that developed around the harbors of Stony Brook, Setauket, Port Jefferson, and Mount Sinai. Englebright chairs the Assembly's Committee on Environmental Conservation, and sits on the following standing Committees: Energy; Higher Education; Science & Technology; and Rules. Trained as a geologist and biologist, his scientific background informs his legislative approach, such as his successful advocacy on behalf of a state ban on the sale of baby bottles and other childcare products containing BPA, bisphenol-A which disrupts estrogen. He pushed successfully for the NYS Pine Barrens Protection Act, authored New York's solar and wind net-metering laws in the 1990s, and successfully worked in 2008 for the expansion of solar net-metering to include all utility customer classes. In addition, he advocated on behalf of advancing the NY-SUNY2020 Challenge Grant Program in an effort to expand research and economic development, as well as increased access to education at Stony Brook. Assemblyman Englebright's previous elective office includes service in the Suffolk County Legislature from 1983-1992. The Georgia-born Englebright holds a BS from the University of Tennessee, and an MS in Paleontology/Sedimentology from SUNY Stony Brook. The father of two children lives in Setauket.

## HARVEY EPSTEIN (D)
*74th - Part of New York County*

107 Avenue B, New York, NY 10009
212-979-9696/epsteins@nyassembly.gov

Legislative Office Building, Room 419, Albany, NY 12248
518-455-5506

Harvey Epstein represents the East Side of Manhattan, including the neighborhoods of the Lower East Side, East Village, Alphabet City, Stuyvesant Town/Peter Cooper Village, Murray Hill, Tudor City, and the United Nations. In the Assembly he is Chair of the Subcommittee on Retention of Homeownership and Stabilization of Affordable Housing and sits on the following committees: Agriculture; Environmental Conservation; Governmental Operations; Higher Education; Housing; and People with Disabilities. He is also a member of the Task Force on People with Disabilities.

Assemblyman Epstein has been a public interest lawyer in New York City since graduating from CUNY Law School in 1994. Throughout his career serving our city, he has worked on critical economic development and housing issues. During the five years he served as a tenant member of the Rent Guidelines Board, he was instrumental in successfully orchestrating the first rent freeze for one-year leases in the 47-year history of the Rent Guidelines Board.

An experienced leader and community organizer for social justice, Epstein has been active in his community and has served as PTA President for his children's elementary school. He resides in the East Village with his wife, Anita, two children, Leila and Joshua, and their rescue dog, Homer.

## PATRICIA FAHY (D)
*109th - City of Albany and Towns of Bethlehem, Guilderland and New Scotland*

Legislative Office Building, Room 452, Albany, NY 12248
518-455-4178/FahyP@nyassembly.gov

Patricia Fahy was first elected to the New York State Assembly in 2012. She is Vice Chair of the Majority Steering Committee. She also sits on the following standing Committees: Codes; Children and Families; Economic Development, Job Creation, and Commerce and Industry; Environmental Conservation; Higher Education; Tourism, Parks, Arts, and Sports Development; and Transportation. In addition, she is a member of the Task Force on Women's Issues and the Legislative Women's Caucus. Prior to running for the Assembly, Fahy served as President of the Albany City School Board for one of her four years on the board. Professionally, Fahy boasts an extensive background in labor-related, legislative issues. She was Associate Commissioner of Intergovernmental Affairs and Federal Policy at the NYS Department of Labor for five years. She co-chaired the Disconnected Youth Work Group of Governor Paterson's Children's Cabinet. Prior to moving to Albany in 1997, she was Executive Director of the Chicago Workforce Board. Prior to that time, she worked as both a Legislative Assistant and a Legislative Analyst on Capitol Hill in Washington, DC, then went on to become the Associate Director for Employment and Training in the US Department of Labor Congressional Affairs Office. The Chicago-area native has been active within her community, including service on the University Albany Center for Women in Government and Civil Society since 2009. She earned a BS from Northern Illinois University and an MPA from the University of Illinois at Chicago. She is married to RPI professor Dr. B. Wayne Bequette. The couple has two children.

## CHARLES FALL (D)
*61st - Part of Richmond County*

853 Forest Avenue, Staten Island, NY 10310
718-442-9932/fallc@nyassembly.gov

Legislative Office Building, Room 534, Albany, NY 12248
518-455-4677

Charles Fall represents New York's 61st Assembly District covering the North Shore of Staten Island, where he has resided his whole life. Fall is the first Muslim and African-American Assembly Member elected from Staten Island. Fall is Chair of the Subcommittee on Consumer Fraud Protection and serves on the following committees: Aging; Cities; Consumer Affairs and Protection; Corporations, Authorities, and Commissions; Governmental Employees; and Tourism, Parks, Arts, and Sports Development. Fall is also a member of the Black, Puerto Rican, Hispanic & Asian Legislative Caucus.

Assemblyman Fall comes from a working-class family of six. His parents immigrated to Staten Island from Guinea, West Africa, and displayed a commitment to improving the lives of those around them. Fall's legislative priorities revolve around comprehensive strategies to ensure stable and healthier communities. This includes expanding resources for teachers, parents, and students to resolve academic disparities; creating affordable housing options; ensuring individuals and families have sufficient health coverage and access to vital services; and improving transportation infrastructure; and other longstanding community concerns on the North Shore.

Fall's priority is to develop and strengthen relationships between community leaders and elected officials and champion solutions for community issues. In 2014, he served as the Staten Island Borough Director and Citywide Islamic Liaison for the Mayor of New York City, working to ensure universal prekindergarten and paid sick leave became realities. Fall then became the Chief of Staff to the Staten Island Parks and Recreation Commissioner with the desire to enhance local greenery to encourage community recreation and create safer neighborhoods. Fall earned his BA from Southwestern College in Kansas and received a master of public administration with honors at Pace University.

Fall's passion for running and basketball causes him to start each morning with a run, and host basketball clinics for young kids in his community.

He resides in his childhood neighborhood, Mariners Harbor, with his high school sweetheart, Alesse, and their two daughters, Maimouna and Naila.

## NATHALIA FERNANDEZ (D)
*80th - Part of Bronx County*

2018 Williamsbridge Road, Bronx, NY 10461
718-409-0109/fernandezn@nyassembly.gov

Legislative Office Building, Room 540, Albany, NY 12248
518-455-5844

Nathalia Fernandez represents New York's 80th District covering a part of the Bronx, which includes Allerton, Pelham Gardens, and Morris Park, among others. In the Assembly, she is Chair of the Subcommittee on Effective Treatment and sits on these standing Committees: Alcoholism and Drug Abuse; Cities; Mental Health; Oversight, Analysis and Investigation; Social Services; and Tourism, Parks, Arts, and Sports Development. She is also a member of the Black, Puerto Rican, Hispanic & Asian Legislative Caucus; the Puerto Rican/Hispanic Task Force; the Task Force on Women's Issues; and the Legislative Women's Caucus.

A daughter of immigrant parents, she was raised to understand the benefit of a strong work ethic. Her father, William, migrated with his family from Cuba to the Bronx at a young age and started his own business painting apartments in his late teens to help his father support the family. Her mother, Sonia, came to the United States from Colombia and found her home in the neighborhood of Bedford Park.

The Bronx has always been a home away from home for her. Upon graduating from Hofstra University, she found herself volunteering for change within the Bronx. Fernandez was driven by her compassion for

her peers and neighbors, and it was no surprise when she served the 80th Assembly District as Chief of Staff to former Assemblyman Mark Gjonaj. During her time in the 80th Assembly District, Fernandez led numerous projects and initiatives. Under her direction, the Assembly office provided internships and numerous volunteer opportunities to high school and college students, organized events and health care services for seniors, and planned numerous community events. Public service became her passion and provided the fulfillment she was seeking in her career.

In early 2017, Fernandez joined the Executive Chamber at the highest level of state government as the Bronx Regional Representative for Governor Andrew Cuomo. She has worked with all sectors of government and community stakeholders to advance projects and services that benefit constituents. In addition to her numerous responsibilities, she educated the borough on the availability of the Excelsior Scholarship and the paid family leave program. She was active in awarding $10 million to the Bronx Civic Center under the Governor's Downstate Revitalization Initiative. In partnership with the Bronx borough president's office, this project allowed her to work closely with community stakeholders and small businesses to create a uniform plan of execution on how best to utilize the grant.

## MICHAEL J. FITZPATRICK (R)
*8th - Part of Suffolk County*

285 Middle County Road, Suite 202, Smithtown, NY 11787
631-724-2929/FitzpatrickM@nyassembly.gov

Legislative Office Building, Room 458, Albany, NY
12248/518-455-5021

Michael J. Fitzpatrick was elected to the New York State Assembly representing the 7th Assembly District in November 2002. His district includes the town of Smithtown and parts of Islip and Brookhaven townships. Fitzpatrick currently holds the leadership position of Vice Chair of the Assembly Minority Conference Program Committee. He is the Ranking Minority Member of the Housing Committee, and also sits on the following committees: Agriculture; Banks; Higher Education; and Ways and Means. Professionally, Fitzpatrick is an Investment Associate with Morgan Stanley in the firm's Port Jefferson branch office. Prior to his election to the Assembly, Fitzpatrick was an elected member of the Smithtown Town Council for 15 years, from 1988 through 2003. Fitzpatrick is Secretary of the New York State American-Irish Legislators Society, and active in his local community. Born in Jamaica, Queens and raised in Hauppauge, Fitzpatrick received his BA in business administration from St. Michael's College in Vermont. He and his wife live in St. James, in Smithtown, and are parents to two children.

## PHARA SOUFFRANT FORREST (D)
*57th - Parts of Queens County*

55 Hanson Place, Brooklyn, NY 11217
718-596-0100/souffrantforrestp@nyassembly.gov

Legislative Office Building, Room 542, Albany, NY 12248
518-455-5325

Phara Souffrant Forrest is serving her first term in the New York State Assembly representing the 57th Assembly District, which consists of the neighborhoods of Fort Greene and Clinton Hill as well as parts of Bed Stuy, Prospect Heights and Crown Heights. The Assemblywoman is Chair of the Subcommittee on Intergenerational Care and sits as a member on the following Committees: Aging; Consumer Affairs and Protection; Higher Education; Insurance; Social Services; and the Task Force on Women's Issues.

As a lifelong Brooklynite, Forrest is a proud product of Brooklyn's public schools system, attending both Phillipa Schuyler Middle School and Benjamin Banneker Academy for Community Development. She then went on to attend SUNY Geneseo, where she majored in political science before moving on to obtain a nursing degree at CUNY City Tech. Before being elected to the Assembly, she worked for a number of years as a maternal child health field nurse, where she would care for new mothers after they gave birth.

In addition to her work as a nurse, Forrest is President of her building's tenant association and has been an active member of the Crown Heights Tenant Union. She credits her run for the Assembly to her work in tenant organizing and her work to help pressure the State Legislature to pass the Housing Stability & Tenant Protection Act of 2019. As part of her work, the Assembly Member participated in a demonstration at the Capitol, where she was arrested fighting for her fellow tenants, and credits this moment to inspire her to run for the Assembly.

---

### CHRISTOPHER S. FRIEND (R)
*124th - Tioga County and Parts of Broome and Chemung Counties*

1250 Schweizer Road, Horseheads, NY 14845
607-562-3602/friendc@nyassembly.gov

Legislative Office Building, Room 938, Albany, NY 12248
518-455-4538

Christopher Friend was elected to the New York State Assembly in 2011. His district includes all of Tioga County; the Town of Maine in Broome County; the city of Elmira; the towns of Ashland, Baldwin, Big Flats, Chemung, Elmira, Horseheads, Southport, and the villages of Elmira Heights, Horseheads, and Wellsburg in Chemung County. He is the Ranking Minority Member on the Committee on Children and Families and the Committee on Local Governments, and also sits on the following committees: Aging; Agriculture; Corporations, Authorities, and Commissions; Economic Development, Job Creation, and Commerce and Industry; Housing; and Science & Technology. A chemist by training, he has published more than 20 scientific papers and symposiums. Friend's public service began with work on advisory boards and commissions for the Town of Big Flats starting in 2004. He moved on to the Chemung County Legislature, to which he was elected in 2006. Assemblyman Friend holds a BS in chemistry from the University of New Hampshire, as well as a master's and PhD in chemistry from the SUNY at Buffalo. He and his wife live in Big Flats with their four children.

---

### MATHYLDE FRONTUS (D)
*80th - Part of Bronx County*

2002 Mermaid Avenue, Brooklyn, NY 11224
718-266-0267 /FrontusM@nyassembly.gov

310 93rd Street, Brooklyn, NY 11209
347-560-6302

Legislative Office Building, Room 324, Albany, NY 12248
518-455-4811

Mathylde Frontus represents the 46th Assembly District, covering all of Coney Island and Sea Gate, as well as parts of Bath Beach, Bay Ridge, Brighton Beach, Dyker Heights and Gravesend. Frontus is the fifth Haitian-American elected to the New York State Assembly, and the second Haitian-American woman elected from New York City. In the Assembly, she is Chair on the Subcommittee on Minority Mental Health and serves on the following committees: Aging; Children and Families; Economic Development, Job Creation, Commerce and Industry; Mental Health; Tourism, Parks, Arts, and Sports Development; and Transportation. She is also a member of the Black, Puerto Rican, Hispanic & Asian Legislative Caucus; the Task Force on Women's Issues; and the Legislative Women's Caucus.

Frontus has lived in Coney Island for over 30 years and is a well-known community leader and advocate, mostly for her role as the founder of three organizations in Coney Island and the architect of various programs in her neighborhood which have positively impacted hundreds of individuals, youth, and families. From 2004-2016, she served as the Founder and Executive Director of Urban Neighborhood Services (UNS), a

one-stop shop social service agency that provides a range of programs and initiatives such as financial literacy, veterans support, health education, LGBTQ resources, legal assistance, college prep, reentry services for the formerly incarcerated, job and housing assistance, mental health services and youth leadership development.

During her tenure at UNS, she also founded two coalitions to address gun violence in the Coney Island community. In December 2009, she created the Coney Island Coalition against Violence and was elected as its Co-Chair. In December 2013, after two back-to-back fatal shootings in the community, she founded the Coney Island Anti-Violence Collaborative and served as the Acting Chair of the group until December 2015. From 2015-2017, she served on the steering committee of the organization.

Assemblywomen Frontus' commitment to public service dates back to high school. As a young student at Edward R. Murrow High School, she was active in Council for Unity, organizing events to promote cross-cultural dialogue. As a college student at NYU, she founded a chapter of Council for Unity on campus and organized various events to promote racial, ethnic and religious tolerance and unity. She served on the Community Advisory Board at Coney Island Hospital, the Community Learning Schools Advisory Board at P.S. 188, and the NYPD 60th Precinct Community Council. She's run a book club at the Coney Island Public Library to promote reading and literacy. Her record of service has earned her various awards including the 2014 Characters Unite Award from the USA Network/NBC Universal. She was one of ten national recipients recognized by the network for combating hate, intolerance, and discrimination and making significant contributions to promoting greater tolerance, respect, and acceptance in their communities.

Frontus received a BSW and MSW from NYU, an MA in clinical psychology from Teachers College, Columbia University, as well as a master's of theological studies from Harvard Divinity School. In May 2015, she received her PhD from the Columbia University School of Social Work where she specialized in social policy & administration. In 2016, she was appointed as an Adjunct Assistant Professor at the Columbia University School of Social Work.

---

### SANDRA R. GALEF (D)
*95th - Parts of Westchester County*

2 Church Street, Ossining, NY 10562
914-941-1111/GalefS@nyassembly.gov

Legislative Office Building, Room 641, Albany, NY 12248
518-455-5348

Sandy Galef was first elected to the Assembly in 1992. Her district covers the Towns of Cortlandt, Ossining, Kent, Philipstown, and the City of Peekskill. She chairs the Real Property Taxation Committee and also serves on the following committees: Corporations, Authorities, and Commissions; Election Law; Governmental Operations; and Health. She has held previous leadership positions, including Chair of the Libraries and Education Technology Committee. Galef also serves on the Assembly Majority Steering Committee and the Hudson Valley Greenway Communities Council. Her recent legislative successes include Assembly passage of legislation to end sexual harassment in smaller businesses and work environments. She has been a leading advocate in the legislature for tax reduction, education, government efficiency, environmental/clean energy, health, voting rights, organ donation, the disability community, and senior citizens. Before her election to the Assembly, Galef sat on the Westchester County Legislature for 13 years, including eight as the Board of Legislator's minority leader. Galef is a former teacher in the Scarsdale school system and has been deeply active in Westchester community affairs for many years. Nationally, she chaired the National Association of Counties' Labor and Employee Benefits Steering Committee, and received an Eastern Leadership Academy fellowship from the University of Pennsylvania Fels Institute of Government. Galef has sat on the boards of directors of numerous health or educational organizations

Biographies

in the Westchester region, and has received numerous awards, including the American Cancer Society, NYS Association of Counties, NYS Federation of Police, Reality Check Organization, and the NY Library Association. She also hosts two TV shows, called "Dear Sandy" and "Speakout with Sandy Galef." She holds a BS from Purdue University and an MEd from the University of Virginia. Galef, a widow, resides in Ossining and has two children.

## EMILY GALLAGHER (D)
*50th - Part of Kings County*

Legislative Office Building, Room 818, Albany, NY 12248
518-455-4477/gallaghere@nyassembly.gov

Emily Gallagher is an activist, organizer, and nonprofit professional who serves as the Assembly Member for New York's 50th District (Greenpoint, Williamsburg Clinton Hill, Ft. Greene, Brooklyn). Gallagher's career has been focused on fostering a relationship of mutual empowerment between local communities and the institutions that serve them. In the Assembly, she is Chair of the Subcommittee on Child Product Safety and sits on the following Committees: Alcoholism and Drug Abuse; Consumer Affairs and Protection; Election Law; Small Business; Transportation; and the Task Force on Women's Issues.

A native of Rochester, New York, Gallagher graduated from Ithaca College in 2006 where she majored in cinema and visual studies with a dual minor in art and art history. This path led her to New York City, where she worked several jobs in art galleries and as an artist assistant. During this time, she struggled to make ends meet, sometimes balancing up to five part-time jobs at once. Gallagher developed a deeper sense of the profound inequalities and challenges confronting working people in New York and became passionately interested in the stories of her Greenpoint neighbors, particularly the district's rich history of local community activism.

Eventually, Gallagher transitioned to work in Museum Education in New York City history, including several years at the Lower East Side Tenement Museum and Brooklyn Historical Society. In 2015, she became the Community Affairs Director for Hostelling International, a federation of youth hostels around the world with an iconic location in Harlem, where she worked to improve environmental sustainability and develop deeper cooperation between the tourism industry and the local communities where it operates.

A passionate lifelong volunteer, Assemblywoman Gallagher spent her free time community organizing in Greenpoint and Williamsburg, eventually becoming the co-chair of the environmental and social justice activist group Neighbors Allied for Good Growth (NAG) from 2008 to 2015, and penning a weekly column for the local paper, the *Greenpoint Star*, beginning in 2015. Gallagher focused on the intersectional nature of the problems facing her community, especially around environmental degradation, health inequality, tenants' rights, and a rapidly gentrifying waterfront.

After participating in the fight against waterfront luxury rezonings in 2008, Gallagher joined several grassroots organizations. That fall, she was appointed as a member of Brooklyn Community Board 1. In 2020, Gallagher was elected North Brooklyn's first new member of the Assembly in nearly 50 years. It is her passion for grassroots activism that brought her to state government, and working for her constituents' needs remains her top priority. Gallagher seeks to bring transformational change to New York, protecting the environment and guaranteeing a dignified life for all.

## JEFF GALLAHAN (R)
*131st - Ontario County and Parts of Seneca County*

70 Elizabeth Blackwell Street, Geneva, NY 14456
315-781-2030/gallahanj@nyassembly.gov

Legislative Office Building, Room 725, Albany, NY 12248
518-455-3979

Jeff Gallahan was elected to the New York State Assembly on November 3, 2020. His district is comprised of Ontario County and parts of Seneca County. In the Assembly, he is a member of the following Committees: Aging; Children and Families; Local Governments; Racing and Wagering; and Tourism, Parks, Arts and Sports Development.

Assemblyman Gallahan believes that his real-world experience is beneficial to the people of his district and throughout New York. As a believer in the "American Dream" he raised his children to be hardworking while leading by example. Gallahan fights to hold the line on taxes and pushes for an end to recently enacted bail reform measures. He believes that in this critical time in history we should ensure law enforcement has all the tools necessary to keep our communities safe. He is committed to standing up for middle-class values, small businesses, and our important agricultural community.

Prior to being elected, Gallahan was a journeyman machinist at the General Railway Signal Company, moved into cutting tool sales with various manufacturers and moved up the ranks, eventually taking on a number of management roles. He and his wife, Lynn, are proud small business owners and founded CR7 Food Trailer and Catering in 2017. The business serves Manchester and surrounding communities. Through this venture, they are able to give back to a variety of causes by donating their time and resources, including the Boy Scouts of America and the Shortsville American Legion. He has also served as the Manchester Town Supervisor for 11 years and 4 years prior as town councilman.

Assemblyman Gallahan is the founder of the Red Jacket High School trap shooting team, teaching local youth about firearms safety. He also volunteers for the Sons of the American Legion, Clifton Springs Area YMCA and is a proud supporter of the Back the Blue movement and local sportsman clubs.

A lifelong resident of Ontario County, he and his wife of 42 years Lynn, are the parents of two children and three grandchildren.

## JARETT GANDOLFO (R)
*7th - Parts of Suffolk County*

859 Montauk Highwat, Suite 1, Bayport, NY 11705
631-5898-0348/gandolfoj@nyassembly.gov

Legislative Office Building, Room 426, Albany, NY 12248
518-455-4611

Jarett Gandolfo was elected to the New York State Assembly on November 3, 2020. The 7th Assembly District includes parts of Suffolk County, including Bay Shore, Brightwaters, Islip, East Islip, Islip Terrace, Great River, Oakdale, Bohemia, West Sayville, Sayville, Bayport, Blue Point, Patchogue, and East Patchogue. In the Assembly, he is a member of the following Committees: Alcoholism and Drug Abuse; Higher Education; Insurance; Mental Health; and Racing and Wagering.

Prior to being elected to the Assembly, Gandolfo worked alongside former Assemblyman Andrew Garbarino as his Chief of Staff. In that role, Jarett dedicated his time to serving the communities and residents of the 7th Assembly District. From working to help constituents, to securing grants for local municipalities, and nonprofits and advocating on behalf of local organizations to support their initiatives, he has a deep understanding of government and its processes. While in Albany, he is eager to continue to work on behalf of his constituents.

Assemblyman Gandolfo is proud of his blue-collar upbringing during which his parents instilled in him the importance of a strong work ethic, the value of education, and the significance of family. He worked at his grandfather's window treatment shop, and as a supermarket cashier and warehouse delivery driver while in school.

As an Assemblyman, he works to advance policies that strengthen the local economy, help businesses, and support law enforcement, and also to repeal recently-enacted bail reform laws.

Dedicated to public service, Gandolfo serves on the Board of Directors of the Islip Community Development Agency, an organization that helps local families buy homes, works to clean up neighborhoods, and provides financial assistance to local nonprofits.

Gandolfo graduated from SUNY Albany where he earned a degree in criminal justice, and then went on to earn a MPA degree and a certificate in city management from Villanova University. He and his wife, Natalia, are residents of Sayville.

## JODI GIGLIO (R)
*2nd - Parts of Suffolk County*

30 W. Main Street, Suite 101, Riverhead, NY 11901
631-727-0204/giglioj@nyassembly.gov

Legislative Office Building, Room 720, Albany, NY 12248
518-455-5777

Jodi Giglio was elected to the New York State Assembly on November 3, 2020. Her district includes the North Fork of Long Island in Suffolk County, portions of the town of Brookhaven, and the towns of Riverhead and Southold. In the Assembly, she is a member of the following Committees: Consumer Affairs and Protection; Economic Development, Job Creation, Commerce and Industry; Governmental Employees; Tourism, Parks, Arts and Sports Development; and the Commission on Water Resource Needs of New York State.

Giglio's experience as a Riverhead Town councilwoman and proud business owner will undoubtedly position her to represent the people of the 2nd Assembly District well. She is committed to fixing Albany and prepared to help address and change the state's current fiscal climate; she understands the importance of finding solutions to reduce the state's significant budget deficit in order to help businesses and taxpayers thrive. She will work to advance legislation that prioritizes the needs of hardworking Long Islanders and ensures taxpayer money is reinvested in Suffolk County. While in Albany, Giglio will fight for measures that cut wasteful spending, make communities safer, create high-paying jobs, and protect the environment.

Prior to being elected to the Assembly, Assemblywoman Giglio served on the Riverhead Town Council for more than 10 years. As a small business owner eager for change in local government, she works on behalf of her constituents; her track record speaks for itself. As councilwoman, she initiated several strategies to save the town and its residents millions of dollars by implementing process improvements and eliminating wasteful spending. In the Assembly, Giglio is focused on addressing the state's crumbling infrastructure, developing initiatives to better train our future workforce, and providing critical care and funding for our most vulnerable residents and veterans.

Giglio is a proud union member of Local 138, International Union of Operating Engineers, and successfully runs a NYS Certified Women-Owned Business Enterprise; she has also been honored by Minority Millennials Inc. as a Woman of Distinction for her positive impact on minorities and youth.

Assembly Member Giglio has been a resident of Baiting Hollow for the last 20 years and is a mother of three. Her experience in the private and public sectors equip her with a unique perspective on how to tackle the state's toughest challenges, particularly in the wake of the COVID-19 pandemic. She promotes commonsense solutions that will restore the power back to the people of New York State and put the economy back on the right track.

## JOSEPH M. GIGLIO (R-C-I)
*148th - Cattaraugus County, Allegany County and parts of Steuben County*

700 W. State Street, Olean, NY 14760
716-373-7103/GiglioJ@nyassembly.gov

Legislative Office Building, Roo 525, Albany, NY 12248
518-455-5241

Joseph Giglio was first elected to the Assembly in 2005. His district includes all of Cattaraugus and Allegany counties, as well as the towns of Greenwood, Jasper, Troupsburg, and West Union in Steuben County. The district also includes parts of three Seneca Nation of Indians reservations. He chairs the Assembly Minority Conference's Steering Committee and is Ranking Minority Member of the Corrections Committee. His other committee memberships are as follows: Correction; Ethics and Guidance; Codes; and Rules. Within the Assembly, Giglio co-chaired the Minority Statewide Forum on Workforce Issues in the Correctional System. As a former State Deputy Inspector General, Giglio focused on investigating criminal and corruption in state agencies and those who do business with the state within the Western New York area. In addition, he worked as a Special Assistant in the State Attorney General's office, and the sheriff's departments for both the Cattaraugus and Erie County sheriff's departments. His many awards include one from the New York State Farm Bureau as a member of their "circle of friends" for his perfect voting record in support of agricultural issues. He holds a bachelor's degree from the State University of New York at Buffalo. He is married, the father of four, and lives in Gowanda.

## DEBORAH J. GLICK (D)
*66th - Part of New York County*

853 Broadway, Suite 2007, New York, NY 10003
212-674-5153/GlickD@nyassembly.gov

Legislative Office Building, Room 717, Albany, NY 12248
518-455-4841

Deborah Glick was first elected to the Assembly in 1990, and is the first openly lesbian or gay member of the New York State Legislature. She chairs the Higher Education Committee and sits on the following committees: Environmental Conservation; Governmental Operations; Rules; and Ways and Means. She is also a member of the Task Force on Women's Issues and the Legislative Women's Caucus. Prior to being elected to the Assembly, Glick owned and managed a small TriBeCa printing business, and later became Deputy Director of General Services for the City Department of Housing, Preservation and Development. Her legislative achievements include passage of the Sexual Orientation Non-Discrimination Act (SONDA), which was signed into law in 2002, as well as the Women's Health and Wellness Act, which became law in 2003. She saw her Hospital Visitation Bill, which gives domestic partners the same rights as spouses and next-of-kin when the loved one is in a hospital or nursing facility, became law in 2004. She also backed the Loft Law, which brings former commercial buildings up to residential code and protects current tenants, many of them artists, from eviction. Additional legislative priorities for Glick are improving conditions in New York City's mass transit system; advocating for pedestrian and driver safety at crosswalks; and protecting animals from others using their fur in novelties. She graduated from the City University of New York's Queens College and holds an MBA from Fordham University.

## JESSICA GONZALEZ-ROJAS (R)
*34th - Part of Queens County*

75-35 31st Avenue, Suite 206B (2nd Floor), East Elmhurst, NY 11370
718-457-0384/ gonzalezrojasj@nyassembly.gov

Legislative Office Building, Room 941, Albany, NY 12248
518-455-4545

In 2020, Jessica González-Rojas was elected to the New York State Assembly representing the 34th Assembly District, which includes the diverse Queens communities of Jackson Heights, East Elmhurst, Woodside, and Corona. She is a social justice leader who has dedicated her life—on both the local and national level—to fight for immigrant rights, racial justice, and gender equity. In the Assembly, she is Chair of the Subcommittee on Human Trafficking; she is also a member of the following Committees: Children and Families; Cities; Corporation, Authorities and Commissions; Environmental Conservation; Social Services; the Asian Pacific American Task Force; the Black, Puerto Rican, Hispanic & Asian Legislative Caucus; the Legislative Women's Caucus; the Task Force on New Americans; the Puerto Rican/Hispanic Task Force; and the Task Force on Women's Issues.

For 13 years, Gonzalez-Rojas served in leadership at the National Latina Institute for Reproductive Justice, the only national reproductive justice organization that is dedicated to building Latina power to advance health, dignity, and justice for 29 million Latinas, their families, and communities in the United States. She has been a leader in progressive movements for over two decades. She successfully forges connections between reproductive health, gender, immigration, LGBTQ liberation, labor and Latinx civil rights, breaking down barriers between movements and building a strong Latina grassroots presence.

Assembly Member Gonzalez-Rojas is a longtime leader in community and electoral politics. Before running for State Assembly in 2020, she was elected to the New York State Committee from 2002 to 2006. She has received proclamations from the New York State Senate, New York State Assembly, New York City Comptroller, and New York City Council for her local and national advocacy. Through a leadership program at the National Association of Latino Elected and Appointed Officials (NALEO), she served as a Community Liaison in two district offices of Congresswoman Nydia M. Velázquez.

Gonzalez-Rojas has held leadership roles in numerous local and national organizations that promote social justice advocacy. For 12 years, she served on the Board of Directors of New Immigrant Community Empowerment (NICE), a Queens-based nonprofit whose mission is to ensure that immigrants can build social, political and economic power. She was appointed as the Queens representative rider advocate for the New York City Transit Riders Council/Permanent Citizens Advisory Committee to the MTA and served in that role for 8 years, advocating for the needs of subway and bus riders from the community. She served as vice chair of the National Hispanic Leadership Agenda, a coalition of the most prominent national Latinx civil rights organizations in the country, and co-chaired its Health Committee and Latina Task Force. She has worked in the field of early childhood education, higher education, disability rights, veterans' health, and racial justice. Gonzalez-Rojas was selected as a Rockwood Leadership Institute Leading from the Inside Out Fellow for the 2016 to 2017 cohort and for the New American Leaders Fellowship program in 2019.

Assemblywoman Gonzalez-Rojas served as an adjunct professor at NYU's Robert F. Wagner Graduate School of Public Service and the City University of New York's (CUNY) City College and has taught courses on Latinidad, reproductive rights, gender, and sexuality. She holds a master's degree from the NYU Wagner School, with a concentration in public and nonprofit management and public policy. Gonzalez-Rojas has bachelor's degree in international relations from Boston University, where she graduated cum laude, and completed a certificate program from the Institute for Not-for-Profit Management at Columbia University's Graduate School of Business. The Assemblywoman was born in Queens and has lived in the community she represents for over two decades. She resides with her partner, Danny, and their young son who attends a local public school in Jackson Heights.

## ANDREW W. "ANDY" GOODELL (R-C-I)
*150th - Chautauqua County*

Fenton Building, 2 E. 2nd Street, Suite 320, Jamestown, NY 14701
716-664-7773/goodella@nyassembly.gov

Legislative Office Building, Albany, NY 12248
518-455-4328

Andy Goodell was elected to the New York State Assembly in 2010. He is Assembly Minority Leader Pro Tempore and is the Ranking Minority member on the Social Services Committee. In addition, he sits on the following committees: Cities; Governmental Operations; Social Services; and the Commission on Administrative Regulations Review. Goodell was the author of legislation for legal services for the disabled, criminal laws against hazardous waste violators, health insurance coverage for midwife services, and illegal evictions. He is managing partner at the law firm of Goodell & Rankin. Goodell's public service includes eight years as county executive for Chautauqua County. As county executive, he cut the tax rate six years in a row. In the community, he is founding member and former officer of the Chautauqua Leadership Network; Past President of the Jamestown Rotary; Treasurer for Bemus Bay Pops; and former President of the SUNY Fredonia Business Administration and Accounting Advisory Board; former Secretary and Board Member of the Chautauqua Area Girl Scout Council; Co-Chair of the Camp Timbercrest Capital Campaign; and former Co-chair of the United Way Professional Division. He is a Fellow of the New York Academy of Medicine, and a member of the American Public Health Association, the New York Civil Liberties Union, the Art Students League, and the China Institute. Goodell has earned numerous awards, including the Ed Crawford Award, the highest honor bestowed by the New York State Association of Counties. He holds undergraduate degrees in political science and mathematics from Williams College and his law degree from Cornell Law School, where he was a member of the Cornell Law Review. He is married with three daughters, a stepson, and several grandchildren.

## RICHARD N. GOTTFRIED (D-WF)
*75th - Part of New York County*

214 W. 29th Street, Suite 1002, New York, NY 10001
212-807-7900/GottfriedR@nyassembly.gov

Legislative Office Building, Room 822, Albany, NY 12248
518-455-4941

Richard N. Gottfried was first elected to the New York State Assembly in 1971 and represents a district that includes Chelsea, Hell's Kitchen, Murray Hill, Midtown and part of the Lincoln Center area in Manhattan. Gottfried is a member of the Assembly Majority Steering Committee and Chair on the Health Committee. He also sits on the Higher Education and Rules Committees and is a member of the Asian Pacific American Task Force. He is the former Deputy Majority Leader and Assistant Majority Leader, and has chaired major committees, including the Assembly Committee on Health since 1987. Gottfried's achievements in his long tenure helming the health committee are numerous; he was a major architect of New York's landmark managed care reforms. His legislative achievements include the passage of the Prenatal Care Assistance Program for low-income women; the Child Health Plus Program that allows low- and moderate-income parents to get free or low-cost health insurance for their children; Family Health Plus that provides free health coverage for low-income adults; and the Health Care Proxy Law. He has advocated on behalf of patient autonomy, especially in end-of-life care, and reproductive freedom. Gottfried introduced the first same-sex marriage bill in the Assembly in 2003, and was a cosponsor of the bill that became law in 2011. He also sponsors the Gender Non-Discrimination Act (GENDA), to prohibit discrimination based on gender identity (transgender); a bill to prohibit New York-licensed health professionals from cooperating in the torture or improper treatment of prisoners; and the bill to legalize the use of medical marijuana. Gottfried is a leading advocate in the legislature for civil liberties, reproductive freedom, and gay rights. He has received numerous awards, including being named to the New York Civil Liberties Union's Honor Roll and the Environmental Legislator of the Year Award from the Environmental Advocates. He is a Fellow of the New York Academy of Medicine, holds an undergraduate degree from Cornell University, and a JD from Columbia Law School. He lives in Manhattan with his wife; they have one child and a grandchild.

## JUDY GRIFFIN (D)
*21st - Part of Nassau County*

74 N. Village Avenue, Rockville Centre, NY 11570
516-561-8216/griffinj@nyassembly.gov

Legislative Office Building, Room 432, Albany, NY 12248
518-455-4656

Judy Griffin was elected on November 6, 2018, to represent the 21st Assembly District, which includes Lynbrook, Rockville Centre, Malverne, South Hempstead, Baldwin and parts of Freeport, West Hempstead, Oceanside, East Rockaway, Lakeview, Hewlett, Hempstead, Franklin Square, and Valley Stream. In the Assembly, she is Chair of the Commission on Toxic Substances and Hazardous Wastes and serves on the following standing Committees: Alcoholism and Drug Abuse; Economic Development, Job Creation, Commerce, and Industry; Environmental Conservation; Governmental Employees; and Higher Education. She is also a member of the Legislative Women's Caucus and the Task Force on Women's Issues.

Directly before she was elected to office, Griffin served for several years as a Senior Advisor and Director of Community Outreach to NY State Senator Todd Kaminsky. As his Director of Community Outreach, she was particularly successful in developing productive relationships with many of the same business and civic leaders in Senator Kaminsky's district whom she will now represent in Albany. As Assemblywoman, Griffin is thrilled that she will be able to continue to dedicate herself to working for, and fighting for, the interests of all of the residents of the 21st District.

Griffin's career in advocacy was initially inspired by her natural interest in her own children's educational experiences. As a mother, she understood the incredible impact that teachers would have on her children and instinctively appreciated the importance of having caring, dedicated and compassionate educators. She advocated for programs that enable all students to thrive, especially those with special education classifications. Her educational advocacy efforts later broadened to tackle many other critical issues that led her to the frontlines as a leader of the nascent "Opt-Out" movement, where she fought to rid school districts of unfair standardized testing practices. She believes students should spend their time in school learning, not merely test taking, and teachers, as professionals, should be evaluated as such.

Assemblywoman Griffin is actively involved in the community. She joined the Rockville Centre Newcomers Club upon moving to Rockville Centre and became President the following year. She was a member of the RVC Mercy League, a Brownie and Girl Scout Leader, and an engaged PTA member who chaired many committees at local schools. She was also an activist in various local issues. In 2016, she was Senator Kaminsky's representative on the Rockville Centre Coalition for Youth, serving as Government Representative from June 2016 to June 2018. As an Assemblywoman, she is now on the Government Sector for the group. Later in 2016, she became a founding member of Raising Voices USA, a civic engagement advocacy group.

Her legislative priorities include: bringing back a fair share of the tax revenue to the district; ensuring government is kept out of women's personal reproductive health decisions; strengthening gun safety measures; expanding voting rights; promoting legislation to protect our environment; and enacting commonsense ethics rules to clean up corruption in Albany. She advocates for a comprehensive approach to the opioid epidemic, with more emphasis on prevention, and is exploring more effective ways to help our veterans, seniors, and young people.

Griffin holds a BS in business economics with minors in political science and communication from SUNY at Oneonta. After graduating from college, she worked in the financial industry at Dean Witter Reynolds, Inc. and Scudder Stevens and Clark, Inc. Subsequently, she graduated from the Institute for Integrative Nutrition in 2009 and became an Integrative Health Coach. Griffin then founded a health coaching business and co-founded a corporate wellness business. She is also the author of *Flourish Beyond 50*.

Assemblywoman Griffin and her husband raised their four children in Rockville Centre, their home for nearly 30 years.

## AILEEN M. GUNTHER (D-I-WF)
*100th - Sullivan and Orange Counties*

Middletown City Hall, 3rd Floor, 16 James Street, Middletown, NY 10940
845-342-9304

18 Anawana Lake Road, Monticello, NY 12701
845-794-5807 GuntheA@nyassembly.gov

Legislative Office Building, Room 826, Albany, NY 11248
518-455-5355

Aileen Gunther was first elected to the Assembly in 2003 to fill the vacancy created by the untimely death of her husband, Assemblyman Jake Gunther. She chairs the Mental Health Committee and Subcommittee on Women's Health. Gunther also sits on the following committees: Agriculture; Environmental Conservation; Health; and Racing and Wagering. Gunther is also a member of the Task Force on Women's Issues; the Legislative Women's Caucus; and the Puerto Rican/Hispanic Task Force. Assemblywoman Gunther is a registered nurse and worked many years at Catskill Regional Medical Center, where she rose to Director of Performance Improvement and Risk Management. Among the legislation she has introduced are measures to enact the New York state nursing shortage correction act; establish the nurse loan repayment program; and create a rural home health flexibility program. She is also a fierce advocate for school funding, fire departments, access to health care for all New Yorkers, and lower middle-class taxes. She holds a nursing degree from Orange County Community College.

## STEPHEN HAWLEY (R-I-C)
*139th - Genesee County, parts of Monroe and Orleans Counties*

121 N. Main Street, Suite 100, Albion, NY 14411
585-589-5780/HawleyS@nyassembly.gov

Legislative Office Building, Room 521, Albany, NY 12248
518-455-5811

Stephen Hawley was elected to the New York State Assembly during a special election in 2006. His district includes all of Genesee County; the Towns of Clarkson, Hamlin, Sweden and Riga in Monroe County; and all of Orleans County except the town of Shelby. He is Deputy Minority Leader and formerly served as Deputy Minority Whip. Hawley is the Ranking Minority Member of the Veterans' Affairs Committee and currently serves on the following committees: Agriculture; Insurance; Rules; Veterans' Affairs; and Ways and Means. In addition, he is a member of the Subcommittee on Women Veterans and a member of numerous task forces, including Economic Development; Education and Infrastructure; Tax, Mandate Relief, and Government Reform; and Public Safety. Professionally, Hawley owned and operated Hawley Farms, and now owns The Insurance Center in his hometown of Batavia. In addition, Hawley sells residential and commercial property in the region. He also served in the Ohio Army National Guard, and the US Army Reserves. Hawley has been highly involved in his community, and his involvement includes former service on the Genesee County Legislature, the Board of Directors of the Genesee Community College Foundation, as President of the Genesee County Empire Zone Development Board, Cornell Cooperative Extension of Genesee County, and many other local organizations. During his Assembly tenure, Hawley has helped develop substantial legislation that prevents registered level two or three sex offenders from working in amusement parks and requires that certain sex offenders' addresses be reported to the Division of Criminal Justice Services. He authored several pieces of legislation that would assist the agricultural industry including exempting owners of farms and the owners of multiple dwellings from the Scaffold Law. He holds a BS in education from the University of Toledo and is father to two sons.

## CARL E. HEASTIE (D)
*83rd - Part of Bronx County*

1446 E. Gun Hill Road, Bronx, NY 10469
718-654-6539/Speaker@nyassembly.gov

Legislative Office Building, Room 932, Albany, NY 12248
518-455-3791

Carl E. Heastie was first elected to the New York State Assembly in 2000 and, in February 2015, was elected to the position of Speaker of the Assembly. He is the first African American to hold the post. His first budget as Speaker made a $1.8 billion investment in education; addressed homelessness; and gave working families resources to achieve financial independence. He retains a seat on the Rules Committee, which he chairs. In addition, he is a member of the Black, Puerto Rican, Hispanic & Asian Legislative Caucus. His legislative achievements prior to ascending to the Speaker position include being a principal negotiator to secure a minimum wage increase that took effect January 1, 2014 and advocating on behalf of increases in unemployment insurance benefits. Other legislative priorities for Speaker Heastie include criminal justice reform, the rising costs of housing, ridesharing, gun safety, child care, climate change, and water quality infrastructure and remediation. He was also instrumental in the construction of a YMCA state-of-art-facility in the Edenwald neighborhood of the Bronx, which opened in 2020. Professionally, Heastie was a budget analyst in the New York City comptroller's office prior to his election to the Assembly. He holds a BS in applied mathematics and statistics from SUNY Stony Brook, and an MBA from Bernard M. Baruch College.

## ANDREW HEVESI (D)
*28th - Parts of Queens County*

70-50 Austin Street, Suite 118, Forest Hills, NY 11375
718-263-5595/HevesiA@nyassembly.gov

Legislative Office Building, Room 844, Albany, NY 12248
518-455-4926

Andrew Hevesi was first elected to the New York State Assembly in May 2005. His district includes Forest Hills, Rego Park, Ridgewood, Richmond Hill, Middle Village, Glendale, and Kew Gardens. He chairs the Committee on Children and Families, and also sits on the following standing Committees: Banks; Codes; Health; and Labor. Other legislative priorities include renewable energy generation, human trafficking, domestic violence, and information technology. He is the former Chairman of the Assembly's Oversight, Analysis, and Investigations Committee. Professionally, Hevesi was Director of Community Affairs for the New York City Public Advocate Betsy Gotbaum, as well as Chief of Staff to former Assemblyman Jeff Klein. He also worked for the Domestic Violence Bureau of the Queens County District Attorney's Office. He holds a bachelor's degree in political science from Queens College and is married with one child.

## PAMELA HUNTER (D)
*128th - East Side of Syracuse and Surrounding Towns*

711 E. Genesee Street, 2nd Floor, Syracuse, NY 13210
315-449-9536/HunterP@nyassembly.gov

Legislative Office Building, Room 553, Albany, NY 12248
518-455-5383

Pamela Hunter is a native of Upstate New York and a US Army Veteran, currently representing the south and east sides of Syracuse as well as the surrounding towns of Salina, Dewitt and Onondaga.

Prior to her election to the New York State Assembly, she served on the Syracuse Common Council, most recently as Chair of the Public Safety Committee. In the Assembly she is Chair of the Subcommittee on Women Veterans and serves on the following committees: Energy; Insurance; Social Services; Transportation; and Veterans' Affairs. In addition, she is a member of the Black, Puerto Rican, Hispanic & Asian Legislative Caucus; the Legislative Women's Caucus; and the Task Force on Women's Issues. Hunter has authored legislation to provide assistance to tenants, protect the environment, and aide veterans in employment. She sat on the board of the Syracuse Industrial Development Agency, working to create jobs and grow the economy. She has a long history of leadership in local nonprofit organizations, including Epilepsy-Pralid, Inc., the Syracuse Community Health Center, Home Aides of CNY, Catholic Charities, Meals on Wheels, and AccessCNY. She holds a bachelor's degree in business administration from Strayer College in Washington, DC. Pamela lives in Syracuse with her husband and son.

## ALICIA L. HYNDMAN (D)
*29th - Part of Queens*

232-06A Merrick Boulevard, Springfield Gardens, NY 11413
718-732-5412/HyndmanA@nyassembly.gov

Legislative Office Building, Room 702, Albany, NY 12248
518-455-4451

Alicia L. Hyndman was elected to the New York State Assembly on November 10, 2015 in the 29th Assembly District, encompassing the neighborhoods of Laurelton, Rosedale, St. Albans, Addisleigh Park, Hollis, Springfield Gardens, and Jamaica. Hyndman is Chair of the Subcommittee on the Commission on Solid Waste Management and sits on the following standing Committees: Economic Development, Job Creation, Commerce, and Industry; Education; Governmental Operations; Higher Education; Small Business; Ways and Means; and Transportation. She is also a member of the Asian Pacific American Task Force, the Black, Puerto Rican, Hispanic & Asian Legislative Caucus, the Legislative Women's Caucus, and the Task Force on Women's Issues. The daughter of Caribbean immigrants, Assemblywoman Hyndman emigrated to the United States from London, England as a young child. Assemblywoman Hyndman served on the NYC Department of Education's Community District Education Council 29 (CEC 29) for ten years, the last four years as President. As a longtime community education advocate, Assemblywoman Hyndman plans to focus on bringing resources and information back into the community to support youth and senior services, alleviate flooding, grow small businesses, and provide access to living wage jobs and entrepreneurial opportunities. Assemblywoman Hyndman holds a BA from the SUNY at New Paltz, and an MPA from Framingham State College. She resides in Rosedale, Queens with her daughters Nia and Nyla.

## CHANTEL JACKSON (R)
*79th - Part of Bronx County*

780 Concourse Village West, Ground Floor, Professional, Bronx, NY 10451
718-538-3829/ jacksonc@nyassembly.gov

Legislative Office Building, Albany, NY 12248
518-455-5272

Chantel Jackson was elected to serve New York State's 79th Assembly District as a first-time candidate in November 2020, representing parts of Concourse Village, Morrisania, Melrose, Belmont, Claremont, and East Tremont. In the Assembly, Jackson is Chair of the Subcommittee on Micro Business; she is also a member of the following Committees: Alcoholism and Drug Abuse; Cities; Education; Mental Health; Small Business; and the Task Force on Women's Issues.

Jackson is a licensed social worker, college professor, author, and dedicated mom. She is extremely proud of her immigrant mom from Belize who is the Vice President of her local-DC37 Local 1655-and her dad who is the CEO of Workshop in Business Opportunities (WIBO). Born in Harlem among six siblings, she attended public school for the majority of her life. She graduated from City College with a bachelor's degree in psychology and later received her graduate degree from Adelphi's School of Social Work. Jackson spent nine years helping low-income first-generation students get into college and secure financial aid while teaching at various colleges and universities. For the last four years before winning her election, she was a NYC public high school social worker and UFT member, assisting students with their mental and physical wellness.

Assembly Member Jackson believes that her Wellness, Housing, Education, NOW! (W.H.E.N.) mission will transform her community. She is focused on reducing high rates of diabetes, obesity, heart disease, and asthma by addressing the environmental factors that cause these issues; on properly funding mental health services and increase insurance for uninsured and underinsured people; and on creating affordable housing, lowering evictions and increasing home ownership. Jackson advocates for the neediest school districts to receive the funding owed to them by New York State and for increasing education in the RBCs: Real Estate, Business, Credit & Stocks.

Being a teen mom and single parent has given her the knowledge necessary to create legislation that will empower the most vulnerable populations, and she looks to be a voice in Albany for Black people, women, parents, social workers, immigrants, union members, the LGBTQIA+ community, and all marginalized groups.

### JONATHAN G. JACOBSON (D)
*104th - Dutchess and Orange Counties*

47 Grand Street, Newburgh, NY 12550
845-562-0888/jacobsonj@nyassembly.gov

Legislative Office Building, Room 628, Albany, NY 12248
518-455-5762

Jonathan Jacobson was elected to the New York State Assembly on November 6, 2018, to fill the seat vacated by the death of Frank Skartados. Jacobson is Chair of the Subcommittee on Election Day Operations and Voter Disenfranchisement; and sits on the following committees: Cities; Election Law; Insurance; Labor; Local Governments; and Transportation.

At the time of his election, Jacobson was a Newburgh City Councilman where he had championed infrastructure repair, especially fixing the terrible streets. Not satisfied with the status quo, he did his homework and found $250,000, which Newburgh did not realize it had coming, from the state for additional street paving.

Early in his career, Jacobson served as an Assistant Counsel to the Speaker of the New York State Assembly and was assigned to the Labor Committee where he researched and wrote legislation. Later, as an Assistant New York State Attorney General, he headed the Consumer Frauds Bureau at the Poughkeepsie Regional Office protecting the people of New York State from fraudulent and illegal business practices. He con-

tinued his public service career as a New York State Workers' Compensation Law Judge.

In the early 1990s, he headed the City of Newburgh Charter Review Commission and wrote a proposed new charter for Newburgh. He also started his own law firm and focused on representing workers in workers' compensation and Social Security disability cases.

Jacobson graduated from Duke University, cum laude, with honors in political science and he went on to graduate from New York Law School.

### JOSH JENSEN (R)
*134th - Parts of Monroe County*

2496 W. Ridge Road, Rochester, NY 14626
585-225-4190/jensenj@nyassembly.gov

Legislative Office Building, Room 722, Albany, NY 12248
518-455-4664

Josh Jensen was elected to the New York State Assembly on November 3, 2020. His district includes a portion of Monroe County, specifically the towns of Greece, Ogden, and Parma and the villages of Hilton and Spencerport. In the Assembly, Jensen sits on the following Committees: Corporations, Authorities and Commissions; Health; Housing; and Libraries and Education Technology.

Jensen believes the state needs to cut unnecessary spending, help create more jobs, and push for the increased protection of our families and neighborhoods through enhanced public safety initiatives.

Assembly Member Jensen graduated from Niagara University and Hilton High School. Prior to being elected to the Assembly, Jensen served the residents of the 3rd Ward as a member of the Town of Greece's Town Board. As a councilman, he supported proposals that lowered taxes and prioritized the maintenance and improvement of vital infrastructure. He previously worked for Senator Joe Robach, serving as Director of Communications and Director of Community Affairs and Public Policy. He has also proudly volunteered with the Hilton Education Foundation and Rochester area chapter of the National Fallen Firefighters.

Jensen resides in Greece with his wife, Casey, and their children, Margot and Brendan.

### KIMBERLY JEAN-PIERRE (D)
*11 - Suffolk County*

640 W. Montauk Highway, Lindenhurst, NY 11757-5538
631-957-2087/jeanpierrek@nyassembly.gov

Legislative Office Building, Room 742, Albany, NY 12248
518-455-5787

Kimberly Jean-Pierre was first elected to the New York State Assembly in 2014. Jean-Pierre is Chair of the Committee on Libraries and Education Technology. She sits on the following committees: Banks; Children and Families; Corporation, Authorities, and Commissions; and Education. She is also a member of the Black, Puerto Rican, Hispanic & Asian Legislative Caucus, the Legislative Women's Caucus, and the Task Force on Women's Issues. Prior to her election she served as Vice President of Properties for the Town of Babylon's Industrial Development Agency. Prior to that, she was a Legislative Aide to Congressman Steve Israel-as Community Outreach Coordinator-and to Suffolk County legislator DuWayne Gregory. She holds an undergraduate degree from Brooklyn College and an MS in public policy from SUNY at Stony Brook.

## BILLY JONES (D)

*115th - Parts of Clinton, Franklin, and St. Lawrence Counties*

202 U.S. Oval, Plattsburgh, NY 12903
518-562-1986/jonesb@nyassembly.gov

Legislative Office Building, Room 551, Albany, NY 12248
518-455-5943

Billy Jones was elected to the Assembly in 2016 to represent the 115th District. He is Chair of the Subcommittee on Agriculture Economic Development and Farmland Protection; He also sits on the following committees: Aging; Agriculture; Economic Development, Job Creation, Commerce, and Industry; Small Business; Tourism, Parks, Arts and Sports Development; and Veterans' Affairs. In the Assembly, his legislative priorities are lowering taxes for middle-class families, improving the education system, and rooting out government corruption.

After graduating from high school in Chateaugay, Billy Jones managed his family's dairy farm. Beginning in 1996 he also worked as a corrections officer for the New York State Department of Corrections. From 2009 to 2013 he served as Mayor of Chateaugay, and beginning in 2010 he was a Franklin County legislator, becoming chairman in 2013. As a county legislator he was able to reform ethics laws to make government more transparent. He is active in various organizations throughout the North Country, including the Chateaugay Rotary Club and the Malone Elks Lodge, and he was a Board Member of the United Way of the Adirondack Region. He is also a member of the North Country Economic Development Council, where he has supported numerous projects that help local businesses boost the region's economy. In the State Assembly, his legislative priorities are lowering taxes for middle-class families, improving the education system, rooting out government corruption, and creating good-paying jobs for residents of the North Country. A resident of Franklin County, he is the father of a daughter, Ella Liberty Jones, born on the Fourth of July.

## LATOYA JOYNER (D)

*77th - Bronx County*

910 Grand Concourse, Suite 1JK, Bronx, NY 10451
718-538-2000/joynerl@nyassembly.gov

Latoya Joyner was first elected to the New York State Assembly in 2014 from a Bronx district that includes Claremont, Concourse, Highbridge, Mount Eden, and Morris Heights. Joyner is Chair of the Committee on Labor and sits on the following committees: Education; Housing; Judiciary; Ways and Means; and Social Services. She is also a member of the Black, Puerto Rican, Hispanic & Asian Legislative Caucus, the Legislative Women's Caucus, the Puerto Rican/Hispanic Task Force, and the Task Force on Women's Issues. Her legislative issues include affordable housing, rent regulation, education, and domestic violence. Prior to her election, she was a member of Community Board 4 and the Neighborhood Advisory Board. She interned with Assemblywoman Aurelia Green, then became a Community Liaison in her district office. She holds an undergraduate degree from SUNY Stony Brook, as well as a JD from the University at Buffalo Law School.

## ANNA R. KELLES (D)

*125th - Tompkins County and Part of Cortland County*

106 E. Court Street, Ithaca, NY 14850
607-277-8030kellesa@nyassembly.gov

Legislative Office Building, Albany, NY 12248
518-455-5444

Assembly Member Dr. Anna Kelles represents the 125th District, including Tompkins County and the southwest of Cortland County. This district includes the metropolitan areas of Ithaca and Cortland as well as seventeen smaller municipal towns and villages in both counties. In the Assembly, Kelles is Chair of the Subcommittee on Agricultural Produc-

tion & Techbology and sits on various Committees, including Agriculture; Correction; Economic Development, Job Creation, Commerce and Industry; Environmental Conservation; Locals Governments; and the Task Force on Women's Issues.

Before becoming a state Assembly Member, Kelles served in the Tompkins County Legislature from 2015 to 2020. She served as chair of the Health and Human Services Committee, the Planning, Development and Environmental Quality Committee, and, for the last several years, as the chair of the Housing and Economic Development Committee. In her tenure on the County Legislature, she crafted legislation and effectively championed many public health issues, including access to affordable housing in walkable communities, immigrants' rights, expanded use of alternatives to incarceration, restricting youth access to tobacco, and funding to end homelessness, expand rural broadband access, and support child care initiatives. She also authored environmental legislation, such as an initiative to block state permitting of a proposed trash incinerator on the shore of Cayuga Lake. She served on the Community Housing Development Fund board, the Downtown Ithaca Alliance, the Strategic Tourism Planning Board, Ithaca Area Economic Development and Southern Tier 8, a regional economic development council.

Kelles earned a dual bachelor's degree in biology and environmental studies at Binghamton University in 1997. Subsequently, she spent four years in Ecuador working with marginalized populations to promote sound nutritional and environmental practices. In Ecuador, she worked as a high school biology teacher and as an ecological guide in the Amazon basin. In 2008, Kelles earned a PhD in nutritional epidemiology from the University of North Carolina at Chapel Hill, exploring the relationship between urbanization and multigenerational health-related behavior patterns in Cebu, Philippines.

Assemblywoman Kelles spent a year following her PhD teaching Sports Nutrition at Ithaca College before becoming the Director of the School of Applied Clinical Nutrition at New York Chiropractic College, where she built a master's program focused on whole foods therapeutic nutrition. She managed the development of the Center for Nutrition Advocacy from 2012 to 2013 and concurrently served as a Director for the Green Resource Hub from 2012 to 2015, a regional nonprofit organization with the mission of supporting businesses, organizations, and entrepreneurs to grow their economic, social, and environmental bottom lines.

In 2015 to 2017 she was a full lecturer at Cornell University in the Division of Nutritional Sciences before leaving to launch a private practice in nutrition and wellness. Kelles served as the Administration Manager for the Certifying Examination for Nutrition Specialists and chair of the Examination Development Council of the Board of the Certification for Nutrition Specialists (BCNS) for 8 years prior to running for the State Assembly.

Kelles was born and raised in Tompkins County. After traveling the world, she returned to the beautiful lakes, waterfalls, and trails and their peerless natural beauty that served as her sanctuary as a child. She lives with her partner and their two beloved puppies.

## RONALD T. KIM (D)

*40 - Part of Queens County*

136-20 38th Avenue, Suite 10A, Flushing, NY 11354
718-939-0195/KimR@nyassembly.gov

Legislative Office Building, Room 824, Albany, NY 12248
518-455-5411

Ron Kim was first elected to the New York State Senate in 2012. Kim is Chair of the Committee on Aging and sits on the following committees: Corporations, Authorities, and Commissions; Education; Governmental Operations; Health; and Housing. He is also a member of the Black, Puerto Rican, Hispanic & Asian Legislative Caucus and the Puerto Rican/Hispanic Task Force. Kim's legislative priorities include raising the age of criminal responsibility for certain crimes, securing equal access to health and human services for limited English-speaking individuals, and regulating and reforming the nail salon industry in New York City. Prior to his election, he most recently worked for The Parkside Group, which he joined after serving as a Regional Director for Government and Community Affairs in the administrations of Governors Eliot Spitzer and David A. Paterson. His other public service positions have included: working for then-Councilmember John C. Liu; as an Aide to then-Assemblyman Mark Weprin; and working for the New York City Department of Buildings and the Department of Small Business Services. He became a National Urban Fellow, where he advised the Chief Education Office of the Chicago Public Schools while earning and Masters in Public Administration from Baruch College. He also holds a BA from Hamilton College. Assemblyman Kim lives in Flushing with his wife and two daughters.

## KIERAN MICHAEL LALOR (R)
*105th - Parts of Dutchess County*

North Hopewell Plaza, Suite 1, 1075 Route 82, Hopewell Junction, NY 12533
845-221-2202/LalorK@nyassembly.gov

Legislative Office Building, Room 531, Albany, NY 12248
518-455-5725

Kieran Michael Lalor was first elected to the Assembly in 2012 to a district that includes Beekman, Dover, East Fishkill, Fishkill, LaGrange, Pawling, Union Vale, Wappinger, and Washington. Lalor is Ranking Minority Member of the Banks Committees and serves on the following standing Committees: Governmental Operations, Corporations, Authorities, and Commissions; State-Local Relations; and Economic Development, Job Creation, and Commerce and Industry. His priorities in the Assembly include tax relief for homeowners, job growth tax incentives for small businesses, school safety, protecting fellow veterans. Professionally, he is the founder of KML Strategies, LLC, a business development and research services consulting firm working with companies that make safety products for military and law enforcement. He served as an infantryman in the Marine Corps Reserve and his unit was twice activated, including in Nasiriya, Iraq. He also helped rescue Gulf Coast residents impacted by Hurricane Katrina. Lalor is involved in numerous local and veteran's organizations. He holds a BA from Providence College and a JD from Pace Law School. The Hopewell Junction resident is married and has four children.

## CHARLES D. LAVINE (D)
*13th - Part of Nassau County*

1 School Street, Suite 303-B, Glen Cove, NY 11542
516-676-0050/lavinec@nyassembly.gov

Charles D. Lavine was elected to the New York State Assembly in 2004.

Legislative Office Building, Room 831, Albany, NY 12248
518-455-5456

He chairs the Committee on Judiciary, and is a member of the following standing Committees: Codes; Ethics and Guidance; Insurance; Rules; and Judiciary. He also co-chaired the New York State Legislative Ethics Commission and the Administrative Regulations Review Commission. He has sponsored the following legislation: increased penalties for those who use high-capacity magazines, as well as legislation to help halt illegal gun trafficking into New York; stripping pensions from corrupt public officials; identifying veterans in need and coordinating necessary services to improve their lives; and marriage equality. He is President of the New York Chapter of the National Association of Jewish Legislators. Prior to being elected to the Assembly, Lavine was appointed to the Glen Cove Planning Board. He later was appointed to a vacancy on the Glen Cove City Council and was subsequently elected.

Professionally, Lavine worked as an attorney in the Legal Aid Society of the City of New York, as well as his own private practice in Queens

County and lower Manhattan. However, he has been a full-time legislator since becoming an Assembly member.

He holds a BA in English literature from the University of Wisconsin and a JD from New York Law School. He and his wife have two children.

## MIKE LAWLER (R)
*97th - Part of Rockland County*

1 Blue Hill Plaza, Suite 1116, Pearl River, NY 10965
845-624-4601/lawlerm@nyassembly.gov

Legislative Office Building, Room 718, Albany, NY 12248
518-455-5118

Mike Lawler was elected to the New York State Assembly on November 3, 2020, and serves the southern portion of Rockland County.

As an Assemblyman, he is working to reduce the state's onerous tax burden, bring fiscal discipline to its budget, provide law enforcement with the resources needed to do its work, and craft legislation to improve public safety. In the Assembly, Lawler sits on the following Committees: Aging; Banks; Education; Governmental Operations; Housing; and the Commission on Critical Transportation Choice.

Prior to being elected to the Assembly, Lawler served as Deputy Town Supervisor in Orangetown under Supervisor Teresa Kenny, and previously worked in the Westchester County Executive's Office as an advisor to Rob Astorino. In those roles, he gained invaluable experience dealing with issues ranging from crafting a disciplined budget to public policy and community outreach initiatives. He also served as Executive Director of the State Republican Party and has helped secure the election of candidates at federal, state, and local levels.

In addition to his public service career, Assemblyman Lawyer is a successful small-business owner and brings his experience and knowledge from the private sector where he founded his own government affairs and public relations firm, to best serve his constituents.

Lawler is a lifelong Rockland County resident and graduate of Suffern High School. In 2009, he earned a degree in business administration with a double major in accounting and finance from Manhattan College. His hard work earned him the distinction of valedictorian of his graduating class. He and his wife, Doina, live in Pearl River.

## JOHN LEMONDES (R)
*126th - Parts of Cayuga, Chenango, Cortland, and Onandaga Counties*

69 South Street, Auburn, NY 13021
315-255-3045/lemondesj@nyassembly.gov

Legislative Office Building, Room 720, Albany, NY 12248
518-455-5878

John Lemondes was elected to the New York State Assembly on November 3, 2020. His district is made up of parts of Cayuga, Chenango, Cortland, and Onondaga counties.

As an Assemblyman, Lemondes works to reduce taxes, create jobs, support our small businesses, and protect Second Amendment rights. He believes agriculture and business are the backbone of our economy and will push to end overregulation for hardworking farmers. In the Assembly, he sits on the following Committees: Banks; Corporations, Authorities and Commissions; Economic Development, Job Creation, Commerce and Industry; and Environmental Conservation.

Lemondes comes from a family of veterans and is a graduate of Paul Smiths College, Penn State University, and Syracuse University, after which he served in the army for 27 years. In 2014, he retired as a colonel after a career that included numerous overseas tours. After his retirement from the Army, he and his family began operating a farm in LaFayette.

Assembly Member Lemondes most recently served as the President of the Farmer Veteran Coalition of New York state, an active member of the American Sheep Industry Association, and served on the Board of Directors of the Onondaga County Soil & Water Conservation District. He is also a proud member of the New York State Farm Bureau. Committed to the environment and its critical role in the agricultural industry, as an Assemblyman, Lemondes will fight to protect the preservation of his region's natural resources as well as its watershed needs. He is also a staunch advocate for public safety.

Lemondes and his wife, Martha, reside in LaFayette with their children.

## JENNIFER LUNSFORD (D)
*135th - Part of Monroe County*

268 Fairport Village Landing, Fairport, NY 14450
585-223-9130/lunsfordj@nyassembly.gov

Legislative Office Building, Room 820, Albany, NY 12248
518-455-5784

Jen Lunsford is proud to represent the good people of the 135th Assembly District, which includes the towns of Webster, Penfield, East Rochester and Perinton on the east side of Monroe County. In the Assembly, Lunsford is Chair of the Subcommittee on Digital Libraries and sits on the following Committees: Children and Families; Economic Development, Job Creation, Commerce and Industry; Environmental Conservation; Libraries and Education Technology; Local Governments; and the Task Force on Women's Issues.

Assemblywoman Lunsford was born on Long Island to a working mom and stay-at-home dad. She graduated from Patchogue-Medford High School and then went on to Hartwick College in Oneonta, where she dual majored in political science and philosophy. After working as a paralegal for a major international law firm, she attended Boston University School of Law where she concentrated in health care law, served as a note editor on the *American Journal of Law and Medicine* and won the Dean's Award for Constitutional Law. Following law school, Lunsford moved to Rochester, where her husband grew up, to begin her legal career. She has spent the past eleven years working as a litigator, focusing primarily on plaintiff's side personal injury, workers' compensation, and Social Security disability.

Lunsford has deep roots as a community volunteer and activist fighting for reproductive justice, criminal justice, and universal health care with organizations like Lawyers for Good Government and If/When/How. She ran for office following the 2016 election, to shape the world into a place of hope and opportunity for her son, and for all the families of the 135th District. Lunsford lives in Perinton with her husband, Scott, and their four-year old son, Mackay.

## DONNA LUPARDO (D)
*123rd - Part of Broome County*

State Office Building, 17th Floor, 44 Hawley Street, Binghamton, NY 13901
607-723-9047/LupardoD@nyassembly.gov

Legislative Office Building, Room 828, Albany, NY 12248
518-455-5431

Donna A. Lupardo was elected to the New York State Assembly in 2004 to represent a district that includes the City of Binghamton and the Towns of Vestal and Union. She chairs the Committee on Agriculture and also sits on the following committees: Higher Education; Economic Development, Job Creation, and Commerce and Industry; Rules; and Transportation. Lupardo is also a member of the Legislative Women's Caucus and the Task Force on Women's Issues. Her legislative achievements include backing the State Green Building Construction Act, tenant notification of environmental testing results, and authorship of the Contract Disclosure Act, which reformed the way state resources are allo-

cated. She is also committed to lead testing of school drinking water, structural inspection of parking garages, and indoor air quality, including radon exposure. Prior to being elected to the Assembly, she was an adjunct lecturer at SUNY Binghamton. She served on the Broome County Legislature from 1999 to 2000. She holds an undergraduate degree from Wagner College and a Master's degree in philosophy from SUNY Binghamton. She is married and lives in Endwell.

## WILLIAM B. MAGNARELLI (D)
*129th - Parts of the City of Syracuse plus Geddes and Van Buren*

Room 840, 333 E. Washington Street Syracuse, NY 13202
315-428-9651/MagnarW@nyassembly.gov

Legislative Office Building, Room 830, Albany, NY 12248
518-455-4826

William Magnarelli was first elected to the New York State Assembly in 1998. He is Chair of the Transportation Committee. In addition, he sits on the following committees: Economic Development, Job Creation, Commerce, and Industry; Education; Oversight, Analysis, and Investigation; Ways and Means; and Rules. Prior to being elected to the Assembly, Magnarelli was Majority Leader of the Syracuse Common Council. By profession, he is a practicing attorney, and was a member of the US Army Reserves where he rose to the rank of Captain. He backed the statewide Amber Plan law, and supported Family Health Plus that provides health care coverage to one million uninsured New Yorkers. In addition, he has secured funding for a variety of Central New York resources, such as $37 million for the Syracuse Center of Excellence, to boost the region's economic development. His community involvement includes serving on the board of the Arthritis Foundation and as President of Our Lady of Pompeii Church Parish Council. He attended Syracuse University and Syracuse University College of Law, where he received his law degree. He was married for over 40 years to his wife Karen, who passed away in 2017, and is the father of three children and four grandchildren.

## ZOHRAN MAMDANI (D)
*36th - Part of Queens County*

24-08 32nd Street, Suite 1002A, Astoria, NY 11102
718-545-3889/mamdaniz@nyassembly.gov

Legislative Office Building, Albany, NY 12248
518-455-5014

Zohran Kwame Mamdani was born and raised in Kampala, Uganda, moving to New York City with his family at the age of 7. A graduate of the NYC Public School System, he attended the Bronx High School of Science and received a bachelor's degree in Africana studies from Bowdoin College. In 2018 he became naturalized as an American citizen.

Prior to representing the 36th Assembly District and its neighborhoods of Astoria, Ditmars-Steinway, and Astoria Heights, Mamdani worked as a foreclosure prevention housing counselor, helping low-income homeowners of color across Queens fight off eviction and stay in their homes. It was this job that led him to run for office. After having spent every day negotiating with banks that valued profits over people, he came face-to-face with the reality that this housing crisis-one which predated this pandemic-was not natural to our lives, but instead a choice. A choice that was the consequence of decades of pro-corporate policies enacted across our country as well as our state. Yet, like with any choice, we always have the opportunity to change and Mamdani is excited to be a part of that.

More than his professional experience, however it was the act of organizing that led to Assemblyman Mamdani becoming politically active in the first place. In high school, he cofounded his school's first ever cricket team, which would go on to participate in the Public School Athletic League's inaugural cricket season. This act, though not ostensibly a political one, taught him how coming together with a few likeminded individuals can transform rhetoric into reality. Taking that lesson with him, he went on to cofound Bowdoin College's first Students for Justice in Palestine chapter and later organize across the country with different progressive organizations seeking to win national elections as well as expand healthcare coverage.

As an Assembly Member, Mamdani fights every day for a future where each and every New Yorker lives a dignified life and where the distribution of that dignity is not determined by the market. At a time when many of his neighbors spend half their income on rent, breathe the most polluted air in Queens, and are profiled at the highest rates of any neighborhood in the borough, he works toward creating a future where housing, energy, and justice are for the many, not just the few. In the Assembly, Mamdani is Co-chair of the Asian Pacific American Task Force; he also sits as a Member on the following Committees: Aging; Cities; Election Law; Energy; and Real Property Taxation.

Assemblyman Mamdani is proud to be the first South Asian man to serve in the NYS Assembly as well as the first Ugandan and only the third Muslim to ever be a member of the body. He seeks to amplify the voices of the unheard across both the district and the state.

## BRIAN MANKTELOW (R-C-I)
*130th - Wayne County, and Parts of Cayuga and Oswego Counties*

10 Leach Road, Lyons, NY 14489
315-946-5166/manktelowb@nyassembly.gov

Legislative Office Building, Room 320, Albany, NY 12248
518-455-5655

Brian Manktelow was elected to the New York State Assembly on November 6, 2018. The district includes all of Wayne County, the towns of Aurelius, Brutus, Cato, Conquest, Ira, Mentz, Montezuma, Sennett, Sterling; Victory in Cayuga County; and the towns of Hannibal, Minetto, and Oswego in Oswego County. In the Assembly, he sits on the following standing Committees: Banks; Environmental Conservation; Local Governments; Small Business; and Veterans' Affairs.

Assemblyman Manktelow served in the US Army, attaining the rank of sergeant after graduating from Williamson High School. He then completed classes at the University of Chicago and Finger Lakes Community College, where he pursued a degree in political science. He has been the Town Supervisor in Lyons since 2009 and has worked to protect the interests of his fellow residents during the dissolution of the village of Lyons in 2015, ensuring a positive impact on the municipality's future. In addition, he served as Vice Chairman of the Wayne County Board of Supervisors, was Chairman of the board's Finance Committee, and also sat on the Government Operations and Human Services committees. Manktelow was instrumental in initializing the Wayne County Land Bank in 2017 to rejuvenate derelict properties, get them back on the tax rolls, and reduce blight.

He has owned and operated Manktelow Farms in Lyons for more than 30 years, and has been an active member of the Wayne County Farm Bureau. Brian's background gives him a unique perspective on the challenges faced by everyday New Yorkers.

As an Assemblyman, he is fighting hard for policies that encourage economic growth, pushing to reduce unfunded state mandates and high taxes, advocating for resources to battle the growing opioid epidemic, as well as addressing the need to protect the natural resources in his district. He works diligently with colleagues to create solutions to the state's economic struggles by creating opportunities for businesses to thrive.

Manktelow currently resides in Lyons with his wife, Crystal, and they have five children.

## JOHN T. MCDONALD III (D)
*108th - Parts of Albany, Rensselaer and Saratoga Counties*

Legislative Office Building, Room 417, Albany, NY 12248
518-455-4474/McDonaldJ@nyassembly.gov

John T. McDonald III was elected to the New York State Assembly in 2012 to a district that includes sections of Albany, Troy and the communities of Green Island, North Greenbush, Rensselaer, Waterford, and Watervliet. He chairs the Committee on Oversight, Analysis, and Investigation and sits on the following committees: Alcoholism and Drug Abuse; Health; Insurance; Higher Education; Real Property Taxation; and Ways and Means. In the Assembly his focus is on local government, health care, small business, job growth and creation, and the heroin/opioid crisis that is ravaging the state. He is President of his family-owned Marra's Pharmacy in his hometown of Cohoes. Prior to being elected to the Assembly, McDonald spent 13 years as Mayor of Cohoes. In this role, he focused on economic development and revitalization or developments in key areas. As a result, 2,000 new residential units arrived in the city, bringing downtown revitalization and improvements to the Cohoes Falls as a regional attraction. McDonald was also actively involved in the New York State Conference of Mayors, including serving as President of the state-wide organization. He also has been actively involved on numerous boards, including chairing the Capital District Transportation Committee, and the Cohoes Industrial Development Agency, as well as sitting on boards such as the State Comptroller's Local Advisory Team. He holds a BS in pharmacy science from Albany College of Pharmacy, as well as an honorary Doctorate of Humanity, and is the married father of three.

## DAVID G. MCDONOUGH (R)
*14th - Part of Nassau County*

404 Bedford Avenue, Bellmore, NY 11710
516-409-2070/mcdonoughd@nyassembly.gov

Legislative Office Building, Room 443, Albany, NY 12248
518-455-4633

David McDonough was first elected to the New York State Assembly in 2002 and is the Ranking Minority member on the Transportation Committee. He sits on the following committees: Consumer Affairs and Protection; Education; Health; Transportation; and Veterans' Affairs. He is also Chair of the Minority Task Force on Public Safety and a member of the Subcommittees on Child Product Safety and Regulated Mortgage Lenders. McDonough is Past President of the Nassau County Council of Chambers of Commerce, a member of the Committee for the Merrick Downtown Revitalization Project, and four-term President for the Merrick Chamber of Commerce. In this role, his achievements included growing the membership ranks by 35 percent. In addition, he is a founding member and former board member of the Bellmore-Merrick Community Wellness Council and a member and Past President of the Kiwanis Club of Merrick. In addition, McDonough served in both the US Coast Guard and the US Air Force. He holds a BA in economics from Columbia University, and is a graduate of the American Academy of Dramatic Arts. The Merrick resident is married with three children and four grandchildren.

## KAREN MCMAHON (D)
*146th - Parts of Erie and Niagara Counties*

5500 Main Street, Suite 216, Williamsville, NY 14221
716-634-1895/mcmahonk@nyassembly.gov

Legislative Office Building, Room 631, Albany, NY 12248
518-455-4618

Karen McMahon was elected in November 2018 to represent the 146th District, which includes the town of Amherst and the village of Williamsville in Erie County, and the town of Pendleton in Niagara

County. In the Assembly, McMahon is Chair on the Subcommittee on Trusts and Estates and serves on the following standing Committees: Higher Education; Libraries and Education Technology; Environmental Conservation; Judiciary; People with Disabilities; and Transportation. She is also a member of the Legislative Women's Caucus and the Task Force on Women's Issues.

McMahon was raised in Snyder and earned both her undergraduate and law degrees at the University of Buffalo. She worked for nearly 30 years as a confidential law clerk to judges of the New York State Appellate Division, Fourth Department, and the US District Court for the Western District of New York. Following her retirement from federal service in 2016, she joined the private practice of her husband, attorney Jeff Marcus, representing parents of students with disabilities in special education cases.

Having spent her legal career administering justice, upholding the rule of law, and advocating for the underrepresented, Assemblywoman McMahon's priorities include quality public education, affordable health care, job growth in Western New York, and initiatives to protect the environment and combat climate change.

She has served on the Village of Williamsville Environmental Advisory Committee and the Village Master Plan Revision Committee. She is also a member of the Women's Bar Association of the State of New York, Western New York Chapter, the Adirondack Mountain Club, and the Adirondack Forty-Sixers.

McMahon lives in the village of Williamsville with her husband, and is the mother of three daughters, Emily, Alison, and Sarah.

## DEMOND MEEKS (D)
*137th - Part of Monroe County*

107 Liberty Pole Way, Rochester, NY 14604
585-454-3670/meeksd@nyassembly.gov

Legislative Office Building, Room 704, Albany, NY 12248
518-455-5606

Assemblyman Meeks entered the political arena to improve the standard and quality of living for all Rochestarians. He is committed to educating, organizing, and mobilizing people around community issues. In the Assembly, he is Chair of the Subcommittee on Insurer Investments and Market Practices in Underserved Areas; he also sits on the following Committees: Children and Families; Cities; Governmental Operations; Housing; and Insurance.

As a servant-leader in the Rochester community, Meeks has been an advocate for quality education, fair wages, workers' rights, and social justice. As an administrative organizer with 1199SEIU, he represents nearly 800 health care sector employees and takes on an array of tasks including bargaining contracts. Meeks has mobilized workers around workplace issues, such as improved wages and benefits, as well as dignity and respect. Shortly after achieving employment with 1199SEIU in November 2010, he became an active member of the Rochester Chapter of the Coalition of Black Trade Unionists.

Since its induction in 2013, Meeks has been an active member of the Parent Leadership Training Institute Civic Design Team, as they're committed to teaching parents how to become practiced change agents for the next generation to improve the lifelong health, safety, and learning of children. He is an active member of the Omega Psi Phi Fraternity Incorporated. He was initiated into the brotherhood in the spring of 2010. Meeks currently assists his fellow fraternal brothers with "Project Stride," a youth mentorship program at School #4 as well as mentorship at the Boys & Girls Club of Rochester.

With the assistance of his family, Assembly Member Meeks commits to braving the elements on Rochester "Cold Blue" weather days and feeding those in need of a hot meal. As a member of the New York Statewide Coordinating Committee of the Poor People's Campaign, he works with groups such as Metro Justice and the Social Welfare Action Alliance (SWAA) to build coalitions as part of "A National Call for Moral Revival."

As a vested member of the Rochester community, Meeks is an advocate for social justice and the empowerment of youth. In 2017, he was awarded the Black Men Achieve Awards Civil & Human Rights and Brother of the Year. In 2018, he was awarded the Frederick Douglass Award from the Coalition of Black Trade Unionists; and in 2019, he was awarded the Civil & Human Rights Activist of the Year. Assemblyman Meeks was also awarded the Dr. Walter Cooper Community Service Award by the Rochester Black Bar Association as well as the Superior Community Service Award from the Omega Psi Phi Fraternity Incorporated.

Demond Meeks is a native of Rochester, New York. He and his wife Cratrina raised their children in the 19th Ward. Meeks and his family worship at Aenon Missionary Baptist Church. His educational background includes an associate degree from MCC and a BA from SUNY Brockport. He has received additional labor-related trainings and certifications from Cornell University.

## JOHN K. MIKULIN (R-C-I)
*17th - Nassau County*

1975 Hempstead Turnpike, Suite 202, East Meadow, NY 11554
516-228-4960/mikulinj@nyassembly.gov

Legislative Office Building, Room 550, Albany, NY 12248
518-455-5341

John Mikulin was elected to the New York State Assembly on April 24, 2018. His district is entirely in Nassau County. Mikulin serves on the following standing Committees in the Assembly: Banks; Codes; Consumer Affairs and Protection; Education; and Election Law.

As an Assemblyman, Mikulin fights to lower taxes, reduce outmigration, combat New York's devastating opioid crisis, and make New York more business friendly. He is focusing on reforming New York's economic development programs and eliminate wasteful spending.

He also supports local control of education and eliminating the haphazardly implemented Common Core Curriculum.

Mikulin was President of the Island Trees Library Board and served as the Deputy Town Attorney in the Town of Hempstead prior to being elected to the Assembly. He is also a member of the Levittown Property Association.

Mikulin has a bachelor's degree and master's degree in government, as well as a JD from Touro Law School. He and his wife, Corinne, reside in Bethpage, in the Town of Hempstead.

## BRIAN D. MILLER (R)
*101st - Delaware, Herkimer, Oneida, Orange, Ostego, Sullivan, and Ulster Counties*

4747 Middle Settlement Road, New Hartford, NY 13413
315-736-3879

14 Central Avenue, Suite 101, PO Box 247, Wallkill, NY 12589
845-895-1080/millerb@nyassembly.gov

Legislative Office Building, Room 544, Albany, NY 12248
518-455-5334

Brian Miller was elected to the New York State Assembly in November of 2016. He sits on the following committees: Agriculture; Consumer Affairs and Protection; Environmental Conservation; Real Property Taxation; and Transportation. As a graduate of Mohawk Valley Community College, he worked for nearly four decades as a mechanical engineer. From 2000 to 2016, he served as an Oneida County legislator in the 16th district. He has also served as Chairman of the Public Works Committee, Assistant Majority Leader, member of the Ways and Means Committee, and member of the Region 6 Fish and Wildlife Management Board, and he served for eight years as the Bridgewater Town Supervisor. He has volunteered as a Little League and youth basketball coach and as a member of the Sauquoit Valley Optimist Club, the Sauquoit Valley Youth Association, Western Star 15 F&AM (Free and Accepted Masons), the Oneida County Law Library Board of Directors, the Oneida County Fire Advisory Board, and the Oneida County Republican Committee. He also assists with the Cornell Cooperative Extension Government Intern Program. As an assemblyman, his goals include reducing taxes and unfunded mandates, overhauling the Common Core education standards, and eliminating the restraints of the SAFE Act (Secure Ammunition and Firearms Enforcement Act of 2013), as well as increasing employment opportunities and mental health services for veterans. He also plans to address the heroin epidemic by increasing treatment options and improving education on the dangers of opioids and heroin. He resides in New Hartford, a suburb outside Utica, with his wife, Dawn, and son, Nicholas, and he has climbed all forty-six of the high peaks in the Adirondacks.

## MELISSA MILLER (R)
*20th - Part of Nassau County*

2001 Park Street, Atlantic Beach, NY 11509
516-431-0500/millerML@nyassembly.gov

Legislative Office Building, Room 439, Albany, NY 12248
518-455-3028

Prior to her election to the State Assembly in 2016, Melissa (Missy) Miller, formerly a medical assistant in a pediatrician's office, was a stay-at-home parent who raised two children with complicated medical issues and who lost a third to a rare disease, an experience that led her to devote much of her life to helping chronically ill children. For more than two decades she worked in professional and volunteer capacities to train hundreds of pediatric residents to handle the challenges of working with chronically ill children. As a leader with Compassionate Care New York, consisting of patients, providers, and organizations that advocate for the relief of suffering of very ill patients, she worked with legislators to pass the state's Compassionate Care Act, which legalized medical marijuana for some ten diseases and syndromes-an effort that in 2015 garnered her the New York State Woman of Distinction award. As a legislator, her goals include advocating for greater accessibility to programs for disabled children and adults, finding more ways to combat a growing heroin epidemic, increasing government transparency, imposing term limits on legislators, and restoring to school districts the power to choose their own curricula. In the Assembly, Miller sits on the following committees: Children and Families; Education; Environmental Conservation; Health; Mental Health; and People with Disabilities. She is also a member of the Legislative Women's Caucus. She lives in Atlantic Beach, where she was born and raised, with her husband, Brandon, and children, Katy and Oliver.

## MARCELA MITAYNES (D)
*51st - Part of Kings County*

4907 4th Avenue, Suite 1A, Brooklyn, NY 11220
718-492-6334/mitaynesm@nyassembly.gov

Legislative Office Building, Room 431, Albany, NY 12248
518-455-3821

Assembly Member Marcela Mitaynes represents Red Hook, Sunset Park, and northern Bay Ridge. In the Assembly, she is Chair of the Subcommittee on Regulated Mortgage Lenders and sits on the following Committees: Banks; Children and Families; Education; Judiciary; Transportation; and the Task Force on Women's Issues.

Mitaynes migrated to New York City from Peru as a child with her family and was raised in Sunset Park, Brooklyn. She is now raising her own family in that same vibrant, beautiful community. She attended elementary school at P.S. 169 in Sunset Park. Her daughter went on to go to the same elementary school and Mitaynes served as President of the PTA at P.S. 169. She has also proven to be an active member of her community as a member of Community Board 7 for ten years.

When Assemblywoman Mitaynes was evicted from her rent-stabilized apartment of 30 years, she began her life's work of empowering her neighbors to know their rights and find their voices to fight to stay in their homes. Through her work with Neighbors Helping Neighbors, and with tenants throughout New York State, she was instrumental in the passage of the historic Housing Stability and Tenant Protection Act of 2019. This legislation dramatically and comprehensively strengthened the rights of tenants in rent-stabilized apartments to defend their homes and communities.

She continues to organize in the district and help build power for working-class people. Mitaynes believes a mass, working-class movement is needed to win a future where working-class people have a chance to live dignified lives.

## MICHAEL A. MONTESANO (R-I-C)
*15th - Part of Nassau County*

111 West Old Country Road, Suite 202, Hicksville NY 11801
516-937-3571/montesanom@nyassembly.gov

Legislative Office Building, Room 437, Albany, NY 12248
518-455-4684

Michael Montesano was elected to the New York State Assembly in 2010. In 2020 he was appointed as Deputy Minority Whip. He sits on the following committees: Rules; Ways and Means; Codes; Ethics and Guidance; Judiciary; and Oversight, Analysis, and Investigation. Prior to his election, he was a police officer and detective for the NYPD for a decade and served as an EMT Supervisor and Investigator for the NYC Emergency Medical Service. In 1990 he started his own private practice law firm and served as Acting Village Justice in Roslyn Harbor. He also was a Village Prosecutor for Roslyn Harbor and adjunct professor at the New York Institute of Technology. He has served as a President, Vice President and Trustee of the North Shore School District Board of Education. Montesano was also the former President of the Nassau County Criminal Courts Bar Association and the Nassau County Magistrates Association. He holds an associate degree from Nassau County Community College, a bachelor's degree in Criminal Justice from St. John's University, and a law degree from CUNY Law School at Queens College. He is married, resides in Glen Head, has two children and two stepchildren.

## ANGELO J. MORINELLO (R)
*145th - Erie and Niagara Counties*

800 Main Street, Suite 2C, Niagara Falls, NY 14301
716-282-6062/morinelloa@nyassembly.gov

Legislative Office Building, Room 404, Albany, NY 12248
518-455-5284

Angelo J. Morinello was born and raised in western New York, and was a combat soldier during the Vietnam War. He earned a bachelor's degree from St. Bonaventure University in 1977 and completed a law degree at the Cleveland State University School of Law in 1973. He served as in-house counsel for the family business founded by his grandfather, Certo Brothers Distributing Company. He also served as an Assistant District Attorney in Nassau County and as counsel to Niagara Falls Community Development. From 1990 to 1998 he was a partner in the law firm of Siegel Kelleher & Kahn. Most recently, from 2001 to 2015, he served as a city court judge for Niagara Falls, stepping down at age seventy despite his term extending to 2022.

Biographies

Morinello was elected to the New York State Assembly in November of 2016. He sits on the following committees: Codes; Economic Development, Job Creation, Commerce, and Industry; Labor; Tourism, Parks, Arts, and Sports Development; Veterans' Affairs; and the Commission on Toxic Substances and Hazardous Waste. One of his principal goals as a legislator is to combat a culture of corruption in Albany, and to that end he is a proponent of term limits. He also wants to foster workforce development programs to help ensure the employability of younger workers, create more jobs, and address the impact of drugs and violence on New York's families.

## YUH-LINE NIOU (D)
*65th - Part of New York County*

64 Fulton Street, Room 302, New York, NY 10038
212-312-1420/niouy@nyassembly.gov

Legislative Office Building, Room 746, Albany, NY 12248
518-455-3640

Yuh-line Niou was the first Asian American to be elected to the State Assembly in 2016 for a district that includes Chinatown and the first for any district in Manhattan. She chairs the Subcommittee on Catastrophic Natural Disasters and is co-chair for the Asian Pacific American Task Force. Niou also sits on the following committees: Banks; Consumer Affairs and Protection; Corporations, Authorities, and Commissions; Housing; Insurance; Libraries and Education Technology. In addition, she is a member of the Black, Puerto Rican, Hispanic & Asian Legislative Caucus, the Legislative Women's Caucus, and the Task Force on Women's Issues.

Yuh-line Niou was born in Taiwan and lived in Moscow, Idaho; El Paso, Texas; and Beaverton, Oregon. While attending Evergreen State College in Olympia, Washington, she served as an intern to Washington State legislators, working on state policy and ultimately taking a position with the Washington State House Health Committee chair. In that capacity, she helped develop policies to expand senior access to prescription medication, improve women's health care, and expand health coverage for low-income families. She then went on to work as an advocate and organizer on antipoverty issues, opposing predatory lending and helping low-income families accumulate assets. In 2010 she moved to New York to earn a master's degree in public administration from Baruch College as a National Urban Fellow. She also served as Chief of Staff to State Assemblyman Ron Kim, where she aided thousands of immigrants, small-business owners, teachers, seniors, workers, and students. She has drafted legislation to expand language access for immigrant communities, fought for more affordable housing, and expanded services for seniors. She lives in the Financial District in lower Manhattan.

## CATHERINE T. NOLAN (D)
*37th - Part of Queens County*

47-40 21st Street, Room 810, Long Island City, NY 11101
718-784-3194/nolanc@nyassembly.gov

Legislative Office Building, Room 739, Albany, NY 12248
518-455-4851

Catherine Nolan was elected to the New York State Assembly in 1984 and represents a district that includes the neighborhoods of Sunnyside, Ridgewood, Long Island City, Queensbridge, Ravenswood, Astoria, Woodside, Maspeth, Dutch Kills, and Blissville. She has chaired the Assembly's Committee on Education from 2006 to 2018; and in that capacity, has spearheaded efforts to achieve class size reduction, universal pre-K, middle school initiatives, and improve high school graduation rates. In the Assembly she is Deputy Speaker and sits on the following committees: Rules; Veterans' Affairs; and Ways and Means. Nolan is also a member of the Assembly Majority Steering Committee, the Legislative Women's Caucus, the Puerto Rican/Hispanic Task Force, and the Task Force on Women's Issues. She has previously chaired the Commit-

tee on Banks, the Committee on Labor, the Real Property Taxation Committee, and the Assembly's Commission on State-Federal Relations. She also represented the Assembly on the MTA Capital Program Review Board. In the Assembly, Nolan has passed legislation to raise the minimum wage; enhance whistleblower protections for healthcare workers; strengthen sweatshop enforcement; tighten enforcement of unpaid wage violations; protect innocent bystanders involved in strikes; and create a special fund to investigate prevailing wage violations. She holds a BA from NYU and resides in Ridgewood with her husband and son.

## MICHAEL J. NORRIS (R)
*144th - Orleans County and parts of Erie and Niagara Counties*

8180 Main Street, Clarence, NY 14221
716-839-4691/Norrism@nyassembly.gov

Legislative Office Building, Room 450, Albany, NY 12248
518-4555-4601

Michael J. Norris was elected in November 2016 and reelected in 2018. As a member of the Assembly, he has fought for stronger ethics laws, including pension forfeiture; supported more transparency in state government by sponsoring the State Contracts Sunlight Act; championed legislation to expand coverage for volunteer fire service; and advocated for a greater emphasis of vocational job training opportunities. Norris has also worked to improve infrastructure, roads, parks, and the library system in the Western New York region. He currently serves as the Ranking Minority member of the Election Law Committees and is also a member of the following committees: Ways and Means; Transportation; Rules; and Judiciary.

Michael J. Norris, a lifelong resident of Lockport, received a BA from Niagara University and a JD from Albany Law School. After he was admitted to the New York State Bar in 2006, he engaged in general practice, concentrating in the areas of real estate, wills and estate planning, and municipal law as a partner in the law firm of Seaman Norris, LLP. He served as the attorney for the towns of Lockport and Somerset and the village of Cassadaga, the Third Deputy Corporation Counsel for Lockport, and the Prosecutor for the towns of Lockport and Hartland. He also worked for the New York State Senate and Assembly, served as a Niagara County Election Commissioner, and interned in the Lockport mayor's office. An active community leader, he is a member and Past President of the Lockport Rotary Club and member of All Saints Catholic Church in Lockport. He is also a past member of the Tony Nemi's Youth Sportsman's League and the Lockport Community Television Board of Directors. He was one of twelve members selected for the Greater Niagara Newspapers' Inaugural Under 40 Class in 2015 and received the Paul Harris Award from Lockport Rotary in 2013. He continues to reside in Lockport.

## DANIEL J. O'DONNELL (D)
*69th - Part of New York County*

245 W. 104th Street, New York, NY 10025
212-866-3970/OdonnellD@nyassembly.gov

Legislative Office Building, Room 712, Albany, NY 12248
518-455-5603

Daniel J. O'Donnell was first elected to the New York State Assembly in 2002 and represents a district that includes Manhattan Valley, Morningside Heights, and parts of the Upper West Side. He chairs the Committee on Tourism, Parks, Arts and Sports Development and Codes Subcommittee on Criminal Procedure. He sits on the following committees: Codes, Education, and Environmental Conservation. O'Donnell is also a member of the Puerto Rican/Hispanic Task Force. O'Donnell is the first openly gay man elected to the New York State Assembly. During his tenure in the Assembly, he has been the prime sponsor of major legislation including the Marriage Equality Act, a bill O'Donnell led to passage in the Assembly five times; it was finally signed into law in June 2011.

He also backed the Dignity for All Students Act, which requires public schools in New York to combat bias-based bullying and harassment. Prior to joining the Assembly, O'Donnell was a public defender in the Brooklyn office of the Legal Aid Society; he then opened his own public interest law firm. His community practice helped clients with tenant representation, as well as civil rights litigations ranging from employee discrimination to First Amendment rights. He earned a BA from George Washington University and his JD from CUNY Law School. Born in Queens and raised in Commack, O'Donnell lives with his husband in Morningside Heights.

### STEVEN OTIS (D)
*91st - Part of Westchester County*

222 Grace Church Street, Port Chester, NY 10573
914-939-7028/OtisS@nyassembly.gov

Legislative Office Building, Room 327, Albany, NY 12248
518-455-4897

Steven Otis was first elected in 2012 to the New York State Assembly to represent a district that includes the Sound Shore communities of Larchmont, Mamaroneck, New Rochelle, Port Chester, Rye, and Rye Brook. He chairs the Assembly Majority Conference and the Committee in Science & Technology; he is also the former Chair of the Commission on Solid Waste Management. Assemblyman Otis sits on the following standing Committees: Corporations, Authorities, and Commissions; Education; Environmental Conservation; and Local Governments. He is also a member of the Puerto Rican/Hispanic Task Force. In the Assembly, his priorities include increased state funding to school districts, legislation to make directing laser pointers at airplane cockpits illegal under state law, strengthening child labor law protections for minors working in the modeling industry, enacting rules to prevent dangerous accidents from falling soccer goals, expanding options for consumers holding annuities, expanding notice of all missing persons cases to the federal database, and increasing the state penalty for stealing a family pet. Otis is the former Mayor of Rye, a post he held for 12 years, the longest in the city's history. He also served for many years as Counsel and Chief of Staff to Senator Suzi Oppenheimer from 1985 until his election to the Assembly. Prior to that, he was a Senate Fellow and Legislative Director to State Senator Jeremy S. Weinstein. He has been deeply involved in his community's civic life-particularly focusing on environment and water-related issues-for many years, including serving as Chair of the City of Rye Conservation Commission, and Vice Chair of the Long Island Sound Watershed Intermunicipal Council. He graduated from Hobart & William Smith Colleges and holds a Master's degree in public administration from New York University and a JD from Hofstra University School of Law. He is married and lives with his wife in Rye.

### PHILIP A. PALMESANO (R-C-I)
*132nd - Schuyler and Yates Counties, Parts of Steuben, Chemung, and Seneca Counties*

105 E. Steuben Street, Bath, NY 14810
607-776-9691/palmesanop@nyassembly.gov

Legislative Office Building, Room 448, Albany, NY 12248
518-455-5791

Assemblyman Phil Palmesano was first elected to the Assembly in 2010. His district includes most of Steuben County, Schuyler and Yates counties, and the following towns in Chemung and Seneca counties: Catlin, Erin, Van Etten, Veteran, Covert, Lodi, Ovid, and Romulus. In 2020 Palmesano was appointed as Assistant Minority Leader, having been the Deputy Minority Whip in 2019. He is the Ranking Minority Member on the Energy Committee, and sits on the following Assembly Committees: Correction; Corporations, Authorities, and Commissions; Energy; Insurance; Rural Resources; and Ways and Means. He is also a member of the Task Force on Demographic Research and Reapportionment.

His public service background includes stints as a Legislative Aide to former State Assemblyman Donald Davidsen; former State Assemblyman Jim Bacalles, and District Director to former Congressman Randy Kuhl, Jr. In addition, Assemblyman Palmesano was the District Director for New York State Senator George Winner, and represented the city of Corning in the Steuben County Legislature. He is active in community organizations such as the marketing committee of Catholic Charities of Steuben County; the boards of Steuben County Community Services; and Chemung, Schuyler, Steuben Workforce NY system. Palmesano also served on advisory committees for Camp Good Days and Special Times, and the Great Corning Chamber of Commerce Corning-Steuben Leadership program. He holds a BA in political science from St. Bonaventure University, and resides in Corning with his wife and two children.

### AMY R. PAULIN (D)
*88th - Part of Westchester County*

700 White Plains Road, Suite 252, Scarsdale, NY 10583
914-723-1115/paulina@nyassembly.gov

Legislative Office Building, Room 422, Albany, NY 12248
518-455-5585

Assemblywoman Amy Paulin was elected to the New York State Assembly in November 2000 and represents a district that includes Bronxville, Pelham, Pelham Manor, Scarsdale, Tuckahoe, Eastchester, and parts of New Rochelle and White Plains. She currently chairs the Assembly's Corporations, Authorities, and Commissions Committee and serves on the following committees: Education; Health; and Rules. Her work in the Energy committee was focused on encouraging renewable energy and ensuring a reliable electricity grid. In addition, she is a member of the Task Force on Women's Issues, the Legislative Women's Caucus, and the Puerto Rican/Hispanic Task Force. Her priorities in the Assembly includes state government reform; children and families; domestic violence; sex trafficking; education; health care; animal welfare; and preventing gun violence. Prior to joining the Assembly, she served as Executive Director of My Sisters' Place and as a member of the Scarsdale Village Board. She also was Founder and Chairwoman of the Westchester Women's Agenda. She is the recipient of numerous awards including the Federated Conservations of Westchester County and the Spirit of Independence award from Westchester Disabled on the Move. She was inducted into the Westchester Women's Hall of Fame by the Women's Research and Education Fund in 2017. The Brooklyn-born Paulin graduated from SUNY-Albany, holds a Master's degree from SUNY-Albany and has completed doctoral coursework in Criminal Justice from the same school. She and her husband reside in Scarsdale and have three children.

### CRYSTAL D. PEOPLES-STOKES (D)
*141st - Part of Erie County*

425 Michigan Avenue, Buffalo, NY 14203
716-897-9714/PeopleC@nyassembly.gov

Legislative Office Building, Room 926, Albany, NY 12248
518-455-5005

Crystal Davis Peoples-Stokes was first elected to the New York State Assembly in 2002. She is Majority Leader and Chair of the Committee on Governmental Operations and the New York State Legislative Women's Caucus. In addition, she sits on the following: Rules Committee; the Black, Puerto Rican, Hispanic & Asian Legislative Committee; the Legislative Women's Caucus; and the Task Force on Women's Issues. She has been actively involved in making sure that minority and women-owned businesses have a fair chance at obtaining state contracts, including being appointed by Governor Cuomo to sit on the Minority- and Women-Owned Business Enterprise Teach Task Force. She also has backed major funding for a number of Western New York projects such as funds for a new home for the Community Health Center of Buffalo and the city's Educational Opportunity Center's new facility.

In the Assembly, Peoples-Stokes has championed a Diversity in Medicine initiative that has promoted entry into the medical field with academic and financial supports for promising students of color. Peoples-Stokes secured resources to start Buffalo's Teacher Diversity Pipeline which will help teachers' aides and assistants obtain the proper training and certification to teach in NYS. Peoples-Stokes also successfully passed a law to decriminalize possession and the expungement of minor marijuana convictions from New Yorkers' criminal records, a critical accomplishment along the path towards the state legalization of marijuana and the reinvestment of disenfranchised communities of color, a bill she has sponsored for the last six years.

She holds a BS in elementary education and a master's degree in student personnel administration from Buffalo State College. She is married and lives in Buffalo, her hometown.

## N. NICK PERRY (D)
*58th - Part of Kings County*

903 Utica Avenue, Brooklyn, NY 11203
718-385-3336/perryn@nyassembly.gov

Legislative Office Building, Room 736, Albany, NY 12248
518-455-4166

N. Nick Perry was elected to the New York State Assembly in 1992 to represent his Brooklyn district. He is the Assistant Speaker Pro Tempore and also sits on the following committees: Rules; Ways and Means; Codes; Banks; Labor: Ways and Means; and Transportation. He also is a member of the Black, Puerto Rican, Hispanic & Asian Legislative Caucus; and Chair of the New York State Association of Black and Puerto Rican Legislators and the Regional Chairman (for NY and PA) of the National Black Caucus of State Legislators. Perry, who emigrated from his native Jamaica, volunteered for the US Army, where he served two years' active duty and four years' reserve. He has long been active in local public service, serving on his local Community Board as Chair. He also served on the Brooklyn Borough Board. In the Assembly, Perry achieved two recent, significant victories with the Cyber Crime Youth Rescue Act and the Taxpayer Refund Choice Act. He holds a BA in political science and an MA in public policy from Brooklyn College. He is the married father to two, and has one grandchild.

## STACEY PHEFFER AMATO (D)
*23rd - Part of Queens County*

9516 Rockaway Beach Boulevard, Rockaway Beach, NY 11693
718-945-9550

162-38 Crossbay Boulevard, Howard Beach, NY 11414
718-641-8755/(fax) 718-835-3190/amatos@nyassembly.gov

Legislative Office Building, Room 827, Albany, NY 12248
518-455-4292

Stacey Pheffer Amato, whose district encompasses the Queens neighborhoods of Broad Channel, Hamilton Beach, Howard Beach, Lindenwood, Ozone Park, and Rockaway, occupies a seat that was previously held by her mother, Queens County clerk Audrey Pheffer, making the two the first mother-daughter team to hold the same seat in the New York State Legislature. Assemblywoman Pheffer Amato sits on the following standing Committees: Veterans' Affairs; Corporation, Authorities, and Commissions; Governmental Employees; Racing and Wagering; and Science & Technology. In addition, she is a member of the Legislative Women's Caucus and the Task Force on Women's Issues.

She holds a bachelor's degree in business economics from SUNY Oneonta and, with her husband, Frank, owns Elegante Restaurant & Pizzeria in Rockaway Beach. She worked as an education paraprofessional for the New York City Department of Education and as a procurement analyst for the New York Fire Department and the New York City Sanitation Department. She was a district leader for the 23rd District, working closely with elected officials and civic groups to get more families involved in the community. She has also been an active member of the Rockaway Beach Civic Association for more than a decade and is a committee member for the New York Rising Community Reconstruction Program, which oversees the state's recovery efforts from Superstorm Sandy. She has also served as President of the parent associations at her children's schools, including during the period when one school was displaced to Brooklyn after Superstorm Sandy. Born in Rockaway, she and her husband live in Rockaway Beach with their two children, Sam and Isabella.

## VICTOR M. PICHARDO (D)
*86th - Parts of New York County*

2175C Jerome Avenue, Bronx, NY 10453
718-933-6909/pichardov@nyassembly.gov

Legislative Office Building, Room 424, Albany, NY 12248
518-455-5511

Victor M. Pichardo was elected to the represent New York Assembly District 86 during a special election held on November 5, 2013. His district includes University Heights and areas of West Bronx. In the Assembly, he is Chair Banks Committee. Pichardo sits on the following Committees: Higher Education; Housing; Small Business; and Social Services. He is also a member of the Black, Puerto Rican, Hispanic & Asian Legislative Caucus and the Puerto Rican/Hispanic Task Force. He formerly served as Staff Assistant to Senator Chuck Schumer, and was promoted to Community Outreach Coordinator/Latino Liaison. He has also held the position of Associate Director of Public Relations at Mercy College, and the Director of Community Affairs for State Senator Gustavo Rivera in the Bronx. He holds a degree in communications with double minors in English and sociology from the University of Buffalo.

## JAMES GARY PRETLOW (D)
*89th - Part of Westchester County*

6 Gramatan Avenue, Mt. Vernon, NY 10550
914-667-0127/pretlowj@nyassembly.gov

Legislative Office Building, Room 845, Albany, NY 12248
518-455-5447

J. Gary Pretlow was elected to the New York State Assembly in 1992 to represent a district that includes Mount Vernon and Yonkers. He chairs the Committee on Racing and Wagering, and also sits on the following standing Committees: Codes; Insurance; Rules; and Ways and Means. In addition, he is a member of the Black Puerto Rican, Hispanic & Asian Legislative Caucus and the Puerto Rican/Hispanic Task Force. Assemblyman Pretlow is responsible for Cynthia's Law, a provision of which makes reckless assault of a child a class D felony. In addition, he has worked to stabilize the finances of the New York City Off Track Betting Corporation; he backs a state takeover. Professionally, he is a financial planner with Moncur-Pretlow & Co. His previous public service includes the Mount Vernon City Council, where he chaired the Finance and Planning Committee, and the Capital Projects Board. He remains active in his local community and has received numerous awards. He holds a BBA from Baruch College, and is the married father of one.

## DAN QUART (D)
*73rd - Part of New York County*

353 Lexington Avenue, Suite 704, New York, NY 10016
212-605-0937/quartd@nyassembly.gov

Legislative Office Building, Room 741, Albany, NY 12248
518-455-4794

Assemblyman Dan Quart was elected in November 2011 to represent a district that encompasses the Upper East Side, Midtown East, Turtle Bay, and Sutton Place. He is Chair of the Administrative Regulations Review

Commission, and sits on the following standing Committees: Alcoholism and Drug Abuse; Consumer Affairs and Protection; Corporations, Authorities, and Commissions; Correction; Judiciary; and Tourism, Parks, Arts and Sports Development. Quart is also a member of the Asian Pacific American Task Force. Assemblyman Quart has made criminal justice reform a central goal of his legislative agenda. After witnessing the harmful effects the failings of our justice system had on New Yorkers, particularly people of color and low income, he introduced legislation that would seek to end cash bail, fairly compensate exonerees, reform our ACD process, and keep big money out of elections of district attorneys.

His previous public office was on Community Board 8, where he co-chaired the Transportation Committee and chaired the 2nd Avenue Subway Task Force. An attorney, Quart has been heavily involved in doing pro bono work for many years. He has served as a volunteer for the Housing Division of the Legal Aid Society, providing free representation for low-income tenants in eviction proceedings, since 2002. In 2003, New York State Chief Judge Judith Kaye awarded him the Pro Bono Publico Award as one of New York City's top pro bono attorneys. He also has been the pro bono attorney for the tenants in the Eastwood Housing complex on Roosevelt Island; and for the Disabled Veterans Consortium, representing a disabled veteran who was denied benefits. Beginning in 2009, Dan has partnered with Eviction Intervention Services to organize and lead a pro bono clinic representing tenants on the East Side who fall just above the monetary threshold for free legal services, but cannot afford an attorney of their own. He holds an undergraduate degree from SUNY Binghamton and a JD from St. John's Law School. He is the married father of two.

## EDWARD P. RA (R)
*19th - Part of Nassau County*

825 East Gate Boulevard, Suite 207, Garden City, NY 11530
516-535-4095/rae@nyassembly.gov

444 CAP, Albany, NY 12248
518-455-4627

Ed Ra was elected to the New York State Assembly in 2010 to a district on his native Long Island that includes parts of the Towns of Hempstead, North Hempstead, and Oyster Bay. He is the Ranking Member on the Ways and Means Committee and also is a member of the Education and Health Committees. Ra is also Vice Chair of the Minority Task Force on School Safety. From 2013-2016, Ra served as Ranking Minority Member of the Education Committee; during that time he spearheaded efforts to reform the state's Common Core Standards and developed the Achieving Pupil Preparedness and Launching Excellence (APPLE) Plan. In addition, he continues to fight for a less test-centric teacher evaluation system and advocates for adequate funding of Long Island schools and better support for special education students.

Additional legislative priorities include emphasizing transparency and accountability in the state budget process, rooting out public corruption, and promoting public safety. Ra has served as the Deputy Town Attorney for the Town of Hempstead and as a Legal Aide in the Office of the New York State Attorney General. He holds an undergraduate degree from Loyola College of Maryland, and a JD from St. John's University School of Law. Ra also holds an LLM in intellectual property law from Benjamin N. Cardozo School of Law. He and his wife live in Garden City South.

## JENIFER RAJKUMAR (D)
*38th - Part of Queens County*

83-91 Woodhaven Boulevard, Woodhaven, NY 11421
718-805-0950/rajkumarj@nyassembly.gov

Legislative Office Building, Albany, NY 12248
518-455-4621

Jenifer Rajkumar made history as the first South Asian-American woman ever to be elected to a state office in New York. In the Assembly, she is Chair of the Subcommittee on Diversity in Law; she also sits as a member on the following Committees: Aging; Consumer Affairs and Protection; Judiciary; Small Business; Veterans' Affairs; and the Task Force on Women's Issues

Assemblywoman Rajkumar is a civil rights attorney and a former district leader with a background working in government. She served as the State's Director of Immigration Affairs and as Special Counsel from 2017 to 2019. She is on the board of Represent Women, on the Legal Advisory Council for Sanctuary for Families, and a member of a number of other organizations for social change. Rajkumar also taught as a professor at CUNY's Lehman College.

Rajkumar was born and raised in New York; the first-generation American in her family.

With early roots in public service and giving back, Rajkumar graduated from Stanford Law School with distinction for her pro bono legal work on behalf of vulnerable individuals. She graduated from the University of Pennsylvania magna cum laude and Phi Beta Kappa, where she received the Alice Paul Award for exemplary service to women and families.

As a civil rights lawyer, Assembly Member Rajkumar stood up for the vulnerable and the disenfranchised throughout her career. She litigated class action cases on behalf of workers, tenants, and women at Sanford Heisler Sharp LLP, a national public interest law firm. She collaborated with the U.S. Department of Justice on several *qui tam* cases combating corporate fraud and excess. The resulting settlements saved millions in taxpayer dollars. She was also part of the legal team of *Velez v. Novartis*, ranked by the United Nations as one of the top 10 cases in the world advancing women's equality. The largest gender discrimination case ever to go to trial, the case took on big pharma on behalf of a class of 5,600 women for their gender pay and pregnancy discrimination claims. She was also originating counsel on an amicus curiae brief filed in the U.S Supreme Court presenting arguments in favor of equality for women in nontraditional fields of employment such as firefighting, construction, and law enforcement.

In 2015 and 2016, she was selected to Super Lawyers' New York-Metro Rising Stars List, a recognition given to no more than 2.5 percent of the lawyers in New York.

Just before being elected to the State Assembly, Rajkumar served as Director of Immigration Affairs & Special Counsel for New York State. She led and built the Liberty Defense Project, a first-in-the-nation, multi-million-dollar state led project to assist immigrants in obtaining legal services. Rajkumar also represented New York State in litigation before Administrative Law Judges. She served as an ethics officer; handling ethics matters for the State. She was a statewide surrogate on the State's signature policy items. She traveled from the farms of upstate New York to her home in Queens to help New York's communities. Inspired by the people of New York, she is now more motivated than ever to dedicate herself to public service as a proud member of the New York State Assembly.

## PHILIP R. RAMOS (D-WF)
*6th - Part of Suffolk County*

1010 Suffolk Avenue, Brentwood, NY 11717
631-435-3214/ramosp@nyassembly.gov

Legislative Office Building, Room 648, Albany, NY 12248
518-455-5185

Phil Ramos was first elected to the New York State Assembly in 2002 to a district that includes portions of the hamlets of Brentwood, Central Islip, Bay Shore, North Bay Shore, and Islandia. He is Deputy Majority Leader, a member of the Subcommittee on Students with Special Needs, and sits on the following standing Committees: Aging; Education; Local

Governments; and Ways and Means. In addition, he was elected Vice Chair of the Black, Puerto Rican, Hispanic & Asian Legislative Caucus and is a member of the Puerto Rican/Hispanic Task Force. Assemblyman Ramos has achieved notable increases in state aid for local school districts, helping both students and taxpayers; worked tirelessly to expand universal pre-K; and secured property tax rebates for homeowners, extending the property tax cap. Ramos is a retired detective who rose through the ranks of the Suffolk County Police Department. During his two decades in law enforcement, Assemblyman Ramos worked undercover in the Narcotics Unit for eight years, then went on to become a detective. He joined with other Latino police officers to found the Suffolk County Police Hispanic Society to address Latino issues in the community, and he also helped organize the Long Island Latino Elected Officials Association. He began his working career as a Therapy Aide and Emergency Medical Technician. He is father to two children.

## MICHAEL REILLY (R)
*62nd - Part of Richmond County*

7001 Amboy Road, Suite 202E, Staten Island, NY 10307
718-967-5194/reillym@nyassembly.gov

Legislative Office Building, Room 428, Albany, NY 12248
518-455-4501

Michael Reilly was elected to the New York State Assembly on November 6, 2018. His district is comprised of parts of Richmond County. Assemblyman Reilly serves on the following standing Committees: Aging; Cities; Codes; Education; Governmental Employees; Higher Education; and Housing.

As an Assemblyman, he is working to improve the state's education system, ensure adequate funding for the schools and programs critical to his constituents, support law enforcement officers, combat the state's devastating opioid crisis, and craft legislation to bolster public safety.

Assemblyman Reilly is dedicated to bringing together principal stakeholders, elected officials, and community partners to solve problems and make improvements to New York State. He served as a volunteer with the NYC Community Education Council (CEC) for Staten Island and has represented CEC 31 since first being elected to the school board in 2009, including serving as President of CEC 31 since 2014. Reilly has also been a mentor and coach for the YMCA youth baseball league and volunteers as a member of the Board of Managers for the Staten Island YMCA.

Reilly is a retired New York City Police Lieutenant and served in the US Army Reserves. He and his wife, Mary, and their three children live in Eltingville.

## KARINES REYES (D)
*87th - Part of Bronx County*

1973 Westchester Avenue, Bronx, NY 10462
718-931-2620/reyesk@nyassembly.gov

Legislative Office Building, Room 325, Albany, NY 12248
518-455-5102

As Assemblywoman of the 87th District, Karines Reyes is Chair of the Subcommittee on Workplace Safety and sits on the following standing Committees: Aging; Alcoholism and Drug Abuse; Health; Labor; and Social Services. She is also a member of the Black, Puerto Rican, Hispanic & Asian Legislative Caucus; the Legislative Women's Caucus; the Puerto Rican/Hispanic Task Force; and the Task Force on Women's Issues.

Reyes has been a Bronxite for nearly 20 years. Born in the neighborhood of Los Minas, Santo Domingo, in the Dominican Republic, she identifies as an Afro-Latina. She is a registered nurse in the Oncology Department at Montefiore Einstein Hospital. Reyes has two young sons and has been

balancing the tasks of being a nurse, union representative, activist and volunteer without neglecting the duties of her most important job-being a mother.

Her family left the Dominican Republic and moved to her father's homeland of Carolina, Puerto Rico, in her early childhood. She immigrated to the United States with her mother when she was 6 years old. Moving to Corona, Queens, to live with her maternal grandfather, she experienced the culture shock of a place that was different and unknown. The challenge of learning English made her apprehensive, but she dove right in and excelled in all areas of her education.

Her love for the arts and music continued to develop as she moved throughout the public school system. During her years at the High School of Art and Design, Reyes focused on visual arts, creating an array of inspiring works of art. She majored in advertising and served as the Account Executive for the student-run advertising agency. After graduating with honors, she attended CUNY Baruch College and studied communications. During that time, she began working at Mount Sinai Hospital in the Health Information Management Department. Three years later, she had her first son, and soon thereafter started working at Aramark at Mount Sinai Hospital, moving to the Physical Therapy Department as an Admissions Coordinator when her second son was born in 2010.

While on maternity leave, Reyes went to nursing school, and volunteered in Haiti after the earthquake, and got her nursing degree in 2013. Shortly after, she began her nursing career at Montefiore Hospital on the In-Patient Oncology Ward. Reyes attained a certification in chemotherapy infusion and worked in the hospital and as an infusion nurse at the Eastchester Cancer Center. She was an active leader and served on the New York State Nursing Association Executive Committee at Einstein Hospital as Vice Chair of the bargaining unit. Additionally, she has participated in lobbying for safer nurse-to-patient ratios and single-payer health care in New York. Her leadership role has led her to address local community boards and build relationships with many of the city's elected officials. She has also traveled around the country attending conferences as a representative with NYSNA to speak about issues affecting communities nationally.

As a Latina of Puerto Rican descent, her interest in the island's economic struggles led Reyes to participate in many demonstrations both in the states and on the island of Puerto Rico, particularly in reference to health equity and human rights issues. After Hurricane Maria hit the island, she served as a volunteer nurse with the first group of medical professionals deployed by New York State. Along with a team of fellow nurses, LPNs, doctors and pharmacists, they staffed medical tents outside San Pedro Hospital in Fajardo, Puerto Rico. They provided much-needed medical services to the community.

## DIANA C. RICHARDSON (D-WF-G)
*43 - Part of Kings County*

330 Empire Boulevard, 1st Floor, Brooklyn, NY 11225
718-771-3105/district43@nyassembly.gov

Legislative Office Building, Room 547, Albany, NY 12248
518-455-5262

Diana C. Richardson was first elected to the New York State Assembly in a special election on May 5, 2015 from a district that includes Crown Heights, Lefferts Gardens, Wingate, and East Flatbush. Assemblywoman Richardson is Chair of the Commission on Government Administration and sits on the following committees: Banks; Corporations, Authorities, and Commissions; Education; Labor; Mental Health; and Small Business. She is also a member of the Black, Puerto Rican, Hispanic & Asian Legislative Caucus; the Task Force on Women's Issues; and is Second Vice Chair of the BLAC Association, which raises funds for college scholarships. Richardson's legislative agenda focuses on civic engagement, education equity, permanent affordable housing, small business enhancement, criminal justice reform, antigun violence initiatives, and community empowerment. She was Director of Constituent Affairs for

NYS Senator Kevin Parker, and has been Executive Member of Brooklyn's Community Board 9. She holds an undergraduate degree from CUNY Medgar Evers, and a master's of public administration from CUNY Baruch College. She is the mother of one.

## JONATHAN RIVERA (D)
*149th - Part of Erie County*

65 Grant Street, Buffalo, NY 14213
716-885-9630/riveraj@nyassembly.gov

Legislative Office Building, NY 12248
518-455-4886

Jon Rivera represents people of the 149th Assembly District. In the Assembly he is Chair of the Subcommittee on Regional Tourism Development and sits on the following Committees: Election Law; Energy; Housing; Local Governments; and Tourism, Parks, Arts and Sports Development.

He is a lifelong resident of Buffalo's West Side, where he resides with his wife, Stephanie, and their young daughter, Ana. Rivera is a proud graduate of the Buffalo public schools, where he went on to earn his bachelor's degree from Buffalo State College in business administration. After graduating, he began his own public service career in the office of Congressman Brian Higgins during his first term in office, where he represented Congressman Higgins in the community and advocated for constituent needs in Washington.

Rivera then turned his career to the private sector, where he worked for HSBC Bank. By the time he was 23, he had moved from Customer Service to Branch Manager and Licensed Sales Professional (LSP). In this role, he managed multiple branches, including the one in his home neighborhood of Grant & Ferry on Buffalo's West Side.

After growing a career in banking, Rivera sought a return to public service and accepted a position in the office of the Erie County Executive Mark Poloncarz as the liaison to the County Legislature. While there, he assisted in the drafting of legislation and the passage of multiple on time budgets. After a few years, he was promoted the Special Assistant to the Commissioner of Public Works in Erie County, where he currently serves.

As a volunteer, Assemblyman Rivera has been an active member of the community, serving as the board Chair of Open Buffalo, a board member of the Massachusetts Avenue Project and Hispanics United of Buffalo, as well as Chair of the Erie County Commission on New Americans.

## JOSÉ RIVERA (D)
*78th - Part of Bronx County*

One Fordham Plaza, Suite 1008, 10th Floor, Bronx, NY 10458
718-933-2204/riveraj@nyassembly.gov

Legislative Office Building, Room 536, Albany, NY 12248
518-455-5414

José Rivera was first elected to the New York State Assembly in 1982, where he served for five years. He then left office and was re-elected in 2000. He is Deputy Majority Whip, and a member of the following committees: Aging; Agriculture; Insurance; and Small Business. He formerly chaired the Task Force on Food, Farm and Nutrition Policy. During his previous stint in the Assembly, he served as Treasurer, Vice Chair, and Chairman of the Black and Puerto Rican Caucus. As the Chair of this committee, he was instrumental in establishing the Martin Luther King holiday in the state of New York. In addition, he is a member of the Puerto Rican/Hispanic Task Force and the Black, Puerto Rican, Hispanic & Asian Legislative Caucus. Rivera also has served on the New York City Council.

## ROBERT J. RODRIGUEZ (D)
*68th - Part of New York County*

55 E. 115th Street, New York, NY 10029
212-828-3953/Rodriguezrj@nyassembly.gov

Legislative Office Building, Room 729, Albany, NY 12248
518-455-4781

Robert J. Rodriguez was elected to the New York State Assembly in 2010. He chairs the Legislative Task Force on Demographic Research and Reapportionment, and is a member of the following standing Committees: Ways and Means; Banks; Corporation, Authorities, and Commissions; Housing; Labor; and Mental Health. He is also a member of the Black, Puerto Rican, Hispanic & Asian Legislative Caucus and the Puerto Rican/Hispanic Task Force. His professional experience includes work as Vice President of a minority-owned public finance firm. He served on Community Board 11, including as Chair. In addition, he sat on the Board of Directors of the Upper Manhattan Empowerment Zone. Other community service includes sitting on the boards of the Terrence Cardinal Cooke Community Advisory Board, Catholic Charities Community Services of New York, and SCANNY, a youth and family services organization. The East Harlem native holds degree BA from Yale University and an MBA from New York University.

## DANIEL ROSENTHAL (D)
*27th - Parts of Queens County*

159-06 71st Avenue, Flushing, NY 11365
718-969-1508/rosenthald@nyassembly.gov

Legislative Office Building, Room 441, Albany, NY 12248
518-455-4404

Daniel Rosenthal is the youngest sitting member in the Assembly to date, having won his special election unopposed in 2017. He is Chair of the Task Force on Food, Farm & Nutrition Policy, and sits on the following committees: Aging; Health; Insurance; Labor; Real Property Taxation; and Social Services. Assemblyman Rosenthal frequently advocates for raising public health awareness, proper medical care for New York citizens, and fully funding area schools. Before his work on the Assembly, Rosenthal worked as a Councilman Aide for six years, serving as District Director under Councilman Rory Lancman. Among Rosenthal's successes are pushing the City's Department of Design and Construction to complete the Kew Gardens Hills Library, and speaking for the district's interests on the Flushing Meadows Corona Park Community Advisory Board. He is a graduate of Lander College for Men and lives in Kew Gardens Hills.

## LINDA B. ROSENTHAL (D)
*67th - Part of New York County*

230 W. 72nd Street, Ste 2F, New York, NY 10023
212-873-6368/RosentL@nyassembly.gov

Legislative Office Building, Room 844, Albany, NY 12248
518-455-5802

Linda B. Rosenthal was first elected to the New York State Assembly in 2006. Her district includes the Upper West Side and parts of Clinton/Hell's Kitchen in Manhattan. She chairs the Committee on Social Services, and sits the following standing Committees: Agriculture; Codes; Health; and Housing. Rosenthal is a member of the Subcommittee on Renewable Energy, the Tuition Assistance Program, and Women's Health. In addition, she is a member of the Task Force on Women's Issues. Among her legislative achievements is the passage of more than 40 laws, including laws that extend orders of protection to companion animals; allowing same-sex couples to adopt non-biological children together in New York State, and banning the sale of electronic cigarettes to minors. She has established herself as a leading advocate on affordable housing, domestic violence, consumer protection, government reform, environmental issues, and animal cruelty. Prior to joining the legislature, Rosenthal served as Manhattan District Director and Director of Special Projects to Congressman Jerrold Nadler. She holds a BA in history from the University of Rochester, and is a lifelong resident of the Upper West Side.

## NILY ROZIC (D)
*25th - Part of Queens County*

159-16 Union Turnpike, Flushing, NY 11366
718-820-0214/RozicN@nyassembly.gov

Legislative Office Building, Room 941, Albany, NY 12248
518-455-5172

Nily Rozic was first elected to the New York State Assembly in 2012 to a district that includes northeast Queens neighborhoods including Flushing, Queensboro Hill, Hillcrest, Fresh Meadows, Oakland Gardens, Bayside, and Douglaston. She chairs the Committee on Consumer Affairs and Protection and sits on the following standing Committees: Labor; Correction; Corporation, Authorities, and Commissions; Consumer Affairs and Protection; and Ways and Means. She is also Chair of the Assembly's Office of State-Federal Relations and a member of the Black, Puerto Rican, Hispanic & Asian Legislative Caucus; the Asian Pacific American Task Force; the Task Force on Women's Issues; and the Puerto Rican/Hispanic Task Force. She is the former Chief of Staff to Assemblyman Brian Kavanagh. Within her community, she served on Community Board 8. She has also been a featured speaker at Running Start's Young Women's Political Summit, the Bella Abzug Leadership Institute, and IGNITE's Young Women's Political Mobilization Conference. The Fresh Meadows resident, who was born in Jerusalem and raised in Queens, holds an undergraduate degree from New York University.

## JOHN SALKA (R)
*121st - Madison County and Parts of Otsego and Oneida Counties*

214 Farrier Avenue, Oneida, NY 13421
315-361-4125/salkaj@nyassembly.gov

Legislative Office Building, Room 529, Albany, NY 12248
518-455-4807

John Salka was elected to the New York State Assembly on November 6, 2018. Assemblyman Salka is Chair of the Committee on Children and Families and sits on the following committees: Aging; Banks; Economic Development, Job Creation, and Commerce and Industry; Health; Higher Education; Social Services; and the Commission on State-Local Relations.

As an Assemblyman, Salka hopes to bring more transparency to his constituents and combat the culture of corruption in Albany. As a small business owner, he understands the challenges facing job creators across the state. He has spent 30 years in the medical profession as a registered respiratory therapist and has an intimate understanding of medicine and rural healthcare needs and will work to increase medical services in those areas. As the supervisor of a family-farming community, he will advocate on their behalf, as he strongly believes agriculture is the backbone of the upstate economy. He staunchly opposes the SAFE Act and will push for its repeal.

Since 2007, Salka has been the Town Supervisor of Brookfield. He has served as a school board member for the Brookfield Central School district for seven years, four of those years as President. He also plans to use the knowledge gained during his time as a board member to help fix issues within the school system, specifically the flaws associated with the Common Core Standards.

Salka and his wife, Erin, have been residents of the town of Brookfield for 27 years; they have two children.

## ANGELO SANTABARBARA (D-WF-I-WE)
*111th - Montgomery, Schenectady, and Albany Counties*

2550 Riverfront Center, Amsterdam, NY 12010
518-843-0227/SantabarbaraA@nyassembly.gov

433 State Street, Schenectady, NY 12305
518-381-2941

Legislative Office Building, Room 654, Albany, NY 12248
518-455-5197

Angelo Santabarbara was first elected to the New York State Assembly in 2012. He chairs the Commission on Rural Resources and the Subcommittee on Autism Spectrum Disorders, and also sits on the following committees: Agriculture; Energy; Governmental Employees; Mental Health; Racing and Wagering; and Veterans' Affairs. Professionally, he is an engineer. He was previously elected to the Schenectady County Legislature where he chaired the transportation committee. In addition, he sits on the Board of Directors for the Autism Society of the Greater Capital Region, Family and Child Services of Schenectady, and the Cornell Cooperative Extension in Schenectady County. He started a cheesemaking company and donates all profits to local children's charities. Santabarbara, a lifelong resident of Schenectady County, served in the US Army Reserves and is the founder and former Commander of AMVETS Post 35. He holds a bachelor's degree from SUNY Albany and lives in Rotterdam with his wife and two children.

## NADER J. SAYEGH (D)
*90th - Part of Nassau County*

35 E. Grassy Sprain Road, 406B, Yonkers, NY 10710
914-779-8805/sayeghn@nyassembly.gov

Legislative Office Building, Room 326, Albany, NY 12248
518-455-3662

Nader J. Sayegh was elected in 2018 as Assemblyman of the 90th District. In the Assembly, he is Chair on the Subcommittee on Students with Special Needs; and sits on the following standing Committees: Banks; Cities; Education; Health; Racing and Wagering; and Real Property Taxation. In addition, he is a member of the Black, Puerto Rican, Hispanic & Asian Legislative Caucus.

A resident of Yonkers for over 60 years, he grew up with seven siblings on the southwest side of the city, which was ethnically and racially diverse. After working his way through college, he dedicated himself to being a spokesperson for community needs in education and in equitable opportunities for all.

This path has guided him to seek and reach success as a teacher, principal, college professor, Captain in the New York State Guard/Militia, and President of the Yonkers Public Schools Board of Education. In addition, he also served as a Trustee for the NYS Board of Elections, where he was on several committees, including the Instructional Affairs Committee and the Big Five Cities Board.

Assemblyman Sayegh's leadership in community service and as an attorney for 28 years, specializing in personal injury, immigration, criminal and real estate law, has resulted in his participation in numerous civic, hospital and nonprofit scholarship committees, including the Spanish Foundation, and the NAACP, to name a few areas where he has, and continues to be, a consistent supporter and advocate for education, labor and human resources.

Sayegh represents the 90th Assembly District, which almost entirely encompasses the city of Yonkers. In this role, he continues to lobby for the redistributing of funds to his city so the school system can build new schools. One of his goals in the Assembly is to fight for changes in the New York State Education Funding Formula, which shortchanges Yonkers students and deprives schools of a fair share of their necessary funding. In the Assembly, he also works toward decreasing taxes for the middle class, while enhancing the job market and the economy in New York State.

Sayegh earned an associate degree from Westchester Community College, a bachelor's degree in history and political science from Lehman College, a master's degree in international affairs from Fairleigh Dickinson University, a professional diploma in administration and supervision from Fordham University, and a JD from Pace University School of Law.

He has been married to his wife, Sana, for 34 years and they have five daughters.

## COLIN SCHMITT (R-C-I)
*99th - Orange and Rockland Counties*

6 Depot Street, Suite 103, Washingtonville, NY 10992
845-469-6929/schmittc@nyassembly.gov

Legislative Office Building, Room 433, Albany, NY 12248
518-455-5441

Colin J. Schmitt was elected to the New York State Assembly on November 6, 2018, to represent parts of Orange and Rockland counties. In the Assembly, Schmitt has been named as the Ranking Member of the Committee on Local Government. He also sits on the following committees: Housing; Insurance; Labor; and Local Governments.

Prior to his election to the Assembly, Schmitt served as Chief of Staff for the Town of New Windsor, where he helped oversee the town's day-to-day operations and delivered real results for local residents. He played a key role in the town's historic ethics reform; wrote legislation to modernize the town ethics code; and revamped its dormant ethics committee.

By bringing together the county, town, and the private sector, he helped secure significant economic development investment for the community and hundreds of thousands of dollars in grant funding for various town projects, including restoration of the historic New Windsor Woodlawn Cemetery and the establishment of a town tree committee and Arbor Day celebration honoring first responders and veterans.

While still in high school, Schmitt joined the staff of then-Assemblywoman Annie Rabbitt as a Volunteer, then an Intern, and eventually the youngest Aide ever hired by the New York State Assembly.

As a college student, he founded and chaired a nonpartisan government reform political action committee (New Dawn NY) that promoted ethics reform, budget reform and job creation. Through New Dawn NY, Colin successfully created the grassroots "Stop NY Double Dip" campaign that garnered local, statewide, and national media attention.

Schmitt earned a degree in politics with a minor in theology and religious studies from Catholic University of America.

After college, he joined the staff of Senator Greg Ball, serving as Director of Operations for the NYS Senate Veterans, Homeland Security, and Military Affairs Committee.

Schmitt is a member of the Army National Guard. He completed Army Basic Combat Training at Fort Benning, GA, and finished as distinguished honor graduate from Fort Lee as a 92A automated logistics supply specialist. He is currently assigned to the 1569th Transportation Company in New Windsor, New York Army National Guard.

He is a member of numerous community, civic, and fraternal organizations. In 2015, Colin was honored by the Lymphatic Education and Research Network and "Connor's Spartans" for his work as a state Senate staff member on behalf of the lymphatic disease community.

Schmitt resides in New Windsor with his wife, Nikki Pagano-Schmitt.

## REBECCA A. SEAWRIGHT (D)
*76th - Part of New York County*

1485 York Avenue, New York, NY 10075
212-288-4607/SeawrightR@nyassembly.gov

Legislative Office Building, Room 744, Albany, NY 12248
518-455-5676

Rebecca Seawright was elected to the New York State Assembly in 2014 from a district that includes Manhattan's Upper East Side, Yorkville, and Roosevelt Island. Seawright is Secretary of the Majority and Chair of the Task Force on Women's Issues. He is also a member of the following committees: Banks; Codes; Corporation, Authorities, and Commissions; Education; Judiciary; and Ways and Means. Assemblywoman Seawright is on the Board of Directors for the Legislative Women's Caucus and the Bipartisan Pro-Choice Legislative Caucus; she is also on member of the Puerto Rican/Hispanic Task Force. Since her election, Seawright has secured $7.5 million of funding for her district's public schools, senior centers, and parks. She is a lifelong advocate for women's rights, gun violence prevention, public health, election reform, criminal justice reform, and government transparency. She is the former Assistant District Attorney in the Brooklyn DA's office and legal counselor to small business owners and entrepreneurs. She is also a former member of Community Planning Board 8. In addition, she is Chair of the Board of Visitors of CUNY School of Law, and Chair of the Board of Directors for the Feminist Press. Originally from Texas, Assemblywoman Seawright was State Director of the National Women's Political Caucus, and Chief of Staff for Texas legislator Bob Melton. She also worked in Washington, DC for former US Senator Lloyd Bentsen, and Congressmen Charles Stenholm and the late Marvin Leath. An Upper East Side resident for more than 20 years, she holds a law degree from CUNY Law School. She is a married mother of one.

## AMANDA SEPTIMO (D)
*84th - Part of Bronx County*

384 E 149th Street, Suite 202, Bronx, NY 10455
718-292-2901/septimoa@nyassembly.gov

Legislative Office Building, Room 819, Albany, NY 12248
518-455-5402

Amanda Septimo represents the people of the 84th Assembly District. In the Assembly, she is a member of the following Committees: Agriculture; Banks; Education; Environmental Conservation; Veterans' Affairs; and the Task Force on Women's Issues.

Septimo is a lifelong Bronx resident with a long, rich history of service to the community. Her spirit of activism and community leadership began in her adolescence and can be traced through the entirety of her career. At just 12 years old, she became aware of the prevailing social, economic, and environmental injustices within our community, and soon began to organize around these causes throughout the South Bronx.

While still in her teens, Amanda began working with the Point Community Development Corporation in its teen activist program, A.C.T.I.O.N. It was during this time that Septimo was able to gain the fine-tuned understanding of what advocacy means for people in the Bronx. Playing an integral role in preventing the new jail at Oak Point, getting the Floating Pool to Barretto Point Park, and extending six bus services exposed Amanda to the power of community activism, and the power of a dedication to change.

In these same years, Assemblywoman Septimo volunteered with various local and international groups, including the New York City Parks Department. There, she concentrated her efforts on tutoring local youth: teaching them to read, write, and offering vital mentorship and guidance. While volunteering with the International YMCA, she traveled to West Africa and helped plant more than 300 various fruit juice trees, creating a much-needed boost to the ailing local economy. These public service efforts would gain her the recognition of Community Board 2 and the New York Yankees, who awarded her the 2005 Youth Leadership Award.

Septimo went on to receive the prestigious Posse Scholarship, which earned her a full-tuition scholarship to Vanderbilt University. There, she remained actively involved on campus and used the skills and knowledge that she learned at home in the Bronx towards correcting the injustices within her surrounding community.

Throughout her college years, Septimo served as an intern with the Legal Aid Society fighting cases of domestic violence, with an emphasis on Spanish-speaking immigrants. She also volunteered with the Metro Public Defenders where she operated as an intern case-work investigator; this work allowed her to plant herself within the community, and tackle cases where defendants were often times victims of a criminal justice system stacked against them.

After her years at Vanderbilt, Assembly Member Septimo brought the work of her youth full circle and went on to work with Congressman Jose 47 84th Assembly District E. Serrano—whom she interned with for two years in high school—as a Community Liaison, before being promoted to District Director at 23 years old. In these four years, she was able to observe the powerful connection between policy and opportunities for progress for people in The Bronx.

With this expanded experience and sharpened perspective of government, Septimo went on to work with the Council of School Supervisors and Administrators (CSA) to ensure that school leaders and students have the resources they need to transform every school into a thriving learning environment. After working with CSA, she fought to bring equity, justice, and true representation to the forefront in the South Bronx by running for State Assembly in the 84th Assembly District. While the campaign was ultimately unsuccessful, the experience allowed her to understand the issues of the community on a granular level and develop common-sense solutions that will ultimately help the South Bronx grow. She won the seat two years later.

## GINA SILLITTI (D)
*16th - Part of Nassau County*

20 Vanderventer Avenue, Suite 100 West, Port Washington, NY 11050
516-482-6966/sillittig@nyassembly.gov

Legislative Office Building, Room 919, Albany, NY 12248
518-455-5732

Born and raised on Long Island, Gina Sillitti has a proven record of public service and will use her government experience to deliver results for the people of the 16th Assembly District. She is a first-time elected official, having won her first election in November 2020. In the Assembly, she is Chair of the Subcommittee on Occupational License; she also sits on the following Committees: Economic Development, Job Creation, Commerce and Industry; Local Governments; Election Law; Tourism, Parks, and Sports Development; Transportation; and the Task Force on Women's Issues.

Sillitti's nearly two-decade career in public service included working at the Nassau County Legislature, where she learned the value of constituent services. For her it was about working hard and getting results for the people she served.

Sillitti worked to secure millions for local fire departments, helped thousands of constituents with issues from repairing potholes to navigating their personal tragedies, worked to get much-needed infrastructure projects delivered for the district, and helped bring hundreds of thousands of dollars in community development block grants to improve local schools.

In 2010, Assemblywoman Sillitti was appointed Deputy Commissioner of the Department of Community Services in the Town of North Hempstead. In this role, she worked with a wide variety of constituency groups, including forming the first Asian-American Festival Committee to promote the growing cultural diversity in our town. She was promoted

to Deputy Chief of Staff and the Director of Legislative Affairs for the Town where she served as liaison to officials at every level to ensure projects, grant requests and legislation received the proper attention. Sillitti was the point person on all special projects for the town supervisor involving the public, including as Chair of North Hempstead's 9/11 Memorial Committee, a group consisting of members of the FDNY and NYPD, victims' families, local volunteer fire departments that responded to Ground Zero, veterans, and local architects.

In 2015, Sillitti was recruited to serve as Director of Human Resources and Compliance at the Nassau County Board of Elections. There, she implemented new policies and procedures to modernize the office and save taxpayer dollars.

Sillitti now utilizes her years of government experience to deliver for her district. As a member of the New York State Assembly, she works to make living on Long Island more affordable. She also understands the importance of increasing state aid for our schools, our town, and our villages so they can rely less on property taxes. Sillitti currently resides in the beautiful Village of Manorhaven in Port Washington with her husband, Kevin Clemency.

## JO ANNE SIMON (D)
*52nd - Part of Kings County*

341 Smith Street, Brooklyn, NY 11231
718-246-4889/simonj@nyassembly.gov

Legislative Office Building, Room 435, Albany, NY 12248
518-455-5426

Jo Anne Simon was elected to the New York State Assembly in 2014. She is the Chair of the Committee on Ethics and Guidance and the Commission on Legislative Ethics and sits on the following committees: Consumer Affairs and Protection; Higher Education; Labor; and Transportation. Simon is also a member of the Legislative Women's Caucus and the Task Force on Women's Issues. Her priorities in the Assembly are affordable housing, street safety, access to education, fiscal responsibility to the public agenda, and environmental justice. She established a disability civil rights firm following positions such as teaching in Hofstra University School of Law's clinical program, and is a nationally-recognized expert in her field. She is also an Adjunct Assistant Professor of Law at Fordham University. She is highly active in the areas of Democratic, civic and community affairs, including as President of the Boerum Hill Association, and has founded or co-founded organizations such as Council of Brooklyn Neighborhoods, Friends of Douglass/Greene Park, Hoyt-Schermerhorn Task Force, the Downtown Brooklyn Traffic Calming Task Force, and the Association on Higher Education and Disability (AHEAD), of which she is general counsel. She also chaired the Gowanus Community Stakeholder Group and Gowanus Expressway Community Coalition. She holds a BA in communication sciences from Iona College, a master's degree in education of the deaf from Gallaudet University; and a law degree from Fordham University School of Law. A Brooklyn resident since 1981, the Yonkers native lives in Boerum Hill, Brooklyn, with her husband.

## MATTHEW SIMPSON (R)
*114th - Essex and Warren Counties and Parts of Saratoga and Washington Counties*

140 Glen Street, Glen Falls, NY 12801
518-792-4546/simpsonm@nyassembly.gov

Legislative Office Building, Room 721, Albany, NY 12248
518-455-5565

Matt Simpson was elected to the New York State Assembly on November 3, 2020. His district is comprised of Essex County, Warren County, and parts of Saratoga and Washington counties. As an Assemblyman, Simpson will work to rein in out-of-control spending, fight for lower taxes, eliminate burdensome unfunded mandates, and improve the state's failing infrastructure. In the Assembly, he sits on the following Committees: Environmental Conservation; Local Governments; Social Services; and Tourism, Parks, Arts and Sports Development.

Simpson grew up in the North Country and was first elected to public office in 2011 when he won a seat on the Town Board in Horicon. Two years later, he was elected Town Supervisor where he served until his election to the Assembly. While Town Supervisor, he also worked double duty by sitting on the Warren County Board of Supervisors. There, Simpson served as Committee Chair of public works, Committee Chair of personnel, committee Vice Chair of public safety, and in a number of other capacities.

Assemblyman Simpson was appointed to the Warren & Washington County IDA in 2015, and served as its chair from 2018 to 2019. During that time, he oversaw many projects designed to advance the economic viability of the area. His volunteer work includes serving as President of the Adirondack Association of Towns and Villages (AATV). The AATV represents more than 100 municipalities throughout the Adirondack Park. In his time there, he has worked alongside members of New York State Assembly and Senate, as well as numerous environmental organizations like the Adirondack Counsel.

Prior to public service, Simpson was a small business owner for more than 30 years in the construction trades industry. There, he learned the value of rolling up his sleeves and working until a job is done. Over the span of three decades, he also learned first-hand what goes into creating jobs, making payroll, and succeeding in growing a business in the North Country despite being faced with challenges. Simpson lives in Horicon with his wife, Judy, and their two children.

## DOUG SMITH (R)
*5th - The towns of Brookhaven and Islip, and parts of North Patchogue, Islandia, and Stony Brook*

991 Main Street, Suite 202, Holbrook, NY 11741
631-585-0230/smithd@nyassembly.gov

Legislative Office Building, Room 545, Albany, NY 12248
518-455-5937

Doug Smith was elected to represent the people of the 5th District in the New York State Assembly on April 24, 2018. His district spans the townships of Brookhaven and Islip, and includes Holbrook, Holtsville, Ronkonkoma, Lake Ronkonkoma, Lake Grove, Centereach, Selden, Farmingville, as well as parts of North Patchogue, Islandia, and Stony Brook. In the Assembly, Smith sits on the following standing Committees: Aging; Education; Energy; Higher Education; and Housing.

Smith is dedicated to public service and fighting for Long Island. A lifelong member of our community, he is a graduate of Sachem High School and St. Joseph's College where he earned a degree in mathematics, adolescent education, and is a NYS certified Mathematics Teacher, for grades 7-12.

For the seven years prior to his election, Smith served as Chief of Staff to Assemblyman Al Graf. Whether it be solving over 2,000 constituent cases, leading the charge against the flawed Common Core curriculum, fighting to give families the tools they need to combat the heroin epidemic, or advocating for changes in the law to protect victims of domestic violence, each day he worked tirelessly on behalf of the people of the 5th Assembly District.

During college, Assemblyman Smith served as an Aide at the Social Security Administration. He also spent nights teaching adult education courses, and on the weekends helped educate homeless and underprivileged youth in the Sachem School District.

Smith is a small business owner who operates a website design and hosting company. He is a member of and previously served on the Board of Directors for the Ronkonkoma Chamber of Commerce. He is also active within the Holbrook Chamber of Commerce and is a member of the Centereach and Ronkonkoma Civic Associations, as well as the Sachem Alumni Association. Smith and his wife, Elizabeth, reside in Holbrook.

## ROBERT SMULLEN (R)
*118th - Fulton, Hamilton, and parts of Herkimer, Oneida, and St. Lawrence Counties*

235 North Prospect Street, Herkimer, NY 13350
315-866-1632/smullenr@nyassembly.gov

41 E. Main Street, Room 108 City Hall, Johnstown, NY 12095
518-762-1427

Legislative Office Building, Room 527, Albany, NY 12248
518-455-5393

Robert Smullen was elected to the New York State Assembly on November 6, 2018. His district is comprised of Fulton, Hamilton and parts of Herkimer, Oneida and St. Lawrence counties. In the Assembly, Smullen sits on these committees: Banks; Economic Development, Job Creation, Commerce, and Industry; Environmental Conservation; and Higher Education; Libraries and Education Technology; and Social Services.

As an Assemblyman, Smullen works to lower taxes, lessen regulations to strengthen the state's economy, and protect our liberty. He is also committed to providing support for veterans and active service military personnel, drafting legislation aimed at protecting vulnerable New Yorkers.

In 2015, Smullen retired from the Marine Corps at the rank of Colonel, with 24 years of service and three combat tours to Afghanistan, including participating in Operation Enduring Freedom after the September 11th, 2001 attacks on New York. He has also served at the Pentagon as a Military Strategist and in numerous command and staff positions around the world. Before election, he was the Executive Director of the Hudson River-Black River Regulating District, a New York State Public Benefit Corporation.

In 2003, he was appointed by President George W. Bush as a White House Fellow, serving at the United States Department of Energy in the Office of the Secretary of Energy. He has a BA in history from The Citadel, an MA from the School of Foreign Service at Georgetown University, and an MS in resource management from The Eisenhower School, where he is a distinguished graduate of the National Defense University.

Smullen is also a proud member of the American Legion and Marine Corps League, and regularly volunteers with the New York Naval Militia.

A lifelong resident of upstate New York, he lives on Matilda Hill Farm in the Town of Johnstown in Meco. He and his wife, Megan, have four children.

## MICHAELLE C. SOLAGES (D)
*22nd - Parts of Nassau County*

1690 Central Court, Valley Stream NY 11580
516-599-2972/SolagesM@nyassembly.gov

Legislative Office Building, Room 619, Albany, NY 12248
518-455-4465

Michaelle Solages was first elected to the New York State Assembly in 2012. Her Long Island district includes North Valley Stream, Valley Stream, South Floral Park, Floral Park, Bellarose Terrace, North Woodmere, Elmont, Stewart Manor, and parts of Franklin Square. She is a past Chair of the Subcommittee on Child Product Safety, the Task Force on New Americans, and First Vice Chair of the NYS Black, Puerto Rican, Hispanic & Asian Legislative Caucus. Solages is also a member of Task Force on Women's Issues; the Asian Pacific American Task Force; and the Legislative Women's Caucus. Assemblywoman Solages sits on the following standing Committees: Health; Libraries and Education Technology; Racing and Wagering; and Social Services. Professionally, she has worked in libraries as a Supervisor of Access Services at her alma mater, Hofstra University, from which she holds a bachelor's degree. She is also the recipient of numerous awards, including the New York Library Association Senator Hugh Farley Outstanding Advocate for Libraries and the New York City Breastfeeding Council's Champion award. She and her husband live in Elmont.

## PHIL STECK (D)
*110th - Parts of Schenectady and Albany Counties*

1609 Union Street, Schenectady, NY 12309
518-377-0902/SteckP@nyassembly.gov

Legislative Office Building, Room 627, Albany, NY 12248
518-455-5931

Phil Steck was first elected to the New York State Assembly in 2012. He chairs the Committee on Alcoholism and Drug Abuse and sits on the following Committees: Health; Insurance; Judiciary; Labor; and Oversight, Analysis and Investigation. In the legislature, among the issues he backs are single-payer health insurance; increased funding for public education; and raising revenue through the stock transfer tax to pay for rebuilding the infrastructure of Upstate New York. Prior to his election to the Assembly, Steck served on the Albany County Legislature for four terms. An attorney by profession, he is a Civil Rights and Employment Law Specialist in the firm of Cooper, Erving and Savage LLP. He also spent two years as Assistant District Attorney in Rensselaer and New York counties. He holds an undergraduate degree from Harvard University and a JD from the University of Pennsylvania Law School. The married father of two lives in Loudonville.

## STEVE STERN (D)
*10th - Parts of Babylon and Huntington in Suffolk County*

95 Broad Hollow Road, Suite 100, Melville, NY 11747
631-271-8025/sterns@nyassembly.gov

Legislative Office Building, Room 919, Albany, NY 12248
518-455-5732

Steve Stern represents the 10th District. In the Assembly, he is Chair of the Subcommittee on Renewable Energy and serves on the following standing Committees: Aging; Banks; Economic Development, Job Creation, Commerce, and Industry; Energy; Insurance; and Veterans' Affairs.

He previously served six terms as Suffolk County Legislator representing the 16th District. In addition to representing our community with distinction and a commitment to providing outstanding constituent services, Steve has also authored several legislative initiatives that have been the first in New York State and even in the nation.

Stern introduced and passed the Housing Our Homeless Heroes Act, an important legislative initiative to end veteran homelessness and ensure that our veterans and their families always have a place to call home.

He also created New York State's first Silver Alert system, which—like an Amber Alert—assists in the safe return of individuals with Alzheimer's and other cognitive disorders. It has been expanded by the Suffolk County Police Department to include those with special needs, such as autism, developmental disabilities and severe mental illness.

In addition, he authored the Protect Our Fallen Heroes Act, which protects military funerals from reprehensible and disrespectful protests while families are grieving the loss of their loved ones to ensure respect for those who made the ultimate sacrifice for our great nation.

Consistently committed to protecting the health and safety of our most vulnerable, he sponsored the Toxin-Free Toddlers and Babies Act, landmark legislation to prohibit the sale of baby bottles and toddler cups containing the hazardous chemical BPA. In addition, he is the co-sponsor of the most aggressive legislation in the nation to protect our children from

violent sexual predators. He has also authored successful legislation to strengthen penalties against illegal dumping and created the Shed the Meds pharmaceutical collection program to protect our environment, our drinking water, and our young people.

Stern assisted in coordinating Congressional hearings for the US House Select Committee on Aging, focusing on issues of elder abuse, long-term care, and health and legal services for Long Island's senior citizens.

He graduated from Tulane University and received his law degree from Western Michigan University TMC Law School, graduating cum laude. He is a Certified Elder Law Attorney (CELA) through the National Elder Law Foundation and is admitted to practice law in New York and Florida. He was also elected a fellow of the New York Bar Foundation.

In addition, Stern has served as Adjunct Professor of law at Touro School of Law, is a past Trustee of the Long Island Chapter of the Multiple Sclerosis Society and a past Vice President of the Suffolk Y JCC. He has been featured in *Newsday*, *The New York Times* and *Long Island Business News*. Stern is also proud to have been chosen as Man of the Year in Government by the Times of Huntington.

## AL STIRPE (D)
*127th - Part of Onondaga County*

7293 Buckley Road, Suite 201, North Syracuse, NY 13212
315-452-1115/StirpeA@nyassembly.gov

Legislative Office Building, Room 622, Albany, NY 12248
518-455-4505

Al Stirpe was elected to the New York State Assembly in 2012. He previously served in the Assembly from 2007 to 2010. He chairs the Committee on Small Business, and sits on the following standing Committees: Agriculture; Alcoholism and Drug Abuse; Economic Development, Job Creation, Commerce and Industry; and Higher Education. Prior to his most recent election, Stirpe served as Executive Director of Synapse Sustainability Trust, an environmental nonprofit. Professionally, he worked for General Electric, then spun off a GE operation to form CID Technologies and became its CFO until the company was sold. Stirpe then formed a new venture, Qube Software Inc., and took it from startup to multimillion-dollar business. He serves on the Board of Directors for Friends of North Syracuse Early Education, Onondaga Citizens League, and New York State Fair. For the past six years, Stirpe has run his LifeSavers Blood Drive in conjunction with the Red Cross. He has received awards including the first SUNY Empire State College Excellence in Environmental Sustainability Award. He holds an undergraduate degree in economics from the University of Notre Dame and is the married father of one and stepfather to two.

## CHRIS TAGUE (R-C-I)
*102nd - Green and Schoharies Counties*

45 Five Mile Woods Road, Suite 3, Catskill, NY 12414
518-943-1371/taguec@nyassembly.gov

113 Park Place, Suite 6, Schoharie, NY 12157
518-295-7250

Legislative Office Building, Room 937, Albany, NY 12248
518-455-5363

Chris Tague was elected to the New York State Assembly on April 24, 2018. His district consists of all of Greene and Schoharie Counties along with parts of Delaware, Columbia, Albany, Otsego, and Ulster Counties. Tague serves on the following Committees: Agriculture; Election Law; Environmental Conservation; Real Property Taxation; and Tourism, Parks, Arts, and Sports Development.

After graduating from school in 1987, Tague started his own successful dairy farm business in 1987 growing from 25 cows to 75 cows upon selling the business in 1992. Soon thereafter, he joined Cobleskill Stone

Products and fell in love with the hard work of the laborer position. He was quickly promoted to Foreman, then again promoted to supervise the maintenance shops and trucking division. He earned the title of Superintendent of the Quarry, overseeing the entire operation and is currently the General Manager, with the responsibility of company-wide health and safety compliance; environmental compliance; political action; education; and community outreach.

He previously was elected Schoharie Town Supervisor in 2015. During this time he was invested in social issues, such as the growing heroin epidemic and the protection and support of firefighters, EMS, and first responders.

As an Assemblyman, he focuses on key issues that affect his constituents, including: access to broadband internet, reducing taxes, providing support for local farmers, and fixing upstate's failing infrastructure. Tague currently resides in Schoharie and has lived there all his life.

## MICHAEL TANNOUSIS (R)
*64th - Parts of Richmond and Kings County*

11 Maplewood Place, Staten Island, NY 10306
718-987-0197/tannousism@nyassembly.gov

7716 3rd Avenue, Brooklyn, NY 11209
718-439-8090

Legislative Office Building, Room 543, Albany, NY 12248
518-455-5716

Michael Tannousis was elected to the New York State Assembly on November 3, 2020. His district represents parts of Southern Brooklyn and the East Shore of Staten Island. In the Assembly, he sits on the following Committees: Again; Cities; Codes; Government Employees; Judiciary; Solid Waste Management; and the Commission on Toxic Substances and Hazardous Wastes.

Assemblyman Tannousis began his career in public service in 2006 when he was hired as an Aide to former New York City Council Minority Leader James Oddo. After graduating law school, he became an Assistant District Attorney in the Bronx District Attorney's Office, where he prosecuted major felony offenses. In 2016, he was hired to a similar role in the Richmond County District Attorney's office. During his tenure at the Richmond County DA's office, he successfully prosecuted serious felony cases involving violent crimes and drug sales. Two of his highest profile cases included the conviction after trial of a double murder in Dongan Hills and the successful retrial of the infamous Ramada Inn murders. Tannousis has also served as counsel to City Council Member Joseph Borelli.

As an experienced prosecutor, Tannousis uses his expertise to prioritize protecting the rights of victims and enact changes to recent bail and judicial discretion reforms. He believes the state government has lost focus on the taxpayers' best interests and is resolved to making Staten Island and Brooklyn better, more affordable places to live through improvements to transportation options, education, and fighting misguided property rights laws.

Tannousis is a lifelong Staten Islander and is the son of Greek immigrants who came to America to seek a better life after being displaced by armed conflict in Cyprus. He is a graduate of Public School 23, Intermediate School 24, and Monsignor Farrell High School. He earned an undergraduate degree from SUNY Binghamton and his JD from Pace Law School. Proud of his Greek and Cypriot community roots, he previously served as a board member of the Cyprus-US Chamber of Commerce and was a delegate for the Cyprus Federation of America. Michael Tannousis currently resides in the Great Kills neighborhood with his wife, Anna, and their morkie, Alex.

## AL TAYLOR (D)
*71st - Parts of New York County*

2541-55 Adam Clayton Powell Jr. Boulevard, New York, NY 10039
212-234-1430/taylora@nyassembly.gov

Legislative Office Building, Room 602, Albany, NY 12248
518-455-5491

Al Taylor was first elected to the New York State Assembly in 2017, his New York County district including portions of Hamilton Heights, Harlem, and Washington Heights in Upper Manhattan. Taylor is Chair of the Subcommittee on Regulated Mortgage Lenders, and also sits on the following committees: Aging; Banks; Cities; Election Law; Education; and Housing. He is also a member of the Black, Puerto Rican, Hispanic & Asian Legislative Caucus and the Puerto Rican/Hispanic Task Force. Taylor is focused on improving public schools, protecting tenants and affordable housing, and fixing public transportation. Taylor works to give people, especially children, a second chance, as his own community gave to him in his youth. Taylor also served in the US Army's military police unit. Taylor served as Chief of Staff to former Assemblyman Herman "Denny" Farrell Jr., working to improve the lives of seniors and provide mentorship for troubled teenagers, among other efforts. He has also been a leader against guns and violence, initiating the Man Up! In Harlem program, which was credited with dramatically reducing violence in the area. It has since been replicated in housing projects throughout Upper Manhattan. He has also fought against anti-LGBT hate crimes in Harlem. Taylor is a pastor of Infinity Mennonite Church, and walked 780 miles to Chicago in a 2016 mission called "It's a Love Thing," whose aim was inspiring others to confront violence and walk towards peace. He has also led a disaster relief mission to Haiti in 2010 after the devastating earthquake. Taylor received a BA in public/group communication from Lehman College and the MDiv with a concentration in church development from Nyack College/Alliance Theological Seminary. He resides in Northern Manhattan with his wife and five children.

## FRED W. THIELE, JR. (D-I-WF-WE)
*1st - Part of Suffolk County*

3350 Noyac Road, Building B, Suite 1, Sag Harbor, NY 11963
631-537-2583/ThieleF@nyassembly.gov

Fred Thiele was elected to the New York State Assembly in 1995 and represents a district at the end of Long Island. Thiele is Chair of the Committee on Local Governments and sits on the following standing Committees: Environmental Conservation; Oversight, Analysis, and Investigation; Rules; and Transportation. He is also a member of the Assembly Majority Steering Committee, the NYS Legislative Aviation Caucus, and the NYS Bipartisan Pro Choice Legislative Caucus. His legislative successes include drafting and sponsoring legislation that created the Peconic Bay Community Preservation Fund Act which authorized the five towns in the region to establish dedicated funds, financed by a 2 percent real estate transfer tax, for land acquisition for open space, farmland, and historic preservation, as well as recreational purposes. This program was overwhelmingly approved in a public referendum in 1998 and has generated more than $150 million for land preservation efforts and has resulted in the preservation of thousands of acres of sensitive lands. He also has backed efforts to create Peconic County from Long Island's five easternmost towns, and has supported efforts to ensure fiscal responsibility at all levels of government. Additional legislative priorities include traffic and transportation issues; government reform; reduction of income taxes; debt reform initiatives; elimination of the state estate and gift tax; and the STAR program to reduce school taxes. Prior to joining the Assembly, Theile was counsel to Assemblyman John Behan, then Southampton Town Attorney. In 1987 he served in the Suffolk County Legislature, and in 1991 he went on to become Southampton Town Supervisor. Theile holds a BA from Long Island University, Southampton College, and a JD from Albany Law School. He is a father to three and has lived in Sag Harbor for his entire life.

Biographies

557

## CLYDE VANEL (D)
*33rd - Part of Queens County*

97-01 Springfield Boulevard, Queens Village, NY 11429
718-479-2333/vanelc@nyassembly.gov

Legislative Office Building, Room 454, Albany, NY 12248
518-455-4711

Assemblyman Clyde Vanel was elected to the New York State Assembly in November 2016. He is Chair of the Subcommittee on Internet and New Technology, and sits on the following committees: Banks; Children and Families; Codes; Corporations, Authorities, and Commission; Racing and Wagering; and Science & Technology. Vanel is also a member of the Asian Pacific American Task Force and the Black, Puerto Rican, Hispanic & Asian Legislative Caucus. As a legislator, he wants to put his experience as an entrepreneur to work in addressing the problem of the high cost of doing business in Queens, especially for small businesses.

Vanel earned an AAS in applied science in aerospace technology and a BS in aviation administration from Farmingdale State College, where he served as the Student Government President. He then earned a law degree at the Boston University School of Law, where he served as the Editor-in-Chief of the Journal of Science & Technology Law. He later served as Chief of Staff for New York State Senator James Sanders Jr. He is the owner and operator of the Vanel Law Firm, focusing on intellectual property law, business law, and wills and estate planning. He is also an Internet entrepreneur, owning and operating TrademarkReady.com, which provides trademark filing and protection services. Additionally, for five years he was the owner and operator of Vanel on First, a restaurant, bar, and lounge in lower Manhattan. He is the founder of the New York Metro chapter of Black Pilots of America, Inc., an organization that exposes the community and youth to the field of aviation and provides preflight and aviation-related training. He has worked extensively in political community empowerment, helping numerous members of the community become involved with and informed about elections and political issues. He has mentored young men with Eagle Academy in the Bronx and Queens and with the Young Men's Rites of Passage at the Allen A.M.E Church in Jamaica, Queens. He is a member of Kappa Alpha Psi Fraternity. His Queens district encompasses the neighborhoods of St. Albans, Hollis, Queens Village, Bellerose, parts of Floral Park, and Cambria Heights, where he was raised with nine brothers and sisters.

## MARK WALCZYK (R-C-I)
*116th - Parts of North Jefferson and St. Lawrence Counties*

317 Washington Street, Suite 210, Dulles State Office, Watertown, NY 13601
315-786-0284/walczykm@nyassembly.gov

3 Remington Avenue, Canton, NY 13617
315-386-2037

Legislative Office Building, Room 940, Albany, NY 12248
518-455-5545

Mark Walczyk was elected to the New York State Assembly on November 6, 2018. His district is comprised of Northern Jefferson and St. Lawrence counties. In the Assembly, he sits on the following standing Committees: Cities; Correction; Energy; Higher Education; Social Services; and Transportation. Walczyk is also a member of the Commission on Rural Resources.

Assemblyman Walczyk is committed to making state investments in aging infrastructure with much-needed repairs to crumbling roads and bridges, as well as protecting precious rivers and lakes located in his district. He is also a strong proponent of policies that empower teachers and gives students the opportunity to be successful in job preparation training at the secondary and collegiate levels.

Walczyk earned the rank of Eagle Scout out of high school and after graduating from the University of Albany began his career in public service with a focus on statewide policy to improving life for residents in Upstate New York. He joined the staff of state Senator Patty Ritchie as her Legislative Director and later as District Director. Walczyk was elected to the Watertown City Council in 2015.

He has proudly served in the armed forces for the last six years as a commissioned officer in the US Army Reserve's 479th Engineer Battalion. For the last two years, he served as Company Commander of the 366th Engineer Company based in Canton.

An active community member and volunteer, Walczyk is a member of the Watertown Noontime Rotary Club, Jefferson County Animal Cruelty Task Force, NRA, American Legion Post 61, Italian American Civic Association, Jefferson County Historical Society, Friends of the MAC Nature Center, and Friends of Thompson Park.

Walczyk is an angler, an avid hiker, and a four-time Ironman Triathlete. He resides in Watertown near his fiancée, Jessica.

## LATRICE MONIQUE WALKER (D)
*55th - Part of Kings County*

400 Rockaway Avenue, 2nd Floor, Brooklyn, NY 11212
718-342-1256/WalkerL@nyassembly.gov

Legislative Office Building, Room 713, Albany, NY 12248
518-455-4466

Latrice Walker was elected to the New York State Assembly in 2014. She serves as Chair for the Committee on Election Law and sits on the following standing Committees: Codes; Correction; Housing; Election Law; Insurance; and Judiciary. Assemblywoman Walker is also a member of the Black, Puerto Rican, Hispanic & Asian Legislative Caucus; the Legislative Women's Caucus; the Puerto Rican/Hispanic Task Force; and the Task Force on Women's Issues. She previously served as Counsel to US Representative Yvette D. Clarke. She supports affordable housing while preserving and advocating on behalf of residents of the New York City Housing Authority. She is a founding member of the Ocean Hill-Brownsville Coalition of Young Professionals. She holds an undergraduate degree from SUNY Purchase College and a JD from Pace University. She lives in Ocean-Hill Brownsville and has one daughter.

## MONICA P. WALLACE (D)
*143rd - Part of Erie County*

2562 Walden Avenue, Suite 102, Cheektowaga, NY 14225
716-686-0080/wallacem@nyassembly.gov

Legislative Office Building, Room 704, Albany, NY 12248
518-4555-5921

Monica Wallace, elected to a district that encompasses the Erie County towns of Cheektowaga and Lancaster and the villages of Depew, Lancaster, and Sloan, was the first person in her family to earn a college degree. She worked her way through college and law school, earning an undergraduate degree with honors from SUNY Binghamton and a law degree, cum laude, from SUNY Buffalo Law School. Before she was elected to the State Assembly, she spent much of her legal career as a law clerk in federal court. She also held a position on the faculty at her alma mater, SUNY Buffalo Law School. She was a Local and State Director for the Western New York Chapter of the Women's Bar Association of the State of New York, an organization dedicated to advancing the status of women and children in the state. She also served as a member of the Lancaster YMCA board and on the Legal Writing Institute's Bar Outreach Committee.

In the Assembly, she sits on the following Committees: Governmental Operations; Judiciary; Local Governments; Science & Technology; Transportation; and Veterans' Affairs. Wallace is also a member of the

Legislative Women's Caucus and the Task Force on Women's Issues. As a legislator, her goals include strengthening public education, promoting the interests of working families, creating jobs by supporting economic development, upgrading local infrastructure, and restoring integrity to government by helping pass ethics reform legislation, including a bill to prevent taxpayer-funded pensions from being paid to public officers convicted of corruption. She also wants to prevent conflicts of interest with regard to legislator's outside income. She lives in Lancaster with her husband, John, and two children, Jack and Claire.

## MARY BETH WALSH (R)
*112th - Parts of Saratoga and Schenectady Counties*

199 Milton Avenue, Suite 3-4, Ballston Spa, NY 12020
518-884-8010/walshm@nyassembly.gov

Legislative Office Building, Room 635, Albany, NY 12248
518-455-5772

Mary Beth Walsh was first elected to the New York State Assembly on November 8, 2016. She earned a law degree at the Albany Law School, and has maintained her own private law practice. She has been a practicing attorney for more than twenty-five years, recently serving as Saratoga Assistant County Attorney and the attorney for the town of Edinburg. Before her election to the State Assembly, she served in a variety of leadership positions in local and county government, including two terms as a councilwoman in the town of Ballston and as a member of the Saratoga County Industrial Development Agency, the Saratoga County Ethics Advisory Council, and the Saratoga County Autism Council. As councilwoman, she helped deliver vital services to residents while promoting fiscal restraint and keeping Ballston free of municipal taxation. In the Assembly, Walsh is the Assistant Minority Leader Pro Tempore as well as a member of the Legislative Women's Caucus. She also serves on the following committees: Education; Judiciary; Libraries and Education Technology; and Mental Health. As a legislator, her priorities include instilling ethics reform in state government, revitalizing the economy and altering the climate for business, promoting the interests of middle-class families, revamping the education system, empowering parents to advocate for their children, and protecting upstate values. She and her husband, Jim, are parents of six children in a blended family.

## HELENE E. WEINSTEIN (D)
*41st - Part of Kings County*

3520 Nostrand Avenue, Brooklyn, NY 11229
718-648-4700/WeinstH@nyassembly.gov

Legislative Office Building, Room 923, Albany, NY 12248
518-455-5462

Helene Weinstein was first elected to the New York State Assembly in 1980. Her district includes the Sheepshead Bay, Midwood, Flatlands, Canarsie, and East Flatbush communities in Brooklyn. She is the former Chair of the Judiciary Committee and chairs the Committee on Ways and Means, the first woman in the state to hold the position. She also sits on the Rules Committee and is a member of the Task Force on Women's issues and the Legislative Women's Caucus. She has sponsored major reforms in the state's jury system and is the leading proponent of ensuring civil legal services for low-income New Yorkers. She is also a leading advocate for women, sponsoring the Family Court Fair Access law of 2008, a reform measure that expanded access to civil orders of protection to domestic violence victims in dating and intimate relationships.

She has written a plethora of laws protecting children from sex offenders, shielded consumers from unfair banking and business practices, championed the landmark "zombie property" law, which improved communities by forcing lenders and banks to maintain properties vacant following foreclosures, and passed a law closing the loopholes that made raising rent and rent decontrol far too easy for landlords who priced families out of their homes. Other major state laws she has sponsored include a law

declaring surrogate parenting contracts void and against public policy and a rape shield extension law to protect crime victims. She has held a number of significant posts and has received numerous awards. Her civic involvement includes sitting on the board of the Center for Women in Government. She holds a BA from American University and a JD from New England School of Law.

## DAVID I. WEPRIN (D)
*24th - Part of Queens County*

185-06 Union Turnpike, Fresh Meadows, NY11366
718-454-3027/Weprind@nyassembly.gov

111-12 Atlantic Avenue, #5, Richmond Hill, NY 11419
718-805-2381

Legislative Office Building, Room 526, Albany, NY 12248
518-455-5806

David Weprin was elected to the New York State Assembly in 2010 and now represents the same district his father, the late Assembly Speaker Saul Weprin, represented for 23 years. His brother Mark Weprin spent more than 15 years in the same seat. Weprin chairs the Assembly Committee of Correction. He also sits on the following committees: Banks; Codes; Judiciary; and Ways and Means. He is also a member of the Asian Pacific American Task Force and the Puerto Rican/Hispanic Task Force. Professionally, Weprin spent many years in the financial services industry. From 1983 to 1987, he was Deputy Superintendent of Banks and Secretary of the Banking Board for New York State, an appointment made by former Governor Mario Cuomo. As Deputy Superintendent, he advised the Banking Department on the formulation of banking standards, and exercised power to approve or disapprove the issuance of bank charters and licenses and the establishment of branch banks. His elected public service began when he was elected to the New York City Council in 2001.

Weprin's organizational affiliations include or have included Northeast Queens Jewish Community Council, Queens Jewish Community Council, Transitional Services for NY, National Conference of Community & Justice, Respect for Law Alliance, National Committee for the Furtherance of Jewish Education, Greater Jamaica Development Corp., Metropolitan Council on Jewish Poverty, American Jewish Congress, Holliswood Civic Association, Economic Education Foundation of the Securities Industry Association, and the Brandeis Association.

He holds a BA from SUNY-Albany and a JD from Hofstra University. He and his wife are parents to five children.

## JAIME R. WILLIAMS (D)
*59th - Part of Brooklyn*

5318 Avenue N, 1st Floor, Brooklyn, NY 11234
718-252-2124/williamsja@nyassembly.gov

Jaime Williams was elected to serve the 59th Assembly District on April 19, 2016, encompassing the neighborhoods of Canarsie, Georgetown, Mill Basin, Marine Park, and Gerritsen Beach. She is Chair of the Subcommittee on Emergency Response/Disaster and is a member of the following standing Committees: Agriculture; Consumer Affairs and Protection; Environmental Conservation; Governmental Operations; Insurance; and Transportation. Williams is also a member of the Black, Puerto Rican, Hispanic & Asian Legislative Caucus; the Legislative Women's Caucus; the Puerto Rican/Hispanic Task Force; and the Task Force on Women's Issues.

Originally from Trinidad and Tobago, she came to the United States in 1999, settling in New York City. She obtained her GED when she first came to the United States and then attended Kingsborough Community College. She has a bachelor's degree in social work from York College and a master's degree in social work from Fordham University and is certified as an alcohol and substance abuse counselor. In 2007, she founded Empowerment = Courage to Heal Inc., an organization devoted to raising awareness against domestic violence. Assemblywoman Williams is a member of the Canarsie Lions Club and the 69th Precinct Community Council.

## CARRIE WOERNER (D)
*113 - Saratoga and Washington Counties*

112 Spring Street, Suite 205, Saratoga Springs, NY 12866
518-584-5493/woernerc@nyassembly.gov

Legislative Office Building, Room 502, Albany, NY 12248
518-455-5404

Carrie Woerner was elected to the New York State Assembly in 2014. She is Chair of the Subcommittee on the Commission on Skills Development and Career Education and sits on the following Committees: Agriculture; Local Governments; Racing and Wagering; Small Business; and Tourism, Parks, Arts, and Sports Development. Woerner is also a member of the Commission on Rural Resources; the Legislative Women's Caucus; and the Task Force on Women's Issues.

In the Assembly, Woerner advocates for responsible spending; focuses on improving the business climate for farms and small businesses; strengthens public schools; and protects the traditions, heritage, and culture of Saratoga and Washington counties. She is Vice President and General Manager of MeetMax Conference Software, a division of The Wall Street Transcript, and established the software division in Saratoga Springs in 2008. She has also worked for Dell/Perot systems and IMB. She is the former Executive Director of the Saratoga Springs Preservation Foundation, where she expanded the organization, published a walking tour guide, and secured $130,000 in state funding to restore historic buildings in the Beekman Street Arts District. She also founded the Historic Saratoga Race Track Preservation Coalition. She served as a Round Lake Village Trustee for three terms, and is a member of the Town of Malta Planning Board and the Malta Sunrise Rotary. She holds a bachelor's degree from Carnegie-Mellon University and an MBA from Santa Clara University.

## KENNETH ZEBROWSKI (D)
*96th - Rockland County*

67 N. Main Street, New City, NY 10956
845-634-9791/ZebrowskiK@nyassembly.gov

Legislative Office Building, Room 625, Albany, NY 12248
518-455-5735

Ken Zebrowski was first elected to the New York State Assembly on May 1, 2007 during a special election held to fill the seat of his late father, Assemblyman Kenneth P. Zebrowski. He currently chairs the Committee on Governmental Operations and is a member of the Subcommittee on Emerging Workforce. He also sits on the following standing Committees: Rules; Ethics and Guidance; Judicary; and Government Employees. In 2013, Zebrowski authored and passed a Hepatitis C testing bill that led thousands of New Yorkers to get treatment for this life-threatening disease. His legislative priorities also include reducing mandates on local governments; preventing reductions and changes to the STAR property tax relief program; increasing funding to schools; protecting businesses from losing tax incentives; bringing full-day kin-

dergarten statewide; increasing voter access, protecting sexual assault and domestic violence victims; preventing gun violence; and regulating student loan companies. Prior to his election, Zebrowski served in the Rockland County Legislature. He founded the law firm of Zebrowski & Zebrowski with his father, and is currently of counsel to the New City law firm of Braunfotel & Frendel, LLC. He holds a BA from SUNY-Albany and a JD from Seton Hall University School of Law.

## STEFANI ZINERMAN (D)
*56th - Part of Kings County*

1360 Fulton Street, Room 417, Brooklyn, NY 11216
718-399-7630/zinermans@nyassembly.gov

Legislative Office Building, Albany, NY 12248
518-455-5474

Stefani L. Zinerman was elected to the 56th District in the New York State Assembly on November 3, 2020, to represent the historic neighborhoods of Bedford-Stuyvesant and Crown Heights in Brooklyn. She joins the Legislature as an experienced government, nonprofit, and small-business professional who has pioneered efforts in workforce development and healthy aging initiatives. In the Assembly, she is Chair of the Subcommittee on Emerging Workforce; she also sits on the following Committees: Aging; Agriculture; People with Disabilities; Tourism, Parks, Arts and Sports Development, and the Task Force on Women's Issues.

Sinerman is a tireless advocate for civil rights and justice and champions education access, food justice, housing stability, and maternal health. As a Silver Life member and member-at-large of the Brooklyn NAACP, she continuously promotes voter rights and is a recognized leader in voter education, engagement, and registration.

Prior to her election to the New York State Assembly, Assemblywoman Zinerman worked in local and state government, beginning as Chief of Staff for the 36th Council District for five years before moving into the role of Director of Special Projects for State Senator Velmanette Montgomery. Her entire career has focused on equity and access as a Program Manager for several human rights organizations, including the Research Foundation/CUNY, the Algebra Project, the Education Development Center, the Community Service Society, and the American Red Cross.

An active member of Community Board 3, the 81st Precinct Community Council, Community Education Council 16, and Boys and Girls High School Community Advisory Committee, Zinerman continues to work on education equity, public safety, and emergency preparedness. During her tenure at the New York City Council, she served as Chair of the Age Friendly Neighborhood Initiative and worked closely with community stakeholders to expand the program, which led to Brooklyn receiving recognition as an Age Friendly City in 2019.

Assembly Member Zinerman is committed to building a better future for the 56th District and works diligently to enhance the quality of life for everyone in her community through coalition building and mission-driven actions. She believes that reliable health care, racial equity, housing stability, and wealth-building is the key to a sustainable future for the people, the businesses and the community institutions of Bedford-Stuyvesant and Crown Heights.

## US SENATE: NEW YORK DELEGATION

### KIRSTEN E. GILLIBRAND (D)

478 Russell Senate Office Building, Washington, DC 20510
202-224-4451/www.gillibrand.senate.gov

780 Third Avenue, Suite 2601, New York, NY 10017
212-688-6262/

PO Box 749, Yonkers, NY 10710
845-875-4585/

Kenneth B. Keating Federal Building, 100 State Street, Room 4195,
Rochester, NY 14614
585-263-6250/

James M. Hanley Federal Building, 100 S. Clinton Street, Room 1470,
PO Box 7378, Syracuse, NY 13261
315-448-0470/

155 Pinelawn Road, Suite 250 North, Melville, NY 11747
631-249-2825/

PO Box 273, Lowville, NY 13367
315-376-6118/

Leo W. O'Brien Federal Building, 11A Clinton Square, Room 821, Albany, NY 12207
518-431-0120/

Larkin at Exchange, 726 Exchange Street, Suite 511, Buffalo, NY, 14210
716-854-9725/

One of Senator Kirsten Gillibrand's top priorities in the United States Senate is to rebuild the American economy. She is fighting every day for better-paying jobs, more products stamped with the words "Made in America" and more new small businesses around New York State. She is determined to make sure that all New Yorkers have the opportunity to reach their potential, and she has consistently been a voice for the voiceless across New York and all around the country.

Throughout her time in the Senate, Senator Gillibrand has been a leader in some of the toughest fights in Washington. She led the effort to repeal the "Don't Ask Don't Tell" policy that banned gays from serving openly in the military; she wrote the STOCK Act, which made it illegal for members of Congress to financially benefit from inside information; and she won the long fight to provide permanent health care and compensation to the 9/11 first responders and community survivors who are sick with diseases caused by the toxins at Ground Zero. Senator Gillibrand brought Democrats and Republicans together to win these legislative victories.

Senator Gillibrand is committed to keeping Americans safe from threats overseas and at home. From her seat on the Senate Armed Services Committee, she has been a vocal advocate for strengthening America's armed services, national security, and military readiness. She has also called for an independent investigation into Russian cybercrimes against our government institutions. Senator Gillibrand's bipartisan bill to keep guns out of the hands of criminals and make gun trafficking a federal crime—the Hadiya Pendleton and Nyasia Pryear-Yard Gun Trafficking and Crime Prevention Act—is one of the only recent gun bills to be supported by both parties and a majority of the Senate.

Senator Gillibrand is leading the fight to reform the justice system for sexual assault survivors in the military and on college campuses. In 2013, as Chair of the Armed Services subcommittee on personnel, she held the first Senate hearing on the issue of sexual assault in the military in almost a decade, and has built a bipartisan coalition of Senators in support of her bill, the Military Justice Improvement Act, which would remove sexual assault cases from the chain of command. She has also built a broad, bipartisan coalition for the Campus Accountability and Safety Act, which would finally hold colleges accountable for sexual assault on their campuses.

As the mother of two young sons, Senator Gillibrand understands the challenges that working families are facing in today's economy. She is a champion for the economic empowerment of women and working families, and she has authored new legislation to rewrite the rules of the workplace so it can keep up with our changing workforce. She is fighting to pass bills that would raise the minimum wage, make quality child care more affordable, create universal pre-K, and ensure equal pay for equal work. Senator Gillibrand also introduced the FAMILY Act, which would create a national paid leave program for all American workers' for about the cost of a cup of coffee a week.

Senator Gillibrand was the first New York Senator to join the Senate Agriculture Committee in nearly 40 years, and she uses that position to give New York's farmers and agricultural producers a voice in Washington. She has fought for programs that would support specialty crop insurance, expand rural broadband access, and improve recovery efforts after natural disasters. She also continues to lead the fight in the Senate to protect access to healthy meals for struggling children, seniors, and veterans.

On the Senate Select Committee on Intelligence, Senator Gillibrand represents the interests of New York, which has been the top terror target in the United States since before 9/11, and works closely with the NYPD and NY Department of Homeland Security to keep our state safe. She is also working to better prepare the nation for the barrage of cyber-attacks that have targeted local institutions and private businesses alike by focusing on hardening both public and private sector cyber defenses.

From her seat on the Senate Aging Committee, Senator Gillibrand is committed to fighting on behalf of seniors. She introduced a bipartisan bill to crack down on senior fraud, and she also wrote bipartisan legislation that would make price gouging of medicines by pharmaceutical companies a federal crime.

After attending Albany's Academy of Holy Names, Senator Gillibrand graduated in 1984 from the Emma Willard School in Troy, New York's "first all-women's" high school in the United States. A magna cum laude graduate of Dartmouth College in 1988, Gillibrand went on to receive her law degree from the UCLA School of Law in 1991 and served as a law clerk on the Second Circuit Court of Appeals. After working as an attorney in New York City for more than a decade, Senator Gillibrand served as Special Counsel to United States Secretary of Housing and Urban Development (HUD) Andrew Cuomo during the Clinton Administration. She then worked as an attorney in Upstate New York before becoming a member of Congress. Born and raised in upstate New York, Senator Gillibrand's home is in Brunswick, New York, with her husband, Jonathan Gillibrand, and their two sons, Theo and Henry.

### CHARLES E. SCHUMER (D)

322 Hart Senate Office Building, Washington, DC 20510
202-224-6542/www.schumer.senate.gov

780 3rd Avenue, Suite 2301, New York, NY 10017
212-486-4430

Leo O'Brien Building, Room 420, Albany, NY 12207
518-431-4070

15 Henry Street, Room M103, Binghamton, NY 13901
607-772-6792

130 S. Elmwood Avenue, #660, Buffalo, NY 14202
716-846-4111

One Park Place, Suite 100, Peekskill, NY 10566
914-734-1532

145 Pine Lawn Road, #300, Melville, NY 11747
631-753-0978

100 State Street, Room 3040, Rochester, NY 14614
585-263-5866

100 S. Clinton Street, Room 841, Syracuse, NY 13261
315-423-5471

In 1998, Charles E. Schumer was elected to the US Senate; he became New York's senior senator when Senator Daniel Patrick Moynihan retired in 2000. On January 20, 2021, Schumer became Senate Majority Leader, and the first Jewish leader of either chamber of Congress. As Democratic Leader, Senator Schumer does not serve on any committees in the Senate. Most recently, he served as Ranking Member of the Committee on Rules and Administration, on the Senate Judiciary Committee as Ranking Member of the Subcommittee on Immigration, Refugees, and Border Security, and the Senate Finance Committee.

A native of Brooklyn and a graduate of Harvard College and Harvard Law School, Schumer was a three-term member of the New York State Assembly from 1975 to 1980. Schumer served in the U.S. House of Representatives from 1981 to 1999, first representing New York's 16th Congressional District before being redistricted to the 10th Congressional District in 1983 and 9th Congressional District ten years later. In 1998, Schumer was elected as a U.S. senator after defeating three-term Republican incumbent Al D'Amato. He was subsequently reelected in 2004 with 71 percent of the vote, and in 2016 with 70 percent of the vote. He served as Vice Chairman of the Democratic Caucus in the Senate from 2007 to 2017 and was Chairman of the Senate Democratic Policy Committee from 2011 to 2017. Schumer won his fourth term in the Senate in 2016 and was then unanimously elected Democratic leader to succeed Harry Reid, who was retiring.

In November 2017, Senators Schumer and Gillibrand announced $1,908,486 in funding for Head Start and Early Head Start programs at the Community Action Organization of Erie County, the federal funding yielding "real results to young students in Western New York by providing them with the resources they need to succeed both in and out of the classroom." In January 2018, Schumer requested the U.S. Department of Veterans Affairs to complete final acquisitions for two 60-acre and 77-acre parcels in Pembroke, New York, and then initiate construction of the New Western New York National Veterans Cemetery.

In March 2018, Schumer said the bipartisan legislation would assist the children of deceased first respondents afford college by increasing the availability of Pell grant funding. In August 2018, Schumer announced the Senate passed 1 million in FY2019 funding for the national firefighter cancer registry as an amendment to the upcoming FY2019 Health and Human Services (HHS) minibus appropriations bill. Schumer said firefighters needed "first-rate medical care and treatment" for the work they did and the registry would help "researchers track, treat, and eventually prevent firefighters being stricken by cancer." After the death of Arizona Republican John McCain that month, Schumer announced in a statement that he would be introducing legislation to rename the Russell Senate Office Building after McCain.

His achievements have also included bringing affordable air service to Upstate New York and the Hudson Valley and securing over $20 billion in aid to New York City following the attacks on September 11, 2001; authored legislation that eliminated barriers that delay low-cost generic medications from entering the marketplace; championed agricultural measures to preserve vital market support programs for New York's dairy farmers and crop growers; worked to retain New York jobs that were at risk of leaving and to attract new firms to create thousands of new jobs; and led the charge to make college tuition tax deductible. Senate Majority Leader Schumer continues the tradition he began in his first term: he visits each of New York's 62 counties each year. Senator Schumer is the married father of two children.

## US HOUSE OF REPRESENTATIVES: NEW YORK DELEGATION

### JAMAAL BOWMAN (D)
*16th - Parts of Bronx and Westchester Counties*

6 Gramatan Avenue, Suite 205, Mt. Vernon, NY 10550
914-371-9220/ bowman.house.gov

177 Dreiser Loop, Room 3, Bronx, NY 10457
718-530-7710

605 Longworth House Office Building, Washington, DC 20515
202-225-2464

Jamal Bowman represents New York's 16th Congressional District. The district covers much of the north Bronx, as well as the southern half of Westchester County including Mount Vernon, New Rochelle and Bowman's hometown of Yonkers. Bowman is a member of the following Committees: Education and Labor; Science, Space, and Technology; the Black Caucus; the Progressive Caucus; and the LGBTQ+ Equality Caucus.

Rep. Bowman is the founder and former principal of the Cornerstone Academy for Social Action, a public middle school in Eastchester, Bronx. Bowman has fought for teachers, students, and families for twenty years. As a leader in the opt-out movement across the state, he connected parents from diverse backgrounds to the fight. He has been a steering committee member for NYSAPE, where his work centered on successfully dismantling Common Core in New York and decoupling teacher evaluations from student test scores. He has also been a member of the New York State Early Childhood Blue Ribbon Committee, where he championed early childhood learning standards. He worked with Bronx Legal and Visiting Nurse Services to push for policy that trains every teacher in New York State in trauma-informed practices. He worked with Avenues the World school, Negus World, and Hip Hop Saves Lives to implement innovative design thinking and social justice curriculum. Bowman has also led efforts to educate elected officials on the impact of toxic stress on health and education outcomes.

Through his work as an advocate and a principal, he has seen the results of inadequate housing, homelessness, mental health, the racist immigration system, the school to prison pipeline, food deserts, and trauma-filled environments.

Bowman received a master's degree in counselor education from Mercy College and an EdD in organizational leadership from Manhattanville College.

Bowman was born and raised in New York City. He spent his early years in public housing and later in rent-controlled apartments. He didn't have much growing up, but his mother provided him all that he needed: love, a stable family, and a sense of community. Rep. Bowman now lives in Yonkers with his wife and three kids, and he works as the founding principal of a top-ranked public middle school.

### YVETTE D. CLARKE (D)
*9th - Part of Kings County*

2058 Rayburn House Office Building, Washington, DC 20515
202-225-6231/clarke.house.gov

222 Lenox Road, Suites 1&2, Brooklyn, NY 11226
718-287-1142

Hailing from central Brooklyn, Congresswoman Yvette Diane Clarke feels honored to represent the community that raised her. She is the proud daughter of Jamaican immigrants and takes her passion for her Caribbean heritage to Congress, where she co-chairs the Congressional Caribbean Caucus and works to foster relationships between the United States and the Caribbean Community. Clarke is Chair of the Homeland

Cybersecurity, Infrastructure Protection and Innovation Subcommittee, under the jurisdiction of the House Committee on Homeland Security, and was Co-chair of the powerful Energy and Commerce Committee during the 116th Congress. Clarke has been a member of the Congressional Black Caucus since coming to Congress in 2007 and today chairs its Immigration Task Force.

As the Representative of the Ninth Congressional District of New York, Clarke has dedicated herself to continuing the legacy of excellence established by the late Honorable Shirley Chisholm, the first Black woman and Caribbean American elected to Congress. In the 116th Congress, Congresswoman Clarke introduced landmark legislation, which passed in the House, the Dream and Promise Act (H.R. 6). This legislation would give 2.5 million DREAMers, temporary protected status, and deferred enforcement departure recipients a clear citizenship pathway.

Clarke is a leader in the tech and media policy space as Co-chair of the Smart Cities Caucus and Co-chair of the Multicultural Media Caucus. Congresswoman Clarke believes smart technology will make communities more sustainable, resilient, and livable and works hard to ensure communities of color are not left behind while these technological advancements are made. Clarke formed the Multicultural Media Caucus to address diversity and inclusion issues in the media, telecom, and tech industries. Clarke is one of the co-chairs of the Congressional Caucus on Black Women and Girls, which develops programs to support the aspirations of Black women of all ages. Congresswoman Clarke is also the Co-chair of the Medicare for All Caucus, where she is fighting for the right to universal health care.

Prior to being elected to the United States House of Representatives, she served on New York's City Council, representing the 40th District. She succeeded her pioneering mother, former City Council Member Dr. Una S. T. Clarke, making them the first mother-daughter succession in the City Council's history. She cosponsored City Council resolutions that opposed the war in Iraq, criticized the federal USA PATRIOT Act, and called for a national moratorium on the death penalty.

Congresswoman Clarke is a graduate of Oberlin College and was a recipient of the prestigious APPAM/Sloan Fellowship in Public Policy and Policy Analysis. She received the Honorary Degree of Doctor of Laws Honoris Causa from the University of Technology, Jamaica, and the Honorary Doctorate of Public Policy from the University of the Commonwealth Caribbean. Congresswoman Clarke currently resides in the Flatbush neighborhood of Brooklyn, where she grew up.

### ANTONIO DELGADO (D)
*19th - Columbia, Delaware, Greene, Ostego, Schoharie, Sullivan, Ulster, and parts of Broome, Dutchess, Montgomery, and Rensselaer Counties*

1007 Longworth House Office Building, Washington, DC 20515
202-225-5614/delgado.house.gov

256 Clinton Avenue, Kingston, NY 12401

111 Main Street, Delhi, NY 13733
607-376-0090

420 Warren Street, Hudson, NY 12534
518-267-4123

59 N. Main Street, #301, Liberty NY 12754
845-295-6020

Antonio Delgado was elected to represent New York's 19th District in the 116th Congress. He sits on the following committees: Agriculture; Transportation and Infrastructure; and Small Business. Delgado is also a member of the Affordable Prescription Drug Task Force; the Gun Violence Prevention Task Force; the Historic Preservation Caucus; the Expand Social Security Caucus; the LGBT Equality Caucus; among others.

Representative Delgado is from Schenectady and lives in Rhinebeck with his wife, Lacey, and their twin sons, Maxwell and Coltrane. His parents worked for General Electric in Schenectady, demonstrating the values of hard work and commitment to community. It is that hard-working spirit that Rep. Delgado has continued throughout his life: he earned a Rhodes Scholarship while he attended Colgate University in Hamilton, New York, and went on to attend Harvard Law School. Rep. Delgado's professional experiences include a career in the music industry focused on empowering young people through hip hop culture, as well as working as an attorney in the complex commercial space, where he also dedicated significant time to pro bono work in connection with criminal justice reform. It's because of these diverse professional and personal experiences that Delgado finds common ground across the aisle and delivers results for the people of New York's 19th Congressional District.

Delgado spends every day in Congress focused on creating a vibrant local economy, working with local, state, and federal partners—regardless of party—to get results for the people here. From improving access to quality, affordable health care to expanding rural broadband to protecting our agricultural interests, he is dedicated to working across the aisle and standing up for what residents need. During the 116th Congress, Representative Delgado received the Chamber of Commerce Spirit of Enterprise Award and the Jefferson-Hamilton Award for his bipartisan legislative work. He takes seriously his responsibility to be a voice for his constituents across the district, and hold himself accountable to them.

Representative Delgado held 50 town halls in his first term, including 33 town halls in 2019, three in each of the 11 counties in the 19th Congressional District. Rep. Delgado is also committed to ensuring transparency and accessibility: he created four bipartisan, locally-based advisory committees on the priorities important to NY-19 including small business, agriculture, health care and veterans and opened five district offices so that everyone can have their questions answered, issues addressed, and voices heard. Delgado is Chair of the House Agriculture Subcommittee on Commodity Exchanges, Energy, and Credit.

## ADRIANO ESPAILLAT (D)
*13th - Parts of Manhattan and The Bronx*

2332 Rayburn House Office Building, Washington, DC 20515
202-225-4365/espaillat.house.gov

3107 Kingsbridge, New York, NY 10027
212-663-3900

726 Exchange Street, Suite 601, Buffalo, NY 14210
716-852-3501

Representative Espaillat is the first Dominican American to serve in the U.S. House of Representatives and his congressional district includes Harlem, East Harlem, West Harlem, Hamilton Heights, Washington Heights, Inwood, Marble Hill, and the northwest Bronx. First elected to Congress in 2016, Representative Espaillat was sworn into office on January 3, 2017, during the 115th Congress and is serving his third term in Congress.

Espaillat currently serves as a member of the U.S. House Committees on Appropriations and Foreign Affairs. He is also a member of the Congressional Hispanic Caucus (CHC), where he serves in a leadership role as the Second Vice Chair, and is a member of the Congressional Progressive Caucus, where he serves as Deputy Whip. Representative Espaillat also serves as a Senior Whip of the Democratic Caucus. Through his committee assignments and caucus leadership positions, Representative Espaillat helps advance and amplify legislative priorities and accomplishments that aim to improve the lives of families around the nation.

Together with his Democratic colleagues, Espaillat worked to pass more than 900 bills during the 116th Congress, including bipartisan legislation to clean up government, defend access to affordable health care, lower prescription drug costs, respond to the COVID-19 pandemic, invest in our nation's infrastructure, and support policies for job creation and economic growth. He also introduced more than 40 bills and resolutions aimed at improving the lives of constituents, helping small businesses be-

come more competitive and recover from the pandemic, protecting the rights of immigrants, securing funds to complete the Second Avenue Subway's extension into East Harlem, and helping to secure federal grant funding for New York's 13th Congressional District.

A steadfast champion for working- and middle-class New Yorkers, Representative Espaillat is a staunch advocate of a fair living wage, immediate and effective investments in affordable housing, meaningful criminal justice reform, infrastructure improvements, expanded youth programs, and better educational opportunities. Throughout the tenure of his career in public service, he has been a vocal advocate for protecting tenants, improving schools, and making serious, smart investments in economic development, job creation, and environmental protection. Prior to coming to Congress, he served as a New York State Senator during which he represented the neighborhoods of Marble Hill, Inwood, Washington Heights, Hamilton Heights, West Harlem, the Upper West Side, Hell's Kitchen, Clinton, and Chelsea.

While in the New York State Senate, he served as the Ranking Member of the Senate Housing, Construction, and Community Development Committee; Chairman of the Senate Puerto Rican/Latino Caucus; and as a member of the Environmental Conservation, Economic Development, Codes, Insurance, and Judiciary committees. Prior to his tenure as a state senator, he served in the New York State Assembly, and in 1996 became the first Dominican American elected to a state legislature. In 2002, Espaillat was elected Chair of the New York State Black, Puerto Rican, Hispanic and Asian Legislative Caucus.

Prior to entering elected office, Espaillat served as the Manhattan Court Services Coordinator for the NYC Criminal Justice Agency, a nonprofit organization that provides legal services to those in need and works to reduce unnecessary pretrial detention and postsentence incarceration costs. He later worked as Director of the Washington Heights Victims Services Community Office, an organization offering counseling and other services to families of victims of homicides and other crimes, and as the Director of Project Right Start, a national initiative funded by the Robert Wood Johnson Foundation to combat substance abuse by educating the parents of preschool children. Representative Espaillat is a father and grandfather.

## ANDREW R. GARBARINO (R)
*26th - Parts of Niagara and Erie Counties*

1516 Longworth House Office Building, Washington, DC 20515
202-225-7896/garbarino.house.gov

1003 Park Boulevard, Massapequa, NY 11762
516-541-4225

Andrew R. Garbaraino represents New York's 2nd District. In the House of Representatives he serves as a member on the following Committees: Homeland Security; Small Business; the Problem Solvers Caucus; the Italian American Congressional Delegation; and the Suburban Caucus.

A lifelong Long Islander, Rep. Garbarino has dedicated his life to family and community. The proud son of a lawyer and small business owner, he went to Sayville High School where he participated in student government and worked at the local hardware store. As a man of faith, Garbarino received his communion and confirmation at St. Lawrence Catholic Church, where he still attends Mass every Sunday. After high school graduation, he went on to receive his BA in history and classical humanities from George Washington University. Garbarino then returned to Long Island where he received his JD from Hofstra University. Upon his graduation from law school, he joined his father at their family law firm in downtown Sayville.

Garbarino's love and appreciation for his family-oriented community in Long Island inspired him to run for a seat in the New York Assembly, where he served the 7th district for four terms. During his tenure in the Assembly, he fought to increase state funding for Long Island school districts, protect our island's environment including the Great South Bay, oppose tax hikes, and support our local heroes in law enforcement.

A proud member of the Sayville Rotary Club and Knights of Columbus, Garbarino has been a leader in his Long Island community following the Rotary Club's motto, "Service Above Self."

## BRIAN M. HIGGINS (D)
*26th - Parts of Niagara and Erie Counties*

2459 Rayburn House Office Building, Washington, DC 20515
202-225-3306/higgins.house.gov

726 Exchange Street, Suite 601, Buffalo, NY 14210
716-852-3501

800 Main Street, Suite 3C, Niagara Falls, NY 14301
716-282-1274

Brian Higgins is a member of the United States House of Representatives serving New York's 26th Congressional District, which includes portions of Erie and Niagara Counties. Widely accepted as the principal architect of waterfront development in Buffalo and Western New York, he led the fight for a quarter-billion-dollar federal relicensing settlement from the New York Power Authority that continues to finance the transformation of Buffalo's long-neglected Inner and Outer Harbor waterfront areas. In our nation's capital, he is an advocate for policies important to our regional and national economies. Representative Higgins is an avowed supporter of increased funding for biomedical research—an area creating jobs throughout the Buffalo Niagara Medical Campus—and remains a strong voice for robust infrastructure investment, for "nation building here at home."

In the 117th Congress, Higgins serves on the House Committee on Ways and Means, where he also serves as a member of the Subcommittees on Health and Trade. In addition, he currently serves as a member of the House Committee on the Budget. Representative Higgins is Co-chair of the Northern Border Caucus, from which he advocates for federal policies that recognize the unique needs of northern border communities—efforts which serve to strengthen economic and security ties with our Canadian neighbors. He also serves as one of four Co-chairs of the bipartisan House Cancer Caucus, and as a Co-chair of the Revitalizing Older Cities Caucus. Additionally, he is a member of the Great Lakes Task Force, the House Manufacturing Caucus, and the Northeast-Midwest Congressional Coalition.

Higgins has traveled extensively through some of the most volatile regions in the world. In so doing, he has met with world leaders to promote peace in Northern Ireland, the Middle East, South Asia and Africa, including Darfur, Afghanistan, and Iraq.

Prior to his election to the House, Representative Higgins made his career serving in state and local elective office, as well as and in education. He served as an instructor in the History and Economics Departments at SUNY Buffalo State College. A graduate of Buffalo State College, Higgins also earned an advanced degree in public policy and administration from Harvard University's John F. Kennedy School of Government. He has been awarded an honorary Doctorate degree in Humane Letters from Daemen College, and an honorary Doctorate degree in Laws from Medaille College.

## CHRIS JACOBS (R)
*27th - Parts of Niagara and Erie Counties*

214 Cameron House Office Building, Washington, DC 20515
202-225-5265/jacobs.house.gov

8203 Main Street, Suite 2, Williamsville, NY 14221
716-634-2324

128 Main Street, Geneseo, NY 14454
585-519-4002

Christopher L. Jacobs representing New York's 27th Congressional District in the United States House of Representatives. In the House of Representatives, he serves on the following Committees: Agriculture; Budget; and the Northern Border Caucus

Jacobs was born in Buffalo, New York as one of five siblings. He earned his undergraduate degree from Boston College, a master's degree from American University, and a JD from the University at Buffalo Law School.

Prior to holding elected office, Jacobs served as Deputy Commissioner of Environment and Planning in the administration of Erie County Executive Joel Giambra. He also worked at the U.S. Department of Housing and Urban Development under then-HUD Secretary Jack Kemp.

Rep. Jacobs served on the Buffalo Board of Education; he was elected as an at-large member in 2004 and was reelected in 2009. Jacobs serves on the Boards of Buffalo Place and the Freedom Station Coalition and was previously a board member at the Catholic Academy of West Buffalo and the Olmsted Parks Conservancy.

On April 19, 2006, Jacobs was appointed as New York Secretary of State by Governor George Pataki. In 2011, Jacobs was elected Erie County Clerk. He was reelected to the post in 2014.

On November 8, 2016, Jacobs defeated Democrat Amber Small for the 60th District State Senate seat. The district was formerly represented by Democrat Marc Panepinto, with Jacobs' victory contributing to the New York State Senate Republican majority. Jacobs won reelection in 2018. He resigned his seat on July 20, 2020 after being elected to Congress.

Prior to his election to the Senate, Jacobs was the first Republican clerk elected in Erie County in 40 years. As county clerk, Jacobs was credited with reforming the operations of the Office's Real Estate Division, which had fallen into dysfunction. Jacobs drove dramatic efficiencies and revenues throughout the Clerk's Office without increasing the number of employees. He was also credited with building the clerk's "Thank A Vet" Program, now the largest veterans discount program of its kind in the entire state. As clerk he also ran the County's Pistol Permit Division, where he received accommodation for his strong defense of 2nd Amendment rights, especially during the passage of the New York SAFE Act.

A small business owner, Rep. Jacobs is the founder and owner of Avalon Development. Founded in 2002, Avalon has redeveloped many vacant and historic buildings in Western New York. He has received numerous awards for bringing older buildings and the communities around them back to life. His projects have focused on providing unique and affordable space for small businesses to thrive. Jacobs' business experience is one reason he believes that small business creation and growth is critical to the region's comeback.

In 1994, Jacobs started the BISON Scholarship Fund, a charity that raised donations to help send children to private and religious schools. BISON will be celebrating its 25th Anniversary this fall, over that time providing scholarships for more than 20,000 children throughout Western New York. Jacobs believes that all children in American, no matter their income or their address, deserve an education of the highest quality. He is married to Martina Jacobs and they have a daughter, Anna.

## HAKEEM JEFFRIES (D)
*8th - Parts of Kings County and Southwest Queens*

2433 Rayburn Office Building, Washington, DC 20515
202-225-5936/jeffries.house.gov

55 Hanson Place, Suite 603, Brooklyn, NY 11217
718-237-2211

445 Neptune Avenue, First Floor, Brooklyn, NY 11224
718-373-0033

Hakeem Jeffries represents the diverse 8th Congressional District of New York, an area that encompasses large parts of Brooklyn and a section of Queens. Serving his fourth term in the United States Congress, Representative Jeffries is a member of the House Judiciary Committee and House Budget Committee.

Representative Jeffries is Chairman of the House Democratic Caucus, having been elected to that position by his colleagues in November 2018. In that capacity, he is the fifth highest-ranking Democrat in the House of Representatives. He is also the former Whip of the Congressional Black Caucus and previously co-chaired the Democratic Policy and Communications Committee where he helped develop the For the People agenda.

During the 115th and 116th Congresses, Representative Jeffries was one of the most effective legislators in Congress, passing multiple bills through the House of Representatives and into law with substantial bipartisan and stakeholder support. They included bills to create a copyright small claims board allowing the creative middle class to protect their works; to expand scholarship opportunities available to Pakistani women; to provide entrepreneurship counseling and training services to formerly incarcerated individuals; to ensure the attorney-client privilege is protected for incarcerated individuals corresponding electronically with their legal representatives; and to measure the progress of recovery and efforts to address corruption, rule of law and media freedoms in Haiti since the 2010 earthquake. In the 115th Congress, Jeffries worked across the aisle as the lead Democratic sponsor of the FIRST STEP Act, a strong, bipartisan criminal justice reform bill that the President signed into law in December 2018. The act provides retroactive relief for the shameful crack cocaine sentencing disparity that unfairly destroyed lives, families, and communities.

In January 2020, Jeffries was selected by Speaker Nancy Pelosi to serve as one of seven House Impeachment Managers in the Senate trial of President Donald Trump, becoming the first African American man to serve in that role. During the nearly three-week trial, Congressman Jeffries argued that President Trump should be removed from office for abusing his power by pressuring a foreign government, Ukraine, to target an American citizen as part of a corrupt scheme to interfere in the 2020 election.

On June 25, 2020, the House of Representatives passed the "George Floyd Justice in Policing Act." Jeffries helped lead the charge with respect to passage of this historic police reform bill, which included legislation authored by the Congressman to criminalize the chokehold and other inherently dangerous tactics such as a knee to the neck. He Jeffries remains dedicated to working with his colleagues to make transformational police reform a reality and breathe life into the principle of liberty and justice for all.

Rep. Jeffries has played a major role in shaping the Congressional response to the COVID-19 pandemic. He has fought hard to assist state and local governments whose budgets have been devastated by the virus, pushed for an extension of the emergency unemployment benefit and supported efforts to keep everyday Americans in their homes. He also worked to secure billions of dollars in funding for the Metropolitan Transportation Authority in the CARES Act (H.R. 748, Public Law No: 116-136), which became law in March 2020.

Prior to his election to the Congress, Representative Jeffries served for six years in the New York State Assembly. In that capacity, he authored laws to protect the civil liberties of law-abiding New Yorkers during police encounters, encourage the transformation of vacant luxury condominiums into affordable homes for working families, and improve the quality of justice in the civil court system. In 2010, Rep. Jeffries successfully led the first meaningful legislative reform of the NYPD's aggressive and controversial stop-and-frisk program. His legislation prohibits the NYPD from maintaining an electronic database with the personal information of individuals who were stopped, questioned and frisked during a police encounter but not charged with a crime or violation.

Representative Jeffries obtained his bachelor's degree in political science from the SUNY at Binghamton, where he graduated with honors for outstanding academic achievement. He then received his master's degree in public policy from Georgetown University. Thereafter, Jeffries attended New York University School of Law, where he graduated magna cum laude.

After completing law school, Jeffries clerked for the Honorable Harold Baer Jr. of the U.S. District Court for the Southern District of New York. He then practiced law for several years at Paul, Weiss, Rifkind, Wharton & Garrison LLP. He also worked as of-counsel at Godosky & Gentile, a well-regarded litigation firm in New York City. He lives in Prospect Heights with his family.

## MONDAIRE JONES (D)
*17th - Parts of Rockland and Westchester Counties*

1017 Longworth House Office Building, Washington, DC 20515
202-225-6506/jones.house.gov

222 Mamaroneck Avenue, Suite 312, White Plains, NY 10605
914-323-5550

Mondaire Jones is serving his first term as the Congressman from New York's 17th District, encompassing all of Rockland County and parts of central and northern Westchester County. In the U.S. House of Representatives, he serves on the following Committees: Judiciary; Education and Labor; and Ethics. Jones is the Deputy Whip on the Progressive Caucus; Co-chair on the LGBTQ+ Equality Caucus; and is a member of the Black Caucus.

A product of East Ramapo public schools, Rep. Jones was raised in Section 8 housing and on food stamps in the Village of Spring Valley by a single mother who worked multiple jobs to provide for their family.

After graduating from Stanford University, Rep. Jones worked in the U.S. Department of Justice Office of Legal Policy, where he vetted candidates for federal judgeships and worked to reform our criminal legal system to make it more fair and equitable. He later graduated from Harvard Law School.

Before running for Congress, Jones worked as a litigator in private practice, where was awarded by the Legal Aid Society of New York for his pro bono service investigating claims of employment discrimination and helping families defrauded during the Great Recession recover funds. Subsequently, he served as a litigator in the Westchester County Law Department.

Rep. Jones began his activism in high school through the Spring Valley NAACP Youth Council. He would go on to serve on the NAACP's National Board of Directors. Rep. Jones is a cofounder of the nonprofit Rising Leaders, Inc., which teaches professional skills to underserved middle-school students in three American cities, and has previously served on the board of the New York Civil Liberties Union.

As a member of the Judiciary Committee, Rep. Jones continues his lifelong advocacy for civil rights and civil liberties, and the strengthening of our democracy. In Congress, he is fighting for COVID-19 relief, a living wage for all, universal health care, racial justice, climate action, and restoration of the SALT deduction.

Rep. Jones was raised in Rockland County and lives in Westchester County.

## JOHN KATKO (R)
*24th - Onondaga, Cayuga, Wayne, and Oswego Counties*

2428 Rayburn House Office Building, Washington, DC 20515, (202) 225-3701/katko.house.gov

71 Genesee Street, Auburn, NY 13021
315-253-4068

7376 State Route 31, Lyons, NY 14489
315-253-4068

13 W. Oneida Street, 2nd Floor, Oswego, NY 13126
315-423-5637

440 S. Warren Street, 7th Floor, Suite 711, Syracuse, NY 13202
315-423-5657

Congressman John M. Katko was first elected to represent the 24th Congressional District in the U.S. House of Representatives in November 2014. He was reelected for a fourth term in November 2020. The 24th Congressional District includes all of Onondaga, Cayuga, and Wayne Counties and the western portion of Oswego County. In Congress, Katko serves as Ranking Member on the House Committee on Homeland Security and as a member of the House Committee on Transportation & Infrastructure.

After graduating with honors from both Niagara University and Syracuse University College of Law, Congressman Katko began his legal career in private practice at a firm in Washington, D.C. It was not long before he embarked on a career in public service, serving first as a Senior Trial Attorney at the U.S. Securities and Exchange Commission and then commencing his twenty-year career as an Assistant U.S. Attorney for the U.S. Department of Justice. Early in his career as a federal Prosecutor, Katko served as a Special Assistant U.S. Attorney in the Eastern District of Virginia and with the DOJ's Criminal Division, Narcotics & Dangerous Drug Section. In this capacity, he served as a Senior Trial Attorney on the U.S.-Mexico border in El Paso, Texas and in San Juan, Puerto Rico.

He and his wife, Robin, ultimately returned to Katko's hometown of Camillus, New York to raise their family. For over 15 years, he served as a federal organized crime Prosecutor in Syracuse for the U.S. Attorney's Office in the Northern District of New York. In this role, Katko led high-level narcotics federal prosecutions, concurrently holding the positions of Narcotics Chief, Organized Crime Drug Enforcement Task Force Coordinator, Binghamton Office Supervisor, Team Leader, and Grand Jury Coordinator. Notably, he served as Supervisor of the Narcotics Section, formulating the Syracuse Gang Violence Task Force and successfully prosecuting the first-ever RICO gang case in the City of Syracuse, which led to a significant drop in the City's violent crime rate.

Congressman Katko has been honored with the top prosecutor award by three separate Attorneys General, both Democrat and Republican, for his work on the Gang Violence Task Force and international drug-trafficking investigations. Katko has lectured at Syracuse University College of Law and Cornell Law School, and has led attorney trainings for criminal investigations and prosecutions worldwide in Moscow, Croatia, Trinidad & Tobago, Brazil, and El Salvador. In 2011, he was selected to be the sole U.S. advisor on a highly sensitive prosecution in Albania. Katko retired from the U.S. Department of Justice in January 2013 to run for Congress.

Congressman Katko has served as President of the Central New York Chapter of the Leukemia and Lymphoma Society and is actively involved in other community organizations, including the Onondaga County Foster Parent Program and the Camillus Youth Hockey Association. Congressman Katko, his wife Robin, and their three children, Sean, Liam, ad Logan, and black lab Sadie, live in Camillus.

## NICOLE MALLIOTAKIS (R)
*11th - Richmond County*

417 Cannon House Office Building, Washington, DC 20515
202-225-3371/malliotakis.house.gov

Congresswoman Nicole Malliotakis was sworn in on January 3, 2021 to represent Staten Island and Southern Brooklyn. Malliotakis is a member of the following House Committees: Agriculture; Appropriations; Armed Services; Budget; Education; Energy and Commerce; Ethics; Homeland Security; Judiciary; Rules; Small Business; Transportation; Veterans' Affairs; and Taxation.

Prior to serving in the U.S. House of Representatives, Congresswoman Nicole Malliotakis was elected to the New York State Assembly on November 2, 2010, defeating a two-term incumbent. In the Assembly, she served as Minority Whip and the ranking minority member of the Assembly Committee on Governmental Employees. For five terms, Congresswoman Malliotakis fought to restore ethics in Albany, expand transit service in her district, improve programs for senior citizens, reform education and improve New York's economic climate by reducing the tax burden on small businesses and residents. A cornerstone of her tenure was helping her community recover and rebuild following the devastation of Hurricane Sandy in 2012.

In addition to advocating for these same issues in Washington, Congresswoman Malliotakis is acutely focused on securing New York's fair share of federal mass transit funding, which would go towards expanding transportation services and easing traffic congestion, while also championing public safety by supporting our nation's law enforcement officers.

Congresswoman Malliotakis is the daughter of immigrants; her father is from Greece and her mother is a Cuban exile of the Castro dictatorship. She is currently the only Republican member representing New York City in Congress, representing a district spanning the boroughs of Brooklyn and Staten Island. She is a passionate advocate for animal rights and the strengthening of animal cruelty laws, and enjoys spending time with her chihuahua, Peanut.

## CAROLYN B. MALONEY (D)
*12th - Manhattan, Queens, Brooklyn*

2308 Rayburn House Office Building, Washington, DC 20515-0001
202-225-7944/maloney.house.gov

1651 3rd Avenue, Suite 311, New York, NY 01028-3679
212-860-0606

31-19 Newtown Avenue, Astoria, NY 11102
718-932-1804

First elected to Congress in 1992, Carolyn B. Maloney is a recognized progressive national leader with extensive accomplishments on financial services, national security, the economy, and women's issues. She is currently Chairwoman of the House Committee on Oversight and Reform and former Chair of the Joint Economic Committee, the first woman to hold both of these positions. In the House Democratic Caucus, she has served as a Regional Whip and as Vice Chair of the House Democratic Steering and Policy Committee.

In Congress authored landmark legislation including; the James Zadroga 9/11 Health and Compensation Act, its reauthorization, and the Never Forget the Heroes: James Zadroga, Ray Pfeifer, and Luis Alvarez Permanent Authorization of the September 11th Victim Compensation Fund Act to make sure all those suffering health aliments associated with 9/11 get the medical care and compensation they need and deserve; the Debbie Smith Act, which increases funding for law enforcement to process DNA rape kits and has been called "the most important anti-rape legislation in history"; and the Credit CARD Act, also known as the Credit Cardholders' Bill of Rights, which according to the Consumer Financial Protection Bureau (CFPB), has saved consumers more than $16 billion annually since it was signed into law in 2009.

As Chairwoman of the Committee on Oversight and Reform, Congresswoman Maloney is leading the fight to protect the 2020 Census from the Trump Administration's partisan, political attacks and to ensure that the United States Postal Service (USPS) is able to operate at its full capacity. She is the author of the Fair and Accurate Census Act, which would ensure that Census Bureau professionals have the time and resources they need to complete a full and accurate count, the Delivering for America Act to restore USPS services to January 2020 standards and ensure they stay at that level through the pandemic, and the Nonpartisan Postmaster General Act to prevent partisan politics from including in the Postal Service.

On the House Financial Services Committee, she has worked to modernize financial services laws and regulations, strengthen consumer protections, and institute more vigilant oversight of the safety and soundness of our nation's banking industry. In the 114th Congress, she was selected by her Committee colleagues to be Ranking Member on the Subcommittee on Capital Markets and Government Sponsored Enterprises and continued in this position in the 115th Congress. In the 116th Congress, up until her election as Chairwoman of the Committee on Oversight and Reform, she served as the Chair of the Subcommittee on Investor Protection, Entrepreneurship, and Capital Markets. She continues to serve as a member of this subcommittee and the Subcommittee on Housing, Community Development, and Insurance.

Maloney served on the historic conference committee for the Dodd-Frank financial reforms, which also created the Consumer Financial Protection Bureau. Her Credit Cardholders' Bill of Rights (the Credit CARD Act) was signed into law by President Obama in Spring of 2009. She is currently working to curb the use of anonymous shell companies that finance illicit drugs, human trafficking, and terrorism and to pass her Overdraft Protection Act, which would protect consumers from abusive overdraft fees.

As cofounder of the House 9/11 Commission Caucus, Maloney helped author and pass legislation that created the 9/11 Commission and, later, to implement all of the 9/11 Commission's recommendations for improving intelligence gathering—described as the most influential intelligence bill in decades. The James Zadroga 9/11 Health Care and Compensation Act, her bill to provide health care and compensation for 9/11 first responders, residents and workers near Ground Zero passed Congress in late 2010 was signed into law by President Obama on January 2, 2011. The Zadroga Act's World Trade Center Health Program was permanently extended by the bill's reauthorization with an allocation of $8 billion in December 2015. The September 11th Victim Compensation Fund was permanently extended with the passage of the Never Forget the Heroes: James Zadroga, Ray Pfeifer, and Luis Alvarez Permanent Authorization of the September 11th Victim Compensation Fund Act in summer 2019.

As a fighter for domestic and international women's issues, Representative Maloney has authored and helped pass legislation that targets sex trafficking, including the first bill that focused on the "demand" side of human trafficking to punish the perpetrators of these heinous crimes. She is Co-chair of the Congressional Caucus on Human Trafficking, and previously served as the Co-chair of the Trafficking Task Force of the Congressional Caucus for Women's Issues.

New York City has no stronger advocate in Congress than Maloney. She has delivered more than $10 billion in federal aid to New York City, including billions of dollars for the two largest transit construction projects in the nation, the Second Avenue Subway and the East Side Access project, both of which run through her district, and have helped create thousands of jobs in New York. Among other projects she has secured federal funding for are: $670 million for replacing the Kosciuszko Bridge, $37.9 million for the Floating Hospital, $4.4 million for new ferries, $20 million for Dutch Kills Green, $27 million for Queensbridge roof repairs, and more than $300 million in federal grants for high-speed rail improvement projects in the Sunnyside Rail Yards.

Maloney has received numerous awards and honors during her time in office, including the TMG-eMedia Thought Leaders in Business Award; the Manhattan Chamber of Commerce Outstanding Service Award; the CUNY Women's Leadership Award; the Eleanor's Legacy Eleanor Roosevelt Trailblazer of Democracy Award; the Humane Society of the United States Humane Advocate Award; the Business and Professional Women's Club of New York State Outstanding Legislator Award; the Center for Women's Policy Studies Jessie Bernard Wise Women's Award; and the Planned Parenthood Responsible Choices Award.

Maloney was recently named one of Women's eNews 21 Leaders for the 21st Century in May 2017. In March of 2020, she was named the first-ever honorary member of the National Treasury Employees Union (NTEU) for her work on behalf of federal employees and her paid parental leave legislation.

Congresswoman Maloney is currently a member of Women's Forum Inc., the Council on Foreign Relations, Women's City Club, Alice Paul Institute, Eleanor Roosevelt Legacy, Financial Women's Association, National Organization for Women, National Association of Business and Professional Women, New York Landmarks Conservancy, and CIVITAS. She is an Eleanor Roosevelt Distinguished Member of the NY Junior League.

She is the founder and Co-chair of the House Caucus on Hellenic Issues and the House Census Caucus.

Maloney attained a first-degree black belt in Taekwondo in January 2007.

## SEAN P. MALONEY (D)
*18th - Orange, Rockland, Putnam, Dutchess, and Westchester Counties*

464 Cannon House Building, Washington, DC 20515
202-225-5441/seanmaloney.house.gov

123 Grand Street, 2nd Floor, Newburgh, NY 12550
845-561-1259

Representative Sean Patrick Maloney currently represents New York's 18th district in the U.S. House of Representatives and was first elected in November 2012. His top priorities include national security, protecting our drinking water, ensuring our veterans get the benefits they earned, and combating the heroin and opioid epidemic.

Maloney currently serves on the House Permanent Select Committee on Intelligence, the House Transportation and Infrastructure Committee, and the House Agriculture Committee.

The House Intelligence Committee is responsible for overseeing the nation's intelligence agencies, including components of the Departments of Defense, Homeland Security, Justice, State, Treasury and Energy.

Representative Maloney serves on the House Transportation and Infrastructure Committee, which has jurisdiction over all modes of transportation: aviation, maritime, and waterborne transportation, highways, bridges, mass transit, and railroads.

Representative Maloney also serves on the House Agriculture Committee, where he fights to protect important and unique programs which benefit local farmers in the Hudson Valley.

He has a distinguished background in business and public service. He served as a senior advisor in President Bill Clinton's White House as part of a team that balanced the budget and paid down the debt, all while creating over eight hundred thousand jobs here in New York. When he left the White House, he built his own business from scratch. His high-tech startup created hundreds of New York jobs.

Maloney then served as a senior staff member to two Democratic governors of New York, focusing on education and infrastructure projects. He oversaw 13 state agencies and departments, including those responsible for all homeland security, state police and emergency management operations. Representative Maloney and his husband, Randy Florke, have three children together and currently reside in Cold Spring, New York.

## GREGORY W. MEEKS (D)
*5th - Part of Queens County*

2310 Rayburn House Office Building, Washington, DC 20515
202-225-3461/meeks.house.gov

153-01 Jamaica Avenue, 2nd Floor, Jamaica, NY 11432
718-725-6000

67-12, Far Rockaway, Rockaway Beach Boulevard, Arverne, NY 11692
347-230-4032

Gregory W. Meeks was first elected to the US House of Representatives in 1998. Congressman Gregory W. Meeks, now in his twelfth term, has devoted his energy and skill to serving one of the most diverse constituencies in the nation. His efforts on behalf of his district, New York City and State, and the nation as a whole have earned Representative Meeks the respect of his constituents, New Yorkers, and Democrats and Republicans alike. He is known for being an effective, principled, and commonsense leader. As a fervent supporter of the Affordable Care Act enacted under President Obama, Congressman Meeks believes that it should be enhanced. Congressman Meeks is part of the forward-thinking, pro-growth Democratic members who comprise the New Democrat Coalition (NDC), the largest ideological caucus in Congress. He co-chairs the NDCC Trade Task Force.

Congressman Meeks is Chairman of the House Foreign Affairs Committee, the first black Member of Congress to serve as Chair of that committee. Meeks is a multilateralist with decades of experience in foreign policy. He believes that the United States should build coalitions around our interests and work with other countries to build a stable and prosperous future. He is a senior member of the House Financial Services Committee, where he serves as the Chairmen of the Subcommittee on Consumer Protection and Financial Institutions which oversees all financial regulators such as, FDIC, Federal Reserve and all matters pertaining to consumer credit and the stability of the banking system.

Congressman Meeks' grew up in a public housing project and knew in his early years that he wanted to be a lawyer. He was inspired by a mother and father who worked hard to ensure that their children would have opportunities for advancement that they never did. Meeks' parents passed on to him a profound sense of social justice, commitment to community, and willingness to extend a helping hand to those in need.

He carried these values with him to Adelphi University where he earned a bachelor's degree in history. At Howard University Law School, Meeks embraced the jurisprudence of his idol, Thurgood Marshall, and of Charles Hamilton Houston. In the years to follow, Congressman Meeks worked as a Queens County Assistant District Attorney, a Prosecutor for a special antinarcotics taskforce, and Chief Administrative Judge for New York State's worker compensation system. In 1992, he was elected to the New York State Assembly, where he served until 1998, when he won a special election to represent the Fifth Congressional District of New York.

Congressman Meeks is focused on revitalizing the economy, creating jobs, and enhancing the resiliency of the Fifth District's transportation, housing and environmental infrastructure, which were hit hard by Superstorm Sandy. Throughout his tenure in Congress, he has fought to make New York City accessible and full of opportunity for all New Yorkers. One result of Representative Meeks' tireless efforts came to fruition in April of 2017, at the groundbreaking ceremony of the Crossing at Jamaica Station. The housing and retail project, which will bring approximately 4,000 construction jobs to Jamaica, includes hundreds of new affordable residential units.

Striving to improve NYC's accessibility, Congressman Meeks strengthened the major regional transportation hub in Jamaica, Queens via the Intermodal Enhancement and Atlantic Avenue Extension—which includes parts of the LIRR and NYC subway system, Airtrain connection to JFK Airport, and a total of 31 bus lines. He secured over $6 million and $10 million through the Federal Transit Administration and Federal Highway Administration respectively, to vastly improve transportation in his district, especially to and from JFK airport. Congressman Meeks also worked with Governor Cuomo to provide a significant $10 billion upgrade to JFK Airport. Ever focused on increasing diversity, Congressman

Meeks advocated for Minority and Women Business Enterprises (MWBEs) in the bidding process.

Increasing diversity in all sectors of the economy is important to Congressman Meeks and in 1999 he secured $250,000 in federal funding to initiate the Science Engineering Mathematics and Aerospace Academy (SEMAA) at CUNY's York College. Meeks collaborated on the monumental Roadmap for Action, introduced in 2016, which will provide $91 million for the revitalization of Downtown Far Rockaway. These funds marked the continuation of Meeks' ongoing effort to increase affordable housing options, improve transportation infrastructure, and boost the local economy.

Additionally, in the spring of 2017, he and New York City launched a new ferry service, "NYC Ferry," in the Rockaways a month ahead of schedule. This critical project had been in the works since 2005, when Representative Meeks procured $15 million in federal funding. For years, Congressman Meeks has introduced a bill to allow for fairness in the recoupment of disaster assistance, to help not only his district rebuild after Superstorm Sandy, but also other districts suffering from natural disasters.

Congressman Meeks is a member of the Allen AME Church in St. Albans, New York and a proud member of Alpha Phi Alpha Fraternity He is married to Simone-Marie Meeks and has three daughters—Ebony, Aja, and Nia-Aiyana.

## GRACE MENG (D)
*6th - Part of Queens County*

2209 Rayburn House Office Building, Washington, DC 20515
202-225-2601/meng.house.gov

40-13 159th Street, Flushing, NY 11358
718-358-MENG

118-35 Queens Boulevard, 17th Floor, Forest Hills, NY 11375
718-358-MENG

U.S. Congresswoman Grace Meng is serving her fifth term in the United States House of Representatives. Grace represents the Sixth Congressional District of New York encompassing the New York City borough of Queens, including west, central and northeast Queens. She is the first and only Asian American Member of Congress from New York State and the first female Congressmember from Queens since former VP nominee Geraldine Ferraro.

Meng is a member of the powerful House Appropriations Committee and is Vice Chair of its Subcommittee on State and Foreign Operations. She also sits on the Appropriations Subcommittee on Agriculture, and the Subcommittee on Commerce, Justice, Science and Related Agencies. The Appropriations Committee is responsible for funding every federal agency, program, and project within the United States government. She also serves on the House Ethics Committee.

Congresswoman Meng is the First Vice Chair of the Congressional Asian Pacific American Caucus (CAPAC), cofounder of the Congressional Kids Safety Caucus, and a Vice Chair of the Congressional LGBTQ+ Equality Caucus. She is also a proud member of the Congressional Progressive Caucus, Democratic Women's Caucus, Gun Violence Prevention Task Force, House Quiet Skies Caucus, Postal Preservation Caucus, and the Sustainable Energy and Environment Coalition.

Meng has passed several pieces of legislation into law. These include laws about religious freedom, making Queens historic sites part of the National Park Service, striking "Oriental" from federal law and protecting public housing residents from insufficient heat. Also signed into law were her measures to assist veterans and members of the military, and provisions to improve consumer protections and safeguards for children. In addition, she has fought to expand opportunities for communities of color, young people and women, and she secured resources to help local small businesses.

Born in Elmhurst, Queens, and raised in the Bayside and Flushing sections of the borough, Congresswoman Meng attended local schools, and graduated from Stuyvesant High School and the University of Michigan. She then earned a law degree from Yeshiva University's Benjamin Cardozo School of Law. Prior to serving in Congress, Meng was a member of the New York State Assembly. Before entering public service, she worked as a public-interest lawyer. She resides in Queens with her husband, Wayne, and two sons, Tyler and Brandon.

## JOSEPH MORELLE (D)
*25th - Monroe County*

3120 Federal Building, 100 State Street, Rochester, NY 14614
585-232-4850

1317 Longworth House Office Building, Washington, DC 20515
202-225-3615/morelle.house.gov

Joseph Morelle was sworn in on November 13, 2018 as Representative for the 25th District, which includes almost the entirety of Monroe County. Congressman Morelle serves as a member of the House Committee on Rules, the House Committee on Budget, and the House Committee on Education and Labor. As a member of the Education and Labor Committee, Morelle was part of the Early Childhood, Elementary and Secondary Education Subcommittee, and the Health, Employment, Labor and Pensions Subcommittee. In addition, he is a member of the following: Pro-Choice Caucus; Buy American Caucus; Congressinoal Career and Technical Education Caucus; Great Lakes Task Force; Sustainable Energy and Environment Coalition; and Gun Violence Task Force, among others.

A lifelong resident of Upstate New York, Morelle is a former small business owner and was previously elected to the Monroe County Legislature as well as the New York State Assembly, where he served as Majority Leader from 2013 to 2018. Throughout his career, he has worked diligently to improve and expand access to healthcare for all people, grow the economy, and protect communities by passing legislation to ban assault weapons, and strengthen gun background checks.

A graduate of the SUNY at Geneseo, Morelle resides in the town of Irondequoit in Rochester with his wife, Mary Beth. They have three children and three grandchildren.

## JERROLD L. NADLER (D)
*10th - Parts of New York and Kings Counties*

2132 Rayburn House Office Building, Washington, DC 20515
202-225-5635/nadler.house.gov

6605 Fort Hamilton Parkway, Brooklyn, NY 11219
718-373-3198

201 Varick Street, Suite 669, New York, NY 10014
212-367-7350

Congressman Jerrold "Jerry" Nadler represents New York's 10th Congressional District, one of the most dynamic and diverse districts in the country. The district includes Manhattan's Upper West Side, Morningside Heights, Hell's Kitchen, Chelsea, Greenwich Village, Soho, Wall Street, and Battery Park City, as well as the Brooklyn neighborhoods of Borough Park, Kensington, and parts of Bay Ridge, Bensonhurst, Dyker Heights, Red Hook, Sunset Park and Midwood.

Representative Nadler began his career in public service in 1976 in the New York State Assembly. Representing the Upper West Side, he served as a Democratic Assemblyman for 16 years and played a significant role in shaping New York State law concerning child support enforcement and domestic abuse, as well as making major contributions to housing, transportation and consumer protection policy in the state. In 1992, Rep. Nadler was elected to the U.S. House of Representatives in a special

election and has served in Congress ever since. He was reelected to his fourteenth full term in 2018.

The Chairman of the House Judiciary Committee, Congressman Nadler served as Chairman or Ranking Member of its Subcommittee on the Constitution, Civil Rights, and Civil Liberties for thirteen years and also served as the Ranking Member of the Subcommittee on Courts, Intellectual Property, and the Internet.

A Vice Chair and founding member of the House Lesbian, Gay, Bisexual and Transgender (LGBT) Equality Caucus, and the first from New York's congressional delegation to openly support marriage equality, Rep. Nadler has been an original co-sponsor of every major piece of LGBT civil rights legislation for the last twenty-plus years.

Representative Nadler is nationally recognized as a staunch defender of women's health, including a woman's constitutional right to access an abortion. As a senior Member of the House Judiciary Committee and a leader in the House Pro-Choice Caucus, he has often taken a central role in standing up to conservative attacks against every American's right to make personal decisions about reproductive health, including devising the strategy to defeat countless anti-choice bills and carrying the movement's signature piece of legislation.

Congressman Nadler serves as a champion in the House for free speech and free expression. He has often taken difficult votes on controversial issues in order to remain true to his principles and the fundamental belief in the rights guaranteed under the First Amendment. He is one of Congress's most vocal defenders of the separation of church and state and of Americans' right to exercise their religion freely, while also denouncing efforts by some to use religion as an excuse to discriminate.

Jerry Nadler has consistently been recognized as one of Israel's strongest supporters in the U.S. House of Representatives—working diligently towards ensuring a safe, secure, peaceful, and democratic Israel—and has often been a leader on the key issues of ever-strengthened U.S.-Israel cooperation and U.S. foreign aid. Congressman Nadler has long been a leading voice in support of a two-state solution, seeing it as critical to protecting Israel's long-term strategic and security interests. As representative of the largest and most diverse Jewish community in any congressional district in the United States, Nadler has also been an outspoken leader against anti-Semitism and continues to lead a variety of efforts to stymie the growing anti-Zionist, anti-Jewish rhetoric, and campaigns that seek to delegitimize Israel on the world stage. This includes authoring a House Resolution in 2014, condemning all forms of anti-Semitism and rejecting attempts to justify such hatred or violent attacks as an acceptable expression of disapproval or frustration over political events in the Middle East or elsewhere.

Representative Nadler has a long and distinguished record working to reduce gun violence, as the author of bills improving the ban on assault weapons and preventing the sale of firearms to sex offenders. He also has been a strong voice on climate change and environmental justice, and has led efforts to ensure that the Environmental Protection Agency (EPA) uses its full federal authority and responds more aggressively to major environmental disasters, such as the BP oil spill, and is the Congressional leader on clean ports.

Congressman Nadler's record has earned him scores of awards and praise from various progressive groups, including the League of Conservation Voters, Planned Parenthood, the NAACP, the Human Rights Campaign, the Brady Campaign to End Gun Violence, Children's Defense Fund, the American Civil Liberties Union, and the American Federation of Teachers. In the 2015 *TIME Magazine Person of the Year* issue, Jerry Nadler was named as a Teddy Award recipient for political courage.

Rep. Nadler is a graduate of Crown Heights Yeshiva, Stuyvesant High School, Columbia University, and Fordham Law School. He lives on the Upper West Side of Manhattan with his wife, Joyce Miller.

## ALEXANDRIA OCASIO-CORTEZ (D)
*14th - Parts of Bronx and Queens Counties*

74-09 37th Avenue, Suite 305, Jackson Heights, NY 11372
718-662-5970

229 Cannon House Office Building, Washington, DC 20515
202-225-3965/ocasio-cortez.house.gov

Alexandria Ocasio-Cortez, also known as AOC, is the US Representative for New York's 14th Congressional District since January 3, 2019. The district includes the eastern part of the Bronx and portions of north-central Queens in New York City. In Congress, she sits on the following committees: Financial Services and Oversight and Reform.
Ocasio-Cortez is also a member of the following Caucuses: Pro-Choice; Democratic Women, Congressional Progressive; LGBT Equality; Quiet Skies; and Congressional Bangladesh.

Throughout her childhood, Representative Ocasio-Cortez split her time between the Bronx and Yorktown. While visiting her extended family in the Bronx, she saw a stark contrast in opportunities based on their respective zip codes. After high school, Ocasio-Cortez attended Boston University and graduated with degrees in economics and international relations. During this period, she also had the opportunity to work in the office of the late Senator Ted Kennedy. Her role in Senator Kennedy's office provided a firsthand view of the heartbreak families endured after being separated by ICE. These experiences led the Congresswoman to organize Latinx youth in the Bronx and across the United States, eventually, she began work as an Educational Director with the National Hispanic Institute, a role in which she helped Americans, DREAMers and undocumented youth in community leadership and college readiness.

Following the financial crisis of 2008, tragedy struck when her father, Sergio Ocasio-Roman, passed away, forcing her family to sell their Westchester home. She pulled extra shifts to work as a waitress and bartender to support her family during this time, deepening her commitment to issues impacting working-class people.

During the 2016 presidential election, she worked as a volunteer organizer for Bernie Sanders in the South Bronx, expanding her skills in electoral organizing and activism that has taken her across the country and to Standing Rock, South Dakota to stand with indigenous communities, then back to New York's 14th Congressional District to launch her people-funded, grassroots campaign for Congress.

Since her swearing-in to Congress in January of 2019, Congresswoman Ocasio-Cortez has remained committed to serving working-class people over corporate interests and advocating for social, racial, economic, and environmental justice.

## TOM REED III (R)
*23rd - Allegany, Cattaraugus, Chatauqua, Chemung, Ontario, Schuyler, Seneca, Steuben, Tioga, Tompkins, and Yates Counties*

2263 Rayburn House Office Building, Washington, DC 20515
202-225-3161/reed.house.gov

89 W. Market Street, Corning, NY 14830
607-654-7566

One Bluebird Square, Olean, NY 14760
716-379-8434

433 Exchange Street, Geneva, NY 14456
315-759-5229

2 E. 2nd Street, Suite 208, Jamestown, NY 14701
716-708-6369

Congressman Tom Reed was elected to the US House of Representatives in 2010. Since 2011, he has sat on the powerful Committee on Ways and Means and three of its Subcommittees: Human Resources; Select Revenue Measures; and Social Security, where he is Republic Leader. He also co-chairs the House Manufacturing Caucus, the Problem Solvers Caucus, and the Congressional Diabetes Caucus.

In the Problem Solvers Caucus, a group of 24 Republicans and 24 Democrats who meet weekly to solve some of the most contentious issues facing our country today, Reed remains committed to being accessible and help anyone in need. Reed and his team have completed more than 13,000 constituent cases, resolving issues with the Internal Revenue Service (IRS), Veterans Administration (VA), Social Security Administration (SSA) and other federal agencies. He has also held more than 250 public town hall meetings to listen to the thoughts and concerns of his constituents, earning him recognition as one of the most accessible members of Congress.

Reed, the youngest of twelve, was raised by a single mother on a social security check. His father, a decorated career military officer, died when he was two but he still learned from his legacy of service and loyalty. These ideals inspired Tom's mission to help people in need.

Before going to Congress, Congressman Reed was the Mayor of Corning, the town where he was raised and still lives today with his wife Jean and their two children Autumn and Will, under the roof of the home his grandfather built. As the Mayor of his hometown, he learned potholes and parking tickets are not partisan issues and that is the approach he brings to Washington. A former All-American swimmer, Reed graduated from Alfred University in 1993 and from Ohio Northern University College of Law in 1996.

## KATHLEEN M. RICE (D)
*4th - Nassau County*

2345 Rayburn House Office Building, Washington, DC 20515
202-225-5516/kathleenrice.house.gov

229 7th Street, Suite 300, Garden City, NY 11530
516-739-3008

Congresswoman Kathleen Rice represents New York's 4th Congressional District, which encompasses the majority of Nassau County, NY, a diverse suburban community located on Long Island.

First elected to Congress in 2014, Rice has become a leading voice on national security issues as a member of the Homeland Security Committee, where she passed legislation to improve airport security screening in her first year and conducted rigorous oversight of the Trump Administration's border policies during her tenure as Chair of the Subcommittee on Border Security, Facilitation, and Operations. As a member of the Veterans' Affairs Committee, she established herself as a fierce advocate for veterans and for accountability at the Department of Veterans Affairs, and she authored bipartisan legislation to expand employment opportunities for veterans, which was signed into law in January 2021. For the 117th Congress, Congresswoman Rice was named to the Committee on Energy and Commerce, which has the broadest jurisdiction of any authorizing committee in Congress, and she remains a member of the Homeland Security Committee.

Prior to Congress, Rice ran for District Attorney of Nassau County in 2005 and shocked the Long Island political establishment by defeating a thirty-one-year incumbent, becoming the first woman elected District Attorney in Long Island history. She served as District Attorney from 2006 to 2014, and received national acclaim for her efforts to combat drunk driving, which led to a statewide overhaul of DWI laws and Long Island's first DWI-related murder convictions. Rice also focused on combating public corruption, launching investigations that led to significant government reforms and the convictions of dozens of officials from both parties who violated the public's trust.

Congresswoman Rice began her career in public service as an Assistant District Attorney in Brooklyn, NY, where she prosecuted cases of domestic violence and gang activity before joining the office's elite Homicide Bureau. In 1999, she was appointed an Assistant U.S. Attorney, where she went on to an award-winning career as a federal prosecutor in the U.S. Department of Justice's Philadelphia office.

Rice resides in Garden City, NY, where she was raised with her nine brothers and sisters, and she is the proud owner of a Maltese-Yorkie rescue named Pearl. She graduated in 1987 from the Catholic University of America and earned her JD from Touro Law Center in 1991.

## ELISE STEFANIK (R)
*21 - Jefferson, Lewis, St. Lawrence, Franklin, Hamilton, Herkimer, Fulton, Saratoga, Washington, Warren, Essex, Clinton, and Franklin Counties*

2211 Rayburn House Building, Washington, DC 20515
202- 225-4611/stefanik.house.gov

5 Warren Street, Suite 4, Glens Falls, NY 12801
518-743-0964

137 Margaret Street, Suite 100, Plattsburgh, NY 12901
518-561-2324

88 Public Square, Suite A, Watertown, NY 13601
315-782-3150

Congresswoman Elise Stefanik proudly represents New York's 21st District in the House of Representatives in her fourth term in office. She is a member of the House Armed Services Committee, the Committee on Education and Labor, and the House Permanent Select Committee on Intelligence. On the Armed Services Committee, Congresswoman Stefanik serves as the Ranking Member on the new Subcommittee on Cyber, Innovative Technologies, and Information Systems, and as a member of the subcommittee on Strategic Forces. On the Committee on Education and Labor, she serves on the Higher Education and Workforce Investment, and Workforce Protections.

Stefanik is also a member of numerous Caucuses, including the Bipartisan Taskforce to Combat the Heroin Epidemic; Servicewomen & Women Veterans Congressional Caucus; Congressional Community Health Center Caucus (Co-chair); Congressional Army Caucus; House Congressional Veterans Jobs Caucus; Northern Border Caucus (Co-chair); Tuesday Group Congressional Assisting Caregivers Today (ACT) Caucus; and Congressional Dairy Farmers Caucus.

Among Congresswoman Stefanik's accomplishments and initiatives, she: successfully led the New York State delegation in saving Fort Drum from up to 16,000 military personnel cuts due to sequestration; authored the Be Open Act, legislation that passed the House of Representatives and was signed into law by the President. This was the largest fix to Obamacare of the 114th Congress and repealed the auto-enrollment mandate that reduces choices in health coverage and has created confusion that can lead to significant tax penalties on both the employer and employee; authored the Flexible Pell Grant for 21st Century Students Act; was the sole freshman negotiator for two consecutive years on the National Defense Authorization Act (NDAA) and fought hard to include language to help protect and strengthen Fort Drum; coauthored U.S./Canadian preclearance legislation that passed the House of Representatives in 2016 and will help grow North Country commerce, tourism and border security; has worked hard on behalf of North Country veterans, helping to recover hard earned benefits from the VA and helping pass critical legislation to support our North Country heroes, including the Clay Hunt Suicide Prevention for American Veterans Act; and helped pass the 21st Century Cures -Act, a critical, bipartisan legislation designed to help accelerate the discovery, development, and delivery of promising new treatments and cures for patients with diseases ranging from Alzheimer's to Lyme.

From -2006 to 2009, Congresswoman Stefanik served in the West Wing of the White House on President George W. Bush's Domestic Policy Council Staff and in the Office of the Chief of Staff, where she assisted in overseeing the policy development process on all economic and domestic policy issues. Congresswoman Stefanik served as the Director of Vice-Presidential Debate Prep to Paul Ryan, and as the Director of Communications for the Foreign Policy Initiative.

Congresswoman Stefanik was born and raised in Upstate New York. Prior to serving in Congress, she worked at her family's small business. Her upbringing in a small business family taught her the hard work and perseverance necessary to build, operate and grow small businesses in the North Country. As the first member of her immediate family to graduate from college, Congresswoman Stefanik graduated with Honors from Harvard University. She lives in Schuylerville, New York with her husband, Matt.

## THOMAS SUOZZI (D)
*3rd - Parts of Suffolk, Nassau, and Queens Counties*

407 Cannon House Office Building, Washington, DC 20515
202-225-3335/suozzi.house.gov

478A Park Avenue, Huntington, NY 11743
631-923-4100

250-02 Northern Boulevard, Little Neck, NY 11362
718-631-0400

Representative Tom Suozzi, trained as an attorney and CPA, is the Congressman representing the 3rd Congressional District in New York. He is a member of the powerful House Ways and Means Committee, the chief tax-writing committee of the House of Representatives, serving on both the Oversight and Tax Policy subcommittees. Congressman Suozzi is also the Vice Chair of the bipartisan Problem Solvers Caucus and Co-chair of the bipartisan Long Island Sound Caucus. In May of 2019, he was appointed to the Congressional-Executive Commission on China. Prior to his assignment on Ways and Means, the Congressman was a member of the House Foreign Affairs Committee and House Armed Services Committee.

Representative Suozzi is a Vice Chair of the Congressional Problem Solvers Caucus, which is made up of 20 Republicans and 20 Democrats working together to get things done. He is also the Co-chair of the bipartisan Congressional Quiet Skies Caucus, which seeks to raise awareness of aircraft noise issues and find solutions to the problem. Suozzi is a Co-chair of the Congressional Long Island Sound Caucus. This bipartisan group seeks to preserve and protect this national treasure and diverse ecosystem. The Congressman is also a member of the following Congressional organizations: Armenian Issues Caucus; Bipartisan Task Force on Alzheimer's Disease; Bipartisan Task Force on Heroin; CPA Caucus; Climate Solutions Caucus; Dietary Supplement Caucus; Estuary Caucus; Fire Services Caucus; Gun Violence Prevention Task Force; Hidden Heroes Caucus; India and Indian Americans Caucus; Military Mental Health Caucus; and Taiwan Caucus.

Congressman Suozzi previously served as Mayor of his hometown, Glen Cove, NY from 1994 to 2001, and as Nassau County Executive from 2002 to 2009. As a reformer and a problem solver, in 2004 Suozzi created FixAlbany.com, exposing and rooting out corruption in New York state politics. In 2005, he was honored as *Governing* magazine's "Public Official of the Year." In 2007, he was appointed by the Governor to lead a state commission that proposed the first property tax cap, which has now become law. In 2008, the New York State League of Conservation Voters (NYLCV) named him "Environmentalist of the Year."

In 2010, Congressman Suozzi returned to the private sector as a senior advisor to investment banking firm Lazard and as of counsel at Harris Beach law firm. Prior to his time in elected office, Suozzi worked as a litigator for Shearman & Sterling, law clerk to the Chief Judge of the Eastern District, and an auditor for Arthur Andersen & Co.

Congressman Suozzi resides in Glen Cove with his wife Helene, and their three children Caroline, Joseph, and Michael.

**CLAUDIA TENNEY (R)**
*22nd - Chenango, Cortland, Madison, Oneida, and parts of Broome, Oswego, and Tioga Counties*

1410 Longworth House Office Building, Washington, DC 20515
202-225-3665

49 Court Street, Suite 210, Binghamton, NY 13901
607-242-0200

430 Court Street, Suite 102, Utica, NY 12502
315-732-0713

Claudia Tenney was first elected to serve as a member of the United States House of Representatives on November 8, 2016, after winning one of the most expensive races in the nation. As a freshman member of the 115th Congress, she served on the House Financial Services Committee. Tenney was elected to the House of Representatives for a second time in November 2020, in what was yet again among the most expensive and competitive congressional races in the country. In the 117th Congress she is a member of the House Committee on Small Business and the House Committee on Foreign Affairs. Tenney's legislative priorities include: our relationship with China, the Second Amendment; healthcare; education; immigration; and protecting Social Security and Medicare.

Prior to her election in November 2016, Congresswoman Tenney served as a member of the New York State Assembly. She was first elected to the Assembly on November 2, 2010. Tenney is an accomplished attorney and longtime small business owner. Tenney was the co-owner and legal counsel to Mid-York Press, Inc., a commercial printing and manufacturing firm started by her grandfather in 1946. Mid-York Press currently employs nearly 70 people in the Chenango County community of Sherburne. She also maintained a private law practice in Clinton, New York.

Tenney graduated from Colgate University and the Taft College of Law at the University of Cincinnati. She is admitted to the bar in New York, Connecticut and Florida. She also is admitted to all federal courts including the U.S. Supreme Court. Prior to opening her private practice, she was a partner in the Utica-area law firm of Groben, Gilroy, Oster and Saunders.

In 1997, Congresswoman Tenney established Tenney Media Group and served as its publisher and corporate counsel. Tenney Media Group, also based in Clinton, published and printed free community newspapers founded by Claudia's parents and grandparents—the Mid-York Weekly and the Pennysaver. These publications covered three Central New York counties with eight separate weekly editions and had a circulation exceeding 100,000 households. This division was sold to Gannett in 2004.

Apart from the influence of Tenney's family and her legal training, sher approach to public service has been shaped by experiences beyond politics. Tenney was the only American employed by the Consulate General of Yugoslavia, which led to her strong relationship with the large Bosnian refugee population in the Utica area. She also published and produced the first Bosnian newspaper in Utica. Tenney remains an active member of her community, serving on numerous boards and volunteer organizations throughout the district.

Congresswoman Tenney is the daughter of the late Honorable John R. Tenney, who served as a Justice of the Supreme Court of New York in the Fifth Judicial District from 1969 through 2003, and the mother of U.S. Naval Academy graduate Trey Cleary, who serves as a 1st Lieutenant in the U.S. Marine Corps.

**PAUL TONKO (D)**
*20th - Albany, Montgomery, Rensselaer, Saratoga, and Schenectady Counties*

2369 Rayburn House Office Building, Washington, DC 20515
202-225-5076/tonko.house.gov

19 Dove Street, Suite 302, Albany, NY 12210
518-465-0700

105 Jay Street, Room 15, Schenectady, NY 12305
518-374-4547

61 Church St, Room 309, Amsterdam, NY 12010
518-843-3400

Congressman Paul Tonko represents New York's 20th Congressional District, including the communities of Albany, Schenectady, Troy, Saratoga Springs and Amsterdam. He represents all of Albany and Schenectady Counties and parts of Montgomery, Rensselaer and Saratoga Counties. He is serving his sixth term, after first being sworn into Congress in 2009.

Tonko serves on the Energy and Commerce Committee, the oldest standing Committee in the House, created in December of 1795. He is the first Upstate New York Democratic member to serve on the committee since Leo O'Brien, who resigned the post in October 1966. He was elected by his peers in the 116th Congress to chair the Subcommittee on Environment and Climate Change. He was also selected to continue his service on the Science, Space and Technology Committee, as well as on the Natural Resources Committee. He has previously served on the Education and Labor Committee and the Budget Committee.

Among his recent legislation is a proposal to ask the Energy Department to carry out a research, development, and technology demonstration program to improve the efficiency of gas turbines used in power generation systems and to identify the technologies that will lead to gas turbine combined cycle efficiency of 65 percent or simple cycle efficiency of 50 percent. Tonko's priorities in the House also include the following issues: addiction and recovery; agriculture; campaign finance; defense, security, and foreign affairs; education, gun violence; health care; immigration; infrastructure and water systems; mental health; voting; and civil rights. He holds a BA in mechanical and industrial engineering from Clarkson University.

**RITCHIE TORRES (D)**
*15th - Part of Bronx County*

317 Cannon House Office Building, Washington, DC 20515
202-225-4361/ritchietorres.house.gov

1231 Lafayette Avenue, L630, Bronx, NY 10474
718-503-9610

Ritchie John Torres is the U.S. Representative for New York's 15th Congressional District. In the House of Representatives, Torres is Vice Chair of the Home Security Committee and serves on the following standing Committees: Financial Services; the Progressive Caucus; and is Co-chair of the LGBTQ+ Equality Caucus.

Previously, Torres served as the New York City Councilmember for the 15th district elected in 2013. He was the first openly gay candidate to be elected to legislative office in the Bronx, and the youngest member of the city council. He served as the Chair of the Committee on Public Housing, and is a Deputy Majority Leader. As Chair of the Oversight and Investigations Committee Torres focused on taxi medallion predatory loans, and the city's Third-Party Transfer Program. In 2016, he was a delegate for the Bernie Sanders campaign.

Ritchie Torres was born in the Bronx. Torres is Afro-Latino; his father is from Puerto Rico and his mother is African-American. He was raised by his mother in Throggs Neck Houses, a public housing project in the Throggs Neck neighborhood of the East Bronx

He attended Herbert H. Lehman High School, served in the inaugural class of the Coro New York Exploring Leadership Program, and later worked as an intern in the offices of the Mayor and Attorney General. He came out while a sophomore "during a schoolwide forum on marriage equality."

Biographies

Torres enrolled at New York University, but dropped out at the beginning of his sophomore year, as he was suffering from depression. He struggled with negative thoughts based on his sexuality. As he recovered, Torres resumed working for council member James Vacca, eventually becoming Vacca's Housing Director. In that role, Torres conducted site inspections and documented conditions, ensuring critical housing issues were promptly and adequately addressed.

At age twenty-five, Torres ran to succeed Joel Rivera as the councilmember for the 15th district of the New York City Council. When he won the Democratic Party nomination for New York City Council, he became the one of the first openly gay political candidate in the Bronx to win the Democratic Party nomination, and upon victory in the general election became the first openly gay public official in the Bronx. He was also the youngest elected city official. Torres also served as a Deputy Leader of the City Council.

Upon his election, Torres requested the chairmanship of the Council's Committee on Public Housing, tasked with overseeing the New York City Housing Authority. In this role, he helped secure $3 million for Concourse Village, Inc. He also played a crucial role in exposing the city's failures to address lead-paint contamination.

In 2019, along with fellow Council member Vanessa Gibson, Torres announced Right to Counsel 2.0, an expansion of legal aid to NYCHA tenants facing eviction. He worked on legislation aimed to compel companies that employ gig workers to be transparent if the worker's tips are diverted to pay base salary. Torres also proposed legislation to address the movement in New York towards cashless business practices of stores and restaurants.

Rep. Torres helped open the first homeless shelter for LGBTQ youth in the Bronx. He also secured funds for senior centers to serve LGBTQ people in all five NYC's boroughs.

In the House of Representatives, Torres' priority is overhauling public housing and focusing on the issues of concentrated poverty. The 15th Congressional District, in terms of median income, is the nation's poorest.

## NYDIA M. VELAZQUEZ (D)
*7th - Parts of New York, Queens and Kings Counties*

2302 Rayburn House Office Building, Washington, DC 20515
202-225-2361/velazquez.house.gov

266 Broadway, Suite 201, Brooklyn, NY 11211
718-599-3658

500 Pearl Street, Suite 973, New York, NY 10007
212-619-2606

Congresswoman Nydia M. Velázquez is currently serving her fourteenth term as Representative for New York's 7th Congressional District. Congresswoman Velázquez is the Chairwoman of the House Small Business Committee is a senior member of the Financial Services Committee and serves on the following Subcommittees: Subcommittee on Financial Institutions and Consumer Credit; Subcommittee on Housing and Insurance. Velázquez is also a member of the House Committee on Natural Resources and serves on the following Subcommittees: Subcommittee on Energy and Mineral Resources; Subcommittee on Indian, Insular and Alaska Native Affairs; In addition, she serves on the following Congressional Caucuses and Task Forces: Congressional Hispanic Caucus; Congressional Progressive Caucus; Congressional Asian American Pacific Caucus; Democratic Caucus; Women's Issues Caucus; and Urban Caucus.

In 1992, she was the first Puerto Rican woman elected to the U.S. House of Representatives. In February 1998, she was named Ranking Democratic Member of the House Small Business Committee, making her the first Hispanic woman to serve as Ranking Member of a full House committee. Most recently, in 2006, she was named Chairwoman of the House

Small Business Committee, making her the first Latina to chair a full Congressional Committee.

Given these achievements, her roots are humble. She was born in Yabucoa, Puerto Rico in 1953, and was one of nine children. Velázquez started school early, skipped several grades, and became the first person in her family to receive a college diploma. At the age of 16, she entered the University of Puerto Rico in Rio Piedras. She graduated magna cum laude in 1974 with a degree in political science. After earning a master's degree on scholarship from NYU, Velázquez taught Puerto Rican studies at CUNY's Hunter College in 1981.

Her passion for politics took hold in 1983, when Velázquez was appointed Special Assistant to Congressman Edolphus Towns (D-Brooklyn). One year later, she became the first Latina appointed to serve on the New York City Council. By 1986, Velázquez served as the Director of the Department of Puerto Rican Community Affairs in the United States. During that time, she initiated one of the most successful Latino empowerment programs in the nation's history, "Atrevete" (Dare to Go for It!). In 1992, after months of running a grassroots political campaign, Velázquez was elected to the House of Representatives to represent New York's 7th District. Her district, which encompasses parts of Brooklyn, Queens and the Lower East Side of Manhattan, is the only tri-borough district in the New York City congressional delegation. Encompassing many diverse neighborhoods, it is home to a large Latino population, Jewish communities, and parts of Chinatown.

As a fighter for equal rights of the underrepresented and a proponent of economic opportunity for the working class and poor, Congresswoman Velázquez combines sensibility and compassion, as she works to encourage economic development, protect community health and the environment, combat crime and worker abuses, and secure access to affordable housing, quality education and health care for all New York City families. As the top Democrat on the House Small Business Committee, which oversees federal programs and contracts totaling $200 billion annually, Congresswoman Velázquez has been a vocal advocate of American small business and entrepreneurship. She has established numerous small business legislative priorities, encompassing the areas of tax, regulations, access to capital, federal contracting opportunities, trade, technology, health care and pension reform, among others.

Congresswoman Velázquez was named as the inaugural "Woman of the Year" by *Hispanic Business Magazine* in recognition of her national influence in both the political and business sectors and for her longtime support of minority enterprise. Although her work on the Small Business Committee and the House Financial Services Committee (where she is the most senior New York Member on the Subcommittee on Housing and Community Opportunity) keeps her busy, Congresswoman Velázquez can often be found close to home, working for the residents of her district.

## LEE M. ZELDIN (R)
*1st - Suffolk County*

2441 Rayburn House Office Building, Washington, DC 20515
202-225-3826/zeldin.house.gov

31 Oak Street, Suite 20, Patchogue, NY 11772
631-289-1097

30 W. Main Street, Suite 201, Riverhead, NY 11901
631-209-4235

Lee Zeldin was first elected to the US House of Representatives in 2014 from a district at the east end of Long Island. Congressman Zeldin serves on two Committees in the House of Representatives: Financial Services and Foreign Affairs, where he serves as Ranking Member of the Subcommittee on Oversight and Investigations. Additionally, Congressman Zeldin serves as Co-chair of the Long Island Sound Caucus and founding member of the National Estuary Program Caucus and as one of two Jewish Republicans in Congress, also serves as Co-chair of the House Republican Israel Caucus, which has over 100 members, and has been a stalwart opponent of the Boycott, Divestment. and Sanctions (BDS) movement, coleading a House-passed resolution to combat it.

Congressman Lee Zeldin grew up in Suffolk County, New York, where he graduated from William Floyd High School in Mastic Beach. Congressman Zeldin graduated from the State University of New York at Albany (SUNY) and then Albany Law School, becoming New York's youngest attorney at the time at the age of 23. After completing the Army ROTC program, Congressman Zeldin served four years on Active Duty. During that time, he served in different capacities, including as a Military Intelligence Officer, Prosecutor and Military Magistrate. While assigned to the Army's elite 82nd Airborne Division, in the summer of 2006, Congressman Zeldin was deployed to Tikrit, Iraq, with an infantry battalion of fellow paratroopers in support of Operation Iraqi Freedom. Following his service on active duty, in 2007, Congressman Zeldin transitioned from Active Duty to the Army Reserve, where he currently serves as a Lieutenant Colonel.

In 2008, Congressman Zeldin opened a successful law practice in Smithtown, New York, which he operated full time until he was elected to the New York State Senate in 2010, representing New York's 3rd Senate District. He served in the New York State Senate from 2010 to 2014, where he chaired the Consumer Protection Committee. As a State Senator Zeldin led the successful effort to repeal the MTA Payroll Tax for 80 percent of employers, a job-killing tax that was hurting New York's small businesses. He also created the PFC Joseph Dwyer Program, a peer-to-peer counseling program for veterans suffering from posttraumatic stress disorder (PTSD) and traumatic brain injury (TBI); the program started in Suffolk County and quickly expanded across the state. Congressman Zeldin also successfully fought to repeal the Saltwater Fishing License Fee; a victory for tens of thousands of fishermen on Long Island.

In 2014, following four years in the State Senate, Congressman Zeldin was elected to the U.S. House of Representatives, representing New York's First Congressional District. Throughout his tenure in Congress, Representative Zeldin has continued to secure important victories for his district. He has championed the successful effort to save Plum Island, steered a $2 billion Electron Ion Collider (EIC) to Brookhaven National Lab (BNL), and ushered into law his Adult Day Health Care Act to aid veterans who are 70 percent of more disabled and his bill to safeguard veterans' homeownership opportunities.

Congressman Zeldin also secured a new veterans health care clinic on the East End of Long Island, saved a vital communications spectrum for local first responders, helped lead the effort to permanently reauthorize the Zadroga Act and Victim Compensation Fund for 9/11 first responders and their families, and advanced several vital Army Corps projects for his district, including the over $1 billion Fire Island to Montauk Point (FIMP) project. His office has also successfully resolved over 15,000 cases in favor of NY-1 constituents. Congressman Zeldin resides in his hometown of Shirley with his wife, Diana, and their twin daughters, Mikayla and Arianna.

# APPENDICES

**CASH DISBURSEMENTS BY FUNCTION**
**ALL GOVERNMENTAL FUNDS**
**(thousands of dollars)**

| | FY 2020 Actuals | FY 2021 Current | FY 2022 Proposed | FY 2023 Projected | FY 2024 Projected | FY 2025 Projected |
|---|---|---|---|---|---|---|
| **ECONOMIC DEVELOPMENT AND GOVERNMENT OVERSIGHT** | | | | | | |
| Agriculture and Markets, Department of | 105,692 | 95,308 | 99,090 | 87,430 | 86,280 | 85,930 |
| Alcoholic Beverage Control, Division of | 10,611 | 12,849 | 31,708 | 39,294 | 42,233 | 42,593 |
| Economic Development Capital | 2,525 | 6,400 | 0 | 0 | 0 | 0 |
| Economic Development, Department of | 66,479 | 84,323 | 70,349 | 70,349 | 70,349 | 70,349 |
| Empire State Development Corporation | 1,031,284 | 1,647,177 | 1,897,705 | 1,607,277 | 1,430,213 | 1,283,457 |
| Energy Research and Development Authority, New York State | 15,646 | 21,569 | 23,129 | 23,758 | 22,607 | 23,731 |
| Financial Services, Department of | 371,795 | 392,285 | 391,379 | 390,679 | 390,679 | 390,679 |
| Lake Ontario Resiliency/Economic Development | 285 | 30,000 | 40,000 | 10,000 | 0 | 0 |
| Olympic Regional Development Authority | 97,106 | 142,652 | 127,542 | 21,542 | 21,542 | 21,542 |
| Power Authority, New York | 10,315 | 65,678 | 500 | 500 | 500 | 500 |
| Public Service Department | 82,388 | 90,039 | 84,299 | 83,175 | 83,175 | 83,175 |
| Regional Economic Development Program | 1,902 | 3,000 | 0 | 0 | 0 | 0 |
| Strategic Capital Resource Assistance Program | 0 | 0 | 23,900 | 21,400 | 21,599 | 21,400 |
| Strategic Investment Program | 1,056 | 2,500 | 0 | 0 | 0 | 0 |
| **Functional Total** | 1,797,084 | 2,593,780 | 2,789,601 | 2,355,404 | 2,169,177 | 2,023,356 |
| **PARKS AND THE ENVIRONMENT** | | | | | | |
| Adirondack Park Agency | 4,443 | 5,448 | 5,773 | 5,028 | 4,966 | 5,037 |
| Environmental Conservation, Department of | 1,243,110 | 1,392,822 | 1,553,486 | 1,621,918 | 1,610,344 | 1,610,349 |
| Hudson River Park Trust | 2,000 | 8,000 | 18,000 | 17,000 | 14,000 | 12,000 |
| Parks, Recreation and Historic Preservation, Office of | 364,604 | 360,335 | 340,148 | 336,357 | 336,357 | 331,357 |
| **Functional Total** | 1,614,157 | 1,766,605 | 1,917,407 | 1,980,303 | 1,965,667 | 1,958,743 |
| **TRANSPORTATION** | | | | | | |
| Metropolitan Transportation Authority | 544,486 | 1,270,000 | 1,534,400 | 1,146,464 | 1,096,464 | 1,096,464 |
| Motor Vehicles, Department of | 362,100 | 422,728 | 433,547 | 433,547 | 433,547 | 433,547 |
| Transportation, Department of | 8,287,877 | 8,774,915 | 9,657,251 | 9,655,741 | 9,766,356 | 9,646,060 |
| **Functional Total** | 9,194,463 | 10,467,643 | 11,625,198 | 11,235,752 | 11,296,367 | 11,176,071 |
| **HEALTH** | | | | | | |
| Aging, Office for the | 254,394 | 245,638 | 245,379 | 250,433 | 255,616 | 260,928 |
| Health, Department of | 72,735,168 | 78,658,757 | 82,982,807 | 82,917,059 | 84,530,500 | 85,433,763 |
| *Medical Assistance* | 61,310,204 | 67,299,317 | 69,702,413 | 70,526,434 | 72,441,354 | 73,417,427 |
| *Essential Plan* | 3,908,166 | 4,460,138 | 5,525,785 | 5,676,150 | 5,573,013 | 5,504,687 |
| *Medicaid Administration* | 1,572,734 | 1,420,019 | 1,487,833 | 1,434,542 | 1,422,213 | 1,428,505 |
| *Public Health* | 5,944,064 | 5,479,283 | 6,266,776 | 5,279,933 | 5,093,920 | 5,083,144 |
| Medicaid Inspector General, Office of the | 45,787 | 47,978 | 46,560 | 46,560 | 46,560 | 46,560 |
| **Functional Total** | 73,035,349 | 78,952,373 | 83,274,746 | 83,214,052 | 84,832,676 | 85,741,251 |
| **SOCIAL WELFARE** | | | | | | |
| Children and Family Services, Office of | 2,612,986 | 3,193,443 | 2,849,241 | 2,827,042 | 2,833,729 | 2,840,874 |
| *OCFS* | 2,575,771 | 3,122,585 | 2,775,004 | 2,752,805 | 2,759,492 | 2,766,637 |
| *OCFS - Other* | 37,215 | 70,858 | 74,237 | 74,237 | 74,237 | 74,237 |
| Housing and Community Renewal, Division of | 525,868 | 836,394 | 933,174 | 975,589 | 751,657 | 570,398 |
| Human Rights, Division of | 15,432 | 14,313 | 13,940 | 13,590 | 13,590 | 13,590 |
| Labor, Department of | 592,123 | 4,765,491 | 647,355 | 595,738 | 595,738 | 595,738 |
| National and Community Service | 11,971 | 16,986 | 17,305 | 17,305 | 17,632 | 17,963 |
| Nonprofit Infrastructure Capital Investment Program | 19,641 | 18,000 | 15,000 | 15,000 | 14,298 | 0 |
| Temporary and Disability Assistance, Office of | 5,085,108 | 5,236,835 | 5,964,944 | 5,365,168 | 5,394,698 | 5,393,279 |
| *Welfare Assistance* | 3,687,464 | 3,948,230 | 3,902,191 | 3,885,552 | 3,876,707 | 3,843,888 |
| *All Other* | 1,397,644 | 1,288,605 | 2,062,753 | 1,479,616 | 1,517,991 | 1,549,391 |
| **Functional Total** | 8,863,129 | 14,081,462 | 10,440,959 | 9,809,432 | 9,621,342 | 9,431,842 |
| **MENTAL HYGIENE** | | | | | | |
| Addiction Services and Supports, Office of | 577,249 | 619,416 | 644,755 | 697,812 | 712,569 | 727,388 |
| *OASAS* | 503,970 | 550,402 | 574,744 | 626,971 | 641,594 | 655,752 |
| *OASAS - Other* | 73,279 | 69,014 | 70,011 | 70,841 | 70,975 | 71,636 |
| Developmental Disabilities Planning Council | 4,636 | 4,200 | 4,200 | 4,200 | 4,200 | 4,200 |
| Justice Center | 45,278 | 46,106 | 44,726 | 45,743 | 46,351 | 46,948 |
| Mental Health, Office of | 3,032,581 | 3,057,458 | 3,227,200 | 3,318,922 | 3,381,273 | 3,460,928 |
| *OMH* | 1,707,107 | 1,927,351 | 1,915,769 | 1,972,887 | 2,011,644 | 2,062,517 |
| *OMH - Other* | 1,325,474 | 1,130,107 | 1,311,431 | 1,346,035 | 1,369,629 | 1,398,411 |
| Mental Hygiene, Department of | 0 | 0 | 0 | 0 | (22,594) | (22,594) |
| People with Developmental Disabilities, Office for | 3,201,373 | 1,919,684 | 3,012,288 | 2,977,806 | 3,519,125 | 3,754,987 |
| *OPWDD* | 511,007 | 497,526 | 453,371 | 456,332 | 472,641 | 517,693 |
| *OPWDD - Other* | 2,690,366 | 1,422,158 | 2,558,917 | 2,521,474 | 3,046,484 | 3,237,294 |
| **Functional Total** | 6,861,117 | 5,646,864 | 6,933,169 | 7,044,483 | 7,640,924 | 7,971,857 |
| **PUBLIC PROTECTION/CRIMINAL JUSTICE** | | | | | | |
| Correction, Commission of | 3,149 | 2,505 | 2,467 | 2,467 | 2,467 | 2,467 |
| Corrections and Community Supervision, Department of | 3,295,148 | 3,858,337 | 2,953,366 | 2,949,635 | 2,950,800 | 2,950,800 |
| *DOCCS* | 3,295,148 | 3,856,337 | 2,953,366 | 2,949,635 | 2,950,800 | 2,950,800 |
| *DOCCS - Other* | 0 | 2,000 | 0 | 0 | 0 | 0 |

**CASH DISBURSEMENTS BY FUNCTION**
**ALL GOVERNMENTAL FUNDS**
**(thousands of dollars)**

| | FY 2020 Actuals | FY 2021 Current | FY 2022 Proposed | FY 2023 Projected | FY 2024 Projected | FY 2025 Projected |
|---|---|---|---|---|---|---|
| Criminal Justice Services, Division of | 231,940 | 256,324 | 276,817 | 225,653 | 226,603 | 228,253 |
| Homeland Security and Emergency Services, Division of | 1,479,767 | 1,678,189 | 1,239,891 | 1,241,013 | 1,236,602 | 1,235,706 |
| Indigent Legal Services, Office of | 90,265 | 213,432 | 226,463 | 276,550 | 290,449 | 290,610 |
| Judicial Conduct, Commission on | 5,748 | 6,266 | 6,444 | 6,550 | 6,550 | 6,550 |
| Judicial Nomination, Commission on | 0 | 30 | 30 | 30 | 30 | 30 |
| Judicial Screening Committees, New York State | 6 | 38 | 38 | 38 | 38 | 38 |
| Military and Naval Affairs, Division of | 197,777 | 192,956 | 229,572 | 175,643 | 142,504 | 120,776 |
| State Police, Division of | 877,304 | 1,114,625 | 897,468 | 909,035 | 912,465 | 912,465 |
| Statewide Financial System | 31,517 | 29,835 | 28,038 | 27,556 | 27,556 | 27,556 |
| Victim Services, Office of | 114,705 | 131,728 | 132,526 | 132,526 | 130,554 | 130,554 |
| **Functional Total** | **6,327,326** | **7,484,265** | **5,993,120** | **5,946,696** | **5,926,618** | **5,905,805** |
| **HIGHER EDUCATION** | | | | | | |
| City University of New York | 1,073,405 | 2,448,760 | 1,596,457 | 1,644,102 | 1,696,686 | 1,746,023 |
| Higher Education - Miscellaneous | 609 | 441 | 441 | 441 | 441 | 441 |
| Higher Education Facilities Capital Matching Grants Program | 5,669 | 6,000 | 12,650 | 14,150 | 14,150 | 6,650 |
| Higher Education Services Corporation, New York State | 990,167 | 799,551 | 827,200 | 840,508 | 849,148 | 862,108 |
| State University of New York | 8,570,332 | 8,557,211 | 8,732,941 | 8,868,639 | 8,958,642 | 9,033,706 |
| **Functional Total** | **10,640,182** | **11,811,963** | **11,169,689** | **11,367,840** | **11,519,067** | **11,648,928** |
| **EDUCATION** | | | | | | |
| Arts, Council on the | 49,048 | 46,202 | 45,452 | 45,299 | 45,299 | 45,299 |
| Education, Department of | 35,975,909 | 36,345,501 | 37,420,153 | 36,503,057 | 36,227,369 | 37,232,547 |
| *School Aid* | 30,047,154 | 30,673,322 | 33,176,355 | 32,235,435 | 31,993,086 | 32,999,649 |
| *School Aid – Other* | 137,708 | 140,000 | 140,000 | 140,000 | 140,000 | 140,000 |
| *STAR Property Tax Relief* | 2,183,689 | 2,030,377 | 586,503 | 489,479 | 404,525 | 318,508 |
| *Special Education Categorical Programs* | 2,070,572 | 2,112,221 | 2,153,740 | 2,221,593 | 2,285,425 | 2,351,037 |
| *All Other* | 1,536,786 | 1,389,581 | 1,363,555 | 1,416,550 | 1,404,333 | 1,423,353 |
| **Functional Total** | **36,024,957** | **36,391,703** | **37,465,605** | **36,548,356** | **36,272,668** | **37,277,846** |
| **GENERAL GOVERNMENT** | | | | | | |
| Budget, Division of the | 28,955 | 32,286 | 29,307 | 29,307 | 29,307 | 29,307 |
| Civil Service, Department of | 15,490 | 14,597 | 14,605 | 14,626 | 14,686 | 14,686 |
| Deferred Compensation Board | 733 | 833 | 837 | 841 | 841 | 841 |
| Elections, State Board of | 22,321 | 41,174 | 29,263 | 24,991 | 21,391 | 18,791 |
| Employee Relations, Office of | 5,880 | 6,431 | 6,288 | 6,289 | 6,289 | 6,289 |
| Gaming Commission, New York State | 165,136 | 239,025 | 169,667 | 177,616 | 191,385 | 195,694 |
| General Services, Office of | 305,353 | 408,705 | 301,991 | 234,360 | 235,692 | 235,692 |
| Information Technology Services, Office of | 622,486 | 743,300 | 809,703 | 609,067 | 590,396 | 579,038 |
| Inspector General, Office of the | 6,381 | 9,045 | 7,816 | 8,044 | 8,044 | 8,044 |
| Labor Management Committees | 37,107 | 37,631 | 38,378 | 39,139 | 39,916 | 39,916 |
| Prevention of Domestic Violence, Office for | 2,984 | 3,075 | 8,022 | 8,022 | 8,022 | 8,022 |
| Public Employment Relations Board | 3,401 | 3,520 | 3,333 | 3,333 | 3,333 | 3,333 |
| Public Ethics, Joint Commission on | 5,217 | 5,435 | 5,622 | 5,731 | 5,731 | 5,731 |
| State, Department of | 133,787 | 152,797 | 193,777 | 227,794 | 213,475 | 240,307 |
| Tax Appeals, Division of | 2,871 | 3,150 | 2,714 | 2,604 | 2,604 | 2,604 |
| Taxation and Finance, Department of | 352,299 | 361,743 | 340,095 | 333,740 | 334,340 | 334,340 |
| Veterans' Services, Division of | 15,500 | 15,732 | 15,583 | 15,374 | 15,467 | 15,556 |
| Welfare Inspector General, Office of | 640 | 768 | 753 | 768 | 768 | 768 |
| Workers' Compensation Board | 198,282 | 228,305 | 230,203 | 203,194 | 196,439 | 196,439 |
| **Functional Total** | **1,924,823** | **2,307,552** | **2,207,957** | **1,944,840** | **1,918,126** | **1,935,398** |
| **ELECTED OFFICIALS** | | | | | | |
| Audit and Control, Department of | 189,172 | 187,110 | 187,460 | 186,822 | 182,095 | 182,095 |
| Executive Chamber | 13,239 | 13,558 | 13,436 | 13,436 | 13,436 | 13,436 |
| Judiciary | 3,153,277 | 3,003,378 | 3,172,817 | 3,159,539 | 3,111,663 | 3,096,771 |
| Law, Department of | 244,393 | 248,978 | 236,838 | 234,838 | 234,838 | 234,838 |
| Legislature | 228,725 | 228,163 | 235,056 | 231,002 | 231,002 | 231,002 |
| Lieutenant Governor, Office of the | 518 | 590 | 590 | 590 | 590 | 590 |
| **Functional Total** | **3,829,324** | **3,681,777** | **3,846,197** | **3,826,227** | **3,773,624** | **3,758,732** |
| **LOCAL GOVERNMENT ASSISTANCE** | | | | | | |
| Aid and Incentives for Municipalities | 662,056 | 630,077 | 630,069 | 660,323 | 660,323 | 660,323 |
| County-Wide Shared Services Initiative | 11,166 | 15,000 | 15,000 | 59,000 | 59,000 | 59,000 |
| Miscellaneous Financial Assistance | 11,998 | 3,562 | 3,562 | 3,562 | 3,562 | 3,562 |
| Municipalities with VLT Facilities | 28,885 | 28,421 | 18,620 | 18,620 | 18,620 | 18,620 |
| Small Government Assistance | 217 | 207 | 207 | 207 | 207 | 207 |
| **Functional Total** | **714,322** | **677,267** | **667,458** | **741,712** | **741,712** | **741,712** |
| **ALL OTHER CATEGORIES** | | | | | | |
| Arts and Cultural Facilities Improvement | 3,456 | 6,500 | 6,500 | 0 | 0 | 0 |
| General State Charges | 6,655,088 | 5,329,841 | 7,830,260 | 8,413,563 | 8,884,319 | 9,964,887 |
| Long-Term Debt Service | 4,952,363 | 10,506,269 | 6,427,245 | 7,410,624 | 8,170,379 | 8,483,800 |
| Miscellaneous | (245,880) | 400,177 | (1,312,269) | (366,598) | (991,589) | (791,708) |
| Special Infrastructure Account | 789,127 | 625,174 | 1,659,027 | 232,684 | 116,255 | 101,000 |
| **Functional Total** | **12,154,154** | **16,867,961** | **14,610,763** | **15,690,273** | **16,179,364** | **17,757,979** |
| **TOTAL ALL GOVERNMENTAL FUNDS SPENDING** | **172,980,387** | **192,731,215** | **192,941,869** | **191,705,370** | **193,857,332** | **197,329,520** |

*Note: This information is excerpted from the New York State FY 2022 Executive Budget Financial Plan. All Governmental Funds combines activity in the four governmental fund types: General Fund; Special Revenue Funds; Capital Projects Funds; and Debt Service Funds.*

# Demographic and
# Reference Maps

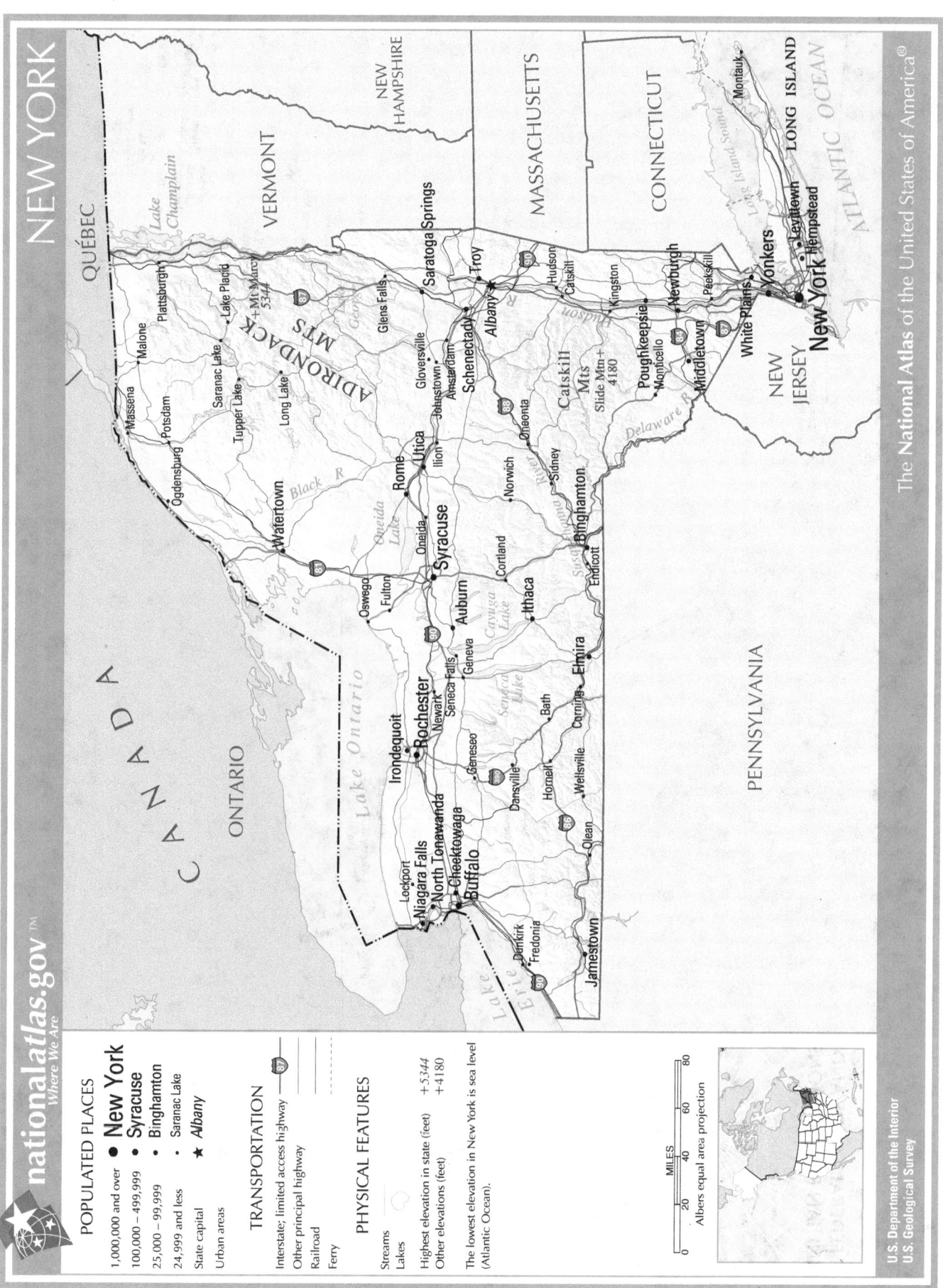

## NEW YORK

### nationalatlas.gov™
*Where We Are*

**POPULATED PLACES**

- ● **New York** — 1,000,000 and over
- ● **Syracuse** — 100,000 – 499,999
- ● **Binghamton** — 25,000 – 99,999
- • Saranac Lake — 24,999 and less
- ★ *Albany* — State capital
- Urban areas

**TRANSPORTATION**

- ⬡87 Interstate; limited access highway
- Other principal highway
- Railroad
- Ferry

**PHYSICAL FEATURES**

- Streams
- Lakes
- Highest elevation in state (feet) +5344
- Other elevations (feet) +4180

The lowest elevation in New York is sea level (Atlantic Ocean).

MILES
0  20  40  60  80

Albers equal area projection

*The* **National Atlas** *of the United States of America*®

U.S. Department of the Interior
U.S. Geological Survey

QUÉBEC
CANADA
ONTARIO
VERMONT
NEW HAMPSHIRE
MASSACHUSETTS
CONNECTICUT
NEW JERSEY
PENNSYLVANIA
ATLANTIC OCEAN
LONG ISLAND
Long Island Sound

Lake Champlain
ADIRONDACK MTS
+ Mt Marcy 5344
Lake Placid
Saranac Lake
Tupper Lake
Long Lake
Black R
Catskill Mts
Slide Mtn + 4180
Lake Ontario
Lake Erie
Oneida Lake
Cayuga Lake
Seneca Lake
Hudson R
Delaware R
Susquehanna River

Massena
Malone
Plattsburgh
Potsdam
Ogdensburg
Saranac Lake
Watertown
Saratoga Springs
Glens Falls
Gloversville
Johnstown
Amsterdam
Troy
Schenectady
*Albany*
Hudson
Catskill
Kingston
Poughkeepsie
Monticello
Newburgh
Middletown
Peekskill
White Plains
Yonkers
Levittown
Hempstead
**New York**
Montauk
Rome
Utica
Ilion
Oneonta
Sidney
Oneida
**Syracuse**
Fulton
Oswego
Norwich
Cortland
**Binghamton**
Endicott
Endwell
Auburn
Ithaca
Geneva
Elmira
Corning
Bath
Wellsville
Hornell
Dansville
Geneseo
Newark
Seneca Falls
**Rochester**
Irondequoit
Lockport
Niagara Falls
North Tonawanda
Cheektowaga
**Buffalo**
Dunkirk
Fredonia
Olean
Jamestown

MILES
0  20  40  60  80

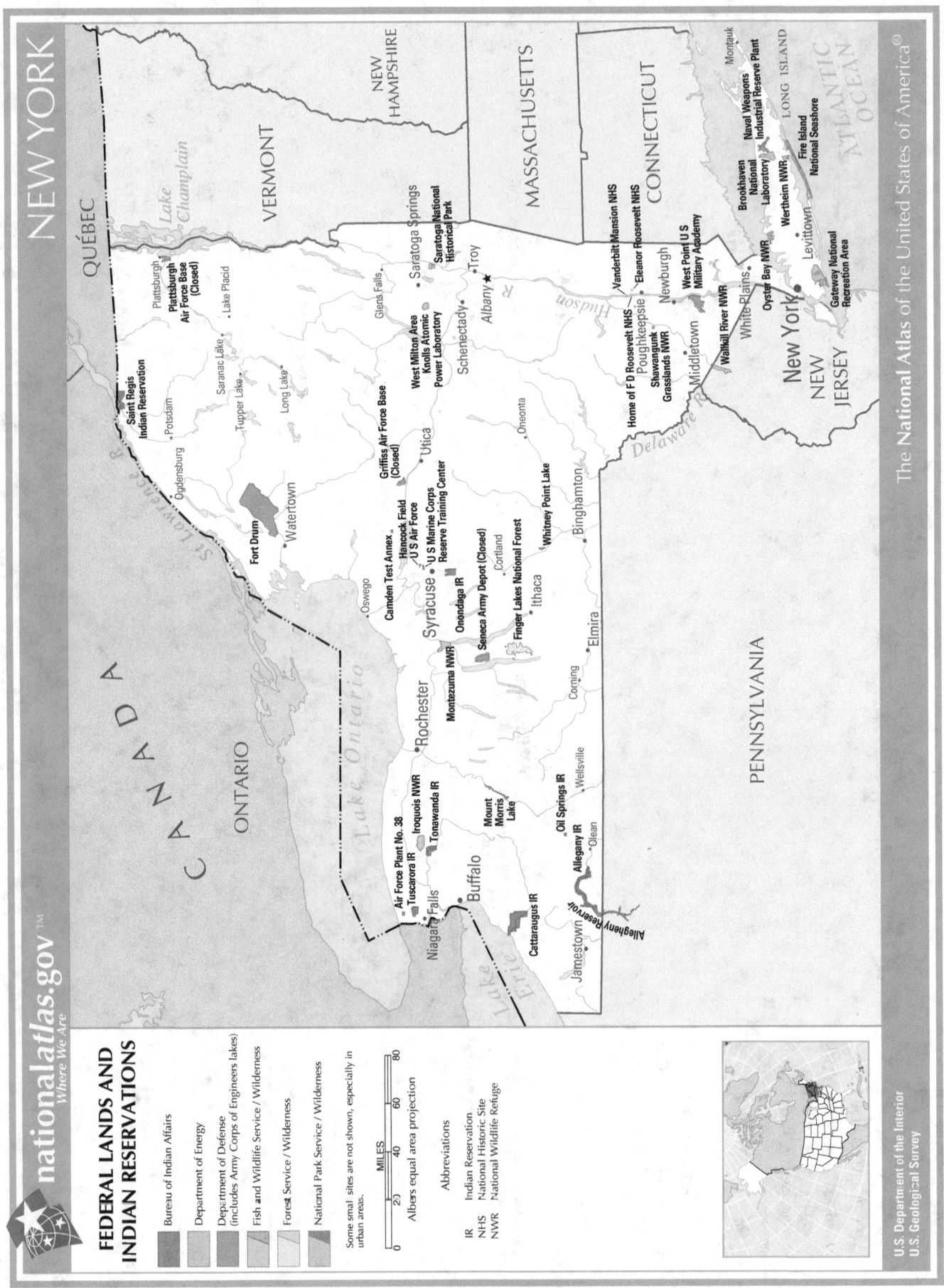

NEW YORK

QUÉBEC

CANADA

ONTARIO

NEW HAMPSHIRE

VERMONT

MASSACHUSETTS

CONNECTICUT

PENNSYLVANIA

NEW JERSEY

Lake Champlain

Lake Ontario

Lake Erie

ATLANTIC OCEAN

LONG ISLAND

Montauk

St. Lawrence R.

Hudson R.

Delaware R.

Allegheny Reservoir

Saint Regis Indian Reservation

Plattsburgh
Plattsburgh Air Force Base (Closed)

Potsdam

Ogdensburg

Saranac Lake
Lake Placid

Tupper Lake

Long Lake

Watertown

Fort Drum

Oswego

Glens Falls

Saratoga Springs

Saratoga National Historical Park

Troy

Albany ★

Schenectady

West Milton Area Knolls Atomic Power Laboratory

Griffiss Air Force Base (Closed)

Utica

Oneonta

Camden Test Annex

Hancock Field U S Air Force

U S Marine Corps Reserve Training Center

Syracuse

Onondaga IR

Seneca Army Depot (Closed)

Cortland

Finger Lakes National Forest

Ithaca

Whitney Point Lake

Binghamton

Montezuma NWR

Rochester

Elmira

Corning

Wellsville

Mount Morris Lake

Oil Springs IR

Olean

Allegany IR

Jamestown

Air Force Plant No. 38
Tuscarora IR

Iroquois NWR

Tonawanda IR

Buffalo

Niagara Falls

Cattaraugus IR

Home of F D Roosevelt NHS
Shawangunk Grasslands NWR

Vanderbilt Mansion NHS
Eleanor Roosevelt NHS

Poughkeepsie

Newburgh

West Point U S Military Academy

Middletown

Wallkill River NWR

White Plains

Oyster Bay NWR

New York

Levittown

Wertheim NWR

Fire Island National Seashore

Gateway National Recreation Area

Brookhaven National Laboratory

Naval Weapons Industrial Reserve Plant

The **National Atlas** of the United States of America®

nationalatlas.gov™
Where We Are

## FEDERAL LANDS AND INDIAN RESERVATIONS

Bureau of Indian Affairs

Department of Energy

Department of Defense (includes Army Corps of Engineers lakes)

Fish and Wildlife Service / Wilderness

Forest Service / Wilderness

National Park Service / Wilderness

Some small sites are not shown, especially in urban areas.

MILES

Albers equal area projection

0   20   40   60   80

### Abbreviations

IR    Indian Reservation
NHS   National Historic Site
NWR   National Wildlife Refuge

U.S. Department of the Interior
U.S. Geological Survey

# Congressional Districts

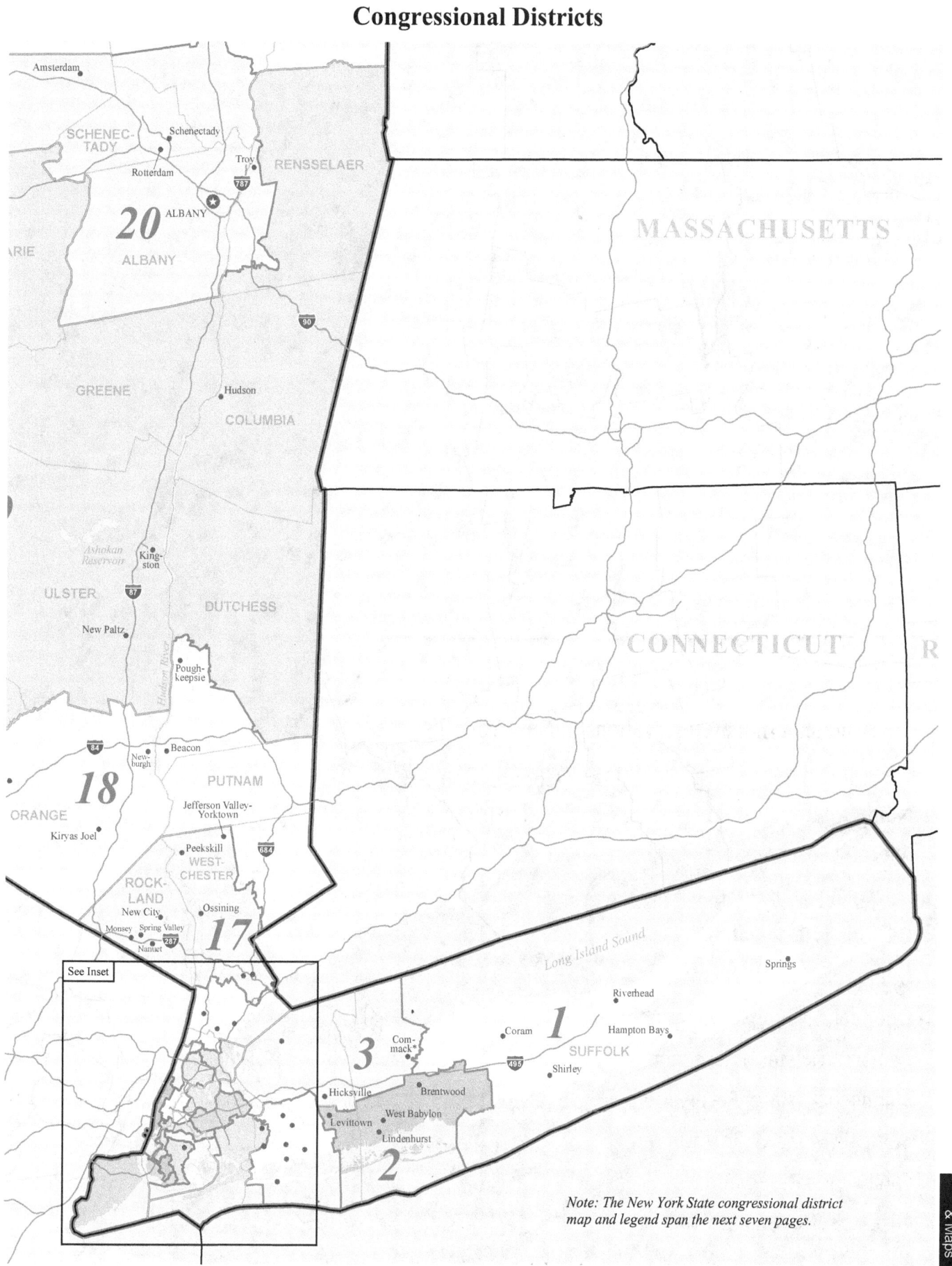

*Note: The New York State congressional district map and legend span the next seven pages.*

585

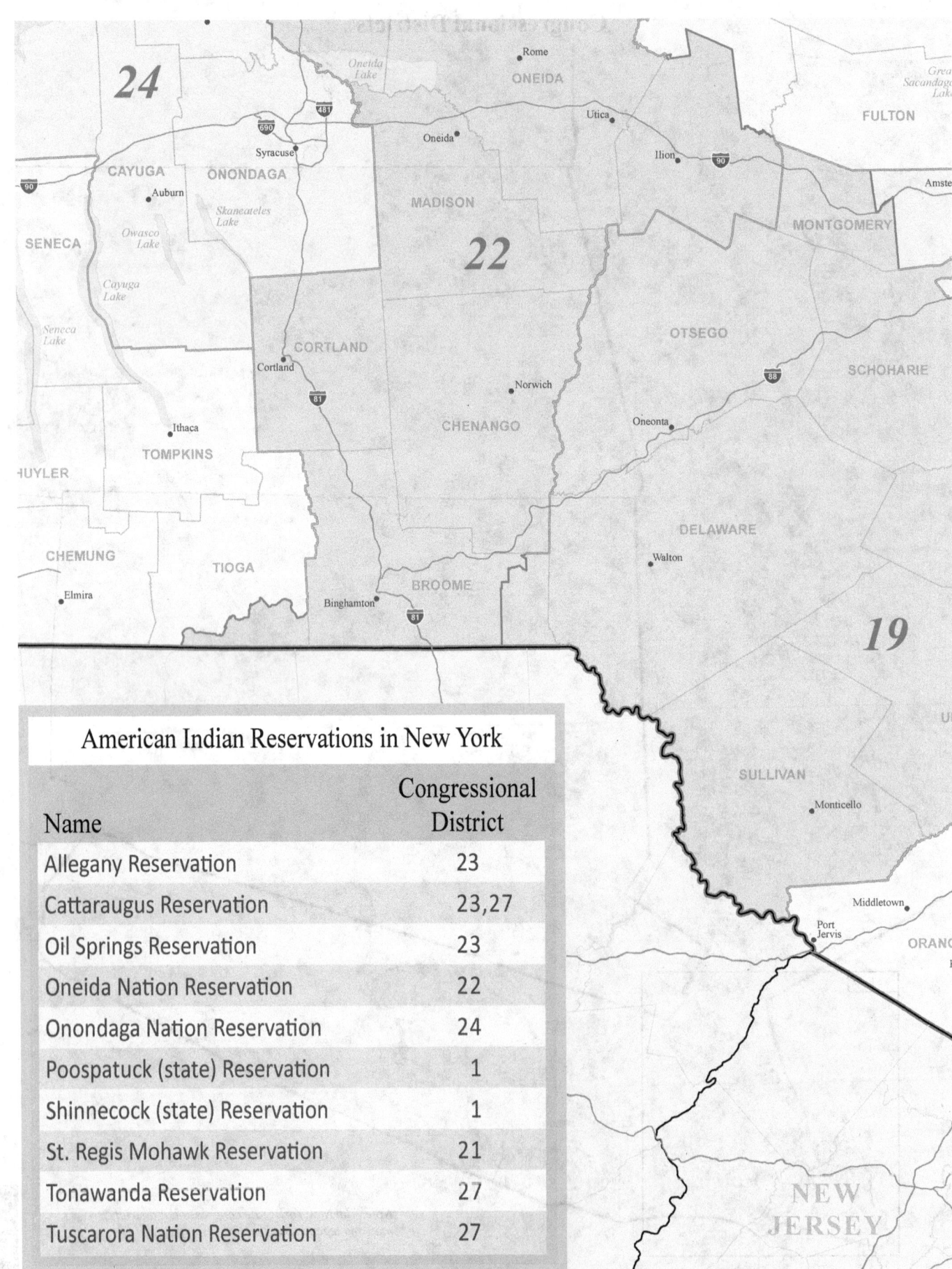

American Indian Reservations in New York

| Name | Congressional District |
|---|---|
| Allegany Reservation | 23 |
| Cattaraugus Reservation | 23,27 |
| Oil Springs Reservation | 23 |
| Oneida Nation Reservation | 22 |
| Onondaga Nation Reservation | 24 |
| Poospatuck (state) Reservation | 1 |
| Shinnecock (state) Reservation | 1 |
| St. Regis Mohawk Reservation | 21 |
| Tonawanda Reservation | 27 |
| Tuscarora Nation Reservation | 27 |

Lake Ontario

*25*

NIAGARA

ORLEANS

MONROE

Niagara
Falls*

Lockport

Irondequoit

Rochester
Brighton

North
Tonawanda

490

190    290    990

GENESEE

90

490

*26*

Buffalo*

Cheektowaga

190

*27*

Batavia

Canandaigua

ONTARIO

Geneseo

ERIE

WYOMING

LIVING-
STON

390

Canandai
Lake

Lake Erie

90

Dunkirk

Fredonia

CHAUTAUQUA

Chautauqua
Lake

CATTARAUGUS

ALLEGANY

Hornell

STEUBEN

86

Salamanca

86

*23*

Jamestown

Olean

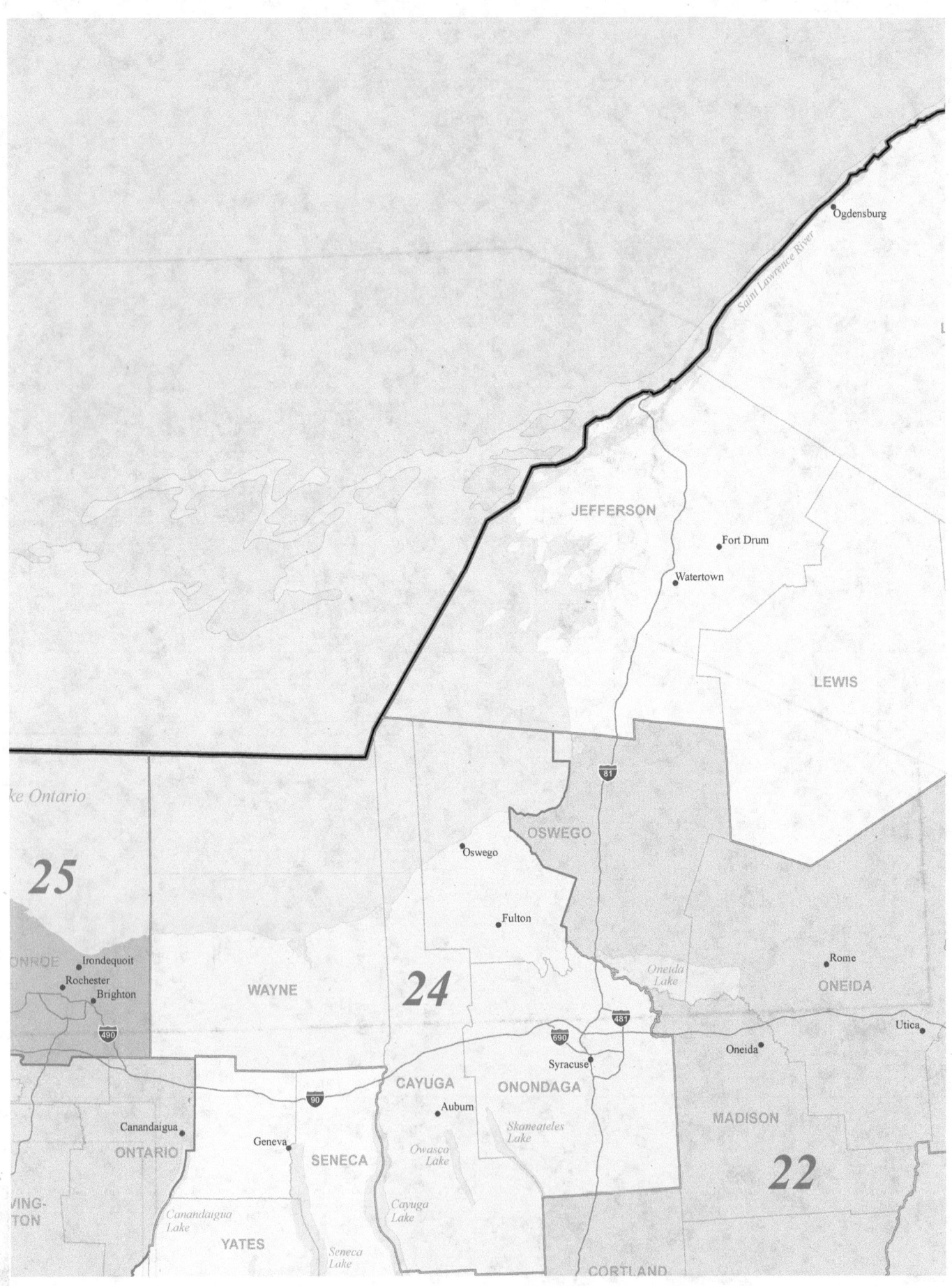

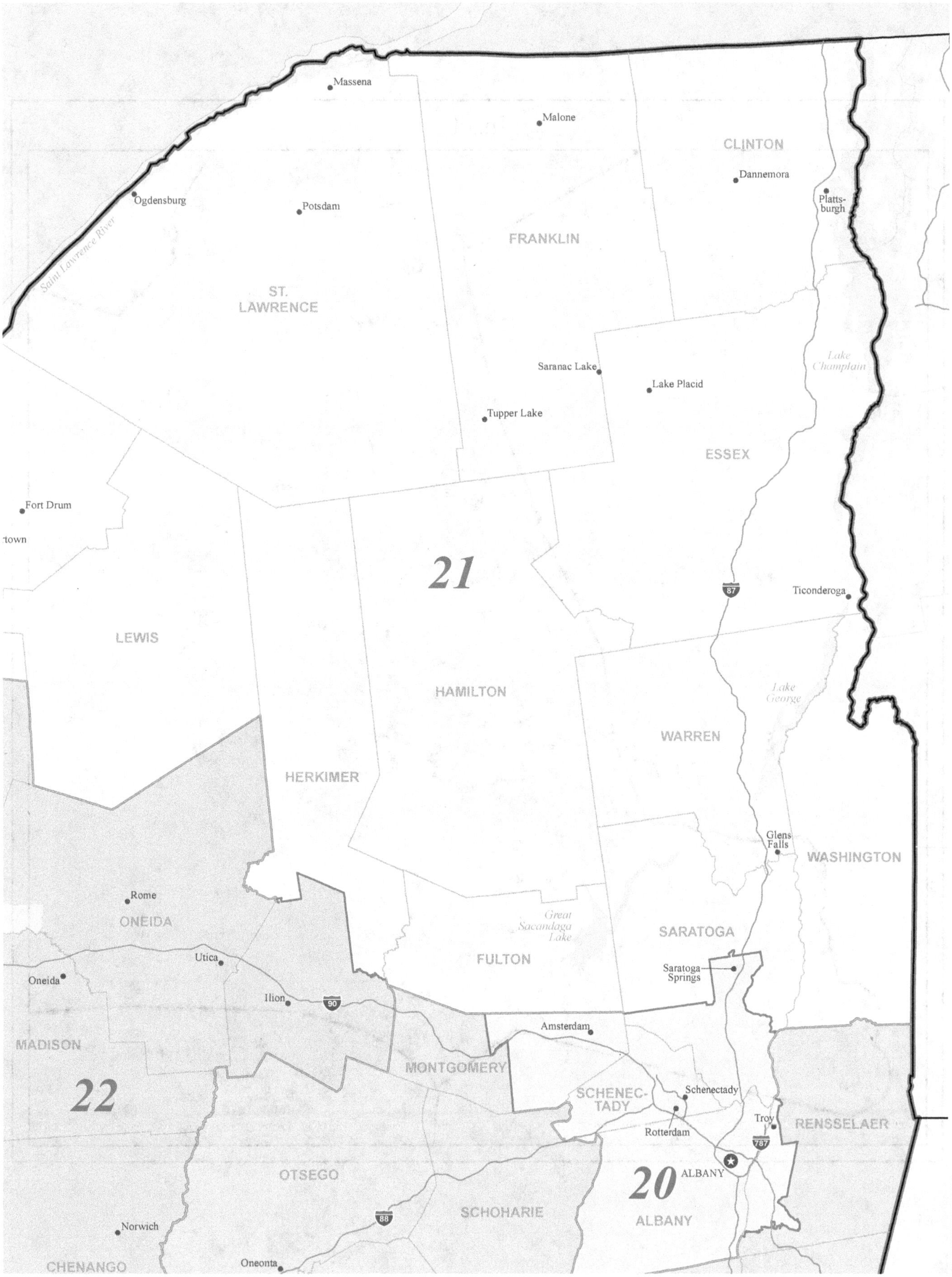
Massena
Malone
CLINTON
Dannemora
Ogdensburg
Potsdam
Platts-
burgh
Saint Lawrence River
FRANKLIN
ST.
LAWRENCE
Lake
Champlain
Saranac Lake
Lake Placid
Tupper Lake
ESSEX
Fort Drum
town
21
87
Ticonderoga
LEWIS
HAMILTON
Lake
George
WARREN
HERKIMER
Glens
Falls
WASHINGTON
Rome
ONEIDA
Great
Sacandaga
Lake
SARATOGA
Utica
FULTON
Oneida
Saratoga
Springs
Ilion
90
Amsterdam
MADISON
MONTGOMERY
22
SCHENEC-
TADY
Schenectady
Troy
RENSSELAER
Rotterdam
787
OTSEGO
20
ALBANY
Norwich
88
SCHOHARIE
ALBANY
CHENANGO
Oneonta

## Inset

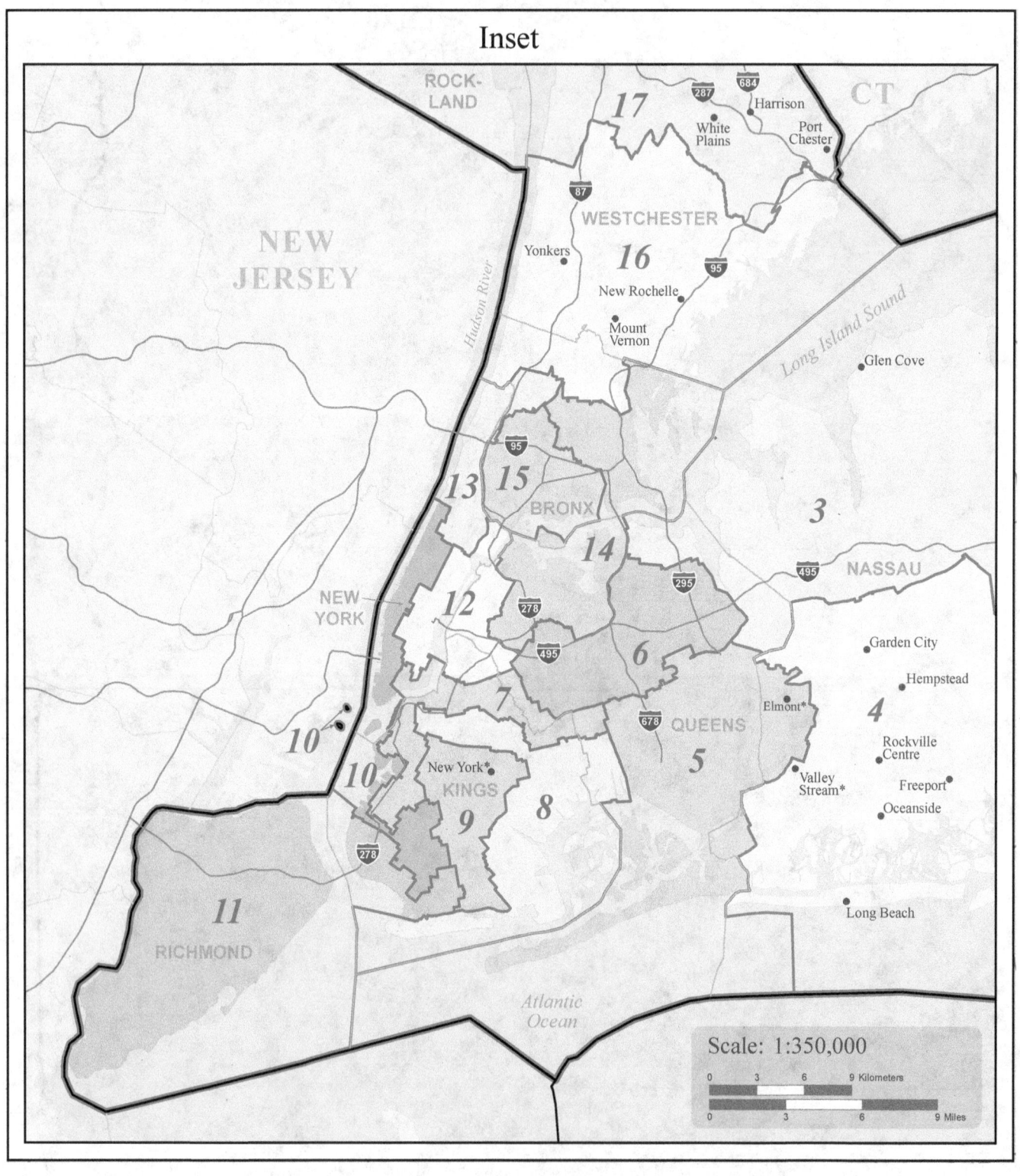

ROCK-
LAND

17

CT

287 684

Harrison

White
Plains

Port
Chester

87

WESTCHESTER

16

NEW
JERSEY

Yonkers

95

New Rochelle

Mount
Vernon

Hudson River

Long Island Sound

Glen Cove

13

15

95

BRONX

3

14

NASSAU

495

295

12

278

Garden City

NEW
YORK

495

6

Hempstead

4

7

678

QUEENS

Elmont*

Rockville
Centre

5

10

New York*

Valley
Stream*

Freeport

Oceanside

10

KINGS

9

8

11

278

RICHMOND

Long Beach

Atlantic
Ocean

Scale: 1:350,000

| 0 | 3 | 6 | 9 Kilometers |
| 0 | 3 | 6 | 9 Miles |

# Map Legend

| | | | |
|---|---|---|---|
| _2_ | Congressional District Boundary | ★ OLYMPIA | State Capital |
| | Congressional District Area | • Collinsville | Selected Place[†] |
| KANSAS | State or Statistically Equivalent Entity | _Lake Champlain_ | Water Body |
| ERIE | County or Statistically Equivalent Entity | 44 | Interstate Highway |

[†]Labels for places located within more than one Congressional District include a '*'.

Congressional districts are those in effect for the 117th Congress of the United States (January 2021-2023); all other legal boundaries and names are as of January 1, 2010. The boundaries shown on this map are for Census Bureau statistical data collection and tabulation purposes only; their depiction and designation for statistical purposes does not constitute a determination of jurisdictional authority or rights of ownership or entitlement.

Source: U.S. Census Bureau's MAF/TIGER database (TAB10)
Projection: State-based Alber's Equal Area

For general information, contact the Congressional Affairs Office at (301) 763-6100. For more information regarding congressional district plans as a result of the 2010 Census, redistricting, and voting rights data, contact the Census Redistricting and Voting Rights Data Office at (301) 763-4039 or www.census.gov/rdo. For information regarding other U.S. Census Bureau products, visit www.census.gov.

## Population

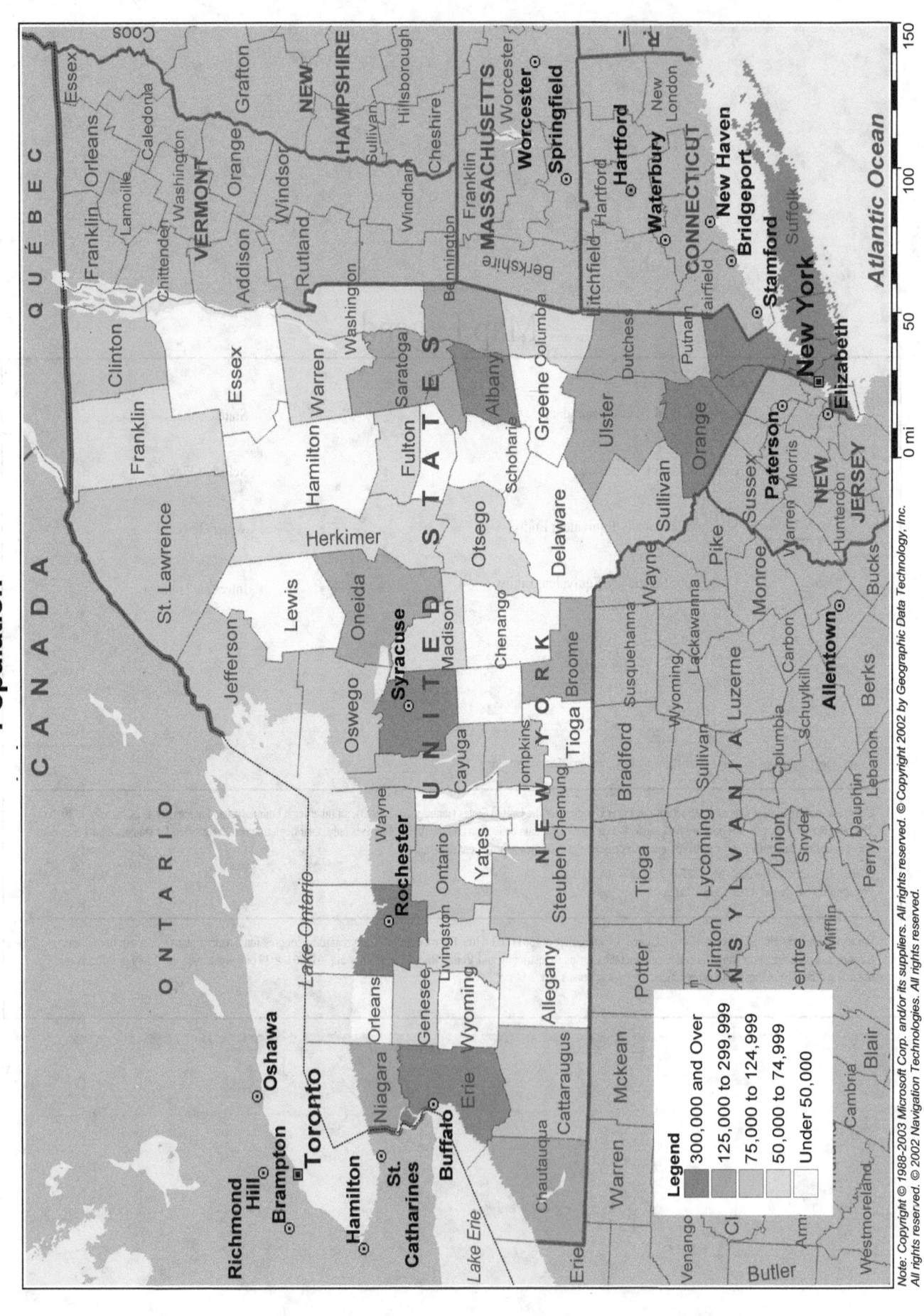

Legend
- 300,000 and Over
- 125,000 to 299,999
- 75,000 to 124,999
- 50,000 to 74,999
- Under 50,000

## Percent White

**Legend**
- 95.0 and Over
- 90.0 to 94.9
- 85.0 to 89.9
- 80.0 to 84.9
- Under 80.0

0 mi   50   100   150

## Percent Black

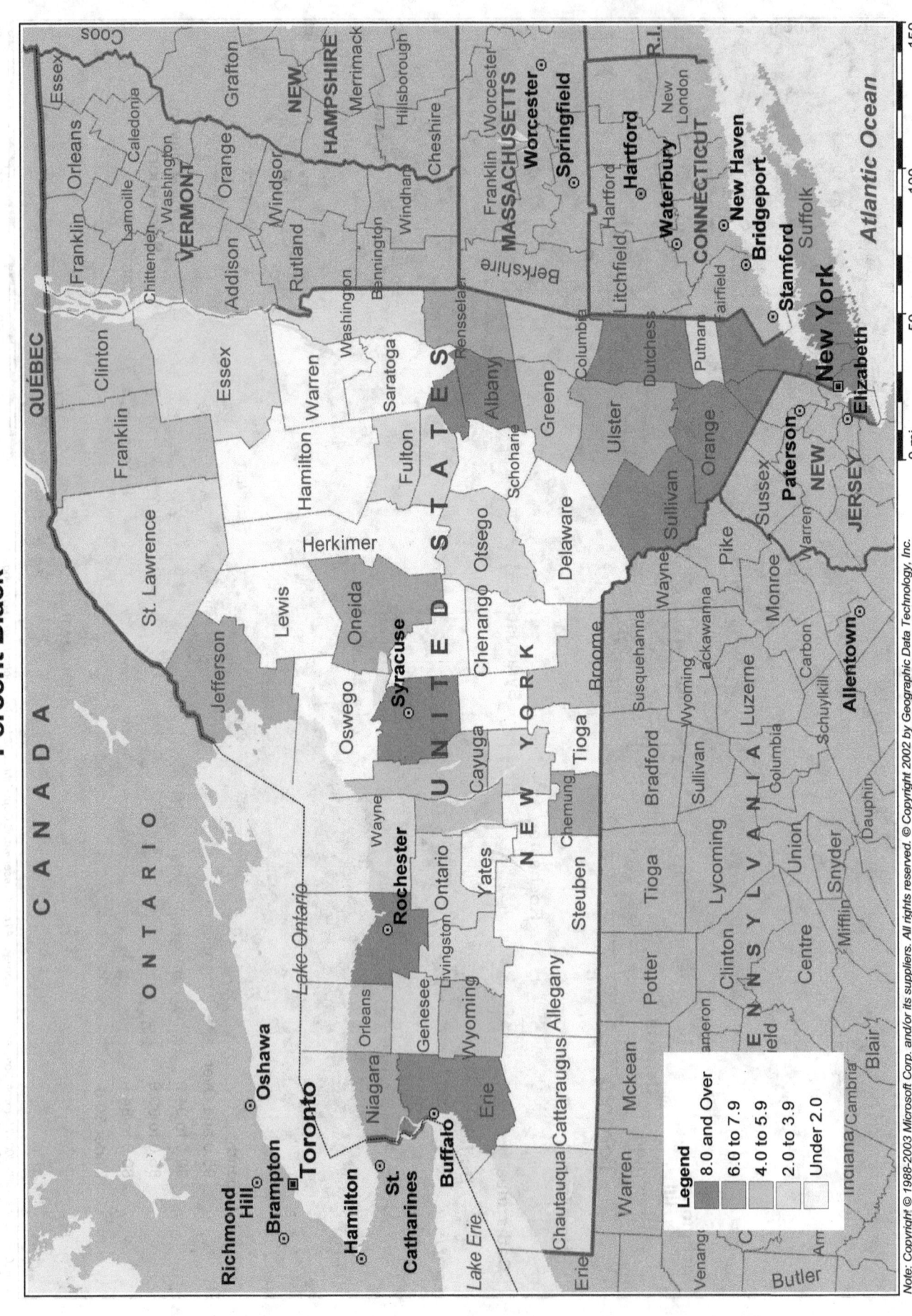

**Legend**
8.0 and Over
6.0 to 7.9
4.0 to 5.9
2.0 to 3.9
Under 2.0

# Percent Asian

Appendices: Financial Plan & Maps

## Percent Hispanic

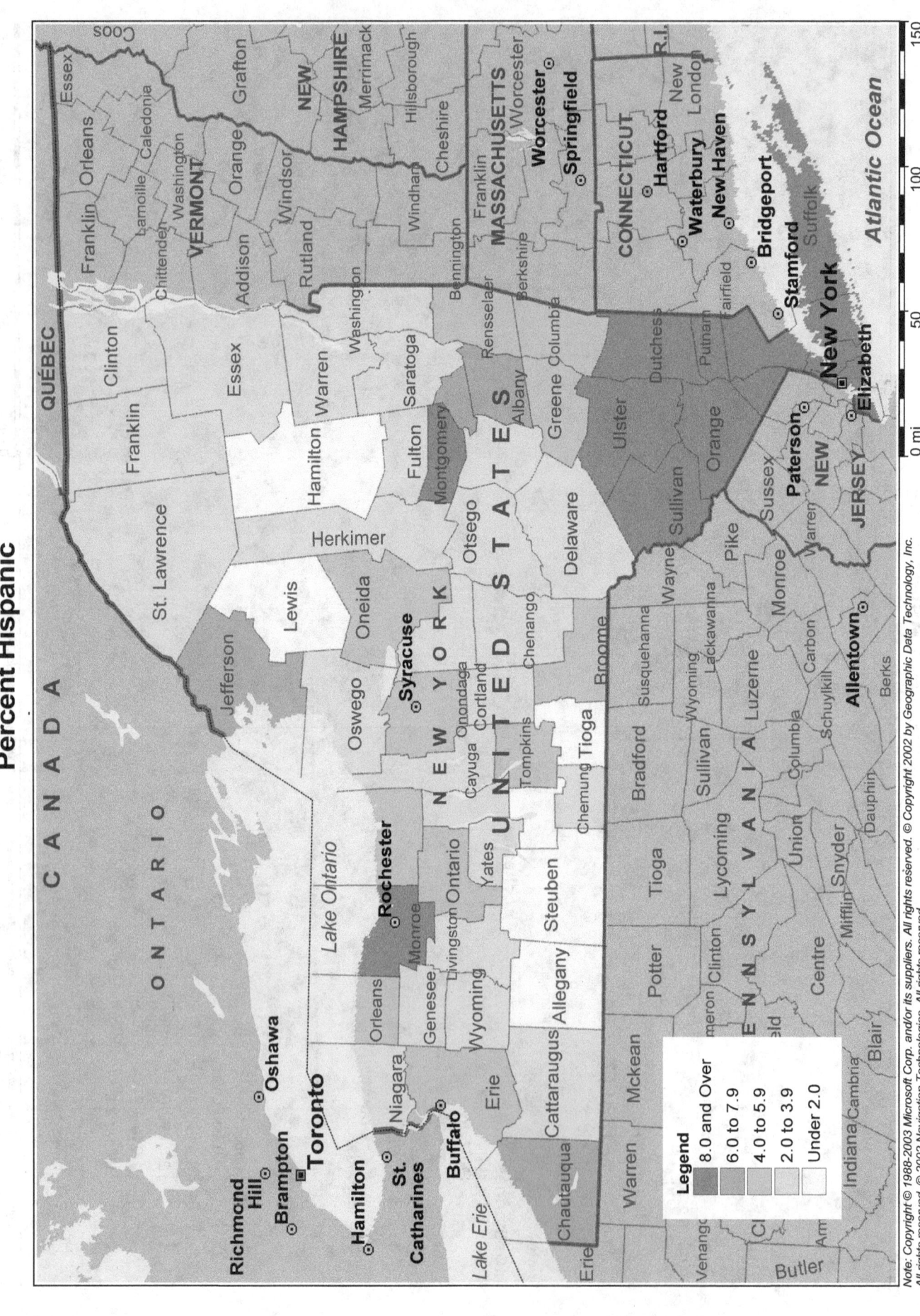

**Legend**
- 8.0 and Over
- 6.0 to 7.9
- 4.0 to 5.9
- 2.0 to 3.9
- Under 2.0

## Median Age

**Legend**
- 44.0 and Over
- 42.0 to 43.9
- 40.0 to 41.9
- 38.0 to 39.9
- Under 38.0

# Median Household Income

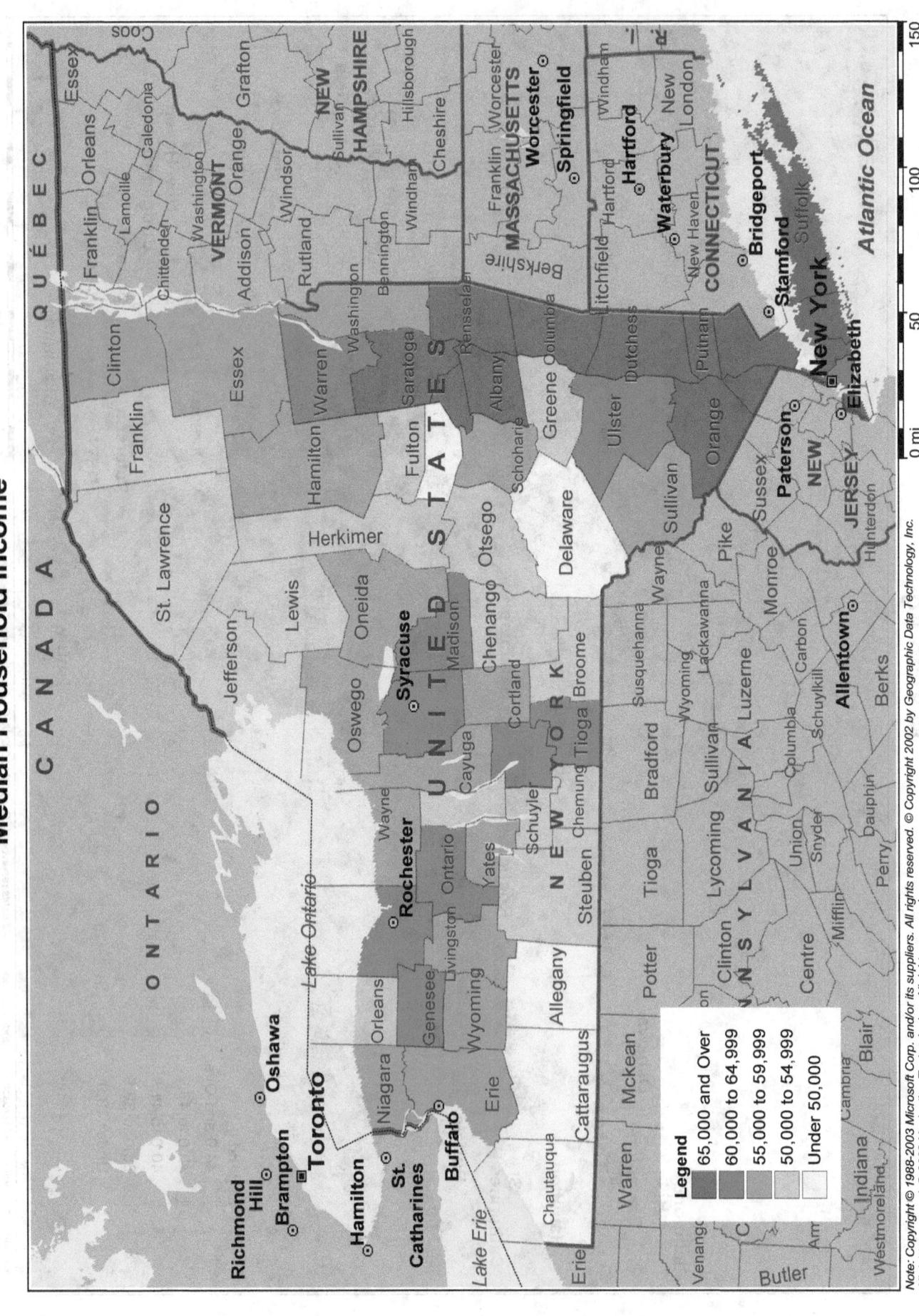

**Legend**

- 65,000 and Over
- 60,000 to 64,999
- 55,000 to 59,999
- 50,000 to 54,999
- Under 50,000

## Median Home Value

**Legend**

- 200,000 and Over
- 175,000 to 199,999
- 150,000 to 174,999
- 125,000 to 149,999
- 100,000 to 124,999
- Under 100,000

## High School Graduates*

**Legend**

- 92.0 and Over
- 90.0 to 91.9
- 88.0 to 89.9
- 86.0 to 87.9
- Under 86.0

## College Graduates*

CANADA

QUÉBEC

Coos

Essex

Franklin
Orleans
Caledonia

VERMONT

NEW
HAMPSHIRE

Lamoille
Washington
Orange
Grafton

Merrimack
Hillsborough

Chittenden
Windsor

Cheshire

Addison
Washington

MASSACHUSETTS

Franklin

Worcester

**Worcester**

**Springfield**

Rutland
Bennington

Berkshire

Hampshire

**Hartford**

Hartford

Windham

New
London

CONNECTICUT

**Waterbury**

Middlesex

**Bridgeport**

ONTARIO

Clinton

Franklin

Essex

Warren

Saratoga

Washington

Rensselaer

Litchfield

Putnam

**Stamford**

Suffolk

St. Lawrence

Hamilton

Fulton
Montgomery

Albany

Greene
Columbia

Dutchess

Orange

**New York**

Atlantic Ocean

Herkimer

Otsego

Delaware

Ulster

Sussex

**Paterson**

**Elizabeth**

Jefferson

Lewis

Oneida

Madison

Chenango

Sullivan

Pike

Warren

NEW
JERSEY

NEW YORK

Oswego

Onondaga

Cortland

Tioga

Broome

Susquehanna

Wayne

Monroe

Lackawanna

Carbon

**Allentown**

UNITED STATES

**Syracuse**

Cayuga

Tompkins

Chemung
Tioga

Bradford

Wyoming

Luzerne

Columbia

Schuylkill

Berks

Lake Ontario

Wayne

Ontario

Livingston

Steuben

Sullivan

**Rochester**

Lycoming

Union

Snyder

Dauphin

Oshawa

Genesee

Wyoming

Allegany

Tioga

PENNSYLVANIA

Perry

Orleans

Potter

Clinton

Mifflin

**Toronto**

Niagara

Erie

Cattaraugus

Mckean

Centre

**Richmond
Hill**

**Brampton**

**Hamilton**

**St.
Catharines**

**Buffalo**

Chautauqua

Warren

Indiana/Cambria

Blair

Lake Erie

Chemung

Venango

Cl

Arm

Butler

Westmoreland

Erie

Legend

- 30.0 and Over
- 26.0 to 29.9
- 22.0 to 25.9
- 18.0 to 21.9
- Under 18.0

150

100

50

0 mi

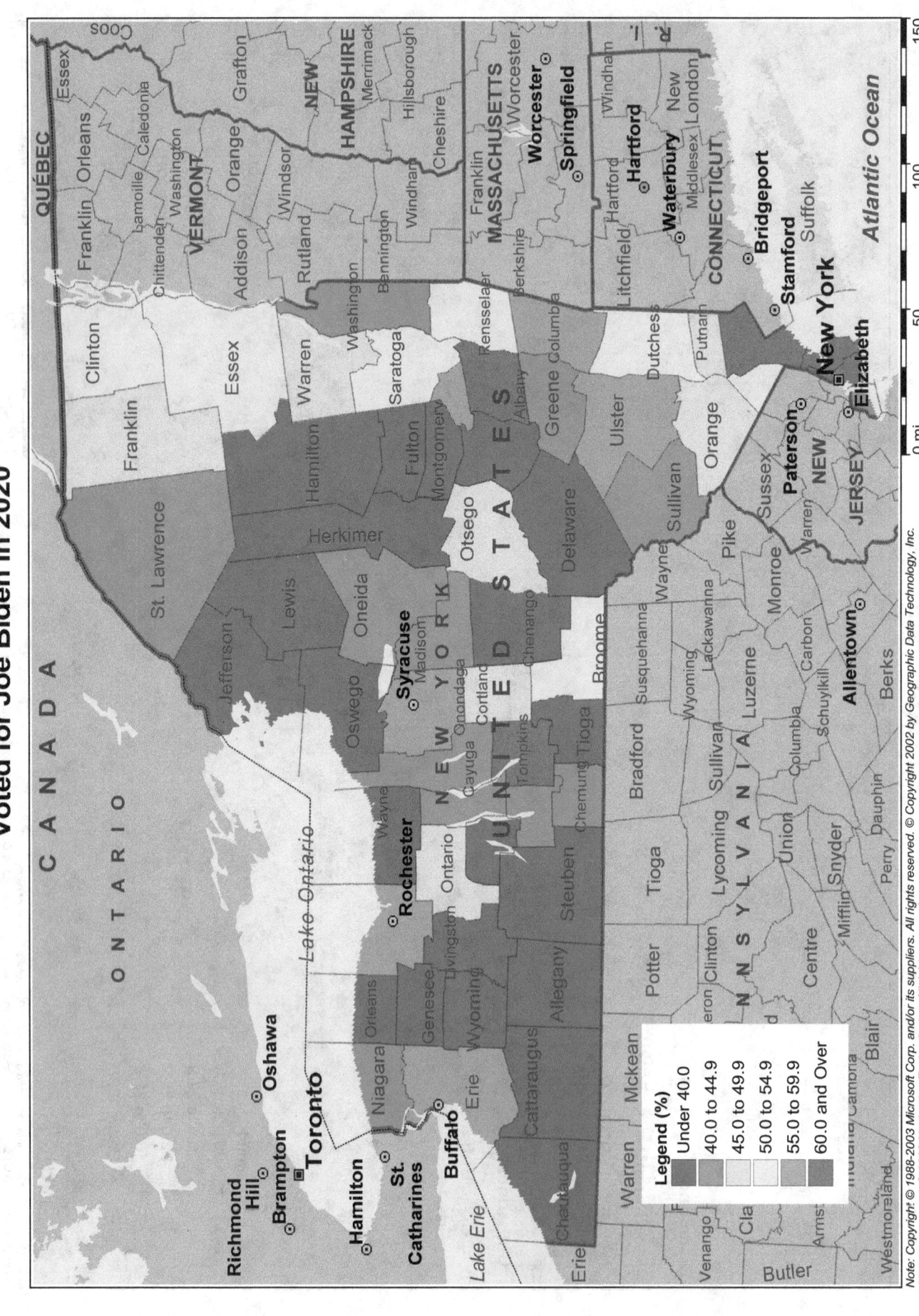

## Voted for Joe Biden in 2020

**Legend (%)**
- Under 40.0
- 40.0 to 44.9
- 45.0 to 49.9
- 50.0 to 54.9
- 55.0 to 59.9
- 60.0 and Over

# NEW YORK - Core Based Statistical Areas (CBSAs) and Counties

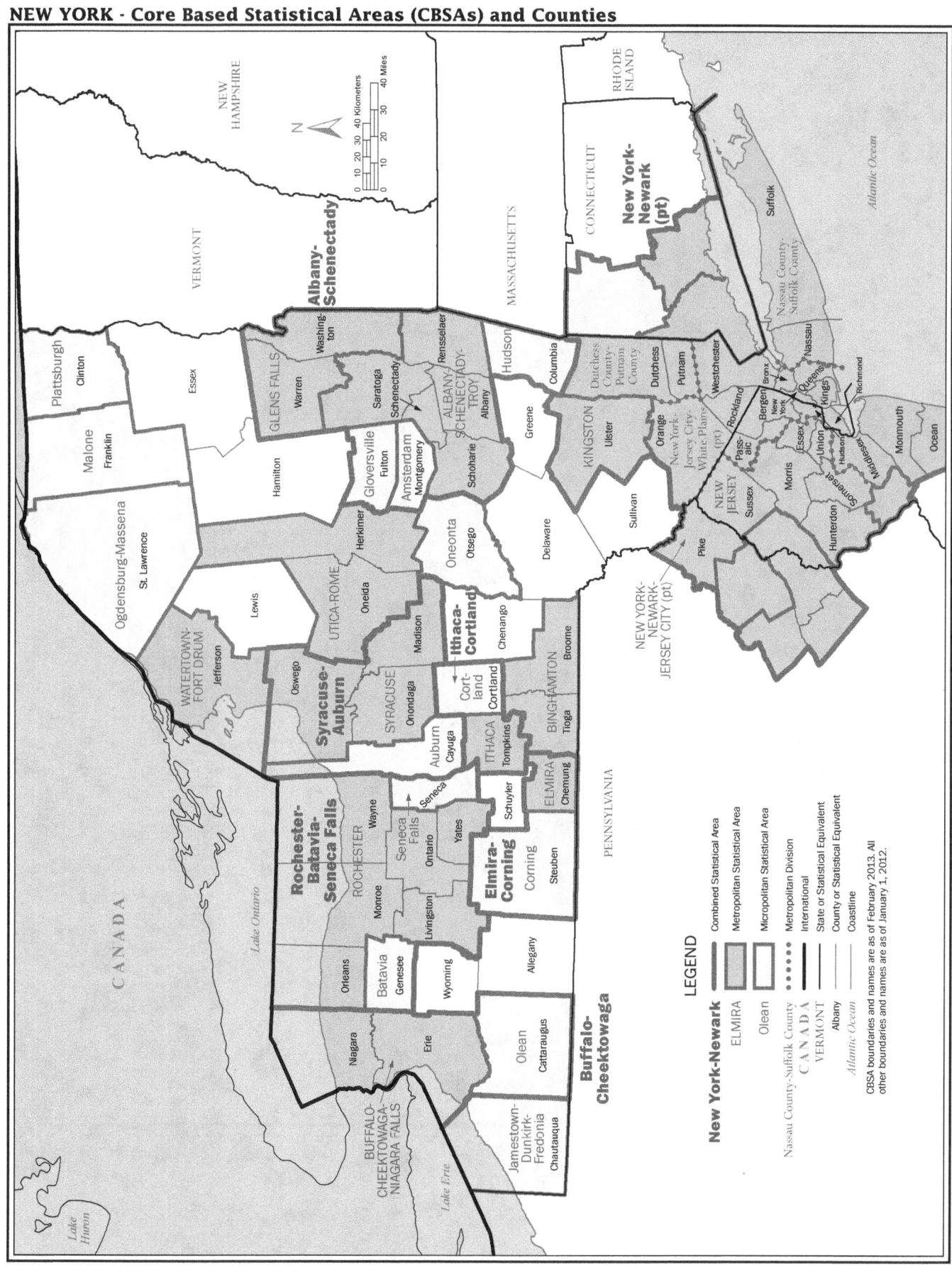

# Name Index

# Name Index

# Organization Index

*Includes the names of the top three levels in all New York State executive departments and agencies; public corporations; authorities; commissions; all organizations listed in the Private Sector sources segment of each policy chapter; lobbyist organizations; political action committees; chambers of commerce; newspapers; news services; radio and television stations; SUNY and CUNY locations; and private colleges.*

# Geographic Index

*Includes the names of the top three levels in all New York State executive departments and agencies; public corporations; authorities; commissions; all organizations listed in the Private Sector sources segment of each policy chapter; lobbyist organizations; political action committees; chambers of commerce; newspapers; news services; radio and television stations; SUNY and CUNY locations; and private colleges.*

*Listings appear in alphabetical order by state, then city.*

*Listings appear in alphabetical order by state, then city.*

# New York

*Listings appear in alphabetical order by state, then city.*

*Listings appear in alphabetical order by state, then city.*

*Listings appear in alphabetical order by state, then city.*

*Listings appear in alphabetical order by state, then city.*

*Listings appear in alphabetical order by state, then city.*

# Geographic Index

Lysander, Town of, 344
WSEN (92.1 FM), 427

**Ballston Spa**
Ballston Spa CSD, 478
Elections, State Board of
*Saratoga, 133*
Saratoga County, 331
*Family Court, 55*
*Supreme, County & Surrogate's Courts, 55*
Saratoga County Industrial Development Agency, 408
US Transportation Department
*Highway-Rail Grade Crossing, 285*
Veterans' Service Organizations
*Saratoga Cnty Rural Preservation Co (Homeless Veterans), 290*

**Barker**
Barker CSD, 472

**Barrytown**
Unification Theological Seminary, 453

**Batavia**
Albany (Northern Region)
*Batavia (Western Region), 242*
Batavia
*Civil & Criminal Courts, 58*
Batavia City SD, 465
Elections, State Board of
*Genesee, 130*
Genesee Community College, 439
Genesee County, 325
*Supreme, County, Family & Surrogate's Courts, 51*
Genesee County Chamber of Commerce, 400
Genesee County Economic Development Center, 400
Health Department
*New York State Veterans' Home at Batavia, 172, 289*
Mancuso Business Development Group, 244
My-T Acres Inc, 73
NYS Vegetable Growers Association Inc, 73
Real Property Tax Services, Office of
*Batavia (Western Region), 232, 260*
US Department of Veterans Affairs
*Batavia VA Medical Center, 292*
Western Regional Off-Track Betting Corp, 104, 270

**Bath**
Bath Area Chamber of Commerce (Greater Bath Area), 395
Bath CSD, 480
Elections, State Board of
*Steuben, 133*
Steuben County, 332
*Supreme, County, Family & Surrogate's Courts, 56*

Steuben County Industrial Development Agency, 410
US Department of Veterans Affairs
*Bath National Cemetery, 291*
*Bath VA Medical Center, 292*
WCIK (103.1 FM), 427

**Bay Shore**
NYSTAR - Division of Science, Technology & Innovation
*Long Island Forum for Technology, 83*

**Bayport**
Bayport-Blue Point UFSD, 480

**Bayshore**
Bay Shore UFSD, 480
Bayshore Chamber of Commerce, 396

**Bayside**
Friends of Austin Shafran, 375
New Yorkers For Katz, 383
Queensborough Community College, 443
Silverstein 2013, 386

**Beacon**
Antalek & Moore Insurance Agency, 78
Beacon
*Civil & Criminal Courts, 58*
Beacon City SD, 463
Corrections & Community Supervision Department
*Beacon Correctional Facility, 106*
*Fishkill Correctional Facility, 107*
Hudson River Sloop Clearwater Inc, 155
WHUD (100.7 FM), 429
WSPK (104.7 FM), 427

**Bear Mountain**
Parks, Recreation & Historic Preservation, NYS Office of
*Palisades Region, 268*

**Beaver Dams**
Corrections & Community Supervision Department
*Monterey Shock Incarceration Correctional Facility, 107*

**Beaver Falls**
Beaver River CSD, 467

**Bedford Hills**
Corrections & Community Supervision Department
*Bedford Hills Correctional Facility, 107*
*Taconic Correctional Facility, 108*
McDonald 2013, 382

**Belfast**
Belfast CSD, 458

**Bellerose**
Mental Health, Office of

*NYC Children's Center - Queens Campus, 226*

**Belleville**
Belleville Henderson CSD, 467

**Bellmore**
Bellmore UFSD, 469
Nassau Council of Chambers, 405
North Bellmore UFSD, 471

**Belmont**
Allegany County, 321
*Supreme, County, Family & Surrogate's Courts, 48*
Allegany County Office of Development & Industrial Development Agency (IDA), 395
Elections, State Board of
*Allegany, 128*
Genesee Valley CSD, 458

**Bemus Point**
Bemus Point CSD, 460

**Bergen**
Byron-Bergen CSD, 466

**Berlin**
Berlin CSD, 477

**Berne**
Berne-Knox-Westerlo CSD, 458

**Bethpage**
Bethpage Chamber of Commerce, 396
Bethpage UFSD, 469
Briarcliffe College-Bethpage, 454
Cablevision Systems Corporation, 141
Cablevision Systems New York PAC, 372
NYSTAR - Division of Science, Technology & Innovation
*Long Island Forum for Technology, 121*
US Department of Homeland Security (DHS)
*New York Asylum Office, 165, 193*

**Binghamton, 204**
Binghamton
*Civil & Criminal Courts, 59*
Binghamton Chamber of Commerce (Greater Binghamton), 396
Binghamton City SD, 459
Binghamton University, State University of New York, 436
Binghamton, City of, 337
Broome Community College, 438
Broome County, 321
*County, Family, 49*
*Surrogate & Supreme Court, 49*
Broome County Industrial Development Agency, 396
Broome-Delaware-Tioga BOCES, 488
Chenango Forks CSD, 459

*Listings appear in alphabetical order by state, then city.*

718

*Listings appear in alphabetical order by state, then city.*

*Listings appear in alphabetical order by state, then city.*

*Listings appear in alphabetical order by state, then city.*

**Camillus**
West Genesee CSD, 474

**Campbell**
Campbell-Savona CSD, 480

**Canaan**
Berkshire Farm Center & Services for Youth, 114, 252
Berkshire UFSD, 462

**Canajoharie**
Canajoharie CSD, 469

**Canandaigua**
Canandaigua
  *Civil & Criminal Courts, 59*
Canandaigua Area Chamber of Commerce, 397
Canandaigua City SD, 474
Canandaigua National Bank & Trust Co, 78
Convention Centers & Visitors Bureaus
  *Ontario County/Finger Lakes Visitors Connection, 271*
Daily Messenger (The), 418
Elections, State Board of
  *Ontario, 132*
Finger Lakes Community College, 439
Messenger Post Newspapers, 418
New York Wine & Grape Foundation, 74, 277
Ontario County, 328
  *Supreme, County, Family & Surrogate's Courts, 54*
Ontario County Industrial Development Agency & Economic Development, 406
US Department of Agriculture
  *Canandaigua Work Station, 69*
US Department of Veterans Affairs
  *Canandaigua VA Medical Center, 292*

**Canaseraga**
Canaseraga CSD, 458

**Canastota**
Canastota CSD, 468
Canastota Chamber of Commerce, 397
Madison County Industrial Development Agency, 404

**Candor**
Candor CSD, 483
NY Farms!, 73

**Canisteo**
Canisteo-Greenwood CSD, 480

**Canton**
Canton CSD, 479
Canton Chamber of Commerce, 397
Elections, State Board of
  *Saint Lawrence, 133*
North Country Savings Bank, 80
St Lawrence County, 332

*Supreme, County, Family & Surrogate's Courts, 55*
St Lawrence County Chamber of Commerce, 410
St Lawrence County Industrial Development Agency, 410
St Lawrence University, 452
St Lawrence-Lewis BOCES, 489
State University College of Technology at Canton, 438

**Cape Vincent**
Cape Vincent Chamber of Commerce, 397
Corrections & Community Supervision Department
  *Cape Vincent Correctional Facility, 107*

**Carle Place**
Carle Place UFSD, 469

**Carmel**
Elections, State Board of
  *Putnam, 132*
Putnam County, 330
  *Supreme, County & Family Courts, 54*
  *Surrogate's Court, 54*
Putnam County Economic Development Corporation, 407

**Caroga Lake**
Wheelerville UFSD, 465

**Carthage**
Carthage Area Chamber of Commerce, 397
Carthage CSD, 467

**Castile**
Parks, Recreation & Historic Preservation, NYS Office of
  *Genesee Region, 268*

**Castle Point**
US Department of Veterans Affairs
  *Castle Point Campus of the VA Hudson Vly Healthcare System, 292*

**Castleton**
Rensselaer-Columbia-Greene (Questar III) BOCES, 489
Schodack CSD, 477

**Cato**
Cato-Meridian CSD, 460

**Catskill**
Catskill CSD, 466
Daily Mail (The), 418
Elections, State Board of
  *Greene, 130*
Greene County, 325
  *Supreme, County, Family & Surrogate's Courts, 51*
Greene County Department of Planning & Economic Development, 401
Hudson Valley Newspapers Inc, 418

**Cazenovia**
Cazenovia Area Chamber of Commerce (Greater Cazenovia Area), 397
Cazenovia CSD, 468
Cazenovia College, 445

**Center Moriches**
Center Moriches UFSD, 481

**Centereach**
Middle Country CSD, 482

**Central Islip**
Central Islip UFSD, 481
Suffolk County
  *1st District Court, Criminal Term, 58*
US Justice Department
  *Central Islip, 113, 210*

**Central Square**
Central Square CSD, 476

**Central Valley**
Monroe-Woodbury CSD, 475

**Champlain**
Northeastern Clinton CSD, 461
US Department of Agriculture
  *Champlain Work Station, 69*
US Department of Homeland Security (DHS)
  *Champlain, Port of, 70, 164, 165, 262*
WCHP (760 AM), 427

**Chappaqua**
Chappaqua CSD, 486

**Chateaugay**
Chateaugay CSD, 465
Corrections & Community Supervision Department
  *Chateaugay Correctional Facility, 107*

**Chatham**
Chatham CSD, 462

**Chaumont**
Lyme CSD, 467

**Chautauqua**
Convention Centers & Visitors Bureaus
  *Chautauqua County Visitors Bureau, 270*

**Chazy**
Chazy Central RSD, 461

**Cheektowaga**
Automotive Technology & Energy Group of Western NY, 286
Cheektowaga CSD, 463
Cheektowaga Chamber of Commerce, 397
Cheektowaga, Town of, 338
Cheektowaga-Maryvale CSD, 464
Cleveland Hill UFSD, 463
US Treasury Department

*Listings appear in alphabetical order by state, then city.*

**Farmingdale**
Farmingdale State College of Technology, 438
Farmingdale UFSD, 470
US Department of Veterans Affairs
*Long Island National Cemetery, 291*

**Farmington**
Farmington Chamber of Commerce, 399
Finger Lakes Racing Association, 274
Northeast Organic Farming Association of New York, 74

**Farmingville**
Brookhaven, Town of, 337
Town of Brookhaven Industrial Development Agency, 396

**Fayetteville**
Farmers' Market Federation of NY, 72
Fayetteville Chamber of Commerce, 400
Manlius, Town of, 344
The Greater Manlius Chamber of Commerce, 401

**Ferndale**
Convention Centers & Visitors Bureaus
*Sullivan County Visitors Association, 271*
Sullivan County Industrial Development Agency, 410

**Fillmore**
Fillmore CSD, 458

**Findley Lake**
Findley Lake Area Chamber of Commerce, 400

**Fishers**
New York Apple Association Inc, 74

**Fishers Island**
Fishers Island UFSD, 481

**Fishkill**
Corrections & Community Supervision Department
*Downstate Correctional Facility, 107*
Fishkill, Town of, 340
New York State Gaming Commission
*Hudson Valley Region, 260*

**Floral Park**
Floral Park-Bellerose UFSD, 470
Friends of Harpreet, 376
New Yorkers For Affordable Housing, 383
Sewanhaka Central HS District, 471

**Florida**
Florida UFSD, 475

**Flushing**
CIDNY - Queens, 253
Evergreen For City Council, 374
Friends For Peter Koo, 375

Friends of John Liu, 376
Friends of Michael Simanowitz, 377
He Gin Lee Committee to Elect For Mayor, 378
International Union of Operating Engineers Local 14-14B Voluntary Political Action Committee, 379
Long Island Business Institute-Flushing, 456
NYC Region 3, 472
New York City
*Environmental Protection, Department of, NYC, 348*
New York Mets, 276
Paul Graziano 2013, 384
Queens College, 443
Sasson For NYC, 386
Sunny Hahn For City Council, 387
Vaughn College of Aeronautics & Technology, 453
Vote Vallone 2013, 388

**Fonda**
Elections, State Board of
*Montgomery, 131*
Fonda-Fultonville CSD, 469
Montgomery County, 327
*Supreme, County, Family & Surrogate's Courts, 52*

**Forest Hills**
Bramson ORT College, 445
Elections, State Board of
*Queens, 131*
Local 1182 Political Action Fund, 380
Plaza College, 457
Re-Elect Koslowitz 2013, 385

**Forestville**
Forestville CSD, 460

**Fort Ann**
Fort Ann CSD, 485

**Fort Covington**
Salmon River CSD, 465

**Fort Drum**
US Defense Department
*Fort Drum, 291*

**Fort Edward**
Elections, State Board of
*Washington, 134*
Fort Edward Chamber of Commerce, 400
Fort Edward UFSD, 485
Washington County, 334
*Supreme, County, Family & Surrogate's Courts, 57*
Washington County Local Development Corporation, 411
Washington-Saratoga-Warren-Hamilton-Essex BOCES, 490

**Fort Plain**
Fort Plain CSD, 469

**Frankfort**
Frankfort-Schuyler CSD, 466

**Franklin**
Franklin CSD, 462

**Franklin Square**
Franklin Square Chamber of Commerce, 400
Franklin Square UFSD, 470

**Franklinville**
Franklinville CSD, 459

**Fredonia**
Fredonia CSD, 460
Fredonia Chamber of Commerce, 400

**Freeport**
Freeport UFSD, 470
Freeport, Village of, 340

**Freeville**
George Junior Republic UFSD, 484

**Fresh Meadows**
Blishteyn For NYC, 371

**Frewsburg**
Frewsburg CSD, 460

**Friendship**
Friendship CSD, 458

**Fulton**
Fulton
*Civil & Criminal Courts, 59*
Fulton City SD, 476

**Gainesville**
Letchworth CSD, 488

**Galway**
Galway CSD, 478

**Garden City**
Adelphi NY Statewide Breast Cancer Hotline & Support Program, 177
Adelphi University, 444
Automobile Club of New York, 273, 286
Cullen & Dykman LLP, 222, 235
Education Department
*Garden City District Office, 119*
Garden City Chamber of Commerce, 400
Garden City UFSD, 470
Garden City, Village of, 340
Law Offices of Frank G. D'Angelo & Associates, 213
Meyer Suozzi English & Klein, PC, 213
NYS Bar Assn, Family Law Section, 215
NYS Bar Assn, General Practice Section, 213
NYS Bar Assn, Resolutions Committee, 213
Nassau BOCES, 489

*Listings appear in alphabetical order by state, then city.*

*Listings appear in alphabetical order by state, then city.*

*Listings appear in alphabetical order by state, then city.*

*Listings appear in alphabetical order by state, then city.*

*Listings appear in alphabetical order by state, then city.*

*Listings appear in alphabetical order by state, then city.*

*Listings appear in alphabetical order by state, then city.*

*Listings appear in alphabetical order by state, then city.*

*Listings appear in alphabetical order by state, then city.*

*Listings appear in alphabetical order by state, then city.*

*Listings appear in alphabetical order by state, then city.*

*Listings appear in alphabetical order by state, then city.*

*Listings appear in alphabetical order by state, then city.*

*Listings appear in alphabetical order by state, then city.*

*Listings appear in alphabetical order by state, then city.*

**Patterson**
Carmel CSD, 476
Patterson Chamber of Commerce, 407

**Pattersonville**
NYS Democratic Senate Campaign
Committee, 383

**Paul Smiths**
Paul Smith's College, 451

**Pavilion**
Pavilion CSD, 466

**Pawling**
Pawling CSD, 463

**Pearl River**
Orange & Rockland Utilities Inc, 143
Pearl River UFSD, 477
Rockland Economic Development
Corporation, 408

**Peekskill**
Hudson Valley Gateway Chamber of
Commerce, 402
Peekskill
*Civil & Criminal Courts, 61*
Peekskill City SD, 487
Peekskill Industrial Development Agency
(City of), 407
Peekskill, City of, 355
State Department
*Region 2 - Peekskill Office, 161*
Workers' Compensation Board
*Peekskill, 199, 218*

**Pelham**
Pelham UFSD, 487

**Penfield**
Penfield CSD, 469
Penfield, Town of, 356

**Penn Yan**
Elections, State Board of
*Yates, 134*
Finger Lakes Economic Development
Center, 412
Finger Lakes Tourism Alliance, 274
Penn Yan CSD, 488
Seneca Flight Operations, 288
Yates County, 335
*Supreme, County, Family & Surrogate's
Courts, 57*
Yates County Chamber of Commerce, 412

**Perry**
Perry Area Chamber of Commerce, 407
Perry CSD, 488
Wyoming County Chamber of Commerce,
412

**Perrysburg**
Garden Gate Greenhouse, 72

**Peru**
Peru CSD, 461

**Phelps**
Phelps Chamber of Commerce, 407

**Philadelphia**
Indian River CSD, 467

**Phoenix**
Phoenix CSD, 476

**Pine Bush**
Pine Bush CSD, 475

**Pine City**
Corrections & Community Supervision
Department
*Southport Correctional Facility, 108*

**Pine Plains**
Election Computer Services Inc, 136
Pine Plains CSD, 463

**Piseco**
Piseco Common SD, 466

**Pittsford**
Campground Owners of New York, 274
D H Ferguson, Attorney, PLLC, 244
Harris Beach LLP, 212
J J Higgins Properties Inc, 244
NYS Bar Assn, Real Property Law Section,
244
Pittsford CSD, 469
Pittsford, Town of, 356
Red Barn Properties, 245

**Plainview**
New York Islanders, 276
Plainview-Old Bethpage CSD, 471
Plainview-Old Bethpage Chamber of
Commerce, 407
WLIW (21) Public Broadcasting, 431

**Plattsburgh, 204**
American Military Retirees Association Inc,
293
Champlain Valley Educational Svcs
(Clinton-Essex-Warren-Washington), 488
Clinton Community College, 439
Clinton County, 323
*Supreme, County, Family & Surrogate's
Courts, 49*
Clinton County, The Development
Corporation, 398
Elections, State Board of
*Clinton, 129*
North Country Vietnam Veterans
Association, Post 1, 295
Plattsburgh
*Civil & Criminal Courts, 61*
Plattsburgh City SD, 461

Plattsburgh-North Country Chamber of
Commerce, 407
Press-Republican, 423
State University of New York at Plattsburgh,
438
US Justice Department
*Plattsburgh, 113, 210*
WPTZ (5) NBC, 431

**Pleasantville**
Mt Pleasant-Cottage UFSD, 487
Pleasantville UFSD, 487

**Poland**
Poland CSD, 467

**Pomona**
Catskill Off-Track Betting Corporation, 94,
269

**Port Byron**
Port Byron CSD, 460

**Port Chester**
Port Chester SD, 487
Port Chester, Village of, 356
Port Chester-Rye Brook Rye Town Chamber
of Commerce, 407
Rye, Town of, 358

**Port Henry**
Moriah CSD, 465

**Port Jefferson**
Brookhaven-Comsewogue UFSD, 481
Greater Port Jefferson Chamber of
Commerce, 401
Port Jefferson Chamber of Commerce, 407
Port Jefferson UFSD, 482

**Port Jervis**
Port Jervis
*Civil & Criminal Courts, 61*
Port Jervis City SD, 475

**Port Washington**
National Marfan Foundation, 181
North Shore Animal League America, 257
Port Washington Chamber of Commerce,
407
Port Washington UFSD, 471

**Portville**
Portville CSD, 459

**Potsdam**
Clarkson University, 445
NYSTAR - Division of Science, Technology
& Innovation
*Center for Advanced Materials Processing
at Clarkson Univ, 82, 120*
*Council for Interntl Trade, Tech,
Education & Communication, 83, 121*
Potsdam CSD, 480
Potsdam Chamber of Commerce, 407

*Listings appear in alphabetical order by state, then city.*

State University at Potsdam, 437

**Poughkeepsie, 204**
Agriculture & Markets Department
*Weights & Measures, 68*
Arlington CSD, 463
Central Hudson Gas & Electric Corporation, 141
Dutchess BOCES, 488
Dutchess Community College, 439
Dutchess County, 324
*Supreme, County & Surrogate's Courts, 50*
Dutchess County Economic Development Corporation, 399
Dutchess County Regional Chamber of Commerce, 407
Education Department
*Mid-Hudson District Office, 119*
Elections, State Board of
*Dutchess, 129*
Gannett Co Inc, 423
Marist College, 448
Marist Institute for Public Opinion, 136
NYS Bar Assn, Judicial Campaign Monitoring Cmte, 214
New York State Association of Family Service Agencies Inc, 257
Ostertag O'Leary & Barrett, 214
Poughkeepsie
*Civil & Criminal Courts, 62*
Poughkeepsie City SD, 463
Poughkeepsie Journal, 423
Poughkeepsie, City of, 356
Poughkeepsie, Town of, 356
Rural & Migrant Ministry Inc, 257
Scenic Hudson, 157
Spackenkill UFSD, 463
Transportation Department
*Region 8, 280*
Vassar College, 453
Veterans' Service Organizations
*Veterans' Coalition of the Hudson Valley, 290*
WPDH (101.5 FM), 429
WRRV (92.7 FM), 429

**Prattsburgh**
Prattsburgh CSD, 480

**Pulaski**
Pulaski CSD, 476
Pulaski-Eastern Shore Chamber of Commerce, 407

**Purchase**
MBIA Insurance Corporation, 79
Manhattanville College, 448
Pepsi Co, 91
Purchase College, State University of New York, 437

**Putnam Station**
Putnam CSD, 485

**Putnam Valley**
Putnam Valley CSD, 477

**Queens**
NYC Region 5, 472
New York Hall of Science, 276
St John's University, 452
St John's University, School of Law, 157
St John's University-Peter J Tobin College of Business, School of Risk Mgmt, 201
US Department of Health & Human Services
*Northeast Regional Laboratory, 251*

**Queens Village**
Friends of Mark Weprin 2013, 377
Mental Health, Office of
*Creedmoor Psychiatric Center, 225*

**Queens Vlg**
NYS Office for People with Developmental Disabilities
*Bernard Fineson Developmental Disabilities Services Office, 226*

**Queensbury**
Adirondack Community College, 438
Queensbury UFSD, 485
Queensbury, Town of, 356
Vietnam Veterans of America, NYS Council, 296

**Quogue**
Quogue UFSD, 482

**Randolph**
Randolph Academy UFSD, 459
Randolph CSD, 460

**Raquette Lake**
Raquette Lake UFSD, 466

**Ray Brook**
Adirondack Park Agency, 93, 148, 268
Albany (Northern Region)
*Ray Brook Satellite Office, 243*
Corrections & Community Supervision Department
*Adirondack Correctional Facility, 106*
Environmental Conservation Department
*Region 5, 146*
Real Property Tax Services, Office of
*Ray Brook Satellite Office, 232, 260*
US Justice Department
*Ray Brook Federal Correctional Institution, 112*

**Red Creek**
Corrections & Community Supervision Department
*Butler Correctional Facility, 107*
Red Creek CSD, 486

**Red Hook**
Red Hook Area Chamber of Commerce, 407
Red Hook CSD, 463

**Rego Park**
Rego Hills Republican Club, 385

**Remsen**
Remsen CSD, 473

**Remsenburg**
Remsenburg-Speonk UFSD, 482

**Rensselaer**
Children & Family Services, Office of, 5, 117, 248
*Council on Children & Families, 5*
*Council on Children & Families (CCF), 249*
*Youth Development, Office of, 249*
Corporation for National & Community Service
*New York Program Office, 251*
Empire State Forest Products Association, 154
Health Department
*School of Public Health, SUNY at Albany, 172*
Healthcare Association of New York State, 180
Healthcare Association of New York State PAC, 378
New York Independent System Operator - Not For Profit, 143
North Greenbush Common SD (Williams), 477
Rensselaer
*Civil & Criminal Courts, 62*
Rensselaer City SD, 477
SUNY at Albany, School of Public Health, Center for Public Health Preparedness, 183

**Retsof**
York CSD, 468

**Rhinebeck**
Rhinebeck Area Chamber of Commerce, 407
Rhinebeck CSD, 463

**Richfield Springs**
Richfield Springs Area Chamber of Commerce, 407
Richfield Springs CSD, 476

**Richmond Hill**
Community For Lynn Nunes, 373
Elaine Nunes 2010, 374
Friends of Nicole Paultre Bell, 377
Mike Duvalle 4 City Council, 382

**Richmond Hills**
People For Leroy Gadsen, 384

*Listings appear in alphabetical order by state, then city.*

*Listings appear in alphabetical order by state, then city.*

*Listings appear in alphabetical order by state, then city.*

*Listings appear in alphabetical order by state, then city.*

*Listings appear in alphabetical order by state, then city.*

*Listings appear in alphabetical order by state, then city.*

*Listings appear in alphabetical order by state, then city.*

*Listings appear in alphabetical order by state, then city.*

**Horsham**
Toll Bros., Inc. PAC, 387

**King of Prussia**
Nuclear Regulatory Commission
*REGION I (includes New York State), 140*

**Newtown Square**
US Department of Agriculture
*Forest Service-Northeastern Area State &
Private Forestry, 151*
*Forest Service-Northern Research Station,
151*

**Paoli**
Friends of Paul Drucker, 377

**Philadelphia**
Cozen O'Connor Empire State PAC, 373
Duane Morris LLP Government Committee -
New York Fund, 374
Fleet Reserve Association (FRA), NE
Region (NJ, NY, PA), 294
NY State Society of Physician Assistants,
181
US Commerce Department
*Philadelphia Region (includes New York),
86*
US Department of Agriculture
*Field Operations-Philadelphia District
Office (includes New York), 175*
US Department of the Interior
*National Park Service-Northeast Region,
152, 272*
US Justice Department
*Audit Division, 209*
US Labor Department
*Wage-Hour Division (WHD)-Northeast
Regional Office, 220*

US Office of Personnel Management
*PHILADELPHIA SERVICE CENTER
(serving New York), 221, 239*

## Tennessee

**Memphis**
Federal Express New York State Political
Action Committee, 374

**Nashville**
US Department of Health & Human Services
*Indian Health Services-Area Office, 251*

## Texas

**Houston**
Service Corporation International Political
Association Committee, 386

**San Antonio**
Air Force Women Officers Associated
(AFWOA), 293

## Vermont

**Montpelier**
National Wildlife Federation - Northeast
Regional Center, 156

**Rutland**
US Department of Agriculture
*Green Mountain & Finger Lakes, 151*

**South Burlington**
Democracy For America - NYC, 373

## Virginia

**Alexandria**
Fleet Reserve Association (FRA), 294
Military Officers Association of America,
294
National Military Family Association
(NMFA), 295
Naval Reserve Association (NRA), 295

**Arlington**
AECOM US FEDERAL PAC, 371
Air Force Association (AFA), 293
Association of the US Army (AUSA), 294
Atlantic States Marine Fisheries
Commission, 93, 148
Military Chaplains Association of the USA
(MCA), 294
Navy League of the US (NLUS), 295

**Falls Church**
Naval Enlisted Reserve Association
(NERA), 295

**Merrifield**
Marine Corps League (MCL), 294

**Reston**
Maximus Inc. Political Action Committee,
381

**Springfield**
Military Order of the Purple Heart (MOPH),
295

*Listings appear in alphabetical order by state, then city.*

# 2021 Title List

Visit www.GreyHouse.com for Product Information, Table of Contents, and Sample Pages.

## Opinions Throughout History

Opinions Throughout History: The Death Penalty
Opinions Throughout History: Diseases & Epidemics
Opinions Throughout History: Drug Use & Abuse
Opinions Throughout History: The Environment
Opinions Throughout History: Gender: Roles & Rights
Opinions Throughout History: Globalization
Opinions Throughout History: Guns in America
Opinions Throughout History: Immigration
Opinions Throughout History: Law Enforcement in America
Opinions Throughout History: National Security vs. Civil &
    Privacy Rights
Opinions Throughout History: Presidential Authority
Opinions Throughout History: Robotics & Artificial Intelligence
Opinions Throughout History: Social Media Issues
Opinions Throughout History: Sports & Games
Opinions Throughout History: Voters' Rights

## This is Who We Were

This is Who We Were: Colonial America (1492-1775)
This is Who We Were: 1880-1899
This is Who We Were: In the 1900s
This is Who We Were: In the 1910s
This is Who We Were: In the 1920s
This is Who We Were: A Companion to the 1940 Census
This is Who We Were: In the 1940s (1940-1949)
This is Who We Were: In the 1950s
This is Who We Were: In the 1960s
This is Who We Were: In the 1970s
This is Who We Were: In the 1980s
This is Who We Were: In the 1990s
This is Who We Were: In the 2000s
This is Who We Were: In the 2010s

## Working Americans

Working Americans—Vol. 1: The Working Class
Working Americans—Vol. 2: The Middle Class
Working Americans—Vol. 3: The Upper Class
Working Americans—Vol. 4: Children
Working Americans—Vol. 5: At War
Working Americans—Vol. 6: Working Women
Working Americans—Vol. 7: Social Movements
Working Americans—Vol. 8: Immigrants
Working Americans—Vol. 9: Revolutionary War to the Civil War
Working Americans—Vol. 10: Sports & Recreation
Working Americans—Vol. 11: Inventors & Entrepreneurs
Working Americans—Vol. 12: Our History through Music
Working Americans—Vol. 13: Education & Educators
Working Americans—Vol. 14: African Americans
Working Americans—Vol. 15: Politics & Politicians
Working Americans—Vol. 16: Farming & Ranching
Working Americans—Vol. 17: Teens in America

## Education

Complete Learning Disabilities Resource Guide
Educators Resource Guide
The Comparative Guide to Elem. & Secondary Schools
Charter School Movement
Special Education: A Reference Book for Policy & Curriculum
    Development

## Grey House Health & Wellness Guides

Autoimmune Disorders Handbook & Resource Guide
Cancer Handbook & Resource Guide
Cardiovascular Disease Handbook & Resource Guide
Dementia Handbook & Resource Guide

## Consumer Health

Autoimmune Disorders Handbook & Resource Guide
Cancer Handbook & Resource Guide
Cardiovascular Disease Handbook & Resource Guide
Comparative Guide to American Hospitals
Complete Mental Health Resource Guide
Complete Resource Guide for Pediatric Disorders
Complete Resource Guide for People with Chronic Illness
Complete Resource Guide for People with Disabilities
Older Americans Information Resource

## General Reference

African Biographical Dictionary
American Environmental Leaders
America's College Museums
Constitutional Amendments
Encyclopedia of African-American Writing
Encyclopedia of Invasions & Conquests
Encyclopedia of Prisoners of War & Internment
Encyclopedia of Rural America
Encyclopedia of the Continental Congresses
Encyclopedia of the United States Cabinet
Encyclopedia of War Journalism
The Environmental Debate
The Evolution Wars: A Guide to the Debates
Financial Literacy Starter Kit
From Suffrage to the Senate
The Gun Debate: Gun Rights & Gun Control in the U.S.
History of Canada
Historical Warrior Peoples & Modern Fighting Groups
Human Rights and the United States
Political Corruption in America
Privacy Rights in the Digital Age
The Religious Right and American Politics
Speakers of the House of Representatives, 1789-2021
US Land & Natural Resources Policy
The Value of a Dollar 1600-1865 Colonial to Civil War
The Value of a Dollar 1860-2019
World Cultural Leaders of the 20th Century

## Business Information

Business Information Resources
The Complete Broadcasting Industry Guide: Television, Radio,
    Cable & Streaming
Directory of Mail Order Catalogs
Environmental Resource Handbook
Food & Beverage Market Place
The Grey House Guide to Homeland Security Resources
The Grey House Performing Arts Industry Guide
Guide to Healthcare Group Purchasing Organizations
Guide to U.S. HMOs and PPOs
Guide to Venture Capital & Private Equity Firms
Hudson's Washington News Media Contacts Guide
New York State Directory
Sports Market Place

**Grey House Publishing | Salem Press | H.W. Wilson** | 4919 Route, 22 PO Box 56, Amenia NY 12501-0056

# 2021 Title List

Visit www.GreyHouse.com for Product Information, Table of Contents, and Sample Pages.

## Statistics & Demographics

America's Top-Rated Cities
America's Top-Rated Smaller Cities
The Comparative Guide to American Suburbs
Profiles of America
Profiles of California
Profiles of Florida
Profiles of Illinois
Profiles of Indiana
Profiles of Massachusetts
Profiles of Michigan
Profiles of New Jersey
Profiles of New York
Profiles of North Carolina & South Carolina
Profiles of Ohio
Profiles of Pennsylvania
Profiles of Texas
Profiles of Virginia
Profiles of Wisconsin

## Canadian Resources

Associations Canada
Canadian Almanac & Directory
Canadian Environmental Resource Guide
Canadian Parliamentary Guide
Canadian Venture Capital & Private Equity Firms
Canadian Who's Who
Cannabis Canada
Careers & Employment Canada
Financial Post: Directory of Directors
Financial Services Canada
FP Bonds: Corporate
FP Bonds: Government
FP Equities: Preferreds & Derivatives
FP Survey: Industrials
FP Survey: Mines & Energy
FP Survey: Predecessor & Defunct
Health Guide Canada
Libraries Canada
Major Canadian Cities: Compared & Ranked, First Edition

## Weiss Financial Ratings

Financial Literacy Basics
Financial Literacy: How to Become an Investor
Financial Literacy: Planning for the Future
Weiss Ratings Consumer Guides
Weiss Ratings Guide to Banks
Weiss Ratings Guide to Credit Unions
Weiss Ratings Guide to Health Insurers
Weiss Ratings Guide to Life & Annuity Insurers
Weiss Ratings Guide to Property & Casualty Insurers
Weiss Ratings Investment Research Guide to Bond & Money
   Market Mutual Funds
Weiss Ratings Investment Research Guide to Exchange-Traded
   Funds
Weiss Ratings Investment Research Guide to Stock Mutual Funds
Weiss Ratings Investment Research Guide to Stocks

## Books in Print Series

American Book Publishing Record® Annual
American Book Publishing Record® Monthly
Books In Print®
Books In Print® Supplement
Books Out Loud™
Bowker's Complete Video Directory™
Children's Books In Print®
El-Hi Textbooks & Serials In Print®
Forthcoming Books®
Law Books & Serials In Print™
Medical & Health Care Books In Print™
Publishers, Distributors & Wholesalers of the US™
Subject Guide to Books In Print®
Subject Guide to Children's Books In Print®

Grey House Publishing | Salem Press | H.W. Wilson | 4919 Route, 22 PO Box 56, Amenia NY 12501-0056

SALEM PRESS

# *2021 Title List*

Visit www.SalemPress.com for Product Information, Table of Contents, and Sample Pages.

SALEM PRESS

# LITERATURE

## *Critical Insights: Authors*

Louisa May Alcott
Sherman Alexie
Isabel Allende
Maya Angelou
Isaac Asimov
Margaret Atwood
Jane Austen
James Baldwin
Saul Bellow
Roberto Bolano
Ray Bradbury
Gwendolyn Brooks
Albert Camus
Raymond Carver
Willa Cather
Geoffrey Chaucer
John Cheever
Joseph Conrad
Charles Dickens
Emily Dickinson
Frederick Douglass
T. S. Eliot
George Eliot
Harlan Ellison
Louise Erdrich
William Faulkner
F. Scott Fitzgerald
Gustave Flaubert
Horton Foote
Benjamin Franklin
Robert Frost
Neil Gaiman
Gabriel Garcia Marquez
Thomas Hardy
Nathaniel Hawthorne
Robert A. Heinlein
Lillian Hellman
Ernest Hemingway
Langston Hughes
Zora Neale Hurston
Henry James
Thomas Jefferson
James Joyce
Jamaica Kincaid
Stephen King
Martin Luther King, Jr.
Barbara Kingsolver
Abraham Lincoln
Mario Vargas Llosa
Jack London
James McBride
Cormac McCarthy
Herman Melville
Arthur Miller
Toni Morrison
Alice Munro
Tim O'Brien
Flannery O'Connor
Eugene O'Neill

George Orwell
Sylvia Plath
Philip Roth
Salman Rushdie
Mary Shelley
John Steinbeck
Amy Tan
Leo Tolstoy
Mark Twain
John Updike
Kurt Vonnegut
Alice Walker
David Foster Wallace
Edith Wharton
Walt Whitman
Oscar Wilde
Tennessee Williams
Richard Wright
Malcolm X

## *Critical Insights: Works*

Absalom, Absalom!
Adventures of Huckleberry Finn
Aeneid
All Quiet on the Western Front
Animal Farm
Anna Karenina
The Awakening
The Bell Jar
Beloved
Billy Budd, Sailor
The Book Thief
Brave New World
The Canterbury Tales
Catch-22
The Catcher in the Rye
The Crucible
Death of a Salesman
The Diary of a Young Girl
Dracula
Fahrenheit 451
The Grapes of Wrath
Great Expectations
The Great Gatsby
Hamlet
The Handmaid's Tale
Harry Potter Series
Heart of Darkness
The Hobbit
The House on Mango Street
How the Garcia Girls Lost Their Accents
The Hunger Games Trilogy
I Know Why the Caged Bird Sings
In Cold Blood
The Inferno
Invisible Man
Jane Eyre
The Joy Luck Club
King Lear
The Kite Runner
Life of Pi
Little Women

Lolita
Lord of the Flies
Macbeth
The Metamorphosis
Midnight's Children
A Midsummer Night's Dream
Moby-Dick
Mrs. Dalloway
Nineteen Eighty-Four
The Odyssey
Of Mice and Men
One Flew Over the Cuckoo's Nest
One Hundred Years of Solitude
Othello
The Outsiders
Paradise Lost
The Pearl
The Poetry of Baudelaire
The Poetry of Edgar Allan Poe
A Portrait of the Artist as a Young Man
Pride and Prejudice
The Red Badge of Courage
Romeo and Juliet
The Scarlet Letter
Short Fiction of Flannery O'Connor
Slaughterhouse-Five
The Sound and the Fury
A Streetcar Named Desire
The Sun Also Rises
A Tale of Two Cities
The Tales of Edgar Allan Poe
Their Eyes Were Watching God
Things Fall Apart
To Kill a Mockingbird
War and Peace
The Woman Warrior

## *Critical Insights: Themes*

The American Comic Book
American Creative Non-Fiction
The American Dream
American Multicultural Identity
American Road Literature
American Short Story
American Sports Fiction
The American Thriller
American Writers in Exile
Censored & Banned Literature
Civil Rights Literature, Past & Present
Coming of Age
Conspiracies
Contemporary Canadian Fiction
Contemporary Immigrant Short Fiction
Contemporary Latin American Fiction
Contemporary Speculative Fiction
Crime and Detective Fiction
Crisis of Faith
Cultural Encounters
Dystopia
Family
The Fantastic
Feminism

# SALEM PRESS

# *2021 Title List*

Visit www.SalemPress.com for Product Information, Table of Contents, and Sample Pages.

# SALEM PRESS

Flash Fiction
Gender, Sex and Sexuality
Good & Evil
The Graphic Novel
Greed
Harlem Renaissance
The Hero's Quest
Historical Fiction
Holocaust Literature
The Immigrant Experience
Inequality
LGBTQ Literature
Literature in Times of Crisis
Literature of Protest
Magical Realism
Midwestern Literature
Modern Japanese Literature
Nature & the Environment
Paranoia, Fear & Alienation
Patriotism
Political Fiction
Postcolonial Literature
Pulp Fiction of the '20s and '30s
Rebellion
Russia's Golden Age
Satire
The Slave Narrative
Social Justice and American Literature
Southern Gothic Literature
Southwestern Literature
Survival
Technology & Humanity
Violence in Literature
Virginia Woolf & 20th Century Women Writers
War

## *Critical Insights: Film*
Bonnie & Clyde
Casablanca
Alfred Hitchcock
Stanley Kubrick

## *Critical Approaches to Literature*
Critical Approaches to Literature: Feminist
Critical Approaches to Literature: Moral
Critical Approaches to Literature: Multicultural
Critical Approaches to Literature: Psychological

## *Critical Surveys of Literature*
Critical Survey of American Literature
Critical Survey of Drama
Critical Survey of Graphic Novels: Heroes & Superheroes
Critical Survey of Graphic Novels: History, Theme, and Technique
Critical Survey of Graphic Novels: Independents and Underground Classics
Critical Survey of Graphic Novels: Manga
Critical Survey of Long Fiction
Critical Survey of Mystery and Detective Fiction
Critical Survey of Mythology & Folklore: Gods & Goddesses
Critical Survey of Mythology & Folklore: Heroes and Heroines
Critical Survey of Mythology & Folklore: Love, Sexuality, and Desire
Critical Survey of Mythology & Folklore: World Mythology
Critical Survey of Poetry
Critical Survey of Poetry: Contemporary Poets
Critical Survey of Science Fiction & Fantasy Literature
Critical Survey of Shakespeare's Plays
Critical Survey of Shakespeare's Sonnets
Critical Survey of Short Fiction
Critical Survey of World Literature
Critical Survey of Young Adult Literature

## *Cyclopedia of Literary Characters & Places*
Cyclopedia of Literary Characters
Cyclopedia of Literary Places

## *Introduction to Literary Context*
American Poetry of the 20th Century
American Post-Modernist Novels
American Short Fiction
English Literature
Plays
World Literature

## *Magill's Literary Annual*
Magill's Literary Annual, 2021
Magill's Literary Annual, 2020
Magill's Literary Annual, 2019

## *Masterplots*
Masterplots, Fourth Edition
Masterplots, 2010-2018 Supplement

## *Notable Writers*
Notable African American Writers
Notable American Women Writers
Notable Mystery & Detective Fiction Writers
Notable Native American Writers & Writers of the American West
Novels into Film: Adaptations & Interpretation
Recommended Reading: 600 Classics Reviewed

Grey House Publishing | Salem Press | H.W. Wilson | 4919 Route, 22 PO Box 56, Amenia NY 12501-0056

SALEM PRESS

# *2021 Title List*

Visit www.SalemPress.com for Product Information, Table of Contents, and Sample Pages.

SALEM PRESS

# HISTORY
## The Decades
The 1910s in America
The Twenties in America
The Thirties in America
The Forties in America
The Fifties in America
The Sixties in America
The Seventies in America
The Eighties in America
The Nineties in America
The 2000s in America
The 2010s in America

## Defining Documents in American History
Defining Documents: The 1900s
Defining Documents: The 1910s
Defining Documents: The 1920s
Defining Documents: The 1930s
Defining Documents: The 1950s
Defining Documents: The 1960s
Defining Documents: The 1970s
Defining Documents: American Citizenship
Defining Documents: The American Economy
Defining Documents: The American Revolution
Defining Documents: The American West
Defining Documents: Business Ethics
Defining Documents: Capital Punishment
Defining Documents: Civil Rights
Defining Documents: Civil War
Defining Documents: The Cold War
Defining Documents: Dissent & Protest
Defining Documents: Drug Policy
Defining Documents: The Emergence of Modern America
Defining Documents: Environment & Conservation
Defining Documents: Espionage & Intrigue
Defining Documents: Exploration and Colonial America
Defining Documents: The Formation of the States
Defining Documents: The Free Press
Defining Documents: The Gun Debate
Defining Documents: Immigration & Immigrant Communities
Defining Documents: The Legacy of 9/11
Defining Documents: LGBTQ+
Defining Documents: Manifest Destiny and the New Nation
Defining Documents: Native Americans
Defining Documents: Political Campaigns, Candidates &
    Discourse
Defining Documents: Postwar 1940s
Defining Documents: Prison Reform
Defining Documents: Secrets, Leaks & Scandals
Defining Documents: Slavery
Defining Documents: Supreme Court Decisions
Defining Documents: Reconstruction Era
Defining Documents: The Vietnam War
Defining Documents: U.S. Involvement in the Middle East
Defining Documents: World War I
Defining Documents: World War II

## Defining Documents in World History
Defining Documents: The 17th Century
Defining Documents: The 18th Century
Defining Documents: The 19th Century
Defining Documents: The 20th Century (1900-1950)
Defining Documents: The Ancient World
Defining Documents: Asia
Defining Documents: Genocide & the Holocaust
Defining Documents: Nationalism & Populism
Defining Documents: Pandemics, Plagues & Public Health
Defining Documents: Renaissance & Early Modern Era
Defining Documents: The Middle Ages
Defining Documents: The Middle East
Defining Documents: Women's Rights

## Great Events from History
Great Events from History: The Ancient World
Great Events from History: The Middle Ages
Great Events from History: The Renaissance & Early Modern Era
Great Events from History: The 17th Century
Great Events from History: The 18th Century
Great Events from History: The 19th Century
Great Events from History: The 20th Century, 1901-1940
Great Events from History: The 20th Century, 1941-1970
Great Events from History: The 20th Century, 1971-2000
Great Events from History: Modern Scandals
Great Events from History: African American History
Great Events from History: The 21st Century, 2000-2016
Great Events from History: LGBTQ Events
Great Events from History: Human Rights

## Great Lives from History
Computer Technology Innovators
Fashion Innovators
Great Athletes
Great Athletes of the Twenty-First Century
Great Lives from History: African Americans
Great Lives from History: American Heroes
Great Lives from History: American Women
Great Lives from History: Asian and Pacific Islander Americans
Great Lives from History: Inventors & Inventions
Great Lives from History: Jewish Americans
Great Lives from History: Latinos
Great Lives from History: Scientists and Science
Great Lives from History: The 17th Century
Great Lives from History: The 18th Century
Great Lives from History: The 19th Century
Great Lives from History: The 20th Century
Great Lives from History: The 21st Century, 2000-2017
Great Lives from History: The Ancient World
Great Lives from History: The Incredibly Wealthy
Great Lives from History: The Middle Ages
Great Lives from History: The Renaissance & Early Modern Era
Human Rights Innovators
Internet Innovators
Music Innovators
Musicians and Composers of the 20th Century
World Political Innovators

Grey House Publishing | Salem Press | H.W. Wilson | 4919 Route, 22 PO Box 56, Amenia NY 12501-0056

SALEM PRESS

# *2021 Title List*

Visit www.SalemPress.com for Product Information, Table of Contents, and Sample Pages.

SALEM PRESS

## History & Government

American First Ladies
American Presidents
The 50 States
The Ancient World: Extraordinary People in Extraordinary
    Societies
The Bill of Rights
The Criminal Justice System
The U.S. Supreme Court

## SOCIAL SCIENCES

Civil Rights Movements: Past & Present
Countries, Peoples and Cultures
Countries: Their Wars & Conflicts: A World Survey
Education Today: Issues, Policies & Practices
Encyclopedia of American Immigration
Ethics: Questions & Morality of Human Actions
Issues in U.S. Immigration
Principles of Sociology: Group Relationships & Behavior
Principles of Sociology: Personal Relationships & Behavior
Principles of Sociology: Societal Issues & Behavior
Racial & Ethnic Relations in America
World Geography

## SCIENCE

Ancient Creatures
Applied Science
Applied Science: Engineering & Mathematics
Applied Science: Science & Medicine
Applied Science: Technology
Biomes and Ecosystems
Earth Science: Earth Materials and Resources
Earth Science: Earth's Surface and History
Earth Science: Earth's Weather, Water and Atmosphere
Earth Science: Physics and Chemistry of the Earth
Encyclopedia of Climate Change
Encyclopedia of Energy
Encyclopedia of Environmental Issues
Encyclopedia of Global Resources
Encyclopedia of Mathematics and Society
Forensic Science
Notable Natural Disasters
The Solar System
USA in Space

## Principles of Science

Principles of Anatomy
Principles of Astronomy
Principles of Behavioral Science
Principles of Biology
Principles of Biotechnology
Principles of Botany
Principles of Chemistry
Principles of Climatology
Principles of Information Technology
Principles of Computer Science
Principles of Ecology
Principles of Energy
Principles of Geology

Principles of Marine Science
Principles of Mathematics
Principles of Modern Agriculture
Principles of Pharmacology
Principles of Physical Science
Principles of Physics
Principles of Programming & Coding
Principles of Robotics & Artificial Intelligence
Principles of Scientific Research
Principles of Sustainability
Principles of Zoology

## HEALTH

Addictions, Substance Abuse & Alcoholism
Adolescent Health & Wellness
Aging
Cancer
Community & Family Health Issues
Integrative, Alternative & Complementary Medicine
Genetics and Inherited Conditions
Infectious Diseases and Conditions
Magill's Medical Guide
Nutrition
Psychology & Behavioral Health
Women's Health

## Principles of Health

Principles of Health: Allergies & Immune Disorders
Principles of Health: Anxiety & Stress
Principles of Health: Depression
Principles of Health: Diabetes
Principles of Health: Nursing
Principles of Health: Obesity
Principles of Health: Pain Management
Principles of Health: Prescription Drug Abuse

Grey House Publishing | Salem Press | H.W. Wilson | 4919 Route, 22 PO Box 56, Amenia NY 12501-0056

# 2021 Title List

Visit www.SalemPress.com for Product Information, Table of Contents, and Sample Pages.

## CAREERS

Careers: Paths to Entrepreneurship
Careers in the Arts: Fine, Performing & Visual
Careers in Building Construction
Careers in Business
Careers in Chemistry
Careers in Communications & Media
Careers in Education & Training
Careers in Environment & Conservation
Careers in Financial Services
Careers in Forensic Science
Careers in Gaming
Careers in Green Energy
Careers in Healthcare
Careers in Hospitality & Tourism
Careers in Human Services
Careers in Information Technology
Careers in Law, Criminal Justice & Emergency Services
Careers in the Music Industry
Careers in Manufacturing & Production
Careers in Nursing
Careers in Physics
Careers in Protective Services
Careers in Psychology & Behavioral Health
Careers in Public Administration
Careers in Sales, Insurance & Real Estate
Careers in Science & Engineering
Careers in Social Media
Careers in Sports & Fitness
Careers in Sports Medicine & Training
Careers in Technical Services & Equipment Repair
Careers in Transportation
Careers in Writing & Editing
Careers Outdoors
Careers Overseas
Careers Working with Infants & Children
Careers Working with Animals

## BUSINESS

Principles of Business: Accounting
Principles of Business: Economics
Principles of Business: Entrepreneurship
Principles of Business: Finance
Principles of Business: Globalization
Principles of Business: Leadership
Principles of Business: Management
Principles of Business: Marketing

Grey House Publishing | Salem Press | H.W. Wilson | 4919 Route, 22 PO Box 56, Amenia NY 12501-0056

# 2021 Title List

Visit www.HWWilsonInPrint.com for Product Information, Table of Contents, and Sample Pages.

## The Reference Shelf

Affordable Housing
Aging in America
Alternative Facts, Post-Truth and the Information War
The American Dream
American Military Presence Overseas
Arab Spring
Artificial Intelligence
The Business of Food
Campaign Trends & Election Law
College Sports
Conspiracy Theories
Democracy Evolving
The Digital Age
Dinosaurs
Embracing New Paradigms in Education
Faith & Science
Families - Traditional & New Structures
Food Insecurity & Hunger in the United States
Future of U.S. Economic Relations: Mexico, Cuba, &
    Venezuela
Global Climate Change
Graphic Novels and Comic Books
Guns in America
Hate Crimes
Immigration
Internet Abuses & Privacy Rights
Internet Law
LGBTQ in the 21st Century
Marijuana Reform
National Debate Topic 2014/2015: The Ocean
National Debate Topic 2015/2016: Surveillance
National Debate Topic 2016/2017: US/China Relations
National Debate Topic 2017/2018: Education Reform
National Debate Topic 2018/2019: Immigration
National Debate Topic 2019/2021: Arms Sales
National Debate Topic 2020/2021: Criminal Justice Reform
National Debate Topic 2021/2022
New Frontiers in Space
The News and its Future
Policing in 2020
Politics of the Oceans
Pollution
Prescription Drug Abuse
Propaganda and Misinformation
Racial Tension in a Postracial Age
Reality Television
Representative American Speeches, Annual Edition
Rethinking Work
Revisiting Gender
Robotics
Russia
Social Networking
The South China Sea Conflict
Space Exploration and Development
Sports in America
The Supreme Court
The Transformation of American Cities
The Two Koreas
U.S. Infrastructure
Vaccinations
Whistleblowers

## Core Collections

Children's Core Collection
Fiction Core Collection
Graphic Novels Core Collection
Middle & Junior High School Core
Public Library Core Collection: Nonfiction
Senior High Core Collection
Young Adult Fiction Core Collection

## Current Biography

Current Biography Cumulative Index 1946-2021
Current Biography Monthly Magazine
Current Biography Yearbook

## Readers' Guide to Periodical Literature

Abridged Readers' Guide to Periodical Literature
Readers' Guide to Periodical Literature

## Indexes

Index to Legal Periodicals & Books
Short Story Index
Book Review Digest

## Sears List

Sears List of Subject Headings
Sears: Lista de Encabezamientos de Materia

## History

American Game Changers: Invention, Innovation &
    Transformation
American Reformers
Speeches of the American Presidents

## Facts About Series

Facts About the 20th Century
Facts About American Immigration
Facts About China
Facts About the Presidents
Facts About the World's Languages

## Nobel Prize Winners

Nobel Prize Winners: 1901-1986
Nobel Prize Winners: 1987-1991
Nobel Prize Winners: 1992-1996
Nobel Prize Winners: 1997-2001
Nobel Prize Winners: 2002-2018

## Famous First Facts

Famous First Facts
Famous First Facts About American Politics
Famous First Facts About Sports
Famous First Facts About the Environment
Famous First Facts: International Edition

## American Book of Days

The American Book of Days
The International Book of Days

Grey House Publishing | Salem Press | H.W. Wilson | 4919 Route, 22 PO Box 56, Amenia NY 12501-0056